THE GLADSTONE DIARIES

Gladstone in 1852, aged forty-two
Engraved from a photograph by Samuel A. Walker

THE GLADSTONE DIARIES

VOLUME IV · 1848–1854

Edited by

M. R. D. FOOT

lately
PROFESSOR OF MODERN HISTORY
IN THE
UNIVERSITY OF MANCHESTER

and

H. C. G. MATTHEW

LECTURER IN GLADSTONE STUDIES
AT
CHRIST CHURCH, OXFORD

CLARENDON PRESS · OXFORD
1974

Oxford University Press, Ely House, London W.1

GLASGOW NEW YORK TORONTO MELBOURNE WELLINGTON
CAPE TOWN IBADAN NAIROBI DAR ES SALAAM LUSAKA ADDIS ABABA
DELHI BOMBAY CALCUTTA MADRAS KARACHI LAHORE DACCA
KUALA LUMPUR SINGAPORE HONG KONG TOKYO

ISBN 0 19 822425 7

PRINTED IN GREAT BRITAIN
BY WILLIAM CLOWES & SONS, LTD.,
LONDON, BECCLES AND COLCHESTER

CONTENTS

VOLUME IV

LIST OF ILLUSTRATIONS

NOTE ON ABBREVIATIONS &c.

Lists of abbreviations used in this volume and an introduction covering its years will be found at the start of volume III.

Jan One 1848. Sat. Circumcision. [*Hawarden*][1]

Church 11 A.M. Wrote to Sir J.G—C.G. Reid (2)—Ld Medwyn—Mr Curtis. Read Huber [2]—Petrarch [3]—Taylor (a golden book: yet I remember him well nigh lost in scepticism; this hath God wrought) [4]—Adv[entures] in Mexico.[5] Lesson to Willy in H.S. Chess with Stephen.

I am struck much by a radical defect in the habit of mind with which I view the comparatively serious personal & domestic anxieties of the last year. I think of them as a load with a latent hope that they are now laid down: but a Christian ought to think of them as a preparation to bear more, even as much as it shall please God to lay upon us according to our strength. Surely it is in this light as a preparation for more that they shd. be viewed: for they must be considered in regard to their fruits: for the trial of your faith worketh patience,[6] a power to bear more trials, & in this, not in the buoyant sense of relief on their cessation, is their real profit.

Let me here make a memorandum about those great treasures our children.

To begin with baby [Mary]: she shows a very placid, & I hope sweet (for it is not a dull) temper: & a great susceptibility to musical sounds in the most unequivocal way.

Jessy is quick, thoughtful, very affectionate; with a strong will which has yet to be broken.

Stephen is the slowest in development of all our children, & the most difficult to understand: but he always makes us think that he has it in him, & that it will come out. He ruminates on what he hears, & then comes out with quaint things. He is beginning to obey: but is only broken in part. He is a very affectionate boy.

Agnes has a gentleness which is very fascinating & makes her easily ruled: but one fears it may partake of *slight*ness in the texture of character: & since her illness her obedience has been less perfect. But when I remember that it came after a great battle, & that she *was* a very proud child, I have no fear but that she will have substance enough: and there is little else to be anxious about for she is a most loving & docile child, loving to God as well as to us; and never *sulks*.

Willy is a noble boy: generous, ingenuous, modest, tender, energetic, reflective & conscientious in a very high degree, indeed well onward as I trust in the way on which his feet were set at Baptism. He has had a good deal to overcome in childhood: and his christian progress is I think astonishing; I mean in practical christianity, the discipline of the will, not in notions & pretensions. Every Sunday he discusses the faults, dangers, advances, of the foregoing week with me, & I hope to his benefit, as it might be to mine, for I have much to learn from those like him.

[1] Lambeth MS 1428 ctd.
[2] Cp. 23 May 44.
[3] Cp. 28 Dec. 47.
[4] Cp. 31 Dec. 47.
[5] Cp. 22 Dec. 47.
[6] I James, i. 3.

2. 2 S. Xmas.

Church 11 A.M. (& Holy C.) & 7 P.M. Conv. with Willy. Read Savonarola—Xtn Remr. on Hampden—Bunsen.[1] Engl. Rev. on Convocation—Hampden—Foreign Intelligence[2]—Also Col. Ch. Mag. on New Zealand.[3]

At 10 A.M. Lavinia[4] had a boy: & all Hawarden was alive with joy on the birth of the heir. Between five & six it died: in the mother's bed—the death was not discovered till past seven. It had not been baptized: but He who spared Nineveh for the sake of the four score thousand who knew not their right hand from their left,[5] has, as I trust & pray, mercies for this poor infant in that mighty Name, not a sound, but a Power, which saves even of them who know it not.

3. M.

Ch. 8½ A.M. Wrote to Mary L[yttelto]n—Lady Wenlock—Hampton—Trying to work out a sketch of Stephen's affairs: & much at the Rectory, where they have more troubles. Nora[6] having convulsions, Cath. transplanted herself & our baby thither. H.S. to Willy. Chess with Stephen—Read Huber—Petrarch—Ruxton's Mexico (finished)—Taylor's Essays—Engl. Rev. on Romish Theories of Unity.[7]

4. T.

Church 8½ A.M. Wrote to R. Barker—Freshfield—Read Huber—Petrarch—Taylor's Essays—Anecdotes of Johnson[8]—Ed[inburgh] Rev. on State of the Nation[9]—Lesson in H.S. to Willy. Much at the Rectory with C. Thank God all goes well there.

5. W.

Church 8½ A.M. Corrected proofs of my Speech & Preface.[10] Lesson in H.S. to Willy. Dined at the Rectory—Walk with C. Read Huber—Ed. Rev. on Kosmos (part)[11]—Taylor (finished)—Milroy on Cholera[12]—Ld Arundel's Remarks[13]—Mayow on Dr Hampden.[14]

[1] *Christian Remembrancer*, xv. 56 (January 1848); review of Gladstone's correspondence with Bunsen.

[2] *English Review*, viii. 289, 430, 489 (December 1847).

[3] *Colonial Church Chronicle*, i. 225.

[4] i.e. Lavinia Glynne.

[5] Six score thousand: Jonah iv. 11.

[6] Honora, da. of Henry and Lavinia Glynne; she d. 1859.

[7] *English Review*, viii. 354 (December 1847).

[8] J. Merry, *The witticisms, anecdotes, jests and sayings of Dr. Samuel *Johnson* (1791).

[9] *Edinburgh Review*, lxxxvii. 138 (January 1848); article by G. C. *Lewis.

[10] Cp. 24 Dec. 47.

[11] Ibid. lxxxvii. 170; article by J. *Herschell.

[12] G. *Milroy, 'The cholera not to be arrested by quarentine' (1847).

[13] H. G. F. Howard, Lord Arundel and Surrey, 'A few remarks on the social and political conditions of British catholics' (1847).

[14] Untraced pamphlet by Mayow Wynell Mayow.

6. Th. Epiph.

Chester Cathedral aftn. Read Huber—Anecdotes of Johnson—Welford on Tobacco Duties.[1] Spent most of the day on O[ak] F[arm] papers & a journey to Chester to see Barker. Wrote to Freshfield—Sir J.G.—Milroy[2]—Locock—Lessons to Willy H.S. & Latin. Chess with Stephen. C's birthday: shamefully forgotten.

7. Fr.

Ch. 8½ A.M. Wrote to Freshfield—Bickers—Malet—Kitton[3]—H. Taylor—Ld Arundel—Hampton—Walked to Buckley with Stephen. Much busied on O.F. papers. Read Huber—Jos. Andrews.[4] breakf. at Rectory where C. is still a prisoner. Today Agnes had a rash which made us uneasy.

8. Sat.

Ch 8½ A.M. Wrote to Sir J.G—Lyttelton—Freshfield—Tyler—Justice Coleridge—J. Murray—F. Rogers—Broadbridge—C.G. Reid. Work on O.F. papers & on correcting Preface acc[ording] to suggestions from my referees—Read Huber—Joseph Andrews—Anecdotes of Johnson—H.S. with Willy. Saw Burnet on the condns. of letting [Hawarden.]

9. 1 S Epiph.

Ch. 11 AM & 3 PM. Wrote to Freshfield. Further corrections of Preface: which I sent off. Read Savonarola—Boos (finished)—Records of a London Clergyman.[5] Agnes thank God seems to get well. Much at the Rectory where C.s cares are heavy.

10. M.

Church 8½ A.M. Wrote to Sir J.G—T.G—E.W. Barlow[6]—Bp of Edinburgh—J.N.G. H.S. with Willy—Read Huber—Anecdotes of Johnson—Jos. Andrews. Worked on a plan for taking my Fathers O.F. claim & mine into Land.[7] Walk with Stephen & Henry. Chess with Stephen.

11. T.

Church 8½ A.M. Wrote to Canning—Ld Arundel—Justice Coleridge (2)—Sir R. Inglis—Freshfield. Read Huber—Joseph Andrews—Anecd. of Johnson (finished)—Ed. Rev. on Kosmos (finished)—H.S. with Willy. Walk with C.—Mr Brewster & Mr Harris[8] dined: two excellent men.

[1] By Richard G. Welford (?1847).
[2] Gavin *Milroy, 1805–86; writer on medicine; see previous day.
[3] John Kitton, 1815–82; Queens', Cambridge; perpetual curate of St. John's, Houghton, 1841–8; headmaster in Hulton 1851–73.
[4] H. *Fielding, *The history of the adventures of Joseph Andrews and his friend Mr. Abraham Adams*, 2 v. (1742).
[5] [J. H. Caunter], *Posthumous records of a London clergyman* (1835).
[6] Edward William Barlow, 1812–69; curate of Rochford, Essex; wrote on theology.
[7] Germ of eventual solution of Oak Farm crisis.
[8] i.e. F. W. Harris.

12. W.

Missed Ch. on account of a tightness on the chest. Wrote to Lyttelton—Sir J.G—Hampton—Parker—Murray—C.A. M'Kenzie[1]—Burnet. Saw Burnet on Estate affairs: & explained at great length to S[tephen] & H[enry] the scheme of commutation[2]—Evg at Rectory.—Read Huber—Ed. Rev. on Irish Crisis[3]—Joseph Andrews (finished)—Mrs Carter's Letters &c[4]—I yesterday reperused my Speech on Univ. Bill in 1834[5] & was glad to find I cd. now nearly speak it over again.

13. Th.

In bed all day. Wrote to Freshfield—Read Huber—Whewell on Cambr. Studies[6]—Martineau's For Each & for all[7]—Ed. Rev. on Ir. Crisis (finished).

14. Fr.

Rose in evg. much better D.G.. Read Huber—Whewell on Cambr. Studies—Martineau's Demerara.[8] Examining the history of the Estate debt by some old mem[oria]ls of account.

15. Sat.

Wrote to Sir J.G—Freshfield—Lyttelton—E.B. Ramsay—Claridge[9]—H.S. with Willy. Read Huber—Quart. Rev. on Ministerial Measures—on Pius IX[10]—Finished Whewell on Cambridge Studies—Memoirs of Geo. IV.[11] Walk with C.—Moved to the Rectory: saw Burnet—further discussion of Stephen's affairs & the steps to be taken.

16. 2 S. Epiph.

Ch. 11 AM & 3 PM. Read Rudelbach's Savonarola—Abp Whately's Letter on Hampden[12]—Records of a London Clergyman—Lyra Apostolica.[13] Much with C. & the children.

[1] Colin A. MacKenzie, 1779–1851, the diarist's great uncle; diplomat and founder of the Traveller's Club; founded a museum in Dingwall.

[2] See two days earlier.

[3] *Edinburgh Review*, lxxxvii. 229 (January 1848); [C. E. *Trevelyan] on the crisis.

[4] W. Palmer, *Selection from the letters, &c. of the late Miss* [*Anna Maria*] *Carter* (1793).

[5] Cp. 28 July 34.

[6] W. *Whewell, *Of a liberal education in general; and with particular reference to . . . Cambridge*, 1st of 3 v. (1845–52).

[7] In H. *Martineau, *Illustrations of political economy*, iv. (1832–3).

[8] Ibid. ii.

[9] Sir John Thomas Claridge, 1792–1868; Kt. 1825; recorder of Prince of Wales's Island 1825–31 when dismissed; Gladstone took up his case, cp. 25 July 48.

[10] *Quarterly Review*, lxxxii. 261, 231 (December 1847).

[11] R. Huish, *Memoirs of George the Fourth*, 2 v. (1830–1).

[12] R. *Whately, 'Statements and reflections respecting the church and the universities . . . the appointment of the bishop of Hereford' (1848).

[13] By [J. H. *Newman] (1836).

17. M.

Ch 8½ A.M. Wrote to Rn. G.—Saw Burnett again on Estate affairs: & family conv. on do. Read Huber—Rudelbach's Savonarola—Records of a L. Clergyman (finished)—Qu. R. on Lodging Houses—on Africa & W.I.[1]—H.S. with Willy.

18. T.

Ch. 8½ A.M.—H.S. with Willy—Wrote to Uncle D.—Freshfield—Queries for Barker & Burnett—Worked on O.F. papers. Walk with C. Read Huber—Petrarch—Woodward on Irish Educn.[2]—Lady M.W. Montagu's Memoirs[3]—Letters—& Transl. of Epictetus.[4] Chess with Stephen. J.N.G. 41 today.

19. Wed.

Ch. 8½ A.M. Wrote to Sir J.G—Freshfield—Scotts—J. Murray—R. Greswell—R.H. Smith (draft for SRG)[5]—Read Huber—Petrarch—Whately on Polit. Econ[6]—Ed. Rev. on Xtn Evidence[7]—Lady M W Montagu—Saw Burnett—A party to Buckley, & luncheon.

20. Th.

Ch. 8½ A.M. Wrote to Jas Freshfield—Rev. C.E. Radclyffe[8]—Badeley—Cardwell—Hampton. H.S. with Willy. Read Huber—Petrarch—Whately on Polit. Economy—Lady M W Montagu—Walk with C. & the children—Chess with S.

21. Fr.

Ch. 8½ A.M. Wrote to Aldrich—M'Kean[9]—Sir J.G—Burnett—Read Huber—Petrarch—Lady M.W. Montagu—Whately's Pol. Econ. H.S. with Willy. To Chester for calls & 1½ hour with Barker on Stephen's affairs. Chess in evg.

22. Sat.

Ch. 8½ A.M. Wrote to E. Badeley—Cardwell—Clarke. Read Huber—Petrarch—Whately—Lady M.W. Montagu—Walk with C.—Chess with S.—Saw Burnett on Stephen's affairs.

[1] *Quarterly Review*, lxxxii. 142, 153 (December 1847).
[2] Cp. 14 June 44.
[3] Cp. 14 July 45.
[4] Ibid. i. 225.
[5] Untraced; probably on the Oak Farm.
[6] R. *Whately, *Introductory lectures on political economy*, 2 v. (1831–2).
[7] *Edinburgh Review*, lxxxvi. 397 (October 1847).
[8] Charles Edward Radclyffe, 1801–62; rector of South Sydenham, Tavistock, 1836–62.
[9] Unidentified.

23. 3 S. Epiph.

Ch 11 AM & 3 P.M. Wrote to Dr Moberly—J. Gurney—Scr. notes—Conv. with Willy. Read Savonarola[1]—Daillé[2]—Newman's Sermons (1) 1–5.[3] They are a great gift: wh he cannot take away.

24. M.

Ch 8½ A.M.—H.S. with Willy. Wrote to Dowbiggin—Northcote—Sir J.G.—Sec. Nat. Debt Office[4]—Mem. on letting Hawarden—on Broughton Lands —and worked much on calculations about Lady G.s annuity. Walk & conv. with S. on do—Saw Blyffil[5] on O.F.—Read Huber—Whately on Pol. Ec. (finished)—Chess with SRG.

25. T. Conv[ersion of] St Paul.

Chester Cathl. 3 P.M. Wrote to Sir J.G.—Judge Coleridge (2)—Read Huber—Lady M.W.M.—Saw Burnett on Stephen's affairs, also went to Chester & saw Barker. Worked on the Annuity &c. Latin Lesson with Willy.

26. Wed.

Ch. 8½ A.M. H.S. lesson to Willy. Wrote to Ld Braybrooke—Freshfield—Barker—Jacobson—Morrell[6]—Pres. of Trinity[7]—Worked much on Stephen's accts & affairs—Read Huber (finished text)—Lady M.W. Montagu—Chess with Stephen.

27. Th.

Ch 8½ A.M. H.S. with Willy. He spoke excellently. Wrote to Sir J.G—Murray—Northcote—Hampton. Walk, conv. on business, & chess, with Stephen. Wrote a memorandum with a general view of his affairs & of the plans. Read Savonarola—Huber—Atty. Generals Speech in Q.B.[8]—and Lady M.W. Montagu.

28. Fr.

Ch. 8½ A.M.—H.S. with Willy. Wrote to Freshfield—White—Moberly. Read Savonarola—Huber (Appx.)—G.A. Bellamy Vol I[9]—Lady M.W.M. Letters & Poems—Badeley's Speech—Walk with S. Chess with C. Saw Burnett on Estate &c. affairs.

[1] Cp. 28 Nov. 47.
[2] Cp. 25 Dec. 47.
[3] J. H. *Newman, *Parochial Sermons*, 6 v. (1834–42).
[4] Samuel Higham.
[5] Otherwise unidentified.
[6] Baker Morrell, solicitor to Oxford University until he d. 1854.
[7] James *Ingram, 1774–1850; president of Trinity College, Oxford, from 1824.
[8] E. L. *Badeley, a speech on the deceased wife's sister controversy delivered to the Queen's Bench on 15 June 1847.
[9] *An apology for the life of George Anne *Bellamy. Written by herself*, 5 v. (1785).

29. Sat.

Ch 8½ A.M. H.S. with Willy. Wrote to R. Barker—Archdn. Hale—Sir J.G—and Messs. Overend.[1] Read Savonarola—Huber (finished)—Lady M W M Poems & Essays (finished) Chess with S.R.G.

30. 4 S. Epiph.

Ch. 11 A.M. & 3 P.M. Conv. with Willy—MS.s on Ev[il][2]—Wrote to Lyttelton—Hawkins—Woollcombe—Freshfield—Read Savonarola—Newman's Sermons—Essay on Internal Evidences[3]—Barbauld's Essays.[4]

31. M.

Ch 11 A.M.—HS. with Willy. Wrote to Bp of London (& draft)[5]—on the course to be taken with regard to nomination of Bps (Saw J.R. Wood.). Saw Willy subdue his temper in the most beautiful way. Then with Stephen all the evening: an ἀκρασία.[6] Read Savonarola & Appx. (finished)—Trial of Sacheverel & Bps Speeches &c.[7]

Tuesday Feb. One. 1848.

Church 8½ A.M. Wrote to Rev. J. Gladstone—and Lord Braybrooke (on S.s affairs & the Annuity. Read Dryden's St Francis Xavier (tr.)[8] Garbett Praelect I. 1[9]—Trial of Sacheverel. Chess with S.—Walk to St John's[10] with him. Willy had a bilious attack.

2. Wed.

Purification. Ch 11 A.M. Wrote to Sir J.G—T.G—J.N.G—Lyttelton—W. Lyttelton—Boydell—Badeley—Claridge—Freshfield—Wilkinson[11]—White—Northcote—Fowke—Tupper. Read Garbett—Dryden's Xavier—Chess with Stephen—Discussing & settling plans.

3. Th.

Ch 8½ AM. HS. with Willy. Wrote to Bp of London—Scott & Co—R. Barker—Read Xavier. Chess with SRG. Conv. on O.F. & Estate matters. Packing & journey arrangements.

[1] Overend, Gurney and Co.; money dealers in Lombard Street; failed in May 1866, one week after Gladstone's budget.
[2] On existing evils: Add MS 44737, f. 1.
[3] By J. *Butler in *Works* (1807); ii. 327; on the evidence for Christianity.
[4] Anna L. Barbauld, *A collection of essays and tracts in theology*, ed. J. Sparks, 4 v. (1823).
[5] Draft in Add MS 44376, f. 46.
[6] 'lack of power'.
[7] Probably *A compleat history of the . . . proceedings of the Parliament . . . against Dr. Henry *Sacheverell* (1710).
[8] *Dryden's tr. of D. Bonhours, *The life of St. Francis Xavier* (1688).
[9] James *Garbett, *De re critica praelectiones Oxonii habitae* (1847); i. 1 is on aesthetics.
[10] J. E. Ellis's church.
[11] See 4 Oct. 36.

4. Fr.

Wrote to Supt Chester Station—Freshfield—Hampton—Journey to Hagley, seeing Barker at Chester, & 3 hours at O.F. with Boydell & with Paterson & Walker. Found W. Lyttelton & spent the evg in conv. with him. Read Xavier—Richelieu's Testament (Political)[1]—Hare's Letter to the Dean of Chichester.[2]

5. Sat.

Wrote to C.G—Scotts—J. Freshfield—Ld Ward—A long day in moving about to see & converse with different persons on the O.F. works, viz. Mr J. Mathews,[3] Mr Amery, Mr Collis,[4] Mr Evers, Mr W. Mathews:[5] with whom I dined at Birm[ingha]m returning late to Hagley.

6. 5 S. Epiph.

Hagley Ch. 11 & 3½. Holy Communion in mg. Wrote to Lyttelton—Freshfield—R. Smith—Hampton. Read Stanley's Sermons & Essays.[6] Also heard & discussed in evg a paper of W. L[yttelton']s on our Lord's great prophecy.

7. M.

Wrote to C.G.—Scotts—Byrne[7]—Goldsmid[8]—E. Smith[9]—Nicolay—Brewer—Palk[10]—R. Scott—Woodgate & 16 or 18 more of the Oxf. Committee inviting them to dinners Left at 8. Reached London at 3. H. of C. 5–6½ and 10–12¾.[11] Saw Lincoln—Campbell—Cardwell—& overdone with a myriad of papers.

8. T.

Wrote to Palk—Judge Coleridge—C.G—Sir J.G—Reid—Kinnaird—Gregory—Darby—O'Callaghan[12]—Torre[13]—Estcourt—Smyth—Ward[14]—Downing[15]—Boydell—Nicholson[16]—Humphreys—Sec. Treasury—Simpson

[1] *Testament politique d'Armand du Plessis, Cardinal duc de Richelieu* (?1643).
[2] J. C. *Hare, 'A letter to the dean of Chichester' (1848); on *Hampden.
[3] An ironmaster, called in to advise on the estate's prospects.
[4] William Blow Collis, Stourbridge solicitor, acting for Boydell.
[5] Agent of the Oak Farm estate, brother of the ironmaster.
[6] A. P. *Stanley, *Sermons and essays on the apostolic age* (1847).
[7] Henry Barnes Byrne, 1824–?81; B.A. 1847; fellow of Queen's, Oxford, 1851–63.
[8] (Sir) Francis Henry *Goldsmid, 1808–78; first Jewish Q.C.; 2nd. Bart. 1859; liberal M.P. Reading 1860–78.
[9] Edmund James Smith, 1823–86; B.A. 1847; scholar of Worcester 1842–53, fellow 1856–65.
[10] Robert John Malet Palk, 1794–1878; uncle of 1st Baron Haldon; barrister.
[11] Disabilities of the Jews: *H* xcvi. 220.
[12] Probably John Cornelius *O'Callaghan, 1805–83; Irish journalist and historian.
[13] Possibly J. L. Torey, coach fitment manufacturer in Spitalfields.
[14] William Ward, 1817–85; 11th Baron Ward 1835; cr. earl of Dudley 1860; a Peelite; chief creditor of the Oak Farm and owner of land around it.
[15] Charles Downing, Temple barrister.
[16] Probably George Stewart Nicholson, proctor in doctor's commons.

—C. Mackenzie—Franklin[1]—& Cotton. Saw Freshfield—Dr Spry—Hardinge—Lincoln on NZ—Palk & Ld Shaftesbury. Working amidst my Chaos in evg. H. of C. 5–6¾.[2] Read Attempt to justify Agitn. agt. Dr. Hampden[3]—NZ papers.[4]

9. Wed.

Wrote to C.G—Dr Hodgkin—Mozley—Hayes—DeVere—James Rogers[5]—Ld Braybrooke—Hays Smith—R. Palk—Messrs. Plumptre and Bowman[6] Saw Lyttelton (to breakf.)—Mr Hawkins—Bp of London—H. of C. 12–6. Spoke 40 m. on NZ.[7] Read NZ papers—Birks, Abp Whately, Sir R. Inglis, & Euphron, on the Jews[8]—Williams on Welch Educn.[9] Wrote Memm. on Pantonian Trust.[10]

10. Th.

Wrote to R. Palk—C.G—Barker—Gooch—Wrote a condensed Mem. on the Panton Fund & examd. the papers. Calls, and commenced house operations in my chaos. H. of C. 5–7¼.[11] Saw R. Palk on Trin. Coll. Bill—Godley—With the Jameses an hour in evg. Read Phillips's Letter[12]—Goldsmid on the Jews[13]—Ld Shrewsbury to MacHale[14]—Ld Arundel & the Nat. Club. on 'in Coenâ Domini[15]—Adler's Sermon[16]—The Church *not* in Danger.[17]

11. Fr.

Wrote to Sir J. Claridge—Jas Freshfield—T.G—Ld Medwyn—Crawford—

[1] Perhaps John Franklin, City merchant.
[2] Foreign policy: *H* xcvi. 290.
[3] 'An attempt to justify the agitation against the appointment of Dr. *Hampden to the see of Hereford: a letter to Archdeacon *Hare; by a Tutor of a College' (1848).
[4] Correspondence with governor *Grey: *PP* 1847–8, xliii. 251–371.
[5] James Edwin Thorold *Rogers, 1823–90; economist and historian; liberal M.P. Southwark 1880–5, Bermondsey 1885–6; from 1854 a frequent correspondent with Gladstone.
[6] Perhaps a slip of the pen for Plumptre and Brodrick, London solicitors.
[7] On Waitangi and land policy: *H* xcvi. 331.
[8] T. R. *Birks, 'Letter to . . . *Russell' (1848); R. *Whately, 'Speech in the House of Lords, August 1833' (reprinted 1848); Sir R. H. *Inglis, 'The Jew Bill' (1848); Euphron, 'Remarks on the proposed Bill . . .' (1848).
[9] William Williams, M.P., 'A letter to . . . *Russell on the . . . state of education in Wales' (1848).
[10] Add MS 44737, f. 5; this trust was set up early in the nineteenth century to provide two episcopalian theology lecturers in Edinburgh; The Trinity College governors hoped to move them to Glenalmond by a private members bill.
[11] Prison discipline: *H* xcvi. 368.
[12] Perhaps R. Phillips, 'A letter to Dr. D. B. *Reid' (1831); on philosophy.
[13] Sir F. H. *Goldsmid, 'Reply to the arguments advanced against the removal of the remaining disabilities of the Jews' (1848).
[14] J. Talbot, earl of Shrewsbury, 'Reply to Archbishop *MacHale's letter to the earl of Shewsbury' (1848).
[15] *Addresses of the National Club*, 2nd series iii. 11 (21 December 1847); on the papal bull and Lord Arundel; the club was an extremist anglican faction. Cp. 5 Jan. 48.
[16] N. A. Adler, 'The Jewish faith. A sermon' (1848).
[17] R. D. *Hampden (1848).

Burges.[1] Read Scholefield's Serm[2]—Rest in the Church[3]—Saw Woodgate—Dined with J.N.G.—H. of C. 10–1¼. Voted in 277:204 for the Jew Bill.[4] Worked on papers books pictures &c.

12. Sat.

A letterless day of work on books, papers, pictures, china, &c. Saw Kinnaird—Tyler—Sir R. Peel & Lincoln on New Zealand. C.G. came at 5.30 with Agnes & baby. Read Dr Mill on Hampden[5]—Benson on the Congé d'Elire.[6]

13. 6 S. Epiph.

St Martin's mg. Marg. Chapel aftn. Read MS on 2 Pet. III. 12. Wrote to Birks—James—Scholefield[7]—Burges—J. Manners. Read La Steyrie Hist. Confession[8]—Rest in the Church—Allies Introdn.[9]

14. M.

Wrote to Sir J.G—G. & Co—Rev. J. Carden[10]—Paterson & Walker—Freshfield—J. Mathews—Cadogan Williams.[11] Saw Dr Harington[12] & Mr Morell—J.R. Hope—Northcote—Lefevre—H. of C. 5–6¾ and 8½–12½. Spoke on NZ.[13] Read La Steyrie—Degradation of Science in England[14]—Hanging pictures & arranging books ornaments &c.

15. T.

Wrote to Jas Freshfield—Uncle Divie—Northcote—G.W. Hope—Bp Russell—& some half dozen more country members of my Election Committee. Read Account of Rabelais & parts of the book[15]—Strauss (began)[16]

[1] George Burges, solicitor in the Strand, about a servant at Christ Church, Oxford; Hawn P.

[2] J. *Scholefield, 'The golden pipes: the word of the Lord to England' (1848); on Zechariah iv. 6.

[3] [E. F. S. Harris], *Rest in the church* (1848).

[4] 2°: *H* xcvi. 537.

[5] W. H. *Mill, 'A letter to a clergyman . . . on the theological character of Dr. *Hampton's Bampton Lectures' (1848).

[6] C. *Benson, 'The congé d'élire; or, the present mode of making English bishops' (1848).

[7] James *Scholefield, 1789–1853; regius professor of Greek at Cambridge from 1825.

[8] C. P. de Lasteyrie du Saillant, *Histoire de la confession sous ses rapports religieux, moraux et politiques, chez les peuples anciens et modernes* (1846).

[9] Cp. 21 Apr. 44.

[10] James Carden, 1819–78; Merton; curate of Oddington, Gloucestershire, 1845–6; no further employment found.

[11] Pamphleteer; wrote on working class annuities.

[12] Richard Harington, 1800–53; D.D. 1842; principal of Brasenose, Oxford from 1842.

[13] On the new constitution: *H* xcvi. 601.

[14] Cp. 24 Dec. 47.

[15] *The works of F. Rabelais, M.D. . . . with a large account of the life and works of the author* [by P. A. Motteux], 3 v. (1693–4).

[16] D. F. Strauss, *Das Leben Jesu*, 2 v. (1837).

—Degradation of Science (finished)—Saw S.R.G. on his matters—Lincoln —H. of C. 4–6¾. Dined at J.N.G's. Worked upon papers, & on accounts &c.

16. Wed.

Wrote to Claridge—Sir S. Canning—Dr Hodgkin—Sir J G—Chr. Darby—C.G. Reid—Dr Giles.[1] Saw Canning—Lincoln—SRG—Read Strauss—Laurence on Dr Hampden's case[2]—Worked on papers &c. H. of C. 12½–6. Spoke on R.C. Relief Bill.[3]

17. Th.

Wrote to Andrew—Bramston—Tabberner[4]—Northcote—Sir J.G.—Griffiths[5]—H. Glynne—Lyttelton—Ld Ward—Smith & Co—Read Strauss—Tabberner on Supply of Water—H. of C. 5–7.[6] Nearly finished getting my books papers &c. into order. C. confined to bed with influenza. Stephen went off: light hearted enough.

18. Fr.

Wrote to Kirkland—Harris. Read Strauss. Saw Aborig. Soc. Deputation—J.R. Hope. H. of C. 5–12¼. A night of important announcements & many signs of rough weather.[7] Still at work on bills, furniture &c. much of the day.

19. Sat.

Wrote to Tyler—Wortley—Bartholomew[8]—Claridge—Kennedy—Cocks & Biddulph—Sir J.G—Boydell—Griffith—Willy—W. Mathews—Finished my Committee invitations—76 in all. Fifteen to dinner: a very cordial party to all appearance. Saw Badeley on Ch. matters—Tyler—Bonham—Heneage—Gaskell—Calls—and business. At work on arranging wine—Parl papers—&c. Read Strauss. This was dearest Anne's day of death, rather of new birth. What a tumult it has been to me, what peace to her blessed spirit.

20. Septa. S.

St Martin's & Holy C. 11 A.M. Marg. Chapel 3.30. Read aloud MS of the day (42). Wrote to W. Mathews. Wrote MS. Theol. Read Newman's S.—

[1] John Allen *Giles, 1808–84; D.C.L. 1838; editor and translator; his 'Christian Records' suppressed by S. *Wilberforce 1854; vicar of Sutton 1867–84.

[2] R. F. Laurence, 'An inquiry into the circumstances attendant upon the condemnation of Dr. *Hampden in 1836 . . . reprinted with some prefatory remarks . . .' (1848).

[3] Supporting it, with qualifications about Jesuits: *H* xcvi. 741.

[4] John Loude Tabberner, pamphleteer, of Walton-on-Thames, wrote 'The past, the present and the probable future supply of water to London' (1847).

[5] John Griffiths or Griffith, agent for the Oak Farm estate after the removal of Boydell.

[6] Deb. on Bank Charter Act: *H* xcvi. 803.

[7] The budget, announcing increased defence estimates and continuation of income tax: *H* xcvi. 900.

[8] John Bartholomew, 1790–1865; archdeacon of Barnstaple from 1847.

Bp Forbes's Consecrn. S.[1]—Strauss—Statement by Chapter of Manchr.[2]—La Steyrie.

Th[eology] Fix steadily in the mind this idea, that what you have first to realise and determine in yourself is not the relation of laymen to the clergy or of rulers to the ruled in the Church, but it is the conception of the Church at large as a visible corporation spiritually endowed i.e. having spiritual powers attached to the legitimate exercise of its organs.

Next compare this conception with the antagonist theory of the Church as a sum total of living and believing minds and you will come to learn that the organic idea destroys nothing of all that is positive true and good in the gratuitous one, but super*adds* to it. And that he who destroys the former to substitute the latter is a plunderer of our privileges who gives nothing in return.[3]

21. M.

Wrote to Freshfield (2)—Lyttelton—Barker—Griffith—Roper—all on O.F. Saw Archd. Thorp—In City to see Freshfield, but missed him. Saw Bp of Exeter—Porter—Northcote & Phillimore—Lincoln. Another Committee dinner party of fifteen. H. of C. 4½–6½.[4] Read Hawkins's Inaug. Lecture.[5] And tried to examine some revenue papers but too much distracted by the O.F. matters & correspondence to make progress. They make it quite impossible for me to discharge my duties properly in Parliament: but there is no escape at hand: and I suppose that to force one would be tampering with the will of God so clearly & wisely manifested in the late calamity.

22. T.

Wrote to C.G—W.F. Campbell—W. Mathews—J. Boydell—W. Gladstone —Dr Greenhill[6]—Miss Browne—(Chester) Railway Supt.—Read account of Emerson[7]—Orlando Forester's pamphlet[8]—Worked on revenue papers. H. of C. 3¾–7 and 10½–12¼.[9] Dined with the Jameses. Worked on house bills & accts.

23. Wed.

St Anne's 8¼ P.M. Wrote to Sir J.G—C.G—J. Griffith—Dr Hume[10]—Rev Messrs. Bell[11]—Gondon—Cheyne[12]—Monro—Smith—Brown—Dr Kehoe.

[1] A. P. *Forbes, 'Jesus our worship: a sermon preached at the consecration of St. Columba's, Edinburgh' (1848).

[2] One of the many pamphlets on the education controversy there.

[3] Dated 20 February 1848; Add MS 44737, f. 11.

[4] Deb. on estimates: *H* xcvi. 987.

[5] E. *Hawkins 'An inaugural lecture upon the foundation of Dean *Ireland's Professorship' (1848); cp. 2 Nov. 47.

[6] William Alexander *Greenhill, 1814–94; physician at Radcliffe hospital, Oxford, 1839–51; practised in Hastings after 1851; on Gladstone's Oxford cttee.

[7] Report of his British tour in 1847.

[8] 'A few words on the *Hampden controversy' (1847).

[9] Budget: *H* xcvi. 1056.

[10] i.e. Abraham *Hume.

[11] Obscure.

[12] Patrick Cheyne, episcopal incumbent of St. John's, Aberdeen, 1816–*ca.* 1860.

Saw Mr Roper—Mr Mathews (breakf.)—Mrs Malcolm—Bonham—Mr Hallam. Accounts & business. Read 'Claims of the Ch. of Rome [1]—Worked on revenue & trade papers.

24. Th. St Matthias.

St James's 8 A.M. Followed however by some cough. Wrote to Sir J.G—Sir R. Broun [2]—Walter [3]—Read Ld Devon's Letter [4]—Shepherd on Game Laws [5]—Faudel's Letter to Inglis [6]—Manchester Ch. Pamphlets [7]—Saw W.F. Campbell—Thesiger—Worked on bills & accounts—H. of C. 5–10: on Window Tax.[8]

25. Fr.

Wrote to Sir R. Inglis—Rev. J. Bartholomew—J.R. Hope—Rev. R. Gregory [9]—J. Finch.[10] 11–1 with Peel (also Goulburn & Cardwell) on the Budget & Income Tax. He does not seem to allow himself to realise his position: but power is surely coming near him, & likely to be forced upon him. He says that he wd. have added the actual deficiency to debt (3½ mill.) & pledged himself to meet the prospective one (1¾ mill) by economy. Saw Bonham—Judge Coleridge—Read Thornton on Peasant Proprietors [11]—Remarks on Quoad Sacra Churches.[12] C.G. ret[urne]d from Brighton, Miss Browne with Willy Stephen & Jessie from Hawarden. H. of C. 5–6 and 7½–11½.[13]

On Friday the 25th [February] I met Goulburn & Cardwell at Sir R. Peel's: & [14] we went through the items of the Budget. At the close Sir R. Peel declared his own view of the state of public affairs to be such that had he had the work to do he would have proposed to add the deficiency caused by extraordinary items of expenditure—viz. [£]1525000 on account of Ireland, £1100000 on account of the Kafir war, & £245000 Navy Excess to the debt of the country, or rather that he would pay them out of the balances in the Exchequer, would renew the Income

[1] [E. S. Appleyard] 'Claims of the church of Rome, considered with a view to unity' (1848).

[2] Sir Richard *Broun, 1801–58; 8th Bart. 1844; pamphleteer.

[3] Probably John *Walter, 1818–94; manager and proprietor of *The Times* from 1847.

[4] W. Courtenay, 10th earl of Devon, 'Letter from an Irish proprietor to the ministers of religion of the district' (1847).

[5] John C. Shepherd, 'The anti-game law prize essay. A statement of some of the evils which arise to the community from the game laws' (1847).

[6] H. Faudel, 'A few words on the Jewish disabilities addressed to Sir R. H. *Inglis' (1848).

[7] 'Reform in the ecclesiastical provision for the parish of Manchester' (1847).

[8] Voted in 160 to 68 against its repeal: *H* xcvi. 1297.

[9] Robert Gregory, 1819–1911; priest 1844, vicar of St. Mary, Lambeth, 1857–73; canon of St. Paul's 1868; chaplain to bp. of Chester 1884.

[10] John Finch, 1783–1857; Liverpool iron merchant and founder of temperance societies.

[11] W. T. *Thornton, 'A plea for peasant proprietors: with the outlines of a plan for their establishment in Ireland' (1848).

[12] Untraced; *quoad sacra* refers to Scottish parishes constituted for ecclesiastical purposes, as opposed to those *quoad civilia*.

[13] Income and expenditure: *H* xcvi. 1334.

[14] Over another word.

Tax at three per cent, & would pledge the Govt. to a reduction of Expenditure so as to bring it within income. He said however that he thought the country would have borne an increase of the penny charged for postage to two pence.[1]

26. Sat.

Wrote to W. Mathews—Sir J. Claridge—Paterson & Walker—Griffith—R. Barker—Dr Rice[2]—Rev. J.L. Ross. Saw Northcote—Porter—T.G. My last Committee dinner: we were 20. Read Ross on Ch. & State,[3] & finished Remarks on Quoad Sacra Churches. Worked on Rev. & Trade Tables.[4]

27. Sexa. S.

St Martins 8½ A.M. (Holy Comm.) & 11.—St James's 3. Read MS of 45 aloud in evg. Conv. with Willy. Saw Ld Braybrooke—J.N.G—Read 'Some Account of the Reasons of my Conversion[5]—Rest in the Ch—Liturgical Doc. of Q. Elis.[6]

28. M.

Wrote to Mr Hallam—Hays—Freshfield—Tourmey[7]—C. Miller—Messrs. G. & Co—Passengers Commee.[8] & H of C. 2½–9¼.[9] Read Correspondence with Jelf Sharp.[10] Worked on Trade & Revenue papers. H.S. with Willy.

29. T.

Wrote to Darwin—Pol. Mem. Passengers Commee. 12½–1¾. H. of C. 4¼–6¼.[11] Read Ross on Ch. & State—Rest in the Church—Kehoe on African Settlement[12]—Walk & chess with C.—H.S. with Willy—Saw Mr Miller—conv. with Goulburn on the Budget.

Yesterday Graham declared the same opinion to me about the penny postage and considered that it had been a great error in the Government not to lay on that impost at the present juncture.[13]

[1] Written on 29 Dec. 48, see that day. Add MS 44 777, f. 275

[2] Edward Rice, 1776–1862; Christ Church; D.D. 1820; rector of Great Barrington, Gloucestershire, 1810–56, of Oddington 1820–62; dean of Gloucester 1826–62.

[3] J. L. Ross, 'Reciprocal obligations of the church and the civil power' (1848).

[4] 'Tables of the revenue, population and commerce of the United Kingdom . . . 1846': *PP* 1847–8, lxii. 1, 131.

[5] Untraced.

[6] W. K. Clay, ed., *Liturgies and occasional forms of prayer set forth in the reign of Queen Elizabeth* (1847).

[7] Possibly Stewart Tournay, solicitor in Walbrook Street, London.

[8] Select cttee. on the North America Passengers Bill: *PP* 1847–8, v. 21–30.

[9] Defence estimates increases: *H* xcvi. 1334.

[10] 'Correspondence between Major Jelf Sharp and the warden of Trinity College, Glenalmond, on four separate occasions' (1848); on Sharp's qualifications for taking holy communion.

[11] Irish poor law: *H* xcvii. 28.

[12] T. Kehoe, 'Some considerations in favour of forming a settlement at the confluence of the Niger and Tchadda' (1847).

[13] '(This must have been written in the end of February. W.E.G. D. 12. 48.)' added. Add MS 44777, f. 275.

Wedy. March One 1848 London.

Marg. Chapel 5 P.M. Wrote to Sir J.G—A.P. Stanley—R. Barker—J. Griffiths—R. Palk—Ld Stanley—E. Manning—Attended Levee at 2—Tithe Redemption Board at 1—Saw Freshfield on O.F.—Hope & Maitland [1] on Panton Trust Bill—Ld Grey—Goulburn—Labouchere—Scotts—Read Strauss—La Steyrie (Vol. 2) [2]—H.S. with Willy.

2. Th.

Wrote to E. Manning—Dr. Ogilvy—Dalhousie—Spottiswoode & Robertson [3]—Dowbiggin—Mrs A.L. Robertson—E. Coleridge—W. Taylor (for C.G.)—Saw Mrs Manning—Miles—Ld Harrowby & Bp of Salisbury—Goulburn—Lincoln—S.B. Clarke [4]—At Public Office for O.F. Business—Called with C. on Aunt J but missed her. H. of C. 4–6¾.[5] Read Strauss—Burlington College papers & Addresses [6]—Lasteyrie [7]—J.L. Ross—H.S. with Willy.

3. Fr.

Wrote to Lefevre—Sir J. Claridge—J. Hays—Dean Barber—Passengers Bill Comm. 1–2. House 4¾–8½ and 10–12. Voted in 316:141 against classified Income Tax [8]—Saw Lefevre & Porter—Read Strauss—Lasteyrie—Goulburn's Financial Statement [9]—The Old Whig.[10]

4. Sat.

Marg. Chapel 5 P.M. Wrote to R. Bentley—E.V. Harcourt—Rev. Dr. Hawkins—Rev. E.S. Foulkes [11]—Dr Morton [12]—Saw Ld Fred. Kerr—Lyttelton—Dowbiggin—Dr Ogilvy—Hamilton—Northcote—H.S. with Willy. Read Strauss—La Steyrie (finished)—Sir P. Maitland's Correspondence with Ld Grey [13]—Dined with the Mildmays.

5. Quinqua[gesima] S.

—St Martin's (& Holy C.) 11 AM—Marg. Chapel 7 P.M. Conv. with Willy.

[1] John Maitland, conveyancer; of Spottiswoode and Robertson; see 2 notes below.
[2] Cp. 13 Feb. 48.
[3] John Spottiswoode and David Robertson, parliamentary agents, dealing with the Panton Trust Bill.
[4] Seymour Clarke, 1814–76, superintendent G.W.R. 1840–50; manager G.N.R. 1850–70; requested Gladstone to arbitrate 1851, cp. 26 Aug. 51.
[5] New palace of Westminster: *H* xcvii. 138.
[6] Probably Burlington College, New Jersey, 'Address of the trustees: prospectus of the preparatory school' (1846).
[7] Cp. 13 Feb. 48.
[8] *H* xcvii. 229.
[9] Probably that of 1845, his last full budget: *H* lxxvii. 573.
[10] *The Old Whig, or the consistent protestant:* a London periodical (1735–38).
[11] Edmund Salisbury Foulkes or Ffoulkes, 1819–94; anglican priest 1849; roman catholic 1855–70; fellow of Jesus, Oxford, 1842–54; vicar of St. Mary's, Oxford, 1878–94.
[12] Edward Morton, 1799–1859; physician to Western Dispensary and to Royal Metropolitan Infirmary for children.
[13] On 'The state of Kafir tribes': *PP* 1847–8, xliii. 11–31.

Read Jewel & Harding[1]—Daillé—Newman's Sermons—Strauss—Claims of the Ch. of Rome (finished)—Read MS of 44 aloud in evg.

6. M.

Wrote to Paterson & Walker—Saw Archdeacon Wilberforce—Dean of Windsor—& JNG who complained of being sorely hurt by my usual manner to him,—which causes me much regret & shame. H.S. & Latin with Willy. Worked on revenue papers &c. H. of C. 4¾–8 and 9–12½.[2] Read Hill on Defences[3]—Prop. Tax v. Income Tax.[4]

7. T.

Wrote to Sir R. Peel—D.M. Perceval—M. Radius[5]—R. Barker—J.S. Brewer[6]—W.R. Farquhar—W. Mathews—E.S. Foulkes—H.S. with Willy —Saw Sir J.G—W. Mathews (O.F.)—Paterson & Walker (O.F.)—Dowr. Duchess of Beaufort—H. of C. 4¼–6.[7] Dined with JNG. Read Strauss—MacCulloch on Succession to Property[8]—Ld Shrewsbury to Ld Arundel—Worked on O.F. (mine) papers.

8. Ash Wednesday.

St James's 11–1¼. Missed Ch Ch Westmr. in evg by change of hour. H. of C. 1½–5¾ on R.C. relief Bill.[9] Wrote to R. Williamson—E. Manning—G. Burnett—Sir J. Hobhouse (& draft)—W.W. Malet—Wainwright. Read Strauss—Biggs on Turkey[10]—De Vere's 'English Misrule'[11] &c. Since the sores in my arms I have not attempted abstinence: nor do I intend it during Lent as respects the quantities of food wh nature may seem to require: but only in the adjuncts or quality—for when these adjuncts or some of them are removed, nature becomes more moderate. It is very sad to feel that the palate has become accommodated to certain luxuries so that they are as necessaries to it.—I continue to use both wine & meat.

9. Th.

Wrote to Ld Shrewsbury—Freshfield—Barker—Stokes—Griffiths—Ld Grey—Sir J. Hobhouse—Ross. 2½ h. with Sir J.G. on O.F. & Stephen's affairs.—Saw Hope—Read with the utmost distress the correspondence

[1] See 29 Mar. 46.

[2] Income tax: *H* xcvii. 235.

[3] F. Hill, 'National Force: economic defence of the country from internal tumult and foreign aggression' (1848).

[4] 'Property tax *versus* income tax, in a letter addressed to the representatives of the United Kingdom' (1848).

[5] Unidentified.

[6] John Sherren *Brewer, 1810–79; professor of English language, Kings College, London, 1855–77; historian.

[7] Misc. business: *H* xcvii. 311.

[8] J. R. *McCulloch, 'A treatise on the succession to property vacant by death' (1848).

[9] Voted in 151 to 119 for it: *H* xcvii. 324.

[10] W. Biggs, 'Never go to war about Turkey' (1847); letters reprinted from the *Leicestershire Mercury*.

[11] A. T. De Vere, *English misrule and Irish misdeeds* (1848).

with Mrs Rawson. I cannot think that matter stands well as it now stands.[1] Conv. with J.N.G. upon it. Read Strauss—English Misrule—H.S. with Willy. Dined at Mr Oliverson's.

10. Fr.

H.S. with Willy. Read Strauss—De Vere—11–1 at Sir R. Peel's on the Debate & subjects of it. I was desired to wait for D'Israeli. H. of C. 4¾–7½ and 8¼–1¼. The last hour & a quarter speaking. Peel was gratified: & that was enough for me—Rising at mid-night I had to throw overboard the chief part of my cargo of figures.[2]

11. Sat.

Marg. Chapel 5 P.M. Wrote to E. Manning—J. & E. Palmer[3]—G.R. Porter—J. Griffith—Sir J.T. Claridge—Saw R Phillimore—Sir J.G—Aunt D.—Sir F. Doyle—Maitland. H.S. with Willy—Read De Vere's 'English Misrule'—Arranging papers &c—Sworn in as special constable[4]—Sir J.G. & nine to dinner—whist.

12. 1 S. Lent.

St Martin's 8½ & 11. St Paul's Knightsbr. 3 P.M.—MS of 44 aloud in evg. Saw Sir J.G—Ld Arundel—Read Vaughan[5]—'The Sure Hope of Reconciliation'[6]—Strauss—Wrote to Manning.[7]

13. M.

Wrote to Cocks & Biddulph—R. Barker—F.J. Brown[8]—J. Griffith—H.S. & Latin Lesson with Willy—Read Strauss—De Vere—Willis on Education Clauses.[9] Sir J.G. Mr Freshfield & Mr Mathews dined & we discussed the O.F. affairs in evg. Worked on O.F. papers. H. of C. 4¾–6½ and 10¾–12½. Voted in 363:138 for 3 years Inc. Tax.[10] An unexpectedly large majority. Finished my Accounts for 1847. Worked on books.

14. T.

Wrote to G. Burnett—Wm. Gladstone—Rev. G. Sandford[11]—Read

[1] A row between Sir J. *Gladstone and Mrs. Rawson of Seaforth, with whom Helen had been staying; cp. Checkland, 326–3.

[2] He followed *Disraeli: *H* xcvii. 438.

[3] i.e. J. H. *Palmer and his partner Edmund.

[4] As part of the precautions against the Chartists. Cp. 10 Apr. 48.

[5] Cp. 7 Nov. and 12 Dec. 47.

[6] By [E. S. Appleyard] (1847).

[7] In Lathbury, ii. 278.

[8] Unidentified.

[9] W. D. Willis, 'Outlines of proposals for the adjustment of the education question between the church and the committee of the privy council' (1848).

[10] *H* xcvii. 532; and spoke on special constables: *H* xcvii. 458.

[11] George Sandford, 1816–98; vicar of St. Jude's, Sheffield, 1846–80, of Eccleshall, Yorkshire, 1880–98.

Strauss—English Misrule (De Vere) (finished)—M'Culloch on Succession—Marriott on V.D. Land[1]—Worked on O.F. papers & prepared a Memorandum on Stephen's affairs: dark, but not hopeless. Saw A. Hope—Blackstone—G[eorge] & Mary (they dined here) on O.F. affairs—H. of C. 5¼–7 and 8½–11.[2]

15. Wed.

Ch Ch Broadway 6 P.M.—& made inquiries about Costello. Wrote to Sir J.G—T.T. Courtenay—Rev. R. Martin—Edwards & Ball—Aunt D.—H.S. with Willy. H. of C. 4¼–6.[3] read Strauss—Lessons to a Young Prince[4]—Le Juif Errant[5]—Corresp. of Educn. Committee of P.C[6]—E. Jones on Welsh Educn.[7]

16. Th.

H.S. with Willy. Read Strauss—Le Juif Errant—Letters to a Young Prince—Worked on O.F. papers—H. of C. 5½–6¾ & after dinner[8]—Dined with the Brownriggs—Saw Sir W. Heathcote—Sir C. Wood—Sir W. James (new Ch).[9]

17. Fr.

Wrote to Whittakers[10]—F. Davis—Sir J.G—G. Burnett—R. Barker—Macray. H.S. with Willy. Saw Sir W R Farquhar—Freshfield—Mr Dalrymple (oculist about Stephen)[11]—Mahon—Attended SPG at 1 to choose the new Abp our President.[12] We have had a great loss. Read Ross on Ch. & State—Nav. Laws Evidence[13]—Strauss—Le Juif Errant. H. of C. 5–7½ and 10½–12½.[14]

18. Sat.

Marg. Chapel 5 P.M. H.S. with Willy. House business & calls. Wrote to R. Barker—Sir J. Claridge—Messrs. G. & Co. Read Strauss—Nav. Laws Ev.—Le Juif Errant.

[1] F. A. Marriott, 'Is a penal colony reconcilable with God's constitution of human society and the laws of Christ's kingdom?' (1847); against transportation.
[2] Voted to retain death penalty: *H* xcvii. 592.
[3] Misc. business: *H* xcvii. 598.
[4] [D. *Williams] *Lessons to a young prince, by an old statesman, on the present disposition in Europe to a general revolution* (1791).
[5] By Eugène Sue (1844–5); see also 25 Oct. 45.
[6] *PP* 1847–8, l. 1.
[7] Evan Jones of Tredegar, *A vindication of the educational and moral condition of Wales in reply to W. Williams* (1848). Cp. 9 Feb. 48.
[8] Medical relief: *H* xcvii. 632.
[9] The Leicester Square project.
[10] Whittaker & Co., booksellers in Ave Maria Lane.
[11] John Dalrymple, 1803–52, of the Royal London Opthalmic hospital.
[12] i.e. J. B. *Sumner, succeeding *Howley.
[13] Cp. 17 Nov. 47.
[14] Irish income tax: *H* xcvii. 701.

19. 2 S. Lent.

St Martins & H.C. 11 AM. Wells St Ch 7 P.M. MS of 44 on Gospel aloud in evg. Conv. with Willy. Wrote on St Joh. VI. 57.[1] Read Vaughan's Serm [2]—Daillé [3]—Sure Hope of Reconc—Strauss—Bp Ridley.[4]

20. M.

Wrote to Rn. G—Cocks & Co—J. Griffiths—J. Macray—W.J. Davidson [5]—T.W. Allies—H.S. and Latin lessons with Willy—H. of C. 5¾–8½ and 9½–1: on the am[oun]t of force for the Navy.[6] Read Strauss—Nav. Laws Ev.—Le Juif Errant. Saw Manson (& wrote notes of pictures)—Ld R. Grosvenor (extension of the Episcopate).

21. T.

Wrote to Sir J G—R. Barker—Mr Braithwaite Poole—Justice Coleridge—Maitland. H.S. with Willy. Commee. on Slave Trade Prevention & H. of C. 12½–6¼.[7] Saw Ld Shaftesbury & Mr Palk, with Hope & Maitland—Ld Redesdale—Freshfields—Bethell—Worked on O.F. Business. Read Strauss—Le Juif—Old Postmaster on Indian Railways.[8]

22. Wed.

Wrote to Sir J.S. Forbes—Miss E. Webley [9]—Mr Usborne [10]—Dowbiggin—Wm Gladstone—H.S. with Willy. Read Strauss—Le Juif—Nav. L. Ev. Attended Chanc. Aff. Office [11]—Saw Ld Hardinge—dined with Ld Abn. meeting M. Guizot & Count Jarnac.

23. Th.

Wrote to R. Barker—Lady Westminster—Dr Greenhill—Saw Lincoln—J.N.G.—Mrs Malcolm—Wm Gladstone (O.F. & SRG.) At Hugh Cholmondeley's marriage 11½:[12] Lady Kinnoul's breakfast at 1—Ld K. spoke to me with much feeling. Read Strauss—Le Juif—Nav. Laws Ev—Hare's Memoir of Sterling [13]—Commee. & H. of C. 2½–4 & 5¾–7.[14] Walk with CG.—H.S. with Willy & now Agnes joins us. Sweeter children I could not desire, scarcely could imagine—Singing in evg.

[1] Cp. Add MS 44780, f. 248.
[2] Cp. 7 Nov. 47.
[3] Cp. 25 Dec. 47.
[4] Cp. 16 Jan. 42.
[5] Of Herries, Farquhar, Davidson, Chapman & Co., London bankers.
[6] Spoke briefly: *H* xcvii. 790.
[7] Misc. business: *H* xcvii. 846.
[8] Not found.
[9] Probably a charity worker at the Rose Street house.
[10] Thomas Usborne, 1810–69; wrote on history and travel.
[11] The chancery affidavit office, Southampton Buildings, London.
[12] He m. as his first wife Lady Sarah, d. 1859, 2nd da. of Thomas Robert Hay 1785–1866, 10th earl of Kinnoull 1804 who m. 1824 Louisa Burton Rowley, who d. 1885.
[13] J. *Sterling, *Essays and tales* (1848); edited by J. C. *Hare, with a memoir.
[14] Repeal of game laws: *H* xcvii. 919.

24. Fr.

Wrote to Sir J.G—S.R.G—T.F. Elliot—F.T. Palgrave—H.S. with Willy & Agnes.—In the city with Mr Pearce[1] & Wm. G. on Stephen's affairs. Then with Freshfield—also saw M'Carthy—E. Coleridge—Pearce (2)—& spoke on Railway Bills. H. of C. 4–8½.[2] Read Strauss—Le Juif—Walpole's Speech on the Jews[3]—Nav. Laws Ev.

25. Annunciation.

Ch Ch Broadway 6 P.M.—H.S. with Willy. Wrote to G. Burnett—R. Barker—Rn. Gladstone—Read Strauss—Le Juif—Nav. Laws Ev—O.F. Statistics[4]—Suggestions on Examn. Statute.[5] The Hopes Lytteltons & Badeley dined. Singing in evg. Saw Dr Worthington.

26. 3 S. Lent.

St Martin's 8½ (H.C.) & 11—St Andrew's Wells St 7 P.M. MS. of 41 aloud.—Conv. with Willy—Read Vaughan—Sure Hope of Reconc. (finished)—Strauss—Daillé—Kennaway's Lent Tract.[6] Saw Sir W. James (new [Leicester Square] Ch).

27. M.

Wrote to T. Turner[7]—Severn—Stooks—H.S. & Latin with Willy. Walk with C. Dined with the Lns. Read Strauss—Le Juif—Nav. L. Ev. Saw Ld Cholmondeley—Pearce & others—Simeon—Sir R. Inglis—H. of C. 4–7 and 10¾–12.[8]

28. T.

Wrote to Pearce—Freshfield—Wm. Gladstone—Sir J.G—Rn. G—R. Barker—D. Perceval—Rev. H. Roberts[9]—H.S. with Willy. Read Strauss—Le Juif—Nav. L. Ev. Commee. 12½–4. House 5¾–8½ & spoke on Railway Commission.[10] Went to Mr Ellison's at 9. Saw Ld Ripon (Claridge)[11] & Ld Hardinge. I had but 3 hours sleep whether from strong coffee or from lack & irregularity in the meals of the day I hardly know. How abundantly is that great blessing permitted to me in general.

[1] George Pearce, underwriter and insurance broker, in Bank Chambers, Lombard Street.

[2] Slave trade: *H* xcvii. 971.

[3] S. H. *Walpole, 'Speech on the 2° of the Jewish Disabilities Bill' (1848); opposing the Bill.

[4] Probably a report from Boydell; sundry in Hawn P.

[5] [B. *Jowett and A. P. *Stanley], 'Suggestions for an improvement of the examination statute' (1848).

[6] C. E. Kennaway, 'Thoughts for the lent season of 1848' (1848).

[7] Probably Thomas Turner, 1804–83; equity draftsman and conveyancer.

[8] Property tax: *H* xcvii. 1021.

[9] Probably Henry Mander Roberts, 1808–67; chaplain of Magdalen, Oxford, 1836–55, of Merton 1852–5; rector of All Saints, Saltfleetby, 1855–67.

[10] *H* xcvii. 1071–5.

[11] See 15 Jan. 48 n.

29. Wed.

Wrote to Wm. Gladstone—Sir J.G—Wrote to Duffy [1]—Gates [2]—Palmer—E. of Lincoln—Principal of BNC—Morpeth—Rev W James—J. Henderson—Redesdale. Read as yesty. H. of C. $1\frac{1}{2}$–$5\frac{3}{4}$.[3] We dined at Sir R. Peel's where were MM. Guizot & Duchatel [4]—Saw Lincoln (R. Commn.).

30. Th.

Wrote to Wm. Gladstone—Abp Canterbury—Lyttelton—Freshfield—Ch Ch Broadway 6 P.M. Saw Ld Redesdale—Gen. Pasley—R. Phillimore—Went to the city: missed Freshfield. Read as yesty. 7 to dinner. H.S. with Willy.

31. Fr.

Wrote to Canning—Bone [5]—Jones—Mrs Keys [6]—Read as Yesty.—& Sterling's Life—H.S. with Willy.—Walk with C. Saw Wm. Gladstone—Haggitt.[7] H. of C. 5–8.[8]

Saturday April One.
1848.

St Paul's Knightsbr. 5 P.M. Wrote to Sir J.G—R. Barker—Lefevre—Dowbiggin—Read as yesty., Louis Blanc for Sterling.[9] Saw General Pasley—Freshfield's Clerk—& others. H.S. with Willy. Walk with C.—dined with the Egertons.[10]

2. 4 S. Lent.

St Martin's 11–2. Marg. Chapel 7 P.M. MS of 43 aloud in evg. Read Strauss—Memoir of Sterling—His Essay on Wiclif [11]—Chr. Rem on Hampden [12]—Engl. Rev. on Ch & St.[13]

3. M.

Wrote to Earl Dalhousie—Ld Braybrooke—R. Barker—G. Burnett—Sir

[1] James Duffy, 1809–71; publisher in Paternoster Row, London.
[2] Perhaps Philip Chasemore Gates, 1824–1914; barrister 1850; Q.C. 1874; recorder of Brighton 1879.
[3] Misc. business: *H* xcvii. 1097.
[4] Charles Marie Tanneguy, comte de Duchâtel, 1803–67; French minister of commerce 1834, of the interior 1841–8; denounced reform in February 1848. Guizot's ministry resigned on 22 February.
[5] Perhaps Henry Pierce *Bone, 1779–1856; society miniaturist and enamelist.
[6] Perhaps the wife of David Keys of Craven Street.
[7] Francis Richard Haggitt, 1824–1911; Peelite M.P. Herefordshire 1847–52; took name of Wegg-Prosser 1849.
[8] Army estimates: *H* xcvii. 1149.
[9] J. J. L. Blanc, *Organisation du travail* (1841).
[10] i.e. the Egerton-Warburtons.
[11] J. *Sterling, *Essays and tales*, i. 30 (1848).
[12] *Christian Remembrancer*, xv. 214 (January 1848).
[13] *English Review*, ix. 157 (March 1848).

J.G—Mrs Keys—C.H. Oakes—J. Barber[1]—Goulburn—Marshall. Saw Sir H. Young—Mrs Larkins—JNG—Northcote. Read Strauss—Le Juif Errant.[2] H.S. & Latin lessons with Willy—H. of C. $4\frac{3}{4}$–$7\frac{1}{2}$ & $8\frac{1}{2}$–12. (Nav. Laws, & Jewish Disabilities.)[3]

4. T.

Wrote to Bone—J. Griffith—Rev. J.H. Woodward[4]—Maitland—H.S. with Willy & A. Read Strauss—Le Juif—Br. Critic on Eccles. Commissions.[5] Commee. & H. of C. 1–4 and $5\frac{1}{2}$–$9\frac{3}{4}$. Spoke on Eccl. Commn.[6] Saw Heathcote —Whittam[7] (Sir JG.).

5. Wed.

Marg. Chapel 5 P.M. Wrote to Ld Braybrooke (& draft) E. Coleridge—Chandos Pole[8]—Seeley—Maitland—Moon—Rowe[9]—Wm. Gladstone—Read Strauss—Le Juif—Merch. Seam. F[inancial] Commn. Report[10]—Saw Beit[11]—Lincoln—H.S. with Willy & Agnes. Attended the very interesting dinner to Hardinge: tho' I cd. have wished it at another season. I sat between Macaulay & C. Wood. Peel's Speech was very nearly a masterpiece.[12]

6. Th.

Wrote to Maitland—Ld Ellenborough—Dodsworth. Worked on the Panton Trust Bill,[13] recasting part of the Preamble. H.S. with W. & A. Commee., Tithe Redemption Trust, & House $12\frac{1}{2}$–$7\frac{1}{4}$.[14] Saw Sir J. Claridge with Goulburn & Thesiger. The Lytteltons dined. Read Strauss—Le Juif—Miall on Church & State.[15]

7. Fr.

Wrote to Sir J.G—R. Barker—Wylie. H.S. with Willy & Agnes. Saw Dr. Harington—J.N.G—Ld Palmerston. Commee at $11\frac{3}{4}$. H. of C. 5–9.[16] Read Strauss—Le Juif—Louis Blanc.

[1] Perhaps John Barber, 1819–83; Gray's Inn barrister from 1843.
[2] Cp. 25 Oct. 45.
[3] Spoke on navigation laws: *H* xcvii. 1207.
[4] J. Henry Woodward, d. *ca.* 1855; curate of St. James's, Bristol.
[5] *British Critic*, xxxiv. 301 (October 1843).
[6] *H* xcvii. 1284; followed and attacked *Bright.
[7] George Whittam, a senior cttee. clerk of the house of commons.
[8] Edward Sacheverell Chandos Pole, 1792–1863; soldier and archaeologist, known as 'The Squire'.
[9] Perhaps Samuel Rowe, 1793–1853; vicar of Crediton, Devon, 1835–53; antiquarian.
[10] Report of the 1846 income and expenditure: *PP* 1847–8, lx. 347.
[11] Dr. Robert Beith, of Greenwich Hospital.
[12] Cp. *The Times*, 6 April 1848, 8c.
[13] Cp. 9 Feb. 48.
[14] Irish waste lands: *H* xcvii. 1356.
[15] E. *Miall, 'The church and state question' (1848).
[16] The chartist petition: *H* xcviii. 4.

8. Sat.

St Andrews Wells St 4 P.M. Wrote to Clowes—Dean of Windsor. H.S. with Willy & Agnes. Read Strauss (which I shall now leave off for a month)—Le Juif—Pietas Oxoniensis [1]—Louis Blanc—Nav. Laws Evidence (finished)—Memoirs of H. Peters.[2] C.G. went to Windsor. Saw Dowbiggin.

9. 5 S. Lent.

St Martins 8½ (H.C.) & 11—St Andrew's 7 P.M.—MS of 34 aloud in evg. Wrote to W. James—Miss Brown. Saw J.N.G—J. Hope (Panton Bill). Read Life of Ricci [3]—of Fletcher [4]—Vaughan's Serm finished—Pietas Ox. finished. Today, the first Sunday for some time my thoughts were not disturbed by the O.F. & Stephen's affairs: but there was a new & sad intrusion in the thoughts of & in conversation about tomorrow.

10. M.

Wrote to Dean of Windsor—Ld Wenlock—Barker—Griffiths—Amery—Read Le Juif Errant. Latin Lesson with Willy. H. of C. 4¾–7 and 9¾–12½.[5] 10–12 to meet C. at the Paddington Terminus with the children. 2–3¾: on duty as special constable. May our hearts feel profoundly the mercies of this very remarkable day.[6]

11. T.

Wrote to S. Ramsey—G. Grant—Roberts—Wylie. H.S. with the children. Finished Le Juif Errant: about wh much might be said. Also read Qu. Rev. on Army—& on French Revn.[7] Saw J.N.G—Wm. Gladstone—Courtenay (on the offers made to him)[8]—Ld Harrowby & Heathcote on do—M. Guizot who came full of congratulations on yesterday. H. of C. 3½–7.[9]

12. Wed.

St James's 3 P.M. Wrote to Sir J.G. H.S. with Willy. Read Young's Letters on Nav. Laws [10]—the Church in Fetters [11]—Ross on Ch. & State—Louis

[1] [Sir R. *Hill], 'Pietas Oxoniensis' (1768).
[2] *The tales and jests of Mr. Hugh *Peters, collected into one volume* (1660).
[3] Cp. 9 May 45.
[4] *The select works and memoirs of the Rev. Joseph Fletcher*, 3 v. (1846).
[5] National security: *H* xcviii. 73.
[6] Feargus *O'Connor's giant chartist demonstration on Kennington Common was washed out by heavy rain.
[7] *Quarterly Review*, lxxxii. 453, 541 (March 1848); on military preparedness, and the French crisis.
[8] Presumably of alternative employment.
[9] National security: *H* xcviii. 153.
[10] A. *Young, *An enquiry into the legality & expediency of increasing the Royal Navy by subscriptions for building county ships* (1783); correspondence with C. Lofft.
[11] Untraced.

Blanc—Grote on Switz[1]—Ellis on Nat. Edn.[2]—Saw Wm. Gladstone—Hon. W. Campbell[3]—Scotts—Conv. with Ashley—saw W. James. H. of C. 5–6.[4] Attended the Carlton dinner to Lord Hardinge.[5]

13. Th.

Wrote to Sir J.G—E.L. Robertson & Co—Barker—Ellis—Macdonald—G. Grant—Griffiths—Elgin—Ld Geo. Bentinck. H.S. with the children. Read Ross on Ch. & State—Commee. 12¾–4. H. of C. 5½–7¼ and 11–12.[6] 10 to dinner incl. M. Guizot. Saw Northcote—also H[elen] in Eaton Place & she came in evg. Her manner is indeed greatly & most favourably changed: let us hope & pray. (see p. 146).[7]

DIPTYCH SEPT. 28. 1847.

The classification is imperfect. Some of the persons are prayed for in mixed regards.[8]

My Father	
Brothers	Thomas Robertson John
Sister	Helen
Sisters in law	Louisa Mary Ellen Elisabeth Mary Lavinia
Brothers in law	Stephen Henry George
Wife...	Catherine
Children.	Willy Agnes Stephen Jessy

[1] G. *Grote, *Seven letters on the recent politics in Switzerland* (1847).
[2] William *Ellis, 1800–81; insurance underwriter; founded schools, and wrote anonymously, *inter alia*, 'A few questions on secular education' (1848).
[3] William Frederick Campbell, 1824–93; lib. M.P. Cambridge 1847–52, Harwich 1859–60; 2nd Baron Stratheden 1860, 2nd Baron Campbell of St. Andrews 1861.
[4] National security: *H* xcviii. 223.
[5] Cp. *The Times*, 13 April 1847, 5b.
[6] Chartist petition: *H* xcviii. 284.
[7] The text breaks off here for the lists, written on 28 September 1847, of people whom the diarist remembered at prayer, and continues on his page 146.
[8] These two sentences up left-hand margin.

Widows.....	Lady F. Hope
	Lady Lothian
	Lady Mordaunt
	Lady Dunmore[1]
	Mrs Wilbraham
	Mrs T. Egerton.
Others in trial or sickness bodily	H. Denison
	R. Neville
	Mrs Lindsay
	[2]Wicklow[3] family
	Lady Vernon
W. Challis	Mr & Mrs Egerton.
L. Cowie[4]	Mr Staniforth
Mrs Sherriffs	Sir J. & Lady H.S. Forbes.
Moore[5]	Arbuthnott family.
On account of spiritual trial, danger, *or* fall	J.H. Newman
	Dr Pusey
	Mr Keble
	Mr Oakeley
C. Christie	Mr Sibthorp
O.B. Cole	R. Williams
Mr Fortescue	J. Williams
Ld Stavordale	
Mr Dyce[6]	W. Palmer (sen)
Lady G. Fullerton	W. Palmer (jun)
W. Hampton	Mr S. Rogers
His wife.	S. Lyttelton
	W.H. Lyttelton.
As friends..	A. Manzoni
	J.R. Hope.
	A. Kinnaird.
	H.E. Manning
	E. Badeley
	W.K. Hamilton
	Dr Hook
	Duchess of Beaufort
	W.R. & Lady J.G. Farquhar.

[1] Lady Catherine Murray, *née* Herbert, d. 1886; da. of 11th earl of Pembroke and sister of Sidney *Herbert; m. Alexander Edward Murray, 1804–45, who succ. as 6th Earl of Dunmore 1836.

[2] 'Let' here deleted.

[3] '& his' here deleted.

[4] Probably of Fasque.

[5] In pencil.

[6] Second col. begins here.

In spiritual offices } Archbishop of Canty.
. . . . York

Bishop of London
. . . . Brechin (vac.)

The Pope

Bishops in the Colonies
especy. Bp Medley [1]
. . Field [sic]
. . Selwyn

and the newly consecrated

Bp Perry
. . Short
. . Gray
. . Tyrrell [2]

Godchildren (ought) [3]
Tyler
Selwyn
Lyttelton
Farquhar
Goalen

In civil authority.
Queen.
Royal family
Ministers
Parliament.

Under the engagement (nightly) }
Aclands, T.D. & A.
Judge Coleridge
F. Rogers
Capt. Moorsom
Mr. Butterfield

M Monsell
Ld Adare
Mr Rhodes
Mr Brett
Mr R. Palmer.

Campbell
Haddan

---

and plans at or in

Fasque
Glenalmond
Leeds

Canterbury
Harrow Weald [4]
Margaret St

St Pancras
Leicester Square
H. of Charity
Engagement &c.

[1] John *Medley, 1804–92; bp. of Fredericton 1845, metropolitan of Canada 1879.
[2] William Tyrrell, 1807–79; bp. of New South Wales 1847–79.
[3] In pencil.
[4] E. *Monro's tractarian church at Harrow.

BOOKS READ AT FASQUE. 1846.

Laing's Notes on the Pilgrimage to Treves.
Scotti's Teoremi di Politica Cristiana Vol. I. II.
Gertrude Vol. II. Vol. I.
Quarterly on Lyttelton's Memoirs & J.G. Phillimore's Reply.
MacCulloch's Adam Smith on the Wealth of Nations Vol. I. II. III. IV.
Casaubon's Epistolae.
Homer's Iliad
Daniel, Réponse aux Provinciales
Dante's Inferno, Purgatorio Paradiso (+)
Döllinger's Kirchengeschichte. Vol. I. II.
Maskell's Dissertations on the Ancient Liturgies &c.
Campbell's Lives of the Chancellors I. II. III.
Homer's Odyssey.
Homeric Hymns Fragments &c.
Dumas' Montecristo I–XII.
Virgil's Æneid (+)
Lady Hester Stanhope's Memoirs I. II. III.
Baup's Précis des Faits Relatifs a la Démission des Pasteurs du Canton de Vaud.
Maurette's Farewell to the Pope.
Gray's Catechism of the Free Church.
Quarty, Chr. Rem., & Engl. Reviews of Octr. divers articles.
The New Timon.
Steinbach on the Punjaub.
Outram's Conquest of Scinde I.
Petrie on the Round Towers of Ireland.
St John on Highland Sports. I. II.
Goliath Slain (by the Author of Pietas Oxons.)
Burnet on the Letter of the French Clergy.
Ld Lindsay's Progression by Antagonism.

April. 1848. London.

14. Fr.

St James's 3 P.M. Wrote to Wm. G—Fraser & Tayleur—H.S. with the children. Saw E. Coleridge—C. Marryat—G. Grant—Ld Harrowby on Edn. Clauses—Bp of Oxford on do—H. of C. before dinner & $10\frac{1}{2}$–$12\frac{3}{4}$.[1] Read Bp Wiseman's letter[2]—Grote on Switzerland—Scrope's Rights of Industry[3]—Worked on my money matters.

[1] National security: *H* xcviii. 340.
[2] N. P. S. *Wiseman, 'Conversion: a letter to Mr. Alexander Chirol and his family on their happy admission . . . to the . . . catholic church (1847).
[3] G. P. *Scrope, 'A plea for the rights of industry in Ireland' (1848).

15. Sat.

Wrote to Godley—Sir J.G. (2)[1]—Reed[2]—Houghton & Co[3]—R. Barker—H.S. with Willy & Agnes. Dined with J.N.G.—Ld Northampton's (last) afterwards. Saw Bp of Oxford—Mr Ricardo—S.H. Northcote—Walpole—Visited the Soup Kitchen & Refuge[4]—Read Grote on Switzerland (finished) —Louis Blanc—Sterling's Essays.

16. Palm Sunday.

St Martins 11–2 (Holy C.)—St James's Evg. Read aloud MS. of 45. Walk with C.—Saw W. James. Read Uffizio[5]—Newman's S.—Ricci's Life—Arnauld, Perpetuité[6]—Grapel's Tract.[7]

17. M.

St Martin's 8 A.M. The Gospel at prayers in mg: evg prayers this week: with Avrillon[8]—H.S. and Latin with Willy. Visited Soup Kitchen with C. & M. Wrote to Wm. Gladstone—Dr. Harington—Dr. Richards—Haddan—Woollcombe—Fraser & Tayleur—Dowbiggin—Lyttelton—Scotts—Griffiths—Amery. Saw Scotts—Ld Ashley—H. of C. $4\frac{3}{4}$–$7\frac{1}{2}$ and $10\frac{1}{4}$–$12\frac{1}{2}$. Spoke on Copper Ores.[9] Read Sterling—Hodgkins L. to Cobden[10]—Watson's Appeal to the Laity.[11]

18. T.

St James's 8 AM. Wrote to Rn. G—R.M. Martin—J.B. Mozley[12]—C. Bond[13] —W. Grapel[14]—Palmer—Freshfield—Wm. Gladstone—Worked on O.F. & S.R.G's. affairs—H.S. with W. & A.—Prayers evg with Avrillon, mg with the Gospel. Read Guizot's Washington[15]—Life of Ricci—Creasy's Sub

[1] Extract from one in Bassett, 75.

[2] Probably sc. Reid.

[3] Stationery manufacturers in Poultry, London.

[4] A plan of Alexis Benoit Soyer, 1809–58, chef, to provide soup kitchens and a hostel for the poor was financed by a picture exhibition; cp. *The Times*, 13 May 1848, 3f.

[5] i.e. the holy office, in Italian.

[6] A. Arnauld, *La perpetuité de la foy de l'église catholique touchant l'eucharistie . . . Deux Dissertations sur le sujet de J. Scot, et de Bertram* (1669).

[7] W. Grapel, 'The church's holy days the only safeguard against the desecration of the Lord's day' (1848).

[8] Cp. 23 Feb. 45.

[9] For the abolition of their duties: *H* xcviii. 440.

[10] T. *Hodgkin, 'A letter to Richard *Cobden on free trade and slave labour' (1848).

[11] Cp. 23 Apr. 42.

[12] James Bowling *Mozley, 1813–78; tractarian; joint-editor of *Christian Remembrancer*; incumbent of Old Shoreham 1856; regius professor of divinity at Oxford from 1871.

[13] Perhaps Charles Bond, 1808–86; bookseller in Covent Garden.

[14] William Grapel, 1821–?86; barrister and author on Roman law.

[15] F. P. G. Guizot, *Washington* (1841).

Rege Sacerdos.[1] Worked on the Treaties, with ref. to Navigation Laws.[2] Saw Hume—Lincoln—Fremantle—Commee. 12–2. House $5\frac{1}{2}$–$7\frac{1}{2}$.[3]

19. Wed.

St Martin's 8 A.M. Prayers mg & evg (Avrillon) & H.S. with Willy & Agnes. Wrote to R. Barker (2)—Sir J.G.—G. Grant—Fraser & Tayleur—Saw Ricardo—Northcote—H. of C. 3–5.[4] Read Life of Ricci—Bunsen's Mema. on Schleswig Holstein[5]—Morning on O.F. & own concerns.

20. Th.

Marg. Chapel & Holy C. $7\frac{3}{4}$–10. MS on the Epistle aloud in evg. Wrote to Freshfield—Sir J. Forbes—Walk with C. & the children. Read Mema. on Schleswig Holstein—Guizot's Washington—European remodellings[6]—Tukes visit to Connaught[7]—Worked on S.R.G.s affairs—Saw Lyttelton—J.N.G—Sir H. Dukinfield.

21. Good Friday.

St Martin's $8\frac{1}{2}$ A.M. (Holy C.)—and 11 A.M. St James's 3 P.M.—Avrillon (with omissions &c. as usual) aloud in evg. Read Things after Death[8]—Arnaud Réponse[9]—Life of Ricci. Wrote Draft Address to H.M. for the parish at Sir H. Dukinfield's request.[10] Wrote also to Sir H.D.—to Barker—G. Grant—Fraser & Tayleur—Rev. J. Bramston:[11] these, most of them, strangely mixed with the appropriate subjects of the day. Indeed these many affairs have been to me during the present week a temptation as well as a necessity. Indeed this solemn time should be passed in retirement to reap the fruit of it, which might be so rich. Deeper and deeper seems to me from year to year the principle of these holy commemorations, as an instrument of our discipline; & God grant that they be not entirely lost, even to such as me.

22. Easter Eve.

St Martin's 11 A.M.—& Margaret Chapel 5 P.M. for that moving service which closes the Church's mourning. Oh may it be granted that we carry

[1] E. S. *Creasy, 'Sub rege sacerdos. Comments on bishop *Hampden's case' (1848).
[2] Probably with reference to the B. of T. memorandum prepared for the select cttee: *PP* 1847–8, xx. 23.
[3] National security: *H* xcviii. 453.
[4] Schleswig Holstein: *H* xcviii. 509.
[5] C. C. J. von Bunsen, *Memoir on the constitutional rights of the duchies of Schleswig and Holstein, presented to Viscount *Palmerston* (1848).
[6] *European remodellings: a plan with a variation* (1848).
[7] J. H. *Tuke, 'A visit to Connaught in the autumn of 1847' (1848).
[8] [J. Miller], 'Things after death; three chapters on the intermediate state' (1848).
[9] Cp. 16 Apr. 48.
[10] An anti-chartist declaration of loyalty to the crown: printed versions in Add MS 44737, f. 27–9.
[11] John Bramston, 1802–89; fellow of Exeter, Oxford, 1825–30; vicar of Baddow, Essex, 1830–40, of Witham, Essex, 1840–72; dean of Winchester 1872–83.

forth with us some of that death of the Lord which is the gate of life, & which she by word & as it were act has been teaching us to realise.

Wrote to Scotts—Fraser & Tayleur—Saw Scotts—Freshfield's Clerk—Read Parad An[imae]—Ricci (finished Vol I)—Avrillon aloud in evg—Cureton's Pref. to St Ath Fest.[1] Helen with J. & E. dined. She is in a state greatly needing guidance & in part at least capable of it: but whence is it to come?

12–2¼. St Martin's Vestry on a congratulatory Address: which was only with difficulty prevented from hauling in Parliamentary Reform.

[1] *The festal letters of Athanasius discovered in an ancient Syriac version, and edited by W. *Cureton* (1848).

[VOLUME XV][1]

[The front fly-leaf contains:—]

Au 49. Owe Bp Oxford 9/6.
Lincoln No 4 D. 12
£7 odd curtain money.
Ap. 11. Not my *last.*[2]

PRIVATE.
WEG.
(NO. 15).

Quisquis bonum majus subire proposuit, bonum minus, quod potuit, sibi illicitum fecit. S. Greg. ap S. Bern. Ep. 94.[3]
Ha poco tempo: e'l poco ch'ha dispensa
con gran misura: e invan nol lascia gire.
Orl. Fur. XLIII. 50.[4]

AP. 23 /48 TO MAY 31. 50.

London.
Easter Day, 1848.
April 23.

St Martin's 8½ A.M. (Holy C.) & 11—Hanover Chapel aft—Wrote MS on Acts 13. 32, 3 & read to servants.[5] Wrote to Sir J.G—Bp of London—W.C. James. Read Newman's S.—Cureton's[6]—Parad. An.—Life of Ricci. Singing.

24. Easter Monday.

Marg. Chapel 5 P.M. H.S. with W. & A. They also breakfasted with C. & me: & we had singing too. Saw Bp of London—Jas Hope—Aunt D—Creswick—Read Guizot's Washington—Ricci—Wrote to Sir C. Pasley—Sir W. James—Fraser & Tayleur—W.K. Hamilton—Wm. Gladstone—Kennedy—Bp of London.

[1] Lambeth MS 1429, 149 ff.
[2] These four lines in pencil.
[3] 'Whoever conceives he may approach a greater good, forbids himself the lesser good that lies within his power.' St. Gregory, on St. Bernard's letters, xciv.
[4] 'He has little time; and what little he has, he lays out with a generous hand; he does not want to wander fruitlessly.' Ariosto, *Orlando Furioso*, xliii. 50. 5–6.
[5] Cp. Add MS 44780, f. 252.
[6] W. *Cureton, *Three Sermons Preached at the Chapel Royal, St. James* (1848).

25. Easter Tuesday: St Mark.

Wells Street Ch 4 PM.—H.S. with Willy. Wrote to Wm. Gladstone—Fraser & Tayleur (P.S.)—Sir J.G—Bp of Edinburgh—E. Badeley. Worked on accounts—& on my books. Saw Mr Maitland.[1] Eight to dinner—singing. Read L. Blanc Org. du Travail[2]—Reginald Dalton[3]—Washington (finished).

26. Wed.

(Found Ch Ch St Giles's shut.) Wrote to Miss Brown—Mr Ellacombe[4]—Jas Alexander—Read Louis Blanc (finished) Ind. Railways. H.S. with Willy. Walk with C—Saw Ld Wenlock on Stephen's affairs. Worked on books & house business. Ten to dinner—singing.

27. Th.

St Andrew's 4 P.M. H.S. with Willy—Wrote to C.A. Wood—G. Grant (Cock St)—Fraser & Tayleur—Saw Wm. G—Palgrave—Scotts—Read Life of Ricci—E.I. Railways (finished)[5]—Reginald Dalton—Osborne's expurgated Horace.[6] Dined with the Jameses.—Music—Walk with C.

28. Fr.

St Paul's Kn[ightsbridge] 5 PM. Wrote to R. Barker (2)—Sir J.G—J. Lefevre—Bp of Edinburgh—J. Maitland—Boyach[7]—Tupper—Ellacombe—Dowbiggin—read Pym on the State of Ireland[8]—Reg. Dalton—Ricci's Life—Publius on Finance & Colonies[9]—H.S. with Willy—Walk with C.

29. Sat.

St George's 5 P.M. Wrote to Sir J.G—G. & Co—G. Grant—Lyttelton—Freshfield—Ellis—Williams & Co[10]—Hamilton—Royal Acad. Exhibn. 2½–4¾, and attended the dinner[11]—Read Now & Then[12]—Pym on Ireland—Ricci's Life (finished) but ill done—H.S. with Willy.

[1] Henry Maitland, Edinburgh stockbroker, through whom Gladstone bought many shares in Scottish railway companies.

[2] Cp. 1 Apr. 48.

[3] [J. G. *Lockhart], *Reginald Dalton*, 3 v. (1823).

[4] Henry Thomas Ellacombe, 1790–1885; vicar of Bitton, Gloucestershire, 1835–50, of Clyst St. George, Devon, 1850–85; authority on church bells.

[5] Cp. 21 Mar. 48.

[6] *Horace: with notes by . . . C. *Girdlestone . . . and W. A. Osborne* (1848).

[7] Probably a pen-slip for Boydell.

[8] J. Pim, *The conditions and prospects of Ireland and the evils arising from the present distribution of property* (1848).

[9] 'Thoughts on finance and colonies, by Publius' (1846).

[10] Chester bankers.

[11] Cp. *The Times*, 1 May 1848, 7f.

[12] Untraced novel; by a tractarian?

30. S. 1 Easter.

St Martins 8½ (Holy C.) & 11—Marg. Chapel 3½. MS. of 43 for the day aloud. singing. Read Flechere's Life[1]—Arnaud's Perpetuité[2]—Col. Ch. Magazine[3]—Worked on Secreta Eucharistica.[4]

May 1. SS. Philip & James. Monday.

Wrote to Sir J.G. H.S. with W. & A—Latin with Willy. Saw Scotts—Lyttelton—Christie—Northcote—Lefevre (Nav. Laws & Annuity)—H. Seymer—Read Pim on Ireland—Now & Then—Blackwood on W.I.[5] H. of C. 5–7.

2. T.

Wrote to Sir R. Peel—Sir J.G—Rev. E. Hawkins—Mr Dickson—Mrs Ellborough[6]—J. Griffiths. Read Pim on Ireland—Now & Then—Danson on Condition of the People.[7]—Saw J.B. Mosley—D. Smith—Warden of H. of Charity[8]—& Lyttelton on Do—Arranging letters & working on accounts.

3. Wed.

Wrote to Lefevre (2)—Sir J.G.—R. Barker—Rev. Mr. Osborne—Dr. Acland—Mr. Aldrich—Fraser & Tayleur—H.S. with Willy & A. Walk with C. A quiet ev[ening] & singing. H. of C. 12¼–2.[9] Saw Lefevre—Read Publius on Finance &c (finished)—Now & Then (finished—an excellent intention but a most indifferent romance—) Sterling on Carlyle[10]—Pim on Ireland.

4. Th.

Wrote to J. Murray—Ashley—F. Davis—Bp of London—Saw Mr Casey[11]—Mrs Henderson—Mr Teed—Dr. Acland[12]—A. Stafford[13]—Sir J. Graham—Sir F. Thesiger—Ld Ashley—Slave Trade Comm. 12½–2½. H. of C. 5–7¼, and 10¼–11¾. Voted with a very clear conscience for the Jews in 234:173.[14]

[1] Cp. 9 Apr. 48.
[2] Cp. 16 Apr. 48.
[3] *Colonial Church Chronicle*, i. 369; more on New Zealand.
[4] Add MS 44834.
[5] *Blackwood's Edinburgh Magazine*, lxiii. 219 (February 1848) on the West Indies.
[6] Unidentified.
[7] J. T. Danson, 'A contribution towards an investigation of the changes . . . in the condition of the people' (1848).
[8] Cp. 6 June 47.
[9] Misc. business: *H* xcviii. 589.
[10] J. *Sterling, *Essays and tales* (1848), i. 252.
[11] Perhaps James R. Casey of Mourilyan & Casey, printers.
[12] (Sir) Henry Wentworth *Acland, 1815–1900; M.D. 1848; professor of clinical medicine, Oxford, 1851, regius professor 1858–94; K.C.B. 1884; cp. Add MS 44091.
[13] Augustus Stafford O'Brien Stafford, 1811–57; tory M.P. N. Northamptonshire 1841–57; sec. to admiralty 1852.
[14] 3°: *H* xcviii. 653. *Inglis spoke against, but abstained. See 16 Dec. 47 and above, iii. xxxiii.

H.S. with W. & A. dined with the R. Nevilles. Read Gioberti's Gesuita Moderno (began)[1]—Sterling on Carlyle.

5. Fr.

Wrote to Rev. H.S. Anders—Fraser & Tayleur—J. Griffiths—M. Welsh—J. Amery—and G. Burnett—H.S. with W. & A.—C. laid up—Saw Dr Hook—J.R. Hope—Judge Coleridge—M. Gladstone—Read Gioberti—Sterling's Carlyle, a very powerful criticism—Loss & Gain[2]—H. of C. 5–7$\frac{3}{4}$.[3]

6. Sat.

Wrote to Sir J.G—Rn. G—JNG—Fraser & Tayleur—N.J. Denison[4]—3–4$\frac{1}{2}$. King's Coll. Prize Distribution. Seconded thanks to the Primate.[5] Saw Ld Harrowby Dr Jelf—Breakf. with Mr Rogers—Ten to dinner—music in evg. H.S. with W. & A. Walk with C. Read Gioberti—Loss & Gain.

7. 2 S E.

St Martin's & Holy C. 11 am—Chapel Royal 5.30 P.M.—MS on Confirmn. aloud. Conv. with Willy. Saw C. Heseltine[6]—Badeley—Wrote to Ld Medwyn—Read Loss & Gain—Gioberti—Life of Fletcher.

8. M.

Wrote to C. Heseltine—Levi Smith[7]—G. Burnett—J. Freshfield—D. Smith & Sons[8]—Read Spanish Correspondence[9]—Loss & Gain (finished)—Reginald Dalton—Gioberti—Pim on Ireland—Kept my bed till noon with a slight influenza.

9. T.

Wrote to Cardwell—Cary[10]—Malet—Maitland—Sir J.G—Northcote—D. Smith & Sons—Laurie—H. of C. 5–7.[11] Lns. dined. H.S. with W. & A. Read Gioberti—Pim on Ireland (finished)—Reginald Dalton—&c.

10. Wed.

Wrote to Dowbiggin—W. Mathews—Sir J.G—H. Maitland—H.S. with W.

[1] V. Gioberti, *Il Gesuita moderno*, 5 v. (1846–7); for notes, cp. Add MS 44737, ff. 42–61.
[2] By [J. H. *Newman] (1848); see above, iii. xlvii.
[3] Public Health Bill: *H* xcviii. 710.
[4] Unidentified.
[5] Cp. *The Times*, 8 May 1848, 3f.
[6] i.e. M. C. Heseltine.
[7] Perhaps a partner in D. Smith and sons.
[8] Daniel Smith and sons, London surveyors and land agents.
[9] On the diplomatic crisis: *PP* 1847–8, lxv. 221.l
[10] Probably Henry Cary, 1804–70; barrister, then curate of Drayton, Berkshire, 1847–1849; went to New South Wales 1849, judge there from 1861.
[11] Misc. business: *H* xcviii. 808.

& A—Saw Alex. Wood—Tupper—& 8–10 attended meeting of the Graphic Society—Walk with C—Read Gioberti—Francis Hist. Bank [1]—Reginald Dalton.

11. Th.

Wrote to J. Foster—J. Freshfield—Sir J.G.—E. Coleridge—Commee. 1½–4. House 4–7 and 10–12¼.[2] Saw Mathews on O.F.—Sir R. Peel, Sir J. Graham, Labouchere, all on Navig. Laws—R. Cavendish, R. Palmer, Sir T. Acland, on the Heresy Clause—Read Gioberti.

Before the opening of the Government plan,[3] I saw Sir R. Peel on the Navigation Laws, having been desirous to converse with him particularly about the question whether we should proceed unconditionally or by way of reciprocity. I explained to him the case of the Swedish Treaty as I conceived it to stand and he on my statement of it agreed with me. He agreed also that if the Govt. should announce an unconditional measure founding it upon the opinion of the Law Officers of the Crown. [sic] On the question whether it would be politic to base our concessions in any manner on reciprocity he gave no further opinion but agreed with me that I should speak to Labouchere & advise against shutting up that question by an official declaration that we were bound by our treaties to proceed unconditionally.[4]

12. Fr.

Wrote to Northcote—Saxton—Fraser & Tayleur—H.S. with W. & A.—Read Gioberti—Reginald Dalton—Goode's Reply to the Bp of Exeter [5]—Francis on the Bank (finished)—H. of C. 4¾–6¼ and 9½–12½.[6] Saw Maitland—R. Palmer—King's Coll. Council 2–3¾.

13. Sat.

(Found St James's shut 3 PM). Wrote to J.H. Parker—Freshfield—Fraser & Tayleur—M. Fitzgerald.[7] H.S. with W. & A.—Rode one of John's horses, by his kind offer: an event for me.—Singing—Saw Mayow—Sir H. Dukinfield—Read Gioberti—Railway Comm[issio]n Report [8]—Reginald Dalton—& Fabliaux.[9] Questo libro comprai perchè avea di dentro il nome del Sig. Grenville cui aveva appartenuto: ed incominciai a leggerlo e vi trovai inqualche parte [10] cose sporche coperte sotto il velo dello linguaggio affatto

[1] Cp. 19 Nov. 47.
[2] Removal of Aliens Bill: *H* xcviii. 851.
[3] 'Today' deleted and this phrase added; probably refers to this day; the govt. scheme was introduced on 15 May.
[4] Finished, initialled and dated 12 December 1848, but written earlier; Add MS 44777, f. 276.
[5] W. *Goode, 'A defence of the thirty-nine articles as the legal and canonical test of doctrine . . . a reply to the bishop of Exeter's remarks . . .' (1848).
[6] Stamford elections: *H* xcviii. 932.
[7] Perhaps Michael Dillon Fitzgerald, London surgeon.
[8] *PP* 1847–8, xxvi. 289.
[9] *Fabliaux et contes des poètes françois des XI–XVe siècles, publiés par Barbazon*, 4 v. 1808; bawdy tales, regarded by Victorians as pornographic. Cp. 19 July 48.
[10] 'del' here deleted.

strano: così,[1] buetti il tossico, peccando, perche vi fu lume benchì oscurato da una nebbia—macchiai la mente e la memoria—che piaccia a Dio purgarmi, che ho bisogno. Ho notato il giorno in nero.[2] Worked on my books.

14. 3 S. Easter.

St Martin's 11 A.M. St James's 7 P.M. Printed S[ermon] aloud in ev.—Walk with C. Read Gioberti—Binney on Nonconformity[3]—Pretyman on Ch. & State[4]—Hares Postscript[5]—King on Gk Church[6]—Saw W. James.

15. M.

Wrote to Mr Hamilton Gray—Sir J.G—W.G—M.F. Tupper—W. Mathews—J. Griffiths—Latin with W—H.S. with W. & A.—Saw Mr Hawes—In the City & saw Freshfield on O.F. Read Gioberti—D'Israeli[7] & Letters to Times on Sleswig[8]—Reg. Dalton—Fabliaux—Anche me altra volta leggendovi ho trovato sotto titoli innocentissimi delle bestialità: doveva aver cirtato le prime presumzioni del male—che sia l'ultima di cotali sperienze vergognose.[9]

16. T.

Wrote to Barker—Reddie—Fraser & Tayleur. Saw Drake—J.N.G—S. Herbert—Read Gioberti—Reg. Dalton—Slave Trade Comm. 12¼–2¼: H. of C. 5–8¼. *Rose* to speak at 8 on Cathedral Establishments:[10] off by Mail Train 8.45 to Birmm.

17. Wed.

Wrote to Fraser & Tayleur—Miss Brennan.[11] Read Gioberti—Reg. Dalton (finished)—In the morning saw Mathews—Griffiths—Coleman. Examined in Court of Bankruptcy 10¾–1½.[12] Off to London at 2½. Dined at Ld Spencer's: Devonshire House afr.

[1] 'però' here deleted.

[2] 'I bought this book because it had within it the name of Mr. Grenville, to whom it had belonged: and I began to read it, and found in some parts of it impure passages, concealed beneath the veil of a quite foreign idiom: so I drank the poison, sinfully, because understanding was thus hidden by a cloud—I have stained my memory and my soul—which may it please God to cleanse for me, as I have need. Have set down a black mark against this day.' Cp. 26 Oct. 45.

[3] T. *Binney, 'Conscientious clerical nonconformity' (1839).

[4] J. R. Pretyman, *Relations of church and state. The church subjugated, not allied to the state* (1848).

[5] Cp. 23 Mar. 48.

[6] Lord Peter *King, *An enquiry into the constitution . . . of the primitive church* (1691).

[7] Probably *Tancred* (1847).

[8] *The Times*, 12, 13 and 15 May 1848.

[9] 'Again, reading in these another time, I have found beastlinesses under the most innocent headings; I should have sheered off at the first hints of evil—may these be the last of such base explorations.' He was perturbed enough by this incident not to record a visit to the commons, where he spoke on the navigation laws (*H* xcviii. 1022–3).

[10] Called for amndt. of 1840 Act: *H* xcviii. 1096.

[11] A companion, first to Lady Glynne, then to Helen Gladstone.

[12] On the affairs of the Oak Farm estate, see *The Times*, 18 May 1848, 7d.

18. Th.

Wrote to Swift—Sir J.G—Saw Campbell—Commee. 12–1¾. H. of Charity 2½–4½. H. of C.[1] Read Gioberti—Huskisson's Sp.[2] Fabliaux: ma bisogna mi pare chiudrei gli ultimi due volumi per sempre avendo caduto anche un altra volta nelle sporcizie: quel male così forte e così sottili in quella età e in questa. Ho letto con peccato benche con disgusto, sotto il pretesto di cercare solamente quello che fu innocente. Ma reo di una prava curiosita, contro tutte le regole di prudenza spirituale e accendendo la guerra tra li migliori parti del uomo e le più basse.[3]

19. Fr.

Wrote to R. Barker—Rev. W. Malet—Fraser & Tayleur—Middleton—H.S. with W. & A. H. of C. 5–8.[4] Queen's Ball afr. Saw Ld Aberdeen—Goulburn —Rev. Sydney Turner.[5] Read Gioberti—Old French poets, (of wh some things good some singular some very bad)[6]—Report of Philanthropic Soc.[7] —Times Articles on W.I. question[8]—Huskisson on Shipping interest.[9]

A sad affair with Henry in evg. and there has been this of Brennans: but both have come as it were to teach me now how I of all men am most bound to gentleness in judging others.

20. Sat.

St Ann's Soho 8¼ P.M. Wrote to Sir J.G—Griffiths—Fraser & Tayleur—Ld Medwyn—Christie & Manson—Sir J. Claridge—Sir H. Dukinfield. Settled with Henry to keep him—& spoke seriously to him: but my words were more due to myself. Saw Mr Vernon's pictures with C.[10]—Lady Arundel's in evg. Read Gioberti—Huskisson—Malden on Universities.[11]

21. 4 S. E[aster]

10½–3½. To Philanthropic Soc's Chapel: luncheon afterwards then meeting

[1] Public Health Bill: *H* xcviii. 1172.

[2] W. *Huskisson, *Speeches*, 3 v. (1831).

[3] 'But it seems to me necessary to shut up these last two volumes for good, having fallen yet again among impurities: how strong and subtle are the evils of that age, and of this. I read sinfully, although with disgust, under the pretext of hunting solely for what was innocent; but—criminal that I am—with a prurient curiosity against all the rules of pious prudence, and inflaming the war between the better qualities of man and the worse.' See also 26 Oct. 45, 22 Feb. 49.

[4] Misc. business: *H* xcviii. 1211.

[5] Sydney Turner, 1814–79; chaplain of philanthropic society for reformation of juvenile offenders 1842–57; prison inspector 1867–75; dean of Ripon 1875–6.

[6] Probably H. F. Cary, *The early French poets* (1846).

[7] *Annual Report* (1848) of the philanthropic society's farm school for the reformation of criminal boys, Redhill, Surrey.

[8] 6 April 1848, 8a.

[9] W. *Huskisson, *Speeches* (1831), iii. 77.

[10] Robert *Vernon, 1774–1849; art patron and collector; presented his collection to the National Gallery in 1847; it was first displayed in 1848.

[11] H. *Malden, 'On the origins of universities and academical degrees' (1835).

in the School & Addresses[1]—St James's evg. MS of 47 aloud in evg. Read Gioberti—Daillé[2]—Wordsw. Sequel to Letters to M. Gondon.[3]

22. M.

Wrote to Sir J.G—R. Barker—C.G. Reid—D. Gladstone—Read Gioberti—Eccl. Commn. Evidence[4]—Chastoiement d'un Fils &c.[5] Latin with W—H.S. with W. & A. Worked much on annuity & money questions. Calls. H. of C. 5–7.[6]

23. T.

Wrote to Lyttelton—Griffiths—Fraser & Tayleur—Isaacson—G.A. Denison. H.S. with the children. Read Gioberti—Eccl. Commn. Evidence—Began D'Azeglio on the Jews.[7] Commee. 12¼–2. H. of C. 5–9½ & 10–11½. Spoke in answer to Ld G. Bentinck.[8]—Saw Sir J. Hobhouse.

24. Wed.

Wrote to Stonhouse[9]—Howis[10]—Neville Jones.[11] H.S. with W. & A. 11–12 at Lincolns with Godley on Sir W. Molesworth's motion.[12] 12–2 Tithe Redemption Trust. King's Coll. to 4: J. Manners's on Sisterhood of Mercy 5–6½. dined with the Hudsons—Duke of Devonshires ball afterwards. Read Gioberti Vol 2—'Cheap Sugar'.[13]

25. Th.

Wrote to Middleton—Barker—Fraser & Tayleur—Dowbiggin—Bowdler—Sewell—Maskell—Ld Shrewsbury. Commee. 12¼–2¼. House 5–7¼.[14] H.S. with W. & A. Dined at Lady Wenlock's. Went into physic for an attack of Engl. Cholera[15] with a slight reappearance (yesty.) of the inflammatory symptoms of last autumn in my right arm. Read Gioberti.

[1] No report found.
[2] Cp. 25 Dec. 47.
[3] Christopher *Wordsworth *fils*, 'Sequel to letters to M. Gondon, on the destructive character of the church of Rome' (1848).
[4] Perhaps the second report of the Ecclesiastical Commissioners: *PP* 1847, xxxiii. 233.
[5] 'Le chastoiement d'un père à son fils' in *Fabliaux et Contes*, ii. 39; cp. 13 May 48.
[6] Misc. business: *H* xcviii. 1236.
[7] M. Tapparelli d'Azeglio, *Dell' emancipazione civile degl' Israeliti* (1848).
[8] On distress and free trade: *H* xcviii. 1265, 1305.
[9] Probably William Brocklehurst Stonehouse, 1792–1862; vicar of Owston, Lincolnshire, 1822–62; ecclesiastical historian.
[10] Perhaps William Howis, gentleman, of Woburn Place.
[11] 1809?–91; vicar of St. George's, Bolton, 1847–91.
[12] *Molesworth's motion on the reduction of colonial expenditure, moved eventually on 25 July 1848, cp. *H* c. 816.
[13] Cp. 6 Nov. 47.
[14] Spanish diplomatic crisis: *H* xcviii. 1410.
[15] Bilious diarrhoea and cramps, usually occuring in late summer and early autumn.

26. Fr.

Kept my bed till near noon. Wrote to Sir J.G—A. Turner—Ld Jermyn—Read Gioberti—Libri[1]—Burke—H. of C. Commees 12¼–4½.[2] Singing with Willy.

27. Sat.

Wrote to A. Turner—A. Williams—Dr Spry—Fraser & Tayleur. Read Gioberti—The Madrid Correspondence.[3] H.S. with the children. Tea with Ld & Lady Somers. Drive with C: & attended the drawingroom. Saw Goulburn—Bp of Bath & Wells.

28. 5 S. E.

St Martins mg—St James's evg. C. read for me—my arm more angry. How gently almost imperceptibly am I touched. Walk with C—Read Gioberti—Libri—Daillé—Newman's Sermons.

29. M.

Wrote to G. & Co—Rn. G—Fraser & Tayleur—Read Gioberti—Libri—Ricardo on Nav. Laws[4]—H.S. with W. & A.—singing—H. of C. 5–8. Put off speaking [on the navigation laws] on acct. of the state of my arm.[5] Saw Goulburn—Northcote—

30. T.

Wrote to Helen—Hutt—Godley. H.S. with the children—Saw Locock—Silvertop—Ld J. Russell. Read Gioberti—Libri—Lords Ev. on Nav. Law.[6] H. of C. 6–8¾ and 9½–10¾.[7]

31. Wed.

Wrote to Fraser & Tayleur. H. of C. 3–6.[8] Dined at Sir R. Inglis's. Up late: & my arm very troublesome—Saw Godley—conv. with Abp of Canterbury—Read Gioberti—& began Kingsley's Saint's Tragedy.[9]

[1] G. B. I. T. Libri Carrucci dalla Sommaia, probably his *Histoire des sciences mathematiques en Italie*, 4 v. (1838–41).
[2] Supply: *H* xcviii. 1422.
[3] Cp. 8 May 48.
[4] J. L. *Ricardo, *The anatomy of the navigation laws* (1847).
[5] *H* xcix. 9.
[6] House of Lords *Journals*, 1848, lxxx.
[7] Spoke briefly about bakeries: *H* xcix. 17.
[8] Roman catholic relief: *H* xcix. 134.
[9] C. *Kingsley, *The saint's tragedy; or the true story of Elizabeth of Hungary* (1848) with an introduction by J. F. D. *Maurice.

Thursday June One.
Ascension Day.

St James's 11 AM. & Holy Communion. The interval since the last has been painful: I have been sorely beaten in fight, and have had too much room to doubt whether I really fought at all in earnest.[1] Better accounts came today of my Father: whose new attacks had given cause for serious uneasiness. Wrote to G. Denison—W. James—Messrs. Williams (skeleton). Read Libri—Ricardo. H.S. with children. My arm thank God began to improve. H. of C. 5–7.[2] Dined at Baron Parke's.[3]

2. Fr.

Wrote to G. Grant—Fraser & Tayleur—Sir J.G—H.J.G—Aunt J. Saw R. Barker—H.S. with W. & A. Commee. 12¼–3. House 4¾–7. Spoke under 1½ hour on the Navigation Laws. House again 11–12.[4] Read Gioberti—Dined with the Kynastons.

3. Sat.

Wrote to Anders—Felton[5]—Thom—A. Turner—Tupper—Dunning—Scott Russell—Freshfield—Saw R. Barker—M. Hutt—Bp of Brechin—Goulburn—Reddie—H.S. with the children—Dined at Ld Arundel's—Read V.D.L. papers[6]—Our dear Willy's birthday: wh brings for the future no other wish than that he may continue to grow as he has grown hitherto in grace & wisdom.

4. S. aft. Ascension.

St Martin's & Holy C. 11–1¾. Marg. Chapel aft. MS of 42 aloud. Walk with C. Conv. with Willy. Read Gioberti—Bensons Fletcher—Newman—B. & F. Rev. on Cathedral Service.[7]

5. M.

Wrote to Dowbiggin—Abp of Canterbury—H. Glynne—Miss Brown—R. Barker—G. Burnett—J. Griffiths—H. Wilberforce—Cocks & Co—V. Chancellor—Prov. Oriel—Pres[ident] St John's—Mast. University.[8] Latin with W.—H.S. with W. & A. Walk with C. Dined at Mr Wynne's. H. of C. 4¾–7 and 11–1¼.[9] Read Gioberti.

[1] Cp. 7, 13 and 18 May 48.
[2] Navigation laws: *H* xcix. 179.
[3] i.e. Sir James *Parke.
[4] *H* xcix. 251–73.
[5] Perhaps John Felton, London coach maker.
[6] *PP* 1847–8, xlvii. 679.
[7] *British and Foreign Quarterly Review*, xvi. 397 (1844).
[8] Frederick Charles Plumptre, 1796–1870; master of University College, Oxford 1838–70; vice-chancellor 1848–51.
[9] Spanish crisis: *H* xcix. 347.

6. T.

Wrote to E.L. Robertson & Co—Lyttelton—Hickey—Felton—Rn. G—Sir R. Bromley—Greswell—H. Maitland—Barker—Fraser & Tayleur—H.S. with the children. Committees & House 12–4 and 5–7. Saw Hutt—H. Wilberforce—& Collis—10 to dinner & party in evg. Read Burke.

7. Wed.

Wrote to T. Williams[1]—H[elen] J. Gladstone—Cocks & Co—T.G. H.S. with W. & Agnes—Saw Walesby[2]—T.D. Acland—Coleman (O.F.). Read Sharpe to Ld Auckland[3]—Bourne on E.I. Railways[4]—H. of C. & N.S. meeting 2¾–6¾.[5] Dined at Ld Arundel's—Ld Foley's afterwards.[6]

8. Th.

Wrote to J. Griffith (2)—Rev. T. Andrewes—Rev. T. Shadforth[7]—Saw Mr Dowbiggin—Freshfield—S.R.G (on his affairs) Read Gioberti—Libri Appx—H.S. with the children—Commee. 12–1½. Took the chair at Spitalfields School of Design meeting 2½–4½.[8] Dined with Ly Wenlock—& House 9¾–12.[9]

9. Fr.

Wrote to Bp of London—Claridge—Sir H. Dukinfield—Sir J.G—H.J.G—Fraser & Tayleur—H. Maitland—Barker—Dunning—Sir J.C. Hobhouse. Went with C. to B[edford] Square where we learned from Mr Tyler that there is no hope of Good & kind Aunt Divie's life. Saw Sir J. Hobhouse—Thesiger. H. of C. 9¾–2¼: voted in 294:177 on Nav. Laws—not over good discipline for my arm.[10] H.S. with the children—Read Gioberti—Libri—Huskisson's Speeches.

10. Sat.

Wrote to Mr Greswell (2)—Ph. Palmer[11]—J. Griffiths—R. Cavendish—Lieut. Sharpe[12]—J. Macdonald—J.M. Macdonald[13]—Evan Lewis[14]—Saw

[1] Probably Thomas Williams, 1801–77; archdeacon of Llandaff 1843–59, dean 1857–77.
[2] Francis Pearson Walesby, 1798–1858; professor of Anglo-Saxon at Oxford 1829–34; recorder of Woodstock, near Oxford, from 1845.
[3] Probably an untraced letter by lieutenant Sharpe, cp. 10 June 48.
[4] J. Bourne, *Railways in India* (1848).
[5] Scottish Worship Bill: *H* xcix. 476.
[6] Thomas Henry Foley, 1808–69; whig M.P. Worcestershire 1830–33; 6th Baron Foley 1833.
[7] Thomas Shadforth, 1816–87; tutor of University College, Oxford, 1846–58; proctor 1848; vicar of Hersham, Surrey, 1861–78, of Beckley, Kent, 1878–87.
[8] No report found.
[9] Navigation Laws: *H* xcix. 510.
[10] *H* xcix. 670.
[11] Philip Hall Palmer, 1802–79; rector of Woolsthorpe, Lincolnshire, 1844–78.
[12] Perhaps William Henry Sharpe Sharpe, lieut. in royal regiment of foot 1847; wanted help in promotion?
[13] Unidentified.
[14] Evan *Lewis, 1825?–69; independent minister; author of pietistic tracts.

Mr Woodward—Sir H. Dukinfield—Mr Tyler in B. Square who told us of my Aunt's peaceful end—she is I trust at rest in God. Kept my bed early in the day. Read Parl. papers—Gioberti—The Saint's Tragedy—Revolution of 1848.[1]

11. Whitsunday & St Barnabas.

St Martins $8\frac{1}{2}$ (Holy Commn.)—and 11—St Jamess 7. P.M. Wrote on St Barn[abas] Day.[2] Read aloud MS of 42. Walk with C. Read Life of Fletcher —Gioberti.—Reviewing my life with reference to the engagement made some years since, I have to note 1. that my feeble efforts at abstinence have been sadly checked since the autumn—by the state of my arm & of the nervous system: 2. that the H. of Charity has become less suitable than it was to affording me ever so little scope for works of mercy: 3. that I have fallen more seriously within the last month than for between 2 & 3 years. Here is cause for much sadness, may it be also fruitful.

12. Whitm.

The day appointed for disturbances: but all was as tranquil as possible thro' God's mercy. I kept at home waiting a summons as spec[ial] constable.[3] Wrote to Sen. Proctor[4]—Jun. Proctor[5]—Sir J.G—R. Barker—Sir R. Peel —Mr Gullick[6]—Fraser & Tayleur—H.S. with W. & A.—Latin with W. Singing. Read Gioberti—Strauss[7]—Kingsley's St Elizabeth[8]—Scott on Prop. Tax[9]—R. Phillimore on Congè d'Elire.[10]

13. Whit Tuesday.

St James's 11 A.M. Wrote to Sir W. James—J.E. Tyler—Poulter—G. & Co —Rn. G—Greswell—Dr Wellesley[11]—Vice-Chancellor—Dr Cotton—J.E. Coleman. Read Gioberti—Bp of St David's Speech[12]—1–$5\frac{1}{2}$ Drove down to

[1] C. R. Cameron, *The revolutions of 1848: a recommencement of the judgments upon the papacy* (1848).

[2] Cp. Add MS 44780, f. 256, and above, iii. xliv. St. Barnabas was the engagement's patron saint and it met on his day, cp. 23 Feb. 45.

[3] A further chartist demonstration, announced for this day, never took place; cp. 10 Apr. 48.

[4] T. Shadforth.

[5] Martin Johnson Green, fellow of Lincoln, Oxford, 1837–49; rector of Winterbourne Abbas, Dorset, from 1848.

[6] Possibly Thomas Gullick, bootmaker in Regent Street.

[7] Cp. 15 Feb. 48.

[8] Cp. 31 May 48.

[9] Probably J. Scott, 'A letter to the Chancellor . . . on his proposed sale of the Land Tax' (1798).

[10] R. *Phillimore, 'The practice and courts of civil and ecclesiastical law, and the statements in Mr. Bouverie's speech on the subject, examined . . . in a letter to . . . Gladstone' (1848).

[11] Henry *Wellesley, 1791–1866; D.D. 1847; principal of New Hall, Oxford, 1847–66; antiquary.

[12] C. *Thirlwall, 'Speech in the house of lords, May 25th' (1848); on the Jewish Disabilities Bill.

Dropmore:[1] we found Lady G[renville] most kind as before, & Sir F. Lewis[2] singularly well informed.

14. W.

Walk with C. & baby. Read Gioberti—Hobhouse (on Troas)[3]—& foraged amid the books—We find Mrs Greville Howard[4] an intelligent & excellent person.

15. Th.

Visited Hedsor & Clifden[5]—what a constellation of beautiful places. Read Gioberti—Hobhouse—Chandler.[6]

16. Fr.

St George's Windsor 10½ A.M. Went round it afr.—Breakfast at the Deanery: having left Dropmore at 8½. Reached town at 3½. H. of Commons 5¼–11. W.I. & Nav. Laws.[7] Wrote to Sir J.G—G.E. Anson—H. Maitland—G. & Co. Read Gioberti—Denman on Afrn. Slave Trade.[8] Saw Thesiger—Lincoln—Sir R. Inglis.

17. Sat.

Wrote to Drake—Griffiths—Cardwell—O.B. Cole—W. Maskell[9]—Christie & Manson—Duke—Bromehead[10]—Wilson & Pedder[11]—Aunt Divie's funeral took place today: at Kensal Green: & occupied me 9½–1. We did not see my Uncle, whom God support. Went up with the Oxford Address at 3.[12] Saw the Provost of Worcester. At Cardwell's on the W.I. question 4½–7¼. Tea at Lady Brabazon's.

18. Trin. S.

—St Martins (& H.C.) 11–2. St James's at 7. MS of 41 aloud in evg. Conv. with Willy. Walk with C. & the children—Wrote to W. James—& draft Address to Sir H. Dukinfield[13]—Read Gioberti (finished Vol 2) and Benson's Life of Fletcher.

[1] Cp. 7 June 45.
[2] i.e. Sir T. F. *Lewis.
[3] J. C. *Hobhouse, *A journey through Albania*, 2 v. (1813); letter xlii.
[4] Mary, *née* Howard, m. 1807 Fulke Greville Upton, 1773–1846, soldier, br. of 1st Viscount Templetown. He took surname of Howard.
[5] Cliveden is 1 mile SW. of Dropmore; Hedsor lies between the two.
[6] J. Chandler, *Horae Sacrae: private prayers and meditations* (1848).
[7] *H* xcix. 729.
[8] T. *Denman, 'A letter from Lord Denman to Lord *Brougham, on the final extinction of the slave trade' (2 ed., 1848).
[9] Copy in Add MS 44367, f. 198.
[10] Probably Joseph Crawford Bromehead, 1810?–1902; Caius, Cambridge, barrister, equity draftsman and conveyancer.
[11] Liverpool shipwrights; Cuthbert Pedder lived in Toxteth Park.
[12] Convocation declared its loyalty to the crown. Cp. *The Times*, 19 June 1848, 8d.
[13] Cp. 21 Apr. 48.

19. M.

Wrote to Sir J.G—Miss G—W. Mathews—Mr Hamilton Gray—Barker—Palmer—Latin lesson to Willy—Meetings at 10 & $3\frac{1}{2}$ on the W.I. relief. Saw Sir R. Peel but no one extracted even an inkling from him. H. of C. $4\frac{1}{4}$–$8\frac{1}{4}$ and $9\frac{3}{4}$–12.[1] Saw R. Neville—Hobhouse—Read Field on Pr. Discipline[2]—W.I. papers.[3]

20. T.

Wrote to Wm. Gladstone—R. Cavendish—Fox Maule—Fraser & Tayleur—Griffiths—Geo. Chance[4]—Dr. Russell—Ld Harris—Saw W. Mathews—Manning—E. Coleridge—Graham—Cardwell, Lincoln, Goulburn, Wortley, on W.I. Debate. Nothing known of Sir R. Peel's intentions. H. of C. & Commee. $12\frac{1}{4}$–$2\frac{1}{4}$, 4–7, and 10–$1\frac{3}{4}$.[5]—H.S. with W. & A. Read W.I. Papers—South Western Case[6]—Guage [sic] Report.[7]

21. Wed.

Wrote to Dean of Windsor—W.M. Church—R. Barker—G. & Co—Rn. G—H.S. with the children—H. of C. & Tithe Red. Trust 12–$2\frac{1}{4}$.[8] Saw Lincoln—Cardwell—Sir W.C. James—Ramsays. Read W.I. papers—Eton Case[9]—Dined at J.N.G.s.

22. Th.

Wrote to Sir J. Claridge—Saw Sir R. Peel on the W.I. Question: he is in real & great difficulty as to the proper measures to be taken about the W.I. as indeed all are. Also Cardwell—Drake. Read Field on Prison Discipline—Jelly on Jamaica[10]—W.I. Commee. evidence. H. of C. 4–8 and $8\frac{3}{4}$–12. Spoke $1\frac{1}{4}$ hour on the W.I. Question[11]—H.S. with the children.

23. Fr.

Wrote to Northcote—Greswell—R. Pennefather[12]—Griffiths—Scotts—Fraser & Tayleur—Mathews—G. Chance. H.S. with the children. Read Jelly on Cond. of England[13]—Field—Kingsley's St Elizabeth (finished)—

[1] Sugar duties and the West Indies: *H* xcix. 811.

[2] J. Field, *Prison discipline. The advantages of the separate system of imprisonment, as established in the county gaol of Reading* (1846).

[3] Probably the 'Reports exhibiting the past and present state of the West India colonies': *PP* 1847–8, xlvi. 1.

[4] George Chance, 1819–1903; Trinity, Cambridge; barrister at Lincoln's Inn from 1846.

[5] National representation: *H* xcix. 879.

[6] *PP* 1847, xxxi. 33.

[7] *PP* 1846, xxxviii. 371, 377.

[8] *H* xcix. 971.

[9] 'Speech of counsel . . . on behalf of . . . Eton against the G.W.R. extension' (1848).

[10] T. Jelly, 'A brief inquiry into the condition of Jamaica' (1847).

[11] *H* xcix. 1014.

[12] Richard *Pennefather, 1773–1849; under-secretary for Ireland 1845.

[13] T. Jelly, 'A cursory glance at the past and present condition of Great Britain' (1848); on sugar.

H. of C. 5–7½ and 11–12¼.[1] Attended Col. Bishoprics' Committee—Saw Hobhouse—& the West Indians. Dined at Ld Hardinge's.

24. St John Baptist. Sat.

Marg. Chapel 5 P.M. Wrote to Sir H. Dukinfield—Sir J.G—T.G—R[obertso]n G—G. Grant—Lyttelton—Miss Lyttelton. Saw Scotts—W. Alexander. H.S. with children—Walk with C.—many calls. Dined with Mr G. Harcourt. Read Woodard's Plea for the Middle Classes[2]—Field—Macgregor[3]—Sir R. Gardiner's Report[4]—Coal Whipper's Report.[5]

25. 1 S Trin.

St Martin's 8½ (H.C.) 11 and 3 P.M.—read aloud MS of 47 for yesterday—Conv. with Willy. Wrote to E. Coleridge—B. Harrison. Read Daillé (finished) Field on the Church (began)[6]—Benson's Life of Fletcher—Dean of West[minste]rs reopening Sermon[7]—Bp NZ Serm. at his College[8]—& Harrison's Charge:[9] the two last most deeply interesting.

26. M.

Wrote to Walesby—Wm. Gladstone—C. Gray[10]—Prickett—Hulland[11]—H.J.G. H.S. with children. Latin with Willy. Read Field—Fane on 'a Minister of Justice[12]—Suffrage Petitions.[13] Saw Thesiger—Aunt J—J. Casey. H. of C. 5–8½ and 9¾–12¼.[14]

27. T.

Wrote to Mr C. Fane—Connor—Shadforth—V[ice] C[hancellor]—Greswell—Raikes—R. Gardner. Saw Northcote. H.S. with the children. Eccl. Comm. Committee 12–2½.[15] Drive with C. & calls—Singing. Read Field—Causes Celebres[16]—Morrison on Railways.[17]

[1] Sugar duties: *H* xcix. 1089.
[2] N. *Woodard, 'A plea for the middle classes' (1848); on education.
[3] Cp. 9 Jan. 43.
[4] Sir R. W. *Gardiner, 'Report on the numerical deficiency, want of instruction, and inefficient equipment of the artillery of the British army' (1848).
[5] 'Receipt and expenditure of the coalwhippers' office', *PP* 1847, xlvi. 69.
[6] Richard *Field, *Of the church five bookes* (1606).
[7] W. Buckland, 'A sermon preached . . . on the reopening of the choir . . .' (1848).
[8] G. A. *Selwyn, 'An idea of a colonial college' (1848); on I Sam xix. 20–24, preached in Auckland.
[9] B. Harrison, 'The remembrance of a departed guide and ruler in the church of God' (1848).
[10] Perhaps Charles *Gray, 1782–1851; Scottish composer and antiquary.
[11] Probably Richard Hulland, sheriff's officer of Lincoln's Inn.
[12] R. G. C. *Fane, *Ministry of Justice; its necessity as an instrument of law reform* (1848).
[13] Untraced.
[14] Sugar duties: *H* xcix. 1217.
[15] He was occasionally consulted by the ecclesiastical commissioners about this time, cp. G. F. A. Best, *Temporal Pillars* (1964), 357.
[16] *Causes célèbres étrangères publiées en France pour la première fois*, 5 v. (1827–8).
[17] James *Morrison, *The influence of English railway legislation on trade and industry* (1848).

28. W.

Ch Ch Broadw[ay, Westminster]. 6 P.M. H.S. with the children. *Wrote* to Dean of Westminster—Bp of N. Zealand—Malet—Maitland—Barker—E. Coleridge—Griffiths—E. Wilmot Chetwode. Dined with Tomline[1]—Queen's Concert afterwards—Saw Lincoln. H. of C. 12–6.[2] Read Field—Bp White on Amn. Church.[3] Helen's birthday recurs with less dark aspect thank God; & the very great mercies of the last year should make us hope & pray for the addition of more.

29. St Peter. Th.

Wells St Ch. at 4 P.M. H.S. with the children—Wrote to Sir J.G—Fraser & Tayleur. Read Harle on Navig. Laws[4]—Field. H. of C. 5¼–7 and 10½–1½: voted in 245:260 agt. ministers.[5] Commee. 12–1½. Visited the Abbey: where too little has been done or too much.[6] Eight to dinner—singing.

30. Fr.

Wrote to Geo. Grant—R. Creed[7]—Fraser & Tayleur—Aunt J.—R. Greswell Mr Twist[8]—Clarke. Eccl. Commn. Commee 12–2½. King's Coll. 3–4½. H. of C. 4¾–7¼ & 10¼–1.[9] H.S. with the children. Dined at Ld Braybrooke's.

Sat. July One. 1848.

St Andrew's Wells St 4 P.M. Wrote to Shannon—J. Griffiths—Cocks & Co—Shadforth. Saw Kinnaird—Bp of Oxford—H.S. with children—Lady Westminster's in evg—Read Field—Woolcombe [sic] on Poor Scholars[10]—Martin on Sugar Question[11]—Northcote (2) on Navig. Laws.[12]

2. S. 2 Trin.

St Martins & H.C. mg—St James's evg. MS of 42/ aloud in evg. Walk with

[1] George Tomline, 1812–89; tory M.P. Sudbury 1840–1, Shrewsbury 1841–7, 1852–68; picture collector; lived in 1 Carlton House Terrace.

[2] Misc. business: *H* xcix. 1289.

[3] W. White, *Memoirs of the protestant episcopal church in the United States of America* (1820).

[4] W. L. Harle, 'The total repeal of the navigation laws, discussed and enforced, in a letter to Earl *Grey' (1848).

[5] Sugar duties: *H* xcix. 1396. The Peelites were completely split, Gladstone, *Cardwell, *Herbert and others voting with the tories, *Peel, and *Graham with the whigs.

[6] Probably G. G. *Scott's restoration of the choir stalls, done this year.

[7] Perhaps Edward Richard Creed, barrister from 1827.

[8] Thomas Kenyon Twist, Liverpool merchant.

[9] Sugar duties cttee: *H* xcix. 1413.

[10] E. C. Woollcombe, 'University extension and the poor scholar question' (1848).

[11] R. M. *Martin, 'The sugar question, in relation to free trade and protection' (1848).

[12] Drafts by S. H. *Northcote for his pamphlet 'A short review of the history of the navigation laws of England' (1849); cp. A. Lang, *Sir Stafford *Northcote* (1890), i. 72–3.

C. Read Benson's Fletcher (finished)—Arch. Wilberforce's Charge[1]—Xtn Rem. on Webb[2]—Eng. Rev. on The Papacy—& on Rest in the Church.[3]

3. M.

Wrote to Williams & Co—Adin Williams—H. Chester—R. Greswell (2)—Ld Campden—Scotts—Fraser & Tayleur. Saw Cardwell & Barkly.[4] Conv. with Willy—H.S.—& Latin. Read Cole on Public Schools[5]—Field—Hist. American Church. Arranged letters & papers.

4. T.

Wrote to A. Williams—C. Gerard[6]—H. Maitland—G. & Co—Sir J.G—Mrs Stürmer[7]—C.G. Reid—Manning—J. Griffiths. Read Field—Ed. Rev. on Strauss's Julian—Academ. Tests[8]—Niccolo de' Lapi.[9] Eccl. Comn. Commee. 12–2¼. H. of C. 5¼–7½. Spoke 20 m. on Railway Commn.[10] Saw B. Moore[11] & C. Saunders[12]—Off at 8½ PM for Nuneham—midnight walk from the Station.

5. Wed.

With scarcely a glance at this pretty place I went off as did a large party after breakfast to Oxford: joined the V.C. and doctors in the Hall at Wadham: and went in procession to the Divinity Schools provided with a white neckcloth by Sir R. Inglis who seized me at the Station in horror & alarm when he saw me with a black one.[13] In due time we were summoned to the Theatre where my degree had been granted with some non placets but with no scrutiny. That scene so remarkable to the eye & mind, so pictorial & so national, was I think trying to Cath. but she has no want of strength for such things. There was great tumult about me mite that I am: the hissers being obstinate & the fautores[14] also very generous & manful. 'Gladstone & the Jew Bill' came sometimes from the gallery, sometimes more favouring sounds. The proceedings lasted till two. Then we went to luncheon & speeches at University: then to a long but interesting concert at

[1] R. I. *Wilberforce, 'Relations of church and state; a charge . . .' (1848).
[2] *Christian Remembrancer*, xvi. 27 (July 1848); on B. Webb's *Sketches of continental ecclesiology* (1848).
[3] *English Review*, ix. 255 (June 1848).
[4] (Sir) Henry *Barkly, 1815–98; Peelite M.P. Leominster 1845–8; governed British Guiana 1848–53, other colonies 1853–70, the Cape 1870–7; K.C.B. 1853.
[5] H. Cole, *A manual of practical observations on our public schools* (?1848).
[6] G. P. Gerard, probably a pauper; Gladstone gave him £1.
[7] Perhaps the wife of Karl Stürmer, 1803–81, fresco painter, especially of religious subjects.
[8] *Edinburgh Review*, lxxxviii. 94, 163 (July 1848).
[9] By M. d'Azeglio (1841).
[10] *H* c. 119.
[11] i.e. J. Bramley Moore.
[12] Charles Alexander Saunders, 1797–1864; secretary of Great Western railway from 1833.
[13] As a new burgess, he was made a doctor of civil law, *honoris causa*, at the Encaenia; attempts to get the Hebdomadal Board not to recommend him had failed, cp. Ward, 146.
[14] 'Supporters'.

4: after this & a rest for C. in New College Gardens to the Provost of Oriel's for tea; finally to town at half past nine & we were in our own house at twelve. Reading the arrivals of the day, & ordinary duties, sent me to bed after half past one.

6. Th.

Wrote to E. Coleridge—Fraser & Tayleur—Miss Robertson—E. of Dalhousie—Messrs. Coutts—Thornton—Williams & Co—Sir H. Dukinfield—Smee—Gerard—Foster—J. Bramston. Saw Fraser Tytler. H.S. with W. & A. Westmr. Abbey 3 P.M. Slave Trade Comm. $1\frac{1}{2}$–3. H. of C. 4–$7\frac{1}{4}$ and 11–1.[1] Dined with the Hopes. Read Field.

7. Fr.

Wrote to Scotts—Amery—R. Barker—J. Griffiths—Phillimore—Waylen—Mills. Eccl. Commn. Commee. 1–3. Saw Northcote—H. of C. $4\frac{3}{4}$–$8\frac{3}{4}$ and $10\frac{1}{4}$–$12\frac{1}{2}$. Spoke $\frac{3}{4}$ hour on W.I. question & finance in particular.[2] Read Field—Niccolo de' Lapi.

8. Sat.

St Andr. Wells St 4 P.M. Wrote to H. Maitland—Fraser & Tayleur—G. Burnett—Sir J.G—J. Griffiths—W.U. Richards—C. Blackwell[3]—G. Chance—R. Warburton—H.S. with W. & A.—Dined at Ld R. Grosvenor's—Read Field—Higgins's 3d Letter to Ld J. Russell[4]—Quarterly on Countess of Ossory & on Sir T.F. Buxton.[5]

9. 3 S Trin.

St Martin's $8\frac{1}{2}$ (H.C.) & 11.—St James's 7 P.M.—MS of 46 aloud to servants—Conv. with Willy—Read Memoirs of Amern. Ch—Manning's Sermons[6]—Reunion des Religions[7]—Eng. Rev. on Madeira Chaplaincy & Willmott's Taylor.[8]

10. M.

Wrote to SR Glynne—C.G. Reid—CA Wood—Freshfield—Williams & Co—Wm. G.—Waylen—Skidmore[9]—H.S. with W. & A.—Latin with Willy—Went with C. to the Exhibition $5\frac{1}{4}$–$6\frac{3}{4}$. House at 5. Dined with the Herberts

[1] National representation: *H* c. 156.
[2] *H* c. 249–59.
[3] C. H. Blackwell, Lord Ward's agent at Dudley.
[4] Jacob Omnium [M. J. *Higgins], 'Is cheap sugar the triumph of free trade? A third letter to . . . *Russell' (1848).
[5] *Quarterly Review*, lxxxiii. 110, 127 (June 1848).
[6] Cp. 24 Nov. 44.
[7] Untraced.
[8] *English Review*, ix. 298, 315 (June 1848).
[9] Perhaps Joseph Skidmore, maltster in Dudley, possibly an Oak Farm creditor.

& House 11–1¾. Spoke on Sugar Importers' Claim.[1] Read Field—Niccolò de' Lapi—Dublin (rejected) Art on Irish Ch.[2]

Yesterday I visited Manning & had conversation about my own political course & the course of his mind with respect to religion. He described to me the searching trial he had undergone in an effort to test his position in the Ch. of England for the sake of others who hung upon him. This trial produced or aggravated illness & illness bringing death into view made the probation more effectual. The result was his full confirmation in allegiance to the Church, and (rather than but) also his increased[3] disposition to dwell on her Catholic & positive character rather than on what is negative, or peculiar, or external viz. the Protestant & the national aspects. I expressed a strong hope that his tone of language would not alter from what it has heretofore been, for such a change wd. compromise his usefulness.[4]—

11. T.

Harrow Weald Ch 11–1½. Went down there by train at 9 and viewed St Andrew's College: a remarkable creation, both materially & morally, when results, thus early too, are compared with means.[5] Returned by train at 3. Calls. Saw Miss Browne. Wrote to Mrs Herbert—Christie & Manson—Fraser & Tayleur—J. Griffiths—C. Blackwell—Read Field—D'Azeglio on the Jews[6]—Quarterly on Cabet[7]—H. of C. in evg.[8]—Singing.

12. Wed.

Wrote to J. Murray—O'Neil[9]—Field—Burnaby—G. Chance. H.S. with W. & A. H. of C. 3–4¼.[10] At Sir R. Peel's picture party, full of Ministers: dined at Grillion's with Sir J. Graham & Tufnell only: Lady Clerk's music (an admirable orchestra) in evg.[11] Finished Field. Read d'Azeglio on the Jews—Life of Aretino[12]—Quarterly (Guizot?) on Religion in France.[13]

13. Th.

Wrote to Sir J.G—Scotts—Fraser & Tayleur—Maitland—Manson—H.S. with W. & A. Saw Farquhar—Bp of Salisbury. H. of C. 5–7¼.[14] Ten to

[1] *H* c. 374–9.
[2] Not traced; given him by *Manning?
[3] 'be' here deleted.
[4] But cp. 30 Mar., 7 Apr. 51.
[5] Edward *Monro's free tractarian boys boarding school. The scheme collapsed when *Monro went to Leeds in 1860.
[6] Cp. 23 May 48.
[7] *Quarterly Review*, lxxxiii. 165 (June 1848), hostile to Cabet and Louis Blanc.
[8] Irish estates: *H* c. 385.
[9] Probably Henry Nelson O'Neil, 1817–80; historical and allegorical painter.
[10] Sunday trading: *H* c. 449.
[11] Lady Maria Clerk, *née* Law, d. 1866; m. 1810 Sir G. *Clerk.
[12] Cp. 27 Dec. 43.
[13] *Quarterly Review*, lxxxiii. 199 (June 1848); article by F. Guizot.
[14] Irish estates: *H* c. 469.

dinner—singing in evg. Read Quarterly on Cretineau Joly[1]—Hist. Amn. Church—Cent Nouvelles Nouvelles (chiefly summary)[2]—G. Denison's Statement.[3]

14. Fr.

Wrote to Fraser & Tayleur—G. & Co—Rn. G—C. Enderby—T.G—Hamilton Gray—Freshfield. Saw Mr G.G. Scott[4]—Inglis—Ashley (Edn. Clauses)—J. Young—H.S. with W. & A. Dined at Ld Crewe's.[5] Walk with C. H. of C. 4½–7½.[6] Read Hist. of Amn. Episc. Church.—The Pope & Revolutionary Italy.[7]

15. Sat.

Wrote to E. Hawkins—Lincoln—J.N.G—A. Williams—H.S. with W. & A. —Saw M. Pearson[8]—Mr Greswell—Mr Hornby—Went to Mrs. Lawrence's party aftn.[9] Read D'Azeglio on Jewish Emann. (finished)—Bancroft's Hist. United States[10]—Canada Parl. Papers[11]—Locke & Stephenson on the Guages.[12]

16. 4 S. Trin.

St Martins (H.C.) 11 am. Marg. Chapel evg.—MS of 47 aloud—Conv. with Willy—also with Agnes on a temptation of yest. evg when she took a bit of sugar, & then tried to conceal it by a 'story'. She is truly & sorely grieved: strength is what she yet wants. Read Wordsworth Sequel[13]—Bp White on Amn. Convention[14]—Gorham's Volume on his case.[15]

17. M.

Wrote to O.B. Cole—Sir J.G—Therry[16]—Barker—Fraser & Tayleur—H. Maitland—Charteris—Sir R. Peel—Sir J. Hobhouse—J. Griffiths. Saw Mr

[1] *Quarterly Review*, lxxxiii. 70 (June 1848); cp. 10 July 45.
[2] *Sensuit la table de ce present livre intitule des Cent Nouvelles Nouvelles* (?1495, often reprinted).
[3] G. A. *Denison, 'Statement, letters and memorial addressed to . . . the Incorporated Society for promoting the education of the poor' (1848).
[4] (Sir) George Gilbert *Scott, 1811–78; gothic revival architect and restorer.
[5] Hungerford Crewe, 1812–93; 3rd Baron Crewe 1835; d. unmarried; lived in Hill Street.
[6] Misc. business: *H* c. 480.
[7] Probably G. Mazzini, *Italy, Austria and the pope. A letter to Sir James *Graham* (1845).
[8] Perhaps Mary Martha Pearson, *née* Dutton, 1799–1871; artist.
[9] She lived in Marlborough Road.
[10] G. Bancroft, *History of the United States, from the discovery of the American continent to the war of independence* (1848).
[11] *PP* 1847–8, lix. 1; governor general's despatch on navigation laws.
[12] Pamphlets by Joseph *Locke and G. *Stephenson.
[13] Cp. 21 May 48.
[14] Cp. 28 June 48.
[15] G. C. *Gorham, 'Examination before admission to a benefice by the bishop of Exeter followed by refusal to institute, on the allegation of unsound doctrine respecting the efficacy of Baptism' (1848).
[16] (Sir) Roger *Therry, 1800–74; attorney-general N.S. Wales 1841; puisne judge there 1846; ed., *Canning's *Speeches* (1828).

Jenkins (OBC)[1]—Mr Parker (RR)—Messrs. Clowes (Clerk)—Graham & Goulburn (Claridge)—Ld J. Russell (oath)—Labouchere—Speaker. H.S. with W. & A.—Dined with the Wortleys. Lady Davy's afterwards. C. went to Hagley. Read White on Amn Church—Worked on Estate Society's Bill[2] —Commee. & House 2–7½. House 11½–12¼.[3]

18. T.

Wrote to Freshfield—Greswell—C.G—L. Evelyn—G. & Co—Shee—R. Barker—H.S. with Willy—Saw Mr Burnaby—Mr Boulton— Freshfield—Claridge—Nicolay—Lincoln. In the City 12½–2½.—Then Eccl. Comm. Commee. & House to 5½.[4] Dined with the Wortleys—Read White Amn. Ch —Parl. papers on Cape[5]—Sale of Beer Bill[6]—Law of Marriage Report[7]—Worked on private affairs.

19. Wed.

Wrote to Maitland—G. Hope—J.N.G—J. Griffiths—C.G—Sir J. Claridge —Lushington—Wrote also at night a separate Mem. on a sad subject. Saw Mr Therry—Mr C.M. Lushington[8]—Mr Hill—Farmer's Estate Soc. Comm. 12–4. Tea at Lady Hope's.

The[9] annexed memorandum—as it stands, scarcely intelligible without a comment—was put on paper at Baden in Oct. 1845. It contained such results as I had been enabled to reach with regard to practical means for the correction of a principal besetting sin, impurity: that impurity which has its seat mainly in the mind: which for some time past I have defined in my prayers as 'dangerous curiosity & filthiness of spirit'; an activity of the intellect on impure subjects, covering itself with the plea of innocent and useful ends.

It may seem that the remedial means here indicated are but mechanical. But then for that very reason they have been plain & palpable, & thus I believe much more useful to me, than if they had been in themselves of a higher order—for on more refined matter the subtle & blinding influences of corrupt sophism, which is my deadly foe, would have operated with greater

[1] i.e. O[xford] B[alliol] C[ollege]; William James Jenkins, 1821–97; fellow of Balliol 1840–52; rector of Fillingham from 1852; prosecuted railway companies; or, possibly, about O. B. Cole.

[2] The Farmers Estate Society (Ireland) Bill (*PP* 1847–8, ii. 397) was, on Gladstone's recommendation, referred to a select cttee., which he chaired; for its report, cp. *PP.* 1847–8, xvii. 363. The intent was to establish Irish small-holders with at least thirty acres.

[3] Business of the session: *H* c. 512.

[4] Misc. business: *H* c. 571.

[5] *PP* xliii. 1.

[6] Its 1° was on 13 July 1848, cp. *H* c. 469 and *PP* 1847–8, vi. 251.

[7] On prohibited degrees of affinity: *PP* 1847–8, xxviii. 233.

[8] Charles Manners Lushington, 1819–64; fellow of All Souls 1843–6; private secretary to president of board of control 1843–54; Peelite M.P. Canterbury 1854–7.

[9] The rest of this day's entry, signed and dated this day, is the contents of a notebook in Lambeth MSS, to which the 'annexed memorandum' (printed, with its list of subsequent entries, at 26 Oct. 45) is fixed with wax. See the introduction, iii. xxiv n., xlvi.

force. When I compare my convictions in religion, and the mercies that have been poured upon me, with the extraordinary tenacity of the evil in me, the fruit without doubt of indulgence, I cannot but deeply believe that my debt to the justice of God is the very heaviest that can be conceived: for have I not after all suffered that sin which I have described to have its habitation & to find its food in me, and could it have been covered by such flimsy pretexts but for an extreme corruption?

The pursuit of knowledge, the desire of estimating different periods & states of the moral and religious life of man, the hope of doing good to persons living in sin: of all these I had utterly failed to discern the proper bounds, and had sometimes perhaps often lost even these from view when once upon the train of thought on imagery of which they might have first effected the introduction. Further if at any time I had discerned those bounds, the vision of them became dim & ineffectual at the time of need, even if resolutions of a solemn kind had been formed, & formed at the most solemn hour—before the Altar.

The question could not but arise in my mind, with regard to many subjects,[1] but to this in particular, do I under pretence of seeking at that Altar the most powerful medicine for my deep disease, really profane the Holiest—or is it in faith & desire towards God, however low & weak, that I repair thither, faith & desire only saved by such resort from total extinction?

It would be of no use to devise elaborate phrases of shame; only this I know that I must hope the feeling of it will deepen ever from day to day: today it has need to be very deep.

In retrospect however, while keenly conscious that none has so awful a debt to the divine Justice, none is driven so exclusively to rest upon that one great feature of the sacrifice of Christ the infirmities of its power—I must also say that without being free from the fear of having profaned the Altar, I yet believe that frequent resort to it, in the midst of my unworthiness, which alas has come after as well as before the great gift there given, has been the principal instrument whereby it has pleased the Lord at all times, and before marriage in particular to prevent my wickedness from reaching to that full maturity by outward acts which in its turn would have deepened my inward blackness. Without that, what should I have been! Whatever sway I have shamefully & abominably permitted to the corrupt action of my mind on impure subjects—in the various forms which the annexed paper indicates, and those not all inward only nor confined to myself—I am anxious that there has been a power within me struggling against the enemy & limiting his fearful ravages, not so as to diminish my demerit, but yet so as to keep open the door of mercy—and I connect that power, as with other religious means, so especially & above all, with the Blessed Sacrament whose very name I am too bold in writing. What then should I otherwise have been when even now "my wickednesses are gone over my head and are like a sore burden too heavy for me to bear.["][2]

[1] Half a page left blank. [2] Psalm xxxviii. 4.

Looking back then over more than twenty years since this plague began, I can discern two periods at which the evil was so to speak materially limited but it may also have been formally, essentially, enhanced. First the period of marriage: and secondly that period of general recollection and prevision, which was vouchsafed me in my retired life at Baden.

It was then I think that I first got a clear view of this sound and reasonable principle: that supposing even the corrupt manners of men may, nay must be studied by some, yet it should be either by those who are distinctly *called* to contact with such objects, in a manner apart from more depraved and clandestine inclination, & who therefore may look to God their Father & boldly beseech Him to neutralise the poison that they drink, or else by those who have got such a command over the particular evil, or have made such a general progress in holiness, that the excitement from without finds no sympathy within and therefore instils no corruption. But it was not so with me, for though I might persuade myself that in my inner heart I carried along with me a perfect hatred and disgust towards the fruit & work of lust, yet this was not genuine, or, if genuine was too weak to defend mind and body from the infection, especially in a case like mine, when the habits of my life, such as being out at all hours, place me peculiarly in the way of contact with exciting causes.

It was then a reasonable proposition to put to myself, that although there might be those that might innocently & without hurt endure that contact, yet if sought by me it must be sought without either a legitimate call, or an inward preparation to defend me—and that therefore I could not hope to escape from the natural law of cause and effect and must by touching this defiled matter contract new defilement in myself and new guilt before God.

I think, however, and Oh may it not be mere wicked presumption, the judicial penalty of former sin, that makes me think, that the rules of avoidance and repression arranged at Baden have been blessed by the mercy of God in a considerable degree up to a late period: that since then for instance there had been more care if I was accosted by one of those poor creatures, so much less sinners than myself, in the streets, to avoid saying anything that would naturally lead to further offence by word or otherwise, and generally less of rash handling of the *irritamenta* which when once touched put an end for the time to our moral freedom.

The days marked on the last side of the annexed paper are those on which I had noted my having offended against [the] sense of the rules noted on it. These offences are far from representing all that I had to deplore during the time, in regard to the particular subject: they represent the occasions on which by some act of mine I had courted evil—not those on which when it came without my seeking I had by infirmity and evil habit suffered from it —and the acts generally fell under one class: they were commonly the perusal of books of which I knew enough to be aware that I ought to avoid them: under the notion of seeing whether any good or instructive end was contemplated, or any peculiar principle illustrated in them; not books of the very worst class or not known to be such, but yet books such as those

'Fabliaux' of which I have spoken in my Journal[1] and which even if the first access to them were innocent yet soon gave indication of their containing sad pollution.

On these occasions I do not doubt that I have trifled with my convictions: i.e. having previously had a clear & strong impression that I was not fit for such things even *if* others were, I had lost the clearness & strength of this impression, and such impressions suffer detriment not by intellectual but by moral defect for they ought to grow into instincts if they are received with an entire honesty of purpose.

But what I have to record against myself deepens in sadness. From former experience I have found that over-exercise and exhaustion of the mind demoralise it: leave it open to attacks of the Evil One, and with impaired means of resistance. Not that a loving and pure soul necessarily suffers from this cause: *all* things work together for good to such, because the sense of weakness within them only leads them to a more heartfelt and lively reliance on their Strength. With me it has been otherwise. This year has not been a year, thus far, of affliction: how often do I ask myself indistinctly what I now put in distinct words on paper, whether if I desire the salvation of my soul I ought not directly to pray for it: but it has been a year of over-pressure upon me, from the combination with my public & usual occupations of a considerable weight of business in itself perplexing[2] foreign to my habits and quite beyond my capacity.[3] Under this I have been sore, feeble, and worried: I have lost courage to look my daily duties in the face: the disposition to turn my back on them lurks within me: and this, without leading me to any such monstrous conclusion, predisposes me to that vague habit of mind which seeks relief in some kind of counter-excitement. Alas am I now describing honestly the particulars of my sad experience so unworthy of a Christian, or am I again weaving the web of false and treacherous excuses in the vain hope to hide from my God my spiritual nakedness?[4]

With this cause however I think the more frequently repeated lapses into temptation & yieldings to it during the present year have been connected; as matter of fact: in that sense only I state it. I know there is here no justification: had I sought strength according to my need, His grace would have been sufficient for me. I state it, not to justify but to condemn: to make clear what follows.

At the Holy Sacrament on Sunday last I asked of myself whether there was not yet one source of evil, which had not been stopped up by any rule or distinct resolution or conviction applicable to it. What profligate conversation, or books known to have that character, or shopwindows presenting corresponding forms to the eye, or exhibitions making the same appeal, or

[1] Cp. 13 May 48.
[2] 'and' deleted.
[3] i.e. the Oak Farm.
[4] 'There has also been the check imposed on my little casual paltry efforts at subjugation of the flesh, by the orders to feed up on account of the late affliction in my arm'. This sentence added in the margin. See 8 and 28 Mar. 48.

trains of suggested thought on impure subjects, required [sic] seemed to have been before me: but there is something beyond this: there are books whose titles do not tell the corruption that is in them, or which are licentious while weak and which contaminate without powerfully moving, or again the eye may range over books which do not contain polluted matter, with an expectation that of itself pollutes: and then a true Christian instinct detects and repells before evil is done: and seeing this subject before me I then made a Resolution, with a consciousness that I must be either the better or the worse for it, to avoid the gratuitous perusal or even glance of all books of which the title suggested that they might probably offer food to depraved appetite.

And yet this night having gone into a bookshop with reference to a work or two which I wished to buy I saw a book of 'Political Pieces' of Charles II's age which I suspected yet I looked into it verifying my own suspicions but distinctly against my resolution: and not to mention other books, harmless at which I looked with the vague curiosity so full of danger and generally related to an indistinct but evil desire, I saw a book marked 'Rochester's poems' and looked at the contents then at some of the verses which were his, and in this I acted against my Resolution though I believe I did not actually read what was evil: but looking on through the rest of the book—which at first appeared more innocent—I found two vile poems, and of these with disgust I hope but certainly with a corrupt sympathy I read parts under that very pretext, repudiated by myself as being *for me* a sheer and wicked delusion, of acquiring a knowledge of the facts of nature & manners of men and I found the consequence of the temper in which I was: for having the opportunity of speaking words of truth to the fallen, I spoiled them in the utterance as if my tongue had failed me.

This might be a less offence for many but for me it is very very great—after so many falls, so much self trial, perceptions proximate to my case, so slowly gained, quickly and repeatedly lost: it seems so like a wilful welcoming of the Evil One, a determination to serve God & Mammon. Even in making this record I know not whether it be for evil or for good: it is however with pain & this is my hope, but Oh! not enough pain, a weak ineffectual pain whereas it should be one piercing the inmost soul. O that I may attain to such a pain. For the present it stings my pride a little: & perhaps though for my own eye only now may lead to what will sting it more.[1] And my poor Resolution—in fragments this very evening, although formed so lately & at the Altar of my God! It may be put together again—but what wondrous mercy if I should be enabled to keep it. Indeed 'O God my heart condemneth me'—condemneth me utterly, hopelessly—'but Thou art greater than my heart and knowest all things.'[2] And as an humble means, it is not wholly without its use, that if it please God my own hand & pen shall continue to be witness against me if I fall anew lengthening the list of my broken vows, if, which God forbid, the fountain of mine iniquity is not even now to be stopped.

[1] His future self-scourgings? [2] Version of I John iii. 20.

20. Th.

Wrote to C.G. H.S. with Willy. Committees[1] & House 11–6½.[2] Dined at Mr Lockharts. Duchess of Norfolk's afterwards. Read Barrington's Letter to Peel, &c.[3]

21. Fr.

Wrote to Fraser & Tayleur—C.M. Lushington—CG—Rev. Mr Haughton[4] —Gen. Pasley—T. Steuart Gladstone—H.S. with Willy. Eccl. Comm. 12¾–2. H. of C. 3¾–9.[5] Read Bancroft U.S.—Dean Hoare on Irish Edn.[6]—Matsell on Slave Trade.[7]

22. Sat.

Wrote to Mrs Wortley—Sir J. Claridge—C.G—H. Maitland—Fraser & Tayleur—J.L. Ross—Williams & Co—Sir J.G—J. Freshfield—Mrs C. Chisholm.[8] Visited Uncle Divie, who was much moved—saw C. Wordsworth. H.S. with Willy. H. of C. 12½–2 and 4¼–7.[9] At Lady F. Hopes in aftn. to hear Mrs Gartshore,[10] with great delight & admiration—dined at Lady Davy's. Read Bancroft—Matsell (finished)—Ld Hervey's Memoirs.[11]

23. 5. S. Trin.

Westmr. Abbey with Willy 10 AM—St James's 7 P.M. Conv. with Willy—wrote to Scotts—Read MS on the Gospel aloud—Wrote to No 22 & cancelled it on change of mind:[12] it had reference to a conversation last night coming home. Read Moullet Comp. Theol[13]—Strauss[14]—Manning's Sermons—Gorham on Inf. Baptism.[15]

24. M.

Wrote to C.G—R. Barker—Fraser & Tayleur—B. Gibbons[16]—Ly E.

[1] The Ecclesiastical Commission and Farmers' Estate Cttees.
[2] Irish estates: *H* c. 583.
[3] 'Letter of Sir Matthew Barrington, bart., to . . . *Peel' (1848); on Irish agricultural improvements.
[4] Probably William Haughton, 1810–83; rector of S. Wootton, Norfolk, 1842–69, of Barton Turf 1869–83, wrote on politics.
[5] Sugar duties: *H* c. 642.
[6] E. N. Hoare, 'A letter to . . . *Stanley on . . . National Education in Ireland' (1842).
[7] Probably H. J. Matson, 'Remarks on the slave trade and African squadron' (1848).
[8] Caroline *Chisholm, *née* Jones, 1808–77; m. 1830 Archibald Chisholm; promoted emigration of families from England to Australia 1846–54; wrote on colonization.
[9] Habeas Corpus in Ireland: *H* c. 696.
[10] Mary, *née* Douglas, m. 1836 John Murray-Gartshore and d. 1851; well known for her singing.
[11] John, Baron *Hervey, *Memoirs of the reign of George II, from his accession to the death of Queen Caroline*, 2 v. (1848); ed., J. W. *Croker.
[12] Untraced; probably a rescue case. Cp. next entry.
[13] C. Moullet, *De l'être en general et de l'être organisé en particulier* (1845).
[14] Cp. 15 Feb. 48.
[15] Cp. 16 July 48.
[16] Benjamin Gibbons, iron-master at Kingswinford.

Ashley[1]—Farmer's Estate Comm. & House 3–7.[2] Read Bancroft—Lowe's Report on the Land Question N.S.W.[3]—Tea at Lady Hopes—Saw Dowbiggin—Campbell—visit to a young sick person, in a place of danger, & convss. there.

25. T. St. James

Wrote to T.G. (his birthday)—Northcote—Mrs Middleton—Haughton. Read Bancroft—Cape Papers—H.S. with Willy—Commn. & H. of C. 12¼–2½, 5–10 and 11–12. Molesworths speech was very clear, full of well arranged facts, & with a great balance of what was true & useful. It was also forcible, & very easy to listen to tho' so full of figures. It was a day of thought on puzzling questions, without sensible progress. This of the Slave Trade is most difficult.—Made my motion for poor Sir J. Claridge—with little fruit but perhaps as much as could be hoped.[4] C.G. returned. Saw Rn. G.

26. Wed.

Wrote to W. Chance[5]—J. Skidmore—Ld Medwyn—J. Murray—Jarvis[6]—Rev. E. Monro—C. Wordsworth. H.S. with W. & A. Walk with C—Lady Fortescue's Concert in evg.[7] Saw Mr W. Browne[8]—Engaged on house & family matters with C. Read Lewis on Govt. of Dependencies[9]—Bancroft.

27. Th.

Jessy's birthday. God bless her: Willy made a little speech at dinner proposing her health. Wrote to Gall[10]—T.S. Gladstone—Sir J G—Nicolay—Dowbiggin—Longmans—Mrs Denison—Dodsworth. Read 2d Sanitary Report[11]—Bancroft—Wilkinson on South Australia.[12] H.S. with W. & A.—Walk with C—H. of C. 5–8:[13] Lady Lawley's Concert in evg. Saw Lincoln—Goulburn *cum* Graham—Courtenay.

[1] Emily Ashley-Cooper, 1810–72; da. of 5th Earl Cowper, m. 1830 Anthony, *Lord Ashley, 7th earl of Shaftesbury.

[2] Irish measures: *H* c. 757.

[3] Robert *Lowe, 'The impending crisis' (1847); printed with comments, in *PP* 1847–8, xlii. 553.

[4] The motion called for a government appointment for Claridge: *H* c. 812; cp. 15 Jan. 48 n. *Molesworth spoke on colonial government.

[5] William Chance & Co., Birmingham and London, merchants trading with America.

[6] Perhaps (Sir) Lewis Whincop Jarvis, 1816–88; banker and solicitor at Lynn; Kt. 1878.

[7] Elizabeth, *née* Geale, 1805–96; 2nd wife 1841 of Hugh Fortesque, 1783–1861, 2nd Earl Fortesque 1841, lord steward of the household 1846–50.

[8] Perhaps William Browne, 1791–1876; 3rd s. of 1st earl of Kenmare; lib. M.P. Kerry 1841–7.

[9] Cp. 18 Nov. 41.

[10] Probably James Gall, 1784–1874; partner in Gall and Inglis, Edinburgh publishers.

[11] Of the metropolitan sanitary commission, *PP* 1847–8, xxxii. 253.

[12] G. B. Wilkinson, *South Australia; its advantages and its resources* (1848).

[13] Misc. business: *H* c. 902.

28. Fr.

Wrote to Freshfield—Dowbiggin—Maitland—Fraser & T. Sir G. Grey—Talfourd—Thesiger—A. Caswall—R. Barker—Twiss—Griffiths—Clowes. Saw Messrs. Chance—do again with Freshfield—Smyth & Jeffers.[1] H.S. with the children. Eccl. Commn. Commee. 1–4. H. of C. 11½–1. Spoke on Farmer's Estate Soc[iety] Bill.[2] Read Bancroft—Lewis on Dependencies.

29. Sat.

Wrote to G. & Co (2)—Haslewood[3]—Claridge—H.S. with the children. Took C. & Willy to the Diorama[4]—he was enchanted. Nine to dinner (Lady Grenville's party). Read Bancroft—Wilkinson—Ld Hervey's Court of Geo. II.

30. 6 S Trin.

St Martins 8½ (Holy Comn.) and 11. St James's evg. MS of 1840 aloud in evg. Walk with C. & the children. Saw Monsell. Read Manning's S. (finished)—Gorham (Finished)—Ross on Ch. & St. (finished)[5]—Amn. Ep. Canons & S. Carolina Convention Reports.[6]

31. M.

Wrote to Dowbiggin—Sir J.G—Freshfield—Col. Barney. H.S. with W & A—Latin with Willy. Worked on accounts—H. of C. 12–3 and 5–10.[7] Saw Ld Spencer. Read Wilkinson—Lewis.

Tuesday Aug. 1. 48.

Wrote to Mr Malet. H.S. with the children. Slave Trade Committee 11–5 & House 6–8¾.[8] Read Wilkinson—Bancroft—House & other arrangements—Saw Alex. Wood—Singing in evg.

2. Wed.

Wrote to Griffiths—W.H. Lowe[9]—Fraser & Tayleur—Haughton. H.S. with the children. Committees 11–6 P.M. Read Wilkinson—Bancroft—Lewis. Tea with Ld Somers. Then Lincoln came in at 11 P.M. & told us the sad news of his wife's clandestine & very sudden journey, a very terrible blow.[10]

[1] Probably William Smythe and G. Jefferys, barristers.
[2] *H* c. 978; cp. 17 July 48.
[3] Ashby Blair Haslewood, *ca.* 1810–?77; curate of St. Mark's, Marylebone, 1845–64; vicar of St. Michael's, Coventry, 1864–6, of Ridware, Staffordshire, 1866–77.
[4] In Regent's Park, representing Mount Etna erupting.
[5] Cp. 26 Feb. 48.
[6] *Canons for the government of the protestant episcopal church in the U.S.A. . . . to which are added the constitution of the church* (1832); also contains sundry convention reports.
[7] Farmers' Bill cttee.; spoke on Sugar duties: *H* c. 1041, 1061.
[8] Church property: *H* c. 1075.
[9] Perhaps William H. Lowe, Birmingham solicitor.
[10] She had fled abroad with her lover, Lord Walpole. See 13 July 49 and Magnus, 92–4.

3. Th.

Wrote to Skidmore—Bp of London—C.K. Murray—Saw S. Herbert—G. Burnett—Hutt and [blank.] Read Lewis—Misc. Estimates Report & Evidence[1]—Wilkinson. H. of C. 1–3 on Farmer's Est. Bill[2]—H.S. with the children—Went to see the Model Lodging Houses.[3]

4. Fr.

Wrote to Barker—Sir J.G—Rn. G—Guazzaroni[4]—Griffiths—H.S. with the children. Saw Godley—Nicolay—Burnett—Macfie—Dowbiggin. Read Navy Estimates Report[5]—Ld Hervey's Court of Geo. II—Wilkinson (finished)—Remarks on Fasting[6]—Letter on Emigration.[7] Saw Lincoln again on his great calamity. He declares this is final: but we must yet hope. Dined with the Hopes. H. of C. 5–6¼.[8]

5. Sat.

(Missed Ch at 7½ finding all shut) Wrote to W. Mathews—Thorpe—Bowen—Huddlestone (G)[9]—Barlow—J. Manners—C.G. went to Red leaf mg—Read Ld Hervey—B. Edwards on Col. Govt.[10]—Nicholson on Cape[11]—Lewis on Dependencies—Worked on papers accts & house arrangements—tea with the Hopes.

6. 7 S Trin.

St Martins 11–2 (H.C.) & St Andrew's 7 P.M.—MS on Transfig. aloud in evg. Walk with the children. Lincoln brought his boys to early dinner. Conv. with him afterwards on V[ancouver] I[sland] & Lady L.—I tried to point out how laudanum goes to destroy responsibility & unfit people for punishment properly so called or for abandonment to themselves: using my sister's case as a parable. Wrote to Sir J.G—Wallace Harvey[12]—Read

[1] *PP* 1847–8, xl. 281.
[2] Though it was not debated: *H* c. 1113.
[3] In George Street, Bloomsbury.
[4] Possibly Antony Lazzaroni, Edinburgh figure maker.
[5] *PP* 1847–8, xxi. 1.
[6] 'Remarks on fasting, and on the discipline of the body; in a letter to a clergyman, by a physician' (1848).
[7] Cp. 26 Mar. 47.
[8] Misc. business: *H* c. 1144.
[9] George James Huddlestone, 1803–77; rector of Tunworth, Hampshire, 1844–77.
[10] Bryan *Edwards, either 'Thoughts on the late proceedings of government, respecting the trade of the West Indies with the United States . . .' (1784) or *The history, civil and commercial, of the British colonies in the West Indies*, 3 v. (1793–1801).
[11] G. Nicholson, *The Cape and its colonists* (1848).
[12] Scotsman training for the bar; requested Gladstone's helping in publishing his book on British diplomacy; Hawn P.

Wordsworth's Sequel[1]—Newman's S.[2]—Strauss—Bp Chapman's Charge[3] —Ogilvy's Address[4]—Liturgical Services (Elis.).[5]

7. M.

Wrote to Ford—Sir J.G—Manning—Divett—Claridge—Amery—Griffiths —Eagar[6]—Chamonozow[7]—H.S. with Agnes. Saw Young—J. Manners—Hutt—Hume—Godley—Goulburn—& our new Vicar Mr M'Kenzie.[8] House 5–6¾.[9] Singing in evg. Read Chamonozow on N.Z—Hervey's Court of Geo II—Manning's Charge[10]—& worked on divers papers.

8. T.

Wrote to Dowbiggin—Lincoln—H.S. with the children—Saw Coleman (O.F.)[11]—Fagan. E.C. Committee 1–3¾. H. of C. 8¾–12. Voted agt. the ballot, in 81:86! I *ought* to have spoken: & would, but could not—my brain would not do the work after my morning's occupation with Coleman.[12] Read Nicholson on the Cape (finished)—Chamonozow. Tried to write on Colonies: but it will I fear be an abortion.

9. Wed.

Wrote to Geo. Chance—Aunt J.—G. & Co—W. James—Burnett—H.J.G—Scotts—Mr L. Walker—Hay—Mrs Trist[13]—H.S. with the children—Walk with C. Saw E. Denison—Bouverie—C. Wood—H. Glynne—Wyld—Christy—H. of C. 5½–9¾. Again I should have spoken if I could: on the Estimates.[14] Read Chamonozow—Lowe's Protest & Appx.[15] Worked on accounts.

10. Th.

Wrote to Ellen Ward. Attended S. Lyttelton's marriage: the most laughing one I ever saw, with perhaps the most cause to be grave. God

[1] Cp. 21 May 48.
[2] Cp. 23 Jan. 48.
[3] James Chapman, 'A charge delivered . . . by James, bishop of Colombo' (1847).
[4] C. A. *Ogilvie, 'Considerations on subscription to the thirty nine articles, submitted for the serious attention of candidates for holy orders' (1845).
[5] Cp. 27 Feb. 48.
[6] Probably John Eager, Liverpool merchant.
[7] Louis Alexis Chamerovzow, novelist and pamphleteer; sec. anti-slavery society 1852–70; wrote *The New Zealand question, and the rights of aborigines* (1848).
[8] i.e. Henry *MacKenzie, cp. 5 Mar. 39; often referred to by Gladstone as 'the vicar'.
[9] Taxation: *H* c. 1181.
[10] H. E. *Manning, 'Charge at the ordinary visitation' (1848).
[11] James Edward Coleman, of Coleman, Turquands, Young and co., was the accountant auditing the Oak Farm accounts.
[12] Resolution in favour of voting by ballot carried by five votes, but no action taken until 1872: *H* c. 1241.
[13] Jane Warren Trist, *née* Devonshire, m. 1848 John Fincher Trist, 1822–90, Devon landlord.
[14] Naval estimates: *H* c. 1320.
[15] R. T. *Lowe, 'Protest against the ministrations in Madeira of the Rev. T. K. Brown, in opposition to episcopal authority' (1848).

grant it may be for good. Ld Spencer with Ly Lyttelton & others dined with us.[1]

Saw our Vicar—J. Hume—Worked most of the day on Hudson's Bay & V.I. papers & correspondence parlty. & MS. House 5–7 and 10½–12½.[2] Read Chamonozow—H.S. with the children.

11. Fr.

Wrote to Felton—Sir J.G. (2)—Lincoln (2)—Fitzgerald—Greswell—H.S. with the children. H. of C. 5–8.[3] Read V.I. Correspondence[4]—Chamonozow—Simpson's Life[5]—Selkirk Narrative[6]—Edwards's W.I.

12. Sat.

Wrote to J.T. Thomson—R. Creed—M & M Wray[7]—Badeley—H.S. with the children. Read Umfreville[8]—Ellis[9]—Robson[10]—Selkirk Narrative—Ld Hervey's Geo. II.—Ch Ch Broadway 6 P.M.

13. 8 S Trin.

St Martins 11 AM St James 7 PM—MS of 44 aloud in evg. Wrote on I Kings Ch XIII (I & began II).[11] Saw Badeley on Bouverie's Bill & wrote Memm.[12] Read Commentaries on I Kings Ch XIII and Wordsworth's Sequel (finished)—Reunion des Religions. The Lytteltons here in evg.

14. M.

Wrote to Sir J.G—E. Badeley—Lincoln—J.N.G—S.H. Northcote—E.P. Bouverie—Jennings—Read A. Smith[13]—Merivale[14]—Ch. Miss Reports[15]—Bp of Montreal's Journal[16]—Nicolay MSS—Hervey's Court of Jas II—Chamonozow—H.S. with W & A—Latin with Willy—they went off with C. at 10½ to Hagley. Saw Bouverie—Christie[17]—H. of C. 5–7½ and 9½–1. Spoke on supply.[18]

[1] Spencer Lyttelton m. this day Henrietta Cornewall of Delbury Hall, Shropshire; she d. 1889.

[2] Spoke on navigation laws: *H* ci. 57.

[3] Misc. business: *H* ci. 84.

[4] Cp. 16 Sept. 47.

[5] A. Simpson, *The life and travels of Thomas *Simpson, the Arctic discoverer* (1845).

[6] T. *Douglas, earl of Selkirk, *A narrative of occurrences in the Indian countries of North America* (1817).

[7] Warfingers, at Downe's warf, East Smithfield, London.

[8] E. Umfreville, *The present state of Hudson's Bay* (1790).

[9] H. *Ellis, *A voyage to Hudson's Bay in 1746* (1848).

[10] J. Robson, *An account of six years residence in Hudson's Bay from 1733 to 1736 and 1744 to 1747*, 2 v. (1752).

[11] Cp. Add MS 44780, f. 260.

[12] The Bill was to amend the Toleration Act: Add MS 44737, f. 37. Edward Pleydell *Bouverie, 1818–89; lib. M.P. Kilmarnock 1844–73; president, poor law board 1855–58.

[13] Cp. 15 Aug. 46.

[14] Cp. 9 Nov. 42.

[15] Probably the Church Missionary Society *Annual Report* (1848).

[16] Cp. 20 July 45.

[17] Altered to Christy or vice-versa.

[18] Gladstone and *Disraeli both vainly opposed a grant to *Trevelyan for his Irish famine work: *H* ci. 139–41.

15. T.

Wrote to Rev. H. Mackenzie—C.G—Chamonozow—Fagan—Saw Mr Fitzgerald—Uncle D—Mr Fortescue—Mr Christy—Shopping, & house arrangements with a view to departure. Read Ld Hervey—Chamonozow (finished)—Isbister's MSS.[1]

16. Wed.

Wrote to Hays—Morgans[2]—C.G—Lincoln (2)—Walkey[3]—Ld Braybrooke—Burnett—Waghorn—Read Dunn[4]—Ld Hervey (finished I)—H. of C. 5–$7\frac{1}{2}$ and $9\frac{1}{4}$–$12\frac{3}{4}$.[5] Worked in packing, arranging papers &c & for journey.

17. Th.

Wrote to Fraser & Tayleur—Sir J.G—Sir S. Scott & Co—Mrs Ward—C.G—W. Chance. In the city & saw Freshfield—Mr George (dentist)[6]—H. of C. 12–$1\frac{3}{4}$, 5–7 and $8\frac{3}{4}$–$12\frac{3}{4}$. Read Turgot[7]—Wilkess Expl. Exp[8]—Dunn's Hist. Oregon Territory. Worked on papers for V.I. debate. Spoke on Dipl. Relations with Rome.[9]

18. Fr.

Wrote to D. Coleridge—Mrs Mildmay—Paterson & Walker—C.G—Scotts (2)—Williams & Co—W. James—Saw D. Robertson—H. of C. $1\frac{1}{4}$–3, 5–$9\frac{1}{2}$, $10\frac{1}{2}$–1. Spoke on Education—on Vote for Univv—& $1\frac{3}{4}$ hour on Vancouver's Island[10]—Read Niger[11]—Eardley Wilmot correspondence[12]—Worked on V.I. & Hudson's Bay books & papers for speech.

19. Sat.

Wrote to Sir J. Stephen—Rev. H. Mackenzie—C.G—W. Chance—Canon Trevor[13]—J.N.G—Ld Grey—Sir W. Denison—Archdeacon Marriott—Lincoln—Packed & sent off my things—arranging books papers &c. for departure. Read Dunn's Hist. Oregon—Ld Hervey Vol II—L & NW. Report &c.[14]—Took Miss B. & Meriel to Euston Square—called on Uncle D—saw Stephy & Jessy off for Fasque, both very happy. Saw Dummert.[15]

[1] A. K. *Isbister's petition on Hudson's Bay, printed on 17 August 1848; copy in Add MS 44565, f. 299.
[2] Perhaps Morgan, Martyn, George and Co., London stationers.
[3] Charles Elliot Walkey, 1780–1865; rector of Collumpton, Devon, 1804–65; wrote on theology.
[4] Cp. 1 Aug. 44.
[5] Misc. business: *H* ci. 145.
[6] John Durance George, M.R.C.S. 1838; dental surgeon to university college hospital.
[7] *Oeuvres de Turgot*, ed. MM. E. Daire and H. Dussard, 2 v. (1844).
[8] C. Wilkes, *Narrative of the United States exploring expedition . . . 1838–1842*, 5 v. (1844).
[9] Supporting them: *H* ci. 229–235.
[10] Strongly critical of the Hudson's Bay Company: *H* ci. 268–89.
[11] *The chronicles of Radulphus *Niger . . . first edited by R. Anstruther* (1844).
[12] Cp. 29 and 30 Apr. 46 nn.
[13] George *Trevor, 1809–88; canon of York 1847–88; rector of All Saints, York, 1847–1868, of Beeford 1871–88; theologian and orientalist.
[14] *PP* 1847–8, xxxi. 399.
[15] Possibly a charity or rescue case.

20. 8 S. Trin.

St Martins 11 AM (H.C.) & Marg. Chapel 7 P.M.—Read aloud MS on Epistle[1]—Finished 2d MS on the Man of God from Judah[2]—Walk with Badeley—Read Nurses Instn. Report[3]—Reunion des Religions—Bp Thirlwall's Introdn. to Schleiermacher[4]—Scandret on Sacrifice.[5]

21. M.

Wrote to C.G—Lincoln (2)—Rn. G—G & Co—A. Chapman—L. Walker—Bp of London—Sir L. O'Brien[6]—Mrs Medlicott[7]—Read Sir L. O'Brien on Ireland—Saw Ld Brougham—Hume—Paterson & Walker—Mrs Tyler. H. of C. 1–3 and 5–8¼. Spoke on NZ and Labuan &c.[8] arranging papers paying bills &c. for departure.

22. T.

Wrote to Freshfield—Off at 5¾ to Birm. Walk to Halesowen,[9] there taken up by C. Found all well: a pleasant evening. Chess with Lyttelton—Read Strauss[10]—Gioberti.[11]

23. Wed.

Wrote to Fraser & Tayleur—Williams & Co—and E. Hobhouse—Read Gioberti—Strauss—Townshend's Facts in Mesmerism[12]—Chess with G. Walk with the party to St Kenelm's[13]—my face better—Lady G. received me very kindly.

24. St Barthol.

Wrote to Sir J.G—10–5 in Birmingham on O.F. business with Collis, Amery, & Freshfield. Chess with G. Read Strauss—Gioberti—Bid goodbye to Ly W[enlock] & S. Lawley[14] who seems very promising.

[1] Cp. Add MS 44780, f. 264.
[2] Untraced.
[3] Of the Nursing Sisters Institute in Devonshire Square.
[4] F. E. D. Schleiermacher, *A critical essay on the gospel of St. Luke* (1825); introduced and tr. by C. *Thirlwall.
[5] J. *Scandret, *Sacrifice the divine service* (1707).
[6] Sir Lucius O'Brien, 1800–?60; 5th Bart. 1837; tory M.P. co. Clare 1826–30, 1847–52; wrote 'Ireland, the late famine, and the poor laws' (1848).
[7] She kept a toy shop near Parliament.
[8] On Labuan in E. Indies: *H* ci. 312.
[9] 4 miles SW. of Birmingham city centre.
[10] Cp. 15 Feb. 48.
[11] Cp. 4 May 48.
[12] C. H. *Townshend, *Facts in mesmerism, with reasons for a dispassionate inquiry into it* (1840).
[13] Cp. 4 Feb. 47.
[14] Stephen Willoughby Lawley, 1823–1905, s. of 1st Baron Wenlock; rector of Escrick, Yorkshire, 1848–68, then of Exminster, Essex; sub-dean of York 1852–62.

25. Fr.

Wrote to W. B. Collis—Freshfield—H. Kynaston—H. Mackenzie—Saw Dunning & Griffiths on O.F.—& worked on papers respecting it. Walk with C. Chess with G—Church 10 A.M. Read Gioberti—Strauss—Hare Townshend—Hodgson's Evidence on Cholera.[1]

26. Sat.

Wrote to Fraser & Tayleur. Rode with G—Whist in evg—Worked on railway papers & figures. Read Gioberti—-Strauss—Hare Townshend. Mr Bouverie came.

27. 9 S. Trin.

Hagley Ch mg & aft. Read Marsh on Interp. & Critm. of Bible[2]—Gioberti—Strauss.

28. M.

Wrote to Sir J.G—Hampton—Godley—C.G. Reid—Fraser—Ivall—Griffiths—Collis—Amery—Freshfield. Worked on O.F. papers & figures. Walk with C.—music in evg. Read Gioberti—Strauss—Townshend.

29.

Wrote to Ld Spencer—Sir J.G—Rn. G—Barker—Fraser & Tayleur—Scotts. Latin lesson with Willy—Read Strauss—Townshend—worked on O.F. papers—Saw J. Mathews—Mr Foster—At the school feast on the hill[3]—party in evg.

30. W.

Wrote to Freshfield—Read Gioberti—Strauss—Townshend—Hervey's Memoirs—Attended the Bowmeeting at Westwood & saw Ld Ward who was perfectly goodhumoured.[4] Church 7¼ P.M.

31. Th.

Wrote to J. Amery—W.B. Collis (2)—W. Chance (with Memm. of arrangement)—Went to Corbyn's Hall[5] to see Messrs. Mathews, Griffiths, & Skidmore—then to O.F. on business—also saw Collis. Read Strauss—Gioberti—Townshend—Ld Hervey.

[1] Joseph Hodgson's evidence to the sanitary commissioners, *PP* 1847–8, xxxii. 1.
[2] E. G. Marsh, *The Christian doctrine of sanctification* (1848); his *Bampton lectures.
[3] On Wychbury hill, ¾ mile N. of Hagley Hall.
[4] As chief creditor of the Oak Farm he had a right not to be. See 7 Aug. 46 for the Bow.
[5] 5 miles NE. of Stourbridge, site of Benjamin Gibbons' furnaces, forge and colliery.

Friday Septr. One 1848.

Church 10 A.M. Wrote to Goodford[1]—R. Barker—Ivall—Bennett—Paskin—Read Strauss—Townshend—Ld Hervey—Wedys debate[2]—Saw Amery—Collis—at Stourbridge. Conv. with WHL. & Mr Arbuthnot.

2. Sat.

Wrote to Sir J.G—J.N.G—J. Griffiths—Hampton—C.K. Murray—Goodford—Cocks. At Himley[3] to luncheon—Saw Mr Burr—Mr Foster—Mr Claughton.[4] Read Strauss—Gioberti—Ld Hervey.

3. 11 S. Trin.

Church 11 A.M. & Holy C—3½ P.M. Read Strauss—Davison Sermm & on Bapt. Regn.—also on Practical Education[5]—Browning's Convict Ship[6]—Gioberti.

4. M.

Wrote to J. Griffiths—J. Freshfield—J. Amery—Earl Dalhousie—Sec. Troon Steamers—Mrs Wadd—Latin lesson to Willy—Walk with C. Read Strauss—Gioberti—Lord Hervey—saw Claughton—Mackarness—Chess with Hussey.

5. T.

Wrote to T.G—M. de Mestral. Read Gioberti—Strauss—Ld Hervey—Townshend—Fraser's Mag. on the first Steam Voyage[7]—Went with L[yttelto]n to Birmingham for the Jenny Lind Concert. Also at Stourbridge on O.F. affairs.

6. Wed.

Church 7¼ P.M. Wrote to Rev. H. Mackenzie—R. Barker—Reid—Tayleur—Maitland—Ivall—Mrs Richardson[8]—Hampton—Walk with C—Chess with Calvert—Read Strauss—Townshend—& Lord Hervey.

7. Th.

Wrote to T.G—H.J.G—W.C. James—Kemp & Co—Hampton—Read Strauss—Townshend—Gioberti—Lord Hervey—making arrangements for journey—Walk with G. & Calvert—Chess with Calvert.

[1] Charles Old *Goodford, 1812–84; assistant master at Eton 1835, head master 1853–1862, provost 1862–84.
[2] *Disraeli's attack on whig handling of session business: *H* ci. 669.
[3] Himley Hall, Lord Ward's seat, 1 mile NW. Oak Farm, 8 miles N. o Hagley.
[4] See 26 Aug. 51.
[5] In J. *Davison, *Remains and occasional publications* (1840), 277, 407.
[6] C. A. Browning, *The convict ship* (1844); moral education and its effects on convicts.
[7] *Fraser's Magazine*, xxxviii. 275 (September 1848).
[8] Perhaps the wife of Thomas Richardson of Woodfield House, Hawarden.

8. Fr.

Church 10 A.M. Wrote to W. Chance—Ld Selkirk—S.R. Glynne—Barker—Read Strauss (finished Vol. 1) and Ld Hervey (finished)—a remarkable but horrible book. Also read Boydell's extraordinary pamphlet.[1] Walk with Ln. & Calvert.

9. Sat.

Wrote to Jas Foster—Rn. G—Cocks & Co—H. Taylor—Read Gioberti—Davison on Ed. Rev. & Oxford—Do on Silk Trade[2]—Townshend on Mesmerism (finished)—I feel that the question ought to be most seriously considered whether the process of mesmerising should not be tried on Lady Glynne. We went off to Birch's Farm & walked over it.[3] Mr Woodgate dined. Journey & money arrangements.

10. 12 S. Trin.

Ch 11 and 3. Wrote to Sir J.G—Fleetwood Steam Co[4]—Read Gioberti—Griselini on F. Paolo[5]—Marsh's Lectures.[6]

11. M.

Wrote to Collis. Saw J. Griffiths—Read Davison—Packed, & off at 10¾ to Wolverhampton & Fleetwood[7] at 7 A.M. where we were most improperly detained till near 12: which renders it impossible for me to attend the Trinity College [Glenalmond] meeting tomorrow. We had a tolerable passage, C., Miss Brown, & baby, not sick. NB. a teaspoonful of brandy made me worse.

12. T.

Wrote to M'Donald—Kemp & Co—Reached Troon[8] 2 P.M.—Glasgow 3½—Perth 7—where we had great difficulty in getting accommodation. Read 'Peerage Jobbery'.[9]

13. Wed.

9½–1¾ to Fasque, leaving the railroad at Montrose. We were very well satisfied with my Father's appearance: & found Jessy & Stephie blooming: Helen also very well—& John with his family. Set to work on unpack & arrange my *pied–a–terre*. Wrote to Maitland—Scotts—G. & Co—Worked on papers—Whist in evg.

[1] J. Boydell, 'A letter to Sir S. Glynne on the suspension of the Oak Farm works written in consequence of remarks made by . . . W. E. Gladstone with notes of the proceedings in the Birmingham court of bankruptcy before Mr. Commissioner Balguy' (1848); criticizes Gladstone's probity and business ability. Copy in Hawn P.

[2] J. *Davison, *Remains,* 641.

[3] 1 mile W. of Hagley.

[4] To arrange the passage to Scotland.

[5] F. Griselini, *Del genio di F. P. Sarpi in ogni facolta scientifica* . . . , 2 v. (1785).

[6] Cp. 27 Aug. 48.

[7] About 8 miles N. of Blackpool.

[8] About 4 miles N. of Ayr.

[9] Untraced pamphlet.

14. Th.

Wrote to Hampton—D.A. Miller[1]—C. Wordsworth—Mrs Chisholm—Rev. J.H. Hill[2]—Rev. E. Hawkins—Stevenson & Son[3]—W.B. Long[4]—Rev. H. Mackenzie—Read Gioberti—Talfourd's Final Memorials of C. Lamb[5]—Fitzgerald on V.I.[6]—Major Court on G.W.R.[7] Called at Fettercairn H.—Drove Sir J.G two hours & stood two batteries on Free Trade—Conv. with J.N.G. on the meditated settlement of property upon us.[8]

15. Fr.

Wrote to Rn. G—G. Chance—J. Griffiths—H.S. lesson to W. & A.—Read Strauss (began Vol 2)—Gioberti—Marshall's Life of Washington[9]—Memorials of Lamb—Drove my Father out. Whist with him in evg. Called on the Irvines & old Tibby.[10]—H.S. with W. & A.

16. Sat.

Read Strauss—Gioberti—Marshall's Washington—Account of Red River[11]—Memoir of Wilson[12]—Memorials of Lamb—Drove my Father out—Whist in evg. HS. with W. & A.

17. 13 S. Trin.

Church 11 & 3. It is a great delight to return to this little Chapel, the fruit of hope against hope. Coming hither also makes me begin to feel some repose of mind, & opportunity for selfexamn. which I trust may come to good. Read Ep. S. Bernard[13]—Gioberti—Tiers Ordre de St François[14]—Luther on the Will (terrible)[15]—Bp of Exeter's Charge[16]—Sydow on the Scottish Church.[17]

[1] A former employee of the Hudson's Bay Company, who had written a long letter on Vancouver Island, cp. Add MS 44367, f. 263.

[2] John Harwood *Hill, 1809–86; rector of Cranoe, Leicestershire 1837–86; archaeologist and antiquarian.

[3] Carpet dealers in Covent Garden.

[4] Property tax commissioners' clerk.

[5] T. N. *Talfourd, *Final memorials of Charles *Lamb, consisting chiefly of his letters not before published* (1848).

[6] J. E. *Fitzgerald, 'An examination of the charter and proceedings of the Hudson's Bay Company with reference to the grant of Vancouver's Island' (?1849), cp. Add MS 44367, f. 241.

[7] H. Court, 'A digest of the realities of the Great Western Railway' (1848).

[8] Cp. 28 Sept. and 19 Nov. 48.

[9] J. Marshall, *The life of George Washington*, 5 v. (1804–7).

[10] Tibby Souter, a villager.

[11] Perhaps J. West, *Substance of a journal during a residence at the Red River colony* (1824).

[12] Joshua *Wilson, *Memoir of the life and character of Thomas* Wilson* (1846).

[13] Cp. 1 Aug. 47.

[14] *La Règle du tiers-ordre des pénitens, instituée par le patriarche et seraphique père S. François pour les personnes seculières* (1663).

[15] Perhaps M. Luther, *The way to prayer*, tr. S. W. Singer (1846).

[16] H. *Phillpotts, 'A charge delivered . . . at the triennial visitation' (1848).

[17] C. L. A. Sydow, *The Scottish Church question* (1845).

18. M.

Wrote to H. Tayleur—Ld Medwyn—Wm. Gladstone. Conv. with Willy—*vice* yesterday. H.S. with him & Agnes. Read Bp of Exeter (finished)—Strauss—Talfourd's Lamb (finished Vol 1)—The Account of Red River—Out shooting with J.N.G. on Balfour: we had much conv. on family & money matters.

19. Tuesday.

Wrote to H. Maitland—Kemp & Co—W. Forbes—Ld Redesdale—Ld Camden—Ld Fielding. Read Strauss—Gioberti—Talfourd's Lamb—Account of Red River &c. (finished). H.S. with Willy & Agnes. Visit to Phesdo. With my Father on family matters.

20. Wed.

Wrote to J.E. Fitzgerald[1]—C.G. Reid (with corrected draft of Circular)—Lyttelton—H.S. with W & A. Read Strauss—Gioberti—Talfourd's Lamb—Walk to the works on Calcott Burn.[2]

21. Th. St Matthew.

Ch 11 A.M. H.S. with W. & A.—Wrote to Collis—Rev. J. Stevenson[3]—John & I [talked] with my Father on his plan of assigning property to us. We urged his making it, as far as its goes [sic] & as between one another, final. Read Strauss—Gioberti—Marshall's Washington—Whist with my Father: & drove out with him.

22. Fr.

Wrote to R. Barker (2)—Rn. G. Read Strauss—Gioberti—Lamb's Talfourd (finished)—Shooting with JNG—Whist in evg. H.S. with children. We were again with my Father on his arrangements about property & are very glad that he is now disposed to make them as far as they go *final.* These days have been days of touching recollection: so different are they from last year! But may they do the same work if in another way.

23. Sat.

Wrote to W.C. James—H. Tayleur—Ed. Montrose Standard—H.S. with children. Visited. Walk with Mr G.—Whist in evg. Read Strauss—Gioberti—Cowper's Task (began)[4]—Marshall's Washington—Campbell's Ld Eldon.[5]

[1] James Edward *Fitzgerald, 1818–96; Trinity, Cambridge; British Museum under-secretary 1849; emigrated to New Zealand 1850; prime-minister there 1854.

[2] $1\frac{1}{2}$ miles SW. of Fasque.

[3] Joseph *Stevenson, 1806–95; archivist 1831–41; curate of St. Giles, Durham, 1847, vicar of Leighton Buzzard 1849–62; edited the Rolls series; became roman priest 1872.

[4] W. *Cowper, *The task, a poem, in six books . . . to which are added . . . an epistle to Joseph Hill, Esq.* . . . (1785).

[5] J. *Campbell, *The lives of the lord chancellors* (1847), vii. 1.

24. 14 S. Trin.

Chapel 11 & 3. Wrote to Bonham. Read St Bernard—Tiers Ordre—Gioberti—Strauss. Saw Forbes—Mr Irvine. John leaves us tomorrow: my Father will miss him. But I have before me a good work of filial love, if grace may be given me to fulfil it. This & what I have [to do] towards my wife's family must for the present stand instead of much else, & by these as well as by other means can the Lord work His work in me.

25 M.

Wrote to Ld Selkirk (2)[1]—W. Chance. John & his party went in mg. Read Strauss—Gioberti—Marshall's Washington—Campbell's Ld Eldon. H.S. with W. & A.—A walk on the hill & visited. John & his party went. C. weans today. Whist with my Father, & a morning as well as evg *sederunt*.—Worked on my own money matters.

26. T.

Wrote to Collis—W. Gladstone—H.S. with W & A.—Latin with Willy. Drove Sir J.G. Conv. on his property plans. Picquet in evg. Read Strauss—Gioberti—Marshall's Washington—Ld Eldon. Worked a little by way of beginning on reducing my Father's books to order.

27. Wed.

Wrote to J.N.G—Hampton—Mr Miller—W. Forbes. H.S. with the children. Worked on the books. Walk. The Glynnes came. Whist in evg. Read Strauss—Gioberti—Ld Eldon—Washington.

28. Th.

Wrote to Dean Ramsay—W. Hampton—Collis—Freshfield. H.S. with Willy. Worked on the books: on O.F. & on my own affairs wh for the present will suffer from my Fathers arrangements as well as from O.F. & S.R.G's necessities: i.e. I expect to decline by £1700, or $\frac{1}{3}$ of my income: only £500 of this, probably, final loss: £860 by conversion into land diminishing annual proceeds: £340 withdrawn by my Father's new arrangements. Read Strauss—Gioberti—Ld Eldon. Went up Glenfarquhar[2] with Willy, & the Glynnes part of the way. Willy is such very good company, with others or alone.—Whist in evg.

29. St Michael. Fr.

Off at 8.15 to Katerline Consecration[3] & Holy Communion with abt. 130 or 140, chiefly of the fishermen & their families: a most devout & edifying congregation. We got back at $5\frac{1}{2}$: the distance 17 to 18 miles. Read Strauss

[1] Cp. Add MS 44367, ff. 280, 306, 317: a quarrel.
[2] About 7 miles NE. of Fasque.
[3] The episcopal chapel in Caterline, on the coast 5 miles S. of Stonehaven.

—Ld Campbell's Eldon. Whist in evg. Willy was of our party at his own earnest petition.

30. Sat.

Wrote to F. Baring—J.E. Fitzgerald—Rn. G—T.G—Bp of Brechin. H.S. with Willy only. With my Father on R. Martin's case[1]—& then a long conversation on his will & arrangements about property. Worked on the books—whist. Read Strauss—Gioberti—Lord Campbell's Eldon.

Sunday Oct. 1. 15 Trin.

Chapel 11 and 3 as usual. Wrote to Mr Stevenson—Lord J. Manners. Wrote on Holy Eucharist.[2] Read Book of Maccabees—St Bernard—Tiers Ordre de S. Francois—Visited.

2. M.

Wrote to H.J.G—Hampton—H. Tayleur—J. Griffiths—Chance—R. Barker—J. Hamilton Gray—M F Tupper—Mrs Chisholm—Rev A. Rankin[3]—E. Badeley. Read Strauss—Gioberti—Campbell's Eldon. Took C & L. the Delaly ride.[4] Whist in evg—& singing.

3. T.

Wrote an explanatory Memorandum on O.F. & S.R.G.s affairs—Latin lesson to Willy—Took the party up the Cairn [O'Mount]. Ld J. Manners came—whist. Read Strauss—Gioberti—D. of Argyle on Eccl. Hist. of Scotland.[5]

4. Wed.

Wrote to J.N.G—H.J.G—Rn. G—W. Hampton—Drove the party to the Burn. The river was most grand today. Read Strauss—Gioberti—Duke of Argyle. Whist in evg—& music.

5 Th.

Wrote to Miller—H. Maitland—and Rn. G. H.S. with Willy. Finished Memorandum on Oak Farm & S.R.G's affairs.[6] Walk with Ld J. Manners—music in evg. Read Strauss—Gioberti—Duke of Argyle—Ld Clarendon.[7]

[1] Robert Martin, the Fasque gamekeeper, was left a year's wages by the second codicil of Sir J. *Gladstone's will.

[2] Not found.

[3] Arthur Ranken, 1806–86; episcopal incumbent of St. John, Portsay, Banff, 1829–34, of St. Drostane, near Aberdeen, 1834–80; dean of Aberdeen 1880–6.

[4] A farm 1 mile W. of Fasque.

[5] G. D. *Campbell, duke of Argyll, '*Presbytery Examined*': *an essay, critical and historical, on the ecclesiastical history of Scotland since the Reformation* (1848); reviewed by Gladstone in the *Quarterly Review*, lxxxiii. 78 (December 1848); MS not traced; cp. Argyll, i. 308–13.

[6] On Oak Farm mortgages; Hawn. P.

[7] The 4th Earl; details at 8 Mar. 53 n.

6. Fr.

Wrote to J. Wood—R. Barker—H.S. with Willy. This morning about 7 I saw the box containing dear Anne's coffin placed in the N. bedroom on the ground floor till the arrangements for finally depositing it together with the other coffins are made—It is now locked up there & inaccessible. Took the party to Fordoun & the Friar's glen.[1] Music in evg. Saw Paterson & Walker on O.F.—& went, for Sir J.G. to inspect the Caldcott burn embankment. Hammered out an air for 'Und ob die wolke' &c.[2]

7. Sat.

Wrote to Rn. G—G. Grant—& Anon. Russian.[3] Read Strauss—Gioberti—D. of Argyle (finished)—Spottiswoode Miscy.[4]—Sage's Life.[5] H.S. with Willy—Walk with Ld J. Manners—music in evg.

8. 16 S. Trin.

Chapel mg & aft.—Conv. with Willy—Visited. Read St Bernard—Abp Spottiswoode's Sermon &c—Strauss.

9. M.

Prevented by sore throat from accompanying my Father to Edinburgh—kept to bed & blue pill—Our party went off with him. Read Strauss—Gioberti—Ld Campbell's Eldon—New M. on Dubarri.[6]

10. T.

Wrote to E. of Lincoln—H. Maitland—Scotts (2)—Sir J.G—G. & Co—Hampton—Masters. Read Strauss—Gioberti—Campbell's Eldon—Cowper's Task—Downstairs today. Saw Forbes—worked on the books.

11. Wed.

Wrote to Sir J.G—J.N.G—Freshfields—Sec. G.N.E. Co—H.S. with Willy—Walk, with C. riding to the Phesdo burn to examine damage: & to see the old folk at the Lodge there—Worked on the books. Read Strauss—Gioberti—Campbell's Eldon—Quarty. on Whiteside's Italy.[7] Wrote on H. Euch[arist].

[1] About 6 miles E. of Fasque.
[2] Untraced.
[3] Untraced.
[4] *The Spottiswoode Miscellany; a collection of original papers and tracts illustrative chiefly of the civil and ecclesiastical history of Scotland*, 2 v. (1844–5).
[5] J. Gillane, *The life of . . . John *Sage* (1714); a Scottish Bishop.
[6] Perhaps *Memoires de Madame la Comtesse Du Barri*, 4 v. (1829).
[7] *Quarterly Review*, lxxxiii. 552 (September 1848), review of J. *Whiteside, *Italy in the nineteenth century*, 3 v. (1848).

12. Th.

Wrote to Sir J.G—Mrs Redford[1]—R. Barker. H.S. with Willy—drove C. to L[aurence]kirk. Worked on the books. Wrote on H. Euch. Read Strauss—Gioberti—Ld C.s Eldon (finished)—Quart. on Penitentiaries: excellent.[2]

13. Fr.

Wrote to Sir J.G. Drove C. to Arbuthnott. Worked much on the books. H.S. with Willy. Read Strauss—Gioberti—Ld Campbell's Loughborough[3]—Cowper's Task. Restraint in food given up on the last irritation in my arms, resumed on coming here, now again nearly given up on account of the circumstances of the time.

14. Sat.

Wrote to Sir J.G—H. Tayleur—Walter James. H.S. with Willy—Visited—Read Strauss—Gioberti—Ld Loughborough—Marshall's Washington—Cowper's Task. calls, & visited—worked on books.

15. S. 17 Trin.

Ch. 11 & 3. Visited +. Wrote to R. Barker—J.N.G—Read S. Bernard—Sydow on Sc. Church—Gioberti—Strauss.

16. M.

Wrote to Freshfield—Scotts—J. Griffiths. H.S. & Latin Lesson with Willy—Read Strauss—Gioberti—Bp Forbes's Sermon on Mr Morse[4]—Ld Loughborough. Sir J.G. returned—in good health & spirits. An evening of conv. Worked on books.

17. T.

Began to write on D. of Argyll's Book.[5] H.S. with Willy. Worked on books. Read Strauss—Gioberti—Ld Loughb. Whist in evg.

18. Wed. St Luke.

Chapel at 11 A.M. H.S. with Willy—Worked on books. Read Strauss—Gioberti (finished Vol 3)—Marshall's Washington—Ld Campbell's Loughborough. Agnes's birthday—it ought to be one of profound thankfulness when we recollect what she had just passed through this day year.

[1] Unidentified.
[2] *Quarterly Review*, lxxxiii, 359 (September 1847), on female penitentiaries.
[3] J. *Campbell, *The lives of the lord chancellors* (1847), vi. 1.
[4] An MS, cp. W. Perry, *A. P. *Forbes* (1939), 197.
[5] Cp. 3 Oct. 48.

19. Th.

Wrote to Hampton—Worked on D. of Argyll. H.S. with Willy—Church conversations with Badeley yesterday & today—Read Strauss—Gioberti—Ld Campbell—Worked on books.

20. Fr.

Wrote to Bp of Brechin—H. Maitland—Scotts. H.S. with Willy—and much consultation on Miss Browne's difficulties with him. Listlessness is the very worst: & all he wants is a more uniform strength of will to fight against it. It is singular, but it is at these times of going wrong, that I am always most struck with the thorough fundamental excellence of character which it has pleased God to give him. Worked much on D. of A[rgyll]. Drove Badeley to the Friar's Glen. Read Strauss—Ld Campbell—A favourable turn in Willy's affairs in the evg.

21. Sat.

Wrote draft to Lees for Sir J.G. Wrote to Mr Lockhart—J.N.G.—C. Wordsworth—Freshfield. Read Marshall's Introd. to Washington. Worked on D. of Argyll.—H.S. with Willy. Drove the party to the Burn—Chess with Lady Brabazon—My Father thank God has had a tranquil & pleasant week.

22. S. 18 Trin.

Chapel 11 & 3. Corrected MS. on D. of Argyll. Wrote to Lyttelton—Read St Bernard—Lael & Chilion [1]—Strauss—Hooker. Conv. with Willy.

23 M.

Wrote to Scotts. Off at nine with Sir J.G., C.G., & our visitors for Edinburgh: arrived at 8. Saw Bp of Brechin 3 h. in Dundee on affairs of our Communion. Saw Helen a moment: she suffers much & her dangers still exist. Saw Miller afterwards on her case.[2] Read Textile Manufactures of G.B.[3]

24 T.

St Columba's Ch 10 A.M.[4] Saw Maitland—Bp of Edinbro'—Mr Ramsay. Attended Railway meeting 1–3¼ with Sir J.G. & spoke.[5] I went there to be with him: but I spoke willingly, on public grounds, since I think it is on

[1] Possibly pamphlet on G. Leale and J. R. P. Chilion, both involved in French church controversy 1845–6.

[2] Cp. 4 Nov. 48.

[3] G. *Dodd, *The textile manufactures of Great Britain*, 6 v. (1844–6).

[4] On Castle Hill, Edinburgh.

[5] A special meeting of the Edinburgh and Northern Railway to issue preference stock for an Aberdeen extension in collaboration with the Aberdeen Railway Company; the Gladstones unsuccessfully moved an amendment against the issue.

those grounds chiefly that the scheme of the Directors for fresh outlay & engagements is to be resisted.
4.15 P.M. off to Perth—Slept at the George in the 'Princess's' Room—Read 'Textile Manufactures.

25. Wed.

At 9¾ off to Trinity College: we were all delighted with its appearance & condition. Back at two to Perth: reached Fasque at 8. Catherine suffering from pain. We got her to bed quickly—& she profited thank God by rubbing, warmth, & then Castor Oil with peppermint water. My Father was most affectionate to her: too much so for his ease. Read Ld Campbell's Loughborough, then Erskine.[1]

26. Th.

Wrote to Northcote—Haughton—Kennedy—Commr. Stamps & Taxes[2]—J. Griffiths. H.S. with Willy. Read Strauss—Gioberti—Campbell's Lord Erskine—Beranger[3]—Corrected MS on D. of Argyll—Worked on the books. Walk with Willy.—C. better but still with much soreness. Of which a little came on me in the night.

27. Fr.

Wrote to E. of Lincoln—G. Burnett. H.S. with Willy. Read Strauss—Gioberti—Wiseman's Letter to Chirol[4]—Ld Erskine. My Father is now generally quiet & in good spirits: but excitable on occasion: seems to lose the power of reading & requires me for conversation three or four times a day, besides Catherine. It ought to be with me a greatly prized opportunity of rendering to him filial duty: & I hope it will be an useful lesson. Much conv. with C. on Lincoln's mournful letter. Whist in evg. Worked on books.

28. Sat. SS. Simon & Jude.

Chapel at 11 A.M. Wrote to Hope—Pelly—Roper—Read Strauss—Gioberti—Washington—Ld Erskine—H. Stevenson—Whist with Sir J.G. Drove with him & examined the Caldcotts Burn.

29. S. 19 Trin.

Chapel 11 & 3: & Holy Communion. Wrote to Dean Ramsay—Visited—Read St Bernard—Lael & Chilion—Bp Salisb. Charge[5]—Bp NZ. College Sermon[6]—Maskell's S. on Absolution.[7] Wrote on Transubstn.—& on Selection of Psalms.

[1] J. *Campbell, *The lives of the lord chancellors*, vi. 367.
[2] Thomas Pender.
[3] P. J. de Beranger, *Oeuvres complètes*, 4 v. (1834).
[4] Cp. 14 Apr. 48.
[5] E. *Denison, 'A charge delivered to the clergy of the diocese of Salisbury' (1848).
[6] Cp. 25 June 48.
[7] W. *Maskell, 'The outward means of grace' (1849); on Psalm cvii. 4.

30. M.

Wrote to S.R. Glynne—Maskell[1]—Scotts. H.S. with Willy—also Latin Lesson. Further correcting MS. on Duke of Argyll. Read Strauss—Life of Erskine—With S. Bateson[2] and at Ross's[3] for my Father.

On Saturday he told me he thought he had not treated me, relatively to my brothers, with justice, in letting me pay half the Oxford [election] Expences: & that he would—some time hence, probably 15 to 18 months—repay me. I told him I could only accept this as an act of generosity, & by no means of justice. I had to oppose his wish today about his letter to the Duke of Buccleuch on the Ferry:[4] he was sore I fear: but I find (31st) from him today that he has happily abandoned the idea. No one ever so freely admitted this kind of interference.

31. T.

Wrote to J.N.G—Burnett—Collis. H.S. with Willy. Drove C. to L[aurence]-kirk—for books, &c. Read Strauss—Gioberti—Lord Erskine's life—Corrected MS. Willy seems again to prosper in the schoolroom. C. has recovered from her indisposition of last week.

Wednesday Nov. One. All Saints.

Chapel at 11 A.M. Wrote to Lindsay—Tayleur. corrected MS. made the arrangements for the removal of the bodies[5]—Walk with Willy—visited. Read Strauss—Ld Erskine (finished)—Whist with my Father.

2 Th.

Wrote to Lockhart—I spent the early part of the day about the removal of the bodies of my Mother (& Uncle R) from Fettercairn, my Sister Anne from the house, to the vault under the Chapel, whither when it was all done my Father went to see them. The day is an appropriate one. It is a seemly and peaceful home for the Christian dead to which they have now come. Their souls are with thee O God: their beloved memory with us: & we are joined in the Church the communion of Saints: may we be found at the last too in that holy fellowship. Finished & sent off my MS. Drove Sir J.G. —Whist with him. H.S. with Willy. Read Strauss—began Ld Campbell Vol IV (Maynard.).[6]

3. F.

Wrote to Rn. G (2)—T.S. Gladstone—H.S. with Willy. Conferences about

[1] Copy in Add MS 44368, f. 22.
[2] Samuel Stephen Bateson, 1821–79, J. N. Gladstone's br. in law; barrister.
[3] i.e. D. Ross.
[4] The Burntisland ferry, cp. Checkland, 327–8.
[5] See next day.
[6] J. *Campbell, *The lives of the lord chancellors,* iv. 1.

him & Miss Browne. Worked on the books. Whist in evg. Read Neal's Hist[1] —Gioberti—Ld Campbell V. 4—Blackwood on Conservative re-union—poor:[2] and finished Strauss, a painful book but wh has its uses as well as its dangers.

4. Sat.

Wrote to Prof. Miller[3]—H.J.G.—W. Hampton—Lincoln—Collis. H.S. with Willy. Read Gioberti—Life of Washington—Ld Campbell—Skinner's Hist Scots Church.[4] Finished arranging the books: a serious matter & I am afraid not now very perfect. Whist with Sir J.G. Conv. with C. about the sad Lincoln affairs: and with my Father about Helen's letter. I advised him to send it to Miller—which he did, by me—to answer it without disputing but particularly without recognising the reality of her impressions—& to have the written evidence put together which shows that they are in short fanatical. It is dismal that true miracle should be brought into discredit by these notions sheer products of a heated imagination. But the thing is important; & some day, which God grant, she may be in a condition to consider the evidence.

5. 20 S. Trin.

Chapel 11 & 3. made tables of the Services of Festivals & Holy days. Read St Bernard—Gioberti—Tiers Ordre—Lael & Chilion (finished) Visited—Read Mr Irvine's Sermon on H[oly] Eucharist aloud to Sir J.G. in evg. A faceache wh had vexed me during the mg & during the day disappeared under the effort of it—

6. M.

Wrote (long) to Freshfield—Amery—Read Gioberti—Ld Campbell—Mr Burnett came: & I spent nearly all day upon some tough matters connected with the O[ak] F[arm] and Hawarden affairs. Also in the evg went through the miscellaneous subjects relating to the Estate with Mr B[urnett] and arranged with him respecting my purchases from Sir Stephen [Glynne]. I think extremely well of him. Latin lesson with Willy—also H.S.

7. T.

Wrote to Barker (2) with the results of yesterday's discussions & on other matters—also to Dowbiggin—Bridle[5]—C.G.—Reid—H.S. with Willy. Saw Burnett (further)—Mr Irvine—on divers subjects—C.G. on Miss Browne's case & H. Glynne's payment—Whist with Sir J.G.—Arranging letters &c—Read Gioberti—Ld Campbell—

[1] Cp. 7 Nov. 47.
[2] *Blackwood's Edinburgh Magazine*, lxiv. 632 (November 1848).
[3] James *Miller, 1812–64; professor of surgery at Edinburgh University from 1842.
[4] Cp. 22 Oct. 44.
[5] Involved with the Oak Farm.

8. Wed.

Wrote to Aunt J.—T.G.—H.S. with Willy—12½–3½. Attended Mackies funeral.[1] Saw Mr Whyte & had also conv with two *Free*ministers there. In the evening my Father much delighted us by offering to ask Mr W. to dinner. With my Father about his affairs and will: on which I made several minor suggestions. Whist with him. Arranging family matters—Read Gioberti—The Pearl of days[2]—Life of Washington—

9. Th.

Wrote to Miss Browne—Hampton—Austine—Dean Ramsay—H.S. with Willy. Read Gioberti—Life of Washington—Ld Campbell.—Rev. Mr Whyte & do Wilson[3] dined: all went off extremely well. Working on my Fathers matters: drove C. to Fordoun.

10. Fr.

Wrote to Barker—Lincoln—Wm. Gladstone—H.S. with Willy—C. laid up. Read Gioberti—Washington—Ld Campbell—Walk with my Father—Picquet in evg.

11. Sat.

Wrote to the Primus—H.S. with Willy—Walk with him—Whist with Sir J.G.—conv. on his will & money matters. Read Gioberti—Washington—Ld Campbell—Goode on Tract 90.[4] C. improved—

12. 21 S. Trin

Chapel 11 & 3. Made entries in Burial Register & copy. Read S. Bernard—Gioberti—Allies[5]—Worked on selecting Psalms—Visited (+).

13. M.

Wrote to Collis—Freshfield—Coleman—J.N.G.—Jos. Price[6]—H.S. with Willy—also Latin—Read Gioberti—Washington—Ld Campbell—Whist in evg. Working on O.F. papers.

14. T.

Worked all mg in abstracting my Fathers will & deed of Tailzie[7] for him as he forgets particulars of their contents. H.S. with Willy. Read Gioberti—Washington—Ld Campbell—Drove C. to Lkirk—Whist with Sir J.G.

[1] Unidentified; probably a villager.
[2] [Barbara H. Farquhar], 'The pearl of days; or, the advantages of the Sabbath to the working classes' (1848).
[3] Presbyterian minister.
[4] W. *Goode, 'Tract XC historically refuted; or a reply to . . . F. *Oakeley' (1845).
[5] T. W. Allies, 'The Church of England cleared from the charge of schism' (enlarged 2 ed., 1848).
[6] Stockbroker in London.
[7] Entail.

15. Wed.

Wrote to R. Barker—H.S. with Willy. Went with my Father to Lkirk & whist with him in evg. Examined books at Lkirk for my article. & corrected the proofs. Read Gioberti—Washington—Ld Campbell—Le Bas' Laud[1]—Rns. birthday: may God bless & keep him. There is now a new & critical phase in his life.[2]

16. Th.

Wrote to M.F. Tupper—T.C. Cowan[3]—Messrs. G. & Co. H.S. with Willy. Walk with him. Whist in evg. Read my Fathers MS prayers of 1818: they have remarkable force & facility: & I think also terseness. Also his MS for will. Read Gioberti—Washington—Ld Campbell—

17. Th.

Wrote to Griffiths (2) and draft—to Roper & dft.—Lincoln—Dr. Guthrie—S.R. Glynne—H.S. with Willy—Visited. Read Gioberti—Washington—Ld Campbell—Whist with Sir J.G.—Worked on my Father's papers—

18. Sat.

Wrote to J. Murray—J. Freshfield—T.G.—H.S. with Willy. Walk with C. Whist with Sir J.G. Read Gioberti—Ld Campbell (finished IV) Washington (finished III)—Cowper's Task (finished)—Finished corrections &c of my Article.

19. 22 S. Trin

Chapel 11 & 2½. Wrote on Luke XIV. 26.[4]—Visited. Read Mr I[rvine's] morning Serm. aloud to Sir J.G.—Saw Dr. Guthrie—Read S. Bernard: Gioberti: Tiers Ordre de St Fr: Smith's Truth as Revealed.[5]

20. M.

Wrote to Tayleur—Mrs Hodges. H.S. with Willy—also Latin lesson. Read Gioberti—Washington—Andersen's Hist. Commerce (began)[6]—Cowper's Tirocinium[7]—Ld Campbell. Whist with Sir J.G. Walk to C's ride.

21. T.

Worked all the forenoon with my Father taking down (& discussing) new directions for his will. He has even pressed me for declarations of opinion &

[1] C. W. *Le Bas, *Life of Archbishop *Laud* (1836).
[2] He had taken over almost all Sir John's Liverpool business.
[3] Thomas C. Cowan, from 1843 perpetual curate of St. Thomas', Liverpool.
[4] Cp. Add MS 44780, f. 268.
[5] George Smith of Birse, 'Truth as revealed, or voluntaryism and free criticism opposed to the word of God' (1847).
[6] Adam Anderson, *An historical and chronological deduction of the origin of commerce, from the earliest accounts to the present time*, 2 v. (1764).
[7] Part of *The Task*; cp. 23 Sept. 48.

I have in general given them with freedom. At my suggestion he altered the arrangement making our Shares equally divisible among our issue—introduced a provision respecting Anne's books—a general power to Ex[ecut]ors to recognise honorary engagements—a nett sum to T.G. in cons[ideratio]n of the burdens charged upon the Estates—right of pre-emption of the Estates for his male descendants—also he increased what he meant for Hayman [1]—& made the new plate an absolute heirloom. I did not advise any substantial change in regard to Helen: but rather encouraged his making her bequeathable portion only £5000 rather than £10,000. I also advised his giving Tom something from my Mother's jewels as an heirloom —and fixing the sum for Asylum. This I think was all of a substantial character that sprang from me: and I make the note of it now because I am at present the only one of his children cognisant of the particulars of his will.
H.S. with Willy. Walk & visits—whist in evg. Read Gioberti—Washington —Ld Campbell—& Waverley: a fresh perusal by way of treat.[2]

22. Wed.

Wrote to J.N.G.—Barker. H.S. with Willy. Mary's first birthday. She is the quickest & most forward of all the children at her age. Yesterday she named the flies 'com' and repeats it whenever she sees one. She has thank God great health, is like her cousin Nora Glynne & her Aunt Mary [Lady Lyttelton], & it seems as if Agnes & she were Catherine & Mary over again. I was again engaged with Sir J.G. about his will—reading the Directions of yesterday aloud & taking down any amendments. I must add to the Memm. I then made, that I advised him to 'direct' arbitration in the last Clause rather than "strongly urge, and recommend". Read Gioberti—Washington —Ld Campbell—Waverley. Whist with Sir J.G.—Chapel music at F. House.

23. Th.

Wrote to T.G.—Rev. Mr Eden—H.S. with Willy. We made an exp. to Mrs Souter with her gown & (after consulting 'Pitnamoon') [3] about her removing to Old Mains: she showed the most beautiful & simple local attachment: & said Willy who had been sitting by her "was very complaisant, and had muckle o' humility.["]

Walk in hall with Sir J.G. & Whist. Also saw him about Tom's notes *both* of which by an unhappy blunder I put in his hands: & he was annoyed through my fault not Tom's: but I trust *only* for the moment—Read Gioberti—Washington—Waverley—Ld Campbell (Vol V)—

[1] He left Richard Hayman, his butler, an annuity of £15 *per annum*.
[2] By Sir W. *Scott, 3 v. (1814).
[3] The laird of the farm of Pitnamoon, owned by Sir John Gladstone, 2½ miles ESE. of Fasque.

24. Fr.

Wrote to H.J.G. & copy—Tayleur. H.S. with Willy—& another disturbance in schoolroom affairs but wh. I trust ended well. Read Gioberti—Washington—(finished Vol IV)—Ld Campbell & Waverley. My letter to Helen was most painful: the subject makes me wish I could find myself even a calumniator. I tried to consider it much, & not act beyond the occasion.[1] Visited—Whist with Sir J.G.

25. Sat.

Wrote to Hampton—Amery—Masters—Freshfield—Merewether—Kingston [2]—Lander [3]—Bosworth [4]—J. Gregory—F. Rogers—H.S. with Willy. Read Gioberti—Washington (Vol. V). Ld Campbell—Waverley—The Irvine family and Mr Robertson [5] dined. Whist in evg.

26. Last S. Trin.

Chapel 11 & 2½. Read Mr I.s morning Sermon aloud to my Father. Visited. Walked with C.—worked on arrangements of Psalms. Wrote on the case of Naaman: part of wh speaks so powerfully to me.[6] Opened the question of Sub[scriptio]n for the Scots Bprics with my Father. Thank God he gave a ready ear. We had grief today from Agnes who told a second story: tho the fault was mitigated by spontaneous confession. Read S. Bernard—Gioberti—Tiers Ordre—

27. M.

Wrote to Mr Balfour—J.R. Hope (2) & copy: this being an account of Helen's case, on which I examined the correspondence, & stated in my letter the result. Again on the Bprics: my Father made & wrote for my guidance his decision. Read Gioberti—Washington—Ld Campbell—Waverley. Private conv. with Willy. Also Latin lesson. Also conv. with poor Agnes, who was restored in evg. Also with C. on her letter to Miss B. Whist in evg.

28. T.

Wrote to C.G. Reid—Ld Medwyn (& made extract)—Earl of Lincoln—Paterson & Walker. H.S. with Willy. Read Gioberti—Washington—Ld Campbell (Vol V)—Waverley—Saw Greig—Whist in evg.

[1] Gladstone had been much shocked to find that his sister had been using books by protestant divines as lavatory paper. See Magnus, 84, for extracts from his letter, in Hawn P.

[2] William Henry Giles *Kingston, 1814–80; edited *The Colonist* 1844, the *Colonial Magazine* 1849–51; sponsored emigration schemes.

[3] John Lander, b. 1817; Pembroke, Oxford; rector of Donnington, Herefordshire, from 1845.

[4] J. *Bosworth; or Thomas Bosworth, 1823?–99, London bookseller and publisher, especially of Irvingite books.

[5] James Robertson, surgeon, of Fettercairn.

[6] On II Kings v. 13; cp. Add MS 44780, f. 272.

29. Wed.

H.S. with Willy. Read Gioberti—Washn.—Ld Campbell—Waverley. 11–5. Drove C. to Kinnaird,[1] on the part of my Father, to ask for Sir J. Carnegie. The Miss C.s[2] are particularly pleasant: & there are some interesting pictures. Whist in evg.

30. St Andrew.

Wrote to H.J.G.—J.R. Hope—Northcote—Wm. Gladstone. Chapel at 11 A.M. at F[ettercairn] House to practice singing. Walk with C. & the children. Whist in evg. Read as yesterday—beginning Gioberti 5th & *last.*

Friday Decr. One 1848.

Wrote to Rn. G—T.G.—Greig—Rev. Mr Whyte—J.L. Ross—Howis: H.S. with Willy. Visited. Walk with C.—Helen returned. Read as yesterday. Whist in evg.—also singing. Wrote on Col. Policy.[3]

2. Sat.

Wrote to Wm. Gladstone—H. Tayleur—J.E. Fitzgerald—H.S. with Willy. Party to dinner & music in evg. Read Sir J.G.s MS drafts (from L & M.)[4] for will & entail—Read Gioberti—Washington—Waverley.

3. Advent Sunday.

Chapel (Holy Comm. mg.) mg & aft. Visited (+). Read the morning sermon aloud to Sir J.G. Wrote to T.D. Acland—worked on Psalms—Read S. Bernard—Gioberti—Tiers Ordre—Smith on the Free Ch &c[5]—

4. M.

Wrote to Bp of Aberdeen—Miss Brown—Sir W. James—F. Rogers—Bp of Oxford. H.S with Willy. Visited. Walk with C. Spent the forenoon with my Father reading his dft will to him discussing particulars. Read Gioberti—S. Bernard—Washington (finished)—Ld Campbell—Waverley finished. As to the last I find the two chapters of the interviews at Carlisle as sublime as I thought them 25 years ago: as to Washington, he is a great man, above the level & the measure of most modern greatness. He is Roman in a wonderful degree.

5. T.

Wrote to Hampton—R. Barker—J. Griffiths. H.S. with Willy—also Latin

[1] Kinnaird Castle, seat of Sir James Carnegie, 4 miles SE. of Brechin.

[2] Sir David Carnegie, d. 1805, 6th Bart. had four unmarried daughters: Christina Mary, d. 1860; Elizabeth, d. 1884; Jane; Agnes, d. 1875.

[3] Start of important series on colonial govt. and commerce; cp. Add MS 44738, ff. 234–64.

[4] James Leighton, Montrose solicitor and town clerk and witness, with his partner, George Cooper Myres, to Sir J. *Gladstone's will.

[5] Cp. 19 Nov. 48.

lesson. Worked most of the morning with Sir J.G. & with Leighton, on the will & appertaining papers. Made up monthly letters. Parted with H. Scarr my footman: tried to advise him. Read S. Bernard (de Consideratione)[1]—Gioberti—Guy Mannering.[2] Walk with C.—Whist in evg.

6. Wed.

Chapel 11 A.M. Wrote to T.G.—J.G. Lockhart—H.S. with Willy. Read S. Bernard—Gioberti—Raynal on Amn. Revolution[3]—Ld Campbell—Guy Mannering. Visited. Walk with C. Music in evg. Worked on Pss. Wrote on Col Policy.

πολ. Those who have denied the doctrine of original sin have been hard pressed to account for all the evil and misery in the world: they have been bound not to impute it to the universality of individual sinfulness. They have very commonly, and naturally enough, fastened the charge upon Government the great organ of collective man. The logical difficulty of thus producing something out of nothing is not indeed thus conquered: but it is put out of immediate view by shifting it a little farther off. This is a way of accounting for it: a fact however stands independently of the justness of every account given of it: and I think it is a fact that the class in question have in a very remarkable degree been opponents of established government and given, except where a love of ease had a preponderating influence over them, to favour innovation.[4]

7. Th.

Wrote to Bp of Glasgow—Mr S. Christy—Rev. Mr Wilson—H.S. with Willy. Read S. Bernard—Gioberti—Raynal on Amn. Revolution (finished)—Ld Campbell (finished)—Guy Mannering. Busy in another misunderstanding with Miss Browne: however, she conquered herself and it ended well. Visited. Walk with Willy. Worked on Psalms: with my scissors. Whist in evg.

8. Fr.

Chapel 11 a.m.[5] Visited. Read S. Bernard—Gioberti—Paine's Age of Reason[6]—Royal Academy Lectures (began)[7]—Guy Mannering. Walk, with C. & the children riding. Worked on Psalms.[8]

[1] Migne, *PL* clxxxii. 727.
[2] By Sir W. *Scott, 3 v. (1815).
[3] G. T. F. Raynal, *A philosophical and political history of the British . . . in North America* (1779).
[4] 6 December 1848; Add MS 44737, f. 62.
[5] 'H.C. with Sir J.G.' here deleted.
[6] T. *Paine, *The age of reason; being an investigation of true and fabulous theology* (1794); notes in Add MS 44737, f. 65.
[7] R. N. Wornum, ed., *Lectures on painting. By the Royal Academicians* (1848); contains lectures by James *Barry.
[8] Sir J. *Gladstone's will was this day signed at Fasque.

9. Sat.

Wrote to J. Griffiths—J.N.G.—Wordsworth—F.W. Brown[1]—Ireland. H.S. with Willy—Worked on Pss. Read S. Bernard—Gioberti—T. Paine's Age of Reason—Barry's Lectures—Guy Mannering—

10. 2 S. Advent.

Chapel mg. & aft—Conv. with Willy—Visited—read aft. sermon aloud to my Father. Worked on Pss. Read S. Bernard—Synode de Pistoie[2]—Tiers Ordre.

11. M.

Wrote to H. Tayleur—G. & Co—R. Phillimore. H.S. with Willy also Latin lesson—worked on Psalms. Walk with C—examined Caldcotts Burn—whist in evg. Read S. Bernard—Gioberti—Barry—Guy Mannering—Case of Canterbury Lay Clerks.[3] Wrote for Exc. Butl.[4]

We drank after dinner to my Fathers health. He is thank God well & tranquil: and he looks onward steadily. A few mornings ago when we had been speaking of some recent arrangement he spoke to me starting I think from the desirableness of getting all his affairs into the clearest form to this effect, that he wished thus to have all settled for he thought it very likely that when he was called away it would be like Sir John Barrow suddenly;[5] that he looked upon death as a mere removal, and regarded it without apprehension, for he had endeavoured to live in the performance of his duty and he placed his trust in the 'compensation' which had been made for our sins: he trusted also he was sensible of the great & peculiar blessings wh God had bestowed upon him.—He also then or lately intimated that until a recent period he had looked forward to living probably some two or three years longer but this incident of Sir J.B.s death has made him view his own as more likely to be within that time.

12. T.

Wrote to Bunsen. H.S. with Willy. Visited. Whist with Sir J.G.—Dinner party. Read S. Bernard—Gioberti—(finished this very long but important work)—T. Paine's Age of Reason—W. Irving's Columbus[6]—Guy Mannering—Wrote Exc. Butl.

[1] Perhaps the governess's father.

[2] Cp. 11 July 47.

[3] C. Sandys, 'The memorial and case of the clericilaici or lay-clerks of Canterbury Cathedral' (1848).

[4] Not found.

[5] Sir John *Barrow, 1764–1848, of Liverpool; second secretary to the admiralty 1804–6 and 1807–45; 1st Bart. 1835.

[6] Washington Irving, *A history of the life and voyages of Christopher Columbus*, 4 v. (1828).

In the early part of the Session those who are called Protectionists offered Goulburn to take him for their leader: which he declined.

Some time after this, Goulburn, Graham, Lincoln, & I, were asked if we should object to meet Bankes & Ld Granby[1] on the subject of our relative political positions, or rather I believe it was to meet Ld Ellenborough & Ld Lyndhurst with a view to the other meeting. Graham I believe declined being determined to do nothing but with Peel. Lincoln also declined. Goulburn made the communication to me, & I was with him of opinion that we could not properly decline to meet our old colleagues from whom we had never been separated, nor did I see any objection to the other meeting, but that it must not be supposed there was any doubt or hesitation in my mind as to our commercial policy in respect to which I thought not merely that we must not retrace our steps but that we must finish what yet remained undone as I was persuaded

1 that it was right on its own merits

2 that until these questions were disposed of there could be no ground cleared for solid & permanent union with many to whose general principles we subscribed.

I heard no more of it. This may have been connected with my endeavours to force the Government to bring forward the Navigation Laws which they were manifestly inclined to avoid: endeavours for which Labouchere afterwards thanked me individually saying I had much helped him.

Not long before the close of the Session of 1848, I observed to Young that the communication of which he had been the organ had dropped rather oddly.[2] He said he had reported to Peel our conversation: and that he thought Peel had shortly after seen Graham upon the subject: he connected the dropping of the suggestion, which it must be remembered had proceeded spontaneously from Peel himself, with that interview & a discussion between him & Graham.

It is singular that Peel should have started such a subject without knowing his own mind upon it, as it seemed that he placed the necessity of some kind on rather high grounds e.g. that without it we could not give effective support to the Govt.[3]

13. Wed.

Chapel 11. a.m. Wrote to Rn. G.—MS Theol. &c[4]—Read S. Bernard—Mr Hallam's Notes[5]—T. Paine, Amn. Crisis[6]—Barry's Lectures—Guy Mannering—Walk with Willy—Whist in evg. My Father has now made up his mind that Sir J. Barrow's case has nothing to do with his, thinking that it was organic disease of the heart—But Q[uer]y? Worked on Psalms.

14. Th.

Wrote to Freshfield—Paterson & Walker (if)—Hampton. H.S. with Willy. Walk with C.G. Col MSS—Read S. Bernard—Hallam—T. Paine—Barry—Guy Mannering (finished).

[1] A leader of the protectionists; cp. 15 June 49 n.

[2] See 7 Dec. 47.

[3] Dated 12 December 1848; Add MS 44777, f. 274 ff.

[4] Not found.

[5] H. *Hallam, 'Supplemental notes to the view of the state of Europe during the middle ages' (1848); Gladstone's notes are in Add MS 44737, f. 69.

[6] T. *Paine, *The American crisis* (?1792); Gladstone's notes are in Add MS 44737, f. 70.

15. Fr.

Chapel 11 a.m. Wrote to Bp of Glasgow—Bp of Brechin—Duthie & Duncan[1]—Music practice. Read S. Bernard—Hallam—T. Paine—Barry—The Antiquary.[2] Storm. Whist with Sir J.G.

16. Sat.

Wrote to T.G.—Hampton—Rev. Mr Annesley[3]—R. Barker—H. Tayleur—H.S. with Willy—Worked on Psalms—Calls at Edzell: drove with Sir J.G.—walk home. Read S. Bernard—Hallam's Notes—R. Phillimore on Eccl. Courts[4]—Paine's American Crisis (finished)—The Antiquary—Scots Episc[opal] Magazine.[5]

17. 3 S. Advent.

Chapel 11 & 2½ Wrote on the parable of the ten talents.[6] Conv. with Willy—Visited—read Mr I.s aft sermon aloud to Sir J.G.—Read S. Bernard—Synode de Pistoie—Tiers Ordre (finished)—

18. M.

Wrote to Dowbiggin—H. Tayleur—N. British Railway Supt.—R. Barker—G. Burnett. H.S. with Willy. Also Latin lesson. Worked on accounts & private affairs—as related to S.R.G. Read S. Bernard—Hallam's Notes—Longfellow's Poems[7]—The Antiquary. Worked on Ps[alm]s. I was in the vault today: it is very calm as it should be. Helen & also Aunt J. were there before me. Out of door errands for Sir J.G.—walk with C. & the children.

19. T.

Wrote to Duthie & Co. Also dft for C.G. to Lady Ln. H.S. with Willy. Worked on Ps[alm]s. Again read over my Father's Will & Entail to him: omitting the purely technical parts. We found but one error. Read S. Bernard—Hallam's Notes. Longfellow's poems (finished. They show decided genius)—Barry's Lectures—The 'Mysteries of London'[8]

20. Wed.

Chapel 11 a.m. Wrote to Lincoln—S.R. Glynne—O.B. Cole—H. Tayleur. Read S. Bernard—Hallam's Notes (with his M[iddle] Ages)—Barry &

[1] Writers to the signet in Great King Street, Edinburgh.
[2] By Sir W. *Scott, 3 v. (1816).
[3] Probably Charles Annesley, 1788–1863; fellow of All Souls, Oxford, from 1813.
[4] Cp. 12 June 48.
[5] It ran for a few months only in 1844.
[6] Cp. Add MS 44780, f. 276.
[7] H. W. Longfellow, either *Poems on slavery, early poems, additional poems, and ballads* (1848) or *The belfry of Bruges and other poems* (1848).
[8] An advance copy of *The mysteries of London* [*a novel*] *translated from the French* (1849). Imitating E. Sue's best-seller on Paris.

Opie's Lectures[1]—Mysteries of London—West Rev. on Ld J. Russell[2]—Worked on Ps[alm]s. Walk with C.

21. Th. St Thomas.

Chapel 11 a.m. Wrote to Leighton & Myers—H.H. Creed—H. Tayleur—Paterson & Walker—Freshfield. Wrote divers MSS. Read St Bernard—Hallam's Notes—Talfourd's Speech for Shelley[3]—Mysteries of London: of wh from what I have read I think it much better, tho' coarser than the French novels. Worked on the Psalms. Whist with my Father.

Rel[igion] It may be that you are tempted to do some certain act in which the mind may be divided thus. A dull black misgiving warns you to stop: a well constructed argument shows that you may, nay even that you ought to go on. Yet often will the former be right, and the latter will be wrong, on account of some false assumption lying at its root which vitiates the whole. But how strange it may be said that the Monitor of Truth should come in a cloudy form should present itself in a shape such as every superstition may assume—while on the other hand the voice of temptation assumes the tones of Reason which man is bound to obey. And yet it is so. But mark this is the sign that all has not been right. Truth only comes thus to minds which have been perverted and of which the habits are not yet thoroughly set right. They are weaker inwardly than those that have never fallen, and their outward difficulties too are greater: murmur not at this: it is the very law of Divine retribution and likewise of natural justice—Sin cannot pass over us and leave us as we were, and every sin we commit has a long train of poison that it draws and sheds behind it, which disastrous sequel is indeed the very & most effectual witness that God hath set his curse upon it & that its paths are the paths of death. And the forgiveness which should reverse that law of Eternal Justice would be a forgiveness not according to the character of God, but one destructive of the basis of moral responsibility, and meet only to work the work of Satan.[4]

22. Fr.

Chapel 11 a.m. Visited.—Drive with my Father. Whist in evg. Dinner party. Music. Assisted Helen with her books. Read S. Bernard—Hallam's Notes (finished)—Ed. Rev. Vol 28 on Annual Parliaments[5]—Goode's reply to Oakeley.[6]

23. Sat.

Wrote to Freshfield—Leighton & Myers—H. Tayleur. Saw Paterson & Walker (O.F.) Engaged with the Company in the forenoon—Helping H. with her books—Read St Bernard—Goode—The Antiquary—Wrote MSS Theol.

[1] Cp. 8 Dec. 48.
[2] *Westminster Review*, xcviii. 1 (October 1848).
[3] T. N. *Talfourd, 'Speech for the defendant, in the prosecution of the Queen v. Moxon, for the publication of Shelley's works' (1841).
[4] Dated this day; Add MS 44737, f. 73.
[5] *Edinburgh Review*, xxviii. 125 (March 1817).
[6] Cp. 11 Nov. 48.

24. 4 S. Advent.

Chapel mg & aft—Conv. with Willy. Visited +. Read Mr I.s morning Sermon aloud to my Father. Worked on Pss. Read St Bernard—Synode de Pistoie—and Goode (finished)—

25. Xmas Day.

Chapel mg (with Holy C.) & aftn—Visited. Wrote to Dowbiggin—Read St Bernard—Synode de Pistoie—Xtn Remembrancer on New Test &c.[1]

26. St Stephen.

Chapel 11 a.m. Latin lesson with Willy. Also walk. Wrote to R. Phillimore —Horsfall—J. Mackenzie—E. Foster[2]—Lewin—Read St Bernard—Phillimore on Eccl Courts (finished)—The Antiquary—Opie's Lectures—Worked on a heavy arrival of papers & letters from London.

27. St John Evang.

Chapel 11 a.m. Wrote to Rn. G.—Palin[3]—Borradaile[4]—Wyld[5]—Neustein[6] —Whitaker[7]—Walk to C.s ride—Visited Wallace[8]—Whist. Read St Bernard—Synode de Pistoie—R.M. Martin on Vancouver's I.[9]—The Antiquary—

28. Innocents.

Chapel 11 a.m. Wrote to W. Wyon—G. Poulson[10]—M.F. Tupper—Buckingham—P. Hall—Monsell—Scotts—Twist—H. Howard—Drive with C.—Whist in evg. Read St Bernard—Synode de Pistoie—Martin's Vanc. I.—Antiquary—

29. Fr.

Wrote to Hampton—E. Hawkins—Everard[11]—Gerard—R.M. Martin—J.N.G.—W.C. James. H.S. with Willy. Read S. Bernard—Synode de Pistoie—R.M. Martin (finished)—Dr Everard's Letter—Chr. Wordsworth's

[1] *Christian Remembrancer*, xvi. 456 (October 1848); on *Gorham.

[2] Probably Edward Ward Foster, 1762–5; landscape and portrait painter, and writer on theology and history.

[3] William *Palin, 1803–82; rector of Stifford from 1834, author and hymnist.

[4] Harry Borradaile, 1800–76; in Bombay civil service 1819–44; wrote on Indian law; member of *Macaulay's law commission.

[5] James Wyld, 1812–87; lib. M.P. for Bodmin 1847–52, 1857–9, 1865–68; bought centre of Leicester Square 1851; geographer.

[6] Unidentified.

[7] Possibly Samuel Whitaker, secretary to sundry railway companies.

[8] A villager.

[9] R. M. *Martin, *The Hudson's Bay territories and Vancouver's Island* (1849).

[10] George *Poulson, 1783–1858; Yorkshire topographer and antiquarian.

[11] Edward Everard, 1786?–1856?; D.D. 1831; curate of Staplegrove, Somerset, 1841–4, of Bishop's Hull 1844–55; sent Gladstone an advance copy of his 'Letter setting forth that baptismal regeneration . . . is no cause for controversy' (1849).

Sermon[1]—Bp of Oxfords Charge[2]—The Antiquary (finished). The evening was dignified with Charades very well got up, & to the intense delight of the children. Whist with Sir J.G.

As I look back upon the course of this year though I would fain hope that in some points of duty it has been a year of improvement, I must feel with shame that in respect to purity it has been one of retrogression. I have been sensible of a weakness and relaxation of mind, a loss of determining and resisting power, from not so much the amount as the kind of business in which this year for the first time I have been so constantly engaged: and the vague curiosity which so often entraps me has thus acquired in regard to reading a greater scope. Yet to trace the ill in any manner to a cause consoles though it does not excuse. There have also been some other circumstances tending to weaken discipline. But it is a grievous and a crying shame: only God yet lets the figtree cumber the ground[3] leaving therefore the door of hope open, and surrounds me with so many blessings which I do not yet believe to be signs of His concealed wrath. Oh may He make me strong in the secret conflict and give me that blessed gift of spiritual *integrity.*

Willy and Agnes presented me with little letters today both most acceptable, diversified according to their years.

30. Sat.

9–7: 95 miles to Dalkeith,[4] with delays. Saw Helen's bust in Ed[inburgh] on the way: a work showing energy in the artist.[5] Read Synode de Pistoie—Herschel's Discourse on Nat[ural] Philosophy[6]—

31. S. Chapel 11 & 3.

The music is most striking: both in execution, & what is better in intention: & the whole very satisfactory. It is really a privilege to see great station so filled as it is here. Walked to Ld Melville's:[7] made acquaintance with the Miss Dundases, & with Lady Lothian, all well worth knowing, but the latter even surpassed my high expectations.[8] Read Synode de Pistoie—B. Noel on Church & State[9]—Bp Jolly on the Church[10]—Slights Letter to Bp of Oxford[11]—Acland's on Oxf[ord] Med[ical] Education.[12]

Wrote to Sir J.G. and so ends the year. My occupations in connection

[1] Christopher *Wordsworth *fils*, 'Righteousness exalteth a nation' (1848); in Prov. xiv. 34.

[2] S. *Wilberforce, 'A charge delivered . . . at his primary visitation' (1848).

[3] See Luke, xiii. 7.

[4] 6 miles SE. of Edinburgh, seat of duke of Buccleuch.

[5] See 14 Apr. 47 n.

[6] Sir J. F. W. *Herschel, *A preliminary discourse on natural philosophy* (1831).

[7] Robert Dundas, 1771–1851; 2nd Viscount Melville 1811; had 2 das., Jane, d. 1862 and Anne, d. 1851. His seat was Melville Castle, 2 miles W. of Dalkeith.

[8] She was then a tractarian, see 2 Sept. 46 n.

[9] B. W. *Noel, *Essay on the union of church and state* (1848).

[10] A. *Jolly, 'Some plain instructions concerning the nature and constitution of the Christian Church' (1840).

[11] H. S. Slight, 'A letter to the . . . bishop of Oxford' (1848); on colonial missionaries.

[12] H. W. *Acland, 'Remarks on the extension of education of the university of Oxford' (1848).

with Stephen's affairs have been a new & marked feature in it to me. Under nothing has my heart oftener sunk: I feel upon me the feebleness of my ignorance & incompetence aggravated by the pressure of very heterogeneous duties. Yet the hand of God I think has clearly pointed me to *this* duty: & immersed as it is in every secular element, I know [1] that had I in me but one spark of the spirit of a saint, or of a son, I should say with all my heart, Even so Lord, be it as Thou wilt, let me walk calmly & earnestly in the way of duty, seeing by Thy light, feeling by Thy Hand, from day to day, from hour to hour, learning Thy lessons in Thy school & striving even from the meanest of Thy creatures to glorify Thy name. O that it may be so, & even this labour sanctified by offering it up to God.

[1] Instead of 'feel'.

Dalkeith Jan. One 1849.

Circumcision

Chapel 11 (with Holy Comm[unio]n) & 3½. The morning house prayers at *nine* were those of the Church: omitting from 1st Lesson as far as the Collect.—The holy office was administered in a most becoming manner in the Chapel. Wrote to Sir J.G.—Freshfield—Ld Wenlock—the Dean of Windsor. Read B. Noel. Walks with Ld Lothian & Mr Meyrick—also with the Dss. & C.G. At night there was a servants ball in wh the Duke took an active & most becoming part. I was a stupid spectator. Agnes had her first lessons [in dancing] from Mr Balfour[1] & the Duke—& kept admirable time.

2. T.

10–8¼. 95 m. to Fasque. Saw C. off for York. Saw Slater, & Helen's bust—C.G. Reid—Mr Ramsay—A.H. Wylie. Read B. Noel—Herschel's Discourse. Engaged with letters & papers in evg after arrival. It is really a privilege to visit such people as those under whose roof they [*sc.* we] have been; their station & wealth do not give them ornament but receive it from them.

3. Wed.

Wrote to C.G.—Hampton—Dowbiggin—R. Barker—(2)—Howis—Cocks & Biddulph—T.G.—G. & Co. H.S. with Willy & his Cousin: who is a quick ingenuous affectionate boy.[2] Poor Willy has been beset by his listlessness: & we had sore ado about it today. But a beginning of improvement thank God was made. And in truth this is nearly his sole fault. Would God that my wounds were such & capable of such healing. Read S. Bernard[3]—Synode de Pistoie[4]—Quarterly on L. & N.W.R.[5] Arranging letters & papers. Whist with Sir J.G.—walk with Johnnie & W. Saw Ly H. Forbes, Servant's Ball in evg.

4. Th.

Wrote to C.G.—G. Tomline—Abp Canterbury—T. Butlin—S.G. Grady[6]—Wm. Gladstone—C. Enderby—E. Hill[7]—H[oly S[cripture] with Willy.

[1] Perhaps James Maitland Balfour of Whittingham, 1820–56; tory M.P. Haddingtonshire 1841–7; A.J.'s* father.

[2] i.e. John Gladstone, Robertson's eldest son.

[3] Cp. 27 Feb. 47.

[4] Cp. 11 July 47.

[5] *Quarterly Review*, lxxxiv. 1 (December 1848); on the working of the L.N.W.R.

[6] Standish Grove Grady, 1815–91; recorder of Gravesend 1848–89; wrote on property and Hindu law.

[7] Edward Hill, 1807–1900; student of Christ Church 1827–50; public examiner at Oxford 1836–7, 1856–7; cp. 26 Jan. 47.

But we had a sad day with him the indolence being hard & dogged. Walk—visited. Read S. Bernard—Synode de Pistoie—Herschel's Discourse—Quarterly on Vanity Fair & Jane Eyre.[1]

5. Fr.

Wrote to Mrs Glynne—Scotts. Wrote on H[oly] E[ucharist]. H.S. with Willy & Johnnie. Read S. Bernard—Synode de Pistoie—Quarterly on Public Instruction[2]—Herschel's Discourse. Saw Lady H. Forbes. Visited. More work with Willy: but improvement again commenced.

6. Sat. Epiphany.

Chapel 11 am. Worked on Psalms. Drove with Sir J.G. Wrote to H. Tayleur—G & Co—Rn. G.—C.G.—Dowbiggin. Wrote on H.E.[3] Read S. Bernard—Synode de Pistoie—Herschel—Quarterly on Lord Castlereagh[4]—Sir C. Grandison which I finished mainly by the contents of Chapters.[5] A brighter day again with Willy. Drove with Sir J.G. to the Burn.

7. 1 S. Epiph.

Chapel 11 a.m. (with H.C.) and 2½ P.M. Conv. with Willy. Visited. Read a Serm. aloud of Mr Irvine's to Sir J.G. Worked on Secr[eta] Euchar[istica]. Read Synode de Pistoie (finished Vol. II. of documents)—Maskell on Absolution[6]—St Bernard.

8. M.

Wrote to C.G.—J. Murray—Mr Maskell. Latin lesson to Willy. H.S. with Willy & Johnnie. Read Maskell (finished)—Crosby Hall Lectures[7]—St. Bernard. Whist with Sir J.G.

9. T.

Wrote to C.G.—Mr. Ireland[8]—Manning—H.S. with W. & J. Read St Bernard—Proceedings in the Hampden case[9]—Herschel's Discourse (finished)—various old Railway & Canal Tracts—Quarty. on Austria.[10] H.S. with the two boys. Out with my Father.

[1] *Quarterly Review*, lxxxiv. 153 (December 1848); reviews of the novels and of the *Governesses Benevolent Institution Report for 1847*.
[2] ibid. lxxxiv. 238 (December 1848); on France under Guizot.
[3] Cp. Add MS 44737, ff. 140–162.
[4] *Quarterly Review*, lxxxiv. 264 (December 1848); review of *Castlereagh's *Memoirs and correspondence*, 4 v. (1848).
[5] Cp. 9 July 47.
[6] Cp. 29 Oct. 48.
[7] *Crosby Hall lectures on education* (1848); mostly by anglican priests.
[8] Perhaps Thomas James Ireland, 1790?–1863; tory M.P. for Bewdley 1847–8, the election being declared void.
[9] *The case of Dr. *Hampden. The official and legal proceedings connected with the appointment of Dr. *Hampden to the see of Hereford . . . with notes and an appendix* (1848).
[10] *Quarterly Review*, lxxxiv. 185 (December 1848); reviews of fourteen books on Austria and Germany.

10. Wed.

Wrote to C.G.—H. Glynne—G. Burnett—Bickers—A. Guthrie (& two notes to make a hoax for Aunt J.) H.S. with Willy & J.—Saw Ly H. F[orbes]. Read St Bernard—Hampden case—Quarterly on Italian Intervention[1]—Education Lectures.[2]

11. Th.

Wrote to C.G.—Sir R. Inglis. H.S. with W. & J. Read St Bernard—Hampden Case—Almon's Life of Wilkes[3]—Dr. Faustus[4]—Lancaster on his Method[5]—Vanity Fair[6]—Crosby Hall Lectures (finished).

12. Fr.

Wrote to Leighton & Myers—Ashe[7]—Gibson—Sedgwick. H.S. with Willy. Read S. Bernard—Hampden Proceedings (finished)—National Distress[8]—Shirley's poems &c[9]—Decline of Historical Painting.[10] Dinner party in evg. Whist with Sir J.G.

13. Sat.

Wrote to C.G.—R. Barker—J. Griffiths—Dean of Windsor. H.S. with the two boys. Read S. Bernard—Twiss on the Duchies[11]—Observations on Decline of Hist. Painting (finished)—Vanity Fair. Whist with Sir J.G.—Lionised Mr Carnegie.[12]

This day having been much tempted during the week I made a slight application in a new form of the principle of discipline: with a good effect at the time, and how thankful ought I to be to God if I should find it so continue.[13]

[1] ibid. p. 222; review of S. Ferrari, 'La Révolution et les Réformes en Italie' (1848).
[2] See note to two days previously.
[3] J. Almon, *The correspondence of the late John *Wilkes . . . [with] memoirs of his life*, 5 v. (1805).
[4] By C. *Marlowe (1604).
[5] Joseph *Lancaster, *The Lancasterian system of education, with improvements* (1821); he used the older children as monitors to impose on the younger a mechanical drill for learning by rote.
[6] W. M. *Thackeray, *Vanity Fair: a novel without a hero* (1848).
[7] Perhaps Thomas Ashe, Manchester cotton manufacturer who became a priest, was vicar of Coppenhall from 1869 and d. 1878.
[8] Perhaps 'Breach of Privilege . . . the evidence of John Bull [at] the secret cttee. on National Distress' (1848).
[9] By James *Shirley (1646).
[10] Possibly B. R. *Haydon, 'Some enquiry into the causes which have obstructed the advance of historical painting for the last 70 years in England' (1829).
[11] Sir T. *Twiss, 'On the relations of the duchies of Schleswig and Holstein, to the crown of Denmark and the Germanic Confederation' (1848).
[12] (Sir) James Carnegie, 1827–1905; 6th Bart. 1849; lord lieutenant of Kincardineshire 1849–56; 9th earl of Southesk 1855 by reversal of Act of Attainder; land owner and art connoisseur.
[13] The start of the use of a scourge: cp. 12 Apr. 49 and above, iii. xlv–xlvii.

It was also a day of difficulty with Willy: & with Miss B[rowne]. I must add apart from Willy: he went to bed early—his naughtiness is always better than my goodness.

14. 2. S. Epiph.

Chapel 11 & 2½. Conv. with Willy: (who had written a *beautiful* note to Miss B.) read Sermon aloud to my Father: visited (+) Wrote to C.G.—saw Sir J.G. (perforce) on S[tephen Glynne]'s affairs. Read Allies[1]—S. Bernard—Bp Patrick's Life.[2]

15. M.

Wrote to C.G.—R. Barker—Thomas—Wm. Gladstone—J.E. Fitzgerald. H.S. with the boys: long Latin lesson with Willy—Walk with him. Read St Bernard—Twiss on the Duchies—Colquhoun's Letters on Ch Reform[3]—Vanity Fair. Saw Mr Irvine on Chapel matters—took Mrs Souter to the Old Mains.[4]

16. T.

Wrote to C.G.—G & Co—J.N.G.—Farquhar—H.S. Thornton.[5] H.S. with Willy. A stiff morning on my accounts with Stephen Glynne. Visited. Saw Sir J. Forbes on Church & local matters.—Whist with my Father. Also he drew me for once into a Free Trade conversation: from wh I could not escape for three quarters of an hour. Read S. Bernard—Twiss on the Duchies—The Wayside Cross (aloud to Helen)[6]—Vanity Fair.

17. Wed.

Wrote to C.G. (2)—Duchess of Buccleuch—Leighton & Myers. H.S. with the boys. Read S. Bernard (finished the last of his works, with sorrow)—Dr. Twiss (finished)—Grimur Thomson[7]—Mir Shahanul Ali[8]—Vanity Fair—The Wayside Cross (aloud to H.). Notes on India.[9] Drove with Sir J.G. Worked on Ps[alm]s.

18. Th.

Wrote to C.G. Also [wrote] MS Theol &c.[10] H.S. with the boys. Read Allies—Grimur Thomson (finished)—The National Distress—Vanity Fair—The

[1] T. W. Allies, *Journal in France in 1845 and 1848, with letters from Italy in 1847* (1849).
[2] Simon Patrick, *Autobiography* (1839).
[3] J. Campbell Colquhoun, 'A plan of church extension and reform submitted to Lord John *Russell' (2 ed., 1849, with extra material).
[4] Farm S. of Fasque.
[5] Henry Sykes Thornton, 1800–82; partner in Williams Deacon's Bank from 1826; F.R.S. 1834.
[6] Untraced tract.
[7] Grímur Thomsen, *Les garanties anglo-françaises, données au Danemark en 1720 pour le duché de Slesvic* (1848); from Danish.
[8] Shahamat Ali, *The Sikhs and Afghans in connexion with India and Persia* (1847).
[9] Perhaps F. J. Shore, *Notes on Indian affairs*, 2 v. (1837).
[10] Add MS 44737, f. 137.

Wayside Cross—Whist with Sir J.G.—commenced arrangements & prepns. for journey.

19. Fri.

Wrote to Burnett (2)—Griffiths—Mir Shanalul Ali.[1] Wrote Mem. for Sir J.G. (S.R.G.). H.S. with the boys, walk with W. Visited. Worked on Ps[alm]s. Read Allies—Notes & opinions on India—Opie's Lectures[2]—Vanity Fair. Wayside Cross (finished)—

20. Sat.

Wrote to Barker—Gibbon—Leighton & Myers—Freshfield—W. Webb.[3]—C.G. (2)—Duthie—A. Williams—H.S. with the boys. Latin lesson to Johnnie—Up the Cairn with them. Read Allies—Bp Gloster on Horfield Manor[4]—Vanity Fair—Opie (finished). Worked on O.F. accounts & papers.

21. 3 S. Epiph.

Chapel mg. & aft. Conv. with Willy—Serm aloud to Sir J.G. Worked on Pss. Wrote to C.G—Greswell. Read Comp. to Prayer Book[5]—Patrick (finished)—Allies.

22. M.

Wrote to C.G.—Marshall (Dundee)[6]—Raisbeck.[7] H.S. with the boys. Latin with Willy. Preparations for dislodgement. Visited the old people & made some arrangements with Sir J.G. about them. Read Allies—Vanity Fair.

23. T.

Wrote to G. & Co—Duthie & Co—M.F. Tupper—Forbes—M.E.G.—C.G—Bush Hotel Carlisle. H.S. with the boys. Finished Vanity Fair: a work of genius, & to be admired in some other respects. A busy day in preparation for departure, giving clothes, visits &c. Saw Lady H. F[orbes]. In the evening my Father was quite broken down at the departure of the children, & not only for a moment but he could not throw it off—

24. Wed.

We all were up early, & my Father & H[elen] astir. We started soon after six, & were delayed & perplexed at Perth by changes of trains; I sent the 'little

[1] Shahamat Ali was secretary to the British Mission in Persia 1832–9, to Peshawar 1839, to the political resident in Malwa in the 1840's.

[2] O. *Opie, *Lectures on painting delivered at the Royal Academy of Arts* (1809).

[3] William Webb, 1775–1856; master of Clare, Cambridge, from 1815; vicar of Littlington, Cambridgeshire, from 1816.

[4] J. H. *Monk, 'Horfield Manor. A letter to each of the rural deans . . . of Gloucester and Bristol' (1848); privately printed, with an appendix. On whether Horfield Manor should be owned by the diocese of Bristol or the Ecclesiastical Commissioners.

[5] Cp. 29 May 47.

[6] Perhaps Marshall & Edgar, machine makers at Lilybank, Dundee.

[7] Unidentified.

ones' & nurses light by Edinburgh, & with Miss B[rowne] & Willy travelled all night by Mail from Perth direct. Read Emerson's Essays.[1] Wrote to Sir J.G.

25. (Conv[ersion of] St Paul) Th.

Willy made out his night (except a transit in the rain) capitally. We arrived in London at one: the 'little ones' at 8: & found all well thank God. Wrote to M.E. G[ladstone]—Capt. Coddington (to complain)[2]—E. Hill—G. Harcourt. Saw Manning—J.N.G.—Dowbiggin. At work among my letters & papers, the chaos usually awaiting arrival in London. Read the Vicar's Letter.[3]

26. Fr.

Wrote to Cardwell—James—Mahon—Maskell—Broster—Burnett—Sir J. Graham—Scotts—Towns.[4] Read Obss. on Ch. & State[5]—Foulkes's Letters to Bp of Oxford.[6] Shopping & domestic business—at 5.15 went down to Oxford. Evening in the rooms of my kind host [John] Hill. Chapel 9.20.

27. Sat.

Chapel 8 a.m. & 4 P.M. Breakf. at Hill's—luncheon at Mr Greswell's—dinner in Hall. The day chiefly occupied in visits: an interesting one to the V[ice] C[hancellor] who gave me a sketch of the forthcoming Statute and of the rather promising state of the poor Scholar question. Wrote to Sir J.G. Read Jelf's Sermons[7]—Longfellow's Evangeline & Poems, Gilfillan's Preface.[8]

28. 4 S. Epiph:

Prayers 8 am Ch Ch 4 P.M. Magdalen. Serm St Peter's mg and Univ. aft. Breakf. with Hill. dinner with Mozley (Magd.) Read Jelf—Emerson—Church of the Fathers[9]—Montague's life.[10] Wrote to C.G.

[1] R. W. Emerson, *Essays* (1841); preface by T. *Carlyle.
[2] Joshua William Coddington, captain R.E. 1841, inspector in railway department of B. of T. 1844–7; secretary of Caledonian Railway from 1847. Gladstone complained he had had to change coaches in the rain; cp. Add MS 44368, f. 76.
[3] H. *Mackenzie, 'A pastoral letter to the Parishioners of St. Martin-in-the-Fields' (1849); known as 'the vicar'.
[4] *Peel's steward.
[5] [J. F. *Ferrier], 'Observations on church and state suggested by the duke of *Argyll's *Essay* (1848).
[6] E. S. Ffoulkes, 'Three letters . . . on marriage with the deceased wife's sister' (1849).
[7] R. W. *Jelf, *Sermons doctrinal and practical, preached abroad* (1835).
[8] H. W. Longfellow, *Evangeline, a tale of Acadie* (1848); introduction probably by G. *Gilfillan, who later wrote on him.
[9] Cp. 7 Nov. 41.
[10] P. Montague, *The West Indian* (1827); an autobiography.

29. M.

Chapel 8 A.M. & 4 P.M. Breakf. with Mr Haddan Trin.—Luncheon Mr Greswell—dinner Mr Pococke, Qu[een's].[1] Many visits: convv. with the Provost of Oriel & with others on the new Statute about which I am hopeful.[2] Read Hussey on the Examinn. Statute[3]—Longfellow's Poems. Wrote to Wm. Gladstone.

30. T.

Prayers 8 a.m. (St. M. Magd.) & 4 P.M. Ch. Ch. Wrote to C.G. Breakf. Dr. Jacobson—Luncheon Rector of Exeter—Dinner Mr Stanley (Univ.). Attended Sermon at St. Mary's. Read Longfellow—Emerson. More visits & conversations: including Dr Bliss about Huber—he much desires it could be done & will consider it.[4]

31. Wed.

Chapel Ch. Ch. 8 a.m. Breakfast Marryat (Oriel)—dinner, Vice Chancellor's. Visits. Went with Bp of Madras[5] & Sewell to Radley: worth a much longer journey.[6] Wrote to Sir J.G.—Read Oxford Pamphlets of the last Century, illustrating its political condition.

London.
Thursday Feb. One 1849

Chapel 8 a.m. By Express to London (37 m[iles, out of 55, in] 38 min.) Wrote to Masterman—Vicar—Bp of Sydney—Doyle—Marryat—G. Roper. Coddington—G. Harcourt. Read Wakefield on Colonisation.[7] H. of C. 4–8 and 9½–12½.[8] Saw Richardson.

Fr. 2. Purification.

Wrote to Copeland—Bannister—Irvine (Jas)[9]—Baines[10]—Lewin—Monro

[1] Nicholas *Pocock, 1814–97; lecturer in mathematics at Queen's, Oxford, 1847; priest 1855; historian and editor.

[2] New examination statute establishing, *inter alia*, the school of modern history; passed after great wrangling 1850; cp. 16–17 Feb. 49.

[3] R. *Hussey, 'Remarks on some proposed changes in the public examinations' (1848).

[4] Victor Aimé Huber, 1800–69; German philanthropist, founder of cooperatives and writer on English Universities; probably to arrange a welcome for him in Oxford. Cp. 23 May 44.

[5] Thomas *Dealby, 1796–1861; chaplain in Bengal 1829; archdeacon of Calcutta 1835; consecrated bp. of Madras 1849, installed February 1850.

[6] St. Peter's College, Radley, by Oxford; founded by *Sewell as a high church boarding school, opened 1847.

[7] E. G. *Wakefield, 'A statement of the principles and objects of a proposed national society, for the cure and prevention of pauperism by means of systematic colonization' (1830).

[8] *Disraeli's amdt. to address: *H* cii. 115.

[9] James Irvine, vicar of Leigh, Manchester, from 1839.

[10] Matthew Talbot *Baines, 1799–1860; lib. M.P. Hull 1847–52, Leeds 1852–9; president of poor law board 1849; chancellor of duchy of Lancaster 1855–8; as such, first dissenter to sit in Cabinet.

—Cobbe[1]—Kingston. Read Macaulay's Hist[2]—Moodie (mad?)[3]—E. Monro on Ed[ucatio]n[4]—H. of C. 4½–7½ and 9–12½.[5] Worked most of the day upon my books papers &c. a fight always to be renewed on return to town. Saw Manning.

Sat. 3.

Wrote to Sir J.G.—Wm. G.—and Miss Pickwoad.[6] Read Macgregor on Finance[7]—Macaulay—Shopping—Arranging papers books &c. Saw Sir J. Pelly—W.C. James (on new Ch)—&, with him, the Vicar—Attended the Baptism of George's Infant.[8]

4. Septua[gesima] S[unday].

St Martin's & H.C. 11 a.m. St And[rew's] Wells St 7 P.M. Read MS. of 1841 aloud in evg. Read Herbert's MS. & accompg. letters on Cathedrals[9]—wrote to him. Worked on Memm. respecting our new Church plan: wh through the Providence of God has wonderfully revived.[10] Read English Rev. (nearly all).[11] I went to H.C. today with a peculiar shame: for the two last days I have to record against myself for very clear offences. but I hope to use again that valuable remedy which may it please God to bless.

5. M.

Wrote to Williams Deacon & Co—Sir W.C. James (2)—Sir J.G.—Mr Tyler—Mr Caparn—Sir A. Gordon[12]—Mr Bannister. H. of C. 4½–6¾.[13] Read Wakefield on Colonisation—Emerson's Essays.[14] Dined with Lady Hope—accounts. & shopping.

[1] Perhaps George Cobbe, 1782–1865; lieutenant royal artillery 1799, colonel commandant 1857, general 1864.

[2] The first vol. of T. B. *Macaulay, *The history of England from the accession of James II*, 5 v. (1849–61).

[3] J. Moodie, *Principles and observations on many and various subjects* (1848); attacks both chartists and 'upper ranks'.

[4] Privately printed pamphlet by Edward *Monro appealing for funds for St. Andrew's College, Harrow Weald; cp. Add MS 44368, f. 81; Gladstone sent £30.

[5] Address carried: *H* cii. 220.

[6] Unidentified; a member of the household?

[7] John *Macgregor, 'Financial reform: a letter to the citizens of Glasgow' (1849).

[8] Lavinia Lyttelton; she m. 1870 Edward Stuart *Talbot, 1844–1934, J. G. Talbot's br., who was 1st warden of Keble, Oxford, 1870–88, bp. of Rochester 1895, Southwark 1905, Winchester 1911–23. She d. 1939.

[9] Sidney *Herbert's pamphlet, 'Proposals for the better application of cathedral institutions to their intended uses', was privately circulated (1849).

[10] Add MS 44737, f. 114; because of the opposition of the Tulk family, it was now hoped to place the church to the east of Leicester Square.

[11] *English Review*, x. 257–500 (December 1848).

[12] Sir Alexander Cornewall Duff-Gordon, 1811–73; 3rd Bart. 1832; treasury clerk 1846–56; chancellor's (Lewis) secretary 1855; commissioner of inland revenue board 1857; scholar and translator.

[13] Deb. on Queen's speech: *H* cii. 258.

[14] Cp. 24 Jan. 49.

6. T.

Wrote to Sir J. Graham—R. Burn[1]—C. Clode[2]—W. Palmer. H.S. with Willy.—more trouble with Miss B[rowne] about his sums: she is *hard*! Calls & business.—Nine to dinner in evg. Read Wakefield—Guizot De la Democratie[3]—Muggeridge on Irish Distress[4]—do Parl. papers.[5] Saw Bouverie—Ld H. Vane[6]—Sir J. Graham—H. of C. $4\frac{1}{2}$–$6\frac{3}{4}$, $11\frac{1}{4}$–$12\frac{1}{2}$.[7]

7. Wed.

Wrote to H.J.G.—Rev S. Isaacson—J. Griffiths—Sir W. James—Smee (form). H.S. with Willy. H. of C. $1\frac{1}{2}$–$3\frac{3}{4}$. Saw W. James—The Vicar—J.N.G. (about Helen). Read Wakefield—Cotterill on Railways[8]—Macaulay—

8. Th.

Wrote to Lyttelton—R. Barker—Sir J.G.—Dr. Mackenzie—Rev. G.E. Murray[9]—C.R. Cotterill[10]—E.L. Ward. H.S. with Willy. Saw J.N.G. (Helen)—Dean of Windsor—J.S. Lefevre (Lay Cl) Maitland (Trin Coll). L[yttelto]n (S.R.G.) Mr Butler. Nine to dinner. Music in evg. Read Wakefield on Colonn. (finished)—Cotterill on Railways. Nash on Colonisation.[11] H. of C. $4\frac{3}{4}$–$6\frac{3}{4}$.[12] Writing up accounts for 1848.[13]

9. Fr.

Wrote to Sir J. Pelly—T. Denman[14]—Rev. W. Palmer—Rev. S. Isaacson. H.S. with Willy. Read Nash on Colonisation (finished)—Martin on Railways[15]—Ansted's Goldseeker[16]—Macaulay's Hist. Bookbuying & worked on Catalogue. Saw Godley[17]—G. Grant. H. of C. $9\frac{1}{2}$–$11\frac{3}{4}$. Peel made an unprepared but most able skilful & graceful speech.[18]

[1] Possibly Ralph Burn, shoe-maker in Piccadilly.

[2] Charles Matthew Clode, 1818–93; London solicitor 1839–58; war office solicitor 1858–76, legal secretary there 1876–80.

[3] F. P. G. Guizot, *De la démocratie en France, Janvier 1849* (1849).

[4] R. M. Muggeridge, 'Notes on the Irish difficulty: with remedial suggestions' (1849).

[5] *PP* 1849, xlviii. 5; on aid to distressed Irish poor-law unions.

[6] Harry George Vane, 1803–91; 3rd s. of 1st duke of Cleveland; liberal M.P. S. Durham 1841–59, Hastings 1859–64; changed surname to Powlett 1864; succ. as 4th and last duke of Cleveland 1864.

[7] Suspension of Irish habeas corpus: *H* cii. 306.

[8] C. F. Cotterill 'The past, present and future position of the London and North Western and Great Western Railway Companies' (1849).

[9] George Edward Murray, 1818–54; fellow of All Soul's, Oxford, 1841–4; rector of South Fleet, Kent, from 1843.

[10] Charles Forster Cotterill, pamphleteer.

[11] R. W. Nash, 'Suggestions on the subject of colonization' (1849).

[12] Misc. business: *H* cii. 439.

[13] In Hawn P.

[14] Thomas Aitchison-*Denman, 1805–94; barrister from 1833; 2nd Baron Denman 1854; took surname Aitchison 1876; supported parliamentary reform and female suffrage.

[15] R. M. *Martin, *Railways—past, present and prospective* (1849).

[16] D. T. *Ansted, *The gold-seeker's manual* (1849).

[17] John Robert *Godley, 1814–61; emigration enthusiast, founded Canterbury, New Zealand 1850.

[18] On Irish coercion: *H* cii. 549.

10. Sat.

Wrote to H. Tayleur—Messrs Williams & Co—Wm. Gladstone. H.S. with Willy. Calls. Dined with the Wortleys: saw Col. Talbot (Canada)[1]—Higgins.[2] Read Ansted—Wright on Synodal Functions[3]—Macaulay. Busy (mg) arranging dressingroom & clothes: I hope now to get quite tidy for the first time in this house.

11. Sex[agesim]a. S.

St Martins mg: St James's evg. MS of 43 aloud. Wrote out fair new Ch. Memm. & saw Lady James (for Sir W.)[4] Read Bp Hampden's Introduction[5]—Denison on Edn question.[6] C. on do—Nat. 'Schoolmr' on do[7]—Xtn Rem. on Marriage Laws—on Penitentiaries.[8] walk with C.—singing.

12. M.

Wrote to Sir J.G.—Welsh—Griffiths. H.S. with Willy. Read C. Buller on Responsible Govt.[9]—Macaulay's Hist—Milnes to Ld Lansdowne.[10] Worked on arranging furniture & books. H of C. 10–1.[11]

13. T.

Wrote to E.L. Ward—R. Barker. H.S. with Willy. A long morning on accounts (chiefly) for 1848—& on furniture & house arrangements. Saw Mr Maskell. Visited the Bath, & Washhouses with Sir H. Dukinfield. Saw Mr Bouverie on Toleration Act Amt. Bill[12]—Sir J. Graham on M.S.F.[13]—Also I spoke to Sir R. Peel & others on the apparent intention, if real most astounding, to make the Nav[igation] Law an open question: at the House 5–7.[14] Dined with the Ellisons.

14. Wed.

Wrote to Bp of London—Dickson—R.M. Milnes. H.S. with Willy. H. of C

[1] Thomas *Talbot, 1771–1853; lieutenant-colonel 1796; founded Port Talbot on Lake Erie 1802, and 27 other settlements.

[2] Matthew James *Higgins, 1810–68; journalist; wrote on colonies, Ireland and social topics under pseudonym 'Jacob Omnium'.

[3] Thomas P. Wright, *Urgent reasons for reviving the synodal functions of the church* (1849).

[4] Add MS 44737, f. 165.

[5] R. D. *Hampden, 'Introduction to the second edition of *Bampton lectures of the year 1832' (1837); published separately.

[6] G. A. *Denison, 'Church education, the present state of the management clause question' (1849).

[7] Untraced.

[8] *Christian Remembrancer*, xvii. 129, 1 (January 1849).

[9] C. *Buller, *Responsible government for the colonies* (1840).

[10] R. M. *Milnes, 'The events of 1848, especially in their relation to Great Britain. A letter to the marquis of *Lansdowne' (1849).

[11] Ireland: *H* cii. 590.

[12] Cp. 13 Aug. 48.

[13] Probably the Merchant Seamen's Fund.

[14] Misc. business, prior to the Navigation Acts deb. the next day: *H* cii. 642.

12–4¼.[1] Read Milnes (finished)—Bp of NZ on Ld Grey's Instructions[2]—Ansted's Goldfinder (finished). Attended the Graphic Society's Meeting.[3] Evening party at home afterwards: & music.

15. Th.

Wrote to Rev. F. Fowke[4]—Northcote—Mrs Lacy[5]—Greswell—Vice Chancellor of Oxf[ord]—Sir J. Johnstone—Vicar of St Martin's. H.S. with W. & Agnes. Worked on Books & house arrangements. Read May on Parl. Business[6]—Argyll Correspondence[7]—Goodhart on Marriage[8]—Richards on Horfield Manor.[9] Saw Matheson—Nicoll—Bonham. Dined at Baron Parke's: Sir W. James's afterwards.

16. Fr.

Wrote to Sir J.G.—Sir J. Kirkland—Williams & Co—Scotts—& G. Lawrence.[10] Worked on accounts & books—also out of door business. Saw Mr Meadows.[11] H. of C. at 4 to 5.[12] Dined at Lady F. Hopes. & again conversed with Col. Talbot on Colonial matters. Read the Argyll Correspondence—Mr Field's Report[13]—Macaulay. Br. Assocn. Report.[14] Wrote Letter to Chronicle on Oxf Statute[15]—with covering note.

17. Sat.

Marg. Chapel 5 P.M. Wrote to J. Walker—White. H.S. with Willy. Saw Bp of London (new Ch & Bouverie's Bill)—G. Harcourt—Mr Rogers—Farquhar—R. Cavendish—Scotts. J.S. Wortley. dined with the Speaker—Jane Lawley's afterwards.—Read Ball on Ireland[16]—Westm. Review on do.[17] My letter (Academicus) in M. Chron.

[1] Spoke briefly prior to cttee. stage of Navigation Acts repeal: *H* cii. 680.

[2] *Selwyn had sent a letter for Gladstone to show to interested parties; cp. H. W. Tucker, *Life of G. A. *Selwyn*, 2 v. (1879), i. 273.

[3] Society for the discussion of rare works of art; lasted until 1890.

[4] Francis Fowke, ?1809–1902; Peterhouse, Cambridge, 1835; vicar of Pensett, Staffordshire, 1844–60; d. in South Africa.

[5] Susannah Lacy, *née* Icboult; wife of Henry Charles Lacy, Peelite M.P. Bodmin 1847–52.

[6] T. Erskine *May, 'Remarks . . . with a view to facilitate the dispatch of public business in parliament' (1849).

[7] G. D. *Campbell, 'Correspondence between the duke of Argyll and the Revd. Andrew Gray, Perth, in reference to his Grace's essay, entitled, *Presbytery examined*' (1849).

[8] C. J. Goodhart, 'The lawfulness of marriage with a deceased wife's sister' (1848).

[9] H. Richards, 'Letter to the lord bishop of Gloucester and Bristol' (1848).

[10] George Lawrence, of Lawrence and Reed, Cheapside solicitors.

[11] Perhaps Joseph Kenny *Meadows, 1790?–1874; R.A. exhibitor and book illustrator.

[12] Irish distress: *H* cii. 784.

[13] John Field, 'A report presented to the magistrates of Berkshire' (1848); on Reading gaol.

[14] Report of the 1848 meeting in Swansea.

[15] Strongly advising convocation to pass the exam. statute, and suggesting for the future something much like the politics, philosophy and economics school; see next day.

[16] John *Ball, *What is to be done for Ireland*? (1849).

[17] *Westminster Review*, i. 436 (January 1849).

18. Quinqu[agesim]a. S.

St Martin's & H.C. 11 A.M.—St James Ev[enin]g. Read aloud MS of 42 in evg.—Conv with Willy. Wrote on the Gospel. Wrote to Sir J.G. Read Bp [of] Oxf[ord's] Headington Serm[1]—Four Ordination Sermons[2]—Hook's on Confession[3]—Barnes to Ld J.R.[4]—Marriage Report.[5]

19. M.

Wrote to T.G—R. Barker—Sir J.G—D. Fergusson—Dean of Windsor—Ld Wenlock—Amery—J.E. Denison—Prof. Ansted[6]—J. Ball.[7] H.S. with Willy. Morning in the city. Saw Wm. G—Gurney—Freshfield—Johnson & Longden[8]—Lady Inglis.[9] H. of C. 4½–8 and 9¼–12. Spoke briefly on Jews.[10] Read Macaulay—Marriage Report—began Ceylon papers[11]—Syngeneia.[12] A day never to be passed without some recollection *whose* birthday into life it was.[13]

20. T.

Wrote to T.G. H.S. with Willy. Saw W. Hamilton on Cathedrals.[14] Nine to dinner in evg. Worked nearly all day on the Ceylon papers, bulky, important, & very painful. Read also [blank.] H. of C. 4½–7½ and 10½–12½ on Ceylon debate.[15]

21. Ash Wed.

St Martin's 11 A.M. Prayers & MS of 40 aloud in evg. Wrote to Sir A. Agnew—Sir J. Forbes—E. Badeley—G. Offor[16]—White & Borrett[17]—

[1] Perhaps S. *Wilberforce, 'Union with Christ' (1848); preached at Littlemore, 2 miles from Headington, Oxford.

[2] *Four sermons preached at the general ordination of the bishop of Oxford, by C. C. Clerke, R. C. French, J. Randall, E. M. Goulburn, chaplains to the Bp.* (1848).

[3] W. F. *Hook, 'Auricular confession' (1848).

[4] Ralph Barnes, 'A letter to . . . *Russell on the commission of inquiry into episcopal and capitular estates' (1849).

[5] 'First report of the commissioners . . . [on] the state and operation of marriage *PP* 1847–8, xxviii. 233, the controversial report on, *inter alia*, the deceased wife's sister question.

[6] David Thomas *Ansted, 1814–80; fellow of Jesus, Cambridge, 1840–51; professor of geology at King's College, London, from 1845.

[7] John *Ball, 1818–89; poor law commissioner 1846–52; liberal M.P. co. Carlow 1852–7; under-secretary for colonies 1855–7; first president of the Alpine Club 1858.

[8] Stock and share brokers in Tokenhouse Yard; Gladstone usually dealt with Thomas Hayter Longden.

[9] Mary, *née* Briscoe; m. Sir R. I. *Inglis 1807.

[10] On parliamentary oaths: *H* cii. 924.

[11] On the rebellion in 1848: *PP* 1849, xxxvi. 1–386. Cp. Morrell, appendix A.

[12] Untraced; perhaps on syngenesia, the 19th class in the Linnean system.

[13] Cp. 19 Feb. 29.

[14] On the reform of their institutions.

[15] *H* cii. 938. He was put on consequent Ceylon and British Guiana cttee.; cp. *PP* 1849, xi. 1, for its report.

[16] George *Offor, 1787–1864; bookseller on Tower Hill; author and editor.

[17] Solicitors firm in Lincolns Inn; John Meadows White, 1799–1863, solicitor to the Ecclesiastical Commission 1842–63, was the senior partner.

Northcote—Cove[1]—Wyndham Harding—Morgan—Pickering—Wright—Griffiths. Saw Sir H. Dukinfield—Seymer—Baillie—Lyttelton. Read Allies's Tour[2]—Pickering on Election Law[3]—Bennett on Marriage Law.[4]

22. Th.

Wrote to E. Hawkins—Bunsen—J. Walker—O. Crease[5]—W. Selwyn. H.S. with Willy. H. of C. 4¾–8½ Marr[iage] Law & Bouverie.[6] Saw Sir W. James—Northcote—S. Herbert—Jay (Snell & Co.)[7]—Bouverie. Read Marriage Law Evidence—Hope's pamphlet[8]—Allies's Tour—Contes et Fabliaux (which I should have let alone).[9]

23. Fr.

Wrote to Rn. G—Sir J.G. (& part draft)—A.B. Strut[10]—R. Phillimore—James—Sumner—Taunton—T.B. Murray[11]—F. Fowke. H.S. with Willy. Saw Dean of Windsor & R. Neville—J.N.G—W. Page Wood.[12] Busy about garden plans. H. of C. 4½–7¼.[13] Read Dawes on Schools[14]—Allies's Tour—T.B. Murray on SPCK[15]—and finished Pickering.

24. Sat.

St Andrew's Wells St 5 PM. Wrote to Wm. Gladstone—H.B. Wilson—J. Griffiths—Sir J.G—Rev. J. Jones—Miss Brown—the Vicar—Mr G. Harcourt. H.S. with Willy. Read Meadows White[16]—Laing[17]—E. Vaughan—Matheson on Mints[18]—Irish Poor Law[19]—Allies. Saw Herbert. dined Dss of Beaufort's.

[1] Edward Cove, rector of Thoresway, Lincolnshire, from 1831.
[2] Cp. 14 Jan. 49.
[3] P. A. Pickering, *Remarks on treating and other matters . . . controverted elections and parliamentary committees* (1849).
[4] H. Bennett, 'A plain statement of the grounds on which it is contended that marriage within the prohibited degrees is forbidden in scripture' (1849).
[5] Orlando Crease of Pentonville, had sent an essay; Hawn P.
[6] Spoke on *Bouverie's motion on clergy and the Toleration Act: *H* cii. 1132.
[7] An employee of William and Edward Snell and Co., house agents in Albemarle Street; cp. 29 May 49.
[8] A. J. B. *Hope, 'The report of her majesty's commission on the laws of marriage . . . in a letter to Sir R. H. *Inglis' (1849).
[9] Cp. 13 and 18 May 48.
[10] Arthur B. Strutt; business unknown, cp. Add MS 44561 (index v.).
[11] Thomas Boyles Murray, 1798–1860; secretary of S.P.C.K. 1835; curate of St. Dunstan in the East from 1837; prebendary of St. Paul's 1843.
[12] William Page *Wood, 1801–81; liberal M.P. Oxford city 1847–53; solicitor-general 1851–2, 1852–3; lord chancellor 1868–72; cr. Baron Hatherley 1868. Cp. Add MS 44205.
[13] Oaths Bill: *H* cii. 1188.
[14] R. *Dawes, 'Observations on the working of the government scheme of education, and on school inspection' (1849).
[15] T. B. Murray, 'Jubilee tract: great success from small beginings' (1849); on S.P.C.K. founders.
[16] J. Meadows White, probably 'Suggestions for the rating of the tithe commutation rent charge' (1845).
[17] Probably David Laing, *Sermons, chiefly resulting from daily experience* (1847).
[18] Untraced pamphlet by G. F. Matheson.
[19] *Irish poor law: past, present, future* (1849).

25. 1 S. Lent.

St Martins mg 8½ (H.C.) & 11 (Mr Melvill preached & quite revived my old impression of him as a very powerful orator.)[1]—St James's 7 P.M. Finished MS. on Quinqu[agesim]a Gospel: & read it aloud in evg. Walk with C. & the children. Read Allies—Goode's Vindication[2]—Ch Miss. Jubilee[3]—Sewell's Sermon[4]—Townsends do.[5]

26.

Wrote to G. Harcourt—Jas Hope—Scotts—Vicar. Latin lesson with Willy. Working on my books. H of C. 5½–8.[6] Read Allies—Statist. Journal[7]—Comn. on Poor Rate[8]—Williams on Welsh Edn.[9]—Emigr. Papers[10]—Mint Report.

27. T.

Wrote to Bp of London—W. Mathews—J. Gladstone—Brogden—Shahamet Ali—Du Fresne.[11] H.S. with Willy—Saw Mr Meadows White—Hope. H. of C. 3¾–7. (Whitechapel Bill)[12] Read Allies (finished)—Minutes of P.C. on Education[13]—Bayle (Luther &c)[14]—

28. Wed.

Wrote to Sir J.G—D. Fergusson—Bp of New Zealand. H.S. with Willy. Attended levee. Also ragged School at 8½. A few came to tea. Saw the Vicar—Mr [J.G.] Hubbard—Read Gray on Museum[15]—Emerson.

London.
Thurs. March One 1849.

Wrote to Hubbard—Bayly—Mansfield—Tupper—Laing—D. of Argyll (dft)[16]—Bouverie—Lyttelton—Dr Harington—Bp of Exeter—Lefevre—Reid—W.C. James—Freshfield. H.S. with Willy. Ceylon Commee 1–2½.

[1] Cp. 30 June 33; a version of part of which is in Morley, i. 100.
[2] W. *Goode, 'A vindication of the "Defence of the xxxix articles" in reply to the recent charge of the bishop of *Exeter' (1848).
[3] 'Church Missionary Society jubilee' (1848); a collection of papers.
[4] W. *Sewell, probably 'Christian communism. A sermon' (1848).
[5] G. *Townsend, *Sermons on miscellaneous subjects, with two charges* (1849).
[6] *Cobden's motion on financial reform: *H* cii. 1218.
[7] *The Statistical Journal and Record of Useful Knowledge*, was published monthly from October 1837 to February 1838.
[8] Poor law commissioners report for England and Wales for 1848: *PP* 1849, xxv. 1.
[9] J. Williams, 'A discourse at the opening of the Welsh Educational Institution' (1848).
[10] Eighth report of the emigration commissioners: *PP* 1847–8, xxvi. 1.
[11] Unidentified.
[12] Spoke on clerical salaries: *H* cii. 1319.
[13] 'Minutes of the committee of council on education': *PP* 1847–8, i. 1.
[14] The entries on Luther and other subjects in P. Bayle, *Dictionaire historique et critique*, 2 v. (1697); English tr. (1710).
[15] J. E. Gray, 'A letter to the earl of Ellesmere, on the management of the library of printed books in the British Museum' (1849); privately printed.
[16] In Add MS 44098, f. 1.

H. of C 4½–9.[1] Saw Meer Shahamet Ali—Mahon—Herbert. Read Guizot (Democratie)—Duke of Argyll's Appx.[2]

2. *Fr.*

Wrote (fair) to D. of Argyll—Sir J.G.—C. Selwyn.[3] H.S. with Willy. Saw Goulburn & Clerk on Nav. Law—Cardwell on do. H. of C. 5–8 and 9½–12.[4] Read Guizot (finished)—Colonial Magazine[5]—Nav. Law (Parl) correspondence.[6]

3. *Sat.*

St Andrew's Wells St 5 P.M. Wrote to Sir J.G.—Wenham. Dined at Mr Harcourt's—a remarkable party. Breakfast at Milnes's: met Guizot. City 12¼–2¾. Saw Gurney—Freshfields—Coleman—Alliance Co[7]—Barry & Co[8]—Johnson & Co.[9] Read Gray on Museum—Macaulay.

4. *2. S Lent.*

St. Martin's 11 (& H.C.)—Marg. Chapel Evg. MS of 43 aloud in evg. Wrote to Williams & Co—Hawkins. Read Bp Hampden[10]—Wilberforce on the Incarnation[11]—Watson on Southey[12]—Engl. Rev. on Loss & Gain.[13] Walk with C.—conv. with her & Stephen [Glynne] to move him towards marriage.[14]

5. *M.*

Wrote to Rose—T.W. Allies—and Dowbiggin. Latin lesson to Willy. Saw Thesiger Clerk & Goulburn & Cardwell on Nav. Law—Lincoln Corry & others on Irish Rate in Aid. Attended Dr Buckland's Lecture on the Layard Antiquities at the Museum.[15] H. of C. 4½–7½ and 9½–12½.[16] Lady F. Hope & others to dinner. Read Young on Nav. Laws.[17]

[1] Irish Poor Law: *H* ciii. 48.

[2] In the second ed. of *Argyll's *Essay*; cp. 3 Oct. 48.

[3] (Sir) Charles Jasper *Selwyn, 1813–69; barrister 1840; tory M.P. Cambridge University 1859–68; solicitor-general and Kt. 1867; lord justice of appeal 1868.

[4] Irish Poor Law: *H* ciii. 100.

[5] The *Colonial magazine and Commercial-Maritime Journal*, ed., R. M. Martin, was published in 1842–3. [B.M. cat. dates wrong.]

[6] *PP* 1849, li. 177–263; contains colonial and foreign correspondence.

[7] The Alliance Life and Fire Assurance Company; Andrew Hamilton was its secretary.

[8] Probably the Cornhill stock-brokers.

[9] i.e. Johnson and Longden.

[10] R. D. *Hampden, *Sermons preached before the University of Oxford, 1836–1847* (1848).

[11] R. I. *Wilberforce, *The doctrine of the incarnation* (1848).

[12] R. *Watson, 'Observations on *Southey's *Life of Wesley*' (1820).

[13] *English Review*, x. 46 (September 1848).

[14] He stayed a bachelor.

[15] The first batch of *Layard's discoveries from Nineveh reached the British Museum in June 1847; cp. G. Waterhouse, *Layard of Nineveh* (1963), ch. vii.

[16] Irish Poor Law: *H* ciii. 170.

[17] G. F. Young, 'Free trade and the navigation laws, practically considered' (1849).

6. T.

Wrote to R. Barker (& Memm)—J. Griffiths—St Leger—J.M. White. H.S. with Willy. At Sir R. Peel's on Nav. Laws 11–1. As usual he is evidently bound as respects his vote. Slave Trade Commee. at $3\frac{1}{2}$. H. of C to $6\frac{3}{4}$ and $10\frac{3}{4}$–$1\frac{1}{4}$. Voted in 164:237 agt. rate in aid. I shd. have spoken had not Lincoln today made up his mind & agreed to do it.[1] Dined at Mr Mildmay's. Read Fitzgerald on H.B. Company.[2] Arranged letters & papers.

On Tuesday the 6th of March Goulburn, Clerk, Cardwell & I met at Sir R. Peel's to discuss the Navigation Law Bill and particularly the question of proceeding by unconditional or by conditional legislation. All of us except Sir R.P. were inclined to the latter course but we passed nearly two hours in conversation chiefly on this part of the plan, also however on some of the others, with no other issue than such as was easy to foresee, namely that he throughout on every point either positively held by the Bill or parried what was said against it. Thus (nearly) it was with the West Indian plan last year, and thus with the rate in aid this year. In point of fact, of all members of Parliament he has the smallest degree of free judgement in regard to the announced measures of the Government. He dare not vote against any of them in any point of importance, and this on account of the weakness of the administration, because through their weakness their existence might be endangered by an hostile vote even though not intended to carry want of confidence, and if he were a party to such a vote he would stand before the world—whatever he might be in his own mind—as a bidder for office, the character he is determined not not [3] to bear. It is a very singular effect in two ways for first on account of his eminence he has lost the privilege which even much meaner men think essential to their position that of judging & voting freely: & the Govt. gains the benefit of this on account of its weakness since if it were strong enough to hold its own way the restraint would cease to operate. It is indeed true that the Govt. would be very ready to follow his suggestions where they knew them beforehand, but I speak of the cases where they proceed without being in concert of any kind with him until their measure is before the world.[4]

7. Wed.

Wrote to Northcote—Sir J.G.—T.G.—and Mrs Bowen.[5] H.S. with Willy. Saw Col Bristow—Dowbiggin—Manson. Read Fitzgerald—Emerson—Fragmenta Liturgica[6]—Scots Church[7]—Building Report. Worked on Catalogue of Books. Walk with C. H. of C. $3\frac{1}{2}$–$4\frac{3}{4}$.[8]

[1] The Peelites were split on the Irish poor law, *Peel, *Graham and *Cardwell voting with the govt., Gladstone, *Goulburn, *Lincoln and *Herbert against: *H* ciii. 314.

[2] Cp. 14 Sept. 48.

[3] Second 'not' at start of a new line.

[4] Dated 15 March 1849; Add MS 44777, f. 283.

[5] Perhaps Katherine Emily, *née* Steele, m. 1834 Christopher Bowen, 1801–90, rector of St Thomas, Winchester.

[6] P. *Hall, ed., *Fragmenta liturgica. Documents illustrative of the liturgy of the Church of England* (1848).

[7] Perhaps 'The episcopal church in Scotland proved to be in full communion with the Church of England' (1849).

[8] Naples and Sicily: *H* ciii. 356.

8. Th.

Wrote to J.E. Fitzgerald—A. Lendrum—Mr D. Gladstone H.S. with Willy. Read Transportation papers[1]—Fitzgerald (finished)—Worked on Book Catalogue &c. H. of C. 4½–9 and 10–12¼.[2] Saw Lincoln. Attended parochial Meeting at 11—went with James to Bedfordbury[3] afterwards.

9. Fr.

Wrote to Wm. Gladstone—Dr Everard—Mr Roberts. H.S. with Willy. Saw Mr Shank—Sir J. Tyrrell—Lincoln. Read Emerson's Essays—Nav. Law Evidence—(& worked figures).[4] H. of C. 5½–7 and 8¼–12: waiting to speak on Nav. Law.[5]

10. Sat.

St Andrew's W[ells] St. 5 P.M. H.S. with Willy. Wrote to W. Forbes—J. Gray—Mr Bennett—Sir J.G.—Duke of Argyll (& draft)[6]—Claridge—Bourdillon.[7] Read Bennett on Law on Marriage[8]—Pusey on do.[9] Worked on books—and on accounts. Dined at J.N.G.s.

11. S. 3 Lent.

St Martin's 8½ (H.C.) & 11. St Jamess evg. MS on Gospel aloud at night—Spoke to Edward on the Confirmn.[10] Saw Wortley—Courtenay—T.S. Gladstone. Read Watson on Southey—Archd. Wilberforce[11]—Kip's Lenten Fast.[12]

12. M.

Wrote to Nicol—Jordan—Rev. R. Williams[13]—H.J.G.—Latin lesson to Willy. Also private conv. with him. Attended the Poor Law Commn. with the Parish Deputation.[14] Saw the Vicar—Lincoln. Read Emerson's Essays—

[1] Transportation to the Cape and Ceylon: *PP* 1849, xliii. 1.

[2] Spoke, accusing *Grey of precipitancy in ending transportation settlements in Australia: *H* ciii. 420.

[3] A chapel of ease, 'a mere little room', in Bedfordbury Street, by Covent Garden, for which some of the Leicester Square Church funds were used. Cp. Add MS 44264, f. 191, 203.

[4] Cp. Add MS 44737, f. 179 ff.

[5] He was called in time to move the adjournment: *H* ciii. 533.

[6] In Add MS 44098, f. 9.

[7] James Dewar Bourdillon, 1811–83; secretary to board of revenue 1843–60.

[8] Cp. 21 Feb. 49.

[9] E. B. *Pusey, 'Marriage with a deceased wife's sister prohibited by holy scripture, as understood by the church for 1500 years' (1849).

[10] Edward Wardell, a servant.

[11] Cp. 4 Mar. 49.

[12] W. I. Kip, *The history, object and proper observance of the holy season of Lent* (1844).

[13] Rowland *Williams, *fils*, 1817–70; fellow of King's, Cambridge, 1839; vice-principal of St. David's, Lampeter, 1840–62; prosecuted for contributions to *Essays and Reviews* 1860; or perhaps his father, d. 1854, canon of St. Asaph 1809–54.

[14] Probably on the poor law school planned for St. Martin's-in-the-Fields; cp. *PP* 1850, xxvii. 15.

Guiana papers.[1] Stokers & Pokers.[2] H. of C. 4½–6¾ Spoke 1⅓ h. on Nav. Law for conditional legislation.[3]

13. T.

Wrote to Sir J.G.—Rev. E. Edwards[4]—M.T. Baines—R. Barker—T. Banister[5]—T.D. Acland. Ceylon &c Commee. 12–4. H. of C. 5–10½ on Church Rates.[6] H.S. with Willy. Read B.G. papers—Surtees on Church Reform[7]—Carmichael Smyth on B.N.A. Railway.[8]

14. Wed.

Wrote to Freshfield. H.S. with Willy, Worked on Nav. Law Clauses & Amendments. Walk with C.—Dined at Ld Ab[erdeen']s.[9] Saw Mrs Howis[10]—Lincoln—E. Ellice—Guizot. H. of C 1¼–4.[11] Read B.G. papers—

15. Th.

Wrote to Sir J.G.—Nicolay—Anders—Bp of Aberdeen—Lowe. H.S. with Willy. Saw Manning on Church matters—Thesiger on Nav. Law Clauses. B.G. Commee.[12] & H. of C. 3–7½ and 11½–2¾. Voted in 280:189 agt. D'Israeli.[13] Read B.G. papers (finished)—Enderby on Auckland Islands[14]—Abate Leone Consp. of Jesuits.[15]

Last night I dined at Lord Aberdeen's where Mr. E. Ellice (sen.) began to speak about the Navigation Laws. He said distinctly he agreed entirely with what I had said, that the only sensible manner of proceeding was that of conditional legislation but that he must vote with his party for he said if one does not vote with one's party when they are in the wrong one might as well not vote with them at all. He said upon my suggesting that the Govt. appeared to be either lukewarm or divided upon the subject that it was not so: but that their measure could not pass & he was very desirous to know whether the Lords under Ld Stanley's auspices would not agree to pass something in the nature of my plan. Indeed he appeared to be fishing on behalf of the government, & this also struck Lincoln to whom he spoke separately.[16]

[1] The Ceylon and British Guiana cttee. members dealt with the latter first; for references to the papers they studied, cp. marginal notes in *PP* 1849, li. 1ff.
[2] [Sir F. B. *Head], 'Stokers and Pokers; or, the London and North-Western railway, the electric telegraph and the railway clearing-house' (1849).
[3] *H* ciii. 540–63; speech notes in Add MS 44651, f. 33.
[4] Probably Edward Edwards, curate of Marsden, Yorkshire, 1823; rector of Pengoes, Montgomeryshire, from 1849; author.
[5] Thomas Banister, barrister of the Middle Temple from 1842.
[6] Spoke for their reform: *H* ciii. 671.
[7] S. F. Surtees, 'Church abuses and church reform. Four letters to E. Horsham' (1849).
[8] Untraced pamphlet by Robert Carmichael Smyth, who published on this in 1850.
[9] See next day.
[10] Wife of William Howis, of Woburn Place.
[11] *Disraeli's petition on local taxation: *H* ciii. 702.
[12] Searching examination of Sir H. Light; Gladstone did not speak: *PP* 1849, xi. 24.
[13] *H* ciii. 858.
[14] C. Enderby, *The Auckland islands: a short account of their climate, soil and production* (1849).
[15] Abate Leone, *The Jesuit conspiracy. The secret plan of the order*, tr. (1848).
[16] Dated 15 March 1849; Add MS 44777, f. 285.

16. Fr.

Wrote to Treasurer Flaxman Fund[1]—Sir W. James—Mr Black[2]—Mr Radcliffe.[3] H.S. with Willy. Worked on Nav. Law Clauses & saw Labouchere —Thesiger—Clerk—Goulburn—The Govt. seem disposed to take them if possible. Read Ab. Leone—worked on books. Saw Godley on Col[onial] Policy—Mansfield on do.[4] H. of C. 4½–8 and 10½–11¾.[5]

17. Sat.

St And. Wells St 5 P.M. Wrote to Col Short[6]—Northcote (2)—Badeley—Saunders—O. Hargreave[7]—Ld Medwyn—Hayden.[8] H.S. with Willy. Saw Coleridge—Monsell—Northcote (on Nav. Law). Read Ab Leone—Hayden on Irish Ch—Evan Jones on Welsh Education[9]—Eneas Macdonnell[10]—Bp of New Zealand's Tour.[11] Worked on Nav. Law Clauses.[12] Helen arrived at night: well & in spirits.

18. 4 S. Lent.

St Martin's mg: St James evg—Conv. with Willy—Finished & read aloud MS on part of the Ep[istle]. Saw Badeley on Bouverie's Bill. Read Watson on Southey (finished).[13] Catena on Gospels[14]—Palmer's appeal to Scottish Church.[15]

19. M.

Wrote to Ph. Pusey—Sir J.G.—Rn. G.—Adie—W. Palin—T.G. Latin lesson to Willy. Read Palmer's Appeal—Slave Trade Comm[16] & House 1–7 and House 10–12.[17] Saw Badeley on Clergy Relief (!) Bill—Bouverie on do—Conferences with Clerk, Thesiger & Cardwell on Nav. Law about wh we have much difficulty—also conv. with Graham—& with Tufnell—Govt. seem to wish for a middle term.

[1] Of the *Flaxman picture collection at University College, London.

[2] Perhaps James Frederick Black, headmaster of Kendal grammar school.

[3] Perhaps John Alexander Radcliffe, Westminster solicitor.

[4] Perhaps Ralph Mansfield, 1799–1880; Australian journalist, on Sydney *Morning Herald* from 1841.

[5] Budget statement: *H* ciii. 877.

[6] Charles William *Short, 1798–1857; in Coldstream guards; chief subscriber to Christ Church, Broadway, and driving force behind the Rose Street house of charity.

[7] Oliver H. Hargreave of Bloomsbury Place; business untraced.

[8] John Hayden, *ca.* 1795–1855; rector of Upper Cumber; archdeacon of Derry 1849–55; wrote 'Observations . . . on the national system of education in Ireland' (1838).

[9] Cp. 15 Mar. 48.

[10] 'My first speech; and my latest advice to my countrymen' (1849).

[11] G. A. *Selwyn, *New Zealand. Part ii. Journal of . . . tour from August to December 1843* (1847).

[12] Notes in Add MS 44737, f. 192.

[13] Cp. 4 Mar. 49.

[14] *Cathena, seu explicatio locorum qui in Pentateucho subobscuriones occurrunt* (1572).

[15] [William *Palmer, of Magdalen], *An appeal to the Scottish bishops and clergy* (1849); on passive communion.

[16] He was on the select cttee for 'providing the final extinction of the slave trade'; it reported first 24 May 1849 and second on 21 June 1849; cp. *PP* 1849, xix. 3, 179.

[17] Army estimates: *H* ciii. 964.

20. T.

H.S. with Willy. Ceylon Commee. 12¼–2. Nav Laws meeting at 2½ (Clerk, Thesiger, Cardwell, Lincoln, S. Herbert) at wh we agreed on a plan & a reference to Peel—then to H. of C. until 6.—Saw Godley. Dined at Lady F. Hope's. Read Wray on Marriage Law[1]—Palmer's appeal to Scots Church.

21. Wed.

Wrote to J. Griffiths—Capt. Davies[2]—Sir S. Scott & Co—Rev. B. King[3]—Murray Gladstone. At 11½ saw Sir R. Peel with Cardwell on Nav. Laws. Then went to B.T. & (a little after) saw Mr Labouchere & after conversing with him determined not to move. Attended House—St Andrew's Wells St 5. P.M. Small dinner at home: Lady J. Russell's afr. Saw Godley—Lincoln.

22. Th.

Wrote to Blewitt—Griffiths—Amery—Swift—Ryland[4]—Sir J.G.—Buckingham—C. Marriott. H.S. with Willy. Read Palmer's Appeal—Canada papers & debates.[5] Att[en]d[e]d Guiana Commee 12¼–3: H. of C. 4¾–7.[6] Dined at Wilson Pattens (conv. with Abp Cant. on Bouverie's Bill). Mrs Malcolms, & Lady Vernons,[7] after. Communicated to such Members interested as I met my intentions about Nav. Laws & reciprocity.

23. Fr.

Wrote to R. Barker—Dean of Windsor—Lyttelton—W.F. Campbell—B. Hawes—Rev. E. Monro—T. Bourdillon—W.C. James. Agnes now D.G. nearly well: Willy ill with a torpid liver: he is so, so good. Saw Godley (Canada)—Murray Gladstone—Maclachlan.[8] Read Palmer's appeal. H. of C 4¾–8 and 9–12¾.: speaking on Nav. Law. D'Israeli assailed me at the end of the Committee.[9]

24. Sat.

Marg. Chapel 5. P.M. Wrote to Sir J.G.—Gurney & Co—and [blank.] Worked on books. Read Virgil &c—V.I. papers[10]—Aylwin on Nav. Law[11]—

[1] G. Wray, 'The sound policy of the existing law of marriage' (1849).

[2] Perhaps Henry Thomas Davies, 1794–1869; captain R.N. from 1814.

[3] Brian King, 1811–95; rector of St. George-in-the-East, London, 1842–63, when he caused rioting through ritualism; vicar of Avebury 1863–94.

[4] George Herman Ryland, dismissed clerk of the executive council of Canada; claimed compensation; his case taken up by *Argyll; cp. *Argyll, i. 314–9, *H* cix. 1049 and cx. 1286.

[5] On the Navigation Acts, with extracts from the legislative assembly's debates: *PP* 1849, li. 168.

[6] Asked two questions on Canadian rebellion: *H* ciii. 1124.

[7] Isabella Caroline, *née* Ellison; she m. as his first wife 5th Lord *Vernon 1824, and d. 1853.

[8] Hubert Maclaughlin, 1805–82; rector of Burford, Shropshire, from 1838, prebendary of Hereford from 1857.

[9] *H* ciii. 1248; speech notes in Add MS 44651, f. 35.

[10] Despatches on Vancouver's Island: *PP* 1849, xxxv. 629.

[11] D. C. Aylwin, 'A series of letters on the Navigation Laws' (1849).

Newdigate on Balance of Trade[1]—Danish War[2]—Palmer's Appeal. Saw Dalrymple on H.s case—Cumming Bruce. Dined with the Herberts—then to the Speaker's levee, & Mr Stephens's to see his noble work of Satan tempting Eve.[3]

25. 5 S. Lent & Annuncn.

St Martin's (& Holy C.) 11 a.m. Whitehall aftn. Conv. with Willy. Wrote on Annunc[iatio]n & read aloud in evg. Read Palmer's Appeal—Wesley's Life[4]—Newmans Serm.[5]

26. M.

Wrote to West—Ross. Latin lesson to Willy. Saw Mr Swift—Mr Wynn. House 4¾–7½ and 9–12:[6] Read Palmer's Appeal—Leone's Plan of the Jesuits —Ross on Dioc. Colleges[7]—Cape Case.[8] Took H. to see Mr Tomline's Pictures.

27. T.

Wrote to Sir J.G.—Walter Farquhar—R. Barker—Trevor. S.P.G. meeting at 11, & spoke—Commee. 12–3¾. House 5–8¼.[9] Lady Waldegrave's[10] & Lady Jersey's in Evg. Read Palmer's Appeal—Leone's Secret Plan. Worked on Guiana Resolutions.

28. W.

Marg[aret Street] Chapel 5. P.M. H.S. with Willy. Worked on my books. Dined with the F. Lewises. Wrote to Leightons—Mr G. Harcourt. Also Mem. of Nav. Law conversations.[11] Read Palmer—Emerson—Macaulay. Saw R. Palmer.

29. Th.

Wrote to Lady Wenlock—Mr Ramsay—T. Bibby[12]—R. Barker. Read Palmer's Appeal—Macaulay. Worked on books. H.S with Willy. Commee. (Clergy Relief) & House 12–5.[13] Saw Bp of London (on the Bill)—S. Herbert —W. Selwyn. Dined at Ld Crewe's.

[1] C. N. *Newdegate, 'Two letters to . . . *Labouchere on the balance of trade' (1849).
[2] 'Who is to blame for the war between Denmark and Germany', tr. (1849).
[3] Edward Bowring *Stephens, 1815–82, sculptor. This work was shown at the 1851 exhibition.
[4] R. *Southey, *Life of *Wesley*, 2 v. (1820); cp. 4 Mar. 49 n.
[5] Cp. 23 Jan. 48.
[6] Spoke on Navigation Bill: *H* ciii. 1305.
[7] J. L. Ross, 'Letters on diocesan theological colleges' (1849).
[8] Transportation to the Cape: *PP* 1849, xliii. 1.
[9] Cape transportation: *H* ciii. 1371.
[10] Frances Elizabeth Anne, *née* Braham, 1821–79; m. 1839 J. J. H. Waldegrave, 1840 7th Earl Waldegrave, 1847 G. G. Harcourt, 1863 Chichester *Fortescue; known as Lady *Waldegrave; society beauty, heiress and hostess.
[11] Add MS 44737, f. 177.
[12] Thomas *Bibby, 1799–1863, Irish Greek scholar and eccentric.
[13] Select cttee. on Bouverie's Clergy Relief Bill: *PP* 1849, ii. 65, and Ireland: *H* civ. 22.

30. Fr.

Wrote to Sir J.G.—Wray—Hussey—Mackenzie Wilson. H.S. with Willy. Saw Barker. Read Palmer's Appeal—Emersons Essays (finished)—Italian Poetry. Walk with C. H. of C. 5–10. I never witnessed anything more singular than the manner in which a (virtual) vote of censure on the Govt. was recorded *nem. con.* It was aimed directly at the Adm[iral]ty who well deserved it.[1]

31. Sat.

Marg Chapel 5. P.M. Wrote to Sir J.G.—T.G.—Dean of Windsor—Wm. Gladstone. Read Macaulay. Saw James—Gurneys—Freshfield—Barker—Hamilton (Alliance)—Spending the morning in the City on O[ak] F[arm] & Stephen's affairs H.S. with Willy. Dined at Sir R. Peel's.

Palm Sunday Ap. One 49.

St Martin's 11 a.m. The new Bedfordbury Service at 7 P.M. May this seed of a new Church & flock be faithfully watered & abundantly blessed. Wrote to W. Palmer—Walk with C. & the children. Read MS of 44 aloud. Saw Hope on Bouverie's Bill & W. James. Read Bp of NZs Charge—his Journal[2] —Palmer's Appeal (finished).

2. M.

Wrote to Bp of Aberdeen—Dean of Ferns—Renton—Sewell[3]—Ellis—Reddie—C.K. Murray—J. Griffiths. Marg. Chapel 8. a.m., Read Synge's Canada in 1848[4]—Reviews. Saw Labouchere on Nav. Law—At Commee. (Clergy Relief) 12–2¾: it is on the whole I think well arranged. Saw Hope on Bouverie's Bill—H. of C. 9–12½. Paired for the Rate in aid.[5]

3. T.

St James's 8. a.m. & Hagley Church evg. Wrote to Mr Hollingsworth. Read Keble on Matrimony[6]—English Review[7] At 11 went with C & 3 children to Hagley.

4. Wed.

Hagley Ch 10 a.m. Latin lesson to Willy. Dear Stephen's birthday: God bless him, & indeed He has blest the boy much. Read Engl. Rev. (except 2

[1] Hume's motion on naval expenditure: *H* civ. 61.
[2] G. A. *Selwyn, 'A charge delivered . . .' (1848); and cp. 17 Mar. 49.
[3] John Campbell Renton, 1814–56; tory M.P. Berwick-on-Tweed 1847–52.
[4] By M. H. Synge (1848).
[5] *H* civ. 161.
[6] J. *Keble, 'Against profane dealing with holy matrimony' (1849).
[7] *English Review*, xi. 1–255 (March 1849).

& 4)[1]—Christian Remr.[2]—Bp Doanes Serm & Addresses.[3] Journey to Siwah.[4] Went to Stourbridge & saw Griffiths—Amery—Collis—Foster jun.[5]—

5. Th.

Hagley Ch 10 a.m. Wrote to Sir J.G.—Dean of Windsor—Finished Chr. Remembr. (except I). 11½–8¼ Went to Birmingham to meet Freshfield for the O[ak] F[arm] Sale which as was to be expected was nominal as to price. Saw Ld Ward's agent afterwards. The purchase of the lease has now placed all in our hands: & there now remains to be coped with the capital difficulty of disposing of the shattered property in the best manner. In this I pray that a spirit of wisdom may be given me, & that I may do it as a religious work, regard being had to the fact that my own money interest in it is small. But certainly these cares do not assort well with the time, though they may be used so as to contribute in some way to its purposes.

6. Good Friday.

Church 11 (with Holy Commn.) and 3½. Wrote to C. Uppington (detaining letter)—Bp of Aberdeen—Mr S. Clarke[6]—Northcote. Read Arnold's Last Sermons[7]—Wesley's Sermons[8]—Monro's Letter on Educn.[9]—W[esley]'s on the 'Assize' is very grand—A[rnold's] bear marks of his passionate hostility to the idea of the Catholic Church & are also tinged with Luthers notion of justification. Conv. on the Marriage Bill.

7. Easter Eve.

Ch 10 a.m. & 7 P.M. It is plainly a want with us that both this day, & the last but one, should receive in our minds greater & more specific notice. Marvellous things are to be spoken of both—This is singular 1. as the day to realise the state of deadness to our sins, lying in the grave with Christ: 2. as the opening of communion between the dead & the living. However my employments were hardly appropriate: the aftn being spent at Stourbridge, with Foster & with Collis. Wrote to W. Mathews—R. Smith—E. Monro. Latin lesson to Willy. Read Australian Handbook[10]—Neander's Leben Jesu.[11]

[1] ibid., he omitted the articles on Florence, and the Girondins.

[2] *Christian Remembrancer*, xvii. 265 (April 1849); probably review of *Grote's *History of Greece*.

[3] G. W. Doane, *Sermons on various occasions; with three charges to the clergy of his diocese* (1842).

[4] E. F. Jomard, *Voyage à l'oasis de Syonah* (1823); or in G. A. Hoskins, *Visit to the great oasis of the Libyan desert* (1837).

[5] An Oak Farm employee.

[6] Sidney Clark or Clarke, 1820?–1908; curate of St. Martin-in-the-Fields and in charge of the Bedfordbury chapel 1849–52 (cp. 8 Mar. 49 n.); chaplain to the forces 1854–78.

[7] T. *Arnold, *Sermons chiefly on the interpretation of scripture* (1845).

[8] J. *Wesley, *Sermons on several occasions*, 8 v. (1787–97).

[9] Untraced letter by E. *Monro on his Harrow Weald school.

[10] S. Sidney, *Australian handbook* (1848).

[11] J. A. W. Neander, *Das Leben Jesu Christi* (1845); English tr. (1846).

8. Easter Day.

Church 11 (with Holy Commn.) and 3½. Read Neander—Wesley's Sermons —Nicole Essais de Morale[1]—Ed. Rev. on Union. & on D. of Argyll.[2] Walk with C. & Baby.

9. Easter Monday.

Church at 10 A.M. Wrote to J.N.G.—Sir J.G.—Chess with G.—& billiards. Read Neander—Persian Letters[3]—Journey to Siwah—Tucker's Letters to Kippis.[4]

10. Easter Tues.

Ch 10 a.m. Wrote to Godley—R. Cavendish—J. Foster. Read Quintilian—Ed. Rev. on Miss Strickland[5]—Journey to Siwah—Chalmers's early Sermons.[6] Chess with G. Went to Stourbridge & saw Collis on O.F. matters.

11. Wed. ♄[7]

8½–3½ To London Read Journey to Siwah—The Nemesis of Faith[8]—Dubl. Rev. on Indian Schism, & on Allies.[9] Godley came to dinner, to talk over Colonial matters—Worked on letters &c. Attended Graphic Society.

12. Th.

St James's 3 P.M. Wrote to Mr Benbow[10]—Treasury—Horsfall[11]—Silk[12]—Bliss—Preston[13]—Freshfield—Ch[urch] Miss[ionary] Soc. Secretary—G. & Co—Rn. G.—G. Burnett—Ward. Worked on O.F. papers. Dined with J.N.G.—Godley's to tea; met Mr Rintoul[14] for a Colonial conversation. Read Nemesis of Faith—Lady Alice[15]—Crashaw &c. at London Library. This

[1] Cp. 27 Aug. 43 n.

[2] *Edinburgh Review*, lxxxviii. 499, 462 (April 1849); on *Argyll's *Essay.*

[3] [C. de Secondat], *Lettres Persanes*, 2 v. (1721); tr. (1722).

[4] J. *Tucker, 'Letters to the Revd. Dr. *Kippis' (1773); on dissenting ministers.

[5] *Edinburgh Review*, lxxxviii. 435 (April 1849); a review of A. *Strickland, *Lives of the queens of England* (1840–8).

[6] Probably the sermons in vol. i. of T. *Chalmers, *Works* (1848).

[7] The use of a scourge on this day; Gladstone occasionally scourged himself from 13 January 1849 onwards; cp. 26 Oct. 45, 19 July 48 and 22 Apr. 49 and above, iii. xlvii. The sign occurs as late as 25 May 1859.

[8] J. A. *Froude's part-autobiographical novel (1848), publicly burned by W. *Sewell.

[9] *Dublin Review*, xxvi. 152, 241 (March 1849); articles on the Portuguese schism in India, and on T. W. Allies.

[10] John Henry Benbow, London solicitor acting as agent in charge of the sale of Oak Farm.

[11] Thomas Berry Horsfall, 1805–78; Liverpool merchant, mayor there 1847–8; tory M.P. Derby 1852–3 (unseated for bribery), Liverpool 1853–68.

[12] Probably John Alexander Silk, solicitor in Brunswick Square.

[13] Probably Robert Berthon Preston, 1820–60; Liverpool merchant, engineer and art patron.

[14] Robert Stephen *Rintoul, 1787–1858; founded *The Spectator* 1828, edited it until 1858.

[15] J. V. Huntington, *Lady Alice or the New Una*, 3 v. Puseyite novel (1849).

week is ever a week of great temptations: I suppose there is a power of reaction [after Lent]. Would that I could feel that I had resisted thoroughly: or punished manfully. Great is my leniency in self-judgment: Oh that I may learn equal & better gentleness to my fellowmen.

13. Fr. ♄

Wrote to Ld Medwyn—C.G.—Read Nemesis of Faith (finished)—Macaulay—Quintilian—Lady Alice. Attended S.P.G. meeting—saw Bp of London—Mr Bowdler.

14. St James 8¼ P.M.

Wrote to Collis—Griffiths—Sir J.G.—C.G.—G and Co. Saw Northcote—Mr Benbow (O.F.) Mr Rogers—Mr S. Clarke—Herbert. Drive with the children & calls. Read Twisleton's Evidence[1]—Fane on Tenant right.[2] Quintilian—Macaulay[3]—Lady Alice.

15. 1 S [after] Easter.

Abbey mg. Bedfordbury evg. MS of 44 for E. Day aloud. Gave a lesson to Stephen & Jessy in wh they were very nice. Wrote draft to Mr Venn.[4] Read Life of Wesley[5]—Hampden's Bampton L.[6]—Harris on Priesthood[7]—Bp N[ew]f[oun]d[lan]d's Journal[8]—

16. M.

Wrote to C.G.[9]—Mr J. Burr[10]—Jas Ward—Bowdler—Lefevre—Breakfast with Mr Rogers. Macaulay, Prof. Miller & others—Saw Mr Wynn—Sir J. Young—Baillie. H. of C. 5–9½. Spoke on Scott's motion for a Colonial Committee.[11] Read Quintilian—Lady Alice—Bp Exeter on Mr Shore's Case[12]—Worked on O.F.

17. T.

Wrote to C.G.—Willy (in French)—Mr Benbow—Griffiths—Heath Barber—James—Hawkins—C. Wordsworth. Guiana Committee & House 12½–

[1] E. T. B. *Twistleton, *Evidence as to the religious working of the Common Schools in Massachusetts*, (1854).

[2] [R. G. C. *Fane], 'Tenant-right; its necessity as a means of promoting good farming' (1849).

[3] Cp. 2 Feb. 49.

[4] Henry Venn, 1796–1873; secretary of C.M.S. from 1841; prebendary of St. Paul's 1846–73; wrote on Africa; Gladstone's drafts in Add MS 44368, ff. 145–53.

[5] Cp. 25 Mar. 49.

[6] Cp. 18 July 45.

[7] Henry Harris, 'An essay on priesthood' (1849); opposing T. *Arnold's theory of the church.

[8] Cp. 20 July 45.

[9] Fragment in Bassett, 76.

[10] John Burr, accountant, had made a valuation of the Oak Farm estate.

[11] The motion was lost, 34 to 81: *H* civ. 352.

[12] H. *Phillpotts, 'The case of the Revd. Mr. Shore' (1849); *Phillpotts had brought an action against James Shore.

5½.[1] Worked on O.F. papers. Read Quintilian—Lady Alice—R. Cavendish to Abp.[2] Dined at John's.[3]

18. W.

Wrote to J.N.G.—Sir J.G.—Northcote—W. Talbot—E.H. Collier[4]—Archd Grant[5]—W. Palmer (Cant)—C.G.—Saw H.J.G.—J. Young—Mr Tyler—Ld Castlereagh[6] & others—Sir L. O'Brien—Higgins—(B.G. Committee)—Lincoln (Vancouver's Island)—Attended Eton meeting at 4½. Mr Monro's party in evg. Read A Barrister on Keble's Tract[7]—Lady Alice. St John, on the Desert.[8]

19. Th.

Wrote to Bp of Exeter. C.G.—P. Slater—Mackenzie Wilson. Committees 12¼–3¾. House 5–8 & 9¼–1.[9] Read Quintilian—Torrens on South Australia & Ireland[10]—Wordsworth on Palmer's Appeal.[11] Discussed Vancouver's Island with Lincoln, Goulburn, & Thesiger.

20. Fr.

Wrote to Benbow—C.G.—Armstrong[12]—Teed. Dined (at Goldsmiths Hall) with Wm. G. Saw Godley—H.J.G.—J.N.G.—Bold & Mann (Nav. Law)[13]—then Lincoln, Goulburn, Thesiger, Wortley & Christie met here on V.I. & the H[udson's] B[ay] Co. H. of C. 4½–6 and 11¼–1. Voted in 146:194 for Irish Income Tax.[14] Read Ceylon & B. Guiana papers.

21. Sat. ♄

St Anne's Soho 8¼ P.M. Wrote to Benbow—Foster—Griffiths—Sir J.G.—C.G.[15]—Bellairs—Torrens—Harris—Sec. R. Academy. Read Quintilian—Northcote on Nav. Laws—Lady Alice—& Slave Trade papers.[16] 12–2 with

[1] Irish land: *H* civ. 382.
[2] R. Cavendish, 'A letter to the archbishop of Canterbury on the actual relations between church and state' (1849).
[3] John Gladstone, then living at 46 Eaton Square.
[4] Perhaps of Edmund Collier & Sons, City merchants.
[5] i.e. Anthony *Grant.
[6] Frederick William Robert Stewart, 1805–72; styled Viscount Castlereagh 1822–54; tory M.P. co. Down 1826–52; 4th marquess of Londonderry 1854.
[7] 'Remarks on a late tract by . . . *Keble' (1849); author unknown; cp. 3 Apr. 49.
[8] John vi. 31.
[9] Spoke on Navigation Bill: *H* civ. 466.
[10] R. *Torrens, 'Systematic colonization. Ireland saved . . . to which is added [a letter on] the South Australian experiment' (1849).
[11] Charles *Wordsworth, 'Address at the . . . special synod' (1849); attacks *Palmer.
[12] John *Armstrong, 1813–56; vicar of Tidenham, Gloucestershire, 1845; started Clewer female penitentiary 1849; D.D. 1853; bp. of Grahamstown from 1853.
[13] Liverpool ship-owners; the shipping interest there was hostile to repeal and encouraged Gladstone's reciprocity scheme.
[14] *H* civ. 540; cp. Hammond, 67.
[15] Fragment in Bassett, 77.
[16] Transcripts of the evidence to the select cttee.; cp. *PP* 1849, xix. 3ff.

Lincoln at Sir R. Peel's. A long & very interesting & free conversation on V[ancouver] Island & from that the Nav. Law, Govt., & Queen. Went to Lady Grey's[1] party in the evg. I noticed there but one woman & no other man of Tory connection or politics.

22. 2 S. Easter.

Chester Square Ch mg, where Mr Harrison preached[2]—Bedfordbury evg, where I precented; all was very orderly only a select few of the ragged school being admitted. MS of 44 aloud in evg. (See separate MS of today) Wrote to Bullock—Dr Pusey—Bp of Edinburgh—Mr Venn.[3] Read Wesley's Life—Pusey's Preface—Letters on Marriage Law[4]—Tyler's Illustr. of Common Prayer.[5]

Secret.[6] Reviewing the recent past with reference to the sin of impurity I have much cause for pain and shame: I do not say that it has come in with the force of last year but I think it has lingered more. I have not found the same power as at first in the remedy which I began to use in January. There is an account of all the times of using it with the mark ɦ.[7] I notice that I have been trusting unduly to this & the fear of it & have been seduced into a neglect of other rules, not to deviate, not to break off upon first presumptions of contamination or excitement from without e.g. by what meets the eye. This I have done under an undue presumption of having strength to keep the enemy as it were at arms length: but it is not warranted for even while the mind dreams that it holds itself aloft & free & keeps the command yet sin finds some lodgment.

I have both last Sunday & this morning abstained from going to the Holy Communion; & I must state the reason—it was because I had not shaken off the foe, had not driven him out. Although (in my self-flattery) I hoped that I had not deliberately put away from me the light or inwardly fled from the Presence of God, yet I had not been faithful to it, had not carried it through the whole man, had suffered myself—in which a clearer Eye than mine must draw the line between infirmity & corruption—to hover in a vague and dreamy state on the border of sin with visions of good before me but without any true vigour for their accomplishment.

I know that two of the rocks on which I may fear to split are 1. the allowing & entertaining positive desire: in regard to which our Lord has left us so

[1] Lady Maria, *née* Hamilton, 1803–79; m. 1832 Viscount Howick, who succ. as 3rd Earl *Grey 1845.

[2] Probably B. *Harrison; Joseph Harriman Hamilton, 1799–1881, was the incumbent of St. Michael's, Chester Square, Pimlico, 1848–71.

[3] Draft in Add MS 44368, f. 165.

[4] The reports on the law of marriage provoked many pamphlets and letters; two examples are 'A letter to Sir R. H. *Inglis . . . by an English woman' (1849); 'An earnest address on . . . the law of marriage' (1849).

[5] J. E. *Tyler, *Meditations from the fathers . . . arranged as devotional exercises on the book of common prayer*, 2 v. (1849).

[6] A memorandum in Lambeth MSS, dated this day.

[7] See 26 Oct. 45 for a list of these, and diary entries.

clear and conspicuous a law.[1] 2. that which is well called *delectatio morosa.*[2] I am aware that either of these is adultery in the heart. It is towards them that the Enemy & my own evil bias of habit would draw me, with the beginnings & incitements of these that they solicit me. Nor would they so solicit me if they were repelled with firmness, singleness, entireness of purpose. Without this nothing avails: reliance on one remedy or safeguard only induces forgetfulness and remissness as to others.

Man as God made him is wonderfully made: I as I have made myself am strangely constituted. An ideal above the ordinary married state is commonly before me & ever returns upon me: while the very perils from which it commonly delivers still beset me as snares and pitfalls among which I walk.

Having that sentiment that I was not ready for the altar, I nevertheless aimed in part at what is called spiritual communion: aware at the same time that to recognise this in such case as a genuine substitute, would be a very perilous error.

23. M.

Wrote to Freshfield (2)—Johnson & Longden—S. Trash[3]—Mr Tyler—Wm. Gladstone—Dr Marsh[4]—Lt. Waghorn[5]—J. Walker—Northcote—Sir J.G. —D. Fergusson—Read Quintilian—Northcote on Nav. Law (finished). Worked on O.F. papers. Saw Kinnaird: a very painful interview on Mr Bouverie's Bill. Saw Bp of Oxford—Lincoln—C & the 3 children returned in aftn.—each as well as I cd hope.[6] H of C. $4\frac{1}{2}$–7 and 10–$1\frac{1}{2}$. Voted in 275: 214 for Nav. Bill.[7]

24. T.

Wrote to Mr Foster—Marx & Millctt[8]—E. Hawkins—Judge Coleridge—Commee. (Ceylon) $12\frac{1}{4}$–3: H. of C. $4\frac{3}{4}$–9 and $10\frac{1}{4}$–$12\frac{3}{4}$.[9] Read Lady Alice (finished)—Marsh on Ch & State.[10] Saw Lincoln—Goulburn—Bp of Oxford. H.S. with Willy.

25. Wed. St Mark.

Ch Ch Westr. 6 P.M. H.S. with Willy. Wrote to Johnson & Longden. Commee. & H.S. [*sc.* H. of C.] $1\frac{1}{4}$–6.[11] Read Macaulay—"Catholic" Poor

[1] 'whosoever looketh on a woman to lust after her hath committed adultery with her already in his heart': Matt. v. 28.
[2] Enjoying thinking of evil without the intention of action; Aquinas, *Summa Theol.* I^{a} II^{aa} *q.* lxxiv. a. 6, taken from Augustine, *de Trinitate* xii. 12(18).
[3] Secretary of the Radcliffe Hospital, Oxford.
[4] William *Marsh, 1775–1864; Oxford D.D. 1839; canon of Worcester from 1848; evangelical preacher and writer.
[5] i.e. Thomas *Waghorn.
[6] Catherine Gladstone was again pregnant; cp. 28 Aug. 49.
[7] Most leading Peelites voted for it: *H* civ. 702.
[8] Perhaps M. Marx, importer of French goods and Thomas Millett, French polisher.
[9] Spoke on the Punjab: *H* civ. 753.
[10] W. N. T. Marsh, 'The church and the state' (1849).
[11] Sunday travelling on railways: *H* civ. 831.

School Report[1]—Dined at R. Cavendish's—Saw Ashley—Christy—Bp of Oxford.

26. T.

Wrote to Neilson's—G. & Co—Robinson—Lendrum—Montgomery—Prince—Collis—Sir J. Forbes. H.S. with Willy. Read Macaulay—Macfarlane (Italy)[2]—Marsh—Toulmin Smith[3]—'A Churchman' agt. Keble.[4] Saw Mr Hodgson—

27. Fr.

Wrote to Sir J.G.—Griffiths—Dr Ogle[5]—Mr Trash—H. of C. 4½–6 Commee. 12½–3.[6] H.S. with Willy. Read Quintilian—Marsh—Macaulay—Jenkinson agt. Keble[7]—Hill's 50 days.[8] Saw Hayward—Bonham.

28. Sat.

Marg. Chapel 5 P.M. H.S. with Willy. Calls & drive with C. Dined at R. Neville's. Wrote to J.N.G. (2)—Rn. G.—Collis—J. Downie—Vice Chancellor (Oxf)—Mr R. Seymour.[9] Read Quintilian—Harrington on Macaulay[10]—Mary Barton[11]—Daly's Correspondence.[12] Worked on books.

29. 3 S. E.

Marg Chapel at 11 (Manning preached—worthily of himself) St Martins 8½ A.M. (H.C.)—Bedfordbury evg. Wrote to E. Manning—T. Bowdler—R. Cavendish. MS of 1840 aloud. Read Bp Forbes on Sisterhoods[13]—Lyon on D. of Argyll[14]—Aitchison on do[15]—Marsh—Life of Wesley.

[1] Probably *PP* 1849, xlii. 199; on the management of non-anglican schools.

[2] C. *Macfarlane, *A glance at revolutionised Italy . . . in the summer of 1848*, 2 v. (1849). Macfarlane later strongly opposed Gladstone's Neapolitan pamphlets.

[3] J. T. *Smith, 'Parallels between the constitution and constitutional history of England and Hungary' (1849).

[4] 'An examination of . . . *Keble's tract against profane dealing with holy matrimony. By an English churchman' (1849).

[5] James Adey *Ogle, 1792–1857, Aldrich professor of medicine at Oxford 1824, clinical professor 1830, regius 1851.

[6] Irish poor rates: *H* civ. 933.

[7] J. S. Jenkinson, 'Marriage with a deceased wife's sister . . . the denunciations employed against it by J. *Keble proved to be unscriptural' (1849).

[8] P. G. *Hill, *Fifty days on board a slave-vessel in the Mozambique channel* (1844).

[9] Richard Seymour, 1806?–1880; rector of Kinwarton 1834–77; canon of Worcester from 1846.

[10] E. C. Harington, *The reformers of the Anglican Church and Mr. *Macaulay's History of England* (1849).

[11] By Mrs. E. C. *Gaskell, 2 v. (1848); describes, *inter alia*, prostitution in Manchester.

[12] 'A correspondence which arose out of the discussion at Carlow between [Robert *Daly] and [William Clowry], to which are annexed Notes . . . by Robert *Daly' (1825).

[13] A. P. Forbes, 'A plea for sisterhoods' (1849).

[14] C. J. Lyon, 'Three letters on the duke of *Argyll's . . . *Presbytery examined*' (1849).

[15] D. Aitchison, 'Strictures on the duke of *Argyll's essay on the ecclesiastical history of Scotland' (1849).

30. M.

Wrote to Johnson & Longden—J. Griffiths—J. Benbow (& draft)—C.G. Reid—JNG—Sir G. Grey—Rev. C. Miller—J. Dunning[1]—D. Fergusson—Rev. R. Lee[2]—Scotts. Latin Lesson to Willy. $1\frac{1}{2}$–5 To the Ceremonial at Phil[anthropic] Society's Farm with C.[3]—House of C. $7\frac{1}{2}$–$8\frac{1}{2}$.[4] Read Marsh (Ch & St)—Macaulay—Mary Barton—Jer. Taylor[5]—Wortley's Speech.[6] I launched my letter to Mr Benbow naming the price of £130,000 for O[ak] F[arm] today in perfect *bona fides* but with fear & trembling.

London
Tuesday—May One 1849.
St Philip & St James.

St James's Ch 3. P.M. Committee B[ritish] G[uiana] $12\frac{1}{4}$–$2\frac{1}{2}$. Read Macaulay—Mary Barton—B.G. papers—V[an] D[iemen's] Land do.[7] H.S. with Willy. Saw Sir R. Peel—Lincoln—

2. Wed.

Wrote to Benbow—Sir T. Fremantle—Treasurer of Grey's[8]—and Bp of London. H.S. with Willy. Saw E. Manning—Walpole[9] on Cl[ergy] Relief Bill—Herbert on do. Lincoln. Read Ryland's Case & papers.[10] Dined at S. Herbert's. Worked on B. Guiana Case. House 12–6: beaten on Clergy Relief Bill, as to the Proviso Protecting the Clergy: Inglis absent!!—This to me is one of the deepest of all Ch. & State questions.[11]

3. Th.

Wrote to Benbow—H. of C. $4\frac{1}{2}$–8 and 9–1. (Marriage Bill)[12] H.S. with Willy. Saw H. Taylor (B.G.)—Dowbiggin. Read Ryland's Case—Mary Barton—Badeley on Marriage Law[13]—Jer. Taylor on Do—Bennett on do.[14]

[1] Probably Joseph Dunning, a prominent Leeds solicitor.
[2] Robert *Lee, 1804–68; minister of Greyfriar's Church, Edinburgh, from 1843; professor of biblical criticism, Edinburgh, 1847; attempted liberalization of the Kirk; Gladstone reviewed his *Erastus* in 1844; cp. 31 Aug. 1844.
[3] *Albert laid the foundation stone of the society's farm school at Reigate; cp. *The Times*, 1 May 1849, 5e.
[4] Supply: *H* civ. 1000.
[5] Jeremy *Taylor, 'The marriage ring; or, the mysteriousness and duties of marriage' (1842).
[6] J. A. *Stuart-Wortley, 'Law of Marriage. The substance of a speech in the House of Commons' (1849); his Marriage Bill: *H* cii. 1101.
[7] Governor's report for 1848: *PP* 1849, xxxiv. 1.
[8] Sir Herbert Jenner–*Fust, 1778–1852; dean of the arches 1834; gave judgement against *Gorham on 2 August 1849.
[9] Spencer Horatio *Walpole, 1806–98; tory M.P. Midhurst 1846–56, Cambridge university 1856–82; home secretary 1852, 1858–9, 1866–7; chairman Great Western railway; chronicler and biographer.
[10] Cp. 22 Mar. 49.
[11] Spoke twice: *H* civ. 1127, 1131.
[12] Interjected: *H* civ. 1238.
[13] E. *Badeley, 'Marriage with a deceased wife's sister prohibited by holy scripture' (1849); cp. 27 Jan. 48.
[14] Untraced letter or sermon by W. J. E. *Bennett.

4. Fr.

Wrote to S.R.G.—Christy & Manson—G. Harcourt—Mozley—Bowdler—Ryland. Saw Mr Burnett 10½–12¾ on Hawarden Estate affairs & my own. B.G. Committee 1–3. House 5–7½ and 10–12¾.[1] Read Fortescue on Citizenship.[2] Mary Barton—B.G. papers. Singing in evg!

5. Sat.

Wrote to Hawkins—Collis—Griffiths—Lincoln—J.D. Coleridge—S.R.G.—Toulmin Smith[3]—Bannister—Warrington[4]—Palmer—Cole—Barnes—E. Manning—Mrs Berry[5]—Teed—Sewell. Breakfasted at John's to see my Father who thank God is well: he is even overfull of energy & says of another person relatively to Free Trade 'Why he is more violent than I am'. Saw Bp of London (Cl[ergy] Relief)—Messrs. Thomas & Mowbray[6]—R. Scott—Fremantle—Burnett—Benbow on O.F. a long & anxious conversation, showing only a glimpse of daylight. At the Exhibition 3–4½ and at the dinner.[7] Saw also R. Scott—Cumming Bruce. Read Campbells Speech[8]—Ogilvy on Nav. Law.[9] Worked on arranging my correspondence—sadly bulky.

6. 4 S. E[aster].

St Martin's & Holy C. at 11—Bedfordbury at 7. MS of 44 aloud. Wrote mem. on Cl[ergy] Relief Bill & sent it, with a note, to Bp of London.[10] Saw Manning on this & on Allies's Case—Saw Sir J.G.—Sir Walter James—

7. M.

Wrote to Benbow (& copy) Butler—Judge Coleridge—Maitland—Reed. Latin lesson to Willy. Read Mary Barton—Blunt on Ecc[lesiastica]l Reform.[11] Attended a meeting at Ld J. Manners's at 3. H. of C. 4¼–6½ and 10–12¼.[12] dined at J.N.G.s—& saw my Father in mg. Saw Godley (Canada, NZ.)

8. T.

Wrote to Dr Fisher[13]—S. Bannister—W.B. Collis—Mrs Scott. H.S. with

[1] Ireland: *H* civ. 1260.

[2] Chichester S. *Fortescue, 'Christian profession not the test of citizenship. An essay for the day' (1849).

[3] Joshua Toulmin *Smith, 1816–69; barrister 1849, publicist and reformer.

[4] Perhaps William Warrington, d.? 1866, artist and stained glass maker.

[5] Unidentified.

[6] Probably Ralph Thomas and John Robert Mowbray, barristers.

[7] The horticultural society's exhibition at Chiswick; cp. *The Times,* 7 May 1849, 5a.

[8] Not found.

[9] T. *Ogilvy, *Statistical evidence affecting the question of the Navigation Laws* (1849).

[10] Draft in Add MS 44566, f. 63.

[11] Cp. 20 Mar. 47.

[12] Oaths Bill: *H* civ. 1396.

[13] William Webster *Fisher, 1798?–1874; M.D. 1825; Downing professor of medicine, Cambridge, from 1841.

Willy—Saw Vicar—Mr Young—H. of C. 4¾–6½.[1] My Father dined here with 8. Lady Arundel's afterwards.[2] Read Mary Barton—(finished)—Sicilian papers[3]—Badeley's Speech.[4] Worked on Law of Marriage.

9. W.

Wrote to Benbow (& copy)—Ld Wharncliffe—C.G. Jones—G. Harcourt—Wrote Mem. on Slave Trade for Mr Hutt[5]—H.S. with Willy. Saw Messrs. Young & Batten[6]—Ld Wharncliffe—Sir J.G.—Hutt—Read Newland on Irish Edn.[7]—Hudson's Bay papers.[8] H. of C. 4½–5¾.[9] Dined at Ld Wenlock's—London Univ. Assembly afterwards.

10. Th.

Wrote to Benbow (& copy)—d[itto] 2°. H.S. with Willy. Saw Bp of Exeter—S. Herbert—S.H. Northcote—B.G. Commee. 1½–3 and House 9–12.[10] Read Hudsons Bay papers—Cui Bono[11]—Hofland's Lecture.[12] Worked on Marriage Law for Speech.

11. Fr.

Ch Ch St Giles 5. P.M. H.S. with Willy & Agnes—Wrote to J. Freshfield—Messrs. Freshfield—Christie & Manson—Mrs Carmichael[13]—Pickering—Dr Beke.[14] Saw Ld Wharncliffe—Uncle D.—at Ld Wenlock's in evg. Read Mrs Godwin's Wrongs of Women[15]—Quintilian—Allen on Extinction of Slave Trade[16]—Dwight on law of Marriage.[17]

12. Sat.

Wrote to Sir J.G.—Freshfield—Bridges—Pickering—Ld Wharncliffe—H.S. with W. & A. Worked on Books, & Catalogue—Read Quintilian—

[1] Joint stock banks: *H* cv. 121.
[2] Lady Augusta Mary Minna Catherine, 1821–86, da. of 1st Baron Lyons; m. 1839 Henry Granville Howard, later 14th duke of Norfolk.
[3] Correspondence on Sicilian and Neapolitan affairs, *PP* 1849, lvi. 193, 205.
[4] Cp. 3 May 49.
[5] Not traced; William Hutt was chairman of the select cttee. on the slave trade.
[6] Edmund Batten, b. 1818; Inner Temple barrister from 1842; took additional surname of Chisholm 1859.
[7] H. Newland, 'Remarks . . . on the state of education in Ireland' (1849).
[8] On the Red River settlement: *PP* 1849, xxxv. 509.
[9] Irish labour: *H* cv. 155.
[10] Public expenditure: *H* cv. 208.
[11] J. *Tucker, '*Cui bono?* What benefits can arise from the war?' (1781).
[12] Probably a lecture by T. C. *Hofland, artist, who d. 1843.
[13] Unidentified.
[14] Charles Tilstone *Beke, 1800–74; Ph.D. Tubingen 1837; explored Abyssinia and Near East; civil list pension 1870.
[15] Mary *Godwin, *née* Wollstonecraft, *A vindication of the rights of woman* (1792).
[16] Capt. W. *Allen, R.N., 'A plan for the immediate extinction of the slave trade' (1849).
[17] S. E. Dwight, *The Hebrew wife; or, the law of marriage examined in relation to . . . polygamy and . . . incest* (1836).

Curzon's Visit.[1] Saw Ld Ashburton—Campbell—10 to dinner: Ld Chandos[2] one of them—we liked his *manliness* much—evening party afterwards. I was low & beaten: much to my dishonour for how great are my blessings.

We settled upon bringing matters to a crisis with Miss Browne [the governess]. wrote accordingly—

13. 5 S. E.

St Martin's mg. Bedfordbury Ev. read aloud MS of 42—walk with C. & the children—Read Dwight—Life of Wesley—Nightingale's Portraiture of Methm.[3]

14. M.

Wrote to Benbow (& draft)—Woodward. Latin lesson to Willy. C[olonial] B[ishops] Fund meeting 2–3½.[4] Read Quintilian—Bamford's Radical[5]—Dwight's Hebrew Wife—H. of C. 4½–7 and 9½–12½.[6] Saw Christie & Manson—Lincoln—Hutt.

15. T.

Wrote to J.N.G.—Dean of Ferns—Rev. W. Blunt—H.S. with W. & A. Read Dean Ramsay on Chalmers[7]—Ed Rev. on Mary Barton[8]—Quintilian—B.G. Commee & E. Counties do 12½–4.[9] H. of C. 4–7.[10] Saw Christie & Manson. Dined with Lady Lyttelton. Hardly any *man* would be so entirely above care for certain petty comforts. She hears the word 'take no thought'.[11]

16. W.

St Georges 5 P.M. Wrote to H. Chester—E. Hawkins—E. Manning—J. Benbow (& copy); Sir J.G.—E. Hill—Collis. H.S. with W. & A. H. of C. & Committee 12–4¾. Spoke briefly on Canada in reply to Roebuck.[12] Saw Cumming Bruce on do. At the Queen's Ball in evg.[13] Read Denison on Law of Marriage[14]—Quintilian—Bamford—Canada papers.

[1] R. *Curzon, Baron Zouche, *Visits to monasteries in the Levant* (1849).
[2] Richard Plantagenet Campbell Temple-Nugent-Brydges-Chandos-*Grenville, 1823–89; styled Lord Chandos until 1861; tory M.P. Buckingham 1846–57; 3rd duke of Buckingham 1861; colonial secretary 1867–8.
[3] J. *Nightingale, *A portraiture of methodism* (1807).
[4] Gladstone was joint treasurer with J. G. *Hubbard.
[5] S. *Bamford, *Passages in the life of a radical*, 2 v. (1841–3); Gladstone's notes in Add MS 44737 f. 197.
[6] Irish land: *H* cv. 391.
[7] E. B. *Ramsay, *Memoir of Thomas *Chalmers* (?1849).
[8] *Edinburgh Review*, lxxxviii. 402 (April 1849); Greg's review of Mrs. *Gaskell's novel.
[9] The select cttee. on the Eastern Counties Railway Company, on which he sat; report in *PP* 1849, x. 649.
[10] Irish emigration: *H* cv. 500.
[11] Matt. vi. 34.
[12] On disturbances in Canada: *H* cv. 565.
[13] Cp. *The Times*, 17 May 1849, 5a.
[14] E. B. Denison, 'Letter . . . on the clause relating to the clergy in the bill for allowing marriages with a deceased wife's sister or niece' (1849).

17. Th. Ascension Day

St James 11 a.m. & Holy Commn. Wrote to Sir J. Pelly—Hawes—Northcote—Badeley. Committee (E.C.) & H of C. 2¼–6½.[1] Read Canada Papers (fresh)[2]—

18. Fr.

Wrote to Mrs Henderson[3]—J. Dunning. H.S. with W. & A. Read Jamaica Papers[4]—Clarkson on the Slave Trade[5]—Malet's Letter.[6] Committee 12¼–3 & House 4½–9 (Parl Oaths.)[7] At Mrs Malcolm's Concert. Saw Archd Wilberforce.

19. Sat.

Wrote to Sir J.G.—Mrs Colman[8]—Collis—Griffiths. In the city at Freshfields & court of Bankruptcy:[9] then went to the Drawingroom.[10] H.S. with the children. Saw Bp of Salisbury—C.G. Reid. Read Clarkson—Palmers supplement to Appeal[11]—Wordsworths Address[12]—Townsend on Ir. Edn.[13] —Curzon's Monasteries[14]—Voyage to Hudson's Bay.[15]

20. S aft. Ascension.

St Martin's & H.C. mg—Bedfordbury Evg. Wrote to Bp of London. Saw Ld Aberdeen (Nav. Law & Scots Ch)—Manning. Read Wesley's Life (finished)—Toulmin's Hist. Dissenters[16]—Nightingale's Methodism—Toleration Statutes.

21. M.

Wrote to Bp of Oxford—Ld Lyttelton—W.P. Pickering[17] R. Barker—S. Baker.[18] Latin lesson to Willy. Committee 1–3. H. of C & L 4½–7¼.[19] Dined at

[1] Irish poor relief: *H* cv. 589.
[2] On controversy over indemnity for losses in the 1837–8 rebellion: *PP* 1849, xxxv. 301.
[3] Unidentified.
[4] *PP* 1849, xxxvii. 205.
[5] T. Clarkson, *The history of the rise, progress and accomplishment of the abolition of the African slave trade by the British parliament*, 2 v. (1808).
[6] W. W. Malet, 'The tithe redemption trust. A letter to Lord Lyttelton' (1849).
[7] *H* cv. 670.
[8] Unidentified.
[9] Perhaps for the bankruptcy hearing on Alexander Prince, patent agent, specializing in railway appliances; cp. *The Times*, 21 May 1849, 8f.
[10] For the Queen's birthday.
[11] A second edition with supplement of W. *Palmer's *Appeal*; cp. 18 Mar. 49.
[12] Cp. 19 Apr. 49.
[13] T. S. Townsend, 'The policy of a separate grant for education in Ireland, considered' (1849).
[14] Cp. 12 May 49.
[15] Cp. 12 Aug. 48.
[16] Cp. 1 June 44.
[17] William Percival Pickering, 1819–*c.* 1905; barrister of Lincoln's Inn 1846; in Canada from 1852.
[18] Probably Stephen Cattley Baker, 1819?–92; vicar of Skenfrith, Monmouthshire, 1846–52; chaplain Usk correction house 1852–60, vicar of Usk from 1860.
[19] Lords on Navigation, Commons on Ireland: *H* cv. 687, 760.

Lady Brabazon's. Saw R. Phillimore—Mrs Henderson—Read Quintilian—Clarkson.

22. T.

Wrote to Foster—Acland—Mrs Larkin—Ld Ward. H.S. with W. & A. Read Quintilian—Layard—Bamford. Committee 1–2 H. of Lords 8–10.[1] Ld J. Manners (H. of Charity) 2½–4½. Saw Bp of Salisbury—

23. Wed.

St James's 3. P.M. Wrote to Lincoln—Sir J.G.—Freshfields—Philip—Teale—Cayley.[2] Arranging wine cellar—Drive & walk with C. Dined at Sir F. Thesiger's—Mrs Mildmays, & then Lady Waldegrave's, afterwards—Read Quintilian—Clarkson—Roebuck on Colonies.[3]

24. Th.

Wrote to Griffiths—Barker—Jacob Ley. Northcote—Pelly. H.S. with W & A. Read Quintilian—Roebuck on Colonies—S. Smith on Ballot,[4]—10 to dinner (for Duchess of Buccleuch & Manning). H. of C. 4½–7¼ and 10¼–12. Spoke & voted for the introduction of Roebuck's Bill.[5] Saw Dowbiggin—Sir R. Inglis.

25. Fr.

Wrote to Mr Cayley—Mr Hawker.[6] Lockhart—Norton—S. Baker—H.S. with W & A. Saw Bp of Edinbro—Bp (designate) of Rupert's Land.[7] Mr Cayley (from Canada)—Manson—Lincoln—& made calls. Read Roebuck (finished)—Shore's Statement of his Case[8]—Bamford.[9] H. of C. 4¼–7¼.[10] Dined at Ld Wenlock's. Lady Essex afr. Conv with one of those poor creatures, a very sad case [R].

26. Sat.

Wrote to Sir J.G.—Griffiths—Christie—Hawes. H.S. with W & A. Saw W.F. Campbell—Clerk—Godley. 3–5 Servant's Provident Meeting where I spoke. Willy was there; & his attention or rather absorption were beautiful.

[1] *Brougham's petition on Scotch episcopalians: *H* cv. 782.
[2] W. Cayley of Canada; otherwise unidentified.
[3] J. A. *Roebuck, *The colonies of England* (1849).
[4] Sydney *Smith, *Ballot* (1839).
[5] To introduce a bill for better government of certain colonies: *H* cv. 958.
[6] Robert Stephen *Hawker, 1803–75; vicar of Morwenstow from 1834; antiquarian and poet.
[7] David Anderson, 1814–85; vice-principal of St. Bee's 1841–7; Oxford D.D. 1849; bp. of Rupert's Land, Canada, 1849–64; perpetual curate of Christ Church, Clifton, 1864–81.
[8] James Shore, 'The case of the Rev. J. Shore . . . with an appendix containing the whole of the correspondence' (1849); a reply to *Phillpotts; cp. 16 Apr. 49.
[9] Cp. 4 May 49.
[10] Spoke briefly on estimates: *H* cv. 978.

Drove out to Lady Hope's at Hampstead in evg. Read Quintilian—Clarkson—Mackay's Crisis in Canada.[1]

27. Whitsunday.

St Martin's 8½ (H.C.) & 11. Bedfordbury 7 P.M. MS of 1840 aloud in evg. Family Walk. Read Horneck's Ascetick[2]—Toulmin's Hist—Nightingales Methodm.—Nicole &c aloud to C.G.

28. M.

St James's 3 P.M. Wrote to Collis. Latin lesson to Willy. Read Macaulay—Prospective Review on Froude &c[3]—Bamford—Dr Lushington's Evidence.[4] Saw Bonham—J. Young—Godley. 10 to dinner—Evg party afr.

29. Whittuesday.

St Paul's Kn[ightsbridge] 5. P.M. H.S. with W & A. Walk with C. & W. The attempted sale of No 13 was a perfect failure, without a bid. So I at once made Mema. for Dowbiggin & Snell to sell either this or that & went to arrange accordingly. Saw Herbert on E[cclesiastical] Commr. Bill—Moorsom. Wrote to Sir J.G. Read Bamford—Humboldt's Kosmos[5]—Macaulay. Six to dinner. Church law conv. with Badeley & Phillimore.

30. Wed.

Wrote to Rn. G—Sir R. Peel. H.S. with the children. Another outbreak with Miss Browne: & wrote a draft of note to quit wh. C. sent up to her. It is sad but must be. Saw Godley—Lincoln—Sir J. Pelly (H[udson] B[ay] Co & V[ancouver] I[sland])—and in (evg.) had a conv. with Ld Ward. I found him too self complacent: but quick & intelligent & extremely interested in Church matters. Lady Aylesbury's in evg. Read Canada papers—Bamford—Quintilian. Attended parish Educn. meeting 12–1½ & spoke.[6] Book buying afr.

31. Th.

Wrote to T.G.—Dowbiggin—Snell & Co. H.S. with W. & A. Saw Cayley—Godley—Read Quintilian—Australian papers[7]—B.N.A. do[8]—Clarkson. Dined at Mr Ellison's—Lady Milton's afterwards. H. of C. 4½–7¼.[9]

[1] A. *Mackay, *The Crisis in Canada; or, vindication of Lord Elgin and his cabinet* (1849).
[2] A. *Horneck, *The happy ascetick: or, the best exercise* (1681).
[3] J. *Martineau, ed., *The Prospective Review; a quarterly journal of theology & literature*, v. 163–83 (1849); reviews of J. A. *Froude, *Shadows of the clouds* (1847) and *The nemesis of faith* (1849).
[4] Stephen Lushington's evidence to the select cttee. on the slave trade on 3 May 1849; Gladstone had missed the cttee. that day; cp. *PP* 1849, xix. 89.
[5] F. H. A. von Humboldt, *Kosmos*, 5 v. (1845–62).
[6] No report traced.
[7] On proposed constitutional alterations: *PP* 1849, xxxv. 1.
[8] Preparing for his question next day.
[9] Spoke on the Mint: *H* cv. 1017.

Friday June One 1849.

Wrote to Freshfields—J. Freshfield—Burnett. H.S. with the children. Saw Scotts—G. Hope—S. Herbert—Ld Aberdeen—Goulburn—Lincoln. (on Canada) A. Kinnaird—Read Clarkson—Bamford. H. of C. $4\frac{1}{4}$–$7\frac{1}{4}$.[1] Queen's Concert in evg.[2]

2. Sat.

St George's 5 P.M. Wrote to G. Harcourt (2)—Ld J. Russell (& draft)—Collis—J. Auldjo[3]—G. Chance—Sir J.G.—Dowbiggins. Landzell (dentist) 9–$10\frac{1}{4}$.[4] Saw Sir R. Peel (Canada)—S. Herbert—G. Hope—Godley. Read H. Gordon on Irish Colleges[5]—Clarkson—M. Seymour's 'mornings'[6] N[ational] Club on Irish Ch.[7]

3. Trin. Sunday.

St Martin's & H.C. mg. Bedfordbury evg. MS. of 42 aloud. Walk with C. & the children. It is Willy's birthday: & we have scarcely any thing to wish but that he may be & grow hereafter just as he has begun. Maxima debetur puero reverentia,[8] in a very high sense, at least to him from me. Read Wilberforce on Incarnation[9]—Horneck's Ascetic—Toulmin's Protestant Dissenters[10]—Nightingale.

4. M.

Wrote to Sir R. Peel—Bp of London—J. Freshfield.—Messrs. F.—Ld Cathcart—Johnson & Longden. Latin lesson with Willy. Arranging letters & papers. H. of C. $4\frac{1}{4}$–$7\frac{1}{2}$ and $9\frac{1}{2}$–12. Spoke on Australian Constn. Bill.[11] Read Bamford—Clarkson. Saw Duke of Argyll—Ramsays. Wrote claims for E[cclesiastical] C[ommission] Bill.[12]

5. T.

Wrote to R. Barker—A. Mackay[13]—T.D. Acland—Cunningham—Nicolay—J.B. Monsell—Sir J.G. At Mr Landzell's 9–10. Saw Mr Riddell from

[1] Asked a question on Canadian rebellion losses report: *H* cv. 1031; cp. 17 May 49.
[2] Cp. *The Times*, 2 June 1849, 5f.
[3] John Auldjo, d. 1857; F.R.S. 1840; mountaineer and sketcher.
[4] William Landzell, dentist in Grosvenor Street.
[5] Hunter Gordon, 'The question of the Irish colleges shortly stated' (1849).
[6] 'Beresford' here deleted. M. Seymour, *Mornings among the Jesuits at Rome* (1849).
[7] Nos. viii–xii of *National Club addresses to the protestants of the Empire*, 2nd series (1848) are on the Irish church and its endowments.
[8] 'The greatest reverence is due to a child' (Juvenal).
[9] Cp. 4 Mar. 49.
[10] Cp. 1 June 44.
[11] Mainly on franchise problems: *H* cv. 1128.
[12] Untraced; the bill was withdrawn after its 2° and reintroduced 1850.
[13] Alexander *Mackay, 1808–52; barrister and journalist specializing on foreign topics; cp. 26 May 49.

U[pper] Canada [1]—Saw Bouverie—Nicholl—Slater. Commee. & House 12¼–6½—& 9½–12½.[2] Read Clarkson.

6. *Wed.*

Wrote to Griffiths—Ranford [3]—C. Christie—H.S. with the children. N.S. meeting 2½–8.[4] Dined at Sir H. Hardinge's. Grosvenor House afterwards. Saw Ld Aberdeen Graham & Goulburn on Canada—Conv. with Cardwell on Church matters. Read Clarkson—Whiston on Cathedral Trusts [5]—Irish papers.[6]

7. *Th.*

Wrote to Sir J.G.—Sec. Radcliffe Hospital—G. Harcourt. 5 to dinner. Landzell's 9–10. Saw Collis on O.F. matters 1–2. Herbert on plan for New Bishops.[7] E.C. Committee & St Mark's meeting (spoke) 2¼–6½.[8] Read Macaulay—Clarkson (finished).

8. *Fr.*

Wrote to Freshfield—Sir J.G.—Phillimore—Bp of London—Mrs Ramsay—M. Lyttelton—Sec L. & N.W.R.—Lady James—Saw Manning—Dowbiggin (No 13)—Lincoln—Goulburn (Canada)—Peel (do)—Brougham (do)—also Palmer on Clergy Relief—Goulburn *do.* H. of C 4¼–7¼.[9] Dined at Lady Wenlock's—Read Whiston (finished)—M. Seymour. This day we received a mercy little short of a miracle. Catherine, with little Mary on her left arm slipped on the back stairs, clung to the child with both arms to save her, fell *headlong* down a flight of 7 steep flag steps, then again down five more, kept by her noble motherly love the babe from injury & received none of a serious nature or such as to hasten her confinement though she struck upon & much bruised the brow & had another severe contusion on the arm. I am amazed at the watchful Providence which has thus delivered us: but yet I think had she been as I am this deliverance perhaps had not been wrought.

She lay up all day absolute quiet being prescribed: & every one was most kind.

[1] Charles James Buchanan Riddell gave him an account of meetings on the rebellion; see Add MS 44566, f. 22.
[2] National representation: *H* cv. 1156.
[3] Perhaps Charles Ransford, 1807?–86; F.R.C.P.E. 1835; professor of medicine and botany at Edinburgh.
[4] The annual meeting of the national society for promoting the education of the poor; cp. *The Times*, 7 June 1849, 8a. There was a row about education, cp. Purcell, i., chapter xx.
[5] Robert Whiston, 'Cathedral trusts and their fulfilment' (1849).
[6] Probably *PP* 1849, xvi. 1019.
[7] The colonial bps. plan.
[8] On the extension of St. Mark's College; cp. *The Times*, 8 June 1849, 3c.
[9] Ireland: *H* cv. 1295.

Tonight Ld Brougham accosted me at Lord Jersey's and gave his views about Canada inquiring as to my intentions as he had seen I was to move in the House of Commons.[1] I found him very reasonable: disposed to admit the principle of responsible government though rather misliking the phrase in which I cannot help concurring: clinging however to the notion that the minority might claim some degree of protection against the majority from us. He however mainly seemed to found himself on this proposition that responsible government in the case of a Colony must be modified by the Colonial relation: which is my ground if it means that there are a certain class of questions imperial of which the Colonial Parliament has no right to dispose in the last resort. Then he went on to observe that the prerogative of the Crown in this matter was a very high one and that it was difficult to interfere except in a case of necessity: so that he did not appear to incline to praying for disallowance. I then told him what I had told Lord John Russell tonight viz. that I meant to argue for one of two alternatives, either an authoritative construction of the Act or else an opportunity to the Legislature to amend & the suspension of allowance in the meantime: of which he seemed to approve. He wished me to see Lord Lyndhurst who had been looking at the legal aspect of the matter with him. I observed to him that in the House of Lords they had a great power in their hands since it seemed clear that anything which it was reasonable to ask could be carried there. Also that I had three reasons for not making a motion now: 1. that it would make it more difficult for the Govt. to resolve firmly: 2. that I was doubtful as to carrying it: 3. that it might embarrass the House of Lords.

On telling Ld John my intentions tonight, which I did with Peel's approval, I found from him that he considered the Upper Canada Act was not intended to authorise the payment of compensation to rebels. Nothing passed from which I could divine his views: as far as a presumption could be raised, it would have been rather unfavourable than otherwise.[2]

9. Sat.

St Anne's 8¼. P.M. Wrote to Rev. S. Clark—H. Seymour—W. Cayley. Landzell's at 9. Sale of Mr Cunningham's pictures 1–3, very interesting.[3] Calls. Drive with the children. Saw Godley—Severn—Read Macaulay—M. Seymour. Last Canadian Parl. papers.[4] C. remained quiet & as well as I could desire.

10. 1 S. Trin.

St Martin's 8½ (H.C.) and 11. (when thanks were returned for C. by name): Bedfordbury evg. MS. of 47 aloud at night. Wrote to Acland—Read M. Seymour (finished)—Horneck's Ascetic[5]—Nightingale (finished). B. Noel on Ch & State.[6]

[1] Cp. 14 June 49.
[2] Initialled and dated 8 June 1849; Add MS 44777, f. 294.
[3] The sale of Italian pictures of William Coningham, 1815–84, at Christie's made 11,000 guineas; cp. *Annual Register*, 1849, 62.
[4] Further papers on the indemnity crisis: *PP* 1849, xxxv. 341.
[5] Cp. 27 May 49.
[6] Cp. 30 Dec. 48.

11. M. St Barnabas.

Wrote to Sir J.G.—T.G.—Aunt J.—Scotts—Kirkland—White—R. Barker—Paterson—Halcomb—Latin lesson to Willy. Landzell's at 9. Saw Dowbiggin (house)—Aclands (the Engagement)—Ld Stanley (Canada) in H. of Lords—Hutt—Nicholl (about Lady L[incoln].)—Read Canada papers—Humboldt[1]—Lang on Australian Constn.[2]—and other pamphlets.

12. T.

Wrote to J.N.G.—Mr Owen[3]—R.W. Rawson—Lady James. Saw Cayley—A.M. Paterson—Archd Manning—Slave Trade Comm. (Report) & House 12¼–6½.[4] Read Humboldt. Worked on Canada question—H.S. with the Children.

13. Wed.

Westmr. Abbey 3. P.M. Wrote to Collis—Barker—Sir F. Smith., H. of C. 12½–6.[5] H.S. with the children., Saw Ld Lyndhurst—R. Palmer—Badeley (Cl. Relief)—Read Canada Acts Reports &c.[6] Humboldt—Queens Ball in evg.[7]

14. Th.

Wrote to Rn. G.—H.S. with Children. Working up Canada papers nearly all day: Saw Mr Gillespie—Mr Hincks[8]—wrote to Mr H. House at 4½. Spoke 2 h on the Canada Act. Home to tea & House again till 1½: we had sad blundering & squabbling wholly caused by Mr Herries's friends.[9]

15. Fr.

Wrote to Bannister—Macarthur—Ld Granby (in H[ouse])[10] Saw Nicholl, Herbert, & Lincoln (Canada)—R. Barker—Godley. Slave Trade Comm & House 12–6½, House 10¾–1½. Voted in 150:291 on the Canada Act, Herries's

[1] Cp. 29 May 49.
[2] J. D. Lang, perhaps his 'Letter to . . . Lord *Stanley . . . on proroguing the Legislative Council of New South Wales' (1845).
[3] (Sir) Richard *Owen, 1804–92, surgeon and naturalist; on 1851 exhibition cttee.; K.C.B. 1884.
[4] *Cobden's motion on international arbitration: *H* cvi. 53.
[5] Spoke on country rates: *H* cvi. 153.
[6] *PP* 1849, xxxv. 341.
[7] Report in *The Times*, 14 June 1849, 5e.
[8] (Sir) Francis *Hincks, 1807–85; Canadian statesman; prime minister there 1851–4; governed Barbados 1855–62, British Guiana 1862–9; K.C.M.G. 1869; Gladstone described the conversation in *H* cvi. 201.
[9] He strongly criticized the home government's failure to intervene early and decisively in the Canadian crisis, regardless of local opinion: *H* cvi. 189–225; speech notes in Add MS 44651, f. 40.
[10] Charles Cecil John *Manners, 1815–88; styled marquess of Granby till 1857; tory M.P. Stamford 1837–52; Leicestershire 1852–7; leader of protectionists after *Bentinck's resignation 1848; 6th duke of Rutland 1857.

motion. The management & the issue fill me with disgust. But I must not hastily assume that I have not myself to thank.[1] Dined at Lady Davy's.

16. Sat.

St James's 3. P.M. Wrote to Ld Aberdeen (2)—Ld Granby—W.F. Campbell—Sir J.G.—Vice Chancellor. Brasier[2]—Arbuthnot—Wm. Gladstone—H.S. with the children. Saw Rawson—Dowbiggin—Lincoln—South Australian Soirée 8–10$\frac{3}{4}$, where I made a speech under sore compulsion. The meeting was remarkably well attended.[3] C.G. went off at one to the sea, with Agnes & baby: to recover her tone after the shock of last week. London Libr. Commee. at 4$\frac{1}{4}$.

17. 2. S. Trin.

St Martin's & H.C. at 11 a.m.—Bedfordbury evg. Walk with the children. Conv. with Willy on the disasters of last week but one—I am pierced with shame when I talk to him about sin & repentance from it. Read MS of 43 on Gospel—Began a new one on do. & wrote on Matt VIII. 20.—Began a Concordance of the Prayer book Psalms.[4] Read B. Noel—Toulmin—Crashaw. Wrote to C. Robins.

18. M.

Wrote to Lincoln—Sec. Lpool Fire & Life Co[5]—Canning—T.G.—Macfarlane—Slater—Palmer—C.G.[6] Latin lesson with Willy. Arranging papers & Railway Certificates. Saw Ld Brougham—Lincoln—(V.I.—he dined with me)[7]—Ld Stanley. Read Roman Papers—Ross on the Oregon[8]—Ceylon papers.[9] Lady Salisbury's in evg.[10]

19. T.

Wrote to C.G. Worked on Vancouvers Island papers. H.S. with Willy. Read Ross—Simpson[11]—Ceylon (Buddhism) papers—Hart on Colonies.[12] Ceylon Committee 12–4. House 4–6$\frac{3}{4}$ and 7$\frac{3}{4}$ to the count out.[13]

[1] *Herries' motion was to nullify the Canadian assembly's Indemnity Act: *H* cvi. 252.
[2] Perhaps James Brasier, 1784–1864; capt. R.N. 1837, vice-admiral 1863.
[3] Cp. Bassett, 77.
[4] Later published as *The Psalter, with a concordance* (1895).
[5] Swinton Boult, 1809–76; chief secretary, 1836–65, of the Liverpool and London Fire and Life Assurance Company; managing director from 1865.
[6] Fragment in Bassett, 77.
[7] Cp. Bassett, 78.
[8] A. *Ross, *Adventures of the first settlers on the Oregon or Columbia river* (1849).
[9] The select cttee. had begun to consider Ceylon; cp. *PP* xi. 475.
[10] Cp. Bassett, 77–8.
[11] Cp. 10 Aug. 44.
[12] Not found.
[13] The Vancouver's island deb. was counted out: *H* cvi. 593.

20. Wed.

Wrote to C.G.[1]—W.P. Pickering—C. Robins—M. Welsh—L. Marshall.[2] H.S. with Willy. Read Simpson. Saw Nicholl—Lincoln—The former disclosed to me new & very painful evidence raising for the first time in my mind the serious fear that poor Lady L. may have committed the last act of infidelity.[3] Dined at Ld Crewe's. H. of C. 12–6. Spoke 1½ hour on Wortley's Marriage Bill & voted in 143:177 agt. it.[4] Worked on the papers in mg.

21. Th.

Wrote to C.G.—Sir J.G.—Scotts—Ld Aberdeen—Dowbiggin—Lincoln—Wainwright. H.S. with Willy. Saw Nicholl—Sir R. Peel (on the same subject [Lady Lincoln]: and it is a great privilege to be able to call in his aid)—Mr Dyke[5]—Alex. Wood—Nicholl again. & then poor Lincoln. Commee. 12½–3½ House (where I took Willy) 4½–6½.[6] Dined at Ld Ashburtons: Carlyle was there in the evg & spoke very painfully about religion, and I must add in a manner the most intolerant. Lady Waldegrave's afterwards. Read Simpson.

22. Fr.

Wrote to Chev. Banero[7]—J. Murray—J. Nicholl—C.G.—Sec. Chief Baron. Saw Logan & de Salis—Pottinger[8]—J.N.G.—Lincoln. Read Simpson—Wynne on Welsh Edn.[9]—Monius on Free Trade.[10] H. of C. 4–7.[11] Dined at Cannings. Worked on Ecc Commn. Clauses.

23. Sat.

Wrote to S. Herbert—Nicholl—Williams Deacon & Co. H.S. with Willy. Worked on Eccl. Commn. (new Bishopric) Clauses. Saw Herbert. Read Quintilian—began Lessings Laocoon.[12] Off at 2 to Eastbourne. There found C.G. & R. Cavendish: we drove & walked on the Downs and enjoyed the glorious evening & almost Italian sea.

[1] During debate: cp. Bassett, 78.
[2] Perhaps Leonard Marshall, desk maker and timber merchant, with various London branches.
[3] She was pregnant in Italy, with Lord Walpole. Gladstone's trip was to bring evidence of this.
[4] He vehemently opposed the bill: *H* cvi. 616; notes in Add MS 44651, f. 53 and annotated division list in Add MS 44566, f. 76.
[5] William Dyke, 1814–80; fellow of Jesus, Oxford, 1845–61; rector of Bagenden, Gloucestershire, 1861–80.
[6] Award of medals to doctors: *H* cvi. 640.
[7] Unidentified.
[8] Probably Henry Allison Pottinger, b. ?1824; fellow of Worcester, Oxford; junior proctor 1853; barrister at Lincoln's Inn from 1860.
[9] R. Wynne, *Essays on Education* (1761), including a chapter on Welsh.
[10] Not found.
[11] The budget: *H* cvi. 740.
[12] By G. F. Lessing (1766); English tr. (1836).

24. Sunday & St. John Baptist.

Church & H.C. 11–2. At Compton Place[1]—walks with C.—Bathe at 8½ a.m. Read Horneck's Ascetic.

25. M.

Wrote to J.N.G.[2]—Pelly—Sir J.G.—Thesiger. Bathe—early dinner, off at 4.45 and reached home at 9. All have profited much by the trip. Read Lessing—Pepys.[3] Saw Hanmer—Nicholl—Peel—Lincoln (priv.). H. of C. 10¼–1¼ Irish Poor Law & Cl[ergy] Relief.[4]

26. T.

Wrote to Ryland—T.C. Huddlestone—Alex. Wood. Ceylon Commee 12½–4. House 6–7¼ & 8½–1. Spoke 1 h. on Molesworths motion.[5] Saw Hill—A. Hope—Sir R. Peel & Thesiger on L[incoln]'s matters—Nicholl—L. himself.

27. Wed.

Wrote to Mayow—D. Hunter—Terry—Ford[6]—Sec. Tithe Red[emption][7]—Sec. King's Coll. Hospital[8]—Churchwardens. H.S. with W[illy] & Agnes. Saw John about our Scots plans: we had a hot altercation on his stating that my letter to him was dictated by selfishness: but we afterwards cooled. I told him I hope truly that he misconstrued it, and that it aimed at providing for my Father's comfort. Saw Sir J. Pelly—Charteris, & Count Changy's converted Flax[9]—Ld Braybrooke—H.J.G.—Read Archd. Hale's Charge[10]—Report of W.I. Committee[11]—Hincks on Canada.[12] 7–9 Ld Mayor's dinner & 10–12½ Lady Westm[inste]rs Concert where the Queen was. At the former I sat by Graham & had an interesting convn.

28. Th.

Wrote to Dowbiggin—Freshfield—Greswell (2)—Pelly (draft)[13]—Larkins—Irvine—Joplin—Sir J.G.—Ld C. Russell.[14] H.S. with Willy—B.G. Commee.

[1] The Cavendishes' house by Eastbourne; cp. 23 Feb. 50.
[2] See 27 June 49.
[3] Pepys's *Diary* was then only available in the unsatisfactory editions by Lord Braybrooke, 2 v. (1825) or 5 v. (1828).
[4] *H* cvi. 830.
[5] *H* cvi. 982, requesting royal commission on colonial administration; speech notes in Add MS 44651, f. 57.
[6] Unidentified.
[7] William T. Young was secretary of the tithe redemption trust.
[8] John Lyon.
[9] Perhaps the chevalier Claussen, then exhibiting process for cottonizing flax.
[10] W. H. *Hale, 'A charge delivered . . .' (1849).
[11] Probably the Liverpool West India Association's *Annual Report.*
[12] F. *Hincks, *Canada; its financial position and resources* (1849).
[13] Add MS 44368, f. 194.
[14] Lord Charles James Fox Russell, 1807–94; 6th s. of 6th duke of Bedford; whig M.P. Bedfordshire 1832–48; serjeant at arms 1848–75.

& House 12½–6½.[1] Saw Serj. Merewether—Hume—Lincoln—J.N.G. Walk with C.—dined at home & songs. Poor dear Helen's birthday must not pass unremembered though it be very sad.

29. Fr. ♄ St Peter.

[2]Wrote to Lincoln—& a new draft to Pelly.—H.J.G. *Ch. Ch. Broadway 6 P.M.*[3] H.S. with children. Saw Dowbiggin—Snell—Hume—Hawes (H[udson's] B[ay] Co)—Goulburn & Wortley (do)—Young (conv. about Peel). H. of C. 4¼–6½.[4] Read Irish Eviction Papers[5]—Lords Railway Audit Report.[6] Quintilian—Simpson—Newman on the Soul.[7] Ly Lansdown[e]'s Concert.

30. Sat.

Saint Georges 5. P.M. Wrote to Sir J.H. Pelly—Sir J.G.—Miss Brown—Scotts—Chaplin—Therry—Lowe—Newbolt.[8] H.S. with the children. Saw Lincoln—J.N.G.—Atty. General. Dined at Ld Aberdeen's where I had much conv. with young Stanley & was struck with his ability. His resemblance to his Father in the details of manner is even ludicrous.[9] House of C. at 3½. Read Quintilian—Simpson.

4. S. Trin—July One. 1849.

St Martin's 11 a.m. & H.C.—Bedfordbury evg. MS of 47 aloud at night. Saw Lincoln. Walk with C. Worked on Concordance. Read Horneck—B. Noel (finished)—Toulmin.

2. M.

Wrote to Burnaby. Latin lesson to Willy. Read Quintilian—Newman (F)—Xt Remembr. on Allies—on Geology.[10] Saw Mr Greswell—Dowbiggin—Rn. G.—Alex Hope. At Lady F. Hope's to hear Mrs Gartshore—who sings with more genius than anyone I have heard. H. of C. 4½–8 and 10¾–11¾.[11]

[1] Ireland: *H* cvi. 1043.
[2] 'J.G.' here deleted.
[3] As he records, he was in the Commons from 4.15 to 6.30 p.m.
[4] Ireland: *H* cvi. 1084.
[5] *PP* 1849, xlix. 279.
[6] Reports from Lords select cttee. on railway audits: *PP* 1849, x. 1.
[7] F. W. *Newman, *The soul, her sorrows and aspirations* (1849); Gladstone's notes in Add MS 44737, f. 201.
[8] Perhaps Thomas John *Newbolt, 1807–50; traveller and servant of E.I.C.: assistant at Kurnool 1843–8, at Hyderabad 1848.
[9] Edward Henry *Stanley, 1826–93; tory M.P. King's Lynn 1848–69; secretary of state for colonies, 1858, 1882–5; India, 1858–9; foreign affairs, 1866–8 and 1874–8; 15th earl of Derby 1869; changed sides twice. A kleptomaniac. Cp. Add MSS 44141–2.
[10] *Christian Remembrancer*, xviii. 151, 226 (July 1849).
[11] Spoke briefly on merchant seamen: *H* cvi. 1141.

3. T.

Wrote to Sir J.G.—R. Barker—Mr Reeves—Sir J.H. Pelly & draft.[1]—Tufnell. Saw Greswell—H.J.G. Committee 12$\frac{3}{4}$–4. Read Quintilian—P.C. Ed's minutes & Correspondence.[2] 10 to dinner (young Stanley & young Peel[3] included)—evg party afterwards. H.S. with W. & A.

4. Wed.

Wrote to Dowbiggin—Sir J.G.—Newbolt—H.S. with W. & A.—Saw Greswell—Rn. G.—Freshfield & Collis—Goulburn—Hawes—Roebuck (Australia & H.B. Co)—Lincoln. H. of C. 1–5. Spoke on Marriage Bill.[4] Read Newman—P.C. Edn. Correspondence. Lady Waldegraves Concert in Evg.

5. Th.

Wrote to Sir J.G.—H.S. with the children. Ceylon Commee. 12$\frac{1}{4}$–3$\frac{1}{4}$: House 6–8. Moved Address relating to H[udson's] B[ay] Co[mpany].[5] Read Huber, & Newman (for Univ. debate expected)[6]—Ballantyne's Hudson's Bay[7]—Q.R. on Wortley's Bill—on Democracy.[8] Worked on private affairs & papers. Saw Goulburn—A. Palmer.

6. Fr.

Wrote to Mr Harcourt—D. Fergusson—Manning[9]—G. & Co (2)—A. Whyte—W.C. James. H.S. with the children. Saw Mr Harcourt—Miss Eyre[10]—Dowbiggin—Godley—Hume—Cayley. Read Quintilian—Ballantyne. H. of C. 1–3$\frac{1}{4}$, 5–7$\frac{1}{4}$ and 9$\frac{3}{4}$–3. Voted in 296:156 agt. Disraeli's vote of confidence in himself as Lincoln properly termed it. Peel spoke like a gentleman a statesman & a Christian: but was ill & rudely treated at the close by the Protectionists. And it was very observable that in all he said of his own feelings & relation to the question he had not a cheer from any minister except C. Wood: but many from the Free Traders behind them.[11]

[1] In Add MS 44368, f. 202.

[2] *PP* 1849, xlii. 83.

[3] (Sir) Robert *Peel, 1822–95, 3rd Bart. 1850; Peelite M.P. Tamworth 1850–80, tory M.P. Huntingdon 1884–5, Blackburn 1885–6; erratic and extravagant.

[4] *H* cvi. 1318.

[5] *H* cvi. 1355, proposing inquiry into legality of the company's powers.

[6] Cp. 23 May 44.

[7] By R. M. *Ballantyne (1848).

[8] *Quarterly Review*, lxxxv. 156 (June 1849), hostile to marriage with a dead wife's sister. ibid. 260, reviewing Guizot, *Democracy in France* (1849) and (hardly before time?) *The people's charter* (1838).

[9] In Lathbury, ii. 281.

[10] Governess to the younger children until her marriage in 1850.

[11] Want of confidence: *H* cvi. 1141, 1398. Cp. Buckle, iii. 212, and Parker, iii. 522.

7. Sat.

St George's 5 P.M. Wrote to Manning. Read Ballantyne—Newman on the Soul—Engl. Rev.[1]—Saw Lincoln & then Peel with him. We talked chiefly on the subject of a Mission. L having said that the only persons whom he would like to send were in circumstances to render it impossible I told him he ought to let them judge of that. He there-upon named Manning & me, I undertook to write to M. & said it might probably be practicable for me—which C. approved. Saw also Miss Eyre about her distressing predicament. Saw H. Fitzroy—Sir E. Codrington.

8. 5. S. Trin.

St Martins 8½ H.C. and Bedfordbury evg. MS on Matt VIII. 20 aloud in evg. Worked on Concordance. Read Horneck (finished)—Toulmin (finished)—began Hamilton on Prophecy.[2] Went with Lincoln to see Thesiger: who strongly agreed as to a private Mission. We discussed some particulars. Also with C.

9. M.

Wrote to Pearson (3)—Freshfield (2)—Sir J.G.—Ryland—G. Graham—Geo. Grant—Collis—G. Chance—Jas. Wilson (Hawick)[3]—Bousfield—Locock—Latin lesson to Willy—Saw Labouchere—Glyn—Lincoln & [blank.] Read Simpson's journey[4]—Ballantyne (finished)—Ross's Oregon.[5] H. of C. 12–4¼ and 10¼–1.[6]

10. T.

Wrote to E. Manning—Ld Grey—(& draft)—C.G. Reid—Fox Maule—V. Chancr. Oxf. Dowbiggin—Saw Ld Kildare[7]—Thesiger—Hawes—Fox Maule—Mary Ln. (about C.) Commee. 12½–4½ and House 10¼–1.[8] Read Newman on the Soul (finished)—Ross's Oregon—Ceylon papers.

11. Wed.

Wrote to Ld Grey—Scotts—Rn. G.—Freshfields—Macarthur—Begg[9]—Griffiths—Caparn—E. Foster—H. Maitland. Read Ensor[10]—Ross's Oregon—Saw Scotts—Dowbiggin—Mr Harcourt—Landzell—M.E.G.—Ld Grey

[1] *English Review*, xi. 255–500 (June 1849).
[2] Perhaps sermon xvii. of R. W. *Hamilton, *Sermons* (1846).
[3] Cp. 28 Feb. 45.
[4] Cp. 10 Aug. 44.
[5] Cp. 18 June 49.
[6] Scottish marriages: *H* cvii. 3.
[7] Charles William FitzGerald, 1819–87, styled marquess of Kildare till he succ. as 4th duke of Leinster 1874; liberal M.P. co. Kildare 1847–52.
[8] Irish church: *H* cvii. 107.
[9] James *Begg, 1808–83; minister of Newington free church, Edinburgh, 1843–83; author.
[10] T. Ensor, 'The case decided: protectionists and free traders reconciled' (1849).

monument (a sign of the times)[1]—Lincoln—Smythe—H. of C. $3\frac{1}{2}$–6.[2] Dined at J.N.G.s—Mrs R. Neville's after.[3] Attended at Peel's in the forenoon where it had been decided to accept my offer to go to Naples. So I had to commence my preparations forthwith. Immediately after came Ld Grey's purchase of No 13 [Carlton House Terrace]—a weight off my time tho' at what wd be called a wretched price.

12. Th.

Wrote to Rn. G.—Huddlestone—Mr F. Peel[4]—Johnson & Longden—Amery—Freshfield—Barker—V. Chancr. Oxford—Chr Wordsworth—Wynne—Le Baron[5]—Greswell. Saw Scotts—M. Drouyn de l'Huys[6]—Prince Castelcicala—Miss Eyre—C. Uppington.—Christie & Manson—Lincoln. H. of C. & Commee $12\frac{1}{4}$–$3\frac{1}{4}$, 5–$7\frac{1}{2}$ and $10\frac{1}{4}$–1. Spoke on Mercantile Marine & on Sir W. Denison's Case.[7] Late at night I made copies of parts of the painful & shameful papers of Lady W.s [*sc.* Lincoln's] Case.

In France. July 49.

13. Fr.

Wrote to H.E. Manning—D. Fergusson—Collis—Griffiths—F. Talbot—Dowbiggin—Ld Kildare—G. Harcourt—Sir J.G.—D. Milne—A. Smith[8]—Saw Lincoln—Dowbiggin—Christie—Coalwhippers Deputation—Busy with arrangements about my mission, departure, & sale of House. H. of C. 5–$6\frac{1}{4}$.[9] C. drove with me to the station & saw me off at 8.30.

14. Sat.

Wrote to C.G. (from Paris) crossed in $2\frac{3}{4}$ hour from Dover to Calais: sick enough. Off by the train at $3\frac{1}{4}$ [A.M.] & 230 miles to Paris done in 7 hours: Arrived $10\frac{1}{4}$.—Saw the Banker—M. Thayer (Directeur des Postes.)[10] called at the Presidents[11]—(found the Assembly did not sit) saw the Madeleine & the Louvre (hurried)—and off by the 7.40 train for Bourges & Marseilles: having got rid of my sickness. Read Orlando Furioso.[12]

[1] It was never erected, cp. G. M. Trevelyan, *Lord *Grey of the Reform Bill* (1920), 368.
[2] Misc. business: *H* cvii. 174.
[3] Julia Roberta, da. of Sir Robert Frankland Russell, Bart.; m. Ralph Neville (Grenville) 1845 and d. 1892.
[4] (Sir) Frederick *Peel, 1823–1906, 2nd s. of 2nd Bart., Peelite M.P. Leominster 1849–52, Bury 1852–7, 1859–65; war under-secretary 1855–7, F.S.T. 1859–65, K.C.M.G. 1869, railway commissioner 1874.
[5] Felix Le Baron, French advocate practising in Leicester Square.
[6] Edward Drouyn de l'Huys, 1805–81; French first minister 1848–9; ambassador in London 1849–51; foreign minister 1852–5, 1862–6.
[7] *H* cvii. 236, 254.
[8] Archibald *Smith, 1813–72; fellow of Trinity, Cambridge, 1836–53; barrister specializing in real property from 1841.
[9] Irish judgments: *H* cvii. 325.
[10] E. Thayer; he gave Gladstone official assistance; cp. 6 Aug. 49.
[11] i.e. Louis Napoleon, president of the republic from December 1848.
[12] By L. Ariosto, English tr. by H. Croker (1755); Gladstone's notes are in Add MSS 44737, ff. 117–36 and 44738, ff. 27–85.

15. 5. S. Trin.

All day in the Malle Poste with the night before & after. We rested a short time at Moulins[1] 10 A.M. & St Etienne[2] at midnight. Harvest & other labour went on & few of the men had Sunday dresses on the road—most of the women. Very few Churches appear. The harvest considered very fine—but not what a Scotch farmer would call so—I feel the pain of a Sunday spent in travelling; but on this occasion I could not doubt as to my duty—Read (by snatches) St Greg[ory] de Cura Pastorali[3]—& went thro' our prayers as well as I could.

16. M.

As yesterday. We came successively into the land of the vine, the mulberry tree, & the olive—much beautiful country particularly about the descent upon the Rhone & Valence.[4] No stoppage for food. Read St Greg. de Cur[a] Past. Reached Marseilles ½ h. after midnight: went to Hotel Beauveau, by no means overtired thank God notwithst[an]d[in]g the great heat.

17. T.

Wrote to C.G.[5]—Wrote up Journal. Saw Banker & Consul Turnbull[6]—Went aboard the Colombo—consulted the Directeur des Postes about my Toulon scheme & decided on remaining here patiently for the Govt. boat on Thursday mg. Dined at the table d'hôte & made talk with an Italian & a Peruvian neighbour. At the Gymnase afterwards.[7] Read Orlando Furioso.

18. Wed.

Wrote to C.G. (to keep)—M. Audibert.[8] Read Lessing's Laocoon[9]—Orlando—Goldoni's Bottega del Café.[10] In the morning walked up to the Notre Dame de la Garde: saw the beautiful view there & the Chapel.[11] Arranged my other matters & among the rest purchased a cask of the wine of the country to send home. Table d'hôte again & heard Lucia di Lammermoor well performed at the Theatre.[12]

[1] 160 miles SSE. of Paris.
[2] 25 miles SW. of Lyons.
[3] Cp. 18 Oct. 40.
[4] 55 miles S. of Lyons.
[5] Part in Bassett, 79–80.
[6] Alexander Turnbull, British consul at Marseilles 1815–58.
[7] The theatre du Gymnase, off the Cannebière.
[8] Antoine Audibert, wine merchant in Marseilles.
[9] Cp. 23 June 49.
[10] By Carlo Goldoni (1755).
[11] Church on a high hill to the S. of the old harbour; rebuilt in 1864.
[12] Donizetti's opera, first performed in Naples, 1835.

19. Th.

Went on board at 9½. Sailed 10¾ in the Scamandre, a roomy, solid, slow boat. There was motion but I was able to read & even eat. I had much conversation with an intelligent American of the Whig party on board.[1] Read Lessing—Goldoni.

20. Fr.

Reached Genoa before 11. Went ashore & spent some time in seeing Churches & otherwise renewing my acquaintance with the city. The main front of the Cathedral is fine, the doorways very fine, the contact & almost fusion, the melting point of the round & pointed arch remarkable—in the arcade of the centre aisle of the nave the round rests upon the pointed.[2] The Annunziata is sadly[3] overgilded & its new white marble portico heavy though very different from the execrable one at the theatre.[4]—But I am on board ship & my head tells me I must not write more: I will only say that the books & portraits in the shop windows (Kossuth, Garibaldi, Mazzini, Charles Albert (rare), Napoleon—no Pius IX.) & writings on the walls are very significant, also the sale of Journals al fresco to the labouring people, & of London printed Bibles at 5 francs in bookshops.—Thus far at Leghorn where the rolling of the Steamer made me leave off: & it effectually stopped all attempts to read—whether light or heavier books. I returned on board at Genoa & dined with a good stock of resolution: but there came on a very rough night wh made me & many better sailors extremely sick.

21. Sat.

Reached Leghorn rather battered in the morning: & wrote to C.G.—but as I have said I was unmanned & took to my back again on starting in the afternoon for Civita Vecchia. But I have reason to thank God who thus restrained me from the temptations of idleness & its wanton thoughts.

22. 7 S. Trin.

Wrote again to C.G at night—to C. Harris[5] mg. Landed between 8 & 9: found the town in great hustle with a multitude of French soldiers.[6] I had at length decided on leaving the Steamer on account of the quarantine at Naples towards the sea. And the town being so unquiet & Inns full & as I

[1] The whigs were from 1834 to 1854 the main opponents of the democratic party in the U.S.A.; supporting men of property, professional men, and the strength of the union.

[2] The cathedral of San Lorenzo, erected in 1100 and subsequently altered in the romanesque, gothic and renaissance styles. The fourteenth-century interior is supported by twelfth-century columns.

[3] Instead of 'really'.

[4] The Teatro Carlo Felice, built 1826–8, one of the largest in Italy.

[5] Englishman resident in Naples.

[6] Garibaldi had retreated from Rome, which the French army entered on 3 July to restore the papacy.

look for the first opportunity for Naples I took the Diligence at 11½ for Rome. With great difficulty we reached it at ten & I went to Serny's[1] where I heard the midnight Cannons of the French warn everybody to bed. I managed the prayers better my eyes being fitter for carriage service than usual: also read S. Greg. de Curâ Past. & Mazzini's Address to the Pope.[2] I had an intelligent & not irreligious Italian for my companion: who was keenly against the Pope. His false position indeed saute aux yeux.

23. M.

Closed & sent off my letter to C.G. Had some trouble in planning my journey to Naples. The Diligence (at 11 A.M.) would not go without a certain number of travellers—& there were not enough to make a quorum. The Courier was full. The next Courier would only arrive on Wedy. at midnight. At last I arranged with the landlord that I shd. pay to release him from the Courier & we post off together tonight. Saw Mr Freeborn & read his dispatches & letters.[3] Made a purchase of bronzes & arranged for dispatching them. Then went to S. Pietro in Montorio & surveyed the ground of the late operations,[4] with the aid & instructions of two ardent little black eyed Roman boys, Romani dal cuore[5]—From thence & P[orta] San Pancrazio[6] to the Vatican—and thence again to St Peters: on which several things occurred to me. I take every opportunity of talking to the people & find the strongest feeling against the Pope only qualified in the minds of some one or two of those who live by strangers that they have diminished sadly since troubles began. I do not talk to that class alone & even the most favourable to the governo de' preti[7] told me the people considered the Pope a traitor & he seemed to agree.

After a busy day of much interest I set off soon after nine with my landlord post to Naples. We travelled all night knocking up the postilions & ostlers from their straw in the stables as usual. On these occasions they are even more than commonly laconic. E.G. Scene W.E.G. (kicks open a door) 'c'è la stalla, questa? Risp. Chè vuol? W.E.G. Cavalli. Risp. Quant? W.E.G. Du. Risp. (not believing me or anxious to put more) Guard un po, Paschal[8]—then Paschal looks & the horses are attached. The night air is moist for some hours from sunset afterwards fresh. If there is no objection on account of health it seems far the best time for travelling in Italy at this season when difficulties of police do not interrupt as at Capua. The men are all in their clothes & horses are put to almost as quickly, or not much more

[1] Cp. 29 Mar., 25 May 1832.

[2] G. Mazzini, 'A Pio IX . . . Lettera' (1847).

[3] John Freeborn, British consular agent in Rome from ?1831; assisted the flight of Garibaldi and his men.

[4] Most of the heavy fighting had taken place near this church on the Janiculum.

[5] 'Out and out Romans'.

[6] Also known as the Porta Aurelia, on the top of the Janiculum.

[7] 'Government of priests'.

[8] W.E.G., 'Is this the stable?' 'Wotcher want?' 'Horses.' 'Ow many?' 'Two.' 'Arf a mo, Paschal.'

slowly: for the quickest here would be slow in England. Read Murray's Handbook[1]—Guadagnoli's Poems.[2]

24. T.

Read Guadagnoli. We stopped nowhere except at Capua for Ices *while* the passport was under visa, & my companion paid doganieri[3] & police for speed much more than my fashion but we were not at the Crocelle till 11½ & recollecting my journey in 38 with Kinnaird[4] I think English perseverance does something towards procuring speed. The country is generally beautiful from Terracina to Sparanisi,[5] both sea & land view. After that the road becomes inclosed. The prospect towards Vesuvius descending after St Agata,[6] with the plain of Naples & Capua between is singularly fine, the whole mountain standing clear & well defined from his base. He was smoking as tranquilly as a Dutchman.

At Gaeta I saw 9 vessels which seemed to be of war: and the Mola was crammed with Neapolitan soldiers. There was a train of I suppose runaway artillery. All the Neapolitans ask if Rome is quiet. These arms by sea & land bristling round the 'Chief Pastor' are no mere figure but a true index of his very unnatural position. We found Naples in illumination.

25. Wed. St James.

Wrote (at night) to Lincoln—and to C. Went to British Library—Mr West[7] —Mad. Unghara[8]—Iggulden[9]—& off at 1½ to Castell.[10] & Sorrento—from which using great speed I got back before 8 in the evening. Then I had a singular conversation (one of two) in the street: & last saw Mr Unghara about Lady L.—& Serny to settle our accounts. Read Guadagnoli—the texture is slight & there is a want of moral tone.

Arranged with Harris that he is to visit me tomorrow—& on finding that Lady L. has certainly gone north, to Milan as her first point, decided on following her thither by the Lombardo tomorrow.

26. Th.

Wrote to Ln. Saw Mrs Unghara—Mr C. Harris—Mr Temple[11]—Serny—

[1] J. *Murray, *Handbook for travellers in Central Italy, including the Papal states, Rome, and the cities of Etruria* (1843); by Octavian Blewitt.

[2] P. Guadagnoli, *Sonetti . . . centuria prima* (1785).

[3] 'Customs officials'.

[4] See above, ii. 443, 495–502.

[5] 22 miles NNW. of Naples.

[6] St. Agata del Goti, on the hills 20 miles NE. of Naples.

[7] Lionel Sackville Sackville West, 1827–1908; attaché in Naples 1849, then other minor posts; ambassador to Argentine 1872, Madrid 1878; envoy extraordinary in Washington 1881–8; 2nd Baron Sackville 1888.

[8] An Englishwoman married to an Italian who kept the Hotel des Etrangers in Naples where Lady Lincoln had stayed in 1848.

[9] Iggulden and Co.; bankers in the Largo Vittoria.

[10] Castellammare, on the coast road between Naples and Sorrento.

[11] (Sir) William Temple, 1788–1856, younger br. of *Palmerston; legation secretary in Stockholm 1814–7, Frankfurt 1817–23, Berlin 1823–8, St. Petersburg 1828–32; envoy extraordinary and minister plenipotentiary at Naples from 1832; K.C.B. 1851.

but got no new light. Arranged for departure & off at 5. Read Ariosto C[anto] V[1]—it is *most* beautiful. Left Naples with good weather & had a tolerable passage of 15 to 16 h. I have even in this hurried time much to write: but then the hurry is an effectual impediment.

27. Fr.

At Civita Vecchia: where I read Ariosto [(]finishing the only Vol. with me) & Goldoni. We took on board Galletti,[2] the Marquis Constabile,[3] a Lombard named Wilmer of English descent who had been fighting at Rome,[4] Cav. Barreri,[5] & on the whole a very interesting party & there was abundance of conversation chiefly but not wholly on the politics of Italy & Rome.

28. Sat.

A good passage to Leghorn where we arrived under 14 hours: four hours delay before any one could land. Then the police required me to pay 3 pauls for entering the city to deliver Mr Temple's letter to the Consul[6]—this I refused & on their being challenged to shew their authority they receded. I went to see the English Church & burying ground, & the principal Ch. & bought some books & shoes. The Church is creditable internally except the *very mean* windows in the Tribune. The burying ground has but heathenish symbols: & one person is commemorated in his Epitaph as the minister of a Meeting at Bristol.[7] But these times have made 'peace' & 'confusion' one thing for so many. I was however rather satisfied, as to the monuments, that there is a *new* cemetery carried outwards beyond the growth of the city, & no monument in this relates to a death within the last 10 years.

I returned on board at 3 read Goldoni and Leopardi (who is very forcible):[8] & even dined with comfort in *port*, started at 6 & had an excellent passage, dishonoured by two drunken men, one English & one Scotch, who were ludicrous to the last degree.

29. 8 S Trin.

Finished & sent off my letters to C.G. & Lincoln from Genoa. Read the prayers & S. Greg de Curâ Past.—Landed in Genoa at 7. Arranged with some difficulty for my departure with the Courier in the afternoon. At the Police & Post—breakfast at the Feder—Attended a Sermon at the Delle

[1] Of his *Orlando Furioso*.
[2] Giuseppe Galletti, 1798–1873; liberal minister in the papal states; minister of police 1848; president of the Roman Republic until its fall.
[3] Otherwise unidentified.
[4] Probably a member of the Lombard brigade, disbanded on 4 July; cp. E. Dandolo, *The Italian volunteers* (1851), 288–9.
[5] Otherwise unidentified.
[6] Frederick Thompson, British consul at Leghorn 1844–52.
[7] The cemetery of the Chiese Anglicana, about 500 yards SE. of the Porto Vecchio.
[8] Giacomo Leopardi; his *Opere* were published in 6 v. (1845–9) and were reviewed by Gladstone in the *Quarterly Review* (March 1850), reprinted in *Gleanings*, ii. 65; drafts in Add MS 44684, ff. 152–203.

Vigne,[1] not very remarkable in matter but animated & not *Popish* properly so called. Then I went to the English Chapel but by an error of time only came in for the Sermon there which was wholly without animation but of exceeding good matter, as I thought, by the Rev. Mr Hussey.[2] A hot & dusty drive across the Appennines but with a fine view.

30. M.

(Wrote to C.G.) Reached Milan at 10½. Breakfasted (luxuriously) at the Albergo della Città & then set out on my search for Lady L. the particulars of which I detailed to C. This kept me till past 3. I was too late for the Brera[3]—went to the Duomo & S. Alessandro, bought some books arranged to go to Como tomorrow morning: dined at the Table d'Hote & then went to work with pen & ink, & my books—S. Greg. de Curâ Past.—Goldoni—

At 8 went to the Teatro Ré and heard the Masnadieri[4] sung with two good basses & good Choruses—home at midnight but my sleep was bitten away.

31. T.

Called at 3½ & off at 4½ to Como: first I was in the Duomo at 4¼ where were others. On the top of a Diligence from Monza, I had two remarkably pleasant Italian companions, one a Milanese artisan (who knew Ariosto and Walter Scott) the other more like a peasant and we seemed all to enjoy the conversation. The last part of the drive was beautiful & pleasant it must always be where the cultivation is so high & nice. After breakfast at Como I set about the sad purpose of my visit. It was a day of great excitement, constant movement, overpowering sadness. I saw the Govr. of the Province —the head of Police—the landlord—the (false) Mrs L[aurence]'s courier— the *levatrice*[5] (at night)—& had the laquais de place incessantly at work— he did it well & we went at the proper time to watch the departure. All this I wrote fully to Lincoln in the evening except the horror reported to me.

Also wrote to C. four letters to Lady L[incoln] or Mrs L[aurence] & drafts —read Goldoni & Leopardi a little—went into the Cathedral which is fine[6] —those piles of statues on one another on the front are bad.

Wed. Aug. One. 1849.

After a short sleep I rose & went in search of Dr Balzari[7] but he was not to be found. Then put up my things & went off by the Steamer to Varena.[8]

[1] Santa Maria delle Vigne in the Piazza delle Vigne, by the E. end of the harbour.
[2] Unidentified *locum*; I. Irvine was the incumbent.
[3] The art gallery.
[4] Opera in 4 acts by Verdi, first performed in Rome, 1848.
[5] Midwife attending Mrs Laurence, *alias* Lady Lincoln, whose flight from Como precipitated her confinement, cp. Add MS 44368, f. 258.
[6] Instead of 'grand'.
[7] The doctor who had attended Lady Lincoln in Como.
[8] Magnus, 93, has 'Verona' which is not on Lake Como. Varena is some 20 miles across the lake, on which Lecco, some 12 miles S. of Varena, also lies.

The contrast between the luxury of a rapid voyage, sweet & cool airs upon the lake, with its beautiful scenery & sky, and the business I was about was really horrible. I fell into conversation with a certain Camuzzi who told me much. Arrived at Varena before 12 made my inquiries dined & waited (Albergo Reale) till 6. Then 6–8 to Lecco where I found 'Mrs L.' had gone through to Bergamo last night. Lune d'Oro at Lecco: a good bed. Read Leopardi. Wrote two further letters to Lady L: the last, inclosing the first, for the Como Post.

2. Th.

5–9¼ to Como: the latter part of the drive, indeed the whole, beautiful. I sought solitude on the top of the Diligence. Passed a picture of the Blessed Virgin with this touching title: Mater Amoris ac Doloris. Then some of those funereal paintings, one of wh, representing the human body under the process of corruption, was most revolting. But it helps to explain the system of religion here & its action through the senses.

At Como I saw Dr Balzari: visited the Villa Mancini:[1] had further conv. with the Servitore di Piazza Carlo Sironi, of whom I incline to think well (& I left him in great good humour); put up my things & came off at 2 with the Mail so called to Varese[2] then took a carriage to Laveno,[3] a lovely drive & spot. Hotel Moro, comfortable. The boatmen great rogues: asked 16 francs, & stood for it: I agreed for 10½. Read Leopardi. Commenced a long & painful letter to Lincoln.

3. Fr.

6–8 crossed the Lake [Maggiore] to Baveno.[4] Breakfasted & bathed there—read Leopardi—wrote up Journal—finished my letter to Lincoln & wrote out fair the drafts No 5 & No 6—in waiting for the Milan Courier who does not pass until 4 P.M. Inn (Posta) good: even to its tea. Many fleas about however as I found to my cost, and theirs. Studied my course homewards which should now be prompt. Worked a little in Vocabulary but alas for the first time: I have been too lazy. I had come within these few days to be very much annoyed by inflammation in my eyelids—it was on this day at its worst.

But all the delights of travelling (and delights there must be in this most lovely region) & all its cares are suppressed by the deadly weight of the subject which I carried out with me & now in a far more aggravated form I carry home. I have but one real comfort: a hope flows in upon me, nay a belief, founded perhaps on the worthlessness & brutality of the seducer in this case, that the day of penitence will come, & that then this journey though for no worthiness God knows of mine may have its fruits.

[1] The villa where Lady Lincoln had stayed.
[2] 12 miles W. of Como.
[3] On the E. side of Lake Maggiore.
[4] On the W. side of the lake, 4 miles from Verbania.

4–9¼. Journey to Domo d'Ossola.[1] The first part, where the valley is close, most lovely. Posta, a respectable Inn. Lay down, & slept during the interval which the coach spends here: when they wakened me at 2½ I could not get my eyes even half open for some time.—I fell in today with an Italian painter: as yesterday with a student. I must say they are a nation who make delightful fellow travellers.

4. Sat.

2¾ AM. Left D[omodossola] and crossed the Simplon. From Iselle[2] for some miles, & then the descent from the top to Brieg,[3] are extremely fine. At the former place I heard the last of the everdear Italian tongue—'questo è l'ultimo paese d'Italia.[4] After 1½ hours at Brieg, travelled on through the night: & rather rapidly. Read Leopardi, sparingly. With assiduous bathing & steaming in hot water (i.e. at the stoppages) my eyes improve.

5. Sunday. 9 Trin.[5]

Reached Lausanne at midday. Went unwashed & unshorn to the Service as I found it only began ¼ hour before noon. Finding there was H.C. notwithstanding the suddenness I staid. There were 23 ladies & 6 men besides the clergyman. Then I went to the Faucon (very clean & good) & before 3 got to breakfast. Read S. Greg. de Curâ Past. and Count Recanati.[6] Determined to proceed by Besançon[7] as more secure. Wrote a P.S. to Lincoln & wrote up Journal from Friday. Found there was no Aft. Service. Thought of going to the Free Church at 7: but learned that it was only a "reunion familiere chez Mesdames Chavannes",[8] being prohibited by law: & thought it better not to go.

Oh that poor miserable Lady L.—once the dream of dreams, the image that to my young eye combined everything that earth could offer of beauty and of joy. What is she now! But may that Spotless Sacrifice whereof I partook, unworthy as I am, today avail for her, to the washing away of sin, & to the renewal of the image of God.

At midnight, started for Besançon.

6. M.

Reached Pontarlier[9] 10½ A.M. Besançon 6 P.M. through much beautiful country on the Jura range. At Besançon by means of M. Thayer's[10] letter I obtained the outside place on the Malle Poste and went off again at 11 P.M.

[1] On the Simplon road, 30 miles NW. of Verbania.
[2] Now the Italian entry to the Simplon tunnel.
[3] Brig, on the Rhône, 30 miles E. of Sion.
[4] 'This is the last region of Italy'.
[5] Late entries till 11 August 1849.
[6] G. B. Recanati, *Poesi* (1717).
[7] 45 miles E. of Dijon.
[8] 'An informal meeting at the house of the ladies Chevannes'; Madame Chevannes was the widow of H. H. Joy; cp. 2 May 33 and Hawn. P.
[9] In France, midway between Lausanne and Besançon.
[10] Cp. 14 July 49.

The descent upon the town is picturesque & it is a nice one: I looked into the Churches & found them well kept: many women, no men—Read Leopardi.

7. T.

Langres[1] at 6 A.M. Tours [*sc.* Troyes] 4 P.M. Fair Inns. Visited the Cathedrals at both places. The first is very late—with old parts. Tours [*sc.* Troyes] is an interesting pointed Church, fine west front & rose windows: the restored one did not please me at all either in tracery or glass. It was here or at Langres that I found *3* men at last among a multitude of women, I mean a hundred or more—I took the opportunity at L. and elsewhere of saying my morning prayers in the Church instead of *en route.* The Malle Poste travels fast & changes quickly but makes very long occasional stoppages for office business. Finished Leopardi.

8. W.

Reached Paris 5 P.M. Went to Hotel Bristol & to bed for two hours: the first since Laveno [on 2 August]. Delivered my dispatches between 8 & 9. Wrote to C.G. Read Count Recanati. Went to the Louvre—from wh I should wish most to remember Raphael's little St Georges, Correggio's Holy Family, Perugino's Nativity. To the Madeleine—and the Assembly: where the debates were uninteresting: but it was a *sight.*[2] Some little purchases.

Dined at the Embassy: where were Changarnier,[3] de Tocqueville,[4] O. Barrot,[5] Count Molè,[6] & others chiefly English including Jacob Omnium. Lord & Lady N[ormanby] both very pleasant: & I had the opportunity I desired of saying something to the former about Rome, in the sense of favour to the poor *people* there. Off at 11 P.M. for Amiens.

9. Th.

Reached Amiens at 4 A.M. Visited the Cathedral on which I should say the West doorways and the exterior of the Choir pleased me most—& the Church impressed me with what I often feel that length & heighth are the great elements of the proper beauty of a pointed Cathedral: that breadth is thrown away: & proportion seems violated by the equality of height in the

[1] 55 miles NNW. of Besançon.

[2] The deb. was on railway construction, and judicial reorganization; cp. *Le Moniteur Universel*, 9 August 1849, 2638.

[3] Nicholas Anne Théodule Changarnier, 1793–1877; French general; put down Paris insurrection June 1849; imprisoned 1851, exiled 1852; returned and elected deputy 1871.

[4] Alexis Charles Henri Clérel de Tocqueville, 1805–59; minister of foreign affairs 1849; historian.

[5] Camile Hyacinthe Odilon Barrot, 1791–1873; promoted 1830 revolution; president of the council 1848–October 1849.

[6] Louis Matthieu Molé, 1781–1855; French foreign minister 1830, 1836; prime minister 1837–9.

two lines of aisle (it is a five aisle Church). There is also overmuch light: but with all this it is a very beautiful Ch.

Breakfasted at the Station. Read Casti's Tartaro[1]—Dr Winslow's Journal.[2] Off at 8 for Boulogne. Thence at 12.30 for Folkestone, & had the comfort of a smooth passage, the first I understand this summer. For travelling companions had Mr Scarth a geologist & ecclesiologist & apparently a very good & agreeable man:[3] also Dr Winslow with whom I conversed across the Channel on his interesting profession. Dined at Folkestone: a little out of conceit with English Inns as compared to the really good ones of the Continent. 6–10¼ Folkestone to London where I found dearest C. waiting for me at the Station: & Willy too wakened up to welcome me. I found Agnes delicate but all thank God well: Would God I had brought to them such tidings as C. brought to me.

I ought to be most thankful for having accomplished such a journey without derangement of health or failure of strength. To some lassitude & exhaustion I must of course plead guilty.

The Statistics are as follows. Time 27 days—of which two in forced idleness at Marseilles.

Distance over 3000 miles.
Of which Steam about.. 950.
Railway about........ 750
Posting & priv. carriage 220
Malle Poste, French.... 600
Italian Courier with
Mail & Swiss ab[out]... 350.
Diligence............. 140

I was in
Paris 1st time............hours 8
Marseilles.....................57
Genoa first time............... 4
Rome...........................22
Naples 1st time................14
...... 2d......................20½
Genoa 2d....................... 7½
Milan..........................18
Como 1st time..................24
..... 2d....................... 5
Lausanne.......................12
Paris 2d time..................18
I was in bed ashore 11 nights altogether about 55 hours.
In steamer 6 nights.
Travelling 10 nights.

[1] *Il poema tartaro di G. Casti*, 2 v. (1803); cp. *Gleanings*, ii. 96.
[2] *Quarterly Journal of Psychological Medicine*, founded 1848 by Forbes Benignus *Winslow, 1810–74, who started a lunatic asylum at Hammersmith 1847.
[3] Harry Mengden Scarth, 1814–90; rector of Bathwick, Somerset, 1841–71, of Wrington from 1871; antiquarian.

With a courier & carriage I should I think have spent more time & four times as much money: tho' I might have gained in bodily comfort somewhat.

10. Fr.

This day was occupied in conversation partly with C. & Mary—chiefly with reading & arranging the accumulation of papers made during my absence, and in writing to Lincoln—Manning—Sir J.G—Sir A. Dalrymple [1] —Mr Bowdler—C.G. Reid. To bed early & had a most sound sleep of 9¼ hours.

11. Sat.

Wrote to Barnes—Young—Vicar of St Martin's—N. Jackson [2]—R. Barker —J. Griffiths—J. Amery—H. Maitland—Nicolay—Sir E. Codrington—Guazzaroni [3]—Huddlestone—Lady Campbell—Lewin—Thesiger—Labouchere. Saw Scotts—Worked on private papers & accounts. Wrote up Journal from Sunday last.

12. 10 S. Trin.

St Martins 8½ H.C. and 11—Bedfordbury Evg—MS of 1842 aloud in evg. Worked on Concordance of Psalms—Wrote to Denison. Walk with C. & the children—Read Manning's masterly Charge [4]—Dr Croly on Marriage Bill [5]—Count Recanati.

13. M.

Wrote to Freshfields—Lincoln—Raikes—Richmond—Sec. House of Charity —A. Nicoll—E. Manning—Shipwash [6]—Sir J.G—Nicolay—Col. Reid—Dr Croly [7]—Dr Lang [8]—Landzell. Latin lesson to Willy. Read Tartaro Poema [9]—Guerazzi's Discourse [10]—saw Christies—Drive with C. & calls.

14. T.

Wrote to Thesiger—H.S. with the children. Saw Sir A. Dalrymple (Sisters of Mercy)—Johnson & Longden—Freshfields—Smiths—Scottish Union—

[1] Sir Adolphus John Dalrymple, 1784–1866; tory M.P. sundry constituencies 1817–41; 2nd Bart. 1830.

[2] Unidentified.

[3] Unidentified; travelling companion in Italy?

[4] H. E. *Manning, 'A charge delivered at the ordinary visitation of the archdeaconry of Chichester in July 1849', largely on education.

[5] G. *Croly, 'Marriage with the sister of a deceased wife; injurious to morals and unauthorised by Holy Scripture' (1849).

[6] Shipwash and Company, English and foreign mineral water suppliers, St. James's.

[7] George *Croly, 1798–1860; LL.D. Trinity, Dublin, 1831; rector St. Stephen's, Walbrook, London, 1835–60; poet and critic.

[8] John Dunmore *Lang, 1799–1878; D.D. Glasgow 1825; active in New South Wales politics, lectured in England on Australia 1846–9; wrote on colonization.

[9] Cp. 9 Aug. 49.

[10] F. D. Guerrazzi, *Discorsi politici* (1849).

(in the city 1–4)—E. Badeley (evg.)—Read Tartaro Poema—Giorini's Chiave to do[1]—Tait's Mag. on Oxford University.[2]

15. Wed.

Wrote to Johnson & Longden—Johnson—Sir J.G.—J.N.G—Drive & walk with C. Mr Landzell's (dentist) at 9. Saw Thesiger & detailed to him the history of my journey as it respects Lady L. he sees no room for doubt, nor for hesitation.

Badeley dined with us. I am glad to find even him antipapal on the Roman question. Read Tartaro Poema—Worked on private papers.

16. Th.

Wrote to Hope—R. Barker—W.B. Collis. H.S. with the children. Read Tartaro but my eyes are going backwards, apparently, under the lotion wh I began this morning. It was not a hard day for them, as most of it was spent with Lincoln, & on his matters with Thesiger, also with Mr Parkinson his Solr.[3] There was no doubt or hesitation as to the facts: nothing to discuss except modes of proceeding. L. & Thesiger dined with us: & in the evg when T. was gone L. sat late & spoke out his whole mind. One noble thing he said that I must not let fall to the ground. "I hope the time may come when I may be able to revenge myself on her by some act of kindness done to her without her knowledge". Though he cannot satisfy himself that he is resigned to the will of God, here is a spirit deeply Christian governing all his movements towards her.

17. Fr.

Wrote to J.E. Denison—J. Amery—MF Tupper—H.S. with the children—Again with Lincoln about his business. Saw Dowbiggin on house. Drive with C & the children—Worked on arranging papers & letters—from the state of my eyes, I did not read except a little 'Tartaro'. Lady Hope & HJG dined.

18. Sat.

Ch Ch Broadway 6 P.M. H.S. with the children. Worked on arranging books &c. Finished Tartaro Poema—Wrote to Sir J.G—D. Coghlan[4]—H. Maitland. Drive with C.—Chess in evg.—Locock went for his holiday.

19. S. 11 Trin.

St Martins 11 AM. (& H.C.)—Bedfordbury 7 PM. MS on Naaman aloud in evg. Worked on Concordance—Read a little S Greg. de Cur. Past. We suddenly changed our plan & are to go to Hawarden tomorrow for C.s

[1] Untraced introduction to an ed. of Casti.
[2] *Tait's Edinburgh Magazine*, xvi. 525 (August 1849).
[3] See 27 Nov. 47.
[4] Unidentified.

confinement. I was moved to suggest it, now that the attraction of Locock's presence has been removed, from her apparent susceptibility to slight attacks of cholera which suggest that in the time of weakness it might be more formidable. Wrote letters in consequence to Ld Palmerston—Mr Addington—Sec L N W RR[1]—Mrs Smith[2]—M. Lyttelton.

20. M.

Wrote to Walter James—Williams & Co—Lincoln—Dowbiggin—Freshfield—Sir R. Peel—Sec. G.N.E. Co[3]—Barker—Christie & Manson. Saw C.G. off at 9 by Express Train, without much fear & thank God she performed the journey with no difficulty. I followed at 5 & rejoined her at the Rectory soon after eleven. To Chester we took 5 hours precisely. Saw Crampton (Dentist)[4]—Northcote—Scotts—Dowbiggin's people—Lincoln, who bade me a moving farewell. Shopping & house business.

21. T.

Church 8½ AM. Wrote to Miss Eyre—Dr Cape—Lady Hope—Northcote—Lincoln — Parkinson[5] — Peel — Barber — Collis — Griffiths — Dowbiggin —Perused the agreement with Chance & that for the Chester Block[6]—Saw Coleridge—Brewster—My eyes continue poorly, & yesterday I failed to find Dalrymple who is out of town. C. read me part of Quarterly on Scots Eccl. buildings.[7]

22. Wed.

Church 8½ AM. Wrote on Clergy Relief Bill—Also on Austr. Govt. Bill.[8] Walk with C.—& Chess in evg.

23. Th.

Church 8½ AM. Wrote to Sir J.G—T.G—Hampton—Barlow—Nicolay—At 9¾ went to Chester. Saw Barker on SRG's affairs—& on the Chester Block agreement—Then went to meet the children who left London at 6¼ AM. & arrived at 1.35 PM—went with them on to Queensferry & Hawarden. We were all rejoiced to reunite: Stephen particularly, & his old friendship with Jessy had suffered no detriment from a separation of near two months. An omen of future fidelity. My eyes suffered from the light today—reading is at an end except the paper—which is a kind of necessary.

Chess with C. Worked on Concordance of Ps[alm]s.[9]

[1] Richard Creed, secretary of the London and North Western Railway from 1833.
[2] A nurse; cp. 30 Aug. 49.
[3] John Law Sparkes, secretary and law clerk of Great North of England Railway from 1845.
[4] In London.
[5] Draft on the extent of evidence in the Lincoln affair in Add MS 44368, f. 225.
[6] He purchased the 'Chester Block', about a thousand acres to the NE. of Broughton Church, from Sir S. Glynne for £46,930. The area was later re-united with the Hawarden estate.
[7] *Quarterly Review*, lxxxv. 103 (June 1849).
[8] Untraced.
[9] Cp. 17 June 49.

24. Fr. St Bartholomew.

Church 11 A.M. Wrote to Sec. G.N.E. Co—Worked on accts & priv. papers. Also on Concordance of Psalms. Saw Coleridge—Walk with C. & the children.—Chess. Our satisfaction in having Miss Eyre increases daily. She seems to have alike tact & enthusiasm, shows no sign of selfishness in any point, works freely & hard & makes nothing of it, is warm & simple in her religion: & with this has all the accomplishments we can want.

25. Sat. Ch. 8½ A.M.

Wrote to Sir J.G.—10¼–3½ Walked with Burnet over the Chester Block Property with which I was generally much pleased as to capability & even cultivation. We discussed a number of questions connected with it & I am more & more highly satisfied with him as Agent here. Called on the Brewsters—Worked on Concordance of Ps[alm]s. Chess with C. My eyes thank God are improving—though slowly. C. still disappoints Locock's prophecies by her long delay. She thought the 5th probable & expected the 10th.

26. S 12 Trin.

Ch mg & evg. Wrote to Lincoln—Worked much on Concordance. Conv. with Coleridge—Read a little of Chalmers's Sermons on Commercial Affairs. They are stamped with his nobleness: but have deep pitfalls in them.[1]

27. M.

Church 8½ A.M. Latin lesson with Willy. Wrote to [George] Harrison in mg: as Catherine had symptoms last night. They continued through the day & evening but she was downstairs till 9½ & in the aftn. we drew her out in the Chair. Mr Harrison came at 3 & again at 11. I lay down beside her. Mr H. also applied a blistering liquid to my temples. I worked on Concordance—but did not read; & was chiefly with C.

28. T.

A fourth daughter was born to us at ¼ before 3 A.M., a very plump & full grown child;[2] and this caused a severe last stage of labour. But C. was very well after it, & as thankful as became her. The infant I thought promising in appearance. Both were well thank God during the day. Wrote (on this event) to J.N.G.—T.G.—Rn. G—Ly Glynne—Ly Wenlock—Ld Braybrooke—Ed. Morn. Post—M. Lyttelton—Dow[age]r Ly Lyttelton—

[1] T. *Chalmers, *Works* (1843–9), vi., 'Commercial discourses', on 'The power of selfishness in promoting the honesties of mercantile intercourse', and other similar themes.

[2] Helen Gladstone, 1849–1925, later vice-principal of Newnham College, Cambridge; named to mark her father's reconciliation with his sister.

D[uche]ss of Buccleuch—Mrs R. Neville—Stephen—C. Uppington—Lincoln—and on other matters to—Scotts—Hubbard—Walter James—Hampton—Macculloch—E. Coleridge—Worked a little on Concordance.

29. Wed.

Church 8½ A.M. H.S. with the children. Wrote to Lincoln—Hampton—C.G. Reid—Jameson—Scotts—G. Harcourt—H. Glynne—Worked on Concordance—2¼–6¾ Went with Burnet over the Shordley property[1] & saw the principal tenants also conversed on the improvements wh ought to be made there. Read B[urnet']s Mem. C. going on well except that the medicine (Senna) did not act.

30. Th.

Church 8½ AM. H.S. with the children. Worked on Concordance—Saw Mr Harrison—Dined with the Coleridges. C. was of course in the meshes of her old difficulties today & the failure of aperient medicines tried several times was against her. Much rubbing however (by Mrs S[mith] & me) seemed to keep the right organ from getting into an obstinate state.

31. Fr.

Church 8½ AM. H.S. with the children—Wrote to Freshfields (with Assignment)—Johnson & Longden—Worked on Concordance or rather *Index* to Psalms. Wrote on Clergy Relief.[2] Saw Mr Harrison (under whose treatment my eyes are improving)—Brewster—Much with C. rubbing & otherwise—the medicine has acted, the rubbing too answers, & except some soreness everything thank God is well.—She had also the aid of a 3 months baby (Humphreys)[3] yesty. & today.

Aug.[4] [*Sc. September*] *One 1849. Saty.*

Church 8½ A.M. Wrote to Sir J.G—Helen—J.N.G—H. Maitland. Operations continued today with C. who thank God goes on very well. Worked on Index to Psalms. Also on private accounts—Read 'The Question answered' (Canada)[5]—Saw Mr Harris—Mr Burnet.

2. 13 S. Trin.

Hn. Ch 11 A.M. (& Holy C.)—Broughton aftn. Conv. with Willy. Wrote to Hampton—G. Anson—E. Badeley—Hatchards. Read (a little) Chalmers. Worked on Index to Psalms. Much with C—who is now in all points prosperous[6] having good nights—except a little obstinacy in resisting aperients.

[1] Shordley Manor is 4 miles S. of Hawarden. [2] Not found.
[3] A servant's or villager's. [4] 'Sept' pencilled in over original 'Aug.'
[5] Untraced. [6] Instead of 'prospering'.

3. M.

Church $8\frac{1}{2}$ A.M. Wrote to H. Tayleur—E. Coleridge—and Mary Ln.—Latin lesson to Willy. Worked on Index. Read (a little) Chalmers. All well thank God upstairs. We have now ceased to rub: & the blue pill has done what was to be desired.

4. T.

Church $8\frac{1}{2}$ AM. H.S. with W. & A. Wrote to Barker—Goodford—J. Burr—G. Harcourt—W. Talbot—Freshfields. Saw G. Burnett—J. Griffiths—Lincoln. Tea at the Castle.[1] Worked (a little) on Index. Willy ill at night partly from not chewing, partly from having eaten peach at tea: his sickness excessive: sal volatile failed, then brandy & water, at last calomel (given in bread $1\frac{1}{2}$ grain) succeeded.

5. Wed.

Church $8\frac{1}{2}$ A.M. H.S. with Agnes. Wrote to H. Tayleur—Dean Torry. Worked a good while on the Index. My eyes thank God improve & I ventured to read a little of Chalmers especially as there was no newspaper today. C. & baby so well! Much with her: & prayers as usual. She spent *several* hours on the couch today—first went there Sunday. Walk to Broughton—

6. Th.

Ch $8\frac{1}{2}$ A.M. Wrote to Jas Freshfield—Messrs. Freshfield (& rewrote)—Sir J.G—R. Barker—Watson—Sir John Forbes—Miss *E.* Uppington (about her sister).[2] Worked on Index to Psalms. Read Chalmers. A batch of letters & papers from London gave me some work. Music with the children.

7. Fr.

Ch $8\frac{1}{2}$ AM. H.S. with children—Wrote to J.N.G—do private—Bp of Brechin—M'Cracken—Jas Watson—H. Tayleur—Saw Burnett & fixed on the outlay for Hammels at Cop House Farm[3]—cost £350. Saw Lincoln. Walk with him & early dinner. We went through the various subjects standing for discussion, some of them of great interest: & an opening was given me to point out that the Eccl. Court & Parlt. together do not really give a complete divorce.[4] Worked on Index to Psalms.

8. Sat.

Ch. $8\frac{1}{2}$ AM. H.S. with children—Wrote to Collis—Mrs Conway—Worked on Index to Psalms. I have passed the halfway: but fear the task will do less

[1] i.e. a picnic in the ruins.
[2] Caroline Uppingham had been given temporary leave because of illness; cp. Add MS 44368, f. 136.
[3] On the river Dee, 2 miles SW. of Chester.
[4] Moral questions remained.

than I had hoped towards enlarging my knowledge of this wonderful book.[1] Singing with the children.

9. 14 S. Trin.

Broughton Ch morng. Hawarden evg. Finished Chalmers on Commercial Affairs &c—Worked on Index to Psalms. Wrote to Sir A. Dalrymple.

10. M.

Ch 8½ A.M. Latin lesson to Willy. Saw Burnett. Wrote to Barker—Singing with the children. Worked on Index. Wrote on Cl. Relief Bill. C. has I find been suffering from night perspirations: today she avoided hot washing & they were much less (at night)—She has had trouble with Mrs Baker our nurse: it was difficult to replace the incomparable Caroline [Uppington].

11. T.

Ch 8½ A.M. H.S. with children. Settled (I hope) matters with Mrs B[aker], after consultation—Wrote to Scotts—Maitland—to Johnson & Longden (for tomorrow)—H. Tayleur (for do)—Worked on Index. Wrote on Clergy Relief Bill. Singing with the children. C. got her feet down. Called on Mrs Cole.[2]

12. Wed.

Church 8½ AM. H.S. with Agnes. Singing with the children. Wrote to J.N.G—H.J.G—Mr Jas Foster—Sir W. Denison (for Mr Box)[3] Wrote on Cl. Relief Bill—Worked on Index—C. walked a little—& played chess with me.

13. Th.

Church 8½ A.M. H.S. with children. Wrote to E. Uppington—O.B. Cole—Messrs. M'Cracken—Messrs. Tatham[4]—Worked on Index to Psalms—Walk with Coleridge & SRG who arrived. Dined at the Castle. C.G. is kept back a little by nervous affection at nights: yet only a little. Baby is now fed all night & *once* in the day.

14. Fr.

Church 8½ AM. Wrote to J. Griffiths—W.B. Collis—J. Freshfield—Messrs. Williams. Went to Chester 9½–2½. Saw Mr Barker, & settled terms of Chester Block Agreement—& to prosecute Chamberlain[5]—also discussed

[1] See 17 June 49.

[2] Wife of captain Thomas Edward Cole, agent at Aston Hall, Hawarden.

[3] Perhaps Stephen Box of Chester wanted a post in Van Diemen's Land.

[4] Either Tatham and Proctor, cp. 9 Mar. 40 n., or Tatham, Upton, Johnson, Upton and Johnson, Lincoln's Inn solicitors; Gladstone dealt with both firms.

[5] George John Chamberlaine of the Groves House, Chester, purchased various lands in Flintshire from Sir S. Glynne 1846–8; there was subsequently a dispute over the completion of the purchase; cp. legal papers from 1849–50 in Hawn. P.

change of mortgages, sale of Queensferry Farm[1] to L[yttelto]n, & other matters. Then went to the Bank & settled with Messrs. Williams the terms of an account there. In & out by the two Railways.[2] Made acquaintance with the Bp & was much pleased with his manner & conversation[3]—Also called at the Deanery & Canon Blomfield's[4]—we saw there the Bp of London looking much worse than in the season. C. down stairs. Singing with the children—Chess with Stephen—Read Wesleyan Preacher's Letter to Mr King[5]—Description of the Tubular Bridges.[6]

15. Sat.

Church 8½ A.M. H.S. with W. & A. Wrote to Sir J.G—T.G—T. Greene—H. Kynaston—Sir A. Dalrymple—Mrs Nealds[7]—J. Griffiths—Northcote—Fitzgerald—Dodsworth—Wm. G—MacCracken—Freshfield—Johnson & Longden. Drew C. out in the Chair & otherwise busy with her. Chess with Stephen [Glynne]. Worked a little on Index.

16. S.

Hawarden Ch 11 & 3. An admirable sermon from Mr Brewster on the present judgments. My cares were heavy upon me today a letter from J.[N.G.] ruffling me inwardly. But the Psalm spoke to me, even to me! in the words "I eased his shoulder from the burden: his hands were delivered from making the pots."[8] Yes surely the day will come. Wrote to J.N.G. draft & letter with some cons[ideratio]n & in the hope it has nothing I shall hereafter wish unwritten: to J. E. Denison—Ffolliott[9]—Parkinson[10]—Hampton—Sec. L. & NW. Worked on Index. Wrote Preface to the plan.[11] Conv. with Willy.

17. M.

Church 8½ AM. Latin with Willy. Drew C. in Chair. Chess with her. Worked on Index—Wrote on Cl[ergy] Relief Bill. Household business. Wrote to H. Maitland. Saw Burnett.

18. T.

Being under blue pill I did not rise early: there were also some threatenings

[1] Near Hawarden Bridge over the Dee.
[2] One by Conah's Quay, the other by Lower Kinnerton.
[3] John *Graham, 1794–1865; master of Christ's, Cambridge, 1830–48; bp. of Chester from 1848.
[4] George Becher Blomfield, 1802–85; br. of C.J.*; curate of Hawarden 1824–7; prebendary of Chester from 1827; canon of Chester; rector of Stevenage 1834–74.
[5] Not found.
[6] 'General description of the Britannia and Conway Tubular Bridges on the Chester and Holyhead Railway' (1849).
[7] Unidentified.
[8] Psalm lxxxi. 6.
[9] John Ffolliott, 1798–1868; tory M.P. Sligo 1841–50.
[10] Draft in Add MS 44368, f. 243.
[11] Of the concordance.

on my arm, but, Mr Harrison tells me, superficial. Wrote to Mr Snape.[1] Worked on Index. Wrote on Cl. Relief Bill. Saw Burnett. Mary Lyttelton came & we talked over the Queensferry plan for making over land to George & Henry. Walk with Willy.

19. Wed.

Ch 7 P.M. H.S. with W. & A.—Also singing. Wrote to Hampton—Mrs Conway—Parkinson—Dowbiggin—Messrs. Tatham—M'Cracken—Mr Hill. Wrote on Clergy Relief Bill. Worked on Index. Drew C. in Chair. Saw Mr Burnett—& Mr Brewster with whom we arranged the Baptism of dear Baby for Friday evening.

20. Th.

Church 8½ AM. H.S. with the children. Wrote to Barker—Freshfield—& to Lyttelton in explanation of my scheme as to land. Worked on Index to Psalms. Drew C. in chair. Much conv. with C. & M. on family affairs & Castle plans. Wrote on Cl. Relief Bill. Read Twelfth Night.

21. Fr. St Matthew.

Church 11 A.M. and & 7 P.M. Wrote to Messrs. Williams—J.N.G—Sir J.G—Supt. Scottish Midland[2]—C.G. Reid—W. Hampton—Collis. Wrote on Cl. Relief Bill. Drove C. out—Chess with Stephen.

At 3½ we had the girl school children and some old people to tea in the garden & they played afterwards. Then in the evg our dear little Helen was baptized and C. returned thanks for her recovery: which has been very prosperous, so are we favoured while the scourge is on many. Not that I am spared because I am worthy, but, I trust, that I may become so. The little ones sat up for Church except Mary: & I tried to explain to Stephen and Jessy.

22. Sat.

Received a letter from Lincoln which made me stagger with admiration, just as I was starting for Queensferry at 8 A.M.—Saw Barker in Chester at 9 on S.R.G's business.—To London by Express 9¾–4. Saw Mr Parkinson—Messrs. Tatham (to whom I delivered the conveyance)—Tubb & Henderson[3] about alterations—inquiries about Manning. Saw Calvert[4] & had farming convn. Wrote to Manning—Rn. G—Ch. Wordsworth—Ballard[5]—

[1] Perhaps Alfred William Snape, 1825–96; curate of Brent-Eleigh 1848–51, St. John, Waterloo Road, London, 1853–5; vicar of St. Mary, Southwark, 1855–74, St. Mary, Bury St. Edmunds, from 1874.

[2] Robert Dow Ker, superintendent of the Scottish Midland Junction Railway from 1845.

[3] Perhaps William James Henderson, joiner and cabinet maker, of Northumberland Street.

[4] R. Calvert, a tenant?

[5] Edward Ballard, 1820–97; London physician, specializing in digestion.

Dodsworth—M'Cracken (canc[elle]d)—Haly. Read Lardner on Steam Engine[1]—S. Greg. de Cur. Past.

23. 16 S Trin.

St Martins H.C. 8½ AM—Westmr. Abbey 10 AM—Marg. Chapel 7 P.M. Read S. Greg. de Cur. Past. Set to music (in my way) & wrote out Verses 1 & 2 of Psalm 42.[2] Revised paper on Cl. Relief Bill. Entered our little Helen's birth & Baptism in the great Bible.[3] MS. for 15 S Trin. aloud in evg.

24. M.

Wrote to Freshfield—Lockhart—Parkinson[4]—M'Cracken (2)—Williams & Co—Hubbard—Johnson & Co—C. Uppington—C.G—Wm. Smith—G.G. Harcourt—Supt. Crewe Station. A very busy day about Stephen's and other matters—Saw Mr Bockett[5]—Officer of the Rock Life Office[6]—Scotts—Dowbiggin—settled with Addis's man about lighting the Wilson[7]—with Henderson about the doors—& did some shopping—Examined accounts. Restless & awake through the night—for an hour (2–3) read St Greg. de Cur. Past.[8]

25. T.

Left home 10 m before 6—reached Chester 10 m to 2—saw Messrs. Barker & Burnett on Stephen's mortgages & on letting the castle—then visited Mr W. Smith's [Cop] Farm & heard him on several matters—saw Mr Harrison about C.s indisposition. Wrote to Mr Bockett—Mr Brewster—draft for Burnett to Ld Seaham[9]—Saw Mr Thom.[10] Read Lardner on Steam Engine. Chess with Stephen.

26. Wed.

Ch. 7 P.M. Up late & conv. with C. on plans for Fasque (altered suddenly in consequence of letters)—& about L[incoln]. Went to Buckley to luncheon & saw the schools. Mr Foulkes is a fine fellow. Read Quarterly on Chess.[11] Wrote to Sir J.G—H.J.G—Lyttelton—H Tayleur—Johnson & Co. Chess with Stephen.

[1] D. *Lardner, *A rudimentary treatise on the steam engine* (1848).
[2] Untraced.
[3] i.e. in the Gladstone family bible.
[4] Draft in Add MS 44368, f. 251.
[5] Daniel Smith Bockett, solicitor to the Law Life-Assurance Society.
[6] The Rock Life Assurance Company, head office in New Bridge Street, London.
[7] Probably William Addis, ironmongers, of Leicester Street, Leicester Square. 'The Wilson' was perhaps the product of Robert and William Wilson and Co., bath and household boiler-makers.
[8] Cp. 18 Oct. 40.
[9] George Henry Robert Charles William Vane (Tempest), 1821–84; styled Viscount Seaham 1823–54; tory M.P. Durham 1847–54; succ. as 2nd Earl Vane 1854, adding Tempest to his surname; succ. his half-brother as 5th marquess of Londonderry 1872.
[10] i.e. J. H. *Thom.
[11] *Quarterly Review*, lxxxv. 82 (June 1849).

27. Th.

Ch 8½ A.M. Wrote to Rn. G (2)—Rev. Mr Cowan—H. Tayleur—Clerk of Lieutenancy (Kincard[ine])[1]—J. Hignett.[2] Wrote out in ink my little anthem. Walked to the Ferry to meet Henry on his return. Chess with Stephen. Singing with the children.

28. Fr.

Ch 7 P.M. Wrote to Lincoln (a difficult letter, even to do ill)[3]—Manning (with the former inclosed)—Hampton—Panizzi—Lockhart—Mayow—Greene. Transposed the anthem into two flats. Read Dermot the Unbaptised (too stimulating for children)[4]—finished Lardner on Steam Engine. Stated to Henry my proposn. for his taking land in lieu of his mortgage. Saw Mr Troughton—Mr Burnett. H.S. with Willy.

29. St Michael.

Church 7 P.M. Latin lesson with Willy. Wrote to Mr Barker—Mr Burnett—Mr Griffiths—Lyttelton—Dalton—T.G—Supt. C. & B. Railway[5]—Messrs. King[6]—Collis—& G. & Co(?) Saw Mr Burnett—Called at Jones's Farm—Chess with Stephen. Worked on Index to Psalms.

30. 17 S. Trin.

Church 11 A.M. 3 P.M. Wrote to Barker—Rn. G—H.J.G—Supt C[hester] & Birkenhead. Worked on Index. Read Burton's Testimonies to the Trinity.[7]

Monday Oct 1. 1849.

Church 8½ AM. Finished Index—it remains to arrange & revise—Finished Burton—Read Ed. Rev. on Macaulay.[8] Wrote to Rn. G—Supt Sc[ottish] Midland—Saw Mr Burnett—Mr Jones—Left Memm. with the former on the various improvements in contemplation—Chess with Stephen—who beat me soundly. Packing & arrangements for departure—Visited the Bennions.[9]

2. Tuesday.

Off at 8¼ by Chester to Liverpool. Saw Mr Gardner[10] in Chester. Rn. G. in

[1] Probably James Christian, W.S., certainly clerk in the 1850's.
[2] John Hignett, solicitor; Richard Barker's partner in Chester.
[3] Cp. 12 Oct. 49 n.
[4] Untraced.
[5] Of the Chester and Birkenhead railway.
[6] Probably King and Attwaters, Oxford Street solicitors.
[7] E. *Burton, *Testimonies of the anti-Nicene fathers to the doctrine of the Trinity and the divinity of the Holy Ghost* (1831).
[8] *Edinburgh Review*, xc. 249 (July 1849); a review of the first vol. of his *History*.
[9] Perhaps John Bennion, Chester tailor, and his wife.
[10] Samuel Gardner, cabinet maker.

Liverpool. Embarked in the Admiral at 11 A.M.—& had fine weather. Had it been otherwise we should still have found a journey with 6 little children a formidable affair.

3. Wed.

Reached Greenock at 6 AM—Glasgow by Railway 8½.—Forfar at 3—detained there near 3 hours from want of correspondence between the Railways—Fasque at 8 PM, all well thank God, C. only tired. My Father had some friends: I was pleased with his vigour and spirits.—Saw Bp of Brechin.

4. Th.

Most of the morning in conv. with my Father. Wrote to Mr Parkinson—Dowbiggin—Collis & Co—All my impressions as to poor Lady L. painfully confirmed by the post of today.[1] My Father laboured hard to work something out of me. He also assaulted me twice about Free Trade but was chiefly on private matters: I endeavoured to discourage HIS embarking further in W.I. property—unpacking & arranging my goods—Went at 2½ with Macinroy to the Stonehaven dinner in honour of the Lord Lieut. Sir J. Carnegie who appeared very courteous well-intending & conscientious. I found Macinroy who is a good practical man not gloomy about the prospects of land. The dinner was pleasant, Capt. Barclay in the Chair who says my Father is the prophet Elijah. I had to return thanks (2°) for the University of Oxford.[2]

5. Fr.

Wrote to Lyttelton—C. Uppington—Worked on her accounts, & my own—not now so simple as they were wont. Walk to C.s ride. Further progress in making a settlement—Whist with Sir J.G.—As I shall have much time to spend with him, leaving little visible note, my journal days here will probably be half days. But that time will be useful to me in many ways unless it be my own fault: particularly in teaching patience & a humble mind. God grant it may be of ever so little use to him. He spoke with much heat about Mr Irvine's very painful affair: we talked the matter over but there is no clear opening or hope of good: yet the spirit of a peacemaker never is without fruit: may that rejoice us.[3] Helen & Aunt J. both seem very reasonable.

6. Sat.

Wrote to G. & Co—Kynaston—J.N.G—Tatham & Co—Hampton—G. & Co—A. Panizzi. Read Leopardi's Memoirs & began prose works.[4] Saw Mr

[1] J. Parkinson had sent news of her confinement; draft to him in Add MS 44368, f. 258.
[2] No report found.
[3] Quarrel about conduct of chapel services.
[4] Cp. 28 July 49.

Irvine—Whist with Sir J.G. Working on accounts—my own & of Aunt E's 'Estate'—Wrote a little on Leopardi.[1]

7. 18 S. Trin.

Chapel 11 AM (& Holy Commn.) & 3 PM. It was very delightful notwithstanding the present drawbacks. Walk with C—with Willy. Wrote to Hampton—Sec. Carlton.[2] Read Leopardi (M.) on the Santa Casa[3]—Maskell's Sermons[4]—Wrote on M. Leopardi—and jotted down music for Ps. 81 verses 6, 7.[5]

8. M.

Wrote to Maitland—Ed M[ontrose] Standard—Innes[6]—Atkins[7]—Hart[8]—Latin lesson to Willy. Wrote out (by request) my recollection of Speeches last Thursday. Read Leopardi—Whist with Sir J.G.—Drove C. to Laurencekirk—for books &c.

9. T.

Wrote to Manning (2)—H.S. with W. & Agnes—Began S. Aug[ustine] in Psalmos, with Bp Horne & the Oxford Translation:[9] & a little Commentary, wh I hope to collect as I go on with the reading.[10] Read Leopardi. Accounts & house business—Not one evg yet have I escaped without a Free Trade Lecture! But it flows pretty calmly, & always in the same channel.

10. Wed.

Wrote to Sec G NE Co[11]—Sec L & NW Co—Lyttelton—Hubbard—Hampton—Bunsen. H.S. with W. & A. Worked on Pss. with S. Aug. & Bp H. Read Leopardi (finished I. began II.) Jotted down music for 'He hath not despised' &c. A long evening conv. with Sir J.G. on O.F. & kindred matters—saw Mr Irvine: but did not touch the point.

11. Th.

Wrote to Mr Griffiths—Collis—Burnett—Dowbiggin—Latin lesson to Willy. Wrote O.F. & S.R.G. Mema. for my Father—conv. with him on them. Worked on Pss. with S. Aug. & Horne—Read Leopardi—Visited. Saw Mr Irvine.

[1] Add MS 44684, f. 152.
[2] William Rainger, secretary of the Carlton Club.
[3] Count Monaldo Leopardi, *La Santa Casa di Loreto* (1841); cp. *Gleanings*, ii. 123.
[4] W. Maskell, *Sermons* (1849).
[5] Not found.
[6] William Innes of Raemoir, 1781–1863; cp. 16 Oct. 49.
[7] William Atkins, 1811–79; rector of Tullyaguish, Donegal, 1844–62, of Gorey, Wexford, 1862–79; dean of Ferns 1862–79.
[8] Probably George Augustus Frederick Hart, 1797?–1873; vicar of Arundel from 1844.
[9] G. *Horne, A commentary upon the book of Psalms, 12 v. (1776).
[10] Add MS 44737, f. 204.
[11] Horace Catley.

12. Fr.

Wrote to Mr Parkinson.[1] H.S. with the children. Latin lesson with Willy. Worked on Pss. & Commentary as usual with S. Aug. & Bp Horne. Read Leopardi. Dined with the Macinroys. Visited.

13. Sat.

Wrote to Tatham & Co—R. Barker. H.S. with the children. Latin lesson to Willy—Read Leopardi—Worked on Pss. with S. Aug. & Bp Horne. Drove C. to L[aurence]kirk—Whist with Sir J.G.

14. 19 S. Trin.

Chapel 11 & 3. Visited +. Read Maskell's Sermon (finished)—Leopardi's Martirio[2]—Prichard on Wortley's Bill.[3] Copied out Psalm Tunes.

15. M.

Wrote to Freshfield (with Mema.)—Griffiths—Hubbard—Examined O.F. accounts. Worked on Pss. with S. Aug. & Horne—Latin lesson to Willy. Read Leopardi. Copied out Psalm Tunes—Examined E.P. & D. accounts[4] & conv. with Sir J.G. on them.

16.

Wrote to H. Tayleur—Lindsay—Read Leopardi (finished II)—Gioberti. Provided Willy with Latin exercises. Packed—& off at 10¼ to Raemoir 20 miles by the Cairn. Found a large party there & were most hospitably entertained. Walk with Mr Innes to see the astonishing efforts made in the reclamation of land: there is scarcely anything in art or manufacture more remarkable. Whist in evg.

17. Wed.

Off at 10½ to Haddo House[5] by Kintore[6] and Inverury[7] 28 miles arrived 4¼. Baby an excellent traveller: we go light in a phaeton and pair. Read Leopardi—Gioberti. Conv. with Ld Abn. particularly on the Q[ueen] & [Prince] about Church matters: of which I made Mema.[8]

[1] Draft suggesting immediate serving of the citation in the Lincoln divorce, in Add MS 44368, f. 260.

[2] 'Il Martirio de' Santi Padri' in his *Opere* (1849), ii. 189.

[3] Not found; on the Deceased Wife's Sister's Bill.

[4] The accounts of the Edinburgh, Perth and Dundee Railway, in which he was a shareholder; cp. Hawn. P.

[5] *Aberdeen's seat, 18 miles NNW. of Aberdeen.

[6] 11 miles NW. of Aberdeen.

[7] 3 miles past Kintore, on the Aberdeen–Elgin road.

[8] On the Queen's support for rationalism, *Hampden and the Kirk: Add MS 44777, f. 296.

18. Th. St Luke.

Agnes's birthday: may she give to God the life so remarkably given back two years ago to her, & may this prayer for her go up from worthier lips than every day, this very day included proves mine to be.
Read Leopardi—with Isocrates, Virgil, and the Odyssey. Walk with Ld Aberdeen & Mr Grant &c. Ld A. is as kind good & delightful as ever. Wrote to Tatham—Sir S. Scott & Co—H. Tayleur.

19. Fr.

Wrote to Lindsay—Dalhousie—Dr Brandreth—S.R. Glynne—Sir J.G—J.G. Lockhart—Read Leopardi—Lorenzo de' Medici—Anacreon—Moschus[1]—the two latter for Leopardi—Music in evg. Ld A. drove me (C. was in another carriage) to Formartine, Woodhead Chapel, & Fyvie.[2] We had much conversation: of parts of wh I made Mema.

I had today a twenty mile drive with Lord Aberdeen in his pony carriage and we had much interesting conversation on various subjects.

Yesterday morning we had been on Peel's political position which I described as false and in the abstract almost immoral—as he, and still more Graham, sit on the opposition side of the House professing thereby to be independent members of Parliament but in every critical vote are governed by the intention to keep ministers in office & sacrifice every thing to that intention. In this Lord A. agreed. He said that they lost the motion on foreign policy last July in consequence of its being brought forward by Brougham & the scandalous manner in which he performed his task which even gave the idea of treachery to those who heard him.[3]

Today we were on the Roman question led to it by an apparently approaching crisis in France. Lord Aberdeen spoke ill of Mazzini, rather ill of Galletti, tolerably of Mamiani[4] but was of opinion that the Pope by his connivance at the Crusade against Austria had entirely lost his own ground as against the movement that took effect last November exciting expectations which he could neither fulfil nor[5] lay—that the exigencies of Roman Catholic Christendom made the question most serious but that they were no sufficient answer to a people claiming the laws franchises and guarantees that are now almost the common birthright of all Europe—that if the Popedom offered any compensation for the loss of freedom it was to the inhabitants of Rome alone and none whatever to those of Bologna & the marches the best & most important part of the Roman population—that it was impossible for the Pope to maintain his *own* ground against his subjects after they had as they now have learned their strength—that he could only be maintained by foreign force, & that force would only be supplied by some Power having selfish purposes in view while on the other hand this would not be long tolerated by the rest—that we could not expect or ask the Romans to submit to have the taxation of the country regulated by a body of priests, while on the other hand it was very difficult to constitute a lay authority, the higher energies of the laity having almost been lost by desuetude—that we were at "*a dead lock*"—at the

[1] Tr. Leopardi (1815); cp. *Gleanings*, ii. 72.
[2] 9 miles W. of Haddo House.
[3] *H* cvii. 616 (20 July 1849).
[4] Count Terenzio Mamiani della Rovere, 1802–85; liberal prime minister of papal states 1848, went to Piedmont where he was later a minister.
[5] 'al[lay]' here deleted.

very beginning of extreme difficulties. He looked to some mediation of the R.C. powers but did not see how it was to be done. The Austrians he said certainly would not have interfered had not France done so—and the Duc de Broglie had told him when Pius IX was elected Pope that he knew the man as an honest & weak one & that it was just the same as if La Fayette had been made Pope for he would give up all for popularity—which was curiously verified.

We went also to Free Trade, upon which I told Lord A. that more for form's sake than anything else I had promised my father to ask him how he felt. He was disposed to go farther into the question and after we had left it he recurred to it: and said that when Peel first made his proposal in October 1845 to open the ports with an intimation that in his judgement the old law would never be restored, he asked the opinions *seriatim* and first came Lincoln's against him—then the Duke's against him—then a third & a fourth—upon this he broke the line & said 'Aberdeen what do you think?'[1]

20. Sat.

Wrote (from Fasque) to Lincoln—Manning—R. Barker (2). Left Ld Aberdeen's at 9. Spent 2¼ hours with Ld & Ly Lindsay at Echt,[2] most pleasantly: each be[ing] alike pleasant in their respective ways & spheres: reached Bridge of Dye soon after 5: posted over the hill & to Fasque at 6¾—dark from the Cairn.—We found a party at home—Music in evg.

21. 20 S. Trin.

Chapel 11, & 3 PM. Wrote to Mr Dalton. Read Rhind's Apology.[3] Read Bp of Exeter's criticism on my C[lergy] R[elief] paper & corrected a portion of the paper.[4] Walk with Mr Safe.[5]

22. M.

Wrote to Mr Lockhart—W. Mathews—J. Griffiths—M'Crackens—H. Tayleur—H. Maitland—Mrs Scott—Greswell—Dr Macbride—Latin lesson to Willy. Read Leopardi—Q.R. on Britannia Bridge.[6] Finished correcting (anew) C.R. paper & dispatched it. Whist in evg. O.F. conv. with my Father who advised me to have the mines worked [at the Oak Farm].

23. T.

Wrote to Collis—Messrs. King (& copy of do to C.)—Lord Aberdeen—W.M. Goalen. H.S. with W. & A. Singing practice with children aftn. Drove

[1] Dated this day; Add MS 44777, f. 298.

[2] James Lindsay, 1783–1869; 7th earl of Balcarres 1825; cr. Baron Wigan 1826; successfully claimed dignities of 24th earl of Crawford and Lord Lindsay 1848; unsuccessfully claimed dukedom of Montrose; m. 1811 Maria Frances Margaret Pennington, 1783–1850, da. of 1st Baron Muncaster. Dun Echt was his seat, 12 miles W. of Aberdeen.

[3] T. Rhind, *An apology for . . . T. Rhind; or, an account of the . . . reason for which he separated from the presbyterian party* (1712).

[4] Not found; earlier draft in Add MS 44368, f. 162.

[5] James William Safe of Devonshire Terrace, London; business untraced; cp. 29 Feb. 56.

[6] *Quarterly Review*, lxxxv. 399 (September 1849); on the tubular bridge to Anglesey.

Sir J.G. to Lkirk. Whist in evg. Read Leopardi—and Bunsen's MS most difficult to decipher.[1]

24. Wed.

Wrote to Sir C. Scott—Scott & Co—H. Maitland—Dr Brandreth—Dalhousie (in line of former)—Gaskell—H.S. with W. & A. Read Leopardi—Col. Hanger on Polygamy &c[2]—Q.R. on Britannia Bridge. With Sir J.G. on his arrangements of property.

25. Th.

Wrote to Burnett—S.R.G—Lyttelton—R. Barker. Latin lesson with Willy. Read Leopardi—Q.R. on Rome.[3] Worked on Leopardi. Walk to C.s ride—whist. My Father still at work on the same subjects. He is a rare example of the desire in one who has accumulated to disperse among his children in his lifetime. In this he shows himself like himself. The only difficulty is to prevent its going too far. Last evg he spoke much more gently about Mr Irvine: indeed very gently.

26. Fr.

Wrote to T.G—dft for Aunt J. to Dr Grant. H.S. with W. & A. Preparing plan of London breakfasts.[4] Working on my own affairs. Read Leopardi—Q.R. on peace agitators.[5] Drove C. to Lkirk—Whist in evg.

27. Sat.

Wrote to Maitland—MacCulloch—Gawthorne[6]—Butler—Rickets[7]—Henderson—S. Clarke—Rowsell. H.S. with W. & A. Walk to C.s ride. Whist with Sir J.G. Read Leopardi—Works, & Epistolario.

28. 21 S Trin. & SS. Simon & Jude.

Chapel 11 AM. & 3 PM. Conv. with Willy. Read one of Mr Atkinson's Sermons[8] to Sir J.G. Read Parish Choir[9]—Q.R. on Methodism in Wales[10]—Leopardi with transln. from Gioberti[11]—Also divers MSS. Precented in aftn. service.

[1] Probably of his German journey; cp. Bunsen, *Memoirs*, ii. 206.

[2] G. *Hanger, *Life, adventures and opinions*, 2 v. (1801); i., ch. 1 is on 'Marriage and polygamy', favouring the latter.

[3] *Quarterly Review*, lxxxv. 563 (September 1849).

[4] The Gladstones' main time for entertaining large numbers in London.

[5] *Quarterly Review*, lxxxv. 452 (September 1849).

[6] Possibly Francis Seeker Gawthern, 1813–*ca.* 1855; Exeter, Oxford; priest, but never an incumbent.

[7] Perhaps Charles Rickets, London manufacturer of gas stoves and cooking appliances; cp. 24 Sept. 49.

[8] One of M. Atkinson's *Practical sermons*, 2 v. (1812).

[9] Untraced.

[10] *Quarterly Review*, lxxxv. 313 (September 1849).

[11] A tr. of a letter by Francesco Scarpa in *Il Gesuita Moderno* (1846), cp. *Quarterly Review*, lxxxvi. 325–7.

29. M.

Wrote to Badeley—Bickers. Latin lesson to Willy. Wrote on Leopardi—Read Leopardi's Epistolario—Walk to C.s ride—Whist with Sir J.G.

30. T.

Wrote to Ld Spencer—Lyttelton—Primate of Ireland. H.S. with the children. Read Leopardi—Op. & Epist. Wrote on do—Drove C. to the Burn—Whist—

31. Wed.

Wrote to Rn. G—G. & Co—H. Maitland. H.S. with the children. Read Leopardi—Epist. & Works. Wrote on do. Walk to Stephy's ride. Whist.

All Saints. Thursday Nov. 1.

Chapel 11 AM. Latin lesson to Willy. Read Leopardi. Wrote on do. Wrote to Collis—J. Griffiths—R. Barker—Out with C. & the children. Whist in evg.

2. Fr.

Wrote to S. Herbert. H.S. with W. & A.—Singing lesson to them in aftn—there being rain. Read Leopardi—Wrote & worked on him—Whist in evg.

3. Sat.

Wrote to Hampton—Panizzi—Sir R. Inglis—Fitzgerald—T. Pearson[1]—Ld Spencer[2]—H. Maitland—Tayleur—H.S. with W. & A. Read Leopardi. Worked on Leopardi. Out with C. & the children. Whist.

4. 22 S. Trin.

Chapel 11 AM & H.C.—3 PM. Serm. aloud to Sir J.G.—& then went on Mr I[rvine']s matter—but with doubtful effect. Wrote on Leopardi—Read-Scots Tracts No VI—No VII[3]—Palmer's Continuation of his Proceedings[4]—Xtn Rem. on Hymnology—Cathedrals—Palestrina.[5]

5. M.

Wrote to S.R. Glynne—J. Parkinson—W.B. Collis—Freshfields—H. Maitland—Rev. D. Wilson[6]—Latin lesson to Willy. Considering with C. her

[1] Perhaps Thomas Hooke *Pearson, 1806–92; Eton; served in India; colonel 1879.

[2] Frederick Spencer, 1798–1857; 4th Earl Spencer 1834; minor office 1846–8, 1854–7.

[3] A continuation of the series *Tracts for all places and all times. Edited by Scottish churchmen* of which only i. and ii. (1839) have been traced.

[4] An expanded version of his *Appeal*; cp. 18 Mar. 49 and Selborne I, ii. 58 n.

[5] *Christian Remembrancer*, xviii. 302, 373, 404. (October 1849).

[6] Daniel Wilson, 1805–86; vicar of St. Mary's, Islington, 1832–86; prebendary of St. Paul's 1872–86; an evangelical.

letter to poor Lady L.—a last effort. Busy on my own affairs. Read Leopardi. Worked on do: the moral part of the subject is perplexing.

Poor Willy's Guy Faux in the evg had an unfortunate effect. I confessed to Aunt J. the excess into which I was betrayed. Singing with Willy.

6. T.

Wrote to Hampton—Bickers—Sec. Ch. Miss. Soc—Lyttelton—R. Barker—Tayleur—Maitland—Cureton—J.N.G—H.S. with W. & A. Read Leopardi's letters—hard. Dined at the Burn. Saw Lady H. Forbes.

7. Wed.

Wrote to Mr Hubbard—Chev. Bunsen—H. Maitland—J. Griffiths—Rev A.P. Stanley. H.S. with W. & A. Read Leopardi (finished the Epistolario)—& Poole on Coal Traffic:[1] Whist with Sir J.G.

8. Th.

Wrote to Rn. G—H. Maitland—J.G. Lockhart—W.F. Campbell—Latin lesson to Willy—Worked on Leopardi—whom I finished reading yesterday. Whist in evg. My Father spoke to me an hour on free trade with not more than 3 or 4 minutes of intervals: 29 minutes by the clock without a break & as usual at the top of his voice. However as he now is little excited about it I am easy.

9. Fr.

H.S. with W. & A. Worked all day, i.e. all my available day on Leopardi: my difficulty now is to controul my material & cut down my work. In evg, read Q.R. on signs of Death:[2] and Sir R. Keith's memoirs.[3]

10. Sat.

Wrote to J.N.G—C. Robins—E. Coleridge—H. Maitland. H.S. with W. & A. Revised & put into shape, abridging, where I could, my Article or paper on G. Leopardi.[4] Read J.T. Smith on Engl. & Hungn. Constitution.[5] Whist with Sir J.G.—Walk with C.—

11. 23 S. Trin.

Chapel 11 A.M. & 3 P.M. Sermon aloud to Sir J.G. in evg. Visited. Wrote to Mr Dodsworth—Mr Baily—Mr R. Jackson[6]—Mr Maskell—Read Scottish

[1] B. Poole, 'A report . . . on coal traffic' (1849); on the L.N.W. Railway.
[2] *Quarterly Review*, lxxxv. 346 (September 1849); review of Fontenelle.
[3] Sir R. M. *Keith, *Memoirs and correspondence*, 2 v. (1849); ed. Mrs. G. Smyth.
[4] Cp. 28 July 49.
[5] Cp. 26 Apr. 49.
[6] Robert Jackson, 1811?–87; fellow of New College, Oxford, 1830–48; sub-warden 1845.

Mag[1]—City Mission Report[2]—Ecclesiologist[3]—Col. Ch. Chron.[4]—Dissenter's Catechism.[5]

12. M.

Wrote to S. Herbert—Lockhart—Latin lesson to Willy. Worked for my Father on calculations & mema. about his distribution of property. Whist in evg. Read Parker Antiq. Brit. Ecclesiae[6]—Edinb. Rev. on Reason & Faith.[7]

13. T.

Wrote to T.G—Rn. G—H. Maitland—E. of Aberdeen—H.S. with W. & A. Read Parker Antiqq. Brit. Eccl—Guerrazzi's Battaglia di Benevento[8]—Ed Rev. on Agriculture—& on Coal Statistics.[9] Walk with Capt. Ramsay & Railway & local convn.

14. Wed.

Wrote to Lockhart—Panizzi—Manning—Sir R. Inglis—Lincoln—Hubbard—Sparkes—Toogood.[10] H.S. with W & A. Walk with C. & others—Whist—music. Read Parker—Guerrazzi—Manning's Sermon on Analogy, in proof, on wh I had to comment for him.[11] Began correction of my article on Cl. Relief—with the aid of Badeley's comments.

15. Th.

The day of Thanksgiving & Robns. birthday. Chapel 11 AM (with H.C.) and 3 P.M. Copied out my part in the Anthem. Finished correcting my proof sheets—& dispatched them to Clowes & Son. Wrote to Fitzgerald—Hampton—Rev. H. Mackenzie—Worked for Sir J.G. on his Mema.

16. Fr.

Wrote to Secretary C.M.S.—Sir W. James—Mr Gell[12]—Mr Church about Willy—The Bp of Brechin about Mr Irvine. Latin lesson to Willy. Read

[1] *Scottish Magazine and Church Review*, ii. 471 (October 1849); an episcopalian journal, took Gladstone's side in dispute with *Wordsworth on synods.

[2] *Annual Report* (1849) of the London City Mission.

[3] *The Ecclesiologist*, x. 169 (November 1849), on the churches of Tours.

[4] *Colonial Church Chronicle*, iii. 161 (November 1849); on British Guiana.

[5] B.R., *The dissenter's catechism* (1703).

[6] M. *Parker, *De Antiquitate Britannicae Ecclesiae et privilegiis Ecclesiae Cantuariensis* (1572); notes in Add MS 44737, f. 205.

[7] *Edinburgh Review*, xc. 293 (October 1849).

[8] By F. D. Guerrazzi, 4 v. (1829).

[9] *Edinburgh Review*, xc. 357, 525 (October 1849).

[10] William Toogood, journalist; cp. Add MS 44383, f. 190.

[11] H. E. *Manning, 'The analogy of nature', on I Cor. xv. 358, printed in his *Sermons* (1850), vi. 152.

[12] John Philip Gell, 1815–98; Trinity, Cambridge; chaplain to bp. of Tasmania 1844–8, curate of St. Martin-in-the-fields, London, 1849, of St. Mary's, 1850–4; vicar of St. John's, Notting Hill, 1854–78.

Parker—Longfellow's Kavanagh.[1] But a return of the inflammatory symptoms in my eye will now very nearly stop my little reading for a time. Walk to C.s ride. Whist in evg. Arranged with Sir J.G. about money to work the O.F. mines & determined to begin it.

17. Sat.

Wrote to Griffiths—Amery—Collis—R. Barker—S.R.G.—a heavy batch, in fulfilment of yesterday's determination [on Oak Farm]. Also to Lyttelton —Adderley—Godley and H. Maitland. H.S. with the children—Singing at Fettercairn House in afn. Whist in evg. Finished 'Kavanagh'.

18. 24 S Trin.

Chapel 11 AM & 3 PM. Serm. aloud in evg to Sir J.G. Visited + Wrote to Bp of New Zealand—E. Badeley—Wrote on Habak. C. 11. v. .(finished) & on Ps. V. v. 8.

19. M.

Wrote to S.R. Glynne—H. Glynne—G. Burnett—W. Hampton—J. Freshfield—Freshfield & Co—Latin Lesson to Willy. Revived my undertaking on the Psalms—quod felix faustumq sit, Te duce, Te auspice, Lux mea, et Vita mea.[2] Read Parker Antiq.—Battaglia di Benevento. Walk with C. Whist in evg. At work on Psalm Index (cutting).

20. T.

Wrote to Porter (G.R)—H. Maitland—A. Lendrum. H.S. with the children. Worked on my accounts. Worked on Pss. Read Parker—Guerrazzi—Worked on Pss. Index—My Father pressed me about Free Trade, still clinging to the hope that I may change. It is very difficult to manage the subject. Silence encourages him in that delusive idea: Counter argument excites him: and any mere plea by way of escape he exposes & protests against with great force. All this difficulty of mine really springs from the strength of his affection.

21. Wed.

Wrote to S.R. Glynne—Mr Hubbard—H.S. with W. & A. Read Parker Antiqq—Guerrazzi—Engl. Rev. on Kneller Hall—The Emerson Mania—& Maskell's Absolution[3]—Walk to C's ride. Worked on Psalm Index. Considering & making preparations for a new will. The complication of my property from the O.F. & S.R.G. affairs renders this necessary.

[1] H. W. Longfellow, *Kavanagh, a tale* (1849).
[2] 'may it be fortunate and prosperous, under your leadership and your auspices, O my light and my life'.
[3] *English Review*, xxii. 107, 139, 196 (September 1849).

22. Th.

Wrote to H. Tayleur—E. Manning. Latin lesson to Willy. Music with the children—& copying. Read Parker's Antiqq—Guerrazzi—Ed. Rev. on Schools of Design (by Northcote).[1] Worked on Index to Pss. Whist in evg.

23. Fr.

H.S. with W. & A.—New arrangements about Willy's Latin—Conv. with Miss Eyre—she is most satisfactory. Worked on Pss. & on Index to do—Read Parker—Guerrazzi—Martineau on the East[2]—Worked at music—Worked on Mema. for Will.

24. Sat.

Wrote to Barker—J.G. Lockhart—Northcote. Latin lesson to Willy. Whist with Sir J.G.—Read Parker—Guerrazzi. T.G. came: conv. with him on Sir J.G.s affairs, & on the sad Irvine business. Visited.

25. 25 S. Trin.

Chapel 11 AM & 3 PM. Visited the Falconers: & learned & went into their temporal distresses: I hope warrantably, on the principle which requires us to pull the ox out of the pit.[3] Read Rhind[4]—Trial of Occasional Conformity[5]—Parker's Antiqq—Engl. Rev. on Seymour—Maitland, Parish Schoolmasters, Cathedrals, & Foreign Intelligence.[6]

26. M.

Wrote to R. Barker—W. Talbot—G. Talbot jun.[7]—H. Maitland. H.S. with W. & A. Read Parker—Battaglia di Benevento. Went to the Falconers again & conv. with Sir J.G. Whist in evg. Conv. with T.G. on family matters &c.

27. T.

Wrote to Sir J. Carnegie. Latin lesson to Willy. Read Parker—B. di Benevento—and Martineau on the East. At work on Falconer's matters with my Father Fergusson & young Mr F.

[1] *Edinburgh Review*, xc. 473 (October 1849).

[2] H. *Martineau, *Eastern life, past and present*, 3 v. (1848).

[3] Cp. 31 Aug. 43: they were tenants of Sir J. *Gladstone.

[4] Cp. 21 Oct. 49.

[5] Untraced.

[6] *English Review*, xii. 30, 65, 88, 223 (September 1849).

[7] Gerald Chetwynd-Talbot, 1819–85; 9th s. of 2nd Earl Talbot; appeared before Ceylon cttee.; applied to Gladstone for a colonial post 1854; became director of Indian military stores; cp. Add MS 44529, f. 159.

28. Wed.

Wrote to H. Maitland—Scotts—do incl. in Maitland—S.R.G.—J. Amery. Read Parker—Guerrazzi—Buxton's Memoirs [1]—9¼–2½ Out on Ld Kintore's [2] & Sir J.F's hills to shoot white hares. Scarcely any were to be had & the snow on the tops W. of the Cairn was full 6 in. deep but I had a most healthful walk & saw the Sloch of Birnie which from the brink is really fine.[3]

Working for my Father on some figures.

29. Th.

Wrote to Bunsen. Corrected the proofs of Leopardi & did all as desired by Mr L[ockhart]. Also read L's poetry &c. Latin lesson to Willy. Read Abp Parker—Guerrazzi—Reading to my Father; who had a very uneasy day, feeble and rather confused. Saw Bp of Brechin abt. Mr I[rvine]. Conv. with Tom about the burdens (by the will) & other matters.

30. Fr. St Andrew.

Chapel 10½ AM. Wrote to Mr Amery. Tom left us at 9 AM. My Father rallied in the middle of the day: but did not quite show his usual strength. Saw the Bp. Read Sir J.G's letters to him: then went to Arbuthnott. Read Guerrazzi—Buxton's Memoirs.

Sat. December One 1849.

Wrote to H. Tayleur—S.R. Glynne—Parkinson [4]—J.E. Denison—J.G. Hubbard. Latin lesson to Willy. Worked on SRG's matters. Also on trade information from London. At 3 went to Farmers' Club dinner & spoke.[5] They received it kindly—I had to present Macinroy's Plate: & then went on their general prospects. Left at 8¾. Whist with Sir J.G.—Read Abp Parker—Guerrazzi.

2. Advent Sunday.

Chapel at 11 A.M. (Holy Communn.) & 2½ PM. Sermon aloud to Sir J.G.—C.G. laid up from yesterday's mistakes—Wrote to Lyttelton—J. Griffiths—Mr Irvine. Read Parker—Bagshawe's Argt.[6]—Danger to Ch. E. (1690) [7]—Newman's S.[8]

[1] T. F. *Buxton, *Memoirs* (1848); ed. C. Buxton.

[2] Francis Alexander Keith-Falconer, 1828–80; 8th earl of Kintore 1844; seat at Inglismaldie, 5 miles NE. of Brechin.

[3] 3½ miles NE. of Fasque.

[4] Draft on a letter from Lady Lincoln, in Add MS 44368, f. 282.

[5] Controversially on free trade, report in *Blackwood's Edinburgh Magazine*, lxvii. 124 (January 1850); cp. 17 Dec. 49 n.

[6] Edward *Bagshaw the elder, 'Two arguments in Parliament, the first concerning the canons, the second concerning the premunire upon those canons' (1641).

[7] 'The danger of the Church of England' (1690); author unknown.

[8] Cp. 23 Jan. 48.

3. M.

Wrote to T.G—J. Calvert—Godley—Hampton—Coutts—Lonsdale—Fagan—Northcote—Dowbiggin—Phillimore[1]—Guthrie—Macinroy. Also wrote four letters for Sir J.G. Read La Battaglia di Benevento (finished)—Hallam & Russell in illustrn.[2]—Parker—Buxton's Memoirs—Went to the ploughing match—Saw Fergusson on Falconer's case[3]—Whist with Sir J.G.

4. T.

Wrote to H. Maitland—Rn. G—G. & Co—Panizzi. Latin lesson to Willy—Working for my Father—Read Parker—Buxton's Mem.—Mauri &c. Opere Burksche[4]—At 2½ PM we went to Kinnaird to dine & sleep—We found Sir J. & Lady C.K.[5] most kind.

5. Wed.

Read Buxton—Parker—Walk with C.G—Off at 11 to Fasque. My Father better: but a Free Trade Lecture rather excited him in evg. Whist in evg—Worked on Ps[alm]s Index.

6. Th.

Wrote to Rn. G—J.N.G—H. Maitland—Lockhart—E. Manning—Parkinson[6]—Adderley—W. Forbes. Latin lesson to Willy. Read Buxton—Parker—Worked for my Father. Whist in evg. Arranging papers.

7. Fr.

Chapel 11 AM. (Mr Teed) Wrote to Paterson[7]—Walker—Geo. Talbot jun—F. Temple.[8] Read Parker—Buxton's Mem.—Ariosto (recommenced—& began an 'Argument' of the Poem).[9] Confined by Rain. Music with the children. Worked for my Father on Schedules of his Appropriation.

8. Sat.

Wrote to Hampton—Lonsdale—Northcote—Barker—Carter[10]—Maitland—Griffiths. Latin lesson to Willy. Read Parker—Buxton—Ariosto (making

[1] Lathbury, i. 95.
[2] H. *Hallam, *The Middle Ages* (1818), i, ch. 3 part 2.
[3] See 25 Nov. 49.
[4] Perhaps A. Mauri, *Opere del Cardinale S. Pallavicino* (1834).
[5] Lady Catherine Hamilton Carnegie, 1829–55, da. of 1st earl of Gainsborough; m. (Sir) James Carnegie 1849. Kinnaird was his seat.
[6] Draft in Add MS 44368, f. 286.
[7] A. M. Paterson, of Montrose, involved in the Oak Farm; cp. Sir J. *Gladstone's letter in Hawn P.
[8] Frederick *Temple, 1821–1902; priest 1846; head-master of Rugby 1857–69; bp. of Exeter 1869; abp. of Canterbury 1896.
[9] Cp. 14 July 49 and Add MS 44738, ff. 27–85.
[10] Thomas Thellusson Carter, 1808–1901; rector of Clewer, Berkshire, 1844, warden of Clewer house of mercy 1849; hon. canon of Christ Church 1870.

argument). Singing at F[ettercairn] House. Worked on Index to Psalms. Finished Schedules for my Father. Whist with Sir J.G: who is by no means right yet.

9. 2 S. Advent.

Chapel 11 & 2½. Sermon aloud to Sir J.G. Conv. with Willy. Also with E. Wardell about his attending the Holy Communion. Worked on Psalm music. Wrote to Bp of Brechin—A.M. Paterson—T.G. Read Parker—Buxton's Memoirs (finished).

10. M.

Wrote to Hampton—Bunsen—Coutts—Dowbiggin—Freshfield—R. Barker—Hubbard—Carnegie—Frewen. H.S. with W. & A. Also conv. with W. who said Papa we ought not to be certain that we are right in religion & those who differ from us wrong, ought we? Worked for Sir J.G. Whist & walk (hall) with him. Read Parker—Ariosto (with arg)—E.P. & D.RR.[1] P.O. Correspondence.[2] Worked on Index to Psalms.

11. T.

Wrote to Paterson—Rn. G. Latin lesson to Willy. Worked & wrote for my Father most of the day.

He is now 85. His prospects of life might be & may be excellent: but from particular causes they are more precarious. May both life & death be peace to him in Christ.

Worked on Will Memoranda. Read Parker—Ariosto (making arg.) Chess with Mr Teed.

12. Wed.

Chapel 11 A.M. Latin lesson to Willy. Wrote to Lincoln—Herbert—H. Maitland—Bp of Brechin—Read Parker—Ariosto—Spencer—Worked on Index to Pss—my Notes have stagnated from want of energy. Walk &c. with Sir J.G. & settling about Mrs Croall.[3]—Chess with Mr Teed.

13. Th.

Wrote to Godley—Mr Eyre—G. Glyn—Rev. H. Venn—H. Maitland. Latin lesson to Willy. Read Ariosto—Parker—Mr Eyre's pamphlet Letter[4]—Spencer—Worked on Psalm Index—Work with Sir JG—& walk.

[1] The Edinburgh, Perth and Dundee Railway, probably its annual report; cp. 15 Oct. 49.

[2] On Sunday labour in the post office, cp. Add MS 44368, f. 316.

[3] She lived on the hill behind Fasque, cp. 17 Dec. 51.

[4] C. Eyre, 'The history of St. Cuthbert' (1849).

14. Fr.

Chapel 11 A.M. Wrote to H. Maitland—Capt. Barclay—JNG. With Guthrie about my Father: whose hours are to be changed. Whist with him —& walk. Read Parker—Ariosto—and Miss Martineau. Latin lesson to Willy.

15. Sat.

Wrote to J. Griffiths. Latin lesson to Willy. Worked for my Father 10½–2. In the evening walk—& whist. Dining at 4 commenced: but he was unsettled & annoyed by the change. Read Parker—Ariosto—Monro on Rents & Profits[1]—Ross's answer to Ld Kinnaird[2]—Spencer.

16. 3 S Adv.

Chapel 11 AM & 3 PM—Sermon aloud to Sir J.G. in evg—I had to precent the organ being disabled. Read Parker (finished)—Jackson's Sermon—M. Leopardi—Newman's Sermons—Divers tracts. My Father *well* after the change of hours but very uneasy.

17. M.

Wrote (dft & fair copy) to Montr. Standard in reply to Barclay[3]—to Ed. Standard—R. Barker—& Rn. G. Latin lesson to Willy.

My Father attacked me about Free Trade in a morning conv. but I think was a little mollified by my representation that even for Protectionists Protection is not *the* question of this moment. Read Ariosto (with arg.)—Caird's,[4] Ld Kinnaird's,[5] Mr Whitmore's pamphlets.[6] Whist & walk with Sir J.G.

18. T.

Wrote to Scotts—Wm. Gladstone—Robt. Gladstone—G.L. Falconer—Rn. G—Latin lesson to Willy. Walk with him & a *history lecture*. He is such good company. Also with C. & 'Bicketer'.[7] Jotted down some music. Read Ariosto—Spencer—Chalmers's Life.[8] Whist walk &c. with Sir J.G.

[1] Untraced pamphlet by E. *Monro.

[2] T. Ross, 'Lord Kinnaird's "Letter to his tenantry on profitable investment" answered'. (1849).

[3] Draft in Add MS 44368, f. 298; Barclay had attacked Gladstone's speech at the Fettercairn Farmer's Club. Cp. 1 Dec. 49.

[4] J. *Caird, 'High farming under liberal covenants the best substitute for protection' (1849).

[5] See note on T. Ross two days previously.

[6] W. W. Whitmore, 'A few plain thoughts on free trade, as affecting agriculture' (?1849).

[7] Unidentified; a pet?

[8] W. *Hanna, *Memoirs of the life and writings of Thomas *Chalmers*, 4 v. (1849).

19. Wed.

Chapel 11 AM. Wrote to G. Burnett (2)—G.C. Glyn—G. Talbot jun—F. Calvert (with corrected proof of Speech—Rev. F. Harris—Macinroy. Latin lesson to Willy. Drove C. to Lkirk to see the Goalens &c. Read Ariosto—Chalmers's Life—Hoskins Hist. of Agriculture [1]—My Father sat talking for 3 h. at night—somewhat confused—but it acted as exercise & he slept well.

20. Th.

Wrote to Hampton—Lockhart—Bunsen—W.W. Clark [2]—Joyce—James—H. Maitland. Latin lesson to Willy. Read Ariosto (much)—Chalmers. Whist with Sir J.G. Went to see the Falconers & arrangements for them.

21. Fr.

Chapel 11 AM. Wrote to Ld J. Russell—& a letter for my Father to sign to Mr Arnott W.S.[3]—Practising with Ly H. F[orbes]—Latin lesson to Willy—Read Ariosto—Hoskins—Chalmers. Visited.

22. Sat.

Wrote to Adderley—Sir W. Farquhar—S. Herbert—J. Walker—T.G. Latin lesson to Willy. Busy abt wine & Xmas arrangements. Read Ariosto—Chalmers—Hoskyns (finished)—Walk with CG—Whist with Sir JG.

23. S. Advent 4.

Chapel 11 & 2½. Arranging Ps[alm]s—My Father was in an uneasy way & wd not let me read a Sermon to him: but got over it late in evg. Visited. Read Chalmers's Life—Chalmers on Necessity.[4] Busy about the two delinquents who cut the ashtree.

24. M. Xmas Eve.

Wrote to J.N.G—Capt. Barclay—W.B. Collis—J.G. Lockhart—J. Arnott —and wrote (for Sir J.G. to sign) to Mr Tindal [5]—Duthie & Co. Latin lesson to Willy. Worked on papers for Sir J.G. & on Falconer's matter & that of the tree purloined. Whist. Read Ariosto—Leopardi's M[oschus]—Letters to Bunsen &c [6]—Spenser. This birthday never can be forgotten: though she [Anne] whom it recalls has had better birthdays since.

[1] C. W. *Hoskyns, *A short inquiry into the history of agriculture* (1849).
[2] William Wilcox Clarke, 1808?–81; Wadham, Oxford; rector of N. Wooton, Norfolk, from 1834.
[3] James Arnott, 1791–1866; writer to the signet in Edinburgh from 1815.
[4] T. *Chalmers, probably his *Five lectures on predestination* (1837).
[5] Unidentified.
[6] Six MS letters; cp. Add MS 44274, f. 13v.

Tues. Xmas Day 49.

Chapel 10½ A.M and 3 P.M. 38 communicants of 48 congr. Edward [Wardell] was there to my great joy.[1] I had indeed two griefs—my own sins, and my Father's absence from the Holy Table which he has been the means of spreading for others. Read Manning's Sermons—Chalmers's Life (finished Vol I)—and Ariosto. Wrote to Bp of Brechin. Visited. My Father cleared up in the evg.

26. St Stephen.

Chapel 11 AM. Wrote to Uncle Divie—Scotts—Hampton—J.P. Larkins. Latin lesson to Willy. Visited. Walk to C.s ride. Read Manning—Ariosto—Spenser. Whist with Sir J.G. Worked for him & tried to explain the case of John's allotment.

27. St John.

Chapel 11 A.M. Wrote to J. Severn. Latin lesson to Willy. Arranging my papers & letters. Read Ariosto—Memoirs of do[2]—Spenser—Elements of Geology.[3] Whist with Sir J.G. Saw Falconer.

28. H. Innocents.

Chapel 11 AM. Latin lesson to Willy. Worked & wrote out new account of distribution for Sir J.G. He finally fixed on adding 10 F. & Clyde Shares to J.N.G. acc to my suggestion.[4] Read Ariosto—Spenser—Elements of Geology. Whist with Sir JG. Singing with Willy.

29. Sat.

Wrote to T.G. (with Memorandum)—G. Burnet (2)—R. Barker—Clowes. Latin lesson to Willy. Read Ariosto—Spenser (Shepherd's Cal.)

Whist with Sir J.G.—& conv. on his affairs & arrangements of them: with wh I hope he is now done—the responsibility of being near him & advising him on any question *between* the interests of different members of his family in his *present* stage of old age is great, & increasing.

And this day I am forty years old. Forty years long hath God been grieved with me—hath with much long suffering endured me! Alas I cannot say better of myself. The retrospect of my inward life is dark. Not such is my common mood: it ought probably to be darker than it is. The best sign I could name of myself is that I think the noted desire of my heart at every moment—whether excited or suppressed—is, 'Even so come Lord Jesus'. But every faithful Christian secures for himself the answer to this prayer by opening the door of his own heart

[1] Cp. 9 Dec. 49.

[2] A. *Panizzi's ed. of Boiardo's *Orlando Innamorata* and Ariosto's *Orlando Furioso*, 6 v. (1830–4), with an essay, memoirs and lives.

[3] By Sir C. *Lyell (1838), a supplement to his *Principles of geology*, 4 v. (1830–4).

[4] Forth-Clyde Canal shares; cp. Checkland, 339–40.

whither the Lord is ever ready to come. This I cannot testify. In some things I may seem to improve a little: but the flesh and the devil if not the world still have fearful hold upon me. Again my soul seems to be still set on doing at some time special things for God: but I utterly fail in preparing myself for them by the things not special, the duties which lie near my hand. How every day teaches me of the manner in which Satan profits by repulses: forthwith making his silent entry at some point left without guard. O that I may profit by them too! in at length *sincerely* casting myself upon Christ and holding back none of my heart from Him, for insincerity and holding back are I fear yet my bane. But it is not my outward so much as my inward life that grieves me.

There are *family* petitions with which I ought to be importunate: but only one personal that I venture to indicate in conditional prayer: it is for the lightening of the load of pecuniary cares & anxieties upon me.

In my public life my heart does not condemn me of failure in integrity of purpose: as a son I hope I may have a little improved: as husband & father I am very unworthy of my office—my heart is not large with love to all Christian men, does not rightly see Christ in them: but the worst is that it is still entangled by selfwoven sophistries in the meshes of impurity ever shifting its forms to evade detection.

'Lead me O Lord in thy righteousness because of mine enemies: make thy way plain before my face'[1]—this seems appointed to be my continual prayer. Yet not only before my face but within my conscience. If I could get back or rather get the spirit of a child, the way would be plain. It may be obtained: whether it will I know not[;] in the meantime seeing the want of it let me at least be humble, & from day to day more & more humble.

These decade birthdays are greater even than the annual ones. How blessed would it be if this should be the point from whence is to spring a lowlier & better life.

30. S. after Xmas.

Chapel 11 A.M. and 2½ P.M. Tried in vain to get my Father to let me read [him a sermon]. Wrote to Manning[2]—Bp of Brechin—Williams & Co (Chester)—M. Wilson. Read Manning—Leopardi (M[oschus])[3]—Life of a Daughter at home.[4]

31. M.

Wrote to Miss Brown—Guthrie[5]—J.R. Hope—H. Maitland—J.E. Fitzgerald. Latin lesson to Willy. Read Ariosto—Spenser. Began to write on Ariosto; as well as the Argument & Notes which I am writing. Whist with Sir J.G.

[1] Psalm V. 8.
[2] Lathbury, i. 95.
[3] Or his father, Monaldo Leopardi's, book, cp. 7 Oct. 49.
[4] [Sarah Stephen], *Passages from the life of a daughter at home* (1845).
[5] Thomas *Guthrie, 1803–73; banker in Brechin 1827–9; minister of Arbirlot, Forfar, 1830–7, of Greyfriars, Edinburgh, 1837, of Free St. John's, Edinburgh, 1843–64; philanthropist.

Tuesday Jan. One. 1850
The Circumcision.

Chapel 11 A.M. Wrote to Cardwell—J.N.G. Read Ariosto—Spenser—Worked on Ariosto. Whist with Sir J.G.—Showed at the servants' Ball. Visited. Latin lesson to Willy.

2. Wed.

Wrote to J.N.G.—T.G.—Mr Bockett. Latin lesson to Willy. Read Ariosto—Spenser. Worked on Ariosto. Working for [Sir] J.G.—& whist with him.

3. Th.

Wrote to Rev. Dr. Paterson[1]—Rev. Dr. Jones.[2] Latin lesson to Willy. Working for Sir J.G.—Whist with him in evg. Read Ariosto—also Introduction to Boiardo & began his Orlando Innamorato.[3] Visited +. Walk with C.

4. Fr.

Wrote to H. Maitland—Duthie & Co—Mrs Scott (Brotherton). Latin lesson to Willy. Read Ariosto—Boiardo. Capt. Barclay & Macinroy dined. Whist & agricultural conversation divided the evening. Worked much for Sir J.G. on meditated changes in his will & other matters.

5. Sat.

Wrote to Robertson G—Bp of Oxford—Judge Coleridge—Archd. Manning—Bp of Brechin—Ld Medwyn. Latin lesson with Willy. Read Ariosto—Boiardo. Agric. conv. with Macinroy. Much morning work for Sir J.G. With Capt. Barclay at the farm. Whist in evg.

6. S. Epiphany.

Chapel 11 AM (with Holy Commn.) & $2\frac{1}{2}$ P.M. Conv. with Willy. C.s birthday—shamefully overlooked by me in my prayers. Wrote to Farquhar—Ed. Guardian. Read Manning's S.—Life of Rowland Hill[4]—Life of a Daughter at home. Visited.

[1] John *Paterson, 1776–1855; congregationalist minister and missionary; D.D. 1817; Scottish secretary of London Missionary Society 1825; latterly lived in Forfarshire.

[2] Hugh Jones, 1796–1866; Jesus, Oxford; D.D. 1844; rector of Llandegran, Anglesea, from 1843.

[3] By Matteo M. Boiardo, first published 1511; Gladstone compiled an 'Argument' of this work in Add MS 44738, f. 7–26.

[4] By E. Sidney (1833).

7. M.

Wrote to Paterson—Griffiths—Joyce—Leighton—Miss Brown—Ramsay—Maitland. Latin lesson to Willy. Read Boiardo—making argument &c. as I go along. Business. Whist with Sir J.G. Arranged for journey with C. to Ed[inburgh].

8. T.

Wrote to Barker. Up at 4.15 AM. Off at 5.10 to Marykirk[1] with C. baby & Baker, also Forbes: some railway troubles & impostures but a prosperous journey. Arrived soon after one. Went to Mackay's Hotel which we found very comfortable.[2] Saw Mr Ramsay—H. Maitland—H. Lees[3]—W. Forbes—& Mr Nasmyth[4] who operated on my teeth & took out a monster admirably. dined with the Ramsays—he is ever the same changeless charming man. read Bojardo at night.

9. Wed.

Wrote (from Fasque) to Sec. Aberdeen Co[5]—Mr Lang—Scotts—G. & Co. Breakfasted with W. Forbes. saw Bp of Brechin—Bp of Glasgow[6]—Mr Ramsay—Mr Maitland—Mr Nasmyth who operated upon me further.

Some shopping—off at 12½, after some more grievances reached Fasque at 6¼. Busy with my own & Sir J.G.s letters—& journey speculations. Whist with Sir J.G.

10. Th.

Wrote to R. Cavendish—R.J. Venables—H.U. Addington—Superintendent Perth Station—S.H. Northcote—(H. Lees for Sir J.G.). Latin lesson to Willy. Conv. with him on divine grace & prayer—constant or *perpetual* prayer. Journey plans discussed with C. Arranged letters &c. Worked for Sir J.G. & read to him. Setting off with a late letter for C. found myself able to keep on the *run* all the way to F[ettercair]n with which being now rather old I was at first pleased only instead of being thankful. Worked on Ariosto. Read Bojardo.

11. Fr.

Wrote to J.N.G—Sir J. Young—Mr Church—Ralph Neville[7]—Latin lesson to Willy. Read & worked on Bojardo &c. Hope & Henderson came. Conv.

[1] Midway between Fettercairn and Montrose.
[2] In Princes Street.
[3] Henry Lees, secretary of the Edinburgh and Northern Railway, later of the Edinburgh, Perth and Dundee Railway.
[4] Robert Nasmyth of George Street; surgeon-dentist to the Queen.
[5] George Reith, secretary of the Aberdeen Railway Company from 1846; the company was arranging a private member's bill, cp. *PP* 1851, xxxi. 33a.
[6] Walter John Trower, 1804–77; bp. of Glasgow 1848–59; D.D. 1849; bp. of Gibraltar 1863–8; rector of Ashington, Sussex, 1871–7; cp. 26 Apr. 31 n.
[7] 'S. R. Glynne' here deleted.

with Hope on Gorham Case & the Colonial Church question.[1] Worked for Sir J.G.

12. Sat.

Wrote to Scotts—Hampton—J. Murray—Dowbiggin—Adie. Latin lesson to Willy. Read Bojardo. Further conv. with Hope—also walk & conv. with him on Lady L[incoln] I supposing him to have been retained—wrongly. He gave me pleasure by reporting from Oswald[2] that Douglas[3] thought I had done fairly by his sister. Tableaux & charades in evg. Whist for Sir J.G.—With him on St Andrew's about which he is now keen again.

13. 1 S. Epiph.

Chapel 11 & 2½. Visited +. Wrote on Colonial Church, for Clauses[4]—& discussion with Hope at night—also on the Gorham Case, a crisis of the Church of England. Read M.A. Buonarroti[5]—Manning's Sermons—Sidney's Life of Hill—Life of Daughter at home (finished).

14. M.

Wrote to Bp of Norwich[6]—J.E. Fitzgerald—T.G.—R. Oliverson—A. Lendrum. Latin lesson to Willy. Further discussion with Hope on the Col. Ch. Clauses & made & copied out the 4th Edn. of them after he was gone.[7] Read Boiardo. Worked for Sir J.G. Whist with him. Walk with C. Busied with a multifarious parcel from London.

15. T.

Wrote to Hampton—Cochrane—Forbes—(dft) letter & statement for Scottish Central Co[8]—S.R. Glynne—Kidd[9]—Davis—Macgillivray[10]—Boler—Hutt—Sec. Aberdeen Co—Hubbard—Miss Harris. Latin lesson to Willy. Read & worked on Boiardo. Read Ld Redesdale on Regeneration.[11] Whist with Sir J.G.

[1] For *Hope's view of *Gorham, cp. Ornsby, ii. 79ff.
[2] Alexander Haldane Oswald, 1811–68; Peelite M.P. Ayrshire 1843–52; director of Caledonian Railway.
[3] i.e. W. A. A. A. *Douglas, Lady Lincoln's brother; cp. 26 Apr. 33 n.
[4] Add MS 44738, f. 1.
[5] i.e. Michael Angelo, the artist; probably his *Life and works*, ed. R. Duppa (1806).
[6] Samuel *Hinds, 1793–1872; bp. of Norwich 1849–57; historian and theologian.
[7] Later sent to bp. of Norwich: Add MS 44738, f. 5.
[8] The Scottish Central Railway, in which the Gladstones held shares; it was under threat from the Caledonian Railway, cp. 20 Jan. 50 n.
[9] Possibly Thomas Kidd, deputy chairman of the St. Helen's Railway.
[10] William Macgillivray, 1796–1852; professor of natural history at Aberdeen from 1841; wrote on ornithology.
[11] J. T. Freeman Mitford, 'Reflections on the doctrine of regeneration' (1849).

16. W.

Wrote to Rn. G—Mr Stirling—Mr Adderley—Mr J. Balfour[1]—& Joint Letter, & Statement, for Sir [JSForbes] & myself to [Scottish] Central [Railway] Co. Latin Lesson to Willy. Read Boiardo—A Lover of Truth on the Leigh Case.[2] Worked on Boiardo.[3] Singing with the children.

17. Th.

Wrote to Forbes—T.G. (for Sir J.G.)—H. Lees (for do)—Lang—& H. Maitland. Latin Lesson to Willy. Worked for Sir J.G.—& saw Mr Leighton on the Codicil to his Will. Whist in evg. Read Boiardo (with Analysis &c)

18. Fr.

Wrote to T.G—Rn. G—J.N.G. (with best wishes on his birthday) and Sir J. Young. Again with Leighton & Sir J.G. about the Codicil. Latin lesson to Willy. Read & worked on Boiardo.

19. Sat.

Wrote to Ld Redesdale—J.D. Coleridge. Latin lesson to Willy. Worked much for Sir J.G. (& about little: but little is enough to make him restless now.) Whist in evg.

Worked with Willy on our new snowhouse. Read Boiardo.

20. 2 S. Epiph.

Chapel closed Mr Irvine announcing himself unwell at 9.

Read prayers & a Sermon of Mannings mg and also aft.—My Father was at the first & heard all. Wrote to Marriott—Aldrich. Read Manning (finished)—Sidney's Hill—Sewells Two Sermons[4]—Bp of Glasgow's Serm[5]—Philopolis[6]—Everard on Baptm[7]—&c. Visited.

21. M.

Wrote to Author of Facts for Curates Fund[8]—H. Maitland—T. Thomson—Earl Waldegrave[9]—R. Neville—Hubbard—Sewell. Latin lesson to Willy. Worked for Sir J.G—& whist. Read & worked on Boiardo. Worked at snowhouse with Willy.

[1] John Balfour of Balbirnie, 1811–95; soldier and director of Caledonian Railway.

[2] Untraced; on Leigh barony, disputed between George and Chandos *Leigh until 1839, when the latter became 1st Baron Leigh of the second creation.

[3] Cp. 3 Jan. 50 n.

[4] W. *Sewell, 'The nation, the church, and the university of Oxford.' (1849).

[5] W. J. Trower, 'An address delivered to the clergy of the diocese' (1849).

[6] Philopolis [T. W. *Peile], *The Christian temple and its representative priesthood* (1849).

[7] E. Everard, 'A letter, setting forth that baptismal regeneration . . . is no cause for controversy' (1849).

[8] 'Facts and thoughts for the additional curates' aid society in . . . the diocese of Manchester' (1849); author unidentified.

[9] William Waldegrave, 1788–1859; whig M.P. Bedford 1815–18, 8th Earl Waldegrave 1846.

22. T.

Wrote to Sir J. Forbes—Sec. Scots Central (joint)—do (separate)—J. Griffiths—A.M. Paterson—Dundee Steam Office [1]—Mr Teed—T. Thomson. Latin lesson to Willy. Worked for Sir J.G—& whist—Saw Mr Irvine. Read & worked on Boiardo—Read Blackwood on California, & on W.E.G.[2]

23. Wed.

Wrote to Mr Leighton—Dowbiggin—Collis—Maitland. Latin lesson to Willy. Worked for Sir J.G. Whist in evg. Read & worked on Boiardo. Arrangements for journey & packing for London.

24. Th.

Wrote to Geo. Knight [3]—T.G.—H. Maitland—Lady Jersey—J.C. Hubbard. Latin lesson to Willy. Worked for Sir J.G. Whist in evg. Read Boiardo (finished) & worked on him—Read Hoggarty Diamond.[4] Paying bills &c.

25. Fr. Conv. St Paul.

Chapel 11 AM. + Visited. A fatiguing walk. ∴ fed much as usual. Latin lesson to Willy. Read Hoggarty Diamond. Worked on Spenser. Wrote to Bp Norwich—Forfar Station Agent.[5] Worked for Sir J.G. Whist in evg.

26. Sat.

Wrote to Hampton—Northcote—J.E. Fitzgerald—Bush Inn Carlisle [6]—Johnson—Scotts—Mr Church—Sec. Caledonian Co. Latin lesson to Willy—Worked much for Sir J.G. on Mema. Read Hoggarty Diamond (finished)—Tassoni.[7] Worked on Spencer. [sic] [8] Saw Mr Irvine about the organ—Mr Falconer. Packing & a press of business. Whist in evg. Wrote a paper to help Willy's Latin.

27. Sept[uagesim]a. S.

Chapel 11 AM and 2½ P.M. Visited. Wrote to T.G (2)—Mr Teed—Mr Irvine. Read Sidney's Hill (finished) Saw Forbes about poor Anne Sherriffs—Sir J.G. about do—Ly H[arriet Forbes] abt the organ. a scene with Miss I.[9] abt the organ. Fresh snow in evg & doubts as to our journey—my Father's fever surpassed all former occasions.

[1] To arrange passage south.

[2] See 1 Dec. 49.

[3] Perhaps George Knight, auctioneer and wine broker, of Crosby Hall Chambers, London.

[4] W. M. *Thackeray, *The history of Samuel Titmarsh and the Great Hoggarty Diamond* (1841).

[5] Untraced.

[6] The Bush family and commercial hotel in English Street.

[7] A. Tassoni, *La secchia rapita* (1627).

[8] Notes on *Spenser's *Faery Queen* in Add MS 44738, f. 86.

[9] Miss J. Irvine, D. A. Irvine's da.

28. M.

Wrote (from Carlisle) to Sir J.G.—Hampton. Read Cosa sono i Francesi[1]—Gioberti.[2] Up at 3¾ A.M.—off at 4¾ to Marykirk, a party of 11 & thence to Carlisle—safe & well. almost no snow on the ground after touching the railway.

29. T.

Called late and off hurriedly from the Bush (very good but somewhat dear) by the 7.45 Train. Reached Birmingham at 5¼: filling (as yesty.) a 2d Class compartment all the way. There poor dear Willy parted from the rest with many tears & went on with me to Blisworth[3] & Northampton. I had some interesting conversation with him.

30. Wed.

We left at 7 AM. for Wellingborough & thence after breakfast went on through a fine country to Geddington[4] where I deposited my dear dear boy feeling as if I left there a piece & a great piece cut out of my heart. But I was delighted with all I saw, Mr C.,[5] Mrs C., the boys, the food, the place, the cleanliness and order (the space a little narrow indoors) and I am most thankful & glad to think that he is left in such care: besides the comfort of believing that he will strive to live as in the presence of God. I was there with him from ten to two: & reached Carlton Gardens at 8.

Spent the evening till midnight on my letters & papers, a formidable heap: particularly perusing the Caledonian Railway papers.[6]

31. Th.

Wrote to M'Cracken—Davis—Maitland—C.G—Sir J.G—Griffiths—U. Sec. Colonies[7]—Macewan & Auld[8]—Sec. Caledonian Co. Saw Scotts—Dowbiggin—Northcote—Manning—S. Herbert—S.H. Walpole. Exhib. Commn. 11¾–4¾.[9] H. of C. 9–11½.[10] Worked on papers.

[1] Not further traced.
[2] Cp. 4 May 48.
[3] A station 5 miles SW. of Northampton.
[4] 3 miles NE. of Kettering.
[5] i.e. W. M. H. Church, cp. 21 June 48. The prep school at Geddington is well described in Sir N. *Lyttelton, *Eighty years* (n.d.), ch. ii.
[6] It had run into financial difficulties, having attempted to take over several minor central Scotland lines. English shareholders, led by Edward Plunkett, ousted the Edinburgh directors; cp. 5 Feb. 50. Plunkett, 1808–89, was captain R.N. 1846 and succ. as 16th Baron Dunsany 1852.
[7] i.e. H. *Merivale.
[8] James MacEwan, 1801–74 and John Auld, 1810–75, both writers to the signet.
[9] The commissioners of the 1851 exhibition, of whom Gladstone was one, decided on Hyde Park as the site; cp. *PP* 1850, xxxiii. 298.
[10] Queen's speech: *H* cviii. 82.

Friday Feb. One 1850.

Wrote to C.G—Miss J. Irvine—Dr Buchanan—R. Oliverson. H. of C. 10–2. Saw Mr Hubbard—J.E. Fitzgerald—Sir W. James—Sir W. Gomme—Miss Eyre—Dr Lang—R. Barker—the Gardener—who together occupied me nearly from ten to five on their various subjects—Mr Blakemore[1]—Wrote up Journal (& Mema. of account. Worked on accounts. Read (part) Xtn Remembrancer on Dante—a noble Article.[2] Voted in 311:192 agt the quasi-protection amendment.[3]

2. Sat. Purification.

Church at 10 A.M. for the Baptism of my new godchild Northcote's son.[4] May he be as good as his father.—St Anne's Soho 8¼ P.M. Saw Bonham—the Herberts—J. Murray. Wrote to T.G—C.G—Rev. D. Robertson—Mr Church—Sir J.S. Forbes—Sec. Central Railway (joint)—Robertson G—H. Tayleur—J.E. Fitzgerald—G.A. Denison—C.B. Dalton—King (Scots Episc. Sch)—A. de Vere—H. Woodcock—&, last not least, my Willy, whose first letter from school most thoughtful affectionate & good I got today. Worked on year's accounts & papers, & domestic affairs. Breakfasted with Northcote. Read Buchanan's History[5]—Hamilton on Educn. & P.C.[6]—

3. Sex[agesim]a. S.

St Martins 11 AM. and Holy C.—Bedfordbury evg. MS of 45 aloud in evg. Saw R. Cavendish—Badeley—E. Stanley—dined with the Jameses—tea with the Herberts. Wrote to J.N.G—Hawkins—Mr E. Macdonnell—Tyler—Manning. Read Fuller's answer to Stapleton[7]—Denison on Nat Edn.[8]—Wright on Servetus[9]—Macdonnell on Gorham[10]—Monro's Sermon.[11]

4. M.

Wrote to C.G—H.J.G—W. Hutt—J.D. Coleridge. Read Xt Rem. on Dante (finished). Dined at Mr Harcourt's. 11½–2½ Clydesdale Junction meeting

[1] Probably Richard Blakemore.

[2] *Christian Remembrancer*, xix. 187 (January 1850); on J. A. *Carlyle's prose translation.

[3] The protectionists moved an amendment on agrarian distress: *H* cviii. 125, 254.

[4] John Stafford Northcote, 3 January 1850–1920; railway engineer in England and India 1867–76; curate, St. Margaret's, Westminster, 1878–81; rector of Upton Pyne 1881–9; vicar, St. Andrew, Westminster, 1889–1916; chaplain to Edward VII and George V.

[5] G. *Buchanan, *The history of Scotland* (1690).

[6] Henry B. Hamilton, 'The privy council and the national society' (1850).

[7] Untraced reply to A. G. Stapleton, 'Suggestions for a conservative and popular reform in the Commons House of Parliament' (1850).

[8] Cp. 11 Feb. 49.

[9] R. Wright, unitarian, 'An apology for Michael Servetus' (1806).

[10] Untraced pamphlet or MS by Eneas Macdonnell.

[11] E. *Monro, 'The fulfilment of the ministry. A sermon' (1848); on Col. iv. 17.

(Temple)[1] then with Manning till 5 on the Gorham case & its consquences. Also saw Oliverson—Miss Eyre (goodbye)—Goulburn. Then H. of C.[2]

5. T.

Wrote to Ld Hobart—Tatham. Read Abp of York's Charge[3]—Richardson on the Slave Trade.[4] Dined with the Jameses. Saw Miss Henderson[5]—then went off to Clydesdale meeting—back to see Messrs. Bate (O.F)[6] 11–12½—then Mr Armstrong (Penity.)[7]—then Add. Curates Committee to 3—Caledonian meeting to 5¾[8]—and House of Commons.[9] Dined with the Jameses. Worked on O.F. papers.

6. Wed.

Wrote to C.G—WHG—Mr Stirling—Bannister—Collis—Bennett—Langley[10]—R. Barker—Bartlett (Mrs)[11]—W.F. Campbell. Read Lyttelton on Colonisation[12]—Knight on Taxation of books.[13] Saw Dowbiggin—Stirling—Wilson Patten—Rev J.G—J. Young—Mr Armstrong. Manufacturers Committee 1–2 Finance do 2–3¾. Dined with the Cannings. Conv. with Oswald.

7. Th.

Wrote to C.G—Sir J.G—Sec. Caledonian Co—Dr Dearle—Tatham—G. Burnett. Bp of Exeter & Mr Hubbard to breakfast. From the conv. of the former I gather plainly that he will not succumb to an anticatholic decision.[14] Saw Mr W.F. Campbell—Exhibn. Commn. 12–3. Saw Scotts—S.R.G—Calls. Got myself sick & unwell in the evg. House 10¼–12. Abstained from voting on Wortley's Bill.[15] Read Morgan on Marriage Law[16]—Gibbon—Adderley on Australian Bill, & other pamphlets.[17]

[1] A special meeting of shareholders on the company's difficulties; cp. *The Times*, 5 February 1850, 8e.

[2] The Greek question: *H* cviii. 273.

[3] T. *Musgrave, 'A charge delivered . . .' (1849).

[4] J. *Richardson, 'The cruisers: being a letter . . . in defence of armed coercion for the extinction of the slave trade' (1849).

[5] Governess, replacing Miss Eyre.

[6] G. Bate and Co. made an unsuccessful offer for the Oak Farm works.

[7] i.e. J. *Armstrong.

[8] An extraordinary meeting to elect new directors; Plunkett became chairman; cp. *The Times*, 8 February 1850, 8e.

[9] Ecclesiastical commission: *H* cviii. 348.

[10] Daniel Baxter Langley, 1797?–1881; vicar of Olney, Buckinghamshire, 1836–56; rector of Yardley-Hastings 1856–81; author.

[11] Cp. 23 May 35.

[12] G. W. *Lyttelton, 'The colonial empire of Great Britain, especially in its religious aspect. A lecture' (1850).

[13] C. *Knight, 'The struggles of a book against excessive taxation' (1850).

[14] In the *Gorham appeal case, then before the privy council judicial cttee.

[15] Deceased Wife's Sister: *H* cviii. 524.

[16] H. D. *Morgan, *The doctrine and law of marriage, adultery and divorce*, 2 v. (1826).

[17] C. B. Adderley, 'The Australian Colonies Government Bill discussed' (1849).

8. Fr.

Wrote to JNG—Hawkins—Rev. Mr Irvine—G. Graham[1]—J. Murray Finance (Commn.) Committee at 11½. Bp of London's 3–4. Saw Manning—Birley.[2] But a poorish day. H. of C. 4¾–10. Spoke in Colonial debate.[3] Then home & arranged for departure. Also worked till 12½ on translations of the prose Extracts in my paper on Leopardi—much agt the grain.[4]

9. Sat.

Wrote to Willy. Off at 5¾ to Hagley. Walk from Birm. Met by C—arrived at 2. Read Morgante Maggiore[5]—Ed. Rev. on Mining Records.[6] Found C. thank God well.

10. Quinqu[agesim]a S.

Church 11 & 3. Singing in Evg. Read English Review[7]—Wilberforce on Baptism[8]—Vaughan's Lectures[9]—Southey's Commonplace book.[10] Singing—Walk with C.

11. M.

Wrote to Stafford—J. Scott Russell[11]—Mr Greswell—Mr Uppington[12]—G. Burnett—Freshfield. At Stourbridge 10¾–2 with Collis, Griffiths, Growcott,[13] & the Messrs. Bate on O.F. matters. Read Morgante Magg.

12. T.

Wrote to Sir J.G—J. Griffiths—Goulburn—Dowbiggin—Jones & Yarrell—MacCulloch. Read Morgante Maggiore—Sequel to the Furioso. Chess with George. Worked on Pulci &c.[14]

[1] Major George Graham, 1801–88; private secretary to his bro. Sir James* 1831–4, 1841–2; registrar general 1838–79.

[2] Probably John Shepherd Birley, 1806?–83; Brasenose, Oxford; rector of All Saint's, Bolton, 1832–43; perpetual curate of Hoghton, Lancashire, 1846–50.

[3] On Australian colonies: *H* cviii. 595.

[4] Cp. *Quarterly Review*, lxxxvi. 295 (March 1850).

[5] L. Pulci, *Morgante Maggiore* (1507).

[6] *Edinburgh Review*, xci. 62 (January 1850).

[7] *English Review*, xii. 288 (December 1849); probably the review of *Palmer's 'Appeal to the Scottish Bishops' (1849).

[8] R. I. *Wilberforce, 'The doctrine of holy baptism; with remarks on . . . W. *Goode's "Effects of infant baptism"' (1849).

[9] Robert Vaughan, *The age and Christianity* (1849).

[10] Ed. in 4 v. (1849–51) by J. W. Warter.

[11] John Scott *Russell, 1808–82; naval architect and engineer; secretary of society of arts 1845–50; Great Exhibition commissioner.

[12] Charles Uppington, father of Caroline Uppington.

[13] John Growcott, mine organizer, of Pensnett, near the Oak Farm.

[14] Cp. Add MS 44738, f. 104.

13. Ash Wednesday.

Church 10 A.M. & 7 P.M. Wrote to J.N.G—Rn. G—G. Bate. Saw Mr Griffiths on O.F. matters—Mr Burnett on do—on Hawarden Estate affairs—also on my own. Read Morg Maggiore—also Boydell's Book.[1]

14. Th.

Ch 10 AM. Saw Mr Paterson—Mr Griffiths—Mr Amery—Mr Collis—Mr Burnett on O.F. affairs—the aspect of which seems to improve. Walk with C. &c. Dined (with G. [Lyttelton]) at Mr Hodgetts's.[2] Read Morg. Maggiore.

15. Fr.

Church at 10 AM. Wrote to Mr Amery (with terms)—Hampton. Saw Griffiths on O.F. matters—Mr Girdlestone—Mr Woodgate. Read Morg. Maggiore—Ruskin's Seven Lamps.[3] Walk with C.—Chess with L[yttelto]n.—singing.

16. Sat.

Church 10 A.M. Wrote to Sir J.G—Willy—J. Griffiths—G. Bate—Edwards & Ball—H. Tayleur. Read and worked on Pulci. Walk with Ln.—Chess with him—with W. Ln. Singing with the school children in Church.

17. 1 S. Lent.

Ch 11 AM. 3 P.M. Walk with C. Read Michel's Bampton Lectures[4]—Trench's Essay on the Star[5]—Alford's NT.[6]

18. M.

Left at 8 for London. Home at 3¼. Wrote to J.N.G—Rector of Exeter—G.A. Denison. Read Ed. Rev. on Dolly's brae[7]—Pulci—Carlyle's Latter day Papers No 1.[8] Saw Goulburn—Inglis—Molesworth—Manson—Oldfield[9]—Labouchere. H. of C. & H. of Lords 4¾–11½.[10]

[1] J. Boydell, *A treatise on landed property* (1849); on how to run an estate profitably!
[2] Thomas Webb Hodgetts of Hagley, b. 1788; a magistrate and land-owner.
[3] J. *Ruskin, *Seven lamps of architecture* (1849).
[4] R. *Michell, *The nature and comparative value of the christian evidences considered generally* . . . (1849).
[5] R. Chenevix *Trench, 'The star of the wise men: a commentary on the second chapter of St. Matthew' (1850).
[6] H. *Alford, *The Greek testament; with a critically revised text* . . . (1849).
[7] *Edinburgh Review*, xci. 87 (January 1850); Dolly's brae was the scene of an Orangemen's demonstration in July 1849.
[8] By T. *Carlyle (1850); number one: 'The present time'.
[9] John *Oldfield, 1789–1863; engineer; at Waterloo; commanded R.E. in Canada 1839–43, in Ireland 1848–54; colonel 1846, general 1862. He was involved in the Dolly's brae affair.
[10] Lords on Dolly's brae, the Commons on Australia: *H* cviii. 886, 976.

19. T.

Wrote to Scotts—Jacobson—J. Griffiths—Sir J. Forbes—C.G—Sir W.C. James. Ceylon Committee 12–2½.[1] H. of C. 5–8½ and 9¾–12¼. Read Morgante Maggiore. Worked upon my books & papers. Much disposition among our friends to vote with D[israeli] in wh Goulburn shared.[2]

20. Wed.

Wrote to Scotts—C.G—Sir J. Forbes—Sir JG—R. Caparn—Freshfields—Michel[3]—H of C. 3½–4½.[4] Saw Molesworth & the C[olonial]Ref [orm Association] Committee on the Church Clause &c—Goulburn—Marriott—S. Herbert—Miles—Ld Harrowby. Dined with J.N.G—Read Townsend on Baptm.[5]

21. Th.

Wrote to C.G. Saw Bp of London—Mr Wodehouse—S. Herbert—Mr Gray—Mr R. Scott—Mr Oliverson. Commission 3–5. H of C. 5–8 and 10½–1¾. Spoke after Graham on the opposite side and voted in 252:273.[6] Read Wilmore on Trial by Jury[7]—Clifton on Manchester Church[8]—Burgess on Foreign Congregations.[9] A hard & longish day.

22. Fr.

Wrote to Rev. Mr Kidd—C.G[10]—T.G—A.M. Paterson. Worked on letters & papers. Saw Mr Wodehouse—Archdn. Manning—Canon Sergeant[11]—Ld J. Russell—Bp of London—Sir R. Inglis. Dined with the J. Wortleys. H of C. 4–7.[12]

23. Sat.

Wrote to C.G—Mr Maskell (on his pamphlet)[13] Read Mr Maskell. Worked on arranging books. Sisterhood of Mercy meeting 2–4.[14] Saw Mr Dodsworth

[1] Cp. 20 Feb. 49 n.

[2] *Disraeli's motion for inquiry into agricultural distress: *H* cviii. 1026; cp. 27 Feb. 50.

[3] Richard *Michell, 1805–77; fellow of Lincoln, Oxford, 1830; D.D. 1868; vice-principal 1848; principal from 1868 of Magdalen Hall, Oxford, later called Hertford College.

[4] Misc. business: *H* cviii. 1119.

[5] G. *Townsend, 'Baptismal regeneration' (1850).

[6] Spoke and voted in support of *Disraeli's motion: *H* cviii. 1204; and see Greville, vi. 207.

[7] G. Willmore, 'Is trial by jury worth keeping?' (1850).

[8] Untraced pamphlet by Robert Cox Clifton.

[9] R. Burgess, 'An enquiry into the state of the Church of England congregations in France, Belgium, and Switzerland' (1850).

[10] Bassett, 80–2.

[11] Oswald Sergeant, 1798?–1854; St. John's, Cambridge; fellow of Manchester collegiate church 1832; canon of Manchester from 1845.

[12] Misc. business: *H* cviii. 1287.

[13] W. *Maskell 'A first letter on the present position of the high church party in the Church of England' (1850), disputing the authority of the privy council; cp. Add MS 44369, f. 38 and Lathbury, i. 97.

[14] i.e. the house at Clewer to which rescue cases were sent.

—W.R. Farquhar—S. Herbert—R. Phillimore—R. Cavendish. Calls. Dined with Mrs Cavendish.[1]

24. 2 S. Lent & St Matthias.

St Martin's H.C. 8½ AM. St Andrew's 11—Bedfordbury 7 P.M. Wrote to (Rev's) Mr Rees[2]—E. Fellows—R. Burgess—Jas Beaven[3]—S W Wayte[4]—G.F. Townsend—E. Monro—D.E. Williams—S. Clark—Col. Short[5]—Archdn. Hale. Read Hale on Deacons[6]—Monro on Purity[7]—Wilberforce on Baptism—Hollingsworth on Prophecy[8]—Manchr. case & opinion.[9] MS. of 44 aloud in evg.

25. M.

Wrote to Sir J.G—R.G—J. Griffiths—Willy—Phipps—King—Dalzell—S. Denison—W. Bridges—Monkland & Co[10]—C.G—Lyttelton—Lincoln—Hollingsworth—Barnes—T. Burnaby—Wright. Read Pulci—Goode's Review of Fust.[11] Saw Ld Powis—Sir A. Dalrymple. Ceylon Commee. 12¼–3½: and H. of C. & H of L. 5–7½.[12] Calls.

26. T.

Wrote to Parkinson—Freshfield—Phillott[13]—J E Gray—Williams & Co—Phillimore[14]—W.F. Campbell. Saw Mr Maskell—Ld Ashburton—Adderley. St Martin's Parish Meeting 11–12½ on Model Dwellings: where I made a proposal.[15] H. of C. 5–7¼.[16] Dined with the Granville Vernons. Read &

[1] Louisa, da. of 1st Lord Lismore, widow of William Cavendish, 1783–1812; mother of 7th duke of Devonshire and (Lord) R.; she lived in Belgrave Place and Compton Place, Sussex, and d. 1863; cp. 24 June 49.

[2] Probably Samuel Rees, 1801–53; St. John's, Cambridge; headmaster of North Walsham school 1835–43; vicar of Horsey, Norfolk, from 1835.

[3] James Beaven, b. 1801; St. Edmund Hall, Oxford; D.D. 1842; professor of divinity, Toronto.

[4] Samuel William Wayte, 1819–98; fellow of Trinity, Oxford, 1842–66, president 1868–78; a secretary of the Oxford commission 1854–8.

[5] See 17 Mar. 49.

[6] W. H. *Hale, 'The duties of priest and deacons in the Church of England' (1850).

[7] E. *Monro, 'Purity of life. A sermon' (1850); on Matt. v. 8.

[8] A. G. H. Hollingsworth, *The holyland restored; or, an examination of the prophetic evidence for the restitution of Palestine to the Jews* (1849).

[9] Perhaps 'Manchester church question plainly stated' (1850); on the relationship of the chapter to the parishes and to Manchester College.

[10] Unidentified.

[11] W. *Goode, 'Review of the judgment of Sir H. J. *Fust in the case of *Gorham . . .' (1850).

[12] Ecclesiastical Commission Bill in the Lords, Irish voting in the Commons: *H* cviii. 1323, 1335.

[13] James Russell Phillott, 1802–65; fellow of Magdalen, Oxford, 1829–35; rector of Ballymoney, Connor, from 1830; precentor of Connor from 1847.

[14] Lathbury, i. 99.

[15] No report traced.

[16] Education: *H* civ. 27.

corrected the Libel in L's case.[1] Read Pulci—Bennett's Sermons [2]—Sewell's Serm [3]—Keble's Ch. matters.[4]

27. Wed.

Wrote to C.G—Duckett—Haly. H. of C. 1½–4¼.[5] Saw Goulburn & Thesiger (on Irish Registration)—Mr Kennaway—Tyrrell—Ly Lyttelton—R. Oliverson. Read Pulci. Calls. Wrote Political Memoranda.

On Tuesday the 19th. [February] when Mr. Disraeli made his motion for a Committee on the Poor Laws, I talked the question over with Mr. Goulburn during the debate: and found him disposed to vote for the motion if there had been a division that night. I determined to do the same & to state my reasons.

The debate however was adjourned & the next day he called on me & said he had been looking into the financial part of the question & was now inclined to resist the motion.

I went in to see Sidney Herbert and found him disposed to favour it as being demanded by justice to the agriculturists, and likewise as the most direct & ready way open to us of affording some relief to the farmer. I agreed to see him again next morning, did so, and then formally decided to vote with Disraeli. He was not well enough to attend tho he wished it.[6]

On Saturday I was with Herbert again & he told me Graham had been to see him: that he had come from Peel's house and probably also from Peel: very uneasy about the Government: uneasy about the Australian bill & the motion for two chambers which he thought likely to be carried: and impressed with some idea that my vote might have been the result of a previous understanding with the Protectionists: to which he had added that if it were so, and if we two together with Lord Aberdeen had such an understanding with them, it altered the case materially as to their succeeding to the Government. But Herbert assured him that my vote was given simply & solely on the ground of the justice of the case: upon which he went away comforted.

Today Sir J. Tyrrell came to me & talked in general terms about the debate of last week & the Farmer's question: then he called me away from the table in the[7] room where I was standing & said he would ask me a question on his own responsibility alone. It was this: whether supposing it were perfectly understood that I took my own course upon protection and other questions with regard to which I had declared an opinion—supposing[8] further that in all respects my personal honour & character was secured—I should be inclined to act with the Protectionists as a party—since in that case he presumed that as 'the throne was vacant' there was nothing to prevent me from leading them. This was the sum of what he said though in very many more words: rather a startling question under all the circumstances.

[1] *Lincoln's first formal plea for divorce.

[2] W. J. E. *Bennett, 'The crown, the state and the church, their junction or their separation. Two sermons' (1850).

[3] W. *Sewell, 'The position of Christ's church in England at this time as a witness to divine truth' (1850); on Acts i. 6–9.

[4] J. *Keble, 'Church matters in 1850' (1850).

[5] Marriage Bill: *H* cix. 81.

[6] This sentence added later.

[7] 'Club' deleted.

[8] 'it' deleted.

I told him in reply that what he had said was more an expression of feeling than a question—that it did not appear to me that up to the present time the Protectionists had been properly an opposition, except with respect to questions of free trade—that there was therefore no line of action drawn by systematic conduct on a series of measures, such as could supply a basis, or a criterion, without which such a question could hardly be framed, or any answer given to it—that my votes since leaving office had been given independently, i.e. upon the merits of each case, and not with a view to keeping the government in office—and had in fact been frequently against them on vital questions—that I thought we were all to a great degree in the hands of the Govt. who by avoiding points of conflict with the Conservative party had prevented their rallying anew in force, and who by an opposite course hereafter might cause such a rally—that I disclaimed for my own part all recollections of quarrels—& thought it was the duty of public men to unite & cooperate with those in whom they could confide, according to the exigencies of the country—that beyond this expression of a general sentiment, & reference to my conduct, I did not think the state of public affairs, of parties, & of men, such at the present moment as to admit of an answer—further that any question, to be practical, must proceed upon grounds more definite, and could not be hypothetically put or replied to—lastly that such inquiries could only be properly made & answered by & through persons responsible.[1]

The fact is I could with truth have gone much beyond my answer to him as regards my disposition not to obstruct Ld Stanley's coming in for obstruction's sake: but I could not say to him, nor to myself, that I saw my way to cooperation. Questions of antipathy must be more subdued, & questions of sympathy more pronounced & worked upon, before that could be, with honour or in fact.[2]

28. Th.

Wrote to Christie & Manson—Pritt & Sherwood[3]—Greenhill—Sir A. Galloway—Griffiths—Monsell—C.G—J.L. Ross—J.W. Joyce—Read Pulci—Saw R. Phillimore—Ld Aberdeen—Freshfield—Williams & Co—Barry—Thesiger & Goulburn, on Irish Registration. H of C. 5–7 and 9½–1.[4] Exhibn. Commn. 3–5.

Friday Mch One 1850.

Wrote to T.G—Newcome[5]—Scotts—J. Murray (2) Campbell—G & Co—Sir J.G—M.F. Tupper. Saw Coleridge—Wm. & R. Gladstone—Christie. Read Pulci. H. of C. 4¼–7¼ & 8½–12. Voted in 144:213 agt Ministers & Graham on the Irish Franchise: with much dissatisfaction in regard to the latter.[6] Calls.

2. Sat.

Wrote to J. Griffiths—A.M. Paterson. Up at 5. 6¼–2 to Hagley, walking

[1] Three paras. omitted.
[2] Dated this day; Add MS 44777, ff. 307, 309.
[3] Pritt, Sherwood, Venables and Grubb, parliamentary agents; cp. 28 May 34.
[4] J. *Hume's motion on parliamentary reform: *H* cix. 137.
[5] Richard Newcombe, 1779–1857; archdeacon of Merioneth 1834–57.
[6] *H* cix. 287.

from Birmingham. Saw Griffiths on O.F. Read Emerson's Representative Men.[1] Chess with W. Lyttelton.

3. 3 S. Lent.

Church 11 (& Holy Commn.) & 3½. Read Wilberforce on Baptism—Petrarch de Sol. Relig.[2]—Goode on P. Martyr's Letter (What a *martyr*!)[3] Xtn Rem. on Cholera—on the Gorham case.[4] Conv. with W. L[yttelton] on do.

4. M.

Church at 10 AM. Wrote to Sir J.G.—J. Griffiths—J. Amery—Collis—H. Tayleur. Read Sequel to Ariosto—Willis on Colonies[5]—Dr Bayford's Speech[6]—Col. Ch. Chronicle.[7] Walk with C.—Chess with WHL. Mr Giles[8] announced an 'ulcer' on (little) Mary's eye. Jessy too is a wreck—we are thankful to be going near the best advice.

5. T.

Church 10 AM. Wrote to Tupper—Parkinson—Supt L. & NW. Station—Mr Church—W.H.G—J. Griffiths. Read Sequel to the Furioso (fin[ished])—Pulci (fin[ished])—Charters of Old Amn. Colonies.[9] Walk with C.

6. Wed.

8½–3½ Hagley to C. Gardens. Wrote to Mr Quirk[10]—Miss Neave[11]—Sec. National Society[12]—Mr Tyner[13]—Mr Brameld.[14] H. of C. 3¾–6: voted agt Wortley's Bill.[15] Worked on Papers &c. Mary's eye did not suffer by the journey & Dalrymple was encouraging.

[1] By R. W. Emerson (1850); lectures given in Britain in 1849.

[2] *De Otio Religioso* or *De Vita Solitaria.*

[3] *An unpublished letter of Peter Martyr . . . to H. Bullinger, written from Oxford just after the completion of the second prayer-book of Edward VI . . . edited, with remarks, by W.* **Goode* (1850).

[4] *Christian Remembrancer*, xix. 164, 1 (January 1850).

[5] N. P. Willis, *Life, here and there; or, sketches of society and adventure at far-apart times and places* (1850).

[6] '*Gorham, Clerk against the bishop of Exeter: the argument of Dr. [A. F.] Bayford on behalf of . . . *Gorham' (1849).

[7] *Colonial Church Chronicle*, iii. 321 (March 1850); on apostolic method of missions.

[8] Henry Giles, surgeon practising in Stourbridge.

[9] S. Lucas, *Charters of the old English colonies in America* (1850).

[10] George Quirk, b. ?1824; Worcester, Oxford; rector of Martinsthorpe, Rutland, from 1849; a pluralist.

[11] Treasurer of Royal Female Philanthropic Society.

[12] James Gylby *Lonsdale, 1818–92; priest 1842, sec. National Society for promoting the education of the poor; professor of classical literature, London, 1865–70.

[13] Perhaps William Tyner, 1763–1854; vicar of Compton, Sussex, from 1806.

[14] George William Brameld, 1817–*ca.* 1870; Lincoln College, Oxford: vicar of East Markham, Nottinghamshire, from 1852.

[15] *H* cix. 455.

7. Th.

Wrote to Ld J. Russell—Sir S. Lushington—B. Hawes—J R Hope—D. of Argyll—Sir JG—Canon Trevor—C.G. Reid—J.L. Ross. Saw Tupper (O.F) —Archdn. Manning & Wilberforce—Molesworth—Walpole. Read Letter to Ld J. Russell on Oxford.[1] Commee. on Ceylon & Exhn. Commn. & House 12¾–6¼.[2] Dined at the Palace: probably (I write this on Saturday) for the last time. H. of C. 11–12.—An uneasy night with little Mary.

8. Fr.

Wrote to Scotts—Scott Russell—Sir JG—Rn. G—Leighton—Hubbard—Jansen[3]—G. Knight—Rev. Mr Howson[4] & see inf.[5] Spent the morning in conference with Hope—Manning[6]—& Archd. & H. Wilberforce, on the Gorham case & its probable consequences. Archdn. Wilberforce (with Doyle & M.L.) to dinner, when we had more conversation. Saw also Wegg Prosser—Adderley. Read Col. Ch. papers. Wrote to Bp of London.

9. Sat.

Wrote to Bp of N. Zealand—Bp of Salisbury—C.J. Abraham[7]—Gladstone & Co. Marg. Chapel 5 P.M. Read 'the Judgment'.[8]—L & NW Report.[9] Saw Archd. Wilberforce—Manning—Farquhar—Wegg Prosser—Alex. Hope—also (in evg) Cavendish, Badeley, Rogers, Mr Kennaway, on the Gorham question. Saw Mr Rogers. Saw Sir S. Lushington[10] on the Col. Church Clauses.[11]

10. 4 S. Lent.

St Martin's H.C. 8½ AM—St Andrew's 11 AM—Bedfordbury 7 P.M. Read Gorham—Buchanan's Ten Years Conflict.[12] Wrote to Bp of Brechin—A. Hope—Sec. C.M.S. Wrote Memm. on the actual position of Churchmen[13]—

[1] 'Letter to *Russell . . . on the constitutional defects of the university & colleges of Oxford, with suggestions for a royal commission of inquiry into the universities. By a member of the Oxford convocation' [C. A. Row] (1850).

[2] Ireland and, later, the ballot: *H* cix. 465, 497.

[3] Probably Thomas Corbyn Janson, 1809–63; partner in Brown, Janson & Co., London bankers.

[4] John Saul *Howson, 1816–85; principal of Liverpool Collegiate Institution 1849–66; D.D. 1861; dean of Chester 1867–85; wrote on theology.

[5] See last sentence of entry.

[6] For *Manning's recollection's of Gladstone's reaction to the judgment, given this day, see Purcell, i. 528. For *Gorham, see above, iii. xxxiv.

[7] Charles John Abraham, 1814–1903; master at Eton 1839–49; *Selwyn's chaplain in New Zealand 1850; bp. of Wellington 1858–70; canon of Lichfield 1870–8.

[8] The judicial cttee. of the privy council's judgment the previous day on the *Gorham appeal case, which reversed *Fust's judgment, thus finding for *Gorham.

[9] Its annual report; the L.N.W.R. had broken off negotiations on administering the Caledonian Railway.

[10] i.e. Stephen *Lushington.

[11] 'Read Perfected [?] judgment' here heavily deleted.

[12] R. *Buchanan, *The ten years' conflict: being the history of the disruption of the Church of Scotland*, 2 v. (1849).

[13] Untraced; cp. resolutions on *Gorham in Add MS 44566, f. 94.

Spent the aftn. in conversation with Manning & we found ourselves still in substantial agreement. Saw Sir W. James. Read a S[ermon] of Manning's aloud.

11. M.

Laid up with cold & physic for it. Up in evg & read Buchanan. Saw (in my bedroom) Bp of Exeter—Ld Aberdeen—Alex. Hope—Manning[1]—R. Cavendish—J.N.G.

12. T.

Up before noon. Wrote to Bp of London—Mr Wodehouse—A. Robertson—Rn. G—Glyde[2]—Sir S. Lushington—P. Buchan.[3] Read Buchanan on the 10 Years Conflict. Saw J.N.G. Worked on letters & papers. Committees & House 2–$5\frac{1}{2}$.[4] Before 8 P.M. Manning came & a party followed him. They went at 12 but Badeley staid until after one explaining to me the position of the question as to a prohibition in the Gorham Case.[5]

13. Wed.

Wrote to Mayow—Sir J.G—Archdeacon Hale—Tupper—C. Uppington—H. Glynne—Sir J.S. Forbes. Read Buchanan—Turner on Manchester Parish Bill.[6] Dined with the Jameses: & afterwards attended the Graphic Society.[7] Saw Bp of London—Ld Powis—Seymer—G. Hope—Manning—on the Gorham case—Mr Wodehouse—Rand[8]—Towgood[9]—on other business.

14. Th.

Wrote to G. Chance—Griffiths—Bp of Brechin—Rev. Mr Abraham—Cavendish—Bp of Exeter. Read Buchanan. Hope Badeley Talbot Cavendish Dr Pusey Messrs. Keble Denison & Bennett here from $9\frac{3}{4}$ to 12 on the draft of the Resolutions.—Badeley again in the evg. also saw Prosser & Ld Powis: on the whole I resolved to try some immediate effort. Commee. $12\frac{3}{4}$–$2\frac{1}{2}$—Diocn. Board $2\frac{3}{4}$–4. H. of C. 5–$7\frac{1}{4}$.[10]

[1] The occasion recollected by *Manning in Purcell, i. 528; *Manning had clearly forgotten the chronology.

[2] Obscure; a slip of the pen for Glynne?

[3] Perhaps Peter Buchan, 1790–1854; Scottish antiquarian and publisher.

[4] Taxation: *H* cix. 738.

[5] Cp. Purcell, i. 528–9. *Badeley was *Phillpotts' advocate before the privy council. Tractarians were concerned at secular jurisdiction on doctrinal questions.

[6] T. Turner, 'A letter on the collegiate parish church of Manchester: with remarks on the bill before parliament for the division of the parish' (1850).

[7] No report found.

[8] William Rand, china dealer in Kensington.

[9] Probably John Towgood, barrister in Chancery Lane.

[10] Factories: *H* cix. 883.

15. Fr.

Wrote to Robn. G—to do, at great length, on the attendance at Fasque—Scotts—Prosser—Cavendish—Kirkland—Tayleur—Read Surtees on Slave Trade [1]—Adderley on Ld J. Russell's Speech.[2] Saw Cavendish Talbot & Mr Kennaway (morning) 10½–1: Talbot & Hope in aftn—Powis—Adderley—H. Fitzroy—S. Herbert—on the Gorham business. H of Commons 5–7¼.[3] Dined at Ld Granville's to meet M. Sallandrouze.[4]

16. Sat.

Westmr. Abbey 3 PM.

Wrote to Kirkland—H. Cole—Valpy [5]—R. Leigh [6]—Marshall—Willy—Mr Church—Williams & Co—Talbot—Redesdale—T.T. Carter—J. Griffiths (2)—Prof. Graham [7]—Mr J.C. Robertson [8]

Saw Herbert—Hope—Dr Pusey—Prosser—H. Fitzroy—Rogers—C.A. Wood—Lyttelton—on the Gorham case. We finally (as I hope) fixed the Address to the Bp of London.[9] The Bp of Exeter & Badeley, with the Lytteltons, came to dinner. Saw Mr Williams (O.F.) [10]—H. Cole—Graham (Cl[ydesdale] Junct.) [11] Denison. Read Girdlestone on Commee. of Council [12]—Scoble on Slave Trade Movement.[13]

17. 5 S. Lent.

St Martins 11 A.M. (with H.C.)—Bedfordbury Evg—MS. of 1841 aloud to servants. Wrote to A. Hope—Dr Jacobson—Saw Sewell & R. Cavendish—W.C. James—on Gorham case. Saw Bunsen. Read Irons [14]—Dodsworth (eheu)[15]—Neale (excellent) [16]—Ordinarium & Canon Missae—Kennaway on Lent & on the Incarnation.[17]

[1] Not found; by S. F. Surtees?

[2] C. B. Adderley, 'Some reflections on [*Russell's] speech on colonial policy' (1850).

[3] *Wood's budget statement: *H* cix. 971.

[4] Charles Jean Sallandouze de Lamornaix, 1809–67; Parisian industrialist and diplomat; promoted sale of French luxuries in England, with a china shop off Hanover Square; a French delegate to the 1851 exhibition. Granville George *Leveson-Gower, 1815–91; 2nd Earl Granville 1846; vice president b. of t. 1848, paymaster 1848; foreign secretary 1851–2, 1870–4, 1880–5; lord president 1852–4, 1859; chancellor of duchy 1854; colonial secretary 1868–70, 1886; cp. Add MSS 44165–80 and Ramm I and II.

[5] Probably Francis Edward Jackson *Valpy, 1797–1882; headmaster of Reading school 1830; rector of Garveston from 1854.

[6] Probably Richard Leigh, 1808–84; rector of Hassall 1843–63, of Walton 1868–84.

[7] Thomas *Graham, 1805–69; professor of chemistry, in Glasgow, and London.

[8] Unidentified.

[9] Add MS 44738, f. 119; urging the bps. to action and leadership. See above, iii. xxxiv.

[10] Perhaps Benjamin Williams, coal dealer, of Kate's Hill, Dudley.

[11] Gladstone stood to lose from the Caledonian and Edinburgh and Glasgow Amalgamation Bill, and opposed it on 18 March; the 2° was delayed 6 months: *H* cix. 1052.

[12] E. *Girdlestone, 'The committee of council on education: an imaginary enemy, a real friend' (1850).

[13] Cp. 10 Mar. 40, or a more recent untraced pamphlet by John Scoble.

[14] W. J. Irons, 'The judgments on baptismal regeneration' (1850); on *Gorham.

[15] W. *Dodsworth, 'The *Gorham case briefly considered' (1850); cp. Liddon, iii. 261.

[16] J. M. *Neale, 'A few words of hope on the present crisis of the English church' (1850).

[17] Cp. 26 Mar. 48.

18. M.

Wrote to Mr Maskell—Swift—Redesdale—Paterson—Burnett—Williams & Co. Read Buchanan—Lord's Report on Slave Trade.[1] H. of C. $3\frac{3}{4}$–7.[2] Saw Seymer—Cavendish—Hope—Castlereagh. Saw Geo. Hope—Mr Oldfield[3]—J.E. Denison—Sir J. Graham. Drs. Mill, Pusey &c. met here in evg. I was not with them.[4]

19. T.

Wrote to Ld Fielding.[5] Saw J.N.G. on family matters—R. Cavendish (Gorham)—S. Herbert. Read Buchanan—& (most of the day) Slave Trade Evidence documents & pamphlets. H. of C. $4\frac{1}{2}$–$6\frac{1}{2}$ & $7\frac{3}{4}$–2. Spoke $11\frac{3}{4}$–$12\frac{3}{4}$ for Mr Hutt's motion: and was much amused with the liberality of the compliments from the radicals who with the Tories were (as it happened) the main supporters, being less under the Whip.[6]

20. Wed.

Wrote to H. Cole—W.C. James—Scotts—S. Herbert—G.C. Glyn—T.G—Rn. G—F. Breedon.[7] Saw R. Cavendish—Ld Feilding—F R Wegg Prosser—on the Address & made arrangments for closing—Stafford. Saw Mr Swift on Railway Rating[8]—Sir J. Graham. Dined at Sir R. Peel's where I had much conversation with W. Patten & Walpole on the Gorham Judgment—Lady John Russell's afterwards. Read Buchanan.

21. Th.

Wrote to S. Herbert—J.R. Hope—Bp of London (& dft)—Sir Ch. Hotham.[9] Saw Mr Allen.[10] Saw Lyttelton—T.D. Acland—Mr Bernard. Read Buchanan. $5\frac{1}{2}$–$12\frac{1}{4}$. To the Banquet at the Mansionhouse. The Prince's Speech while it filled me with even more respect, was like a 5th Gospel, a new Evangel.[11] Much conv. with Ld Granville & Baron Rothschild. I greatly like Ld G.

[1] Report of the Lord's select cttee., with evidence and appendix: *PP* 1850, ix. 1.

[2] Caledonian Railway Bill, *Gorham: *H* cix. 1050, 1054.

[3] Thomas Oldfield, a barrister, advising on Scottish Railway affairs; cp. 7 May 50.

[4] He refused to sign the declaration, according to Manning because of his privy councillor's oath; cp. Purcell i. 530, who compares him to Judas! In 1896 Gladstone wrote 'I entirely disavow and disclaim Manning's statement *as it stands*' (to Purcell, in Lathbury, ii. 338).

[5] 'Saw J.N.G.' here heavily deleted.

[6] *Hutt's motion to expedite the abolition of the slave trade: *H* cix. 1110.

[7] Unidentified.

[8] i.e. John Swift; cp. 18 Mar. 44.

[9] Sir Charles *Hotham, 1806–55; captain R.N. 1833; K.C.B. 1846; governed Victoria 1854–5.

[10] Thomas Allen, house agent acting for Lord Grey who purchased 13 Carlton House Terrace from the diarist.

[11] The dinner was for *Albert to meet promoters of the 1851 exhibition; cp. *The Times*, 22 March 1850, 5a.

22. Fr.

Wrote to T.G—C.A. Wood. Saw Jas Hope—J.N.G—W. Page Wood—R. Cavendish—Northcote. Willy came home & made us a joyful day. Read Buchanan—Mackay on Australian Bill [1]—Am[erica]n Charters [2] & Bancroft.[3] Attended Commission mg. House of Commons 5½–8¼ and 9¼–1¼. Spoke 11¾–12¾ for the double chamber & voted in 147:198. It was a noble subject.[4]

23. Sat.

Ch Ch Broadway 6 P.M. Wrote to Ld Wenlock—Huddlestone—J. Griffiths—Rn. G—C.G. Reid. Read Buchanan—Hook's Letter (!!)[5] Saw R. Cavendish—De Tabley—Wegg Prosser—Northcote—on the Address. Saw Mr Parkinson—Mr Allen (& settled with Ld Grey!)[6] The Phillimores & Hope dined.

24. Palm S.

St Martin's & H.C. 11 AM. Bedfordbury Evg. MS. of 1840 for the day aloud in Evg. Saw James (& his picture) Wrote out & corrected afresh Col. Ch. Clauses.[7] Sent paragraphs to Chronicle & Post abt the address to Bp of London.[8] Read Anderden on the Last Words [9]—Hussey, Pref. & Serm [10]—Dr Buchanan.

25. Annunc[iatio]n.

Marg. Chapel 9 AM. Wrote to Lincoln—R. Neville—Lyttelton—R. Palmer—J.R. Hope—R.R. Dean [11]—H.S. with W. & A. Latin lesson with Willy. Read Buchanan—Bp of Exeter's letter to Abp [12]—Claughton's Sermon [13]—Chr. Wordsworth's do.[14] Saw R. Cavendish—Wrote out copies of Col. Ch. Clauses. Commee. & House 12½–6.[15]

[1] A. Mackay, 'Analysis of the Australian Colonies Government Bill' (1850).
[2] Cp. 5 Mar. 50.
[3] Cp. 15 July 48.
[4] On the Australian Colonies Government Bill: *H* cix. 1333.
[5] W. F. *Hook, '*Gorham v. the bishop of Exeter: a letter to Sir Walter Farquhar, Bart., on the present crisis in the church' (1850); *Hook argued that the tractarians 'exaggerated' the difficulties raised by the *Gorham case.
[6] Grey's delay in settling had almost led to the withdrawal from sale of 13 Carlton House Terrace.
[7] Add MS 44738, f. 91.
[8] In Add MS 44566, f. 101; on *Gorham.
[9] W. H. *Anderdon, apostate, *The words from the cross; a series of Lent sermons* (1848).
[10] R. *Hussey, *Sermons, mostly academical: with a preface* (1850); refuting W. *Cureton's views on St. Ignatius' *Epistles*.
[11] Richard Ryder Dean, 1810–85; Christ Church; barrister from 1836; director of London North Western Railway.
[12] H. *Phillpotts, 'A letter to the abp. of Canterbury' (1850); on the *Gorham case.
[13] T. L. *Claughton, 'Our present duties in regard of holy baptism' (1850).
[14] Christopher *Wordsworth, *fils*, 'Beautiful scenery' (1850); on Col. i. 16–18.
[15] Misc. business: *H* cix. 1361.

26. T.

St James's 11 AM. Wrote out copies of Bp's letter for the newspapers. H.S. with W. & A. Latin with Willy. Read Buchanan (finished)—Report on Intramural Interment[1]—Toplady[2]—Jefferson. Saw R. Cavendish—Lyttelton—& went with them to the Bp with whom we had a long & interesting conversation. Shopping.

27. Wed.

St James's 11 A.M. Wrote to Sir J.G—Stibbs[3]—Thring[4]—Leighton—Mackay—Hawes—Newland—Valpy—Causton. [H.]S. with W. & A. [La]tin lesson with Willy[5]—Read Jefferson's Life[6]—Saw[7] Christy & Bell—J.N.G—Mr Dodsworth (Gorham)—and A.P. Stanley. Wrote on Colonies[8]

28. Th.

St Martin's 8 AM. MS. of 1840 to servants at night. H.S. with W. & A. Wrote to H. Tayleur—Col. Light—W.F. Campbell. Worked much on my books. Read Jefferson—Qu. Rev. on Ireland—Qu. College—Son's Diary—Facts in Figures.[9]

29. Good Friday.

St Martins (with H. Commn.) at 11—Marg. Chapel at 5 P.M.—Avrillon[10] at prayers in evg. Saw J.N.G. Read Anderden's Last Words—The Eastern Churches[11]—Bp Forbes's Considerationes Modestae[12]—Crisp on Christ Made Sin.[13] Dear little Jessy's illness which has long been tedious, looked serious today: there was a total loss of appetite now for the 3d day, & of energy, and apparently some unconquerable obstruction in the bowels.[14]

30. Easter Eve.

Marg. Chapel 5 P.M.—Avrillon aloud in evg. H.S. with W. & A.—Latin with Willy. Read Xtn Remembrancer on Church & State[15]—Jefferson.

[1] *PP* 1850, xxxiii. 369: on interments in St. Margaret's, Westminster.
[2] Cp. Mar. 45.
[3] Probably Edward Cambridge Stibbs, bookseller in the Strand.
[4] Henry Thring, 1818–1907; barrister 1845; home office counsel 1860; parliamentary counsel 1869–86; cr. Baron Thring 1886; *d.s.p.*; cp. Add MS 44332, ff. 1–158.
[5] Top of page slightly torn.
[6] S. C. Carpenter, ed., *Memoirs of the Hon. T. Jefferson, president of the United States*, 2 v. (1809).
[7] 'Lyttelton' here deleted.
[8] Probably Add MS 44738, f. 87.
[9] *Quarterly Review*, lxxxvi. 480, 364, 449, 437 (March 1850).
[10] Cp. 23 Feb. 45.
[11] [E. S. Appleyard] *The eastern churches: containing sketches of the Nestorian, Armenian, Jacobite, Coptic and Abyssinian communities* (1850).
[12] W. *Forbes, *Considerationes modestae et pacificae controversiarum de justificatione purgatorio, invocatione sanctorum Christo mediatore, et eucharistia* (1658, reprinted 1850).
[13] By Samuel *Crisp the quaker (1691).
[14] She was dying of meningitis.
[15] *Christian Remembrancer*, xix. 471 (March 1850).

Worked most of the day on arranging letters & papers—Wrote on the Day. Jessy was worse this evg: there being a good deal of fever today.

31. Easter Day.

St Martins 8½ (H. Commn.). St Andrews (Wells St) at 11 with Willy—Marg. Chapel at 7 with C. MS. of 42 aloud in evg. Wrote to Bp of Aberdeen—Roundell Palmer—W.P. Wood—Masters [1]—Twist [2]—Hope—Mitchinson [3]—Jas Ross.[4] Read Ecclesiologist [5]—Colon. Ch. Chronicle [6]—Xtn Remembrancer on Eusebius.[7] Jessy thank God better in the night under C's affectionate & unwearied care.

Easter Monday April One 1850.

St Andrew's 5 P.M. H.S. with W. & A.—Latin with Willy. Saw R. Phillimore—Lyttelton—Baldock. Dined with the Mildmays. Wrote to Bp of Glasgow—J. Griffiths—Mr Johnstone.

Examined 3½ hours (by a most tedious process) on Lady Lincoln's wretched case.[8] Calls &c. Jessy had much pain last night & we sent to Locock about 4 A.M. who when he came cheered us. In the morning thank God she was better.

Ap 2. Tues.

St Andrews 5 PM. Latin lesson with Willy. Wrote to Sir J.G—J.N.G—T.G—Rn. G—H.J.G—Redesdale—Mary Ln.—Canning—De Tabley—Ly Brabazon (to put them off)—Lady H. Forbes—Mr C. Uppington. Saw Messrs. Oldfield & Baylis [9]—E.L. Robertson—Lyttelton. Read Watts on the Gorham Case [10]—Q.R. on Grote.[11]

It was a day of much anxiety & pain. Last night the brain was in a fearful state of irritation & dear little Jessy spent it tossing, moaning, & screaming, chiefly in C.s arms, the rest in mine. With day came some diminution of the excitement: & Locock in the morning still held it most probable that the stomach was the cause. But at night he declared the head symptoms unequivocal. The moaning was much less but the head moved very constantly from side to side. The pulse was low, which he much disliked. The eyes very heavy. He says it is tubercular inflammation of the membranes of the brain, a most insidious form of disease: the danger imminent but the case "far

[1] Joseph Masters, 1795–1863; London bookseller; published *Ecclesiologist* 1842–63.

[2] Joseph Wilding Twist, 1810–65; Queen's, Oxford; priest 1842; curate of Christ Church, Liverpool, 1855, later of St. Michael's, Kingston, Jamaica.

[3] Thomas Mitchinson, 1792–1862; curate of Carrington, Lincolnshire, 1819–62; vicar of Helpringham 1836–54.

[4] Gentleman, lived in Brompton Row; Hawn P.

[5] *Ecclesiologist*, x. 361 (April 1850).

[6] *Colonial Church Chronicle*, iii. 361 (April 1850); on the church in Tinnevelly.

[7] *Christian Remembrancer*, xix. 331 (March 1850).

[8] Private examination prior to that in Lords; cp. 28 May 50.

[9] Thomas Henry Baylis, Temple barrister.

[10] Untraced pamphlet, perhaps by John Watts.

[11] *Quarterly Review*, lxxxvi. 384 (March 1850).

from hopeless": 48 hours he thinks will bring it to a point so as to make the issue clear. And now O Father can we readily yield her up to Thee? O how much better will she be cared for than in this sad & evil world. His will be done. My Catherine bears up wonderfully.

Wed. Ap 3.

Marg. Chapel 5 P.M. H.S. with W. & A. Latin lesson to Willy. Wrote to H.J.G—Lockhart—J. Murray—Tupper—Ly Brabazon—Miss Brown—H. Tayleur. 12–3¼. Examn. finished at Doctors Commons. Saw the Vicar—Phillimore. Read Wiseman,[1] A Voice from the North,[2] Denison, on the Gorham Case.[3]

And now for dearest Jessy. The improvement in the night was steady: the faculties returned, the excitement diminished. Dr L.s report in the morning was so materially changed as to make hope preponderate: and tonight he says that ground has *not* been lost during the day. The rolling of the head & the shivering has ceased though the pain indicating the evil is still seated there. The distressing exterior symptoms have now disappeared. Let us with God's grace in our patience possess our souls until He declare His will.

4. Th.

St Anne's 8¼ P.M. Wrote to Manning—Bp of Glasgow—Lady Kerrison—J.N.G—The Vicar. H.S. with W. & A. Saw R. Phillimore & Ld Ashburton on Gorham case &c. Saw JNG on L & NWR. Calls during the afternoon & business.

This was a day of cheerfulness until about 3 and afterwards of retrogression. Jessy had much discomfort connected partly with action of the bowels & partly perhaps owing to so much as 18 hours without the Dover's powder.[4] However thank God tho' discomfort, and loss of faculties marked the latter part of the day, all those bad symptoms which returned were in a mitigated form & the pulse *held* its improvement.

5. Fr.

St James's with C. 3 P.M. Wrote to Northcote—H. Cole—Sir J.G—H.J.G—Sir J. Forbes—Ly H. Forbes—Broster—Col. Short—Mr Church. Saw Mr Norton—T.G—J.N.G. Prepared my separate copies of Leopardi to send out: & got an ill report of it through Mr Cochrane of the L[ondon] Library.[5]

[1] N. P. S. *Wiseman, 'The final appeal in matters of faith' (1850); on John xviii. 36.

[2] [S. B. Harper], 'A voice from the north; an appeal to the people of England on behalf of their church' (1850).

[3] G. A. *Denison, 'An appeal to the clergy and laity of the Church of England to combine for the defence of the church and for the recovery of her rights and liberties' (1850).

[4] A sudorific made of opium, and sulphate of potash; cp. *DNB* xv. 382.

[5] i.e. J. G. *Cochrane.

Read Jefferson—Panizzi's Essay on Italian Romance[1]—Leslie on Tillotson's Sentiments.[2]

For the 24 hours up to tonight upon the whole I trust there is some slight improvement: the pulse keeps its ground: the consciousness comes & goes: there is less excitement on the whole. Our hopes keep uppermost: tho' not without a struggle.

6. Sat.

Marg. Chapel 5 P.M. H.S. with W. & A. Latin lesson with Willy. Wrote to Geo. Dalton[3]—Worked on accounts & business. Saw R. Palmer (Australian Ch)—R. Cavendish (Gorham)—Ld Kinnaird & A. Kinnaird—Mr Peel, Mr Zinn,[4] about the pictures.

Jessy seemed to get pretty well through the day as Locock to whom we sent in the aftn was not afraid of the action of the bowels (it had occurred thrice); but the night was uneasy & not long after I had gone to bed i.e. a little before 3 she had for the first time a sort of convulsive affection: followed at an interval by a slighter one. I went up to Dr L. who did not seem to regard them as of vital consequence: though in combination with other signs they show that we have I fear fallen to a point as low as that of Tuesday night. We enlarged the blisters & kept up the Dover's powder with the $\frac{1}{2}$ grain only of calomel. My poor C. was more cut up & tried tonight than I have yet seen her.

7. 1 S. Easter.

St Martins at 12$\frac{3}{4}$ (after Litany & Psalms at home) for Holy Communion. Westmr. Abbey in afternoon. Conv. with Willy on his personal matters of religion & duty. I was obliged to put gently into his mind how likely it is that he may no more return home to Jessy. Read aloud MS of 44 for the day. Read Lechler's Englische Deismus.[5]

At night, chiefly while watching in Jessy's room, began a sort of journal of her illness.[6] Also wrote to HJG—Sir J.G—& Lady H.S. Forbes. This was a day rather of gain as we trust than loss: but the risks are still fearful.

8. M.

St Andrews 5 P.M. H.S. with W. & A. Latin lesson to Willy. Wrote to Miss Lyttelton—S. Herbert—Cooke—Linton[7]—Mr Church—Locock (in evg)—M. Lyttelton—Sir J.G—H.J.G—Lady H. Forbes. Saw Walpole Hope & R. Phillimore, who were afterwards joined by Palmer on the Australian Church Clauses.

[1] A. *Panizzi, *Orlando innamorato di Bojardo; Orlando furioso di Ariosto: with an essay on the romantic narrative poetry of the Italians* (1830).

[2] [C. *Leslie], 'The charge of socinianism against Dr. *Tillotson considered' (1695).

[3] Perhaps George James Dalton, who ran an academy in London.

[4] Unidentified; reading uncertain.

[5] G. V. Lechler, *Geschichte des englishen Deismus* (1841).

[6] Later inserted into a general account of Jessy's life: Add MS 44738, f. 134.

[7] (Sir) William *Linton, 1791–1876; landscape painter; exhibited at Royal Academy until 1859; K.C.B. 1865. See entry of 2 days earlier and 5 Apr. 51.

While they were here Locock came: and found Jessy in a state almost hopeless. We were deluded yesterday as to convulsions: for I now find Mrs Baker observed some. But without knowing this Catherine perceived through a mother's divining instinct that her darling had begun to give way in the deadly struggle. In the afternoon I prepared some little things by anticipation.

As the evening drew on all the signs grew worse, and our hearts again very sick yet I trust neither of us are so blindly selfish as to murmur at the Lord's being about to raise one of our children to Himself. Dr Locock's last visit left us no hope. C. and I with Mrs Baker sat in the room of death and watched the beloved child in her death battle, powerless to aid her. In the intervals of the thickening convulsions I read Mr Munro's excellent Letter,[1] & wrote the necessary letters for the morning: until latterly when there were scarcely any spaces of repose between the tearings and tossings of the conflict.

9.[2] *T.* (*St Anne's Soho 8¼ P.M*).

It is all over, and all well. The blessed child was released at two o'clock in the morning compassionately taken by her Saviour into the fold of His peace. I dwell on it no longer in this place: I must try to put together a few recollections of her little life. C. & I got to rest between 3 & 4. I was wakened in the morning by her weeping. The day was occupied with the communications & arrangements necessarily following the Death.
Saw J.N.G—T.G—Sir W. James—Dr Locock—Mr Clemence (for the coffin)[3]—Lyttelton—Lady Brabazon.

Wrote letters to

H.J.G.	Lady Brabazon	D. Robertson
Sir J.G.	James	Rn G.
Ly H. Forbes	Canning	E.L. Robertson
Mr Irvine	Dss Beaufort	R. Neville—
Mr Goalen	The Vicar.	Wm Gladstone
Hayman	J.N.G.—	J. Griffiths
Fergusson	Mrs Wadd.	Mr Maskell
	Bp of Glasgow	Mrs Malcolm
Lady Hope	Mrs Herbert	

I read the Innocent's Day Epistle[4] at prayers: and tried to explain it to the three elder children. C. is heavily pressed in body: yet not too heavily.[5]

[1] E. *Monro, 'A few words on the spirit in which men are meeting the present crisis in the church. A letter' (1850).
[2] The whole of this entry is surrounded by a heavy black line.
[3] John Clemence, carpenter in the Strand.
[4] Revelations, xiv.
[5] This and the next entry do not betray the severe emotional crisis through which Gladstone passed immediately following Jessy's death; cp. Magnus, 94 and Add MS 44738, ff. 122–46.

10. Wed.

St Anne's 8¼ P.M. Saw J.N.G—Jane Wortley—Jas Hope—Lady James—Mr Tyler—Latin lesson to Willy. Wrote to H. Tayleur—Sec. L. & NW. Railway Co—Wm. Gladstone—Mrs Hagart—C. Wordsworth—Rector of Exeter—Dr Booth—Mr Irvine—Mr Church—Northcote—Larkins—Cavendish—Cole—Maguire[1]—G.A. Denison—Col. Light.

Today we had Jessy in the Boudoir. Flowers came from Scotland: and C. put them about her.

I wrote today this little inscription perhaps for the stone floor of the Chapel over her.

Underneath
Sleep the mortal remains of
Catherine Jessy Gladstone
Born July 27. 1845
Died April 9. 1850
'And in their mouth was
found no guile: for they
are without fault before
the throne of God.
Rev. XIV. 5.[2]

Catherine showed nervous weakness a little: but was much comforted by having Jessy near: I mean her body near: for of her spirit we know not: but that may be also near.

11. Th.

St Andrew's Wells St 5 P.M. H.S. with W. & A. Latin lesson with Willy. Wrote to Mrs Egerton—Mr Maskell—Rn. G—Mr Church—Brighton R. Superintt.—Blisworth do—Kate G. Saw J.N.G—Dean of Windsor & Lady C.N. Grenville—Registrar.[3] Read Mr Maskell's 2d Letter[4]—& Anti-tractarian Barrister.[5]

In the evening came the closing of the coffin & the last kiss upon the cold features of our Jessy. It was a pang for me; a deep one for a mother—who is going too to part from her sooner.

12. Fr.

Left C.G. at 5¾ AM: & went from Euston Square in a Coupee with the dear remains. Took Willy as far as Blisworth & there *consigned* him for Geddington. Closed my blind to have no other company than the thought of her who seems incessantly to beckon me & say 'Come Pappy Come': & of the land whither she is gone.

[1] John M. Maguire, anglican chaplain to the Boyle Poor Law Union; cp. 12 Apr. 50 n.
[2] Now inscribed on the floor in the centre of the transept of St. Andrew's chapel, Fasque.
[3] i.e. G. Graham.
[4] Cp. Add MS 44369, f. 141.
[5] Probably 'The morality of tractarianism' (1850); signed 'A.B.'.

Read T.A Kempis[1]—Maguire.[2]—Notwithstanding precautions & assurances I had to pay in five parts and to make three changes of carriage.

13. Sat.[3]

Reached Fasque between 8 & 9 AM. Welcomed by Helen with deep emotion: & by all: particularly Hayman.[4] At Eleven we had morning prayers, the funeral office, & Holy Communion: after which I saw the coffin set right under the spot where she used to kneel in infant prayer.[5]

Wrote to C.G—Hampton—H.K. Seymer.

Read T.A Kempis—Acland's Daily Steps.[6]

My Father did not converse much on business: & having slept ill went to rest after dinner.—I conversed with Aunt J. & again with Helen about our darling's life and illness.

Read a multitude of Sir J.G.s letters and papers. I kept the key of the vault and was able to visit my Jessy there.

14. Sunday.

Chapel mg & aft. Wrote to C.G.—Hampton—Visited. Much Conv. with my Father: also with H. on the manner of providing for his comfort: the matter now stands very ill. Short visits he declared are worse than none. Began Account of my Jessy.[7] Read a little de Imitat[ione Christi].

15. M.

Wrote to Bp of Glasgow. Worked over 7 hours on letters & papers for Sir J.G: with the effect of pleasing him as if it had been of use which I cannot say generally it was. I fear it should be said that he is now under a mild form of mental disease beginning: & our[8] great study should be to keep it mild. At F[ettercairn] House: and visited the poor & old who remembered and loved Jessy. Worked on account of her & other memoranda. Read a little De Imit. Xti. Whist with Sir J.G.

I could only pay one last visit [to the vault] being with my Father so much. Oh that I may carry away with me the seal of that Chamber.

16. T.

Round early by order of my Father to speak to him again about my work

[1] Cp. 1 Apr. 47.

[2] J. M. Maguire, *Letters in vindication of the Church of Ireland* (1850); much of it a gloss on Gladstone's writings.

[3] This entry is surrounded by a heavy black line.

[4] See the draft inscription to Hayman, dated this day, on the fly leaf following 31 May 50.

[5] Gladstone later severely criticized D. A. Irvine's conduct of the burial service: cp. Add MS 44369, f. 180.

[6] [A. H. D. Acland], *Daily steps towards heaven; or, practical thoughts on the gospel history* (1849); a best-selling pietistic guide.

[7] Add MS 44738, f. 123–141, with additions by Catherine Gladstone.

[8] Instead of 'the'.

upon his papers last night, which, so much is his mind altered, he contemplates with uneasiness & even with some suspicion. Left at ¼ to 9. Reached Edinburgh ¼ to 4. Saw Dean Ramsay—Mr Reid. Found Bp of Glasgow was absent. Left at 6 for London. Read Maguire—De Imit. Xti.

17. Wed.

Reached home about noon—Worked upon my letters—Saw J.N.G—S. Herbert—Molesworth—Went to the House quietly in case of a vote on Fox's Bill—which there was not.[1] Wrote to R. Phillimore—J. Griffiths—Bp of London—W. Palmer—C. Luxmoore—Goulburn—Borthwick[2]—At 7 went down to Brighton. Found C. better & Mary I hope advanced a little. Finished Maguire.

18. Th.

Wrote to T.G—Sir J.G. Read The Aristocrat on Protection[3]—Jefferson's Sermon[4]—The Federalist[5]—Leon Faucher[6]—Pratt's answer in the case of Wagstaff.[7] Walk with.—[*sic*] Carried Mary out. Dinner & evg with the Lytteltons.

19. Fr.

Wrote to R. Cavendish—Bp of Salisbury—Mr Jefferson[8]—Jas Freshfield—Willy—Mr Jefferson. Walk with C. Read Allies on the Supremacy[9]—Hare's Letter to Cavendish[10]—Lechler's Geschichte des Engl. Deismus (began)[11]—The Federalist. Wrote a little on the Gorham case.[12]

20. Sat.

Wrote to Rn. G—Major Beresford.[13] Read Lechler—the Federalist—Bradford's Letter to Meredith.[14] Wrote on Gorham. Dined with the Lytteltons.

[1] W. J. *Fox's Education Bill: *H* cx. 437.
[2] Peter Borthwick, 1804–52; barrister; tory M.P. Evesham 1835–47; edited *Morning Post* 1850–2.
[3] [J. L. Elliott], *A letter to the electors of Westminster. From an aristocrat* (1850).
[4] J. D. Jefferson, 'A sermon . . . upon the occasion of the deaths of two infants' (1850).
[5] By [A. Hamilton], 2 v. (1788).
[6] Probably his *Histoire financière. De la situation financière et du budget* (1850).
[7] Not found.
[8] Joseph Dunnington Jefferson, 1807–80; vicar of Thorganby, Yorkshire, from 1832, prebendary of York from 1852; cp. previous day's entry.
[9] T. W. Allies, 'The royal supremacy, viewed in reference to the two spiritual powers of order and jurisdiction' (1850).
[10] J. C. *Hare, 'A letter to the Hon. R. Cavendish, on the recent judgment of the court of appeal' (1850).
[11] But see 7 Apr. 50.
[12] Add MS 44738, f. 147.
[13] i.e. (Sir) G. de la P. Beresford.
[14] S. D. Bradford, 'Letters to . . . W. M. Meredith . . . on his recent treasury report' (1850). Reprinted from the *Boston Post.*

21. Sunday 3 S. Easter.

St Paul's (& H.C.) 11–2.—St Mary's aftn. Mr Elliot[1] preached without book: neat but really very superficial: I am told it was a bad specimen. Read Lechler—T.A Kempis—Dr Mills admirable Sermon.[2] Wrote to Dr Mill. Wrote on Gorham Case.

22. M.

St Paul's 7 P.M. Wrote on Gorham case. Walk with C. Dined with the Lytteltons. Read the Federalist.

23. T.

Wrote to C.G—Wm. Gladstone—Vice Chancellor of Oxford—Dr Saunders. Read T.A Kempis—Oxford Remarks on Letter to Ld J.R.[3] Came up by the train at 11: saw Sir R. Inglis—Mr Goulburn—Manning—Cavendish—Walpole—J.G. Hubbard—Wm. Gladstone. H of C. 4¾–12½: on the University motion which brought me very reluctantly to town.[4]

24. Wed.

Dined with the Wortleys (alone). Saw Archdn. Wilberforce—Manning—W. Palmer—R. Phillimore—J.N.G—T.G—C.G. Nicolay—Sir R. Inglis—S.H. Northcote—the Police. Prepared & sent off the little presents for Fasque with notes to W.M. Goalen—Mr Irvine—Hayman—H.J.G. Also wrote to R. Barker—Sir J.G—C.G—Mr Gell. And worked on my arrear of letters and papers: accumulated during the last three weeks.

25. Th. St Mark.

St James's 7 P.M. Read Salomons on Oaths[5]—Oaths Report[6]—Macrobius[7]—Wilberforce on the Sacramental System.[8]

Wrote to C.G.—Griffiths—Sir J. Pakington—Peers[9]—Jervis[10]—D. of Wellington—W.K. Hamilton—Nussey[11]—Dr Rice—Mr Johnstone.

H. of C. 3¾–6.[12] Finished my mournful task, the account of dearest Jessy. Saw Mr Thring on Col. Ch. Clauses—Sir R. Inglis—Mr Goulburn—& (called on) the Duke of Wellington, on Universities—also Tufnell. [Also

[1] Henry Venn *Elliot, 1792–1865; curate of St. Mary's, Brighton, from 1827; a strict evangelical and sabbatarian.

[2] W. H. Mill, 'Human policy and divine truth' (1850); on Luke xxiii. 34.

[3] Not found, but cp. 7 Mar. 50.

[4] *Inglis spoke for Oxford unsuccessfully against the motion for inquiry into university reform: *H* cx. 697.

[5] Untraced pamphlet by Sir David Salomons, Bart.

[6] Select cttee. report on oaths of members: *PP* 1850, xv. 137.

[7] A. M. Macrobius, *Somnium Scipionis ex Ciceronis libro de republica excerptum* (1483).

[8] R. I. *Wilberforce, 'The sacramental system; a sermon on I John iv. 2' (1850).

[9] Probably Charles Peers, 1774–1853; recorder of Henley; sheriff of Oxfordshire 1821.

[10] Sir John *Jervis, 1802–56; lib. M.P. Chester 1832–50; attorney general and Kt. 1846; lord chief justice of common pleas from 1850.

[11] John Nussey, d. 1862; apothecary to the crown, and to the Gladstone children.

[12] Australian Colonies Government Bill: *H* cx. 797.

saw] Badeley—Archdeacon Wilberforce—on Gorham's Case. J. Young—S. Herbert—Major Beresford—J. Manners—on Irish Franchise[1]—Christy on Vancouver's Island.[2] Mr Sydney Turner—Mr Richson[3]—& Ld Kinnaird—on other subjects.

26. Fr.

Wrote to H.J.G.—Robn. G—G. Grant—Chamerozow—Harting[4]—Vicar of Bexhill[5]—Blunt—Farquhar—D. Fergusson—W.F. Campbell—Webster. Breakfasted with Bp of Oxford & Archdn. W. when we discussed the Court of Appeal at much length. Afterwards saw Bp of Exeter, & Bp of Bath & Wells—then from 5 P.M. to 7¼ was with Bps of Exeter & Oxford, Archdeacon W., Page Wood[6] & Palmer, on a plan which seems very good for the Court of Appeal. Also saw the D[ivie] Robertsons—J.N.G.—& Mr Hawkins on Colonial Church. Worked on accounts (house & tradesmen's Bills) Wrote out cards of thanks (112): a mechanical duty, but for much real kindness. Got late to bed.

27. Sat.

Wrote (Brighton) to Sir J.G—H.J.G—T.G—J. Griffiths—M.F. Tupper. Went by the 6 A.M. train to Brighton. Found little Mary now nearly for 3 months a great invalid, had been going back again. I had a letter from my Father calling me to Fasque which was most distressing as evincing I fear an increasing instability of mind. Read Bp of Sydney Correspondence[7]—Cawdrey's Case.[8] Wrote on Gorham a little. Dined with the Lytteltons. Corrected my account of Jessy.

28. 4 S. E[aster].

St Paul's mg. & Holy C. St George's aftn. Wrote to Bp of Oxford. Wrote on the Supremacy.[9] Saw Phillimore. Finished Cawdrey—read Bp of Salisb. Sermon[10]—T.A Kempis.

[1] Cp. *H* cx. 1281.
[2] Samuel Christy, 1811–89; Peelite M.P. for Newcastle-under-Lyme 1847–59; added surname of Miller 1862.
[3] Charles *Richson, 1806–74; clerk of Manchester Collegiate church 1844–54; rector of St. Andrew's, Ancoats, from 1854; educationalist, influenced 1870 Act.
[4] James Vincent Harting, 1812–83; Lincoln's Inn solicitor from 1836, dealing mainly with roman catholic business.
[5] Henry Winckworth Simpson, 1792–1876; rector of Bexhill 1840–76; prebendary of Chichester 1841–76.
[6] Sir John Page Wood, 1796–1866; chaplain to Queen *Caroline 1822; rector of St. Peter's, Cornhill, London, 1824–66; succ. as 2nd Bart. 1843.
[7] W. G. *Broughton, 'Correspondence between . . . [Broughton] and the Revs. F. T. C. Russell and P. T. Beamish, deacons' (1849).
[8] Cp. *Gleanings*, v. 225 n.
[9] The start of his 'Remarks on the royal supremacy as it is defined by reason, history, and the constitution: a letter to the bishop of London' (1850); cp. Add MS 44684, f. 203 and *Gleanings*, v. 173.
[10] E. *Denison, 'Sorrow and consolation' (1850).

29. M.

Wrote to Manning.[1] Walk with C. Wrote on the Supremacy. Read Australian Ch. papers[2]—A Layman on the Independence of Oxford.[3]

Dear little Mary has for many days occasioned uneasiness to Catherine: especially as reflecting the stealthy approach of our Jessy's disease. Mr Taylor[4] however encourages us to believe that the great irritability of her constitution & her weakness are referable to temporary causes the whooping cough in particular. But C. thinks they must all stay here longer on her account. Returned to London by the train at 6.30.—worked at home on papers: and H. of C. 11¾–1¼ (Eccl. Commn. Bill.)[5]

30. T.

Wrote to C.G Rn. G—Mr Grant—Dr Hawkins—Mr Wilkinson—Sir J.G—Saw Rev. Mr Fry[6]—Mr Oldfield—Mr Parish (mad)[7]—Sir J. Pakington—Mr Greswell—Mr W. Forbes—Mr Webster—Sir J. Young—H. of C. 5–7¼. Dined with the Jameses. H. of C. 10½–12. I did not feel enough *in* the question to vote (Henley's motion).[8] Read Blackstone[9]—Irons's Sequel[10]—Sewell on Univ. Constitn.[11] Wrote Mem. on Clydesdale Junction case.[12]

Wed. May One. SS. Philip & James.

St Anne's Soho 8¼ P.M. Wrote to C.G—W.H.G—Chancellor of London University[13]—Saw the Vice Chancr. of Oxford—Redesdale—R W Rawson—Mr. Tyler—A.B. Hope—Read Anderson's Sermons[14]—Redesdale's Observations[15]—Webster's Speech on Slavery (the last part very masculine & fine).[16] House of Commons 2¾–6. Spoke on Railway Traffic Bill—& on Pluralities Bill.[17]

[1] Lathbury, i. 100.
[2] On ecclesiastical sees and jurisdiction: *PP* 1850, xxxvii. 545, 591.
[3] 'The independence of the universities and colleges of Oxford and Cambridge, by a layman' (1838).
[4] Probably Charles Taylor, 1815?–94; surgeon to Royal South London Dispensary and expert on infant fevers and hydrocephalus.
[5] *H* cx. 938.
[6] Probably James Fry, 1817–? *ca.* 55; vicar of Sompting, Sussex, from 1837.
[7] Perhaps John Parish, who lived by the Oak Farm.
[8] On public service salaries and wages: *H* cx. 981.
[9] W. *Blackstone, *Commentaries on the laws of England*, 4 v. (1765–9).
[10] W. J. *Irons, 'Sequel to a pamphlet on the royal supremacy . . . in reply to the Rev. W. *Maskell and the Rev. T. W. Allies' (1850); cp. 19 Apr. 50.
[11] W. *Sewell, 'The university commission; or, Lord John *Russell's post-bag of 27 April 1850' (1850).
[12] In Hawn. P.; on railway amalgamations.
[13] William *Cavendish, 1808–91; 5th earl of Burlington 1834; 7th duke of Devonshire 1858; chancellor of London university 1836–56, of Cambridge 1861–91.
[14] J. S. M. Anderson, *Sermons on various subjects* (1837); or his 'Trials of the church' (1850); two sermons on the *Gorham case.
[15] J. T. Freeman *Mitford, 'Observations on the judgment in the *Gorham case: and the way of unity' (1850).
[16] D. Webster, 'A speech . . . on the subject of slavery'; made in the Senate on 7 March 1850, denouncing peaceable secession.
[17] *H* cx. 1079, 1083.

2. Th.

Wrote to J. Parkinson—R. Williams—Tupper—Eneas Macdonnell—T. Oldfield. Saw R. Phillimore (Gorham)—Archdn. Manning (do)—W.F. Campbell—E. Badeley—Archdn. Wilberforce—Adderley—Molesworth. H. of C. 5¼–7.[1] Dined with JNG. Read Coke's Inst[2]—Dr Hook's Letter[3]—Goode's do to Bp of Exeter.[4] Business. Conv. at night with an unhappy woman [R].

3. Fr.

St Andrew's 5 PM. Wrote to H. Tayleur—W.E. Jelf—C.G—Scotts—Parkinson—Rowsell.[5] Saw Manning (Gorham &c) (to breakfast)—Mr Gell (Austr. Ch.)—Hildyard (Railway purchase).[6] Read Goode to Bp of Exeter (finished)—Dublin Rev. on Gorham Case[7]—Whiston Extract on Jurisdiction of Convocation[8]—Westm[inste]r Rev. on Ch. (began)[9] Calls &c. Arranging letters & accounts.

4. Sat.

Wrote to Messrs. Sir S. Scott & Co—Wm. Forbes—Peel (Golden Square)[10]—Sir J.G.—C.G.[11] Breakfast at Grillions: & dinner at the Royal Academy: there I sat by Disraeli who was very easy & agreeable. A gap on the other side for Graham.[12] 11¼–12¾ with S. Herbert & Mr Reed about the Chapter Clauses.[13] 2¼–5 at the Exhibition: there was much to see. Read Lewis on Supremacy (began)[14]—Westm[inste]r & For. on Church (finished)—Found again the same poor creature at night. She has a son to support: & working *very* hard with her needle *may* reach 6/ per week as a maximum: pays 5/ for lodging—sends her boy to school at 6d a week [R]. Lives No 6 Duke's Court.

5. 5 S. Easter.

Savoy Ch mg. Bedfordbury evg. MS for 4 S. E[aster] aloud to servants.

[1] County Courts Bill: *H* cx. 1110.
[2] By Sir E. *Coke, first published in four parts 1642–4. Used for his 'Supremacy' article.
[3] Cp. 23 Mar. 50.
[4] W. *Goode, 'A letter to the bishop of Exeter' (1850); on *Gorham.
[5] Thomas James Rowsell, 1816–94; vicar of St. Peter's, Stepney, 1844–60; rector of St. Margaret's, Lothbury, 1860–72; a very popular preacher.
[6] George Hildyard, solicitor in Holborn.
[7] *Dublin Review*, xxviii. 234 (March 1850); by *Wiseman; Gladstone found the article 'astounding'; cp. *Gleanings*, v. 242.
[8] W. *Whiston, *Several hundred texts of holy scripture . . . with an extract from the former preface . . . to which is added, the censure of both houses of convocation passed upon him* [Whiston] (1807).
[9] *Westminster Review*, liii. 165; on the condition of the Anglican Church.
[10] John Peel lived in Golden Square, London; possibly the 4th son of the 2nd Bart.
[11] Paragraph in Bassett, 82.
[12] Cp. ibid. 83.
[13] Of the Australian Colonies Government Bill.
[14] J. Lewis, 'Defence of ecclesiastical establishment' (1850).

Tea with the Jameses. Read Lewis (finished)—Chambers [1]—Pusey [2]—Stephen (Eccl. Law) [3] & worked on paper from them.[4] Discussed a new proposal of the Vicar's with James: which will hardly do.[5] Nor do we wish to make any great move at present.

6. M.

Wrote to C.G—Laing—Treasurer Guy's Hospital—E.C. Woollcombe—C. Marriott—Geo. Grant. Saw J.S. Colquhoun & Mr Oldfield (Cl[ydesdale] Junction)—Beresford—Bernard—Mr Lake (Oxf. Comm[issio]n) [6]—Duke of Argyll. Read Parl. Papers on Australian Ch [7]—Caledonian RR. Case & opinion [8]—D. of Argyll on Riland's Case.[9] H. of C. 5–11¾ (Home to Coffee). Spoke briefly on Molesworth's motion and at length on the *just* claim for the freedom of the Church in the Colonies.[10]

7. T.

Wrote to Lincoln—C.G—C.B. Adderley—D. of Buccleuch. Lady Lincoln's divorce pronounced this day in the Eccl. Court. Saw G. Hope (to breakfast—about his brother)—Messrs. Johnstone, Colquhoun & Oldfield (C. J[unction] Shares) & prepared Memorandum [11]—S. Herbert & Reed (Cathedral Clauses)—Duke of Argyll (Riland's Cse)—A. Stafford (Irish Registration)—Archdn. Hale (Subdiaconate.) D. of Buccleuch on Irish Registration. Ld Stanley on do (at his home)—Young, Herbert, Thesiger, & Jocelyn on do—Molesworth Adderley & others on Australian Bill. H. of C. 5½–7¼.[12] Dined quietly with the Herberts. Read Pusey—& Wilson's (half-mad) pamphlet.[13]

8. Wed.

Wrote to C.G. Dined at [Sir G.] Grey's—Then to Graphic Society [14]—& Devonshire House—but left at 10½. S.R.G. & Lyttelton to breakfast. Saw Adderley on Austr. Bill—Simeon,[15] on do—Beresford, on Irish Franchise—Capt. Plunkett, on Caledonian RR—J.N.G. on family matters—Redesdale,

[1] J. D. Chambers, 'A review of the *Gorham case' (1850).

[2] E. B. *Pusey, 'The royal supremacy not an arbitrary authority but limited by the laws of the church of which kings are members' (1850).

[3] A. J. Stephens, *Ecclesiastical statutes*, 2 v. (1845); cp. *Gleanings*, v. 187ff.

[4] Cp. 28 Apr. 50.

[5] On the Leicester Square church.

[6] i.e. W. C. *Lake.

[7] Cp. 29 Apr. 50 n.

[8] Not found; under Plunkett the company's affairs improved and payments to debenture holders were renewed; cp. 30 Jan. 50.

[9] Cp. 22 Mar. 49.

[10] Moving a new clause and several provisos: *H* cx. 1195.

[11] In Hawn P.

[12] Moved an amndt. to the Australian Colonies Government Bill to permit the meeting of episcopal chapters: *H* cx. 1207; the amndt. was defeated in 187:102.

[13] F. Wilson, 'A letter to the Rev. William Gresley' (1850); violently anti-tractarian.

[14] Cp. 14 Feb. 49.

[15] See 26 July 50 n.

on Gorham Case—Sir G. Grey on Ch Clauses—Goulburn—Stafford—Worked on Australian papers & Bishop's Clauses.[1]

9. Ascension Day.

Wells St (& H.C.) at 11 A.M. SRG.—J.N.G—Sir J. Young—dined. Saw Mrs Larkins—calls—Saw Ld Aberdeen—J. Young—Sir F. Thesiger—Stafford—House 4½–6½.[2] Read & worked on Australian papers—& framed motion for Monday.[3] Read Wilberforce's Sermons—The Federalist—Strena Poetica.[4] Wrote to C.G—Sir JG—T.G—Sir W. James—Manning—H. Taylor—Warner—Clarke—Mr Kennaway.

10. Fr.

Wrote to C.G—Dr [J.L.] Richards. H. of C. 4¼–7¼ and 9¼–12½. Voted in 186:254 agt Irish Franchise Bill.[5] 11½–2 with Messrs. Colquhoun & Oldfield, also Capt. Plunkett, endeavouring the adjust the Clydesdale Junction affair: & drew Mema.[6] Saw S. Herbert—Goulburn—Sir G. Grey & Hawes on Col. Ch. Clauses. Read The Federalist. Much dissatisfied with Sir J. Graham's Speech: but I did not like to repeat the part that fell to me on Disraeli's motion.[7] H.S. with Agnes & Stephen.

11. Sat.

St Anne's 8¼ P.M. Wrote to Ld Brooke[8]—Paterson—Ld Aberdeen—Ld Kinnaird—Riddell—Hildyard—Hartung[9]—Rev. Mr Haddan—Rev Mr Chaplin[10]—Rev Mr Phillips[11]—Rev Mr Hoskin[12]—Dr Jelf—Mr Anderson—(Capt?) Hope.[13] Saw Ld Aberdeen (Irish Franchise, & Buxton's motion)[14]—J. Young—G. Grant (my affairs)—W.F. Campbell—R. Lowe (from N.S.W.)—J.N.G. Calls. H.S. with Agnes & Stephen. Read the Federalist—Story on Amn. Constitution[15]—Cavendish's letter to Hare[16]—Grinfield's Letter.[17]—Taylor's Virgin Widow.[18]

[1] Cp. Add MS 44738, ff. 87–95.
[2] Irish voters: *H* cx. 1281.
[3] A further attempt at amndt; cp. 2 days previously and *H* cx. 1398.
[4] By [H. Kynaston] (1849).
[5] *H* cx. 1369.
[6] Hawn P.
[7] Cp. 21 Feb. 50.
[8] George Guy Greville, 1818–93; styled Lord Brooke until 1853 when he succ. as 4th earl of Warwick; tory M.P. Warwickshire 1845–53.
[9] *Sc.* Harting.
[10] Edward John Chaplin, 1812–53; fellow of Magdalen College, Oxford, 1836–52.
[11] Cp. 13 Apr. 34.
[12] Peter Charles Mellish Hoskin, 1816–95; curate of St. Peter's, Regent Square, 1842–5; vicar of Whittlesford, Cambridge, 1845–62, of Great Malvern 1862–8.
[13] Unclear which; perhaps involved in the Clydesdale arbitration.
[14] E. N. Buxton's motion on sugar protection; not moved until 31 May 1850: *H* cxi. 528.
[15] J. Story, *Commentaries on the constitution of the United States*, 3 v. (1833).
[16] R. Cavendish, 'A letter to Archdeacon *Hare on the judgment in the *Gorham case' (1850); cp. 19 Apr. 50.
[17] E. W. *Grinfield, 'An expostulatory letter to . . . *Wiseman . . . on the interpolated curse in the Vatican Septuagint' (1850).
[18] By Henry *Taylor (1850); a play.

12. S. after Ascension.

St Andrew's 11 AM—St Martins 3. PM. MS of 42 aloud.

I did not go to Holy Commn. for I have had much wicked negligence to reproach myself with of late as respects particular temptations: & though desiring that heavenly food I thought reverence required a longer consideration. Worked much on the Supremacy papers & Extracts. Read Wilberforce's Sermons[1]—Wordsworth Trin Coll Sermon[2]—Cranoe Church Sermons.[3]

13. M.

Wrote to T.G. (2)—J. Griffiths—Greswell. Read Story on Constn. of U.S. H.S. with A. & S. Saw Adderley—J.N.G—Farquhar—Wrote some verses about Jessy: almost the first for 12 years.[4] H. of C. 4½–7¾ and 9–12. Spoke 1½ hour on Austr. Col. Bill: to an indifferent & inattentive House. But it is necessary to speak these truths of Colonial policy even to unwilling ears.[5] C.G. returned: Mary thank God much better.

14. T.

Uncle Divie died 2½ A.M. Wrote to D. Robertson—Rev. A.W. Haddan—H. Tayleur. Saw A. Kinnaird & Mr Swift—Mr T. Oldfield—Lyttelton & E.G. Wakefield—Sir F. Thesiger & W.P. Wood—Simeon—R. Cavendish & M.W. Mayow—Read Corry on Visi[ta]torial power[6]—& Letter on Assessed Taxes.[7] The Lytteltons & S.R.G. dined. H. of C. 4½–6¾ and 10½–2¼. Voted in 298:184 agt. Committee on Corn Laws.[8] H.S. with Agnes.

15.

Wrote to R. Neville—Scotts—Dean of Windsor—R. Barker—& saw Ld Wenlock & Lyttelton—on S.R.G.s affairs. Dined with the Wenlocks. Saw Archd. Hale—J.N.G—Messrs. Tatham—S.R.G—W.C. James—Ld Wenlock. H.S. with Agnes. Wrote also to JNG—Sir J.G—D. Fergusson—D.A. Irvine—Earl Grey—W. Forbes—Sir J. Forbes—E. Hawkins—Mr. F. Harris.

[1] R. I. *Wilberforce, *Sermons on the new birth of man's nature* (1850).

[2] Charles *Wordsworth, 'A sermon preached on the occasion of the offertory directed to be made throughout the dioceses of . . . Scotland, on behalf of Trinity College, Glenalmond' (1850).

[3] Sermons preached at the consecration of Cranoe church, Lincolnshire, founded 1849 by J. H. *Hill.

[4] Add MS 44738, f. 143.

[5] He proposed an amndt., seconded by *Roebuck, to allow Australians to consider the bill before its enactment. Gladstone and *Roebuck were the tellers in the amndt.'s defeat in 128 to 226: *H* cx. 1384.

[6] G. L. Corrie, *Brief historical notices of the interference of the crown with the affairs of the English universities* (1839).

[7] Not found.

[8] *H* cxi. 97.

16. Th.

Wrote to S.R.G—Scotts—Rob. Phillimore—Kynaston—H.S. with Agnes. In the City: saw Freshfield—Overends—: saw also Page Wood—J. Young. H. of C. 4½–5½ and 9½–1.[1] Dined at Ld Mahon's: Antiquarian Society afterwards.[2] Read Williams to the Provost of Eton[3]—Virgin Widow (finished)—

17. Fr.

Wrote to Freshfield—Lyttelton—R. Barker—Sir J.G—T.G—T.C. Huddlestone—D. Robertson. Saw S. Herbert—Ld Aberdeen—Goulburn—G. Burnett—W.F. Campbell. Attended S.P.G.[4] H of C. 4½–7.[5] Read Whewell II on Cambridge Edn.[6]—J. Manners's Ballads.[7] Gave notice of Bps' Clauses in Eccl Commn. Bill. Whether the thing will be done this way I do not feel sure: but I think it will be done in no other.[8] A few songs at night: the first during this anxious winter & spring.

18. Sat.

Wrote to Freshfield—Hoares—Overends—Dr Hawtrey—Ch. Ch. Broadway 6 P.M. The Lytteltons dined. Chess with George. S. Herbert came in, & we conversed on Church & public affairs till past midnight. Read Mr Venn's Letter to Sir R. Inglis.[9] Worked through most of the morning & day on my accounts for 1849, waiting till this date. H.S. with Agnes.

19. Whitsunday.

St Martin's & H.C. 11–2. Bedforbury evg.—MS of /47 aloud in evg. Wrote draft to Mr Venn—also Draft of proposed engagement[10]—Saw Cavendish on Gorham Case—engagement—Simeon, on do—W.C. James on Leicester Square Church—& on Engagement.

20. M. Whitmonday.

Wrote to R. Barker—G.C. Lewis + (2)[11]—W.F. Campbell—Sir R. Inglis—H. Venn (copy fm dft)[12] H.S. with Agnes. Worked further on draft Engagement—& on Colonial Church Claims. Saw Lyttelton (Engagement)—

[1] Marriages Bill: *H* cxi. 112.
[2] C. W. Martin, M.P., read a paper on crucifixion nails; cp. *Proceedings of the society of antiquaries of London*, ii. 78.
[3] Untraced.
[4] Report on the *Colonial Church Chronicle*, iii. 480 (June 1850).
[5] Ireland: *H* cxi. 171.
[6] The second volume of W. *Whewell, *Of a liberal education in general*; cp. 13 Jan. 48.
[7] Lord J. J. R. *Manners, *English ballads and other poems* (1850).
[8] Gladstone's amndt., moved and withdrawn on 15 July 1850, enabled the commissioners to endow new Bishops with limited incomes and no seats in the Lords: *H* cxi. 1406.
[9] H. *Venn, 'Colonial church legislation; a letter to Sir Robert *Inglis, Bart.' (1850).
[10] Amongst tractarians to delay action on *Gorham for two months; cp. Purcell, i. 538; different from the engagement brotherhood, cp. 23 Feb. 45.
[11] '+ No 2 cancelled' added at foot of page.
[12] Draft in Add MS 44369, f. 212.

Monsell (do)—Wegg Prosser (do)—Mr Bennett (do)—Oldfield. St Paul's Knightsbridge at 5 AM [*sc.* PM] for the Baptism of John's twins, I being godfather to the elder, Constance Edith.[1] Went to his house for *Caudle*[2] after the service: wh was performed most impressively by Mr Bennett. Dined at Lady Vernon's—Began Allen on the Royal Prerogative (& reviews &c. of do).[3]

21. Whittuesday.

St Andrews 5 P.M. At 9½ went to Uncle D[ivie']s funeral at Kensall Green. To me it was Jessy's over again: & I was at Fasque. But I have a grateful affection for him. Wrote to T.G—Sir J.G—B. Hawes—De Tabley—Willy—Mozley—Knight—Saw Powis—Cardwell—Read Hastings's Letter to Claughton[4]—Allen, & Berenger on do[5]—Le Maistre (la France)[6]—

22. Wed.

Wrote to H.J.G—Aunt J.—Freshfield—Hoares—H.S. with Agnes—Worked upon my Will—In the City: saw Longden[7]—J.N.G—W.C. James & Mr Walker—Mr Tyler. Dined with the Wenlocks—Read Allen on Prerogative.

23. Th.

Wrote to Manning—F.R. Wegg Prosser—Simmons[8]—Rn. G. Six to dinner—for the Macinroys. H.S. with A. & Stephen. Saw De Tabley—Cavendish—F.R. Wegg Prosser—Badeley—H.W. Wilberforce (on *Rome* & the Gorham Case) H. of C. 4½–6½.[9] Read Greek Blue Book[10]—Allen—Morality of Tractarianism.[11] Attended Parish Meeting for a Visiting Association.[12]

24. Fr.

Wrote to J.N.G—Sir J.G—Sir R. Inglis—E. Hill—W. Dyke—P. Black[13]—

[1] He had conflated his godchild's name from Constance Elizabeth, d. unmarried (his godchild) and Edith Helen, 1850–1941, who m. 1870 William Alexander Dumaresq, 1839–80, Inner Temple barrister from 1858.

[2] A warmed, spiced gruel with wine.

[3] J. *Allen, *Inquiry into the rise and growth of the royal prerogative in England* (1830); the 1849 ed. has comments by, *inter alia*, M. Bérenger; cp. *Gleanings*, v. 245.

[4] H. J. Hastings, 'Reasons for not signing the proposed address to the bishop of Worcester . . . in a letter to T. L. *Claughton' (1850); on the *Gorham case.

[5] See n. on previous day.

[6] Joseph, comte de Maistre. *Considerations sur la France* (1796); cp. *Gleanings*, v. 288.

[7] Thomas Hayter Longden, stockbroker.

[8] (Sir) John Lintorn Arabin *Simmons, 1821–1903; sec. to railway commissioners 1847–54; commissioner in Turkey 1854; sundry military and diplomatic posts; field marshal 1890.

[9] Greece: *H* cxi. 237.

[10] The original Blue Book on *Pacifico was published in February 1850, and supplemented in April, May and June: *PP* 1850, lvi. 43–857.

[11] By [Augusta T. *Drane] (1850); sometimes wrongly attributed to J. H. *Newman.

[12] No report found.

[13] Patrick *Black, 1813–79; Christ Church; physician at St. Bartholomew's from 1842; wrote on chloroform.

Taunton—J.P. Gell—H.S. with W. & A. Worked on accounts of property & expenditure: now finished. Finished my draft of a Will. Saw R. Phillimore—Sir G. Grey—Sir J. Young—Mr Goulburn. H. of C. 4½–6¾. Read Row's Letter to Inglis[1]—Allen on the Prerogative (finished)—Dyce Sermon.[2]

25. Sat.

Wrote to G. Dundas[3]—Bowdler—Highfield[4]—Peers—De Tabley. H.S. with Agnes. Saw Lyttelton—Courtenay & Wakefield on N.Z[5]—Mr C. Uppington—Mr J. Parkinson—R. Cavendish—Wodehouse. Dined at Ld Wenlock's. Looked into Phillimore's notes & books & began to *re*write on the Supremacy.[6] Read Bisset on Univ. Reform[7]—Ceylon Committee 12¾–3½.

26. Trin. S.

St Andrew's Wells St 11–2. Bedfordbury evg. Ms of 40 aloud to servants. Mary's fourth daughter born.[8] Saw S. Herbert—Sir W. James & Lady James on a family matter & after convn. wrote a draft proposed to be sent to Mr Edwardes.[9] Worked on the Supremacy: and fear that I must re-re-write.

27. M.

Wrote to Lady James. H.S. with the children. Ceylon Committee & House 12½–6½.[10] Read Greek papers—Bp Wiseman (2d) on the Supremacy[11]—Saw W.C. James mg & evg & worked on his matter—saw Sir J. Young—Worked on the Supremacy.

28. T.

H.S. with the children. Read Mr E. Stanley[12]—Pusey on Suprem.[13]—Randall.[14] Saw W. James—the Uppingtons—Lyttelton—Mr L. Walker—

[1] C. A. Row, 'Letter to Sir R. H. *Inglis, Bart., in reply to his speech on university reform' (1850).
[2] Untraced.
[3] George Dundas, curate of Myton-on-Swale, Yorkshire, curate of St. Matthew's, Nottingham, from 1855.
[4] Perhaps George Highfield, London hatter.
[5] Cp. Morrell, 324ff.
[6] Cp. Add MS 44684, ff. 203–8.
[7] T. Bisset, 'Suggestions on university reform. A letter' (1850).
[8] Mary Catherine Lyttelton, d. unm. 1875.
[9] Perhaps the start of the procedure by which Gladstone became guardian to James's children, cp. 31 Aug. 53; perhaps Edwin Edwards, 1823–79, proctor and notary.
[10] Spoke on the Chester Railway: *H* cxi. 385.
[11] Cp. 3 May 50.
[12] E. H. S. *Stanley, 'Claims and resources of the West Indian Colonies. A letter to . . . W. E. Gladstone' (1850).
[13] Cp. 5 May 50.
[14] J. Randall, 'A letter to the Ven. E. Berens . . . on the constitution of the ultimate court of appeal in causes ecclesiastical' (1850).

Lord Aberdeen—De Tabley. House of Lords 3–5 to be examined on poor Lincoln's Divorce Bill[1] H. of C. afterwards.[2] Worked on the Supremacy—but at mere fragments & scraps of time.

29. Wed.

Wrote to H. Tayleur—Johnson & Longden—R. Phillimore—Wilson Patten—Bennett—Cubitt[3]—Finished Stanley—H.S. with A. & Stephen—Saw Sir R. Peel—Thesiger—Parkinson—on the provision for Lady Lincoln: which we have now to settle of necessity on our own responsibility.[4] Also Sir W. James—Lord Mansfield—on this affair with Mr E[dwardes].[5] Also Mrs Chisholm—Mr E. Wodehouse—Goulburn. Dined with the Kerrisons. Worked a good deal & with more advance on the Supremacy.

30. Th.

Wrote to Sir J.G—Scotts—Ld Aberdeen—Mr Chalmers[6]—H.S. with the children—Saw W. Forbes—Parkinson—Goulburn—Sir R. Peel (Lincoln's Divorce)—Lefevre—Wilson Patten (L's Divorce)—H. of C. 12–2 and 5–8.[7] Worked on the Supremacy—and references connected with it.

31. Friday.

Wrote to Sir J.G. H.S. with the children. Saw R. Phillimore (on my MS.)—Monsell & De Vere (on the proposed engagement)[8]—Goulburn Cardwell & S. Herbert on Buxton's motion—also Lord Aberdeen—Mr Ellison—Worked on The Supremacy—Attended meeting at St Paul's Knightsbridge respecting a projected Church engagement. 8½–9¼: obliged to go back to the H. of Commons. Attended H. of C. 5¼–7¾ and 9½–1½. Spoke (1½) for Sir E. Buxton's motion: not now a very easy or pleasant subject. Voted for it in 234:275.[9]

Home with Herbert after the division: tea & conv. on parties: we agreed that they are essentially *two*: & that Govt. must be carried on in this country by the less pronounced portion of each in turn: as matters now stand. Worked on W.I. facts & figures.

In concluding this month I will put down a new rule which suggested itself to me on Monday to help me in that important & difficult work keeping guard in respect of impurity. My practice of marking days of failure has become ineffective & I trust it may be less so if I try to avoid the cause viz. an indefiniteness & uncertainty [of] what ought to be marked. I now think of marking days in two classes: one those of distinct offence against my rules:[10]

[1] The bill's 1° and 2°; not reported in *H*; copy of evidence in Hawn P. Gladstone quoted from this journal to establish 2 August 1848 as date of Lady Lincoln's elopement.

[2] Misc. business: *H* cxi. 437.

[3] William Cubitt, 1791–1863; builder; Peelite M.P. Andover 1847–61, 1862–3.

[4] A dispute over whether she should have £900 *p.a.* from her husband; cp. Add MS 44369, f. 283.

[5] See entry four days previously.

[6] Perhaps Patrick Chalmers, 1802–54; lib. M.P. Montrose 1835–42; antiquarian; seat at Auldbar, by Brechin.

[7] Spoke briefly on universities: *H* cxi. 457.

[8] See 19 May 50.

[9] Cp. 11 May 50, and *H* cxi. 580.

[10] See list before 1 June 50 and 26 Oct. 45.

the other that of ill impressions without such distinctness of offence. Thus I hope to cover the debateable ground—which may God prosper in me.

[The back fly-leaf contains:—]

To Richard Hayman
Fasque April 13
1850
from W.E. Gladstone
in token of his regard,
and in acknowledgement of kindness
........rendered to his daughter Catherine Jessy
while living, and when dead.

[and in pencil:—]

James on the Collects

Learn to Die

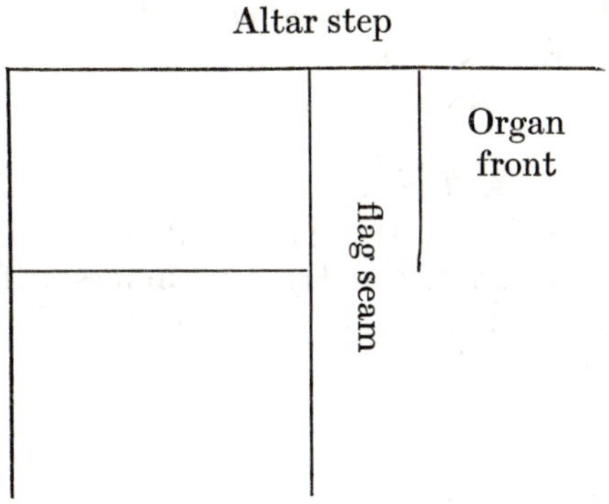

Altar step

Organ front

flag seam

[VOLUME XVI][1]

NO. 16.

JUN. 1. 50 TO FEB. 29. 52.

June 1 + 4 + 6 + 7 + 10 + 11 + 13 ♄ + 19 + 20 + 21 + 22 ♄ + [2]

SATURDAY JUNE ONE 1850. LONDON.

H.S. with W. & A. Wrote to H. Tayleur—Rn. G—J.P. Gell—Mirfield—Randall—Edmonstone—Lawn[3]—Sproule[4]—H.E. Manning[5]—Bp of Glasgow. Read Collier—The Questioner questioned.[6] Saw R. Phillimore—R. Cavendish—Mr Chaffers[7]—Acland. Irish Franchise meeting at 5¾ (S. Herbert's)—Dined with the Wenlocks. Correcting, but slowly, MS. on supremacy.

2. 1 S. Trin.

St Martins & H.C. 11–2. Bedfordbury evg. Saw Archd. Manning—R. Cavendish—Capt. Barclay—the Jameses (Edwards) Wrote to Bp of London. Worked all spare time in correcting my paper on the Supremacy: & finished it. MS of 1840 aloud in evg.

3. M.

Wrote to Bp of Oxford (2)—J. Murray—Rev. J. Gladstone—Willy—Lady Kerrison—Finch—Dr Whewell. H.S. with Agnes. Saw Mr Swabey[8]—S. Herbert—Mr Gell—Parkinson (twice)—Mr Ranken—Wilson Patten—Phillimore. Read Baron Alderson's Letter[9]—Searching Strype,[10] Gibson,[11] &c. and further correcting my MS. 5 to dinner. H. of C. & Commee. 2–7¼ and 10¼–12½.[12] Afterwards heard the disastrous news of the division in the Lords 84:51. I heard the most important parts of the debate: greatly pleased & not less shocked.[13]

[1] Lambeth MS 1430, 136 ff.

[2] This line, faintly in pencil, at top of inside fly-leaf. It indicates days of 'distinct offence against my rules'; cp. 31 May 50. Table continued below, iv. 398.

[3] Perhaps Benjamin Lawn, Cheapside bootmaker.

[4] George Thomas Paterson Sproule, lecturer at St. Leonards-on-sea; from 1855 rector of St. Olave, Southwark.

[5] In Lathbury, ii. 26.

[6] 'The questioner questioned: or, a few inquiries concerning the commission of inquiry: by a member of convocation' (1850).

[7] Thomas Chaffers, 1813–?60; fellow of Brasenose, Oxford, 1836–60; proctor 1846.

[8] Henry Swabey, 1826–78; curate in London 1849, rector of St. Aldate's, Oxford, 1850–6; secretary S.P.C.K. 1863–78.

[9] [Sir E. H. *Alderson], 'A letter to the bp. of Exeter' (1850); on the *Gorham case.

[10] John *Strype, *Life of *Grindal* (1710); cp. *Gleanings*, v. 264.

[11] E. *Gibson, *Codex Juris Ecclesiae Anglicanae* (1713).

[12] Misc. business: *H* cxi. 709.

[13] The rejection of the 2° of *Blomfield's bill to amend the law of appeal to the privy council on matters of doctrine: *H* cxi. 598.

4. T.

Wrote to Murray—Wade—Mackenzie—Coutts—Lake—Tupper—R. Wilberforce—C.D. Hope[1]—(Rev. Mr) James. Saw W.K. Hamilton—R. Cavendish—Mr Jas Edmonstone—(Hon & Rev) F. Grey—Goulburn—G.C. Glyn—Ld Hardinge. H.S. with Agnes. Read Pusey on the Supremacy. H. of C. 4¼–7 and at night.[2] Calls.—Arranging letters & documents.

5. Wed.

Wrote to V.C. Oxford—Robn. G—J. Murray—J.P. Gell. H.S. with the children. Saw Bp of Toronto—S.H. Northcote—S. Herbert—Freshfield (C.)—Johnson & Longden—(in the city). H. of Commons 2¾–6.[3] Went to Ld Wenlock's in evg. And at night had a long & interesting conv. with S. Herbert on the very menacing affairs of the Church. Read Whewell—Pusey on Supry.[4]—Hoare's Letters to Sir G. Grey.[5]

6. Th.

Wrote to Orger & Meryon[6]—W. Wainwright—W.C. James—L. Walker (draft)—S.H. Northcote—Ed. Times.[7] H.S. with the children. Attended Servant's Prov. Meeting 3¾–5½. Ceylon Commee. 12¼–3. House 9½–11¼.[8] Saw Bonham—Oldfield—Lowe. Dined at Ld Wenlock's. Commenced correcting proof sheets. Read the Donoso Cortes.[9]

7. Fr.

Wrote to E. Hill—H. Tayleur—Mr Hoare—Capt. Simmons—T. Goalen—Bp of Oxford. Corrected my proof-sheets. Saw Lyttelton—Manning—R. Barker—Capt. Plunkett & Mr Graham—E.L. Robertson—Mr Pritt's Clerk. Conv. with E. Bruce on Gorham Case[10]—Cardwell on Finance—Sir A. Dalrymple & Major Whyte.[11] H. of C. 9¼–12¼. I gave a vote for the Burial Tax in 126:88 as thinking it just yet with reluctance for it places the endowment on a most invidious & precarious footing: and it seems to be trying to lay fresh foundation stones when the ground is so nearly cut away.[12] Read Bp of Ossory's Charge.[13]

[1] Unidentified.
[2] Irish poor law: *H* cxi. 723.
[3] Education Bill: *H* cxi. 756.
[4] Cp. 5 May 50.
[5] By W. H. *Hoare (1850); on baptismal regeneration.
[6] Booksellers in Fenchurch Street.
[7] Probably not printed, but possibly the letter by 'Oxoniensis' on Oxford fellowship reforms, printed on 10 June 1850, 5c.
[8] Factories Bill: *H* cxi. 823.
[9] *Coleccion escojida de los escritos del Sr. D. Juan Donoso Cortés*, 2 v. (1848).
[10] i.e. Lord E. A. C. B. Bruce.
[11] Perhaps Robert Dennis White, major 1846, London agent for E.I. army.
[12] *H* cxi. 927.
[13] No charge traced for J. T. O'Brien in this year; perhaps his 'Speech [to] the church education society for Ireland' (1850).

8. Sat.

St Andrew's Wells St 5 P.M. Wrote to J.N.G—J. Murray—W.C. James—Napier—Ld Aberdeen. H.S. with the children. Saw R. Barker & Mr Ford—Mr Greswell—J.S. Lefevre on Univv.—S. Herbert on my pamphlet in which at his instance I made some further corrections to stop alarm. Ceylon Committee 12½–4. Read Pusey on Supremacy.

9. 2 S. Trin.

St Martin's H.C. 8½ A.M.—St James's 11 A.M—Bedfordbury 7 P.M. MS. for St Barnabas aloud. Saw Bp of Brechin—H.E. Manning—W.C. James. Read Donoso Cortes—Prayerbook of the Oratorians.[1] Walk with C.G. Corrected Revises.

10. M.

Wrote to E.G. Wakefield—J. Murray. H.S. with the children. Commee. 2–4. H. of C. & Lords 5–7½.[2] Saw T. Goalen—J.G. Hubbard—Bp of Salisbury—Bp of Oxford—Mr Oldfield—Capt. Plunkett—Mr Beachcroft—Mr Hodgson—Mr Richards. Read Whewell Cambr. Edn. (finished)[3]—Harrison's Charge[4]—Lady Dysart's in evg.

11. T. St Barnabas.

Late for the Consecration.[5] Went to St James's at 11. H.S. with the children. Wrote to Rn. G—G. & Co—Bp of London—S. Herbert—T. Stephen—Johnson & Longden—T. Goalen—Sec. L. & NW Co. Visited Mr Metcalfe's pictures. Ceylon Commee. 2½–4¼. Saw Mr Page Wood—Bp of Oxford. Dined at Merch. Tailor's Hall.[6] Read Ld Wharncliffe to Sir J. Graham.[7] The Age.[8]

12. Wed.

Wrote to Archdn. Manning—Sir J.G—J. Moss. H.S. with the children. Saw R. Cavendish—S. Herbert—Simeon—Mr J A Smith with Mr Aglionby—Mr Bernal. Ceylon Commee. 12–3. 8 to dinner. Read Bp Selwyn's Letter to Coleridge[9]—Fielding.

[1] Probably 'The primitive liturgy and eucharist . . . for the use of the oratory' (1726), reprinted in P. Hall, *Fragmenta Liturgica*, iv. (1848).
[2] In the Commons, the new Houses of Parliament, in the Lords the Australian Bill: *H* cxi. 956–82.
[3] Cp. 13 Jan. 48.
[4] B. *Harrison, 'The church the guardian of her children' (1850).
[5] Of St. Barnabas, Pimlico, to which the Rose Street house of charity was attached.
[6] Report in *The Times*, 12 June 1850, 8c.
[7] Probably an MS.
[8] [P. J. Bailey], *The Age* (1829); a poem.
[9] Untraced letter by G. A. Selwyn.

13. Th.

Wrote to W. Forbes—T.G—Mr Pascoe.[1] H.S. with Agnes. Read Montaigne[2]—Lewis on Supremacy[3]—Eccl. Courts Reports[4]—M'Lean on Hudson's Bay Territory[5]—Genin's Memoir of Marguerite de Valois.[6] Committees 12–2. Canada Univ. meeting to 3. H. of C. 11¼–1.[7] Dined at Ld R. Grosvenor's.

14. Fr.

St Barnabas 11–2 A.M. [*sc.* P.M.] Wrote to Johnson Longden & Co—Glyn Halifax & Co[8]—R. Williams—E. Monro—L. Walker[9]—G. Finch (and draft)[10] Read M'Lean's Hudson's Bay. Dined at Lyttelton's. Saw J.N.G—Factory Delegates.[11] H. of C. 4¾–7 and 9–11¼.[12]

15. Sat.

St Barnabas 7 P.M. H.S. with children. Exhibn. Commee &c 2¼–3¾. Worked on Statutes & Palmer[13]—for the great Church question: began a new MS.[14] Read Ld Lindsay's pamphlet.[15] Saw J.N.G—S. Herbert—D. Robertson. Wrote to T.G—Mr Hallam[16]—G. Finch—G. Burnett. Walk with C.

16. 3 S. Trin.

St Martin's & H.C. 11–2. Bedfordbury evg. MS of 1842 aloud in evg. Tea with the Jameses. Walk with C. & the children. Saw Bp of Brechin—Lyttelton—Read Strype[17]—'Controv. on Interim State'.[18] Wrote on the present controversy.

17. M.

Wrote to Mr Swabey—H.J.G—Messrs. Glyn & Co—Dean Barber—Mr G.C. Glyn—Mr L. Walker. H.S. with the children. Saw R. Phillimore—

[1] Francis Polkinghorne *Pascoe, 1813–93; made large entomological collection.
[2] M. de Montaigne, *Essais* (1850).
[3] Cp. 4 May 50.
[4] For England: *PP* 1850, xiii. 886; for Ireland: *PP* 1850, li. 395; for Australia: *PP* 1850, xxxvii. 591.
[5] J. *McLean *Notes of a twenty-five years' service in the Hudson's Bay Territory*, 2 v. (1849).
[6] F. Génin, *Lettres de Marguerite d'Angoulême* (1841); with an introduction.
[7] Marriages Bill: *H* cxi. 1179.
[8] The London banking firm of Sir Richard Plumptre Glyn, 1787–1863; 2nd Bart. 1838.
[9] Draft on the Leicester Square church: Add MS 44369, f. 258.
[10] Add MS 44369, f. 264 and in Lathbury, i. 108.
[11] Presumably on the Factories Bill.
[12] Factories Bill: *H* cxi. 1234.
[13] Probably *sc.* Parker; cp. *Gleanings,* v. 184 n.
[14] Cp. 29 Apr. 50 n.
[15] A. W. C. Lindsay, 'A brief analysis of the doctrine and argument in the case of *Gorham v. the bishop of Exeter' (1850).
[16] Lathbury, i. 110.
[17] Cp. 3 June 50.
[18] Not found.

Mr Cattley [1] (from Mr Swabey—Mr Hawes. Committee 7 H. of C. & L. 1–8. Ld Stanley made on the Greek question the finest speech I ever heard from him—H. of C. and H. of L. 10¼–1¾.[2] Read Dodsworth's Letter to Pusey [3]—M'Lean's Hudson's Bay Territory.

18. T.

Wrote to Woods & Works [4]—Johnson Longden & Co—Manning—Sir J.G. H.S. with the children. Saw Mr Oldfield—Mr Hubbard—E.L. Robertson—Mr Parkinson—Mr Adams (Woods)—Mr Hawes—Lyttelton—Goulburn—Sir R. Peel. H. of C. 4¼–7¼.[5] Read Bp of Ripon's Pastoral Letter.[6] Fane on Minr. of Justice [7]—M'Lean.

19. Wed.

Wrote to Dr Richards—Rev. W.U. Richards—Mr Strong—A. Watson—Willy. Saw Dr Mill, Mr Hubbard, Jas Hope, on the Gorham case—S. Herbert—H. of C. 12–4½ (& Committees).[8] Dined at Ld Wenlock's. Read Greek papers—Jordan's Appeal [9]—Keyser on Stock Exchange.[10]

20. Th.

Wrote to Sir J.G—C.G—T.G. H.S. with children. Saw Alex. Hope. Went out to breakfast with Milnes to meet Mr Prescott [11]—Saw Young evg. Worked on Greek papers. H. of C. 4½–7½. C.G. went off unexpectedly to Hagley to nurse Lady G. Read Watson's reply to Goode [12]—Greek papers.

21. Fr.

Wrote to Manning—Scotts—Glyn & Co—Parkinson—Ld Seymour—Mrs Bowyer.[13] H.S. with children. At 10 to Ld Abns (Green) [14]—11–1 Sir R. Peel's (Lincoln) [15]—also saw [16] Young—Herbert. Exhib. Commn. & House

[1] Stephen Read Cattley or Catley, b. *ca.* 1805; Queens', Cambridge; rector of Baythorpe, Norfolk, 1832–57; chaplain to Lambeth female lunatic asylum 1842–57; curate, St. John's, Clapham, 1857–68; rector, Fittleworth, Sussex, 1868–76.

[2] In the Lords, *Pacifico, in the Commons, Ireland: *H* cxi. 1293, 1405.

[3] W. *Dodsworth, 'A letter to . . . E. B. *Pusey on the position which he has taken in the present crisis' (1850); cp. Liddon, iii. 262.

[4] William Adams, principal clerk of Woods and Works.

[5] Indian cotton: *H* cxii. 10.

[6] C. T. *Longley, 'A pastoral letter to the clergy . . . of Ripon' (1850).

[7] Cp. 26 June 48.

[8] Scottish schools: *H* cxii. 75.

[9] J. Jordan, 'An appeal to the . . . evangelical clergy' (1850); on *Gorham.

[10] H. Keyser, *The law relating to transactions on the stock exchange* (1850).

[11] Probably Henry James Prescott, 1802–56; director of the bank of England 1836–56, governor 1849–50.

[12] A. *Watson, 'An apology for the plain sense of the doctrine of the prayer book on holy baptism, in answer to . . . W. *Goode' (1850).

[13] Charlotte, *née* Wells, m. 1844 William Henry Wentworth Bowyer, 1807–72, rector of Clapham; she d. 1864.

[14] i.e. the Peelite M.P.

[15] Report in Add MS 44369, f. 283.

[16] Instead of 'with'.

3–8. Heard young Stanley who argues his speech admirably tho' with some disadvantage from a rather thick utterance.[1] Read Robertson on the Gorham Case[2]—Engl. Greek papers—French do.

22. Sat.

Wrote to Robertson G—C.G—C. Wordsworth. dined with the Gaskells. Deputation to Ld Seymour 11–1. Mr Masson with me 1½–3½.[3] Read Greek papers—Lords' Debate.[4] D'Haussonville on Swiss affairs.[5]

23. 4 S. Trin.

St Andrew's Wells St (H.C.) 11–2. Bedfordbury evg. MS for St J.B. aloud at night. Read Tennyson's In Memoriam[6]—'Time's Best Blessing'[7]—R. Wilberforce's Charge.[8] Saw Canning—James—HJG. Wrote to Manning[9]—Mr Hallam—Archdn. Wilberforce—J.E. Gladstone—Mr Macfie.

24. M. St John Baptist.

Read all day on the Greek papers. H. of C. through the debate except an hour.[10] Read D'Haussonville. Wrote to Rn G—Mr Monro—Sec. Prov. Society.[11]

25. T.

H.S. with children. Dined at Sir J. Pakingtons. Saw HJG.—CG retd. with good accts. Read Parl. papers—a Greek Merchant[12]—Mr Bracebridge.[13] Committees 12½–4. H. of C. 4–6¼ and 10½–2½ hearing Ld Palmerston's speech an extraordinary & masterly effort.[14]

26. Wed.

Wrote to Manning[15] H.S. with children. H of C. & Commee. 12½–6. Baptism of G.s infant at 12. Saw Mr Oldfield—Northcote—JNG—J. Murray—Hildyard. Read Ld Stanley's Speech,[16] & (French) Greek papers.

[1] E. H. *Stanley on Irish education: *H* cxii. 172.
[2] J. C. *Robertson, 'The bearings of the *Gorham case: a letter to a friend' (1850).
[3] George Joseph Gustave *Masson, 1819–88; educated in France; tutor in England from 1847; French master at Harrow 1855–88.
[4] i.e. *H* cxi. 1293.
[5] J. O. B. de Cléron, Count d'Haussonville, *Switzerland. A history of the French and English diplomacy in that country during the last three years* (1850).
[6] Published this year.
[7] Untraced.
[8] R. I. *Wilberforce, 'The practical effect of the *Gorham case' (1850).
[9] Lathbury, i. 102.
[10] *Roebuck's motion on foreign policy principles and *Pacifico: *H* cxii. 255.
[11] '25. T.' here deleted.
[12] Untraced; on *Pacifico.
[13] C. H. Bracebridge, 'A letter on the affairs of Greece' (1850).
[14] Defending his handling of the *Pacifico affair: *H* cxii. 380.
[15] Lathbury, i. 104.
[16] A reprint of his speech in *H* cxi. 1293.

27. Th.

Wrote to Sir J.G. (late) Worked again on on Greek papers. Saw Ld Aberdeen —J.R. Hope—Dr Twiss—MM Rangabè[1] & F. Peel. Meeting of Commissioners 1–2½. H. of C. 4½–6 and 8–2. Spoke 2¼ hours in the debate on Foreign Policy.[2] Read Tennyson's Poems.

28. Fr.

Wrote to Wade—Murray—Michell—G. Burnett—Vice Chancellor. Up late —arranging papers wh had fallen into confusion. Ceylon Commee. & House 3–7¾. Dined at Mr Ellison's. H. of C. 10½–4. Sir R. Peel made a sound & good speech: with less however of physical vigour than is or was usual. Disraeli was below his mark though he seemed in earnest. Lord John about par. The division was disgusting, not on account of the numbers simply but considering where they came from.[3]

29. Sat. St Peter.

Wrote to Mr Griffiths. Up late. Meeting of the Exhibition Commission at 11–1. At two started for Eton & Windsor: met Sir J. Graham at the cricket match which I watched with great interest.[4] From thence to the Deanery. Saw Hawtrey—Coleridge. The Dean though so feeble is hospitable as ever. Read T.A Kempis.

30. 5 S. Trin.

St George's mg. Eton Chapel aftn. Walk with C.—Music in evg. Read Bp Forbes Cons. Modestae[5]—T.A Kempis.

Monday July One 1850.

Wrote to J.[6] Murray—Col. Grey—S. Herbert. Morning Service at 10½. Visited the Windsor Schools. Saw the Provost—Dr Hawtrey—& (evg) Bp of Oxford—Ld Aberdeen—E. Cardwell. Reached H of C. from Windsor at 5½. Remained for the University Vote till 10¼.[7] Then went to the Concert at the Palace. The Queen spoke to me with the most simple earnestness about the sad accident to Sir R. Peel. We were much shocked on learning its true character this morning at Windsor. May God sustain him & restore him.[8]

[1] Alexandros Rizos Rangabé, 1810–92; professor at Athens 1844–56; Greek foreign minister 1856–9; wrote on literature and archaeology; ed. *Spectateur d'Orient*, which he sent to Gladstone.

[2] Opposing *Palmerston on *Pacifico: *H* cxii. 543–90; full text in Bassett, *Speeches*, 109. The public start of his long conflict with *Palmerston.

[3] *Roebuck's motion was carried in 310 to 264; cp. *H* cxii. 739, and see 23 Nov. 50.

[4] Marylebone beat Eton by five runs. F. Lillywhite thought this season 'the greatest for cricket ever known' (*The guide to cricketers* (1851), 34).

[5] Cp. 29 Mar. 50.

[6] 'S. He' here deleted.

[7] Supply of professors to Oxford and Cambridge: *H* cxii. 804.

[8] *Peel's horse threw him and fell on him on Constitution Hill on 29 June.

2. T.

Wrote to J. Murray—Vice Chancellor of Oxford (2)—Sir J.G—A.W. Haddan—Barker—Phillott—Christie. Saw Northcote—R. Phillimore—Bonham—Beresford—J.N.G. H.S. with the children. H. of C. & Commees. 3–6.[1] Then went to Sir R. Peels & received before seven the deplorable account of the change in his state: which sent me away almost without hope. We dined with Ralph Neville: & afterwards heard the great calamity which the nation has suffered in the death of its greatest statesman. Peace be to him. I remember with joy with how pure true and vigilant a conscience he always seemed to act. Read Bp of Glasgow's Letter.[2] Began to write out a corrected Report of my Speech.

3. Wed.

Wrote to S.H. Northcote—Rev. R. Greswell—Ed Mg Chron.[3] Saw (a rare event) all my three brothers—S. Herbert—Sir Geo. Grey—R. Phillimore. Six to dinner. Worked on writing out my Speech. H of C. at 12 when taking us all by surprise Hume moved the adjournment suddenly in token of respect to Peel, and I after consulting Patten made the best of it & seconded him.[4] Corrected proof of my remarks for the M. Chronicle: they needed it, having been indeed scarcely audible.[5]

4. Th.

Wrote to Sir J.G.—H.S. with Agnes. Saw J.N.G.—S. Herbert—W. Patten—Wodehouse. Commee. $12\frac{1}{4}$–$3\frac{1}{4}$, House $4\frac{1}{2}$–$10\frac{3}{4}$. The public funeral proposed and declined: I regretted the wish which made refusal necessary. On asking Goulburn if I might see the honoured remains I found it had been necessary to close them. Spoke on the Exhibition Site. Wrote (by request) an article for M. Chronicle about Sir R.P. to correct the Times. Worked on Speech MS. Saw Mr J.A. Smith. Commee. $12\frac{1}{4}$–$3\frac{1}{2}$ and H of C. $4\frac{1}{2}$–$10\frac{1}{2}$.[6] My Article appeared in the Chronicle of today: with a preface & some amendments.

5. Fr.

Wrote to G & Co—H. Tayleur. H.S. with the children. Worked all day on my MS which I finished: & on correcting proofsheets. H. of C. $10\frac{1}{2}$–$1\frac{1}{2}$.[7] Walk with C. Saw S. Herbert.

[1] Misc. business: *H* cxii. 850.
[2] W. J. Trower wrote two letters to the bp. of London on *Gorham, privately printed later published. Cp. Add MS 44369, f. 83.
[3] 'H.S. with the children' here deleted.
[4] Quoting *Scott on *Pitt: *H* cxii. 857.
[5] See next day's entry.
[6] *H* cxii. 923.
[7] Malt tax: *H* cxii. 982

6. Sat.

Wrote to Archd. Wilberforce—J. Griffiths—J.D. Coleridge—A. Brandram[1] —Dr Vaughan—H. Raikes—Ch[urch]wardens. H.S. with the children. Saw Dr Hook—Mr J.A. Smith—Sir J. Graham—J.N.G—Jocelyn—Town (Sir R. Peel's Steward).[2] Commission 3¼–5½. With C. at R. Academy 5¾–7. Eight to dinner. Arranging papers & letters.

7. 6 S. Trin.

St Martin's & H.C. 11–2. Bedfordbury evg.—MS for the day aloud. Walk with C. Read Consid. Mod—Monro's Parochial Work[3]—Sermons by Harvey,[4] Townsend,[5] 'a Minister of Christ'.[6]

8. M.

Wrote to Goulburn—Glyn & Co—R. Barker—C. Mackenzie—Col[onial] Reform Society—H.E. Manning—L. Walker. H.S. with children. Commee 12½–3. House 5–12½. Spoke on Eccl. Commn. Bill Clauses.[7] Saw Wilson Patten—Parkinson—Badeley—Herbert—South [R]: in whose case there are some very touching & shaming circumstances. Read Keyser[8]—Westmr. Rev. on Prostitution.[9]

9. T.

Westmr. Abbey at 3. About this hour Sir R. Peel will have been interred. I mourn to be absent. H.S. with the children. Wrote to Sir J.G—Parry & Co[10]—Ld Redesdale—Collis (2)—Rev. Mr Jordan[11]—Churton—Hopkins—Manning—J. Severn—T.G[12]—Bp of Toronto—Hawkins. Corrected proof sheets of Speech. Read Manning's Letter in proof[13]—Dubl. Rev. on Achilli[14] —Agricultural Reports.[15] H of C. & Commee. 12½–3. H of C. midnight to 2½. Spoke on P.O. question.[16]

[1] Andrew Brandram, 1791–*ca.* 1855; Oriel, Oxford; rector of Beckenham, Kent, from 1838.
[2] *Sc.* Towns.
[3] E. *Monro, *Parochial work* (1850).
[4] Probably W. W. *Harvey, 'The Love of God and of his earthly sanctuary' (1845); on Psalm xxvi. 8.
[5] Cp. 25 Feb. 49.
[6] Untraced.
[7] *H* cxii. 1115.
[8] Cp. 19 June 50.
[9] *Westminster Review*, liii. 448 (1850). See above, iii. xliv.
[10] Robert S. Parry and Co., London publishers.
[11] John Jordan, 1804–74; vicar of Enstone, Oxfordshire, from 1840; poet and pamphleteer.
[12] For 'Sir J.G.'
[13] H. E. *Manning, 'The appellate jurisdiction of the crown in matters spiritual; a letter to the bishop of Chichester' (1850); cp. Lathbury, i. 111.
[14] *Dublin Review*, xxviii. 469 (June 1850); on Dr. Giacinto Achilli.
[15] For 1849: *PP* 1850, lii. 409.
[16] On Sunday labour in the post office: *H* cxii. 1213.

10. Wed.

Wrote to E. Griffiths—J.S. Conway [1]—Ld Aberdeen—Archdeacon Grant—Mrs Pakenham [2]—Mrs Tennant. Saw Phillimore—Bp of Toronto—Lyttelton—Mr Hawkins. U. Canada Meeting at 1½. H. of C. 3–6: on Marriage Bill.[3] C. entertained the schoolgirls here in House & Garden: rather to astonishment of the community, but much to her honour. Jane Wortley's party in evg. Read Binney on Marriage Law—his curious Letter.[4]

11. Th.

Wrote to de Vere—Beldam—Napier—M. Jones—G. [5] & Co—Rn G. H.S. with the children. Commn Commee & House 2¼–6¼.[6] Saw Sunday P.O. Labour Deputation—Northcote. Domestic matters. Went with C. Agnes & Stephen in evg to the Overland Exhibition.[7] Read Barnes's Letter [8]—Ullathorne on Educn.[9]—Beldam on Do [10]—Wood's Acct of Oxford Visitation [11]—Preface to King's Coll. Statutes &c.[12]

12. Fr.

Wrote to Wm. Gladstone—Manning—Downes [13]—Harris—E. Hawkins—G.R. Denison—W.S. Pratten [*sc.* Patten]. Saw Phillimore—Farquhar—Bonham—De Salis & Logan—Sir J. Graham—Mr Parkinson—Cardwell. Ceylon Commee 12¼–2½. Exhibition Committee 3–4. H. of C. 5–7¼ and 8¼–9½.[14] Read Ward's Memoirs.[15] H.S. with children.

13. Sat.

Wrote to C. Wordsworth—T. Lathbury—C.A. Wood—M. Guizot—Ld Harris—J.N.G—Sir J.G—Jos Wood.[16] Saw Mr Ryle Wood [17]—Oldfield—

[1] Son of J.; cp. 9 Aug. 25 and 6 Jan. 53 n.

[2] Frances Julia, *née* Peters, d. 1894; widow of Felix Thomas Tollemache; m. 1845 as his second wife John Pakenham, 1790–1876, 4th s. of Sir Thomas *Pakenham, captain R.N. 1826, admiral 1864. Cp. 20 July 50.

[3] *H* cxii. 1220.

[4] T. Binney, 'An argument in relation to the Levitical marriage law' (?1850).

[5] Perhaps Michael Jones, 1774–1851; barrister from 1809; bibliophile and antiquarian.

[6] Abolition of death penalty: *H* cxii. 1252.

[7] A diorama of the overland mail route to India.

[8] R. Barnes, 'A letter to Lord John *Russell on the first report of the episcopal and capitular revenues commissioners' (1850).

[9] W. B. *Ullathorne, 'Remarks on the proposed education bill' (1850).

[10] J. Beldam, 'A letter to Lord John *Russell on national education' (1850).

[11] *The history of the visitation of the university of Oxford by a parliamentary commission in the years 1647, 1648. Abridged from the annals of Antony à *Wood* (1837).

[12] J. Heywood, *Collection of the statutes for the university and the colleges of Cambridge* (1850).

[13] John Downes, secretary of working man's cttee. for Peel memorial; Hawn P.

[14] Misc. business: *H* cxii. 1289.

[15] H. Ward, *Five years in Kaffirland*, 2 v. (1848).

[16] Probably Joshua Wood, 1804?–78; sundry curacies 1835–45; headmaster Kirkby-Ravensworth school 1845–72; vicar of E. Crowton, Northallerton, 1872–8.

[17] i.e. John Ryle Wood.

Severn—Lyttelton—Freshfield—Johnson (J.L. & Co)[1]—Pickersgill[2]—Mrs Wadd—J.S. Wortley. H.S. with Agnes. Inscription Commee. 4–5.[3] In the City &c. on business. Read Pym on the Jews[4]—M'Lean's Hudson's Bay Vol I[5]

14. 7 S. Trin.

St Martins (H.C). 8½ AM & 11—St James evg. MS of /45 for the day aloud at night. Walk with C. Wrote to Mr Hawkins. Saw Hope. Read Monro's Parochial Work—Bp of Melbourne's Letter[6]—Newman's Six Lectures on Difficulties of Anglicans.[7]

15. M.

Wrote to Griffiths—W. Chance—Ld Ellesmere—Greswell—Dr Locock—Sir R. Inglis—Johnson Longden & Co—and [blank.] Saw Mr Dalrymple—Towns—Sir G. Grey—Wortley. H.S. with the children. Read Remarks on Eccl. Jurisdiction (1689)[8]—Lyttelton's Speech[9]—Westhead on XIX Leviticus.[10] Commission 3–5¼. House to 6, & 8–12. Spoke on Bps Clauses &c. We made a little way.[11]

16. T.

Wrote to Johnson L. & Co—C. Uppington—J.H. Parker—Rn. G—Rev Mr Dodd—Mr Downes—Ld Campden. Also corrected & copied out & sent dft letter to Bp of London.[12] H.S. with the children. Saw Severn—S. Herbert. H. of C. & Commn. 2–6.[13] Went to see Ld Ashburnham's pictures.[14] C. went off with the children at noon. Attended the Chisholm meeting in the evg:[15] & tea at Lady Pembroke's afterwards.[16]

[1] i.e. of Johnson, Longden & Co.

[2] Henry William *Pickersgill, 1782–1875; Royal Academician and society portrait painter: Gladstone did not sit to him.

[3] Preparing the 1851 Exhibition medals.

[4] W. W. Pym, 'The Jew an important member of the body of Christ' (1843).

[5] Cp. 14 June 50.

[6] C. *Perry, 'A letter . . . to the hon. secretary of the special committee of that diocese [Melbourne]' (1849).

[7] J. H. *Newman, *Lectures on certain difficulties felt by Anglicans in submitting to the Catholic Church* (1850).

[8] Not found.

[9] On 3° Australian Colonies Government Bill: *H* cxii. 972.

[10] J. P. B. Westhead, 'The xviiith chapter of Leviticus not the marriage code of Israel' (1850).

[11] Ecclesiastical Commission Bill: *H* cxii. 1402–13.

[12] On the *Gorham judgment: Add MS 44369, f. 335, and Lathbury, i. 105.

[13] Misc. business: *H* cxii. 1425.

[14] Cp. 20 July 50.

[15] Probably on the *Chisholm plan for female emigration. Cp. 22 July 48.

[16] Ottavia Herbert, *née* Spinelli, 1793?–1857, da. of the duke of Laurino, widow of the prince of Butera de Rubari, d. 1814; m. 1814 Robert Henry Herbert, 1791–1862, 12th earl of Pembroke 1827.

17. Wed.

St Mary's Crown St 8½ PM. Wrote to J. Severn—C. Stewart—Mrs Pakenham—G. Burnett—Rev. C.D. Reade[1]—Judge Coleridge—C.G. Saw Ruttley[2]—Sir A. Dalrymple. Visited Moore's picture, a supposed Raphael: exquisitely beautiful[3]—Inscription Committee 5–6¾: & wrote Report.[4] Read Huber[5]—Corry on Visitatorial power[6]—Worked on Parliamentary records (precedents)—Read Bowyer's Readings.[7] Conv. with two unhappy women in the streets at night [R].

18. Thurs.

Wrote to J.N.G—C.G (2)—Mr Shiel [*sc.* Sheil]. Ceylon Commee. 12–4. H of C. 5¼–8 and 8½–12¼. Spoke 1½ hour on Univ. Commission. Lord John very flat: the tone of the House favourable to the Univv.[8] Read & made extracts relating to them.[9]

19. Fr.

Wrote to C.G.—Parkinson—Fisher[10]—Mr G. Grove[11]—E. Monro—J. Griffiths—Williams & Co—E. Hawkins. Saw Lyttelton—Barker—Manning—R. Phillimore—Sir J. Graham—Thesiger—S. Herbert—W. Patten—Duchess of Beaufort (evg). Ceylon Commee. 2–5. H of C. 5–8. and 10¼–12¼.[12]

20. Sat.

Wrote to C.G. Christie's (Ld Ashburnham's picture Sale) 1–3¼. Saw Capt. Pakenham—Archd. Wilberforce—Ld Radstock—Hope—Cardwell: with whom I had much interesting conversation on our political condition. Also he with Archdn. W[ilberforce], A. Stanley, & Mr Marshall, Ch Ch,[13] breakfasted with me. Dined at Wilson Patten's. Private affairs.

[1] Charles Darby Reade, 1821–?65; rector of Wishford, Salisbury, 1848–50, of Stow Bedon, Norfolk, 1850–60.

[2] Thomas Rutley, picture dealer in Great Newport Street.

[3] Belonging to Morris Moore, 1812–85, connoisseur of Raphael and art dealer; from 1830 lived mostly in Rome; cp. 15 July 51.

[4] Not traced.

[5] Cp. 23 May 44.

[6] Cp. 14 May 50.

[7] (Sir) G. *Bowyer, *Readings delivered before the honourable society of the Middle Temple, in the year 1850* (1850).

[8] Hostile to the commission: *H* cxii. 1495; published with alterations as 'Speech on the commission of inquiry into the state of the universities of Oxford and Cambridge'; draft in Add MS 44684, f. 209.

[9] ibid.

[10] 'Johnson Longden & Co' here deleted.

[11] (Sir) George *Grove, 1820–1900; engineer, then secretary to society of arts 1849, to Crystal Palace 1856; wrote *Dictionary of music and musicians*, 4 v. (1878–89).

[12] West Africa: *H* cxiii. 37.

[13] George Marshall, 1818–97; student of Christ Church 1837–58; censor 1849–57; proctor 1850; rector of Pyrton, Oxfordshire, 1857–75.

21. 8 S. Trin.

St Mary's Crown St mg. Bedfordbury evg. MS. on 1st mg lesson aloud at nt. Wrote to C.G—H. Glynne. Saw Archdn Wilberforce—& Manning for a good long while. Read Monro's Par. Work (finished)—Xtn Rem on do—on Synods—on Supremacy [1]—Fortescue's Serm.[2]—Henry's Lecture (Belfast) [3]

22. M.

Wrote to Severn—W.H.G—Mr Church—J. Griffiths—Messrs. Williams & Co—Tupper—J.L. Ross—Ld C. Clinton—Baron—Duchess of Beaufort. Read Leake on the Greek Islands [4]—M'Lean on Hudson's Bay—Ceylon Committee & House 1½–6.[5] Saw Rangabè. Saw E. Hering, at night [R]—(address No 6 [blank] St M Lane) & stood opposite Argyll Rooms.[6]

23. T.

Wrote to Maskell—Severn—Dearle [7]—Dean of Lincoln—Cooke (Peace Soc.) [8]—Jackson—Walker—C.G. Read pamphlets—Petronius. Peel Memorial Meeting at one.[9] Exhibn. Commn. at 3. H. of C. afn.[10] Dined at Grillion's. Saw Ld Hardinge—Goulburn—Cardwell. Saw E[mma] Clifton [11] evg. Arranging my books for departure.

24. Wed.

Ch Ch St Giles's 5 P.M. Wrote to C.G.[12] and to..... Johnson Longden & Co. Saw Manning—Sewell—Mrs Barrable [13]—Greswell—Freshfield—Glyns. In the City in afternoon. Saw E. Clifton 6–7½ [R]. Went to the Concert at Lansdowne House. Worked on arranging Parl. books & papers.

25. St James.

St James's 3 PM. Wrote to C.G—Sir J.G—J.N.G—Ld Granville—T. Walker—R. Barker—W. Mathews—Sec. G.N.E Co—Mr Masters—O.B. Cole—Rev. T. Bowdler—M. Wigram [14]—J. Griffiths—Col. Stewart—Freshfields

[1] *Christian Remembrancer*, xx. 203, 234, 185 (July 1850).

[2] R. H. Fortescue, 'The Tudor supremacy in jurisdiction unlimited' (1850); on John xviii. 36.

[3] Probably untraced lecture by James *Henry, Dublin physician and Virgil scholar.

[4] W. M. *Leake, *Travels in the Morea*, 3 v. (1830).

[5] Supply: *H* cxiii. 96.

[6] The notorious centre for aristocratic dissipation in Great Windmill Street.

[7] Edward Dearle, 1806–91; D.Mus. Cambridge 1842; organist at Newark 1835–64, then in London; composed oratarios.

[8] Untraced official of the Peace Society, founded 1816, with offices in New Broad Street, which held congresses in various English towns in the autumn of 1850.

[9] Cp. *The Times*, 24 July 1850, 8b.

[10] Ionian islands: *H* cxiii. 175.

[11] A rescue case, about to occupy much of the diarist's attention: cp. 27 July, 1–2 and 15–16 Aug., 2–5 Oct. 50, 28 Feb. 51 etc.

[12] At half-past one next morning: paragraph in Bassett, 83.

[13] Mrs. Amelia G. Barrable, artist with a studio in Oxford Street.

[14] Money Wigram, 1790–1873; London merchant and shipowner.

—Wordsworth—V.C. Oxford—Mr J. Parkinson. Read Ward's Memoirs.[1] Adelphi Theatre at 9¼: an amusing farce with some social morality in it.[2] Dined with the Herberts. H. of C. 12–2¼.[3] Saw Wilson Patten—Mr Carpenter—Worked on papers & accts.

26. Fr.

Wrote to Y N B. Co[4]—C.G[5]—J. Simeon[6]—Rev W. Gray[7]—S. Herbert—Saw Bp of Oxford—S. Herbert—Hume—House of Commons & Commission 12–7¼: again 12–2.[8] Worked on accounts. Read Sanitary Report[9]—H.B. papers.[10] At Mad. Bunsen's party.[11] Saw E. Clifton [R]

27. Sat.

St Mary's Crown St 8½ PM. Wrote to C.G—Bowdler—J.N.G—H. Chester—Mrs Caravia[12]—Johnson Longden & Co—Saw Bust of Peel at Hogarths[13]—Baron Brunnow. Saw E. Clifton [R] at night and made I hope some way—But alas my unworthiness. Worked on letters papers & accounts: & on draft of will. My cough very bad & headach almost unmanageable. Read Smith on China.[14]

28. 9 S. Trin.

Spent most of the day in bed (after physic). Read Wilberforce's Sermons—Wrote to Mr Carter—Bp of New Zealand. MS. meant for E. C[lifton] [R].

29. M.

Wrote to Sir J.G—C.G—Gaspey—Rennie—Moncreiff—H. Tayleur—Capt. Peers—R. Thorp—H. Lees. In the City with Freshfield about my will. Also saw Mr Longden—Williams & Co—H. of C. 3½–6¼.[15] Cough still bad: head middling: but I was out perforce. Read Railway Commns Report[16]—Clark on Climate.[17] Lyttelton came at night. Saw Simeon.

[1] Cp. 12 July 50.
[2] 'The emigré's daughter'.
[3] Misc. business: *H* cxiii. 214.
[4] The York, Newcastle and Berwick Railway, with offices in York; under threat of take-over by the Caledonian Railway.
[5] Fragment in Bassett, 83.
[6] (Sir) John Simeon, 1815–70; liberal M.P. for Isle of Wight, 1847–51, 1865–70; 3rd Bart. 1854.
[7] William Gray, 1785–1863; vicar of Brafferton from 1822; canon of Ripon 1828.
[8] Spoke briefly on the Ceylon report: *H* cxiii. 344.
[9] Report on the cholera epidemic of 1848–9: *PP* 1850, xxi. 3.
[10] Papers on the Health Bill: *PP* 1850, iii. 149ff.
[11] Frances *Bunsen, *née* Waddington, 1791–1876; m. 1817 the Chevalier Bunsen and later wrote on him.
[12] Unidentified.
[13] A marble bust by Christopher Benini, exhibited at Hogarth's gallery in Haymarket.
[14] George *Smith, bp. of Victoria, *A narrative of an exploratory visit to each of the consular cities of China* (1847).
[15] Jewish members' oaths: *H* cxiii. 397.
[16] Report for 1849; *PP* 1850, xxxi. 1.
[17] Sir J. Clark, *The influence of climate in the prevention and cure of chronic diseases* (1829).

30. T.

Wrote to C.G—G.F. Young—Adderley—Manning[1]—Dr Wiese[2]—Mrs Tennant[3]—Freshfield. Read Cochrane's Young Italy[4]—divers pamphlets. Saw E.L. Robertson (Bonds liquidation)—Ld C. Hamilton & H. Herbert—Goulburn. H. of C. 1–4½ & 7½–9½. Paired for £12 franchise.[5] Saw E. Clifton [R].

31. Wed.

Wrote to C.G—R. Cavendish—J.N.G—My head & cough D.G. better. Nothing from Mrs Tennant. Saw Parkinson—Ruttley & Manson. Read Exp. of Lord's Prayer[6]—Serm. on Sir R. Peel.[7] In the city—saw Freshfield—Johnson Longden & Co. Went to the Olympic at nine: thought on the question of the drama with a question as to my course hitherto. But I cannot justify being accessory to the profession of the ballet.[8]

Thurs. Aug. One 1850.

Wrote to Freshfield—Locock—Tatham—Severn—Harper—Johnson Longden & Co—Bentley[9]—Mrs Tennant. Saw Hubbard—Simeon—Sir J. Graham. Worked on letters, accounts, & general preparation for departure. H. of C. 12¼–2¼. Spoke on Amendments to Austr. Col. Bill—again 5–7.[10] Gave notice about Hudson's Bay. Visited the Vernon Gallery 3–4.[11] Before nine I went to find E.C: but failed [R]: after 1¼ hour came home & finished matters with Hampton: went again at 11½ to O. Street, & again failed. Resolved to go to E.C.s lodgings: I found her there: & left her with the resolution declared of going in the morning by my advice & with her child at once to Mrs Tennant.[12] I therefore wrote to aid her: I hope[13] and even think I am not deceived, while I am sure that I deserve to be.

2. Fr.

After 2½ hours in bed rose & came by the early train to Birmm.—met by dearest C. & Willy on my way from thence & found all the children well at Hagley except that Mary's eye has still the same formidable spot not much

[1] Lathbury, i. 112.
[2] Ludwig Adolf Wiese, Prussian historian; wrote on Britain; introduced to diarist by Abeken, cp. Add MS 44369, f. 296.
[3] She had resigned as superintendent of the rescue home at Clewer and had to be persuaded to return; cp. 28 Sept. 43.
[4] By A. D. R. Cochrane (1850).
[5] *H* cxiii. 574.
[6] Many; perhaps that by bp. R. Leighton (?1830).
[7] Probably J. S. M. Anderson, 'The dead yet speaking. A sermon preached after the death of . . . *Peel' (1850).
[8] 'The Malcontent', followed by 'A Roland for an Oliver'.
[9] Richard *Bentley, 1794–1871; publisher; founded his *Miscellany* 1837 and *Young England* 1845.
[10] *H* cxiii. 626.
[11] T. *Vernon's studio; cp. 20 May 48.
[12] At Clewer.
[13] Instead of 'trust'.

changed for the better. Read Life of Peel[1]—Montaigne. Walk with C. & told her of the proceedings of last night—which she approved & with much interest. My cough better.

3. Sat.

Wrote to Sir J. Graham—Ld Brougham—Scotts. Remained in bed till the afternoon my cough being obstinate. Read Rolliad[2]—White on Et[ernal] Pun[ishmen]t.[3]

4. 10 S. Trin.

H.C. at one—Aft. Ch. at 3½. Rose at midday. Read Mr White's work wh suggests some painful reflections.

5. M.

Wrote to Sir J.G—H.J.G—Latin lesson to Willy. Chess with George. Read Life of Peel—Moeurs des Turcs[4]—Lyells Elem. Geology.[5] My cough a little mended: & I was down to breakfast. Dear Mary's eye has made but little progress. We discussed travelling plans.

6. T.

Wrote to Mrs Tennant—E. Clifton—Ld Brougham—G.A. Hamilton—Hampton—Lincoln—Latin lesson to Willy. Saw Griffiths on O.F. matters. Chess with Lyttelton. Read James on Italian Schools[6]—Life of Sir R. Peel.

7. Wed.

Wrote to J.N.G—J. Griffiths—J. Dalrymple. Latin lesson to Willy. Read Sir R. Peel's Life (finished)—Brand's Lectures on Geology[7]—began Mansfield Park. Chess with George. Mary kept to the house for her eye.

8. Th.

Wrote to Williams & Co—Rich. Smith—Lincoln—Hampton—Bar. Brunnow—Dr Greenhill—Miss F. Uppington[8]—H. Tayleur—Messrs. Johnson Longden & Co. Latin lesson to Willy. Chess with George. Saw Griffiths. Read Brand's Lectures—Mansfield Park—Cuvier Theory of the Earth.[9] Both Little Mary & I improved—(si magna licet [componere parvo].)[10]

[1] 'The life, political career and death of Sir Robert *Peel' (1850); a pamphlet.
[2] [J. *Richardson *et alia*], 'Criticisms on the Rolliad, a poem, being a more faithful portraiture of [*Pitt] than any extant' (1784).
[3] E. White, *Life in Christ* (1846), discourse ii.
[4] J. A. Guer, *Moeurs et Usages des Turcs*, 2 v. (1746–7).
[5] Cp. 27 Dec. 49.
[6] J. T. *James, *The Italian schools of painting* (1820).
[7] W. T. *Brande, *Outlines of geology* (1817); a course of lectures.
[8] Caroline Uppington's sister.
[9] G. L. C. F. D. de Cuvier, *Essays on the theory of the earth* (1813); tr. R. Kerr.
[10] 'if one may compare great things with small'.

9. Fr.

Church 10 A.M. Wrote to T.G—Watson—Readman.[1] A party to dinner. A painful conv. on the Gorham Case & its adjuncts. Out with C. Latin lesson with Willy. Saw Paterson. Read Mansfield Park—Cuvier.

10. Sat.

Wrote to Mrs R (No 7 R. Pl) [2]—Mrs Tennant—Sir J.G. Latin lesson to Willy. Saw Mr Chance—Mr Collis with Mr Griffiths (at Stourbridge)—Finished Mansfield Park—'Old Poz' acted in the evg by the children with much deserved applause. A repeat of last Thursday. Music from Mr Yorke: a treat.[3]

11. 11 S. Trin.

Ch 11 & 3. Read Cuvier (finished)—Colonial Ch. Chron.[4]—Ecclesiologist.[5] Walk with C. & Agnes. Music in evg.

12. M.

Wrote to Hampton. 8¾–2¾. Journey to Hawarden: where we found all well & the little Glynnes very sweet children (2 & 3 especy.), much come on.[6] Read James on Ital. painting (finished)—Staunton on Chess [7]—Wm. Lyttelton's Sermon & appx.[8] Chess with Stephen.

13. T.

Church 8½ AM. Wrote to Sir J.G—Rn. G. Latin lesson to Willy. Chess with Stephen. Read Engl. Review [9]—Staunton on Chess—Lyell's Geology. Went with C. to the Castle to examine Mr Nesfield's [10] doings: he has *not* app[aren]tly been too bold.

14. Wed.

Church 8½ A.M. Wrote to Lincoln—Lady Manvers—J. Watson. H.S. & Latin lesson to Willy. Drive with C.—Chess with S.—Read Introduction to the Study of Gothic Architecture [11]—Pepys's Memoirs & Diary.[12]

[1] R. Readman; not otherwise identified.
[2] Mrs. Ruff, a bawd. Cp. 16 Aug. 50.
[3] Unidentified.
[4] *Colonial Church Chronicle*, iv. 4 (August 1850); on Natal.
[5] *Ecclesiologist*, xi. 73 (August 1850); article on the controversial Scotch prayer book.
[6] i.e. Henry Glynne's daughters Honora, Mary and Catherine who d. February 1854.
[7] H. *Staunton, *The chess-player's handbook* (1847).
[8] W. H. *Lyttelton, 'Dangers to truth . . . with an appendix on the controversy on baptism' (1850).
[9] *English Review*, xiii. 257 (June 1850).
[10] William Andrews *Nesfield, 1793–1881; landscape gardener and water colourist.
[11] By J. H. *Parker (1849).
[12] Cp. 25 June 49.

15. Th.

Church 8½ A.M. Mrs Tennant's letter this morning showed that matters had not moved with respect to E. Clifton: and after consulting with C. I thought it my duty to go to town [R]. I reached my house at 8 P.M.—failed in finding E.C. for the evening, though I did all I could. Latin lesson to Willy—also H.S.—Wrote to Burnett—& in evg to Mr Glyn—Freshfield—Amery—Mrs Tennant—Scotts—J.R. Hope—Read Mrs Vidal's Woodleigh Farm.[1]

16. Fr.

Wrote to S.R.G—C.G—Ld F. Somerset—Scotts—C. Mackenzie—Hon. E.H. Stanley—Magee[2]—Morris—Mosse[3]—Sec. Y.N.B. Co—Read Woodleigh Farm—Parker's Intro to Goth. Archit (finished)—Saw Lincoln—Mr Rogers—Mrs Barber[4]—Mr Longden—Bonham—Mr Talbot[5]—Mrs Ruff—& the same person with the poor victim—Mr Field, agent of the Socy. Mr F. will carry on the matter so as really I hope to neutralise Mrs R.s influence.—I failed in getting at night a separate commun[icatio]n.

17. Sat.

Wrote to Lady Manvers—Sir J.G—R.G—5¾–2½ from my door to Hawarden: where thank God C. gave me a good account of little Mary—Read Woodleigh Farm. A tired & sleepy evg. Worked on a large batch of letters.

18. 12 S. Trin.

Church 11 & 3. Walk with C. Read Horsley's Sermons[6]—Massingberd's Reformation[7]—Woodleigh Farm (finished)—Ward's Letter.[8]

19. M.

Church 8½ A.M. Wrote to Readman—Griffiths—Macintyre. H.S. & Latin lessons to Willy. Out with C.—Chess—Read E.H. Stanley's South America[9]—Saw Burnett & long Conversations on Estate affairs.

[1] M. T. Vidal, *Cabramatta, and Woodleigh Farm* (1850).
[2] William Connor *Magee, 1821–91; livings in England and Ireland 1845–64; dean of Cork 1864–8; bp. of Peterborough 1868; abp. of York 1891.
[3] Probably Henry Moore Mosse, curate of Christ Church, Liverpool, 1849, of Heneage, Belper, from 1855.
[4] Receiving charity payments from the Gladstones; she possibly kept lodgings for rescue cases.
[5] James Beard Talbot, 1800?–81; founder and secretary of London society for protection of young females and the prevention of juvenile prostitution from 1835; Field also worked for this society, which had an asylum in Tottenham.
[6] S. *Horsley, *Sermons*, the 3rd ed. in 3 v. (1812).
[7] F. C. *Massingberg, *The English reformation* (1842).
[8] W. G. *Ward, 'The Anglican establishment contrasted . . . with the Catholic Church of every age' (1850); from *The Guardian.*
[9] E. H. S. *Stanley, 'Six weeks in South America' (1850).

20. Tues.

Detained in bed mg by sore throat. Wrote to Sir J.G—T.G—W.P. Ward—Maitland—C. Uppington—Johnson L. & Co—Sec. Y.N. & B. Co—Latin lesson to Willy. Saw Burnett 11½–1½—Foulkes. With C. at the Castle and speculations on the possibility of establishing a joint concern there next year.[1] Went with S. to dine at Mr Cooke's.[2]

21. Wed.

Church 8½ AM. Latin lesson to Willy. Wrote to Barker—Collis—Richardson. Read T.A Kempis—Pepyss Diary. Went with C. at 11 to Rhyl[3] where we found little Mary's eye somewhat improved. Bathed & walks there.

22. Th.

Despite the weather we all bathed & walked: also moved little Mary to a real sea-lodging. Read Pepys (finished Vol I) Returned home at 7.

23. Fr.

Wrote to

Lincoln	Hampton.	Watson.
Mrs Tennant	Mrs H[ampto]n.	Maitland.
Rn. G.	Freshfield.	R. Barker.
Rev. T. James	J.L. & Co.	R. Gladstone.
Scotts.	Readman.	Sir A. Edmonstone.

Church 8½ AM. H.S. & Latin lesson to Willy. Walk with C. & with S.R.G.

24. Sat. St Bartholomew.

Church 8½ A.M. Latin lesson to Willy. Visits (incl. Jane Roberts)[4] with C. Chess with Stephen. Read Pepys—Lyell. Wrote to Lyttelton—J.N.G—Aunt J.—Ld Harris—Claud Hamilton.

25. 13 S. Trin.

Church 11 A.M. 6½ P.M. Wrote to Manning.[5] Read Scott on Restoration of Churches[6]—Horsley's Sermons.

[1] Sir S. Glynne was able to return to the castle in 1852. Despite various proposals, it was never let.

[2] Philip Davies-Cooke, 1793–1853; of Gwysany, Mold, Flintshire; land-owner, much involved in tory politics in the county.

[3] On the North Wales coast, about 25 miles NW. of Hawarden.

[4] A villager.

[5] Lathbury, i. 113.

[6] G. G. *Scott, 'A plea for the faithful restoration of our ancient churches' (1850).

26. M.

Church 8½ A.M. Wrote to Freshfield—E.L. Robertson—J. Murray—Jas Watson—Scotts—W.P. Ward—Griffiths—H. Tayleur. Latin lesson to Willy. Spent the forenoon with Barker & then Burnett—Chess with Stephen—Read Pepys. Cricket (hat) with Willy—walk with C. & ruminated on Stephen's affairs which still present nothing but the prospect of an arduous & protracted though not hopeless struggle.

27. T.

Church 8½ A.M. Wrote to Robert Gladstone—Rangabe—Ed. Morn. Chron[1] —Ed. Engl. Rev.[2]—Latin lesson to Willy. Saw Burnett & discussed with him a new scheme of relief for S. to the extent of £500 p.a. or more—mg & evg. Read Pepys—Stanley. Chess with Stephen.

28. Wed.

Chester Cath[edra]l 10 A.M. Saw Mr Slade—Mr Barker—do with Mr Townshend—Mr Burnett—Wrote to J.N.G—Sir J.G—Jas Watson—H. Tayleur—W. Chance—J. Griffiths—A M Paterson—Rev W. Church. Latin lesson to Willy. Conv. with Stephen on his affairs: I am now at the bottom I think of his difficulties: which though lessened are still frightful. Chess with him. Read Mayow's 2d to Maskell.[3] Our darling baby has this day closed her first year: which leaves nothing for us to wish except that by God's grace such [years] as are to come may be, in due proportion, like it.

29. Th.

Church 8½ A.M. Latin lesson to Willy. Packing & preparations. Wrote to Fagge[4]—Cole—Hampton—Maitland—Mrs Tyler—Lord Braybrooke (draft)—Call at Cath. Farm[5]—Mary Farm—saw Mr Brewster—Mr Burnett.

30. Fr.

Church 8½ A.M. Started at 9¾ for Liverpool—where I saw Robn.—Tayleur —Kelso—Mr Moss. Wrote (after revision) to Ld Braybrooke—R. Barker—Manning—J. Watson—Tayleur—Sec Lpool & Crosby [and Southport railway] Co. Left Lpool at 4 for the North—by Fleetwood. Read 'In Memoriam'. A fine passage.

[1] John Douglas *Cook, 1808–54; edited *Morning Chronicle* on its purchase in 1848 as a Peelite organ by *Lincoln, *Herbert and *Cardwell, and *Saturday Review* from 1855.

[2] William *Palmer of Worcester College.

[3] M. W. Mayow, 'A second letter to the Rev. W. *Maskell . . . Thoughts on the position of the Church of England as to her dogmatic teaching' (1850).

[4] John Frederick Fagge, 1814–84; vicar of Aston Cantlow, Warwickshire, from 1849; fathered 11 children.

[5] Mary's Farm and Catherine's Farm were ¼ and ¾ mile NE. of Broughton church, and were named after the sisters Glynne about 1835.

31. Sat.

Wrote to C.G. Reached Glasgow at 12¾. Breakfast there & called at Mr Watson's for business. 2–10½ Journey to Fasque. Conv. with JNG.

Fasque Sunday Sept. One.

Chapel mg (& Holy Commn.) & aft. Read Edmonstone[1]—Robins.[2] Much conv. with my Father who is in all respects visibly much more *aged* but calm & generally well. This however it seems is a *good* day.

2. M.

Wrote to Mayow—C.G—Lyttelton—R. Barker. Read Cotterill on Agric. Distress[3]—Sterne (whose 30th Sermon is a singular picture)[4]—Mayow's Letter (finished). Visited at Fettercairn House. Saw Croal about the inscription.[5] Two long conversations with my Father who tho' weaker in mind & body is more tranquil & composed, & more manageable on matters where it is needful that he should be managed.

3. T.

Wrote to C.G—W. Forbes—Leighton & Myers—Jas Hope—Mrs Long—A M Paterson—R. Readman. Convv. with my Father: who has passed 3 days without sending off a letter. Calls. Read Tassoni Secchia Rapita[6]—Boccaccio Decam.—Cotterill (finished)—Swift's Poems.

4. Wed.

Wrote to Ld Fortescue—Jas Watson—Collis—Tayleur—C.G—J.H. Parker. Calls & visits. Read Swift—Tassoni—Boccaccio. My Father requires now more of conversation than anything else: the days of whist as well as letter writing are gone. His hearing is not materially worse.

5. Th.

Wrote to C.G[7]—Lawson. Read Vicar of Wakefield—Tassoni—Boccaccio. The Secchia is rather heavy: & I press on with it because I am tempted to turn over to the less vulgar but more dangerous pages of the Decamerone—which is a book that some should know: but they should be better men than I. Began—malgrado mio[8]—to write out my Univ. Commn. Speech.[9] Walk with John & on the hill.

[1] Sir A. *Edmonstone, 'A letter . . . on the present aspect of church matters' (1850).
[2] S. *Robins, 'Some reasons against the revival of convocation' (1850).
[3] C. F. Cotterill, **Agricultural distress, its cause and remedy* (1850).
[4] L. *Sterne, *Works*, iv. 123 (1769); a 'Description of the world' based on 2 Peter iii. 11.
[5] On Jessy's tomb, carved by Croall, a local craftsman.
[6] Cp. 26 Jan. 50.
[7] Lathbury, i. 117.
[8] 'despite myself'.
[9] Cp. 18 July 50 n.

6. Fr.

Wrote to C.G—R. Barker (2)—E.L. Robertson—Jas Watson—Chas Wordsworth. Read Tassoni (finished)—Boccaccio—Swift's Poems—Vicar of Wakefield. Worked a little on Speech. Walk & visits. My Father today has his itch for doing supposed work among his papers.

7. Sat.

Wrote to C.G—Rev. S. Robins—W.C. James—Hampton—Lawson. Read Swift—Vicar of Wakefield—Lessing's Laocoon (recommenced)[1]—& Béranger.[2] Walked up the hill & found that thank God this air has restored my strength. Worked on Speech.

8. 15 S. Trin.

Read the Morning service to my Father who attended with fervour through a large part of it. Chapel afterwards & again at 3. Wrote to Manning[3]—Bp of Oxford—Dr Hawkins—J.R. Hope. Wrote Mem. on my Father's affairs: such a lesson do they seem to convey.[4] This paper was the fruit of a conv. with John last night. Read Forbes' Cons. Mod[5]—De Imitatione—Visit +.

9. M.

Wrote to Lees (cancelled)—G. Burnett—C.G.—Worked on S.R.G's papers: & have now I hope a clear view of his affairs: now, a prospect of mixed alarm & hope: 3 years ago, of hidden ruin. Worked with my Father on his papers. The occupation is bad for him & utterly useless: but to make resistance would be worse. Read Swift—Laocoon—Béranger (who seems to respect nature no more than revelation.) Hudson's Evidence.[6] John went to St Andrew's: discussed with him the possibility of relieving my Father of St Andrew's.[7] Walk & visit.

10. T.

Wrote to C.G—Lyttelton—Jas Watson—Overends. Worked on Speech. Worked long on S.R.G's affairs. The release from the jointure-security is absolutely requisite. Read Laocoon—Swift.

11. Wed.

Wrote to C.G[8]—R. Palmer—Ch. Wordsworth—Sec. Y.N.B. Co—W. Hampton—H. Tayleur—W.B. Collis—Jas Watson. Worked on Speech—Rode to the Burn—saw the Arbuthnotts. A long evening conversation with my Father at his best. Read Laocoon—Swift—C. Wordsworth.[9]

[1] Cp. 23 June 49.
[2] Cp. 26 Oct. 48.
[3] Lathbury, i. 335.
[4] Cp. Checkland, 368 and n.
[5] Cp. 30 June 50.
[6] *Report of his* [George *Hudson's] *evidence on the trial of the cause of Richardson versus Wodson* (1850); a libel action.
[7] The building project; cp. Checkland, 342.
[8] On suicide, in Lathbury, ii. 282.
[9] Christopher *Wordsworth, *fils, Is the church of Rome the Babylon of the book of revelation?* (1850).

12. Th.

Wrote to C.G—A.M. Paterson—J. Griffiths—W.B. Collis. Worked on Speech. Hill walk. My Father had a day of great confusion: all his symptoms are those of approaching failure in the brain. Read Laocoon—Swift—Longfellow's poems: the Ship is indeed noble.[1]

13. Fr.

Wrote to C.G—W.H.G—H. Tayleur—Jas Watson—Messrs. G. & Co—E.L. Robertson. Worked on Stephen's affairs—& my own. Worked much on my Speech and finished that worse than tedious business. Read Laocoon—Drove Aunt J. to Laurencekirk. Saw the Goalens, Mr Gibburn,[2] Capt Barclay. Again visited dear Jessy's Vault.

14. Sat.

Wrote to C.G—Geo. Grant—J. Griffiths—R. Cavendish—Jas Watson—Leighton & Myers—H. Tayleur—J.S. Lawson[3]—Sec. YNB Co. Read Swift—finished Longfellow. Hill walk. Finished correcting MS. of Speech—corrected also proofsheets.

15. 16 S. Trin.

Read morning Service to my Father: then to the Chapel: & again in aftn. Wrote to W. James—Wordsworth. Walk with J.N.G.—Visited the Vault. Read Bp Forbes—T.A'Kempis. Corrected a proof—to catch the press tomorrow.

16. M.

Wrote to C.G—Ld Fortescue—Ld Braybrooke—R. Barker—Sir S. Scott & Co—Maitland—Jas Watson—Sec. Y.N.B. Co, with plan—Jas. Hume. Wrote heads of plan for release of S.R.G.s Estate from Jointure. Wrote Memoranda for Codicils for Sir J.G. Read Laocoon—Swift. Conversations with Helen about the Phesdo codicil (not satisfactory)[4] & with John. My Father was in his best health today: which only made more evident the doubtful condition of his mind & how his acts *might* be questioned.

17. T.

Wrote to C.G—Bp of Oxford—H. Maitland—Jas Watson. Went to the Slogh with Helen 11½–2¼: it is really grand: over much so for my giddy

[1] H. W. Longfellow, *The seaside and the fireside* (1849) in which 'The building of the ship' was the principal poem.

[2] Unidentified.

[3] Printer to the *Montrose Standard*, printing the university speech.

[4] The third codicil, signed on 19 September 1850, gave Helen the option of occupying Phesdo house and part of its estate.

head.[1] Aftn got flowers for Jessy's coffin: which I visit daily. Read Laocoon —Forbes Cons. Mod.—Lavater[2]—Swift—Lyell's Geology.[3]

18. Wed.

Wrote to C.G—Gurneys—J. Amery—J. Griffiths—Lawson—Mayow—T.H. Taunton—Bellairs. Saw Paterson. Read Laocoon—Bp Forbes Cons Mod—Swift. Corr. Proofs. Hill walk—Visit to the Vault as usual.

19. Th.

Wrote to C.G—Jas Watson—W.K. Hamilton. All the morning with my Father, or Mr Myers, respecting the new codicil executed today. Hill walk—&c. Dined with the Forbeses. Read Bp Forbes—Laocoon—Swift—Memoirs of Duchillon.[4]

20. Fr.

Wrote to C.G—Rn. G—Lees—Maitland—Watson—Sec. Y.N.B. Co—H. Tayleur. Wrote for my Father. Worked on my affairs. Walk with John—visits. Read Bp Forbes—Laocoon—Aytoun's Lays of the Cavaliers[5]—Swift—Memoirs of a Traveller.[6]

21. Sat. St Matthew.

Chapel 11 A.M. Wrote to C.G—Rn. G—Jas Watson—H. Maitland—C.B. Adderley—W. Yool[7]—Alex. Gibbon.[8] Corrected proofsheets. Read Bp Forbes—Laocoon. Walk with J.N.G. Dinner party: my Father kept to his room: & all seemed unnatural in consequence. No man was ever more the life of his own hospitalities. Hope came in evg. Conv. with him. Preparing for departure.

22. 17 S. Trin.

Chapel 11¼ & 3. Reading service to my Father. Wrote to Manning. Read Bp Forbes—Melville's Letter to me[9]—Caled[onian] RR. papers (for a cause).[10] Walk with Hope and conversation on the case of the Church. All his old doubts & dispositions have revived; but he seems disposed to think & act steadily. Finished packing. My Father bid me a most affectionate farewell. In the middle of the day he said 'I *may* perhaps be alive when you

[1] The slogh of Birnie, 3 mile NE. of Fasque.
[2] One of J. C. Lavater's *Werke*, 6 v. (1834–38); on physiognomy.
[3] Cp. 5 Aug. 50.
[4] J. M. Dutens, known as Duchillon, *Memoires sur les travaux publics de l'Angleterre* (1819).
[5] W. E. *Aytoun, *Lays of the Scottish cavaliers, and other poems* (1849).
[6] i.e. Duchillon.
[7] William Alexander Yool, 1826–83; actuary to ecclesiastical commission from ?1854.
[8] Financial pamphleteer.
[9] D. Melville, 'A practical question about Oxford, considered in a letter to . . . Gladstone' (1850).
[10] Hawn P; further amalgamations.

return. At night he was in higher spirits. I rejoice to think that the thankful & tranquil tone is now predominant in his mind.

23. M.

Wrote to Watson—Sec. Y.N.B. Left Fasque at 5¾ A.M: reached St Andrew's 10¾. Inspected the houses & building ground there: then went to the Cathedral &c. Reached Edinbro at 3. Saw Mr Maitland—went to E.P.D. Office[1] for business—called on Mr Ramsay whom I missed—gave up Glasgow—walk round Arthur's seat—read Lessing's Laocoon. Off at 9¼ P.M. for Lpool.

24. T.

Reached Broad Green at 7¼. Went with Rn. to Lpool & Seaforth at 9½—Went over the property & through the House—Saw Mr Grant—Mr Staniforth—the latter with much sympathy & concern but he seems to have a Christian fortitude given him—Ret[urne]d to Broad Green to see M.E.—Off to Chester at five: saw Messrs. Barker & Burnett there on Stephen's matters—then to Hawarden, & well tired to bed. Saw Lavinia: rather too soon I thought for baby is but 9 days old: a really *pretty* child.[2]

25. Wed.

Church 6½ P.M. Wrote to Sir J.G—Ld Braybrooke—Mr Oldfield—Mr W.U. Richards—Bp of London—Rev. D. Melville.[3] Read Laocoon. Saw Mr Griffiths—Mr Brewster. The Brabazons came: walk with him.

26. Th.

Wrote to Lincoln—Rn. G—E.L. Robertson—Scotts—Hampton—T.G.—Sec. Y.N.B. Co. Saw Mr Burnett on the proposed purchase. Walk with C. Read Laocoon—Pepys. Church at 8½ A.M.

27. Fr.

Church at 8½ A.M. Wrote to G. Burnett—R. Barker (with Memorandum of proposed proceedings)[4]—Grant (Bahamas)[5]—Grant (Oxford)[6]—Jas Watson—C.B. Adderley. Worked on Guides & Handbooks. Read Laocoon (finished)—Pepys. Walk with C. & to meet Mary from Rhyl: much better thank God yet most susceptible & in a state clearly showing the need of the measure we propose.

[1] Of the Edinburgh, Perth and Dundee Railway.

[2] Gertrude Jessy, diarist's god-da., and 4th da. of Henry Glynne, m. as his second wife George Sholto Gordon Douglas-*Pennant, 1836–1907; tory M.P. Carnarvonshire 1866–8, 1874–80; 2nd Baron Penrhyn 1886; controversial quarry-owner. She d. 1940.

[3] David Melville, 1808–1904; tutor at Durham University 1842–51; principal of Hatfield Hall 1846–51; canon of Worcester 1851, dean 1881; D.D. 1882; cp. 22 Sept. 50.

[4] Hawn P.

[5] Probably G. Grant.

[6] i.e. Anthony *Grant.

28. Sat.

Church 8½ A.M.

Wrote to	Mahon (Lt)[1]	Mahon (Lord)
J. Griffith	Mansel	T.G.
J. Amery	O'Brien	Jas. Watson
R. Smith	Scotts	R. Ward.

Swan (W[olver]hampton) (susp[ende]d).

Read Pepys—Caled. Report & Debate. Chess with Stephen. Walked with him to the field of the ploughing match. Discussing & considering routes.

29. St Michael & 18 S. Trin.

Church 11 and 3. Baptism of my little goddaughter Gertrude Jessy Glynne whom God bless. Wrote to Lyttelton—W. Lyttelton—R. Cavendish—A. Acland—W.C. James. Read Horsley's Serm (finished Vol 3)[2]—Daily Steps to Hard Heaven[3]—Forbes, Cons. Mod. Vol I (finished)—Cabramatta Store.[4]

30. M.

Church 8½ A.M. Wrote to Jas Watson (2)—Sec. Y.N.B. Railway. Read Laocoon. 10–6. Journey to Grove Park:[5] where I was most kindly received (every thing warm but the rooms) & found Louisa pretty well, Tom's girls much come on & possessing among them a very uncommon share of good looks.[6]

Tuesday Oct. One. 1850.

Wrote to Ld Aberdeen—C.G—Sec. Y.N.B. Co—Jas Watson. Went with Tom over the place mg—then rode to Warwick—aftn walk to the Lunatic Asylum[7]—spent the evg, as last night, in conversation on family matters.

2. Wed.

Wrote to C.G—Jas Watson—H. Tayleur—H. Maitland—Mr Lamond—Sir J.G—HJG—Mr Bockett. Left Grove Park at 6¼. Reached London at 12. Went to work on letters & papers. Called on Mr Tyler—Mr Bockett. Manning with me 7–11. Looked about for poor E. Clifton: but in vain [R].

[1] Perhaps Thomas Mahon, 1832–79; lieut. R.A. 1850, later colonel.
[2] Cp. 18 Aug. 50.
[3] Cp. 13 Apr. 50.
[4] Cp. 15 Aug. 50 n.
[5] Seat 2½ miles W. of Warwick, then occupied by the diarist's elder brother.
[6] Thomas and Louisa Gladstone had six daughters, none of whom married: Louisa (cp. 6 Aug. 37); Anne, 1839–85; Mary Selina, b. 1842; Evelyn Marcella, 1847–52; Ida, 1849–74; Frances Margaret born in November 1850, d. 1853.
[7] Warwick County Lunatic Asylum with 300 beds.

3. Th.

St Paul's 3¼ PM. Wrote to G. Burnett—J. Griffiths—C.G—Gurneys—Williams & Co—Dr Fergusson[1]—Spent the forenoon in seeking Dr Fergusson & Mr Hodgson to see whether in case of need one of them cd. go down to see Lavinia who alas lies very dangerously ill. Aftn in city—Saw Johnson & Longdens—Williamses—Overends (on S.R.G.'s matters). Manning came to dine & staid 7–11. His conversation on these two evenings opens to me a still darkening prospect. Alas for what lies before us: for my deserts it cannot indeed be gloomy enough: but for the sheep & lambs of Christ! Read Scottish Presbyter's Letter to Bp of Glasgow.[2] At 11 PM. Lavinia [Glynne] died. When *I* went to look for E.C.—in vain [R].

4. Fr.

Wrote to

C. Stewart	T.G.	J. Masters
D.S. Bockett	C.G.	Rn. G.
R. Barker (2)	Burnett	
Scotts (2)	R.H. Smith	
Collis	J. Watson	
E.L. Robertson	O.B. Cole	

Saw Towns—R. Phillimore, on Church Affairs—D.S. Bockett, on mortgages—Bonham—S. Scott—G. & W. Lyttelton who between one and two brought the sad account of their sister's death. Lavinia was a soul singularly pure and sweet though quite mature: she was infancy and womanhood together. It is well with her: Earth has lost, and Paradise has gained. I went with the Brothers to the Station. Read Q.R. on California[3]—Allies on the See of Peter.[4]

5. Sat.

Wrote to J.L. and Co—C.G.—Sir J.G.—Lawson—Lincoln. Arranged my letters of ¾ of this year—Worked I think 5 hours on accounts for myself & S.R.G's matters. Saw Phillimore—De Tabley—C.A. Wood—Mr Oldfield—the Lytteltons, on their way back, & went with them to Euston Square.[5] Also saw Jane Tyler. Sought E.C. (as yesty.) but in vain [R]. Could I do otherwise in common humanity? Read Allies.

6. 19 S. Trin.

St Andrews 11 A.M. & H.C.—Bedfordbury 7 P.M. Read Allies (finished)—Bp Berkeley—Christian Remembrr.—Ch. Miss[ionary] Report.[6] Wrote to

[1] i.e. R. Ferguson.
[2] 'A letter to . . . . the bishop of Glasgow. By a Scotch Presbyter' (1850).
[3] *Quarterly Review*, lxxxvii. 395 (September 1850).
[4] T. W. Allies, *The see of St. Peter, the rock of the church, the source of jurisdiction and the centre of unity* (1850). Gladstone was upset by it, cp. Add MS 44369, f. 411.
[5] As now, the terminus for trains to the north-west.
[6] *Christian Remembrancer*, xx. 488 (October 1850); on North American missions.

Manning [1]—Allies—Alex. Hope—H. Mackenzie [2]—E. Hawkins—Sec. Tithe Red. Trust.[3]

7. M.

Wrote to Lincoln—Cocks & Co—Dowbiggin—Mrs Tennant—St Martin's Churchwardens—J.H. Parker—Rev Mr [O.] Tennant—Jas Watson—Scotts. In the City with Overends & Johnson Longden & Co—then shopping. Read Lessing. Went by the evening Express to Hawarden: conv. with Ward & with Charteris on the way. Reached Hn. before midnight: & in a long conversation afterwards received from C. the harrowing details of Lavinia's death. She was worn with her pious services: but the recollection of them is sweet for this world & the next.

8. T.

Wrote to Lincoln—Hampton—Miss Brown—Hodgson—Hinde—R. Barker. The day was chiefly passed in the conversations & arrangements of a time & scene like this. Saw Burnett. Drive & walk with C.

9. Wed.

Church 8½ A.M. Wrote to S. Gurney [4]—Willy—Sir John Forbes—copied & sent letter to Allies after submitting it to Stephen.[5] Went to Chester with Burnett & made with him the necessary arrangements for the correspondence in relation to the mortgages during my absence. We have I think now a great opportunity of improving Stephen's position. Read Pepys's Diary—Engl. Rev. on Hungary—& on Church Emancn.[6]

10. Th.

Church 8½ A.M. Wrote to J.N.G—H. Maitland. Read Pepys—Engl. Rev. Walk with W. Lyttelton. We feel ourselves too large a party & the interval before the funeral too long. I if any am one of the intruders: but C. wished me here soon, & she is the prop & centre of all the rest. But every one seems to feel the approach of the funeral.

11. Fr.

Church at 11 (Funeral & Holy Communion) A.M.: & 7 P.M. Wrote to Hampton—Oldfield—and Walter James.

The morning was chiefly occupied in preparations for the funeral. We (the men who were mourners) walked behind the coffin: six clergymen bore the pall: a few friends followed us, then the servants & others: the whole

[1] Lathbury, i. 117.
[2] A few letters deleted here.
[3] W. T. Young; cp. 27 June 49.
[4] Samuel *Gurney, 1786–1856; partner in Overend and Gurney.
[5] Draft in Add MS 44369, f. 411.
[6] *English Review*, xiv. 1, 93 (September 1850).

population seemed to attend: the church was crowded & 200 communicated. It was a moving and an edifying scene. The death of a young mother, when caused by her maternal office, is always touching: and few people touched so deeply as the lost Lavinia. But lost she is not—except to sight. Would that we were well with her or may well follow her. Went to the vault to arrange the coffins after the services were over. Walk with Stephen. Saw Barker. Read Plain Sermons[1]—Pepys.

12. Sat.

Church 8½ A.M. Wrote (draft) to Bockett. Walk with Stephen & W.L.—Chess with Stephen. Read Lessing—Pepys.

13. 20 S. Trin.

Church 11 A.M. an admirable Sermon, of course hav[in]g reference to Lavinia, from Mr Brewster—& 7 P.M. when Mr Ffoulkes preached well on the same matter. Wrote to Manning—Harris. Read Lyra Apostolica[2]—Engl. Review[3]—Manual of Devotions.[4] went off immediately after evg Ch[urch] & travelled all night to London.

14. M.

Reached London 5 A.M.—To bed for 2½ hours. Wrote to Parker—Watson—Elliot—Addington—Mahon—Ld Mayor of York[5]—Johnson L. & Co—Simson[6]—Barlow—Mrs Tennant—A. Good[7]—City Remembrancer—Pr. Castelcicala. Worked on S.R.G.s money matters. Saw Messrs. Oldfield & Baylis—Mr D. Wyatt—& Mr Fox at the Exhibition Works which I visited in the aftn[8]—also Scotts. Read Monro's 'Reasons'.[9] Shopping.

15. T.

Wrote to S.R. Glynne—Mr R. Barker—Mr D.S. Bockett—T.G—Sir J.G—Mary Lyttelton. Shopping.

C.G. arrived while I was in the city & found a new inflammation in Mary's eye from the cold & journey yesterday. We saw Dalrymple, but late: & cannot now go Thursday. But there has been a cessation for many weeks now: & thank God this is much in her favour. Her general appearance too is good: her spirits high: and she is quick lively & captivating in the highest degree. Her illness has however interrupted discipline. Saw Fairman[10]—

[1] [G. C. Perceval], *Plain sermons preached in a village church*, 3 v. (1831).
[2] Cp. 16 Jan. 48.
[3] *English Review*, xiv. 1 (September 1850).
[4] Cp. 7 Sept. 45.
[5] George H. Seymour.
[6] Probably James Simson, d. 1876; M.D. Edinburgh 1816; Edinburgh surgeon.
[7] Possibly August Good, London cork manufacturer.
[8] (Sir) Charles *Fox, 1810–74; engineer; with John Henderson and *Paxton designed and erected the buildings for the 1851 exhibition in Hyde Park; kt. 1851.
[9] E. *Monro, 'Reasons for feeling secure in the Church of England' (1850).
[10] Perhaps John N. Fairman, customs searcher, about the journey.

E. Hawkins—then, in the City, Overends—Johnson Longden & Co—& settled (I hope) S's money affairs so far as needful for the time of my absence. Saw Dalrymple: we must put off our journey. Busy upon letters, accounts, & other preparatory arrangements until between one & two.

16. Wed.

Wrote to Jas Watson—H. Maitland—Johnson Longden & Co—J.C. Colquhoun—Willy—J.N.G (2)—Lyttelton. Saw Bp of Toronto—R. Phillimore—Mr Dalrymple. Shopping & walk with C. Continued busy with arrangements for our journey. Read Ward's (2d) Pamphlet[1]—Wilson's Appeal[2]—Scott's Letter to him.[3]

17. Th.

Wrote to Scotts (2)—Mrs Ward—R.B. Lawley[4]—D.S. Bockett—R. Barker—J.D. Coleridge—E. of Lincoln—Bp of Salisbury—Ed. Morn. Chronicle (2)[5]—J. Murray—Rev. S. Clarke. Read Keble's No II.[6] In the City about my passport: & again a busy day of preparation & clearing up. But even preparation must end, when departure comes. Saw Phillimore—Mr S. Clarke. Gave Agnes her Bible Lesson. Late to bed.

18. Fr.

Set out at a quarter past eight for the Boulogne boat leaving London Bridge at 9. We had a beautiful passage until we reached the chops of the Channel when all but Edward[7] were sick, C. suffering much beyond her wont, & little Mary giving way last. We arrived between eight & nine. I was much incensed at the impudence of the captain in kissing & hugging Agnes: & was very hot. I saw the baggage through the custom-house where it was sadly rummaged. We put up at the H. des Bains: & there I met Dr Begbie(?)[8] who spoke to me of Naples, from Jany. onwards. Read Lessing, Lit. Letters.[9] Wrote to the Captain of the Steamer, *warning* him.

Sat. 19.

Mary's eye showed a red spot today. But she was in high force & spirits. Walk with C. & A. in Boulogne—Went off by the midday train: reached Paris at 6½: went to the hotel Victoria: rather at a venture. I left my card

[1] W. G. *Ward, 'The Anglican establishment . . . a second letter to *The Guardian*' (1850); on *Gorham; cp. 18 Aug. 50.

[2] Daniel Wilson, 'Appeal to the evangelical members of the Church of England' (1850).

[3] 'Letter to the Rev. D. Wilson . . . by Mr. W. Scott' (1850); cp. *Christian Remembrancer*, xx. 517 (December 1850).

[4] *Sc.* B. R. Lawley.

[5] To announce departure.

[6] J. *Keble, 'Church matters in 1850. No. 2.' (1850).

[7] The servant.

[8] James *Begbie, 1799–1869; Edinburgh physician; president of Medico-Chirurgical Society 1850–52; Queen's physician 1853.

[9] '19. Sat.' here deleted.

at the Embassy & Elysée.[1] The servants followed us by a later train: & C. had much work in the case of Mary. Wrote up accounts &c.

20. 21 S. Trin.

Church Rue d'Aguesseau[2] 11½ & 4. Madeleine Sermon at 9½: Abbe Laine or Paine. I was at some distance & the echo almost prevented my hearing, except that the general strain was upon authority as essential to a religious community. Again in aftn Abbe Watrin: on reason & faith: the first must, after examining the motives for belief, surrender itself: but in order to be rehabilitated. The doctrine was however rather rigidly & jarringly stated. In the evg inquiries about our journey southwards. Dinner at table d'hote; interminable. We are taken in as to our hotel: though not uncomfortable in rooms or food. It is filled with English not of a high order of travellers. Prayers in evg: & made a comment on the Epistle of the day.[3]

21. M.

Much trouble about the Passport: which is reported not arrived from Boulogne. Went with C. to Notre Dame: & after that to a dinner at a Palais Royal Restaurant. Called on MM. Guizot & Montalembert: both out of Paris. At the Bankers' for money. Opera in the evening: Bremond was Edgar in Lucia: a good actor.[4] Afterwards Cerito[5] danced in a pantomime ballet: she is a wonderful work of art, a statue made alive. She is most graceful & most remarkable of all I think in gesticulation with the arms where there is no muscular feat to perform. Also St Leon's violin playing was very notable: both in feeling when he chose & for *tours de force*. Read 'La Madone de Rimini'.[6]

22. T.

Breakfast café & dinner Restaurant with C.—We went to Versailles & lost ourselves for two hours amidst the bewilderments of that wonderful palace.[7] I spent the early part of the day 11–1½ in doing myself the work of my passport, apprehensive from yesterday's failure. Theatre François in evg.[8] Madlle Brehan (Marguerite)[9] Samson (Charles V)[10] and Geffroi

[1] Then, as now, the president's official residence.
[2] The Anglican chapel off the Faubourg St. Honoré.
[3] Eph. vi. 10.
[4] Bremond is unidentified. The opera was Donizetti's *Lucia di Lammermoor* (1835).
[5] Francesca Cerrito, 1817–1909; Neapolitan dancer known as 'the fourth grace'; m. to Charles Victor Arthur Saint-Léon, 1821–70, French violinist, dancer, choreographer and composer. The ballet was probably 'Le Violon du diable', choreographed by St. Léon (1849), in which he danced and played the violin.
[6] 'La Madone de Rimini, ou relation de l'évènement miraculeux qui vient d'avoir lieu à Rimini' (?1850).
[7] 10 miles WSW. of the centre of Paris.
[8] The play was 'Les contes de la reine de Navarre' by E. Scribe and E. Legouvé, first performed in 1850.
[9] Madeleine Brehan, French actress.
[10] Joseph Isidore Samson, 1793–1871; French comedy actor; retired 1863.

(Francis I)[1] excellent: the last particularly tho' it was the smallest part. Read 'Les hommes politiques du jour jugès d'après Lavater['][2] &c. Notwithstanding the bitter cold, in which little Mary was out yesterday, her eye has not suffered.

23. Wed.

Wrote to Sir J.G—T.G—Hampton. We found this morning that little Mary's eye had suffered notwithstanding the confinement to the house yesterday & this induced us to forfeit our places, change our plans & buy the carriage of our friends the Warburtons with whom we breakfasted & spent the forenoon upon the question. In the evening we all dined at Vefours' and had coffee at the Rotonde[3] altogether: passing the time very agreeably. In the afternoon we went to the Louvre where only the French School was to been seen. It has many Claudes & Poussins, and is strong in Vernets. Of the other French painters I admire Le Brun most though not very warmly. Of the Poussins none equalled Ld Ashburnham's: but a small Assumption by the door is very remarkable considering the artist for its *grouping* & the rape of the Sabines agreeable because being a picture of dispersion one does not as in so many of his works while admiring the excellence of the figures singly miss unity in the composition as a whole.[4]
Read Les hommes politiques &c. & began Reybaud's Jerome Paturot.[5] We have fixed to have prayers wherever we have a fixed morning.

24. Th.

Another busy day upon the repairs of the carriage & preparations for departure. Dined with the Warburtons again at Vefour's[6]—No time in the day for any sights. Shopping—getting money &c. In the evening the carriage came home & we were busy in getting ready for an early start. I went through the Bourse in the forenoon & heard the astounding but as it seems daily din of the auction of the Rentes. Finished 'Les hommes Politiques'. The Warburton's saw us home in the evening: & we bid them farewell with much regret.

25.

For most of my occupations from this time, see Journal of my Tour.[7] Here I shall still note down what I may write, or read, with other matter more

[1] Edmond Aimé Florentin Geffroy, 1804–95; actor, mostly at the Comédie Française, author and painter.
[2] Untraced; a work assessing contemporary politicians after the system of the phrenologist J. C. Lavater; cp. 17 Sept. 50.
[3] Véfour's restaurant and the Café de la Rotonde were both in the Palais Royal.
[4] 'L'enlèvement des Sabines', painted 1637–9.
[5] M. R. L. Reybaud, *Jérôme Paturot à la recherche d'une position sociale* (1842) and its sequel *Jérôme Paturot à la recherche de la meilleure des républiques*, 3 v. (1848); satires on the July monarchy.
[6] In the Palais Royal.
[7] Add MS 44818E; entries from it until 25 December 1850 follow the daily entry from the Lambeth diary after a break of one line. Sometimes the travel diary was not written. It is headed 'Paris Octr 1850'. Catherine Gladstone also kept a diary of this expedition, in Hawn P.

inwardly personal as it may occur. No study today but of handbooks, maps, and the Livre de Poste:[1] accounts at night.

As our journey is undertaken for the health of our little Mary, and as that object governs the whole of our movements, we pass by on the right and on the left what is most interesting without even a glance, and can therefore have little of the material at command which fills an ordinary journal. Still as some things will even [*sc.* ever] force themselves on the view of the merest passer by, and as all foreign travels should show men and manners even without the deliberate search for them, I shall separate what relates to our tour henceforward from my private Journal.

We left Paris *Friday Oct. 25* by the Orleans train of 7.45 A.M. Our hotel the Victoria was all we had a right [to] expect: we had clean rooms and very eatable victuals: the general conveniences belonging to superior hotels we had not a right to expect there.

One hundred & ninety miles of Railway to Nevers cost 254 francs or £10.3 for the carriage and ourselves in it: or about 13 pence a mile for the vehicle and five third class places. This I think is dearer than in England. The Orleans line however is less liberal than the Centre: which includes 3 tickets in the carriage fare. We did not quite cover 20 miles an hour. We had however a good stoppage at Orleans: and I went off at a venture to see the Cathedral[2] which pleased me a good deal. The stone is in a state of singular sharpness and freshness. There are beautiful though not very large rose windows: & many of them: some with a star pattern. The whole exterior surface is deeply pierced with light & shade, contrasting well with the extreme flatness of the sides at (for example) Notre Dame & Strasburgh. The transepts are singularly short, much shorter than Notre Dame, and the nave is I think the shorter limb of the Cross. There are five aisles as at N.D. and with the same (as it seems to me) grave defect that the four outer ones are of uniform height, against the law of progression as applicable to a pointed building, but the eye reaches into them more than at N.D. where they are almost lost, and the only way I found to appreciate at all the magnitude of the Church was by standing at the extreme West end. At Orleans the Choir is very nobly lofty: and the triforium is sized more like ours than Notre Dame. The West front is very fine. But the exterior view like that of the (few) other French Cathedrals I have seen, even Amiens has not the changing but homogeneous & unbroken harmony which the general view of our best Cathedrals gives at whatever distance & from whatever point of view.

I scudded back to the Railway in some fear: & found the buffet at the Gare[3] pretty good but not very cheap.

We were obliged on the principle I have named to scud past Bourges[4]

[1] The French government's guide to posting, published annually, giving official distances and charges.

[2] The cathedral of St. Croix, built in the seventeenth century, but in the gothic style.

[3] Railway station.

[4] 69 miles SE. of Orleans.

and reached Nevers[1] at dusk. At six we got off and reached Moulins,[2] notwithstanding abundant entreaties, some objurgations, & pay well raised whenever I could get any thing like service, only at half past eleven.

In the sandy district before reaching Orleans, we found the grapes hanging thick on the trees, the leaves deadbrown beside them, & the snow at mid-day still lingering on the ground.

Before this we traversed a great corn district, where indeed there was scarcely a sign of any thing else. The ploughs heavy, with large useless wheels that might relieve the man a little & burden the horses much. The ploughing shallow, & mere turning over of the land without any setting up. Most of it however was with horses two abreast. But it was odd to see within two hundred yards six harrows with one horse to each & two men for all, and one harrow with three horses & two persons. But there were probably half a dozen different estates between. The sheep were among the stubbles with little appearance of food, hardly any green crops, mangel-wurzels where any.

At Moulins faithful to Murray[3] I drove to the Hotel d'Allier[4] despite the postillion who pooh-poohed it as not meant for voitures en passe but only Diligences.[5] Independently of other considerations there is great advantage on arriving late in going to a place where you find people alive with coach work, instead of unbarring a great gate to enter upon cold, desolation, & infinite delay of supper. But the Hotel d'Allier is also a good one & a moderate.

Our evening & morning were occupied with necessary work.

I was ill satisfied indeed with this commencement of French posting: sluggish heavy & extortionate were the epithets most applicable to those who drove us.

26. Sat.

Wrote (from Roannes)[6] to the Director of Posts. More work on Murray and the Livre des Postes. Mary is most fascinating but with strong self will: with affections I believe equally strong which will aid much in the battle with it. Agnes is most patient yielding and unselfish: but there is room for more energy, which we hope this journey may develop. The characteristic qualities of each have started out very clearly.

Saturday, Oct. 26. After our long journey of 226 miles yesterday lasting 16 hours, we gave the children a long rest and only started at half past ten from Moulins. We travelled somewhat better, always through a well cultivated country till we got among the high lands after passing La Palisse.[7]

[1] 35 miles ESE. of Bourges.

[2] 30 miles S. of Nevers.

[3] John Murray, *Handbook for travellers in France* (many editions, probably that of 1849).

[4] On the bank of the Allier, the only hotel recommended by Murray.

[5] The French stage coach, 'a huge, heavy, lofty, lumbering machine, something between an English stage and a broad-wheeled wagon', Murray, op. cit., xxv.

[6] 50 miles SE. of Moulins.

[7] Midway between Moulins and Roanne.

I may mention that the Post Inn there is reputed to be good; as also at St. Pierre le Moutier[1] which we passed last night.

Regularly as we move southwards the standard of agriculture is lowered. We were yesterday with horses, today with oxen.

We found difficulty in getting horses & the post masters pleaded the English mail.

At St. Germain l'Espinasse[2] I had a row with a stripling of that very unsatisfactory & greedy race the French postilions. It was of constant occurrence on the road that they disputed my reckoning for the horses: and they always either were in a blunder or intended fraud. This lad of whom I now speak tried to get 12 sous more than was due for the horses and failed: & then as I paid him a trifle under the 50 sous per myriametre[3] (being ill satisfied with his pace) he raised a debate about the children wanting to make me pay for them as a person in the teeth of the law. He was abetted by the succeeding postilion & kept me half an hour in debate putting again & again the same question & demanding to see the children & judge of their age. At last the post master appeared & put an end to this impudent proceeding. I promised to complain to the Director of Posts: & on reaching Roanne about half past eight I wrote to him accordingly.

27. 22 S. Trin.

Morning Prayer at 12: interrupted however (after being first delayed by minor matters) by a violent sickness of Agnes who was put to bed & in the evening had fever. Thank God we are in a fair Inn, nay a good one. Prayers in evg at nine: & a comment from Notes previously made on the Gospel. Heard two Sermons in the Churches of the town & lost another by misinformation. Read Gerbet on the Dogme Générateur.[4]

Little Mary inimitable in her fun. When the two were left together in the morning, she said she was taking care of Agnes. Then got her dolls made up and averred 'I am a Mama, I'm nursing': & when C. wanted tea, she said 'I'll go down to the kitchen, as well as I can'. I don't know how she looks when thus put on paper but she really is the very best company oftentimes. Worked on Journal.

Sunday, Oct. 27. Roanne (Hotel de la Poste).[5] I tried without prejudice to our own private proceedings at the Inn, to turn today to account in the way of Churches and Sermons: but it is really most difficult to find out, unless one hits upon the official persons, what sermons and when there are to be. I however fell in the morning upon a prône[6] to schoolchildren after the monthly Communion at the lower paroisee[7] which was in the nature of a

[1] Midway between Nevers and Moulins.

[2] 8 miles NE. of Roanne.

[3] Ten thousand metres; since 1840 substituted with kilometres for 'postes' as the official measurement of coaching distances.

[4] O. P. Gerbert, *Considérations sur le dogme génèrateur de la piété catholique* (1829).

[5] 'Bad and dirty' according to Murray's *Guide to France* (1847), 371.

[6] 'Sermon'.

[7] 'Parish church'.

general exhortation to manifest gratitude to God for His precious gifts & His love, in the way of attendance (as well as I could make out not being very near) on divine Ordinances. There were no men, except one, and the schoolchildren. So again at a Sermon in the College Church[1] in the afternoon. But at the Mass without Sermon in the principal Paroisee the men were perhaps a fourth.

C. and I got well placed at the College Church, & heard the Sermon of (as I understood) M. Garrabè, who is 'Principal, aumonier, et tout',[2] to the Establishment. He preached with energy on earnestness & in a Gallican tone, quoting Bossuet,[3] highly commending Gerson[4] as the father in Christ of many souls, and glancing distinctly at the Jesuits when he thus asserted the dignity of the Catholic morality 'Je dis la morale Catholique, je ne dis pas des particuliers, mais la morale de l'Eglise', taken in its '*ensemble*'.[5] His subject was the reasonableness of believing, generally considered: the certainty of the historical facts of our Saviour's existence and work, His miracles, His doctrine, & His appointment of an Organ for the continuing & propagation of that doctrine. He dwelt upon Mahometan, heretical, & external testimonies to the facts of religion as well as that of Christians: upon the moral and social evidences of the mighty work done by the Church in the world, society transformed, all laws, all life & manners, impregnated with the new spirit from the Gospel. He dwelt upon the new trophies and certain ultimate triumph of the Church: there is England he said, view that protestant people: our exiled priests went among them and were seen and known by them: les opinions sont adoucies, les prejudices [*sc.* préjugés] ont tombès, et aujourdhui après tant de temps l'Angleterre retourne au sein du catholicisme.[6] The doctrine to which he invited his people lay in the Gospels, the Epistles, the works of the Fathers: its corruption was morally impossible as the testimony of Christendom would have cried down the innovator: il y a tous [*sc.* toutes] nos doctrines, tous nos Eveques, tous nos Archevêques, et le Pape;[7] who indeed came in rather as the tail than as the climax. It was in the main I thought a thoroughly well meant & honest Sermon, full of fervour; but behind the age in reference to the modern forms of infidelity.

The chief parish Church[8] is a modern Cruciform: built I understand by the town: of good interior effect, but indefensible detail without, & a shabbiness in having the front of one stone & the main part of the body & the Choir of another & inferior kind. There are many painted windows, with the figures well drawn but in the general effect having French defects, glare and want of repose and solemnity.

Though there is a Churchgoing class here, Sunday seems miserably kept.

[1] In the college, by the Rue de la Côte; rebuilt later in the century.

[2] 'Principal, chaplain and everything'.

[3] Jacques Bénigne Bossuet, 1627–1704; French bp. and theologian.

[4] Jean Charlier de Gerson, 1363–1429; French philosopher and theologian.

[5] 'I speak of Catholic morality, I do not speak about particular aspects of it, but of the morality of the Church' taken 'as a whole'.

[6] 'Opinions are softened, prejudices have been abandoned, and today after so long England is returning to the bosom of catholicism'.

[7] 'There are all our doctrines, all our Bishops, all our Archbishops, and the Pope'.

[8] Notre Dame des Victoires, built in the style of thirteenth century.

Every shop was open, as my eyes can bear too confident witness, from morning to night. I am not sure whether I did mark *one* exception: if so it was only one.

28. SS. Simon & Jude. Monday.

Agnes thank God better. No literature beyond Murray & the Post Book, and in the evening the French Guide[1] (faute de Murray) save a little Jerome Paturot. C. has very hard work & I shall rejoice when she can rest a little. Both Edward & Emily[2] shape well & have good courage. Wrote to my Father—the Postmaster at Avignon.

Monday, Oct 28. 8½–4½ Roanne to Lyons, 88 kilom., with the old half poste Royale at the Lyons end, deprived of course of its distinctive name.

We left our Hotel at Roanne, La Poste, with regrets being very well treated there. The beds we found excellent, the kitchen very superior; only one department was faulty, which may be guessed, & I took the liberty of speaking to the landlady about it, in the interest of the house, when I came away.

The last half of the stage to S. Symphorien[3] being the early part of the Tarare ascent has much beauty: as has the view up the Rhone at the Roanne Bridge.[4]

As we get Southwards agriculture still degenerates for we now come to the most miserable little ploughs held by *one* hand of the ploughman while with the other he has a long staff to lick his oxen!

The country is high & rather cold on the whole but with some extensive prospects. Soon after leaving Salvagny[5] we got a noble view of the Alps: the only fine one, as we afterwards found, that we were to enjoy on their northern side. The environs of Lyons are seen from some distance but not the body of the town.

For the last stage we were visited with a second postilion as well as a fourth horse—the allegation was that this was necessary on entering and quitting Lyons. I was incredulous but did not know that I could help myself.

Upon arriving there I set about information respecting these routes—

1. Grenoble to Nice & Genoa
2. Avignon to do
3. Chambery[6] to Genoa

and concluded in favour of the last, which is new to Catherine & offers us the quickest access to an Italian climate. The evening was occupied with matters of money & business.

[1] Perhaps *Guide pittoresque du voyageur en France*, 6 v. (1838).
[2] Servants accompanying the party.
[3] St. Symphorien en Lay, 10 miles SE. of Roanne.
[4] The new stone bridge at Roanne on the St. Symphorien road, over the Loire (not the Rhône).
[5] About 10 miles from Lyons on the Roanne–Lyons road.
[6] In Savoy, then independent, 50 miles ESE. of Lyons.

We were at the Hotel de Provence[1] and thought it decidedly good, with an intelligent & attentive landlady.

The steamers to Avignon are not cheap for passengers & for carriages so dear that they save hardly anything as compared with posting. At this season there is it appears great uncertainty about reaching Avignon within the day: and thus the advantage vanishes.

29. T.

Wrote to Postmaster at Nice—Landlady Hotel de Provence. Read Jerome Paturot. Worked on accounts, route, &c. in evg.

Oct. 29. Tuesday. We started at seven & reached Chambery at the same hour. Today we had no clear view of the Alps & saw nothing of the pure snowwhite tops, but only of some that for the moment wore hairpowder.

At Pont de Beauvoisin[2] I recovered 100 francs from the custom house on the carriage which I had purchased from Mr. Warburton. I should have failed to get this as the entry was in his name, had it not been for an indorsement which we made signifying that the interest in the carriage was transferred to me & signed by him.

The people of the Sardinian custom house simply looked into my passport and set me free to go without a word about searching except asking whether I had anything to declare. They did not seem to wait for money and I only gave a couple of francs to one who seemed of the lower order among them.

Though we had not a very fine afternoon, we enjoyed and admired exceedingly the two passes of the two first stages in Savoy, on either side of the Station Les Echelles.[3] The tunnel of the second, exchanging the sides of the mountain, heightens the effect of the grandeur & beauty of the ascent by a surprise.

Both on this and following days we found the horses more readily and actively served at the station after crossing the frontier than in France. In both countries we experienced occasionally delay from want of them. The Savoy Tariff follows the old French post equal to 8 kilom. or 4/5 of the myriameter. It is lower therefore *per horse*: but to us it becomes higher because the two children are charged as a person, which we just escaped in France by Mary's wanting a few weeks of being three years old.

I am therefore liable for five horses: and I also find the postmasters, when they are entitled to charge a cheval de renfort,[4] trying to count the fourth harnessed horse in that character and make me pay two petits chevaux or unharnessed horses: but this I refused steadily, and will not pay for any *extra* horse until all the regular horses have been put to. And as I have five persons, and we *never* go beyond five horses, the cheval de renfort only turns my petits chevaux into actual horses.

[1] The second best hotel in Lyons.
[2] The last village in France on the Chambéry road.
[3] So called because of the ladders and tunnels of the old roads built to avoid mountain torrents.
[4] Trace horse.

30. Wed.

The day nearly as yesterday. Read Jérome Paturot a little: but 12 hours en route and the arrangements before & after pretty nearly fill my time.

Oct. 30. Wednesday. 7 A.M. to 8 P.M. 14½ posts. Chambèry to Modane.[1] But we were at S. Michel[2] before 5: and should have been at Modane before seven but for a horse who as they said fell ill on the road and kept us over three hours on the last stage.

The Inn at Chambèry we found very good: & moderate in charges.

The drive of today was much finer than from my recollections of February 1832[3] I had supposed we should find it: which shows the gain of even the latest autumn over dead winter for scenery. Indeed no part of it was without interest. It was particularly fine soon after quitting Aiguebelle:[4] for the whole distance generally from Grande Maison[5] to near St. Jean: and again soon after quitting St. Jean. My French Guide book is a good deal too much horrified and repelled by the sternness of the rocks. Stern indeed they are but very noble and grand in form and much relieved by wood as well as by cultivation.

At St. Jean a large fair or market was going on, where there appeared to be considerable dealings in cattle and sheep for consumption, as I inferred from the fact that the latter, bought probably from feeders on the remoter tracts, were going off for the most part one by one, & the sheep in very small lots indeed, often one two or three, to be fattened. This looks at least like considerable consumption of animal food among the peasantry.

About a mile or little more beyond St. Jean, on the left hand, a small stream trickles down into the road, scarcely more than a thread, which seems to have raised for itself a stalagmite bed projecting some feet from the general plane of the hillside, and itself tumbling down a little channel scooped like a groove along this projection. It is a good example on a small scale of the way in which great rivers like the Mississippi raise themselves above the level of the adjoining country.

The ascent from St. Michel to Modane is very decided. Modane itself is the coldest and most ungenial in character, and from the nature of the vicinage, of all the stations of the ascent. Lans le Bourg[6] for instance though considerably higher has more cultivation about it and is more cheerful and liveable in appearance. The valley is more open there.

We were at the Hotel des Voyageurs: which announces itself on its board as 'for English for travellers'. The beds were not bad but the eating indifferent and very dear. This is in some degree a necessity when everything must be brought from a distance. No grain for example is grown about Modane except rye. But I should not say the Inn was to be recommended.

[1] Midway along the Chambéry to Turin road. [2] 5 miles W. of Modane.

[3] Cp. 29 Feb. 32.

[4] 20 miles E. of Chambéry.

[5] Between Aiguebelle and St. Jean de Maurienne, the latter being the chief town in the valley, known for its wine.

[6] The village at the foot of Mont Cenis and at the start of the ascent to the Col du Mont Cenis. This road was built by Napoleon 1803–10.

31. Th.

We arrived early: I went to the Parochia[1] where was a Benediction. Set Agnes to work on Italian Vocabulary. Busy with accts & Journal. Read Guide for Turin,[2] & Jerome Paturot.

Oct. 31. Thursday. 8–5. 11¾ posts from Modane to Susa.[3] We were detained ¾ of an hour at Lanslebourg for want of horses: so that the distance might easily be done in 8½ hours: and 4½ more would finish the journey to Turin or nearly so.

Tomorrow begins the winter scale of charges, adding 10 sous per post to the charge for horses. For my party as it was the stage from Lanslebourg to Mount Cenis[4] cost 34½ francs: tomorrow it would have been 42, besides the 20 for the barrier: that is over 2/6 per mile. But we must consider what it is that we are doing, crossing with ease & comfort the huge barrier that so long seemed all but invincible.

Within 20 years I cannot doubt but that the railway will surmount or pierce the Alps.[5]

The ascent of Mont Cenis on the Savoy side is very long and tedious as far as mere ascent is concerned, so much is lost in intermediate descents. The route is ill kept too, much worse (on both sides,) than when I passed in 1832. The number of feet surmounted between Pont de Beauvoisin & the top,[6] is I should think much greater than the Splugen,[7] if we do not deduct those again lost by descent, perhaps equal to that of the Stelvio.[8] On the other hand the descent on the Italian side is as in other passes sharp and short: and this greatly heightens the almost magical effect of the change of scene and climate on getting down to Susa.

On the other hand the Savoy side presents a very long range of fine and even grand scenery. To say nothing of the passes below Chambery, how favourably does the road upwards bear comparison with the valley of the Simplon below Brieg,[9] or with the Italian side of the Stelvio below Bormio.[10] Grand forms of mountain, noble & awful walls of rock, intermixture of foliage in which natural beech[11] appears to predominate, and the work of human hands struggling gallantly for every inch of soil, combine to give great interest to the scenery. The views of the *tops* are not generally grand: and it must be admitted that the pass itself, above Lanslebourg, yields the palm to others. It is less grand in the critical points, with more of what is great in the secondary parts.

Nothing can be more picturesque and Alpine than the rapidity with which the eye having just lost Lanslebourg comes from a commanding

[1] San Guisto, eleventh-century church.
[2] Untraced.
[3] In the valley, 32 miles W. of Turin.
[4] The post house at the summit of the col.
[5] The Mont Cenis railway tunnel was begun in 1857 and opened in 1871.
[6] The summit of the pass is at 6,835 ft.
[7] The pass, at 6,814 ft., from Grisons into Lombardy.
[8] At 9,174 ft. the highest pass in Europe suitable for carriages, from the Tyrol into Lombardy.
[9] On the Rhône, 30 miles E. of Sion; see 4 Aug. 49.
[10] 23 miles E. of St. Moritz.
[11] ? birch.

point upon Susa: while still at a great distance. The whole descent to Susa is very fine. Still the road from Lanslebourg to that point fails in this that it is not of the first order of Alpine grandeur: it cannot compare with the Via Mala—with the Swiss prospect in the descent of the Simplon—with the huge flank of the Ortler Spitz[1]—or with the astounding zigzags of either the Splugen or the Stelvio.

Though my Guide book (which I took at Lyons having left my Handbook at home and being unable to replace it there) denounces the *Poste* at Susa as mauvaise et chère,[2] I distinctly aver it to be good and moderate: with a reservation for the beds, which were middling: I was bitten for the first time since our start, in the key of B not in that of F.

Functions were going on in the Churches of Susa when we arrived for the Eve of All Saints. I found that there were to be sermons on the morrow, but not early enough for me.

Friday Nov 1. All Saints.

Wrote to Sir J.G—R. Phillimore. Heard two Sermons after arriving in Turin. Called on Marquis d'Azeglio[3] and the Br. Minister[4]—Worked on Journal & Accounts. Read Jerome Paturot.

Friday Novr. 1. 8½–1½. 7 Posts to Turin. The descent of the valley, very gradual, offers fine scenery on all hands: and in particular the ascent of [blank][5] which crowns the last hill on the right & seems to be the key of the valley is a very noble object.

The people were all in costume for the Festa, and well dressed: the beggars not many: some frightful goitres still.

Nothing can exceed the wearisomeness of the long unbroken avenue of trees which leads nearly the whole distance from Rivoli[6] to Turin: in length it must be 8 miles,[7] in wearisomeness it must be reckoned eighty. Notwithstanding that the Superga[8] closing the vista on its proud elevation makes the perspective a very fine one: and the light vapour that broods even over an Italian city of 120000 people tells that Turin is between it and the eye.

We drove to the Europa[9] which we find as of old an excellent Inn. It indeed is not free from the noxious smells which abound in this capital, though its drainage might one should suppose be excellent: and it fails in another point that of aspect as its principal face is to the north & the western rooms get little of the sun. We are on that side: and we find the beds & kitchen alike admirably good: the service not quite so perfect.

[1] In the Tyrol; its summit of over 14,500 ft. the highest in the Austrian empire.

[2] 'bad and expensive'.

[3] Massimo Taparelli, Marchese d'Azeglio, 1798–1866; romantic novelist; president of the Piedmont council of ministers 1849–52, when replaced by Cavour.

[4] Ralph Abercromby, 1803–68; minister to German confederation 1839–40, to Sardinia 1840–51, to the Hague 1851–8; succ. as 2nd Baron Dunfermline 1858.

[5] Probably the Monte di Roccia Melone, 11,000 ft., dominating Susa.

[6] About 7 miles W. of Turin.

[7] It was 6 miles long.

[8] The basilica on the top of a steep hill, built in 1706.

[9] The best hotel in Turin, in the Piazza Castello.

I went out to make calls and attend to some necessary matters: and went also to some Churches. On S. Filippo Neri [1] I found a curious advertisement giving notice that the same pious person who had caused Remigio's (Cycle of) Epistles & Gospels in 'Lingua Toscana' [2] to be sold at 4 francs instead of six had now arranged, in order yet more effectually to stimulate Christian souls to become possessed of this instalment of edification, to deliver with it a copper plate engraving of the genealogy of the Royal family of Savoy, which sold separately at two francs. It was interesting to notice 1. the benevolent purpose—2. I fear, the slackness of the people about real instruction in the substance of the text of the Scripture—3. the means of subvention, a genealogical tree of that house, to which they are so much attached, as all events and all signs, the printshops, the women's broaches, and the like, demonstrate. I have made the purchase. The conjunction is too like Jerome Paturot's last and successful expedient for selling the *Aspic*.

Having discovered two Sermons we went to hear both. The first was at San Lorenzo, preached by a Canonico ([blank]) with great energy and considerable rhetorical power. The doctrine was in the coarse and material strain of the popular purgatorial system. "Idem ignis cruciat impios in inferno, et justos in purgatorio": so, *according* to the preacher, says St. Cyprian.[3] His great effect was to heighten the description of the tortures there suffered by the just: his great regret, that no words of his could adequately represent them, or give more than the slightest glance at the interior of their awful prison. The face of God is hid from them, while they absolutely burn with love towards Him: this last indeed was the one softening and refining touch in the picture, all else was writhing and scorching: and oh! the wickedness of those who could not exert themselves by prayers and good works but especially by alms for the relief of the parents, helpmates, brothers, sisters, children, whom they had lost: or of those who being in the enjoyment of fortunes left to them by the dead, used no part of them for the mitigation and shortening of their pains. Only to think of the moment when the Angel of Peace appears in Purgatory to liberate some soul that has been helped by the faithful upon earth: around that Angel crowd a multitude of souls each hoping that it may be he, and bewailing that it is not—and if there are any who say that these representations [4] are an invention of the priests such persons can know nothing of the divine character of Christian Charity the queen of all virtues.

It was a painful Sermon. The intensity of the strain of sin is the redeeming idea of the purgatorial system: but it is also that which least comports with vicarious removal: nor was this dwelt upon: it was pain which was continually pressed, not defilement. The general tone was like an inversion of Scripture: for these dead then do not rest from their labours but come into far sharper sufferings than on earth. Again is not their language In

[1] Opposite the Accademia delle Scienze.

[2] Remigio Nannini, ?1521–8; Dominican author. His translation, *Epistole e Evangeli* (1575) was often reprinted.

[3] 'The same fire burns the sinners in hell and the just in purgatory'. Not from Cyprian; probably from one of the many sermons wrongly ascribed to him.

[4] These two words written over an illegible deletion.

la sua volontade è nostra pace:[1] but they are represented as in agony from which they are impatient to be delivered. But if there were pain in the intermediate state it must be as the necessary instrument of loving correction, and those souls which hate sin alone would love the pain which wipes away the marks of it.

The second Sermon was preached in a Church under the Cathedral:[2] the same doctrine from an inferior man. He however told us that to believe in the sin of Purgatory was not of necessary faith: but indubitable according to the Scriptures and Fathers. His sermon spoke also of the pangs of exclusion from the vision of God for those who love Him: but this was not the basis, it was an exceptional idea, and fire, fire, fire, was the staple. He urged 'until he shall have paid the uttermost farthing': the doom of the impenitent as the measure of the destiny of the redeemed. And he quoted the reward of the just for good done to our neighbours as a proof *a fortiori* of the reward of what we do for the soul in Purgatory, which is indeed *il prossimo il più necessitoso che esiste*.[3] Such a shifting of the basis of the idea given us of the state of the dead must work most powerfully upon moral action here: and must surely have a powerful tendency to set aside the idea of thorough conversion in the mind of the mass of men. (Marked reference was made to those who had received Purgatorial bequests & not paid them.)

There were *two* collections made during each of these Sermons. The subterranean one[4] did not appear to draw much money from the audience.

2. *Sat.*

See Journal of Tour. Read Jerome Paturot—Worked on Journal & Accounts. Made some purchases of books, a kind of winters stock—Little Mary now goes to the window without her bonnet or veil: and no inflammation appears in the eye but only the film, & weakness.

Saturday Novr. 2. I could not find any preaching today: but the office for the dead was going on. Shops however were open which was not the case yesterday: & the town had its ordinary appearance.

The Churches here require no particular comment. St. Filippo Neri has grandeur of space—S. Lorenzo[5] a very elaborately constructed compound of (I think) octagons by way of dome—the Mère Dieu,[6] a miniature Pantheon with great effect—the Cathedral very little worthy [of] note: but with what seemed a good copy of the Cena.[7]

[1] 'In his will is our peace': Dante, *Paradiso*, iii. 85.
[2] The cathedral of S. Giovanni Battista, built 1498–1505.
[3] 'the nearest, the most necessitous that exists'.
[4] i.e. that in the church below.
[5] In the Piazza Castello, built by Guarini (1687) with a spectacular dome balanced on ribs, each of which is the chord of $\frac{3}{8}$ of a circle.
[6] On the right bank of the Po, built 1818–40 as a memorial to the restoration of the royal family.
[7] A copy of Leonardo da Vinci's 'Cenacolo' ('Last Supper'), at the west end of the church.

I visited the Collection of Pictures in the Palazzo Madama[1] and found it very strong in the Flemish School. In particular there is a most beautiful Vandyck of three children of Charles the First, sold by Cromwell: an exquisitely finished small Rembrandt of a Burgomaster: a number of small landscapes by an artist whose works were not before known to me Greffier[2] (?) with most admirable perspectives and minute graduations of ground distance: a magnificent portrait of Paul III by Titian, a truly wonderful picture:[3]

The so called Raphael[4] seems a highly finished & carefully got up picture: the style has none of that almost divine elevation which belongs to his earlier works: nor did the execution of it seem to me like that of his later ones.

Homer singing his own verses to the violin by Spagnoletto[5] is a forcible painting: but the violin is against the Homeric idea, and the manner of execution is hard without being natural. I liked a picture of St. Peter with a Cardinal by Gaudenzio di Ferrara better than anything I have seen of that artist.

There are also specimens of Giovan Bellini, Francia, Albert Durer, Ludwig von Leyden, Holbein: so the older & more masculine manners are not wanting.

And I noticed one very fine Canaletti & capital specimens of Teniers: a Paul Potter,[6] good, as always: he is so sure a card.

The account in my French Guide Book is very bad; both as to fact & taste.

I conversed long with the keeper of the pictures about Piedmontese affairs. He is one of five intelligent men with whom I have spoken of them. All were in the same sense: liberal, but not republican: without any irreligious tone (at least four of them) but entirely with the Government and against the Pope in the present struggle,[7] & announcing it to be understood that with or without the Pope's assent, the Government would persevere. This keeper of the pictures was one: two were booksellers: one a medical man whom I met at the theatre: lastly one very intelligent well mannered young man, whose profession I do not know.

I am much struck with the very bad pronunciation. One preacher whom I have heard gave the French u, very nearly, in *uno* and other words, besides

[1] A thirteenth-century castle in the Piazza Castello, altered to hold the royal picture collection. In the late nineteenth century it was used for political assemblies, but since 1935 it has been the Museo Civico, again a picture gallery.

[2] Jacques Greffier, *floruit* 1520; painter and sculptor working at Châteaudun.

[3] Titian first painted Paul III when he was present at the meeting of Charles V and the Pope at Ferrara, in 1543. There were many copies of this portrait, showing the Pope bare-headed. The original, and other portraits of him by Titian, is in the Capodimonte, Naples. Gladstone saw a copy of this.

[4] 'La Madonna della Tenda'; an important copy.

[5] Jusepe de Ribera, called Lo Spagnoletto, 1588–1652; Spanish artist who worked mainly in Naples.

[6] 1625–54; Dutch artist, known best for rural and animal pictures.

[7] On 9 April 1850 all ecclesiastical jurisdiction was abolished in Sardinia by the Siccardi law; on 4 May the abp. of Turin was arrested for issuing regulations opposed to this law; on 14 May the Pope protested against his imprisonment.

the more common corruptions of Piedmontese pronunciation. Another, a Canon of the Cathedral, actually said coluia maia, voia, poia,[1] and so forth. I cannot make the people of the lower class understand me. This might fairly be ascribed to my bad Italian: but I do not find it the case in other parts of Italy. I even heard here what I never heard before, an Italian, a Canon preaching in S. Lorenzo, who could not pronounce his *r* and said nearly Sag-gha-menti etc.—so different from that rrringing r which nearly every Italian knows how to sound.

I bought some books in various shops: in moderation, this has the advantage of giving one the means of intercourse with an intelligent class: but one among whom in Italy sneers at the prevailing religion are common, without much evidence of discrimination between the true in it & the adventitious.

I saw a specimen of the National Guard: it is a *new* institution and being new such a body can hardly be well organized or disciplined. Of military we have plenty: & some good bands.

In the afternoon we went out shopping & in the streets of this city I observe a strange contrast with the year 1832, when I was last here. Then one could not walk down the Strada del Po[2] without meeting perhaps an hundred friars. *Now* in three days stay at Turin, constantly out, I have scarcely seen half a dozen. I inquired of some persons in conversation why this was: & I am told that there is no diminution in the number of them, but, *non escono:*[3] they are, or are reputed to be, with the Archbishop & agt. the Govt. in the matter of the Siccardi Law, and therefore think it best to keep at home.

In the evening we went to the Teatro Gerlino,[4] as the title of the play promised to show us something of the national feeling. It was *La Suora di Carità Torinese in Roma*[5] and the scene laid in 1848. It did so: though it contained no reference to the events of that year. In one point of view it was very painful: for the *Suora,*[6] who had escaped from the *Sacro Cuore*[7] and the Jesuit influence in that institute to the Order of Charity, appeared in it as the subject of a reviving passion which ends in her removal from the Order and her marriage to a person between whom & her there had been a former attachment. This did not however seem unacceptable to the audience: a crowded one. But the really remarkable points of the evening were the passages that electrically struck the people: these all turned upon the corruptions of the priesthood, or aristocratical tyranny, or the ill fame of the Jesuits, setta infame, setta maledetta.[8] Nothing could be more distinct than the course of popular feeling: nothing more vehement than its movement. A priest was the popular old man of the play: but his language

[1] A dialect: 'that fellow, ever, your, after'.

[2] The Via Po, an arcaded street, main thoroughfare of E. quarter of Turin, running from the Piazza Castello.

[3] 'they do not go outside'.

[4] A diurnal theatre open to the sky.

[5] 'The sister of charity from Turin in Rome'; author untraced.

[6] 'Sister'.

[7] 'Sacred Heart'.

[8] 'infamous sect, accursed sect'.

was pretty much limited to philanthropy. Maledetti coloro fra i miei colleghi che vivono delle lor decime e non fanno etc.[1] The house rang to passages like these. I was rather surprised to see benediction acted, & confession all but acted.

The appointments of the theatre were poor but the acting good in this & in a comic piece which followed.

This day was not kept as a *festa* and the streets were quiet, whereas on Friday and Sunday they were very noisy.

Turin has the gaity of a capital, excellent kitchens, and amusements: but the smells are vile as if the town had no drainage at all: and the air in all the shaded streets is more dank than in any Italian city I know.

3. 23 S. Trin.

Prayers 9½ A.M. and 7½ P.M. without Comment. Heard one Sermon (Cathedral) & parts of two more in S. Lorenzo. Read Gerbet's Dogme Generateur.[2] Went with C. on an expedition to Superga: but our time was short and the view was shut up in haze. I regretted this the less because I am not very sure that the excursion was within *my* Sunday liberties, as I hold it prudent to measure them for myself without any pretence to think for those who are less in need of law. Interrupted in evg by preparations for journey & a trip to the Railway Station.

Nov. 3. 23 S. Trinity Turin. I have heard today a whole Sermon & two halves. The entire one was in the Cathedral from the Canon who has just been appointed to the cure of souls connected with it. It was apparently a practical discourse, though rather dialectic in form, from an earnest man. He trembled when ten years ago God who chooses feeble instruments to work His designs appointed him to a cure of souls: much more now when called to one so arduous. But He whom He sends a duty always sends the strength to fulfil it: and hence he was consoled. He had also much confidence in the protection of the B.V.M.—St. John the titular of the Church & the Saints tutelary of Turin: also in the venerable Chapter that had chosen him (there was not the slightest reference made to the Archbishop:) and lastly in the people themselves. But great was the work, and great the needs of the human soul. They had for instance a great need for instruction. This was necessary to them 1. as Christians—for how could they be Christ's disciples without knowing and accepting his commands. 2. as rational beings—for in that capacity it is the business of man to look to his latter end. 3. as social beings because out of this property arise a multitude of relations which without knowledge we cannot observe aright.

On all these grounds therefore he besought them to attend his instructions which he would give to the best of his power. Not that he would teach them new things: but would strive to renovate and refresh their old impressions. Not belief only but light also was necessary to them. Nor had religion

[1] 'Cursed are those among my colleagues who live on their tithes and do nothing etc.'
[2] Cp. 27 Oct. 50.

anything to fear from abundance of light, her only danger was from its scanty & partial distribution.

Of the part sermons that I heard one was an exhortation to trust in the promises of Christ that the soul of the just should come to peace: as if by way of relieving the sombre teaching of the anniversary just past. The other was a dry exposition in the most formal terms of the doctrine of Seven Sacraments: of their matter, form & the intention of the priest, as together making them valid: and a sort of *a priori* argument from the nature and state of man to show how & why they could not be more or less than seven.

We tried the Superga[1] today. It is indeed a superb situation: but except the Alpine tops into & almost upon which one seemed to look, all was covered with a dense haze: the outline of Turin was covered with a dense haze. The fall of the ground away from this great structure on all sides is most striking. C. did not go to the building, & I did not go in. In mere distance it must be six miles from Turin, 1000 to 1200 feet above the level of it: & with the interior objects, a good day's work. We were only 3¼ hours away.

We had most of our usual proceeding in our rooms: but I was obliged to go out at night about the fare of the carriage as our landlord told me there were only two [railway] trucks, and nothing but payment could make sure.

4. M.[2]

A long day on the road. In evg, Teatro Carlo Felice:[3] a failure: Worked accounts, & read Jerome Paturot.

Monday, Nov. 4. We left the Europa at 5½ A.M.—Turin at 6.10 and reached Novi[4] (I suppose over 80 miles) about 10, in fog nearly all the way. We saw considerable traffic on the line: a great traffic too all the way to Genoa: & I shall be surprised if this railway through the Appennine, formidable as are its works, shall fail to pay. Its charges are lower than the French: but a carriage pays more than 6 first class passengers. Those however who go in it are only charged as 3d class.

We breakfasted comfortably at the Europa in Novi.

And here I was obliged to take the Bollettone[5] which had only been a phantom to me before. If it were given instead of requiring to be sought at some cost of time, it would be really useful. But it was not asked for or shown, all the way from the Savoy frontier to the Mediterranean. It only cost 15 sous.

The state of the road from Novi till very near the top of the Appennines is disgraceful to any civilized country: & it is no excuse that the railway is in

[1] Cp. 1 Nov. 50.

[2] This day, and the next two, originally mis-dated by the diarist, who corrected himself.

[3] The opera house of Genoa opened in 1828, in the piazza of the same name.

[4] 25 miles N. of Genoa.

[5] A document valid for 24 hours issued by the post office giving the route, without which post-horses were unobtainable.

course of being made (to Ronco[1] they say it will be open in two months). But it may be owing to the burden of the war: and that alas is no frivolous excuse.

From Ronco the ascent begins. The scenery is very beautiful though it falls short of absolute grandeur: and it has the purely Italian character, which is quite distinct from that of the Alps. The point, where the Stone dividing the provinces of Novi and Genoa rises on the left, gives a fine view into the mountains: and after passing the summit the downward prospects are fine also. The audacious works of the railway accompany the road all along, and add much to the interest of the scene.

It was not until between half past seven and eight that we reached our Inn at Genoa. We just caught the Mediterranean after passing the summit.

Between Novi and Ronco we met Mr. Hallam: and I was much grieved and shocked to learn from his servant the death of his son at Siena a fortnight back.[2] How he has been smitten!

Genoa. Hotel Feder. On arrival while C. had some necessary food, I went off to the Carlo Felice and saw half of a *pasticcio*[3] thoroughly uninteresting. There were I suppose scarcely fifteen pounds in the house. But I heard great things of Madlle Cruvelli[4] who did not play.

5. T.

Wrote to Mr Jas Watson—Sir S. Scott & Co—Mr R. Barker—J.N.G. Worked on my papers & accounts to this date: & the usual troubles of post, money, passport, & means of further progress. Read Jerome Paturot. Mary is inimitable: enters at once into every kind of joke, & makes them: for instance an oddly dressed man who has brought C. her velvets she declares positively to be Punch & has shaken hands with him in that capacity.

Tuesday, Nov. 5. This was a day chiefly of business: the ordinary & necessary business of a travelling family party, and the accessory business of shopping. The silverwork of Genoa is indeed almost incredible for beauty and cheapness together. C. dealt in velvets and I in books, which abound here.

We found the *table d'hote*, *tavola rotonda*, at 5 P.M. excellent: attendance on the rest of the house rather starved by it: the stairs grievous as in all these hotels: & the view of the sea could not induce us to mount from the second floor to the third.

In the evening C. and I went to the Carlo Felice whose Madlle Cruvelli played in *Linda di Chamounix.*[5] She is both a great singer and great actress and if she lives must make herself well known in London and all over Europe. The people here have a *furore* for her & no wonder. They brought her five times on the stage after the Opera. The Barytone is a fine voice, the Tenor fair, the Buffo bad, the Contralto very bad. I understand that this theatre is insufficiently aided by the city and the Choruses are weak as well as many members of the Company. Though the Opera is good music it does not abound in airs for the memory.

[1] 12 miles N. of Genoa.
[2] Cp. Morley, i. 230.
[3] 'pastiche'.
[4] Jeanne Sophie Cruvelli, 1826–1907; German soprano.
[5] By Donizetti (1842).

6. Wed.

See Tour Journal. Prayers mg. Wrote to Lincoln—Manning—W. Hampton—Mr Hallam—Read Orsini's Repubblica Romana [1]—Busy in considering & arranging plans: accounts: journal (evg).

Wednesday Nov. 6. Genoa. Went with C. to the Church of the Annunziata [2] and S. Siro.[3] The former is very highly ornamented, the latter has better forms in the interior. The arch is too small, it appeared to me, in the Annuniziata, for the intercommunication: too narrow & too low. The gold is new and glares painfully. There is a lofty dome & a fine portico.

The beggars of Genoa are beyond anything numerous and forward: some of them fat, some well dressed, all most urgent. They are more or less of the sturdy kind & will not take a first or second refusal. I do not remember so much & such diffused begging in any town.

I find that having crossed the Cenis & avoided Marseilles in order to escape the Quarantine at Naples, I am no better at Genoa. Naples is very logical, and not only quarantines Marseilles because she does not impose restraint on vessels from Malta, but likewise Genoa, Leghorn, & Civ. Vecchia, because they give free pratique [4] from Marseilles. I had therefore to examine today cost and other questions connected with the various land routes as well as different stages of the sea. The charge by the steamers is certainly enormous: yet relatively I do not suffer from it as much as others for my carriage will only pay one first class place, & will not have to pay the *nourriture obligatoire* [5] or the *spese di sanità*.[6]

In the evening I went to the *Teatro delle Vigne*,[7] and found it a puppet show. The puppets however were made to talk, i.e. the opera *words* of Ernani [8] were recited and one puppet killed himself in the last scene. The price of entrance was about $2\frac{1}{2}$ pence. The seats were not more than one-third full. Even at this low price there was a most respectable orchestra of about 10 performers—and a military guard. The recitations were tolerable: the appointments of course but mean.

I hear it said that the Genoese given to business do not effectually support their places of amusement. I should however from the number of bookshops judge them to be great readers.

7. Th.

See Tour Journal. The day occupied except what is there described occupied in arranging for departure.

[1] F. Orsini, assassin, *Memorie e documenti intorno al governo della repubblica Romana* (1850).

[2] Originally a private church, built in the seventeenth century by the Lomelli family; the roof was regilded in the early nineteenth century.

[3] Originally the cathedral of Genoa; virtually rebuilt in the seventeenth century.

[4] From *avoir libre pratique*, 'to be out of quarantine'.

[5] The meal compulsorily included in the price of the ticket; cp. 8 Nov. 50.

[6] 'health charges'.

[7] Untraced.

[8] By Verdi.

Thursday Novr. 7. This morning having had a desire to go by the *Anglo* Italian boat rather than the Sardinian, I went on board her (the Levantine) and was obliged to give up the idea and make my arrangements as well as I could with the Castor.

To refresh my recollections of the general character of Genoese palaces, I went to the Brignola.[1] It is strange and rather sad to begin on the third floor: but I suppose these are the best rooms. In one of the principal ones, pictures were exposed for sale. There are some beautiful marble floors. The collection is not first rate: especially what they called Vandycks seemed to me inferior—but there were two or three satisfactory Titians, one of Bonifazio in which the Blessed Virgin is the central figure, one Andrea del Sarto:[2] a portrait at least a professed one by Francia:[3] one or two of Bellini: one which I liked of Luca d'Olanda (as here called).[4] The union of Flemish and Venetian pictures with the (very inferior) Genoese, and the comparative absence of other schools bears witness to the intercourse and union among the ancient centres of European commerce.

I am exceedingly struck by the readiness and speed with which, even now, accounts are made out here.

In the afternoon we drove to the *Buro*[5] for the view of the sea and city, which is beautiful: we obtained it by entering with leave a private Garden. There was haze on the sea which materially limited the eye in that direction: but the city upon the bosom of the Appennine to the front and right looked glorious.

We went also to the Cathedral which boasts of a Baroccio:[6] the nave is very interesting as well as (what we call) the west front: the latter for its rich and deeply recessed doorways: the former for its structure. The main arches are just pointed. Over them those of the triforium are round, but higher, in proportion to breadth, than our round arches generally.

We embarked in the evening about seven: and I must not forget to notice that the Feder while it is one of the best hotels is likewise one with the most moderate & conscientious charges.

The tariff here for embarking my carriage is 20 francs: and nearly 1 franc each for ourselves, in fact I paid 5 francs. These are monstrous charges. For the carriage however I paid five francs less as an out of door batelier[7] had offered to do it for that money.

We were exceedingly crowded in the Castore: 130 passengers. The obligatory dinner is not only a task but almost an imposture: it turned out to consist of a piece of roast veal, and some fruit! to which was subjoined roast chicken, I apprehend in consequence of our criticisms. But we had

[1] The home of the Brignole-Sale family, presented with its contents to the city of Genoa in 1874, and subsequently named Palazzo Rosso.

[2] The Holy Family (now regarded as a copy) by Andrea del Sarto (1486–1530), Florentine painter.

[3] Probably Francesco Francia, 1450?–1517, Bolognese painter.

[4] By Lucas van Leyden, 1494–1533; Dutch painter and engraver.

[5] Probably the Burlo, a hill WNW. of the city.

[6] 'The Crucifixion with Three Saints' painted by Barocci in 1596, now placed on the right of the altar.

[7] Ferryman.

good weather & an easy passage though we rolled a little at times: they profess to do it in 7 hours, & I imagine were not over 8. The French Scamandre[1] I think took 11 to 12, with rather bad weather.

8. Fr.

Staid on board. Wrote up Journal & accts. Read Orsini—Jerome Paturot.

Friday, Nov. 8. A quiet day on board in the harbour of Leghorn: until 4½ o'clock when the boat sailed for Cività Vecchia.[2]

The regular *songs* of the gangs at work on the ships here are curious and I have not heard them elsewhere.

Leghorn always seems to take one backwards: it is the least Italian looking of all Italian towns which I know.

We understand the Quarantine is taken off at Naples: if this be so, it will give us another (a third) night in the steamboat, and bring us to our destination I hope on Sunday morning.

9. Sat.

Ashore with C. at Civita Vecchia. Journal & accts.—Intention to read, disappointed by a ground swell which lasted for six hours.

10. S 24 Trin.

[Naples] Ch mg & aft.—Sermon afterwards in S. Caterina.[3] Read Gerbet—Tamburini's Vera Idea della S. Sede.[4] How thankful should we be to have reached all well the point of our destination: the view was perfectly ravishing, & the air, when we reached the 2d floor drawingroom of the Hotel des Etrangers: they were redolent of health and joy.

Sat. Nov. 10 [*sic*, and Sunday, conflated]. Between 13 & 14 hours sail brought us to Cività Vecchia. The boat was excessively crowded: but the good weather made everything easy. We had some pleasant companions and there was general good humour, increased as far as we were concerned by the strengthening expectation that the quarantine is off at Naples. It is but just to these extravagantly dear boats to add we had today an excellent dinner: & that they stand well in point of cleanliness. *This* is I imagine the quickest boat that runs between Naples and Marseilles: in the Lombardo I spent (with even better weather) 2 or 3 more hours on each of the stages between Genoa & Naples; & in the French Steamers (Govt.) considerably more. The *Castore* is however very low in the water and they say that with sea running the crew cannot keep the fore part of the ship and that she is washed from stem to stern.

[1] Cp. 20 July 49.

[2] The port 40 miles WNW. of Rome.

[3] The church of S. Orsola, at the junction of the Strada San Caterina and the Strada di Chiaja; cp. 17 Nov. 50.

[4] P. Tamburini, *Vera idea della Santa Sede; operetta divisa in due parti* (1818).

C. and I landed for breakfast, which we got and *good* in the main at the Hotel Orlandi.[1] I then went about my passport and its three necessary *ordinations* in order to get on to Naples. Having understood from Capt. Johnson[2] a fellow passenger that there might be abatement from the Tariff prices I offered 150 fr. to go on to Naples, the full amount being 187½: but after a message to the Captain it was declined and they giving me a fair choice I went with them, rather pleased at their sticking to their point.

The port of Cività Vecchia is worth seeing: there is so visible in stone the hand that traced all Michael Angelo's designs.[3] And the main *place*[4] of the town is good. That is all. We landed 109 passengers for Rome. Pretty work they seemed to have in getting away. Although we were in port about six, none, not even an Italian family favoured with a special order to land (who left the ship at 8 or half past) got away till long past eleven. But few had started at a little before one, when I re-embarked. Not one I think could reach Rome with daylight, some at midnight, some would fail altogether. The dispatch of the Neapolitan Consul[5] satisfied me finally that we have nothing to fear from quarantine.

Many ladies slept on deck last night. Today we are thin.

We started from Civ. Vecchia at half past three and were in port at Naples before half past seven: but I believe they slackened their engines in the latter part of the voyage. We had six hours of most disagreeable ground swell which laid us on our backs and the dinner party, I *heard*, came down to three. The mountain of Terracina[6] is very grand at night, rising like an island as the low coast beside it is not seen.

We did not land at Naples until past nine: and I took as little baggage as possible, not as yet aware that here the general rule is inverted & that everything ought to be separated from the carriage. We drove to the Hotel des Etrangers[7] where we found a party of fellow passengers whom we had recommended to it: we both settled temporarily in one set of rooms too large for either separately. I was able to get out for the morning Church: I found a good congregation & pains taken with the Church music. Mr. Pugh[8] the Chaplain preached in the morning, & a young stranger very well in the afternoon.

I went to a Church in the Strada S. Caterina and heard a Sermon there. The subject was the destruction by Jehu of the worshippers of Baal. The narrative 2 Kings X. 18–28 was expanded I think into at least half an hour

[1] The chief hotel.

[2] John Samuel Willes Johnson, 1793–1863; entered R.N. 1807, captain 1846; Peelite M.P. Montgomery 1861–3; author of guide to Italy, Switzerland and France.

[3] Michelangelo completed the Forte del Sangallo in the harbour; largely destroyed during the 2nd World War.

[4] The Palazzo communale, then containing a museum of Etruscan antiquities.

[5] Captain Thomas Gallwey, R.N.; British consul in Naples from 1834.

[6] The Monti Ansoni, inland from Terracina, which is on the coast 60 miles NW. of Naples.

[7] In the Strada Chiatamone, opposite the Castel dell'Ovo, with an unimpeded view of the sea.

[8] Giles Pugh, 1804–75; chaplain to British embassy in Naples 1846–61; vicar of Shapwick from 1864.

of[1] detail. This detail was most elaborately got up with all manner of accessories: and it was acted with great skill and effect by the very fat preacher: the church was full and I never saw more attentive listeners. I have before observed with how much interest sermons purporting to give the facts of the Scripture text are heard in R.C. countries. Occasionally the preacher said he was quoting not the Sacred text but the sense of some exposition. On the whole however the people must have supposed a multitude of particulars to be from Scripture which were added to fill up and to enhance the history. I must add that these particulars were in no way out of harmony with the actual selection. Of comment there was little, but that little pithy. The preacher discussed the conduct of Jehu. He was slaying the enemies of God & by the Divine Command: but he did it by fraud. Was his action good? He answered unequivocally, no: quoted S. Augustine & other authorities to the effect that evil must not be done in order that good may come of it: not even if it were to release from Purgatory all the souls that are in it, should we tell a semplice bugia.[2] A good lesson for a Neapolitan Congregation. He showed that to make an action good it must be done with a certain intention: but Jehu's intention only was to be released from the curses which God had inflicted on those who tolerated the worship of Baal. After Jehu, the preacher went on to the account of Hezekiah & the prophet's death bed:[3] with the purpose of illustrating the secret of peace at our latter end: but this did not not connect very well with the foregoing part.

Today for the first time in a foreign city I saw a man reduced to a bestial state in the street: he was a sailor indescribably drunk, and he spoke alas! English: being an Englishman in the American service, or an American, I do not know which. As he was reeling & bellowing on his way a funeral came by: with the crucifix carried at the head. He cried out 'Jesus Christ' and he with a companion who was half guiding him after a few moments were certainly overawed and stood by against the wall. One of the torch-bearers in the meantime, in the white hood, poked his torch well in the face of the fellow. Next morning I saw more of these drunkards also belonging to the American service (the Cumberland): and an Italian came up to me & said 'Gli Inglesi sono una bella e brava nazione, ma gli Americani tutt 'altro'.[4] Whether this was for my English ear I know not.

11. M.

Calls—business of necessity—read the Guardian in evg & Jerome Paturot. See Tour Journal. Tomorrow we hope to decide the main question, *where* & how we are to live. Saw Mr Hubbard.[5]

Naples. Monday Nov. II. The early part of the day was occupied chiefly about my luggage, which after all I had to fetch away from the carriage.

[1] 'simple narrative' here deleted. [2] 'single lie'
[3] II Kings xiii. recounts Elisha's death.
[4] 'The English are a fine and handsome nation, but the Americans far from it'.
[5] i.e. J. G. *Hubbard.

The expence and trouble of landing a carriage here are great. Ten dollars of duty must be paid outright. Four dollars more for landing. A Guarantee must be given for a further payment of duty after a year. This introduces the Banker: who takes the matter into his own hands & so the 'trouble' but I apprehend at a charge. Then there are the baggage boatmen, the sailors, the coaches, the facchini for carrying the baggage, the custom house officers of all sorts and sizes. *Vedi Signore come noi siamo stati gentili, non abbiamo guardato niente, mezzo piastra e poco Signore*;[1] and the small ones *bottiglie*[2] without end.

It seems that Naples is considered a good market for the sale of an English carriage, & that the State views with a wise jealousy the introduction of such a formidable engine. But this jealousy touches only carriages coming by sea: no cognizance whatever is taken of those which come in by land. The traveller on arriving by steam with a carriage should immediately strip it of all baggage and carry this through the baggage custom house. The carriage must go into the great custom house: and everything in it is liable to be treated as merchandise, & practically I understand many legitimate articles of luggage are made to pay duty as when sent in a package by sea, while books are likely to be detained for the 'revisione'[3] which is in the hands of a Priest of Sorrento.

Our excellent landlord & landlady have introduced into Naples the innovation of a table d'hôte: & as I now testify from two days experience, a very good one.

In the evening I went with Mr. Halsey[4] to the Fiorentini.[5] It seems to thrive & and is much smarter than when I saw it in 1838. The play was the Conte di Montecristo:[6] and the acting admirable. Aliprandi[7] as Dantes, Senora Alberti[8] as Mercedes, Suzzi[9] as Pendon, [blank] as Faria, acted admirably: and others too were good but less prominent. The house was full: and it is now the first in Naples for *plays*.

12. T.

Saw Mr Hubbard—Sir W. Molesworth—Ld Leven[10]—Mr Temple—discussed plans with our landlord, and with the landlord of the rooms No 5 Chiatamone. Mr Temple was very courteous, & we agreed well about the

[1] 'Look, sir, how kind we have been, we haven't looked at anything, [give us] half a piastra and a little more, sir'.

[2] 'Bottles'.

[3] 'censorship'.

[4] Probably Thomas Plumer Halsey, 1815–54; tory M.P. Hertfordshire from 1846; drowned off Villa Franca.

[5] The Teatro Fiorentini, in the street of that name; the oldest theatre in Naples, specializing in drama.

[6] An adaptation of Dumas' novel (1844–5).

[7] Luigi Aliprandi, 1817–1859, son of a Mantuan artisan; specialized in romantic rôles at Teatro Fiorentini.

[8] Giulia Alberti, *ca.* 1810–1872, one of a family of actors, she worked at the Teatro Fiorentini with the actor P. Monti, whom she m. in 1835.

[9] Unidentified.

[10] David Leslie-Melville, 1785–1860; 10th earl of Leven 1820; rear admiral 1846; m. 1824 Elizabeth Anne Campbell, d. 1863, 2nd da. of Sir Archibald Campbell, 2nd bart.

Roman Govt. On the Bull of Pius IX[1] he said it would be an useful warning to those in our Church who had been disposed to draw near to the Church of Rome: but he does not see that the sole means of defence must be found in strengthening the organisation of the Church of England which is the thing decried & denounced as approximation to Rome. I complimented him on Ld Palmerston's June Speech:[2] to wh he replied that it was a very satisfactory debate: oddly said to me. We, or rather I, have been imprudent in putting up here with our present room-partners: for I find *he* is a Clergyman[3] who sinks & has sunk for many years his clerical character, & to this class I have a most pointed objection. C. was obliged to come home from the Teatro Nuovo[4] by the smell. Read Jer. Paturot. Began Colletti.[5]

Naples. Tuesday Nov. 12. Busy about our plans, balancing hotel against private apartment.

In the evg we dined, extremely well though amid the perfume of cigars, at the Europa Cafè & Restaurant:[6] and then went to the Teatro Nuovo where was a good orchestra, a bad opera company, and an odd version of the patois *spoken* with the music.

13.

Wrote to Ungaro—Dagna.[7] Read Jerome Paturot—Colletti—Went to tea at Lady Leven's & met Mr Lacaita[8] a very accomplished man—he knew Leopardi. After inquiring & reckoning as well as I could, & chiefly on account of C.s preference for freedom, space, & no stairs, I took the apartments No 5 Chiatamone[9] from Sig. Dagna and we 'extended' & signed our agreement in duplicate. Busy in the aftn. about supplies and in taking the consegna[10] of the moveable & perishable part of the effects.

14. Th.

Wrote to Sir J.G—Willy—Walk with Mr Hubbard—Read Tamburini's Vera Idea—Colletti—Jerome Paturot—Pio IX e l'Italia[11]—Moved into our new abode & arranged our goods there—dining with C. at the Europa.

[1] *Litterae Apostolicae SS. Domini Nostri quibus hierarchia episcopalis in Anglia restituitur*, issued on 29 September 1850, restoring Roman Catholic dioceses in England; called a Bull, though not technically one.

[2] On *Pacifico, cp. 25 June 50.

[3] Unidentified.

[4] Built in 1724, off the Via Roma, specializing in comic opera.

[5] Pietro Colletta, *Storia del reame di Napoli dal 1734 sino al 1825*, 2 v. (1832).

[6] In the Largo di S. Ferdinando, famous for its ice cream.

[7] His prospective landlord.

[8] (Sir) James Philip *Lacaita, 1813–95; b. in Italy; advocate 1836; legal advisor to British legation in Naples until 1852; professor of Italian, London, 1853–6; Gladstone's secretary in Ionian Isles 1858; in Italian politics from 1861; K.C.M.G. 1859. Cp. Add MSS 44233–4. For this meeting, wrongly dated by *Lacaita, see C. Lacaita, *An Italian Englishman* (1933), 25.

[9] Opposite the Castell dell'Ovo, to the west of the Porto Militaire.

[10] 'delivery'.

[11] M. L. A. de Lamartine de Prat, *L'Italia e Pio nono* (1847).

Nov. 13. 14. Most of our time occupied in considering & then effecting our change of domicile, and the many little arrangements connected with it.

The English grocery shop, kept by Stanford,[1] offers great advantages in point of convenience, & on being challenged by Mr. Hubbard with the question whether they allowed a commission to servants, the woman answered that the prices as they now are would not admit of it, being at the lowest point. But my impressions are not wholly in favour of these English purveyors in foreign cities: if their object had been to do business at mere market rates of profit, I apprehend they would have staid at home.

15.

Robertson's birthday: God bless him—Resumed morning prayers I hope not to be again interrupted while we stay here. H.S. with Agnes. Read Tamburini—Guide des Voyageurs—Pio IX e l'Italia—Colletti's History—Jerome Paturot.

Nov. 15. A day of obstinate and cold rain until the afternoon had made some progress. There was snow upon Vesuvius and the mountains over Castellammare. We thought it cold: but my thermometer without any fire was between 65 & 70.

16. Sat.

We have still much to do in making our very slight household arrangements: the consequence of not feeling able to *trust* people freely. Walk with C. Saw Mr Lacaita. Read Tamburini—Pio IX—Jerome Paturot—Colletta. Lady Leven's in evg.

Sat. Nov. 16. I called on Mr. Lacaita who conversed most intelligently on the state of education & on the legal profession. He considers that both are lower now than before the French domination, although there is a greater surface covered as far as the elementary acquirements of reading & writing are concerned. The education of the last century was founded wholly on the classics: this has now ceased, a disastrous change in his view. The law of Naples is the Code Napoleon somewhat modified: a bad exchange for what it displaced, tho' some of the forms of proceeding are simplified. Here the Avvocato discharges all the functions which with us are assigned to[2] special pleaders, and conveyancers and most of those of the attorney, whom he chooses instead of being chosen by him. The advocato also looks to the drawing of bills & answers and is responsible in chief for the whole conduct of the case at every point.

I find Mrs. Trollope's mysteries of London[3] translated into Italian here: & announced as by 'Sir F. Trollope'.

[1] He kept a warehouse with British goods in the Largo di Vittoria.

[2] 'Among' here deleted.

[3] A London version of E. Sue, *Les mystères de Paris* (1842–3); almost certainly not by Frances *Trollope; cp. 19 Dec. 48.

The information we collected in England was in favour of the climate of Naples for the closing month of the year, & against it for the opening ones: but Mr. Lacaita tells me that there is no such distinction but in general a cycle of sharp, then wet, & then fine and warm weather. But he adds that March is *often* remarkable for bitter winds.

17. 24[1] Trinity Sunday.

Church 11 & 3. A well meant but perfectly dismal Sermon on unity among ourselves & avoiding questions of words. Sermon in Church of [blank] afterwards. Read the Epistle & comment at evg prayers. Wrote notes. Read Tamburini—Pio IX—Pascal. Wrote to Sig. Lacaita. Catechism with Agnes.

Sunday Nov. 17. I again went to a Sermon in the Sant Ursula[2] at 4¼ P.M. It was today a recital of the defeat of Sennacherib–bo, and the illness of Hezekiah,[3] *dressed* in the same way as last Sunday. The acting was certainly in excess: but it moved the people & kept their attention up. At times the preacher would say 'attenti adesso'.[4] At times there proceeded from them mixed sounds difficult to describe, as if venting their general excitement when he had stirred it to the utmost. As for instance in the account he gave of the death of Julian the Apostate who as he said spat blood in torrents: and when the physician told him there was no cure, & he must die in two hours, he caught in his hand a quantity of the blood that poured from his mouth, flung it at the heavens & cried 'Ahi Nazzarino hai vinto',[5] & so expired. His close was as follows, in the middle of Hezekiah's illness. 'Now you will wish to know what was the answer of the prophet. Well, come next Thursday, & I will tell you'. They received this with a laugh. It was a curious illustration however of the total absence of *direct* knowledge of the Scripture text, except so far as morsels of it are made known in the ordinary services.

18. M.

H.S. with Agnes—Read Tamburini—Colletta. Fiorentini in Evg with C.G. —Busy on the *consegna* & other household matters which are now I hope likely to get into order. Saw Sir W. Molesworth—Mr Hubbard. Read Ld J. Russell's letter to the Bp of Durham.[6] All human influences, from all quarters, seem to combine against the poor Church of England. But He that sitteth on high is mightier: & we know not yet His purpose.

Monday Nov. 18. The following detail may show how strangers are regarded at Naples as a prey to be fought for.

Not being satisfied with the milkman's prices (I speak of him who serves the house) I called on Saturday to see Mr. Hubbard's man and told him to send me yesterday morning a piece of butter & a caraff of milk by way of

[1] Instead of 'Ch. A.M.' [2] Cp. 10 Nov. 50. [3] II Kings xx. 1–14.
[4] 'Attend now'. [5] 'Ah, Nazarene, you have conquered'.
[6] (1850); text in *English Historical Documents*, xii. (1), no. 121; hostile to the Pope's restoration of Roman Catholic sees in England.

trial. None reached me: and I went to complain. 'Mio marito', said the wife 'andò alla casa Dupont[1] e il guardaporto l'ha ributtato, gli ha ricusato l'entrata.'[2] Well I said send again this evening, and tomorrow morning: I will speak to the Porter: at any rate let your husband demand to see *me*. On returning home I challenged the porter who wholly disclaimed interference. He said the man had come, after the rival (or original) one had left the milk and butter for the day: that he asked my servant whether it was right: that as the servant does not speak Italian, he could only make out that milk and butter had been left, so thought it right to tell the man not to leave any more. Well said I there has been a mistake: we will say no more about it: but the man comes again tonight & tomorrow morning, there will be no mistake now. The night and morning came but no milk or butter from the new man. In the meantime the old one with whom after having asked him what was his ultimo prezzo[3] I made no attempt to bargain volunteered to reduce his terms on both to those of the other dealer: which I believing the other to have neglected me accepted. I was telling the story thus far to Mr. Hubbard in the presence of Sir T. Carmichael[4] whose family employ the *new* man. He said 'that man has been complaining grievously to our servants that he had been to your house this morning & had been refused admittance.' Having heard this I again challenged the porter—who is one of the most creditable looking people to be seen in Naples and he distinctly & positively assured me that since the mistake of yesterday morning the new milk man had not presented himself here at all!

I know not whether there will be a sequel to the story: it is already long, but characteristic.

I was in my egg-man's shop this morning: he came up to me as I was quitting it and said "Monsieur, Gesù Cristo". It was the Host, on the way to a sick person. The carriages stopped: every one uncovered: but the manner of every person in the procession except the Priest seemed careless & irreverant and we may well question the wisdom[5] of treating the mystical as if it were a simply natural Presence.

This evening we went again to the Fiorentini where Montecristo was the play. Of it I have already spoken: it was followed by a loathsome Comedy *La Gobba*[6] where the main interest was made to turn upon the humpbacks of two principal personages. I came away in the midst of it: but left the audience with ranks hardly at all thinned after 4½ hours too of hot entertainment. I think it is often remarked that the Italian taste and character where they degenerate at all have a very gross and materialistic tone: I thought this an instance. Compare with this the Punch of London who never introduces anyone's deformity into his caricatures.[7]

[1] His neighbour.
[2] 'My husband went to the Dupont house and the concierge turned him away, he refused him entry'.
[3] 'final price'.
[4] Sir Thomas Gibson Carmichael, 1817–55; capt. R.N. 1846; 9th bart. 1850; *Lacaita's brother-in-law.
[5] 'Of teaching the people thus their language' written in the margin, unconnected.
[6] 'The Hump'; author untraced.
[7] Though Mr. Punch always had a hooked hump on his back on the cover from 1849!

19. T.

Wrote to J.N.G. H.S. with Agnes after prayers: & Italian in evg. Read Tamburini—Pio IX—Jerome Paturot—Colletta. Saw Mr Halsey.[1] Singing, and trying to learn the Fra poco (transposed). Wrote on H[oly] S[scripture].[2]

Tuesday Nov 19. Here is the sequel to the milkman's romance. The sister of the excluded came here today about washing: and assured me her brother had been here according to my orders, & had fallen in with the old *lattajo*[3] who said to him if you bring your milk & butter to the Signore, *io vi ammazzo.*[4]

Rain kept me indoors most of the day: of the nine days since we have been here three have been like this: two or three more have felt cold: but I see the thermometer in my room, without a fire below 65°. It blew hard too: and we walked to the projection in the Chiaja Garden for sea air which we got very good with some spray. still as S.R.G. observes the sea air of the Mediterranean is not that of the Atlantic.

20. Wed.

H.S. with Agnes. Wrote MS. Theol. Read Tamburini—Pio IX—Jerome Paturot (finished)—Colletta. Singing. And chess with C. Also walked Mary: whose eyes thank God do not suffer from the violent wind. Saw the Molesworths: shopping with C.

21. Th.

Wrote to Hampton—T.G—Sir S. Scott & Co—Mr Temple—Willy. H.S. with Agnes. Singing. Went with C. to Sermon. Read Tamburini (finished)—Pio IX—began Philarete Chasles.[5] The Greenes[6] dined with us: & took up their quarters here: wh sounds odd but there was some mistake on their part wh led to it without our meaning it.

Wdy Nov 20. Thurs. Nov 21. In vain I attempt to find in the booksellers' shops any tolerable *plan* of the City of Naples. There appears to be no such thing as a *good* one for sale here: but in London & Paris no doubt there are plenty.

Thursday being a Festa—the announcement of, or an addition to, a Jubilee!! of 15 days appointed by the Pope in celebration of his return to Rome—there was preaching & we went at 4¼ to the [blank] in the Str. Santa Caterina. We heard here too a Sermon chiefly consisting in Scripture narrative, filled in with details, and expressively acted. The subject was Moses in the bulrushes and the moral drawn was the duty of *women* being

[1] 'Mr. Hubbard' here deleted.
[2] Add MS 44738, f. 182.
[3] 'the milkman'.
[4] 'I kill you'.
[5] V. E. Philarète Chasles, perhaps his *Etudes politiques* (1846) on eighteenth century England.
[6] Cp. 5 May 38.

mothers to bring up their children carefully & keep them from contact with evil. For as he told them it is given to you to rear offspring who are to augment the family of men on earth & the family of God in heaven, & then, changing his tone & manner *e forse anche la famiglia del diavolo in inferno.*[1] Without being generally remarkable, the Sermon as I thought showed considerable tact and address in the appeal to womanly feelings: and it was entirely free from what may be called Roman peculiarities.

22. Fr.

Little Mary's birthday. May God make us duly thankful for His great mercy in bringing us here on her account & our hopes of her health: & may He cause her to grow in grace as in stature. Read Colletta—Pio IX e l'Italia—Borgianelli's Gesuitophobia [2]—Leopardi's Ultime Poesie.[3] Singing mg & evg. Went with C. to S. Ferdinando [4] for a Sermon: but having been misinformed about the time we lost it.—Walk & saw Churches. H.S. with Agnes. The Greenes in evg: conv. on Ch. matters.

Friday Nov 22. Went to the Trinità Maggiore [5] & other Churches: the one I have named is a good example of the fine effect of breadth in the *Italian* style, like length in the pointed.

Went at 6 PM to San Ferdinando for a Sermon after having made particular enquiries about the time: but it had taken place we found at 5. It is not an easy matter in Naples to get any *exact* account of times: the answer generally is *verso le . . .*[6] with a considerable margin.

I read the Archbishop's Jubilee Address.[7] Its tone was not triumphant & spoke of the occasion rather as one of deprecation. It was full of the matter of Indulgence & the like & therefore pleased me not.

I often think of Dr. Dollingers assurance to me—expressing I am sure his own conviction—that the Church had no judicial function, no authority beyond the grave. I wish this were the real Roman doctrine. But can anything be clearer than the following inscription copied from the Pedestal of the Image in the Largo Trinità Maggiore:

Benedetto XIV Pontefice Massimo concede Indulgenza Plenaria a chiunque venira questa santa Immagine *toties quoties*: e però libera una anima del Purgatorio, per ogni volta che onora questa Immacolata Madre.[8]

[1] 'and perhaps also the family of the devil in hell'.

[2] Enrico Borgianelli, *Discorso sull' Antica e Moderna Gesuitofobia ossia delle vere cagioni dell' Odio in Europa contra la Compagnia di Gesù*, 2 v. (Naples, 1850).

[3] Cp. 28 July 49.

[4] By the San Carlo theatre.

[5] S. Trinita Maggiore, in the street of that name, also known as S. Gèsu Nuovo, built in 1584 in the shape of a Greek cross.

[6] 'Roughly . . .'

[7] By R. Sforza.

[8] 'Benedict XIV, Supreme Pontif, grants plenary indulgence to whoever comes to this Holy Image as often as occasion arises: and thus delivers a soul from purgatory for each time that he honours this Immaculate Mother.'

23. Sat.

Italian lesson to Agnes. The Capo di Monte[1] drive with C. & walk. Dined with the Hubbards. Read Pio IX (finished P.S.)—Borgianelli's Gesuitophobia—Colletta—the Guardian (by Mr Hubbard's favour). After breakfast I declaimed against the "Peelites" who voted with Govt. or staid away on the Palmerston [Pacifico] division: rather vehemently: having quite forgotten, that Greene was in the latter class.[2]

Saturday Nov. 23. In the afternoon we drove the Capo di Monte road and enjoyed exceedingly both the very Italian character of the near view, & the remarkable beauty of the commanding prospects which at various points the descent offers of the bay, Vesuvius from top to base, and the Appennines rising sharp & sheer from the brown plain of Naples. One should however be on the lookout to catch these fine views for the road twists and the prospect shifts continually.

24. Preadvent Sunday.

Church 11 & 3. A *painful* Sermon in the mg: by way of being a summary of religion & of the New Testament! with a new *Credo*. Yet well meant: & neither "Evangelical" nor Calvinistic. In evg read (the Greenes being still here) from T. AKempis. To Italian Sermon at 4¼ PM. Read Gerbet's Dogme Generateur[3]—Borgianelli—Ventura's Oration on Graziosi.[4]

Sunday Nov. 24. I went to Sermon at 4¼ in the same Church as on Thursday. The preacher continued the story of Moses to his marriage with Jethro's daughter.[5] It was filled in as usual with supposititious particulars: but advantage was taken of points in the narrative to moralise. For instance from the priest's daughters feeding the flock he took occasion to pronounce an eulogium upon labour as honourable to all men. He interpolated thus that one of the daughters went to call Moses, that it was probably la più snella, la più curiosa,[6] and also graziosa.[7] The relation with the acting was certainly very like a nurse's tale to children & had not the dignity of sacred narrative: but it was done so as to be remembered and the direct instruction interspersed made one feel it was a sermon. He explained for instance that priests were allowed to marry under the old law which was only a shadow (I pass by the obvious exceptions which might be taken to his mode of putting it) and that when we hear of speaking with God it ordinarily means with His angels.

The preacher closed his Sermon by an explanation of the Jubilee and the conditions of Indulgences: traced the former from the Old Testament:

[1] The palace and art museum on the hill to the N. of the city.
[2] *H* cxii. 742. The other Greene, also a Peelite, voted with the government.
[3] Cp. 27 Oct. 50.
[4] G. Ventura da Raulica, *Oraisons funèbres d'O'Connell et du Chanoine Graziosi* (1848).
[5] Exodus, ii. 11–22.
[6] 'The slenderest, the most inquisitive'.
[7] 'Gracious'.

stated that ordinarily certain sins were reserved to the Pope, others to the Bishop: that during this Jubilee these reservations were suspended: the condition was to visit one of the Churches where the Holy Sacrament is exposed, & to recite five Credos, five Paters, five Aves: that they must remember the distinction between Absolution which removes sin and Indulgence which removes the temporal penalties of it either in this life or in Purgatory. He severely blamed those who would not use these opportunities, not he said that I mean you, voi siete tutti santi, tutti, ma, se c'è forse qualche impertinentuccio intrato fra noi, he spoke for such.[1] This is not well worth recounting for the manner of it: but I was struck with the clear, simple, methodical, *way* of inculcation.

25. M.

H.S. with Agnes: also Italian. Read Ventura on Graziosi—on O'Connell—Colletta. C. had a party to tea in the evening: with singing. It lasted from 8½ to near 11½. We spent most of the day on an exp. to St Martino:[2] & dined with the Greene's at the Europa.

Monday. Nov. 25. We went with the Leven party to San Martino. They had an order from the Pope, necessary for ladies: 'arbitrio & prudentiae superioris ammittimus Pius PP. IX.'[3] Great difficulty was made about their entrance because the signature was not witnessed by the Archbishop or Nuncio: but they gave way.

The cloister is extremely light and simple. The Church most elaborately rich in marbles: particularly the high altar rail, & one altar in *pietra dura:*[4] also fruit carved like Gibbons's[5] wood. The Guido of the Nativity is unfinished & has not fair play.[6] But no one I suppose sees Spagnoletto well who does not see him here.[7] Both the Dead Saviour & the Moses are remarkable: the latter grand: the Statue of the dead Angelo put into the plane, the horns made ambiguous & looking like rays. In the other picture the figure of our Lord is the masterpiece: most elaborately finished: very death like and yet not ghastly. I do not like the lights on the figure at the feet: & did not find anything except the one figure very striking.

The monks have plenty of space: they are now 6 priests, 4 novices, 19 conversi[8] where there *were* three times as many: they eat no meat, no eggs & cheese in Lent & Advent: have 5000 ducats a year only.

[1] 'You are all saints, all of you, but if perchance there is some impertinent fellow entered among us'.

[2] A suppressed Carthusian monastery and church situated within the Castel Sant' Elmo, on a hill dominating the W. of Naples. Founded in 1325, it was rebuilt in the seventeenth century.

[3] 'We admit them by the will of our superior judgment, Pius Pater Patriae IX'.

[4] Literally 'hard stones'; semiprecious stones, used in sixteenth century for altar frontals.

[5] i.e. in the manner of Grinling *Gibbons, 1648–1720, who designed and carved the wood in St. Paul's cathedral and other English buildings.

[6] Guido Reni, 1575–1642.

[7] Jusepe de Ribera, known as Lo Spagnoletto, restored Stanzione's 'Deposition from the Cross' in S. Martino, adding Moses and Elias below it.

[8] 'Lay brothers'.

Of the three views, embracing together perhaps three quadrants of the circle, any one would be worth mounting for.

As we looked at the Ships one of the monks asked us if *Lormint* was not still somewhere about here with his *fleet.* A token of the impression which Lord Minto's Embassy has left.[1]

26. T.

Wrote to T.G—R. Phillimore[2]—Bp of Salisbury—H.S. with Agnes: also Italian. Calls: business: visited Santa Chiara.[3] Mr Monsell's[4] in evg: he is excellent: but his illness makes it painful to converse with him, he seems to suffer so. Read Ventura on O'Connell (a romance)—Colletta. Wrote up Journals:

Tuesday Nov. 26. Visited Santa Chiara. It is most curious to observe the remains of the old painted fabric and the immense labour that has been misapplied in its metamorphosis. The tombs are beautiful:[5] very elaborate: great feeling & even sometimes much grace in the figures carved upon them. The bassi rilievi[6] on the pulpit & at the west end should also be noticed. Among the figures on the tombs (which I understand are Massuccio's work) there appeared to be great diversity of execution.

27. Wed.

H.S. with Agnes. Visited the Studio. Bookshops & stalls afterwards. Read Colletta—Farini's Stato Romano da 1815–1850[7]—Borgianelli—Practised music. Saw Mr Hubbard—Lady Malcolm.[8]

Wednesday Nov. 27. Visited the Studio.[9] I paid the driver (2 horses) for the course from the Vittoria 2 carlines. He was furious: I would neither debate nor add, but gave him my address & left him storming. When we came out, he appeared in the same place bowing & smirking & foremost in the competition to carry us back again! Such is Naples.

[1] Cp. 4 Mar. 47 n.

[2] Part in Morley, i. 409.

[3] In the Strada Trinità Maggiore. A very long gothic church, restored and decorated in 1732 when Giotto's frescoes were whitewashed to make the church lighter.

[4] Charles Henry Monsell, 1815–29 Jan. 1851; prebendary of Aghadoe 1840; m. 1839 Harriet O'Brien, 1812–83, who became a sister of mercy 1851, superior of house of Clewer 1852–75. A high churchman, he lived in Naples for health reasons.

[5] Of many of the Anjou dynasty, including those of Robert the Wise (a 42 ft. high monument), of his son Charles, duke of Calabria, (both by Tommaso Masuccio the younger, 1291–1388, Neapolitan sculptor), and his wife, Mary of Valois.

[6] 'Bas-reliefs'.

[7] L. C. Farini, *Lo Stato Romano dall' anno 1815 all' anno 1850*, 3 v. (1850–1); tr. by Gladstone as *The Roman State from 1815 to 1850*, 4 v. (1851–4); the fourth vol. being tr. under Gladstone's direction by his cousin Mrs. A. R. Bennett. Cp. 21 Dec. 50, 3 June 51 and Add MS 44685, ff. 89–255.

[8] Lady Mary Malcolm who m. 1829 Sir M. Malcolm, 6th bart., and d. 1897; she was in Naples with her son and two unmarried daughters (correction to note at 23 June 32).

[9] The museum, built 1586, taken over as the Regnii Studii by the university 1616, by the Bourbons and renamed Museo Reale Borbonico 1816, by Garibaldi and renamed Museo Nazionale 1860.

We spent our time among the pictures & chiefly the Capi d'Opera.[1] It is a delightful room, of such varied & on the whole well sustained excellence. Nothing is grander there than Sebastian del Piombo's Alexander VI.[2] His holy family is very sweet & pure.[3] Giov. Bellini's Transfiguration has a German truth & force with the richness of Venetian colour. I suppose the grace of the Madonna del Coniglio[4] is not surpassed by any picture in the world. Into the Holy Family called Raffaelle's there enters a strong dash of Giulio Romano.[5] Yet the *Gatto* picture,[6] Guilio's admitted work, is again a great way below.

I greatly delight in the B. Virgin & Child of Pietro Perugino[7] in the adjoining Sala: & I wonder whether some of the small background figures which are very graceful & marked in attitude may be the work of Raffaelle.

28. Th.

H.S. with Agnes. Shopping & working up the newspapers: when a projected ride had proved abortive. Saw Mr Monsell—Mr Sinapi[8] (& chose drawings to be executed)—to Lady Malcolm's in evg: where I had an interesting conv. with Baron Brockhausen the Prussian Minister.[9] Read Farini (whom I like much)—Colletta—Borgianelli. C. not well in the evg: did not accompany me. Mr Lacaita whose kindness is indefatigable promised me introductions to ecclesiastics.

Thursday Nov. 28. I heard the Military Band today before the Palace & saw the troops defile. Bands are rare here though soldiers abound: & this one was not first rate by any means. The soldiers look well. Mr. L. says the Gvt. now trust the nation as well as the Swiss force, i.e. since the Sicilian war.

It is odd & characteristic to find the different prices asked here for the same (new) book. For Curci's answer to Gioberti[10] I am asked in 3 different shops, 2 piastres, 2 ducats, 18 carlines.

I must name the price of umbrellas. In the Toledo they appear marked *Prezzi fissi*.[11] The rates for cotton are from 3 to 4 ducats: the articles appear to be such as would scarcely fetch two shillings ($\frac{1}{5}$) in England.

[1] On the eastern wing of the upper floor, which was completely rearranged in 1909.

[2] In fact Clement VII by Sebastiano del Piombo, 1485–1547; born in Venice; after 1513 lived in Rome holding sinecure of the eponymous lead seal ('piombo').

[3] After Raphael, unfinished.

[4] Also known as the Madonna la Zingarella, by Antonio Allegri (Correggio), 1494–1534; so called because of the rabbit ('coniglio') in the foreground.

[5] 1499–1546; architect and painter. The picture, 'Madonna and child with St. Elizabeth, St. Joseph and the Young St. John', is known as the 'Madonna del Divin'Amore'. Raphael's contribution to the picture is disputed, cp. L. Dussler, *Raphael* (1971), 49.

[6] Picture of the holy family, called 'Madonna del Gatto'.

[7] Pietro Vanucci Perugino, 1446–1524.

[8] Neapolitan art dealer and picture restorer; Gladstone spells him variously.

[9] Adolf, Freiherr von Brockhausen, 1801–58; s. of Karl Christian von Brockhausen who d. 1829; Prussian legation minister in Stockholm 1834, in Naples 1842, in Brussels 1852.

[10] C. M. Curci, *Una Divinazione sopra le tre ultime opere di Gioberti* (1849). Gioberti had attacked the Jesuits in his *Prolegomeni del Primato* (1845).

[11] 'fixed prices'.

29. Fr.

Wrote to M.F. Tupper—A.M. Paterson—J. Griffith—H.S. & Italian with Agnes—Sermon 5½ P.M. S. Ferdinando—Dined at Mrs Hope's:[1] singing afterwards. Read Farini—Borgianelli—Colletta. Went with Mr Halsey up to San Martino.

Friday Nov. 29. Sermon in S. Ferdinando. See note of it.[2]

30. Sat. St Andrew.

H.S. with Agnes. Sermon 5½ A.M. S. Ferdinando. Singing in evening. Went to see the Marquis Dragonetti's[3] pictures, now for sale: and Barone's[4] shop & house where are many interesting things, some very beautiful. These took up the afternoon. Read Farini—Borgianelli—La Prima Sett. di Agosto in Torino[5]—Made up my accounts for the month.

Saturday. Nov. 30. The same. See note of it.

Went with Mr. Lacaita to see a collection of pictures belonging to the Marquis [Dragonetti] one of the late Ministers of Foreign Affairs. The prices marked appeared to range from 300 to 700 ducats: the values to less than a tenth part. We spent the afternoon at Barone's. His house is full of interesting objects: and he is himself so very Neapolitan, which means amusing, in manner & address, that he is well worth a visit. His pictures of which he does not profess to be a judge are far cheaper than those we saw this morning.

Advent Sunday Decr. One.

Church 11 A.M. (H.C.) and 3. Sermon 5½ P.M. in St M. degli Ang. Epistle aloud in evg: & comment. Mr Lacaita brought Padre Tosti:[6] with whom I was greatly pleased. Read La Prima Settimana (finished)—Sulle Attualità Ecclesiastiche.[7]

Advent Sunday Dec. 1. Sermon in S.M. Degli Angeli. See note.

2. M.

H.S. & Italian with Agnes. Went to Barone's & finished my transaction. To the Studio with Mr Hubbard. Shopping. To the 'Independence' with a

[1] Ellen, *née* Meredith; m. 1835 Frederick William *Hope, 1797–1863 priest, entomologist and benefactor of Oxford University; lived in Naples for health reasons.

[2] Reports of sermons heard between 29 November 1850 and 19 January 1851 are in Add MS 44738, ff. 183–209.

[3] Luigi, Marquis Dragonetti, 1791–1871; Neapolitan minister of foreign affairs 1848; Italian senator 1861; writer and connoisseur.

[4] Raffaele Barone, fine art dealer in Strada Trinita Maggiore.

[5] *La prima settimana di agosto nella città di Torino* (1850).

[6] Luigi Tosti, 1811–97; monk in abbey of Monte Cassino; wrote many works on Italian ecclesiastical history; much influenced by Gioberti.

[7] Perhaps T. P. G. Massimo, *Sulla proprieta ecclesiastica e sul modo legale . . .*' (1850).

party in aftn. To Lady Leven's in evg. The servants went up Vesuvius: we had therefore more occupation at home. Read Farini—Colletta—Ld Shrewsbury[1] having called several times I went to see him. Lady S. is singularly unreserved. I wish we could have seen the same zeal spread among English Church people of rank for their Church—at least when & while they knew what they had to fight for.

Monday Dec. 2. I offered Barone a sum for the *objects* I wished to purchase & left him to digest it. He begged me to add *un altro poco.*[2] Impossible I said: but that if he did not like to accept I wd. then take a small print (wh I had noted separately). Oh no he did not wish to refuse: but would like un altro poco: which he found hopeless & so desisted. He is I believe safer to deal with than his brethren & altogether the best.

At the Studio we compared Mr. Hubbard's miniature of the Raphael Holy Family, for which he is to pay 120 p., with the original & it seemed very satisfactory. The lights are much more marked & all the edges far sharper but this I suppose is required by the reduction in size & change from oil to water.

Mr. Herbert[3] took a party of ladies on board the Independence an American 56 [gunner]: & I accompanied them. We were most kindly received. The officers appeared to like the visit. The cleanliness was wonderful. Great solidity & mass about the ship: everything of the best: they serve out nothing but sperm candles. The prison was *full.* I saw a Carabine without ramrod which appeared a great improvement. Mr. H. thought so too: & was not aware why we had it not. The view of Naples from the deck was very fine. A good band played: they gave us God save the Queen with great energy. They are chiefly Neapolitan: are temporarily engaged & not borne on the ship's books: which is the American system.

3. T.[4]

Wrote to Sir J.G—Scotts—Mr Jas Watson—H.S. with Agnes. Saw Madame Faluolti[5] & arranged with her for her daughter (of 12 years old nearly) to come here & make a trial of the effect of her conversation & what little else she can do in giving Agnes, & even Mary, Italian. Dined early with Mr Monsell, to meet Father Costa:[6] who presented to me his translation of Allies. He is able & pleasant: but I felt when with him, that a Jesuit is as it were shut up against the access of truth in those things in which he has it not. Called on Mr Knudtzen.[7] Shopping. Got home from Barone my works

[1] John Talbot, 1791–1852; m. 1814 Maria Theresa Talbot, 1797–1856; 16th earl of Shrewsbury 1827; lived in Naples 1850–2; a Roman Catholic.

[2] 'a little more'.

[3] Probably William George Herbert, Lieutenant R.N. 1845, then serving on the Mediterranean station; cp. 18 Dec. 50.

[4] No travel journal this day.

[5] Unidentified.

[6] G. Costa, a Jesuit priest connected with the Vicaria prison, cp. L. Fagan, *Life of *Panizzi* (1880), ii. 105. He tr. T. W. Allies on St. Peter as *La cattedra di S. Pietro, fondamento della chiesa* (1850); cp. 4 Oct. 50.

[7] Unidentified.

of art &c. & arranged them. C.s party to tea in evening, & music. Also practice. Read Farini—Costa's Preface—Colletta.

4. *Wed.*

From $8\frac{1}{2}$ to $5\frac{3}{4}$, expedition to Vesuvius. Sermon. See Notes. Dined at Lady Malcolm's. Read Farini.

Naples Wednesday Dec. 4. We went to Vesuvius. The new drive to the Hermitage[1] lessens labour without saving time: rather otherwise. The time taken was as follows.

Naples to Hermitage	3 hours. 9–12
To the top and back	$3\frac{1}{4}$ hours. 12–$3\frac{1}{4}$.
Luncheon &	$\frac{1}{2}$ } $3\frac{1}{4}$–$5\frac{3}{4}$
Back to Naples	2 }

Mr. Lacaita made great speed & went by the old road in $1\frac{1}{2}$ hours from Naples to the Hermitage. The day was fine but rather hazy: we had a tolerable view of the landward basin: & the stream & small craters at the foot of the cone, belonging to the last eruption. At the top all was sulphurous vapour over the crater & we saw nothing. Two of the ladies walked up: the ascent detestable, worse than of old: the descent as of old amusing. I brought down the little Lady Emily[2] who had been (chiefly) dragged up. C. and Agnes prudently staid at the observatory.

As we returned to Naples the old Naples gigs passed us in numbers laden with from 10 to about 16 persons each: going back from work & business to their homes. There was a kind of stand where they were taking passengers. One I saw with twelve or more on it not yet satisfied and waiting for a fuller cargo.

I went to Sermon on my return.

5. *Th.*

H.S. with Agnes. Saw Madame Faluolti: & her daughter came to stay for certain till Saturday. Went with Ly Malcolm to see Marchese S. Angelo's[3] pictures & vases: see Journal. Then S. Severino.[4] Read Farini—Wiseman's Appeal to the people of England.[5] Sermon. See Notes. Dined at Mr Temple's: & saw his collection in the evening, which he showed most kindly & patiently. Singing practice.

Thursday Dec. 5. Lady Malcolm took us to the Marchese St Angelo's Strada Maddaleni (or in the line of it) & we saw his pictures vases &

[1] A tavern on the shoulder of Vesuvius; the new road was destroyed by lava in 1858.

[2] Presumably the servant, cp. 28 Oct. 50.

[3] A Neapolitan art connoisseur; cp. N. W. *Senior, *Journals kept in France and Italy 1848–52* (1871), ii. 18.

[4] See note in travel diary for this day.

[5] N. P. S. *Wiseman, 'An appeal to the reason and good feeling of the English people on the subject of the catholic hierarchy' (1850).

bronzes: a very interesting collection. Of the pictures I should *wish* to recollect many: especially

The noble twin-portrait of Vittoria Colonna & her husband by Sebastian del Piombo.

The Holy Family with S. Mary Magdalene of Ghirlandajo.[1]

Small Holy Family of Victor Carpaccio[2]—especially the Face of the Virgin.

Small Holy Family of [blank] (Venetian)

Small Holy Family by Parmiggiano.[3]

A Descent from the Cross?

Its pendant by Baroccio:[4] a beautiful little work, wholly free from his mannerism & affectation, with which his more conspicuous & celebrated picture the St. Francis is a little tinged.

We have here Giovan Bellini, Salvator Rosa, Spagnoletto, Gaspar Poussin,[5] Ruysdael,[6] Berghem[7] (probably) & many others in great force: especially the Castel Nuovo picture by Salvator is to be remembered. There is also the sketch of M. Angelo's Last Judgement. And The Adoration of The Virgin by St. Andrew & St. John, a work of Fabrizio Santa Fede,[8] does great honour to the school of Naples: especially the figure of St. John.

In the Ghirlandajo the most beautiful parts are the two heads of Mary & Mary Magdalen.

There are interesting pictures by living Neapolitan artists: for instance the Crucifixion by Morani,[9] & the picture from Boccaccio by Morelli[10] a very young man I understand. The work abounds in fancy. Observe also a head by [blank] a Roman who I understand has more than any other taken Camuccini's[11] place.

The vases were also interesting and extremely numerous: the mosaics in relief are said to be unique.

But in the evening after dinner Mr. Temple showed us his treasures, which certainly appeared to be even more remarkable though fewer. He has two little female heads in Terra Cotta, of *different* beauty but both quite exquisite. He is very rich in the drinking cups which have heads of animals for their base, i.e. his specimens are admirably wrought.

[1] Dominic Ghirlandajo, 1449–1494; Florentine painter.

[2] Vittore Carpaccio 1460–1523?, Venetian painter.

[3] Girolamo Francesco Mazzola, called Parmigiano, 1504–40; Emilian painter, influenced by Correggio and Raphael; ruined himself by alchemy.

[4] Federigo Baroccio, 1535–1612; Italian painter.

[5] Gaspard Dughet, called Poussin; artist, born in Rome of French extraction; br.-in-law and pupil of Nicolas Poussin.

[6] Jakob van Ruysdael, 1630–82; Dutch landscape painter: worked in Haarlem.

[7] Nicolaes Berchem, 1620–83; Dutch painter.

[8] Fabrizio Santafede, 1560–1628; Neapolitan painter.

[9] Vincenzo Morani, 1813–70; historical and portrait-painter; worked mainly for the court of Naples and the Benedictine convent of Trinità della Cava.

[10] Domenico Morelli, 1826–1901; painted historical scenes, portraits and landscapes; senator of Italy from 1886.

[11] Vincenzo Camuccini, 1771–1844, historical painter.

We went today likewise to the San Severino[1] and saw the three veiled Statues: modesty, the Dimiganno & the dead Saviour: the works of three different artists: the last by far the most beautiful for with the triumph over mechanical difficulties the artist has combined a higher feeling.

Sermon. See notes.

6. Fr.

H.S. with Agnes. Worked at the Italian with the Faluolti girl who I am afraid has not the needful *pluck* in her. C. too laboured much. To the Studii with Mr Hubbard. Walk with C. Read Farini—Civiltà Cattolica[2]—Mystagogue.[3] Dined at Sir T. Carmichael's—music in evg. Sermon—See Notes. Another evening conv. with Mr Lacaita. Each one makes me like & admire him more.[4]

Friday Dec. 6. Went to the Studii: a rapid glance at the mosaics & wall paintings, the rest among the pictures. The room of the Capi d'Opera certainly repays repeated visits. Of the two little Correggios I prefer the Coniglio.[5] Marcello's Last Judgement, Giov. Bellini's Transfiguration, Alexander VI, are among the pictures here which are likely to attract less notice than they seem to me to deserve.[6] The last named is a superb work.

In the chamber of the Roman School, the so called Raphael is surely not finished by his hand.[7]

In the left hand picture gallery the Greek works are well worth attention: some of them have along with solemnity distinct grace & beauty. For instance No. 86.[8] In the fourth gallery the works of Cosimo Roselli,[9] Ghirlandajo,[10] Lorenzo da Credi,[11] and Masaccio,[12] are well worth picking out.

Sermon. See Notes.

[1] He had confused the SS. Severino e Sosio in the Largo S. Marcellino, which contained the Neapolitan archives, with the S. Maria della Pietà dei Sangri, known as S. Severo, in the Calata di S. Severo. The latter contains several veiled allegorical statues, often regarded as in very poor taste, including 'Modesty' by Corradini, and the 'Dead Christ', represented lying covered with a sheet adhering to the skin by the sweat of death, by Giuseppe Sammartino.

[2] 'Alla civilta cattolica: riposta di un prelato romano' (n.d.).

[3] Possibly Cleidophorus Mystagogus, *Mercury's Caducean rod*, 2 v. (1704).

[4] These two sentences and extracts from some subsequent days are printed in C. Lacaita, *An Italian Englishman* (1933), 33.

[5] Cp. 27 Nov. 50.

[6] ibid.

[7] Now regarded as a copy of Raphael's 'Bridgewater Madonna' in the National Gallery of Scotland.

[8] 'The child Hercules' by Spinello Aretino, 1373–1411; cp. *Nouveau guide du musée royale Bourbon* (1854), 112.

[9] Cosimo Rosselli, 1439–1507; his 'Marriage of the Virgin with Joseph'.

[10] He had several paintings in this room, notably his 'Holy Family'.

[11] Lorenzo di Credi, 1459–1537; his 'Nativity'.

[12] 'Virgin with the infant Jesus, supported by two angels'; now attributed to Botticelli.

7. Sat.

H.S. with Agnes. Read Farini Wrote up Journal. Sermon—See Notes. Calls, & shopping. We were perplexed about the little parlatrice, (che non parla):[1] but arranged to try her again on Monday. In evg went with Mr Lacaita to the Cardinal's:[2] then to Mr Monsell's; then to Lady Malcolm's. We were alone with the Cardinal: his manner is singularly artless & straightforward. With Mr Monsell I had a very interesting conversation. He deeply appreciates the great practical evils of the actual system of the Ch. of Rome.

Sat. Dec. 7. Sermon. S. Ferdinando. See Notes.
Went with Mr. Lacaita at 7½ to visit, by permission, the Cardinal Archbishop. He was out when we arrived, visiting his Seminary, as he afterwards told us. His palace is spacious: we saw a good many servants: but the furnishing was of great simplicity, not greater however than the manners of the master, which are most artless & straightforward.

His age seems to be under rather than over forty. We talked of (Lord Shrewsbury—Bp. Spencer—) Sir R. Peel (whom he admired much) Guizot, the English Parliament, Oxford, the Exhibition. I thought he did not wish to touch the question of the present excitement: but Mr. Lacaita judged otherwise.

8. 2 S. Advent.

Ch mg 11 & aft 3. Bp Spencer preached both times: & confirmed in the afternoon service. Sermon S. Caterina at 4½ PM. Prayers in evg: wrote notes on the Epistle, & explained it from them. Also with Agnes. Read Curci's Divinazione[3]—Memoires d'un Prêtre Russe.[4]

Sunday Dec. 8. Sermon in S. Caterina Martin. See Notes.

9. M.

H.S. with Agnes. To Carelli's[5] Studio & pictures mg. San Carlo evening. Early tea with Mr Monsell. Read Farini. 2½ hours at the Times: reading about the movement in England. There are good elements in it: but with what strange, fearful, & I apprehend *dominant* admixture.[6] We let the Faluolti girl go home: partly because she has not all we might wish; partly because we hope to do better with a grown up person.

[1] 'Talker (who does not talk)'.

[2] Sisto Riario Sforza, 1810–77; cardinal and abp. of Naples 1845; supported Bourbons; hostile to Italian unity; expelled from Naples 1861; supported the *Syllabus* and papal infallibility. Cp. W. E. Gladstone, *Two Letters . . . *Aberdeen* (1851), 57.

[3] C. M. Curci, *Una divinazione sulle tre ultime opere di Vinc. Gioberti*, 2 v. (1848).

[4] Untraced.

[5] Gabrielli Carelli; still living in 1880; architect and painter; later worked in England. His studio was, like most others in Naples, in the Riviera di Chiaja.

[6] The announcement of roman catholic bps. with British titles provoked widespread hostility and rioting of which *The Times* had long reports, especially on 22 and 23 Nov. 1850.

Monday Dec. 9. Visited Carelli's Studio. His highly finished picture of the interior of St. Giovanni, Malta is to be sold for 500 ducats, *ultimo prezzo*,[1] if it goes to England: and indeed it is a beautiful work.

There was also a view of Palermo by his brother Gonsalvo,[2] very good at 200 pi.: and clever water colour drawings. But I thought less of them after seeing in the evening one of Gigante's[3] of which the aerial effects were most pure and beautiful, leaving nothing to be desired.

At San Carlos in the evening we heard Tadolini[4] & Bassini[5] in the Schiava Saracina.[6] The latter [sc. former] did not seem to me to sing with nearly so much spirit as in the Theatre at Oxford: the latter is a grand voice but the part seemed difficult for a bass (Ismaello). Ferasis[7] danced with the ballet: she has all the muscular feats of Cerito, but not the grace, which seemed to me (in the last named) all but superhuman and really spread an atmosphere of exceeding purity around her.

10. T.

H.S. with Agnes. Read Farini. Practised singing with Miss Hope:[8] Saw Sinepi: who examined my late purchases with me, reports well on the whole, & is to restore the large landscape. Shopping. The Hubbard's came to dinner: C's tea party & music in evg.

Tuesday Dec. 10. Sinepi visited me bringing home his Panorama from San Martino, and examined the pictures I bought last week: showing me where the restorer had been at work. It was he told me his old trade: & I agreed that he should clean & restore the large landscape which he says (after inspection) is Matthew Brill,[9] the brother of Paul[10] (after restoring it, he says certainly Paul Brill).[11] The Madonna on copper is his favourite: Florentine, according to him, & by Salviati.[12] The small circular landscape by Orizzonte.[13] (Romano).[14] The still smaller one by Domenico Brandi[15] (Napoli) un bel quadrettino, graziosetto.[16] The orange flower portrait has been it seems all restored & is in the best state it can be: he thinks it is of some Neapolitan princess. The woman in adultery he thinks well done: of the school of Rubens.

[1] 'last price', i.e. his last offer.

[2] Gonsalvo Carelli, 1818–1900; Neapolitan painter in the school of Posillipo.

[3] Giacinto Gigante, 1806–76; Neapolitan painter; employed all over Europe, famous for his water colours.

[4] Eugénie Tadolini, 1810–?; soprano; one of her last performances; she retired in 1850.

[5] Achille de Bassini, 1819–81; leading bass-baritone at San Carlo 1849–52, then at St. Petersburg.

[6] Probably Pacini's *La Schiava in Bagdad*, first performed in Turin, 1820.

[7] Unidentified.

[8] Probably F. W. *Hope's sister, he had no daughter.

[9] Matthew Brill, 1548–83; Flemish landscape painter.

[10] Paul Brill, 1556–1626; also a Flemish landscape painter.

[11] Passage in parentheses added later in the margin.

[12] Francesco Salviati, 1510–63; Florentine painter.

[13] Jan Frans van Bloemen, called Orizonte, 1662–1749; Dutch landscape painter.

[14] This word, and the next sentence, added in the margin.

[15] 1683–1736; painter to the viceroy of Naples; best known for his landscapes.

[16] 'a beautiful little picture, full of elegance'.

11. Wed.

My Father's 86th year ends today. I shall rejoice to hear that it has passed over well. Great, though undefined, uncertainty, now hangs over his life: but I trust he has a tranquil mind & an eye fixed on heaven. Read Farini—The Guardian—Memoires d'un Pretre Russe. H.S. with Agnes. Conv. with C. on our infirmities. 'Cleanse thou me from my secret sins'.[1] Visited Capo di Monte gardens. The Monsells came to dine: conv. till night was on us.

Wedy Dec. 11. Went to the Capo di Monte Gardens:[2] admission by Order, to be had at the Mission. They are parklike grounds laid out in the English manner with considerable success & with the additional advantage of the cypresses & stone pines, & standard magnolias.

There is a flat resemblance between the forms of the King's Palaces at Caserta,[3] here, & in the city below.

12. Th.

Read Farini (finished)—Prêtre Russe—Processo della Republica di 1849.[4] A walk & interesting conversation with Father Tosti. I also saw Mr Lacaita: & tried to obtain from both clues to information about Farini. Sinepi commenced his work on the Brill picture: in my room, to which I held him, choosing the lesson & the smell together. Lady Leven's at night. Singing.

Th. Dec. 12. I was glad to see some fifty persons (of whom perhaps $\frac{1}{3}$ were clergy) reading in the rooms appointed for the purpose at the Biblioteca. Padre Tosti told me earlier in the day there were from 100 to 120.

13. Fr.

Wrote to T.G—H.J.G—Iggulden—Scotts—Lyttelton. Read Republica di 1849—Curci's Divinazione—the English papers. H.S. with Agnes. Sermon. See Notes. Mrs Hope's in evg—music. Shopping & calls.

Fr. Dec. 13. Sermon—See Notes.

The end of my story of the milkman stands thus. I asked the successful one his opinion of his rival in these terms è galantuomo davvero?[5] but notwithstanding my leading question, he replied Ah! Eccellenza, quello lì, è un assassino![6]

[1] Psalm xix. 12.
[2] The grounds of the Capodimonte; Cp. 23 Nov. 50.
[3] Eighteenth-century palace built by Charles III of Spain, 7 miles ESE. of Capua.
[4] Not found.
[5] 'Oh he's a fine fellow, isn't he?'
[6] 'Ah! your Excellence, that one there is an assassin.'

14. Sat.

$8\frac{1}{2}$–$6\frac{3}{4}$. Expedition to La Trinità:[1] see Journal. Tea at Lady Malcolm's after. Read Mem. d'un Pr. Russe—Wrote Journal.

Saturday Dec. 14. We started at half past eight for La Cava and the Monastery of La Trinità under Lady Malcolm's hospitable auspices. The railway still makes it 13 or 14 miles an hour: $1\frac{1}{2}$ hour brought us to Nocera.[2] The swelling roofs at Torre dell Annunziata[3] on which corn is dried & many household operations performed are well seen from it.

We got carriages amidst a great tumult at Nocera: & stopped on the way to La Cava at Santa Marià Maggiore[4] to see the ancient Baptistery now in a state of sad dilapidation. It is most venerable from antiquity, its form is interesting & its pillars have been splendid but are splitting and crumbling in the damp. It has all the air of a Christian structure though the pillars it is supposed may have been appropriated from some ancient temple. Its form is circular and an aisle surrounds the main space, divided from it by a double row of sixteen pillars, thirty two in all. One of the circular arches which part them faces the entrance & is wider than the rest: a singular architectural arrangement as it is not a multiple of the width being a little less than double. It seems to mark the place of the altar. The light is from the top. Ribs from the pillars outwards forming parts of radii, run across the roof of the aisle. The Baptistery is in the middle & has had a roof or canopy supported by pillars three of which have been removed it seems by a Neapolitan general to adorn his gardens. The pillars of this Church are of very fine marbles & other fine stones.

Less than three quarters of an hour suffices for the drive to the Albergo di Landia[5] at La Cava: which is a clean nice Inn. From hence the ladies went on donkeys the remaining distance, I suppose near three miles to the Monastery of the Trinità, under Monte Finestra. The whole outline of the hills on the right is most grand: the *spur* of the Appennine being in fact nobler here in character than the main chain. Especially Monte Finestra (the *window* is still visible from some points on the way) is a worthy twin to the grand St. Angelo. In front rises the sharp form of the Liberatore, and there are views both of the gulf of Salerno & the plain of Paestum including the site of the ruins.

The Monastery itself is in a most lovely spot, withdrawn & hidden from the valley by a shoulder round which we wound. It overhangs a deep ravine & is overhung itself by the rock of which indeed a part has been allowed to remain protruding in the transept of the Church. The front is recent: the buildings appear to be in excellent order. There are 22 professi, 12 conversi, 16 alumni, and I think 64 seminarists, the Abbot being Bishop & having

[1] The Benedictine monastery founded in 1025 at La Cava, about 28 miles from Naples on the road to Salerno. It contained one of the finest libraries in Italy, later removed to Naples.

[2] About 22 miles along the road to Salerno.

[3] On the coast, about 10 miles SE. of Naples.

[4] Between Nocera and La Cava; a temple converted by early Christians into a baptistry.

[5] In the town of Corpo de Tirreni, to the NE. of the monastery.

here his Seminary. Among the Alumni we saw two little Australians from the Colony of Swan River.[1] The Church is generally plain: the Organ singularly placed behind the altar, but the Choir comes between. There are three rich modern tombs of the three first Abbots, in inlaid marbles; and here again the rock & church join & the cell of the Founder a hollow in the mountain is visible. The organ is said to have 6000 pipes: we heard it play & were much disappointed.

We went with Father Cornè the intelligent keeper of the Manuscripts—now the property of the Govt.—to see them. He showed me the most beautiful works: the Chronicle of the 12th Century, the French missal of the 14th, and the Beato Angelico's own work,[2] the smallest but most interesting of all. The first of these three is a specimen of Greek art & there are beautiful figures, & beautiful heads, especially in the marriage of the Emperor Maurice.[3] We saw also most curious Lombard documents one as early as the 7th Century, being marriage settlements, only made the day *after* nuptials, granting ¼ of the husband's goods as dower: a fine one of the 10th with the names in gold: Roger's[4] gifts of land in Sicily—which the Convent possessed it seems before the French came to the enormous amount of 300000 crowns a year—so he said: and also a copy of the Lombard laws in the 9th Century[5] with a most curious & very rude picture of the presentation of their favourite dish a young pig in milk to the King. The character of this was in no way akin to the Chronicle.

The Seminarists here all learn Greek as well as Latin which P. Cornè told me is considered necessary in this College though disgraziatamente[6] not in all such establishments.

The manuscripts are 60000: & those of the Lombards are more abundant & valuable here than in any other establishment.

We were very unwilling to part from this most lovely & interesting spot, a true image of that retirement for study teaching & devotion to which it is dedicated. But we had to return to Naples which we reached by the evening train and had an excellent tea—supper at Lady Malcolm's.

15. 3 S. Advent.[7]

Church 11 & 3. H.S. with Agnes. Prayers in evg: comment on Epistle. Read Divinazione—Prêtre Russe—Bennett's Letter to Ld J. Russell (as in the M. Chronicle).[8] Walk with C.

16. M.

Wrote to Dagna. Sermon. See Notes. Visited Churches with Mr Hubbard.

[1] Now Western Australia.
[2] Now regarded as by his pupils.
[3] Flavius Tiberius Mauricius, 539–602; emperor of the East from 582.
[4] Roger of Sicily, 1097–1154; duke of Sicily 1127, king 1129.
[5] The *Codex Legum Longobardorum* (1004).
[6] 'Unfortunately'.
[7] No travel diary this day.
[8] W. J. E. *Bennett, reprinted as 'A first letter to . . . *Russell . . . on the present persecution of a certain portion of the English Church' (1850).

See Tour. Read Curci—Prêtre Russe (finished).—Dined with Mr Hubbard: unbroken conv. on Church matters. Shopping & accounts.

Monday Dec. 16. Sermon. S.M. degli Angeli. See Notes.

I went with Mr. Hubbard to the Cathedral[1] in the forenoon: & found that the Miracle[2] stands over until Sunday when the labouring classes can attend: & that this change is commonly made. It adds another feature of strangeness to the case.

The Cathedral is effective in its general character: the arches pointed, almost everything else was mongrel: the piers are blocks of building with granite pillars stuck into them. The late archbishop restored & gilt the Church at his own cost. The throne and pulpit should be observed: & especially the picture of the Assumption by Perugino[3] which is going to ruin from neglect & may have been much tampered with already but is of beautiful design in the best spirit & manner of that great master.

In the Sotterraneo[4] we saw the fine Statue of Caraffa,[5] fine that is in the head & hands & the design: by Michael Angelo: & the strange Pagan bassi rilievi[6] which were brought they say from Pozzuoli & have been fitted into the walls, the character of the rest being made in a degree to correspond with them. This was the corrupt work of Caraffa: who by the bye is represented kneeling & in the act they said of adoring the Statue of San Gennaro.[7] Exterior. NB. the flanking towers: Angioina.[8]

In the Gerolomini or S. Filippo Neri[9] are very noble granite columns & a singularly rich & gorgeous roof,[10] all, as one may say, of Gold, yet so tempered by age or taste as to have a good effect. Guido's St. Francis[11] seems a good specimen. His picture in the Sacristry of the meeting of our Lord & St. John Baptist is in the extreme of naturalism. The other pictures are too high: but I like the Andrea di Salerno as to its general design. They showed us a very beautiful ivory crucifix.

S. Paolo Maggiore.[12] The torsi of Castor and Pollux in the front are very fine, especially the one most contracted: so also the pillars, relics of the old temple.

[1] In the Strada de Duomo, dedicated to St. Januarius, begun in 1272; frequently reconstructed and restored.

[2] The liquefaction of the blood of St. Januarius, martyred in 305, took place annually on the first Saturday of May and on 19 September and 16 December. Cp. 5 May 32.

[3] Pietro Vanucci Perugino, 1446–1524.

[4] 'The crypt' of St. Januarius, also known as Capella Carafa, perhaps the masterpiece of renaissance art in Naples, by Tomaso Malvito da Como, 1497–1508.

[5] Cardinal Oliviero Carafa, founder of the cathedral.

[6] 'Bas-reliefs'.

[7] i.e. St. Januarius.

[8] i.e. of the house of Anjou.

[9] In the Largo Gerolomini; the church, built 1592–1619, is also known as de' Gerolomini.

[10] By Francesco Solimena, 1657–1747.

[11] In the 5th chapel, now in Pinacoteca dei Gerolomini.

[12] Built in 1590 in the Strada de' Tribunali on the site of a temple to Castor and Pollux. An earthquake in 1688 destroyed the remains of the temple save the Castor and Pollux incorporated in the font.

17. T.

Sermon Gerolomini.[1] See Notes. Saw Tosti—Lacaita—Hubbard—Reid. Read Curci—D'Aloe's Guide[2]—The Guardian—Gordon's Reasons of Commission.[3] Party in evening. Singing.

Tuesday Dec. 17. Sermon. See Notes.

I visited Padre Tosti in the Sacristy of S. Severino: then in his room, full of the signs of *work.* Prayers to Gesù Bambino were being offered in the Church. After each so many Paters, Aves, and Glorias were repeated: the first half said by the priest the rest by the people. Then followed music the singing professional and operatic, I must say in the superlative degree.

At the Gerolomini the sexton, not a cleric, conversed with me a good while before the Church. A child with the mother came up kissed his hand & received from him a roll of bread. He told me it was his Sopranipote.[4] I remarked the child's eyes were diseased. He said yes: it was a miserable family: God takes away the bread from those who disregard Him, and gives it to those who serve Him. I asked if the parents were bad people? He said yes. 'Did they not go to confession'? Rarely.

18.

Wrote draft of a letter to Signor Galeotti (Florence).[5] Saw Iggulden—Barber.[6] Walk with Lt Herbert & Mr Scott.[7] Mad. Obrischkoff's[8] in evg: a party of foreigners, exceedingly well managed by the hostess & her daughters. Read Curci—Rivoluzione del 1849—English papers. Chess with Mr Monsell in evg.

Wed. Dec. 18. Walked up the Strada Nuovo with Lt. Herbert & Mr. Scott: turning to the right a little past Cablachi's house: where we gained the crown of the eminence & commanded the view alternately each way at the openings. The villas along the sea have beautiful grounds, only wanting large trees to complete their natural advantages.

At Mad. Obrischkoff's I had a long conversation with the Russian Chargè d'Affaires Baron Schepping[9] about Free Trade: his creed is protection but he did not seem to rely very profoundly on it. The Ducatessa [blank] complimented the English as speaking Italian well: at least said many did so. I am afraid the instances are comparatively rare.

[1] i.e. S. Fillipo Neri.

[2] S. d'Aloe, *Guide pour la gallerie des tableaux du musée Bourbon*, 2 v. (1842–3).

[3] Possibly Osborne *Gordon's pamphlet, cp. 23 July 47.

[4] Probably a mishearing of 'pronipote', great-grandson or great nephew.

[5] Leopoldo Galeotto, editor of the liberal newspaper *Statuto*, published in Florence. Draft in Italian in Add MS 44369, f. 433.

[6] L. J. Barber, vice consul in Naples; helped Gladstone tr. Farini.

[7] Unidentified.

[8] A member of the Russian community, but not attached to the embassy.

[9] Baron von Schöppink, chargé d'affaires from 1850.

19. Th.

Wrote to J. Murray (2). Wrote out fair my letter to Galeotti & showed it to Mr Lacaita. H.S. with Agnes. Walk with C. Read Curci. Worked on money & accounts. Sermon 5½ PM. Sinepi finished his restoration of the Brill: all done in my room. Wrote a quasi Preface to my projected translation of Farini.[1]

Thursday. Dec. 19. Sermon. See Notes.

20. Fr.

Wrote to Lincoln—H.E. Manning—W.C. James[2]—Hampton—Adderley—Willy—J.N.G—Phillimore. H.S. with Agnes. Tea & evg with the Levens. Arranged my letters. Read Curci—English papers—Ashley's Speech at Freemason's Hall!! Lord Chichesters is temperate, Christianlike, refreshing.[3] Sermon at 5½. More inquiries about an Amanuensis. I now only wait the return of my book to begin if with my own hand or C.s wh she gallantly offers.

Friday Dec. 20. Heavy storm from the south. Sermon. See Notes.

Two sentinels stood in front of the Altar where the Exposition was: and they were relieved at short intervals.

21. Sat.

H.S. with Agnes. Sermon. See Notes. Dined at Mr Temple's. Went to the drawing of the Lottery. Got back first Vol. of Farini from Mr Lacaita, & *began to translate*. Saw Manning, another possible amanuensis.[4]

Saturday Dec. 21. We went to the Tribunali[5] to see the drawing of the lottery. It is in a great hall of the building, which was the Vice Regal Palace. The hall is crowded and when the drawing takes place the people are wound up to an intense excitement. Some fifteen or twenty of the judges sit around a horse shoe table. A boy of three or four years old, in a white satin vestment embroidered with gold, is chosen to take the numbers out of the box which contains them. A priest attends to bless him with holy water which he does just before the drawing: a ceremonial painful to witness. The numbers (one to ninety) are shut up in little oval boxes of wood such that his hand takes one at a time. He hands it to a functionary who opens it & gives it to the chief Judge, the chief Judge to one of the lazzaroni[6] who stands behind him and proclaims the number to the people as it is supposed

[1] Cp. 27 Nov. 50.

[2] Lathbury, i. 122.

[3] Huge meeting against ecclesiastical titles; *The Times*, 6 December 1850, 5c.

[4] Unidentified; not H.E.*, who cancelled his visit, cp. Purcell, i. 591.

[5] The Castel Capuano, built by William I; used for courts of justice from 1540. The prison of La Vicaria was opposite.

[6] 'beggars'.

that in him they will have confidence. He did it in a tone indescribably drawling yet drole too, and with Sybilline contortions of his person. Five numbers only are drawn. Those who have bought one number get a prize I think six fold if their number appears: the odds against it are 18:1! Those who have taken more than one only win if more than one of their numbers are among the five. The prizes are higher: but the odds against them immense. The tickets I was grieved to hear are as low as 2½ grains: the proceeds of the tax 13 to 14,000,000 ducats annually: according to Mr. Brown,[1] the Correspondent of the Daily News, 3,000,000. But it is a tax the people bear with eagerness. The charges of so many offices must be very heavy.

Thence we went into the appeal court: a crucifix faces the chief Judge: the portraits of the King & Queen[2] are behind him. The ceiling is very rich. The very highest judicial salary in this country I understand from Mr. Lacaita is 4,000 ducats. The suitors state their cases to the Judges privately: and they are charged by the Procurator General & then retire to vote as our juries for their verdict.

The lower storey is full of prisoners who are unclassified: they sit and beg at the windows.

22. 4 S. Advent.

Church 11 & 3. Prayers in evg—read T. A Kempis. Mr Hubbard to tea & Church conv. Sermon S. Ferd.—with C.—Read Curci—Bellarmini's Gemitus Columbae.[3] Went to the Cathedral: see T[our] Journ.

Sunday, Dec. 22. Before one I reached the Cathedral to see the Liquefaction: which took place when I was here in May 1832.[4] The blood had been borne out in procession when I arrived: & shortly afterwards it was brought back, the Statue of San Gennaro being likewise carried with it. It was placed on the High Altar: the Cardinal went up, viewed, and knelt before it. He then retired as did many of the officiating priests. After half an hour or more occupied in chanting it was carried back to its Chapel: & then at the principal altar exhibited to the people, and turned over before each [altar] to show that the miracle had not occurred on this day. I saw it clearly over the heads of those who were kneeling. The semi-opaque fluid came about three fourths up the circular part of the glass bottle in which it was contained: it was not liquefied. The weather had changed to a colder temperature today which some think affects it. What one does not well see is how they can arbitrarily fix the day, or after having fixed it know before two o'clock that the miracle is not to take place, & lock it up accordingly, which they were on the point of doing when I came away.

Sermon. See Notes.

[1] Edward Noyce Browne, Neapolitan correspondent of the *Morning Post* and *Daily News*; collected money for families of Neapolitan political prisoners.

[2] Mary Theresa, archduchess of Austria, who m. Ferdinand II as his second wife 1837, and d. 1867.

[3] St. Robert [Bellarmino], *De gemitu Columbae, sive de bono lacrymarum* (1617).

[4] Cp. 5 May 32.

23. M.

H.S. with Agnes. Saw Messrs. Barber & Manning—settled with the former—Sermon S. Ferdinando (part) also S.M. degli Angeli—notes. Mad. Delafield's concert at night—her own singing, Fedor[1] the new Tenor, and Bassini, *all* delightful. Saw Mr Brown: & had a conv. then two with the Duca Cajaniello[2] whom I liked much. Worked on the translation of Farini.

Monday Dec. 23. Sermons. See Notes.

The concert at Madame Delafield's was delightful. De Bassini—Fedor the new Tenor, a Russian as I understand—& Mad. Delafield herself—anyone of these three would have made it worth hearing: together they rendered it admirable. De B. is wonderful in the strength of his upper notes and in carrying the *basso* quality up to the highest baryton region.

I was introduced to the Duca Cajaniello & in a short conversation with him [was] exceedingly pleased.

24. T.

H.S. with Agnes. Worked on translation of Farini, dictating to Mr Barber 4–7 P.M., and also by myself. Saw Mr Brown—Senapi & bought an abbozzo,[3] alleged Murillo. Sent the little library I have gathered off for binding which is done here well and cheaply. Drive through the market streets. conv. with Mr Monsell.[4] Lady Malcolm's in evg.

Tuesday Xmas Eve. We had a drive up the Toledo[5] then round by the Vicaria,[6] down to the Basso Porto—through the market Streets. I never witnessed such masses of provision for human beings. They lay in now for the great supper of tonight, & for tomorrow when all shops are shut. Then so much being done in the open air, & so much larger a share of the diet of the city vegetable than with us, all combined to make the show wonderful. Every kind of strange fish was here: but the largest quantity was the Capitone eel which I understand comes from Comacchio.[7] In the Basso Porto wherever two Carriages met the street though for Naples a very wide one was blocked up.

25. Christmas Day.

Church 11 A.M. (and Holy C.)—3 P.M. Read Gemitus Columbae—English papers—H.S. with Agnes. Dined at Mr Monsell's. Translated a little of Farini.

[1] Not further identified.
[2] Gaetano del Pezzo, duke of Caianello, 1833–89; m. Angelia Caracciolo.
[3] 'a rough sketch'.
[4] For this drive and other meetings of the Monsells and Gladstones at this time see T. T. Carter, *Harriet Monsell* (1884), 17–19.
[5] The main street running north to south.
[6] The prison opposite the Castel Capuano.
[7] On the east coast, 50 miles S. of Venice.

Wed. Xmas D[*ay*].[1] In the afternoon I could not find a Church open. Every shop was shut—most even of the provision shops. But there is no merriment in the streets—there was none at the Mole.[2] Naples is changed in this respect.

26. Th. (*S. Stephen*).

H.S. with Agnes. Mr Barber 4–7 on Farini. Worked on it alone. Inspected Senapi while he restored my Abbozzo. Shopping for the evening & busy about Edward who is ill since Tuesday & we fear it may be erysipelas. C.s Xmas tree party at night: managed by the servants of our friends: the people seemed to enjoy themselves.

27. Fr.

Wrote to Dagna. (St John)[3] Dined at Lady Malcolm's. We had to work in restoring order after last night's party. Calls & shopping. Worked on Farini alone & with Mr Barber.

28. Sat.

H. Innocents. Wrote to J.N.G. Purchased another Abbozzo through Senapi: and superintended his cleaning and touching it. Worked on Farini —alone—with C.G—& with Mr Barber. Saw Mr Senior[4]—Mr Reid—Dr Jackson[5]—Mr Hubbard: also told me of his brother in law's[6] having under some pressure joined the Church of Rome. Dined at Mr Temple's. Found *110* pages of Farini done: but only the *first* labour. I do not know how much more there must be.

29. 1 S. Xmas.

Church 11 & 3. At divers Sermons—See Notes. Prayers in evg. with T. AKempis. Walk with C. Read Gemitus Columbae—Ep. Hebrews—the Bennett Correspondence[7] &c—Finished Gordon's 'Reasons'—My forty first year has closed. It has been one of anxiety and of labour, of the last as much and of the first more than most years of my life. I would to God I could add it had been one of progress in obtaining the mastery over my most besetting sins which I think are impurity and lukewarmness. It has

[1] Last entry of the travel diary (though see 13 Feb. 51). Discontinued under stress of the Farini translation?

[2] The Molo Angioino, a pier by the Castel Nuovo, or the Molo Piccolo, to its north.

[3] 'H.S. with Agnes' here deleted.

[4] Nassau William *Senior, 1790–1864; professor of political economy at Oxford 1825–36, 1847–52. His *Journals kept in France and Italy from 1848 to 1852* were published (1871). Cp. 30 Dec. 50 and 12 June 52.

[5] An English surgeon practising in Naples.

[6] Francis *Napier, 1819–98, *Hubbard's wife's br.; 9th Baron Napier in Scottish peerage 1834; secretary to legation in Naples 1846–9; ambassador to U.S.A. 1857–8, to Russia 1860–4, Prussia 1864–6; governed Madras 1866–72 and, temporarily, India 1872; cr. Baron Ettrick 1872.

[7] W. J. E. *Bennett's letter to *Russell, cp. 15 Dec. 50, and 'A letter to W.J.E. *Bennett . . . by a lay-impropriator' (1850).

sorely taught me beyond what I before had realised how little even sorrow has in *itself* a virtue to overcome sin & how far less mere care or anxiety however trying and oppressive. My blessings indeed in domestic life are richer still as my children grow: Both Willy & Agnes are advanced this year in all I most desire: and Jessy is advanced far more, dear dear blessed Jessy. My pecuniary cares for S.R.G. & otherwise are likely to diminish. Outwardly things are well with me: but the State of the Church is a crushing care and affliction. But Above the wave I see the Banner of the Faith high and clear in air. If only God in His boundless mercy will cleanse me with fire from heaven to make me worthy of the arduous labours to which we of this day are called.

I greatly fear & note it here that before another year closes my two dearest friends with whom I had but one heart for the Church of England will have ceased to be *here*.[1] This is heavy. But where will she be? This is even yet heavier far.

30. M.

H.S. with Agnes. 11–2½ C.G. & I to Villa di Lucullo[2] with the Seniors. Read Mr S's Journals in Paris—Tosti's Uriel translated by Mr Reid.[3] Worked on Farini—alone—by C.G.—& by Mr Barber. Went to the Academia in evg: where I was introduced to several Neapolitans.[4]

31. T.

Read Senior's Journals. Worked on Farini by self—C.G.—& Mr Barber—most of the day. Went to Lady Leven's party in the evg. They were most kind: & nothing could in itself be simpler: but I do not like any rejoicings on the death of an old year.

[1] Cp. 7 Apr. 51.

[2] The excavations below Posilippo, on the site of the villa of Lucullus.

[3] L. Tosti, *Uriele*, this tr. untraced. Reid was a friend of the Monsells, cp. T. T. Carter, *Harriet Monsell* (1884), 19.

[4] The Academia Reale di Canto e Ballo, an aristocratic club in Naples.

Naples—January—1851.

Wedy. Jan One 1851. The Circumcision.

The Swiss Chapel open! ours closed![1] Sermon $4\frac{1}{4}$ P.M. See Notes. H.S. with Agnes. Read Senior's Journals. Worked on Farini alone & by C.G. Walked with C. Made up accounts. Dined at Ld Holland's[2]—conv. with various Italians: our host & hostess very kind. Ly Strahan[3] made an attempt to *know* C. wh she effectually resisted.

2. Th.

Little Mary early in the morning had serious threatenings of croup. Strong measures were used: 3 doses of calomel: Dr Strange at his 3d visit thought her better: & thank God she slept comfortably in the evg. At $10\frac{1}{2}$ with Mr Senior to the Archivio—& Marg. St Angelos.[4] At $1\frac{3}{4}$ I had to take Agnes to a picnic by the sea: returned at 4. Worked on Farini with Mr Barber, & alone. Lady Malcolm's in evg. Saw Sig. d'Aloe[5]—Sig. Manna.[6]

3. Fr.

Mary thank God much better: & we were all at ease. Worked on Farini by Mr Barber, C.G. & self. Finished Mr Senior's Journals—very interesting they are. Breakfasted (at 11) with the Senior's to meet De Tocqueville—then to the Vicaria[7]—Saw Mr Brown—& in evg Mr Reid who told us of the imprisonment of our friend Lacaita.

4. Sat.

Wrote to T. Greene—T.G. Worked on Farini—by Mr Barber, & myself. Dined at Lady Malcolms—Vicaria—heard Poerio.[8] Saw Mr Fagan[9] & others about Lacaita: how fruitlessly! One grows wild at being able to do nothing.[10] Went to S. Severino about Tosti.

[1] Church of England services were normally held at 217 Chiaja.

[2] In the Palazzo Roccella.

[3] Mary Ann, *née* Elton, m. 1844 Sir John Strachan, 8th bart.

[4] The head of the Mormile family, prince of Castel San Angelo; owned a large art collection.

[5] Stanislas d'Aloe, director of the Bourbon museum.

[6] Chevalier Giovanni Manna, son-in-law of general Sabatelli and friend of *Lacaita; minister of commerce in constitutional govt. 1848, of finance 1859.

[7] The notorious prison in the Castel Capuano, residence of the Hohenstaufen, since 1540 seat of the Neapolitan law courts. He did not go inside the prison, but attended the trials.

[8] Baron Carlo Poerio, 1803–67; Neapolitan politician; imprisoned for conspiracy 1828–38; Naples prefect of police 1848; sentenced to 24 years imprisonment 1851; escaped to London 1859; vice-president of Italian parliament 1861.

[9] George Fagan, diplomat, unpaid attaché at Naples legation 1837, paid clerk 1839, paid attaché May 1851.

[10] *Lacaita had been arrested.

5. 2 S. Xmas.

Church 11 & H.C. In aftn. I took Mary out. T. aKempis aloud at evg prayers. Missed Italian Sermon—Read Guardian & M.C.—& Rosmini's Cinque Piaghe.[1] Saw Mr Monsell.

6. M. Epiphany.

C's birthday: may it ever come round with blessing on its wings. H.S. with Agnes. Worked on Farini—by C.G., Mr Barber, & myself. We went to the Ellesmeres on board their yacht—business afterwards. Dined at Ld Holland's—Baron Brockhausen's Ball afterwards.

7. T.

11–2 At the Museum. 4–7 Mr Barber: also worked on Farini alone. Saw Sig. Manna—Duke Atri(?).[2] C. was tired at the Museum. dined well at 2¼ PM. slept 3 hours afterwards, got up for her tea party—which lasted from 9 to 11½. When it was over she complained of much pain. Laudanum with the white of egg applied to the back soothed it materially: but it returned. She then took 20 drops of laudanum without much effect. We sent for Dr Strange or Dr Roskelly[3] at 3¼: by that time symptoms of probable miscarriage had just appeared. Dr S. came at 4¼ and found it inevitable: Dr Roskelly at 4¾. C. was however as well in all respects as could be hoped: & when it was over both the doctors were (separately) of opinion that the mischief was not done today although today's exertions brought it out: but that it is of some days or even a fortnight's date. C. refers it with much reason to the shock she got a fortnight ago from a clumsy rider on the ground opposite the house who went past her at a rapid pace very nearly knocking her down.—We got snow with great ease at 4½ A. M.[4]—& then Mrs Bonesi an English nurse. So that we have every comfort: & the occurrence of fatigue today has been a distinct & special mercy.—She soon went to sleep after being put to rights: & slept well. I got to bed at 6½.

8. Wed.

Up at 10½. A cloud of notes to write. C. was very well thank God: & so continued thro' the day. The doctors say a few days' rest only will be required. Read D'Arlincourt's Italie Rouge:[5] a shameful book I think. Calls—shopping—Worked on Farini by Barber, & by myself.

9. Th.

H.S. with A—Also prayers with C. Read D'Arlincourt—Worked on

[1] A. R. Serbati, *Delle Cinque Piaghe della Santa Chiesa . . .* (1849).

[2] Carlo Acquaviva d'Aragona, duca d'Atri.

[3] Both surgeons serving the British community in Naples; the latter had been there since 1805.

[4] To freeze the pain.

[5] C. V. P. d'Arlincourt, *L'Italie rouge, ou histoire des révolutions de Rome, Naples, Palerme, Messine* (1850).

Farini by Mr B. and myself. Mrs Hope's in evg. C. suffered much from faceach though well otherwise.

10. Fr.

Prayers with C. Read D'Arlincourt. Saw Dr Strange—Dr Roskelly—Worked on Farini with Mr B—& by myself. Shopping & business. C. again suffered from faceach but still well in other respects. Towards midnight she had some relief. Agnes too was laid up.

11. Sat.

Worked on Farini by Mr Barber & myself—a hard day. Dined at Mr Temple's—Lady Malcolm's afterwards. Mr T. told me Lacaita is to be out tomorrow!! At 12¼ to Studio. Then to the Jesuit's College. Retd. 3¾. C. free from face ach.

12. 1 S. Epiph.

Church 11 AM. Sermon S. Cath. Mart. 4¼ PM. Wrote notes on part of Ep. & evg. prayers with Comment. Wrote Sermon Notes. Read Theiner's Introd. del Protestantismo in Italia [1]—Walk with Agnes. Found Lacaita at Mrs Monsell's in evg. He is out: *one* of about 150 arrested here within the last three weeks!

13. M.

Wrote to Sir J.G—H.J.G—Canning—Lincoln—Phillimore—Coleridge—J. Murray—Hampton—M. Lyttelton. H.S. with Agnes—walk with her & alone. Worked on Farini: but slowly amid many interruptions. Accounts &c in plenty—Dined at Ld Holland's.

14. T.

Wrote to Cumming & Wood. Worked on accounts &c. Worked on Farini—by Barber & myself—Saw Consul Gallway. Read Agresti [2]—Engl. papers.

15. Wed.

H.S. with Agnes. Worked on Farini—by Barber; C.G. & myself. A good day: got through 27 pages. Shopping—& house matters. Lady Holland's in evg.

16. Th.

Worked on Farini—by Barber—C.G—& self. At the Gesuiti 2–4.[3] There were no Schools today: & Father Costa talked Theology. Dined at Sir G. Baker's.[4] Music in evg. Then to Mrs Gallway's.

[1] A. Theiner, 'Dell'introduzione del Protestantismo in Italia' (1850).
[2] Probably M. Agresti, *Il Senato Conservatore delle Reggi* (1845).
[3] The Jesuits' theological college.
[4] Sir George Baker, 1816–82; 3rd bart. 1830.

17. Fr.

Worked on Farini by the three pens—as yesterday. Walk with Lacaita 2½–5½. We visited Leopardi's tomb.[1] Our conversation was on his matters: his history—present position—& possible prospects in England. I admired him more than ever. Read Regnier.[2] C. drove out for the first time. Saw Mr Brown.

18. Sat.

John's birthday. God bless him. H.S. with Agnes. Saw Ld Ellesmere—Tosti (who is hunted)—Wrote to D'Aloe—Senior—Accounts, &c. Worked on Farini by the three pens.

19. 2 S. Epiph.

Church 11 & 3. C. at the latter. Read T. A'Kempis at evg prayers. Serm. S. Ursula 4¼ P.M.—Notes—Read Gemitus Columbae—Trap for a Sunbeam.[3] Saw Mr Hubbard—Duke & Duchess of Sabriano[4]—Cav. Aloe came in evg about my pictures—& had tea.

20. M.

Wrote to Sir J.G—T.G—Burnett—Scotts. A heavy packing day—for sea. Saw Cav. d'Agresti[5] at his house. Worked on Farini—recension. I find Mr Barber's MS. very middling. Dined at Prince Cimitile's.[6] Worked on accounts. C.G. thrown back from yesterday's work: & will again need some rest.

21. T.

H.S. with Agnes. Recension of Farini—Worked a little on translation—Dined at Baron Rothschild's[7] where I met several of the Ministers but got no real conversation out of any of them. P. San Giacomo[8] pleases me exceedingly. *Wrote* to Dagna.

22. Wed.

A sore throat menacing since Monday evg now broke out fairly with some fever & C. & I were invalids in the same room. Continued in bed my recension of Farini: under smart physic. Read Poliziano.[9]

[1] He d. at Naples 1837, buried in the church of San Vitale by the bay.
[2] Probably J. A. Regnier, *Traité de la formation des mots dans la langue grecque* (1850).
[3] M. A. Planché, *A trap to catch a sunbeam* (1850).
[4] Not further identified.
[5] D. Michele Agresti, procurator-general of Naples.
[6] Prince Prospero Cimitile, Neapolitan noble.
[7] Baron Carl Meyer de Rothschild, 1788–1855, the 4th brother; founded the Neapolitan branch of the bank 1820; m. 1818 Adelheid Herz who d. 1853. Gladstone also met their 1st s., Meyer Carl, 1820–86, who later lived in Frankfurt. Cp. lists following 29 Feb. 52.
[8] Prince of San Giacomo, Neapolitan ambassador to London 1848.
[9] Probably A. Poliziano, *Poesie Italiane* (1825).

23. Th.

Wrote to J.N.G—Phillimore—Jackson—Dagna. Up in the evening with my throat somewhat improved. We both like Dr Strange extremely. Recension of Farini—And a little translation—We had much conference on our plans today; & have pretty nearly given up Rome: I hope rightly, as it was much against the grain with both. But every week *here* is a gain for Mary: & it is now very uncertain when C. could move with perfect prudence.

24. Fr.

Up in the forenoon. C. better but still on her back. Out for calls & business. Our delightful friend Mr Monsell still lies in extreme danger: but God is with him. Worked on translation of Farini—by C.G.—Barber—& myself.

25. Sat. Conv. S. Paul.

C. better. I got out. We discussed plans. Worked on Farini by Barber & myself. Read Guardians—Saw D'Aloe about my pictures—Prince Cimitile—the Jesuit schools with P. Grossi [1] & Dr Gaffney.[2]

26. 3 S. Epiph.

Ch. 11 & 3. T. A'Kempis aloud in evg. Saw D[uche]ss of Sabriano—the Ellesmeres. Wrote to Manning.[3] Read Gemitus Columbae.

27. M.

Wrote to S. Herbert. H.S. with Agnes. Worked on Farini by Barber & self. Drove with C.G. Saw Lacaita—Tosti. Academia in evg $10\frac{3}{4}$–$1\frac{3}{4}$: pretty active conversation all the time with Italians & English.

28. T.

Wrote to Jackson. Worked on Farini alone & by Barber. C.G.[4] went to see Mrs Hubbard.[5] In the evening we had the Ellesmeres here.

29. Wed.

Mr Monsell died: a man rare even among rare men. H.S. with Agnes. Read Poerio's Alcune Liriche [6]—Saw Manna—Worked on Farini, alone—Went with Lacaita up to Camaldoli:[7] & down the steep. Dined at Ld Hollands. Made a sort of clean breast about the Government to the Duchess of Sabriani: wh was not very agreeable to either of us.

[1] Pasquale Grossi, friend of Carlo Poerio, and head of the Neapolitan secret department.
[2] Probably George Gaffney, army physician, who served in several European centres.
[3] Parts in Morley, i. 385–6, 403.
[4] 'began [three words illegible] & had to take to her' here deleted.
[5] Maria Margaret, d. of 8th Baron Napier, m. J. G. *Hubbard, 1st Baron Addington, 1837; she d. 1896.
[6] In MS.; perhaps included in A. and C. Poerio, *Liriche e lettere inedite* (1899).
[7] Hill to W. of the city.

30. Th.

Wrote to Jackson. Saw Mr Brown. Worked on Farini. Attended Mr Monsell's funeral. Dined with the Malcolms. Mrs Story's in evg.

31. Fr.

Worked on Farini—by myself, & by Barber. Read Liriche—Poerio's MS. Saw Strange—Css. Lebzeltern.[1]

Naples
Saturday Feby One 1851.

Wrote to Dr Strange—Ly Malcolm. Worked on Farini by Barber & myself. My last sitting with B. With him I have done 303 pages in $71\frac{3}{4}$ hours: but I fear it is very rough work. The rate is $4\frac{2}{9}$ pages an hour. Made up letters & accounts—On a suggestion from Mr Reid, I went to see Mrs Monsell. Nothing could surpass her demeanour: a perfect harmony of affection, piety, and firmness. Mr Reid & the Malcolms in evg. Shopping &c. Read Alcune Liriche. We have determined under Dr Strange's advice that C. & the rest shall stay here longer than I fear I can.—She is still on her back.

2. 4 S. Epiph. & Purification.

Church (Holy C.) 11–2. Prayers in aftn with C. & went to Sermon—Read T. A'Kempis B. IV. aloud at night. Wrote to Iggulden. Walk with Agnes; Sermon (part) in. Read Gemitus Columbae—Church Papers—M. Chronicle —Saw Garden—Hubbard—Barber.

3. M.

Wrote to Mr Barber—Worked on Farini, both in translation and revision. Read Alcune Liriche—Poerio MS. finished. Accounts. Shopping. San Carlino.[2]

4. T.

Worked on Farini as yesterday. Dined at Mr Hubbard's. Madame Waleski's[3] afterwards. Read Alcune Liriche—Saw Lacaita—Graziosi[4]—Barber, who told me of the King's exercise of mercy: loathsome! I lay awake at night thinking what is my duty in this matter: & got up at $3\frac{1}{2}$ to work, for a chance of sleeping. Visited Osped. Pelligrini[5]—Pace & the Zingaros at S. Severino.[6]

[1] Zénaide de Laval, 1827–?1900, a French émigrée and naturalized Russian. She m. Ludwig Joseph de Lebzeltern, 1774–1854, diplomat and friend of Metternich; Austrian minister in St. Petersburg 1816–26, in Naples 1830–43, where he afterwards lived.

[2] Small theatre noted for the performance of Neapolitan dialect comedies.

[3] Marie Anne, *née* de Ricci, wife of André-Florian-Joseph Colonna, Count Walewski, 1810–68; natural son of Napoleon I, French minister at Naples 1850–51, ambassador in London 1851–56.

[4] A Roman refugee; see next day.

[5] Hospital attached to the church of Trinità de'Pellegrini.

[6] Paintings by Michelangelo Pace, d. 1670, and Pietro Negrone, known as Il Zingaro, d. 1565.

5. *Wed.*

Worked on Farini alone: & on revision with Signor Graziosi a Roman refugee whom I liked. Saw the Lebzelterns—P. Belmonti.[1] Read Nisco's Costituto.[2] Dined with Baillie[3] & Knudtzen—Lady Holland's in evg. Got my boxes (sea) ready for departure. We expected Stephen & were in agitation accordingly.

6. *Th.*

Wrote to Dagna. Worked on Farini—alone & with Graziosi—Lady Malcolm's in evg. Saw Lacaita. Read Napoli e la Costituzione[4]—Ward's letters on the Jesuits.[5]

7. *Fr.*

Wrote to Dagna. Stephen [Glynne] & Seymour Neville arrived.[6] Busy in domestic matters. John's letter set me ablaze about my Father.[7] Walked with C. Dined at Mr Temple's. Calls. Saw Carlo Troja[8] an hour or more. Worked on Farini.

8. *Sat.*

Wrote to Hampton—Phillimore—J.N.G—W.P. Ward[9]—Bp of Exeter—Directeur des Postes. Worked on Farini alone & with Graziosi. Lady Malcolm's in evg—Saw Mr Fagan. Walk with C.G.

9. *5 S. Epiph.*

Church 11 & 3. Read Gemitus Columbae. H.S. with Agnes. Lacaita came in evg with fresh distress & told me of his interview with Peccheneda.[10] We agreed he could not give the names, & certainly could not fly. Made notes of Poerio's case & on other like points. Saw Sir J. Pakington.

10. *M.*

Wrote to Mr Addington—the Duchess!! at Pal. Ischiatelli.[11] Graziosi 9–12. Worked on Farini. In evg to the Cardinal's: I sat an hour, talking chiefly on the Papal aggression—he did not see any *lesion* of territorial rights—& did

[1] Marchese Granito, prince of Belmonte, keeper of the archives at Naples.
[2] *Costituto di N. Nisco* (1850).
[3] i.e. Alexander Baillie, M.P., cp. 13 Oct. 43; he wrote on 'Young Italy' (1850).
[4] (1848); quoted in 'Second letter to *Aberdeen', *Gleanings*, iv. 56.
[5] W. H. P. Ward, 'Defence of the Jesuits: a letter to ... *Lacaita upon the recent expulsion of the Jesuits from Naples' (1848).
[6] Seymour Neville, 1823–1905; fellow of Magdalene, Cambridge, 1845; minor canon of Windsor 1848; vicar of Wraysbury 1856; rector of Ockham 1869–99.
[7] News of his father's declining health.
[8] Carlo Troja, historian and prime minister of Naples in constitutional govt. 1848.
[9] i.e. W. H. P. Ward.
[10] Gaetano Peccheneda, Neapolitan royalist and prefect of police. For the interview, cp. C. Lacaita, *An Italian Englishman* (1933), 29.
[11] The wife of Cesare Francesco del Tufo, 1802–86; Prince Ischitella 1829; Neapolitan minister of war and of the navy, 1848, and from 1849.

not like the *exequatur*.[1] Then to the Academia where I saw Acquaviva—Count Mirepoix[2]—P. San Giacomo (with whom I talked long on my intentions about the govt. & I was *dissuaded* by him for fear of making matters worse—) Lady Farnham[3] & others—Saw Mr Fagan. Discussion on plans. I wait only the moment of a certain degree of convalescence in C. to fix my departure—

11. T.

Worked on Farini. Saw Manna—D. Antonio Reale[4]—Mr Lacaita, on his affairs—he told me I was watched here by spies! Finished Alcune Liriche.

12. Wed.

C. worse—after two day's rest. At 8 I went out to Mr Fagan's, thence with D. Ant. Reale to the Vicaria where I was admitted by an unknown process. I believe as the avvocato of a prisoner Don Gaetano Golia.[5] We then went to Nisida[6] & were refused it being the wrong day.. I came home at noon & found C. had had to send for Dr Strange who was here three times—It is a recommencement of the haemorrhage. Most of my aftn. & evg I was nurse—but [blank.] Saw Lacaita—& went to Lady Holland's—Worked on Farini.

13. Th.

Wrote to Miss Campbell—Dagna (2)—7½–1. Went out to Dr Strange then with the party of yesterday to Nisida where I had a long half hour's conversation chiefly with Poerio. C. though dispirited & weak was thank God declared better. I had to consider our plans. Ly Malcolm's & Mr Iggulden's in evg. Worked on Farini—a little: it was chiefly a nursing day. Saw Lacaita—Mr Clowes—Fagan.

Thursday Feb. 13. 1851.[7] About thirty or forty persons gathered in front of the door of the Bagno of Nisida at eleven today. For half an hour before noon on Thursdays perhaps rather more the prisoners may come out to see their friends, or rather relations. About ten of the political prisoners came out chained two & two. One of them however, Romeo, a master printer, imprisoned for some offence of the press I believe printing the Protesta was chained to a common malefactor a youth of a countenance very far worse than is ordinary among the criminals here. My conductor signified to Poerio in part who I was, & he then came aside to me. We conversed most

[1] Right of temporal authorization for Papal exercize of episcopal functions.
[2] Count Sigismund de Levis-Mirepoix, 1821–86, br. of 2nd duc de San Fernando-Luis.
[3] Anne Frances Esther, *née* Stapleton, 1805–68, m. 1828 Henry Maxwell, 1799–1868, 7th Baron Farnham.
[4] Probably a lawyer; see next day.
[5] Not further identified.
[6] Prison in the fortress on Nisida Island, S.W. of Naples.
[7] Written in a separate notebook, now unbound, in Add MS 44739, f. 1. Descriptive sections of the 'First letter to Aberdeen' are taken from this account.

of the time: for the rest of it I spoke with Pironte[1] to whom he was chained and Braico the nephew of Madame Dekker as whose friend or escort I went in. The name she gave for me at the door was Michele di Santo: and she afterwards told me she described me as half-witted per far men sospetto—'La testa un po' scema' (or un po' scemo di testa) pointing with her finger: 'e un uomo da non capirci niente'.[2]

Sixteen prisoners as I was told by Poerio & Pironte are confined in a room of about 16 palms in length by 10 or 12 in breadth & 10 in height. All have beds: when the beds are down there is no space between them. They cannot get out except at the foot. In this room they cook anything sent by their friends. We saw the soup going in (it was described to me as *stinking* to such a degree as to turn the stomach). On one side the level of the ground is above the top of the room. In consequence it is very damp & from this they said they suffer greatly. There is one window: of course unglazed.

The chains are as follows. Each man has a strong leather girth around him above the hips. To this are secured the upper ends of two chains. One of four long links descends to a kind of double ring going round the ancle. This ring is never undone: the trousers are buttoned all the way up so as to be taken off without disturbing the chains which remain on day & night. The second chain is of eight links of the same length & united the two prisoners together. This likewise is never loosened. The weight of them I understand is sixteen or eighteen rotolos. They limped very much in walking with them. The words that the chains are never loosened are to be understood *strictly*.

Poerio looked worse than at the Vicaria. Braico looked about 36: he is 26. His Aunt said he had a youthful appearance & colour a few weeks ago: she wept at seeing him.

A certain Margherito when in prison denounced the parties inculpated in this case. This man is now in the same Bagno with them: at the moment he was in the hospital: but before he had been chained to Cavaliero one of those whom he denounced! and I understood he would probably be so again.

Poerio declared solemnly his entire innocence of the charges on which he was condemned: I told him it was unnecessary as far as Jervolino's[3] testimony went & I asked if there was any other of moment against him. He said none. He observed that Jervolino on his own showing was deeper in the sect[4] than he Poerio. His own opinions he said were constitutional not republican: he thought Italy in its present corrupt state of society could not have a republic: & the example of France was altogether discouraging. He greatly admired the institutions of England & dwelt at some length on the political condition of his own country: all agreed in this that matters are far worse in the provinces than in Naples. He said a terrible & bloody reaction is in preparation: it will not be worked by us but by other

[1] Michele Pironti, Neapolitan judge and journalist, sentenced with Poerio to 24 years imprisonment.

[2] 'to make it less suspicious—"his head is a bit shrunk" (or "a little shrunk in the head") . . . "and a man who understands nothing up there"'.

[3] An informer, cp. Add MS 44739, f. 15 and *Gleanings*, iv. 22.

[4] The *Unità Italiana* group.

men of very different opinions from ours. He told me that of his Judges three the President included voted for the punishment of death: two for 24 years irons: and 3 for acquittal. The two former sections combined together.

They all wore the dress of common malefactors: a rough red jacket and trousers nearly black of the same material. Over it they wore their great coats. I understood they had not been obliged to have their hair cut: but only to shave away the beard under the chin.

There are about 800 prisoners in this Bagno. The custom of it has been only to put on the single irons. But the regulation has just been altered by an order from P. Luigi the King's Brother.[1]

Poerio complained that he was put into irons under a law of Prince Canosa[2] about 1822, which had previously gone into desuetude. (Don A. Reale told me that a law of Charles III forbade irons for political offences).

Pironte assured me that at the Vicaria while yet uncondemned he was put with two others into a cell eight feet square, with no light except a small grating at the top of the wall out of which they could not see, below the level of the ground I think; and out of this hole they were *never* allowed (even for Mass) to come except to attend the Court of Justice on their trial between the 7th of Decr. and the 3rd of February—being then uncondemned. Within the space of it *every* thing was to be done!!

But they told me that in the Maschio of Ischia 24 feet below the level of the sea is confined the Baron Porcari on account of the Calabrian Insurrection, not yet tried but never allowed to quit this dungeon, which is without light, nor is anyone permitted to visit him there except his wife once a fortnight.

Poerio is apprehended that his case had been made worse by Mr. Temple's intervention: not in the least as blaming Mr. T. or considering it officious. But he said to speak without reserve the King had a great hatred of the English generally.

No one is admitted here under any pretence within the prison.[3]

Poerio was about 16 months in prison before his condemnation. The accused of the September affair have been 26 months & are yet untried.

I was particularly desirous to have Poerio's opinion on the expediency of making some effort in England to draw general attention to these horrors & dissociate the Conservative party from all suppositions of winking at them: because I had had from a sensible man one strong opinion against such a course.[4] I said to him that in my view only two moves could be thought of, the first amicable remonstrance through the Cabinets, the second public notoriety and shame. That had Lord Aberdeen been in power the first might have been practicable, but that with Ld Palmerston it would not because of his position relatively to the other Cabinets, (Yes he said Ld. P. was isolated) not because he would be wanting in the will. Matters standing thus I saw no way open but that of exposure; & might that possibly

[1] Rest of para., amplifying this, omitted.

[2] Prince Antonio Capece Minutolo di Canosa, 1763–1838; minister of police under the restored Bourbons.

[3] 'Seen by Mr. Fagan to this point. Feb. 16' added in margin.

[4] See 10 Feb. 51.

exasperate the Neap. Govt. & increase their severity? His reply was 'as to us, never mind: we can hardly be worse than we are—but think of our country for which we are most willing to be sacrificed. Exposure will do it good. The present Govt. of Naples rely on the English Conservative party. Consequently we were all in horror when Ld Stanley last year carried his motion in the H. of Lords. Let there be a voice from that party showing that whatever Govt. be in power in England, no support will be given to such proceedings as these—it will do much to break them down. It will also strengthen the hands of a better & less obstinate class about the Court. Even there all are not alike—I know it from observation. These Ministers are the extremest of extremes. There are others who would willingly see more moderate courses adopted'. On such grounds as these (I do not quote words) he strongly recommended me to *act*.

I ought to have mentioned that he & most of the other political prisoners wore the felon's red cap.[1]

Had the case been one of illegality alone—had there been no other charge against the Government of Naples than that every day and in every act of its existence it breaks the fundamental law of the land, I for one should certainly have said whatever feelings we as Englishmen may entertain about such a state of things, it is not our business to rectify illegalities simply as such in other countries: we are not propagandists, we have no mission, we had better trust to the progress of events under the controul of Providence to rectify this great evil.

But this illegality gross flagrant & universal as it is becomes totally insignificant in comparison with the other features of this case: features which in my view convert every man into a Propagandist and give every man a mission, to expose if he cannot otherwise amend a gigantic iniquity such as has rarely in the history of man trampled upon Earth or lifted its audacious front to heaven.

There is a bond of flesh which unites man to man, there is a community of nature and of lot, of thought and feeling, of hope and aspiration, of weakness of sorrow and of suffering, which under certain rare circumstances obliges us with a power superior to that of ordinary rules of conduct ever framed with reference to the supposition of an average standard of behaviour among men, with certain limits of deviation this way and that. The present is one of these exceptional cases, for which no ordinary rules can provide.

My position is this that this illegal Government is struggling to protect its utter illegality by a tyranny unparalleled at this moment, and almost without a rival amidst the annals of older atrocities. To say unparalled at this moment is saying little. That might be true were it in point of cruelty corruption and iniquity only a little more than *primus inter pares*. My belief is on the contrary that it stands in a class, & constitutes a *genus*, by itself separated by an immense distance from any other known case even of Italian tyranny.[2] The class persecuted as a whole is the class that lives and

[1] The text breaks off, followed on separate pages by a series of comments, of which the rest of this entry forms part. [2] Few lines omitted.

moves, the middle class, in its widest acceptation, but particularly in that upper part of the middle class which may be said embraces the professions, the most cultivated and progressive part of the nation.[1]

14. Fr.

Wrote to Hampton—T.G.—M. Lyttelton—W.H.G. H.S. with Agnes. Worked on Farini. Dined with Dr Strange. Much about C. who on the whole was better but had returns of the nervous symptoms aftn & evening. Arranged with Dagna.

15. Sat.

Wrote to Duchess of Sabriano—Mons. Apuzzi[2]—Cav. d'Aloe. H.S. with Agnes. Worked on Farini—Accounts, & shopping—Dined with Lady Malcolm—at Marchesa Rendi's[3] later in evg. Saw Pr. Torelli[4]—& others. Went with Stephen to see the Incoronata Giottos.[5]

16. Septua. S.

Church 11 AM. Aftn prayers to C.—T. A Kempis aloud in evg. Saw Fagan—Lacaita—Tosti—D'Ungaro. Read Gemitus Columbae—La Religione Dimostrata.[6]

17. M.

Wrote to Roskelly—E.N. Browne—Kept in bed some hours by a stiff cough: but C. better. After further convn I arranged for her to spend the 4th month in these rooms. Busy on accounts &c. Dined at Lady Malcolm's. Worked on Farini—Saw Tosti (a delightful specimen)—Mr Temple—Lacaita—Read Morier on Schleswig Holstein & Fieri Ital.[7]

18. T.

Packed—settled accounts & Mema.—saw Dr Strange, Lady Malcolm, Mr Barber, Mr Fagan, Messrs. Iggulden—Bid farewell to C. at ½ past 3 & started from Naples soon after five by the Vesuvio. My last sight of it was almost the loveliest: but I could have wished to carry away those dear to me. The night was fine. I dined in the Cabin; & read Tosti's Lega Lombarda.[8]

19. Wed.

Reached Civ. Vecchia at 5, about 13½ hours—Read Tosti—and translated 20 p. of Farini.

[1] Rest, mostly of uncertain date, omitted.

[2] Canon Apuzzi of Naples, author of the *Catechismo Filosofico*. Cp. 23 Feb. 51.

[3] Not identified.

[4] Not identified.

[5] S. Maria dell 'Incoronata, a church in the Strada Medina noted for its Giotto paintings.

[6] Untraced.

[7] Probably R. B. D. *Morier's tr. of a German pamphlet as 'The policy of Denmark towards the duchies of Schleswig Holstein', or one of his articles at this time in the *Examiner*.

[8] L. Tosti, *Storia della Lega Lombarda* (1848).

20. Th.

Reached Leghorn between five and six A.M.—under 11½ hours—swell the first half but I was able to eat. *Wrote* to C.G. for the French Mail tomorrow: would I could as readily hear of her. But how thankful we must be for the great success God has given us in the main purpose of our journey. Worked on Farini—22 pages, & *finished* i.e. the *first* operation. These took me I think near *six* hours.

21. Fr.

Reached Genoa ½ h. A.M.—having run from Leghorn through swell, rain, wind, & fog, in 7 hours exactly. Breakfasted at the Feder (having had no solids yesterday)—bought books & Brooch. Wrote up accts & Journal. Read documents of the Neapol. Constitution[1]—Massari's Casi di Napoli.[2] Started at four for Marseilles.

22. Sat.

Wrote to C.G. Reached Marseilles at 11½: & left at ½ past 3 for Avignon. Remained at Hotel d'Europe through the early part of the night: after a resolute attempt to lionise the outside of the Palace in the dark. Finished Massari—Read Documents in the case of Poerio—& his Constituto.[3]

23. Sexa. S.

A day of travelling. Read some of Apuzzi's Catechism.[4] 4 A.M.–7¾ P.M. Avignon to Lyons. Off again at 9.

24. M.

Reached Nevers at 4 P.M. Saw Moulins & Nevers Cathedrals. Failed at Bourges.[5] On to Paris in the night.

25. T.

Wrote to C.G. Paris at 4 AM. Hotel Windsor at 5. Rose between 8 & 9. On going to the P.O. for my letters I was astonished at the accounts of a ministerial crisis in England so soon.[6] Though for no definite purpose of course I go on to London at once. Missed Ld Normanby & M. Guizot. Saw & dined with the Warburton's. Off to London by the Mail train at 8.

[1] *La Costituzione politica del Regno di Napoli* (1849); cp. *Gleanings*, iv. 58.
[2] G. Massari, *I Casi di Napoli dal 29 gennaio 1848* (1849).
[3] 'Costituto [interrogation] di C. Poerio al parlamento di Napoli' (1850).
[4] Canon Apuzzi, *Catechismo Filosofico per uso delle Scuole Inferiori* (1850). Cp. his first 'Letter to *Aberdeen' in *Gleanings*, iv. 59.
[5] The cathedral of Notre Dame at Moulins is fifteenth century; that of Saint-Cyr at Nevers is thirteenth century, as is Saint-Étienne at Bourges.
[6] *Russell had resigned on 21 February.

26. Wed.

Wrote to Sir J.G—M. Lyttelton. 3 AM reached Calais: 7 AM Dover after a very rough passage quickly made by the Vivid. 10½ AM. London where I was met by my kind friend R. Phillimore at the Station. C[arlton] G[ardens] soon after 11—Saw D. of Newcastle[1]—J.N.G—Beresford—then went to Stanley: & I could not but feel an intense relief at the very first moment when he spoke of a duty on corn & so put me out of the question. Saw Ld Abn.—went to the Levee at two & saw Stanley again. Also Canning—J. Murray—Farquhar. Dined with the Herberts. In the bustle of today I could scarcely even survey the great heap of papers waiting me.

I reached London on the 26th February and found that I was wanted, to see Lord Stanley. Phillimore met me at the London Bridge Station with the Times, when I arrived by the train at half past ten. I had not any idea until that time that my coming would be so opportune.

Lincoln (Duke of Newcastle) reached Carlton Gardens very soon after me. The object of his visit was to dissuade me from accepting office with Stanley: with the notion that though he might *mean* to abandon protection, he would be so damaged in character by it that alliance with him would not be safe, and further that if we held off now the crisis must end shortly in placing the *summa rerum* in our hands. I, under the idea, like him, that there was no intention of proposing a duty on corn, replied that I should have to consider my course carefully but that of course it was a very different thing to take office with him individually, and to join him as one of a body, & that the[2] former might be improper even if the latter were practicable.

By this time Beresford had arrived with a message from Stanley who was now (more or less) suspending his proceedings to see me. (A note from him had been awaiting me some days.) I promised to go directly after seeing Lord Aberdeen. But he came back with a fresh message to go at once & *hear* what he had to say. I did not like to stickle & went.

He told me his object was that I should take office with him—*any* office (his own being by implication out of the question), subject to the reservation that the Foreign Department was offered to Canning but if he declined it open to me, along with others of which he named the Colonial Office & the Board of Trade. Nothing was said of the leadership of the H. of Commons but his anxiety was evident to have any occupant but one for the Foreign Office. I told him I should ask no question and make no remark on these points, as none of them would constitute a difficulty with me, provided no preliminary obstacle were found to intervene.

He said that he proposed to maintain generally the system of free trade and specified the Navigation Law: but he meant to modify it in regard to sugar—which he thought I agreed with him in treating as out of the category of Free Trade—and to corn. The advocates of the change in 1846 spoke of a price of 45/– as below the point at which wheat would stand under Free Trade. It was now at 38/– and if he imposed a duty of 5/– or 6/–, it would not raise the price by the whole of that amount and so would leave wheat cheaper than the Free Traders had prophesied that it would be under their system. He seemed to dwell more upon his own pledges and consistency, than upon an independent conviction of the necessity of a change.

[1] Lincoln had succ. as Newcastle on 12 January 1851.
[2] 'all' deleted.

I heard him pretty much in silence, with surprise, but with an intense sense of relief: feeling that if he had put Protection in abeyance I might have had a most difficult question to decide, whereas now I had no question at all—his announcement decided everything.

I thought however it might be well that I should still see Lord Aberdeen before giving him an[1] answer: and told him I would do so. I asked him also what was his intention with respect to Papal Aggression. He said that this measure was hasty & intemperate as well as ineffective: & that he thought something much better might result from a comprehensive & deliberate inquiry. I told him I was utterly against all penal legislation & against the Ministerial Bill, but that I did not on principle object to inquiry: that on general as well as on personal grounds I wished well to his undertaking and that I would see Lord Aberdeen but that what he had told me about corn constituted I must not conceal from him 'an enormous difficulty'. I used this expression for the purpose of preparing him to receive the answer it was plain I must give. He told me his persevering would probably depend on me.[2]

I then went to the Levee, saw Lord Normanby and others and began to bruit abroad the fame of the Neapolitan Government. Immediately after leaving the Levee (where I also saw Canning, told him what I meant to do and gathered that he would do the like) I changed my clothes and went to give Lord Stanley my answer at which he did not show the least surprise. I was not I think five minutes with him this second time.

The real question with me is this, why did he waste time in proposing to me to join a Cabinet which was to propose a fixed duty on Corn? My vote against local burdens in 1849 was accompanied with the strongest declaration against anything of the kind.[3] I believe the case to be this: that when Lord Stanley wrote to me his note (of Feb. [space]) he meant to try a Govt. with Corn duty in abeyance: that he was compelled to change this intention by the resolution of a section of his supporters whom he could not disregard: & that having invited me to confer with him he was obliged to go through.

I told him that either my convictions, or my pledges, were enough singly to bring me to the conclusion which I announced to him in equal conformity with both.

He said he would still persevere though with little hope. I think I told him it seemed to me he ought to do so.[4]

27. Th.

Saw Sir J. Graham & conversed fully with him on the current proceedings. Dined with the Jameses where I saw Ld Hardinge & found him rather leaning to Ld John's [Ecclesiastical Titles] Bill. Today I opened my letters & began to get the mass into order. I hope to write a few Mema. of some of the conversations of these days. Saw Tufnell—C. Greville—Cavendish.

28. Fr.

Wrote to J. Watson—H. Tayleur—T.G—Johnson Longden & Co. Dined

[1] 'Final' deleted.
[2] Para. reporting this to *Aberdeen omitted.
[3] Cp. 15 Mar. 49.
[4] Initialled and dated at Fasque, 22 April 1851, but written from 27 February; Add MS 44777, f. 322.

with the J.N.G's—House $4\frac{1}{2}$–$7\frac{1}{4}$ listening to the explanations: *troppo.* Walked in search of E. C[lifton] without effect [R]: saw Tupper & others. Read papers from Prosser on overtures to the Eastern Church.[1] Saw Ld Aberdeen with Graham Herbert & Cardwell: on the explanations to be made.

Saturday Mch One 1851.

Wrote to C.G—Oldfield—Wodehouse—Blair[2]—Mrs Curzon[3]—M. Lyttelton—Breakfast &c. with Herbert—Saw Graham & others—F. Wegg Prosser—Mr Addington—Ld Aberdeen—Peel Memorial Meeting at Ld Aberdeen's at 1 P.M.[4] Again went in search of E.C. [R] Read A W Pugin on the Hierarchy[5]—Twiss on Papal Brief[6]—Robins on Supremacy.[7]

2. Quinqua[gesima] S.

St Paul's Kn. mg—Bedfordbury evg. Dined & tea with the Jameses—Saw Manning (Papal Aggr. &c. *only*)—Hope—Cavendish—Wrote to Marriott—Haddan—Robins—Twiss—Chr Wordsworth—B. Powell—Burton—Read the Tracts & Sermon of the three first[8] & two last[9]—also M'Kenzie's & Maberly's Letter.[10]

3. M.

Wrote to T.G—H.J.G—Mr Church—WHG—Mr Burgess—R. Barker—(Telegr. Watson).[11] Saw Mr Bockett—Sir R. Inglis—J. Swift—Mr Tyler—Alick Wood—Clydesdale men. Breakfasted & dined with the Herberts—H of C. $4\frac{3}{4}$–$6\frac{1}{2}$.[12]

4. T.

Wrote to C.G[13]—M. Lyttelton—Rn. G—Messrs. G & Co.—Hodgson Hinde[14]

[1] Cp. 10 Apr. 51.
[2] Perhaps William Fordyce Blair, director of the Glasgow, Paisley Railway.
[3] Emily Julia, *née* Horton, m. Robert Curzon 1850 and d. 1866.
[4] At Argyll House.
[5] A. W. *Pugin, 'An earnest address on the establishment of the hierarchy' (1851).
[6] Sir T. *Twiss, 'The letters apostolic of Pope Pius IX, considered, with reference to the law of England and the law of Europe' (1851).
[7] S. Robins, *An argument for the royal supremacy* (1851).
[8] C. Marriott, 'The true cause of insult and dishonour to the Church of England' (1851); on Isaiah xliii. 26 and A. W. Haddan, 'The church patient in her mode of dealing with controversies' (1851).
[9] B. Powell, 'The state church, a sermon on 1 Cor. iii. 11' (1850) and C. H. Burton, 'The royal supremacy' (1850); on Eph. i. 22.
[10] C. Mackenzie, 'Individual responsibility: a sermon on Matt. xxv. 15' (1850). T. A. Maberly, 'A letter to the Revd. Henry Wellesley, D.D., on the occasion of his visitation sermon' (1850).
[11] (Sir) James Watson, 1801–89; Glasgow stockbroker, dealt with much Gladstone family finance; lord provost there 1871–4; kt. 1874.
[12] *H* cxiv. 1074: the ministerial crisis.
[13] Fragment in Morley, i. 393, on interview with *Aberdeen.
[14] John Hodgson-Hinde, *né* Hodgson, 1806–69; tory M.P. Newcastle 1832–4, 1836–47; took name of Hinde 1836; historian of Northumberland.

—Farquhar—Hawkins. Saw Swift—Oldfield—Freshfield—Johnson L. & Co—Ld Aberdeen—Scotts. Dined with the Mahons—Lady Aylesbury's afterwards.[1] Saw M.A. Crowther [R] who declared she would go to Mrs Tennant's at Clewer. Read De Vere's 'Is the Hierarchy an Aggression'?[2]—St German's Reasons.[3] Worked on accounts.

5. Ash Wedy.

St James's at 11. Tea with the Hopes. Saw Mr Oldfield—Lang (Caled.)[4]—Waterloo House people—Exhibn. Commn. 3–5¾. Wrote to Manning—Mr Church—Jas Watson. Worked on arrears of papers & letters. Search again at n[igh]t without avail.

6. Th.

Dined with the Hopes. Lady Granville's[5] afterwards: & further search. Saw J.N.G. (on my Father's matters)—R. Barker—Rev. E. Hawkins—Mr Oswald. Caledonian RR. meeting 2–5½. We came substantially to an agreement of the Guaranteed interests.[6] At Lady Granville's I was made to hold forth on Neapolitan horrors, with Hope I had a sad conversation that came yet nearer home. 'Manning's mind I think is made up: I am not very far from the same' What piercing words. We argued for two hours, but what am I for such high work?[7]

7. Fr.

Wrote to T.G—W.H.G—Johnson Longden & Co—H. Tayleur—Chairman Caled. Co[8]—Brameld[9]—Barthorp[10]—Fowle—Saw Archdn. Harrison—Herbert (breakfast)—Barker—A. Wood—R.M. Milnes. Attended S.P.G. meeting & moved a Resolution to prevent shirking the real matters in issue in the N[ova] S[cotia] Bpric matter.[11] H of C. 5–7¾ Papal Aggr. Bill.[12] Dined at Ld Granville's. Saw E. Watson [R].

[1] 41 Grosvenor Square.

[2] Written by brother of Aubrey De Vere of Currah Chase, Adare, Ireland. Cp. Add. MS 44370, f. 19.

[3] E. G. Eliot, 3rd Earl St. Germans, 'Reasons for not signing an address to Her Majesty, on the subject of the recent so-called papal aggression' (1850).

[4] Gabriel H. Lang, parliamentary agent for the Caledonian Railway.

[5] Granville m. first 1840 Maria Louise Pelline, da. of duke of Dalberg, widow of Sir F. R. E. Acton and mother of the historian. She d. 1860.

[6] The Caledonian Railway Company's directors were negotiating with the guaranteed and preferential shareholders to secure a reduction of the latter's claims upon the company. These shareholders had petitioned Parliament against the Caledonian Railway Arrangements Bill of 1851. Agreement was reached on 26 May 1851. Cp. 14 March 51 etc.

[7] Cp. 7, 8 Apr. 51.

[8] John Duncan.

[9] Probably George William Brameld, b. 1817; Lincoln College, Oxford; vicar of East Markham, Nottinghamshire, from 1852.

[10] A coalwhipper, see 14 May 51.

[11] On its endowments, cp. *Colonial Church Chronicle*, v. 36, 76.

[12] Spoke on Ecclesiastical Titles Bill 2°, which was deferred: *H* cxiv. 1144.

8. Sat.

Wrote to J. Murray—E.B. Ramsay—Burnett (2)—J.H. Hinde—Saw S. Herbert (breakfast)—Waterloo House people—Capt. Neville—Caledonian Meeting 3–5. Dined with J. Wortleys—Lady Palmerston's afterwards.[1] Read Twiss. Worked on MS. of Farini Trans. for press.[2]

9. 1 S. Lent.

St Andrew's W[ells] St & Holy C. 11–2. Bedfordbury Evg. MS. on the Temptn. aloud in evg. Dined with the Jameses. Saw Talbot—Bp of Salisbury—Manning for 3 hours of discussion in which I found him unsatisfactory in his grounds as well as apparently fixed in his conclusions. Wrote to T.G—Hamilton—Mrs Tennant—Burgess. Began my Letter to Ld Aberdeen.[3] Read Wiseman's Lectures—Wordsworth, Watson, Bosanquet, & Burgess's Tracts.[4]

10. M.

Wrote to M. Lyttelton—T. Newcome[5]—Mrs Perry[6]—Thomas—Sweet—Morris—A. de Vere—Saw Herbert—R. Cavendish—Hamilton—Mrs Church—W.E. Blair—Dined with the J.N.Gs. Read Twiss—& tracts on the Papal Aggression—Worked on the MS. of Farini.

11. T.

Wrote to Pugin—Revs T. Maberly[7]—A. Watson—Malet—James—J. Murray—E. Wakefield—Hayes—Parton & Co[8]—Kingscote—Will—Good. Saw Rev. E. Hawkins—Alex. Hope—and Bp of Exeter—who told me the Bps had determined not to move in the Appeal matter this year & showed me a paper, very ruinous in my judgment, wh they are meditating.[9] Read Twiss—Worked on Farini—Dined with the Jameses.

12. Wed.

Wrote to Ly Canning—Tatham & Co—Rev.s Williams—Stevenson—Burton—Provost of Oriel—Holmes. Breakfast with Milnes: conv. on Papal

[1] At 4 Carlton Gardens.
[2] Cp. 27 Nov. 50.
[3] 'A letter to the earl of *Aberdeen on the state prosecutions of the Neapolitan government', dated 7 April, published in July 1851.
[4] N. P. S. *Wiseman, 'Three lectures on the catholic hierarchy' (1850); C. *Wordsworth, 'On the inspiration of holy scripture' (1851); A. *Watson, 'The church's own action: the safeguard of the church and realm of England against romish aggression: a sermon' (1850); S. R. *Bosanquet, 'The romanists, the established church and the dissenters, his speech on the papal aggression, together with an explanatory letter to the Rev. Robert Jackson' (1851); R. Burgess, *Sermons for the times* (1851).
[5] Perhaps Thomas Newcome, a licenciate; vicar of Tottenham, Middlesex.
[6] Lodging house keeper, on rescue work.
[7] Thomas Astley Maberly, 1804–77; Christ Church, Oxford; vicar of Cuckfield, Sussex, from 1841.
[8] J. Parton, Pimlico linen draper and silk mercer.
[9] Gladstone hoped the bishops would take the lead in attacking the privy council's constitutional position on *Gorham.

Aggression with Mr Trench & others. $2\frac{1}{2}$–$4\frac{1}{4}$. Heard Padre Gavazzi.[1] His exterior is very great: & he seems to have had theological education but to be in a confusion as to principles & his *tone* is not satisfactory. Dined at R. Cavendish's & conv. with him & Phillimore. Ly John Russell's afterwards where I had conversations with divers of the Ministers & with Bunsen & Panizzi about Farini. Saw Lady Brabazon. House matters. Worked on Farini.

13. Th.

Wrote to Mr Hawkins—Sir J.G—E. Webber[2]—Mansfield & Co[3]—Vice Chanc. Oxf.—Finlason[4]—Saw A. Wood—Mr Dalzell[5]—Mr J. Swift—J.N.G—Mrs Barrable—Dined with the Hopes: Mr Lockhart was there & I had less conv. with Jim. Went afterwards (by the advice of the Hopes) to Mrs Hudson's—thence to Lady Granville's—Caledonian Meeting $3\frac{1}{2}$–$4\frac{3}{4}$: Commissioned Mr Oldfield. Worked on Farini.

14. Fr.

Wrote to C.G—Williams Deacon & Co—Freshfield—Overends (2)—Rn. G—Watson—Johnson Longden & Co—Entwistle.[6] Worked on Farini. Read on Papal Aggression. H. of C. $4\frac{1}{4}$–$7\frac{1}{2}$ and $9\frac{1}{2}$–$12\frac{3}{4}$.[7] Spoke on Caledonian RR Bill.[8]

15 Sat.

Wrote to H. Tayleur. Worked on accounts. Attended Caledonian Meeting—Saw Coalwhippers Deputn.[9]—Herbert (breakft)—Bush (Publisher's Monopoly)[10]—Panizzi—Dined with the Jameses to meet Ld Blandford[11] who is an interesting person. Lady Palmerston's afterwards. Read Berington[12]—Parl. Debates, &c.

[1] Alessandro Gavazzi, b. 1809; priest and Italian republican; became an anti-papal preacher in Britain and U.S.A.

[2] Edward Alexander Webber, 1805–72; St. John's, Cambridge; rector of Runnington from 1836 and of Bathealton, Somerset, from 1836.

[3] G. Mansfield & Son, builders, of Mecklenburg Square.

[4] William Francis Finlason, 1818–95; barrister, *Times* law reporter and writer on land tenure. Cp. 21 March 51.

[5] Slip of the pen for (Sir) Robert Alexander Osborne Dalyell, 1821–86; lawyer on Kent circuit 1849; in consular service 1855–74; 8th bart. 1865.

[6] William Entwistle, 1808–65 tory M.P. S. Lancashire 1844–7; chairman of Leeds and Manchester Railway; banker.

[7] Ecclesiastical Titles Bill 2°: *H* cxiv. 1312.

[8] *H* cxiv. 1313.

[9] The coalwhippers discharging coal on the London docks sought better working conditions. See 10 May, 6 June 51.

[10] Gladstone supported the campaign for free trade in books. Cp. J. J. Barnes, *Free trade in books* (1964), 25.

[11] John Winston Spencer *Churchill, 1822–83, styled marquis of Blandford 1840–57, tory M.P. Woodstock 1844, 1847–57; succ. as 7th duke of Marlborough 1857; lord steward of the household, 1866; lord lieutenant of Ireland, 1866–80.

[12] *Memoirs of Gregorio Panzani, giving an account of his agency in England in the years 1634, 1635, 1636*, tr. J. *Berington (1813).

16. 2 S. Lent.

St Barnabas & H.C. mg. Bedfordbury Evg. MS. of 41 aloud in evg. Read Berington—Panzani—Martineau on the Battle of the Churches[1]—With Manning 2–5. He said he had got at my meaning about the Judge in the early ages & wd consider it.[2] Dined with the Jameses.

17. M.

Wrote to M. Lyttelton—Jas Watson—J.N.G—G.F. Matheson—Mrs Tennant. Saw R. Cavendish—Bp of Exeter—J. Manners & others about Baillie. Read Alton Locke[3]—Twiss's Appx (finished) & worked on Papal Aggression. also on Farini. H. of C. 4½–7¼ and 8½–12¼.—Papal Aggression Debate.[4]

18. T.

Wrote to W.C. James—Mr Parish—H. Tayleur—Rn. G—Miles—Moody[5]—T.G. Saw the Manchester School Rate Deputation[6]—Baron Brunnow. Worked on Farini. Read Owen's Letter.[7] Dined at Lady Aylesbury's. H. of C. 5–7¼ and 11¼–12½.[8]

19. Wed.

Wrote to W.H.G—Mr Church—Leighton & Son—Glyn & Co—Scotts—Rankin—Maunsell.[9] Worked on Farini. Dined at Bp of Exeter's: where we talked much upon the threatened Episcopal manifesto (two Hopes, Badeley, R. Cavendish) wh is outrageous.[10] Saw Dr Twiss. Lady Truro's party in evg. Read C.P. Cooper[11]—Chas Buller[12]—& Alton Locke.

20. Th.

Wrote to H. Glynne—my little Stephen—Scotts—Leighton & Son. Worked on Farini—Breakf. & dined with Herbert. H. of C. 5–6¼ and 9–1.[13] Read Butler—Barnes[14]—&c.

[1] A. Martineau, *No need of a living infallible guide in matters of faith: a series of sermons in Whitkirk church* (1851).
[2] Perhaps the occasion recalled in Purcell, i. 617.
[3] C. *Kingsley, *Alton Locke, tailor and poet. An autobiography* (1850).
[4] Titles Bill 2°: *H* cxv. 33.
[5] Nicholas James Moody, 1821–58; Oriel, Oxford; rector of St. Clements, Oxford.
[6] No papers found.
[7] R. Owen, 'An apology for the "High Church" movement on liberal principles, in a letter to John Williams' (1851).
[8] Ecclesiastical Titles Bill 2°: *H* cxv. 125.
[9] Probably William Thomas Maunsell, 1883–62, barrister.
[10] Cp. 11 Mar. 51.
[11] C. P. Cooper, 'The Act of Settlement and the Pope's apostolic letters' (1851).
[12] C. *Buller: 'Speech in the House of Commons on systematic colonization, April 6, 1843' (1843).
[13] Ecclesiastical Titles Bill 2°: *H* cxv. 220.
[14] R. Barnes, 'The papal brief considered with reference to the laws of England' (1850).

21. Fr.

Wrote to Bp of Oxford—J.R. Hope (inclosing the former)—Manning—Ld Kinnaird. Saw Lyttelton—Arundel—Ld Aberdeen & Sir J. Graham—R. Palmer. Worked upon historical & other Extracts for Papal Aggr. Debate. H. of C. 6–7 and 9–12½.[1] Read Alton Locke—& pamphlets by O'Dwyer—Bp Gillies—Bowyer (Roman Documents). Finlason.[2]

22. Sat.

Wrote to A.P. Saunders—copy to Bp of Oxford (& sent my Letter).—Nina (Helen) arrived. Saw Mr Hallam—Bp of Salisbury. Worked on proofs of Farini. Read Alton Locke. Dined at Ld Carlisle's—the Speakers Levee afterwards.

23. 3. S. L[ent].

Pimlico Chapel (H.C.) mg. Bedfordbury evg. I tried to cultivate Nina's acquaintance. Of course she will not own me as papa. (she says no, when meaning *yes* also) MS aloud in evg. Dined with the Jameses. With Manning 2½–4½. Not at close quarters. Saw EHG.[3] Wrote to J.N.G. Read Xtn Remr.[4]—Trevor[5]—Molesworth[6] (Rev.)—Lawrence.[7]

24. M.

Wrote to Bp of Oxford—C.G.—Landlady at Avignon—R. Cavendish. Worked on Papal Aggression, & made Mema. for Speech.[8] Worked on Farini proofs, & preparing MS. Read Alton Locke. Saw Ld Aberdeen—Ld Arundel—E.V. Harcourt. H. of C. 7¾–12½: *waiting*—wh so much prolonged produces great nervousness.[9]

25. T. The Annunciation.

St James, morning. Wrote to M. Lyttelton—H. Glynne—Mr Church—W.H.G.—J.E. Gladstone. Read Alton Locke—Ld Holland's Reminiscences[10]

[1] Ecclesiastical Titles Bill: *H* cxv. 334.

[2] C. O'Dwyer, 'The catholic question of 1851 considered' (1851). J. *Gillis, 'A discourse on the mission and influence of the Popes' (1850). G. *Bowyer, 'The roman documents relating to the new hierarchy, with an argument' (1851). W. F. Finlason, 'The catholic hierarchy vindicated by the law of England' (1851).

[3] i.e. Edith H. Gladstone.

[4] *Christian Remembrancer*, xxi. 1 (January 1851).

[5] G. Trevor 'Party spirit: a serious expostulation with the vicar of St. Peter's, Sheffield' (1851).

[6] 'Correspondence between W. S. Crawford M.P. for Rochdale and Dr. Molesworth . . . on papal aggression' (1851).

[7] C. Lawrence: 'A letter on agricultural education' (1851).

[8] Add MS 44651, f. 186.

[9] Ecclesiastical Titles Bill; he was not called: *H* cxv. 428.

[10] H. R. V. *Fox, 3rd Baron Holland, *Foreign reminiscences* (1850).

—Eden's[1] & Lingard's[2] pamphlets—The Govt & Ir R.C. Members.[3] Breakf. & dinner with the Herberts. Saw the Bp of Oxford & conv[ersed] long on the proposed Address, wh we went over, & on Church affairs. H. of C. 5–6½ and 8¼–3. A.M. Spoke 2¼ hours from 10¾ to 1 A.M. & voted in 95 (only!): 438 agt. the Eccl Titles' Bill.[4] My head being hot I poured water over it with a large sponge before dinner, & this seemed at once to clear the brain.

26. Wed.

Wrote to Panizzi—Mr Church—W.H.G.—Mary Lyttelton—J.N.G.—E. Hawkins—Mr Spranger. Read Alton Locke—Bp of Toronto's Letter (MS)[5] Saw T.G.—Ld Aberdeen—R. Cavendish. Gavazzi's Lecture 2½–4½. Wonderful acting especially at the close.[6] Dined at Lady F. Hope's.

27. Th.

Wrote to A. Watson—R. Mansfield & Co—Panizzi. Dined with the Greenes. music. Saw Mr Currie[7]—Rev. J.E. Gladstone—H.E. Manning—Scots Ch Deputation (on Educn. Bill)[8] J.L. & Co—Freshfields. In the City & book-buying on my way back. H. of C. 4¾–7¾.[9] Read Alton Locke—Freeman on the Cape.[10]

28. Fr.

Wrote to Hayes—J.L. & Co—H. Tayleur—Peters[11]—Sewell—Robertson—Mayow—Monsell—Hendy.[12] Finished Alton Locke—Read Neapolitan political MSS—Settembrini's Address[13]—Wakefield's MS on Col Policy.[14] Saw Doyle—Aldis[15]—and P.L. [R] a singular case indeed.[16] H of C 5¼–7¾.[17]

[1] R. Eden, 'The sin and danger of faithlessness and impatience in the present crisis of the church' (1850).

[2] J. Lingard, 'Observations on the laws and ordinances which exist in foreign states relative to the religious concerns of their roman catholic subjects' (1817, reprinted 1851).

[3] C. P. Cooper, 'The government and the roman catholic members of parliament' (1851).

[4] *H* cxv. 565: seventh night of deb. on Ecclesiastical Titles Bill 2°.

[5] Not found, unless that of 1850 in Add MS 44369, f. 318, or his appeal in ibid. 44566, f. 169.

[6] From January to March 1851 Gavazzi lectured in Italian on papal usurpation in the Princess's Concert Room, Oxford Street; published in English as *Twelve orations on papal usurpation and intolerance* (1851).

[7] i.e. Raikes Currie.

[8] No papers found.

[9] *H* cxv. 650.

[10] J. J. Freeman, 'The Kaffir war; a letter to Earl *Grey' (1851).

[11] Probably Michael Nowell Peters, 1790–1800; vicar of Madron, Cornwall, from 1838.

[12] Francis Paul James Hendy, d. ?1904; St. John's College, Cambridge; curate of Par, Cornwall, 1848–57, of Wolborough, Devon, 1857–62; vicar of St. Neot 1862–74.

[13] 'Difesa di Luigi Settembrini' (1850).

[14] E. G. *Wakefield, 'A view of the art of colonization, with present reference to the British Empire, in letters between a statesman and a colonist' (1849).

[15] Probably Charles James Berridge *Aldis, 1808–72, s. of Sir Charles*; physician and sanitary reformer.

[16] P. Lightfoot, another rescue case; cp. 29–31 Mar., 9 May, 16 June 51.

[17] *H* cxv. 720: debate on army estimates.

Yesterday Hume asked me to let[1] him have my speech for publication to circulate among the Dissenters who as he says know nothing about religious liberty.[2] Wrote a little on Neapol. affairs. Lady Jersey's party in evg. & a philosophico-political convn. with Ly Clanricarde. She gave up Ld John's Letter [on Ecclesiastical Titles].

29. Sat.

Wrote to Panizzi—C.G.—Mrs Warburton. Saw Ld Aberdeen—D. of Newcastle—Wegg Prosser—& [blank.] Worked much on proofs of Farini. Searched for P.L. [R] Dined at Norreys: forgetting proh pudor![3] my engagement to the Cavendishes. Read Settembrini.

30. 4 S. L[ent].

York St Chapel mg[4]—Bedfordbury evg. Townsend on Gospel aloud. Wrote a paper on Manning's question & gave it to him: he smote me to the ground by answering with suppressed emotion that he is now upon the *brink*: and Hope too.[5] Such terrible blows not only overset & oppress but I fear also demoralise me: which tends to show that my trusts are Carnal or the withdrawal of them would not leave such a void. *Was* it possibly from this that thinking P.L. would look for me as turned out to be the fact, I had a second interview & conversation indoors here: & heard more history: yet I trusted without harm done [R]. Wrote to Wordsworth. Read Hussey on Supremacy[6]—Bowyer's Observations[7]—Scotch minutes on Edn. Bill.[8]

31. M.

Wrote to W.C. James—M. Chron. Reporter—J.L. Ross—G. Grove—Ld Kinnaird—L. Mackenzie[9]—T.G.—Mr D Gladstone—C.G. Reid—Illustrated News. Saw Panizzi & worked further with him on the proofs of Farini. Also worked on preparing MS. & on Table of Contents. Saw Mr Sewell on NZ.[10] H. of C. 4–6¾:[11] went to Dr. Dss. of Beauforts at 9, & then to Lady Fremantle's. Saw P.L. again indoors [R] & said I thought it must be the last time: as I fear lest more harm was done than good. There seems to be little guilt, & good affections, but an ill-informed conscience, & a want of depth & strength in impressions. I was certainly wrong in some things & trod the path of danger.

[1] Instead of 'send'. [2] Cp. 25 Mar. 51. [3] 'for shame'.

[4] York St., St. James's, London. Thomas Tunstall Haverfield, 1786–1866, fellow of Corpus, Oxford, from 1812, was its incumbent from 1842.

[5] Version of this sentence and first half of next in Morley, i. 386.

[6] R. *Hussey, *The rise of papal power traced in three lectures* (1851).

[7] G. *Bowyer, *Observations on the arguments of Dr. Twiss respecting the new Roman catholic hierarchy* (1851).

[8] Cp. *PP* 1851, vi. 33 and ibid. 1851, xliv. 1.

[9] Probably the Glasgow oculist attending his sister Helen.

[10] Henry *Sewell, 1807–79, secretary and deputy chairman of Canterbury Association for colonization of New Zealand 1850, member of house of representatives for Christchurch 1854–61, prime minister 1856 and sundry minor offices 1856–72.

[11] *H* cxv. 792: debate on army estimates.

Tuesday Ap. One 1851.

Wrote to Rev. J. Miller[1]—Cocks & Biddulph—Miss Brown—Willy—M. Lyttelton—J.N.G.—J. Griffiths—Nagle—Lyon—Manning. At Br. Museum 2–4¼ with Mr P[anizzi] on my proof sheets. Worked on the Contents & MS of Farini. H. of C. 4¾–6¾. Dined at R. Cavendish's: Bunsen's & Lady Waldegrave's afterwards. Saw Mr Bowyer[2]—& others—

2. W.

Wrote to Lacaita—Lady Malcolm. Saw Manning again: He says we differ in premisses & he will not in reality discuss. Worked with Panizzi on proof sheets. Also alone: & made up the remaining MS. of Vol 1. for press. Read Ullathorne on Lacy's Bill.[3] Mr Smith on Papal Aggra.[4] Dined with Mr Sandars:[5] we discussed Hudson after dinner.[6]

3. Th.

Wrote to E. Coleridge—H. Tayleur—B. Smith—E. Smythe—Read & worked on the Neapolitan case: and wrote a good deal more of my Letter to Ld Aberdeen. Dined with the Hopes. Read Bowyer's Cardinal Abp of Westminster.[7]

4. Fr.

Wrote to Panizzi (2)—B. Smith. Read and wrote on the Neapolitan Case. Finished & corrected my letter & sent it to be transcribed. Saw Phillimore on Ch. matters. H. of C. 5–8¼.[8] Read Bp of London's Charge.[9] Prepared for correcting my Speech. This is little Stephen's birthday. God bless him.

5. Sat.

Wrote to M. Lyttelton—J.N.G.—H.J.G.—C.G.—Mrs Warburton—H. Tayleur—G. Griffiths—Uwins[10]—Cooke—and H.E. Manning, in answer to his note showing me that the blow is to fall tomorrow.

[1] John Cale *Miller, 1814–80, evangelical rector of St. Martin's, Birmingham, canon of Rochester 1873.

[2] Sir George *Bowyer, 1811–83, reader in law at Middle Temple 1850; liberal M.P. for Dundalk 1852–68, for co. Wexford 1874–80; 7th Bart. 1860.

[3] W. B. Ullathorne, 'A plea for the rights and liberties of religious women, with reference to the bill proposed by Mr. Lacy' (1851).

[4] G. Smith of Trinity chapel 'The right of private judgment' (1850), or an MS from B. Smith, otherwise unidentified (see next day).

[5] George Sandars 1805–79; tory M.P. Wakefield 1847–57; auditor of the South Staffordshire railway.

[6] Cp. Add. MS. 44744, f. 183.

[7] G. *Bowyer, 'The cardinal archbishop of Westminster and the new hierarchy' (1851).

[8] *H* cxv. 1030: debs. on Puseyism and the budget.

[9] C. J. *Blomfield, 'A charge delivered to the clergy of the diocese of London, at the visitation in Nov. 1850' (1850).

[10] Thomas *Uwins, 1782–1857, painter; librarian of Royal Academy 1844, surveyor of pictures to the Queen 1845, keeper of the National Gallery 1847.

Dined with the Oswald's. Worked on the Report of my Speech. Attended meeting at Ld Aberdeen's 1–3½: where we had a very interesting conversation. Business and calls. Saw Mr Linton's pictures. Saw Canning.

On the fifth of April we had again a very interesting conversation at Lord Aberdeen's: the new edition of the Budget having now been published.

We all agreed upon the financial aspects of the question. That we must calculate on losing the Income Tax at some probably early day: that the means of dispensing with it are economy, the elasticity of taxes on consumption, economies already prospectively effected in the debt, and lastly & essentially a productive House Tax; that Wood's House Tax from its narrow basis is essentially an unproductive one: that to oppose the exemptions & vote for a wider basis in Committee would be futile: that the choice lay between accepting the House Tax & giving away a necessary resource, and striking at the Budget, with the risk of disturbing the Government.

This question I said was a grave one: but for my own part I should not be deterred from thus aiming at the House Tax by the mere consideration of the danger of the Government, since I looked upon the accession of the Protectionists to power as an event attended with some inconveniences but yet to be encountered as absolutely necessary in order to purge the great aristocratic party of this country from its connection with a cause which is false & grows more and more false every day.

Sir J. Graham stated admirably, & most strongly, his conviction of the State-necessity for Stanley's coming into power: he considered that in this way only could the natural and needful constitution and equilibrium of parties be restored, and evidently implied that there could be no permanent junction on Conservative grounds between our section and the Whig Ministry.

Yet when the other side of the question was presented to him, namely the idea of a vote, which in order to save a financial principle might be given by us, and might put Stanley into Government, he at once shrunk back from it.

I said it was time for us to consider what this practically meant and came to: the upshot of it was that we need deliberate upon nothing: that no *principle* of politics was ever to carry us against the Ministry, therefore we had only to listen to their plans and if we could not privately dissuade, then publicly support. That I knew this course had had the sanction of Sir R. Peel's & Sir J. Graham's example—a most weighty & authoritative sanction.

Yes, said Graham, Peel had followed the Government for the sake of keeping out the Protectionists, 'against his own feelings & his own opinions'.

I rejoined that I never had been able to take that course: that I not only believed in the impossibility of restoring Protection, but that I likewise believed Stanley, who though rash in speech when in opposition is not rash as a minister, (here appealing to Graham who emphatically confirmed this & said he was rather timid of the two—) would not carry the attempt at restoring it to such a point as to do any great harm by it. That on every occasion I had voted according to the merits of questions & never in order to put out the Govt. or to keep them in. That I could not profess to be satisfied with the results of the opposite course: for keeping the Government had now brought us to the very brink of a new Reform Bill.

Yes, Graham said, but if Lord John is in office he will propose as little reform as will enable him to keep it: whereas if he is out he will propose as much as he may find needful in order to recover it—that you may rely upon it will be Lord John's course.

I avowed no such great fears of him in opposition with respect to Reform: & a sense of total insecurity in respect to it with him in Government, looking upon the financial feebleness & the extravagance of his administration as the sure means of generating successive demands for reform. Had Peel been still in office I said reform would not to this day have revived.[1]

6. 5 S. Lent.[2]

St Mary's Crown St & H.C. mg. Bedfordbury evg. Dined & had tea with the Jameses. Townsend aloud. Saw Jos. Hume—R. Cavendish—Ly Ln. Wrote to Mr Mackenzie—

A day of pain! Manning & Hope! Read Chr. Remembrancer wh is manful & good:[3] Bp Oxf. on Confirmation[4]—The Eucharistic month[5]—Città della Filosofia.[6]

7. M.

Wrote to Ld Aberdeen—Ashley—J. Hume. Worked on & concluded correction[7] of my Speech & gave it over to Mr Hume. Worked on Farini with Panizzi: & learned his communications at Claremont. Reviewed[8] my transcribed letter to Aberdeen & dispatched it.[9] Saw the Herberts—Rn. G.—

Hope too is gone. They were my two props. Their going may be to me a sign that my work is gone with them. God give us daily light with daily bread. One blessing I have: total freedom from doubts. These dismal events have smitten but not shaken.[10]

H. of C. 5½–7½: & late.[11] Voted in 278:230 agt. Herries.[12] *But.*

Dined at the Palace: when I had most interesting conversations especially with the Queen about Naples.

8. T.

Wrote to Bockett (2)—Spottiswoodes—C. Wordsworth—Harrison—Smith & Co—Baxter—Walker—Toomes[13]—T.G.—R. Owen—Good—Eden—Wm. G.—Carter. Wrote Mem. on the Budget (House Tax)[14] Saw the Herberts (Ch. & pol.). H of C. 5–7.[15]

Off at 8 by Mail to Paris: after a very busy day. Read Gualterio.[16] Executed a codicil to my will striking out Hope as Ex[ecuto]r: & with a general provision.[17]

[1] Rest omitted; initialled and finished at Fasque, 23 April 1851, Add MS 44777, f. 327.
[2] Next four entries in facsimile in Masterman, at 112.
[3] *Christian Remembrancer*, xxi (April 1851).
[4] Samuel *Wilberforce, 'An address delivered at the confirmation at Eton College' (1851).
[5] *The Eucharistic Month*, a manual of devotion (1850).
[6] Cp. 23 Feb. 51?
[7] instead of 'correcting'.
[8] instead of 'revised'.
[9] Add MS 44684, ff. 236–258.
[10] Part in Morley, i. 386.
[11] Spoke on the budget: *H* cxv. 1202.
[12] An amndt. on income tax.
[13] Perhaps Robert Tomes, Magdalen Hall, Oxford; vicar of Coughton, Warwickshire, 1831–73.
[14] Add MS 44777, ff. 314–21.
[15] *H* cxv. 1226: Church rates, lodging houses, state of Ireland.
[16] F. A. Gualterio, *Gli Ultimi Rivolgimenti Italiani, memorie storiche,* 2 v. (1850); cp. *Gleanings*, iv. 54.
[17] Cp. Morley, i. 386–7. *Northcote succeeded *Hope.

9. Wed.

Reached Paris at 9 A.M. Six hours from Calais. Found C. looking thin but otherwise better than I had hoped: Mary's eye showing the marks of weakness which it had not when I left her. Went to the Sainte Chapelle[1]—St Germain des Prés[2]—St Germain Auxerrois[3]—the first of these exquisite in beauty. Saw Guizot. Went to the gigantic Exposition of Pictures. I thought it less satisfactory than the English, tho' there was abundance of power in it. Portrait, landscape, *genre* pictures, animals, all inferior to ours.[4] Dined with the Warburtons at the Poissonnière.[5]

10. Th.

Off at 7½: reached Boulogne at 2. 3 P.M.–5.25 to Folkestone. Got the luggage through & off to London at 5.50. Reached No 6 before 10½. At work on letters &c: & went to the House for Molesworth's motion till one.[6] Read Prosser on Eastern Ch.[7]

11. Fr.

Wrote to Hodgkin—C.M. Lushington—Baker—Sec. S.E. Railway[8]—R. Wilberforce—G. Denison—Sir G. Prevost.[9] Saw Lyttelton—T.C. Parr—Adderley—Hubbard—J. Young. Read Agr. Distress Debate of last year:[10] & was much puzzled about tonight: but D'Israeli's Speech decided me as all my financial objections tell with enhanced force agt. his plan. H. of C. 4¾–8¾ and, 10–2. Spoke & voted in 273:260 agt. Disraeli.[11] Willy came home.

12. Sat.

Wrote to H.J.G.—J. Hume. Dined with the Herberts. Visited the Crystal Palace—Saw Hubbard—Oldfield—G. Hope—Panizzi—Mahon—Ld Hardinge—G. Bankes (to whom I spoke freely)[12]—Ld Ashley, about Church organisation. Lady Palmerston's in evg. Stephy came home much grown & good. Corrected proofs of Speech on Papal Aggression. Arranged my Deed Chest.

[1] Sainte Chapelle, built in 1243–48 by St. Louis as a shrine for relics; restored 1837–57.

[2] Eleventh-century church by the Sorbonne; used as a saltpetre factory 1794–95, drastically restored 1822.

[3] St. Germain l'Auxerrois, Gothic church of thirteenth–sixteenth centuries; used as a granary, a printing works, and as the 'Temple of Gratitude' during the revolution; sacked by mob 1831, poorly restored 1838.

[4] Masterman's facsimile ends here.

[5] Café Poissonnière, a restaurant in Boulevard Poissonnière.

[6] *Molesworth's motion to reduce colonial expenditure: *H* cxv. 1353.

[7] Perhaps an advance copy or MS of F. R. Wegg-Prosser, *The branch-church theory, a dialogue* (1852); privately printed.

[8] G. S. Herbert.

[9] Sir George *Prevost, 1804–93; 2nd bart. 1816; tractarian; perpetual curate of Stinchcombe 1834–93, archdeacon of Gloucester 1865–81.

[10] *H* cviii. 1026, 1179.

[11] *H* cxvi. 118.

[12] George *Bankes, 1788–1856, barrister; tory M.P. for Corfe Castle 1816–23, 1826–32, Dorset 1841–56; minor office 1829–30; judge advocate general 1852.

13. Palm Sunday.

St Martin's mg. Bedfordbury evg. MS of 1846 aloud. The Jameses came to tea. Saw Cavendish & Talbot—G. Hope. Busy with the children &c. Walk with Willy. Saw Ld Aberdeen: chiefly about the Neapolitans; & made an addition to my letter at his suggestion, with some small changes. Read Kebles Preface[1]—Scots Eccl. Magazine.[2]

14. M.

Bedfordbury 7. P.M. Wrote to Spottiswoode—Ld Aberdeen—Lloyd[3]—Panizzi—T.G.—Clarke—H.J.G.—H. Tayleur—G. & Co—Wainwright—Griffith. Saw Burnett 10–12 & again, on S.R.G.s matters—Napier—Bp of Exeter—J.N.G.—Ld Aberdeen.—Herbert. Latin lesson to Willy. Dined with the Herberts. Finished 'Contents' for Farini. Correcting the other MSS of my letter to Ld Aberdeen.

15. T.

Wrote to Panizzi—J.N.G.—Miss Stürmer[4]—Mrs Ley[5]—Freshfield—Wakefield Grant & Son. Worked on Farini. Latin lesson to Willy. Read on the Cape—Dubl. Review.[6] Saw Northcote—G. Hope. Took Willy to the Crystal Palace: attended meeting of Commission. H. of C. 8–12½. Spoke agt. Ld J. Russell's Committee.[7] Got to bed at 3. a.m.

16. Wed.

Off by the train at 6½. a.m. for the North. Read Bp of Exeter's Pastoral Letter[8]—Gualterio's Ultimi Rivvolgimenti.

17. Th.

Wrote to C.G.—Bockett (& draft) Reached Laurencekirk at 7 & Fasque at 8. Much pleased with my Father's general state tho' he was a little querulous before rising: which he does now about half past ten: going to bed by nine or a little later. He had this day five hours conversation with me. Chapel at 11 a.m. Arranging my things. Read Gualterio—Lays of the Scottish Covenanters.[9]

[1] To his ed. of *Hooker, cp. 5 Sept. 44.
[2] Probably the *Scottish Episcopal Magazine*; cp. 16 Dec. 48.
[3] John Augustine *Lloyd, 1800–54; surveyor-general in Mauritius 1831–49; British chargé d'affaires, Bolivia, 1851; acted as special commissioner, with James Lyon *Playfair, in procuring industrial products for 1851 exhibition.
[4] Miss L. Stumme, attached briefly to the Gladstone family.
[5] Mrs. Linny Ley of Southampton had requested assistance.
[6] *Dublin Review*, xxx. 1 (March 1851).
[7] Against a cttee. of inquiry of South African troubles: *H* cxvi. 260.
[8] H. *Phillpotts, 'A pastoral letter . . . on the present state of the church' (1851).
[9] W. E. *Aytoun, *Lays of the Scottish cavaliers and other poems* (1849).

18. Good Friday.

Chapel 11 & 3. My Father continued well: I spoke to him of his receiving the Holy Communion. Read Gemitus Columbae—Dr Pusey's Letter to the Bishop of London[1]—Ballerinius de Primatu.[2] Q.R. on the Ministry & the Pope.[3] Conv. with Helen on the *Bill.*[4]

19. Sat. Easter Eve.

Chapel 11 a.m. Wrote to C.G.—Willy—S.R.G.—T.G. (2)—Bishop of Exeter—J.N.G.—J. Griffiths—J. Walker. Read Aytoun's Lays—Dubl. Rev. on the Hierarchy[5]—Ld Ellesmere's Transl. on the War in Italy[6]—Gualterio's Ravvolgimenti—& Gemitus Columbae. My Father had a good but dozy day.

And now ends another Lent. My small abstinence of this week has been made smaller still by my journey on Wednesday & Thursday. I am more & more convinced of the blessings of discipline. But I must write a bitter thing against myself. Whether owing (as I think) to the sad sad recent events (of the 6th) or not, I have been unmanned & unnerved & out of sheer cowardice have not used the measure which I have found so beneficial against temptations to impurity.

Therefore they have been stronger than usual in Lent: and I had no courage! It is a strange frame of mind that I seem to have a strong desire for the glory of God with a weak one for my personal sanctification: as though God's first command to me for His glory were not that I should study that sanctification which is His will (Thess).[7] As to abstinence I am beset with coughs, sore throats & weakness of the eyes almost at the threshold: but not quite.

20. Easter. Sunday.

Read the Mg. service to Sir J.G. Chapel 11 a.m. (& H.C.) 3. P.M. My Father had a fair day, a good evening. Macinroy here. I walked with him. Read Scots Eccl. Journal[8]—Pusey's Letter to Bp L—Gemitus Columbae—Ballerinius.

21. Easter. M.

Chapel 11 a.m. Wrote to C.G.—Dean of Moray[9]—T.G.—Rn. G. Read

[1] E. B. *Pusey, 'A letter to the bp. of London in explanation of some statements contained in a letter by the Rev. W. *Dodsworth' (1851).

[2] Petrus Ballerinius, ed. E. W. Westhoff, *De vi ac ratione primatus Romanorum pontificum* (1845).

[3] Review of pamphlets on ecclesiastical titles: *Quarterly Review*, lxxxviii. 247.

[4] Ecclesiastical Titles Bill.

[5] *Dublin Review* (March 1851), xxx. 176.

[6] M. Amari, tr. by Lord F. Leveson Gower, earl of Ellesmere, *History of the war of the Sicilian Vespers*, 3 v. (1850).

[7] I Thessalonians, iv. 3–7.

[8] Cp. 13 April 1851.

[9] Hugh Willoughby Jermyn, 1820–1903; dean of Moray 1851–4; archdeacon in West Indies 1854; rector of Nettlecombe 1858; bp. of Colombo 1871–5; primus of Scotland 1886–1901.

Ellesmere Translation—Lays of Scots Cavaliers. Worked on Farini MS: began preparation of Vol II for press. Calls at F[ettercair]n House &c. My Father continued well & comfortable.

22. Easter. T.

Chapel 11 a.m. Wrote to C.G. Wrote Political Memoranda.[1] Worked on Farini MS. Walk and visits. Read Gualterio—Aytoun (finished)—Quarterly on Ceylon.[2] My Father continued well.

23. Wed.

Wrote to C.G.—E. Wardell[3]—G. Burnett—H. Tayleur—G.C. Myers (for Sir J.G.) Wrote Pol. Memoranda—Worked on Farini. Walked in the hill woods. Read (Ellesmere) War in Italy—Gualterio. My Father a little more restless: Fettis here and made an excellent report.

24. Th.

Wrote to C.G.—E. Coleridge—G.C. Myers (2) (for Sir J.G.)—Western Bank Montrose (do)—Dr Robertson. Visits +. Worked on Farini. Read Gualterio —cardinal Pacca.[4] A good day again with my Father. His mental state is that of *ordinary* incapacity for business: but only *just* incapacity: & with periods of exception.

25. Fr. St Mark.

Chapel 11 a.m. Wrote to C.G.—W.H.G.—Sir J. Young—Wm. Gladstone. Visits: & at F. House. Worked on Farini. Read Gualterio—Gregory on Animal Magnetism (began)[5]—Cardinal Pacca—War in Italy. My Father slightly below yesterday: passionately for my setting off tomorrow mg. that I may be in time for the opening on Thursday. But please God I shall not go *there*.

26. Sat.

Wrote to C.G.—Rn. Gladstone—and Mrs Forbes. Walk on the hill. Worked on Farini. Read Gualterio—Pacca—War in Italy—Gregory on Magnetism. My Father quite as well as yesterday.

27. 2. S. Easter.

Chapel 11–12¼: and at 3. Read the morning Service to my Father. He attended almost throughout. Wrote to Bp of New Zealand—J. Murray. Read Pusey's Letter to Bp London. (finished)—Gemitus Columbae. And the Guardian &c.

[1] Finishing that at 26 Feb. 51.
[2] 'The mysteries of Ceylon', *Quarterly Review* (December 1850), lxxxviii. 100.
[3] Wife of William Wardell of Broughton, a J.P.
[4] B. Pacca, *Historical memoirs*, tr. Sir G. *Head, 2 v. (1850).
[5] W. Gregory, *Letters to a candid inquirer on animal magnetism* (1851).

28. M.

Wrote to C.G.—Hampton—Lyttelton—D.S. Bockett (& draft)—Sir F. Thesiger—R. Barker—Sec. Royal Academy[1]—Rev. J. Gladstone. Worked on Farini MS for press & revises. Read Memoirs of Pacca—War in Italy—Gualterio. My Father still keeps well though his drives are shortened by bad weather.

29. T.

Wrote to J.N.G.—Lindsay & Walker[2]—J. Murray—C. Wordsworth—Mrs Hallewell—W. Malcolm[3]—Adderley (most of these for Sir J.G.) also Farquhar & Gill (J.G.)—Johnston (do)—R. Readman. Worked on Farini. Visits—& at F[ettercairn] House. Read Pacca—Gualterio—War in Italy. My Father ditto.

30. Wed.

Wrote to Rn. G—Mr G. Grant—C.G.—S. Herbert—Miss Scott[4]—Miss Marshall.[5] Worked on Farini. Read War in Italy (finished). Put up my things, set off at 2.40 for Luncarty, & walked thence (8 or 9 m) to Trin. Coll. [Glenalmond] carrying my bag for lack of any other porter. Evening with [Charles] Wordsworth & those assembled.

Thursday May One SS. Philip & James.

Chapel for the Consecration from 11 to 3.40 and again 5–6½. At Holy Communion we had a large number: Scots Office. The chanting was of a noble vigour. Two earnest sermons: but Dean R[amsay']s seemed to proceed on the supposition that the custody of the Deposit is not the first thing; & Wordsworth was on his respectable but impracticable ground of the old Church & State system.

Conversations with Wordsworth (Ch & State)—Bp of Aberdeen (Papal Aggression)—Bp of Argyll (Laymen in Synods)—and others. Wrote to Bp [of] Argyll with extract from Bp of New Zealand about Synods. Set out at 11½ P.M. & walked down to Perth.

2. Fr.

Off at 4. P.M. [*sc.* A.M.]: walked from Laurencekirk & home at 8½ a.m. 18 m between supper & breakfast. Wrote to Mr Myers—Wm. Gladstone (Sir J.G.) —C.G.—D. Caldwell[6] (self). Found my Father more restless, & he was at work talking, asking, dictating or under the process of reading, all his short day—except the drive. Read Pacca—Gualterio. Worked on Farini.

[1] J. P. *Knight. Cp. 15 Jan. 39 n.
[2] Western Bank of Scotland Montrose agents.
[3] Perhaps William Elphinstone Malcolm, b. 1817, Dumfriesshire landowner.
[4] Appointed governess.
[5] Another applicant for governess?
[6] David Caldwell, parliamentary agent and secretary to Forth and Clyde Navigation Company.

Attended Hall's Funeral at Fettercairn.[1] Visited my little Jessy's dear remains.

3. Sat.

Wrote to C.G.—T.G.—P. Work[2]—J. Manners—G.C Myers. Worked on Farini. Read Pacca (finished)—Quarterly on Ld J. Russell (trumpery)[3]—Gualterio—Gregory. Visited the vault: a cold & repulsive name.[4]

4. 2 S. Easter.

Chapel 11 (Holy C.) and 3. Read the service in aftn. to my Father: he was uneasy in mg. Wrote to C.G. Visited as yesterday that calm retreat. Read Hussey on the Papal Power (finished)[5]—Gemitus Columbae (finished) and Ballerinius. These last three have been less tranquil days with my Father: the change appears to be owing to a slight derangement of the stomach.

5. M.

Wrote to C.G.—Capt. Hornby[6]—Duncan & Flockhart[7]—R. Barker. My Father more easy in the day: let me read prayers to him. He can attend only to these & the newspaper (accidents) generally speaking. He was restless at night. Fettis found him well. Visits: & walk on the Garrol. Worked a good deal on Farini. Read Gualterio—Gregory. Visited Jessy's home.

6. T.

Wrote to J. Murray—E. Hawkins—Rn. G—R. Grant & Son—C. Wordsworth—Myers—Bp of Argyll. Read prayers to my Father. Saw Lady H. Forbes. Worked on Sir J.G.s accounts &c. Finished the preparation of the Farini MS. for the press. Read Gualterio—Gregory—& Pacca Vol II. My Father uneasy in the day—much better at night, after prayers read.

7. Wed.

Wrote to Wm. Gladstone—Dr Robertson—Packing up my things & making inventory &c. Visited at the Old Mains: I left Mrs Smith[8] at the point of death. Tibbie Sowter at 83 took her turn with other charitable souls in sitting up through the night with Mrs S.! I read prayers to my Father & had the comfort of leaving him in a satisfactory state. He bid me a most affectionate farewell: & spoke strongly of our coming bodily in July. Left Fasque at 2.40: & travelled by Mail to town. Read Gualterio.

[1] A villager.
[2] 'and' here deleted; Work is otherwise unidentified.
[3] Review of 'Lord John *Russell' (1851): *Quarterly Review*, lxxxviii. 564.
[4] Jessy's burial place below the chapel.
[5] Cp. 30 Mar. 51.
[6] (Sir) Phipps *Hornby, 1785–1867; captain, R.N., 1810; controller of coastguards 1841–6; commanded the Pacific 1847–50; lord of the admiralty 1852; admiral 1858; K.C.B. 1852.
[7] Edinburgh chemists.
[8] A tenant.

8. Th.

Wrote to Sir J.G. Reached home before two. C.G. & the children looked so well. Read Gualterio. H. of C. $4\frac{3}{4}$–$7\frac{1}{4}$. & $9\frac{1}{2}$–$1\frac{1}{4}$. Saw Graham & others & we objected, but in vain, to the Committee on the Income Tax.[1] Went to work upon my mass of letters & papers.

9. Fr.

Wrote to J. Griffiths—Collis—G. & Co—Watson—Rickets—Fayerman[2]—Rev. Mr Andrew.[3] Catherine went to Hagley. Customs Commee.[4] & H. of C. $12\frac{1}{2}$–7.[5] Dined at Herberts with D. of Newcastle & Young: we agreed on leaving Urquhart's motion to itself.[6] Saw G. Hope—Rev. J. Gladstone—Mr G. Harcourt—Setting out about P. L[ightfoot] for whom it seems an obligation to inquire & if possible act, I fell in with Walters[7] in evg [R]: as well as others & I hope one act of evil was stopped. But for me there is a great blank to be filled.

10. Sat.

Wrote to T.G.—M. Wilson—Northcote—Walker—& Saunders. Northcote to breakfast. Saw Mr Green (Coalwhippers)[8]—T. Hayes (do)—Ld Aberdeen—Ld Blandford—Bp of Oxford (Col Ch) Saw also Archdn. Wilberforce. Commission (Exhib) 3–7. Worked on proofs of Farini. Searches & inquiries: with ill result, or none. Worked on my papers &c.

11. 3 S. Easter.

St Martin's mg. Bedfordbury Evg. Townsend on Gospel aloud. Wrote to Mr Church—W.C. James—Dr Döllinger—Mrs Craven—Rev. Mr Thomas. Saw Archdeacon Wilberforce—E. Badeley—Dr Döllinger— & crossed J. Hope on his stairs. Having mentioned that name I must here record the saddest effect wrought on me by the disasters crowned by his & M[anning']s secession: the loss of all *resolution* to carry forward the little self-discipline I ever had. Saw Walters [R]: without apparent result. Read H.J.G.s Tr. of Devotions for the Quarantore[9]—N. Brit. Rev. on Supremacy[10]—Mrs Craven's 'Mot'[11]—Alderson's Letters.[12]

[1] Opposed *Hume's motion for a select cttee. on income tax: *H* cxvi. 726.
[2] Unidentified.
[3] Probably John Chapman Andrew, b. 1822; fellow of Lincoln, Oxford, 1846–60; headmaster of Nelson College, New Zealand, 1860.
[4] The select cttee. on customs, which produced two reports and four volumes of evidence in 1851: *PP* 1851, xi. parts 1–4.
[5] *H* cxvi. 769: Ecclesiastical Titles Bill.
[6] *Urquhart's motion blamed the govt. for encouraging the Pope.
[7] A rescue case, but not Catherine Walters ('Skittles'), 1839–1920, who did not come to London until the late 1850s, and met Gladstone about 1865.
[8] Charles Green, Chairman of coalwhippers commission; opened evidence to cttee (6 June 51).
[9] An MS tr. of the devotional commemorating the period Christ's body lay in the tomb.
[10] *North British Review*, xv. 254 (May 1851); review of *Pusey, cp. 5 May 50.
[11] The MS of P. M. A. A. *Craven, 'Un mot de vérité sur la vie religieuse des femmes' (1855); a close friend of Helen, cp. Oct. 45.
[12] E. H. *Alderson published two letters to *Phillpotts (1851).

12. M.

Wrote to Rev. R. Eden—Overend Gurney & Co—Mr Browne. H.S. with the children. Worked on Farini Proof sheets. Exhibn. Commission at 3. House 5–7¼: & spoke briefly.[1] Dined at Bp of Oxford's. Queen's Concert afterwards.

13. T.

Wrote to H. Tayleur—A. Panizzi—J. Hays—Mansfield & Co—H. Lees—Mrs Gillow.[2] H.S. with Agnes & Stephen. House & family affairs. Saw A. Gladstone—Father Ignatius (Mr. Spencer) a long & singular conversation. worked on Farini. Dined at the Charterhouse & attended the Concert there.

14. Wed.

Wrote to J. Murray—G. & Co—R. Barker—Dean of Ch. Ch.—S.R.G.—Dalhousie—Heathcote—Flood[3] (2)—H.J.G.—G.C. Lewis—Andrew. H.S. with Agnes & S. R. Phillimore to breakfast & discussion on Oxford politics. Worked on Farini: alone, & with Panizzi at Br. Museum. H. of C. 3½–5½.[4] Saw C. Wood, Sir J. Graham, Herbert, on Income Tax Committee. 6¼–12. Went to Shadwell to Coalwhippers Meeting. Those Men were delightful to see & hear: apart from the excess of their grateful feeling towards me—which made me much ashamed. I spoke at some length. There was a great burst from me about Papal Aggression. Three working men made very powerful speeches: Newell, Barthorp & Applegate.

15. Th.

Wrote to Barker—Gaetano Feroce[5]—Lacaita—Fagan—Ld Eddisbury—V[ice] C[hancellor] Oxford—Jas Watson—H. Tayleur—Rev. J. Jones. Our first attempt at a breakfast in honour of Dr. Döllinger, we were eight & it did pretty well. H.S. with A. & S. Saw Mr Green—Mr Labouchere—Mr Hubbard—Mr Panizzi—Napier—Mr R. Barker—Sir J. Young—& attended at Cardwell's where we decided to refuse serving on the I. Tax Committee.[6] Saw Wood afterwards. H of C 4¾–7.[7] Dined at Ld Granville's: where Hope was. Lady Waldegrave's afterwards. Conv. with Duke of Argyll.

16. Friday.

Wrote to G.C. Lewis—Jacobson—R. Greswell—C. Marriott—J.B. Mozley—E. Stanley—Overends—J.A. Jackson—Rector of Exeter—E.C. Woollcombe—W. Pococke—R. Hussey—E. Monro—Carew O'Dwyer.[8]

[1] On Ecclesiastical Titles Bill: *H* cxvi. 882.

[2] Mary Anne, *née* Eyston, m. 1845 Richard Thomas Gillow, Lancashire landowner, and d. 1890.

[3] Perhaps John Flood, b. 1809; at Irish bar from 1834; cp. 11 Aug. 52.

[4] Religious Houses Bill: *H* cxvi. 938.

[5] Unidentified Italian.

[6] Cp. 8 May 51.

[7] Ecclesiastical Titles: *H* cxvi. 993.

[8] Andrew Carew O'Dwyer, 1800–77; barrister; liberal M.P. Drogheda 1832–4; much involved in catholic relief movement.

Read Stoddart on Supremacy. H.S. with A. & S. Saw Phillimore & Jefferies—Lincoln (on two political interviews). Exhibition for less than an hour. Customs committee 12¼–3½. H of C. & H of L. 5¼–6½[1]. Dinner & conv. alone at home. Worked on Farini

17. Sat.

Wrote to J. Murray. H.S. with the Children. Worked much on Farini proofs: & at B. Museum with Panizzi &c. 1–4. Ly F. Hope & others to dinner. Read Byng on Smithfield[2]—Corresp. on Govt. Books[3]—&c. Saw Mr Hubbard—Dr Döllinger. House of Mercy meeting 4½–6½.

18. 4. S. E[aster].

St Martins 11–2 (H.C.) & Chapel Royal 5.30—by Ashley's favour. Saw Dr Döllinger & had 2½ good hours conv. Dined with the Lytteltons Wrote to Hussey—E. Coleridge (2), and Willy. Read Meyrick on Ch. of Rome[4]—Tyler's Address to his Parishioners.[5] Read Townsend aloud in evg.

19. M.

Wrote to Kynaston—E. Hawkins—Aylwin[6]—Jacobson—Dean Moir—T.G.—Grant of Monymusk—A. Turner—D. Gladstone—Rev. Mr Henderson[7]—Spencer Phillips.[8] H.S. with W. & Agnes. House business & bills: but I go on from hand to mouth & am still in chaos. Saw E. Hawkins—S. Herbert—Lady Peel who broke once into a state of highly excited grief & seemed to use all her physical force with herself to keep it down. H. of C. 4¾–8¼ on Eccl. Titles Bill.[9] The Lytteltons dined here. Worked on Farini.

20. T.

Wrote to J. Murray (2). H.S. with A. & S. Worked on Farini—alone & with Panizzi. H. of C. 5½–7½.[10] Worked 'some' on accounts. Saw Hubbard—Mr & Mrs Andrew—Sir W. Heathcote—Mrs Tyler—J. Young—Ld Aberdeen (on finance Resolution).

[1] Ecclesiastical Titles: *H* cxvi. 1045.
[2] F. Byng, *Smithfield and Newgate markets* (1851).
[3] Perhaps *PP* 1851, liv. 124.
[4] F. Meyrick, *What is the working of the church of Spain? What is implied in submitting to Rome?* (1851).
[5] J. E. *Tyler, 'St. Giles-in-the-Fields: the rector's address to his parishioners' (1851).
[6] Possibly Aylwin, Bevan, Cole & Harris, produce brokers and warehouse keepers in Lower Thames Street.
[7] William George Henderson, 1819–1905; fellow of Magdalen, Oxford, 1847–52; junior proctor 1850–1; headmaster in Jersey 1852–62, in Leeds 1862–84; dean of Carlisle from 1884.
[8] William Spencer Phillips, 1795–1863; fellow of Trinity, Oxford, 1822–9; vicar of New Church, Isle of Wight, from 1830.
[9] Spoke: *H* cxvi. 1104.
[10] *H* cxvi. 1162.

21. Wed.

Wrote to Willy—J. Murray. H.S. as usual. Morning spent chiefly in bodily labour on my books. Exhibn. Medal Commee. at 2¼: & then went into the Exhibition, which is overwhelming. Read Dyce's proof to Ruskin.[1] Dined at Mr Greene's. Ld Londesbrough's[2] & then Lady Ashburton's afterwards. Saw J.N.G. about Tom's money matters.

22. Th.

Wrote to Overends—J.D. Coleridge—Sir G. Prevost—C. Stewart—W. Charnock[3]—W. Dyce—J. Hurtley[4]—Sir J. Forbes—D.E. Griffiths[5]—R. Barker—Watkin. H.S. with the children. 2d breakfast: 11 persons including Baron Dupin.[6] C. had an evening party. Meeting of Commission at 12. Exhibition afterwards. Worked much on my books: & reduced them at last to some order. H. of C. 9¼–11¼.[7] Worked on Farini revises. Saw Mr G. Burnett—Mr Labouchere.

23. Fr.

Wrote to Dr Russell[8]—H. Tayleur—Northcote—Bp of Salisbury—Williams & Co (Chester)—H.J.G. H.S. with A. & S.—Customs Commee. & House 1–7. I examined part of the Statistics of the two Oxford contests 1829 & 1847: the results are curious.[9] House again 11¾–1. Worked on Farini. Dined at Ld Ashburton's. Saw Ld Aberdeen—Canning.

24. Sat.

Wrote to J. Murray (2)—Bp of Oxford (for consn.) H.S. with A. & S. Worked on Farini. Read Ld Torrington's Speech[10]—Answer to Quarterly[11]—Pusey's Letter in MS.[12] Breakfasted with the Herbert's: conv. with Bp of Oxford on Papal Aggression. Saw Mr Oldfield on Caledonian affairs. Ld Aberdeen & S. Herbert on finance, & amended a draft Resolution. Read Virgil &c for Medal Inscription Committee wh met here at 4 P.M. Dined with the Wegg Prossers—Lady Palmerston's afterwards.

[1] W. *Dyce, 'Notes on shepherds and sheep: a letter to J. *Ruskin' (1851).

[2] Albert *Denison, *né* Conyngham, 1805–60, s. of 1st Marquis Conyngham; secretary of legation at Florence 1826, at Berlin 1829–31, liberal M.P. Canterbury 1835–41, 1847–50, took surname of Denison 1849; cr. Baron Londesborough 1850. Lived at 144 Piccadilly.

[3] A shopkeeper in Chester.

[4] Unidentified.

[5] Perhaps one of the Griffiths family involved in the Oak Farm.

[6] François Pierre Charles Dupin, 1784–1873; French economist and engineer; chaired French jury at the exhibition; senator 1852.

[7] *H* cxvi. 1234.

[8] John *Russell, 1786–1863; Christ Church; headmaster of Charterhouse 1811–32, D.D. 1820; rector of St. Botolph's, Bishopsgate, from 1832; president of Sion College 1845–46, treasurer of S.P.G.

[9] In 1829 *Inglis defeated *Peel, despite the latter's support from professors, first class men etc.; cp. Ward, 73.

[10] G. Byng, Lord Torrington, 'Speech . . . on the affairs of Ceylon in the House of Lords, April 1, 1851; with an appendix' (1851).

[11] Cp. 4 Dec. 47.

[12] Cp. Add MS 44370, f. 109: Philip *Pusey sent Gladstone an address for publication in the *Morning Chronicle* or *The Times*.

25. 5 S. E[*aster*].

Pimlico Chapel mg. St James's evg. MS. of Ascn. Day aloud in evg. Wrote to Hawkins—J.S.M. Anderson—& after showing my letter for Bp. of Oxford, dispatched it. Saw R. Cavendish—C. Marriott—Ph Pusey—D. of N[ewcastle] & S. H[erbert]—Walk with C. & the children. Read Hawkins's Sermons [1]—Andersons Sermons [2]—Peile's Letter [3]—Reformatio Legum.[4]

26. M.

Wrote to Dr Hawtrey—Hurtley—J. Griffiths—E. Bowring (with Medal Report) [5]—Mr Thomas.[6] H.S. with A. & S. Customs Commee. $12\frac{3}{4}$–$2\frac{1}{4}$. H. of C. $5\frac{1}{4}$–$7\frac{1}{4}$.[7] Dined at R. Cavendish's. Worked on Farini. Saw J.S. Wortley.

27. T.

Wrote to Ld Aberdeen. Read on Ceylon. H.S. with A. & S. Saw Hussey—Lyttelton—Murray. Worked on Farini—alone, & with Panizzi at B. Museum. H. of C. $4\frac{3}{4}$–$9\frac{3}{4}$ and $10\frac{3}{4}$–$12\frac{1}{4}$ on the Ceylon Debate.[8]

28. Th. [sc. *W.*]

Wrote to Ld Abn.—W.F. Larkins—Bp of Sydney—Berkeley—Burgess—Ld St Germans. H.S. with A. & S. Breakfasted with Mr [Samuel] Rogers: who is well & cheerful, his memory impaired for certain purposes. H. of C. $1\frac{1}{2}$–6.[9] Dined at Sir R. Inglis's: an University party. Saw P. Lightfoot [R] Worked on Farini. Read Roman papers &c.[10]

29. Th. Ascension Day.

St James's & H.C. 11–$1\frac{1}{2}$. Saw Mr Selby[11] Worked on Farini with Panizzi. Wrote to H. Tayleur—Bp of Oxford—H.J.G.—T.G. H. of C. $4\frac{3}{4}$–$7\frac{1}{4}$ and $8\frac{1}{2}$–$2\frac{3}{4}$ on Ceylon.[12] Spoke 1h. I have never returned home with an easier conscience & a more perfect conviction of having acted according to justice. Recommenced Farini Preface: the 3d or 4th.

[1] E. *Hawkins, *Sermons on scriptural types and sacramentals* (1851).

[2] James Anderson, *The present crisis: four sermons preached before the Society of Lincoln's Inn* (1851).

[3] T. W. Peile, 'The Church of England not high, not low, but broad as the commandment of God; a letter to Lord John *Russell' (1850).

[4] *Reformatio Legum Ecclesiasticarum, ex authoritate primum Regis Henrici VIII* (1571) or *Reformatio Legum proposita* (1650), heads of proposals of February 1649.

[5] Edgar Alfred Bowring, 1826–1910, s. of Sir J.*; librarian to B. of T. 1848–63; commissioner and occasional secretary to 1851 exhibition commission; liberal M.P. Exeter 1868–74.

[6] Perhaps George Fuller Thomas, tutor of Worcester, Oxford; vicar of Butler's Marston, Warwickshire.

[7] Ecclesiastical Titles: *H* cxvi. 1411.

[8] *H* cxvii. 6.

[9] *H* cxvii. 100: Audit of Railways Account Bill.

[10] Perhaps *Giornale di Roma* (1850). Cp. *North British Review*, xvi. 319 (February 1851).

[11] Cp. Add MS 44651, f. 228.

[12] *H* cxvii. 204; cp. Add MS 44651, ff. 225–30.

30. Fr.

Wrote to J. Young—Mr Temple—Scotts. Saw Herbert—Newcastle—Scotts—R. Cavendish. Meeting at Ld Aberdeen's on a Financial Motion. Exhibition Commission at 3 P.M. We took Stanley down to H. of L. & thought he looked old.[1] H. of C. 5–7½ and 10¾–11¾.[2] Worked a little on Farini.

31. Sat.

Wrote to H. Tayleur—Hurtley—Wm. G. H.S. with A. & S. Went to the birthday Drawingroom with C.[3]—Saw J.N.G. on Tom's matters &c—S. Herbert & Young—and two hours after midnight with them & Newcastle on the same subject. Went to Amateur Drawing's Exhibition.[4] Dined with the Herberts. Worked on Farini.

S. after Ascension June One.

St Martin's mg. & H.C.—St James's evg. MS of 42 aloud in evg.[5] Saw Duchess of Somerset about her brother Patrick's death.[6] We were awakened about four a.m. on acct. of Mary's having a fresh attack of croup. When Cape came about five, C. had already taken the right measures & procured vomiting. 3 doses of Calomel each two grains were given afterwards. She improved rapidly. There was however some return in evg. Read Wordsworth's Sermons.[7]—Wrights Letter[8]—Devotions.

2. M.

Wrote to O.B. Cole H.S. with A. & S. Worked on Farini—alone & with Panizzi. Breakfasted with the Herberts to meet Bp of Oxford & Mr Carter. 10 to dinner at home & evening party. Saw Ld Aberdeen—Ly Jersey. H. of C. 5–7½.[9]

3. T.

Wrote to Willy—B. Harrison—Mr Church—T.G.—Overends—Robbins. H.S. with A. & S. Saw J.N.G.—T. Moss—Bp of Oxford—on the Pusey fulmen.[10] House of Mercy meeting at Ld J. Manners's. Dined with the

[1] *Stanley was 52.

[2] Voted in 62 to 214 on first clause of Ecclesiastical Titles Bill: *H* cxvii. 259.

[3] Cp. *The Times*, 2 June 1851, 8a.

[4] An exhibition of sketches in the Hogarth Gallery in the Haymarket.

[5] Add MS 44779, ff. 234–38.

[6] Margaret, da. of Sir Michael Shaw-Stewart, 5th bart., m. 1836 as his 2nd wife Edward Adolphus *St. Maur, 1775–1855, 11th duke of Somerset; she d. 1880. Her brother, Patrick Maxwell Shaw-Stewart, had d. 30 October 1846. Cp. 31 July 33.

[7] C. *Wordsworth, *Occasional sermons preached in Westminster Abbey*, 2nd series, (1851).

[8] T. P. Wright, 'A letter to Christopher *Wordsworth, D.D., on the difficulties of his synodal theory in reference to his sermon on the authority and uses of church synods' (1851).

[9] Ecclesiastical Titles Bill: *H* cxvii. 344.

[10] *Wilberforce had censured *Pusey in November 1850 for his part in the *Dodsworth affair, and the row had continued with *Keble attempting to mediate; cp. Liddon, iii. 302ff.

Mildmays. Our little Mary's illness has now the character of gastric fever & is serious though I trust not quite alarming. Read Harrison's Charge[1]—Challis on Smithfield[2]—&c.[3]

4. Wed.[4]

H.S. with A. & S. Worked on Farini. Saw Bp of Argyll—the F. Nevilles[5]—J.N.G.—M.A. Larkins—Ld Aberdeen. This was a day of much anxiety about little Mary whose fever & sickness continue obstinate. In the evening thank God she was better. I dined with Ld Aberdeen.

5. Th.

Wrote to H.J.G.—Ramsbotham.[6] H.S. with A. & S. We had no less than twentyone to breakfast in the Drawingroom. Worked on Farini, alone & at B. Museum.—Saw Marriott. Read on Water Supply.[7] H. of C. 5–7½ and 10¾–1.[8] The improvement of last night thank God continued & became more decided.

6. Fr.

Wrote to Provost of Oriel—Warden of All Souls—Jos. Bennett—Rev. W.J.E. Bennett—R. Cavendish—H. Tayleur—Parker. Mary again striding on. Committees Customs & Coalwhippers 12½–3½.[9] At the Exhibition & business there. H of C. 9–11.[10] Read Heyworth's Pamphlet[11]—Worked on Farini.

7. Sat.

Wrote to Mr Macaulay—Freshfield—H.S. with S. & A. House business. Breakfast with Milnes to meet M. de Metz[12]—Saw Ld Aberdeen—Mr Bennett—Mr Woodgate. Finance Committee Exh[ibitio]n at 4—and Exhib[itio]n afterwards. Read Prize Essay.[13] Worked on Farini. Dined with the E.I. Co & home late. Spoke after dinner. Saw—Seymour [R].

[1] B. *Harrison, *fils*, 'The present position of the Church of England, and the consequent duties of her ministers' (1851).

[2] T. M. Challis, 'Smithfield and Newgate markets, as they should and might be. An answer to the Hon. F. Byng' (1851).

[3] The preface to the first volume of Gladstone's translation of Farini is dated this day.

[4] 'Wrote' here deleted.

[5] i.e. W. F. Neville and his wife Fanny Grace.

[6] Francis Henry *Ramsbotham, 1801–68, obstetrician at London hospital.

[7] Various reports on the London water supply are in *PP* 1851, xxiii. 67ff.

[8] Misc. business: *H* cxvii. 449.

[9] Select cttee. on Coalwhippers (Port of London) Bill: *PP* 1851, x. 1. Gladstone often lead the questioning.

[10] Ecclesiastical Titles Bill: *H* cxvii. 553.

[11] Probably L. Heyworth, 'On economic fiscal legislation' (1845).

[12] Frédéric Auguste de Metz, 1796–1873; French penal reformer; founded reformatory system 1840, campaigned for its introduction in Britain.

[13] Untraced.

8. Whitsunday.

York St Chapel & H.C. 11–1½, St James's evg. MS of 42 aloud. Saw Mr Fagan on Borneo. Walk with C. Read Mr Bennett's Farewell Letter.[1]

9. M.

St Andrews Wells St 5. P.M. Wrote to Panizzi—Macaulay—Mrs Cross[2]—W. Forbes—H. Tayleur. Saw Rn. G—& J.N.G. on Tom's matters. H.S. with A. & S. Worked on Farini. Worked on my mass of letters for the year wh are still in Chaos. Dined with the Wenlock's.

10. Whit. Tues.

St James's 11 a.m. Wrote to Mr Baxter—R. Cavendish—H.J.G.—Duke of Newcastle—Fayerman—Miss Watkins[3]—Mayor of Birm[ingha]m.[4] Worked on Farini: alone & with Panizzi: my last visit to him on that matter. Saw C. Christie—J. Murray—people about my dress for Friday. At 5½ went to see the Haddos[5] & Ld Aberdeen at Blackheath: where we passed a very quiet & pleasant evening. Read some of the Judicial papers come from P. Castelcicala.

11. Wed.

Wrote to Ld Aberdeen. Morning's conv. & walk with him chiefly. Read the Neapolitan papers—Wilberforce on Erastianism.[6] Back to town at 6: attended the Merch[ant] Tailors' dinner. Ld Stanley made I think the best after dinner speech I ever heard. Saw Collins[7]—Seymour—& a person from Stourbridge—in the first I was much interested [R].

12. Th.

Wrote to R. Wilberforce—Mrs Dawson—Tayleur—Jas Watson—Preshaw—Liddell. H.S. with Stephen. Breakfast party—dinner party—evening party—at home! Saw D. of Newcastle—Macaulay—Freshfield—Rn. G—J.N.G.—Scotts. Worked on Farini.

[1] W. J. E. *Bennett, 'A farewell letter to his parishioners' (1851).

[2] Perhaps Katherine Matilda, *née* Winn, m. 1846 William Assheton Cross, 1818–83, Lancashire landowner; she d. 1871.

[3] Mrs. Anne Watkins, who lived with Helen Gladstone.

[4] William Lucy, mayor of Birmingham 1849–51.

[5] George John James Gordon, 1816–64, styled Lord Haddo until 1860 when he succ. as 5th earl of Aberdeen; m. 1840 Mary Baillie, sister of 10th earl of Haddington; she d. 1900.

[6] R. I. *Wilberforce, *A sketch of the history of Erastianism together with two sermons on the reality of church ordinances and on the principle of church authority* (1851).

[7] E. Collins, another protracted rescue case.

13. Fr.

Wrote to H. Tayleur—Mr Denton[1]—Silk—Tathams—Lamond—H.S. with A. & S. Railway Arbitration first meeting at 11½ & H. of C. Committees to 4 P.M. H. of C. 7¼–9¾. but I was baulked of the Caffre debate.[2] Sent Murray the very last revises of Farini. Some little work about my dress: resisted moustaches, & the imperial dropped off. Got fairly mounted about 10½. We remained till the end, about two a.m.[3]

14. Sat.

Wrote to Hawkins—R. Baxter[4]—Sir J. Young—Mr Church—Mr Bennett—Sir J. Claridge. H.S. with the children. Read Tennyson. Saw T.S. Gladstone—W. Forbes—Ld Aberdeen—Clerk—S. Herbert—Newcastle. Went to the Exhibition with C. Dined at Sir J. Johnstones—Lady Palmerston's afterwards.

15. Trin[*ity*] *S.*

St Martin's & H.C. 11–2—MS of 41 aloud at night.[5] Bedfordbury at 7 P.M. Conv. with A. & S. C went off to Windsor at 2. Wrote to Bp of Argyll—Marshall—Hawkins. Read Bennett's Farewell (finished)—Bp of Argyll's Sermon[6]—Zincke on Education.[7] Saw E. Collins a second time & with the same feeling [R].

16. M.

Wrote to S.C. Denison—T.G.—Peer Ibrahim Khan. H.S. with the children. read Gualterio.[8] Worked on my letters. H. of C. 4¾–7.[9] Dined with the Cannings. Sad case of some flowergirls at night [R]. Meeting at Ld Aberdeen's 11–1: unsatisfactory indeed. Saw Newcastle afterwards—also Ld Aberdeen—Mr Currie.

17. T.

Wrote to J. Murray—Hathaway[10]—Taunton—V.C. Oxford—Peer Ibr[ahim] Khan—Twiss—Colonel Grey. Saw Hayman—J. Griffiths—Jas Watson—Mr Johnston (Alva). Worked on my letters. arranging for entertainments.

[1] William Denton, 1815–88; curate of Shoreditch 1847–50; vicar of St. Bartholomew, Cricklegate, from 1850.

[2] *H* cxvii. 737: debate on expenses of Kaffir war. Adderley withdrew his amendment.

[3] State ball at Buckingham Palace; the guests wore restoration costumes. Gladstone went as Sir Leoline *Jenkins, 1623–85, principal of Jesus, Oxford, and diplomat, with a reputation as a great stickler for forms.

[4] Robert Baxter, 1802–89; philanthropist; head of Baxter, Rose and Norton, parliamentary solicitors, 1845; founded Great Northern Railway 1846. His firm acted for the Tichborne claimant 1871.

[5] Add MS 44779, ff. 123–126.

[6] A. *Ewing, 'The Lamb of God, a sermon [on St. John i. 29]' (1849).

[7] F. B. *Zincke, 'Why must we educate the whole people? And what prevents our doing it' (1850).

[8] Cp. 8 Apr. 51.

[9] Misc. business: *H* cxvii. 778.

[10] Perhaps Edward Penrose Hathaway, barrister.

Coalwhippers Committee $1\frac{1}{4}$–$4\frac{1}{2}$. Walk with C. Dined with the Lindsays—Lady Colborne's and Mad. Bunsen's in evening. Got my first copies of Farini. Sent No 1 to the Prince: & wrote with sad feelings in those for Hope and Manning.[1] I also directed one to go to Mr Hume among others.

18. Wed.

Wrote to Willy—Mr Richardson—Mr Andrew—E. orfew.[2] H.S. with A. & S. Saw Mr Fagan—P. Ibrahim Khan & his Moonshee[3]—Mr Higgins—Sir J. Young. H of C. at 3. Went with C. to see pictures. Began the Scarlet Letter.[4] Dined with the Braybrookes: came home, put on Sir L. Jenkins once more & went with C. to Lady Ashburton's Ball.

19. Th.

Wrote to Col. Bowles[5]—Rector of Exeter—Mr Butlin—J. Walker—A. Maclean[6]—H. Tayleur—G and Co—Edouart.[7] H.S. with A. & S. A breakfast party of sixteen: incl. the Orientals. Saw Fergusson—Bp of Oxford—J. Griffiths—Dr Mill—D.G. Coleridge—J.N.G. H of C. 6–$7\frac{3}{4}$: Univ. motion. Counted out.[8] Music in evg. Read the Scarlet Letter.

20. Fr.

Wrote to Mr Lewis—Mahon—Liddell—Dawson—J.N.G.—H. Tayleur—Chr. Wordsworth. H.S with S. & A. Finished the Scarlet Letter: an extraordinary work full of poetry: it breaks down morally at the *end*. Read pamphlets. Committees $1\frac{1}{2}$–4. House 5–$7\frac{1}{4}$ and at night.[9] Dined with the Hoggs. Lady Molesworths Music afterwards. Miss Pym sang wonderfully.

21. Sat.

Wrote to Panizzi[10]—W.H. Richards. H.S. with A. & S. Music practice at 12. Saw Mr Parkinson—Ld Ingestre (Fulham)—Rn. G & J.N.G. on T.G's affairs & wrote memm.[11] Willy came up: an Exhibition visit: looking well: not much grown. Took him to Burford's Panorama.[12] Dined at Bp of London's, Fulham. I meet a squadron of Bishops now with much altered feelings. Lord Palmerston's afterwards: met Pantaleoni.[13]

[1] These two sentences in Morley, i. 405.
[2] This name apparently added later; unidentified.
[3] i.e. his secretary, Syed Abdullah.
[4] N. Hawthorne, *The scarlet letter: a romance* (Boston 1850, London 1851).
[5] (Sir) George *Bowles, 1787–1876, served in Peninsula; colonel of 1st West India regiment; master of Queen's household 1845–51; K.C.B. and lieutenant of tower of London 1851.
[6] Possibly Alexander Maclean, Lloyd's insurance broker.
[7] Augustin Gaspard Edouart, 1817–1905; curate of St. Paul's, Blackburn, 1841–50; vicar of St. Michael's, London, 1850–62, of Leominster 1862–96.
[8] Motion on religious tests: *H* cxvi. 1000.
[9] Spoke on Ecclesiastical Titles Bill: *H* cxvi. 1025.
[10] Part in Morley, i. 402.
[11] In Hawn P.
[12] Robert *Burford, 1791–1861, artist, exhibited in London panoramic views of chief places of interest in Europe.
[13] Diomede Pantaleoni, 1810–85; Roman physician and politician; involved in making of 1848 constitution; after 1849 toured Europe as propagandist for unity.

22. 1 S. Trin.

St Martin's mg. Bedfordbury evg. MS of 1840 aloud at night. Wrote to T.G.—and drafts & letters to Hope & Manning. Music. Read Xtn. Remr.[1]—Defence of Priv. Mass [2]—finished Helen's Translated Devotions.

23. M.

Wrote to T. Acland—Dr Hook [3]—Mr Macintyre [4]—Bennett—Hartley—Wickes [5]—Bowring—Kelly—Buckingham. Exhibition at 9 with Willy: till. In aftern. took him to Mr Wyld's Globe.[6] Saw Murray—Rn. G—S. Herbert—Cardwell—Clerk. Committee 1-3. Read the Seven Gables.[7] Lady Jersey's crush in evg.

24. T. St J. Baptist.

Titchfield St Chapel [8] 5. P.M. Wrote to Ld Aberdeen—Scott & Co—Dr Hawtrey. 9-11½ Exhibition with Willy. We left him there alone. Saw Mr Fletcher's pictures.[9] H of Charity Anniv. 3½ P.M. Coalwh[ippers] Commee. & House 1-3.[10]

25. Wed.

Wrote to C. Wordsworth—Mr M'Kenzie—Mrs Dawson—M. Macintyre. Off at 9 to the Exhibition with Willy & a family party. Chiefly among moving machinery. At 11½ went to the Mansion House to the Peel Models.[11] Thence to H. of C. & voted agt. Scots Univ. Bill on certain grounds.[12] Thence to Penit[entiar]y meeting.[13] A Gentleman dinner of 13. C.s evening party & music afterwards. Meeting of Medal Inscr. Committee at 5½. Mr Bennett at 6½—Wm. Gladstone.

[1] *Christian Remembrancer*, xxi. 241 (June 51); perhaps the review of C. *Merivale, *History of the Romans under the Empire* (1850).

[2] T. *Cooper, *An answer in defence of the truth against the apology of private mass, to which is prefixed the work answered, entitled 'An apology of private mass' ed. W. *Goode* (1850).

[3] Cp. Lathbury, i. 122-3.

[4] Perhaps William MacIntyre, 1792-1857; Harley Street specialist on diabetes.

[5] Perhaps William Wickes.

[6] James *Wyld, 1812-87; geographer; liberal M.P. for Bodmin 1847-52, 1857-62, exhibited his 'great globe' in London 1851-62.

[7] N. Hawthorne, *The house of seven gables* (1851).

[8] W. U. *Richards' Margaret Street chapel was in Titchfield Street while *Butterfield was building All Saints.

[9] Ralph Fletcher, 1791-February 1851; Gloucester surgeon; his pictures were auctioned by Christie's, cp. *The Times*, 24 June 1851, 12b.

[10] Misc. business: *H* cxvii. 1140.

[11] For a memorial statue.

[12] *H* cxvi. 1210.

[13] About the Clewer house of mercy.

26. Th.

Wrote to Tayleur—G. & Co—Murray (& copy)[1]—Bickers—J. Young—& J. Griffiths. 17 to breakfast. Then off to Harrow Speeches. Back at five: & to H. of C.[2]—Dined with Ld Robert Grosvenor. Saw Mr Kennaway—Bp of Oxford—Ld Aberdeen—Wilson Patten—E. Hawkins—C.A. Wood. Read Denarius.[3] In evg. walks this week I have seen several to whom I have offered advice: but slightly [R].

27. Fr.

Wrote to J. Murray (& copy)[4]—Dr Hook—Jas Watson—R. Barker (2)—C.B. Adderley—J.N.G.—E. Collins [R]. Saw Christie (& gave him certain commissions)—J. Young—D. of Newcastle—E. Collins 1½ h. Dined at Ld Manvers's. Coalwh[ippers] & Cust[oms] Commee. 1½–4: House to 7¼.[5] Read Denarius—Seven Gables.

28. Sat.

Wrote to J. Murray & copy.[6] H.S. with the children. Read the Seven Gables. Saw Mr Bushe—Mr J. Paxton.[7] Exhibition (agric. implements with Mr Miles) 12–3. Dined with the W. Egerton's. Physicians afterwards—then Lady Waldegraves.

29. 2 S. Trin.

St Martin's H.C. 8½ a.m.–11 a.m.—York St 3. P.M. Read Townshend aloud (S. Peter) at night. Read Palin[8]—Cooper on Priv. Mass. Saw W.C. James—J. Talbot—Dined with the Wenlock's.

30. M.

Wrote to Mr G. Burnett—G.A. Denison—Mr Hyatt. Exhibition 9–12½: sitting to Mr Selous during some part of the time.[9] Read Robins's Speech[10]—Bp of Glasgow's Letter.[11] H of C. 4¾–7½ and 8½–12. Spoke for Disraeli's Resolution, and voted in 129:242.[12] Saw [blank.]

[1] Part in Barnes, *Free trade in books*, 76–77.
[2] Voted in 126 to 49 against *Roebuck's motion on Danish claims: *H* cxvi. 1253.
[3] Denarius, 'Shall we keep the Crystal Palace and have riding and walking in all weathers among flowers, fountains, and sculpture?' (1851).
[4] Part in Barnes, op. cit., 77–78.
[5] Ecclesiastical Titles Bill: *H* cxvi. 1313.
[6] Part in Barnes, op. cit., 78.
[7] (Sir) Joseph *Paxton, 1801–65; gardener at Chatsworth 1826, architect of Crystal Palace 1850.
[8] W. Palin, *History of the Church of England, 1688–1717* (1851).
[9] Henry Courtney Selous, 1803–93; artist; his painting of the opening of the 1851 exhibition is in South Kensington Museum.
[10] S. Robins, 'Speech delivered at the meeting of the National Society, June 4, 1851' (1851).
[11] W. J. Trower, 'A pastoral letter to the clergy of the diocese of Glasgow and Galloway' (1851); on Scottish bps. and presbyterians.
[12] *Disraeli's motion was on the Inhabited House Duty Bill: *H* cxvii. 1446.

Tuesday July One 1851

Wrote to Davies—Goodfellow[1]—J. Griffiths—J. Bennett—Laurie—A. Gordon[2]—Dr Weedall[3]—W.H. Readett. Coalwh[ippers] Comm. & House $2\frac{1}{2}$–$6\frac{3}{4}$ and $8\frac{1}{4}$–12.[4] Worked on arranging my letters since last summer to this date: wh are now at length in order. Read Cape papers.[5] H.S. with the children.

2. Wed.

Wrote to H. Glynn—C.B. Adderley—E. Collins—Sir J.G.—H.J.G. Exhibition (with C.s Bedfordbury people &c) 9–$10\frac{3}{4}$. Saw Mr R. Barker—E. Collins 2 hours [R]. H. of C. $12\frac{1}{2}$–$1\frac{3}{4}$.[6] At Lady Londonderry's party: saw the pictures & Statues: Canova's fine Theseus.[7] Dined with the Wenlocks. Busy hanging pictures.

3. Th.

Wrote to [blank.] H. of C. $4\frac{1}{2}$–$6\frac{1}{2}$.[8] H.S. with the children. Eighteen to breakfast. Conv. with Mr Rintoul: & then till 2. P.M. with A. de Vere on the Church. Dined with M. de Sallandrouze[9] the French Commr. a large party almost all foreign. In the evg. we heard a boy of the name Jullien, a Parisian, play wonderfully on the Violin.[10] Read Bp of Glasgow's Letter.

4. Fr.

Wrote to Northcote—E. Collins [R]—Medicine & in bed during the forenoon. H. of C. $4\frac{3}{4}$–7 and 9–$10\frac{1}{2}$.[11] Spoke on Eccl. T. Bill, after the surprise; & went off immedy. to meet E. Collins who did not come then or later in evg [R]. Attended & spoke at the Clewer House of Mercy meeting. Saw Coleridge. Finished Seven Gables.

[1] Perhaps Stephen Jennings Goodfellow; physician and lecturer at Middlesex hospital.

[2] (Sir) Arthur Charles Hamilton-*Gordon, 1829–1912, *Aberdeen's youngest son; private sec. to his father 1852–5, to Gladstone 1858; succ. F. Lawley as Peelite M.P. Beverley 1854; fruitlessly loved Agnes Gladstone; governed colonies 1861–90; K.C.M.G. 1871; cr. Baron Stanmore 1893; biographer of his fa. and S. *Herbert. Cp. Add MSS 44319–22, some printed in *Transactions of American Philosophical Society* (1961), n.s. li, part 4.

[3] Henry *Weedall, 1788–1859; president of St. Mary's College, Oscott, 1826 and from 1853; D.D. 1829; occasional vicar-apostolic for various English regions.

[4] Misc. business: *H* cxviii. 22.

[5] On the annexation of the Orange River: *PP* 1851, xxxvii. 341.

[6] Misc. business: *H* cxviii. 104.

[7] By Antonio Canova, 1757–1822; neo-classical painter and sculptor; carved his 'Theseus and the Minotaur' 1787, now in the Victoria and Albert museum.

[8] *H* cxviii. 142: misc.

[9] He invited the commissioners to the 1851 exhibition to attend the Paris fête in August 1851.

[10] Jean Lucien Adolphe Jullien, 1845–1932; b. in Paris of a musical family; later a musicologist and composer.

[11] *H* cxviii. 260. He followed *Russell.

5. Sat.

Wrote to Pemberton. Exhibition & Commission 9–3. Ten to dinner at home & evg. party—Lady Hollands at 6 P.M. Saw Newcastle on various questions for the H. of Lords. (My journal has lagged a little & is consequently lean) Read Bowen on Ionian Islands.[1]

6. 3. S. Trin.

York St mg—H.C. at St Martins afr. Bedfordbury in evg. & a visit to two of C.s old people. MS of 46 aloud at night. Read Palin—Wilberforce's Charge[2]—do on Erastianism—Xtn Remembrancer.[3] Wrote on Wilberforce.[4]

7. M.

Wrote to E. Collins (2) Earl of Aberdeen[5]—Prince Castelcicala—Panizzi—Mr Durham[6]—Wm. Gladstone—Bp of Oxford—C. Marriot—Mr Stooks—Wordsworth. Exhibition 8¾–11¼: with another Bedfordbury Batch. Calls. saw Mr Tyler: I much doubt of his recovery.[7] H. of C. 5½–6½.[8] Saw E. Collins at night: and closed with advising a day visit & appeal to C for advice [R]. Finished & sent off to C. Wordsworth my hurried paper on Wilberforce

8. T.

Wrote to Mr Hallam—Jas. Watson—J. Murray—G. & Co—Farquhar—E. Hawkins—Dr Jacobson—Bickers & Bush—E. Collins. 8¼–10¼ at the R. Academy. 1–3 Coalwhippers Committee. 10½–12. Breakfast with Milnes & the Bride[9]—Dined with the Wenlock's. Lady Arundel's[10] afr. & saw him. Then saw E.C. but did not advance in the matter [R]. Read Gambardella on the Glass Palace[11] &c.—Worked on accounts.

9. Wed.

Worked on accounts. H.S. with the children. 10½–4 to Harrow Weald with C., S. Herbert, & Mr A Court; a great interest & a great wonder. Saw E. Hill. Went at 7¼ to the Guildhall party.[12] Back at 2¼. I committed this error from having been told the Emperor of Russia wd be there: as I reckon him a sight worth much.

[1] G. F. *Bowen, *Mount Athos, Thessaly, and Epirus: a diary of a journey from Constantinople to Corfu* (1850).

[2] R. I. *Wilberforce, 'The evangelical and tractarian movements: a charge to the clergy of the East Riding' (1851).

[3] *Christian Remembrancer*, xxii. 1 (July 1851); probably the review of W. Hanna, *Life of *Chalmers*, 2 v. (1849–50).

[4] Not found.

[5] Part in Morley, i. 399 n.

[6] Joseph *Durham, 1814–77, sculptor.

[7] *Tyler d. three months later.

[8] Misc. business: *H* cxviii. 286.

[9] On 31 July 1851 *Milnes married Lady Annabel, da. of 2nd Baron Crewe; she d. 1874.

[10] At 3 Cork Street.

[11] S. Gambardella, 'What shall we do with the glass palace? A letter addressed to the commissioners of the great exhibition' (1851).

[12] An entertainment to celebrate the success of the exhibition.

10. Th.

Wrote to H.J.G.—C. Marriott—Sir W. Temple—Col. Malcolm—Mr Clowes—Mr Murray—Earl of Aberdeen. Saw Dr Pusey 9–10: not to me satisfactory about conciliatory steps.[1] Saw Ld Abn. & agreed to put off the publication till Tuesday. Some 24 to breakfast. Sir C. Eastlake[2] & others were pleased with the new Wilson[3] & other things. Corrected the proofs of my letter to Ld Abn. Read Borneo papers.[4] Dined with the J. Wortley's. H. of C. 5–7¾ and 9½–12¾: spoke on the Borneo affair, a sad one to me.[5]

11. Fr.

Wrote to Ld Aberdeen—Mr C. Butler[6]—Mr Carrington[7]—Dr Hawtrey. H.S. with the children. Saw Ld Aberdeen (Naples) Dined at Ld Aylesbury's. H. of C. 5–7½ and 11–12. Spoke on Education Vote.[8] With C. at Great Exhibition. (Journal defective)

12. Sat.

Wrote to Mrs Kiernan.[9] C. & the children went. Exhibition, after breakfast in B. Square, to 11½. Dined at Mr Harcourt's. Looked for E.C. afterwards [R]: but non inv[eni].[10] Began my Second Letter to Ld Aberdeen.[11] Saw Pr. Frederick of Holstein[12] (Journal again defective)

13. 4 S. Trin.

Breakfast with the Wortleys—Mr Richards's Chapel & H.C.—then to Ld Aberdeen's about Naples. & perused Fortunato's Dispatch[13]—thence to St Paul's at 3.15 & home. Saw S. Lawley—Panizzi—Read Bp of Ripon's letter.[14] Worked a little on my letter. Townsend aloud in evg. Dined with

[1] Cp. 3 May 51 n.

[2] Sir Charles Loch *Eastlake, 1793–1865, keeper of National Gallery 1847, director from 1855; kt. 1856; president of Royal Academy from 1850; an 1851 exhibition commissioner.

[3] Cp. 11 Apr. 32.

[4] On British reprisals in Borneo: *PP* 1851, lvi. 145ff.

[5] Spoke and voted in 230 to 19 against *Hume's motion on *Brooke's conduct in Borneo: *H* cxviii. 484. Cp. Add MS 44651, f. 231.

[6] Probably Charles Robert Butler, 1805?–78; Worcester, Oxford; curate of Catherington, Hampshire; vicar of Porchester 1857–70, of Newchurch from 1870.

[7] Probably Henry Carrington 1814–1906; Caius, Cambridge; dean and rector of Boching, Essex, from 1845; painter and musician.

[8] *H* cxviii. 615, 619.

[9] The wife of Francis Kiernan, 1800–75; physiologist; F.R.S. 1836; collected religious engravings.

[10] 'did not find her'.

[11] W. E. Gladstone, 'A second letter to the earl of *Aberdeen on the state prosecutions of the Neapolitan Government', published on 17 July 1851.

[12] Prince Frederick Christian Augustus of Schleswig-Holstein-Sonderburg-Augustenburg, 1829–80, duke of Augustenburg; protested against Danish succession laws 1849; proclaimed himself Frederick VIII of Schleswig-Holstein 1863, precipitating a crisis; opposed by Bismarck, he left the duchies 1866. He m. *Victoria's half-sister.

[13] Cp. Bassett, 84.

[14] C. T. *Longley, 'A letter to the parishioners of St. Saviour's, Leeds, with an appendix of documents' (1851).

the Herberts: in B. Square. Went with a note to E.C.s—received (unexpectedly) & remained 2 hours [R]: a strange & humbling scene—returned & ℏ[1]

14. M.

Wrote to J. Murray—Prince Castelcicala—C.G.—Ld Palmerston—Panizzi. 10 to breakfast—my last. Worked much on my second Letter—& finished & corrected it. Saw Bp of Oxford—Ld Aberdeen. H. of C. 5–$7\frac{1}{4}$[2] and at home in evg. except a short time looking for E.C.[R].

15. T.

Wrote to Ld Aberdeen—Ld Hobart[3]—C.G.—Tayleur—Swift—Monro—Haddan—J. Griffiths—Rn. G. H. of C $1\frac{1}{2}$–3.[4] Saw Mr Green—Sugar Reforms—Mr Morris Moore (& his picture).[5] At Br. Museum to peruse the Modena Edict.[6] Attended board of Parish overseers about my house. Attended the Dentist & saw the D[owage]r D[uche]ss of Beaufort. Milnes Gaskell dined with me. Corrected proofs. Fell in with E.C. & another mixed scene somewhat like that of 48 hours before [R]— ℏ afterwards.

16. W.

Wrote to P. Lightfoot—Panizzi—C. Marriott—Oxenham—C.G.—Adams (Office of Woods). 9–$11\frac{1}{2}$ Exhibition, with the Braybrookes. Mr Crampton dentist at 3. Saw J.N.G.—Mr Monro—(& arranged with him!) Dined at Grillion's Saw P. L[ightfoot] in evg: who has refused to have any more to say to Mr B., lives at home in regular work under a person named Simpson at 25/ per week, & promised me to go to the service at Bedfordbury [R]. This is a great blessing. Corrected the proofs of my Second Letter to Ld Abn. Read N. Br. Rev. on Italy.[7]

17. Th.

Wrote to J. Murray—J.R. Godley—C.G.—Ld Ellenborough—Phillimore—Panizzi—Bourne—Lear—Westhead[8]—Hayward—Bowdler. Saw Mr Hogg—B. Rothschild. Wrote on the Roman question. H of C. $4\frac{1}{2}$–$9\frac{1}{2}$. Spoke on the Horfield case.[9] Went to Mr Ellison's in the evening. Read Bowen on Ithaca[10]

[1] See above iii. xlvii.
[2] Spoke on the Horfield Manor case: *H* cxviii. 660.
[3] Vere Henry *Hobart, 1818–75, eldest son of 6th earl of Buckinghamshire, clerk in B. of T. 1840–61, governed Madras from 1872.
[4] Misc. business: *H* cxviii. 777.
[5] He wished to show Gladstone a Madonna believed to be by Michelangelo.
[6] 'Edict of 18 April 1832' dealing with the punishment accorded to political prisoners; cp. Add MS 44739, f. 24.
[7] 'Rome and the Italian revolution', *North British Review*, xiv. 319 (February 1851).
[8] Joshua Procter Brown-Westhead, 1807–77; liberal M.P. Knaresborough 1847–53, York 1857–65, 1868–71. Cp. 13 July 51.
[9] He defended the bp. of Gloucester: *H* cxviii. 946.
[10] G. F. *Bowen, *Ithaca in 1850* (1850).

Sir John Gladstone, bart., in old age
calotype by D. O. Hill and R. Adamson

Sir Robert Peel in 1842
from a portrait by John Wood

James Hope (-Scott) and Henry Edward Manning
both drawings by George Richmond.
'. . . the rending and sapping of the Church, the loss of its gems . . .'

London July 1851. 83.

15. T. Wrote to Ld Aberdeen—Ld Har-
dinge—C.G.—Taylor—Swift—Mur-
ray—Haddan—J. Griffiths—V.G.
H. of C. 1½–3.
Saw Mr Green—Sugar Reforms.
Mr Munro's Swan (this pattern)—
At Br. Museum to peruse
the modern Edict—
Attended Board of Parish Over-
seers about my house—
Attended the Dentist Hawke
S. Dss of Beaufort—
Mrs Gaskell dined with us.
Corrected proofs—
Fell in with E.C. Hamilton
wicked read somewhat like
that of 48 hours before—& after-
wards.

16. W. Wrote to P. Lightfoot—
Panizzi—C. Marriott—Ken-
ham—C.G.—Adams (Office
of Woods)—
9–11½ Exhibition, with the
Braybrookes.
The Crampton dentist at 3.
Saw J.N.G.—the money (& arranged with him!)
Dined at Grillion's
Saw P. Lacey: who has refused
to have any want to say to the
B., lives at home in regular
work under a prison warrant
Simpson at 25/ per week, &
promised me to go to Mr Ser-
ter at Bedfordbury. This is
a great blessing.
Corrected the proofs of my
second letter to Ld Abn.
Read N. Br. Rev. on Italy.

17 Th. Wrote to J. Murray—J.
R. Godley—C.G.—Ld Ellenborough—
Phillimore—Panizzi—Bruce—
Lear—Whitehead—Hayward—Bowd-
ler—
Saw Mr Hogg—B. Rothschild.
Wrote on the Roman ques-
tion—
H. of C. 4½–9½. Spoke on
the Hatfield case.
Went to Mr Ellison's in the
evening.
Read Brown on Ithaca.

18 Fr. Wrote to A. Munro—Ld
Aberdeen—C.G.—J.G.—Rev. J.
Gladstone—G. Burnett—C.
Butler—Jones—Ludlam—
Bowen—Swift—
Saw Ld Aberdeen—Bp of Ox-
ford—J. Murray—Harrison—Ph. Pusey
Read Pyrrho—Q.R. on Mac-
farlane—on Ld Beaumont—
H. of C. 4¼–6½.] Salmons—
9–11½ with the Jameses at the
Great Exhibn.

15–18 July 1851
facsimile of Lambeth MS 1430, f. 83

Agnes
drawing by G. Richmond

Catherine Jessy, died April 1850
portrait by G. Hayter

Mary
drawing by K. Hartmann

Helen (Lena)
drawing by K. Hartmann

18. Fr.

Wrote to A. Munro[1]—Ld Aberdeen—C.G.—T.G.—Rev. J. Gladstone—G. Burnett—C. Butler—Jones—Ludlam—Bowen—Swift. Saw Ld Aberdeen —Bp of Oxford—J. Murray—Horseman—Ph. Pusey. Read Pycroft[2]—Q.R. on Macfarlane[3]—on Ld Beaumont[4]—Salomons.[5] H. of C. 4¼–6½.[6] 9–11½ with the Jameses at the Great Exhibn.

19. Sat.

Wrote to F. Adams[7]—Coleridge—B. Wilson[8]—Adderley—C.G.—Rev. J.G. (O.S.)—J. Murray.

Mr Cantwell (Surveyor) at 8½. Mr Hubbard's to breakfast about Harrow Weald—then sat to Mr Selous in the Exhibition at 10—at 11 went to Mr Swifts about the railway arbitration[9]—at 12 to H. of C.—spoke about the Chapter of Windsor, & the Colonial Church[10]—home at 2¾.—Saw T.G. Read Q.R. on Ld Beaumont—on Rome.[11] Dined at Dowr. D[uche]ss Beaufort's[12]—Lady Palmerston's afterwards. Saw nothing of E.C. on looking [R].

20. 5 S. Trin.

St Martin's & H.C. mg. Chapel Royal evg. Townsend aloud at nt. Wrote a paper of points agt. the E[cclesiastical] T[itles] Bill for Ld Aberdeen.[13] Saw Newcastle—J.N.G.[14] Read Moral & Rel. Guide to Exhibn.,[15] Miss Smiths Five years a Catholic; & Beguilement to Romanism.[16] Dined with the Herberts.

[1] Alexander *Munro, 1825–71; sculptor, exhibited portrait-busts including Gladstone at Royal Academy from 1849. Gladstone commissioned work from him which was exhibited at the Royal Academy, cp. 12 Feb. 52 and 13 Oct. 54.

[2] J. W. Pycroft, 'The Oxford University Commission. A letter addressed to Sir *Inglis . . .' (1851).

[3] *Quarterly Review*, lxxxiv. 501 (March 49), 501–48; review of C. MacFarlane, *A glance at revolutionised Italy*, 2 v. (1849).

[4] ibid. lxxxv. 225 (June 1849); review of Lord Beaumont, *Austria and Central Italy*, 2 ed. (1849).

[5] One of the many pamphlets on the *Salomons case; see next n.

[6] *Salomons' refusal to take the oath of abjuration: *H* cxviii. 979.

[7] Frederick Morice Adams, 1828–71; Exeter, Oxford: curate of Stoke Cannon, Devon; rector of Teffont Ewyas, Wiltshire, from 1866.

[8] Benjamin Wilson, b. 1810; Magdalen Hall, Oxford; curate of Fordham, Middlesex, 1850; published sermons and tracts; corresponded with Gladstone until 1874; d. *ca.* 1880.

[9] i.e. John Swift; cp. 26 Aug. 51.

[10] *H* cxviii. 1035, 1040.

[11] *Quarterly Review*, lxxxv. 563 (September 1849).

[12] 45 Grosvenor Square.

[13] *Aberdeen opposed the bill in the Lords on 21 July 1851: *H* cxviii. 1072.

[14] Instead of 'T.G.'.

[15] *The theology and morality of the Great Exhibition as set forth in certain leading articles in the 'Times' and 'Record' newspapers* (1851).

[16] Eliza Smith, *Five years a Roman catholic with incidents of foreign convent life* (1850) and *Progress of Beguilement to romanism: a personal narrative* (1850).

21. M.

Wrote to D[owage]r Dss. Beaufort—Ld Aberdeen—Clowes—C.G.—G. & Co—Supt. S.E. Railway. At 8½ to Exhibn. Thence at 10½ to Newcastle's. Home at 11½ to see Dr Todd & others on attorney's Bill—then T.G. & J.N.G. on business—Adderley—Chairman of L.N.W,[1] Mdd,[2] & G.N. Companies.[3] Prepared some things for departure. H. of C. 3¾–8¼ and 9½–10½. again at 11.[4] Saw E.C. again in the same manner: and did not ℏ afterwards: thinking there was a change [R].

22. T.

Wrote to Ed. M. Chronicle—Mr Pycroft[5]—Mr Clarke—Mr Hudson (Manchr.)—Linton—Dean Torry—C.G.[6]—Rn. G—W.R. Farquhar—E. Collins [R]—Dowr. Dss. Beaufort—J. Lefevre. At 8½ to Exhibn.—thence at 10½ to Dentist. Saw E. Coleridge. H of C. 5–8¼ and 10¼–1: on the Jew admission.[7] Read Quarterly, Italian Articles.[8] Worked on arranging books &c.

23. Wed.

Wrote to E. Monro—J. Murray—Ed M.C.—Mrs Wadd.[9] Saw Newcastle on N.Z.—on his Divorce question—then Mr Sewell & others on N Zealand Bill—then shopping. Saw Phillimore—about Canning. Visited Mrs Wadd. At Botan. Garden Conversazione. Read Q.R. on B. Cochrane—Louis Philippe[10]—Address &c of the Friends of Italy.[11] Dined with Mr B. Westhead at the Clarendon[12] to meet the Am[erica]n Minister[13] & Ld Palmerston. I did not think the former very wise. I returned thanks for H. of C.: Cardwell better for the law. At half past twelve I came away; the first to do so.[14] I then in a singular way hit upon E.C.: two more hours, strange, questionable, or more [R]: followed by ℏ. Whether or not I have been deluded in the notion of doing good by such means, or whether I have sought it through what was unlawful I am not clear. God grant however not for my sake that the good may be done.

[1] George Carr Glyn. Cp. 11 Mar. 41 n.
[2] George *Hudson, chairman of the Midland railway. Cp. 10 July 44.
[3] E. *Denison; on the arbitration, cp. 26 Aug. 51.
[4] *Salomons' case: *H* cxviii. 1143.
[5] Probably James *Pycroft, 1813–95; perpetual curate of St. Mary's, Barnstaple, 1845–56; cricketer.
[6] Part in Bassett, 84.
[7] *H* cxviii. 1320.
[8] *Quarterly Review*, lxxxvii. 533, 557 (September 1850); review of Baillie Cochrane, *Young Italy* (1850).
[9] And a note to his wife, fragment in Bassett, 84.
[10] *Quarterly Review*, lxxxvii. 274 (June 1850).
[11] Not found.
[12] The Clarendon Hotel, New Bond Street.
[13] Abbot Lawrence, 1792–1855; endowed Harvard science school 1847; U.S. ambassador in Britain 1849–52.
[14] No report traced.

24. Th.

Wrote to C. Butler—C.G.—Dr Pusey—Mr Urquhart—J. Murray—Mr Kilburn [1]—E. Wardell—J.H. Thomas—Supt. S.R. Railway [2]—Durham—Whytock—Wakeman—Masson—Panizzi. Saw Mr Fox (N.Z.) [3]—W.C. James—Lord Aberdeen—Cardwell on NZ—Mr Hawes on do. Read Col Rawden on N[ational] Gallery [4]—Pacca—& pamphlets. H. of C. 5–7½ and 10–3. Spoke on N.Z. Bill.[5]

25. Fr. St James.

Wrote to C.G.—Rev. R. Wilson—Count [U.] Marioni [6]—Jas Watson—Mr Trahern.[7] H. of C. 12–2.[8] Saw Newcastle—Scotts—Mrs Tyler. Examined South Australian Acts.[9] Arranged papers &c. Dined at Stafford House: & found the elder as well as the younger Duchess [10] very agreeable. Lady Grey's afterwards. Read Medical Man on Cr. Palace.[11] Saw Dudley Gallery.

26. Sat.

Wrote to C.G.—Stephen—Marioni P.S.—Sallandrouze. Saw J.A. Smith. Read Stanley on W.I.[12] At 10½ to Crystal Palace to meet the D[owage]r Duchess of Beaufort. Again at 2 for the Commission—at 4 to Holland House. At 8 dined with the Wortleys—Lady Palmerston's afterwards. Saw Panizzi. Calls.

27. 6. S. Trin.

York St & H.C. mg. Chapel Royal aft. Townsend aloud evg. Wrote to Dr Pusey—Dr Mill—Col. Reid.[13] Saw Newcastle—R. Phillimore—Ph Pusey. Dined with J.N.G.s Read Wilson's Sermons [14]—Davies Morgan (Vol II) on Laws of Divorce.[15] Plagued since last [16] nt. with a return of neuralgia.

[1] Possibly William Edward Kilburn of the Isle of Wight, a later correspondent.

[2] James Hunter Tasker, superintendent of Scottish and Midland Junction Railway.

[3] (Sir) William Fox, 1812–93; barrister; emigrated 1842; political agent at Nelson, New Zealand 1843; prime minister of New Zealand 1856–62, 1869–72, 1873; K.C.M.G. 1879.

[4] J. D. Rawdon, 'Letter to the Trustees of the National Gallery' (1851).

[5] *H* cxviii. 1389.

[6] Friend of Sir W. James and involved in Neapolitan politics; had written on Nisida prison; Hawn P.

[7] John Montgomery *Traherne, 1788–1860, antiquary; chancellor of Llandaff from 1843.

[8] Misc. business: *H* cxviii. 1531.

[9] Probably those in the governor's report for 1850: *PP* 1851, xxxiv. 99.

[10] The duchess of *Sutherland's 1st. daughter, Elizabeth Georgiana, 1824–1878, m. 1844 8th duke of *Argyll.

[11] 'A medical man's plea for a winter garden in the Crystal Palace' (1851).

[12] E. G. G. Smith-*Stanley, *Farther facts connected with the West Indies: a second letter to W. E. Gladstone* (1851).

[13] (Sir) William *Reid, 1791–1858, in royal engineers; governed Bermuda 1839–46, Windward Islands 1846–8, Malta from 1851; K.C.B. 1851; major-general 1856.

[14] Benjamin Wilson, 'Plain sermons on the doctrine and offices of the Church of England', 2 v. (1850–53).

[15] Cp. 7 Feb. 50.

[16] Instead of 'Friday'.

28. M.

Wrote to Scotts—Rev. J. Gladstone—C.G.—Kay Shuttleworth—Rev. B. Wilson—G. Burnett—and [blank.] Worked on Extracts from Pacca. Saw Mr Moore of the I.L. News to be Catechised & sat to Mr Claudet the Daguerrotypist[1]—Saw Pusey—Newcastle—Fox. Worked on books, papers &c. preparing for departure. Finished Stanley's letter. H. of C. 5–7½ and 12–2¼. Spoke on the N.Z. & Railway Bill.[2] Dined at Holland House: conv. with Ld Clancarty,[3] & Mrs Norton.

29. T.

Wrote to C.G.—Collis (Telegraph)—Rn. G.—J. Swift. Saw E. Nelson.[4] Read Gualterio—Ruskin's Stones of Venice.[5] Willy arrived to be examined. Saw Coleridge. Took Willy to H. of L. and H. of C. Busy arranging papers.

30. Wed.

Wrote to C.G.—H. Tayleur—Ld Shaftesbury (2)—Col Reid—Mrs Wadd—Dr Beaven—E.G. Wakefield—Archd. Churton—G. Sumner[6]—W. Clarke—F. Petruccelli.[7] Read Churton's Charge.[8] Coleridge busy with Willy in the forenoon. Took him to Exhibn. in afternoon 4–6½. Saw Mrs Wadd—Colin MacKenzie[9]—Ld Nelson—Rintoul & others on N. Zealand. H. of C. 12–3½ on Ch. building Bill &c.[10] We got the N.Z. matter I hope settled. At College of Physicians in evg.[11] Much dismayed at 11 P.M. by a renewed invitation to Paris to help to represent the Commission.[12]

31. Th.

Wrote to C.G.—Ld Aberdeen—H. Tayleur (cancelled). Read Gualterio. Saw Swift & Baxter mg. Railway arbitration business 4½–6¾. Saw Ld Abn.—J.N.G. In the morning at 9½ went with Willy to Mr Georges[13] where he had a most severe bout: & I no slight one, but what I was worst

[1] Antoine Francois Jean *Claudet, 1797–1867; b. in Lyons; daguerrotype photographer in London from 1840. This photograph engraved, with others of the exhibition commissioners, in *Illustrated London News*, xix. 508 (18 October 1851).

[2] *H* cxviii. 1632, 34.

[3] William Thomas Le Poer Trench, 1803–72; 3rd earl of Clancarty 1837.

[4] Edward Hamilton Nelson; Trinity, Dublin; curate of Hunstanworth, Durham, 1842–9, of St. Stephen's, St. Mary-le-bone, from 1849.

[5] 1st v. (1851).

[6] George Henry Sumner, 1824–1909, 4th s. of C.R.*; rector of Old Alresford, Winchester, 1850–85; archdeacon of Winchester 1884–1900; suffragan to bp. of Winchester 1888–1908.

[7] Ferdinando Petruccelli della Gattina, 1815–90, Italian author and politician exiled after 1848 rising in Naples; friend of Mazzini. Wrote *La Rivoluzione di Napoli* (1850).

[8] E. Churton, 'The church's claim to self-government, a charge delivered at his visitation' (1851).

[9] Colin A. Mackenzie, 1779–November 1851, the diarist's great uncle; diplomat; founded Traveller's Club 1815 and, by his will, a museum at Dingwall.

[10] Spoke on it: *H* cxviii. 1753.

[11] In Pall Mall East; its president was John Ayrton *Paris, 1785–1856.

[12] Cp. 3 July 51.

[13] i.e. J. D. George.

up to was sitting by him. Neuralgia came on me in the afternoon. I dined at John Talbot's: but it wd. not go, & grew worse at night.

Friday August One 1851.

At 3 I ceased to sleep & at 4 gave up the idea of going to Paris:[1] rose & arranged to go at once in search of repose to Hagley. Wrote to M. Sallandrouze—Mr Scott Russell. Arranging bills &c. with H[ampto]n. By 6½ train left for Birmingham. The Euston staff was completely overdone. Walked from Birmingham reached Hagley at 3. P.M. & slept—found C. & the children well, except Nina middling. Read Petruccelli. Chess with George.

2. Sat.

Wrote to G. Burnett—Panizzi—Ld Aberdeen (2)—Tatham's—Jane Tyler—Hampton—E. Cardwell—H. Glynne—Bp of Oxford—Mr Keble. Read Petruccelli—Mure.[2] Chess with G.—Music. Family affairs with C. A partial but slight return of the pain today.

3. 7 S. Trin.

Ch mg. (with H.C.) & aftn. Read Pollen's Narrative[3]—D. Wilson[4]—Needham[5]—An Aged Curate[6]—A Few Words about Dioc. Synods[7]—Döllinger's Luther.[8] Much & rather obstinate pain today.

4. M.

Wrote to Jas Watson. Read Petruccelli—Fox's Six Colonies of N.Z.[9] Drive & walk with C. Chess with George. & heard his recitations of the Glynnese Glossary.[10] Nursed myself today & had little pain.

5. T.

Wrote to R. Baxter—A. Panizzi—H.J.G. Worked on the Railway Arbitration papers. Greek & Latin lesson with Willy. Read Canada Cl[ergy] Reserve papers[11]—Caledonian Auditor's Report[12]—Petruccelli—Second

[1] With the exhibition commissioners.
[2] W. Mure, 'Remarks on two appendices to the second volume, third edition of Mr. *Grote's history of Greece' (1851).
[3] J. H. Pollen, *Narrative of five years at St. Saviour's, Leeds* (1851).
[4] Daniel Wilson, 'A revival of spiritual religion the only effectual remedy for the dangers which now threaten the Church of England' (1851).
[5] R. W. Needham, 'The church and the synod: a letter to the bishop of Exeter' (1851).
[6] Not found.
[7] One of the many pamphlets on convocation and synods.
[8] By J. J. I. von Döllinger (1851).
[9] William Fox, 'The six colonies of New Zealand' (1851).
[10] G. W. *Lyttelton, *Contributions towards a glossary of the Glynne language, by a student* (1851).
[11] *PP* 1851, xxxvi. 227.
[12] Not found.

Reformation[1] Ease all day thank God: only the after thought of pain. On Clent Hill.[2]

6. Wed.

Church 8 P.M. Wrote to Bp of Salisbury.—V.C. Oxford—Rev. J. Gladstone—Rev. Mr Richings[3]—L.N.W. Manager.[4] Conv. on Theology mg. with Lady L[yttelto]n I spoke over freely. Read Baines's Liverpool[5]—Petruccelli (finished)—Farini Vol. III. (began)—Fox. Worked on arbitration papers.

7. Th.

Wrote to Marq. d'Azeglio—Baxter—Barker—Iggulden. Greek lesson with Willy. Worked on arbitration papers.—Rome. Read Farini—The Simple Story[6]—Fox on N.Z (finished). Walk with C. I now really hope my neuralgia has left me: I hope: while often feeling how needful some pain must be for me: or perhaps some sharper trial. Chess with G. & more Glossary.

8. Fr.

Church 10. a.m. Wrote to Newcastle—Gourlay[7]—Burnett—Jas Watson. Greek lesson to Willy. 11–1. Griffiths on O.F. Read Farini—Ld Shrewsbury's MSS.[8] Chess with G.—Glossary read. Worked on a Memm. about the Hawarden Estate:[9] & walk & conv. with C.

9. Sat.

Wrote to Rn. G—R. Barker—C. Shaw.[10] Greek lesson with Willy. Worked on Stephen's arrangements: & conv on them. Read Farini Walk with C. & cricket. Dinner party here.

10. 8[11] S. Trin.

Ch mg. & aft. Read Döllinger's Luther—Pollen's St Saviours (finished)—W. Lyttelton's Ordination Sermon[12]—Thayr—Smith on Tractarianism.[13] Walk with C.

[1] Untraced tract.
[2] By Clent village, three miles SE. of Stourbridge.
[3] Probably Frederick Hartshill Richings, 1809?–88; Queens', Cambridge; vicar of Atherstone, Warwickshire, from 1841.
[4] M. Huish; cp. 4 Aug. 44.
[5] T. *Baines, *History of commerce and town of Liverpool* (1851).
[6] By Elizabeth *Inchbald (1791).
[7] Possibly D. A. Gourlay, chairman of the local Great Yarmouth committee for the 1851 exhibition.
[8] Probably the additional material for the 2nd ed. of his *Letter to . . . *Russell* (1851), on ecclesiastical titles.
[9] Hawn P.
[10] Perhaps Sir Charles *Shaw, 1795–1871; fought at Waterloo; brigadier-general 1836; chief commissioner of police at Manchester 1839–42.
[11] 7 altered to 8 in pencil.
[12] W. H. Lyttelton, 'Some reasons of want of success in the Christian ministry' (1851).
[13] T. T. Smith, 'Remarks on the influence of tractarianism; or church-principles so, called, in promoting secessions to the church of Rome' (1851).

11. M.

Wrote to Hampton—R. Baxter—R. Barker. Read Gli Ultimi 69 Giorni.[1] Went off at 12¾ to Hawarden with H[elen] & Miss L[yttelto]n. Saw Griffiths on O.F. &c. 11–12—& Burnet on the Railway & other business 8 P.M. to past midnight—Saw MacCulloch.

12. T.

Wrote to Panizzi—Scotts. Off at 8¼. Saw Barker in Chester—& some shopping. Reached W[olver]hampton at 3 & looked at the Church.[2] Hagley at 6: to act as G.s substitute at dinner. Chess with Granville Vernon. Read the 69 Giorni. My journey was satisfactory: the time is an important one & we have now much at work on Stephen's behalf.

13. Wed.

Church 8. P.M. Wrote to C. Wykeham Martin[3]—Sir W. Temple—W. Hampton—Mr E.N. Brown—Robn. G.—Rev. J. Gladstone—H.J.G.—Precenter Hodnet[4]—T.W. Perry[5]—Rev. W. Cooke[6] (for 20th)—J. Benbow—R.F. Gourlay—G. Burnett—Capt. Huish—Jas Watson. Greek with Willy. Read the '69 Giorni'.

14. Th.

Wrote to Swift—E. Wardell. Greek with Willy. Read Col. Mure—69 Giorni. Saw Collis on O.F.—Mr G. Talbot (at Kidderminster)—calls. Chess with George.

15. Fr.

Church 10 a.m. Wrote to J.N.G.—Swift—H. Tayleur—Rn. G.—Read Col Mure—Corsini's Torracchione[7]—finished[8] Gli Ult. 69 Giorni. Busy with letters & papers from London. Chess with George—also walk & on the hill. Greek lesson with Willy.

[1] *Gli ultimi 69 Giorni della Republica in Roma* (Naples, 1849).

[2] Collegiate Church of St. Peter. In June 1851 the town council memorialized the ecclesiastical commissioners on its decayed condition, and it was subsequently restored.

[3] Charles Wykeham-Martin, 1801–70; Peelite M.P. Newport 1841–52, 1865–8.

[4] *sc.* Alfred *Hackman, 1811–74; precentor at Christ Church, Oxford, from 1841; sub-librarian of Bodleian from 1862.

[5] Thomas Walter Perry, 1815–91; curate of All Saint's, Margaret Street, 1850–7, of Addington, Buckinghamshire, 1857–62; vicar of Ardleigh, Essex, from 1872; wrote on anglican law.

[6] William Cooke, 1821–94; sundry curacies 1844–50; vicar of St. Stephen, Hammersmith, 1850–6; hon. canon of Chester from 1855; vicar of Gazeley, Newmarket, from 1856; ed. *The church hymnal* (1853).

[7] B. Corsini, *Il Torracchione desolato*, 2 v. (1768).

[8] For once, word written in full in original.

16. Sat.

Wrote to W. Hampton—Northcote—J. Swift—Ed. M. Chronicle—J. Murray—G. & Co. Greek with Willy. Drove with C & M to Mr Rufford's.[1] Read Torracchione—Col. Mure. Chess with G. in evg: & [Glynnese] Glossary.

17. 9 S. Trin.

Ch mg. & aft.—Read Newmans Five Lectures.[2] Quarterly on Rubrical usage.[3] Wrote to H.J.G.—E. Collins [R]. Apprehension of smallpox for Meriel: & discussion about our plans.

18. M.

Wrote to T.G.—Panizzi—Captain Huish. Read Torracchione. Set out at 8. reached London at 3. At Euston Square till 6¼ on the arbitration with Messrs. Swift Baxter Huish & Clarke. Then calls—& saw Panizzi. Dined with the Wortley's. Looked for E.C. but in vain [R].

19. T.

Wrote to E. Collins—G. Talbot—A. Monro—Sir M. Cholmeley[4]—H.L. Baker—Mr R. Burgess—W. Clarke[5]—Sig. Ricciardi[6]—M'Cracken & Co—Mrs Monk[7]—Mrs M'Donald—C.G.—Mr Danoon[8]—D. Masson—& Ld Aberdeen—part of a longish letter on Macfarlane. Saw Panizzi (to breakf.)—J. Murray—Carpenter—Northcote. Read Macfarlane.[9] 11–4. Finance Committee & Commission (Exhibition). The Prince stated his plan to a certain number. Bills & other business.

Vidi un altra volta E.C. da lei stessa: dalle 9¼ fin alle 11½. Le cose andavano in parte come prima. Ella nondimeno si trovò risoluta non aver mai più a fare con altrui ma fedelmente aspettare qual Osborne[10] il quale secondo le sue lettere brama sposarla appena tornato. Adesso ci sono due in quest anno che ho veduto, risolute siccome spero di non far più male: ed io sto coperto di macchie brutte assai. Se la grazia di Dio si sia servita di me indignissimo, con tanta e tanta nuova colpa mia, per ajutare quelle anime,

[1] Francis Rufford, d. ?1854; Stourbridge banker and glass manufacturer; tory M.P. Worcester 1847–52; chairman of Oxford, Worcester and Wolverhampton railway. His banking firm failed July 1851.

[2] J. H. *Newman, *Lectures on the present position of catholics in England* (1851).

[3] *Quarterly Review*, lxxxix. 203 (June 1851); review of R. *Mant, *Horae liturgicae* (1845).

[4] Sir Montague John Cholmeley, 1802–74; 2nd bart. 1831; liberal M.P. for North Lincolnshire 1847–52, 1857–74.

[5] Perhaps William *Clark, 1821–80, civil engineer and inventor, responsible with Sir Goldsworthy *Gurney for the warming and ventilation of the new houses of parliament.

[6] Count Giuseppi Napoleoni Ricciardi, 1808–85, Italian nationalist.

[7] Jane Monk, *née* Hughes, wife of bp. of Gloucester.

[8] Perhaps Alexander Denoon, merchant in Old Broad Street, London.

[9] Charles Macfarlane, 'The Neapolitan government and Mr. Gladstone: a letter to the earl of *Aberdeen, being a reply to two letters recently addressed to his lordship by the Right Hon. W. E. Gladstone' (1851). Answered by Gladstone in his 'Examination' (see 31 Dec. 51).

[10] Her lover.

per conto loro stia sempre lodato, ed anche in me miserabile glorificato in eterno. Oh quanto ho veduto della sua grandezza, della sua misericordia, quanto anche delle meraviglie del cuore umano: ne ho altresì un sentimento vivo, una coscienza la parte più interna di me la più immedesimata meco: essendo pure fra gli colpevoli colpevolissimi. Questi due anni terribili hanno in verità sloggiato e sradicato il mio cuore dalla Chiesa Angl. in quanto è Chiesa personale e *vivente* nel *corpo* di suoi Pastori e membri: e nel istesso tempo gli due amici soli sostegni, io posso dire, della mia mente, mi si sono strappati lasciandomi lacerato e posso dire moralmente semianime: questi accidenti mi sono quasi stati, ovvero se non sia la grazia di Dio che gli impedisca possono ancora riuscire, la[1] rovina di me in quanto all' anima ed al corpo. Ma quella grazia, quel amore e senza limiti: altrimenti non mai basterebbe per me.[2]

20. Wed.

Wrote to Huish—Ld Aberdeen (finished)—Mrs Tyler—Panizzi. Set out 11½. Reached Hagley 7¾. Willy in measles but doing well & kindly thank God. Read Torracchione. Moving room & on plans.

21. Th.

Wrote to Scotts—Rn. G—H.J.G—Ld Aberdeen—H. Hornby[3]—Mr Burr—J. Walker.[4] Saw Griffiths on O.F. Read Mazzini's Political Writings,[5] &c. Walk with Mr Herbert. Busy with family matters. Willy doing well.

22. Fr.

Church 10 A.M. Wrote to T.G—K. Morrison[6]—G. Talbot jun. Read

[1] 'mia'—my—here deleted.

[1] 'Saw E.C. again by herself; from 9¼ until 11½. Things went partly as before. She nevertheless finds herself determined to have nothing more to do with anyone else, but to wait faithfully for Osborne; who, according to his letters, longs to marry her the moment he returns. Now there are two whom I have seen this year, who are I hope resolved to do no more evil; and I am covered with many foul stains. If God's grace has made use of most unworthy me, with how very much new guilt for me, to help these souls, may it ever be praised on their account, and glorified eternally even in my miserable self. Oh how much have I seen of his grandeur and of his mercy, how much also of the marvels of the human heart; of him too I have a living awareness, a knowledge right in the very inmost parts of myself: that I am, even among guilty ones, the guiltiest [cp. 15 Nov. 29]. These two terrible years have really displaced and uprooted my heart from the Anglican Church, seen as a personal and *living* Church in the *body* of its Priests and members; and at the same time the two friends whom I might call the only supports for my intellect [cp. 7 Apr. 51] have been wrenched away from me, leaving me lacerated, and I may say barely conscious morally: these misfortunes have almost come upon me, or else if they have not, may it be God's grace that prevents them. They may yet succeed in bringing about my ruin, body and soul. But that grace, that love is boundless; otherwise, it would never suffice for me'.

[3] Hugh Hornby, 1792–1875; leading Liverpool merchant; mayor there 1838.

[4] Joseph Need Walker, 1790–1865, Worcestershire landowner; see next day.

[5] G. Mazzini, *Scritti Politici* (1848–9).

[6] Unidentified.

Torracchione—Mazzini's 'Prose'—Ld Mayor's Visit to Oxford.[1] Saw J. Walker. Worked on Arbitration papers.

23. Sat.

Wrote to J. Murray—Rn. G.—Rev. J. Gladstone—A. Oswald—Mad. Rovero[2]—Scotts—Sig. Massari. Walk with G. accompanied by Wakefield & Sewell. Stephen laid up with measles. Read Mazzini—Il Torracchione—The Mormons.[3] Chess with George.

24. 10 S. Trin.

Ch. 11 & 3. Read the Mormons—Arnold's Life.[4] Walk with C. Stephen's case questionable whether measles or nothing.

25. M.

Wrote to A. Panizzi—B. Quaritch[5]—J. Griffiths—Bickers & Bush—Hon. S. Lyttelton—Jones & Yarrell—Gladstone & Co—J. Murray—Jas Watson—Scotts—G. Talbot jun.—Guardian—MacCulloch—Mr Higginson. Construed some Greek to Willy now convalescent. Walk with C. & with G. Read Il Torracchione. Chess with George. Worked on Arbitration papers.

26. T.

Wrote to Huish—H.J.G.—Greek with Willy. Walk with C. Conversed with M[ary Lyttelton] & her about the plans for residing at Hawarden on which we are all agreed. Saw Mr Claughton[6]—& Mr Griffiths on O.F.: not over well pleased. Made, wrote out, & sent my Award (in the form of a memorandum) in the R.R. case.[7] Read Torracchione.

27. Wed.

Church 8 P.M. Wrote to Guizot[8]—J. Murray—Lyttelton—Knight—Mansell—H.J.G.—Northcote—J. Walker—S.R. Glynne. Read The Mormons (finished)—Il Torracchione—Greek lesson to Willy—Calls—Saw Griffiths & Growcott on O.F. matters & gave instructions as I best could.

[1] Untraced.

[2] Madame Adeodata Rovero of Ranelagh Street had written on Naples; Hawn P.

[3] G. Sexton, *Portraiture of Mormonism* (1850).

[4] Cp. 4 July 44.

[5] Bernard Alexander Christian *Quaritch, 1819–99, bookseller near Leicester Square, after 1860 in Piccadilly.

[6] Piers Claverly *Claughton, 1814–84; fellow University, Oxford, 1837–42; rector of Elton, 1845–59; bp. of St. Helena 1859–62, of Colombo 1862–70; archdeacon of London from 1870.

[7] Arbitration for G.N.R. on dispute about London–Yorkshire routs; cp. C. H. Grinling, *History of the Great Northern Railway* (1898), 99–109.

[8] In 'Seven letters of Gladstone to Guizot', *Journal of Modern History*, xi (1939).

28. Th.

Wrote to Mad. A. Rovero.—Supt. L.N.W. Station.[1] Bible lesson to the children—Greek do to Willy. Read Il Torracchione—Mazzini. Cricket with the children. Directions &c for C. Left Hagley at 8. Birmm. at 12. Travelled all night.

29. Fr.

Wrote to C.G. Reached Laurencekirk before 6. Fasque (on foot) at 7. Found my Father thank God wonderfully well: & without fear. Read Mazzini.

30. Sat.

Wrote to C.G.—R. Barker—H. Tayleur. Read Mazzini—Morte d'Orlando. Unpacking & arranging books & papers: & some pretty long conversations with my Father. Calls on Mr Irvine & the Teeds. I again found myself in the Library: with a branch in the dining-room for the forenoons.

31. 11 S. Trin.

Chapel 11 & 3. Wrote to C.G.—Scotts—Editor of the Guardian. Read Robins's Letter to Denison[2]—Russell's Introdn. to Leibnitz.[3] Conv. with Rob[ertso]n on taking over his duty.[4]

Monday Sept. One. 1851.

Wrote to Grote—Bickers—Murray[5]—Wm. Gladstone—Scotts—Mrs Kerr. Robn. & his people went at 9. Read Mazzini—Morte d'Orlando—Gibbon on Taxation.[6] The attendance on my Father is lighter now than it was: his mind is perceptibly less vigorous than in the spring: not his body. Gave directions at F[ettercairn] House.

2. T.

Wrote to T.G.—Rn. G.—Col Reid—Knudtzen—Mrs Higginson[7]—Sec. Cal. Railway—& Sig. Ricciardi. Read Mazzini—Morte d'Orlando. Went at 4. to fetch C. who arrived 1½ hour after time, very tired but the party all well thank God. We sent Willy to F[ettercairn] House to sleep. My Father received C most affectionately: & was keen to see the children but we put him off it till tomorrow.

[1] M. Huish.
[2] S. Robins, 'A letter to G. A. *Denison' (1851).
[3] G. W. von Leibnitz, *A system of theology* . . . tr. with introduction by C. W. *Russell (1850).
[4] Of looking after their father.
[5] Part in Barnes, *Free trade in books*, 78–9.
[6] A. Gibbon, 'Taxation: its nature and properties, with remarks on the incidence and expediency of the repeal of the income tax' (1851).
[7] A member of the Gladstone household until 1854; cp. 12 Aug. 54.

3. Wed.

Wrote to Rn. G.—J.N.G.—Ld Palmerston—Jas. Watson (2)—Capt Huish. Read Mazzini—Mrs Bennett's Transl. Iphigenia [1]—Morte d'Orlando—Report of Bible Society's meeting.[2] Visited: & out with Willy.

4. Th.

Wrote to A. Finlay—A. Lindsay—J.R. Hope—Mr D. Gladstone. Lesson to Willy in Homer. Read Mazzini—Mrs Bennett's Poems (finished)—Morte d'Orlando. More troubled with faceache. C. too was weak & poorly in mg. Calls.

5. Fr.

Wrote to R. Barker (2)—Sir S. Scott & Co—Millingen—T.G.—Surengar [3]—Jas Watson (2)—Merighi [4]—Clydesdale Directors G. Burnett—J.D. George (about my face wh gave me more trouble) Read Mazzini (finished)—Ernesto di Ripalta [5]—Morte d'Orlando—Drive with C. & hill walk.

6. Sat.

Wrote to Forbes—Lyttelton—Mr Jas Lord. Greek & Latin lessons to Willy. Examd. Caled. Railway Act.[6] Went up the Cairn [7] with C. & the children. Reading, conv. & attendance on my Father does not now practically reach two hours a day on the *average*. Read Farini Vol 3.—Morte d'Orlando—Ernesto di Ripalta—and Report of Copyright meeting.

7. 12 S. Trin.

Chapel 11 a.m. & Holy Commn.—& 3 P.M. Read the Service to Sir J.G. in aft.—He *heard*, & was pleased. Read Archd. Thorpe's Charge [8]—Vita di Maria S.S.[9]—Wordsworth on Apoc.[10]—Hornecks Sirenes [11]—The Great Exhibn.[12]

8. M.

Wrote to Jas Watson—R. Barker—R. Lamond [13]—W. Clarke—(draft to) Prof. Mancini.[14] Greek lesson to Willy—& singing in evg. Also a conv. with

[1] Mrs. A. R. Bennett, the diarist's cousin, *Iphigenia in Tauris, from the German of Goethe. With original poems* (1851).
[2] Untraced.
[3] Probably Willem Hendrik Suringar, Dutch writer; cp. 17 Dec. 51.
[4] Perhaps Pietro Merighi, poet living in Palermo.
[5] [H. Geale], *Ernesto di Ripalta: a tale of the Italian revolution*, 3 v. (1849).
[6] The Caledonian and Dumbartonshire Junction Railway Act was passed on 26 June 1846; for a summary of its terms, cp. *PP* 1847, xxxi. 155.
[7] Cairn O'Mount, behind Fasque.
[8] Perhaps C. Thorp, 'A charge . . .' (1844), or a later, untraced charge by him.
[9] C. Massini, *Vita della Santissima Vergine Maria* (1788).
[10] Christopher *Wordsworth, *Lectures on the apocalypse* (1849).
[11] A. *Horneck, *The Sirenes, or, delight and judgment* (1690).
[12] Vates Secundus [G. A. H. Sala], *The great exhibition 'wot is to be'* (1850).
[13] Probably of the stockbrokers' firm; cp. 6 May 43.
[14] Pasquale Stanislao Mancini, 1817–88; Neapolitan lawyer; defended political prisoners and fled 1850; later a Sardinian and Italian minister.

him wh is always a treat. Read Farini—Morte d'Orlando—Ernesto di Ripalta. Called at Phesdo &c.

9. T.

Wrote to J.R. Hope—Rev. F. Harris—S.R. Glynne—Col Lloyd—J. Murray—H. Chester—Sir W.C. James. Greek Lesson to Willy. Walk to C.s ride. Read Farini—Morte d'Orlando—Ernesto di Ripalta. Commenced translating 3d Vol of Farini—on which I must work slowly.

10. Wed.

Wrote to Archdeacon Churton[1]—Jas Watson—Johnson Longden & Co—G. Burnett. Greek Lesson to Willy. Walk to the Burn & visits. Read Farini—Ern. di Ripalta—M. d'Orlando. Read also the Shannon & Chesapeake Action (James)[2] to Sir J.G. directly after dinner wh I find drives blood to the head.

11. Th.

Wrote to Collis—J. Griffiths—Rn. G.—J.N.G. Read Farini—M d'O—& E di Ripalta—also Farquhar's Letters & Verses—Richardson.[3] Began writing notes of facts to Illustrate our Church History during the 18th Century. Boat with C.[4]

12. Fr.

Wrote to Rn. Gladstone—Scotts—H. Tayleur—(& for Sir J.G. to Scotts) Greek lesson to Willy. Cricket with him—& chess. Visits. Worked on transl Farini. Read Farini—M. d'Orlando (finished)—Ern. di Ripalta (finished). Letter to N. Staffordshire Shareholders.[5] My Father very deaf indeed, & uneasy though not ill.

13. Sat.

Wrote to Sig. Mancini—Mr Church—T.G.—Walk with C. & the children's ride by Delaly deer [dyke]. Visited darling Jessy's remains. Read Farini—Boswell's Johnson—Assedio di Firenze (began).[6] Greek & Latin lesson to Willy. Worked on transl. of Farini.

14. S. 13 Trin.

Chapel 11 & 3. Read the service to my Father in the aft. Visited Geo. Moir.[7] Made a little music. Read Horneck—Leibnitz. Arranged for Willy's

[1] Edward *Churton, 1800–74; rector of Crayke 1835, archdeacon of Cleveland from 1846; church historian.

[2] W. *James, *The naval history of Great Britain from 1793 to 1820* (1824), vi. 36.

[3] S. *Richardson, *Clarissa Harlowe, or the history of a young lady* (1748).

[4] On the lake in the grounds of Fasque.

[5] Untraced; railway business.

[6] By F. D. Guerrazzi, 5 v. (1836).

[7] George *Moir, 1800–70, professor of rhetoric at Edinburgh 1835–40; sheriff 1855–68; professor of Scots law 1864; wrote on drama and witchcraft.

Journey. Wrote to Mr Church. Took Willy, with his own will, to see Jessy's last resting place: & the stone.

15. M.

Wrote to Lindsay & Walker[1] J. Bennett. Jas Watson—J. Griffiths—Archdn. Wilkins—Rn. G.—Wm. Gladstone—J.N.G.—J. Henderson. Willy went off at 8 to the Burn thence to start for School with Mr Holland.[2] Read Farini—Boswell's Johnson—A Word to the Wise.[3] C. better but not strong. Visits. Worked on transl. of Farini.

16. Tues.

Wrote to J.N.G.—Ld Clanricarde—Jas Watson—Messrs. Williams Deacon & Co—Lord Aberdeen.[4] H.S. with Agnes. A delightful hill walk by Friars Glen[5] & over to Slack of Birnie. Read Farini—Behn's Widow Ranter[6]—Boswell's Johnson. Worked on Transl. of Farini—

17. Wed.

Wrote to T.G.—Rn. G.—Lindsay & Walker—G. Burnett—Jas Watson. H.S. with Agnes. Visited the Vault. Worked on Farini. Read Farini—Assedio di Firenze—& began Clarissa Harlowe. Visits—Walk with C. & on Garrol.

18. Th.

Wrote to Newcastle—Rev. Mr Lowe.[7] H.S. with Agnes. Worked on Farini. Read Farini—Assedio di Firenze—Clarissa Harlowe. Ride with Agnes.

19. Fr.

Wrote to A.C. Mill—M. Guizot (& draft). H.S. with Agnes. Worked on Farini Transl. Read Farini (finished Vol III)—Assedio di Firenze—Sardinian Constitution[8]—Clarissa Harlowe. Visited the Vault. Walk with C.

20. Sat.

Wrote to Sig. Farini (Itn.) (& draft)—Jas Watson—Johnson & L—Jos. Bennett—J. Griffiths—A. Panizzi—J. Hume—Sard[inia]n Minister.[9] H.S.

[1] See 29 Apr. 51.
[2] Edward Holland, Macinroy's factor.
[3] 'A word to the wise; or a means of protecting against the heavy snow storm of cheap tracts, which is now being poured on the subject of Christian baptism.' (1847).
[4] Cp. Morley, i. 398.
[5] Four miles NE. of Fettercairn; vestiges of a Carmelite friary.
[6] A. *Behn, 'The widow ranter, or, the history of Bacon in Virginia' (1690).
[7] Henry Edward Lowe, 1814–95; Trinity, Cambridge; sundry curacies 1837–50; taught at Atherstone 1858–67, curate of Wilmcote, Warwickshire, 1871–8.
[8] 'Constitution of the kingdom of Sardinia . . . [4 March 1848]' (1851).
[9] Vittorio Emanuele Taparelli, Marchese d'Azeglio, Sardinian minister in London from 1850.

with Agnes—Worked on Farini. Began Balbo's History[1] & read Clarissa Harlowe—Assedio di Firenzi. Walk to C.s ride—Visited the Vault.

21. 14 S. Trin & St Matthew.

Church 11 & 3. Read Service to Sir J.G. Wrote (for him) to Mr Hume—cancelled. Visits. Read Leibnitz—C. Wordsworth's Sermon[2]—Chr. Wordsw. on Apocalypse. This is a day to be remembered ever for God's signal in Agnes's deliverance. More so this year: for she has a slight hurt of the very same kind on the knee, with slight symptoms about it which are no doubt relics of that fearful disease.

22. M.

Wrote to Mr Holland—J. MacCulloch—Mrs Higginson—Pulford—Nicholls—Chr. Wordsworth—C.A. Wood. Worked on Farini. Read Balbo—Clar. Harlowe—A. Gibbon on Taxation. Walk to C.s ride—Visit to the Vault. My Father conversed well today about O.F. & S.R.G. matters.

23. T.

The Anniversary of my blessed Mother's death. We have not needed to mourn for HER. Wrote to J.R. Hope—Willy—A. Gibbon—Jas Watson. Worked on Farini. Read Balbo—Clarissa Harlowe and Assedio di Firenze. Roman MSS.[3]

24. Wed.

Wrote to Panizzi—J. Murray—J. Thomson—Bp of St Andrews—Jas Watson—G.C. Glyn. Worked on Farini. Rode with C.—Music in evg. Read Balbo—Clarissa Harlowe (finished Vol 2)—

25. Th.

Wrote to Ld Feilding—Lacaita—Col Reid—Aunt J.—Bavarian Commissn.[4]—Mr P.E. Wodehouse—H. Chester—J. Thomson—Willy—Willy for Sir J.G. H.S. with Stephen. Read Balbo—Cl Harlowe—& Ass[edio] di Firenze. Worked on Farini. Looking into railway matters. Walk to C.'s ride.

26. Fr.

Wrote to T.G.—R.G.—Ass. Sec. G.P.O.—Jas Watson—G.F. Bowen—H. Stanley.[5] H.S. with the children. Worked on Farini. Read Balbo—Cl

[1] Cesare Balbo, *Della Storia d'Italia fino all'anno 1814 sommario* (1846).
[2] Charles *Wordsworth, 'National Christianity an article of the Christian faith' (1851); on Matt. xxviii. 18.
[3] Not found.
[4] B. J. Schubarth was Bavarian commissioner for the 1851 exhibition.
[5] Henry Edward John Stanley, 1827–1903; précis writer at foreign office 1847–51; appointed to British mission in Constantinople 1851; 3rd Baron Stanley of Alderley 1869.

Harlowe—Lord Monteagle's Letter[1]—Albarella's Letter to W.E.G.[2]—Poerio (transl.).[3] An uneasy day with my Father about money affairs: always in the same sense, anti-avaricious. Worked on a bundle of papers letters &c. from London. A storm last night split the bush between the road & the sunk fence.

27. Sat.

Wrote to H. Tayleur—Dr Beaven—J.N.G.—M.F. Tupper—Scotts. H.S. with Agnes. Worked on Farini. Read Balbo—C. Harlowe—V. Albarella. Arranged my letters. Visits.

28. 15 S. Trin.

Chapel 3¼ P.M. Morning prayers indoors at 11. Read them again at 4½ to my Father: & at a happy moment arranged (as I trust) for a daily Psalm & Prayer. Wrote to Johnson L & Co—Williams & Co—W.C. James. Read Döllinger's Luther (finished)—Arrowsmith's Sacrilege[4]—Cases of Conscience[5]—Crystal Palace.[6] We were all thrown out by Mr Irvine's bilious attack & no provision made.

29. St Michael M.

Wrote to J. Thomson—H. Lees—Jas Watson. H.S. with A. & S. The Psalms & Prayer with my Father after his breakfast began successfully: & will I trust in God continue. Little Mary had another feverish attack we trust less strong than in London. Worked on Farini. Read Balbo—Clar. Harlowe—Assedio di Firenze. Saw Lady Harriet [Forbes].

30. T.

Wrote to Mr Arrowsmith[7]—"Pascal the Younger"[8]—G. Burnett (2)—S.R. Glynne—Mr Caldwell. H.S. with the children. Prayers & Ps. Sir J.G. Worked on Farini. Read Balbo—C. Harlowe—Caleb Field.[9] Mary somewhat better: at night Agnes had a feverish attack.

[1] T. *Spring-Rice, Lord Monteagle, 'Letter to his grace the archbishop of Dublin, on the subject of the Ecclesiastical Titles Act, and the charge delivered to the clergy of Dublin in 1851' (1851).

[2] 'L'Italiano Vincenzo Albarella fra le pene dell'esilio questa lettera narrando del populo di Napoli a Sir Guglielmo Gladstone scrivera.' (1851).

[3] 'Speech of C. Poerio, late minister of public instruction' (1851).

[4] Untraced sermon by J. Arrowsmith; see 30 Sept. 51.

[5] Pascal the Younger [Pierce Connelly], 'Cases of conscience . . . extracted from the moral theology of the romish church' (1851) with prefatory letter to Gladstone.

[6] Several pamphlets of this title published in 1851, one by the Religious Tract Society.

[7] James Arrowsmith, incumbent of Stoke Row, Oxfordshire, from 1850; had sent a sermon.

[8] Pseudonym of Pierce Connelly of Albany Heath, Guildford.

[9] *Caleb Field: A tale of the puritans* by the author of *Passages in the life of Mrs. Margaret Maitland* (1851).

Wednesday Oct. One. 1851.

Wrote to D. of Newcastle—J. Thomson—Jas Watson—T.G.—Miss Hoare[1]—Mrs Goalen. H.S. with Stephen. Psalm &c. Sir J.G. Mary much, Agnes somewhat better thank God. Worked on Farini. Read Balbo—Caleb Field—Gondon's Reply.[2]

2. Th.

Wrote to W.C. James—E. Cardwell. H.S. with S. Prayer & Ps[alm] with Sir J.G. Hill walk round the shoulders & back of Arnbarrow.[3] The children better. C. laden with cold. Worked on Farini. Read Balbo—Cl Harlowe—A. Balleydier[4]—J. Gondon (finished) My Father full once more of a journey to Liverpool & London.

3. Fr.

Wrote to Ld Aberdeen[5]—Lyttelton—M. Lyttelton—J. Murray—A. Panizzi—E. Cardwell. H.S. with Stephen. Worked on Farini. Visits. Cardwell came very kindly to call & left me Sir R. Peel's Memoirs on Emancipation & Corn Law Repeal.[6] I set to about half past seven & finished a little before five in the morning. They were deeply interesting: & infinitely suggestive. Read also Balbo.

4. Sat.

Wrote to J. Quin[7]—J. Griffiths—S. Griffiths[8]—Jas Watson—M.F. Tupper (2)—H. Cole. H.S. with Stephen: Ps. & Pr, Sir J.G. Out with C. & hill walk on Strathfinella.[9] Worked on Farini—little: & wrote memorandum on the Peel papers. Read Richardson.

. . .[10] And here I must repeat, or put into words, the opinions which I silently formed in my room at the Colonial Office in June 1846 when I got the Circulation Box with Peel's own Memorandum not only arguing in favour of resignation but intimating his own intention to resign which if I remember he declared outright in Cabinet—and with the Duke of Wellington's in the opposite sense. The Duke in my opinion was right and Peel wrong: but he had borne the brunt of battle already beyond the measure of human strength & who can wonder that his heart & soul as well as his physical organisation demanded rest?[11]

[1] Perhaps Frances Mary Hoare, da. of Peter Richard Hoare, 1772–1849, banker; she d. 1869.
[2] J. Gondon, 'A letter to . . . Gladstone in answer to his "Two letters to . . . Aberdeen"' (1851); refuted in *Gleanings*, iv. 107–8.
[3] Hill of 1,060 ft., three and a half miles N. of Fettercairn.
[4] A. Balleydier, *Histoire de la révolution de Rome: tableau religieux, politique et militaire des années 1846, 1847, 1848, 1849, et 1850, en Italie* (1851).
[5] Cp. Morley, i. 394 n.
[6] Published as *Memoirs of Sir Robert *Peel*, ed. Lord *Mahon and Edward *Cardwell 2 v. (1856).
[7] Perhaps John Quin, commission agent of Bow Lane, Cheapside.
[8] Probably a relative of J. Griffiths, the Oak Farm agent.
[9] Hill of 1,358 ft., two miles W. of Fordoun.
[10] Follows an analysis of *Peel's *Memoirs*.
[11] Rest omitted; dated this day; Add MS 44777, f. 332.

5. S. 16. Trin.

Chapel 11 & 3. Read the service for my Father. He really hears & enters into it. Wrote to Archdeacon Denison—Mr Timins.[1] Read Vita di Maria SS. Leibnitz Syst. Theol.—Denison's Sermons[2]—Sc. Ep. Soc. Tracts.

6. M.

Wrote to J.N.G.—Mr Stewart—Mr D. Hill.[3] H.S. with Stephen. As usual with Sir J.G. Walk to C.s ride. Worked on Farini & translated (for the M. Chron.) a paper from Rome).[4] Read Balbo—Cl. Harlowe—& Assedio di Firenze

7. T.

Wrote to Ed. M. Chron.—Jas Watson—Padre Ferrara[5]—A. Foote[6]—E. Badeley. H.S. with St[ephen] & al sol.[7] Sir J.G.[,] Willocks[8] having two holidays my reading to Sir J.G. is a little increased. W. Lyttelton came to visit Fasque incog. to my Father: conv. with him. Read Balbo.—Cl. Harlowe. Worked on Farini.

8. Wed.

Wrote to T.G.—H. Tayleur—C. Nicholson[9]—J. Walker—H.S with Stephen. Al sol. with Sir J.G. Gave Billy [Lyttelton] our best hill walk: Friar's Glen, & across to the bottom of the Slack of Birnie, & then down by the Nose & over Hunter's hill back. Worked on Farini. Read Balbo—Ass[edio] di Firenze (finished I)—Cl Harlowe, wh is without doubt an extraordinary book: Gouland's Letter.[10] Agnes & Mary out again. C. an invalid with cold caught in nursing. Billy told me he had scruples about subscription.

9. Th.

Wrote to S. Griffiths—J. Griffiths—Jas Hope—Jas. Watson. H.S with St. —Sir J.G. al sol. Worked on Farini. I am too slow & must sacrifice some reading to get up to 10 pages a day which with my correspondence reading to my Father visiting or going out with C. &c will be as much as I can hope.

[1] John Henry Timins, 1813–97; vicar of West Malling, Kent, 1842–94; found not guilty of murder by poisoning 1883.

[2] G. A. *Denison, 'The church and the school. Two sermons . . .' (1851).

[3] David Octavius *Hill, 1802–70, landscape and portrait painter; in 1850 appointed one of commissioners of board of manufactures in Scotland.

[4] On oppression, *Morning Chronicle*, 9 October 1851.

[5] Abbot Francesco Ferrara, Sicilian geographer and economist.

[6] A. R. L. Foote, Scottish priest, formerly episcopal incumbent at Brechin.

[7] *al solito*, as usual.

[8] John Willox of Edzell, Sir John's secretary; see 25 Sept. 53.

[9] (Sir) Charles *Nicholson, 1808–1903, speaker of New South Wales legislative council 1846–56; a founder of Sydney university; kt. 1852, bart. 1859; returned to Britain 1862; businessman and connoisseur.

[10] H. G. Gouland, 'Place of a proposed new colony, to be called Britannia' (1851).

Read Massari's Raccolta di Scritti [1]—Clarissa Harlowe. Hill walk with W.L. C.G. in bed.

10. Fr.

Wrote to Coachman—Ed. Guardian—E. Ellice—C. Wordsworth. H.S. with St.—Sir J.G. al sol. Worked on Farini. Took W. Lyttelton to Laurencekirk: calls there. Read Ed. Rev. on Naples [2]—Massari (finished)—Parker's Sermon of Merchants.[3] Saw Bp of Brechin.

11. Sat.

Wrote to Ld Aberdeen—T.G.—J. Byrne [4]—Aunt J.—Col Reid—Rev. Mr Timins. H.S. with Stephen—Sir J.G. *al sol.* Worked on Farini. Read Clarissa Harlowe. Calls.

12. 17. S. Trin.

Chapel 11 & 3. Service with Sir J.G.—Walks with W. Ln. & two conversations on his letter & difficulties.[5] Read the various MSS. from the Neapolitan Priests.[6] Also read Ludlow's Christian Socialism [7]—Ed. Rev. on Ap. Succession.[8] Wrote to M.F. Tupper.

13. M.

Wrote to Mr W. Fox—Lord Palmerston (covering)—Caledonian Secretary —Willy for Sir J.G. H.S. with A. & S.—Sir J.G. al sol. Worked on Farini—Read Cl. Harlowe. Ride to Laurencekirk with letters. Four hours reading the Neap. reply in the Journal des Debats & making notes, & Queries to send to Naples.[9]

14. T.

Wrote to Jas Watson—Willy—E. Badeley. H.S. with the children—Sir J.G. al sol. Worked on Farini. Ride with Agnes. Read Cl. Harlowe—Barbarin's Defence.[10]

[1] G. Massari, *Il signor Gladstone ed il governo Napolitano; raccolta di scritti intorno alla questione Napolitana* (1851); tr. of Gladstone's 'Letters to *Aberdeen', *Macfarlane's reply and several tracts and newspaper articles.

[2] *Edinburgh Review*, xciv. 490 (October 1851); review of the 'Letters to Aberdeen' and consequent pamphlets; favourable to Gladstone.

[3] T. Parker, 'A sermon of merchants (1847); on Eccles. xxvii. 2.

[4] John W. Byrne, accountant in Holborn.

[5] Cp. 8 Oct. 51.

[6] Add MS 44370, f. 273.

[7] J. M. Ludlow, 'Christian socialism and its opponents: a lecture' 1851.

[8] *Edinburgh Review*, xciv. 527 (October 1851); review of *Argyll, 'The two-fold protest' (1851).

[9] A French version of the Neapolitan government's reply ('Rassegna degli Errori e delle Fallacie pubblicate dal Sig. Gladstone . . .') appeared in *Journal des Débats* on 27, 28, 30 September 1851.

[10] Cardinal A. Barbarin, 'Ordonnance . . . portant defence de lire, vendre, et debiter une traduction du Nouveau Testament [by Le Maistre]' (1668).

15. Wed.

Wrote to H.G. Gouland[1]—Robn. G.—J. Byrne—G. Burnett. H.S. with the ch[ildre]n—Sir J.G. al sol. Worked on Farini. Visited the Douglases (+): & conv. with H. on their case.[2] Read Clarissa Harlowe—Reports on Endowment Scheme: not over good.

16. Th.

Wrote to J. Murray—Prince Castelcicala—J. Balfour (& draft)—Rev. Jas Robertson (for Sir J.G.)—Jas Watson—Lyttelton—J.R. Godley—Scotts. H.S. with A. & S.—Sir J.G. as usual. Worked on Farini. Read Cl. Harlowe: Magazines. Aunt J. arrived: *through* from London. I set to work on the bundle she brought me of books letters & papers. Walked to Stephen's ride.

17. Fr.

Wrote to Rev. A. Whyte—Rev. Mr Kidd[3]—Mr H. Drummond—Ld Mandeville[4]—Noirsain[5]—Papanicolas[6]—J.W. Cunningham—Watson—Monro. H.S. with A. & S.—Sir J.G. as usual. Worked on Farini. Worked on my arrivals from London, wh I disposed of. Read Cl. Harlowe—Fraser on Italy.[7] Drive with C.

18. Sat. St Luke.

Chapel 11 a.m. Sir J.G. al sol. Wrote to Mr Rule[8]—Mr A. Munro—Mr Gresley. Worked on Farini. Read Clar. Harlowe. Part of the Quart Articles on Papal Pretensions & Revolut. Literature.[9]

19. 18. S. Trin.

Chapel 11 & 3. Service (shortened) with Sir J.G. Read Q.R. on Puritanism[10] —Chr. R. on Quakerism[11]—Caswall's Tract[12]—Col. Ch. Mag. & Scottish Ch. Mag.[13]—

[1] Henry Godfrey Gouland, senior magistrate and collector of customs at Lyttelton, Port Victoria, New Zealand. Cp. 8 Oct. 51.

[2] Villagers.

[3] Probably Thomas George Kidd, 1803–62; Caius, Cambridge; rector of Catwick, Yorkshire, from 1835.

[4] William Drogo Montagu, 1823–90; styled Viscount Mandeville 1843–55; tory M.P. Bewdley 1848–52, Huntingdonshire 1852–5, when he succ. as 7th duke of Manchester.

[5] Unidentified; could read Noirsaire.

[6] Georgios Dracatos Papanicolas, Ionian publicist.

[7] *Fraser's Magazine*, xliv. 237 (September 1851); review of Farini; or ibid. xliv. 437 (October 1851), description of Naples.

[8] William Harris *Rule, 1802–90; Wesleyan minister abroad 1826–42, at home 1842–68; joint editor, Wesleyan conference office 1851–7.

[9] *Quarterly Review*, lxxxix. 451, 491 (September 1851); on papal aggression, and the French crisis.

[10] *Quarterly Review*, lxxxix. 307 (September 1851); review of *Ruskin, 'Notes on the construction of sheepfolds' (1851).

[11] *Christian Remembrancer*, xxii. 319 (October 1851); a review of 'Quakerism . . . by a lady' (n.d.), which precedes a review of Gladstone's tr. of Farini.

[12] H. Caswall, 'A brief account of the method of synodical action in the American church' (1851).

[13] *The Scottish Magazine and Churchman's Review*, n.s. i. 461 (October 1851); on daily prayer.

20. M.

Wrote to Jas. Hope—Williams & Co—Jas. Watson—Ed. M. Chronicle—Mr D. Gladstone—Sig. Galleano.[1] H.S. with the children—Sir J.G. al sol. Worked on Farini translation. Conv. with C. about party organisation—& saw Mr Whyte on the Scots clergy stipends. Revised 1st. Chap. Farini. Read Clar. Harlowe. Wrote for consn. draft of a letter to Newcastle.[2]

21. T.

Wrote to Spottiswoode & Shaw—Jas Watson. H.S. with S. & A.—Sir J.G. al sol. Read Cl. Harlowe. Worked on Farini—Revised Chap 2 and Chap. 3 in part. Visits.

22. Wed.

Wrote to D. of Newcastle—Mr Timins—Mr Whyte—Scotts—J.N.G. H.S. with A. & S.—Sir J.G. al sol. Drs Guthrie & Fettis met: agreed in reporting very well. Worked on Farini Read Cl Harlowe. Walk to C. & Agnes's ride.

23. Th.

Off at 6 A.M. to Trin Coll. arrived at 11¼. Council meeting at 1–3½.[3] Conv. with the Warden—Bishops—Dean Ramsay—Sir A. Edmonstone—Mr Barry.[4] Chapel 5 P.M. Choral service. Saw young Warburton[5]—Read Ricciardi's Histoire de La Revolution D'Italie.[6]

24. Fr.

Off at 8¾ home by Luncarty with Bp of Aberdeen—Reached Fasque at 2¼. Conv. with my Father on Trin Coll. (am[on]g other subjects) in evg. It was agreeable to him: but now he does not well bear the excitement wh seizes him even from agreeable conversation. Worked on Farini Revision. Read Ricciardi's History.

25. Sat.

Wrote to Ld Palmerston—Spottiswoodes (cover)—Jas. Watson. H.S. with A. & S.—Sir J.G. as usual. Worked on Farini—Translation & revision. Read Cl Harlowe. Shot in Balbegno wood.[7]

[1] A. L. Galleano, Italian politician then in London; cp. Add MS 44730, f. 347 and Hawn P.

[2] On course to be taken about the ministry.

[3] Report in *Scottish Magazine*, n.s. i. 553 (November 1851).

[4] Alfred *Barry, 1826–1910; sub-warden of Trinity College, Glenalmond, 1849–54; headmaster in Leeds 1854–62; principal of Cheltenham College 1862–8, of King's, London, 1868–83; abp. of Sydney 1884–9.

[5] See 4 Aug. 46.

[6] G. N. Ricciardi, *Histoire de la révolution d'Italie en 1848* (1849).

[7] One mile SW. of Fettercairn.

26. 19. S. Trin.

Chapel 11 & 3. Shortened service with Sir J.G.—30 min. He was *most* attentive: and in the Litany referred to the Neapolitan prisoners. He was not well: from errors in diet. Read Newman's Lectures VI to IX.[1]—Leibnitz Syst. Theol.—Wrote to Jane Tyler—Rev. Mr White.

27. M.

Wrote to J. Balfour—W.C. James—Austine P. Master—Col. Fraser. H.S. with A. & S.—Sir J.G. as usual. Worked on Farini—translation and revision. Read Clar. Harlowe.

28. T. SS. Simon & Jude.

Chapel 11 a.m. Sir J.G. as usual. Worked on Farini. Translation & revision. Read Clar. Harlowe. Rode with H. Forbes & Agnes to Drumtochtie Fordoun & the Braes.

29. Wed.

Wrote to T.G.—Rn. G.—Jas Watson—Rev. Mr Timins—Rev. Mr Fisher[2] (Sir J.G.)—Jos. King[3]—J. Griffiths—Capt. Barclay. H.S. with the children. Worked on Farini transl. Read Ricciardi's Histoire. 12–6. Journey with C. to Haddo H[ouse] where we found a family party & all the old kindness.

30. Th.

Wrote to H.J.G.—Capt Barclay, as I am seduced into staying a day more. Worked on Farini. Read Ricciardi—Music. Two walks & a sitting with Lord Aberdeen & much interesting conversation on home politics as well as Naples.

31. Fr.

Wrote to Willy—A. Gordon—Duke of Newcastle (which Ld Aberdeen perused) on the course to be taken as to the Ministry. Two more walks with Ld Abn. Worked on Farini.[4] Music in evg: & farewells—reluctant enough. Conv. with Adam G.—& with Ld Haddo.

Sat Novr. One 1851. All Saints.

Wrote (from Fasque) to J.N.G.—J. Griffiths—R. Barker—Sec. P.O.[5]—Jas Watson—& [blank.] Also part of a letter for C. to Mrs [W.]F. Neville

[1] J. H. *Newman, *Lectures on the present position of catholics in England: addressed to the brothers of the Oratory* (1851); lectures iv–ix are on the prejudices and assumptions of protestants.

[2] Perhaps George *Fisher, 1794–1873; astronomer and priest; chaplain to *Parry's expedition 1821–3; headmaster at Greenwich 1834–60.

[3] Joshua King, 1798–1857; fellow of Queens', Cambridge, 1820, president from 1832.

[4] Written over a short erasure.

[5] W. L. Moberly; cp. 22 Sept. 45.

about Lady Newry.[1] Read Ricciardi. Left Haddo at ¼ to nine. Saw the Bishop in Aberdeen & conversed on laymen in Synod: missed Church. On at 2½ to Stonehaven. Visited Capt Barclay at Urry & went about that beautiful place.[2] In several points I like the owner much. On at 5¾ to L[aurence]kirk & made the acquaintance in the carriage of one of the Clergy going to Lkirk for the Winter. Found Sir J.G. better: but not in mind. Worked on letters &c.

2. 20 S. Trin.

Chapel 11 AM (and Holy Communion) & 3 P.M.—Short 35 min. service read with Sir J.G.—Wrote to Rev. D.T. Gladstone—J. Griffiths—Sec. Clydesdale Co. Began project of letter to the Bp of Aberdeen.[3] Read Horneck's Ascetic[4]—Report of Leeds Rural Deanery.

3. M.

Wrote to C. Wordsworth—Laurencekirk Postmaster[5]—Collis—J. Griffiths—Geo. Bennet.[6] H.S. with A. & S.—Sir J.G. al sol. Worked on Farini—transl. & revis. Worked on Sir J.G.s accounts—Arranged my letters & papers up to Oct. 31.—Saw R. Martin &c ab[out] poacher. My Father caught with hoarseness. H[elen] is now most kind both to C. & all the children.

4. T.

Wrote to Spottiswoodes—Jas Watson—Wr. James—A. Galleano—P. Master L.kirk H.S. with A. & S. Worked on Farini—Transl. & Revn. Read Ricciardi—finished. My Father in bed with cold. Visits.

5. Wed.

Wrote to Mrs Wadd—E. Coleridge—P.Mr. Brechin[7] or Edzell—My Father improving: at dinner. H.S. with A. & S. Worked on Farini—Transl. & Rev[ise]d. Read Clar. Harlowe. Saw Falconer.

6. Th.

Wrote to Spottiswoodes—Rev. D.T. Gladstone—Rev Mr Foulkes. H.S. with the children—Sir J.G. al sol. Worked on Farini transl. & finished revision of the Fourth Book. Drove C. to the Burn. Read Cl. Harlowe.

[1] Anne Amelia, da. of Sir C. *Colville, m. 1839 Francis Jack Needham, 1832–May 1851; styled Viscount Newry; tory M.P. Newry from 1841. She d. 1900.

[2] Urie House, two miles NE. of Stonehaven.

[3] Add MS 44684, f. 275. Published as 'A letter to the right reverend William *Skinner, D.D., bishop of Aberdeen and primus, on the functions of laymen in the church' (1852); reprinted in *Gleanings*, vi. 1. On the importance of synods.

[4] Cp. 27 May 49.

[5] John Watt.

[6] Perhaps George Bennett, solicitor in Coleman Street, London.

[7] William Low.

7. Fr.

Wrote to G.C. Myers—J. Stuart[1]—J. Griffiths. H.S. with S. & A.—Prayers with my Father: but he was low spirited & impatient. Worked on Farini—Read Clar. Harlowe—Visits +.

8. Sat.

Wrote to C.G. Reid—Mr Empson[2]—O.B. Cole—Edzell P.Mr. H.S. with the children. Sir J.G. as usual. Worked on Farini. Read Clar. Harlowe & began Italian text of the Neapol. Reply (received on Thursday).[3] Walk round Arnbarrow.[4]

9. 21 S. Trin.

Chapel 11 & 3. Prayers (35 min) with Sir J.G. Wrote to E. Badeley—Marg. Wood—Willy. Read Vita della B.V.M.[5]—'The Royal Exchange & Exhib. Building'[6]—Horneck's Ascetic.

10. M.

Wrote to Jas Watson—Myers—Lady Lyttelton—Jane Wortley H.S. with A. & S.—Sir J.G. as usual. Worked on Farini. Read Clar. Harlowe. Rode with Agnes to Laurencekirk. My Father's bad nights begin to be a serious circumstance, as there is no sufficient cause of a palpable or temporary kind: conv. with Fettis on them.

11. T.

Wrote to Sec. L.N.W.—Rev. E. Hawkins—J. Murray—Bickers & Bushe—Macculloch—T.G.—Mr Irvine—Dr Fergusson. H.S. with A. & S.—Sir J.G. al sol. But he is suffering from want of sleep. Worked on Farini. Read Clar. Harlowe. Hill walk Garrol to Delala deer [dyke]: there is much beauty unopened by the Upper line.—Visits.

12. Wed.

Wrote to Marchese d'Azeglio—Sec. Ed. P.O.—H.S. with S & A. & Sir J.G. al sol. 12½–4 to Arbuthnott with C. Worked on Farini Read Clar. Harlowe.

[1] John *Stuart, 1813–77; Scottish advocate, editor and genealogist; cp. Add MS 44371, f. 3.

[2] William *Empson, 1791–1852, professor of law, East India College, Haileybury, from 1824; edited *Edinburgh Review* from 1847.

[3] Text sent to diarist by the foreign office on *Palmerston's orders, cp. Add MS 44370, f. 358 and 13 Oct. 51 n.

[4] Hill 2 miles N. of Fasque.

[5] Cp. 7 Sept. 51.

[6] 'The Royal Exchange and the palace of industry, or, the possible future of Europe and the world' (1851).

13.

Wrote to Lindsay & Walker—E. Coleridge—G. Burnett—C.G. Reid—W. Shaw. H.S. with A. & S.—Sir J.G. al sol. My Father had a somewhat better night. Worked on Farini—Worked on private accounts. Read Clar. Harlowe —Out with C. & Arnbarrow walk.

14. Fr.

Wrote to Jas Watson—A. Williams—W. Mackenzie W.S.—H.S. with A & S.—Sir J.G. al sol. Worked on Farini—Finished Tr. of Third Volume. Finished Clar Harlowe, on the whole both a great & good book—began F. Torre[1]—Visit. +.

15. Sat.

Wrote to Tatham—J. Hignett—Scotts—Overends—H. Tayleur—J. Macculloch—Mrs Higginson—Mr Irvine. H.S. with A. & S.—Sir J.G. as usual. Worked on papers about Rome with a view to Ed. Rev.[2] Read F. Torre—Papa Nicolas on[3] the Ionian Islands.[4]

16. 22 S. Trin.

10¼–2. To Laurencekirk with C: where we *much* liked Mr Haskell[5] in the service & the Sermon. Prayers at 3 for the household: & Sermon. Prayers at 2½ with my Father: & again at 9 in evg. by his own request when he suggested Bible reading too & said he should like to be at prayers twice a day. Worked on letter to Bp of Aberdeen. Wrote to Mr Stuart. Read Horneck's Sirenes[6]—Sir W. Dunbar papers[7]—Vita della B.V.M. The two little ones sat perfectly quiet through 50 m. of prayers & Sermon.

17. M.

Wrote to T.G.—Rev Mr Woollcombe—Jas Watson. H.S. with A. & S.—morning & evg with my Father. Read Torre. Worked on MS. for Ed Rev.

18. T.

Wrote to Lyttelton—Timins—Lindsay & Walker. H.S. with A & S.—Evg. prayers only with my Father. Mr Stuart came at 11: we tried to reach Fordoun but the drifts wd. not let us. He staid till 4: & we spoke of Church

[1] F. Torre, *Memoire storiche sull'intervento franchese in Roma nel 1849*, 2 v. (1851).
[2] The start of his review of Farini for the *Edinburgh Review*, xcv. 357 (April 1852), reprinted in *Gleanings*, iv. 139; cp. Add MS 44685, f. 40.
[3] These three words smudged; 'papers' next deleted.
[4] 'Ionian', 'The Ionian Islands . . . in reply to a pamphlet entitled "The Ionian Islands under British protection"' (1851).
[5] Joseph Haskell, 1819–71; Clare, Cambridge; curacies in England 1843–8; canon of St. Ninian's, Perth, 1850–6; incumbent at Laurencekirk 1853–4; rector of Barkwith, Lincolnshire, from 1854; close friend of J. M. *Neale. Cp. 1 Dec. 51.
[6] Cp. 7 Sept. 51.
[7] Sent to diarist by C. G. Reid; cp. Add MS 44370, f. 357.

matters with much "content" on my part in him. Read Torre—Bowen on Ionian I.—Worked on Roman MS. finished. C. ill at 11 P.M. with threatening pains, but thank God all went off.[1]

19. W.

Wrote to Ld Granville—Jas. Watson—J. Griffiths—W. Empson. H.S. with A. & S.—prayers with Sir J.G. morning & night. Saw Forbeses—Irvines—Fergussons—Conv. on Sir J.G's matters with H.—Read Torre—Bowen (finished)—Papanicolas.

20. Thurs.

Wrote to Mr Barry—Sig. Galleano—Mr Buchanan[2]—J.N.G—Jas Watson—Ld Lansdowne. H.S. to the children—prayers mg & evg with Sir J.G. Read Torre & Appx—Pantaleoni's All'Europa[3]—Papanicolas on I.I.—St Ninian's Report.[4] Walk with C. & hill walk.

21. Fr.

Wrote to R. Baxter—Ligertwood—Lady Lyttelton—Dean Fortescue. Prayers mg & evg with Sir J.G. Visits. Read Papanicolas on I.I.—Vaudoncourt on do.[5] Revised & corrected my MS. on Rome for Ed. Rev.—

22. Sat.

Wrote to M F Tupper—Jas Watson—Williams Deacon & Co—A. Williams—Mr Irvine. Prayers Sir J.G. mg—H.S. with A & S. Our little Mary is four today. God be thanked for her restored health, with discipline too she is grown a manageable girl. Began correcting MS. (B.V.) of Farini. Wrote on Naples. Read Elliot's Life[6]—Arbitn. Corresp. Drove with C. to Mr Haskell's to make some provision for tomorrow.

23. Pre-advent S[unday].

Chapel 11 & 2½. Dean of Brechin officiated. Abridged my prayers with Sir J.G. Wrote to Mr W.P. Dundas. Conv. with Dean of Brechin: a most pleasing person. Read Pascal the Younger No 2[7]—Doane's 2d Address[8]—

[1] She was again pregnant: cp. 2 Apr. 52.
[2] Perhaps George *Buchanan, 1790–1852, classicist and civil engineer.
[3] *All'Europa. Annotazioni storiche retrospettive dei Costituzionali Romani* (1851); reviewed by Gladstone in *Edinburgh Review*, xcv. 357 (April 1852).
[4] Probably a report from Haskell. Cp. 16 Nov. 51 n.
[5] Cp. 9 Dec. 46.
[6] J. Watkins, *Life, poetry and letters of Ebenezer *Elliot, the corn-law rhymer, with an abstract of his politics* (1850).
[7] 'Petition of Pierce Connelly, Clerk' (1851); requesting that the Commons order the suppression of convents.
[8] One of the many *Addresses* given by bp. G. W. Doane in the U.S.A.

Liguori's Glorie di Maria[1]—Civiltà Cattolica—(No's 35 & 36).[2] Wrote on my Letter to Bp of Aberdeen.

24. M.

Wrote to Spottiswoode & Shaw—Dean of Brechin—Scotts—H. Tayleur. H.S. with A. & S.—Prayers with Sir J.G. He was very restless in mind today: & perhaps the more so from my being obliged to name to him the subject of rents: on which he spontaneously & repeatedly said he would do nothing as to any payment already made. And the time for considering future payments is not yet come. Worked on Farini Revision. Also on Neapolitan Letter.[3] Read Life of Elliott. Walked to Hawhill & Kirton.[4]

25. T.

Wrote to Mr Empson—Jas Watson—Newcastle—Mr J. Stuart. H.S. with A & S.—Sir J.G. kept his bed (chiefly sleeping) except 3 hours in evg. Worked on Farini Revision—And on Neap. Letter. Visits +. Read Elliott's Life—Bowen (C.E.) on E.I. Rail & Steam.[5]

26. Wed.

Wrote to Lyttelton—Jas Watson—G. Burnett (2)—W. Fox. H.S. with A. & S.—Prayers mg & evg with Sir J.G.—Worked on Farini revision—And on Neap. letter. Saw Forbes. Arrangements discussed with C. Read Elliott's Life.

27. Th.

Wrote to H. Tayleur—Robn. Gladstone—Williams Deacon & Co—Mr Grant—also Mr Grant & Rn. G for Sir J.G. H.S. with children. Prayers as usual with Sir J.G. Worked on Neap. Letter. Finished revision 3d Vol Farini. Read Elliott's Life (finished)—Irish Land Tenures[6]—Poetry Antijacobin.[7] Walk round Arnbarrow.

28. Fr.

Wrote to Rn. G—J.N.G—Jas Watson—Mr J.T. Mackenzie.[8] H.S. with A. & S.—Prayers with Sir J.G. morning & evg. Walk with C.G—with Stephen—

[1] Saint Alphonso Maria de Liguori, *Le Glorie di Maria,* tr. into English (1852); argued that it is not always sinful to lie; much consulted by tractarians tending towards Rome.

[2] *La Civiltà Cattolica,* a Jesuit periodical, whose headquarters had just been moved from Naples to Rome.

[3] Probably the start of work on his 'Examination', originally conceived as a third letter to *Aberdeen, cp. 28 Nov. and 31 Dec. 51.

[4] Farms three miles W. of Fettercairn.

[5] Probably an untraced MS.

[6] Series of measure on leasehold, leading to an important bill in 1852: *PP* 1850, ii. 587, 603, 1852–3, iv. 56.

[7] A. Watson, *The anti-jacobin: a hudibrastic poem* (1794).

[8] (Sir) James Thompson Mackenzie of Aberdeen, 1818–90; made fortune in India 1835–50, returned to Britain and bought estate by Ballater; stood unsuccessfully as a Peelite 1851, 1859; bart. 1890.

visits. Read Pamphlets from London—Also Gondon[1] Macfarlane[2] & Naples official Reply. Worked on Letter to Ld Abn. Arrival from London of letters & papers—worked on it.

29. Sat.

Wrote to T.G—Jas Watson—J. Griffiths—Sir C.E. Wilmot[3]—Messrs. Kelly & Slater.[4] H.S. with A. & S.—Prayers with my Father as usual mg & evg. He said afterwards 'very good' & was most devout. While musing in his chair he asked 'Does not the Scripture say "rend your hearts & not your garments"?'[5] Would have it paraphrased: & on hearing of 'to obey is better than sacrifice' made me by repeated questions read him the history of Saul & the Amalekites.[6] God was marking for him the way he had to tread. No sign however had then appeared: the day was a good one with him in every point: the Dr reported favourably: but I write this on Monday morning.

(Read Memoir of Ld Aberdeen—Lang on Railways[7]—Neap. MS. History[8]—&c.) Worked on Letter. Went for 2½ hours to the hill to join the tenants' party. And for 1½ to F. House in the evg to meet the Bp of Brechin.

30. S. Andrew & Advent Sunday.

Chapel 11 A.M. (but called away after the Venite) & 2½ P.M. Read Horneck —Leibnitz—Hook[9]—Bp of Salisbury.[10]

Called down at 7 to see my Father who had been sick with unusual stress & exhaustion. He got to sleep & I left him quiet at half past seven. Dr F[ettis] had been sent for. I heard no more until 9½ & then that he had had more fits of sickness: Helen thought it very serious & had sent very properly for Dr Guthrie. Dr F. came at ten. The hands & feet were cold: pulse good: an injection administered: sickness usually came on after nourishment had been given, or after he had been raised or which he pressed much for taken out of bed for any necessary purpose. There was little result from the measure taken. He was reluctant to take anything. He slept steadily at the intervals: but without seeming refreshed. Twice we observed his eye balls distorted. Before four he had a calomel & scammony pill given to act on the bowels if the evil were there. It did nothing: & he kept next to nothing down

[1] Cp. 1 Oct. 51.

[2] C. *Macfarlane, 'The Neapolitan government and Mr. Gladstone' (1851).

[3] Charles Octavius Eardley-Wilmot, 1824–86, 8th s. of Sir J. E. E. Wilmot, 1st bart.; soldier.

[4] Edward Robert Kelly, 1817–96; attorney and partner in W. Kelly and Co., publishers of Post Office directories from 1840. Isaac Slater, 1803–83, also published directories.

[5] Joel, ii. 12, 13.

[6] I Samuel xv.

[7] G. H. Lang, 'Reasons for the repeal of the railway passenger tax' (1851).

[8] Brought by *Panizzi from Naples; cp. Add MS 44371, f. 64ff.

[9] W. F. *Hook, 'The duty of English churchmen, and the progress of the church in Leeds' (1851).

[10] E. *Denison, 'A charge delivered to the clergy of the diocese of Salisbury . . .' (1851).

of the brandy & stimulants. At 1 A.M. another pill was given him with a drop of croton oil. He was violently & repeatedly sick & seemed to bring it all up. Between five & six there was some failure of pulse—no action of bowels but of the u[rinary] organs good—and his breath began to labour more. A little before seven he took a mouthful of chicken tea & kept it. Again about half past seven several mouthfuls. The extremities had been warmer in the night, pulse 80. They were now inclining to cold and the pulse weaker & slower. He threw the clothes off him. Another injection was tried but did not operate. He both spoke, sneezed, & moved with considerable muscular force: of which Dr F. saw a great collapse yesterday morning.

Monday December One 1851.

At 6 coachman was sent to Broughty[1] & Port on Craig to telegraph for all my brothers & for Dr Miller or Dr Simpson[2] from Edinburgh. Dr Guthrie who went at 5 P.M. yesterday was sent for express: at 7½ I read the prayer of 'small hope' and at 8 sent to Laurencekirk for the Bishop.

Between nine & eleven he had violent fits of sickness & he brought up a bulk larger than the stomach had received in food the excess being made up by bile. This seemed to relieve the stomach and there was no more sickness after about the hour I have named. He took liquid food at intervals in the shape of chicken tea: sometimes a little brandy in old cherry brandy: once a piece of pear, with great relish. He made a decided rally from the time of the last sickness & passed the day generally with comfort. There were also signs of movement in the intestines late in the afternoon & in the evening which gave us hope. But on the other hand there were signs of fever in the waters which came from him. The pulse was good & the breathing had since the morning become easy. He spoke without[3] difficulty, sometimes of his own accord—was unwilling to take his pill & did it as under authority—once addressed me saying 'What shall I do' (his usual phrase) 'William'. But it has of late been very unusual with him distinctly & spontaneously to identify the person he addresses & the use of the name may have been an accident.

Mr Haskell having arrived, after some consultation with the doctors & (by their advice) at an interval when he was roused up I said to him 'Father' —& obtained a sign of his consciousness—'I am afraid you are very ill'— 'Indifferently' he said with imperfect articulation (which afterwards rallied)—'you remember that a little while ago you wished to receive the Holy Sacrament—you can have it now where you are'—'No' he said 'I am not able—it is impossible'.

On the whole from noon to midnight it was a comfortable day. There were proofs of this in the way in which he spoke. For instance when Dr Simpson

[1] Instead of 'Dundee'. Broughty Ferry is on the N., Port on Craig (Tayport) on the S. bank of the Tay.

[2] (Sir) James Young *Simpson, 1811–70; Edinburgh physician; introduced chloroform in obstetrics; cr. bart. 1866.

[3] Instead of 'for'.

came from Edinburgh I think before eleven, & they were about him, he said 'Who's there?' 'The Doctor'. 'The Doctor? I don't want him'.

With respect to the H.C. I refrained from pressing it further partly out of deference to the doctor partly because I knew that in my Father's view it might seem to require a considerable mental effort duly to receive & that accordingly his refusal was perhaps an expression of inability to make it. All through he has been equal to physical efforts but hardly more, & some of those under pressure.

Wrote to Ld Aberdeen[1]—Milnes—D. Robertson.

Dec. 2. Tues.

Wrote to Jas Watson—H. Tayleur—Lady Lyttelton—Mr D. Gladstone—Mrs Nimmo—Louisa—W.C. James—Geo. Grant.

I went to bed from one to four. Dr S. after trying aperient medicine used an injection & succeeded. On going away at 9 A.M. he told me he did not give up all hope—there was the fever & the constitution—we had only to support & restore. He was dissatisfied with the close atmosphere last night & forbade more than four to be in the room at once. Robertson & John arrived between two & three. We passed through the day favourably: the food was albumen with a small quantity of brandy in cherry brandy occasionally. During the day say 18 hours I think my Father had the white of 13 eggs. By the evening he had revived much & showed it by asking 'who speaks'—first to Hayman. Then I went to him on hearing him speak & said what do you wish? 'Who speaks?'. William. 'William? What has been the matter with me?' 'You have been very ill Father you have had first sickness then fever but it is a great mercy that you are better: only you must take the greatest care & do all the doctors bid you'. 'Then I have had sickness & fever'. 'Yes sickness & fever but thank God you are better'.—'Thank God' he promptly replied. He afterwards asked 'how am I?' & on being told he said what does Hayman think? Having been in bed 1–4 last night & 3–6 the night before, I went off at 1½ tonight with a lightened though not quite light heart & was not called until 11.

3. Wed.

Wrote to Capt. Barclay. Read my Neapolitan MS. Tom came. Walked with him & John to Phesdo. Family prayers were omitted this morning for the first time. Little M[ary] told me she had prayed for Grandpapa & wanted to know if he was better because people had prayed for him? I was much out of the room today. The hall has been made a sittingroom to keep the bed-room clear: & I gave way to my brothers just arrived. The albumen diet continued with excellent effect.[2] Even the critical hours this morning passed without drawback. In the evening there was a fresh access of strength. Among other things he asked 'What does Master William think of me?' mixing Willy & me in his ideas. I went to bed at 10½ after we had passed a

[1] One sentence in Morley, i. 402.
[2] 'The bowels were very slight' here deleted.

comfortable evening in domestic conversation. I read only the short (Sick Communion) Collect at prayers.

4. Th.

I rose & came down at 5: had coffee & read in the hall, performing service in the bedroom when needed, until a quarter to 8 when Helen called me in to help in raising him. He lay on his right side with an expression & air that made us uncomfortable. Before this he had actually called 'Get me some porridge' & Dr Guthrie who was with him this night said he might have it. In the night he had had tea & toast twice, & some beef tea with milk in it. At ¼ to 8 he was raised to be fed when the mouth was drawn & he could not articulate. Mustard plasters & blisters were used: the egg put into the mouth but a very small part swallowed: the injection used but with inadequate success. At 11.40 it having also appeared he could not swallow he was laid down & at 12.30 death appeared imminent. Yet he rallied & held on through the night which none of us spent in bed.

Wrote to Dean Ramsay—J. Griffiths.

I read both the prayers at 12.15 & 12.30 respectively in his bedroom.

5. Fr.

Wrote to Northcote—Haskell—R.M. Milnes—Dr Strange.

My Father in the early part of the day showed little change. At 1.40 he had a kind of slight convulsion—rallied again—& we dispersed. The death sweat came freely from this morning onwards. The face had been cold & hot again: so the left hand wh was exposed. He coughed at night: usually closed the lips when wetted. We walked out in front of the house—& C. caught from nervous excitement perhaps a violent tooth ach at night. Dr Guthrie left us last night. I read some of the Neapolitan MSS—Barborisi &c Hist.[1]—Also worked on some little compilations from the Psalms oh! what companions at this time. Ps. 130 was my staple in my dearest Father's room: it is the Psalm of charity which puts each man in the place & self of each other man. C. came down to the library: where I lay & slept from midnight to 5¾.

6. Sat.

Wrote to Reids—Jas Valentine[2]—J. Griffiths—Willy. Read Mayhew on the Street folk.[3] At nine we had a slight fresh alarm, from decaying pulse & strength. The respirations had now increased to past 30 at a time. Again he seemed to rally a little through the day. Once the eyes opened but there was no other sign of convulsion. The lips were wetted from time to

[1] Papers on Saverio Barborisi, who led Neapolitan crowd in 1848 demonstrations and was subsequently imprisoned.

[2] English merchant with a house on the Marina near Palermo; cp. *Senior, *Journals*, ii. 54.

[3] H. *Mayhew, *London labour and the London poor*, 2 v. (1851).

time. By evening the left hand face & left knee were cold: & at night the pulse very weak so that we did not like to go to bed. About nine his pillows & upper bedclothes were shifted. At this time the respirations passed forty with intervals perceptibly shortened.

My Father's Death.[1]

7. 2 S. Advent.

Chapel at 11 A.M. & 2½ P.M.

At 2 A.M. respirations reached 60—the intervals short—the exposed hand cold & becoming livid—the left knee cold—still the metal bed quivered to the strong heave of the chest.

But by five in the morning the greater part of his strength was gone. The face & head were cold. The respiration continuous & feeble. Then a little interval began to creep between each two & three breaths. At length between each one. His face was smoothed: his head so masculine & noble: he looked not more than sixty. There was no rapid decline: all was by steps till the very last—an effort at breathing, weaker than a dying infant might have made, air entering the mouth but not reaching the lungs: not a sound of pain. About an hour before there was the very faintest rattle, but it soon subsided. And so he died, upon the morning of the Lord's rest: oh what a day of meeting for him with his best beloved: his angelic daughter, his high hearted wife. My little Jessy too has she not seen them meet?

The Te Deum 80th Psalm & Advent Hymn were overpowering. Wrote to Willy—Mr Church—Andrew Robertson—E.L. Robertson—Rev. D. Robertson—Robert Gladstone—Adam Gladstone. Read Carter's Letter[2]—Liguori on BVM—Denison[3] on Educn.

8. M.

Wrote to Rev. Mr Jones—Dr Locock—Rev. Mr Rawson—Dr Simpson—Chas Wordsworth—Capt. Barclay—Mr Church—Jas. R. Hope—J. Henderson—Jas Watson—Robn. G.

Mr Tapp[4] & others came over & the funeral arrangements were made. I think the day too soon. I proposed the Holy Communion. John was willing & Tom I think would not have opposed: but from fear of stronger disapproval elsewhere. I did not press it, but it is a great loss to me. Walk with my brothers. Read Protestation du Peuple des Deux Siciles.[5] Preparatory conversations with my brothers on the property arrangements: which are far from simple in aspect.

[1] Headline on p. [112] of original, which contains all but the first and last few lines of this entry.

[2] T. T. Carter, 'Rome catholic and Rome papal. A letter to H. W. Lloyd' (1850).

[3] G. A. *Denison, 'A reply to the committee of the promoters of the Manchester and Salford education scheme' (1851).

[4] The undertaker.

[5] Tr. G. N. Ricciardi (1848).

9. T.

Wrote to Rev. Mr Irvine—Mr Sainthill[1]—Rev Mr Conolly—Mr O Brien—Rev. Mr. Duffield[2]—Mr F. Davis—Mr Harding. Drew up (in consultation) a skeleton of dates & facts for Mr Kaye of the Liverpool Courier (next day extended to the Montrose Standard also.) Also Memoranda of my Father's last days.[3] Walk with John. In the evening we discussed the question whether as proposed by Tom Mr Whyte was to offer his prayer in the Presbyterian manner before all those invited to the funeral in the dining room. Aunt J. approved of this & stated Helen's approval which was not well received. John & I disapproved: and Tom with great & laudable self-controul abandoned it. There were also (indirectly) other uneasy indications on Helen's part towards Catherine. But I hope this will be for us an house of peace. H.S. with the children.

10. Wed.

Wrote to Robertson—Provost Calvert[4]—Jas Watson—Largie[5]—Lindsay & Walker. Finished 'Protestation du Peuple des 2 Sic. H.S. with the children. Corrected & sent off the Skeleton for Montrose & Liverpool.[6] Saw D. Fergusson. Worked on the Memoranda. Visited the Vault. Tom unfortunately examined today into certain complaints between Mrs Harpur[7] & our nurse: & sent for me to my great regret. But I had no choice: & I was much distressed at the woman's gross misconduct & utter want of sense & understanding as shown towards Mrs Bovey[8] & otherwise. Tom was much displeased I regret to add at my naming my Father's latest & rather remarkable declaration about Sir R. Peel & Free Trade.[9] He likewise objected to my reading the Litany, or rather a part of it at family prayer: & determined (on my renewed offer) to take over the prayers into his own hands. Last night I conversed with John about Phesdo & other matters.

11. Th.

Wrote to Dr Thorn[10]—Newcastle—Ld Wenlock—& Mr H. Geale.[11] H.S. with the children. Visited the Vault. Read H. Geale on Ireland. In the morning we discussed not very satisfactorily Mr Ramsay's remaining over

[1] Richard Sainthill, 1787–1869; Irish antiquarian and numismatist.

[2] Matthew Dawson Duffield 1790?–1866; Caius, Cambridge, 1810; vicar of Stebbing, Essex, from 1842; chaplain to duke of Cambridge.

[3] Add MS 44739, f. 104.

[4] James Calvert, Montrose stockbroker and provost.

[5] George Largie; otherwise unidentified.

[6] See *Montrose Standard*, 12 December 1851, 4d and *Liverpool Courier*, 17 December 1851, 8d.

[7] Housekeeper?

[8] The nurse.

[9] Cp. Checkland, 372.

[10] Dr. Alexander Thorn of Banchory, Kincardineshire.

[11] Hamilton Geale, b. 1820; Trinity College, Dublin, 1834; at Irish bar from 1839; wrote on Italy; had probably sent an unpublished MS on Ireland. Cp. 5 Sept. 51 n.

Sunday. At night some conv. on property arrangements. I am driving for what I think very strong reasons at division as opposed to joint interests. Finished my Memoranda respecting my Father: & wrote a little of the MS. to the Bp of Aberdeen.[1] My Father's birthday.

12. Fr.

Wrote to C. Shaw—R. Phillimore—Rev. H. Mackenzie—H.S. with the children. Visited the Vault—took A. & S. there, also Mary.—And I had a last view of the honoured remains which I also showed to Willy (he wishing it) on his arrival. Walk with C. We discussed the question of dining with the funeral guests: it ended in my doing so, alone, but on the part of the family. From 10 to 1 A.M. we four discussed matters of business: as Robertson is obliged to go off tomorrow aftn. Read Irish Land Tenures.

13. Sat.

Wrote to Mr Empson—Lindsay & Walker—Supt. at Perth—J.R. Hope.

This was the day of my Father's funeral. There was a full & solemn attendance. Dean Ramsay read the service. He was laid by my mother's side. Willy knelt beside me in the vault. The order did not satisfy me: & as to what depended upon man the scene was not like Jessy's. But as to the inward & unseen the substance thank God is good. Most of our people went off immediately, or in the afternoon. John & Tom with me had three hours & upwards with Mr Myers. There is a great deal to be done & not all of it very easy. The inheritance besides the entail exceeds *gross* £200000: nett I should think it is £130000 besides the reversion of £40000: Mr Ramsay Mr Grant Goalen & Ogilvy remained. We dined & spent the evening with them. Also saw H.—John is unfortunately (at night) summoned by his wife.

I kissed thrice my Father's cheek & forehead before & after his death: the only kisses that I can remember. In the evening we discussed several questions: among others a suggestion from Tom that I & mine should move from hence earlier than we intended (i.e. than the 26th) to allow him to leave after us & be at Leamington before Christmas. I explained that our staying need not detain the servants.

14. 3 S. Advent.

Chapel 11 A.M. & 2½ P.M. Holy Communion mg. Walk with Mr Ramsay & conversations with him: especially on the lay element in Synods. Also conv. with T. Ogilvy. I tried my MS. to Bp of Abn. but my head is not clear: I am troubled at some things which have occurred. 'Make thy way plain before my face'.[2] But I myself darken it by my inventions. The services & holy song today were a great joy: & what was it to remember before the altar of God four such dear ones as lay beneath. Read a little Liguori. I rather

[1] See 2 Nov. 51.
[2] Psalms v. 8.

invert the method of the Bonaventura Psalter while reading such a book.[1] Wrote to Mr Haskell.

15. M.

Wrote to Sir John Forbes—Bp of Aberdeen—Rn. G—Jas Watson—Williams Deacon & Co (2)—Scotts. H.S. with the children. Visit to the Vault. Walk with C—& T. With Helen on Anne's books. And about pictures. Read Richson on the Manchr. Education Scheme[2]—& finished Barborisi. Busy with Tom on the arrangements.

16. T.

Wrote to Rev. C. Hume.[3]—J. Eveleigh[4]—Visc. Mahon—C. Stewart.—Peer Ibrahim Khan.—Rev. Mr. Dowding.[5]—G.A. Esson[6]—Sowerby.[7]—T. OBrien.[8]—P. Maitland.—Capt. Scott.—J. Lefevre. H.S. with the children. Prepared lists &c. for the division of the Silver & Plate under my Father's will: & we spent all the afternoon & evening in dividing.

17. Wed.

Wrote to Dean Ramsay—Rev. Mr Fisher—Rev. R. Scott—Mr Greig—(Vid. inf[9]) Mr H. Roberts. H.S. with the children—& visit to the Vault. Read Mure on Grote[10]—Suringar on Mettray[11]—Scottish Episcopal Canons.[12] Busied with arranging my letters. Walked up the hills: mist on the top but I had the same pleasure as in seeing an old friend though soiled with a journey. I noted these distances & put them down that if I look back upon this page I may love the old hills as I see them.

By West Garrol to last gate 1½ mile	20 min
Through the gorge to the stream, ¾ mile,	10 min

[1] *The psalter of the Blessed Virgin Mary illustrated; or a critical disquisition and enquiry concerning the genuineness of the parody on the psalms of David . . . ascribed to St. Bonaventure* (1840); in Latin and English.

[2] C. *Richson, 'A sketch of some of the causes which in Manchester induced the abandonment of the voluntary system in the support of schools, and the introduction of the Manchester and Salford Education Bill' (1851).

[3] Charles Hume; licentiate; rector of St. Michael, Wood Street, London, from 1849.

[4] Perhaps John Eveleigh, linendraper, of Hampstead Road, London.

[5] William Charles Dowding, b. ?1819; Exeter, Oxford; secretary of S.P.G.; vicar of St. Thomas's, Scarborough, from 1870.

[6] George A. Esson, accountant, of Great King Street, Edinburgh.

[7] George Brettingham *Sowerby, 1788–1854; conchologist and artist.

[8] Sir Timothy O'Brien, 1790–1862; liberal M.P. Cashel 1846–59; railway financier; cr. bart. 1849.

[9] *Vide infra*, see below: i.e. further list of letters at end of entry.

[10] W. Mure, 'Remarks on two appendices to the second volume, third edition, of Mr *Grote's History of Greece' (1851).

[11] W. H. Suringar, *My visit to Mettray in 1845*, tr. (1851).

[12] Probably 'The Scottish prayer book and the Scottish canons', *The Scottish Magazine and Churchman's Review*, i. 476, 521, 590 (October–December 1851).

Shank of Cairdown to top 1½ mile	24 min
Down, to point of East Garrol[1] road. 1¾ mile (say 12½)	13 min
To Annie Croals 1¼ mile	14½ min
Back to Fasque 1¼ mile	12½ min

Total eight miles & 1 h. 36 min.

Wrote also to A. Panizzi—S. Gurney jun.—Rev. R. Brett[2]—Barrack Serj. Lamont.[3] With Helen on Will affairs & arrangements—Tom, on do.

18. Th.

Wrote to J.N.G.—A. Williams—W.C. James—Scott & Co—Sir R. Inglis—Lindsay & Walker—G. Taylor—R. Wilberforce—R. Cavendish (2)—Robn. Gladstone—Jones & Yarrell. H.S. with the children. Latin verses with Willy. Walk with C—Then with Tom to Douglas's about a drain—There I found old Mrs Douglas very ill, apparently near to death, & + by her. I was so glad to know it. Busy on arrangements—set Willox to work on my Father's papers. Read a part of one of the (very trying) MS. letters from Naples.[4] They are[5] of great length in fact pamphlets but this one very remarkable.

19. Fr.

Wrote to . . . J.N.G.—James Watson—MacCulloch—H. Grant (Ch Ch)[6]—H.S. with A. & S.—Read Neapolitan MS. Revised the Lyttelton & Milnes corrections of 5 sheets of Farini, to send them to Panizzi with my own adoptions. Walked over Hunter's Hill to the Camp & examined that beautiful spot: then to Mrs Macintyre[7]—Gall—Mrs Croal—the Falconers—& lastly the Douglases—Found Mrs D. a little better & +. Accounts &c. Lesson to Willy in Gr. Grammar & verses.

20. Sat.

Wrote to Panizzi—G. Grant. H.S. with A. & S. Latin & Greek lessons with Willy—Mr Myers 3 hours on Executorship affairs 11–2. Walk with C—Worked on *reading* Neapolitan MS. a little more such would soon dispose

[1] 'peat' here deleted.

[2] Robert *Brett, 1808–74; physician; founded tractarian Guild of St. Luke for medical-clerical cooperation; wrote religious tracts, though never ordained; member of the 'engagement', cp. 23 Feb. 45 n.

[3] Obscure.

[4] Cp. 29 Nov. 51 n.

[5] Instead of 'It is'.

[6] Henry Grant, 1823?–76; the college butler, then in charge of rooms and a considerable entrepreneur, cp. E. G. W. Bill and J. F. A. Mason, *Christ Church and reform* (1970), 134–5.

[7] A tenant?

of my eyesight. Also worked 3½ hours on my Father's old letters. Unfortunately he destroyed all before 1812 except a few which escaped by chance.

21. S. 4 Adv[*ent*].

& St Thomas. Chapel 11 & 2½. Visited Mrs Douglas (+) & others. Walked with Mr Fergusson. Read Liguori Glorie—Armstrong. Wrote to Clarke—E. Badeley (long)—and worked a little on Letter to Bp of Aberdeen.

22. M.

Wrote to C. Wordsworth—Bp of Abn. (for consn.)—H.J.G.—Jas Watson—and [blank.] H.S. with W. and A. Worked on Latin &c. with Willy. He brought me his first original Latin verses as follows

> Fertiles terras summo de monte videtis
> Fasquae felicis, ruraq culta manu,
> Arvaq, jam nutrita cito currentibus undis
> Jucundos fructus tempore quaeq ferunt.[1]

I think there is promise in them. Drove C. to the Burn for farewell visit. Finished Letter to Bp of Aberdeen. Worked 4 h on Sir J.G's letters. Busy on wages &c. with Tom.

23. T.

Wrote to Jas Watson—Wm. Forbes—Rn. G—Supt Lkirk. H.S. with W. & A. Greek & Latin with Willy. Business matters with Tom. Walked Willy to the top of the hills by Garrol & back by Delaly: 8 or 8½ miles under 2 hours. He was very fresh in body & most *worthy*. Revised & corrected my MS. to the Bp of Aberdeen. Finished work upon Sir J.G's letters. Some of his Father's to him give me a high idea of the writer's moral tone & mild Christian wisdom. Preparations for departure.

24. Wed.

Wrote to Pritt (Lancaster)[2]—W. Forbes—Ld Aberdeen—Rev. Hutchins.[3] H.S. with W. & A. Visited the Vault. Many visits of farewell in the village & neighbourhood. Greek & Latin with Willy. Began to copy out my letter fair. Finished the Neapolitan MSS. Packing & preparations for departure. Engaged upon the household accounts.

[1] 'From the top of the mountain you can see the fertile lands of happy Fasque, and the country cultivated by the labourer's hand, and the fields now nourished by the swift-flowing waters and which bear pleasant fruits in season.'

[2] Cp. 28 Feb. 50.

[3] William Horace Hutchins, episcopal incumbent of St. James's episcopal chapel, Dingwall, where Sir J. *Gladstone had owned almhouses.

25. Christmas Day.

Services 11 with H.C. & 2½ P.M. Wrote to Mr Panizzi—Mr Falconer—Jas Watson—T.G—Many visits (making 29 in all with yesty.—Mr Whyte the highest)—saw Mrs Douglas & +. Dined with the Forbeses. Copied a little of my MS. Farewell visit to the Vault. Some dregs of packing still remained for today and evg.

26. Friday. (St Stephen).

At 6 A.M. we bid our final adieu to Fasque as a home: the thought of it must for me ever be full of moving recollections. We left Laurencekirk at 7¼: and prosperously reached Lancaster in 12 hours. At 7.35 we reached the Kings Arms, where all was ready & *most* comfortable. I copied a little MS. to Bp of Aberdeen. Oh the irksomeness of that labour. But it enables me to emend.

27. Sat. (St John.)

Wrote to G.C. Tyler[1]—T.G. Reached (Union Court) Lpool at 11. Took C. & the party to the Ferry: & remained for business of the Executorship: occupied most of the day with Robn., Brackenridge[2] & Stanistreet. Dined & slept at Courthey. Copied more MS.

28. S. aft Xmas & H. Innocents.

Came into Liverpool by Rail for morning Church at St Thomas's Toxteth. After service I introduced myself to the clergyman Mr Powell.[3] I noted some things with pain. Crossed to Chester & walked thence to Hawarden for dinner & evening Church. I saw a young girl I am afraid on the way to ruin. Copied more MS.

29. M.

Church 8½ A.M. Wrote to J.N.G. Saw Burnett & went over the draft Railway agreement with him. Pressed S. & H. on the subject of the Grammar School now vacant. Read up papers & letters. Chess with S.

The children (3) wrote to me birthday letters, very acceptable gifts. Would that I were worthier of these & all mercies. But it has been to me a sad year. Almost utterly overthrown, almost a mere wreck of what might have been a Christian. If I have had in my soul any consolatory token it is this that the thought of God's presence & judgment is ever dear to me. But what things have I not done or trodden on the edge of while entertaining that thought. In truth the religious trials of the time have passed my capacity & grasp. I am bewildered, & reel under them. And this does not

[1] George Griffiths Tyler, J.E.'s* son by his 1st (non-Robertson) marriage.

[2] Edward Brackenridge, Seaforth farmer and friend of the Gladstone family; sometimes spelt Breackenridge by Gladstone.

[3] Joseph Ormsby Powell, licentiate; curate of St. Thomas', Toxteth Park, Liverpool, from 1850. The diarist inherited the patronage of the living from his father.

purify but relaxes me & leaves me more open to the invader. So spurious & false a thing I am O God. But I am in thine hand: & Thou wilt show forth thy wisdom and justice, which is all one with thy long-suffering mercy, in me, whether as I think & wish, or whether other & better wise. Amen.

30. T.

Church 8½ A.M. Latin & Greek with Willy. With C. at the Castle. Farther conv. on the School. Wrote to H.J.G.—Bp of Oxford—Robertson—Bp of Aberdeen (recast my covering letter). Finished my transcription to Bp of Aberdeen.

31. Wed.

Ch. 8½ A.M. Wrote to Panizzi—J. Murray—Mahon—W. Ford.[1] Greek & Latin with Willy. Went to work on Neapolitan MS. & my new pamphlet (in posse).[2] Saw J. Shaw. Read Shakespeare. With C. at the Castle—& at Broughton. Chess with Stephen.

It has been a sad year: I do not mean the event of the last month. He that sleeps, sleeps well. I mean the rending & sapping of the Church, the loss of its gems, the darkening of its prospects; as well as the ill fruit this has had in me individually.[3] But the life is in me yet: nor can I even say it is weakened though all outward & earthly influences are against it.

[1] Probably William Ford, 1812–89; London solicitor, in firm of Ranken and Co.

[2] Add MS 44685, f. 1, published as 'An examination of the official reply of the Neapolitan government' (1852), reprinted in *Gleanings*, iv. 71.

[3] Cp. 19 Aug. 51.

Hawarden
Thursday January One 1852
Circumcision.

Church 11 A.M. Lessons with Willy. Wrote to Sir J. S. Forbes—T.G.—Bp of Aberdeen—A. Panizzi—Jas Watson—G. Burnett—R. Cavendish. Read (resumed) L'Assedio di Firenze[1]—Lushington on Neapn. Defence.[2]. Chess with Stephen. Saw Mr Burnett—on Railroad, & farm Rents & management. Wrote Mem. for settlement with the residue.[3]

2. Fr.

Church 8½ A.M. Wrote to Duke of Newcastle—J. Murray—Alex. Oswald—F. Lygon ChCh[4]—R. Baxter. Lessons with Willy. Read Irish Tenures[5]—Assedio di Firenze. Walk with Stephen. Chess with C.G.

3. Sat.

Church 8½ A.M. Wrote to Earl of Aberdeen—Scotts—Mrs G. Malcolm—C. Gerard—J.D. Acland[6]—A. Panizzi. Lessons in Gr[eek] & Lat[in] with Willy. Read the new Quarterly on Farini—on the French Revolution—on Heron's Notes—& part on Junius.[7] Chess with Stephen. Walk with S. & H.

4. 2 S. Xmas.

Church 11 A.M. with Holy Commn.—& 7 P.M.—Read Christian Remembrancer on Jansenism—on Carlyle's Sterling[8]—Bp Forbes on Te Deum—[9] Knott's Letter[10]—Ffoulke's Manual.[11]

[1] Cp. 13 Sept. 51.
[2] H. *Lushington, *A detailed exposure of the apology put forth by the Neapolitan government in reply to the charges of Mr. Gladstone* (1851).
[3] Hawn P.
[4] Frederick Lygon, 1830–91; Christ Church, Oxford, 1848–52; fellow of All Souls 1852–1866; tory M.P. Tewkesbury 1857–63, Worcestershire 1863–6; 6th Earl Beauchamp 1866; minor office 1859, 1874–80; had requested a subscription for new Oxford Union building; Gladstone sent £20.
[5] Cp. 27 Nov. 51.
[6] John Barton Arundel Dyke Acland, 1823–1904; 6th s. of Sir T. D. Acland, 10th bart.; barrister, later in New Zealand.
[7] *Quarterly Review*, xc. 226, 257, 206, 91 (December 1851); articles by E. Cheney, *Croker and D. T. Coulton.
[8] *Christian Remembrancer*, xxiii. 89, 153 (January 1852); reviews of S. P. Tregelles, *The Jansenists* (1851) and T. *Carlyle, *Sterling* (1851).
[9] A. P. *Forbes, *A commentary on the Te Deum* (1850).
[10] John W. Knott, 'A letter to the parishioners of St. Saviour's, Leeds' (1851).
[11] E. S. Ffoulkes, *A manual of ecclesiastical history, from the first to the twelfth century* (1851).

5. M.

Wrote to Jas Watson—T.G.—D. Fergusson—J.N.G.—J. Griffiths—H.J.G.—Provost of Oriel—A. Williams [1]—Bp of Oxford. H.S. with A. & S. Greek & Latin lessons with Willy. Saw Burnett on Railway—Finished Quarty. on Junius—read Clements on Farmers Sons' Education.[2] At night we discussed the arrangements for joint residence in the Castle—please God.

Henry's Children are about the best I ever saw: & Nora a perfect sylph. They do honour to all who have been concerned with them: most of all to her who is gone. Church 8½ A.M.

6. Epiphany.

Church 11 A.M. C.G.s birthday: may God crown her with every gift—but few indeed are wanting yet. Children to tea, cake, & snapdragon in evg. Greek & Latin with Willy (for whom I have translated some Cicero that he may retranslate). Planning journies. Memoranda on jointure arrangement & on residence. Saw Mr Burnett. Visited St John's—admirable.[3] Wrote to M. Lyttelton—Robn. G—G. Burnett—Scotts—R. Wilberforce—J. Murray—Mr Moffat—Jones & Yarrell. Chess with S.R.G. Read Xtian Rem[embrance]r on Coplestone.[4]

7. Wed.

Church 8½ A.M. & at Buckley 6½ P.M. Wrote to J. Griffiths—J. Amery—Wm Chance—Sir J. S. Forbes—Bp of Aberdeen—D. Fergusson—E. Coleridge—W.M.H. Church—Ld Braybrooke—Wm Griffiths. Greek & Latin with Willy. His verses improve. e.g.

Et riget amissâ spina relicta rosâ.[5]

Drove C. to Broughton—Read De Bary's Travels [6]—Col. Ch. Magazine for materials. Dined with Mr Ffoulkes [7] at 4½. After Church, by request from him delivered an address on Missions, chiefly Colonial.[8] By order, over an hour. An attentive auditory. Home by 10. Sent my MS.'Letter to Bp of Aberdeen' away to press.[9]

[1] Probably Alfred Williams, 1818–77; fellow of King's, Cambridge, 1841; curate of Stourbridge 1846–50, of Spon Lane, Birmingham, 1850–54, and sundry other charges.

[2] J. Clements, *The farmers' case with regard to education, plainly stated in a letter addressed to the farmers & other parishioners of Upton St. Leonards* (1851).

[3] St. John's church, Hawarden; cp. 23 July 46n.

[4] *Christian Remembrancer*, xxiii. 1 (January 1852); review of W. J. Copleston, *Memoir of Edward Copleston* (1851).

[5] 'And once the rose is gone, the thorn left behind turns hard'.

[6] T. De Bary, *Notes of a residence in the Canary Islands, the south of Spain, and Algiers* (1851).

[7] i.e. H. P. Foulkes.

[8] No report traced.

[9] Cp. 2 Nov. 51.

8. Th.

Church 8½ A.M. Wrote to Earl of Aberdeen—C.G.—Provost of Oriel—Anderson—Dean Ramsay. Latin & Greek lessons with Willy. Began to correct proofs of Farini. Read Cowley[1]—Sedley.[2] Saw Mr. Burnett ab[out] Moor Farm.[3] Arranging clothes &c. to be left in depot here. Arranged letters.

9. Fr.

Ch. 8½ A.M. Wrote to H. Tayleur—C.G.[4]—J. Griffiths—J. Murray—Bp of Oxford—J.N.G.—Mr J. Swift. Gk & Latin with Willy. Worked on proofs of Farini. Saw Mr Burnett on RR—Mr Baxter on RR Arbitration. Chess with Stephen. Read Assedio di Firenze.

10. Sat.

Church 8½ A.M. Wrote to Jas Freshfield—R.G.—J. Murray—J.N.G. H.S. with A. & S.—Verses, Cicero Transl & Retr[anslation], & Gk Grammar, as us[ual] with W. Examined Freshfield's accounts. Saw Burnett on Railway & Moor Farm. Drew skeleton Schedules for Landed property Accounts.[5] Walked to Moor Farm with S. & H.—Read Assedio di Firenze. Chess with Stephen.

11. 1 S. Epiph.

Ch. 11 A.M. 6½ P.M. Wrote to Bp of Brechin—C.G.—Jas Watson. Corrected proofs of Letter to Bp of Abn.—Read Chr. Rem.—Xtn Year—Glorie di Maria[6]—Robertson's Sermon & Addresses.[7]

12. M.

Chapel 8½ AM. Wrote to Bp of Aberdeen—S.M. Peto[8]—J. Murray—A. Panizzi—C.G.—Hugh Scott—Robt. Gladstone—Mr J. Kendall[9]—Scotts—Sir F.H. Doyle. Worked on Letter & abridged the Primus's for the 'Advertisement'.[10] Greek & Latin lessons with Willy. Archdn. Wilberforce came in aftn. We conversed anxiously much & late. He has sunk since we last met, I

[1] A. *Cowley, *Poems . . . with life by Dr. *Johnson*, in A. Chalmers, *Works of the English poets* (1810), vii.

[2] Sir Charles Sedley, the rake, *Works*, 2 v. (1722).

[3] One mile NE. of Hawarden; arrangements had been made for it to be sold, cp. Gladstone to his wife, 9 January 1852, Hawn P.

[4] Bassett, 85.

[5] Hawn P.

[6] Cp. 23 Nov. 51.

[7] F. W. *Robertson, 'The Israelite's grave in a foreign land. A sermon . . .' (1850); and 'An address delivered at the opening of the working men's institute [at Brighton]' (1849).

[8] (Sir) Samuel Morton *Peto, 1809–1889; railway constructor; lib. M.P. Norwich 1847–54, Finsbury 1859–65; cr. bart. 1855 for constructing Balaclava railway; bankrupt 1866.

[9] John Robinson Kendall, accountant in Toxteth Park, Liverpool.

[10] W. *Skinner to Gladstone, 9 January 1852, printed as an 'Advertisement' in Gladstone, *Letter to *Skinner*, 3.

mean in his stedfastness to Ch[urch of] E[ngland]: but I hope may yet hold.[1]—I gave him mine to Bp of Abn. that I may get his opinion.

13. T.

Church 8½ A.M. Wrote to C.G. T.G. R.Greswell G. Lacaita. H.S. with A. & S. Greek & Latin lessons with Willy. Read Assedio di Firenze. Went to Chester with the Archdn.[2] & our conversations renewed mg & evg. Saw Mr Burnett—Mr Barker—Mr Williams (Bank)—and Mr Raikes at the Registry where I exam[ine]d the St Thomas Seaforth & St Th[omas] Toxteth Consecration Deeds & papers.[3]

14. Wed.

Church 8½ A.M. H.S. with A. & S. Greek & Latin lessons with Willy. Wrote to Mr J. Freshfield—J. Swift—Mr. G. Burnett—Scotts. Chess with Stephen. Arranging for departure. Saw Mr. Burnett.

15. Th.

Off at 8.10 for Broughton. Liverpool (U[nion?] Court)[4] at 10. Saw Mrs Dummert—G. Grant—H. Tayleur—E. Brackenridge. Spent 3 hours with the latter (chiefly) on the Seaforth valuation. On to Manchester at 2: joined Willy there & went on to Clumber which we reached at 7¼ and found a kind welcome & many friends with whom the evening passed right pleasantly. At night, late, I went to work to draw definitively my Memorandum for settle-with my Brothers: & explanations.[5]

16. Fr.

Wrote to Williams & Co—J. Murray—Clowes—J. Griffiths Robn. G. In the forenoon Newcastle detailed & read his proceedings with Ld J. Russell.[6] Conversation with Ld Aberdeen afterwards. We then walked in the Park & to N's very large, I fear too large & costly farm. In aftn a long convn. with N. & Lyttelton on the N. Zealand draft bill:[7] no easy matter. At night & in mg. conversation with Young. Read 'Qui nous sommes'.[8]

17. Sat.

Wrote to Panizzi. Resumed working on the Neapolitan Rassegna and other *relative* papers: having in a conv. with Ld Abn. arranged that I should pro-

[1] He became a roman catholic in 1854.
[2] i.e. R. I. *Wilberforce.
[3] Churches in which Sir John Gladstone had had a controlling interest.
[4] Business untraced.
[5] Hawn P.
[6] For this, and the Peelite conference at Clumber, see J. B. Conacher, *The Peelites and the party system 1846–52* (1972) 94–7.
[7] The New Zealand Government Bill, 1° in *H* cxxi. 299; see *Newcastle's question on 10 February 1852 in *H* cxix. 323.
[8] Not traced; this year Gladstone read a number of mildly titillating French books, cp. 28 May, 21 June etc.

ceed.[1] In the forenoon N., Ld Ab., C[ardwell]., S.H. & I, discussed the reply to Ld J.R. & our political position generally. I fear we are not agreed on the practical course to be taken in regard to the Govt. Read Berni[2] & the Rassegna afresh. Conversation with Young in evg. Greek & Latin with Willy.

18. 2 S. Epiph.

Church service in the Chapel 11½ A.M. Walk with the party in aftn (except Bonham) & a long conversation afterwards including all. We were upon what might follow a break up of the present Govt. & were at one. Also I discussed with S. Herbert Ld Blandford's Church Bill.[3] Worked on the Naples Pamphlet: & [blank] Wrote to Murray—with part of the MS. It was not pleasant to be off Sunday occupations so much today. But the cause of humanity was clear: & the other subject I thought demanded the sacrifice. At night by sitting up till 3 AM finished the Naples Pamphlet: then read (Willy's) Devotions for School Boys.[4] Read Specchio della Pen[itenz]a.[5]

19. M.

Wrote to Bp of Oxford. Left Clumber at 9½: by Eckington[6] with C. to Derby then on with Willy to London. On the way, I amended the MS. for press—corrected two proof sheets of Farini—& then schooled Willy a little in Grammar, & talked to him on many serious matters—he was very satisfactory & in excellent spirits. Reached London about 5 P.M. With Panizzi on Naples, & on Farini's proofs, till near 7. Then to No 6, made arrangements saw Mary & at 8 came on to Eton—wh we reached at ¼ to 10, & supped with the Coleridges. I afterwards read a multitude of letters.

20. T.

(Chapel evg Cuddesdon[7]—a shortened service, with exposition of the lesson) Wrote to J. Murray—T.G.—Vice Chan. Oxf—C.G.—& [blank.] Read Meyrick on Ch. of Spain.[8] Saw Mrs Harris[9]—Conv. with E.C[oleridge]—Took Willy to Dr Hawtrey: he was then examined but quite oppressed & broke down sadly, as compared with what he could do. I left him a little before three after trying to talk him *up*. Saw Cardwell in RR. Cuddesdon at 6. The Vice Chancellor & an elder party from Oxf. dined. Conv. with Dr Acland on Univ. matters late at night.

[1] With his 'Examination', cp. 24 Nov. and 31 Dec. 51.
[2] Probably Francesco Berni, poet, *Opere burlesche*, 3v. (1823–4).
[3] On episcopal and capitular revenues, cp. *H* cxx. 1317.
[4] *Daily devotions for young persons* (1844).
[5] Untraced pietistic work.
[6] Railway station six miles SE. of Sheffield.
[7] The bp. of Oxford's palace. For Gladstone's visit, cp. R. G. Wilberforce, *Life of *Wilberforce* (1881), ii. 134–6.
[8] F. Meyrick, *The practical working of the church in Spain* (1851).
[9] Katherine Lucia, *née* O'Brien, m. 1837 Charles Amyand Harris, 1813–74, 3rd s. of 2nd earl of Malmesbury; prebendary of Salisbury 1841–63; archdeacon of Wiltshire 1863–8; bp. of Gilbraltar 1868. They lived for part of the year in Windsor; she d. 1865.

21. Wed.

Chapel mg & night—Church (full s[ervice] & serm) 6 P.M. Wrote to Rev. S. Andrew[1]—Ph. Pusey—E. Coleridge—Dr Pusey—Hon & R[ev]. E. Howard[2]—Willy (2). Rev. F.W. Russell[3]—Dr Jelf—C.B. Adderley[4]—J.N.G.—Miss C. Weale.[5] A very unhappy note from Willy. I shall be uneasy unless the next is better: his sorrows cut me to the soul for I know that for the time they are sharp enough. Walk & much conv. with the Bishop—over old & loved scenes. And the large & pleasant Oxford party to dinner. Saw Dr Acland. Read Meyrick.

22. Th.

Palace Chapel mg 9 A.M. Wrote to E. Brackenridge—C.G.[6]—G. Burnett—Willy. Wrote & copied out after conv. with Bp Memorandum of main points in the picture of the Church as it stands.[7] Read Bp Exeter to Archdn. of Totnes (part).[8] Rode & walked with the Bp into Oxford—2 good hours on Church policy: read him my Memm. From 4¼ to 6¼ with the LNW. and GN Agents at the Star. I *hope* they are now brought together.[9] A Party to dinner at Oriel. I got conv. about the Commission & College Reforms, particularly with the V.C. & the Princ[ipal] of BNC.

23. Fr.

Ch Ch Prayers 4 P.M. Wrote to Dow[age]r Lady Lyttelton—C.G.—Henry Glynne—Willy—G.F. Mathison—Mrs Hampton. Breakfast Provost of Oriel's. Dinner Vice Chancellor's where we discussed the bookseller's monopoly.[10] Made many calls. Read Brevi Risposte[11]—Catechismo contro le Rivoluzioni.[12]

24. Sat.

(Missed prayers at Magd. they not having begun). Breakfast at Mr Greswell's—Dinner at Oriel. A day of calls, from Pres. of Magd[alen] downwards.

[1] Samuel Andrew, 1817–89; curate of Brackley 1840–1; headmaster of Truro grammar school 1852–5; rector of Halwell, Devon, 1853–89.

[2] i.e. H. E. J. *Howard.

[3] Frederick William Russell, d. *ca.* 1875; B.A. Durham 1847, fellow there; chaplain of Charing Cross hospital from 1867.

[4] Encouraging him to move his Cape motion, which effectively felled the govt.; cp. 20 Feb. 52 and W. S. C. Pemberton, *Life of Lord Norton* (1909) 103–4.

[5] Charlotte Weale, known as sister Doratea, of the Clewer house of mercy.

[6] Bassett, 85.

[7] Add MS 44740, f. 1 and in Lathbury, i. 88.

[8] H. *Phillpotts, 'A letter to the archdeacon of Totnes in answer to an address . . . on the necessity of episcopal ordination' (1852).

[9] An amalgamation dispute, cp. O. S. Nock, *The great northern railway* (1958) 29ff.

[10] Cp. 12 May 52.

[11] 'Brevi riposte alle lettere di Sir W. E. Gladstone indiritte al conte *Aberdeen intorno al governo e al popolo Napoletano' (1851). The pamphlet knights Gladstone *passim.*

[12] In G. Massari, *Il signor Gladstone* (1851); cp. 9 Oct. 51.

Read the 'Losanna' Collection[1]—Ed. Rev. on Bp of Exeter[2]—Description of Vicaria.[3]

25. 3 S. Epiph. & Conv. St Paul.

Ch Ch 8 AM—Magd. 4 P.M. Univ. Sermon 10½ A.M. (Mr Jowett,[4] very remarkable, but unsettling)—& 2 P.M. Walk with Prov. Oriel. Breakfast with Dr Jacobson. Dinner Rector of Exeter in Hall. Worked[5] at night on the Documents in the Case of May 15[6]—and read Babbage[7]—Meyrick.

26. M.

Chapel[8] at Oriel 8 A.M. Wrote to C.G.—T.G: on hearing of the unexpected death of his little Evelyn.[9] Breakfast party at Mr Haddan's. Saw Mr Lacaita. Off at 10.45 (met Lady Norreys) & reached Eton at 1. Spent an hour with Willy & Coleridge. Reached London at four. Saw Panizzi on Neap. pamphlet. Read 'Castel Capuano'.[10] Visited E.C. & spent a long time —tea there [R]. Matters have gone pretty well there: yet mine is a wretched part. Worked on books & papers late at night.

27. T.

Wrote to C.G.—Willy—T. Goalen—J. Murray—and Tupper. Saw Lacaita —Lyttelton (NZ.)—S. & H. Glynne (the Castle)—M.Ln. Dined at Mr G. Harcourts. Worked most of the day & at night on the proofs of my 'Examination' adding divers passages. Read a Colonial Dignitary[11]—Gondon's Introdn.[12]

28. Wed.

Wrote to C.G. Read Reports from South Australia[13]—Cecile.[14] Saw Panizzi —Calls. Worked long & hard among books papers & miscellanies: but I am not yet out of Chaos, or near it.

29. Th.

Wrote to J. Lacaita—Jas Watson—Saw Mr Murray—Calls. 11–2. To B.M. with Panizzi on the Revises of my pamphlet about Naples. Worked

[1] Untraced, unless the collection of documents read next day.

[2] W. J. *Conybeare on *Phillpotts in *Edinburgh Review*, xcv. 59 (January 1852).

[3] Probably MS; cp. 3 Jan. 51.

[4] Benjamin *Jowett, 1817–93; tutor at Balliol 1842–70, master there 1870–93; regius professor of Greek 1855; vice-chancellor 1882–6; contributor to *Essays and reviews* (1860); controversial Oxford 19th century figure, much involved in civil service reforms 1853–4.

[5] Instead of 'read'.

[6] 'Atti e documenti del processo di maesta per gli avvenimenti del 15 Maggio 1848 in Napoli' (1851); the case against Barbarisi *et al.*

[7] C. *Babbage, *The exposition of 1851* (1851).

[8] Instead of 'wrote to'.

[9] Cp. 30 Sept. 50n.

[10] i.e. on the Vicaria prison.

[11] Not found.

[12] Jules Gondon's preface to the English tr. of his *La terreur dans le royaume de Naples* (1851).

[13] Annual reports for 1850 on South Australia, *PP* 1851, xxxiv. 99.

[14] [J. La Vallée] *Cécile, fille d'Achmet III Empereur des Turcs*, 2v. (1787); a romance.

on proofs of Farini. Saw pictures at Christie's. Dined with J.N.G. & conv. Worked further on pamphlets letters & Parl. papers.

30. Fr.

Wrote to C.B. Adderley—Bp of Aberdeen—Mr Panizzi—Bp of Argyll—W.H.G.—Editor of Guardian—M.F. Tupper—Signor Massari[1]—Ld Shaftesbury. Saw Lady Hope—H.J.G. & her House Agent; & visited three houses with her. Saw J. Young—Goulburn. Worked on letters & Bills. Dined with the Norreys's: talked on his strange politics.[2] Went to the Farquhars afterwards: urged him to cooperate in the matter of lay functions. My Naples pamphlet came out today. C. arrived in evg. with Lena thank God better at least for the time. Worked on proofsheets Farini.

31. Sat.

Wrote to Mr Bates—G. Burnett (2)—Ld Granville[3]—G. Grant—Sir W. Temple—Mr E.N. Brown—Hon S. Lyttelton—Mr Hyatt—Mr F. Peel. Dined with Lady Hope—We met Badeley: not gone? It is a wonder. New Zealand party 11–2½: drew rough draft of Resolutions on the whole subject.[4] Went horse hunting with M'Culloch.[5] Saw Ld Aberdeen—H.J. G. (ab. houses)—Hayward, in evg. Locock saw Lena & reported her case delicate & one for care. Meantime she is much better.

1. Feb. 4 S. Epiph.

St Martins & H.C. mg. Bedfordbury evg. Wrote to Bp of Edinburgh.—Mrs E. Peel[6]—Rev. P. Connelly—G.F. Mathison. Townsend aloud in evg. Read Bp of Oxford's Charge, & Appendix[7]—Bp of Exeter's Letter to[8] the Archdeacon of Totnes. Saw W.C. James.

2. M. Purifn.

Titchfield St Chapel 5 P.M. Wrote to Ricciardi—Milnes—Carré[9]—W. Gray—Williams & Co—H. Tayleur—Stanistreet—Newcastle. Saw Newcastle & S. Herbert—Christie—Panizzi (on Farini at B[ritish] M[useum]).

[1] Giuseppi Massari, 1821–84; Italian politician and writer; translated Gladstone's Italian pamphlets; cp. 9 Oct. 51.

[2] Jephson Norreys, a Whig, voted intermittently for and against the corn laws.

[3] Sending copies of Neapolitan pamphlets, cp. Fitzmaurice, **Granville* i. 78.

[4] Add MS 44568, f. 12.

[5] Robert MacCulloch, the coachman.

[6] Perhaps Emily Peel, *née* Swinfen, who m. 1812 Edmund Peel, 1791–1850, younger brother of the prime minister.

[7] S. *Wilberforce, 'A charge . . . at his second visitation, November 1851'; with an appendix on education.

[8] 'Sir R. Inglis' here deleted.

[9] Probably Collings Mauger Carré, 1809–54; Magdalene hall, Oxford; from 1828 an Irvingite evangelist.

Dined with the J. Talbots.[1] Worked on Farini proofsheets. Busy on accounts & papers.

3. T.

Wrote to . . . J. Murray—Bishop of Exeter. House of Commons 4¼–12, on the Address.[2] Saw Sir G. Clerk—S. Herbert & Duke of Newcastle—W.F. Campbell—Mr Peto. Read Bp of Exeter's Letter to Sir R. Inglis.[3]

4. Wed.

Wrote to Mr Jas Watson—Mr F.R. Davis[4]—Mr S.M. Peto—G and Co—Rev. J. Wilson—Rn. G—Rev. F.G. White[5]—Rev. H. Hayman[6]—Cath. Frost[7]—Mr R. Cottle[8]—Miss Weale—Mr G. Burnett—Hyatt—Mrs H. Spencer—Mrs Willes[9]—C.A. Wood—J. Griffiths—Rev. E. Hawkins. Saw J. Lefevre—Lyttelton—A. Oswald—Panizzi. Worked on letters & accounts. Dined with the Cannings—Lady Granville's afterwards. Started the new horses. Read Mr Connelly to Ld Shrewsbury (proof)[10]—Cécile.

5. Th.

Wrote to Spottiswoodes—J. Murray—Herries & Co[11]—Brewster—Flower[12]—Galleano—Tupper—Parker—Dr Jelf—Masson. Saw Mr Adderley (Cape)—Bp of London (Ct of Appeal Bill)[13]—Rt Gladstone & Mr Richson on Manchr. Education—Ld Harris. Worked on Farini Revises. Read Cape papers.[14] Eight to dinner at home. Read Cécile—Disraeli's Bentinck.[15] H. of C. 4½–6½.[16] Saw Mr Goulburn on W.I. motion.

[1] John Chetwynd Talbot m. 1830 Caroline Jane, da. of 1st Lord Wharncliffe; she d. 1876. Cp. 4 Feb. 33.

[2] Interjected on France: *H* cxix. 93.

[3] H. *Phillpotts, 'A letter to Sir R. *Inglis . . . on certain statements in an article of the Edinburgh Review, No. 193, entitled "Bishop Phillpotts"' (1852).

[4] Of Hoxton; Gladstone sent him £2 to assist his education.

[5] Francis Gilbert White, 1824–95; chaplain to bp. of Newfoundland; headmaster in South Africa 1857–60; vicar of Leusden, Devon from 1879.

[6] Henry Hayman, 1823–1904; fellow of St. John's, Oxford 1844; headmaster of various schools 1855–69, of Rugby 1869–74; rector of Aldingham, Leicestershire 1874–1904.

[7] Involved with D. Weale in sisters of mercy?

[8] Perhaps Robert Cottle, 1774–1858, author on religion and founder of the Cottleite sect at Putney.

[9] Perhaps the wife of James Shaw Willes, Temple barrister.

[10] By Pierce Connelly, published as 'Reasons for abjuring allegiance to the see of Rome. A letter to the earl of Shrewsbury' (1852).

[11] Herries, Farquhar, Davidson, Chapman and co., bankers in St. James's street.

[12] Probably William Balmber Flower, 1819–68; missionary, then a master at Christ's hospital 1847–50; sundry curacies 1850–5; author and editor.

[13] *Blomfield intended to revise his 1850 bill on the ecclesiastical jurisdiction of the judicial cttee. of the privy council; cp. *H* cxxi. 427 (10 May 1852).

[14] On a representative assembly at the Cape: *PP* 1852 xxxiii. 181.

[15] *Disraeli, *Lord George *Bentinck: a political biography* (1852).

[16] Misc. business: *H* cxix. 185.

6. Fr.

Wrote to Mrs Labalmondière—Rev. T.H. Greene [1]—Mr F. Peel. Dined with the Jameses. Saw Bp of Exeter (breakfast)—J. Young—Dr Reid—Mr Sewell & Co (N.Z.)—Mr J.H. Parker—Lord Harris. Read Cécile (finished)—Dandolo's Italian volunteers.[2] H. of C. 5–6½.[3] Worked on papers & accts.

7. Sat.

Ch Ch Broadway 6 P.M. St Martins Baptm. of the Lyttelton baby 11½ A.M.[4]

Wrote to

Rev. Mr Fagge
Craig
J. Ley[5]
Stephen
W. Rogers
Rev. Mr Hansell[6]
J.P. Gell
J. James
Archd. Hayden
Mr Townsend
Mr Roddam Tate.[7]

Saw Geo Hope—Bp of Oxford—JNG—J.D. Coleridge—T. Baring [8]—Panizzi. Dined with the Farquhars—Mr Lushington's & Lady Palmerston's afterwards. Worked [9] on papers & accts.

8. Septuagesima S.

Pimlico & H.C. 11–2. Chapel Royal aft.—Ms on Gospel aloud. Wrote to Bp of Tasmania. Saw Newcastle—R. Cavendish. Dined with the R. Lawleys.[10] Read Launceston Proceedings [11]—Bp Tasmania's Charge & Appx [12]—Archd. Garbett's charge.[13]

9. M.

Wrote to Bp of Sydney—Bp of Tasmania—Miss Nicholson. New Zealand discussion 11¾ to 2½—saw Newcastle on his correspondence (bis)—R.

[1] Thomas Huntley Greene, 1824–87; Balliol, Oxford; chaplain to bp. of Gibraltar 1848, to Grey's Inn 1850–6; sundry rectorships 1856–87.

[2] E. Dandolo, *The Italian volunteers and Lombard Rifle brigade* (1849, tr. 1851).

[3] Chancery Relief Bill: *H* cxix. 201.

[4] Arthur Temple *Lyttelton, 1852–1903; 5th s. of 4th Baron Lyttelton; tutor at Keble, Oxford, 1879–82; master of Selwyn, Cambridge, 1882–93; bp. of Southampton 1898; archdeacon of Winchester 1900.

[5] John Ley, 1805–?92; fellow of Exeter, Oxford, 1831–51; rector of Waldron, Sussex, 1850–80.

[6] Edward Halifax Hansell, 1814–84; tutor of Merton, Oxford, 1845–9; fellow of Magdalen, Oxford, 1852–6; rector of Ilsley, Berkshire, 1865–84.

[7] James Roddam Tate, secretary of the Church of England scripture readers' association.

[8] Thomas *Baring, 1799–1873; financier, tory M.P. Yarmouth 1835–7, Huntingdon 1844–73; refused the Exchequer 1852, 1858.

[9] Instead of 'Read'.

[10] Probably B. R. Lawley and his wife.

[11] On Bible Society activities in Launceston, Tasmania.

[12] F. R. Nixon, 'A charge delivered . . . in May 1851 (1851).

[13] J. Garbett, 'Diocesan synods and convocation' (1852).

Palmer (Col. Ch.)—Herbert (M. Chron.)[1]—Adderley (Cape)—R. Barker (S.R.G.). Read Roebuck on the Whig Ministry[2]—Foreign Refugee Papers.[3] H. of C. 4½–8¼ on Reform Bill.[4] The Herberts dined with us.

10. T.

Wrote to Miss Brown—Williams Deacon & Co—Ld John Thynne—Rev. H. M'Kenzie—S.H. Northcote—Bp of Brechin—J. Phillips—J.H. Parker—J. Griffiths—Mayor of Newark.[5] Read NZ papers—Stuart of Dunleath.[6] In the City aftn.: saw Longden—Wm Gladstone—Williamses—Freshfields &c. Also saw Walter James—Adderley (Cape)—Lacaita. H. of C. 3¾–7.[7] Eight to dinner.

11. Wed.

Wrote to T.G.—W. Craig[8]—Ratliffe[9]—J. Walker. Saw Galleano—C.A. Wood—Bp of Salisbury—G. Hope—W.F. Campbell—Adderley—Newcastle—Ld Abn. H of C. 12–3½. Spoke for postponing Manchr. Education Bill.[10] Read 'Finances & Trade'[11]—Roebuck's History. Dined with the Herberts.

12. Th.

Wrote to G. Burnett—Mr A. Perceval—G. Bennett—Edrs West. Review[12]—Dean Ramsay. Read Mahon's Hist[13]—Stuart of Dunleath—Trade & Finance in 1852. Saw S. Herbert—Adderley—Mr Jackson (Railway)[14] Sir W. James (B[edford] B[ury] Ch.)—Jocelyn. Worked on accounts—Visited Mr Munro & my Francesca in his hands.[15] Dined with the Jameses. H. of C. 4¾–7.[16]

[1] Sidney *Herbert wrote occasional articles for the Peelite *Morning Chronicle*, cp. Stanmore, i. 110–2.

[2] J. A. *Roebuck, *History of the whig ministry of 1830 to the passing of the Reform Bill*, 2v. (1852).

[3] On refugees in London: *PP* 1852 liv. 47.

[4] Introduction of *Russell's Reform Bill: *H* cxix. 252.

[5] William Newjam Nicholson, mayor of Newark 1851–early 1852.

[6] A novel by Caroline *Norton, 3v. (1847).

[7] Irish tenant rights: *H* cxix. 333.

[8] Sir William Gibson Craig, 1797–1878; liberal M.P. Edinburgh 1837–52; treasury lord 1846–52; 2nd bart. 1850.

[9] Of Ratliffe and sons, Hawarden iron and brass founders.

[10] *H* cxix. 387.

[11] *Finances and trade of the United Kingdom* (1852).

[12] John *Chapman, 1822–94; bookseller in the Strand; published and edited *Westminster Review* from 1851. Cp. 22 May 52n.

[13] P. H. *Stanhope, Lord Mahon, *History of England from the peace of Utrecht to the peace of Versailles*, 7v. (1836–53).

[14] (Sir)William Jackson, 1805–76; railway contractor; director of Chester and Holyhead railway; lib. M.P. Newcastle-under-Lyme 1847–65, North Derbyshire 1865–8; cr. bart. 1869.

[15] Gladstone had commissioned 'Paolo et Francisca', a model of which was exhibited at the 1851 exhibition, and the final version at the 1852 Royal Academy exhibition. Cp. 1 May 52.

[16] Misc. business: *H* cxix. 437.

13. Fr.

Wrote to Archd. Denison—R M Milnes—Ld Ellesmere—Mr Connelly—Sir Jno Owen—Mr Panizzi. Read Stuart of Dunleath—Mahon's Hist.—Corrected the proofs of Art. on Rome for the Ed. Rev.[1] Dined with the Cannings. C.G. went to Escrick. Saw Mr F. Peel—Newcastle—Labouchere—Sir J. Graham. Met E. C[ollins] in walking home: 2½ h. here: ended pretty well: not so in the middle [R].

14. Sat.

Wrote to C.G[2]—Williams & Co. Worked on Farini proof sheets. Went to Br. Museum to revise them with Panizzi—& for other matter with him. Calls afterwards. Read the painful MS from Rome.[3] Saw Wm. G & Mr S. Turner—the Vicar. Dined with the S. Herberts. Lady Molesworths afterwards: had an useful lecture from him.

15. Sex[agesim]a S.

St Marys (Crown St) mg; & a most pleasing Sermon. St James's (prayers) evg. At the Baptism of Hampton's child at 4¼: to whom I am godfather. (Henry).[4] Wrote MS. and read it aloud in evg. Saw Mr Connelly: an interesting person, of very singular intellectual formation. Read Meyrick—Garbett's Sermon[5]—W. Lyttelton's do[6]—Bethune's Speech.[7] Noted down an air in sevens.[8]

16 M.

Wrote to Sir J.S. Forbes—C.G.—J. Griffiths—T.G.—A. Panizzi—E. Ellis—Jas. Watson. Drafted my Col. Ch. Bill & saw Roundell Palmer on it.[9] Saw Adderley on Cape Motion[10]—also Newcastle—S. Herbert—Goulburn—Young. Worked on accounts. H of C. 4½–7½.[11] Tea at Lady Lyttelton's—Corrected 4 sheets Farini Revises. Saw Archd. Denison. Read Stuart of Dunleath.

17. T.

Wrote to Rev. H. M'Kenzie—C.G.—J.H. Parker—Willy—Rev. Mr Wilson. Did three sheets Farini Revises & two sheets proofs. Arranged pictures &c.

[1] Cp. 15 Nov. 51.

[2] Bassett, 85.

[3] Not found; perhaps about Lady Lincoln; cp. 21 Feb. 52.

[4] But see list at 31 Dec. 56.

[5] James Garbett, 'The church and the age. A sermon preached before the diocesan association' (1851); on Luke xvi. 25.

[6] W. H. Lyttelton, 'The leaven of the Kingdom of God' (1852); with a preface.

[7] Probably G. W. Bethune, 'The claims of our country on literary men. An oration . . .' (1849).

[8] Not found.

[9] The bill was to give self government to the anglican churches in the colonies; cp. *H* cxx. 1265 (28 April 1852).

[10] Adderley's vote of censure on *Grey's handling of the South African war was not moved, since *Russell resigned rather than face it, cp. 20 Feb. 52.

[11] Bill to disenfranchise St. Albans: *H* cxix. 605.

Read Stuart of Dunleath. H of C. 5–7.[1] Saw E. Collins [R]. Worked on accounts.

18. Wed.

Wrote to C.G.—E. Brackenridge—E. Davenport[2]—G & Co's Bookkeeper—Ricciardi—Canon Sergeant—Mr Callendar[3]—J.D. Coleridge. Saw Mr Davison[4]—Oswald—Ld Hardinge—Panizzi—F. Peel. Dined at Sir F. Thesigers. Lady Granvilles afterwards. Drive & calls with the children. Wrote out my Col. Ch. Bill afresh.[5] At night I saw two persons, one named Burton [R] whom I think it an obligation to make more inquiry about. Worked on accounts.

19. Th.

Wrote to Ed Guardian—Mr Stalham[6]—Mr Bennet—Mr Ethelstone[7]—J. Griffiths—C.G.—G. Denison—Miss Lyttelton. Worked on Farini proofs & revises. Worked on my books—weeding a little. Read Stuart of Dunleath—H of C. 4½–8. I intentionally (for once) absented myself from the division.[8] Lady Ellesmere's & Lady Truro's[9] in evg. Saw Newcastle. I visited the poor woman Burton & gave such advice & encouragement as I could to her kind friends the Burnetts[10]—notable people they seemed [R]. Shopping.

20. Fr.

Wrote to H. Tayleur—Mr Furnivall[11]—C.G.—Rev. E.L. Ward—O.B. Cole—Rev. P. Connelly—Messrs. Maples[12]—Mr G.F. Bowen. Worked on Farini. SPG meeting at 10¼—Custom's Committee at one. Saw Lawley—Burnett (Railway &c)—Cochrane—Adderley—Oswald—Newcastle. Read Spurrell (Rev.!!)[13]—Carm. Smyth[14]—Church State & Bible[15]—Stuart of Dunleath.

[1] Misc. business: *H* cxix. 651.

[2] Perhaps of Davenport Brothers, Liverpool import and export merchants.

[3] William Romaine Callendar, wrote on commerce.

[4] Christopher Davison, secretary of the Great North of England Junction railway, involved in negotiations with the Caledonian.

[5] Add MS 44740, ff. 320–2; printed versions, with notes, in *ibid.*, f. 11 and Add MS 44568, f. 116.

[6] Probably Henry Heathcote Stalham, Liverpool solicitor, cp. 5 Mar. 52.

[7] Charles Wicksted Ethelston, 1798–1872; rector of Uplyme, Devon, 1842–?72; owned land in Cheshire.

[8] From the division on the Irish gvnt. and the *World* newspaper: *H* cxix. 825.

[9] Lady Augusta Emma D'Este, 1801–66; da. of Augustus Frederick, duke of Sussex; m. as his 2nd wife 1845 1st Baron Truro.

[10] Mrs. Burton, a prostitute, was taken in by the Burnetts (otherwise unidentified) pending a decision on her application to enter the Rose street house of charity, which was refused; cp. Add MS 44371, f. 206, 216.

[11] Frederick James Furnivall, 1825–1910; barrister at Lincoln's Inn 1846; a Christian socialist; founder *inter alia* of Early English Text society; editor of *Oxford English Dictionary*.

[12] Maples, Maples and Pearse, solicitors in Old Jewry.

[13] James Spurrell, 'Miss Sellon and the "Sisters of Mercy"' (1852); denounces sisterhoods.

[14] R. Carmichael Smyth, 'Memorandum on the necessity of a secretary of state for our defence and war establishments' (1852).

[15] 'The church, the state, and the bible: a trinity in unity' (1852).

H. of C. 5–9½. Voted in 136:125 for Ld Palmerston's motion: a resignation followed: of course to escape the Cape motion. So in Nov. 30.[1]

21. Sat.

Wrote to W. Jackson (2)—C.G.—Col. Maberly—Mr Dorington[2]—Jos. Fletcher[3]—Mr G. Burnett—F.R. Grey.[4] Saw Mr Burnett—A. Panizzi—D. of Newcastle (politics—& Miss H.)[5]—J.N.G.—J.L. & Co—Wms & Co—Gurney—Maples. Finished Stuart of Dunleath. 10 to dinner: all Parliamentary men. Lady Palmerston's afterwards. Worked on Farini.

22. Quinqu[agesim]a S.

St Mary's Crown St and H.C. mg. Dined with the Jameses, Bedfordbury & discussed & Mema. made about our Church plans in evg 5¾–9¾.[6] Wrote to Mr Hawkins—C.G.[7] Saw Jim Wortley—Claude Hamilton[8]—Warden House of Charity[9]—the Burnetts &—Burton[R]. Read Bp Thirlwalls Charge[10]—the Missal—Robins's Letter.[11]

23. M.

Wrote to Mr Perceval—C.G.[12]—Jas Watson. Worked on Farini proofs alone & with Panizzi at B.M. H. of C. 4½–6½.[13] Saw R. Phillimore (2)—Mr Geo. Bennet—S. Herbert—Sir C. Wood—Oswald—R. Cavendish. Dined at Sir J. Harington's[14]—Lady Ellesmere's in evg. Read 'Dry Leaves from Egypt'.[15]

24. T. St Matthias.

Marg. Chapel 5 P.M. Read Kaye's Affghanistan[16]—Mr Cheyne's Letter.[17]

[1] *Palmerston's 'tit for tat' with *Russell, whose gvnt. was defeated by 11 votes on *Palmerston's amndt. to the Local Militia Bill: *H* cxix. 874. *Russell then resigned, and Gladstone introduced his Colonial Bishops Bill: *H* cxix. 880. See 17 Nov. 30.

[2] John Dorington, principal clerk in the public business office of the house of commons.

[3] Joseph Fletcher, 1813–Aug. 52; barrister; inspector of schools from 1844; wrote on pauper education.

[4] Francis Richard Grey, 1803–90; sundry curacies 1836–42; rector of Morpeth 1842–90.

[5] After the divorce Lady Lincoln was so described: 'I think Harriett (which is the *real* second name) without a surname is in the Italian manner' (Gladstone to Parkinson, Add MS 44368, f. 263v.).

[6] Not found.

[7] Bassett, 86.

[8] Lord Claude Hamilton, 1813–84; bro. of 1st duke of Abercorn; tory M.P. co. Tyrone 1835–7, 1839–74; minor office 1852, 1858–9, 1866–8.

[9] William George Tupper, 1825–54, son of M. F.*; Trinity, Oxford; warden of the Rose street house of charity from 1849.

[10] C. *Thirlwall, 'A charge delivered . . .' (1851).

[11] Sanderson *Robins, 'A letter to the Revd. G. A. *Denison' (1851); on education.

[12] Bassett, 87.

[13] *Russell's statement on resignation: *H* cxix. 887.

[14] Sir James Edward Harington, 1821–77; Christ Church and Coldstream guards; 10th bart. 1835; m. 1846 Jane Agnes, da. of J. S. Brownrigg; she d. 1891.

[15] [E. B. *Eastwick] *Dry leaves from young Egypt; being a glance at Sindh, before the arrival of Sir Charles *Napier* (1849).

[16] Sir J. W. *Kaye, *History of the war in Afghanistan*, 2v. (1851).

[17] P. Cheyne, 'A letter to the congregation of St. John, Aberdeen' (1852); on ritualism.

Worked on Farini Revises. Wrote to C.G.[1]—Col Short—T.H. Greene—Mr Kennaway—Ed. Guardian (2)—J.W. Wilson—Scotts.

1850.[2]
June 1–21. 11.x ♄2.
To July 7. + 3.
To July 21 + 3.
To Jul 28. + + + + +
Sept 2[3] 18.13.x.1.x
0. 1–5. 3.x

Saw R. Phillimore—H.J.G.—Spent most of the day in long conversations (1) with Lord Aberdeen—(2) Sir J. Graham, joined by Cardwell—(3) Ld Hardinge—(4) Newcastle. Ten to dinner: a Peelite party—*is* that name to dic.

. . .[4] I went to visit Lord Aberdeen: for I conceived that the present period was very critical for the character and usefulness of our section of politicians in particular, and I look to his weight, his prudence, & his kindliness of disposition, as perhaps our main anchor.

His tone has usually been, during the last few years, that of anxiety to reunite the fragments & reconstruct the Conservative party. But yesterday [i.e. this day], particularly at the commencement of our conversation, he seemed to lean the other way: spoke kindly of Lord Derby & wished that *he* could be extricated from the company with which he is associated: said that though called a despot all his life he had always been & was now friendly to a liberal policy: seemed to think that he was ready to join the liberal party as the audition of this liberal policy: & when I referred to his vote about the Jews told me in confidence he was prepared to change it. He did not however like the Reform question in Lord John's hands: but he considered I thought (and if so he differed from me) that on Church questions we all might co-operate with him securely.

It appeared to me that an influence had been excited in his mind: and that this could be no other than that of the Court; that probably Stockmar had been to him and had intimated that his cooperation with Lord J. Russell to be ready to replace this probably short-lived Cabinet would be acceptable.[5] For it is plain that the Court are commonly anxious to have a ministry in prospect as well as one *in esse*: the consequence of the dislocation of party and feebleness of Governments.

I however put it to Lord Aberdeen that our duty plainly was to hold ourselves clear & free, so as to be prepared to take whatever course might when the time arrived seem most honourable after that defeat of Lord Derby's Corn Bill to which I look forward as a matter of certainty: without at all pretending at this moment to say whether our duty may then be to attempt Conservative reconstruction, or to try single-handed, or to form a junction with the liberals—our least natural position—for, I also urged, we may be liberal in the sense of Peel, working out a liberal policy through the medium of the Conservative party. He was as usual very accessible and kind—with no bitterness or passion—& we parted without any declared difference of opinion. I pressed him to aim at bringing us together for

[1] Bassett, 88.

[2] These seven lines are enclosed in a thick black rule at the corner of the vol.'s last page but one.

[3] '+ ?+4+' here deleted.

[4] 'Yesterday forenoon' omitted.

[5] See *LQV* Is. ii. 435.

common counsels as I thought the time for serious action was now coming and that we ought to act together unless we found that our convictions separated us. I raised the question of our seats: he said he would keep his old one in the House of Lords & Graham the same in the Commons.[1]

I went shortly after to Sir James Graham who was also most kind and frank but whose conservation indicated something nearer a matured resolution to join with Lord John Russell & the liberal party as such.[2]

By invitation, he had called upon Lord John Russell just before: and had told him that though while he was in Government he held aloof from him, *now* he recurred to the relations in which they stood more than twenty years ago when in opposition together. Lord John said he would on Friday move the abandonment of the Reform Bill but would reserve to himself the right of moving a Resolution in favour of Reform generally if he should think fit. He said also that the state of Foreign relations and the likelihood of an invasion of Belgium by France were such as to make a Dissolution of Parliament at this moment most improper: accordingly he thought Lord Derby would not dissolve.

Sir James Graham said the question of Free Trade would be lost in that of Reform & the Constitution: for the people, if their bread were taxed afresh, would lay the blame on the present constituency & demand new institutions.

I said very true if you have a Protectionist majority nor can I say how far it may be necessary to go in such a contingency: but surely it is a mere dream: there is not the smallest likelihood or practical possibility of a Protectionist majority.

He seemed rather to blink this most important point & treat the question as one arguable. He told me however that Roche of Cork had been with him to offer him that county & had told him that the Irish hierarchy would he had no doubt vigorously oppose Lord Derby at the Election.[3]

Sir James Graham appeared to admit that except through the aid of the [Irish] Brass Band or Brigade as they are called, there could be no Protectionist majority.

Cardwell came in during our conversation. I stated that the views which presented themselves to my mind were succinctly these: That we had a right to expect & were bound in case of need to demand that Lord Derby's Government should after despatching only necessary public business proceed to carry the question of Protection to a speedy issue. That that issue must be unfavourable to Protection & would probably be so to Lord Derby's Government.

That the important juncture to contemplate & prepare for was that which would arise immediately after the defeat of Lord Derby's proposal to re-enact a Corn Law.

That the time had come for either a closer communication and cooperation among us of the Peel Government, or else that if we took different courses it should be on the ground of distinct convictions. That no exertion must be spared, in order to overthrow the project of Protection, that might be needful for the purpose.

That our main duty was to preserve our own separate & independent position and not to forestall the question which will arise after Lord Derby's failure but be free & ready then to pursue whatever course in point of party connection the interests of the country might seem to require.[4]

Later in the afternoon I saw Lord Hardinge who told me he had taken the Ordnance as a Military Office & showed me the letter. I told him I thought we

[1] Gladstone and most Peelites sat below the gangway on the opposition side (see 12 Mar. 52).

[2] Initialled and dated here 25 February 1852.

[3] Initialled and dated here 26 February 1852.

[4] Section on *Graham omitted.

seemed to be in danger of sliding into the general mass of the Liberal party: of which result he had a great horror: and I urged his going to Lord Aberdeen & using any influence in his power with a view to averting such a result. He also wished to go to Lord Derby & to use my name but this use at my request he gave up nor do I know whether he meant to go or for what specific purpose but I told him in general terms it seemed to me his position would be a very advantageous one as between Lord D. & us in case the public interest should require it to be used.

I told him also that what I longed for was to maintain our own separate and independent position that we might be in a condition to take our own line after Lord Derby's failure.

The Duke of Wellington had approved of what Lord Hardinge had done & considered that they both stood on the same footing.

After leaving him I met Newcastle and found him extremely incensed with Hardinge whom he declared to be a shabby fellow adding that he meant to tell him so when he met him. I told him I could in no manner join in this censure.

We then spoke of the Govt. & I expressed my apprehension that Graham, & as with him Cardwell, contemplated entering the Liberal party.

He spoke with great asperity against Lord Derby and his party: & believed they would endeavour to evade the question of protection. I said that clearly they had no right to do this, that I really believed Lord Derby would not pursue any such course: and lastly that even if they were so disposed there would be plenty of people to prevent him. I said, as I had at the former conversations that I thought we ought to keep ourselves aloof and free that we might take any course we might find right, as to party conviction, after the defeat of Lord Derby's protection project, to which I looked forward as a certainty. He said that he would make no vows as to junction, not even that he would not join Disraeli; but that he thought this Government must be opposed & overthrown—that those who led the charge against them would reap the reward—that if we did not place ourselves in a prominent position, others would—that my proposal was to adopt again a negative & neutral course,[1] or to support the Govt. I answered that I had no idea of support or connection with the Government—that I did not propose any negative or neutral course but that we should stand by our principles both on free trade & on all other matters—that we should if necessary with others require the Govt. to make their proposal of protection, and do everything to defeat it: as I quite agreed that they had no right to procrastinate the issue although I could not agree with the strong opinion he had expressed that the whole process of adaptation would be suspended, no rents adjusted, no leases taken, until Lord Derby's scheme was tried. I said that it appeared to me on the other hand he was arguing in favour of outright opposition from the first—& he replied 'I certainly think we ought to take every fair opportunity of opposing them.' These were his words.[2]

25. Ash Wednesday.

St James's 11–1 A.M.—St Mary Soho 8½ P.M. Wrote to C.G.—Ld Derby—C. Jenkins[3]—E.G. Wakefield (2)—J. Stuart—J. Griffiths—W. Callendar——W. Entwistle[4]—R. Phillimore. Saw Ld Hardinge—Entwistle & Peel—

[1] 'I said so' deleted.
[2] Add MS 44778, f. 5ff.
[3] Perhaps Robert Charles Jenkins, 1815–96; curate of Turnham Green 1843–54; vicar of Lyminge 1854–96; ecclesiastical historian.
[4] One name—? Roundell—here deleted.

S. Herbert—Jocelyn—Hayward. Read Ld R. Grosvenor's Tour[1]—Sewell's MS. on the Cape.[2]

On Ash Wednesday afternoon I saw Jocelyn: who told me he had declined on grounds of Free Trade only and had expressed to Lord Derby his good will in all other respects. He told me that Palmerston had in like manner declined cooperation on that ground only and was otherwise well disposed to Lord Derby.[3]

26. Th.

Wrote to C.G.[4]—J. Young—Sir R. Inglis—Sec. LNW. Co—Rev. Jas Smith—Jas Watson—R. Phillimore—E. Badeley—R. Palmer. Saw W.C. James—Sir F. Smith—J.N.G— Ld Ellesmere (Levee)—De Tabley (do)—Newcastle. Levee at 2¼ P.M.[5] At 11 calls—& took Helen to the Crystal Palace—Dined with the Herberts. 2½ hours after dinner on politics: then with Ld Abn. till past one.—Wrote Pol. Mema.

27. Fr.

Wrote to R. Palmer—E. Bruce—Wilson Patten—Sir J. Pakington—Mr Bateman—Dr Lundy[6]—Forbes (Sir J.S.)—Mr Tupper—JNG. Saw Cardwell (2)—Wilson Patten—Goulburn & Clerk—E. Bruce—S. Herbert—Canning—R. Palmer. Dined at H. Fitzroys[7] where Newcastle & Ld Lyndhurst met: we had some smart conversation. Read on Nav. Laws (Lindsay).[8] Wrote Pol. Mema.

Yesterday evening I had a further conversation with Newcastle at the Carlton Club. He said to me 'I do not think you will feel much difficulty: I think that you will find the question will be settled for you by the Protectionists.' He then told me that Beresford had sent out orders to their newspapers to run us down—that the same worthy had said 'the Peelites, let them go to hell' and that they were to oppose Wilson Patten in North Lancashire.[9]

I said that Beresford's language was a most severe & unequal test of the feelings of his party: and that his violence and that of others was fed & stimulated by what they imagined or heard of us. (I had heard that very day of Newcastle's own language to my eldest brother as having produced a very irritating effect. My brother said to him 'You only differ from them on one point'—he replied 'I differ from them on every point': so at least the story went—more or less exaggeration usually creeps in).

I said nothing could be more outrageous than their opposing Patten but I did not suppose that any mere abuse or misconduct towards us as individuals or as a

[1] [Lord Robert *Grosvenor] *Leaves from my journal* (1852); a journey to Carlsbad in 1851.

[2] Perhaps that on the Canterbury Association's progress: Add MS 44568, f. 109.

[3] Dated 27 February 1852; Add MS 44778, f. 11.

[4] Bassett, 88.

[5] Cp. *The Times*, 27 February 1852, 5e.

[6] Probably Francis James Lundy, D.C.L.; rector of Grimsby, Toronto, Canada.

[7] Henry Fitzroy, 1807–59; 2nd s. of 2nd Baron Southampton; Peelite M.P. Lewes 1837–59; minor office 1845–6, 1852–5; chaired Commons cttees. 1855–9.

[8] W. S. *Lindsay, *Letters on the navigation laws reprinted from the Morning Herald* (1849).

[9] Patten was unopposed in 1852.

body would of itself justify our placing ourselves in opposition. He thus inveighed against the baseness of which he had no doubt the new Government were about to be guilty. Eglinton and others he said had declared that they would not propose protection to this Parliament—would not unless compelled to do it dissolve—would not think themselves bound on meeting the new Parliament to propose protection at all if they knew the sense of it to be adverse but would still continue to hold office as a simply Conservative Government.

I said we ought not to assume this—we had a right to expect a different course from Lord Derby's character but if unhappily he should not make my expectations good there would be plenty of people to force him—he must bring the question of Protection to an issue and if he did not he would not escape defeat but would join to it dishonour.

He not only held that they could thus indefinitely postpone protection but likewise that they would work upon the Protestant cry against Maynooth and Irish Education. On this subject I said I was disposed to place confidence in Lord Derby.

During this conversation, held on a sofa at the Carlton, we were rather warm: and I said to him 'it appears to me that you do not believe this party to be composed even of men of honour or of gentlemen.' He on the other hand insisted that I was advising a negative policy or a virtual support of Government, and said he was afraid I should separate from the rest of the Peelites if I acted on my opinions: to which I demurred & said I believed they thought as I did. I mentioned that I had seen De Tabley & Ld Ellesmere at the Levee that day; had asked both the question as to our seats, but without declaring my own opinion: & the first had replied we should go below the gangway while the latter said we ought to sit where Ld Palmerston had been sitting—i.e. below the gangway but on the Government side! I quoted this but without adopting it as my own opinion distinctly was that if we sat on the Govt. side we should do wrong: but I saw Newcastle's heat from this, that in a later part of the conversation he imputed to me that I had declared we should sit below the gangway on the Government side supplying of himself a link that was wholly wanting in what I had said. My doctrine from my first conversation with Lord Aberdeen had been the necessity of maintaining our separate and independent position, & of doing all that might be necessary for that end. He did not on this day absolutely repeat the declaration of the previous day about opposition on every fair opportunity: but he evidently clung to the idea that we were hereafter to form a party of our own containing all the good elements of both parties to which I replied the country cannot be governed by a third or middle party unless it be for a time only, and then it can only be under the influence of strong public exigencies acting at the moment of and commanding the formation of such a party. He then glanced at the duty of joining with the party with which his sympathies chiefly lay, namely the Liberal party as such[,] to which I replied in the old strain that I had used to Lord Aberdeen & to Graham that on the whole I thought a Liberal policy would be worked out with greater security to the country through the medium of the Conservative party and I thought a position like Peel's on the liberal side of that party preferable—comparing all advantages & disadvantages—to the Conservative side of the Liberal party. And when he spoke of the Tories as the obstructive body I said not all of them—for instance Mr. Pitt, Mr. Canning, Mr. Huskisson, and in some degree Lord Londonderry & Ld Liverpool.

We then met at dinner at Sidney Herbert's whither I carried him—we found there Lds Aberdeen & Canning, Graham & Cardwell. We set to immediately after Mrs. Herbert left the room & discussed the matter till half past eleven. Sidney

Herbert threw off by declaring our position to be that of men who differed from the Government & held aloof from them on one great question: and who therefore should not sit on the opposition Bench as their adversaries but as men perfectly independent of them below the gangway on the same side of the House. Thus he made his start freely enough but the opinion he had stated he did not vigorously or toughly sustain in our ensuing debate.[1]

28. Sat.

Wrote to Jas Watson—C.B. Adderley—Mr Berkeley—Archdeacon Allen.[2] Attended a meeting at Ld Aberdeen's. Saw Adderley & Sewell—Newcastle—R. Lawley—Sir J. Johnstone—Sandars—Charteris—Cardwell—Ld Powis. Dined at the Speaker's—Ly Palmerston's [afterwards]. Worked on books &c. preparing for the Binder. Worked on Farini Proofs & Revises.

29. 1 S. Lent.

St Martin's mg—Chapel Royal aft. MS of 40 aloud in evg. Saw Ld Aberdeen—Granville Vernon—W.C. James. Read Meyrick—Balmez[3]—Tracts on Catholic Unity.[4] Cath. laid up with influenza: & Lena falling back.

Finis.

Neapolitans &c. whom I met at Naples 1850–1.

Mr Lacaita.
The Cardinal Archbishop.
Padre Tosti
Padre Costa.
Rector of the Jesuits' College 5
Baron Brockhausen.
Count Wachtmeister.[5]
Baron [blank] Russ. Chargè.[6]
Count Waleski.
Prince Cimitile 10
M. d'Obrischkoff
Duca di Cajaniella
Principe San Giacomo
Sig. Behr[7]
Principe di Belmonte 15

[1] Initialled and dated 27 February 1852; Add MS 44778, f. 13. He added more comments later.

[2] John Allen, 1810–86; archdeacon of Shropshire from 1847; edited theological manuscripts.

[3] J. L. Balmes, *Protestantism and catholicity compared in their effects on the civilization of Europe* (1844, tr. 1849).

[4] 'The church, the state and the bible, a trinity in unity' (1852), cp. 20 Feb. 52.

[5] Count Hans Wachtmeister of Johannishus, d. 1905; Swedish diplomat, temporary chargé d'affaires at Naples 1852.

[6] i.e. von Schöppingk.

[7] Italian liberal and friend of Lord Holland, cp. Senior, *Journals*, ii. 18–21.

March. St Angelo
Cavaliere St Angelo[1]
St Angelo
Conte di Monte St Angelo
Cavaliere Agresti . . . 20
Sig. Giov. Manna
Cavaliere d'Aloe.
Principe Ischiatelli
Duca Carlo Acquaviva
Capit. Carlo Merlo[2] . . . 25
Baron Rothschild
Prince—Cimitile
Princess Cimitile.
Duchess of Sabrino
Duchessa di Cajaniella 30
Countess Ludolf[3]
Mad. Obrischkoff
Mad. Rechten
Mad. Delafield.
Mesdlles Obrischkoff 36
Marchese Gentile (Engl).
Duca di Sabriano.
Prince Comitini[4]
General Sabbatelli[5] . . . 40
Marchese Fortunato.
Countess Lebzeltern
Padre Grossi
Cav. Durso Min Finance[6]
Baroness Rothschild . . . 45
M. Rothschild
Count Waleski [*sic*]
Countess Waleski
Count Lebzeltern
Madlle Lebzeltern . . . 50
M. Dupont
M. de Dumreicher[7]
Marchesa Rendi (Torelli)
Marchesa Sonera[8]
Marchese Salvi[9] . . . 55

[1] Nicolo Santangelo; Neapolitan minister for internal affairs 1848.
[2] Formerly in Neapolitan navy, a liberal from Palermo.
[3] Wife of Count Giuseppi Constantino Ludolf, formerly Neapolitan ambassador in London.
[4] Michele Gravina e Requesenz, Prince of Comitini, Neapolitan minister 1848.
[5] Felice Sabbatelli; Neapolitan general and frustrated diplomat, whose fall encouraged him to hostility to Bourbons, cp. Acton, *The last Bourbons* (1961), 298–9.
[6] Pietro D'Urso, minister of agriculture 1849, of finance 1851, prime minister 1851.
[7] A. von Dumreicher; secretary to Austrian legation at Naples 1851–2.
[8] Unidentified. [9] Unidentified.

Sig. Graziosi
Don Carlo Troja.
Count Mirepoix.
Marchesa Salvi (Engl.)[1]
Carlo Poerio . . . 60
Sig. Pironte[2]
Sig. Braico[3]
Baron Uzkull[4]
Duc de Polignac[5]
Prince Torella . . . 65
Duca di Lavello[6]
Mesdlles Agresti
P. Dentrici[7]

[The inside of the back cover is filled with faint traces of writing in pencil, almost completely erased. The following lines are clearly written in pencil, apparently over the top of the other:—]

di Pisseldorf—sui casi d'Austria[8]
Trap to catch a Sunbeam Wright Pall Mall[9]
Precis de l'Hist. de France. Colas. Rue Dauphin[10]
1840. Ends p. 192
Coleridge—Rom. Hist?
Plato Propn. 132. 1.3.

[and in ink:—]

C. Uppington Dunster Somerset

Mr A. Munro.[11]
Mr Jos. Durham 26 Alfred Place. Bedf. Square.

[1] Unidentified.
[2] See 13 Feb. 51.
[3] See 13 Feb. 51.
[4] Jakob Johann Wordemar, Baron von Uexküll, 1823–85; soldier in Russian army.
[5] Jules Armand Jean Melchior, duc de Polignac, 1817–90; soldier in Bavarian army.
[6] Unidentified.
[7] Antonio Dentrici, a member of the Frasso family; procurator general under Poerio.
[8] Probably F. X. von Pillersdorff, *Austria in 1848 and 1849*, tr. G. Gaskell (1850).
[9] Cp. 19 Jan. 51.
[10] Perhaps L. S. Colart, *Histoire de France* (1825).
[11] Five words here deleted, the last two of them 'Regents Park'.

[VOLUME XVII][1]

[On front fly-leaf:]

Erat illi aeternitatis perpetuaeq famae cupido; sed inconsulta. Seut. Ner. c. 55.[2]

W.E. Gladstone

1852.

Private.

Intra fortunam qui cupis esse tuam
IV. Prop. *III*.9.2.[3]

πῶς δ' οὐκ ἔμελλον ἀνδρὸς ὑπομνήματα πάσης αἰδοῦς ἄξια καὶ τιμῆς κτήσεσθαι;

Longin. de Plot.
Fragm. VI.[4]

NO. 17.

MARCH 1. 52 TO AUG. 31. 53.

MONDAY MARCH ONE 1852.

Wrote to Jas Watson (2)—Johnson Longden & Co[5]—H. Caswall—Mr A. Millar[6]—W.G. Tupper—Mr D. Tanish[7]—Willy—W.U. Richards. Saw D. of Newcastle—Pusey—Hayward. Worked on Farini proofsheets—the last—alone & with Panizzi. Attended Exhibn. Commn. meeting. Conv. with the Prince (on agric) & [Philip] Pusey afterwards. Read Neapolitan MS.—Lindsay on Nav. Law.

2. T.

Marg. Chapel 5 P.M. H.S. with A. & S. Wrote to Johnson Longen & Co—T.G.—Scotts—Jas Watson—D. of Newcastle. Dined with the Hoares.[8] Saw

[1] Lambeth MS 1431, 137ff.
[2] 'he had a longing for immortality and perpetual fame—but an ill-considered longing'.
[3] 'You whose wish it is to stay within the bounds of your fortune'.
[4] 'Was it likely that I should fail to acquire the man's writings, deserving as they are of all reverence and honour?'
[5] 'H. Tayleur' here deleted.
[6] Alexander Millar, superintendent of the Dundee railway, then being absorbed by the Caledonian railway.
[7] Perhaps Robert D. Tainsh of Chester, inspector of the Chester and Holyhead railway, or David Tainsh, secretary to Glasgow episcopal church union.
[8] Henry Hoare, 1807–65; landowner, sheriff of Kent from 1842; enthusiast for synods and church expansion; town house was in New Street. He m. 1836 Lady Mary Marsham, da. of 2nd earl of Romney; she d. 1871. Cp. 8 Mar. 52.

Railway Arbitration people[1]—Mr Chance—Mr Sewell—Ld E. Bruce—Mr S. Herbert—H.J.G.—Wegg Prosser. Read Aytoun's Letter[2]—Ld R. Grosvenor.[3]

3. *Wed.*

Wrote to Bp of Oxford—J. Griffiths—Mr Haughton—G. Burnett—Mr Fitzgerald—J. Swift—Sir J. Young—Rev Mr Baker—Sir J. Pakington—Mr Currie MP.—Lyttelton. H.S. with the children. Worked most of the morning upon my books. I am weeding my library—for the binder & finally. The Ralph Nevilles dined. Saw also H. Fitzroy—Panizzi—Mrs Craven—H. Hardinge. Lady John Russell's in evg. Read Pusey's Agric. Report[4]—Fabliaux.[5]

4. *Th.*

Wrote to C.P. Villiers MP.—W.F. Larkins—(& draft)—J. Griffiths—Sec. L.C.S. Co—W.C. Lake—Wm. Forbes—W.C. James. H.S. with the children. Saw Mr Villiers—Mr Bennet (Wimbourn)[6]—Ld Mahon—Goulburn—Charteris—Damer[7]—Cardwell. Worked on Farini Revises. Dined with Mr Hayward to meet Thiers.[8] Read Pusey's Report—wrote Pol. Mema.

5. *Fr.*

Wrote to D. of Newcastle—G. Talbot jun.—Rev. Mr Buckley[9]—Mr Statham—Col. Rice Trevor[10]—Bp of St Asaph—Chas Wordsworth. Read Pusey (finished)—Leaves from Young Egypt—Ld R. Grosvenor. Saw H. Corry—Clerk—Worked on my books—H.S. with the children.

6. *Sat.*

H[oly] S[cripture] with A[gnes] & S[tephen]—Wrote to G. Burnett—Dr Lundy—Mr Fanshawe—Mr Shank—J. Murray—Messrs. Leighton. Read Risposta di un Italiano[11]—Leaves from young Egypt. Shipped off my books

[1] Arbitration on railway amalgamations in Scotland.
[2] Perhaps James Aytoun, 'To the independent electors of Edinburgh and its vicinity' (1832).
[3] Cp. 25 Feb. 52.
[4] P. *Pusey, 'The improvement of farming. What ought landlords and farmers to do?' (1851). Reprinted from the Royal Agricultural Society *Journal*, no. 26.
[5] Cp. 13 May 48.
[6] Reading uncertain.
[7] George Lionel Dawson-Damer, *né* Dawson, 1788–1856, s. of 1st earl of Portarlington, added name of Damer 1829; Peelite M.P. Dorchester 1847–52, tory M.P. Portarlington 1857–80.
[8] Louis Adolphe Thiers, 1797–1877; French politician and historian; minister of the interior 1832–4; prime minister 1836–9; assisted Louis Napoleon, but banished 1852; toured Europe but failed to obtain assistance against Germany 1870, president of France 1871–3.
[9] Theodore Alois William Buckley, 1825–56; chaplain of Christ Church, Oxford, 1851–4; historian and editor.
[10] Perhaps a pen-slip for Arthur Hill Trevor, d. 1863; lieutenant colonel of 59th foot 1844, of 4th foot 1852.
[11] 'Riposta di un Italiano a due lettere del signor Gladstone a Lord *Aberdeen' (1851).

to the binder with all directions. Saw Sir James Graham—Oswald—Ld Ellesmere—Ld Aberdeen—Ld Malmesbury—Mr Walpole. Dined at Ld Aberdeen's—Duchess of Northumberland's afterwards.[1]

7. 2 S.L.

St Martins & H.C.—Bedfordbury evg—MS of 46 aloud at night. Wrote to J. Hume—Sir J.S. Pakington—Mr Lathbury. Saw T.G—W.C. James—Wortley. Last midnight C. had an alarm & Locock came. All became calm again thank God. He predicted the 3rd April. Today she kept well. He told us sad facts about Lady Lincoln & we discussed the new marriage or no-marriage.[2] Read Abp Whateley's Charge[3]—Bp Guiana's Charge[4]—D. of Argyll's Letter[5]—Scudamore's Letters to a Seceder.[6]

8. M.

Wrote to J. Griffiths—Castlereagh—D. Ross—H. Currie—B. Wilson—Collis—Lendrum—Rev. Jas Murray.[7] Saw Messrs. Hoare & Biber[8]—A. Wood—Castlereagh—E. Ellice—W.H. Barber.[9] Lady Salisbury's in evg. Read Ld R. Grosvenor (finished)—Ld Holland's Memoirs of the Whig Party.[10] H.S. with the children.

9. T.

H.S. with the children. Wrote to Duke of Newcastle—G. Grant—E.J. Carter[11]—T.G.—S.R. Glynne—Jas Watson—W.C. James. Read Ld Holland. Saw E. Ellice—Rev. Mr Murray—J.N.G. Nine to dinner: & work with S. Herbert afterwards. Drive with C. & business. Busy arranging my things mg.

[1] Eleanor, da. of 1st duke of Sutherland; m. 1842 Algernon Percy, 1792–1865, 4th duke of Northumberland 1847. She d. 1911.

[2] She remarried in 1860, but not to Walpole with whom she had eloped; cp. 4 Dec. 32.

[3] R. *Whately, 'Protective measures in behalf of the established church, considered in a charge . . .' (1851).

[4] W. P. Austin, 'A charge delivered to the clergy . . . of Guiana' (1852).

[5] G. D. *Campbell, 'The twofold protest. A letter from the duke of Argyll to the bishop of Oxford.' (1851); on ecclesiastical titles.

[6] W. E. *Scudamore, *Letters to a seceeder from the Church of England to the communion of Rome* (1851).

[7] James Fitzgerald Murray, 1811–62; curate of St. Andrew's, Wells street, London, from 1847.

[8] George Edward *Biber, 1801–74; German theologian; Lutheran convert; vicar of Holy Trinity, Roehampton, from 1842; ed. *John Bull* 1848–56; principal contributor to the *English Review.*

[9] William Henry Barber, 1815–72; Magdalene, Cambridge; priest, but never held a cure.

[10] *Memoirs of the whig party during my time, by Henry Richard Lord *Holland. Edited by his son, Henry Edward Lord Holland,* 1st v. (1852).

[11] Eccles James Carter, 1812–71; vicar of Kingston, Somerset and minor canon of Bristol 1851–71.

10. Wed.

St. James's 3 P.M. Wrote to Archdeacon Brooks—Rev. Mr Eyre [1]—Rector Campbell—Jas Watson—Rev. J. Jones—Robn. G. Saw W. Beckett—W. Egerton—Hayward—Ld Hardinge. Dined with the Herberts—Ly Malmesbury's Evg.[2] Read Nott's Lectures [3]—Dry Leaves &c—Dept of Art papers.[4] Arranged my letters up to date.

11. Th.

Wrote to Justice Therry—J. Murray—Sir Jas Graham—A. Wylie—Hon W.F. Campbell—W.B. Collis. H.S. with the children. Dined at Ld R. Grosvenor's: Mad. Van de Weyer's afterwards. Saw[5] Goulburn, Herbert, Young—Hayward—G. Vernon jun. Wrote Pol. Mema.[6] Read Nott's Lectures—Latham on Man [7]—Cautus's Letter [8]—Acland on Medical Edn.[9] &c.

12. Fr.

H.S. with the children. Wrote to Sir J. Kirkland—Mr J.H. Parker. Customs Committee 12¼–3¾.[10] House to 7½.[11] Saw Sir J. Graham—J. Young. Wrote Pol. Mema. Read Hinton on Manchr. Edn.[12]—Girdlestone on do [13]—Italian Volunteers [14]—Nott's Lectures (finished).

Sir James Graham called me out of the House (where he had been sitting on the Opposition Bench and the bulk of Sir R. Peel's friends below the gangway) to say that he had seen Lord John Russell this morning and heard from him the account of yesterday's meeting very much according to the report in the Morning Chronicle. Villiers is to speak on the *Corn Laws* before supply.

Lord John Russell requested him to say to "Mr. Gladstone & others" who are Conservative in policy but friendly to Free Trade that in his judgement the future would depend on the cordiality with which all sections of the majority now act together. If such cordiality prevailed, then he thought it might be possible to check & controul[15] the movement for Reform in a conservative sense: but not otherwise.

[1] William Thomas Eyre, 1795–1868; Brasenose, Oxford; vicar of Padbury from 1830.
[2] James Howard *Harris, 1807–89; 3rd earl of Malmesbury 1841; protectionist whip in lords; as foreign secretary 1852, 1858–9, cooperated with Napoleon III; lord privy seal 1866–8, 1874–6; m. 1st Corisande Emma, da. of 5th earl of Tankerville. She d. 1876.
[3] E. Nott, *Lectures on temperance* (1847).
[4] *PP* 1852–3 liv. 1.
[5] The wife of Sylvain Van de Weyer, 1802–74; Belgian minister in London 1831–67.
[6] See 27 Feb. 52.
[7] R. G. *Latham, *Man and his Migrations* (1851).
[8] 'A letter to . . . William *Skinner . . . on the subject of . . . W. E. Gladstone's proposal to admit the laity into the synods of the church in Scotland. By Cautus' (1852).
[9] Cp. 30 Dec. 48.
[10] Gladstone was on the select cttee. on the constitution and management of the board of customs which reported on 21 June 1852: *PP* 1852 viii, parts 1 and 2.
[11] Misc. business: *H* cxix. 961.
[12] J. H. *Hinton, 'The case of the Manchester educationists; a review of the evidence taken before a cttee. of the House of Commons' (1852).
[13] E. Girdlestone, *The education question* (1852).
[14] Cp. 6 Feb. 52.
[15] Word smudged; ? 'curtail'.

Sir James Graham said that he hoped Lord Derby would still take a manly & explicit course & bring the question of Free Trade to issue with all reasonable dispatch. Such he was persuaded was Lord D's own inclination: But Disraeli's influence was the other way, Delane the Editor of the Times (this evidently came from Lord John) was with Disraeli daily: and in reference to a remark in that paper that Christopher[1] might be treated as the Duke of Buckingham was treated in Sir Robert Peel's Cabinet, Disraeli said 'yes it was very well to deal so with one Duke of Buckingham but in our Cabinet we have six Dukes of Buckingham.[']

I said are we to meet at Lord Aberdeen's tomorrow to consider about Monday (when supply will be moved)? He said that both he and Lord A. thought we should not meet till after Monday 'as much might depend on the tone of ministers in the two houses on that occasion[']: and that when we met we should consider the larger question of a meeting of Peel's friends. I was well pleased to find that he was now worked up to such a point as to be able to contemplate such a meeting. I asked whether he meant that if Lord Derby spoke out & meant to bring the question to issue then there would be no meeting? He said by no means & plainly showed that his idea of such a meeting was in a sense friendly to Lord Derby. He said that at such a meeting his tone would be very different according as Lord Derby might take the manly or the less honourable course. Nothing but demonstration would cause him to expect anything but the former from one for whom he had so much regard. He had told Lord John this morning how important he thought it with a view to the public welfare that Lord Derby's honour should be kept pure & that nothing should occur to disqualify him for the public service.

I could not but admire (& said so) the fairness & candour with which he was disposed to judge Lord Derby. I said 'you might in strictness complain already, & attack him for not having already declared in his first speech that he meant to fight the battle: our business however was not to expose the Government for doing wrong but to bring them if possible to do right—it was an evil that there should be a party favourable to protection but there being such a party the best thing for the country, for all its interests, & for the honour of public men, was that we should settle the question, have it solemnly adjudged, & see Protection dead & buried[']. He assented to all this.

I remarked[2] that the plan adopted at Lord John Russell's evidently put him out of the first place. He said yes, & that no doubt it was shaped with that result full in view. I said I hoped he would speak very early on Monday night & he promised to take the first opportunity he could get.[3] I also intimated an intention of availing myself of an early opening to speak and show that there was no want of cordiality as to Free Trade.

I asked him what he thought as to the Income Tax—and he said that on reflection he was confirmed in the intention to vote it for a year if asked.

Lord John's idea was he said to give the navy and army effective service for the year, the non-effective for six months: *in case* a coercive motion should be found necessary.

He also said he had told Hume he regretted to find that H. had declared ballot to be the test of sincerity in reform: as he had the greatest objections to it: & that in distributing numbers after any measure of disfranchisement numbers alone could not be regarded, to which Hume *agreed*.[4]

This is much the best conversation with Graham I have yet had. May the breeze keep steady.[5]

[1] See 10 Nov. 41. [2] 'pointed out' deleted. [3] *H* cxix. 1081 (15 March 1852.)
[4] This sentence added below. [5] 12 March 1852; Add MS 44778, f. 1.

13. Sat.

Ch Ch Broadway 6 P.M. Wrote to Rev. Spencer Phillips[1]—Bickers—D. Whishas[2]—T.G.—W.P. Pickering—Bp of Argyll—S.R. Glynne. Saw A. Oswald—S. Herbert—Mr Sewell & Mr Wakefield—Mr Gibson & Manchester Deputation[3]—Ld Hardinge—Sir J. Young—Bonham. H.S. with the children. Dined with the Clerks—Duchess of Northumberland's afterwards. Lond. Libr. Comee. 4¼ P.M. Read Italian Volunteers—N.Q. Rview.[4]

14. 3 S. Lent

St Martins H.C.—8½. York St 11—Chapel Royal 5½. Wrote MS on Luke 18.8. & read it aloud. Read Scudamore[5]—Casauboni Ephemerides[6]—Balmez[7]—Meyrick's Church of Spain.[8] Singing.

15. M.

H.S. with the children. Wrote to Lord Malmesbury—Panizzi—R. Taylor—W. Forbes. Customs Commee. 12½–3¾. House 5–12. Spoke in the Debate.[9] Read Pitt Debates[10]—Sir C. Napier on Military Life.[11]

16. T.

H.S. with A & S. Wrote to Johnson Longden & Co—S.R. Glynne—Rev. N. Oxenham[12]—Williams & Co—Sir J. Pakington—E.G. Wakefield. Lord Aberdeen's 12–3. Saw Newcastle—Oswald—J. Young—Pakington. Read Italian Volunteers—(Glasgow) Strang's Report[13]—Ch. Wordsworth's Letter[14]—N.Z. papers.[15] H. of C. 5–8.[16]

17. Wed.

H.S. with A. & S. Wrote to Rev. E. Coleridge—Wm. Fox—A.H. Wylie—H. Tayleur—J. Griffiths—G. Bennett—Greg. Burnett—Rev. Mr Wright—

[1] i.e. W. S. Phillips.
[2] Unidentified.
[3] Thomas Milner-*Gibson, 1806–84; tory M.P. Ipswich 1837–9; lib. M.P. Manchester 1841–57, Ashton 1857–68; prominent leaguer; vice-president of board of trade 1846–8, president 1859–66. The deputation was on the education question.
[4] *New Quarterly Review*, i. 1 (March 1852); a digest of books published in 1851.
[5] Cp. 7 Mar. 52.
[6] I. *Casaubon, *Ephemerides* (1850); his diary, kept from 1597.
[7] Cp. 28 Feb. 52.
[8] Cp. 20 Jan. 52.
[9] On ministerial policy on free trade: *H* cxix. 1102; notes in Add MS 44652, f. 1.
[10] W. *Pitt, the younger, *Speeches . . . in the House of Commons*, 4v. (1806).
[11] Sir Charles Napier's edition of A. de Vigny, *Lights and shadows of military life* (1840).
[12] Nutcombe Oxenham or Oxnam, 1811–59; Oriel, Oxford; vicar of Modbury, Devon, from 1834.
[13] J. Strang, 'Report on the mortality bills of the city of Glasgow and suburbs for 1851' (1852).
[14] Charles *Wordsworth, 'A letter to W. E. Gladstone on the doctrine of "religious liberty" as propounded in his letter to the bp. of Aberdeen' (1852): very strongly hostile.
[15] *PP* 1851 xxxv. 381, on New Zealand political institutions: he moved for further papers, which were presented on 22 March 1852, *PP* 1852 xxxv. 1.
[16] Irish outrages: *H* cxix. 1171.

Archdn. Shortland [1]—Hayman—Mr Callendar. Read Col. Ch. Mag. H of C. 12–3 Manchr. Edn. Bill.[2] Saw Jas Wortley—Mr Home Drummond [3]—Sir Jas Graham & Cardwell—Peto—Wakefield & Sewell—Ld Hardinge (aft & at night)—Ld Aberdeen—Wm. Egerton—T.G—Hubbard—Mr Baxter. Dined with the Herberts (Parlty.)—Clerk—Lady Derby's [4] afterwards: a very mixed & pleasing party. Wrote a draft Memm.[5]

18. Th.

H.S. with the children. Wrote to Mess[rs] Williams (Chr.)—Jas Watson—Mr Dowding. At one [6] we met at Lord Aberdeen's. Saw in the morning Ld Hardinge—Messrs. Swift & Baxter—Archdeacon Shortland—& after, Newcastle—Ld Hardinge agn—Ld Aberdeen again—Bonham—J. Young—Mr Home Drummond. Thirteen to dinner: incl. Lady & Miss Peel.[7] The former seems greatly recovered: the latter charming. Worked on Col. Ch. Bill. Wrote Mema.—H. of C. 4–7.[8] Read Pitt & Melville Correspce.[9]

19. Fr.

H.S. with the children. Wrote to Secretary Walpole [10]—S. Herbert—Chevalier Bunsen—W. Nicol—Earl of Ellesmere—Dr Saunders—Sheriff Fraser [11]—Mrs E. Peel. Saw Messrs. Wylie & Robertson—Ld Hardinge—C. Hardinge—H. Corry—Wakefield & Sewell—E. Hawkins—Johnson Longden & Co—Ld A. Paget—Sir J. Graham—E. Cardwell—Goulburn—Ld Hardinge—E. Ellice—Charteris & H. Seymer. Read Miss Sellon's beautiful reply.[12] H. of C. 3¾–8 and 10–1.[13] Conv. afterwards which was a snare: the consequence of a stray turn, a lesson to avoid them [R].

20. Sat.

St Paul's Kn[ightsbridge] 5 P.M. H.S. with the children. Miss Pearson [14] left us. Wrote to S.M. Peto (& copy)—W.P. Young [15]—R. Williams—Jas Watson

[1] Vincent Shortland, 1803–80; in Bengal European regiment; ordained 1832; archdeacon of Madras 1847–59; retired to Guernsey.

[2] 2°: *H* cxix. 1195.

[3] Henry Home Drummond, 1783–1867; Peelite M.P. Stirlingshire 1820–31, 1840–52.

[4] Emma Caroline Stanley, 1805–76, da. of 1st Baron Skelmersdale; m. 1825 14th earl of Derby.

[5] Not found.

[6] Instead of 'twelve'.

[7] Eliza Peel, 1832–83; da. of the statesman; m. 1855 Francis Stonor, 1829–81, clerk of the house of lords.

[8] Misc. business: *H* cxix. 1244.

[9] P. H. *Stanhope, Lord Mahon, ed., *Secret correspondence connected with Mr. *Pitt's return to office in 1804* (1852); chiefly correspondence between *Pitt and *Melville.

[10] i.e. S. H. *Walpole.

[11] Andrew Fraser, 1805–73; sheriff-substitute at Fort William from 1838.

[12] Priscilla L. *Sellon, 'Reply to a tract by the Rev. J. Spurrell' (1852); cp. 20 Feb., 11 Apr. 52.

[13] Spoke on army estimates: *H* cxix. 1402.

[14] She had taken over as governess from Miss Brown in 1851, and went to Hagley.

[15] Unidentified.

—A.H.D. Acland—Sir Jas Colvile[1]—Earl Spencer. Saw prints at Colnaghi's[2]—shopping. Saw R. Phillimore—Hubbard—G. Hope—Bonham—Newcastle. Worked on accounts. Dined with the Cannings—Sir R. Murchison's afterwards. Read Italian Volunteers—N. Dublin Union Correspe.[3]

21. 4 S. Lent

York St mg—St James (prayers) evg. Read MS of 49 on Epistle aloud. Wrote on Miracle of Loaves. Singing. Read Scudamore—Meyrick—Channing's Life[4]—Freeman's Letter[5]—Elizabethan Prayers.[6] Saw Oswald—Bonham—F. Charteris—R. Cavendish.

22. M.

Wrote to Sir J.S. Forbes—Mr J. Amery—Rev. H. Venn—Rev. P. Freeman.[7] H.S. with the children. Saw Cardwell—Newcastle—Charteris—Monsell—Young—Wilson Patten—Castlereagh. Mr Panizzi brought young Settembrini[8] to breakfast: a nice intelligent youth.[9] Six to dinner. Ly Salisbury's in evg. Worked on a new Entertainment List—Also on accounts. Read Dandolo, It. Volunteers. H. of C. $3\frac{3}{4}$–$7\frac{1}{4}$.[10]

23. T.

Wrote to G. Burnett—Rev. Mr Wayte—R. Barker—Jas Watson—E.F. Deman[11]—W.C. James—Mr Andrew. H.S. with the children—Worked on my affairs—Saw Mr Say's pictures[12]—Mr Rucker's[13]—also at Colnaghi's. Saw Ld Hardinge—Ld Aberdeen—F. Charteris—Labouchere—J.N.G.—Ld Sydney. H. of C. $4\frac{1}{2}$–7.[14] Dined with the Cavendishes—Lady Hogg's[15]—then Lady Jersey's, afterwards.[16]

[1] i.e. Sir J. W. *Colvile; cp. 14 July 26.
[2] Printsellers to the queen; in Pall Mall East; then run by Dominic Paul *Colnaghi, 1790–1879.
[3] *PP* 1852 xlvi. 59; on the dismissal of C. S. Stanford as chaplain there.
[4] *Memoir of William Ellery Channing, with extracts from his correspondence and manuscripts*, 3v. (1848).
[5] P. *Freeman, 'A plea for the education of the clergy, in a letter to the . . . bp. of Exeter' (1851).
[6] Cp. 27 Feb. 48.
[7] Philip *Freeman, 1818–75; principal Chichester theological college 1846–8; canon of Cumbrae college, Bute 1853–8; vicar of Thorverton 1858; archdeacon of Exeter 1865.
[8] Raffaele Settembrini, educated in Britain, officer in British and Italian navies; assisted Jan. 1859 in dramatic rescue of his father, Luigi, 1813–77, Neapolitan professor, imprisoned by the Bourbons 1851–8, senator 1873.
[9] This sentence added at foot of page.
[10] Army and navy estimates: *H* cxix. 1426.
[11] E. F. Deman, technical instructor to the royal flax society in Ireland, and writer on agricultural subjects.
[12] Frederick Richard *Say, *floruit* 1826–58; portrait painter and Royal Academician.
[13] Probably by Michaelangelo *Rooker, 1743–1801; painter and engraver.
[14] Hop duties: *H* cxx. 19.
[15] i.e. Mary Hogg; cp. 15 June 46.
[16] 'Read' here deleted.

24. Wed.

Wrote to H. Lees—Robn. G—and J. Murray. H.S. with the children. Read Dandolo's Ital. Volunteers (finished)—Kay's Affghanistan War [1]—Deman on Flax.[2] Saw Rev Mr Venn—Rev Mr Andrew—Charteris—Young—Johnson Longden & Co. City 2–4. Domestic business & affairs.

25. Th. Annunc[iatio]n.

St James's 3 P.M. H.S. with A. & S. Wrote to E. Collins[R]—Rev. J.L. Walley [3]—S. Herbert—W.C. James—E. Coleridge—M.F. Tupper—T.G.—Dean of Llandaff [4]—Rev. Mr Caparn [5]—Rivington's—Bp of London—D. of Newcastle—R. Barker. Saw Newcastle—Pakington—Ld Granville—JNG—W. F. Campbell—J. Phillips. H. of C. 3¾–7 and 8¼–1: to vote agt Hume's motion.[6] Read Kay's Affghanistan—Llandaff Memoir.[7] Wrote Pol. Mema.[8]

26. Fr.

Wrote to E. Collins—J. Griffiths—Ld Hardinge—Jas Watson—Col. Grey [9]—Rev. Mr Raine [10]—Johnson L. & Co—J. Griffiths—Ed. M. Chron. H.S. with A. and S. Dined at Ld H. Vane's to meet Thiers & Remusat:[11] I liked the latter much. H. of C. 3¾–6½.[12] Searched & at length found E.C. late [R]. Matters are not worse there. Read Kay—Colonial Ch. papers and Tracts [13]—Saw Mr Andrew.

. . .[14] The truth is these last weeks have been spent in an endeavour to keep the House of Commons together and prevent its coming into a state of crisis by means of a body which does not cohere spontaneously but only holds any kind of unity by constant effort. There are at least four distinct shades among the Peelites. Newcastle stands nearly alone if not quite in the rather high flown idea that we are to create and lead a great virtuous powerful intelligent party, neither the actual Conservative nor the actual Liberal party but a new one. Apart from these witcheries, Graham was ready to take his place in the Liberal ranks: Cardwell

[1] Cp. 24 Feb. 52.

[2] E. F. Deman, 'Flax; its cultivation and management' (1851); on Belgian flax-growing methods.

[3] Perhaps John Master Whalley, 1793?–1861; Balliol, Oxford; rector of Slaidburn, by Clithero, from 1838.

[4] William Daniel *Conybeare, 1787–1857; vicar of Axminster, Devon 1836–44; dean of Llandaff 1845–57; wrote on geology.

[5] William Barton Caparn, 1817–?75; Brasenose, Oxford; vicar of West Torrington, Lincolnshire, 1847, of Draycot, Somerset, 1861–75.

[6] Motion on parliamentary reform and the ballot defeated in 89 to 244: *H* cxx. 169.

[7] 'First annual report of the society for providing additional pastoral superintendence and church accommodation in the diocese of Llandaff' (1852).

[8] Finished next day.

[9] i.e. Charles *Grey, cp. 11 May 35; also colonel 1833 and private secretary to Prince *Albert 1849–61.

[10] James *Raine, 1791–1858; rector of Meldon, Northumberland, 1822–58; antiquary and topographer.

[11] Charles François Marie, comte de Rémusat, 1797–1875; French liberal statesman and author; supporter of Thiers; retired from the assembly after the *coup* of 1851.

[12] Charitable trusts: *H* cxx. 213.

[13] Advance copy of *PP* 1852 xxxii. 7, on colonial church legislation.

[14] Follows description of meetings at *Aberdeen's.

Fitzroy & Oswald would I think have gone with him: as F. Peel and Sir C. Douglas went before him. But this section has been arrested, not thoroughly amalgamated owing to Graham. Thirdly there are the great bulk of the Peelites from Goulburn downwards more or less undisguisedly anticipating junction with Lord Derby and avowing that Free Trade is their only point of difference. Lastly I myself, & I think I am with Ld Aberdeen & S. Herbert, have nearly the same desire, but feel that the matter is too crude & too difficult & important for anticipating any conclusion & that our clear line of duty is independence, until the question of Protection shall be settled.

Newcastle's speech in the H. of Lords was solid & good;[1] & more moderate than I had expected. He told me a [*sic*] next day a person had said to him 'The Government understand you are going to make a violent attack upon them, & I can tell you they wish it too.' 'So' he said 'I soon saw what my game was & determined to disappoint them', or words to that effect.[2]

27. Sat.

Wrote to E. Hawkins—Mr Amery—Sir J. Graham (copy to do)—Jas Watson—Melville—Purden[3]—Ld Hardinge. Saw Ld Abn.—Bp of London—Newcastle—Sir R. Murchison. Dined at the Palace—Lady Palmerston's afterwards. Read Kay's Affghanistan—&c. 1½ hours with Dr Leger & his Magnetoscope. Most of the results in figures seemed to me very true.[4]

28. 5 S. Lent

York St mg & H.C.—Bedfordbury Evg—MS. of 42 on Epistle aloud in evg. Wrote to Abp of Canterbury. Saw Wortley—Archdn. of Durham—W.C. James. Read Balmez—Meyrick (finished). The Jameses came to tea.

29. M.

Wrote to John Phillips[5]—S. Herbert—Sir J. Pakington—Miss Brown—Mr J. Dickson[6]—C.G. Reid—Rev. J. Bramston—Jas Buzzard[7]—Saw Ld Harrowby—do with J.S. Wortley—J. Young—G. Hope—J. Phillips—A. Munro—Lord Aberdeen with Newcastle—& (as on Saty.) several members of Parlt. on Graham's Speech.[8] House 3¾–7¼ and 11–12.[9] Six to dinner. H.S. with A. & S. Read Kay's Affghanistan—Col[onial] Ch[urch] papers &c.

30. T.

H.S. with A. & S.—Wrote to Sir Jas Graham—Rev. C. Wordsworth—Bp of London—J. Griffiths—G. Burnett—Sir R. Murchison. Saw Murchison—

[1] *H* cxix. 1261 (19 March 1852).
[2] Initialled and dated 26 March 1852; Add MS 44778, f. 30.
[3] Possibly William John Purdon, nonconformist minister in Liverpool.
[4] Théodore Leger, 1799–1853; mesmerist and phrenologist; held séances and examined heads in Gerrard street, Soho, 1852; used magnetoscope to define 'magnetoid characteristics' mathematically.
[5] i.e. J. H. Philipps.
[6] Perhaps J. Dixon, of Old Swinford, involved in the Oak Farm.
[7] Perhaps the vestry clerk for Westminster, cp. 30 Jan. 41.
[8] A whiggish speech at Carlisle, cp. C. S. Parker, *Sir James *Graham*, ii. 156.
[9] Militia Bill: *H* cxx. 267.

Dr Leger—Jas Wortley—Ld Harrowby—J. Young—C. Villiers—Ld Aberdeen—Sir J. Pakington—Adderley—W. Fox—E. Cardwell. 12–2—Met Newc[astle] & Goulburn at Lord Aberdeen's. Dined with the Sandarses. Met Sir J. Graham! H. of C. 4–7 and 11–12½: to vote agt. Ballot: no Graham.[1]

31. Wed.

Ch Ch Broadway 6 P.M. Wrote to Johnson Longden & Co—S. Herbert—Bp of Aberdeen—Rev. G. Shand[2]—Rev. Sir E. Williams.[3] Worked on Col. Bps Bill—& got my papers ready. H. of C. 12¼–6—in waiting.[4] Dined with the Lefevres. Lady Derby's afterwards. Saw Mr Bright—Newcastle—Bonham—Cardwell—Ld Palmerston—M. Gaskell—Adderley—Roebuck—Beckett Denison—J. Young. C. had warnings during the night.

Yesterday morning we met at Lord Aberdeen's: Newcastle, Goulburn, and I. N. said he thought our duties were 1. still to keep together—even more 2. to do nothing to mark the separation [from Graham].[5] I agreed in the first differed from the second: for I was sure—giving this among other reasons—that the least which would be required in order to enable the Peelites of the H. of C. to keep together was a manifestation on our part that such a speech as that could not be an open question among us.

I mentioned that some of them were coming to No. 5 Carlton Gardens[6] in the course of the afternoon: & my first wish was that soon Lord A. himself would go & tell them how we stood upon Graham's speech. To this they were all opposed: & they seemed to feel that as we had had no meeting yet, it would seem ungracious & unkind to an old friend to hold one by way of ovation over his departure.

It was therefore agreed that I should acquaint Young it was their wish that he should tell any one who might come that we who were there present looked upon our political connection with Graham dissolved by the Carlisle speech.[7]

Thursday April One 1852.

H.S. with A. & S.—Wrote to Bishop of Oxford—Ld Hardinge—C.G. Reid—S.M. Peto—C. Uppington—Jas Watson. Saw Mr Bennett—Sir J.E. Tennent—Newcastle—Mr C. Villiers. Worked on accts. H. of C. 4¼–6¾.[8] Read Exhib. Commn. Report[9]—Burke on Amn. Taxation[10]—Refugee papers.[11] C. made on the whole little progress during the day: more seemingly in the evening: and Dr L. came a second time: but to no effect, & late at night she got sleep.

[1] *H* cxx. 436.

[2] George Shand, 1817–?89; Queen's, Oxford; vicar of Guestwick, Norfolk, 1847–61, of Heydon 1861–88.

[3] Sir Erasmus Henry Griffies-Williams, 1794–1870; 2nd. bart. 1843; rector of Rushall, Wiltshire, 1829–70; chancellor of St. David's cathedral from 1858.

[4] His bill was delayed by the Tenant Right (Ireland) Bill 2°: *H* cxx. 440; cp. 28 Apr. 52.

[5] 'Resumed Ap. 19.' added in margin.

[6] *Herbert's house.

[7] *Aberdeen's comments omitted. Initialled and finished 19 April 1852; Add MS 44778, f. 34.

[8] Foreign refugees: *H* cxx. 477.

[9] First report of 1851 exhibition commissioners: *PP* 1852 xxvi. 1.

[10] Cp. 27 Mar. 45. [11] Cp. 9 Feb. 52.

2. Fr.

Up late. H.S. with W. & A. Wrote to H. Tayleur—J. Griffiths—Dr Leger—M[orning] Post.[1] Attended Exhibn. Commee. & Commn. $2\frac{1}{2}$–$4\frac{1}{2}$. House to 6.[2] Came home in time & found C.s labour progressing rapidly. At 6.40 a little boy was born:[3] about half Lena's weight at the same stage: but very vigorous. This diminution too was a great mercy because two deranged nights had left C. much exhausted. Read Westr. Rev. on Book Trade.[4]

3. Sat.

Wrote to Mr Yeates[5]—Lady Glynne—Sec. Carlton Club—Rn. G—Lady Wenlock. H.S. with W. & A. Virgil with W. Went with Mr Lefevre to Dr Leger's. Dined with the Ashburtons. Ly Palmerston's afterwards. Saw Lyttelton—Mr J.H. Parker—T.G.—Mr Marshall (Studio)[6]—Mr A. Munro—E.H.G—Mr Andrew. Council Stat. Soc. at $4\frac{1}{2}$.[7] Worked on House Accounts. Read [blank.]

4. Palm S.

St Marys Soho 11 AM. Chapel Royal aft.—MS. of 44 aloud in evg. Dined with the Herberts. Read Caswall's Letter[8]—Xtn Remembr. & other Periodicals.[9]

In the aftn. C.s flood of milk troubled her—& a long rubbing at night in some sort brought it round.

5. M.

Virgil with Willy. Wrote to J. Griffiths—H. Tayleur—J. Cunningham—E A Bowring—J. Sandars—Mrs Proby—the Vicar—W. Hollis. Saw E. Coleridge—Ld Harrowby *cum* Mr Muir[10]—W.F. Campbell—L.N.W. Agent—Mr G. Bennett—S. Herbert. Exhibn. Committee $4\frac{1}{2}$–$5\frac{1}{4}$: House to 10. Spoke on Kafir Vote.[11] C. got on with diminished difficulty: another good rubbing at night—& prayers as usual. Read Adderley on Cape.[12]

[1] A short deletion. The letter was to announce the birth.
[2] Ireland: *H* cxx. 602.
[3] Henry (Harry) Neville Gladstone, d. 1935; merchant; cr. Lord Gladstone of Hawarden 1932.
[4] *Westminster Review*, new series i. 511 (April 1852); on the financing and taxation of the book trade.
[5] Perhaps George Yeates, bedstead maker in Blackfriars road; cp. 19 Apr. 52.
[6] Thomas Falcon *Marshall, 1818–78; portrait and historical painter.
[7] To prepare for the ordinary meeting on 19 April 1852; cp. *Journal of the Statistical Society*, xv. 184 (June 1852).
[8] H. Caswall, 'Synodal action necessary to the church. A letter to . . . W. E. Gladstone' (1852). Supports Gladstone's proposals.
[9] *Christian Remembrancer*, xxiii. 249 (April 1852); probably the review of Huc.
[10] Probably James Muir, city commission agent.
[11] Demanding 'local liberty' for the Cape, with 'first responsibility for its own self defence': *H* cxx. 744.
[12] C. B. Adderley, 'Statement of the present Cape case' (1851); an address to the society for the reform of colonial government.

6. T.

St Mary's Cr[own] St. 8½ P.M. Virgil with Willy. Wrote to Rev. T.H. Greene—Mr R. Barker. Saw Bp of St Asaph—Mr Dowding. Worked on Invitation Lists.[1] Read Baxter to Milnes[2]—Kaye's Affghanistan[3]—Ed. Rev. on Reform (part).[4] H. of C. 4½–7. Spoke on Ballastheaver's Bill.[5] C. continued on the whole to thrive: more rubbing at night gained its purpose.

7. Wed.

St James's 11 A.M. Virgil with Willy. Saw Coalwhippers' Depn.[6]—Mr A. Munro. Finished my entertainment List. Wrote to Sir J. Colvile (P.S.)—J. Griffiths—Mrs T. Goalen—Mr Herries. Read Kaye—Ed. Rev. on Reform (finished)—Quarterly on the Administration.[7] Attended Mr Blackett's interesting Lecture on the Iron Trade.[8] C. kept her ground: more rubbing: the difficulty not yet ended.

8. Th.

Marg. Chapel 5 P.M. Virgil with Willy. Read Kaye—N.B. Review on Principles of Taxation.[9] Saw J.N.G.—Bank. Saw Bp of Argyll—& wrote Mem. on Scots Clergy disqualification.[10] Wrote to Bishop of Argyll—Smith & Co—Jas Watson—Geo. Largie—E.L. Robertson & Co[11]—W.R. Greg[12]—Rev. J.L. Ross—R. Barker—Dr Binney[13]—Miss Brown.

Continued the rubbing with C: who also laboured under some soreness: but better than at any time since 42. Prayers as usual.

9. Good Friday.

York St Chapel & H.C. at 11.—Marg. Chapel 5 P.M.—MS for Easter Eve aloud at night. Prayers as usual with C. Finished 2 MS. Saw Lacaita. Read N.B. Review on German Ch[14]—Newman[15] & Greg[16]—Foulkes's Manual[17]—

[1] Add MS 44782, ff. 7–16 lists all Gladstone's breakfast and dinner guests in 1852.

[2] Untraced pamphlet by Robert Baxter, which provoked R. M. Milnes' 'Answer . . . to R. Baxter on the South Yorkshire Isle of Axholme Bill' (1852).

[3] Cp. 24 Feb. 52.

[4] W. R. *Greg on 'The expected reform bill', *Edinburgh Review*, xcv. 213 (January 1852).

[5] On ballast-heavers and coalwhippers: *H* cxx. 787.

[6] In support of his speech the previous day.

[7] *Croker on the old and new ministries, *Quarterly Review*, xc. 567 (March 1852).

[8] Probably by John Fenwick Burgoyne Blackett, 1821–56; fellow of Merton 1845–7; liberal M.P. Newcastle 1852–6.

[9] *North British Review*, xvi. (49 November 1851); review of J. S. *Mill, *Principles of political economy*, 2v. (1848).

[10] Not found.

[11] His cousin's wine firm, then in the Strand; cp. 15 July 26.

[12] William Rathbone *Greg, 1809–81; a mill owner and essayist on political, social and Christian topics.

[13] Hibbert Binney, 1819–87; fellow of Worcester, Oxford, 1846–53; D.D. 1851; bp. of Nova Scotia from 1851.

[14] *North British Review*, xvi. 279 (November 1851).

[15] J. H. *Newman *Discourses on the scope and nature of university education* (1852).

[16] W. R. *Greg, *The creed of Christendom; its foundations and superstructure* (1851).

[17] Cp. 4 Jan. 52.

Eucharistic Devotions—Kaye. C. improving pretty steadily: rubbing, perhaps the last needed. This was our blessed little Jessy's birthday into rest.

10. Easter Eve.

St James's 11 A.M. St Paul's Kn. 9 P.M. Read Kaye's Affghanistan. Wrote to Wm Gladstone—R. Barker—Aunt J—C. Stewart—Mr Furnivall—E. Collins [R]—J.W. Cunningham. Worked on House Accounts. Shopping. Saw Ld Meath. Dined with the Herberts.

And so ends my Lent. Even such as it is I bless God for it. It in some degree reins me up. The abstinence of this week (somewhat altered as to times) costs me a good deal in the increased sleepiness which it produces.

C. proceeds to my heart's content.

11. Easter Day

York St & H.C. 11 am. St Andrew's Wells St Evg. Wrote to Bp of Oxford. Read MS for Easter Tuesday aloud to servants—& again to C. Read Colles,[1] Spurrell No 2,[2] & Miss D. Campbell's pamphlets[3]—the beautiful Appeal from Wantage[4]—Bp Doane's Reply[5]—& others. Saw R. Cavendish. Discussed again with C. the name & godfathers for our little fellow.

12. Easter Monday

St James's 11 A.M. Virgil with Willy. Wrote to Bickers & Bushe—Jas Watson—Mrs J. Lefevre[6]—Robn. G—Johnson Longden & Co—H. Goulburn—E.L. Robertson & Co—T. Flynn[7]—Mrs Bennett—J. Graham. Saw Bp of Oxford—W. Malling[8]—Mr Hubbard—Bp of Capetown—J.N.G. —Mrs Bolton. The Lytteltons dined. Read Kaye's Affghanistan—D. of Newcastle's Speech. C. moved to (quasi) sofa.

13. E. Tuesday.

St Andrews 5 P.M. Virgil with Willy. Wrote to A. Galleano—G. Burnett —Earl of Aberdeen—J.L. Ross. Read Kaye's Affghanistan (began II)—& saw the infamous work of (Pseudo) Meursius.[9] Saw Chev. Bunsen—Rev Mr Pound[10]—J.N.G.—& in evg E. Watson, who had I hoped escaped: & still desires it [R]. I did not act well. Ten to dinner: for Mrs Nimmo.

[1] W. M. Colles, 'Sisters of mercy; sisters of misery; or, Miss *Sellon in the family; with some remarks on "A reply to the Rev. James Spurrell"' (1852).

[2] J. Spurrell, 'A rejoinder to the reply of the superior of the society of the sisters of mercy' (1852).

[3] Diana Campbell, 'Miss Sellon and the sisters of mercy' (1852).

[4] Probably 'Some account of St. Mary's Home at Wantage . . . by the chaplain' (1851).

[5] G. W. Doane, 'The reply of the bishop of New Jersey in reply to the paper, read before the court of bishops, . . . by the bishops of Ohio and Maine' (1852).

[6] i.e. Mrs. John Lefevre; cp. 20 Sept. 41.

[7] Thomas Flynn of Shadwell wrote on behalf of the coalwhippers and ballast-heavers to thank Gladstone for his speech; cp. 6 Apr. 52.

[8] Unidentified.

[9] *Satyra sotadica de arcanis amoris et Veneris* (1680); pornography by N. Chorier but passed off by him as by J. Meursius, Dutch philologist and theologian.

[10] William Pound 1807–81; priest 1834; head master of Old Malton grammar school, Yorkshire, 1839–66, of Appuldurcombe school, Isle of Wight, 1866–76.

14. Wed.

H.S. with W. & A. Virgil with W. Wrote to Wm Gladstone—J.T. Hudson[1] —Bp Capetown. Read Kaye's Affghanistan. Saw F.R. Bonham: in evg E. Collins & endeavoured tho' with much to blame to secure the relation to Osborne [R]. Paid a set of visits, & shopping. Again saw 'Meursius' which in the Preface professes a moral aim.

15. Th.

H.S. with W. & A. Virgil with Willy. Seven hours with Mr Burnett on Hawarden matters: chiefly the Railway & Hancock[2] affairs. Drafted a Memorandum of proposal.[3] Saw J.N.G. Read Kaye's Affghanistan. Wrote to Comte Zucchi[4]—W.C. James—Jas Watson—Rev W. James—Rev Mr Armitstead.[5]

16. Fr.

H.S. with W. & A. Virgil with Willy. Wrote to Rev Mr Bennett—Mad. Ad. Rovero—Mr Walker. Saw Mr Andrew—Mr Haddan—Sir J. Paxton—R. Phillimore—J. Phillips—Bp of Capetown. 5–10¼ P.M. Dined at the Vicar's: then attended & spoke at Parochial S.P.G. meeting.[6] Walk at night. Read Kaye's Affghanistan—Bennett's Letter.[7]

17. Sat.

St Mary's Crown St 8½ PM. H.S. with W. & A. Virgil with Willy. City 11–1½. Saw Gosling (Proctor) to administer:[8] Johnson Longden & Co. Saw Mr Rogers—W.C. James. Attended Owen's Lecture on Epizoa &c: very remarkable.[9] Visited the Hunt[erian] Museum.[10] Wrote to Rev. Mr Blackwell. Read Kaye's Affghanistan.

18. 1 S. E[aster].

Marg. Chapel 11–2 (Holy C.) and 7 P.M. with Willy. Wrote on Zech IX.17 & read it aloud to servants—& then to C.[11] Wrote to P. Lightfoot—Read

[1] John Thomas Hudson, optician; wrote on right use of spectacles.
[2] The firm Rigby and Hancock constructed tramways on the Hawarden estate, in this case probably the railway to Buckley.
[3] Hawn P.
[4] Carlo Zucchi, 1777–1863; Neapolitan general.
[5] John Armitstead, ?1801–65; Trinity, Oxford: vicar of Sandbach, Cheshire, from 1828.
[6] No account traced.
[7] W. J. E. *Bennett, 'A letter to the parishioners of Frome' (1852).
[8] William Frederick Gosling, proctor in doctors' commons; presumably to administer an oath, on his father's will?
[9] Unpublished lecture by Sir Richard *Owen.
[10] *Owen was then its conservator.
[11] And wrote on 'habits', cp. Add MS 44740, f. 5.

Cruttwell's Letter [1]—Scottish Magazine [2]—Foster's School of the Future [3]—Ranke's Reformn.[4]

19 M.

H.S. with W. & A.—Virgil with W. Wrote to Sir R. Murchison—Yeats—Col. Gliamas [5]—Geo. Coode [6]—H. Tayleur—Lyttelton—C.E. Stewart—Mr Blackwell—Rev. Mr Aspinall.[7] Wrote Pol. Mema.[8] Read Kaye's Affghanistan. Saw Thesiger—failed to find P. Lightfoot [R]—Saw E. Scott: who went home late to be alone [R]. Commee. & House 1 to 6½:[9] with a walk to Phillimore's house between.

20. T.

H.S. with W. & A. Virgil with Willy. H. of C. 4½–9¼: on Horsman's motion.[10] Wrote to Bp of Bath & Wells—J. Griffiths and W.C. James—Marchss. of Bath.[11] Sir A. Dalrymple—Rev. R. Greswell. Finished Kaye's remarkable & painful book. Read Zincke's School of the Future. Business & calls. Called late on E. Scott: out [R].

21. Wed.

H.S. with W. & A. Virgil with Willy. Wrote to Jas Watson—Sec. King's College [12]—Read Zincke's School of Future. Saw E.G. Wakefield—W.B. Collis—Page Wood—Oswald—Greswell—. Worked on accounts. H. of C. 1–4¼.[13] Wrote Pol. Mema. Dined at Grillion's: when we talked over the Horsman Debate. Saw E. Scott afterwards 10–1: another Chapter in life [R].

22. Th.

H.S. with W. & A. Virgil with Willy. Wrote to Dean of St Paul's [14]—S.M. Peto—Mr Hallam—Bunsen—Bp of Bath & Wells—Dr Twiss—Wm Gladstone—Ph. Pusey. My first breakfast for the year, only seven *came*.[15] Saw

[1] W. C. Cruttwell, 'A churchman's letter to the parishioners of Frome' (1852); a reply to *Bennett, cp. entry two days previously.

[2] *Scottish magazine and churchman's review*, ii. 160 (April 1852); on ritualism.

[3] Foster B. *Zincke, *Some Thoughts about the School of the Future* (1852).

[4] L. von Ranke, *Deutsche Geschichte im Zeit alter der Reformation*, 5v. (1839); tr. by Sarah Austin, 3v. (1845–7).

[5] Not identified.

[6] A barrister of the Inner Temple from 1833.

[7] George Aspinall; Ph.D. at Heidelberg 1840; curate of St. Matthias, Liverpool, ?1849, later of St. James's, Toxeth Park (not Gladstone's church).

[8] Finishing 31 Mar. 52.

[9] E.I.C.'s charter: *H* cxx. 806.

[10] Spoke on Horsman's motion on the Frome affair: *H* cxx. 932; cp. 24 Apr., 10 June 52 nn.

[11] Harriet Baring, 1804–92; da. of 1st Lord Ashburton; m. 1830 Henry Frederick Thynne, 1797–1837, 3rd marquess of Bath 1837.

[12] John William Cunningham, 1818–1901; s. of J. W.*; St. John's, Cambridge; secretary to King's college, London, 1845–95.

[13] Spoke on church building: *H* cxx. 962.

[14] Henry Hart *Milman, 1791–1868; dean of St. Paul's from 1849, ecclesiastical historian.

[15] Cp. 6 Apr. 52n.

Mr Greswell—Ld Ashburton—Cardwell—Lacaita—Lyttelton—S.M. Peto. Manchr. Edn. Comm. & House 1¼–7.[1] The dropping of the debate prevented me from speaking on Finance & the booktrade. Read Smee's Lectures[2]—Dr Forbes Winslow's Journal[3]—Myst. London.[4] Saw E. Scott—for a few minutes [R].

23. Fr.

H.S. with the children. Virgil with Willy. H of C. 4½–7¼ (took Willy) & 9¾–12½.[5] Wrote to R. Barker—T.T. Carter—Gerard—Murchison—Ly F. Hope. Saw R. Phillimore—Mr Greswell—Dr Binney—Bp of Capetown—S. Herbert & Cardwell—Ld H. Lennox—Mr Bennett—Mr Yorke[6]—Lyttelton—& (n[igh]t) E. Scott briefly [R]. Read Ed. Rev. on Roebuck's Hist—on the Ministry.[7]

24. Sat.

Up at 4¾: walk to London Br. Station with a very fine view of the City. Reached Brighton at 8½. Breakfast & conv. with the Bp of Bath & Wells on the Frome Affair.[8] He was moved to tears. Saw Lady de Tabley: Reached Reigate at 12 & went to the Philanthropic:[9] made a short address to the boys. Reached London 3.45 & home 4.20. Read Layard.[10] Wrote to Dr Pusey—J.L. Ross—Bp of Glasgow. C. in the drawingroom. Willy detained on account of a rash. Dined with the Larkinses: Northumbd. H. afterwards.[11] Saw Newcastle—& (at nt.) E. Scott—and M. Horton: interesting[12] [R].

25. 2 S. E[aster] & St Mark

Chapel Royal mg—Bedfordbury evg—MS. of 44 for the day aloud. Wrote to Lacaita. Began MS. on the Festival.[13] Read Churchman's Year Book[14]—Bp of Ossory's Charge[15]—Prayers for the young.[16] Conv. with Willy—& C. about him.

[1] Resolution for repeal of paper duties: *H* cxx. 983.
[2] A. *Smee, *Principles of the human mind . . . with the lecture on the voltaic mechanism of man* (1849).
[3] F. B. Winslow, *Physic and physicians* (1842).
[4] Cp. 19 Dec. 48.
[5] Militia Bill 2°: *H* cxx. 1035.
[6] Eliot Thomas Yorke, 1805–85; tory M.P. Cambridgeshire 1835–65.
[7] *Edinburgh Review*, xcv. 517, 569 (April 1852); cp. 9 Feb. 52.
[8] Five of the clergy of Frome had signed a petition against the induction of W. J. E. *Bennett, an anglo-catholic.
[9] The reform school built 1849 by the Philanthropic Society.
[10] A. H. *Layard, *Nineveh and its remains*, 2v. (1849).
[11] Town house of duke of Northumberland, at Charing Cross.
[12] She soon married, see 6 July 52.
[13] Not found.
[14] *The churchman's year-book for 1852; or, the ecclesiastical annual register* (1852). A record of ecclesiastical events in 1851.
[15] James T. O'Brien, 'A charge delivered . . . in September 1851' (1852).
[16] *Prayers for the young* (1851).

26. M.

Wrote to Jas Watson—W.R. Farquhar—E. Coleridge—Rev. C. Robins—Dr Hawtrey—Rn. G—Mr Cox[1]—Ed. N. British R.[2]—Longmans—Ed. Westmr. R. Saw T.G. and J.N.G.—Ld Ashburton—Rev. Mr Whitford[3]—Mr Andrew—Mr Fox with Mr Wakefield—Mr E. Ellice—Bp of Oxford—M. Van de Weyer—Newcastle & Herbert—and, late, E. Scott—E[dash]& M. Horton [R]. H. of C. 4¾–7¼ and 11–12¼: voted in 315:165 for 2d reading of the Militia Bill.[4] Willy went off to Eton for the 2d time.

27. T.

H.S. with A. & S. Read Mr Greg's paper on Reform[5]—H. of C. & Commees. 1¾–7¼.[6] Saw B.R. Lawley—Clemence—S. Herbert—H.J.G.—Ld Aberdeen—Bp of Oxford—Cardwell—Goulburn—Peto. Wrote to Ld Hardinge (& draft)[7]—J. Griffiths—Mr Davidson—Rev.[8] Mr Cureton—Dr Pusey. Worked on accounts. Evening with C. (part).

28. Wed.

H.S. with A. & S. 9 to breakfast. We then went to Church where C. had her service (after part of mg prayer) & then our little 'Henry Neville' was baptized by Mr S. Clark: a great joy. H. of C. 12¾–6¼. On Scots Univ. Tests, & then Colonial Church on which I put in my speech, about an hour.[9] Saw Sir J. Pakington (morng)—Bp of Exeter (evg). Dined at D. of Newcastle's where I took the bottom of the table: Lady Ashburton's afterwards: where Ld J. Russell accosted me. Wrote to J. Griffiths—W.R. Greg—Capt. Salt[10]—Bp Bath & Wells—Rev. Mr Bennett.

29. Th.

H.S. with A. &. S. Wrote to Dean of Christ Church—R. Barker—Rev. H. M'Kenzie—J. Mozley—Mrs Irvine—Dr Jelf—Mr Woollcombe—Mr Hobhouse. Twelve to breakfast—partly invited for Lacaita. Committee & House 1¾–7¼ & 10–11¼. Voted for taking down the Crystal Palace.[11] Saw Ld Hardinge—J.N.G. Lady Hardwicke's in evg. Saw a person [R] at night who opened a new chapter of human calamity to me.

[1] Perhaps Robert Cox, 1810–72; writer to the signet; interested in Sabbatarianism.

[2] Alexander Campbell *Fraser, 1819–1914; free church minister and professor from 1844; ed. *North British Review* 1850–7; philosophical theist.

[3] Robert Wells Whitford, 1804–79; St. Edmund hall, Oxford; sundry curacies 1831–1858; chaplain H.E.I.C.S. 1839–51.

[4] *H* cxx. 1185.

[5] In the *Edinburgh Review*, cp. 6 Apr. 52.

[6] County franchise: *H* cxx. 1200.

[7] On income tax: cp. Add MS 44371, f. 352.

[8] 'Rev. Mr. Carr' here deleted.

[9] *H* cxx. 1263; notes in Add MS 44652, f. 8.

[10] Perhaps Samuel Salt, who wrote on railways and canals.

[11] *H* cxx. 1383. It was moved to Sydenham later in the year, and was burnt down in 1936.

30. Fr.

Wrote to Willy—Northcote—Phillimore—Mrs Ellison—J. Griffiths. Breakfasted at Ld Mahon's. Saw Ld J. Thynne & Mr Davies. King's Coll. at 1½.[1] Then to H. of C. seeing E. Scott [R] on my way. Commee. & House 3–9. Spoke shortly on the Budget.[2] Saw E. Collins [R] in evg. Settling as to parties with C.

Sat. May One. St Philip & St James.

H.S. with children. Saw R. Phillimore—Mr Balfour with Mr Ellice. Wrote to Jas Watson—G. Burnett—H. Tayleur—Mr W. Empson—Johnson L.[ongden] & Co—W.H. Barber—Gladstone & Co—Mr [?W] C. Lake. Went at two to the annual treat of the Exhibition: very interesting but not quite at par. Mr Munro's group was vilely placed.[3] From thence to the Amateur Water Colour. The Dinner 6¼–9¼.[4] Lord John R. very happy in following Disraeli. From the dinner I went to join C. under the hospitable roof of the Haddos at Blackheath.[5] Read N. Br. Review on Political Prospects.[6]

May 2. 3 S. E[aster].

Greenwich Churches[7] mg & aft.—Read Bp of Ossory's Charge & Appx (finished)—N. Br. R. on Dr Chalmers.[8] Walk with Ln. & Haddo.

3. M.

Morning walk with C: then returned to town. Wrote to Mr Kennaway—Mr Dalzell—Collr. Sc. Ep. Sch.[9]—Mr Hutt—Jas Watson—Rev. Dr Wolff[10]—W.M. Goalen—Robn. G.—Mr Greswell. Saw Mr Gurney—J.L. & Co—S. Herbert & others about Hutt's Resolution[11]—J.N.G.—Oswald—De Tabley —& at night another person, lightly & wrongfully [R]. Read Mamiani on the Papal Power.[12] H. of C. 5–8¼ and 10–12¾.[13]

[1] Report in *The Times*, 3 May 1852, 7f.
[2] *H* cxxi. 51; notes in Add MS 44652, f. 13.
[3] Cp. 12 Feb. 52n.
[4] Speeches reported in *The Times*, 3 May 1852, 8a.
[5] At Ranger's House, Blackheath.
[6] *North British Review*, xvii. 1 (May 1852); review of J. A. *Roebuck, *History of the whig administration of 1830* (1852).
[7] There was a parish church and five subsidiary churches.
[8] *North British Review*, xvii. 205 (May 1852); review of *Hanna's **Chalmers*.
[9] Probably the college attached to St. Ninian's, Perth.
[10] Joseph *Wolff, 1795–1862; missionary in Asia and India 1821–30; priest 1838; rector of Linthwaite, Yorkshire, 1838–45, of Ile Brewers, Somerset 1845–62.
[11] Probably an unmoved motion on the New Zealand Bill, debated that evening; *Hutt was a leading member of the New Zealand company.
[12] T. Mamiani della Rovere, *Sul papato* (1851).
[13] Spoke supporting the New Zealand Constitution Bill: *H* cxxi. 120, 135.

4. T.

H.S. with Agnes. Wrote to Mr Lacaita—J.L. Ross—J.D. Coleridge—J. Chapman—Bp of Salisbury—T. Nimmo—Sign. de Pompeo [1]—J. Murray—E. Hawkins (BM).[2] Saw Newcastle—Bp of Rochester—Mr Hincks—Home Drummond—Sir G. Clerk—J. Griffiths/ Indian Commee. 2–3¾. House 9–12¾.[3] Saw Hayter—B. Rothschild—S. Herbert & others on the pending questions of the Jews & the four seats.[4]

5. Wed.

H.S. with Stephen. Wrote to Visc. Hardinge—Robn. G (& draft)—G. Burnett—Hayter—(& draft)[5] J.C. Crampern.[6] Saw R. Barker & ex[ecute]d Mortgage[7]—Mr Goulburn—Mr Childers—G.C. Lewis—Milman. Meeting at my house at 4. Lord Aberdeen came afterwards. Attended Guy's Hospital Dinner: & spoke for the House of Commons.[8] Saw E. Scott [R]. C. went to the Ball with Mary.[9]

6. Th.

H.S. with the children. Wrote to Rev. Mr Williams—H. Sewell—R.T. Lowe[10]—Dr Leech[11]—M.W. Mayow—Ed. N. Br. Review. A day of entertainments: breakfast & dinner parties of 16 each: followed by an evening party of C's. Saw E.P.D.R. Deputn.[12]—Rev Mr Kennaway. Educn. Commee. & House 1¾–7.[13] Spoke[14] to Denison, Ld J.R, Ld Palmerston, about Monday, as well as Young & others.

7. Fr.

H.S. with the children. Wrote to R. Phillimore—T.G.—Rev Mr Berry—G. Grove—Rev. C. Crofts[15]—Mr Greswell—M.F. Tupper—Ld C. Russell—H.J.G. Saw Bonham—Rev Mr Lowe—R. Barker—Mr Greig.[16] Committee &

[1] Niccola de Pompeo, Neapolitan banker.
[2] Edward *Hawkins, 1780–1867; keeper of antiquities at British Museum 1826–60; numismatist.
[3] Militia Bill: *H* cxxi. 199.
[4] A bill to assign the four disenfranchised seats for Sudbury and St. Albans to the West Riding of Yorkshire and the southern division of Lancashire; cp. 10 May 52n.
[5] On the disenfranchised seats; cp. Add MS 44372, f. 52.
[6] John Callis Crampern, gentleman, lived in Jermyn Street.
[7] Part of the Hawarden and Ewloe estate was mortgaged for £12,500 to George Price Lloyd of Bala, Merioneth.
[8] No report traced.
[9] The state ball at Buckingham palace, cp. *The Times*, 6 May 1852, 5c.
[10] Richard Thomas *Lowe, 1802–74; anglican chaplain on Madeira 1832–54; naturalist.
[11] Perhaps John Leech, Liverpool physician.
[12] A deputation about the Edinburgh, Perth and Dundee railway, in which Gladstone was a shareholder.
[13] Militia Bill in cttee: *H* cxxi. 299.
[14] Instead of 'saw'.
[15] Christopher Crofts, 1804–94; priest 1828; headmaster Collegiate school, Camberwell, 1846–54, of Sevenoaks grammar school 1854–79.
[16] Probably John James Greig, 1806–82; head constable of Liverpool 1852–81.

H. of C. 3–7 and 10–12½.[1] Dined with the Ellisons. Saw E. Collins: bad: & there must be a change [R].

8. Sat.

H.S. with A. & S. Wrote to R. Barker—J. Walker. Christie's Sale 2–3¼. London Libr. Comm 4–5¼. Saw Bp of Argyll—Lyttelton—Lacaita. Worked on accounts. Read Philanthropic [Society] Reports—& presided at their Dinner at the London Tavern. 5¾–11½. Lady Palmerston's afterwards.

9. 4 S. E[aster].

St James's mg. Chapel Royal aft. MS of 42 on the services aloud. Saw D. of Newcastle. Wrote to Bp of Oxford—Lord Palmerston (& copy).[2] Read Mamiani (finished)—Heygate on the care of the Soul[3]—Account of Kaiserswerth[4]—of Rauber Haus.[5] Walk with C.

10. M.

Wrote to Ld Derby (& draft)—Scotts—R. Phillimore—J. Murray—Archd Sandford—Robn. G—Archd. Harrison—J.S. Wortley—Hon & Rev A. Perceval—Jas Watson—Provost of Oriel—W.C. James—Rev. R. Greswell. Saw Mr Bennett—Bonham—& Monsell, Sir J. Graham, Ld J. Russell, Osborne, at H. of C. about Maynooth: also the Pres. Dr Renehan.[6] Commee. 1–3¼. House 4½–9¾. Spoke 35 m. on moving the Order of the Day & voted in 234:148.[7] Wrote Pol. Mema. On account of Lord Wenlock's death yesterday (requiescat) we put off our parties for Wed. & Thursday—except my breakfast.

11. T.

H.S. with A. & S. Wrote to G. Burnett—Geo. Hancock.[8] Attended M. Thomas's Conference.[9] H. of C. 4½–7½ and 9–12½. Spoke on the Maynooth Grant.[10] Read on do. Saw Saintsbury. Arranged letters & papers.

[1] Militia Bill: *H* cxxi. 371.

[2] In Guedalla, *P*, 85.

[3] W. E. Heygate, *Care of the soul; or sermons on some points of christian prudence* (1851).

[4] [F. *Nightingale] *The institution of Kaiserswerth on the Rhine, for the practical training of deaconesses* (1851); her first publication.

[5] Untraced.

[6] Laurence F. *Renehan, 1797–1857; president of Maynooth college from 1845.

[7] Spoke on the disenfranchised seats: *H* cxxi. 453; notes in Add MS 44652, f. 17.

[8] Of the firm of Rigby and Hancock, Hawarden.

[9] The first of a series of 'Conférences sur l'histoire de l'établissement monarchique en France', given in Willis's rooms by Alexandre Gérard Thomas, 1818–57; cp. *The Times*, 12 May 1852, 8b.

[10] Supporting a motion for a select cttee. of inquiry: *H* cxxi. 567; notes in Add MS 44652, f. 20.

12. Wed.

Wrote to Bp of Cape Town—Sir W.P. Wood—G. Burnett—R. Sainthill—Mr Salomons [1]—Rev Mr Zincke [2]—Rev Mr Bazely.[3] Saw Mr Andrew—Sir C. Wood. Began Mariotti.[4] H. of C. 12¼–2¾. Spoke on the Book Trade.[5] Then to the City: & saw J.L. & Co.—After that shopping. Six to dinner.[6] Then to Graphic Society: and saw M. Malvina.[7]

13. Th.

Wrote [8] to Robn. G—H.J.G.—Mr Shirley Brooks—Jas Watson—C. Butler—S.M. Peto. Sixteen to breakfast. (This we did not put off.) Saw Bp of Argyll—Archd. Wilberforce—Ld Aberdeen—Ald. Salomons—Mr Chabot [9]—MG & TG. Read Mariotti—Adam on Retaliation.[10] Walk at night with C. & Mary for the illuminations:[11] & afr. Worked on accounts.

14. Fr.

H.S. with the children. Wrote to Rev E. Coleridge—F. Adams—Ld Ellesmere—Mr Nicolay—J.H. Parker—Mr Ashford.[12] Went out to breakfast at Mr Hallams. Committee & H. of C. 2–6¾ & 10–11¾.[13] Saw Spottiswoodes—Mildmays. Music in evg. Read Grenville Corresp.[14] Annoyed by one at night [R].

15. Sat.

H.S. with the children. 9¾–11½. At the Exhibition with C. Saw Phillimore—Nicolay—S. Herbert—Sir J. Johnstone—Cardwell—Bonham. Wrote to E.G. Wakefield—Rn. G.—Dean Milman—Rev. R. Burkitt [15]—Rev. A.W. Haddan. Drive with C. Evg at home. Music. Read Mariotti—Parker on the Book Trade [16]—Rev B. Addison.[17]

[1] (Sir) David *Salomons, 1797–1873; Jewish financier; lib. M.P. Greenwich 1851 (fined for voting without being sworn a member), 1859–73; cr. bart. 1869.

[2] Forster Barham *Zincke, 1817–93; vicar of Wherstead 1847–93; Queen's chaplain from ?1852; antiquarian and author. Cp. 18 Apr. 52.

[3] Francis Ley Bazeley, 1805–77; Queens', Cambridge; rector of St. Dominick, Cornwall, 1835–53, of Bideford, Devon, 1853–77.

[4] L. Mariotti, *Italy in 1848* (1851).

[5] On the excessive price of books: *H* cxxi. 593.

[6] But see entry for two days previously.

[7] An artist? Cp. 14 Feb. 49.

[8] Instead of 'H.S. with'.

[9] Probably Philip James Chabot, 1801–68; barrister 1830; merchant and silk dyer.

[10] W. P. Adam, *Thoughts on the policy of retaliation, and its probable effect on the consumer, producer and ship-owner* (1852).

[11] Ministers' houses were illuminated for the Queen's birthday, cp. *The Times*, 14 May 1853, 5d.

[12] Perhaps John Ashford, poet, who wrote on Italy; d. ?1867.

[13] Militia Bill: *H* cxxi. 633.

[14] Instead of 'Mariotti's Italy', *The Grenville papers, being the correspondence of R. *Grenville, Earl Temple, and rt. hon. G. *Grenville, their friends & contemporaries*, ed. W. J. Smith, 4v. (1852).

[15] William Burkitt, curate at Maidstone, Kent; signed letters 'R', not 'W': Hawn P.

[16] J. W. *Parker, a prospectus for the publishing association; copy in Add MS 44372, f. 144.

[17] Berkeley Addison, perhaps his 'Earnest and solemn remonstrance' (1843).

16. 5 S. E[aster].

St Mary's Cr[own] St. & H.C. at 11—Chapel Royal 5½. MS. of 42 aloud at night. Walk with C. Music in evg. Wrote to O.B. Cole. Read Heygate on Care of the Soul—Ed. Rev. on Edn. & on Knox's Liturgy—Knox's Liturgy [1]—Balmez.[2]

17. M.

H.S. with the children. Wrote to Tatham Upton & Co—R. Barker—Rev. Mr Heavyside [3]—H. Chester—Rev. Mr Greswell—H. Sewell—Bp Bath & Wells (2)—Geo. Grove—Mr Disraeli (cancelled) [4]—Mr J. Anders—Mr Rutledge [5]—Capt Williams [6]—Mr Howell [7]—Rev. Dr Binney—Jas Watson. Saw Sir W.P. Wood—H.K. Seymer—E. Ellice—Ld Shaftesbury. Worked on accounts. Ch. Buildg Soc.—Commee.—and House 12¼–7¾.[8] Singing in Evg. Saw E. Reynolds [R]—late.

18. T.

H.S. with the children. Wrote to H. Chester—Sir J. Pakington (two, & copies) [9]—J.L. & Co.—Rev. F. Litchfield.[10] Read NZ. Bill.[11] Drive & calls with C. Saw E.G. Wakefield—Bonham—R. Phillimore—Rev W. Scott. Attended Marlborough House Exhibition[12]—M. Thomass Conference. Evg at home: music: but I was downhearted about my poor Bill & could not sing.[13]

19. Wed.

H.S. with the children. H. of C. 12–6: on Col. Ch. Bill[14]—Saw Bethell,[15] & Sir W.P. Wood, on the subject.—The reverse of fortune was trying: but by me well deserved. Such a steward of such things! Wrote to Tatham & Procter with Certificates. Saw J.N.G—Cardwell. Dined at Sir R. Inglis's to meet the Dean of Ch. Ch. &c. Saw one in evg who made reference to E. Clifton: poor soul [R]. Here till 1¼.

[1] *Edinburgh Review*, xcv. 321, 453 (April 1852); on national education, and a review of J. *Knox, ed. J. *Cumming, *Book of Common Order* (1840).

[2] Cp. 29 Feb. 52.

[3] James William Lucas Heavyside, 1808–97; Trinity, Cambridge; priest 1833; professor of mathematics, Haileybury, 1838–57; canon of Norwich from 1860.

[4] On the Frome case, in Add MS 44652, f. 130.

[5] Perhaps John Young Rutledge, 1824–72; fellow of Trinity, Dublin, from 1850; D.D. 1860; rector of Armagh from 1865.

[6] Of the royal engineers, perhaps John Williams, designing Hawarden tramways?

[7] Perhaps Thomas Howell, 1802–83; businessman; director of war office contracts 1855–74; kt. 1876.

[8] The Frome affair: *H* cxxi. 685.

[9] Add MS 44372, f. 38.

[10] Francis Litchfield, 1792–1876; Merton, Oxford; rector of Elham, Kent, 1830, of Great Linford, Northamptonshire, 1836–76.

[11] The New Zealand Government Bill; cp. 21 May 52.

[12] The board of practical art's exhibition.

[13] The gvnt. had decided to oppose the 2° of his Colonial Bishops Bill, cp. *H* cxxi. 739.

[14] *H* cxxi. 738: notes in Add MS 44652, f. 28.

[15] Notes of conversation in Add MS 44740, f. 8.

20. Th. Ascension Day.

St Martins 11 A.M. Wrote to H. Kynaston—Robn. G—T.C. Huddlestone—W. Longman—J.D. Coleridge—W. Hancock.[1] Worked on Col. Ch. Bill.[2] Saw Mr Andrew—Bonham. Commee. & H. of C. 2–7¼ and 10½–1½: on Maynooth postponement.[3] 10 to dinner.

21. Fr.

Breakfasted with the Dean of St Pauls. Dined with the S. Herberts. Saw J.D. Coleridge—Bonham—Young—R. Cavendish—Archd. Wilberforce—Christy—Ebrington. Worked on N.Z. Bill—B.N.A. Charters. H. of C. 10¼–1½. Spoke 1½ hour on NZ. Bill.[4] Wrote to C. Wray[5]—Robn. G—B. Harrison—G. & Co.—J.P. Norman[6]—J[ohnson] L[ongden] & Co—R. Greswell—R. Barker.

22. Sat.

H.S. with the children. C. went to Brighton. Took her to the Station. Saw J.L. & Co—Mr J. Chapman[7]—Duke of Newcastle—Bp of Oxford. Attended Lond. Libr. Commee. Wrote to Abp of Canterbury (& copy)[8]—Mr Bellairs—Mr Greswell—A.P. Saunders (p[ar]t)—Mr Andrew—J.D. Coleridge—Mr Gordon (Ellon)[9] Read Le Petit Fils d'un Grand Homme[10]—Saw E.C. at night: & had tea there [R]. I am surely self-bewildered.

23. S. after Asc[ensio]n.

Chapel Royal mg—Bedfordbury Evg. Wrote on Ps. V. 8. & read aloud in evg. Saw Newcastle—Oswald—Goulburn. Finished letter to Saunders[11]—Read Hoffman on Am. Ch[12]—Scots Eccl. Journal.[13]

[1] Of Rigby and Hancock, Hawarden.

[2] Add MS 44740, f. 9.

[3] Spoke of Maynooth: *H* cxxi. 845.

[4] *H* cxxi 951; published as 'Speech . . . on the second reading of the New Zealand Constitution Bill' (1852); notes in Add MS 44652, f. 30.

[5] Cecil Wray, 1805–78; vicar of St. Martin-in-the-fields, Liverpool, 1846–75; established sisterhood of holy women; or perhaps his father, Cecil Daniel, 1778–1866, dean of Manchester 1847–66.

[6] John Paxton Norman, 1819–71; barrister and special pleader from 1852; judge of Bengal high court 1867–71, when he was assassinated in Calcutta.

[7] *Chapman had organized a cttee. to inquire into protected profits of London booksellers; cp. Add MS 44731, f. 368.

[8] Add MS 44372, f. 56.

[9] George John Robert Gordon, of Ellon, Aberdeenshire, chargé d'affaires in Stockholm 1845–51; ambassador to Switzerland 1854, to Hanover 1858, to Baden 1859.

[10] Untraced.

[11] No copy found, but see Saunders' reply in Add MS 44372, f. 94.

[12] M. Hoffmann, *A treatise on the law of the protestant episcopal church in the United States* (1850).

[13] On dispute on synods between Gladstone and *Wordsworth; cp. *Scottish Magazine*, n.s. ii. 576 (December 1852).

24. M.

H.S. with Agnes. Wrote to Mr J.P. Lacaita—J.L. & Co—Lord Braybrooke—Mr Greswell—Mr N. Macdonald[1]—J. Ashford—Dr Harington—Sir S. Lushington. Read La Loge du Portier.[2] Dined with the Charterises.[3] Lady C. Denison's ball in evg. Saw C. Wynn[4]—Mrs Phillimore—Mr W. Longman—Bonham—Woodgate—H.J.G.—Mr Fox—W.C. James—J.D. Coleridge. H. of C. 4¾–7½.[5] Went over the amendments in the Col. Bps. Bill with Sir W.P. Wood.

25. T.

H.S. with Agnes. Wrote to Mr Sangster[6]—Capt Lake[7]—Mr N. Macdonald—H. Glynne—Sir Pakington and copy—Rev. T. James—Rev. Mr Lundy—Sir S. Lushington. Saw Mr Greswell—G.W. Hope—Archdn. Harrison—Ld Hardinge. H. of C. 2–6½ (Maynooth)[8] Dined with Ld Carlisle.[9] Read Theatre de Madame:[10] the reason that it[11] is a délassement.[12]

26. Wed.

H.S. with Agnes. Wrote to Mr S. Andrew—Mr Riordon[13]—Bp of Brechin—Dean Ramsay—Sir J. Pakington (and copy)—Northcote. Saw anon: late: advice [R]. Saw Thesiger—Bonham—R. Cavendish—Woodgate—Heneage. Attended St Paul's School Speeches.[14] Shopping—Began to correct my NZ Speech. Dined with S. Herbert. Lady Molesworth's concert afr. Read Buchanan on Pictures[15]—Newman's Lectures on Univ. Education.[16] This day was deeply saddened to us by the news of J. Talbot's death[17] in the night at Brighton: a most heavy loss; except for himself.

27. Th.

H.S. with Agnes. Breakfast party—reaching twenty or thereby. Saw Messrs Best & Stephens[18]—Bonham—R. Phillimore—H.K. Seymer—Sir J.

[1] Norman Hilton MacDonald, d. 1857; fellow of All Souls from 1828; controller of lord chamberlain's department from 1852.
[2] Not found.
[3] Lady Anne Frederica, da. of 1st earl of Lichfield, first wife (1843) of F. R. C. *Charteris, 8th earl of Wemyss; she d. 1896.
[4] Charlotte Williams-*Wynn, 1807–69; da. of C. W.*; diarist.
[5] Misc. business: *H* cxxi. 1048.
[6] Perhaps William Sangster, 1808–88; umbrella maker in Fleet street; won prize at 1851 exhibition for umbrellas; wrote on them.
[7] Edward Lake, 1808–64; captain R.N.
[8] Spoke on Maynooth, *H* cxxi. 1150.
[9] i.e. the seventh earl.
[10] Not found.
[11] 'Plain' here deleted.
[12] 'relaxation'.
[13] James Riordan, of Reeks and Riordan, law writers in Cursitor street.
[14] Cp. *The Times*, 28 May 1852, 5d.
[15] W. Buchanan, *Memoirs of painting, with a chronological history of the importation of pictures by the great masters into England since the French revolution*, 2 vols. (1824).
[16] Cp. 9 Apr. 52.
[17] i.e. John Chetwynd Talbot, cp. 4 Feb. 33.
[18] John Best, 1821–65; barrister from 1846; tory M.P. Kidderminster 1849–52 and Archibald John Stephens, cp. 17 June 45.

Graham (NZ.)—Sir C. Wood. Wrote to Mr C.B. Dalton—Rn. G.—Rev. Mr Wilkinson [1]—G. & Co.—Lord St Leonard's—Lady Glynne—Mr J. Hignett —Mr Troughton—Warden of Durham. Dined with the Warburtons. Read Oxf. Univ. Commn. Report.[2] Worked on correcting my NZ. Speech.

28. Fr.

H.S. with Agnes. Saw Mr Dalton—Commn. & House $2\frac{3}{4}$–7.[3] Wrote to Mr G.F. Bowen—Col. Grey—Rev. E. Hawkins—J.L. Ross—Mr Rendall [4]—H. Floyd [5]—Mr Litton. Read D. at Argyll's Address [6]—Les Premieres Amours [7]—Univ. Commn. Report. Worked on my books with Mr Leighton the Binder.

29. Sat.

H.S. with Agnes. Wrote to Rev. Mr Greswell—Mr Woodgate—Mr Burkitt —Mr Skirving [8]—Banting & Sons.[9] Saw Parker (Solr.)[10]—Leighton—Scotts —Bonham—Ross—Dr Phillimore. Attended L[ondon] lib. Committee & Meeting. Dined at Sir E. Kerrison's—Ld Londesborough's afterwards. Worked most of the day on my books. Saw E. Watson [R] at night: who is going to Australia. Worked on my Speech.

30. Whitsunday.

York St (Holy Comm.) 11–2: and Bedfordbury Evg. MS. of 1840 aloud in evg. Wrote to Bp of Glasgow—Bp of Brechin—Geo. Applegate. Saw R. Cavendish—Mr Senior—Jas Wortley—Settembrini. Walk with C. Read Heygate —Balmez.

31. M.

St Mary's Crown St $8\frac{1}{2}$ P.M. Wrote to Supt. Traffic LNW[11]—Rev. Mr Hughes—Rev. C. Marriott [12]—Jas Watson. Drove with C. Duchess of Grafton's party in evg.[13] Read pamphlets. Worked ab. 8. hours (from 7 AM.) on my books.—Saw Mr Andrew—Lacaita.

[1] John Wilkinson, 1817–76; Wadham, Oxford; rector of Broughton Gifford, Wiltshire, from 1848; wrote on bp. *Butler.

[2] *PP* 1852 xxii. 1. Start of his work on university reform, leading to 1854 bill.

[3] Maynooth: *H* cxxix. 1293.

[4] Henry Rendall, 1818–97; fellow of Brasenose, Oxford, 1840–56; rector of Great Rollright, Oxfordshire, 1855.

[5] Probably Sir Henry Floyd, 1793–1868, *Peel's br. in law; major general, served at Waterloo.

[6] A paper given by him to the London geographical society on fossil leaves on Mull; cp. Argyll, i. 349.

[7] M.D.S. [Deschamps de Saucourt], *Les premières amours, ou Zémire et Zilas* (1784).

[8] John Skirving, engraver and stamp cutter in Artillery place, London.

[9] William Banting and sons, upholsterers and cabinet makers in St. James's.

[10] Parker, Hayes, Barnwell and Twisden, solicitors firm in Lincoln's Inn.

[11] H. P. Bruyere.

[12] In Lathbury, ii. 18.

[13] Mary Caroline, da. of Sir George Cranfield Berkeley; m. 1812 Henry Fitzroy, 1790–1863; 5th duke of Grafton 1844; she d. 1873.

Tuesday June One 1852.

Wrote to Mr Hopkinson—Lt Mahon—S. Langley [1]—Dr Wolff—J. Griffiths —Dr Saunders. Saw Miss Shedden [2]—Ld Jocelyn—Ld Hardinge—Panizzi —Phillimore. Attended M. Thomas' Lecture. Dined with the Oswald's. Mrs Milnes Gaskell's party afterwards. Worked on my books—& on 1847 Election papers. [3]

2. Wed.

H.S. with A. Wrote to Dr Hawtrey—Ed. M. Chronicle—Parker Hayes & Co.—Finished work on my books: now in tolerable order. 3–6 Exhibn. Commn. Meeting at the Palace. The Prince was most sorely disturbed. [4] 16 to dinner—Parliamentary. Breakfast at Tom's and at the Baptism of his little boy 'John Robert' afterwards. [5] Saw Scotts—T.G. & JNG—Mr Hubbard—R. Phillimore. Read my Univ. Commn. Speech (to test it) [6] and pamphlets. Shopping.

3. Th.

H.S. with the children. Ten to breakfast (10–12). Saw R. Phillimore—Bonham—Lacaita—Miss Wynn—Messrs. Fox, Sewell, Wakefield—Ld Hardinge—Corrected proofs of N.Z. Speech. Wrote to Mr J.W. Parker.—

Rev. Mr Greswell
A. Baker [7]
M. Bayley [8]
W. Selwyn
J.S. Pakington
Mayor of Cork [9]
A. Galleano—
Sir F. Rogers

H. of C. 4–7. 17 to dinner: incl. Lord & Lady Palmerston—C.s evening party afterwards. In bed by 1¼.

4. Fr.

Up at 6.30 & to Eton by 7.40 train. Breakf. with Dr Hawtrey—& attended the Speeches wh were much improved as compared with the olden time. Saw my Willy for some while: also Coleridge—Dean of Windsor—Johnnie. Home at 4. House of Commons 4½–9¼ on N.Z. Bill. [10] Then to the Queen's Concert. [11] Read Marquis Montagu's Etudes. [12] Saw Sir J. Graham on NZ.

[1] Samuel Langley kept a fleet of London cabs.
[2] Caroline Goodrich Shedden, da. of George Shedden of Paulerspury park, Northamptonshire, and Bedford square, London; or one of her four unmarried sisters.
[3] See 12 May 47 ff. The dissolution was on 2 July.
[4] Cp. 5 June 52.
[5] T.G.'s. only son: (Sir) John Robert Gladstone, 1852–1926; 3rd bart. 1889; a bachelor.
[6] His speech of 18 July 50, which had opposed the setting up of the commission.
[7] Arthur Baker, 1817–68; Wadham, Oxford; curate of Aylesbury.
[8] Montagu Bayly, b. 1824; Christ Church, Oxford; domestic chaplain to earl of Jersey.
[9] James Lambkin; business untraced.
[10] Spoke on it: *H* cxxii. 41.
[11] Cp. *The Times*, 4 June 1852, 5e.
[12] A. L. C. de Montagu, *Etudes sociales d'après la révélation* (1851).

Wrote to the Lord Chancellor—Dr Dewhurst[1]—Mr C. Foster[2]—Rob. Gladstone—A.P. Saunders.

5. Sat.

Wrote to Rev. Mr Andrew—J. Griffiths—Robn. G—Ld Hardinge—G. & Co—Mr Greswell—J.N.G—Mr J.P. Tweed[3]—J.D. Cook—Mr Ashford. Palace (Surplus Commee.) 11–1½: we got I think out of the scrape.[4] Col. Grey told me at night he had never seen the Prince so agitated as on Wednesday: he did not sleep that night: the Queen tried to encourage him. Saw Mr Rogers—Herbert—St German's. Attended Thomas's Lecture. Then the Talbot Memorial Meeting. It is now no slight daily task to read the newspaper articles & letters on the Oxford Election. Dined with the Adderleys. Lady Palmerston's afterwards.

6. Trin. S.

Spr[ing] Gardens Chapel (& H.C.) 11 A.M.—Chapel Royal aft. MS of 1840 aloud in evg. Read Heygate[5]—Scots Ep. Mag.[6] & Periodicals. Worked on St M[artin's] Church papers.[7] Wrote to J. Mozley—Bp of Glasgow—Mr Teale—Gordon of Ellon—Mr Hawkins—Archdn. Sandford—Vicar of St M[artins].[8]

7. M.

H.S. with S. & A. Wrote to Mr H. Bennett—W. Pusey—Sig. Casto[9]—J. Mackie—M. Czarniawski[10]—T. Nimmo—Amer. Minister—Ld Hardinge—M.W. Mayow. Read Mather papers[11]—and Introd. to Hirscher by Coxe.[12] Customs Comm. 12¾–3¼. H. of C. 9¾–12½.[13] Saw Goulburn & Herbert on Frome[14]—Phillimore on Oxford. Saw E. Scott & E. Lee: the former going to marry & bound for Australia [R].

[1] Henry William Dewhurst, physician and phrenologist.
[2] Charles J. Foster, secretary of a cttee. on new universities; Hawn P.
[3] James Peers Tweed, 1819–90; fellow of Exeter, Oxford 1841–63; rector of Little Waltham 1863–90; wrote on university affairs.
[4] Purchase of the S. Kensington site with the surplus from the exhibition, cp. T. Martin, *Life of the Prince Consort* (1877) ii. 446.
[5] Cp. 9 May 52.
[6] *Scottish Magazine* n.s. ii. 265 (June 1852); supported Gladstone against *Wordsworth.
[7] The St. Martin's church endowment fund; cp. Hawn P.
[8] i.e. H. Mackenzie.
[9] Julius Casto, writer on Italian affairs.
[10] Probably Jan N. Czarnowski, Polish historian.
[11] *The collections of the Dorchester antiquarian and historical society*, 3v. (1844–50) dealt with the Mather family.
[12] J. B. von Hirscher, *Sympathies of the continent, or proposals for a new reformation* (1852); translated and edited, with an introduction, by A. C. Coxe.
[13] Misc. business: *H* cxxii. 101.
[14] On *Horsman's motion for a select cttee., moved the next day.

8. T.

Wrote to Rev. Mr Andrew—Capt Scott—Rev Mr Burkitt—B. Price—Mackenzie Wilson—T. Ramsay[1]—Bp of Bath & Wells.[2] Wrote draft for Mr Greswell to Dr Wynter.[3] Saw Phillimore—Bonham—Archdn. Sandford—Greswell with Seymer, Coleridge, Bernard (12–2). Read Gordon's Letter to Bp of Oxford[4]—Coxe's Introduction. H. of C. 6–1½. Spoke 1¾ hour on the Frome case for the Bishop.[5] Worked on the case.

9. Wed.

Wrote to Jas Watson—Willy—Bp of Moray—Ld Wenlock—J.L. & Co. We dined with the J.N.G.s. Saw my brothers 11–2 on the Residuary Estate affairs[6]—Lacaita—Mr Wenham[7]—Mr Mostyn. House 2¾–6.[8] Read Hirscher—Goulburn's draft Report.[9] Wrote tentatively for an Oxford Address: but I do not think it will do.[10]

10. Th.

Wrote (after midnight at 3 A.M.) to Mr Greswell—priv. & for publication.[11] Twenty to breakfast (ab.) H. of C. 2½–7 and 9–2½. Saw Mr Haddan & Mr Lake on Oxford matters—Dr Beaven—Mr Wegg Prosser—Mr Hubbard—Mr Wenham? Spent much time in examining the Journals & considering, as well as in stirring up others, on the proceedings to be taken about Horsman's motion. Spoke on N.Z. and on the Frome Committee.[12] Mr H.s courage is a little cooled.

11. Fr. (St Barnabas).

Rose at 10. Wrote to Sir W.P. Wood—Warden of New College[13]—G. Harcourt. Saw Mr Davis—C.A. Wood—S. Herbert—Read the Lond. Lib. Testimonials.[14] Dined at Merchant Tailors' Hall: some conv. with Dr

[1] Thomas Ramsay, geographer and educationalist; had sent a pamphlet.
[2] 'Rev. S. Andrew' here deleted.
[3] Not found.
[4] Robert A. Gordon, 'The church's claim and archdeacon *Denison's resolution compared. A letter to the bishop of Oxford' (1852).
[5] The start of his speech was spoilt by the naming of Feargus *O'Connor for disorderly behaviour; *H* cxxii. 274; notes in Add MS 44652, f. 32.
[6] The winding up of his father's will.
[7] Probably John George Wenham, 1820–95; anglican priest, became Roman catholic 1846; rector of St. Mary Magdalen, Mortlake, 1850–95.
[8] Misc. business: *H* cxxii. 332.
[9] Probably *Goulburn's 1837 counsel to Cambridge on statute reform, discussed in correspondence later this year: Add MS 44162, f. 63ff.
[10] Add MS 44740, ff. 15–24.
[11] Sending his Oxford address for publication.
[12] *H* cxxii. 433, 465. He refused to serve on the select cttee. on the Frome affair proposed by Edward *Horsman, 1807–76; liberal M.P. Cockermouth 1836–52, Stroud 1853–1868, Liskeard 1869–76; Irish sec. 1855–7; an Adullamite leader 1866.
[13] David Williams, 1786–1860; headmaster of Winchester 1824–35; warden of New college, Oxford 1840–60; vice-chancellor 1856–8.
[14] See note after next.

Wynter. H. of C. 2–4.[1] Examined Journals. My brothers came here on Resid[uary] Estate business: 11–1.

12. Sat.

Wrote to Mr Lacaita—M.F. Tupper—J. Griffiths—& Customs Commee. 12¾–2½. Saw Chev. Bunsen—Rn. G—Newcastle. Drive with C. & calls. Lond. Libr. Comm. Meeting 3–4¾. Mr Donne elected.[2] Dined with the Denisons. Read Seniors MS Journal.[3]—Worked on O.F. draft Agreement for Furnaces.[4]

13. 1S. Trin.

Pimlico Chapel[5] with H.C. 11–1¾. Bedfordbury evg. MS. on St Barnabas aloud at night. Wrote to Bp of Fredericton—Rev Mr Low—W.C. James—Dr Jacobson. Saw Herbert & Goulburn—Newcastle—W. Palmer & Adm. Poutiatin. Read Hirscher—D. of Argyll on Combe.[6] With C.

14. M.

Wrote to E. St Germans—J.B. Mozley—Rev. D. Robertson—Lady Harington—Rev. W. Scott[7]—Sir C. Eardley—Mr H. Miller[8]—Mr Gres-well—Saw Mr Swift. Exhibn. meeting at the Palace 11¾–1½. My brothers met me here on Residuary Estate at 11. Cust. Comm. & House 1¾–7½. House 11–3.[9] Read Handbook of London. Home by broad day.

15. T.

Wrote to J.C. Robertson—Archdn. Thorp—A. Galleano—W. Graham. Saw my Brothers on Res[iduary] Estate business—Went to Doctors Commons on do.[10] Saw Mr Andrew. Helen's Madrigal party at 4. St James's (Jubilee) 8 P.M. Saw E. Watson & gave the best advice I could about emigration & the means [R].

16. Wed.

Wrote to J.W. Warter—T. Matsey[11]—G.B. Sandford—J. Griffiths—J.B.

[1] Misc. business: *H* cxxii. 509.
[2] William Bodham *Donne, 1807–82; declined editorship of *Edinburgh Review* 1852; librarian, London library 1852–7; lord chancellor's examiner of plays 1857–74.
[3] Cp. 28 Dec. 50n.
[4] Hawn P.
[5] St. Peter's chapel, Charlotte street, Pimlico.
[6] See G. *Combe, 'Secular instruction, or the extension of church endowment? A letter to the duke of *Argyll' (1852).
[7] William *Scott, 1813–72; curate of Christ Church, Hoxton 1839–63; co-editor, *Christian Remembrancer* 1841–68; president, Sion college 1858; vicar of St. Olave's, Jewry, 1862–72.
[8] Mr. Henry Miller of Frome.
[9] Spoke on Frome: *H* cxxii. 614.
[10] The college of doctors of civil law where probate, marriage and divorce business was done.
[11] Unidentified.

Westhead. Shopping. Saw R. Phillimore—W. Palmer—Mr Lyon (Solr.)[1]—Duke of Buccleuch—Dss. of Buccleuch—Chapman (Overends)[2]—Johnson Longden & Co—In the City 1–$2\frac{3}{4}$. Saw E. Scott & E. Lee late: the former looking to marriage & Australia [R]. Read J.B. Westhead on Col. Baronage[3]—Senior's Journal MS—Money on Cotton in India[4]—Prefaces to Rejected Addresses.[5] Evg. at home.

17. Th.

Wrote to Judge Coleridge—Mr Thos Baring—Signor Galleano—& [blank.] Saw one Welsh late: advice [R]. Saw R. Phillimore—Hubbard—G. Hope—D. of Argyll— J.D. Coleridge & M. Bernard[6]—Jocelyn. J.N.G. & R.G. on Residuary Estate affairs. 14 to Breakfast. $1\frac{1}{2}$–$4\frac{1}{2}$ Customs Committee. 6–$7\frac{1}{2}$ and $11\frac{3}{4}$–1 H of C.[7] Dined at Lord Crewe's: Countess Walewska's afterwards.[8] Read 'The Position of Curates'[9] and worked on accounts.

18. Fr.

Wrote to J.E. Fitzgerald—Jas Watson—J.R. Godley. At Bookshops. Saw Phillimore—Northcote—Archdeacon Hale. H. of C. 6–$8\frac{3}{4}$: spoke on Frome Committee—a finale.[10] Lady Zetland's Concert,[11] & Lady Salisbury's ball,[12] in evg. Read Statement of facts on Jamaica[13]—&c.

19. Sat.

Wrote to Collis—Northcote—Scotts—Bp of London—Sec.s U[niversity] C[ommission,] University [College].[14] Eleven to breakfast. Exhibn. Finance Commee. 1–3. Sig. Galleano's Lecture $3\frac{1}{2}$–$4\frac{1}{2}$. Statist[ical] Soc. Council $4\frac{1}{2}$–$5\frac{1}{2}$.[15] E.I. Company's Dinner with S. Herbert at $6\frac{1}{2}$. Lady Palmerston's afterwards. Saw one, & two: advice: but unsatisfactory behaviour [R]. Read [blank.]

[1] James Wittit Lyon, head of solicitor's firm of Lyon, Barnes and Ellis in Westminster.

[2] i.e. D. B. Chapman.

[3] Untraced MS by J. P. Brown Westhead.

[4] E. Money, 'A letter on the cultivation of cotton . . . and other matters connected with India' (1852).

[5] By H. and J. Smith (1812). Cp. 19 Nov. 41.

[6] Mountague *Bernard, 1820–82; Lincoln's inn barrister 1846; 1st professor of international law, Oxford, 1859–74; member of many commissions and tribunals.

[7] Spoke on Australia: *H* cxxii. 863.

[8] The French embassy, at Albert Gate House, Hyde Park.

[9] 'The position of curates of the Church of England: a letter to Edward *Horsman by a curate' (1852).

[10] *H* cxxii. 945.

[11] Sophia Jane Dundas, *née* Williamson, 1803–65; m. 1823 2nd earl of Zetland.

[12] Mary Catherine Cecil, 1824–1900; da. of 5th Earl De La Warr; m. 1st 1847 2nd marquess of Salisbury, as his 2nd wife; m. 2nd 1870 15th earl of Derby.

[13] 'A statement of facts relative to the island of Jamaica' (1852).

[14] A. P. *Stanley and Goldwin *Smith, 1823–1910; fellow of University 1846–54; assistant sec. of Oxford commission; regius professor of history 1858–66; lived in N. America from 1868. Cp. Add MS 44303.

[15] To prepare for the Ordinary Meeting on 21st June; cp. *Journal of the Statistical Society*, xv. 276.

20. S.

Went off early to Windsor. St George's mg. Eton Chapel aftn. We stay at the Deanery: a most hospitable house: where Willy runs tame. Saw Dr Hawtrey—E. Coleridge—Read Hayman[1]—Hirscher (finished)—Amoris Effigies.[2]

21. M.

St George's 10½. Conv. with Willy. Returned to London at 11½. Committee 12½-3: House 6-8½. Spoke briefly on Educn. Minute.[3] Wrote to A.P. Stanley (draft)—G. Burnett—Secs. LNW.RR.—Overends—J. Griffiths—Newcastle—R. Phillimore—Rn. G. Read Amoris Effigies—Empire des Nairs[4] —Dined with the Herberts—Saw one & one after: advice—almost always with some gift [R]. Saw Bonham.

22. T.

Wrote to N.W. Senior—Mr J. Strong[5]—A.P. Stanley (fair)—Miss Reynolds —Tathams—Rev. R. Gregory. Saw D. Robertson—S. Herbert—J.N.G.— R. Phillimore. Shopping. Went to Chelsea & saw E. Reynolds [R]. Ended by recommending to live by drawing: & gave £1 to purchase materials &c. House at 7½. Evg at home. Read the 'Empire des Nairs'—Massaniello Revolution.[6] Wrote out for printing my corrected Col. Ch. Bill.[7]

23. Wed.

Wrote to Mr R. Morier[8]—Rn. G—S.H. Northcote—G. & Co—H. Munro[9] —Jas Anderson. Saw Ld Ashburton—Mr Fagan—Mrs Talbot: who was admirable.[10] H of C. 12-3 Spoke ¾ h on Col. Ch. Bill & made up my quarrel with Pakington wh I *cannot* carry on): and 4¾-6.[11] Dined with the Herberts: then Lady Wilton's ball[12]—& Mrs Packe Reading's concert. Saw & advised one [R].

[1] H. Hayman, *Dialogues of the early church, i Rome, ii Smyrna, iii Carthage* (1851).
[2] Latin verses by [R. *Waring] (1648).
[3] *H* cxxii. 1105.
[4] Le chev. L. [James Lawrence], *L'empire des nairs, ou le paradis de l'amour*, 4v. (1814).
[5] Perhaps John Strong, stereotyper in Chancery Lane.
[6] One of the many books on Masaniello's revolution in Naples in 1647; perhaps A. Saavedra, *Insurrection de Naples en 1647* (1849).
[7] See next day's entry.
[8] (Sir) Robert Burnett David *Morier, 1826-93; sundry diplomatic appointments at German courts 1853-76; minister at Lisbon 1876-81, Madrid 1881-4; K.C.B. 1882; ambassador at St. Petersburg 1884-93; developed strong antipathy to Gladstone.
[9] Hugh Andrew Johnstone *Munro, 1819-85; Kennedy professor, Cambridge, 1869-1872; leading Victorian Latin scholar and editor.
[10] Cp. 26 May 52.
[11] Successfully introduced his bill in cttee. by a procedural device: *H* cxxii. 1204.
[12] Mary Margaret Egerton, 1801-58; da. of 12th earl of Derby; m. 1821 Thomas Egerton, *né* Grosvensor, 1799-1882; 2nd earl of Wilton 1814; took name of Egerton 1821; he m. secondly 1863 Susan Isabella Smith, 1832-1916.

24. St Joh. Baptist.

H[ouse] of Charity Chapel 5–6 after meeting (at wh I was made to speak) 3–5. H. of C. 1¾–2½.[1] Fifteen to breakfast. Saw R. Phillimore—R. Lowe—Mr Allen (Canada)[2] Wrote to Archd. Denison—Mr Fagan—R. Phillimore—Rev. J. Douglas[3]—Stanistreet. Lady Farquhar's party in evg. Saw E. Watson—whose voyage to Australia is arranged [R]—& E. Collins [R]. Read Macaulay on Croker[4]—Empire des Nairs.

25. Fr.

Wrote to H.G. Liddell (& draft)—Robn. G.—J. Yeats[5]—Mr Greswell—Alex. Low[6]—Mr Colton[7]—Mrs Talbot—Mr Vizetelly.[8] E.I. Committee & House of C. 1½–7.[9] Dined with the Cholmondeleys: Ld Lansdowne's concert afterwards. I was seized there with violent pain in the bowls & nausea, near the end: I was but just able to controul it. Saw R. Lowe (Col. Ch)—J.D. Coleridge—Mr Morier—Bp of Bath & Wells. Read the last day's proceedings in Queen's Bench. Proh pudor. Read Empire des Nairs. Saw one Welsh (3°):[10] & advised [R].

26. Sat.

Wrote to G. Burnett—Scott & Co—J. Griffiths—J. M'Glashan[11]—Prichard & Collette[12]—J. Murray—Sig. Montuoro[?][13]—C. Butler—Lady F. Cole—H. Flood—Rev. Mr Dodd—J.W. Wilson—Rev Mr Owen[14]—Sir W. Heathcote[15]—Manch Trustees[16]—Saw Mr Brown Westhead—J.N.G.—Lord Bath. Read Empire des Nairs. Worked on accounts & papers. Walk with C. Mrs Herbert & Jane W[ortley] to dinner—Bath House in evg.

27. 3 S. Trin.

St Martins H.C. at 8½—Pimlico Chapel at 11—Bedfordbury evg. MS. on St J. Baptist aloud. Wrote to P. Lightfoot—Bp of Oxford—R. Wilberforce.

[1] Misc. business: *H* cxxii. 1269.
[2] Perhaps J. Antisell Allen, priest in Toronto diocese.
[3] Probably John James Douglas; Trinity, Cambridge; curate of Wrawby-*cum*-Brigg, Lancashire, 1846; late rector of Kirriemuir, Angus.
[4] *Macaulay's hostile review of *Croker's ed. of *Boswell's *Life of *Johnson*, in the *Edinburgh Review*, liv. 1 (September 1831) and often reprinted.
[5] Probably James Sebastian Yeats, stockbroker in Bank chambers.
[6] Alexander Low, 1800–73; presbyterian minister of Keig, Banff, 1834–73; wrote on Scottish history.
[7] William Charles Colton, 1812–84; Queen's, Oxford; vicar of Baston, Lincolnshire, 1836–58, rector of Leaden Roding, Essex, 1864–84.
[8] Henry *Vizetelly, 1820–94; engraver, journalist, and publisher.
[9] Corrupt Practices Bill: *H* cxxii. 1301.
[10] Altered from '2°.'
[11] John *McGlashan, d. 1866; wrote on civil law; emigrated 1855.
[12] Attorney's firm in Lincoln's inn.
[13] Perhaps Carlos F. Monteiro of Fonseca, Monteiro and Co, London wine merchants.
[14] Robert Owen, b. 1820; dean of Jesus, Oxford, 1849; lecturer in modern history from 1858.
[15] One more name here deleted.
[16] Probably representations on the Manchester education question.

Read Archd. Grant's Sermon[1]—Wilberforce's Charge[2]—Bp of Glasgow's Serm[3]—Hayman's Dialogues—Heygate's Sermons. Saw J. Talbot:[4] he promises to be worthy of his Father.

28. M.

Wrote to Smith & Son—Jas Watson—Coutts & Co—Rev. M. Bayly—Dr Hawtrey—Jas Anderson. Read Emp. des Nairs. Went off at 9½ to Shoreditch & Hayleybury for the examination.[5] Saw Professors Empson—Buckley[6]—and Wilson.[7] Saw Newcastle—Mahon—Mr Mangles[8]—C. Ross—Phillimore. Dined at Bath House.[9] Lady Jersey's afterwards. Saw one late: & advised: a broken creature [R].

29. T. St Peter

Tennison's Chapel at 7 P.M. Wrote to Coutts & Co—Rev. N. Wade—Ld Lyttelton—C.A. Wood—J.R. Mowbray[10]—Dr Knollis[11]—Horatio Owen[12]—A. Kunkler[13]—Archd. Hale—W. F. Thurland[14]—E.G. Sadler[15]—Dr Jacobson—& E. Coleridge. H. of C. and Exhibition Committee & Commn. 12–4½. Saw Mr Lindsay—Ld R. Grosvenor—Duke of Newcastle—Dined with the Wortleys. Read Empire des Nairs. I took £2 with a copy of Jer. Taylor Holy Living to E. Watson's—my promised aid [R].

30. Wed.

Wrote to G.H.G. Anson[16]—Johnson L[ongden] & Co—Ld Courtenay—Rev. B. Wilson—Rev. Mr Keble—Rev. F.B. Zincke—Jas Glover—J.P. Lacaita—Dined at Grillion's—Read Empire des Nairs: (finished Vol II:

[1] A. *Grant, 'The Ramsden sermon on the extension of the church in the colonies and dependencies of the British empire' (1852).
[2] Cp. 1 Feb. 52.
[3] W. J. Trower, 'Defence of the city of God committed to his ministers' (1852); on Psalm xlviii. 12.
[4] Cp. 17 June 40n.
[5] Cp. *The Times*, 29 June 1852, 5f.
[6] William Edward Buckley, 1817?–92; priest 1850; professor of Anglo-Saxon at Oxford 1844–9; professor of classics at Haileybury 1850–7; rector of Middleton-Cheney, Banbury, 1853–92.
[7] Horace Hayman *Wilson, 1786–1860; professor of Sanskrit at Oxford from 1832; external examiner at Haileybury.
[8] Ross Donelly *Mangles, 1801–77; director East India company 1847, chairman 1857–8; liberal M.P. Guildford 1841–58; on council of India 1858–66.
[9] In Piccadilly; London house of Lord *Ashburton.
[10] (Sir) John Robert Mowbray, *né* Cornish, 1815–99; took name of Mowbray 1847; tory M.P. Durham 1853–68, Oxford university 1868–99; cr. bart. 1880; father of commons 1898.
[11] Francis Minden Knollis, 1816–63; fellow of Magdalen, Oxford, 1839–63; D.D. 1851; rector and curate of sundry parishes from 1840; wrote on pastoral topics.
[12] Bookseller in Noble street, Cheapside.
[13] Unidentified.
[14] Unidentified.
[15] Perhaps E. & G. Sadler, tailors in Hanover Square.
[16] George Henry Grenville Anson, 1820–98; rector of Birch-in-Rusholme 1846–98; chaplain to bp. of Manchester 1848–59, 1870–98; archdeacon there 1870–90.

quite enough)—Exh[ibitio]n Commn. 2d Report. Shopping—at Mr Say's who succeeds beyond my expectn.—calls & drive with C. Saw J.N.G.—& others. (Dr Wellesley) Bonham. Settling accts &c. with C. Saw one late: advised. At Grillion's we were unanimous about the Achilli Verdict.[1]

Thurs. July One. 1852.

Wrote to
H. Tayleur—
Coutts & Co—
Overends—
Rev. Greswell
Mr Woollcombe
Dr Binney
H. Caswall.

Saw Jane Tyler—Ld Aberdeen—Sir W. Heathcote & Mr Bernard—Duke of Newcastle—C.M. Lushington—Ld Haddington—G.H. Vernon. Went with C. to the Station. Read Upham's Washington[2]—Engl Rev. on WEG.[3] At At the House of C for clearing up odds & ends. 9–11.[4] Saw E. Collins: la metà di una statua bellissima, bella oltre misura [R].[5]

2. Friday.

Wrote to J.L. & Co—J.L. Ross (& copy)[6]—E. of Aberdeen—C.G.—J. Griffiths—G. Godfrey—S. Herbert—Capt. Neville—Dr Jacobson—S.R. Glynne. Saw Bonham—A. Kunkler—C.M. Lushington—Rev. Mr Browne —D. Millions[7]—J.N.G.—Bp of Oxford—Scotts. Calls—worked on accounts —& in arranging papers. Read Thoughts on Church matters[8]—Graham's Corresp. with B. of T.[9]—The Baroness V. Beck[10]—Called to see Horton & Malins[11] but failed [R].

3. Sat.

Wrote to
C.G.
Willy
Mrs Greene.
Jane Wortley.
C. A. Wood.
E. Coleridge.
J. Murray
Rev. Mr Browne
R. Greswell.
H. Mackenzie
G. C. Berkeley

[1] J. H. *Newman was found guilty of libelling in his *Lectures on the present position of catholics in England* (1851), Giovanni Giacinto Achilli, a Dominican converted to protestantism. A new trial was refused, but Newman was let off with a warning, Achilli being revealed as an adulterer; cp. *Annual Register*, (1852), 381 and (1853), 13.

[2] *The life of General Washington, . . . ed. C. W. Upham*, 2v. (1852).

[3] *English Review*, xvii. 337 (July 1852); a denunciation of Gladstone's *Letter to *Skinner*.

[4] *H* cxxii. 1429. Parliament this day prorogued and dissolved.

[5] 'Half of a most lovely statue, lovely beyond measure.'

[6] Add MS 44372, f. 222.

[7] David T. Millions kept the Grapes at Covent Garden.

[8] Probably 'Letters on church matters; by D.C.L.' (1851).

[9] T. Graham, 'Report made to the board of trade on the loss of the Amazon' (1852).

[10] 'The persecution and death of the baroness von Beck, at Birmingham, in August 1851. Refutation of Mr. Toulmin *Smith's defence of the disgraceful proceedings against that defenceless exile' (1852).

[11] Or 'Malvin'; a rescue case.

In the city. Saw J.L. & Co—Overends—Hubbard—G.W. Hope—W.C. James. Dined at Ld Hardinge's. Read Paget on Reserve Force[1]—Small on Crystal Palace[2]—MS letter from Naples. I got some conversation with Ld Hardinge on Political prospects: he too desponds for Ld Derby. Walk senza frutto[3] a while.

4. 4 S. Trin.

St Philip's mg. late, & missed Holy C.—having been repelled from Chapel Royal)—St Andrews W[ells] St. aft. Wrote to Bp of Capetown—Rev. B. Wilson—G. Hodgkinson—Archd. Wilberforce—Ass. Sec. S.P.G.[4] Read Wilson's Sermon[5]—Caswall on Jubilee[6]—Warter on Synods[7]—Scots Episc. Magazine &c.[8]—Heygate's Sermons: an admirable book. Wrote on the Scotch Synodical question (a scheme of a draft Letter to the Dioc. Synods)[9] Dined with the Wortley's to meet Lady Wenlock: with whom I had a pleasing conversation.[10]

5. M.

Wrote to Pizzala & Co[11]—C.G.—Ld Braybrooke—S.R.G.—S.H. Northcote. Saw Phillimore—Sankay (Officer of Woods)[12]—Lushington & Ross. A hot & hard day's work on my letters, papers, & documents in various forms. Dined at Dr. Duchess of Beaufort's—Lady Willoughby's[13] afterwards. Saw E. Watson [R] who goes on the 20th. Read Hartley on Amn. War[14]—Fraser's mag. on book Trade.[15]

6. T.

Wrote to M. Bernard—C.G.—Archd. Hale—Mr Trevor—& Norreys—Rev. R. Greswell—Mr Dodsworth. A round of calls. Luncheon at Lady Alice Peels.[16] Dined with the Heywoods & got an hour with Robn. on busi-

[1] Lord G. *Paget, 'A letter to . . . *Russell containing suggestions for raising a reserve force' (1852).

[2] J. *Small, 'Caution!!! to the Brighton shareholders and the public at large, against the Crystal Palace removal to Sydenham' (1852).

[3] 'Fruitlessly.'

[4] William Thomas Bullock, 1818–79; assistant secretary of S.P.G. 1850, secretary 1865; chaplain at Kensington palace from 1867.

[5] Cp. 27 July 51.

[6] H. Caswall, 'The jubilee [of the S.P.G.]; or, what I heard and saw in London in . . . June 1852' (1852).

[7] J. W. Warter, 'Clerical synods' (1852).

[8] *Scottish Magazine and churchman's review*, ii. 329 (July 1852); probably on the laity and synods.

[9] Not found; cp. 22 July 52.

[10] Cp. 10 May 52.

[11] Alabaster and glass sellers in Regent street.

[12] Unidentified.

[13] Margaret, *née* Williams, m. 1829 Henry Peyto-Verney, 1773–Dec. 1852, 16th Baron Willoughby de Broke 1820, an Eldonian tory. They lived in Hill street; she d. 1880.

[14] D. *Hartley, *Letters on the American war* (1778).

[15] *Fraser's Magazine*, xlv. 711 (June 1852); on 'underselling' in the book trade.

[16] Lady Alicia Jane Peel, d. 1887, da. of 1st marquis of Ailsa; m. 1824 Jonathan *Peel. They lived in Park place, St. James's.

ness. Fell in with A. Loader [R] who went to 6 C.G. Of these cases I must make a review shortly.[1] Read Hartley. The heat extreme since Sunday: sleep hard to get. Saw C. Ross—Hon. A. Gordon—Mrs Freeman (née Horton) [R].

7. Wed.

Wrote to J.D. Coleridge—A. Gordon—R. Greswell—C.G.—P.D. Cooke—Surveyor of Taxes. Saw Goulburn—J.D. Coleridge—Archd. Wilberforce—J.N.G. Calls.—House Bill &c. cleared. Col Bprics Fund Commee. 2½–4. Visited A. Loader & learned something there [R]. Read Hartley. Busy all morning on my clothes & effects. Lady Aylesbury's party in evg.[2]

8. Th.

Wrote to J.D. Coleridge—H.J.G.—Mr Hamilton Gray—C.G.—Hoares (date 13.)—S.R.G.—Eden & Stanistreet—J.L. & Co—Ed. M. Chronicle & others.[3] Saw Ld Braybrooke—Lady Jersey—Lady Wenlock—J.N.G.—Bonham. Voted for Ld Maidstone.[4] Payments & other arrangements for departure. Off at 5.30 to Didcot: where I found Mr Greswell waiting. We had much conversation & tea in the open air. Off again at 11 for Bristol—arrived after 1½. Went to the *George*: a clean house.

9. Fr.

Wrote to Provost of Oriel. Off at 9½ for Steamer: at 10½ for Tenby:[5] arrived 10¼ evg. The sail down the Avon very beautiful. A short motion after crossing the channel: I became[6] sickish & very chilly. Read Life of Washington.[7] Went to the Coburg Hotel: very tidy.

10. Sat.

It seems odd to be apart from all mankind on my Election day. But I am quiet about it: not chiefly from duty, or from certainty; it is from the conviction that the matter is in the hands of those whose affair it is far more than mine. God sends the issue as may best suit Oxford.[8]

Wrote to C.G.[9]—Bathe in morning. Walk to Manorbier[10]—direct one way by Penally,[11] & the other round. It is a picturesque ruin in good order.

[1] Lists of rescue cases, in Lambeth MSS.

[2] Gertrude Florinda, *née* Gardiner, 1809–92; m. 1833 as his 2nd wife Charles Brudenell-Bruce, 1773–1856; cr. marquess of Ailesbury 1821.

[3] These two words in pencil.

[4] George James Finch-Hatton, 1815–87; styled Viscount Maidstone 1826–58; tory M.P. North Northamptonshire 1837–41; stood unsuccessfully for Westminster 1852; 11th earl of Winchilsea 1858.

[5] Port nine miles east of Pembroke.

[6] 'a little' here deleted.

[7] Cp. 1 July 52.

[8] Cp. 13 July 52n.

[9] Bassett, 89.

[10] Village with a Norman castle, 5½ miles ESE. of Pembroke.

[11] 1½ miles SW. of Tenby.

Met Emlyn[1] here in evg. & joined company with him in his room—Read Life of Washington—Wrote to C.G. Studied the polls.

11. 5. S. Trin.

Tenby Ch. mg. & evg. The Rector[2] preached mg. on the unpardonable sin:[3] meant well: but said some very strange things. Bathed in mg. Walks on the shore both ways. Read Barnes's Catholico-Romanus Pacificus[4]—Jones & Freeman's account of St David's.[5] Went over the Church & curious monuments.

12. M.

Wrote to Jas Watson. After bathe & breakfast, off at 8½ to Bagelly.[6] Thence walked 16 miles to Haverfordwest:[7] the last 8 excessively hot & I was rather overdone. From thence I went on to St. David's[8] (arr. 1¼ left at 2)—reached St D. 4¼—went to Mr Melville's[9] & with him over all the ruins & the Cathedral. Left at 8½: & reached Hav[erfordwes]t at 11 tired enough.

13. T.

Wrote to C.G.[10]—Rev. Mr Marriott. Went from H[averford]West to Carmarthen:[11] there I found Stephen who kindly came to pilot me. In the evg. we walked to a neighbouring Church on a hill for a view of the Towi vale.[12] Read Life of Washington—Browne Willis on St David's.[13] Got the Oxford poll of Saty.: the effect of this folly will be to weaken Inglis greatly.[14]

14. Wed.

At 8¾ off by Mail to Brecon a lovely drive. Then car to Bruntlys.[15] Then walk 14 m. to Builth:[16] all beautiful. Arrived at 8½. Read Barnes. He is on some points *very* Lutheran?

[1] John Frederick Vaughan Campbell, 1817–98; styled Viscount Emlyn 1827–60 when he succ. as 2nd Earl Cawdor; tory M.P. Pembrokeshire 1841–59.

[2] John Hunter Humphreys, 1786–1856; Trinity hall, Cambridge; rector of Tenby 1831–52.

[3] Presumably on despair.

[4] J. *Barnes, *Catholico-Romanus Pacificus* (1680).

[5] W. B. Jones and E. A. *Freeman, *The history and antiquities of St. David's*. Perhaps an MS or privately printed edition; the first edition traced is 1856.

[6] Kilgetty, 5 miles north of Tenby.

[7] 9 miles NNW. of Pembroke.

[8] 14 miles NW. of Haverfordwest.

[9] Edmund Melvill, 1797–1857; prebendary of St. David's cathedral from 1841, chancellor from 1847.

[10] Bassett, 89.

[11] 32 miles east of Haverfordwest.

[12] The valley of the Towy, which flows through Carmarthen.

[13] Browne *Willis, *A survey of the cathedral church of St. David's* (1717).

[14] The final poll on 14 July was *Inglis, 1368; Gladstone, 1108; Robert Bullock Marsham, 758. Marsham, warden of Merton 1826–80, was persuaded by heads of houses to stand as a 'protestant' candidate against Gladstone.

[15] Bronllys, a village 9 miles NE. of Brecon.

[16] Builth Wells, a spa 16 miles N. of Brecon.

15. Th.

Fly and walk to Rhayader.[1] Then Mail at 12½ to Hereford: in all 58 m. & very beautiful. An intelligent fellow passenger too was on the Mail. Went to see the Cathedral &c. in Hereford. Finished Barnes—Read Washington finished V. 1. A voracious meal upon election news in the Times.[2]

16. Fr.

Wrote to G. Burnett. Morning prayers Hereford Cathedral 11. Off at 11.45 for Ludlow.[3] Saw the glorious old castle & the Church: then off to Shrewsbury: where we went to the walls & S. pointed out to me the Churches &c. Read Life of Washington.

17. Sat.

Off at 6.45 & reached Hawarden 9¾. Morning spent in reading letters & papers.

Wrote to J. Watson—J. Griffiths—V.C. of Oxford[4]—Rev. F. Temple—A.W. Haddan.

Cath. & the children arrived before four. We were all happy to meet at this sweet place with auspices somewhat less unhopeful for the family. Read Life of Washington—Wilson's 21 Reasons.[5] Lena has quite the appearance of health & vigour after this heat—thank God.

18. 6 S. Trin.

Church 11 & 3. Wrote to E. Badeley. Read Maitland on the Reformation[6]—Perrone Praelectiones[7]—Bp of Oxford Jubilee Sermon[8]—Quart. Rev. on New Reformn. in Ireland.[9]

19. M.

Wrote to Mr Chermside[10]—D. of Newcastle—Scotts—Williams & Co—Robn. G.—Jones & Yarrell—W.B. Smythe[11]—W. Wilmott. Read Westr. Rev. on Sir R. Peel.[12] Bp of O. & Archd. Wilberforce came: we had much conversation. C. had a feverish attack from halfabortive vaccination. Baby thank God did not suffer. Arranging my goods: & some hours with Burnett on Stephen's affairs—also my own.

[1] 15 miles NNW. of Buith Wells.

[2] *The Times*, 15 July 1852, 3e, announcing the final Oxford result, *inter alia*.

[3] 22 miles north of Hereford.

[4] Draft in Add MS 44372, f. 258; Plumptre had supported Gladstone in the Oxford election.

[5] Benjamin Wilson, *Twenty-one reasons for the re-election of Mr. Gladstone, respectfully addressed to the members of convocation* (1852).

[6] S. R. *Maitland, *Essays on subjects connected with the reformation* (1849).

[7] J. Perrone, *Praelectiones theologicae*, 8v. (1840–3); or Migne's 2v. ed. (1842).

[8] S. *Wilberforce, 'The planting of nations a great responsibility' (1852).

[9] M. *O'Sullivan's article in *Quarterly Review*, xci. 37 (June 1852).

[10] Richard Seymour Conway Chermside, b. 1820? rector of Wilton from 1848.

[11] William Barlow Smythe, squire, of Barbavilla, co. Westmeath.

[12] *Westminster Review*, n.s. ii. 205 (July 1852); review of W. C. *Taylor, *Life and times of Sir R. *Peel* (1848).

20. T.

Church 8½ a.m. Wrote to Canon Melvill—C.A. Wood—G.G. Harcourt—R. Greswell—Sir W. Heathcote—R. Phillimore. Walk to St John's & much of the day in conv. on matters of the Church & religion with the Bp & Archdeacon—including Convocation—Court of Appeal—Scotch Synods & laity—the Doctrine of the Real Presence. Oh what hands are mine to be laid upon such objects! Henry & Mr Troughton dined. Read Washington's Life.

21. Wed.

H.S. with the children. Wrote to Watson—Willy—Bonham J.N.G.—Northcote—Tayleur. Our guests went to the Britannia Bridge[1] & returned in evg. when we resumed. 2½ hours with Mr Burnett. Saw Mr Peel with others. Also friends of his in evg. I explained to him my intention to take no part.[2] Read Life of Washington.

22. Th.

Church 8½ a.m. Conversed further on the question of Lay Functions: & amended by MS. in regard to wh both the brothers [Wilberforce] will act.[3] Walk with them. Read Hoffmann on the Law of the Church[4]—Life of Washington. Our closing conversations on the Ch.—with a spice only of politics.

23. Ch.

8½ a.m. Wrote to E. Badeley—J. Chapman—Miss Lyttelton. Read Life of Washington (Upham—finished)—Piozzi's Anecdotes of Johnson.[5] Worked on my Bank Books & accounts. Chess with Stephen. The Bp & Archdeacon went off.

24. Sat.

Ch 8½ a.m. Wrote to E.C. Woollcombe—Scotts—H. Tayleur—R. Savill[6]—Sir J. Young. Began Latin with little Stephen. Read Cibber's Nonjuror[7]—Piozzi's Anecdotes.—Old Epitaphs & Songs.[8]

An extraordinary sleepiness has been upon me since I came here: either from the warmth—or a reaction of nature after the closing time in London. Saw Mr Harris—Mr Ffoulkes.

[1] Built by *Stevenson over the Menai Straits; opened 1850.

[2] Edmund Peel; of Brynypys, Flintshire, 1826–1903. On 7 July 1852 P. D. Cooke had requested Gladstone's help in Peel's election as a tory for Flintshire. The result was E. Lloyd Mostyn (liberal) 1276, E. Peel (tory) 910.

[3] Cp. Wilberforce, ii. 143ff. for the upshot.

[4] Cp. 23 May 52.

[5] Hestor L. *Piozzi, *Anecdotes of the late Samuel *Johnson* (1786).

[6] Robert Savill, 1807–?88; assistant secretary of L.N.W.R. 1849–72; originated system of payment of railway dividends by warrants.

[7] Cp. 13 July 41.

[8] Not found.

25. 7 S Trin & St James.

Ch. 11 & 3. Singing Psalms with the children. Read the Account of Valentinus Gentilis[1]—Maitland's Reformation—Bellairs's Sermon.[2]

26. M.

(Rain.) Latin lesson with Stephy. Wrote to Lady Norreys—T.G.—Bp of Aberdeen—Robn. G.—Sir Jas Hogg—G. & Co—Sir W.C. James. Saw Burnett. Willy came: well: not grown. Walk & talk with him. Read Oxf. Commn. Report.[3] Propertius[4]—Achilli & Newman Report.[5]

27. T.

Church 8½ a.m. Latin lesson with Stephy. Wrote to R.B.D. Morier—J.N.G. —D. of Newcastle. Read Oxf. Commn. Report—Advice to Clergy[6]—Propertius—Pope's Pastorals &c.[7] Drive & walk with C.

28. Wed.

Church 8½ a.m. Latin lesson with Stephy. Wrote to Jas Watson—J.N.G. —Rev. A. Watson. Read Propertius—Oxf. Univ. Commn. Report—Advice to Clergy—Pope's Poems—& Miscellanea. Out with C.—Music in evg.

29. Th.

Ch 8½ a.m. Latin with Stephy. Wrote to D. Robertson—H. Flood—E. of Aberdeen—(part). Read Propertius—Oxf. Univ. Report—The Guardian's instruction.[8] Walk & car with C. Saw Burnett. Music in evg.

30. Fr.

Church 8½ a.m. Latin with Stephy. Corrected Verses for Willy. Wrote to E. of Aberdeen (finished)—A.B. Hope—Tupper—Sir J. Graham & copy—J. Walker—D. Robertson.—F.R. Bonham. Drove to visit the Cooks[9] with C.—Worked on Bonham's [election] returns.[10] Read Propertius—Oxf. Univ. Report—Guardian's Instruction—Pope's Poems.

[1] B. Aretius, *A short history of Valentinus Gentilis the tritheist* (1696); perhaps tr. by Robert *South.

[2] H. W. Bellairs, 'Work. The Law of God, the lot of man . . . with an appendix . . . on manual industry' (1852).

[3] Cp. 27 May 52. [4] Cp. 25 Aug. 45. [5] Cp. 30 June 52n.

[6] Not found.

[7] Published in J. Tonson, ed., *Poetic Miscellanies* (1709).

[8] [S. *Penton] 'The guardian's instruction; or, the gentleman's romance' (1688).

[9] Probably P. Davies-Cooke and his wife.

[10] Cp. J. B. Conacher, *The Peelites*, 119.

31. Sat.

Church 8½ a.m. Latin with Stephy. Wrote to

Rev. J.H. Gray	J.N.G.
A. Watson	J. Litton
Sir W. Heathcote	T. Ogilvy.
G.C. Lewis.	

and draft for Mr Burnett to Rigby & Hancock.[1] Saw Burnett. Read Propertius—Univ. Commn. Report—Pope's Poems.

Sunday August One 1852.

Church 11 (& H.C.) and 6½. Read Wordsworth on Synods[2]—Archd. Sandford's Charge[3]—Raine on Tithes[4]—Arguments of a Rom. Pr. Answered[5]—Bp of London letter on Earthquakes (1745).[6]

2. M.

Ch 8½ a.m. Latin lesson with Stephy. Virgil with Willy. Wrote to Archdn. Hale—Fr. Adams—J.D. Thackerbery.[7] 3½–7 with Burnett on Estate accounts & business. Read Propertius—Oxf. Commn. Report—Pope's Poems. Worked on H. of C. returns.

3. T.

(Rain mg.) Latin Gr[ammar] with Stephy. Conv. with Miss Scott on his case. Also Agnes had another outbreak which required me to be called in today. Virgil with Willy. Wrote to Lord Monteagle—J.N.G.—Mr D. Gladstone—Marrable.[8] Saw Mr Burnett—Mr Harris. Seven to dinner. Singing. Read Propertius—Oxford Commn. Report. Worked on Estate & accounts.

4. Wed.

Church 8½ a.m. Latin lesson with Stephy. Virgil with Willy. (He does H.S. with his Uncle Stephen.) Wrote to Jas Watson—W.C. James—Sir F. Smith—F. Adams. Read Propertius—Oxf. Commn. Report—Ld Baltimore's trial[9]—Introd. to the Monastery.[10]

[1] On the tramways being constructed on the Hawarden estate; Hawn P.
[2] Cp. 16 Mar. 52.
[3] J. *Sandford 'A charge delivered to the clergy . . . of Coventry' (1852).
[4] J. Raine, 'The origin, progress and evils of alienation of tithes from the church' (1852).
[5] [T. *Comber], 'The plausible arguments of a romish priest answered by an English protestant' (1686).
[6] Perhaps E. *Gibson, 'Pastoral letter to the people of his diocese . . . with a postscript [on] the danger and mischief of popery' (1745).
[7] Unidentified.
[8] Frederick *Marrable, 1818–72; superintending architect to metropolitan board of works 1856–62; designed many London buildings.
[9] *The trial of Frederick *Calvert, Esq., baron of Baltimore . . . for a rape on the body of Sarah Woodcock* (1768).
[10] The 'introductory epistle' to *Scott's novel, 3v. (1820).

5. Th.

Ch. 8½ a.m. Latin Gr. with S. Wrote to Earl of Aberdeen and draft—S. Herbert—Overends—Williams & Co. S.H. Northcote. Saw Mr Burnett: finished accounts for Crop 49 & 50, & made other progress. Read Propertius—and 'The Monastery'.

6. Fr.

Ch. 8½ a.m. Latin Gr. with Stephy. Virgil with Willy. Wrote to D. of Newcastle—Mr Browne—Dr J. Borrett[1]—Rev. G. Fagan[2]—Conte de Cavour[3]—Saw Mr Burnett—Read Propertius—Oxf. Commn. Report—The Monastery—Plowdens 20 months.

7. Sat.

Church 8½ a.m. Lat. Gr. with St. Virgil with Willy. Wrote to Mr W. Gorton[4]—Sir J. Young—Mr F. Jackson—Read Propert[ius]—Oxf. Report—Monastery. Justice Talfourd—C. Wynn—& J. Talbot came. The first as fresh as ever.[5]

8. 9 S. Trin.

St John's mg. Hawarden ch evg. Lesson & conv with Willy on the Mammon of unrighteousness. Read Maitland—Woodleigh Farm[6]—Wilson's Sermons on the Incarnation.[7]

9. M.

Chester Cathedral 10 a.m. Off to Chester at 8½. Two hours with Messrs. North & Lee on the Brickwork & Railway[8]—Also saw Williamses—Burnett—Mr Slade.

Wrote to Jas Watson—Mr D. Gladstone—Rev. B. Wilson—R. Greswell—H. Flood.

Dinner party—& singing. Read Propertius—The Monastery.

10. T.

Latin with Stephen. Willy did a little Theme on the Gospel of last Sunday. Wrote to W.C. James. Read Propertius—Oxf. Com. Report. 10¾–3¾.

[1] Perhaps James Borrett, physician practising in Great Yarmouth.

[2] George Hickson Urquhart Fagan, 1817–75; Oriel, Oxford; rector of King Weston, Somerset 1849–59, of Stoke Rodney 1859–75; prebendary of Wells 1853.

[3] Count Camillo Benso di Cavour, 1810–61; founded journal *Il Risorgimento* 1847; president of Piedmont council 1852–9, 1860–1; Italian prime minister 1861; visited Britain 1852.

[4] William Henry Gorton, 1824–86; Trinity, Cambridge; sundry curacies 1829–36; vicar of Portesham 1837–86.

[5] Talfourd was only 14 years older than Gladstone.

[6] See 15 Aug. 50.

[7] W. W. C. *Wilson, *Christ revealed* (1851).

[8] North was probably an employee of Rigby and Hancock; Charles Lee, Chester estate agent.

Went to Chester: three hours there with Mr Burnett & the Rigby & Hancock party on the railway brickwork wharf &c. Dinner party; & singing. Saw Mr Barker—conv. with young Talbot[1]—Hanmer. J.N.G. came. late.

11. Wed.

Ch 8½ a.m. Lat. Gr. with St[ephen]. Virgil with Willy. Wrote to R.B.D. Morier—J. Litton—W.B. Hancock—W. Brown—C. Wykeham Martin—W. Cromdell.[2]—J.N.G. went—Saw Mr Flood from Ireland. Read Propertius—Oxf. Report—Monastery.

12. Th.

Ch. 8½ a.m. Lat. Gr. with S. Messrs. Barker & Burnett 11–2½. Virgil with Willy. Wrote to Dr Wolff—S.M. Peto—T.G.—and Overends. Read Propertius—The Monastery. 11 to dinner. The Talbots (family) came.

13. Fr.

Ch. 8½ a.m. Lat. Gr. with Stephy. Virgil with Willy. Wrote to J. Griffiths. Read Propertius—Oxf. Report—Monastery. 2–6. went to see the working of Mr Burnett's reaping machine.[3] Good: except where the crop was very heavy & the clover also. But there is still room for improvement.

14. Sat.

Ch. 8½ a.m. Wrote to Mr Haddan: & made copy of Extract. Lat. Gr. with Stephy. Virgil with Willy. Read Propertius—Oxf. Report—The Monastery—&c.

15. 10 S. Trin.

Ch mg. & (St John's) evg. Wrote to Bp of Oxford. Read Maitland—'Enter into thy Closet'.[4] Worked on Psalmody. Singing with the children.

16. M.

Ch. mg as usual. Lat. Gr. with St. Virgil with Willy. Wrote to R[obertso]n G.—H.J.G. Second visit to the Reaping Machine. Music in evg. Read Propertius—Oxf. Report (Appx)—The Monastery (finished).

17. T.

Ch. mg. Lat. Gr. with Stephy. Virgil with Willy. Wrote to D. of Newcastle—(& copied part)—R. Barker—G. Ainslie[5]—Bp Moray & Ross—C.A. Wood

[1] i.e. J. G. Talbot.
[2] William Cromdell of London had written on church and state; Hawn P.
[3] Most reaping machines in Britain were imported from America; McCormick's American machine won a gold medal at the 1851 exhibition.
[4] [E. *Wetenhall] *Enter into thy closet; or, a method and order for private devotion* (1670).
[5] Probably George Ainslie, d. 1875; clerical assistant to additional curates fund; curate of St. Philip's, Clerkenwell 1851–4, then secretary of the church building society.

—Rev. J.O. Powell—Rev. F. Kilvert.[1] Singing with the children. Read Propertius—Oxf. Report (Appx.)—The Monastery—Raikes on the Constn.[2] Called on Mr J. Harris.

18. Wed.

Ch mg. Lat Gr. with Stephy. Wrote to M. Lyttelton—T.G.—W.C. James—Lady Wenlock—Bp of Moray. Drew a new Scheme of Agreement for Brickwork & Railway. Read Propertius—The Abbot[3]—Oxf. Report. Worked on accounts.

19. Th.

Ch 8½ a.m. Lat. Gr. with Stephy. Virgil with Willy. Wrote to M. Hazelhurst[4]—& Mr Ashton.[5] Saw Mr Burnett 12–2 & went with him to Buckley 2½–5 about the Brickwork. Wrote draft for him to Mr Lee. Read Propertius—Persecn. of the Protestants[6]—Abbot. Conv. with Mrs Talbot about the Bond of Resignation.[7] Singing in evg.

20. Fr.

Ch mg. Lat. Gr. with Stephy. Virgil with Willy. Wrote to Rev. Dr Wynter.[8]—J.N.G. also draft—J. Griffiths. also copy—Sir W. Heathcote—E. of Aberdeen. Worked on O.F. Mill & Forge agreement.[9] Read Propertius—Burn's Eccl. Law.[10]—Monastery. C.s warnings (bad nights) grew. Saw Mr Ashton.

21. Sat.

Ch 8½ a.m. Lat Gr. with St. Virgil with Willy. Wrote to Mr W.R. Greg. Saw Mr Burnett. Read Propertius—Longinus—(finished P. began L.)—The Monastery—Ld Beaumont's Pamphlet.[11] Music with the children. C. yet more distressed at night. Moffat came & gave sensible advice, to wean: which is to be done.

22. 11 S. Trin.

Ch mg. & evg. Up late from broken nights. Read Neale's Church Diffi-

[1] One name here deleted. Francis Kilvert, 1793–1863, was curate of Claverton from 1816; tutored private pupils in Bath and edited historical works.

[2] H. *Raikes, *A popular sketch of the origin and development of the English constitution*, 1st. v. (1851).

[3] By *Scott (1820).

[4] Mary Hazelhurst, otherwise unidentified.

[5] Richard Ashton, brick manufacturer in Buckley.

[6] 'Persecution of protestants in the year 1845 . . . a report of the trial at Tralee . . . for a libel of the rev. Charles Gayer' (1845).

[7] On the settlement of her husband's will.

[8] Copy in Add MS 44372, f. 299. Wynter had chaired Marsham's cttee. in the Oxford election.

[9] Hawn P.

[10] R. *Burn, *Ecclesiastical law*, 2v. (1763–5).

[11] M. T. Stapleton, Lord Beaumont, 'France and Austria in central Italy' (1852).

culties[1]—Goulburn's Devotions.[2] We had a good deal of (evg. & day) conv. with Mrs Talbot who is thoroughly genuine & good.

23. M.

Ch 8½ a.m. Lat. Gr. with St. Wrote to Bp of Aberdeen—Mr G. Brown[3]—Bp of Exeter—Rev. S. Clark—M. Hazelhurst—Mr Filmer[4]—Overend & Co—Ld Beaumont[5]—Rev. R. Greswell—Bickers & Bush. Virgil with Willy. Read Propertius—Neale—Conv. with Mrs Talbot on her affairs—Henry, on Stephen's. C.s night again very much disturbed. I lost ½.

24. T.

St Barthol. Ch.[6] 11 a.m. Wrote to Williams & Co—J. Murray—Rev. Mr Humble[7]—Mahon—Sir J. Young—W. Craig. Virgil with Willy. Called at Broughton. Drive with C. Music with the children. Read Tibullus[8]—Raikes on Const[itutio]n.

25. Wed.

Ch 8½ a.m. Lat. Gr. with Stephy. Wrote to H. Tayleur—Rn. G—W.C. James—Rn. & J.N.G.—Rev. R.T. Lowe—Hon. Mrs Talbot. Virgil with Willy. Saw Mr Harris. Read Tibullus—Raikes on Constn.—The Abbot. Put down some *words* the possible germ of a Dictionary of Synonyms or Homoionyms.[9]

26. Th.

Ch 8½ a.m. Lat. Gr. with Stephy. Virgil with Willy. Saw Mr Burnett—Wrote to Rev. Dr. Wynter & draft.[10]—Bp of Oxford (o)[11]—T.G. Read Tibullus—Dined with Mr Raikes. Saw Mr Burnett—H. Glynne.

27. Fr.

Ch 8½ a.m. Lat. Gr[ammar] with Stephy. Wrote to Williams & Co—Scotts & Co—J. Binger. 11½–6. In Chester & walked back thro' my land. Saw Mr R. Barker—A. Banks[12]—Mr Ashton. Read Tibullus—The Abbot. My days are rather mutilated just now from broken nights.

[1] J. M. *Neale, *Lectures principally on the church difficulties of the present time* (1852).
[2] E. M. *Goulburn, *Short devotional forms for morning and night* (1851).
[3] Perhaps George Hilary *Brown, 1786–1856; roman catholic priest 1810; bp. of Liverpool from 1850.
[4] Francis Filmer, unbeneficed priest, who d. 1859.
[5] Miles Thomas Stapleton, 1805–54; wounded in a duel 1832; 8th Baron Beaumont 1840; wrote on Italian politics.
[6] At Sealand, down the hill towards the Dee.
[7] Michael Maughan Humble, 1811–89; Emmanuel, Cambridge; rector of Sutton Scarsdale, Derbyshire, from 1839; pamphleteer.
[8] 'The Abbot' here partly scored through.
[9] *Sc.* Homonyms; not found.
[10] Add MS 44372, f. 308.
[11] (o) presumably means not sent.
[12] Arthur Banks, proprietor of the Green Dragon Hotel, Eastgate, Chester; later worked for Gladstone in elections.

28. Sat.

Ch 8½ a.m. Lat. Gr. with Sephy.

Lena's birthday: requires the record of two special mercies, first the seeming restoration of her health owing to season, codliver oil or both: secondly that her frightful fall out of the car on her head, last Thursday evg. while I was away, causing slight concussion of the brain, *appears* to have left no indication of substantial injury.

Virgil with Willy. We finished the fourth Book of the Æn.—What a great holiday performance this would have been in my time! Wrote to Sir W. Heathcote—J.N.G.—D. of Newcastle—Capt. Williams—Rev. S. Clark—Johnson L. & Co—[1]—J. Chapman—Sir S. Scott & Co—Bp of St. Asaph[2]—Serj. H. Smith[3]—McKenzie Wilson. Also wrote draft in *rebus* Rigby & Hancock—Read Tibullus—The Abbot. The Greswells[4] were here from one to 6½. Much with them: consulted him on my Wynter correspondence.

29. 12 S. Trin.

Ch mg. & evg. Conv. with Willy. Languid after a broken night. C. still quite off her sleep. Read 'The Gentile Sinner'[5]—Neale on Ch. difficulties' (finished)—Maitland's Reformation.

30. M.

Ch 8½ a.m. Lat. Gr. with Stephen. Virgil with Willy. (Ecl[ogue] 1) Wrote to Dr Wynter[6]—J.D. Cook—(and draft) Jas Watson—Bickers & Bush—Wms. Deacon & Co. Read Tibullus—The Abbot—Singing with the children. Drove with C. Saw Mr Burnett (mg. & aft.)

31. T.

Ch. 8½ a.m. Lat Gr. with Stephy. Virgil with Willy. finished 1st Eclogue. Saw C. & Willy off to Rhyl.[7] Saw Mr Burnett—conference with the Rigbys & Hancock's on the questions with them. Rewrote draft of proposals & letter. Wrote to Mr Ashton. Read Tibullus—Abbot (finished)—Kenilworth (began)[8]—Plowden's History.[9]

Wedy. Sept. One. 1852.

Ch 8½ a.m. Lat Gr. with St. Wrote to J. Griffiths—C.G.—Robn. G. Saw Mr Burnett (mg. & aft) & drove into Chester to find Mr Binger[10] but failed. Read Tibullus (finished)—Petronius—Kenilworth—Plowden.

[1] 'Wms. Deacon & Co' here deleted.
[2] Cp. 8–10 Sept. 52.
[3] Not further identified.
[4] R. *Greswell, Gladstone's Oxford cttee. chairman, m. 1836 Joanna Julia Armitriding.
[5] By [C. *Ellis] (1660).
[6] Copy in Add MS 44372, f. 321.
[7] On the coast, 21 miles WNW. of Hawarden.
[8] By *Scott (1821).
[9] Cp. 18 Aug. 45.
[10] James Owen Binger, manager of the Chester Holyhead railway.

2. Th.

Ch 8½ a.m. Wrote to Williams & Co—W.P. Young—W.R. Greg—Jas Young—Rev. Dr. Wynter—Jas Watson—C.G.[1]—Saw Mr Burnett (bis)—Mr Binger—endeavouring to push on the R.R. & Brickwork arrangements: the toughest job I ever had of its kind. Read Longinus—Oxf. Report—Kenilworth: a most enchaining book.

3. Fr.

Ch 8½ a.m. Lat. Gr. with Stephy. He told an untruth & confessed it with bitter tears. Wrote to F.R. Bonham—J. Watson—C.G.'s Trustees[2]—C.A. Wood—Scotts—C.G.—J.N.G.—E. Coleridge—M. Hazelhurst. Read Longinus—Oxf. Report (Evidence)—Kenilworth. Willy returned in evg: & Henry came to tea. Saw Burnett

4. Sat.

Ch 8½ a.m. Wrote to W.P. Young—C.G.—Rev. Dr Wynter and draft—S.R.G.—J. Amery—G. Burnett—W. Hancock—Went to Chester to see dear Willy off: hard to say which of us liked it worst. Saw Mr Binger & the C[hester] H[olyhead] Goods Manager[3]—Mr Roberts (Wms. & Co)[4]—Mr Raikes. Read Longinus—Kenilworth (finished)—which makes my head reel again.

5. 13 S. Trin.

Ch. mg & evg (H[enr]y). Conv. with A. & S.—Wrote to Tupper—Cavendish. Read Webbs Ecclesiology[5]—Courbon on Mental Prayer[6]—Bertram on the Eucharist.[7]

6. M.

Ch. 8½ a.m. Lat. Gr. &c with Stephy. Wrote to E. of Aberdeen (& copy)—C.G.—V.C. of Oxford—Bp St Asaph—Williams & Co—Mr Binger—G. Burnett. Saw Mr Burnett. Read Longinus—Oxf. Commn. Report—Plowden's History.

7. T.

Ch 8½ a.m. Lat. Gr. with Stephy—Wrote to Rich. Ashton—T.G.—R.G. 2–4½ With Rigby & Hancock & Mr Burnett at Q[ueen's] F[erry].—Read

[1] Bassett, 90.
[2] Of her marriage settlement; cp. *Calendar of Hawarden deeds* (1931), 404.
[3] William Comber.
[4] i.e. of Williams and Co., Chester bankers.
[5] B. *Webb of Sheen, *Sketches of continental ecclesiology; or, church notes in Belgium, Germany and Italy* (1848).
[6] W. U. *Richards, ed., *Familiar instructions on mental prayer, from the French of Courbon* (1852). Courbon was a 17th century *curé* of Saint Cyr.
[7] Cp. 4 Sept. 42.

Longinus—Leben u. Reden Sir R. Peel's[1]—Financial Reform Tract III.[2] Went to Rhyl by Tr[ain] 4.50—dined with the Talbots—found C. still broken in sleep; & such was the night

8. Wed.

Wrote to R. Barker—Mr J. Binger. Read Mariotti's Italy[3]—Leben Sir R. Peel. Sea walk to C.s ride. Called on Miss Lloyd—& went to the Palace at St Asaph[4] where we met a party to dinner.

9. Th.

St Asaph Cathl. 10¼ a.m. Read Mariotti—Peel's Leben—Bp of Norwich, Charge (pt).[5] The Bp who is most kind drove us to the Miss Luxmoore's[6] then to Denbigh[7] where we saw the Castle & then back by the narrow & very beautiful vale that descends upon the Elwy.[8] Walk with him. A smaller party in evg. We talked Oxford Comm[issio]n & Church matters. Wrote to Hampton—Miss Scott.

10. Fr.

Cathedral 10¼ a.m. C. had a good night. About noon we returned to Rhyl: had plenty of sea air: bathed: dined with Mrs Talbot. Read Mariotti—Peel's Leben.

11. Sat.

Returned to Hawarden by the early train. Lat. Gr. with Stephy. Wrote to F.R. Bonham—Mrs Talbot—Jas Watson—C.G.—Willy. Read Peel's Leben—Quentin Durward[9]—Worked on S.R.G.s accounts.

12. 14 S. Trin.

Ch mg. & evg. Wrote MS Theol.[10] Wrote to Bp of Oxford[11]—Rev. E.H. Browne. Read Maitland on the Reformation—Caswall's Pilgrimage[12]—Perrone's Praelections[13]—Bp of Argyll Sermon on Emigration[14]—Mr E.H.

[1] By H. Künzel, 2v. (1851).

[2] On taxation, published (1848) by the Liverpool financial reform association, of which Robertson Gladstone was president.

[3] Cp. 12 May 52.

[4] 5 miles south of Rhyl.

[5] S. *Hinds, *A charge delivered to the clergy of the diocese of Norwich, at his visitation* (1852).

[6] Elizabeth Mary, d. 1862, Mary, d. 1865, Frances Ann, d. 1879; all unmarried das. of John *Luxmoore, 1757–1830, bp. of St. Asaph. They lived at Bryn Asaph, by St. Asaph.

[7] 10 miles south of Rhyl.

[8] Flowing NE. to the Clwyd, below St. Asaph.

[9] By *Scott (1823).

[10] Add MS 44740, f. 115.

[11] Wilberforce, ii. 143.

[12] H. Caswall, *A pilgrimage to Canterbury in 1852* (1852).

[13] Cp. 18 July 52.

[14] A. Ewing, '"Che til ma tuille". A sermon on emigration from the highlands and islands of Scotland to Australia' (1852).

Browne on Convocation.[1] Conv. with young J. Talbot on Hymnody. He is morally very forward indeed.

13. M.

Ch 8½ a.m. Lat. Gr. with Stephen. Wrote to J. Griffiths—C.G.—J. Amery—Mrs Talbot—H. Tayleur. Saw Mr C. Davison[2]—Mr Burnett—(12–2) Wrote MS.[3] Read Longinus—Peel's Leben—Quentin Durward.[4] Went to meet S. & apprised him of the state of affairs.[5]

14. T.

Ch 8½ a.m. Lat. Gr. with Stephy. Wrote to C.G.—R. Ashton. Read Longinus—Plautus—part of the Lysistrata & the Eirene of Aristophanes; of wh the extraordinary licentiousness & the mode of using it suggests many thoughts. Plowden's Hist. (finished) Walk with Stephen.

15. Wed.

Ch 8½ a.m. Wrote to Capt. Williams—C.G.—Mr Binger. Lat. Gr. with St. Saw Mr Burnett. Read Longinus—Homer on Roads[6]—Juvenal—Quentin Durward—Peel's Leben. Worked on Arbitration papers.[7]

16. Th.

Ch 8½ a.m. Lat. Gr. with St. Wrote to C.G.[8]—Mrs Howlett—Wrote MS. Read Longinus—Arist. Rhet on ῥυθμος[9]—Qu. Durward—Whitworth on Inland Navigation[10]—Walk with S. Buckley way.[11] Saw Mr Harris. We were astounded in the morning with the news of *the Duke's* death.[12]

17. Fr.

Ch 8½ a.m. Lat Gr. with Stephy. Wrote to W. Comber[13]—G. Burnett—Rev. T. Ainger.[14] Read Longinus περὶ ὕψ.[15] (finished)—Whitworth on Navign. (finished)—Oxf. Commn. Evidence—& Q. Durward. The Herberts came 1½–4½. Walk & conversation with him.

[1] E. H. *Browne, 'Convocation. A letter to . . . S. H. *Walpole' (1852).
[2] Charles Davison, of the King's Ferry carrying company; he lived in Hawarden.
[3] On Agamemnon; Add MS 44740, f. 119.
[4] See 11 Sept. 52.
[5] Presumably about the improvements to the Hawarden estate.
[6] H. S. Homer, *An enquiry into the means of preserving and improving the public roads of this kingdom* (1767).
[7] Disputes about N. Wales railway postal charges etc., see P. Baughan, *Chester–Holyhead railway* (1972) i. 164 ff.
[8] Bassett, 90.
[9] *Rhetoric*, iii. 8.
[10] Richard Whitworth, *The advantages of inland navigation* (1766).
[11] i.e. a walk with Stephen towards Buckley, 2 miles west of Hawarden.
[12] *Wellington had died on the afternoon of the 14th. See 18 Nov. 52.
[13] William Comber, manager of Chester–Holyhead railway goods department.
[14] Thomas *Ainger, 1799–1863; curate of St. Mary's, Hampstead from 1841; prebendary of St. Paul's from 1859; energetic in pastoral work.
[15] *On the sublime;* now only notionally attributed to him.

18. Sat.

Ch 8½ a.m. Lat Gr. with Stephy. Wrote to J.W. Patten[1]—Williams & Co —A. Munro—Rev. W. Sewell—Jos. King—Mr Walcot.[2] Read the Fragments of Longinus[3]—Peel's Leben—Q. Durward. Worked on Letters &c. from London.

19. 15 S. Trin.

Ch. 11 a.m. & 6½ PM. A shortened day after a broken night. Read Maitland on Refn. (finished)—Dissertation on Bertram[4]—State of Virginia Clergy[5] —Serm. on Peace[6]—Lectures on H.C. Ch.[7] Walk with C.

20. M.

Ch 8½ a.m. Lat Gr. with Stephy. Wrote to Rn. G. Rev. J.H. Gray—Wm. Comber—Mr Goulburn—G. Grant—Rev F. Fowke. Began the Bacchides of Plautus—read Quentin Durward. Wilson Patten was here 11–4. on the Chairmanship of Committees.[8] We also discussed the aspect of general politics.

21. T. St Matth.

Ch 11 A.M. Lat Gr. with Stephy. Agnes went with Mrs Herbert to Rhyl. I spoke to her [Agnes] about her great deliverance this day five years: & she wept in gratitude. Would I could as effectually speak to myself. Wrote to D. of Newcastle—Rn. G—M.G. Tupper—(Hon. & Rev.) G. Wellesley—Rev. W. Sewell. Read Bacchides—Quentin Durward—Lucian. Walk with C.

22. Wed.

Ch 7 Evg. Lat Gr. with St. Read Plautus—Q. Durward—Oxf. Report. Wrote to A. Williams—C.G. Reid—E. Collins. Dinner & evg at Rectory to meet Bp Spencer. Walk to Q[ueen's] F[erry] Station—to try two distances; by Mancot[9] & Moor Lane.

23. Th.

Ch. 8½ A.M. Lat Gr. with Stephy. Wrote to Vice Chancr. of Oxford—D.

[1] Copy in Add MS 44372, f. 341.

[2] Charles Walcot, 1795–1875; Trinity, Oxford; rector (and patron) of Bitterley, Herefordshire, from 1834.

[3] The 2v. ed. (1724) by Z. Pearce contained an appendix of fragments.

[4] Cp. 16 Apr. 48.

[5] 'The state of the clergy in Virginia, before the American revolution' (n.d., *ca.* 1800).

[6] Not found.

[7] Two anonymous 'Lectures on the holy catholic church' were published by J. H. *Parker (1852).

[8] Cp. 26 Sept. 52. Wilson *Patten chaired house of commons cttees. November 1852–April 1853.

[9] A mile north of Hawarden.

Ross[1]—J.S. Wortley—R. Barker—Rev. R. Greswell—Jas Watson—Rev. E.C. Woollcombe—H. Tayleur—J. Griffiths. Read Plautus (Stichus)[2]—Oxf. Commn. Report—Uncle Tom's Cabin.[3] Saw Mr Burnett. Dined at Mr Eaton's, Northop.[4]

24. Fr.

Ch. 8½ A.M. Lat Gr. with Stephy. Wrote to Sir J. Young—Willy[5]—Rev W. Sewell. Read Stichus (finished)—Suetonius (began)—Oxf. Report—Wilson on Univ. Tests[6]—F.C. on Free Trade.[7] Saw Mr Burnett & worked on R.R. papers.

25. Sat.

Ch. 8½ A.M. Lat Gr. with Stephy. Wrote to Rev Mr Stevenson—Sir W. James—J. Griffiths—Mr Jos. King—Mrs Howlett.[8] Read Suetonius—Oxf. Report. Went to Chester to meet the C[hester] & H[olyhead] Committee[9]—they knew nothing, but I made all the way I could in conv. with Mr Binger. Walked back. The Herberts & Woodgates[10] came—also W. Patten.

26. 16 S. Trin.

Ch 11 AM—St John's 3 P.M. Read Ellis's Gentile Sinner[11]—Bennett's 2d Letter[12]—Walks & conv. with H. & W. Patten. also with Woodgate—on Ch. matters—also with P[atten] on his Chairmanship. Music in evg.

27. M.

Ch 8½ AM. Lat Gr. with Stephy. Wrote to W. Pitt Dundas—H. Lees—Sec. Bd. Works[13]—J.N.G.—Mrs Talbot. Conv. with Wilson Patten—Herbert: to whom I spoke with a special meaning about some qualities of Lord Aberdeen. We went over to see Eaton: it is really incurable & too much

[1] David Ross of Montrose; Gladstone assisted his passage to Australia 1853.
[2] Notes in Add MS 44740, ff. 159–63.
[3] By H. E. B. Stowe, 2v. (1852); at least a million copies sold in Britain in 1852.
[4] 5 miles WNW. of Hawarden.
[5] In Lathbury, ii. 150.
[6] George *Wilson, *The grievances of the university tests* (1852); on Scottish professors.
[7] 'Free trade: its moral, social, commercial, agricultural, and political results . . . by F.C.' (1852).
[8] Perhaps Mary, wife of John Henry Howlett, 1781–1867, reader of the chapel royal from 1809; founder and secretary of Kensington grammar school.
[9] Of the Chester and Holyhead railway.
[10] H. A. Woodgate and his wife; he was then rector of Belbroughton by Stourbridge; cp. 14 Mar. 30.
[11] Cp. 29 Aug. 52.
[12] W. J. E. *Bennett, 'A second letter to . . . *Russell on the present persecution of a certain portion of the English church' (1852).
[13] i.e. T. W. Phillipps.

we thought has been laid out.[1] Read Suetonius—Mariotti's Italy.[2] We dined at the Rectory: & were exceedingly amused by S. H[erbert] by Curzon's extreme drollery.[3]

28. T.

Ch. 8½ A.M. Lat Gr. with Stephy. Wrote to Mr E.H. Baily R.A.[4]—M.F. Tupper—Capt. Williams R.E. Read Suetonius—Mariotti's Italy—Oxf. Evidence. Worked on Arbitr[atio]n papers.[5] Our numbers at dinner rose to eleven.

29. Wed. S. Michael & All Angels.

Church 11 A.M. Lat Gr. with Stephy. Wrote to Mr A.W. Haddan—& part copy. Read Suetonius—Oxford Evidence—Mariotti's Italy. Walk with Herbert to the Home Farm.

30. Th.

Ch. 8½ A.M. Lat Gr. with Stephy. Wrote to V. Chancellor of Oxford. Read Suetonius—Oxford Evidence. Saw E. Wright.[6] walk with C.—Chess with Stephen. Saw Mr Burnett, on Home Farm & Railway.

Friday October One 1852.

Church 8½ A.M. Lat. Gr. with Stephy. Wrote to G. Grant—H. Tayleur. Attended Agnes's playing: with great satisfaction. Read Suetonius—Oxf. Univ. Evidence. Chess with Stephen.

2. Sat.

Ch 8½ A.M. Lat Gr. &c. with S. Wrote to Messrs. Overend—W.C. James—J. Griffiths. Saw Mr Burnett mg—Mr B. with Mr Comber aft. on the Brick-work & Railway—(&c.) Read Suetonius—Univ. Commn.

3. 17 S. Trin.

Ch. 11 A.M. (H.C.) and 6½ P.M. At H.C. we had to remember old E. Wright, who is gently and[7] gladly dying. Wrote to Bp of Glasgow—Bp of Oxford.[8] Wrote M.S.[9] Read 'Enter into Thy Closet'[10]—Ecclesiastic on Mad. de La

[1] Eaton hall, 3 miles south of Chester; seat of the Grosvenors, rebuilt after 1802 as 'a vast pile whose exterior embraced every known Gothic style'; cp. G. Huxley, *Victorian duke* (1967), 3.

[2] Cp. 12 May 52.

[3] *Curzon was noted for 'his natural talent, varied experience, and lively wit'; cp. *Notice of Lord *Zouche* (n.d.) 23–4.

[4] Edward Hodges *Baily, 1788–1867; sculptor; R.A. 1821.

[5] Cp. 15 Sept. 52.

[6] A villager; cp. 3 Oct. 52.

[7] Instead of 'dyi'.

[8] Wilberforce, ii. 144–5.

[9] On pride, Add MS 44740, f. 164.

[10] Cp. 15 Aug. 52.

Vallière—do. on Ld Shaftesbury—&c.[1] We had much conv. on the children. I have got more insight into Stephen since I began to teach him Latin. His reasoning powers are good, though his memory is far from ready,[2] & his perceptions slow. What is more important is the remarkable tenderness, delicacy, & humility of his character: of which I was previously by no means fully aware.

4. M.

Ch 8½ A.M. Latin with S. as usual. Wrote to Sir T. Gladstone—W. Forbes—S. Herbert—J. Binger—H. Tayleur. Read Suetonius—Oxf. Evidence—Mariott's Italy. Dinner party in evg. Singing.

5. T.

(Rain detained me, mg) Latin with S. as usual. Wrote to Capt Williams—J. Griffiths—Jos. King. Wrote Award (& draft) on the P.O. Arbitration case.[3] Read Suetonius—Oxf. Evidence—finished). Saw Burnett (2).

6. Wed.

Ch. 8½ A.M. Stephy as usual. Wrote to H.E. Brown,[4] J.R. Hope—J. Murray—Mrs E. Strutt[5]—H. Tayleur—H. Lees—W.R. Farquhar. Read Suetonius—Strutt's Artt. on Roman affairs—Mahon's History Vol V—Mariotti. Chess with Lyttelton.

7. Th.

Ch. 8½ A.M. Stephy as usual. Saw Burnett—and W. Rigby who came with proposals. Wrote to J. Amery. Read Suetonius—Mahon's Hist.—Mariotti (finished) Chess with Lyttelton. Walk & measurements.

8. Fr.

Ch 8½ A.M. Stephy as usual. Wrote to M. Hazelhurst—Fr. Adams—Rev. E. Hawkins—H. Tayleur—Rector Festiniog[6]—J. Binger. Read Suetonius—Calhoun on Govt.[7] Saw Mr Burnett—Mr Sheppard jun.[8] (at Buckley)—whither I walked—The Farquhars & Cavendish came. Singing in evg.

9. Sat.

Ch. 8½ A.M. Stephy as usual. [Saw] G. Burnett. Wrote to Earl Spencer—

[1] *The Ecclesiastic and Theologian*, xiv. 133, 165 (July 1852); reviews of *Réflexions sur la miséricorde de Dieu, ouvrage de Madame de la Vallière* (1852) and *Letters of Dr. *Pusey to *Shaftesbury and Sir J. *Romilly* (1852).

[2] Instead of 'strong'. [3] Not found.

[4] Henry Edwards Brown, Parliamentary agent.

[5] Elizabeth Strutt, *floruit* 1827–60; novelist, and, doubtless, author of the untraced articles referred to this day. She was given a gvnt. pension in 1863.

[6] John Jones, rector of Festiniog and Maentwrog, Merioneth, from 1822.

[7] J. C. Calhoun, *Disquisition on government* (1850).

[8] Son of W., a tenant.

H. Lees—Jos. King. Conference with W. Rigby—with Burnett—also with W. Farquhar on the state of Lyttelton's affairs & engagements (sought by him) & afterwards with Catherine. Read Suetonius—Mahon—Q.R. on Parl. Prospects.[1] Music in evg: & much conversation.

10. 18 S. Trin.

Ch. mg—& (St John's) aftn. Much of this day in conv. Read Nitzsch's Babylon & Jerusalem[2]—Perrone[3]—Tasmanian proceedings.[4]

11. M.

Ch. 8½ A.M. Latin with Stephy. Wrote to Earl Spencer—Jas Watson—Ld Hardinge—Mr Shepherd—J.O. Binger—M. Hazelhurst—Bickers & Bushe—P.O. Liverpool—A. Loader [R]. Read Suetonius. Prepared for my visit to Althorp[5] & London. Saw Burnett—Sheppard & Callwall[6]—Miss Scott.

12. T.

Off at 6¼ a.m. for Chester: by W[olver]hampton & St. Valley to Birm[ingham] Weedon[7] & Althorp. Staid 1½ hours, & stated the Canterbury case[8] to Ld Spencer who was most kind. I then went on & reached Carlton Gardens at nine. Went to T.St. then to Anne St. & saw A.L[oader] who went to C.G.: lives with mother, works, and looks to marry [R]. I may be enough ashamed but there is cause to hope for wretched! A.L. The Jer. Taylor had[9] proved most acceptable. Read Uncle Tom's Cabin.

13. Wed.

Wrote to H.J.G.—E.A. Bowring—C. Rickets—J. Broster—Mrs Long—Mrs S. Walker[10]—R. Barker—Mrs A Burgoyne[11]—Mrs Barber. Worked on my papers. Calls & shopping. Saw Ld Hardinge—D. of Newcastle—Bonham—Sir J. Tyrrell—Aunt J.—Scotts. A rather busy day. In evg saw E.C. —& remained some time mainly I hope to muse but ever with shame. Afterwards P. L[ightfoot] who once extricated has married & has (from *his* emigration been again entangled [R]. Read N. Br. Rev. on Crisis of Parties.[12] Bed at 1½.

[1] *Quarterly Review*, xci. 541 (September 1852); *Croker on free trade and papal aggression.

[2] 'Babylon to Jerusalem: a letter addressed to Ida, countess of Hahn Hahn', (1851); attributed to C. I. Nitsch or Abeken.

[3] Cp. 18 July 52.

[4] Report on Van Diemen's Land in 1851, in *PP* 1852 xxxi. 1.

[5] Seat of the Spencers, 6 miles NW. of Northampton.

[6] Involved in the estate improvements.

[7] 7 miles west of Northampton.

[8] Probably the difficulties of the Canterbury settlement in New Zealand.

[9] Instead of 'was'.

[10] Unidentified.

[11] Unidentified.

[12] *North British Review*, xvii. 559 (August 1852); review of J. Moseley, *Political elements* (1852).

14. Th.

Up at 4½—& came off by the 6 A.M. Train: reached Birm. 8.45 Chester 11.45—saw Mr Hignett & came on to Q[ueen's] F[erry] where I waited with C. & saw the Queen's blinds as she flew by.[1] Read Uncle Tom's Cabin. Wrote to Wm. Rigby—Rn. G.—Dean Torry.

On arriving I received the sad news of the death, most sudden, of Rob[ertso]ns eldest son.[2] A child & boy of sweeter dispositions could hardly be. May the rest of God be his portion.

Explained to Mary in full the cause of my journey. Also discussed with Mrs Wilbraham[3] her embarrassments about Eton.

15.

Kept the house in evg. on account of some sorethroat. Latin with Stephy. Wrote to Pres. of St John's—Ld Spencer (& drafts)—Jas Watson—Sir W. Farquhar—and . . . . J.G. Hubbard. Walk with Cavendish & C. Wynn. Read Suetonius—Uncle Tom—which I finished: it is a *great* book, but scarcely denies exaggeration which under the circumstances wd. be a serious error. Long conference with Lyttelton on his affairs (Canterbury). Also with R. Cavendish on the Canterbury engagements. Also consulted to him on the Resolution from Oxford.

16. Sat.

Kept the house. Latin with Stephy. Wrote to Mr J. Broster—J.N.G.—Mrs Barber—W. Rigby—Mr Empson—Woollright[4]—Mary Hazelhurst—and . . . E. Breackenridge. Read Suetonius—Slaughter's R.R. Intelligence[5] Quart. Rev. on Ld Langdale[6]—The White Slave.[7] 9 to dinner.

17. 19 S. Trin.

Buckley Ch. 11 a.m. Kept the house in aft. for my throat. Wrote to Robn. G. Read Synodus Anglicana[8]—Sellon's Contradiction[9]—Jones's Sermon[10] —Qu.R. on Chalmers.[11] Conv. with Cavendish.

[1] She had been visiting the Britannia bridge and Anglesea, and was returning to Windsor.

[2] John; cp. 5 May 38n.

[3] Jessy Bootle-Wilbraham's eldest son Edward, 1837–98, was at Eton 1850–4; he succ. his grandfa. as 2nd Baron Skelmersdale 1853 and was cr. earl of Lathom 1880.

[4] Probably Woollright, Chidson and Wait, Liverpool silk merchants and haberdashers.

[5] *Railway intelligence . . . compiled by M. Slaughter* (1849).

[6] *Quarterly Review* xci. 461 (September 1852); review of T. D. Hardy, *Life and Letters of Lord *Langdale* (1852).

[7] Probably [R. Hildreth] *The white slave; or memoirs of a fugitive* (1852); there was also a 3v. novel of this title by [C. F. Henningsen] (1846).

[8] By E. *Gibson (1702).

[9] W. B. Sellon, *Miss Sellon and the sisters of mercy. A contradiction of the alleged acts of cruelty exercised by Miss Sellon* (1852); with an appendix.

[10] W. H. Jones, 'The temple of pleasure and the Lord's day: a sermon' (1852).

[11] *Quarterly Review*, xci. 402 (September 1852); on W. Hanna, *Life of Thomas *Chalmers*, 4v. (1849).

18. M. St. Luke.

Ch. 11 a.m. Latin with Stephy. Wrote to Rev. Mr Powell—Ld Spencer—Rev. V. Chancellor—Bickers—M. Hazelhurst. Saw Mr Burnett. Read Suetonius—Calhoun on Government. Arranged letters & papers. Agnes's 10th birthday. I gave over to her the watch from her Grandpapa, & spoke to her on the day, in conjunction with her Cousin Johnnie's death. She is a child of sweet dispositions & I have little to wish but that God should keep her such as He has made her.

19. T.

Left Hn. at 6 for Liverpool & Courthey. Relations only, with partners, attended: & the doctor. We saw Robertson: he was like a stately tree rocked & rent by the hurricane. The dear boy Johnnie was buried at Knotty Ash:[1] in a vault outside the Church: he, the especial image of Life as he was, is now its first tenant. Robertson was composed after the funeral. John & I are to[2] remain for the night.

I went into Liverpool at 12½—saw Rev. Mr Powell—Mr W. Rigby—do with Mr Hancock—H. Tayleur—Mr Young Sec. L.C.S.[3]—Breakenridge—& failed with some. Wrote to C.G.—and Willy. Back to Courthey for the evg. M.E. was not well enough to see us. Discussion on family affairs with John. Read K[ing] Lear.

20. Wed.

Walked out with Robn. & bid him a sad farewell about noon. Amidst his sorrow he was kind & considerate as ever.

Afternoon in Liverpool: chiefly with Cunningham[4] & Breakenridge on the Seaforth valuation. Also saw Stanistreet. Off at 5¼ to Birmingham: & thence at midnight to London. Wrote to C.G.—Read K. Lear—The White Slave.

21. Th.

Reached C[arlton] G[ardens] soon after 5 a.m.—Out at 10. Wrote to Provost of Oriel—C.G.—Herries & Co—Coutts & Co—J. Lefevre—Jane Wortley—E.A. Bowring—Mr Lansley[5]—Ed. N.B. Review. Saw Wortley—Lady Wenlock—Mrs Heywood—Mrs Wadd—(Miss) Munro[6]—Sir R. Inglis—F. Bonham. 1¾–3½ Attended the Installation.[7] Ld Derby's Speech was excellent. Shopping. In evg saw E.C. & C. Morgan: with *better* conduct than heretofore [R]. Gave each an Uncle Tom.

[1] 4 miles east of Liverpool.
[2] Instead of 'were'.
[3] Secretary of the Liverpool Charitable Society, of Slater street, Liverpool.
[4] John Cunningham, Liverpool architect and land surveyor.
[5] Draft in Add MS 44373, f. 24.
[6] Perhaps one of the Lanceley family, which owned Chester shops.
[7] In Downing street; an Oxford deputation came to tell *Derby of his election as chancellor as successor to *Wellington.

Made arrangements for my suddenly determined journey to Oxford tomorrow.

22. Fr.

Went by G[reat] W[estern] Express to Oxford—in 68 minutes: stopping at Didcot. Saw Provost of Oriel & put up at his house. We then went forth with the Dean & Sir R.I. & made the usual *giro* of some 50 visits nearly. Found among others Dr Marsham at home. Saw also Greswell—Archd. Wilberforce—Marriott—& others in evg. Wrote to Housemaid at No. 6. Read Phrontisterion:[1] & studied the Poll book.[2] My journey to Oxford was with Sir R.I.: he was very good company: & made auricular confession to me about ices at Ld Derby's luncheon yesterday.

23. Sat.

Oriel Chapel 8 a.m. Wrote to C.G.—R. Barker—Bp of Oxford—Mr Chadwell.[3] Attended the Convocation at 12: the new V. Chancellor[4] made an oration with good heart & bad Latin. Saw Prov. of Oriel—The Bishop—Dr Jacobson—Greswell—Hussey—Mr Haddan—Mr Woollcombe—the (new) V. Chanc[ello]r—the Master of University. Dined at the Deanery. Read Tweed's Three Letters[5]—Rev. E. Greswell's do to D. of W.[6]

24. 20 S. Trin.

New Coll. Chapel 8 a.m.—Ch Ch 4 P.M.—Ch. Ch morning Sermon: St Mary's aft. Saw Mr Lake—Dr Jacobson—Dr Pusey. Dined in Ch Ch Hall & only left the Commonroom when Tom tolled.[7] Read Cloister Life of Charles V[8]—Bunsen's Hippolytus.[9]

25. M.

Oriel Chapel 8 a.m. Wrote to W.C. James—Bp of Oxford—Chadwell—Rev. Mr Tweed. Read Cambridge Univ. Report.[10] Breakfast with Mr Haddan at Trinity—luncheon Mr Clifford at All Souls[11]—dinner with the

[1]. [H. L. *Mansel] 'Scenes from an unfinished drama, entitled Phrontisterion, or, Oxford in the 19th century' (1852).

[2] *An authentic copy of the poll for two burgesses to serve in parliament for the university of Oxford* (1852).

[3] C. B. Chadwell, cutler in Grove street, Oxford.

[4] R. L. Cotton.

[5] [J. P. Tweed] 'The Oxford commission and the memorial for a "Delegacy". Three letters to W. E. Gladstone' (1852).

[6] 'A letter to . . . *Wellington on . . . convocation' (1837); on a controversy between convocation and the hebdomadal board.

[7] The bell of Tom Tower, Christ Church, which tolls 101 strokes at 9.05 p.m.

[8] Sir W. *Stirling *The cloister life of the emperor Charles the fifth* (1852); only 25 copies printed.

[9] C. C. J. von Bunsen, *Hippolytus and his age*, 4v. (1852); written in English.

[10] In *Extracts from the report of the university commissioners* (1852).

[11] (Sir) Charles Cavendish Clifford, 1821–95; fellow of All Souls 1843; *Palmerston's private secretary 1850–7; liberal M.P. Isle of Wight 1857–65, Newport 1870–85; 4th bart. 1892.

Vice Chancellor. Saw Master of Univ.—Mr Sewell—Dr Acland—Mr Stokes —Chadwell—made many calls. Packed &c for departure. Saw Union Soc.s rooms & A[ll] S[ouls] Library.

26. T.

Oriel Chapel 8 a.m. A closing conv. with my kind host the Provost: & a large breakfast party at Balliol with Mr Lake. 10.25–4.15 Journey to Chester. To Birm. I had Ld Stratford de Redcliffe & his party for company. At Chester saw Mr Barker on Stephen's affairs: & came on to Hawarden. Children all well: C. but weak. Read The White Slave.

27. Wed.

Morning wet. Latin with Stephen Wrote to Rev. Dr Cursham[1] Jacobson —Chev. Bunsen—S. Herbert—E. of Aberdeen.—W. Hancock. Read White Slave (finished)—Mahon's Hist—Suetonius—Clergy Reserve Debates.[2] Drove C. to Mold.[3]

28. Thurs. SS. Simon & Jude.

Ch 11 a.m. Latin with Stephen Wrote to M. Hazelhurst—Mr Coller—Mr. Cunningham—Lyttelton—J. Griffiths—Mrs Scott—B. Oliveira[4]—Bp of Oxford. Read Suetonius—Lord Mahon's History. Worked on the Seaforth papers.

29. Fr.

Ch $8\frac{1}{2}$ a.m. Latin with Stephen. Wrote to Lord Spencer—W. Hancock—G. Burnett—W. Shone.[5] Read Suetonius—Greswell on the Initiative[6]—Ld Mahon. Music in evg. Felling of the three Beeches.

30. Sat.

Ch. $8\frac{1}{2}$ a.m. Latin with Stephen. Wrote to J.N.G.—& draft—P.D. Cook—Mrs J.S. Lefevre. Worked most of the day on the Seaforth Estate papers. Read Suetonius—Mahon's Hist. The Stratfords came in evg.[7]

31. 21 S. Trin.

Ch mg. & evg. Read Stirling's Charles V—Bunsen's Hippolytus—Caswall

[1] Thomas Cursham, 1787–1868; Lincoln, Oxford; D.C.L. 1825; vicar of Blackwell, Derbyshire, from 1825.

[2] Probably those in the Canadian assembly, cp. Morrell, 457.

[3] 8 miles west of Hawarden.

[4] Benjamin Oliveira, 1806–65; liberal M.P. Pontefract 1852–7.

[5] William Shone, Chester coachmaker.

[6] Untraced letter by E. or R. *Greswell on the proposed Initiative Board for Oxford university; cp. 3 Feb. 54n.

[7] Eliza Charlotte Canning, *née* Alexander, d. 1882; m. 1825 as his 2nd wife Sir Stratford *Canning, who was cr. Viscount Stratford de Redcliffe in April 1852. Cp. 13 July 32n.

on Convocation[1]—Music in evg. Walk with Ld Stratford & much conversation mg. noon & night: he is my kind friend of near 18 years standing.

Monday Nov. One. All Saints.

Wrote to Archdeacon Sandford. Latin with Stephen. Saw W. Rigby & W. Hancock. Church 11 a.m. Read Suetonius—Mahon's Hist—got into Vol. VI. Chess with S.R.G.

2. T.

Church 8½ a.m. Latin with Stephy. Wrote to Bp of Oxford. Saw Mr Parry—also Mr R. Barker—Worked on a statement of Stephen's affairs. Read Suetonius (finished Nero)—Mahon. Dinner party in evg: the Hancocks[2] here, a sequel of the late arrangements. Singing.

3. Wed.

Ch 8½ a.m. Latin with Stephy. C. & I talked over his prospects & the sending him to Mrs Church. Wrote to Williams & Co—R. Barker—Earl Marshall[3]—Willy—Rev. W.H. Jones[4]—Jas Watson—Robn. G. Read Mahon's Letter to Sparks[5]—Mahon's Hist (finished Vol VI.)—& Stirling's Cloister life of Charles V. Made preparations for departure & sat through the night.

Nov. 4. Th.

3.40 a.m. Drove to Chester—reached No 6. C[arlton] G[ardens] at 1—went direct to the House to show at the Election of Speaker.[6] Saw Mr C. Villiers—Ld J. Russell (in H. of C.). Dined with the Wortleys. Wrote to Mr Goulburn C.G.—M.F. Tupper—W. Wilson—Capt. H. Scott—Rev. F. Teed. Read Stirling.

Stanotte vidi una innominata di 18 anni bellissima e l'accompagnai in casa sua dove ci siam intrattenuti parlando: odia la sua maniera di vivere pure senza coraggio per li spezi e i sacrifizii necessarii per[7] staccarsene. Iddio la compatisca. Vidi anche A. Loader per caso nella strada ed ebbi un discorso assai lungo con lei riguardo principalmente alle nozze sperate e al tempo di mezzo.[8]

[1] H. Caswall, 'The Jerusalem chamber; or, convocation and its possibilities' (1852).

[2] Of Rigby and Hancock.

[3] The 13th duke of *Norfolk, arranging the funeral.

[4] William Hartwell Jones, 1828–58; rector of Llandow, Glamorganshire from 1852; cp. 17 Oct. 52.

[5] P. H. *Stanhope, Lord Mahon, 'A letter to Jared Sparks: being a rejoinder to his "Reply to the strictures of Lord *Mahon . . . on the mode of editing the writings of Washington"' (1852).

[6] The opening of *Barry's new house of commons: *H* cxxiii. 3. *Lefevre was re-elected Speaker.

[7] 'la' and then 'de', here deleted.

[8] 'Tonight I saw a most beautiful unnamed girl of 18. I accompanied her to her house, where we lingered over a talk: she hates her way of life, yet lacks the courage for the expense and sacrifices of detaching herself from it. God have pity on her. Also saw A. Loader by chance in the street and had a somewhat lengthy conversation with her, principally on the marriage hoped for and on the mean time.'

5. Fr.

Marg. Chapel 5 P.M. Up late. Saw Sir J. Young—S. Herbert—W.C. James—Ld Hardinge. H. of C. 2–4 hoping to be sworn. Dined at Ld Hardinge's. Calls. Worked among my effects but without any visible good yet. Wrote to Jas Wortley—J. Griffiths—J.H. Parker—C.G.—Rev. Mr Caswall—J.N.G.—Jas Mozley.

6. Sat.

Wrote to C.G.—Rev. Mr Haddan. Saw R. Phillimore—Jas Mozley—Sir Jas Walmsley[1]—D. of Newcastle—Mr Hayward—Marquis of Blandford—Mr T. Duncombe—Sir W.C. James—Mr A. Munro (& his beautiful work)[2]—E. Cardwell (on Finance)—Lady Peel. Calls. Read N. British on Oxf Commn.[3] Dined at S. Herbert's.

7. 22 S. Trin.

Chapel Royal & H.C. 11 A.M.—St Barnabas 7 P.M. A noble congregation: without a wheel.[4] Wrote dft of letter to Shaftesbury.[5] Read Bunsen's Hippolytus—Montalembert Int. Catholiques[6]—Cumming's Sermon[7]—Sermon on H.E.[8]—Moore's do on Crystal Palace.[9]

8. M.

Wrote to Ld Shaftesbury (fair)—R. Lawley—Rev. Mr Ainger—C.G.—Mr Birch[10]—Rn. G.—Miss Scott. Read Montalembert—Household Words.[11] Lord Aberdeen's 12¼–2. Calls. Shopping. Dined at Canning's & sat till twelve.

9. T.

Wrote to Mr J.G. Lockhart—J.N.G.—Mr W. Hancock—Mr Rae[12]—Mr E.A. Bowring—Miss Crump[13]—Mr Griffiths—Rev. E. Neale.[14] Read

[1] Sir Joshua *Walmsley, 1794–1871; Liverpool corn merchant and anti-corn-law campaigner; founded National Reform Association 1847; kt. 1840; liberal M.P. Bolton 1849–52, Leicester 1852–7.

[2] Cp. 12 Feb. and 10 Nov. 52.

[3] *North British Review*, xviii. 1 (November 1852); review of the Royal Commission *Report* (1852).

[4] i.e. without a carriage; they had all come on foot.

[5] On convocation, in E. Hodder, *Life of *Shaftesbury* (1886) ii. 404–6.

[6] C. de Montalembert, *Des intérêts catholiques au XIXe siècle* (1852); cp. 10 Nov. 52n.

[7] J. Cumming, Scottish minister, 'The Christian nursery. A sermon' (1852).

[8] Perhaps *Pusey's; cp. 30 June 43.

[9] D. Moore, 'Our Sabbaths in danger' (1852); hostile to opening it on Sundays.

[10] Probably Henry Mildred Birch, 1820–84; fellow of King's, Cambridge, 1841; taught at Eton 1844–9; tutored Prince of Wales 1849–51; rector of Prestwich, Lancashire, from 1852.

[11] *Household Words*, vi. 145 (30 October 1852); periodical ed. by *Dickens.

[12] Perhaps John *Rae, 1813–93; surgeon and explorer employed by the Hudson's Bay company.

[13] Mary, da. of George Hamilton Crump of Cheshire, m. 1863 T. Lewis Wilkinson, physician, and d. 1885. Probably the Miss Crump who was governess at Hagley 1848–51.

[14] Erskine *Neale, 1804–83; vicar of Exning from 1854; wrote on theology.

Debates of last March & made Extracts.[1] Read Cardwell's NBR Finance Article[2]—Montalembert's Int. Cath. (finished). Dined at Mr Hayward's: a Peelite party salted with C. Villiers. Jane Wortley's marriage festival afr.[3] C.G. came up: but poorly.

10. Wed.

Wrote to Rev Dr M'Caul (and draft)[4]—Rev Mr Lake—G. Burnett—J.S. Wortley—Lyttelton—Williams Deacon—Johnson Longden. Saw Ld Spencer—& wrote Dupl. Memm. on the Q.F. transaction[5]—Saw Mr Munro & had his group placed on its pedestal in my room—to my delight.[6] Attended R. Lawley's marriage—Saw F. Doyle—J.H. Parker—Lord Aberdeen alone, & with the Duke of Buccleuch. Dined at S. Herbert's. Went afterwards to Ld Abns: we did not get the [Queen's] Speech till near 12 & we discussed matters till past one. It was condemned on all hands.[7] Worked on Montalembert.[8]

11. Th.

Wrote to Lord Aberdeen—Aunt J—R. Phillimore—Dr M'Caul—and copy. Saw Wilson Patten—Rev Mr Lake—D. of Newcastle—H. Corry. Read Liverpool Prize Essay[9]—Vaughan on the Crystal Palace.[10] H. of C. at the time for the Speech: then to Ld Aberdeen's: to whom I had sent a form of motion on Free Trade.[11] Thence to the House until 9½ P.M.—Spoke on the Address. Matters turned out better than I anticipated.[12] Home with A. Kinnaird. Worked on Montalembert.

12. Fr.

Wrote to E. of Aberdeen. Saw Sir W. Heathcote—Lord Mahon—J.N.G—Phillimore—the Speaker—Sir J. Graham—S. Herbert—C. Wood—and others.—Read Hubbard on I. Tax.[13] H. of C. 3¾–6½. Worked on Montalem-

[1] Probably the free trade debs. at the start of *Derby's ministry: *H* cxix. 1039ff. Extracts untraced.

[2] *North British Review*, ix. 269 (May 1848); cp. *Wellesley Index*, ii. 1200.

[3] A party for her brother, Robert Neville Lawley, 1819–91, of the life guards, who next next day m. Georgiana Emily, da. of Lord Robert Edward Henry *Somerset. She d. 1891.

[4] Add MS 44373, f. 38.

[5] Perhaps in Hawn P.: on Queen's Ferry, 2 miles north of Hawarden.

[6] Cp. 6 Nov. 52.

[7] The speech claimed that recent legislation had 'inflicted unavoidable Injury on certain important Interests', i.e. agriculture, and called for consideration on how 'to mitigate that Injury'; cp. *H* cxxiii. 20.

[8] The first draft of his review of Montalembert's *Des intérêts catholiques au XIXe siècle*, published in the *Quarterly Review*, cxii, 137 (December 1852). Cp. Add MS 44685, ff. 67–81.

[9] Not found; probably awarded by the Liverpool Collegiate Institute.

[10] C. J. *Vaughan, 'A few words on the Crystal Palace question' (1852).

[11] Add MS 44740, f. 167.

[12] He followed *Disraeli and denounced the section of the speech quoted above: *H* cxxiii. 91.

[13] J. G. *Hubbard, 'How should an income tax be levied?' (1852), a letter to *Disraeli.

bert. Went with C. to the lying in state at Chelsea wh was very solemn:[1] yet no Xtn sign. Saw Aunt J.[2]

13. Sat.

Wrote to A. Williams—Magdalen Ringers—Dr McCaul—R. Barker—C.G. Reid—J. Griffiths—T. Gladstone—C.J. Foster—Rev. J.O. Powell—Dr M'Caul and 2 copies[3]—J.D. Cook. Read Cochrane 'Who are the Liberals?'[4] To Lord Abns at ½ past 12: discussing Villiers's notice.[5] Saw Sir J. Graham there & afterwards alone—also Newcastle. Saw Mr H. Lindsay—Mrs Tyler—Directors Prov. Instn.[6]—F.R. Wegg Prosser. Dined at Phillimores. Worked on Montalembert.

14. S. 23 Trin.

St James mg. & aftn. Wrote to Wegg Prosser. Read M[orning] Chron[icle]. Report of Convocation[7]—Scots Ch. Magazine[8]—Wegg Prosser on Branch Church Theory.[9] Saw Bp of Oxford. Dined with the Herberts.

15. M.

Wrote to G. & Co—Rev. G.H. Forbes—Willy. Saw Mr Horsfall—Sir J. Graham—Cornwall Legh—Ld Hardinge. H. of C. 4–5½.[10] Visited St Paul's lighted up.[11] Dined at Lady Wenlock's. Worked on Montalembert.

16. T.

Wrote to Mr Lockhart—Mr C. Villiers (2) & copies[12]—T.G.—Willy—M.W. Mayow—Rev. E. Stokes[13]—Rev. T. Collis[14]—Col. Maberly—Rev. A. Hackman—Rev. Dr Todd. Saw Mr R. Barker—Mr Hayward—Corry—Young—Herbert *cum* Graham. Dined with the Farquhars: at Lady Aylesbury's[15]

[1] Of *Wellington.

[2] These two sentences added at the bottom of the page.

[3] Cp. Add MS 44373, ff. 38–54, printed in the *Morning Herald*, 15 November 1852; on Gladstone's reported secession to Scottish episcopalianism.

[4] By A. D. R. Baillie-Cochrane (1852).

[5] *Villiers had given notice that on 22 November he would propose a motion to clarify the ministry's position on free trade: *H* cxxiii. 74. It was moved on 23 November, cp. *H* cxxiii. 351.

[6] The Provident Clerks' Assurance Association in Moorgate street.

[7] 'Representation as introduced into the lower house of the convocation of the province of Canterbury, 12 November 1852' (1852).

[8] *Scottish Magazine and Churchman's Review*, ii. 520 (November 1852); probably the obituary of bp. *Torry.

[9] F. R. Wegg-Prosser, 'The branch church theory' (1852); on high-anglican views on church unity. Cp. 10 Apr. 51.

[10] Misc. business: *H* cxxiii. 145.

[11] The interior of St Paul's was illuminated by gas in rehearsal for the funeral.

[12] In Add MS 44373, f. 62.

[13] Edward Stokes, 1823–63; student of Christ Church 1842–60; reader in Greek 1852, proctor 1854; Whitehall preacher 1850–2.

[14] A slip of the pen for John Day *Collis, 1816–79; fellow of Worcester, Oxford, 1839–47; headmaster and vicar 1842–79; wrote classical text books.

[15] 41 Grosvenor square.

afterwards. Finished & sent off my papers on Montalembert. Read Lord Denman on Marriage Law.[1]

17. Wed.

Wrote to C.G. Reid—F. Wegg Prosser—Mr Riordon[2]—G. Burnett (*or* Mr Baillie)[3] H. of C. & Commee. 11–1¾.[4] Then to the City to see J[ohnson] L[ongden] & Co & to St Pauls on an exploring Expn. for C. & Mary to whom on my return I made known the results. They resolved to go.[5] Saw H. Baring—Sir C. Wood—R. Phillimore. All the West and in our part seems one vast beehive: the stir immeasurable. I went out late to witness the spectacle. At Jane Wortley's in evg. C. had gone to Doctors Commons to sleep. Willy arrived at 9. Conv. with him on his mathematical troubles.

18. Th.

We were all moving pretty early. Willy went to Ld Northampton's: Henry & Stephen with W. Lyttelton & J. Talbot to the Cathedral. I to Jane Wortley's from whence I saw the whole solemn & magnificent procession, in which the grandest thing was the double band of the Guards & the most touching the led horse of the Warrior gone. Thence I went to the H. of C. arriving at 10½: & we all passed rapidly by water to Thames Wharf & so into St Pauls. The procession 2½ m long had to travel 4m. at the calculated rate of 1½ m per h. This was accomplished exactly except a stoppage or two with the car. Notwithstanding long delays at the door & by the grave from bad machinery or arrangements,[6] the service was over at 2.40, taking about 1¼ hour. The spectacle was magnificent in the highest degree: the Mendelsohn Anthem[7] at the end sublime in effect almost beyond anything I ever heard: but the most nobly & touchingly conceived part of all was the slow lowering of the coffin, surmounted by the Duke's coronet & baton, his Military hat & sword, while the organ played the dead march. I sat by E. Ellice. At the close I brought C. & Mary away to Dr Kynaston's & then by water to Westminster & so home. Dined with the S. Herbert's. Read Stirling's Charles V[8] finished—& E.I. Missionary Petition.[9]

19. Fr.

Wrote to E. Collins [R]—Mr Boothby Barry—E. Coleridge. Saw Ld Abn. —Graham—Young—Christy—R. Wilberforce—Newcastle—Tomline—H. Corry—Mr Roberts of Jamaica[10]—Wortley—J N G. Meeting at Ld Abns.

[1] T. *Denman, 'Reasons for legalising marriage with a deceased wife's sister' (1852).
[2] Sc. Riordan.
[3] David Baillie, b. 1827 in Scotland; book-keeper in the Hawarden estates office.
[4] Misc. business: *H* cxxiii. 219.
[5] To *Wellington's funeral.
[6] The railings of St. Paul's had to be cut to let the funeral car in; there was then one-and-a-half-hours delay while the coffin was removed from the car.
[7] 'Sleepers awake!' from the oratorio *St. Paul.*
[8] Cp. 24 Oct. 52.
[9] Not traced.
[10] Henry Roberts, 1812?–74; education commissioner in Jamaica 1845–53; Newcastle's private secretary 1853–4; under-secretary for war 1854–5; revenue commissioner from 1855.

12½–2 on Villiers's motion. H of C. 4½–7½.[1] Wrote Pol. Mema. Willy went off to Eton in the forenoon; C. to Brighton.

Tea with E. Collins & remained till 11 nearly [R]. Remember Hooker's Torch.[2] ♄ Read Cambr. Report—Barry on Cath[edra]l Institutions.[3]

20. Sat.

Wrote to Sir S. Scott & Co—Overends—Sir J. Graham (& two copies)—J.W. Patten—Lord A. Hervey—Wm. Forbes. We met at Ld Abns. at 1½: & decided on a representation. Saw J.N.G—Herbert—C. Villiers—Charteris—C. Ross—& others. Dined with the Herberts. Read Madiai documents[4] & other pamphlets.

21. PreAdvent S[unday].

S. Mary Magd. & H.C. mg. Bedfordbury Evg. Wrote MS on Jer. XXIII & read aloud in Evg. Wrote draft of letter to Manning[5]—to Ld Palmerston, & copy.[6] Composed a Response for the Commandments.[7] Read Bunsen—Social Aspects[8]—& Campbell on Convocation.[9] Saw S. Herbert—Seymer—Geo. Hope—R. Wilberforce.

22. M.

Wrote to Mr J. D. Cook—Mr B. Denison—W.C. James—Mr Morier—Mr R. Lowe—Mr C.G. Reid.—J.N.G. At twelve we met at Ld Abns. From thence H[erbert] & I went to Ld Palmerston's: saw him again in evg.[10] Saw Ld Aberdeen—D. of Newcastle—C. Ross—E.G. Vernon[11]—Evelyn Denison. H. of C. 4–7½.[12] Dined at Herberts. Lady Palmerston's[13] afterwards. Read Napoleon Le Petit.[14] C.G. returned: better D[ei] G[ratia].

23. T.

Wrote to Jas Wortley—J. Griffiths. Read Napoleon le Petit. In the morning I thought over our position, & considered it with Goulburn & Herbert. At 1½ we met at Tomline's, near 30. I made an expln. of our views wh took ¾ hours: some very friendly observations followed. Sat through the debate

[1] Misc. business: *H* cxxiii. 243.

[2] Perhaps a reference to R. *Hooker, 'Sermon on justification', often reprinted, or to one of T. *Hooker's sermons on sexual control. The phrase is used again in connection with scourging, cp. 29 Dec. 53.

[3] H. B. Barry, 'Thoughts on the renovation of cathedral institutions' (1852).

[4] J. C. Evans, 'Translation of the act of accusation, and of the sentence pronounced by the royal court of Florence upon F. and R. Madiai, for the so-called crime of "impiety" (1852), and *PP* 1852–3 cii. 635.

[5] But see Purcell, ii. 161.

[6] In Guedalla, *P*, 87.

[7] Not found.

[8] By J. S. *Smith (1850).

[9] A. Campbell, 'Convocation: a letter to the clergy of the archdeaconery of Liverpool' (1852).

[10] Extensive negotiations on a free trade motion; see Conacher, *Peelites*, 152ff.

[11] See 28 Dec. 52.

[12] Irish land: *H* cxxiii. 305.

[13] Lady Emily Mary, 1787–1870; da. of 1st Viscount Melbourne; m. firstly 1805 5th Earl Cowper, secondly 1839 3rd Viscount *Palmerston. A great social hostess.

[14] By Victor Hugo (1852); written in exile, published in London.

$4\frac{1}{2}$–$12\frac{1}{2}$[1]—saw Macaulay—Lord J. Russell—Herbert—Ld Monck[2]—Sir R. Peel. The prospects after Ld P.s speech tolerable.

24. Wed.

Wrote to Sir J. Graham—(& copy)—Dr J. Casto—J.A. Addison—M'Burnie. Saw Jane Wortley—Farquhar—J.E. Denison—Ld Carlisle—Macaulay—Young—Seymer. Meeting at Ld Aberdeen's 2–$3\frac{3}{4}$. Graham came in. Went thence to Ld Palmerston's. St Paul's at noon & went over the Galleries with the Dean. Then to H. of C.[3] Dined with Jas Wortley—Parliamentary.

25. Th.

Read Income Tax Evidence[4]—Tennyson's Ode[5]—Parl. Debates. Saw S. Herbert. H. of C. $4\frac{3}{4}$–$12\frac{3}{4}$. Spoke on Sir J. Graham's motion: with a view to pacification.[6]

26. Fr.

Wrote to Stephy—Rev. T. Lathbury—W. Forbes—Mrs Cosserat[7]—Rev. J. Jones—A. Turner. Conv. with Ld Aberdeen on the Palace & ministerial contingencies. Saw Graham—Herbert. Read Income Tax Evidence—Wilkinson on Education.[8] H of C $5\frac{1}{2}$–$2\frac{1}{4}$. Spoke in answer to Cobden: I am *glad* I had not to say out what was in me about Disraelis Speech of Tuesday. Divided in 336:256 and in 458:53. So ends the great controversy of Free Trade.[9]

Nervous excitement kept me very wakeful: the first time (after speaking) for many years.

27. Sat.

Chapel[10] Titchfield St 5 P.M. C.G. went off. Wrote to C.G.—Jas Watson. Breakfasted with Sir T. Acland to meet Mr Nobbs.[11] Dined with the

[1] *Villiers' motion on free trade: *H* cxxiii. 351.
[2] Charles Stanley *Monck, 1819–94; 4th Viscount Monck in Irish peerage 1849; liberal M.P. Portsmouth 1852; governed Canada 1861–8; cr. Baron Monck of Ballytrammon 1866; on Irish Land Act commission 1882–4.
[3] County Elections Polls Bill: *H* cxxiii. 461.
[4] First and second reports of the select cttee. on income and property tax, *PP* 1852 ix. 1, 463.
[5] 'Ode on the death of the duke of *Wellington', published on the morning of the funeral. At first much abused in the press.
[6] *H* cxxiii. 484, notes in Add MS 44652, f. 159. *Graham had moved the adjournment of the House.
[7] The wife of George Peloquin Graham Cosserat, b. 1816, rector of Abbots-Kerswell, Devon, 1847, and of Winfrith Newburgh, Dorset from 1851; cp. 3 Jan. 53.
[8] John Wilkinson, 'Popular education. The national society. The two Manchester schemes. The committee of the privy council' (1852).
[9] *H* cxxiii. 680; notes in Add MS 44652, f. 163. The first division was to prevent the modification of *Villiers motion, and was defeated. The second was on the modified motion, and was passed: *H* cxxiii. 698.
[10] Instead of '9'.
[11] George Hunn *Nobbs, 1799–1884; in Chilian navy, then a missionary on Pitcairn island; returned to London for ordination 1852, then led Pitcairn islanders 1853–84.

Farquhar's: conv. on Nat. School Society. Lady Derby's in evg.—where I saw Ld D—Ossulston—Canning—Mr Ball—& others. Wrote Pol. Mema. Read on Income Tax—& Casti Novelle.[1] Saw Duke of Argyll—Lord Aberdeen—Newcastle—Bonham.

This evening I went to Lady Derby's evening party where Lord Derby took me a little aside and said he must take the opportunity of thanking me for the tone of my speech last night which he thought tended to place the discussion on its right footing.

It was evident from his manner & Lady Derby's too that they were highly pleased with the issue of it. I simply made my acknowledgments in terms of the common kind, upon which he went on to ask me what in my view was to happen next? The great object he said was to get rid of all personal questions and to consider how all those men who were united in their general views of government might combine together to carry it on with effect. For himself he felt both uncertain and indifferent: he might be able to carry on the Govt. or might not: but the question lay beyond that by what combination or arrangement of a satisfactory nature in the event of his displacement the administration of public affairs could be conducted.

To this I replied that it seemed to me that *our* situation (meaning that of Herbert Goulburn & others with myself) in relation to his Government remained much as it was in March and April last; for although most important progress had been achieved for the public by the decisions to which we had come about free trade yet according to the plan that he had laid down for his Government they were to stand or fall by the measures they might introduce with reference to finance and the kindred subjects. Therefore I said we have to expect your Budget and the production of it is the next step.

He replied that he much desired to see whether there was a possibility of any *rapprochement* and seemed to glance at personal considerations as likely perhaps to stand in the way.

I said in reply that no doubt there were many difficulties of a personal nature to be faced in conceiving of any ministerial combination when we looked at the present House of Commons: many men of power & eminence but great difficulties arising from various causes, present & past relations, incompatibilities, peculiar defects of character or failures, in bringing them into harmony.

I said that as to relations of parties circumstances were often stronger than the human will; that we must wait for their guiding, and follow it; that no good could arise from any forced or artificial effort to work without their aid; that until they had reached certain stages of development it must constantly happen in life that we could only[2] sit still, and that unsatisfactory as this was to one's own impatience ever craving for a well defined position yet it was the only safe and warrantable ground on which to rest.

He said rather decidedly that he assented to the truth of this doctrine.[3]

28. *Advent Sunday.*

St Martins H.C. at 8½ A.M. St Stephen's 11. Chapel Royal 5½. MS. for the day aloud. Saw Graham. In evg meditated on possible arrangements with

[1] See 23 Jan. 43. [2] 'abide their' deleted.

[3] Rest, on a speech by *Herbert, omitted. Initialled and dated this day; Add MS 44778, f. 48.

the materials at hand. Wrote to Christopher (& draft.)[1] Also wrote out for post my letters to Manning. Read Wilson's Spiritual Catholicity[2]—Smith's Social Aspects.

29. M.

Wrote to Jas Watson—H. Tayleur—Rev. Mr Wilkinson—A.W. Maclean[3]—Rev. R.L. Tyler[4]—C.G.[5]—Rev. E. Monro—J.G. Lockhart—W.F. Campbell. Corrected MS. on Montalembert.[6] Saw Goulburn. H. of C. 4¼–7½.[7] Dined with the Herberts: & discussed political prospects with him & N[ewcastle]. Read Wilkinson on Education—Mathew on U.S. Policy.[8]

30. T. St Andrew.

Wrote to G.B. Mathew—C.G.—Ld Aberdeen—Jas Watson—H. Tayleur. Saw Farquhar on N[ational] S[ociety] & Ch matters—Monsell—Ld Monck. H. of C. 4½–7¼.[9] Worked on accounts. Dined with Mrs Talbot & conv. Read Inc. Tax Evidence, &c. At night saw Loader—Morgan—one from Norwich [R].

Wed. Decr One. 1852

Wrote to Rev. Mr Lonsdale—C.G.—Johnson Longden & Co—Mr Lake—Lyttelton—J. Griffiths. Saw Lady Peel—Cardwell—The Speaker—Mr Hayman—Mr M'Kenzie—Graham. Dined at Grillion's. Madam Bunsen's afterwards. Read Income Tax Debates.[10]

2. Th.

Wrote to W.R. Farquhar—C.G.[11]—C.G. Reid—Miss Scott—Rev. Mr. Warter.—W. Hampton. H. of C. 4½–6.[12] Lady A. Peel's to luncheon—i.e. early dinner. Saw Canning. Read all I could find on Income Tax in old Debates, Ann[ual]. Regr., Pitt's Life,[13] Sinclair's Hist. Revenue.[14] Read Webster on Ireland.[15]

[1] Marked 'private and confidential', on politics; in Add MS 44373, f. 89.
[2] Thomas Wilson, 'Catholicity spiritual and intellectual: an attempt at vindicating the harmony of faith and knowledge' (1850).
[3] Alexander Walker Maclean, wrote on monetary circulation.
[4] Probably Roper Trevor Tyler, 1802–85; University, Oxford; rector of Llantrithyd, Glamorgan from 1838.
[5] 'Willy' here deleted.
[6] See 10 Nov. 52.
[7] The Derby election: *H* cxxiii. 717.
[8] Probably an MS from G. B. Mathew, cp. 6 Apr. 44; he was at this time charged with incompetence in the Bahamas.
[9] 'Ministers Money' in Ireland: *H* cxxiii. 781.
[10] See next day.
[11] Some in Bassett, 91.
[12] Ionian isles: *H* cxxiii. 826.
[13] Cp. 15 Mar. 52 and *H* cxxiii. 985.
[14] Sir J. *Sinclair, *History of the public revenue* (1784).
[15] W. B. Webster, 'Ireland considered as a field for investment or residence' (1852).

3. Fr.

Wrote to Johnson L. & Co—Scotts—Mr Willis—C.G.[1] We met at Lord Aberdeens at 12½ and determined on an immediate protest *in case*. H of C. 3¾–11¼.[2] Read I.T. Debates Pitt's Life &c—Thackeray's Esmond.[3] Breakfast with Milnes. Saw Scotts—Herbert—Dukes of B.[4] & N[ewcastle] [in] Evg at the Club.

4. Sat.

Wrote to W.B. Hancock—Johnson Longden & Co—Mr Cook. Saw Young & Monsell—Senior Proctor[5]—Messrs. Swift & Laing—Ld Monck—Canning—Molesworth. We met at Ld Abns. at 2½ & sat till 5½. Graham came in upon us. Read Casti, Animali—Englishman's Letter to Lord Derby.[6]

5. 2 S. Adv.

Chapel Royal & H.C. at Noon—St Stephen's Evg. MS of 41 aloud. Saw S. Herbert. Read Bunsen's Hippolytus—Armstrong[7]—Warters Sermons[8]—Col. Ch. Magazine—Bp Forbes on Nicene Creed.[9]

6. M.

Wrote to Overends—C.G[10]—W.H.G. In the City: saw Overends—Freshfield. Read on Inc. Tax &c.—Nap. le Petit. H. of C. 3¾–7 and 11–1¾. Spoke on Income Tax.[11] Dined with the Farquhars.

7. T.

The anniversary of my dearest Father's death. I feel a great reluctance to put off my mourning. *It is the last earthly link.*

Read Inc. Tax Debates—Bp of Quebec[12]—Riddell on the Artillery.[13] H of C. 4½–7½.[14] Saw Sir C. Wood—Graham—Panizzi—J.E. Denison—Newcastle—W. Harcourt[15]—J.N.G. Wrote to Mr J.D. Cook—T.G.—

[1] Some in Bassett, 91.
[2] *Disraeli's Budget: *H* cxxiii. 836.
[3] 3v. (1852).
[4] Probably *Buccleuch, cp. Conacher, 30n. 3.
[5] W. C. Lake.
[6] [Sir W. V. *Harcourt] 'The morality of public men' (1852): a famous squib, contributing to the government's fall. For Gladstone's reaction, see Gardiner, i. 70.
[7] Probably G. Armstrong, '"The Duke": some outlines of his character' (1852); a funeral oration.
[8] J. W. *Warter, 'The high-churchman of the old school, and the good dissenter of the old school' (1852); two sermons.
[9] A. P. *Forbes, *A short explanation of the Nicean creed* (1852).
[10] Fragment in Bassett, 91.
[11] On *Pitt and the income and house tax: *H* cxxiii. 981; notes in Add MS 44652, f. 166.
[12] G. J. *Mountain, perhaps his *Journal* (1849).
[13] C. J. B. Riddell, 'Remarks on the organisation of the British royal artillery' (1852).
[14] 2° Tenants Compensation (Ireland) Bill: *H* cxxiii. 1089.
[15] (Sir) William George Granville Venables Vernon *Harcourt, 1827–1904; president of Cambridge union 1849, wrote in daily press as 'Englishman' and 'Historicus'; *Whewell professor of international law 1869–87; liberal M.P. Oxford city 1868–80, Derby 1880–95, Monmouth 1895–1904; solicitor-general 1873–4, home secretary 1880–85, chancellor of the exchequer 1886, 1892–5. Hostile to ritualism and imperialism. Latterly known as 'Jumbo'. See Add MS 44196–44203.

Rev. C.B. Jackson[1]—C.G.—Mr W. Forbes—W.B.Hancock. Dined at Mr Harcourt's.[2]

8. Wed.

Wrote to Bp of Aberdeen—C.G.[3]—J. Griffiths—J.E. Denison. Saw Mr Hubbard—Mr Bennet—Earl Spencer—Lord Aberdeen: we conversed long on political contingencies. Dined at S. Herbert's. Saw Sir J. Graham—Mr Ellice—Young—Mahon. Read Maitland on Income Tax.[4]

9. Th.

A conversation not as it should have been evg & ♄. Wrote to Rev. E. Hawkins—C.G.—Ld Drumlanrig[5]—R. Barker—Dr Dearle—C.A. Wood—Lyttelton—Rev. A. Whyte. Saw Rev Mr Mackenzie—Sir W. James—Bp of Sydney—Graham—Sir C. Wood—G. Harcourt—Goulburn—Pat. Talbot.[6] Breakfast with M Van de Weyer—dined with the Norreyses—Lady Granville's afterwards. Worked on I. Tax.

10. Fr.

Wrote to Rev. Dr Binney—C.G.—J.G. Maitland[7]—Mr J. Tilly[8]—W.R. Farquhar—W.B. Riddell—W.M. Goalen. Saw Sir C. Wood—Chev. St André[9]—Mr Tufnell—J.E. Denison—S. Herbert—Mrs Malcolm—Aunt J. H. of C. 4½–9 and 10–12¾.[10] I sat up for the night: & fell to work on my arrear of letters & papers.

11. Sat.

Off by six o'clock train to Birm. & Hagley which I reached before one: falling in with a nice boy on the road, Nanny's grandson. Saw Griffiths in evg: but was sleepy enough. Read Trench &c.[11] Found C. pretty well, baby out of sorts, Willy & M. very flourishing.

[1] Charles Bird Jackson, 1821–?; Brasenose, Oxford; vicar of Northwood, Staffordshire, 1848–75, rector of Wold Newton, Lincolnshire, from 1875.

[2] Then sharing rooms in St. James's Place.

[3] Some in Bassett, 92.

[4] An advance copy of J. G. *Maitland, 'Property and income tax, Schedule A and Schedule D' (1853); the first of two pamphlets; on the taxation of public fund dividends.

[5] Lord Archibald William Douglas, 1818–58; styled Lord Drumlanrig 1833–56, when he succ. as 7th marquess of Queensberry; Peelite M.P. Dumfriesshire 1847–56; comptroller of the household 1853–6.

[6] (Sir) Wellington Patrick Manvers Chetwynd-Talbot, 1817–98; brother of J. C.-Talbot; *Derby's private secretary 1852; sergeant at arms in the Lords from 1858, K.C.B. 1897.

[7] John Gorham *Maitland, 1818–63; barrister from 1843; secretary of the civil service commission until 1863; wrote on taxation, cp. two days earlier.

[8] (Sir) John Tilley, 1813–98; assistant secretary of the post office 1848, secretary 1864–80; K.C.B. 1880.

[9] Jules St. André, French politician; exiled 1849; allowed to return 1854; cp. *The Guardian*, 18 October 1854, 801.

[10] Spoke on income and house tax: *H* cxxiii. 1232.

[11] R. C. *Trench, *On the Study of Words* (1851).

12. 3 S. Adv[ent].

Ch. mg & aft. Walk with G & with C. Conv. with Willy: also with W.H. L[yttelton] & Mr Oxley[1] in Evg. Read Stephen on the Evangelical Succession.[2]

13. M.

I looked into Willy's work. conversed with C. on G.s wishes in the event of a change: came off with W.H.L. discussing his plans, & having Neville[3] in charge at 1½. Reached 6 C.G. at 9 and the House before 10. Staid[4] to the end[5] & saw Young on the attitude of parties & future possibilities. Read on the Restoration of Belief.[6]

14. T.

Wrote to R. Barker—C.G.—Sir F. Doyle—Rn. G. Saw Ld Abn. on the possible crisis—Bonham—Herbert—J.N.G.—Jocelyn—Ld J. Russell—Goulburn. Railway Comm. 2½–3½.[7] Dined with the Wortleys. H of C. 3¾–7 and 9–1.[8]

15. Wed.

Wrote to J. Griffiths—C.G.[9]—Mr Bogue[10]—Rev W. Hall—C. Wood—Tufnell. I spent the afternoon 3–7 at the H. of C. with the Speaker—Patten—Young—Tufnell—Waldegrave—& on the Journals, trying to unravel the mystery of the question to be put.[11] I saw Bright afterwards. Dined at H. Fitzroy's where we sat until pretty late. My morning too was busy with Mr Hubbard & a visit to Lord Aberdeen before[12] he went to Woburn.[13] Read Oxf. Tutors' Report[14]—the new Reform Bill[15]—Badnall on Col. Church.[16]

[1] John Swaby Oxley, d. *ca.* 1893; ordained 1842, curate of Leeds 1842–7, of Wilburton, Cambridgeshire, 1851–2, of Hagley 1852–5; vicar of Clent 1855–60, of Long Bennington 1860–78.

[2] Sir J. *Stephen, *Essays in ecclesiastical biography* (1849), ii. 65–202; reprinted from the *Edinburgh Review*, lxxxvi.

[3] i.e. N. G. *Lyttelton.

[4] Instead of 'stayed'.

[5] Budget deb.: *H* cxxiii. 1315.

[6] By I. Taylor (1852).

[7] He was on the select cttee. on railway bill amalgamation, which made five reports between December 1852 and May 1853, in *PP* 1852–3 xxxviii *passim.*

[8] Budget deb.: *H* cxxiii. 1435.

[9] Some in Bassett, 92.

[10] David Bogue, 1814–56; publisher and bookseller in Fleet street from 1843.

[11] *Disraeli hoped to gain Irish and radical support by procedural devices; cp. Blake, 341–3 and Bassett, 92–3.

[12] These six words instead of '& other current business &c.'

[13] Bedford held a whig-Peelite conference at Woburn, 15 to 17 December; cp. Conacher, 9.

[14] Advance copy of number 1, on university extension, of the Oxford Tutors' Association *Papers* (1853).

[15] *The New Reform Bill: leading clauses* (1852).

[16] Untraced pamphlet, probably by Hopkins Badnall, 1821–92; priest who wrote on South African churches.

16. Th.

Wrote to C.G. Saw Wood—Cardwell—Graham—Herbert—on the question-affair: also worked up the Exchequer Loan business & made notes for speaking.[1] Read Huc's Travels[2]—in evg. H. of C. $3\frac{3}{4}$–7 and 9–4. Rose at one & spoke till past 3 in answer to Disraeli.[3] I had also taken part in the very exciting debate early in the evening about putting the question. I went to the C[arlton] & wrote to Northcote after the House.

17.

Wrote to Ld Aberdeen—C.G.—H. Tayleur—Jas Watson—Rev. Mr Rawlinson. I conversed long with Young on the Parliamentary & ministerial crisis. Saw J.N.G.—Ld Norreys—Mr Harcourt—Ld Jocelyn—Jas Wortley—J.E. Denison—J.D. Cook—Geo Smythe—Col. Peel—Sir F. Lewis. Dined with the Wortley's. I had but two hours sleep. My nervous system was too powerfully acted upon by the scene of last night. A recollection of having mismanaged a material point (by omission) came into my head when I was half awake between 7 & 8 & utterly prevented my getting more rest. Broadway Church at 6 P.M.

18, Sat.

Marg. Chapel 5 P.M. Wrote to Mr Archer—C.G.[4]—Rev. Mr Burgon. Wrote a Memorandum on the *situation* & read it to Ld Abn. at a conversation in the aftn. Saw Jocelyn—Young—Bonham—R. Phillimore. Saw, with Herbert, Mr J.D. Cook & Mr Venables.[5] Dined at Herbert's where we were except Ld Abn. & C[annin]g the same party as in the last interregnum—but much better agreed.[6] Walk home & long conv. with Cardwell. Arranged my letters.

The exigencies of the present crisis cannot be met by the formation either of a Government representing simply the Liberal party, or of one representing simply the Conservative party.

The Liberal party is perhaps not prepared to take office without the friends of Sir Robert Peel: they are not ready to take office as members of the Liberal party: and if they were they would be encountered by an Opposition numerically too strong for them in the present Parliament and one which they could not weaken by a Dissolution.

Of the Conservative party a portion at least & a considerable portion will adhere to the outgoing Ministers, and those who may be willing to pursue a different course, however useful and needful for the support of the government now to be formed, cannot possibly form its sole support.

[1] Add MS 44652, f. 179.

[2] E. V. Huc, *Travels in Tartary, Thibet, and China, during the years 1844–5–6*, 2v. (1852).

[3] The end of the budget deb.; Gladstone intervened after *Disraeli's concluding speech with an unexpected but, as entries above show, carefully prepared attack: *H* cxxiii. 1523, 1666. Full text of main speech, which felled govt., in Bassett, *Speeches*, 155.

[4] In Bassett, 94.

[5] George Stovin *Venables, 1810–88; barrister, journalist and colleague of J. D. *Cook.

[6] See Conacher, 7, 13–14 and 26 Feb. 52.

The only remaining alternative would therefore seem to be a mixed Government.

The formation of a mixed Government can only be warrantable or auspicious when its members have the most thorough confidence in the honour, integrity, and fidelity of each other: when they are agreed in principle upon all the great questions of public policy immediately emergent: and lastly when a great and palpable exigency of State calls for such a formation.

Such an exigency exists at the present moment, and this not only with respect to contingencies which may happen in connection with our foreign affairs: but more visibly and immediately with regard to a subject on which the public mind is always accessible, ready, and receptive; with reference namely to finance.

The law under which near six millions of the public revenue is levied will expire on the 5th of April.

This large amount of direct taxation, of the most direct of all direct taxation, has hitherto from 1799 to 1815 and from 1842 to 1852 been levied equally from all classes of incomes.

There has been considerable revulsion in the mind of a portion of the public & that not a small one against the principle of equal levy.

Stimulated by the public journals, this revulsion has hitherto been borne down only by the firm union and combination, continued for half a century, of political authorities: all persons who have been responsible for the Government of the country having, whether on the same or on differing grounds, agreed in charging the tax equally on all incomes.

But now an Executive Government has promulgated the principle that a distinction is to be drawn between realised and precarious incomes . . .[1]

This amounts to a proclamation to all classes that their relative position is to be changed:[2] an invitation to them to enter into conflict upon the terms of that change:[2] an assurance from the Executive Government to a large part of them that they are *unjustly* taxed at the present moment and a distinct encouragement to resist the continuance of such taxation.

A view of the question itself & the state of parties at once suggests, that by this course the Income Tax is placed in jeopardy, and the whole financial system & public credit along with it.

There is therefore a resistless call for a vigorous and united effort to settle and secure the finances of the country.

All the strength that can be brought to the task may prove inadequate; none of it can be superfluous.

And further, is it not in the most temperate portions of both the Conservative and the Liberal parties, that support for such an effort is chiefly to be sought?

Thus then the third condition of a mixed government is realised. As to the two former I assume and I thoroughly believe in their existence.

By a mixed Government I mean something different from a fusion of parties. A mixed Government may honourably be formed, but a fusion of parties could not, with a reserve upon political questions more remotely impending, such as that upon Parliamentary Reform: a reserve to this extent, that upon all the particulars and details of such a measure, which must in reality determine its sense and spirit, every man will retain an entire freedom.

It will require the earliest and most serious consideration what course a new Government should pursue with respect to a differentiated Income Tax.

[1] Rest of para. omitted. [2] 'and' deleted.

That which has been bequeathed to them as an abstraction they must either reduce to form, or, at the proper moment, deliberately and definitively reject.

The question in its new position is too large for merely departmental consideration & the responsibility of a single Minister even *with* the Head of the Government.

Might not a Committee of Cabinet be appointed to examine it thoroughly:[1] to consider whether a plan can be devised, consistent with the public faith and sufficiently adjusted in details to have a reasonable chance of passing; and to recommend it to the Cabinet if the result be affirmation; with the fullest understanding however that, if no such plan can be devised, the whole Cabinet will unitedly resist all attempts from whatever quarter to differentiate the Income Tax and will stand or fall upon the fate of a strenuous endeavour to make full provision upon some other basis for the wants of the Exchequer. That basis will probably be found to include of necessity an equally rated Income Tax. But it is needless now to enter upon the question by what arrangements the difficulties in the way of such a measure may be best mitigated and removed.[2]

19. 4 S. Adv[ent].

Marg. Chapel 11 A.M. & H.C.—Chap[el] Royal aft. Ms. of 41 aloud. Dined w. Herberts. Saw Herbert—Newcastle—Arthur Gordon—Goulburn—J. Wortley. Read Manning's Lect[3]—Dill on Ireland[4]—Col. Ch. Bill Proceedings.[5]

20. M.

Wrote to Bp of Sydney—R. Cockerell[6]

C.G.[7]	T.H. Baylis
J.D. Cook	Rev D. Melvill
J. Clarke	J G Lonsdale
Jer. Spencer[8]	F.O. Morris.[9]
Robn G.	S.H. Northcote.

With Ld Abn. 12–2¼ on the J. Russell difficulty. H. of C. 4¼–6 (and H. of L.).[10] Saw Scotts—E. Monro—Young—Fitzroy—Newcastle—Herbert—Ld Stratford—Jocelyn. Dined with Herbert & Newcastle.

At the Carlton afterwards I found myself in a lion's den & was obliged to say something.[11] It all ended well—I found Forester[12] kind & reasonable in a detailed conversation I had with him.—Wrote an Article on the Budget for the Chronicle.[13]

[1] Cp. 29 Dec. 52.
[2] Initialled and dated this day; Add MS 44778, f. 66.
[3] H. E. *Manning, *The grounds of faith* (1852); four lectures.
[4] E. M. Dill, *The mystery solved: or, Ireland's miseries; the grand cause, and cure* (1852).
[5] Various annotated drafts in Add MS 44568.
[6] Probably C. R. *Cockrell, cp. 18 Feb. 45.
[7] In Bassett, 95.
[8] Unidentified.
[9] Francis Orpen *Morris, 1810–93; vicar of Driffield 1844–54; rector of Nunburnholme, Yorkshire from 1854. An anti-Darwinian and anti-vivisectionalist ornithologist.
[10] Ministerial statements of resignation in both Houses: *H* cxxiii. 1698, 1709.
[11] See Magnus, 110–1 and Bassett, 97.
[12] George Cecil Weld Forester, 1807–86; tory M.P. Wenlock 1828–74; minor office 1852, 1858–9; 3rd Baron Forester 1874; a strong protectionist and a Carlton club member.
[13] Printed in the *Morning Chronicle*, 21 December 1852; draft in Add MS 44685, f. 82.

21. T. St Thomas.

Wrote to C.G.[1]—J. Macgregor (and copy)[2]—J.N.G.—Lyttelton—Rev. R. Jones[3]—J.W. Campbell. These are anxious days: but sleep & appetite (save in mg) hold. Saw Northcote—Goulburn—E. Bruce—Ld Palmerston. Ld Aberdeen's 12–2¼ on the formation of a Govt. Then I went to Ld P. to say he wd. call. From thence he came with a negative & we talked with S. H[erbert] on further proceedings. Dined with the Mahons. Went afterwards to S.Hs and discussed official arrangements. Read R. Phillimore's Preface to his Int. Law.[4]

22. Wed.

Wrote to R. Dalyell—C.G.[5]—J.W. Patten—Rn. G—R. Phillimore (2)[6]—S. Herbert—G.B. Mathew—F. Lawley (2). Read Thomas Ld Cromwell.[7] Saw Northcote—Phillimore—Young—Wortley—Panizzi. At Lord Aberdeen's on the formation of a Govt. 12–3½.[8] Dined with Herbert; Ld Abn. came in with good news; we remained (without him) discussing offices & persons until 2 in the morning.—Wrote Memm.[9]

23. Th.

Wrote to D. of Buckingham and copy[10]—C.G.[11]—J. Litton[12]—Provost of Oriel and copy—H. Butler Johnstone[13] and copy—Dr Worthington—Lord Chandos.

This day I had an interview with Messrs. Travers & Crawford[14] about Customs' Reform in the City of London: in the capacity of C[hancellor of the] E[xchequer] designate.[15]

Saw Phillimore & Northcote—J. Young—Bonham. Went to Herberts at 12½. Heard the tidings of Palmerston's accession & Ld J.R's yielding.[16] Ld J. came to us & we discussed a number of offices & persons. Broke up before 4. I went with Graham to C[arlton] Gardens when he called on Lord P. I fol-

[1] In Bassett, 95.
[2] In Add MS 44373, f. 127.
[3] Perhaps Robert *Jones, 1810–79; vicar of All Saints, Rotherhithe, from 1841; Welsh tutor to Lucien Bonaparte; ed. Welsh documents.
[4] R. J. *Phillimore, *Commentaries upon international law*, 4v. (1854–61).
[5] In Bassett, 96.
[6] Published by Phillimore in *The Guardian.*
[7] Probably *The true chronicle historie of the whole life and death of Thomas Lord *Cromwell . . . by W.S.* (1602).
[8] After this talk, *Aberdeen went to Windsor, and suggested that Gladstone should go either to the exchequer or the colonial office. According to *Albert, the crown tipped the balance in favour of the former; cp. *LQV* 1 series, ii. 512, and Bassett, 96–7.
[9] On the Common's leadership, Add MS 44777, f. 341; cp. Conacher, 19.
[10] Add MS 44373, f. 129; on the Carlton club incident.
[11] In Bassett, 97.
[12] Probably John Litton, law agent.
[13] Henry Butler Johnstone, on the Carlton club affair: cp. Add MS 44373, f. 139.
[14] John Ingham Travers, of Joseph Travers and son, wholesale grocers in St. Swithin's Lane; Crawford, Colvin & Co, East India merchants.
[15] This sentence on a later page (72) by itself, with a cross-reference heading: 'Note to p. 67.'
[16] *Palmerston took the home, *Russell the foreign office.

lowed in a few minutes—to congratulate. Dined at Ld Stratford's: conversed on politics with him, & announced the new Govt.

24. Fr.

Wrote to Ld Chandos—C.A. Wood—T. Cubitt[1]—C.G.[2]—Sir J. Young—Provost of Oriel—Mr Haddan. Saw Northcote—F. Lawley—R. Phillimore—Bonham—Jno Young—H. Butler Johnstone—Stuart Knox[3]—E. Cardwell. At 12 a note summoned me to Herbert's suddenly—I went and found another *hitch.* Ld Abn. came with his ultimatum[4] to which we adhered. We broke up at half past three: doubtful as to the result. Met again at 5½ (Argyll House). Ld J. had given in. We went through the minor offices. I left at 7¾, went home dined packed & came off by the Mail at 8.45.—Saw Sir R. Peel—and Mr Kane Income Tax Commissioner.[5]

25. Sat. Xmas Day.

Chester 5 A.M. Hawarden 6¼. C. & Willy had actually slept in Chester & met me. It blew a hurricane. Bed till 10½. Church & H.C. 11–2. Evg 7. Wrote to Vice Chancr. Oxford—T. Gladstone—Earl of Aberdeen[6]—E. Coleridge—Aunt J.

It was a great treat on this of all days to find myself by force with my wife & children. I found Lena the very picture of health & much come on in intelligence. Her habit of order is something strange. She had moved a chair to look at some things. We all left the room and left her in pitch dark. She began to cry loudly. When we returned and asked the cause she said amidst her tears 'I can't get this chair put back'.—To this I must append one of Mary a few days ago at Hagley. 'Mary do you love your Cousin Winny[7] very much?' 'Not very much papa for she is not always good'. 'Do you love *May*[8] much?' 'Yes, very much; she is very good'. Then after reflection 'Papa I think Winny should be put in the fire, & then May & I could play together very nicely'. 'In what fire, Mary?' 'In the fire under the Church papa; you know there's a fire under the Church for naughty children'.

My day was short: for I could not sleep in the RR but had time for thought.

26. S. after Xm[as].

Church 11–1¼ (& H.C.): and 6.30. Wrote to Mr Woodward—R. Phillimore.

[1] Thomas *Cubitt, 1785–1855, brother of William*; made fortune out of construction work in London, including east front of Buckingham palace.

[2] Bassett, 99.

[3] William Stuart Knox, 1826–1900; 2nd son of 2nd earl of Ranfurly; tory M.P. Dungannon 1851–74; household office 1852–3. On the Carlton club incident, cp. Add MS 44373, f, 145.

[4] On the distribution of offices between whigs and Peelites, see Conacher, 22 and Bassett, 100.

[5] Edward Cane, a special commissioner of the property tax.

[6] Cp. Conacher, 25.

[7] Nickname for Lavinia Lyttelton.

[8] i.e. Mary Lyttelton.

Read Newland on Tractarianism.[1] At night I lay down a while & rose to read.

27. M.

Off at 3.40. Train delayed by flood & hurricane. I reached No 6 at 1. Went to see Ld Chandos & took him to Herberts. Saw Herbert—Graham—Young—F. Lawley. Attended the H. of Lords 5–7.[2] Dined at Herbert's. Wrote to Archd. Denison—C.G.—Rev. W.E. Buckley—Robn. G—Archd. Sandford—Sir C. Wood—Sir C. Trevelyan—Mrs Wadd—Rev. R. Greswell. Again during my absence this course of true love has not run smooth.[3]

28. T.

Wrote to Prov. Oriel—C.G.—Sir W. Heathcote (& copy)[4]—Rev. W. Brock[5]—Rev. H. M'Kenzie—W.F. Larkins—J. Wilson Patten—Sir A. Spearman[6]—R. Lowe—Rev. J.L. Ross—A. Oswald—J. Macgregor MP.—Geo. Moffatt MP.[7] Saw F. Lawley (& began work)[8]—Earl of Aberdeen—J. Young—Ld A. Hervey—Rob. Lowe—R. Phillimore (2)—E. Granville Vernon[9]—H. Fitzroy—Mr Dugdale—Ld Drumlanrig. $1\frac{1}{2}$–$6\frac{1}{2}$. Went to Windsor & kissed hands on receiving the seals of office. Saw Ld J. Russell, Graham, & Ld Abn. respecting the Financial Secretaryship.[10] Applied to Ld Lansdowne & Ld Granville about the Income Tax: & had a good deal of conversation about it with them, Ld J. Russell, & C. Wood. I got a good evening of work.

29. Wed.

Wrote to G.B. Mathew—C.G.—W.B. Hughes—J.N.G—G.L. Conyngham—Ld Aberdeen—M.F. Tupper—Rev. J.H. Gray—Rev. D. Robertson—Mrs Fellowes—Rev. R. Greswell. Saw Mr J. Wood—Sir C. Trevelyan—Ld De Tabley—F.R. Bonham—Ld Hardinge—R. Lowe. I had a long conversation with Canning on the question of his accepting office.[11] Went over the Downing St House.[12] Cabinet dinner at Ld Aberdeen's. It went off very well. I got a Committee of Cabinet appointed on the I. Tax.[13]

[1] H. G. *Newland, *South church union lectures* (1852); four lectures on tractarianism.

[2] Statement by *Aberdeen: *H* cxxiii. 1721.

[3] Further rows about minor offices.

[4] Fragment in Conacher, 47–8.

[5] William Brock, 1805–?1875; rector of Bishop's Waltham from 1833.

[6] Sir Alexander Young Spearman, 1793–1874; assistant secretary to treasury 1836–1840; controller of national debt office 1850–73; cr. bart. 1840.

[7] George Moffatt, 1810–78; tea merchant and iron dealer; liberal M.P. Dartmouth 1845–52, Ashburton 1852–9, Honiton 1860–5, Southampton 1865–8.

[8] F. C. Lawley became his private secretary; cp. 10 Jan. 47.

[9] Granville Edward Harcourt Vernon, 1816–61; *Lincoln's private secretary 1845–6; Peelite M.P. Newark 1852–7.

[10] They appointed James *Wilson on 5 January 1853.

[11] He became postmaster-general outside the cabinet.

[12] No. 12; no. 11 was then a dummy door. For the dispute with *Disraeli about the valuation of the furniture, cp. Buckle, iii. 476–80.

[13] Cp. Argyll, 385–6.

And so passed my birthday till past midnight. Then too a vague curiosity misled me & gave me more matter for repentant concern. The year which closes on me closes in one spiritual respect darkly: I have made no progress against the besetting sin often mentioned: & I have often too failed in the courage such as it is needed for self-discipline. Yet I trust my ultimate aim has not been wholly corrupt: & in some other matters my life might seem less unhopeful; but I commend it only to the all-embracing mercy of God in Christ & beseech Him to look on me in Him & not as I am clad in my own works or deservings.

30. Th. X

Wrote to Ld Monteagle—Mrs Davenport—Sir J. Graham—Sir R. Inglis—B. Price (2)—T.G.—Rev Mr Browne—Rn. G—Sir F. Smith—G. & Co[1]—C.G.—Canning. Saw Mr Woollcombe—Phillimore—Sir A. Spearman—Lord Aberdeen—Mr Arbuthnot[2]—Mr Temple—Sir C. Trevelyan—Lord St German's—Duke of Newcastle. Dined at Lord J. Russell's—a semi-Cabinet, with ladies. In evg I had a conv. & was guilty of weakness wh shd. be recorded here: nor can I truly say mere weakness [R]. 'O let not my heart be inclined to any evil thing'.[3] Certainly these cases are most singular exhibitions of human nature: poor human nature.

31. Fr.

Wrote to Capt Scott[4]—Mr Laing—Northcote—Dr Hook—C.G.—Ph. Pusey—Jane Tyler—Panizzi—J.P. Larkins—R. Phillimore—Mr Anstey—Mr A. Hayward—Rev. E.S. Ffoulkes—Mr Lane Fox[5]—Canon Tevor—Mr G.C. Glyn—Dr Saunders—Mr D. Gladstone—Lord J. Russell—Rev. T. James—Mr Hubbard—Dean of Ferns. Saw Mr Wood & Mr Pressly[6] for two hours—Sir T. Fremantle one—Sir C. Trevelyan one—F.R. Bonham—Mr Hayter—F. Charteris—Mr Elliot. Read Dean Newland—Mr Hubbard on I.T. in MS.[7] Dined with Norreys—went to Lady Granville's afterwards. Almost all the conversation was (for me) Income Tax.

[1] 'Ld. Monteagle' here deleted.

[2] George *Arbuthnot, 1802–65; secretary in the treasury 1823–46, to chancellor 1846–50; advisor on currency questions.

[3] Paraphrase of Psalm cxli. 4.

[4] See 22 Jan. 53.

[5] See 4 Jan. 33. He was also tory M.P. Beverley 1840–1, 1847–52, and Ipswich 1842–7.

[6] (Sir) Charles Pressly, 1794–1880; secretary to consolidated stamp and tax board 1833; commissioner of excise 1849, deputy chairman inland revenue 1855, chairman 1856–63; K.C.B. 1866.

[7] J. G. *Hubbard, 'Reform or reject the income tax. Objections to a reform of the income tax considered, in two letters to *The Times*, with additional notes' (1853); the first letter was printed in *The Times*, 8 January 1853.

Saturday Jan One 1853. (*London–Hawarden*)
Quod felix faustumque sit.[1]

Wrote to Earl of Aberdeen—T.G.—Dr Hawtrey—Capt. Huish—Rev. Mr Greswell—Ld St Germans—Sir W. Farquhar—Scotts—Rev. Mr Burkitt—Hayter[2]—J.N.G.—Ld. A. Hervey—Cardwell—and minutes for letters. Read Newland's Lectures[3]—Weekes on Art.[4] Saw R. Phillimore—Bonham—Sir F. Smith—Mr Cox[5]—Mr Stephenson[6]—Mr Crafer—Sir C. Trevelyan. 2½–3¾ presided at the Meeting of the Commissioners of the National Debt.[7] Past four, came home to dine and order packing: then came off by the Express at 5. Only reached Chester at 11 Hawarden at 11¾: all well thank God: unworthy that I am to find them so.

2. 2 S. [*after*] *Xmas*

Church with Holy C. mg: again in evg. Conv. with Willy on 'redeeming the time'. Read Newland—Chr. Remembrancer on Convocation—& on Bunsen (part).[8] Walk with C. By order from Phillimore wrote an Address to be used at Oxford in case of a contest. I made it direct to Convocation.[9] Wrote to Lyttelton—Mr Haddan—Sir W.R. Farquhar.

3. M.

Wrote to F. Lawley—W. Monsell—Breakenridge—Jas Wilson—Rev. Mr Cosserat—Sir A. Gordon[10]—E. Macdonnell—D. of Argyll—G.A. Jamieson[11]—H.Readett—Mr Hubbard—Smith & Co—W.Milner M.P.[12]—R. Phillimore—& minutes. Worked on papers: & especially on a paper by way of prolusion about the Income Tax.[13] A contest at Oxford more confidently announced today. Dinner party in evg; convn with W. Egerton on Income Tax. Church 8½ a.m.

[1] Cp. 19 Nov. 49.

[2] (Sir) William Goodenough Hayter, 1792–1878; whig M.P. for Wells 1837–65; financial secretary to the treasury 1849–50, whig whip 1850–8; bart. 1858.

[3] Cp. 26 Dec. 52.

[4] H. Weekes, 'The prize treatise on the fine arts section of the great exhibition of 1851' (1851).

[5] Probably C. T. Cox.

[6] Henry Frederick Stephenson 1789?–1858; commisioner of inland revenue from 1849.

[7] They met in Old Jewry.

[8] *Christian Remembrancer* xxv. 140, 213 (January 1853).

[9] Not found; apparently unpublished, despite the contest; Dudley Perceval (cp. 3 Apr. 45) stood as a protestant, claiming that Gladstone had ceased to be an anglican communicant; the Gladstone cttee. denied this and other charges.

[10] Declining Sir A. D. Duff-Gordon's offer to be his private secretary; copy in Add MS 44528, f. 75.

[11] Edinburgh wine merchant.

[12] (Sir) William Mordaunt Edward Milner, 1820–67; liberal M.P. York 1848–57; 5th bart. 1855. Copy in Add MS 44528, f. 75.

[13] Add MS 44741, ff. 1–32; cp. Conacher, 61–2.

4. T.

Wrote to Mr Arbuthnot—Rev. E. Muckleston[1]—W.C. James—Ld Chandos—D of Newcastle—W.R. Farquhar—Rev. R. Greswell—Mr Geo. Coode—Mr Goulburn—Rev. Mr Berkeley[2]—F. Lawley—Bp of Salisbury—H. Drummond—Mr W. Rowntree[3] and minutes. Church 8½ a.m. Pursued further & corrected my paper on I.Tax. Again on the subject with Egerton. Dinner party in evg. Walk (short) with C. Read[4] Income Tax Committee's Report[5]—Worked on Canterbury Association papers.[6]

5. Wed.

Ch 8½ a.m. Wrote to Earl of Aberdeen—Mr Greswell—Duke of Argyll—Mrs Ley—Ld Lyttelton—Mr Portal M.P.[7]—Sir A. Spearman—F. Lawley (2)—Archd. Denison—C.B. Chadwell—W.R. Farquhar—Rev. G. Rawlinson[8]—R. Phillimore—T.G. and minutes.[9] Walk with C. Dinner party in evg: and singing in evg. Reperused & dispatched my paper on the Income Tax. Read Babbage on Inc. Tax.[10]

In the evg I heard by telegraph the days poll. Gladstone 171 This is very
Perceval 170
unfavourable & though the numbers are small makes me think it rather likely that I shall be defeated. Unless there is a rally tomorrow I shall look upon that issue as nearly certain. And if so, it will be on political not religious grounds: witness my election in summer. I doubt if this will be a wise act on the part of the University: but it may improve my hope of rendering any poor service in my power to the Church generally. Whatever God shall ordain in it I am perfectly content: though I never can forget my anxiety not to lose the battle in 1847.

6. Th Epiph.

& dearest C.s birthday: a worried one, but such is the wholesome law of life. Church 11 a.m. Attended the Rent dinner 2–4 and spoke on Stephen's behalf, who was off to Oxford. The children wrote charming letters to C. Dinner party in evg: and music afterwards wh helped us on. In the morning my letters led me to determine on going off: but just in time came a

[1] Edward Muckleston, 1820–?; Worcester, Oxford; vicar of Ford, Shropshire 1852–60, rector of Haseley, Warwickshire, 1865.

[2] George Campion Berkeley, b. 1820; Pembroke, Oxford; vicar of Southminster, Essex, from 1839. Copy in Add MS 44528, f. 76.

[3] Joseph Rowntree, merchant on chicory and coffee, cp. Add MS 44570, f. 118.

[4] 'on' here deleted.

[5] Cp. 25 Nov. 52n.

[6] *Canterbury papers*, 12 numbers (1850–52); information on the New Zealand settlement published by the Canterbury association.

[7] Melville Portal, 1819–1904; Christ Church; tory M.P. North Hampshire 1849–57; high sheriff of Hampshire 1863.

[8] George *Rawlinson, 1812–1902; fellow of Exeter, Oxford, 1840, *Camden professor of ancient history 1861–89; rector of All Hallows, Lombard street, from 1888; prolific editor and historian. Cp. Add MS 44282, ff. 209–375.

[9] PRO, T 29/550, f. 15.

[10] C. Babbage 'Thoughts on the principles of taxation', 3rd ed. (1852).

message from F. Lawley who soon appeared & went off again for Oxford with a missive of mine, a letter to Heathcote, for publication.[1]
Wrote to Mr G. Moffatt—Mr Greswell (2) one for publication R. Phillimore—Sir W. Heathcote (2) one for do.—Rev. G.C. Berkeley—F. Lawley—Miss Conway[2]—Mr G. Arbuthnot—and minutes.

7. Fr.

Wrote to Mr Hamilton Gray—G. & Co—
Rev. R. Greswell
H. Caswall
H. Lefroy Baker
Dr Pusey
J. Wilson Patten
Bar. Charles Dupin
A. Symonds[3]
H. Denison
Capt. Huish
F. Wegg Prosser
Rev. R. Burgess
Mr Blakesley
& minutes.

Walk with C. Dinner party in evening; & music afterwards. 11½–2. Saw Mr Barker, Mr Burnett, & Mr Griffiths: discussed the state of Stephen's affairs, now thank God materially improved, and made arrangements for devolving on them the *ordinary* conduct of the business. After midnight Henry [Glynne] arrived; with news of a majority. This pleased me more than I was aware it would: & all faces seemed brighter. Read Mill's Pol. Economy.[4] Prepared for departure.

8. Sat.

Off at 3.50 a.m. Reached C[arlton] G[ardens] before noon. Read Weekes's Prize Treatise;[5] French Treaty papers.[6] Wrote to Judge Coleridge—C.G.—G.W. Hayter[7] & minutes. Saw Phillimore & others—Arbuthnot—Trevelyan—Goulburn—F. Lawley. Dined with the Wortleys. Cabinet 2–5¼. After dinner 10–12 at Phillimore's on the Lempriere Correspondence.[8] Majority 87 today.

9. 1S. Epiph.

St And. (W[ells] St) in mg. with H.C.—Chapel Royal aftn. An Armstrong Sermon aloud at night. Wrote to Lord Chandos and copy[9]—C.G.—J. W.

[1] 'Oxford university election. Mr. Gladstone's cttee. room . . . 7 Jan. 1853'; correspondence with *Greswell and Heathcote; annotated copy in Add MS 44570, f. 83.
[2] Miss E. Conway, da. of J. (cp. 9 Aug. 25) requested a post for her brother, J.S.
[3] Perhaps Alfred Radford Symonds, 1815–83; missionary in India 1841–72, then a curate in London; wrote on missions and liturgy.
[4] J. S. *Mill, *Principles of political economy, with some of their applications to social philosophy*, 2v. (1848).
[5] Cp. 1 Jan. 53.
[6] Perhaps on the 1851 copyright treaty with France, *PP* 1852 li. 527.
[7] i.e. W. G. Hayter.
[8] 'Oxford university election. Dr. Lemprière's letter' (1853); correspondence about the announcement of Lord Chandos as an opponent to Gladstone when the former had already declined candidature.
[9] In Add MS 44373, f. 244.

Barker & Son[1]—Rev. Mr Richards—Draft for Committee (to Perceval Commee)[2] Read Maurice on Sabbath[3]—Scottish Magazine. Much conv. with Northcote. And 2½ hours with Heathcote, N., P., & others on the singular disclosures of Mr Perceval.

10. M.

Wrote to Lyttelton—R M Milnes—F.R. Bonham—M.F. Tupper—E. Cardwell—G. Denison—Ld Courtenay—C.G.—Mr Greswell—Rev. J.H. Gray—Dr Jacobson. Dined at Ld Aberdeens; diplomatic chiefly. Worked on Treasury papers[4] at night. Saw Heathcote—Northcote—Arbuthnot—Sir A. Spearman—Mr Moffatt—Ld St Germans—Phillimore—Dr Smyth. Looked for E.C[lifton]—& ascertained another E.C[ollins]s departure to Australia[R].

11. T.

Wrote to Geo. Denison—J. Swift—Rev. R. Greswell[5]—E. Cardwell—Rev. H. Hall[6]—Lyttelton—R. Phillimore—Rn G—S.H. Northcote—J. Hume—& minutes. Read Q.R. on Budget.[7] Saw Sir W. Heathcote—Mr Coleridge—Sir C. Trevelyan—Judge Roberts[8]—Ld Chandos—Canon Trevor—J.N.G.—E. Granville Vernon. C. came in evg with 4 children. Worked until late late on Treas. papers.

12. Wed.

Wrote to E. Cardwell—Robt. Gladstone—M'Cracken—Jas. Gladstone—T. Vardon[9]—D. of Newcastle—Ld J. Russell—Archd. Sinclair—Provost of Oriel—and . . . & minutes. Read Canada Cl[ergy] Res[erve] papers.—Q.R. on Museum.[10] Saw Ld Aberdeen—Cardwell—Hayter—Arbuthnot—Bank Deputation. Went into the City & saw Freshfield—Gurneys[11]—Ward the Surgeon[12] who bound up my he[el?].[13] Worked on Treas. papers—Off at 6.15 to Windsor & dined there. I had a long conv. with the Prince till past 11 about Finance & the Universities. Also with the Duke of Cambridge on Politics.

[1] Probably W. J. Barker & co., London brokers.
[2] See 2 Jan. 53 n.
[3] J. F. D. *Maurice, *Sermons on the sabbath day; on the character of the warrior; and on the interpretation of history* (1853).
[4] Cp. Add MS 44570, f. 137.
[5] In Lathbury, ii. 18.
[6] Henry Hall, 1813–78; student of Christ Church 1834–57; rector of Semley, Dorset, from 1856.
[7] *Croker on *Disraeli's budget, *Quarterly Review*, xcii. 236 (December 1852).
[8] Thomas Quellyn Roberts, sheriff of Chester 1853.
[9] Thomas Vardon, d. 1857; librarian to house of commons from 1831.
[10] *Quarterly Review*, xcii. 157 (December 1852); *Croker on the British Museum, the article following Gladstone's review of Montalembert.
[11] See Morley, i. 461.
[12] Thomas Ogier Ward; Queen's, Oxford; D. M. 1834; surgeon to the Kensington dispensary.
[13] An accident, cp. 22 Jan. 53.

13. Th.

Chapel in mg. Wrote to D. of Newcastle—Lord Chancellor—Sir T. Fremantle (2) and minutes. Went to London with Sir J. Graham—saw Freshfield—Arbuthnot—Coleridge—Trevelyan—Wood. Reviewed my letter to the Provost of Oriel: and sent it to R. Phillimore.[1] Cabinet 2½–5½. Returned to Windsor for dinner. Read Thomson on the Laws of Thought.[2] Evg. conv. chiefly with the P[rince], Ld Lansdowne, & Graham.

14. Fr.

Chapel mg. St George's aftn. Wrote to Rob. Phillimore—Lyttelton—Mr D. Gladstone—Rev. H. Hutton[3]—Sir C. Trevelyan—J. Wood—Rev. Mr Greswell—S. Herbert—Rev. Mr Warter—F. Lawley & minutes.—Rev. Mr Cholmeley[4]—J. Murray—Ld Canning—Dr Molesworth. Walk with C. to Eton—with Ld Lansdowne—& alone in aftn. Early dinner & play. Two pieces rather too nearly of the same character: very well acted: but the first rather below the mark in morals, & the second in taste.[5] Read Q.R. on Price's Candles Manufactory.[6]

15. Sat.

Chapel 9 AM. Wrote to Earl of Aberdeen—Rev. Mr Owen—Sir T. Fremantle—Ld Raglan—Lord J. Russell—Mr T. Cooper[7]—Mr Stephenson—Rn G—Mr Hallam—Sir A. Spearman—A. Michelangioli[8]—Provost of Oriel—Wm Forbes—Sir J. Forbes—minutes. Saw Sir C. Trevelyan—Arbuthnot—Stephenson—Wilbraham—Woodifield[9] & Messenger[10]—Crafer—Mr Hallam. Saw the new Armoury: left Windsor at 11.45. Read Weekes's Essay.[11] At night read D. of Argyll[12] & worked on Income Tax.[13]

16. 2 S. Epiph.

St Martins mg, & Holy Commn—Bedfordbury evg. MS. for Epiph. aloud at night. C. obliged to leave Church by a sudden faintness: saw Locock. Saw Sir W. James—Mr Grant. Wrote to Rev. Mr M'Kenzie—R. Phillimore—

[1] In reply to E. *Hawkins, 'Letter . . . upon the future representation of the university of Oxford' (1853).

[2] W. *Thomson, *An outline of the necessary laws of thought; a treatise on pure and applied logic*, 2nd ed., much enlarged (1849).

[3] Henry Hutton, 1808–63; curate of Lidlington, Bedfordshire, 1834–49; rector of St. Paul's, Covent Garden, from 1849.

[4] John Cholmeley, 1827–95; curate of Wainfleet St. Mary, Lincolnshire, 1852–9; rector of Carleton-Rode, Norfolk, from 1859.

[5] *The captain of the watch* by J. R. Planché, and *The windmill* by E. Morton; both farces.

[6] *Quarterly Review*, xcii. 1 (December 1852); on the *Special report by the directors to the proprietors of Price's patent candle company* (1852).

[7] Thomas Cooper, senior clerk of the general register office.

[8] Unidentified.

[9] Robert Denby Woodifield, inspector-general of imports and exports.

[10] John Alexander Messenger, clerk to Woodifield, later to the customs board.

[11] Cp. 1 Jan. 53.

[12] Memorandum on income tax, cp. Argyll, i. 386.

[13] Add MS 44741, f. 51.

Archdn. Harrison—Rev. E. Monro—Dean Fortescue[1]—Rev. A. Watson—Rev. H. Randolph[2]—minutes—Bishop of Oxford. Read Chr. Rem. on Domestic Worship[3]—Maurice on Sabbath &c (finished.)[4]—Newland's Lectures (finished).

17. M.

Wrote to[5] Bp of Exeter—J.D. Cook—Sir C. Trevelyan—S. Herbert—Rev. R. Greswell—Mr Smyth MP. minutes. Busy with C. about our house & on accounts. worked on Treasury papers. Cabinet 2½–4½ on Defences. Saw Phillimore—Heathcote—W. Tyler—Jas Wilson—Mr Wood—Mr Pressly—Bonham—Ld Granville—Sir W. Molesworth. Read Le Chevalier on Gold[6]—Ball on Income Tax.[7]

18. T.

John's birthday: may all good attend him. Wrote to Rev. H. Mackenzie—Mr J. Ball—Sir T. Fremantle—Mr Jas Wilson—S. Herbert—Robn. G.—Mr Hubbard—F.B. Portman—Rev Mr Shannon—G. Arbuthnot—Sir W. Molesworth—Rev. Dr Todd—Rev. Mr Lake and minutes. Saw Arbuthnot—G.C. Lewis—Mr Goulburn—Mr Pressly—the Museum Deputation[8]—Mr Hallam—Ld Wenlock—Kinnaird. Worked on Treas. papers. Read Heming on Income Tax[9]—Wrote on do.[10] Herbert dined: & we had much conversation.

19. Wed.

Wrote to Mr Hallam—Ld Overstone[11]—Sir A. Spearman—Sir W. Molesworth—Sir Jas Graham—Lord Talbot—Mr Greswell—Prov. of Oriel—J.D. Cook—Rev. Dr Jacobson—Rev. Mr Hardy—Rev. Dr Molesworth and minutes. Saw E. Cardwell—Mr Wilson—Mr Arbuthnot—Governor of the Bank[12]—E.L. Robertson. Dined with the Farquhars. A conclave on Canterbury NZ afterwards. Read Treasury & Custom's papers at night. Began work on books & effects with a view to removal: C. having yesterday let my house to the Vernons.

[1] E. B. K. Fortescue was dean of St. Ninian's college, Perth, an episcopalian establishment, and resigned January 1853.

[2] Herbert Randolph, 1808–87; vicar of Abbotsley, Huntingdon, 1839–49; incumbent of Holy Trinity, Melrose, 1849–55, curate of Pulham, Dorset, 1867–70, of Ringmore, Devon, 1872–4; edited works by Sir R. T. Wilson.

[3] *Christian Remembrancer* xxv. 29 (January 1853); on 'Household religion and worship'.

[4] Cp. 9 Jan. 53.

[5] One name here deleted, perhaps 'Revd. Mr. Caswall'.

[6] M. Chevalier, tr. D. F. Campbell, *Remarks on the production of the precious metals, and on the depreciation of gold* (1853).

[7] An MS by John Ball, M.P., whose opinion on it had been requested; summary in Add MS 44741, f. 52.

[8] Papers untraced.

[9] G. W. Hemming, 'A just income tax' (1852).

[10] Add MS 44741, f. 56.

[11] Samuel Jones *Loyd, 1796–1883; head of London and Westminster bank 1844; the Bank Act of 1844 was based on his principles; cr. Baron Overstone 1850; wrote much on money.

[12] T. Hankey, cp. 2 July 35 n.

20. Th.

Wrote to Judge Coleridge—W.H. Lyttelton—Sir F. Smith—Capt Lake—Sir W. Heathcote—Dr Jacobson—Sir C. Trevelyan—Mr Cowan—D. of Argyll—Rev. G.H. Forbes and minutes. Worked with Willy on his Latin Verses wh are creditable. Saw Mr Hallam—Lord John Russell (on Education &c.)—Mr Cox—Sir Jas Graham—Mr Merivale. Worked on my books &c. Cabinet $2\frac{1}{2}$–$5\frac{1}{2}$. Dinner party of 18: all of or from Oxford. The fight is really over: & the numbers are G . . . 1022
P . . . 898

21. Fr.

Wrote to Rev. E. Coleridge—V.C. of Oxford (2)—Dr Jacobson—Rev. Dr Pusey—Prov. of Oriel (2)—E. of Aberdeen—Principal of B.N.C.—Mr Hubbard—Tatham & Co—J.H. Parker—Ld J. Russell—Mr Disraeli [1]—Ld Henniker—Mrs Austin—J.N.G.—Le Chev. St André and minutes. Saw Mr Bowring—Mr Macgregor—Lord Aberdeen—the Esquire Bedell [2]—Mr Monsell—Mr Pressly—Lord Hardinge. Dined with the Jameses. Sat up as usual until not far from two busy upon Official papers & the like. Arranged my letters in some degree.

22. Sat.

Wrote to Mr Hallam—Mr Hodges [3]—Mr Wm. Brown—Mr J. Wood—Mr J. Lefevre—T.S. Gladstone—Scotts—Lady M. Ross—Sir J. Young—Mr Greswell—Rev. B. Wilson—Capt H Scott [4]—Sir T. Fremantle; and minutes. Worked on Treasury papers.[5] A little on house matters. Saw Sir C. Trevelyan—Mr Wilson—Ld St Germans. Went with C. to Mr Hodgson & found my leg damaged by Mr Ward's treatment. Fifteen to dinner: Treasury Bank Revenue Boards &c. with the Patriarch Mr Goulburn at the head. It seemed to go off well. Worked on Customs' Report.[6]

23. Sept[uagesim]a. S.

St James's mg(for short walk)—Titchfield St Evg—Armstrong aloud to family.[7] Wrote to Sir C. Trevelyan—Miss Weale—Rev. Mr Laurence [8]—

[1] The start of the correspondence on the chancellor's robe and the Downing street furniture, cp. Buckle, iii. 476 ff.

[2] Henry Forster, 1809?–57; New college; esquire bedel of divinity in Oxford. There were also esquire bedels of law and medicine and arts.

[3] Thomas Law Hodges, 1776–1857; liberal M.P. Kent 1830–2, west Kent 1832–41, 1847–52; cp. Add MS 44570, f. 160.

[4] Henry Young Darracott *Scott, 1822–83; instructor in royal engineers; built the Albert hall 1866; secretary to 1851 commissioners 1873–82.

[5] Draft on hop duties, Add MS 44570, f. 243.

[6] Cp. 12 Mar. 52n.

[7] Probably J. *Armstrong, *Sermons on the festivals* (1845).

[8] Robert French Laurence, 1807?–85; student of Christ Church, 1824–33; vicar of Chalgrove, Oxford, from 1831.

Mr Grueber.[1] Read Bp Glasgow's Serm.[2] Bp Salisbury's do[3]—Bp Exeter's Letter[4]—many more pamphlets or Sermons—La Mennais sur l'Indifférence.[5] Saw Mr Hubbard on Harrow Weald.[6]

24. M.

Wrote to Lord J. Russell

Robn G(2)	Lord Carlisle
Rev. H. Wall[7]	Lord Talbot
J. Husband	Sir J. Harington
G. Rawlinson	Wm Gladstone
Dr Jacobson	Lord Monteagle
Mr Lake	R. Phillimore
O.B. Cole Esq.	E. Cardwell
T.C. Anstey.	C.W. Wynn.

Education Committee 12¾–3. Saw Messrs. Lancaster & Shaw on the Wine Trade.[8] Dinner party & evening party at home. Too much standing damaged my leg. Conv. with Newcastle.

25. T.

Wrote to Prov. of Oriel—Robn. G.—Dr Jacobson—Lord R. Grosvenor—AHD Troyte—W. Beckett—W.R. Greg—Sir W. Molesworth—& minutes. Saw Chicory Deputation[9]—Ld Torrington[10]—F. Charteris—S. Herbert—Ld Overstone—Mr Leeman.[11] Dined with the Herberts alone—We talked Education minute.[12] Worked late on papers. Saw Mr Hodgson—my surgeon.

26. Wed.

Wrote to R. Williams—Rev. G.S. Robertson[13]—G.E. Vernon—Mr Goulburn

[1] Charles Stephen Grueber, 1815–94; curate of Westport, Somerset, 1844–50, of Hambridge, Somerset, 1850; vicar there from 1868; a leading ritualist.

[2] W. J. Trower, 'Defence of the city of God committed to His ministers' (1852); on Ps. xlviii. 12.

[3] E. *Denison, 'Difficulties in the church' (1853); preached in December 1852.

[4] H. *Phillpotts, 'A letter to the archdeacon of Totnes in answer to an address from the clergy of that archdeaconry on the necessity of episcopal ordination' (1852).

[5] H. F. R. de Lamennais, *Essai sur l'indifférence en matière de religion*, 4v. (1817–23).

[6] Cp. 19 June 46n.

[7] Henry Wall, 1810–73; fellow of Balliol, Oxford 1839–71; bursar 1844; *Wykeham professor of logic from 1849.

[8] Henry Lancaster, London wine merchant and Thomas George Shaw, London and Manchester wine merchant; cp. Add MS 44373, f. 204.

[9] Papers presented by it in Add MS 44571.

[10] Sir George Byng, 1812–84; 7th Viscount Torrington 1831; household office 1833–4, 1837–41, 1853, 1859–84; governed Ceylon 1847–50.

[11] Probably George Leeman, 1809–82; solicitor in York 1835; lord mayor of York 1853, 1860, 1870; chairman of north-eastern railway 1874–80; liberal M.P. York 1865–8, 1871–80.

[12] After discussion the tory minute of 12 June 1852 was cancelled by a minute of 2 April 1853, in *PP* 1852–3 lxxix. 490; for a printed draft with Gladstone's comments, cp. Add MS 44570, f. 263.

[13] George Samuel Robertson, 1825?–74; Exeter, Oxford; curate of Sywell, Northamptonshire, from 1850. Copy in Add MS 44528, f. 86.

—Mr Cox—Mrs Boulting[1]—Bp of Oxford—and minutes. Saw Sir C.E. Trevelyan—S. Herbert[2]—Read Sir C. Trevelyan's MS Book on the Permanent Civil Services & Public Accounts[3]—MacCulloch on Taxation.[4] Went to Oxford at 2.45. Dinner party of friends at Dr Jacobson's. Heard Sir F. Ouseley[5] on Piano Forte.

27. Th.

Ch.Ch. service 10 A.M. Wrote to Mr Hayter—F. Charteris—W.B. Hughes—Rev. Mr Zincke—Sir C. Trevelyan. Read MacCulloch. Went in a carriage with the Provost of Oriel to perform the round of visits. I lay up & he did the labour. It only took 1½ hour. Luncheon in Balliol Hall, a mixed party with[6] ladies: & a speech. Visited ChCh common room at 4¾. Dined at Oriel with the Provost. By much care my leg improved. Saw Provost of Oriel—Mr Greswell.

28. Fr.

ChCh service 10 a.m. Wrote to Archdeacon Clerke—Mr Goulburn—Lord John Russell—Rev. H. Surtees—Sir A. Spearman—Mrs Davenport—T.S. Gladstone—Mr Burnett—C.M. Lushington—C. Marriott—Sir C. Trevelyan —Overends—Bp of London—S. Gurney—Jas Atherton[7]—G.F. Bowen—Duke of Newcastle and minutes. Saw Mr E. Palmer[8]—Dr Cardwell—Dr Pusey—Mr Greswell—Mr Lake—Dr Jacobson—Vice Chancellor—F. Lawley. Walk and calls with C.—Dinner party at Dr Jacobson's & a brisk evening. Worked on Treasury papers.

29. Sat.

Wrote to Robn. G.—D. of Newcastle—Mr Arbuthnot—Sir C. Trevelyan (2)—Lord Torrington and minutes. Read MacCulloch on Taxation. Worked on Treasury papers. Breakfast in Exeter Bursary.[9] Dr Acland's afterwards. Off by the train at 12.15: after a very active & pleasant visit generally & a most hospitable entertainment by the Jacobsons. C. was as I expected much pleased with them. We reached Moor Park at half past four: and admired both drive & house (built by Leoni 1720) much.[10] Found the R. Grosvenors quiet: all the better: singing in evg.

[1] Unidentified. [2] 'W' here deleted.
[3] Not published; not seen in Trevelyan MSS when in Bodleian library.
[4] J. R. *McCulloch, *A treatise on the principles and practical influence of taxation and the funding system* (1845).
[5] Sir Frederick Arthur Gore *Ousely, 1825–89; 2nd bart. 1844; curate of St. Barnabas, Pimlico, 1849–51; professor of music at Oxford from 1855; composed from the age of eight.
[6] Instead of 'of'.
[7] James Atherton, of Manchester, in reply to Gladstone's queries on chicory: Add MS 44570, f. 302.
[8] Edward Palmer, 1824?–95; fellow of Balliol 1845–67, of Corpus 1870–8, vice president there 1877; professor of Latin literature 1870–8; archdeacon of Oxford from 1877.
[9] i.e. in Exeter college, in the Turl.
[10] The seat of Lord Robert *Grosvenor, to the SE of Rickmansworth, Hertfordshire.

30. Sexa[gesima] S.

Ch mg & aft. Music in evg. Conv. on Crystal Palace with our kind hosts. Read La Mennais—V[an] D[iemen's] L[and] Edn. papers.[1] Wrote to J. Masterman—J. Griffiths—D. of Newcastle—G. Bennet—Rev. Mr Haddan—M. Bernard—Sir W. Denison—and minutes.

31. M.

Wrote to S. Herbert—T.G.—Sir Eardley Wilmot—J.N.G.—Commr. 67th foot[2]—Dr Smyth—Rev. H. Le Baker—Bp of Oxford and minutes. Saw Mr Harrison—Sir C. Trevelyan—Ld Aberdeen—Mr Wilson—Mr Arbuthnot—Mr Brickwood *cum* Mr Barnes.[3] Dined at Mrs Talbot's. Saw E.C. afterwards: gave £1 [R]. Mr O[sborne] expected back in April. A residue less satisfactory. Came up to town at noon from Moor Park with Lord R. Grosvenor. Worked on Coinage and on Education Papers.

Tues. Feb. One 1853.

Wrote to Rev. J. Skinner—Sir C. Wood—J. Griffiths—Sir J. Young—Mr Wilson—G.C. Myers—Rev. Mr Daniell[4]—W.C. James—Rev. R. Swayne[5]—J. Freshfield—Mr W. Rigby—Bp of Oxford—F.R. Bonham—Lord J. Russell—and minutes. Saw Sir A. Spearman—C. Ross—Archd. Harrison—Mr Goulburn—Ld J. Russell. Dined at Granville's, to prick the Sheriffs.[6] Income Tax conv. with Herbert—D. of Argyll—also conv. with Graham—Molesworth. Worked on papers in evg. A most dense fog.

2. Purif[icatio]n. Wed.

Wrote to Sir W. Heathcote—Robn. G—M.F. Tupper—Canning—J. Griffiths—G. & Co—G. Burnett (2)—Ld Devon—Mr T. Baring—Rev. E. Monro—Rev. A.W. Haddan, and minutes. Saw Sir C. Trevelyan—Mr J. Wood—S. Herbert—Sir W. Herries.[7] Attended Audit Board (45 millions—112 signatures!)[8] Received Manchr. Educn. Deputation.[9] Wrote Minute on Estimates for Gross Revenue.[10] Dined with the S. Herberts. We discussed Defences. Occupied on arrangements for moving: body as well as mind.

[1] On its expansion, cp. *PP* 1852–3 lxii. 443.

[2] John Frederick Ewart, 1786–1854; ensign 1803; lt. colonel 1814; colonel of 67th foot from 1852.

[3] John Strettell Brickwood, secretary to the public works loan office and to the exchequer bill office for West Indies relief, and Henry Hickman Barnes, solicitor to those offices.

[4] Raymond Samuel Daniell, b. 1819?; Magdalen hall, Oxford; priest 1845; curate of Totteridge, then of St. Paul's Shadwell.

[5] Robert George Swayne, 1821?–ca. 1880; Wadham, Oxford; perpetual curate of Bussage, Wiltshire, 1852–9, of St. Edmund's, Salisbury, 1863–77; prebendary of Salisbury 1870–7, canon there 1877.

[6] Report in *The Times*, 3 February 1853, 4f.

[7] Sir William Lewis Herries, 1785–1857; br. of J. C.*; lost a leg in French campaign 1814; kt. 1826; chairman of board of commissioners for auditing public accounts.

[8] In Somerset House; commissioners for auditing public accounts were appointed from 1785.

[9] No papers found.

[10] Add MS 44636, f. 1.

3. Th.

Wrote to E. Cardwell—J. Wood—Rev. L.W. Owen[1]—J. Murray—R. Barker—R.G. Traill—Sir C. Trevelyan. This day we moved to our new abode in Downing Street: busy with arrangements attending the change. Saw Mr Finlaison[2]—Wilson—Sir T. Fremantle—Mr Crafer—Monsell. W.I. Loan meeting 2–3¼.[3] Cabinet to 5½. Read Ranke's Ferdinand I[4]—Sir C. Trevelyan on Consolidated Annuities.[5]

4. Fr.

Wrote to Overends—Ld Aberdeen—Ld Chamberlain—Rev. J.H. Gray—E. Cardwell—R. Barker—Sir C. Trevelyan—G. Grant—The Speaker & minutes. Saw Freshfield—Mr Hayter—Sir C. Trevelyan. Education Committee 1¼–3½.[6] Dined at Mrs Talbots. Worked (as usual) till between one & two in evg on Papers. Read Fergusson on Defences.[7]

5. Sat.

Wrote to Mr Freshfield—Rev. A. Whyte—Overends—T.G.—R. Barker—Rn. G.—G. Burnett—Mr Hoffmann[8]—Mr Stephenson—Sir J.E. Tennent—Mr Ingersoll[9]—Mr Masterman—E. Cardwell—Sir C. Trevelyan—Mr Pennington—& minutes. Saw Coachmaker's Deputn[10]—Hops Deputn.[11]—Ld Aberdeen—Mr Wickham.[12] Cabinet 2¾–6¼. A debate on reducing the force in the Pacific. Ld Abn. Granville Molesworth & I were for it. We failed.

6. Quinqua[gesima]. S.

Whitehall Chapel mg—ChCh Broadway Evg—Holy Commn. at the former. MS. on the Gospel aloud. Saw G. Hope—Walter James. Read Br.Quart. on Univ[ersity] Comm[issio]n—& on Convocation[13]—also divers Rel[igious] pamphlets & periodicals.

7. M.

Wrote to Rev. J.H. Gray—Mr Cowan—Mr Mozley—H. Fitzroy—Mr Jas

[1] Lewis Walsh Owen, 1813?–84; fellow of Balliol, Oxford, 1836–9; rector of Holy Trinity, Colchester, 1839–68, of Wadingham, Lincolnshire, 1868–70, of Wonston, Hampshire, from 1870.

[2] Alexander Glen Finlaison, 1806–92; clerk in national debt office 1823–51, actuary there 1851–75.

[3] Papers in Add MS 44571, f. 201.

[4] First published in the *Historisch-politische Zeitschrift* (1832).

[5] Untraced memorandum.

[6] From 4 January he was a member of the privy council cttee. on education.

[7] J. *Fergusson, 'The peril of Portsmouth; or, French fleets and English forts' (1852).

[8] Probably Henry Hoffman, merchant, of Broad Street Buildings.

[9] Joseph Randolph Ingersoll, United States ambassador in Britain 1853.

[10] Led by J. Masterman, M.P.; on the taxes of carriages, cp. *The Times*, 7 February 1853, 4f.; many papers in Add MS 44570.

[11] Led by H. Brand, M.P.; minute in Add MS 44571, f. 11.

[12] John Wickham, of Batcombe.

[13] *British Quarterly Review*, xvi. 289, 544 (November 1852).

Robertson—Rn. G—T.C.Anstey—John Wood—T.B. Horsfall—Ld A. Hervey —Wm. Bell[1]—& minutes. Saw Wine Duties Deputn[2]—Stamp Duties Depn.[3]—Bp of London & Mr Cotton—Mr Wood & Mr Pressly—Mr Hodges (Hops)—Mr AB Hope—Mr T. Baring—Bp of London 2° on Edn. minute. A party of 14 to dinner: our housewarming. Got 40 min. of walk & drive. Sat working till 2½—in consequence got no sleep till near 8. Read Book 1 of the Prelude.[4]

8. T.

Slept by C.s care into the forenoon. Wrote to Lord Aberdeen—Mr Leslie[5]—Sir J.E. Tennent—Mr Monsell—D. of Newcastle—Mrs Ramsay—Dean Ramsay—Rev. C. Marriott—Sir T. Fremantle—Mr G. Anson—Warden of Durham. Sir J. Graham 12–2 with his myrmidons on the Navy Estimates.[6] Then Cabinet to 5¼. Saw Mr Wilson—Sir C. Trevelyan—Fourteen to dinner: men. Afterwards I went to Lady John Russells: conv.[7] with the Brazilian Minister[8] there. Read on Gold & I. Tax.

9. Wed.

Whitehall Chapel 11–1. Wrote to Sir J. Patteson—Elgin—J.G. Hubbard—G. Moffat—Sir Jas Graham—Robn. G—Earl Beauchamp—M.F. Tupper—Sir J. Graham—Mr D. Milne—Rev Dr Beavan and minutes. Saw R. Phillimore—Bp of Quebec[9]—Mr Reynolds[10]—Mr Cardwell. 2½–4¾ at Home Office on Ordnance Estimates.[11] Read MacCulloch on Funding:[12] dined at home: worked till 1 on Treas. papers &c.—Wrote on Income Tax.

I here note that I shall not during this Lent, at any rate until the end attempt restraint in quantity of food.

10. Th.

Wrote to Sir J. Graham—Mr W. Brown—Ld Goderich[13]—Mr W. Cotton—

[1] Had sent statistics on family finance; Gladstone requested more: Add MS 44528, f. 91v.

[2] From the cttee. of the association for the reduction of wine duties; cp. *The Times*, 8 February 1853, 4f. and notes in Add MS 44741, f. 68.

[3] Cp. Add MS 44741, f. 71.

[4] By *Wordsworth, written 1799–1805, published 1850.

[5] Lewis James Leslie, coachmaker.

[6] Preparing for debate in *H* cxxiv. 311 (18 February 1853); see also *H* cxxiii. 997 (6 December 1852).

[7] Instead of 'saw'.

[8] Sergio Teixeira de Macedo, Brazilian ambassador in London from 1852.

[9] George Jehosophat *Mountain, 1789–1863; rector of Quebec 1817; suffragan bp. of Montreal 1836; bp. of Quebec from 1850.

[10] Henry Revell Reynolds, 1800–66; grands. of H.R.*; Trinity, Cambridge, 1818; barrister from 1826, joint solicitor to the treasury from 1852.

[11] Cp. PRO, T 29/550, f. 319.

[12] Cp. 26 Jan. 53.

[13] Lord George Frederick Samuel *Robinson, 1827–1909; styled Viscount Goderich 1833–59; as a youth a Christian socialist; liberal M.P. Huddersfield 1853–7, West Riding, Yorkshire, 1857–9; 2nd earl of Ripon and 3rd earl de Grey 1859; under-secretary at war office 1859, 1861–3, at India office 1861; secretary for war in the cabinet 1863–6, for India 1866; lord president 1869–73; cr. marquess 1871; became roman catholic 1873; governed India and provoked European hostility 1880–4; 1st lord of admiralty 1886; colonial secretary 1892–5; lord privy seal 1905–8. Cp. Add MSS 44286–7.

Ld Canning—Rn G.—Provost of Oriel—Mr Hubbard—D. of Newcastle—Mr J.B. Mozley—Sir T. Fremantle—C.A. Wood—S. Holme and minutes. Saw Sir C. Trevelyan—Mr Lichfield[1]—Mr Goulburn—H. Fitzroy—Sir J. Graham—S. Herbert—Mr Hayter—Ld Aberdeen. Read Bineau's Report[2]—MacCulloch on Funding—Worked on Educn. Schedule. H. of C. $3\frac{3}{4}$–$6\frac{1}{4}$. Took the oaths. Ld John [Russell] after his statement[3] asked Ld P[almerston] if it was right: he answered very good. Ld J. came & asked me the same: I gave the same answer.[4]

11. Fr.

Wrote to Sir J. Graham—Ld Canning—Rev. J.L. Ross—Mr G.E. Vernon—Ld Drumlanrig—Sir C. Wood—Rev. A. Hanbury—Duke of Argyll—Mr Litchfield—T.G.—J.N.G.—and minutes. Walk & a little shopping. Saw Mr Reynolds—Mr Cotton—Mr Wilson Sir C. Trevelyan—Bp of Oxford—Sir A. Spearman. Dined at Lady Wenlock's. Read Symons on Taxn.[5]—Duke of Buckingham's new work.[6]

12. Sat.

Wrote to Sir J. Graham—Lord Mayor[7]—Lord J. Russell—Robert Gladstone—Govr. of Bank—Rev. R. Greswell—Ld Canning—S.H. Northcote—Mr Roberts—Sir T. Fremantle (2)—Prov. of Oriel—Sir C. Trevelyan—Sir J. Buller[8]—Rev R.C. Trench—Mr Severn—Mr Senior—Rev. E. Monro—Mr Ewart—and minutes. Saw Mr Wilson—Ld Canning—Mr Herbert—Ld Goderich—S. Herbert & Ld Palmerston—Sir C. Trevelyan—Mr Leslie Foster.[9] Cabinet $2\frac{1}{2}$–5. Dined at Duke of Newcastle's. Latin lesson to Stephy—the first for months. Read Prov. of Oriel on Oxf. Election[10]—and other pamphlets. Gave 5/ to one, at night, to go home[R].

13. 1S.Lent.

Whitehall mg: Ch Ch aft: MS. of 44 aloud at night. Saw Cardwell—Wrote to Willy—Bp of Oxford. Read Cookesley's anti-Sellon pamphlet[11]—Mr

[1] Charles Litchfield, a senior treasury clerk.

[2] J. M. Bineau, 'Rapport fait au nom du comité de finances, sur le projet du budget rectifié des dépenses et des recettes de l'exercice 1848' (1848).

[3] 'after' here deleted.

[4] On public business: *H* cxxiv. 29.

[5] J. C. *Symons, 'A scheme of direct taxation for 1853' (1853).

[6] R. P. T. N. B. C. *Grenville, duke of Buckingham, *Memoirs of the court and cabinets of George III from original family documents*, 2v. (1853).

[7] Thomas Challis, 1794–1874; London skin broker; lord mayor 1852–3, his procession cancelled for Wellington's funeral; liberal M.P. Finsbury 1852–7.

[8] Sir John Buller Yarde-Buller, 1799–1871; tory M.P. South Devonshire 1835–58; cr. Baron Churston 1858.

[9] Perhaps of Foster and Braithwaite, city brokers.

[10] E. *Hawkins, 'Letter . . . upon the future representation of the university of Oxford' (1853).

[11] W. G. *Cookesley, 'A letter to the . . . abp. of Dublin, on the nature, government and tendency of Miss Sellon's establishment at Devonport . . . with the abp.'s reply' (1853).

Carter's too: what a contrast![1] Archd. Johnson on Convocation[2]—W. Palmer's Dissertations[3]—La Men[nais]. Made out my Education Schedule.[4]

14. M.

Wrote to E. of Beauchamp—Mr Vardon—Mr Oliveira—Mr T. Hankey—Mr T. Baring—Sir J. Duke[5]—Sir A. Spearman—Mr Hayter—& minutes. Saw Sir J.K. Shuttleworth—Mr Stafford—Sir J. Graham—Mr Greene MP—Sir J. Young—Ld A. Hervey—E. of Aberdeen—Mr Wilson—Sir C. Trevelyan—Mr Tupper—Mr Deedes[6] &c.—Mr Hayter—Mr Ross (U[pper] C[anada])[7] Also Govr. & Dep. G. Bank[8]—Mr Cotton—Mr Anderson[9]—Mr Wilson—Sir C. Trevelyan—on the Interest of Exchequer Bills. Dined at Mrs Talbot's. H of C. 4½–7¼. Brought in Metrop. Impr[ovement] Advances Res[olutio]n.[10] Read Bethune on Clergy Reserves[11]—Dyce on National Gallery.[12]

15. T.

Wrote to Ld Aberdeen—Attorney Gen.[13] D. of Newcastle—Mr Scholefield—Mr Lefevre—Solr. General[14]—V[ice] C[hancellor] Oxford—J. Wood—Ld A. Hervey—J.D. Coleridge—Robn. G and minutes. Seven to dinner. Saw Ld Canning—Ld A. Hervey—Sir A. Spearman—Col. Jebb[15]—Mr Hodgson—Sir C. Trevelyan—and Mr Glyn, also A. Kinnaird after the City hours were over—Mr Wood & Timm.[16] H. of C. 4¾–7½.[17] A few minutes' work today on putting my things in a little order: wh can only be done piecemeal. Read

[1] T. T. Carter, 'Objections to sisterhoods considered, in a letter to a parent' (1853).

[2] Untraced pamphlet by J. Evans Johnson, a colonial archdeacon.

[3] W. *Palmer, of Magdalen, *Dissertations on subjects relating to the 'Orthodox' or 'Eastern Catholic' communion* (1853).

[4] Add MS 44374, f. 57.

[5] Sir James Duke, 1792–1873; coal factor and insurance broker; kt. 1837, lord mayor of London 1848–9; whig M.P. Boston 1837–49, city of London 1849–75; cr. bart. 1849.

[6] William Deedes, 1796–1862; fellow of All Souls 1818–33; tory M.P. East Kent 1845–57, 1857–62.

[7] Probably G. Macleod Ross, rector of Drummondville, Quebec.

[8] i.e. J. G. *Hubbard.

[9] (Sir) William George Anderson 1804–97; assistant paymaster 1841; principal clerk in treasury 1854–65, auditor of duchy of Cornwall 1851–91; assistant comptroller and auditor of exchequer 1865–73; K.C.B. 1870.

[10] A technical resolution, switching payments from one fund to another: *H* cxxiv. 90.

[11] A. N. Bethune, 'The clergy reserve question in Canada' (1853).

[12] W. *Dyce, 'The national gallery its formation and management considered in a letter . . . to Prince *Albert' (1853).

[13] Sir Alexander James Edmund *Cockburn, 1802–80; liberal M.P. Southampton 1847–56; solicitor general 1850–1; kt. 1850; attorney general 1851–2, 1852–6; judge 1856; lord chief justice from 1874; presided at Tichborne trial 1873–4; 10th bart. 1874.

[14] (Sir) Richard *Bethell, 1800–1873; liberal M.P. Aylesbury 1851–59, Wolverhampton 1859–61; solicitor general 1853–56; kt. June 1853; attorney general 1856–8, 1859–61; lord chancellor and Baron Westbury 1861; acquitted defendants of *Essays and Reviews* 1864; resigned after house of commons censure 1864; renowned for sarcasm.

[15] (Sir) Joshua *Jebb, 1793–1863; served in Canada, lieutenant colonel 1847; administered sundry prisons from 1841, a Pentonville commissioner 1849; chairman of convict prisons from 1850; K.C.B. 1859.

[16] Joseph Timm, solicitor to the inland revenue board.

[17] *Drummond's Land Bill 1°: *H* cxxiv. 125.

Maitland on I.T.[1]—Dyce on Nat. Gall. (finished) Latin lesson to S. Saw Williams & gave 10/: I hope in some sense rescued[R].

16. Wed.

Wrote to Ld Clanricarde—Mr Wilson—Duke of Argyll (2)[2]—Sir A. Spearman—Ld J. Russell—Provost of Oriel—Ld Talbot—Mr Freshfield—Ld Emlyn—Archd. Harrison & minutes. Cabinet dinner at Ld Aberdeen's. Cabinet agreed to grant the I. Tax Committee if asked. Saw Mr Brown—Mr Wodehouse—Northcote—Mr Monsell—Lord J. Russell—Bp of Oxford Sir C. Trevelyan—Newcastle—the Chancellor—D. of Argyll—Ld Palmerston. Went to Court at one: when the Convocation Address was presented.[3] Saw the Prince afterwards: & had a few minutes with the pictures. Saw P. Lightfoot & got hold of means of evil wh after seeing I burned[R]. Latin lesson to my little S. Saw Univ. London Deputation.[4]

17. Th.

Wrote to Mr Jas Wilson—Mr Dyce—J.G. Maitland—Canning—J.B. Mozley—Rev. Jos Hilton[5]—Sir C. Wood—Rev. H. Churton—J. Kingsmill[6]—Sir F. Fremantle—Mr Hayter—Mr M'Culloch—Rev. T. Snow—and minutes. Began work on an Index of Subjects and progress.[7] Saw Northcote—Wilson—Bp of Cape Town—Ld Clanricarde—Archd. Sandford—Lord Advocate[8]—Sir W. Herries—Sir J. Graham—Sir C. Trevelyan with Monsell—Lawley—Chicory Deputation—Hop Deputation. H of C. 4½–7¼: agt. Frewen's motion.[9] Eight to dinner. Worked till past 2 a.m.

18. Fr.

Wrote to Scotts—J. Wood (2)[10]—Williams & Co—Earl Nelson—Baron Alderson[11]—Lord St Germans—E.A. Bowring—Sir W. Herries and minutes. Latin lesson to Stephy. Dined at Ld Stratford's. H of C. 4½–7¾ and 10¾–1¼.[12] Saw Sir A. Spearman—Mr Hayter—Ld Cowley—Northcote—Cardwell—

[1] J. G. *Maitland, 'Property and income tax. The present state of the question' (1853); his second pamphlet; cp. 8 Dec. 52.

[2] Written over another name.

[3] The address from the convocation of the clergy of the province of Canterbury; report in *The Times*, 17 February 1853, 3 f.

[4] No papers found.

[5] Probably Joseph Hilton, b.? 1791; Pembroke Cambridge, 1810; priest 1815, lived at Walton on the Hill, Lancashire from 1841. But see J. A. Venn, *Alumni Cantabrigienses*, 2nd series, iii. 378 and Add MS 44528, f. 98.

[6] Sir John Kingsmill, 1798–1859, a Dublin magistrate who was knighted 1830; cp. 7 Mar. 53.

[7] Not found.

[8] James *Moncrieff, lord advocate 1851–2, 1852–8, 1859–66; cp. 19 Apr. 28.

[9] C. H. Frewen's motion against hop duties: *H* cxxiv. 186.

[10] Copy in Add MS 44374, f. 43.

[11] Sir Edward Hall *Alderson, 1787–1857; judge of court of common pleas 1830, baron of exchequer from 1834.

[12] Deb. on relations with France: *H* cxxiv. 246.

Canning—Muntz—Brotherton.[1] Read Blackwood on I. Tax.[2] Yesterday I had 15 h[ours] work: today not much over 13.

19. Sat

Wrote to Messrs. Deacon & Co—W. Craig—Johnson Longden & Co—Northcote—Sir A. Spearman (2)—Mr Gilstrap—Sir C. Trevelyan—Mr J. Wood—Rev. Mr Ratclyffe—Rev. T. W. Barlow[3]—J.S. Buckingham—and minutes. Latin lesson to Stephy. Cabinet 2½–5. Dined at the Speakers. Saw Sir A. Spearman—Mr Greenwood[4]—Govr. of the Bank *cum* Sir A.S.—Cardwell—Mr Abbiss[5]—J.N.G. Wrote a long Memorandum on my providing resp. Exchequer Bills.[6] Also a Mem. of Plan of reduction for the 3 per Cents.[7] Read Remarks on For. Relations.[8]

20. 2.S.L[ent]

Whitehall mg. Chapel Royal aft.—MS of 43 aloud at night. Conv. with Stephy, whose intelligence grows well. Saw Herbert—W. James—Jas Wilson—G.C. Lewis. Read Pamphlets by Humphreys, Archd. Hoare, Walkey, C. Molyneux, Taylor[9]—Convoc. Report, & Twiss on Bp of Cape Town's claim.[10] Wrote to Archd. Harrison—E. of Aberdeen[11]—M.F. Tupper—and minutes. Today too I got a *walk*.

21. M.

Wrote to D. of Newcastle (3)—Sir C. Wood—Mr Freshfield—Robn. G (2)—Sir F. Fremantle—Canning—Sir Ch Fitzroy—H.S. Smith[12]—Dr Jacobson—Lord Cowley—& minutes. Latin lesson with Stephy. Saw Mr Alpass[13]—Mr M. Cross[14]—Sir C. Trevelyan & Mr Gardner—Mr J. Wood—Mr Dugdale—

[1] Joseph *Brotherton, 1783–1866; Manchester cotton manufacturer, radical M.P. Salford from 1832.

[2] *Blackwood's Edinburgh Magazine*, lxxiii. 246 (February 1853); on 'Income-Tax Reform'.

[3] Thomas Wotton Barlow, rector of Little Bowden from 1843.

[4] John Greenwood, 1800–71; assistant solicitor to the treasury 1851, solicitor from 1866.

[5] James Abbiss, 1812–82, London coffee and tea merchant, sheriff of London 1860–1.

[6] Add MS 44741, f. 76.

[7] Add MS 44741, f. 81.

[8] Possibly [W. Parry], 'Remarks on the present aspect of the Turkish question' (1853); a report of visits there in 1850 and 1851.

[9] E. R. Humphreys, 'The dangers and duties of the present time: being the substance to two lectures' (1853); C. J. *Hoare, 'A charge delivered to the clergy of Surrey' (1851); C. E. Walkey, 'One hundred queries for the consideration of the clergy and laity of the Church of England concerning the convocation' (1852); C. Molyneux, probably 'Is it expedient? or, the Sabbath question' (1852); perhaps E. E. L. Taylor, 'The Christian sanctuary in its relations to human interests and the divine glory' (1853).

[10] The start of R. *Gray's long dispute with J. W. Colenso on the former's appointment as African metropolitan bp. 1853.

[11] Attempting, and failing to get *Tupper a pension, cp. Hudson, **Tupper*, 151–2.

[12] Henry Stooks Smith, 1808–81, chief clerk of parliament office, house of lords, 1840–74.

[13] Thomas Alpass, translator of foreign books.

[14] Probably Maurice Cross, secretary to the commissioners of national education in Ireland.

S. Herbert—Ld D. Stuart[1]—Solr. Genl. R. Phillimore—Sir J. Young. H. of C. 5–7 and 9–1.[2] Read Senior's Thiers Journal (No 2).[3] Worked late on Treas. business.

22. T

Wrote to Ld St Germans—Mr J. Wood—Rev. Dr Richards—Overends—Govr. of Bank—M.F. Tupper—Coles Child & Co[4]—Sir C. Trevelyan (2) & minutes. Read Northcote on Oxford Election[5]—Kingdom on Railways.[6] saw Consol. Annuities Depn.—Soap Deputation.[7] Saw Sir C. Trevelyan—Mr Wilson—Masterman. H. of C. $3\frac{3}{4}$–$7\frac{1}{4}$ and 10–$1\frac{3}{4}$.[8] Worked on Treas. papers late.

23. Wed.

Wrote to Rev. E. Hawkins[9]—Thesiger—Ld St Germans—Overends—E.B. Denison—Mr J. Wood—F. Charteris—Mr Baines—Lord Clarendon & minutes. At H. of C. for Maynooth Division.[10] Chancellor's Cabinet Dinner. Countess Colloredo's party afterwards.[11] Saw Canning—Northcote—Monsell—Sir C. Trevelyan—F. Charteris—Granville (on Edn.)—Mr Muntz. Wrote Mem. on Income Tax[12]—Informn. questions on Ordnance Survey[13]—Packet. Instructions (began).[14] Latin lesson to Stephy.

A few minutes of private affairs: my stable has been much perturbed.

24. Th. St Matthias.

Wrote to Duke of Argyll—Canning—Baron Alderson—Earl of Aberdeen—Sir W. Clay—Sir W. Herries—Mr Ricardo—Sir C. Trevelyan—Mr J. Wood—Dean of Carlisle—Sir W. Temple—Archd. Thorp—S. Herbert—Dr Molesworth—Mrs Hibbert—and minutes. Walk as far as Christies, & a few minutes there. Saw Sir S. Northcote—Mr Wood—Mr Hodgson (Surgeon)—

[1] Lord Dudley Coutts *Stuart, 1803–54, 8th s. of 1st marquess of Bute; liberal M.P. Arundel 1830, 1831, 1833, 1835, Marylebone 1847–54; advocated Polish independence.

[2] Spoke on stamp duty: *H* cxxiv. 351.

[3] N. W. *Senior's conversations, published as *Conversations with M. Thiers, M. Guizot and other distinguished persons, during the Second Empire*, ed. M. C. M. Simpson, 2v. (1878).

[4] Child, Coles and co., coal merchants and warfingers with several wharfs on the Thames.

[5] S. H. *Northcote, 'A statement of fact connected with the election of . . . W. E. Gladstone . . . in 1847, and with his re-elections in 1852 and 1853.' (1853).

[6] W. Kingdom, 'Suggestions for improving the value of railway property and for the eventual liquidation of the national debt' (1850).

[7] On soap duties, from Manchester and Bradford, led by *Bright and *Cobden; cp. *The Times*, 23 February 1853, 8a, and *ibid*, 4 March 1853, 6a.

[8] Answered questions: *H* cxxiv, 403, 405.

[9] Copy in Add MS 44374, f. 69.

[10] Voted in 192:162 against motion to end the Maynooth grant.

[11] Marie Thérèse, b. 1818, da. of Alfred de Lebzeltern, m. 1841 Joseph François Jerome, prince Colloredo-Mannsfeld, Austrian ambassador in London.

[12] Several undated in Add MS 44572, f. 141.

[13] An inquiry into the appropriate scale for the ordnance survey; correspondence in *PP* 1854 xli. 189ff.

[14] PRO, T 29/550, f. 505, and see Add MS 44374, f. 63.

Mr Wilson—Mr Brickwood—Charteris. H. of C. $4\frac{1}{2}$–$6\frac{1}{2}$ and 11–$1\frac{1}{4}$. Voted in 234: 205.[1] Wrote draft Instructions for Packet Commission Inquiry. Saw divers.

25. Fr.

Wrote to Mr Wilson—W.W. Woollcombe[2]—T. Baring MP—Canon Trevor Jas Heywood—T.S. Gladstone—Rev. B. Price[3]—Rev. P.C. Claughton—Canning—Sir C. Trevelyan—Hon. F. Charteris—and minutes. Saw Sir C. Trevelyan—J.N.G.—H.J.G.—Cardwell—Charteris—Sir W. James *cum* Rev. Mr Randall[4]—Hastie.[5] Worked on Income Tax. H. of C. 5–$7\frac{3}{4}$ and $10\frac{3}{4}$–$11\frac{1}{2}$.[6] Latin lesson to Stephy. Sworn before the Lord Chancellor in his private room.[7] Went in evg. to see A.L[oader] who has migrated[R].[8] Read Hamilton on the Nat. Debt.[9]

26. Sat

St Martin's $11\frac{1}{2}$ a.m. for the baptism of my new Godson Wm. Talbot S. Wortley:[10] God bless him. Wrote to Sir F. Thesiger—Solr. General—Mr M'Kellar[11]—Canning (3)—T.M. Gladstone—A. Clark (N.Z.)[12]—Jas Watson—G.P.R. James—W. Ewart—and minutes.[13] Cabinet $2\frac{3}{4}$–$5\frac{1}{4}$. Malt Spirits Deputation. Post Horse Deputation.[14] Saw R. Phillimore—Ld A. Hervey—J. Griffiths—Govr. Bank—Sir C. Trevelyan—D. of Argyll—Ld Clarendon. Dined at the Palace. Lady Molesworths afterwards. Read M'Calmont on Packet Contracts, &c.[15]

27. 3.S.Lent

H.C. at St Martin's $8\frac{1}{2}$ a.m. Whitehall 11. Chapel Royal $5\frac{1}{2}$ P.M. MS of 41

[1] For relief of Jewish disabilities: *H* cxxiv. 622.
[2] William Wyatt Woollcombe, 1813?–86; fellow of Exeter, Oxford, 1834–54; sub-rector 1852; rector of Wootton, Northamptonshire, 1854–82.
[3] Bartholomew *Price, 1818–98; fellow of Pembroke, Oxford, 1844, master there from 1891; professor of natural philosophy from 1853; secretary to the *Clarendon press 1868–84.
[4] Probably Henry Goldney Randall, 1809?–81; fellow of St. John's, Oxford, 1834–41; perpetual curate of St. Peter, Bishopworth, 1853–65, vicar in Bristol 1865–77.
[5] Archibald Hastie, 1791–57; director of the East India docks and liberal M.P. Paisley from 1836, or Alexander Hastie, 1805–64; Glasgow merchant and liberal M.P. Glasgow 1847–54.
[6] Army estimates: *H* cxxiv. 670.
[7] To the exchequer court.
[8] i.e. moved house: see 2 Mar. 53.
[9] R. *Hamilton, *Inquiry concerning the rise and progress, redemption . . . and the management of the national debt* (1813); very influential attack on *Vansittart's use of the sinking fund.
[10] William Talbot Stuart-Wortley, 1853–63, 3rd s. of J. A.*
[11] Perhaps William George M'Kellar, London coal merchant.
[12] Archibald Clark, mayor of Auckland, New Zealand; cp. Add MS 44371, f. 222.
[13] Draft on hops, Add MS 44571, f. 209.
[14] A large deputation to request parity of taxation for coaches and railways; cp. *The Times*, 28 February 1853, 8c.
[15] R. MacCalmont, 'Some remarks on the contract packet system, and on ocean penny postage' (1851).

aloud at night. Read Farini's Letter[1]—Opinions on Convocation[2]—Wrote on St. Luke XI. 24–6. Walk with C. Visited Aunt J.

28. M.

Wrote to E. of Aberdeen—Mr Pressly—Mr Disraeli—Canning—H. Maitland—Mr W. Gladstone—H. Tayleur—Rev. H. M'Kenzie—Ld Granville—Ld R. Grosvenor—& minutes. Latin L[esson] with Stephy. Saw Sir C. Trevelyan—Mr Litchfield—Sir J. Graham—Ld A. Hervey—C. Wood. H. of C. 4¾–8 and 9–12.[3] Saw two and spoke: but ill[R]. Read Gibbon on I. Tax.[4]

Tuesday Mch. One 1853.

Wrote to Marq. d'Azeglio—J. Hirons[5]—Mr Gardner—Mr Pressly—E. of Aberdeen—Earl Talbot—Mr Panizzi—and minutes. H. of C. 4½–8 and 9–1¼. Spoke on Legacy & Probate Duties.[6] Saw Mr Wilson—Ld Canning—Mr Wood *cum* Mr Trevor. Worked on Income Tax.

2. Wed.

Wrote to Mr Panizzi—Lord J. Russell—Ld Lyttelton—Sir C. Wood—Bp Fredericton—Rev J.L. Ross—Rev Mr Rawlinson—Bp of Moray—Ld Stratford—Mr C. Trevor—Lt Govr Eyre. Deputn at 1½ on Indentures.[7] H of C. 12¼–1 on Mr Frewen.[8] Saw T.S. Gladstone—Sir T. Fremantle—Bp of Cape Town—Duke of Cambridge—E.H. Gladstone—Mr Gardner *cum* Mr Phillips. Attended the Levee.[9] Dined with the Jameses. At night worked on Income Tax & Probate Duties. Latin lesson to Stephen. Went to see A. Loader: a truly singular case[R].

3. Th.

Wrote to Bp of Brechin—Robn. G.—Ld Palmerston—C. Pressly—Ld A. Hervey—Sir W. Molesworth—and minutes. 11–12¼. Visited Nat. Gallery with W.C. James. Found Col. Thwaites[10]—also Mr Morris Moore. Saw Mr Hayter—Mr Wilson—Sir C. Trevelyan—Sir J. Young—Molesworth—Graham—Canning—Col. Mure[11]—Mr W. Brown—J.E. Denison—J.S. Wortley. H. of C. 4½–11¾. Spoke on Hume's sham motion: turned into a

[1] Perhaps P. Farini's *Letters* (1853), or an MS letter from L. C. Farini.
[2] 'Convocation: opinions of Sir Frederick *Thesiger, Sir W. Page *Wood and Dr. Robert *Phillimore . . .' (1853).
[3] Answered questions, then spoke on ordnance estimates: *H* cxxiv. 735, 746.
[4] Cp. 1 Sept. 51.
[5] Possibly John Hiron, London boot manufacturer.
[6] *H* cxxiv. 815; repeatedly interrupted by W. Williams; notes in Add MS 44653, f. 1.
[7] Papers untraced.
[8] Frewen's Union of Benefices Bill: *H* cxxiv. 884.
[9] Cp. *The Times*, 3 March 1853, 8a.
[10] George Saunders Thwaites, 1778–1866; captain in 48th foot, 1805–17, colonel 1846, lieutenant general 1861; secretary of national gallery trustees 1835–54.
[11] William Mure, 1799–1860, colonel of Renfrewshire militia from 1831; Peelite M.P. Renfrewshire 1846–55; wrote on Greece and the Ionian islands.

real one by Mr Disraeli's trick, wh was baffled by 159:101.[1] Read on Australian Mints[2]—& Tennent on Wine Duties.[3]

4. Fr.

Wrote to Mr Gardner—Mr C. Fane[4]—Sir J.E. Tennent—Ld Carlisle—V. Chanc. Oxford—O.B. Cole—Baron Alderson—Rev Mr Lathbury—Ld Granville and minutes. Wrote Memm. on Australian Mints.[5] Saw Mr Wilson—Mr Gardner—Earl of Aberdeen. H. of C. 4½–7 and 7¾ to 1. Spoke on Can[adian] Cl[ergy] Reserves & voted in 275:192 for 2d reading.[6] Read Hamilton on Nat. Debt—and Can. Cl. Reserve Papers.[7] Drive with C. *Latin with St*[*ephy*].

5. Sat.

Wrote to Sir T. Fremantle—Mr Wilson—Mr Arbuthnot—Sir W. James—Mr Bramley Moore—Sir J. Young—Mr Goulburn . . . & minutes. Worked on Legacy & Probate Duties.[8] Saw Sir A. Spearman—Mr Wood—W.I. Deputation—Tobacco Deputation.[9] Cabinet 3¼–7. We settled the Cape Constn.[10]—Manning Clause[11]—& other matters: I was not much inclined to suspend writs without special report from Committees. Twelve to dinner—Speaker's Levee—Evg party at home. Herbert & Granville sat late.

6. 4 S.Lent.

Whitehall (H.C.) mg. Chap. Royal aft. Walk with C. Wrote (draft) to Mr Disraeli: (I did it purposely *today*):[12] Mr W. Forbes—Rev Mr Aitkin.[13] MS of last Sunday aloud in Evg. Read Trevor on Convn.[14]—Wilkinson, Grey, & other pamphlets[15]—Ch periodicals.[16]

[1] Gladstone opposed *Hume's free-trade motion not on principle, but as a motion 'as being in the nature of a promise'. *Disraeli, at the end of the deb. announced that the tories would vote with the radicals against the coalition: *H* cxxiv. 1014.

[2] Cp. PRO, T 29/550, f. 717.

[3] A draft of Sir J. *Tennent, *né* Emerson, 'Wine, its use and taxation. An inquiry into the operation of the wine duties on consumption and revenue' (1855).

[4] Probably R. G. C. Fane; cp. 14 July 47.

[5] Add MS 44741, f. 93.

[6] *H* cxxiv. 1138. Cp. Conacher, 100; speech notes in Add MS 44653, f. 3.

[7] *PP* 1852–3 lxv. 515.

[8] Cp. Add MS 44572, f. 62.

[9] No papers found.

[10] Cp. Add MS 44572, f. 94.

[11] Of *Cardwell's Merchant Shipping Law Amnd. Bill, then in preparation; cabinet report in Add MS 44571, f. 142.

[12] Cp. Buckle, iii. 478 and Morley, i. 458.

[13] Probably Robert (known to some as Charles) Aitken, 1800–75; minister in Liverpool and Glasgow, then vicar of Pendeen, Cornwall, from 1849.

[14] G. *Trevor, *The convocation of the two provinces, their origin, constitution and forms of proceeding, with a chapter on their revival* (1852).

[15] Perhaps, M. Wilkinson, 'School sermons at Marlborough college' (1852) and S. Grey, 'True churchmen: their position and duties in the present day' (1853).

[16] '(Ch)' here deleted; previous 'Ch' inserted above caret.

7. M.

Wrote to Signor Dassi[1]—Mr Disraeli—Mr Uwins—Mr Hubbard—Robn. G—Mr H. Woodcock[2]—Ld Harris—Bp of London—Mr Trevor—Rev. G. Rawlinson—Sir J. Kingsmill and minutes. Wrote Mem. on Legacy & Probate Duties.[3] Saw Molesworth—Wilson. Latin lesson to Stephy. Education Commee. (& conv. on Oxford) 12–2½. H. of C. 4¾–7 and 10–1.[4] Walked afr. & saw one, without any real good[R]. Read Hamilton on N. Debt—Kingsmill on Taxation of Ireland.[5]

8. T.

Wrote to Sir A. Spearman—Northcote—Mr Pressly—Freshfield—S. Herbert—Fremantle—Mr Goulburn—Robn. G.—Dr Daubeny[6]—and minutes. H. of C. 4½–8¼.[7] Saw Mr Uwins—Govr. Bank—Mr Cardwell—Bps of London & Quebec—Ld Clarendon—Marquis d'Azeglio—Panizzi. Dined with the De Tableys. Lady Clarendon's party afterwards.[8] Visited Christie's. Worked on Revenue subjects.

9. Wed.

Wrote to Ld Aberdeen and minutes. H. of Commons 2½–6. (Metr[opolitan] Adv[ances] Bill).[9] H. of C. Fee Commrs. meeting afterwd.[10] Dined at Newcastle's. Read Exr. Loan papers. Saw Mr Brickwood—Mr Salmons (his messenger)[11]—Ld Aberdeen—Newcastle—Wilson Patten—Bp of Oxford—Mr Hubbard. Re-wrote Mem. on Conversion &c. of Funds. At night saw W[illia]ms No 2: a case for pity & aid if there were a right heart to set about it[R]. Latin lesson to Stephy.

10. Th.

Wrote to E. Cardwell—Mr Uwins (see over)—Mr C. Trevor—Messrs. Tatham & Co—Mr Hayter—D. of Newcastle—J. Wood—Jas Wilson—Sir C. Wood—T.C. Parr—Sir T. Fremantle—and minutes. Read Hamilton on

[1] Giuseppe F. Dassi, Italian economist.

[2] Perhaps Henry Woodcock, attorney general of St. Christopher 1848–50, chief justice of Dominica 1850–56, of Tobago 1862–67.

[3] Add MS 44741, f. 95.

[4] Spoke on the mint: *H* cxxiv. 1223.

[5] Sir J. Kingsmill, 'Taxation in Ireland in connection with the extension of the property and income tax acts to that kingdom' (1853).

[6] Charles Giles Bridle *Daubeny, 1795–1867; professor of chemistry at Oxford 1822–55, of botany 1834, of rural economy 1840.

[7] Spoke on the national gallery: *H* cxxiv. 1317.

[8] Lady Catherine Villiers, 1810–74, da. of 1st earl of Verulam; m. 1st John Foster Barham, 2nd in 1839, George William Frederick *Villiers, 1800–70. He succ. as 4th earl of Clarendon 1838, and was lord privy seal 1840–1, chancellor of duchy of Lancaster 1840–41, 1864–65, president of board of trade 1846–7, lord lieutenant of Ireland 1847–52, foreign secretary 1853–8, 1865–6, 1868–70. Cp. Add MSS 44133–4.

[9] Spoke on it: *H* cxxiv. 1360.

[10] On fees charged on commissions of deputy lieutenants; a report was made on 13 May 1853; *PP* 1852–3 lix. 505.

[11] At the public works loan office.

the Debt. Saw Mr Brickwood & Mr Barnes—Ld A. Hervey—S.H. Northcote—Mr Pressly—Mr Hodgson—W.C. James. H. of C. 4½–12: working on a variety of subjects.[1]

11. Th[sc.F].

Wrote to Mrs Cracroft—Mr Pressly—Archd. Harrison—S. Herbert—Rev. W. Rawson—Sir J.S. Forbes—Sir T. Fremantle—Mr J. Wood—and minutes. Wrote Mem., with outline of plan, on Customs' Duties.[2] H. of C. 9¾–12.[3] Saw J.N.G.—Mr Gardner—Mr Herbert—Mr Goulburn—Mr Wilson—Mr C. Trevor:[4] with whom I discussed largely the Probate & Legacy Duties plan. Visited Christie's.—Latin l[esson] to Stephen. Walk at nt & spoke to two[R].

12. Sat.

Wrote to E. Cardwell—Rev R. Hussey—Lord Monteagle—Mr J. Wood—Sir W.C. James—Mr P. Norton[5]—Sir A. Spearman—T. Ogilvy—Mr Hayter & minutes. Saw Mr Wilson—Mr Salomons. Customs Reform Deputation[6]—Advertisement Duty Deputn.[7] Attended Cabinet 3–5¼. We gave up the last Clause in the C[anadian] C[lergy] R[eserves] Bill. Dined at home. Went to Lady Mary Wood's party.[8] Worked until 2½ on Income Tax (Sir C. Wood's paper &c.)[9]

13. 5 S.Lent.

Whitehall mg & Chapel Royal aft. MS. of 43 aloud in evg. Saw Cavendish—D[owage]r Duchess of Beaufort—Newcastle—Henley[10]—Jas Wortley. Read Shuttleworth on Edn. in Scotland[11]—Purgatorio—Hancock on Yeovil case.[12] Wrote Mem. on Treasury Bonds.[13]

14. M.

Wrote to Mr Geo. Christie—Mr Cardwell—Mr Reynolds—Ld Granville—Sir C. Wood—Mr Goulburn—Sir J. Shuttleworth—Mr G. Glyn—Mr W.

[1] Spoke on gold, attorneys, oaths, Indian territories, and metropolitan improvements: *H* cxxiv. 1385 ff.; notes on attorneys in Add MS 44653, f. 5.

[2] Add MS 44741, f. 115.

[3] India: *H* cxxv. 37.

[4] Charles Trevor, 1800–88; solicitor for legacy duties 1827, controller of legacy duties 1839–65; prepared the Succession Duty Act 1853.

[5] Of Soho Square; otherwise unidentified.

[6] From most large cities; cp. *The Times*, 14 March 1853 5a, ibid. 15 March 1853, first leader, and Add MSS 44374, ff. 134–8, 44572, f. 118, and report at ibid. f. 15.

[7] Notes on it in Add MS 44741, f. 122.

[8] At 35 Chesham place.

[9] Cp. Add MS 44572, f. 122, 141; and wrote long mem. on it in Add MS 44741, f. 123.

[10] Joseph Warner Henley, 1793–1884; tory M.P. Oxfordshire 1841–78; president of the board of trade 1852, 1858–9.

[11] Sir J. *Kay-Shuttleworth, *Public Education* (1853), ch. vii.

[12] G. Hancock, 'The pew question. A case, decided at Yeovil' (1851, expanded ed. 1853).

[13] Add MS 44741, f. 144.

Cotton—Mr J. Wood—and minutes. Latin l[esson] to Stephen. Saw Sir C. Trevelyan—Mr Hawes—Ld Lyndhurst—Col. Mure—Sir J. Graham—Mr Bruce. Wrote & revised on I. Tax.[1] Also amendment of Educn. minute. Attended Commee. on Edn. 12½–2½. House 4½–7.[2] Eight to dinner. Evening party afterwards.—I went also to Lady Lyndhursts,[3] not wishing to seem to slight them. Worked on Revenue afterwards.

15. T.

Wrote to
Mr Greswell
Mr Haddan
Miss Conway
Sir C. Wood—
Mr C. Trevor
Rev. Mr Ffoulkes
Gordon
Marriott
Hext[4]
Mozley
Mr Bowen
Ld Palmerston
Master of Pembroke[5]
Sir R. Inglis
Rev. E. Coleridge
Mr J. Wilson
Messrs Overend.
Ld Aberdeen
Rev Mr Hobhouse[6]
Woollcombe
W Woollcombe
Hedley[7]
Price
and minutes.

Saw Mr Wilson—Mr Brickwood—Sir A. Spearman—Sir J. Graham. H. of C. 4½–8 and 9½–11.[8] Read Hamilton on the Debt. Saw (late) Harford: a true case for sympathy[R].

16. Wed.

Wrote to Mr Pressly—Sir W. Heathcote—do, & others[9]—Ld Lansdowne[10] —E. Cardwell—Mr Franks[11]—Wm. Gladstone—Ld Granville—Mr Hastie MP.—Mr A. Smollett—Ld Aberdeen—Ld Clarendon—Rev. C. Marriott—Sir F. Smith—T.G.—& minutes. Dined at Sir C. Trevelyan's. Exhibn. Commn. 12–1¼. H. of C. 1–2.[12] Saw Sir A. Spearman—Mr Goulburn—Mr

[1] Add MS 44741, f. 146.

[2] Spoke on *Dickens's *Household words* and the stamp duty: *H* cxxv. 159.

[3] They lived at 25 George street, Hanover square.

[4] George Hext, ?1819–1900; fellow of Corpus, Oxford, 1847–58, bursar 1853; vicar of St. Veep, Cornwall, 1857, of Steeple-Langford, Somerset, from 1873.

[5] Francis *Jeune, 1806–68; fellow of Pembroke, Oxford, 1830–7, master there 1843–64; on Oxford commission 1850; vice-chancellor 1858–62; dean of Lincoln 1864, bp. of Peterborough from 1864. Cp. Add MS 44221.

[6] Edmund *Hobhouse, 1816?–1904, fellow of Merton, Oxford, 1841–57 D.D. 1858; bp. of Nelson, New Zealand, 1858–65; assistant to bp. of Lichfield 1869–81; an antiquary.

[7] William Hedley, 1819?–84; fellow of University, Oxford, 1844–62, dean 1851; rector of Beckley, Sussex, 1861–78.

[8] Election petitions: *H* cxxv. 204.

[9] A long letter on Canadian Clergy Reserves Bill, to Heathcote and *Keble; copy in Add MS 44528, f. 113.

[10] 'Ld Aberdeen' here deleted.

[11] Charles Franks, sub-governor of the South Sea Company, which was wound up by the 1853 budget.

[12] Country Rates Bill: *H* cxxv. 258.

Reynolds—Ld Overstone—Sir C. Wood—Ld Aberdeen—Ld Granville—Mr Trevor—Mr B. Price—Northcote—Mr Rich.[1] At night saw Williams (2) [R]. Farther off than Harford. Read Wilson on I. Tax.[2]

17. Th.

Wrote to Sir C. Trevelyan—Mr Wilson—Mr Reynolds—Sir C. Wood—D. of Newcastle—Sir J. Young—Mr Pressly—Mr Fagan—Sir J. Graham—Jas Freshfield—Mrs Cracroft—Mr Franks—Mr Goulburn and minutes. Wrote Memm. on Alderney Harbour.[3] Saw Mr Archer[4]—Sir C. Trevelyan—Mr Cotton—Mr Franks—Governor of the Bank—Ld Overstone—Mr Ellice—Sir J. Graham—Mr Glyn. H. of C. $4\frac{1}{2}$–$7\frac{1}{2}$ and $10\frac{1}{2}$–$1\frac{1}{2}$.[5] Worked on Treas. papers.

18. Fr.

Wrote to Mr M'Culloch—Mrs Goalen—Ld Lansdowne—Mr J. Wood—Ld Aberdeen—and minutes. H. of C. $4\frac{1}{2}$–$7\frac{1}{4}$ and 8–$1\frac{1}{4}$: on Canada Cl. Res. Bill &c.[6] Printing Commee. $12\frac{1}{4}$–$1\frac{1}{4}$.[7] Saw Mr Hubbard—Sir A. Spearman—Mr Dorington—The Speaker—E. Cardwell—Mr Wilson—Mr Wood cum Mr Pressly on measures of taxation—Duke of Newcastle—Deputn. of African Association. Children's French play at $7\frac{1}{2}$: I saw but little.

19. Sat.

Wrote to Mr Masterman—Mr Labouchere—Mr Litchfield—Mr Cardwell—Ld St Germans—Ld Harris—Sir T. Fremantle—Rn. G—& minutes. Dined at Duke of Somerset's. Income Tax Commee. Lansdowne House $12\frac{1}{4}$–$2\frac{1}{4}$. Most satisfactory. Cabinet $2\frac{1}{2}$–$4\frac{1}{2}$ and $4\frac{3}{4}$–6. Saw Cardwell—Graham—Sir C. Trevelyan—Newcastle—Dr Cook cum Mr Cairns.[8] Read Report on Divorce.[9] Worked on Treas. Papers.

20. 6 S.Lent.

Whitehall Chapel mg. Titchfield St evg. MS. of 40 aloud at night. Saw Bp

[1] (Sir) Henry Rich, 1803–69; whig M.P. Knaresborough 1837–41, Richmond 1846–61; minor office 1837–41, a whip 1846–52; cr. bart. 1863.

[2] James Wilson's confidential cabinet minute in Add MS 44572, f. 122.

[3] Not traced, but see PRO, T 29/550, f. 523–4 for the case.

[4] Henry Archer, d. 1863, had invented a machine for perforating postage stamps; the patent was purchased by the treasury for £4000 in 1853; cp. PRO, T 25/551, f. 414.

[5] Answered questions: *H* cxxv. 314.

[6] Spoke on it: *H* cxxv. 492.

[7] A select cttee. was later set up on cost of printing parliamentary papers: *PP* 1854 vii. 303.

[8] i.e. John *Cook and John *Cairns, 1818–92; minister in Berwick-on-Tweed 1845–76, moderator of united presbyterian synod 1872; theologian.

[9] First report of the royal commission on divorce: *PP* 1852–3 xl. 249.

of London—Mrs Hartford.[1] Read Lamennais—Daly's Sermons[2]—Sc. Ch. Mag[3]—Tasmanian Church Tracts.[4]

21. M.

Wrote to Sir C. Trevelyan—Mr Pressly—Sir E. Fillmer[5]—Sir C. Wood—Sir T. Fremantle—Mr Cotton—& minutes. Marg. Chapel 5 P.M. Worked on materials of Budget. Saw Mr Cardwell—Mr Wilson—Mr Litchfield—D of Newcastle *cum* Mr Ross.[6] & Mr Jackson.[7] Worked on materials of Budget—Read B. of Trade Report—Hamilton on National Debt. Worked on arranging my letters & papers. Mr Church came on a visit to see & consider about Stephy.

22. T.

Marg. Chapel 8 P.M. Wrote to Duke of Argyll—Mr W. Forbes—Rev. W. Trollope[8]—Mr C. Franks—Major Macinroy—Mr H. Lees—Mrs Malcolm—Mr J. Litton—Earl of Aberdeen—S. Herbert—D. of Newcastle and minutes. Saw Mr Wilson—Sir C. Trevelyan—Mr H. Hope[9]—Mr Wood *cum* Mr Pressly 3–6 on Budget. Read Hamilton—Tory Radical—X+Y—& other pamphlets.[10] Worked on I.T. papers.

23. Wed.

ChCh Broadway 6 P.M. Wrote to Sir A. Spearman (2)—Sir T. Fremantle—S. Herbert—Sir C. Trevelyan—Rev. F. Teed—Mr Scholefield—Mr Wilson Mr Goulburn—G.P. Scrope MP—Rev E. Coleridge and minutes. Worked today principally on Customs and I[ncome] T[ax]: as yesterday on Inland Rev. & I.T. Saw Ld Aberdeen—Mr Lushington—Sir T. Fremantle.—Read Hamilton on N[ational] Debt—Parl. Debates.

24. Th.

St Mary's Crown St 8½ A.M. Wrote to Rev. F. Meyrick—Mr J. Wood—Sir S. Northcote—Mr Goschen[11]—Solr. General—Sir T. Fremantle (2)—Amn. Minister—Mr Wilson—and minutes. Worked on I. Tax Customs & Treas.

[1] Unidentified.

[2] R. *Daly, *Lectures on a few portions of scripture* (1850).

[3] *Scottish magazine and churchman's review*, iii. 105 (March 1853); on *Kingsley's *Phaethon*.

[4] Perhaps the *Report* of Van Diemen's Land home missionary and Christian instruction society (1852).

[5] Sir Edmund Filmer, 1809–57; 8th bart. 1834, tory M.P. West Kent from 1838.

[6] Probably Charles Ross, then a commissioner of the audit board; cp. 20 Dec. 34.

[7] Probably Henry Bates Jackson, clerk in commissariat branch of the treasury.

[8] William *Trollope, 1798–63, vicar of Great Wigston, Leicestershire, 1834–58, of St. Mary's, Tasmania, from 1858. Copy, on the colonial church, in Add MS 44528, f. 117.

[9] Henry Thomas Hope, 1808–63; whig M.P. East Looe 1830–2, Gloucester 1833–41, 1847–52; architectural patron and china collector.

[10] 'Elements of taxation' by X+Y (1852).

[11] 'Rev. F. Meyrick' here deleted. William Henry Goschen, 1793–1866, fa. of G. J.*; founded the city baking firm of Fruhling and Goschen 1815; involved in 1853 in reducing Russia's debts; cp. A. D. Elliot, *Life of G. J. *Goschen* (1911) i. 37–8.

papers. Saw Mr Wilson—Mr Goulburn—Duke of Newcastle—Sir T. Fremantle *cum* Mr St John[1]—2½–7. Read Hamilton on National Debt.

25. Good Friday & Annuncn.

Whitehall Chapel & Holy Commn. mg.—ChCh Broadway Evg. Read part of one of Anderden's Sermons aloud in evg.[2] Wrote to Sir C. Trevelyan—E. Cardwell—Earl of St Germans—Mr Pressly (2)—Mrs Cracroft—Mr Wilson—Mr B. Osborne[3]—and minutes. Saw Duke of Argyll—Sir S. Northcote. Read Hamilton on Debt (finished)—Two Cantos of the Paradiso—Monro's 'Parish'.[4]

26. Easter Eve.

Westmr. Abbey 10 A.M.—Marg. Chapel 5 P.M. Wrote to Provost of Oriel—R. Phillimore—E. of Clarendon—Rev Mr Lake—Mr R.B. Osborne—and minutes. Worked on Customs' Reform Minutes.[5] Cabinet 2½–5. Saw Ld Canning—Mr Pressly—Mr Wilson—Ld Clarendon—Ld J. Russell—S. Herbert. Read & worked on I. Tax &c.

27. Easter Sunday.

Whitehall & H. C. mg. St Andrews evg. MS of 44 aloud. Read the Counter Theory[6]—Buxton on Irish Edn.[7]—Cox on Boarding Schools for the Poor.[8] Saw Sir J. Graham—Wm. Tyler.[9]

28. M.

Marg. Chapel 5 P.M. Wrote to Sir W. Molesworth—T.G.—Mr D. Gladstone—Mr G. Moffatt—Sir Jas Graham—Sir J. Young (2)—Mrs Austin—and minutes. Saw Mr Wilson—Sir A. Spearman—Mr Wood *cum* Mr Pressly. Went with C. to the Lord Mayor's dinner—a lamentable hole in my evening 6½–12. Came home & worked until four on Budget Plans of Finance of all kinds—and on Customs' Reform Minute.[10]

29. T.

Wrote to Sir T. Fremantle—Mr Litchfield—& minutes. Saw Mr Wood *cum* Mr Pressly—Chev. Bunsen—Mr Trevor—Mr Jas Wilson—Sir A. Spearman.

[1] Frederick St. John, 1809–63; surveyor general of customs from 1853.
[2] One of W. H. Anderdon's many sermons. He became a roman catholic in 1851.
[3] Ralph Bernal Osborne, *né* Bernal, 1808–82, took name of Osborne 1844; liberal M.P. Chipping Wycombe 1841–7, Middlesex 1847–57, Dover 1857–9, Liskeard 1859–65, Nottingham 1866–8, Waterford 1870–4; Admiralty secretary 1852–8.
[4] E. *Monro, *The Parish, a Poem* (1853).
[5] In Add MS 44573, f. 52.
[6] Not traced; cp. perhaps 15 Oct. 41.
[7] C. *Buxton, 'A survey of the system of national education in Ireland' (1853).
[8] J. E. Cox, 'The right training of children' (1850); a sermon preached for a masonic charity.
[9] Probably William Tyler, stationer and deputy of the city council.
[10] Add MS 44741, f. 160.

Revised Customs Reform minute. Left at 4½ for Wilton & arrived at nine: where we were received with the utmost warmth.[1] Read Ed. Rev. on the Govt & Finance[2]—Thring on Colonies.[3]

30. Wed.

Wilton Ch 10½ A.M. Viewed it afterwards: it is a noble monument. Wrote to Lord Aberdeen—Mr G. Moffatt—Lord J. Russell—Mayor of Manchr.[4]—R. Wilbraham—Mr C. Litchfield. Saw something of the house. In aftn. drove up the hill & saw the lie of the country. Read Rickards's Lectures[5]—Travers on Tea Duties[6]—Bagot on Spirits in Bond.[7]

31. Th.

Wrote to Ld J. Russell—Rev Mr Lake—Mr R. Wilbraham—Mr Panizzi—D of Newcastle—Mr M'Gregor—Sir T. Fremantle—and minutes. Saw some of the pictures, wh are very interesting. Read Rickards—& the New Quarterly on Gold,[8] &c—Wrote on Income Tax.[9] Conv. with Herbert on do—The Hamiltons[10] came to dinner: another treat. We drove to see Stonehenge—It is a noble & an awful relic, telling much, & telling too that it conceals more.

Friday April One 1853.

Wilton Church 10½ A.M. Wrote to Sir T. Fremantle—Jas Wilson—Provost of Oriel—Dr Jacobson and minutes. Wrote on Income Tax. Read pamphlets. Drove to Salisbury & saw the Cathedral. The exterior is on the whole a wonder of harmony & beauty, especially from the South. We saw more at Wilton: but the Cathedral was the absorbing object of the day. Wrote on Income Tax & Funds.[11]

2. Sat.

Baby's first birthday: God bless him. Wrote to Sir T. Fremantle—Mr Muntz—Mr Jas Wilson—Mr Franks—Newcastle & minutes. Wrote Mem.

[1] *Herbert's father's house, 3 miles NW. of Salisbury.

[2] *Edinburgh Review*, xcvii. 240 (January 1853); on J. G. *Hubbard, 'How should an income tax be levied' (1852).

[3] Henry, Baron Thring, 'The supremacy of Great Britain not inconsistent with self-government for the colonies' (1851).

[4] Robert Barnes, 1800–71; cotton spinner and Wesleyan philanthropist; mayor of Manchester 1851–3.

[5] Sir G. K. Rickards, *Three lectures delivered before the university of Oxford* (1852); on political economy.

[6] John Travers, 'A letter to the author of remarks [in a *Courier* leading article] . . . upon the tea duties' (1834) or his 'Letter to the editor of the *Courier* . . . upon the tea duties' (3 eds. in 1834).

[7] J. Bagot, 'Observations on the present state of the law affecting home made spirits in bond' (1853).

[8] *New Quarterly Review*, i. 143 (April 1853); review of publications on gold.

[9] On *Russell's letter on income tax, Add MS 44741, f. 176.

[10] Bp. W. K. *Hamilton and his wife.

[11] See previous day.

on Oxford Reforms.[1] Another on the Wine Duties.[2] Left Wilton 7½: in Downing St 11¼. Arranged about entertainments: one of the petty but rigid necessities of my position. Edn. Commee. 12½–2. We settled the affair of the Derby Minute of June 12.[3] Saw Cardwell cum Symons—then with Anson & Swift. Cabinet 3–6. Got authority for my Exchequer Bond &c Resolutions.[4] Fifteen to dinner. Read on I. Tax (Horsman Debate)[5]—Brown on RR Accidents.[6]

3. 1 S.E[aster]

Whitehall (& H. C.) mg. Titchfield St (with Willy) aftn. Sermon aloud in evg. Saw Sir F. Rogers. Read The Counter Theory—Dean of Bristol's Letter[7]—Ed. Rev. on Ch. in Wales—do on Disraeli[8]—Chr. Remember.[9]

4. M.

Wrote to D of Newcastle—Mr Jas Wilson (2)—Mr Richardson—A. Hayward—C. Marriott and minutes. Saw Sir T. Fremantle—Sir A. Spearman—Mr Jas Wilson. Meeting National Debt Commee. 3½ P.M. We changed the form of dealing with the Surplus. H. of C. 4½–9½: Spoke on Edn. Bill and Oxford.[10] Worked till 2½ on Finance.

5. T.

Wrote to V. Chancr. of Oxford—Lyttelton—Sir J. Young—Mr Pressly—S. Herbert—Mr Richards—J.D. Cook and minutes. H. of C. 4½–9¾. Spoke on Wine Du[ties].[11] Saw Fremantle & Custom's Officers on Tariff 11–1½. Wood & Pressly on Inl. Rev. measures 1½–3¾. Drove a little with C: & at 10 went to join the children at Astley's.[12] Worked late on I. Tax &c.

6. Wed.

Wrote to Mrs Bennett—Mr C. Marriott—Mr G. Moore[13]—Rn. G.—Jas Wilson—F. Charteris—G. Moffat—Chev. Bunsen & minutes. Wine Duties meeting 4½–6½. Graham & Granville carried it. Saw Panizzi—Mr Anderson

[1] Add MS 44742, f. 3; part in Conacher, 333–4.
[2] Add MS 44742, f. 5.
[3] Minute by *Derby of 12 June 1852 on appeal to bps. on school management; cp. Add MS 44742, f. 1 and 25 Jan. 53.
[4] On creation of large issue of debentures at 2½%; cp. Add MS 44742, f. 11.
[5] *Horsman's motion for income tax differentiation: *H* xcvii. 162 ff. (3 March 1848).
[6] Untraced pamphlet, perhaps by George Brown of Barnard Castle, author of *A treatise on the Railway and Canal Traffic Act, 1854* (1859).
[7] G. Elliot, 'A letter to J. S. Harford' (1851); on papal aggression.
[8] *Edinburgh Review*, xcvii. 342, 420 (April 1853); W. J. Conybeare on the church, and a review of G. H. Francis, *Benjamin *Disraeli, a critical biography* (1852).
[9] *Christian Remembrancer*, xxv. 289 (April 1853); perhaps the review of W. J. Conybeare, *Life and epistles of St. Paul.*
[10] On *Derby's minute, and Oxford reform: *H* cxxv. 576.
[11] *H* cxxv. 633; he hedged on Oliveira's motion to reduce the duties, which remained until 1860, cp. Buxton, *Finance and politics*, i. 232 ff.
[12] Astley's Amphitheatre in Bridge street, Lambeth.
[13] Probably George Henry Moore, 1811–70, liberal M.P. co. Mayo 1847–57, 1868–70; a leader of the tenant right movement.

—Mr J.D. Cook—do cum Mr Goldwin Smith—Mr Shelley[1]—Sir A. Spearman—Cardwell. Cabinet dinner at Ld Lansdowne's & *Cabinet* afterwards. I came home when C.s party was over & worked till 2½ a.m. as (now) usual.

7. Th

Wrote to Sir C. Wood—G.A. Denison—Mrs Wimpole[2]—Sir T. Fremantle—J. Wood—and minutes. A Prince born[3]—my Palace dinner will [be] put off—Council at 3 to order Thanksgiving. Worked on my Financial Plan. Saw Mr Greswell—Mr Trevor—Sir J. Graham—H. Fitzroy—Sir C. Trevelyan. Read Ed Rev.[4] Worked on Treas. papers. Dined at Mrs Talbots. H. of C. 4½–8¼ and 9½–12¼. Spoke on Consold Annuities.[5]

8. Fr.

Wrote to Ld Monteagle—Prince Albert—Mr Uwins—Lord Aberdeen . . . . and minutes. Saw Sir A. Spearman—Mr Wilson—Sir J. Young—Christie. Worked upon my Resolutions in producing the amended Edition.[6] H. of C. 4½–8½ and 9–10½. Spoke 1¾ h. in explaining the plan of Ex[cheque]r Bonds & Conversion of Debt.[7] 11–2 to the British Museum: to inspect ground & plan[8]—& to read Pamphlets & Speeches on Income Tax. Saw one afterwards[R]—and worked late on Finance papers & I. Tax pamphlets.

9. Sat.

Wrote to Sir A. Spearman—Wm. Gladstone—Mr L. Conyngham—Jas Freshfield—Capt. Barclay—Sir J. Graham—Mr C. Trevor. With the Prince 1–2 on Financial Plans. Cabinet 2¾–6½.[9] Wrote Mema. in evg.[10] Worked upon my figures & got all ready just in time. Saw Mr Shelley—Sir A. Spearman. My darling Willy went off—I had scarcely three minutes to speak to him in the day. Eighteen to dinner: & more in evg. Worked late into the night on remainder of plan.

10. 2 S.E[aster]

Chapel Royal mg. Bedfordbury in evg. Printed (Parker) S[ermon] aloud.[11]

[1] Spencer Shelley, 1813–1908, 4th s. of Sir John Shelley, 6th bart.; treasury clerk 1830–54, senior 1854–6, principal 1859–67.

[2] Unidentified.

[3] Prince Leopold George Duncan Albert, *Victoria's 4th s., duke of Albany 1881, d. in Cannes, 1884.

[4] He also read sundry leaders that day on him, cp. Add MS 44742, f. 13.

[5] With respect to Ireland: *H* cxxv. 754. Notes in Add MS 44653, f. 7.

[6] Of bonds, Add MS 44742, f. 46.

[7] *H* cxxv. 810; notes in Add MS 44653, f. 9.

[8] Of *Panizzi's reading room; the plans were submitted to the trustees in May 1852 and it was opened May 1857.

[9] To explain his budget plans; see Argyll, i. 422–6, who 'never heard a speech . . . which so riveted my attention and that of all my colleagues'.

[10] On effect of 1853–4 proposed tax reductions, Add MS 44742, f. 80.

[11] One of many sermons published by J. H. *Parker.

Read Lamennais—The Counter Theory. Walk with Herbert. Saw E. Collins[R].

11. M.

Wrote to Chev. Bunsen—Canning—W.R. Farquhar—A. Hastie—Mr Oliveira—Robn. G—A.H. Wylie—Mr Cotton—Mr Hubbard—Mr Panizzi—Sir C. Trevelyan—Mr Wood and minutes. Cabinet 2¼–5 on Budget. Wrote Mema. in evg. Saw Sir A. Spearman—Mr Wilson—Mr Goulburn—Mr Trevor. H. of C. 5–6 & 10–12½.[1] Dined at Lady Wenlock's. *Worked on I. Tax until 3 a.m.*

The Cabinet met today at two to consider further the Financial Plan which I had submitted to them.

Sir C. Wood began by stating his objections to the extension of the Income Tax to Ireland & to Incomes between £100 and £150. He thought the balance was cast too much against Ireland . . .[2]

I pointed out how in my view the figures stood with regard to Ireland & showed that by remitting any portion of the Consolidated Annuities we might adjust with Ireland the account as we thought fit. By giving up 1/5 of the capital of the annuities & allowing redemption at 5 per Cent we should give her a million and a half: by giving up a fourth: £170000.

Ld Palmerston followed and said my plan was a great plan & admirably put together, perfectly just too in itself: but it opened too many points of attack: Disraeli was on the watch, all the Irish would join him & so would the Radicals: the Legacy Duty, to which he had individually great objections though mitigated by the form of the proposal, would estrange many of the Conservatives.[3] He did not distinctly declare for Wood but spoke in the sense of reducing the plan.

Lord John Russell then fell in & said, it appeared to him that I had had a task of great difficulty to perform[4] . . . he was disposed to abide by the plan as it stood.

Sir James Graham then fell in & stated that he had spoken in December very strongly against the lowering of the line of exemption:[5] that he considered that the extension of the area of the tax was quite inconsistent with the idea of a *bonâ fide* intention that it should be temporary: and he agreed with Sir Charles Wood that we should drop these two items and only take away half the soap tax.

Wood had quoted his own opinions expressed last December against extending the Income Tax to Ireland.

Lord John said he thought we might make the whole remission of Consolidated Annuities equal to what we are to levy under the Income Tax. To this I agreed saying that every step towards the equalisation of taxation had a value over & above what money it might bring.

Lord Lansdowne said that without communication with Wood he had on reflection come to the same conclusions: and was also of opinion that the remission of Consolidated Annuities would be regarded in Ireland as a matter of right not as a boon nor as a set off against the Income Tax.

[1] Clergy Reserves: *H* cxxv. 923.
[2] Further objections from *Wood omitted; cp. Argyll, i. 428. Ireland had hitherto been exempted from the income tax.
[3] Exemption of real property from legacy duty was abolished.
[4] Details of *Russell's views omitted.
[5] The budget reduced the limit of exemption from £150 to £100.

The Duke of Argyll declared himself favourable to the extension to Ireland and to the whole measure except the extension downwards.

Lord Aberdeen said he considered that the most doubtful part of the whole plan.

I asked Wood about the balance for the year & he said he would give up the exemption on Life Assurances and would also raise the addition to Irish Spirit duty to 1/-.

I urged with respect to Parliamentary difficulty that I considered it would be enormous in whatever way we might think fit to treat these proposals: but that it would be by no means alleviated through the withdrawal of the proposal to tax Ireland and to extend downwards to incomes of £100. That indeed we must expect the Irish members generally to work against us: but that the position in which we were was one of a peculiar nature: that we could only carry our measure by dint of a strong feeling, & could not have that feeling with us if we impaired the proposal to reduce above five millions of taxes. These proposals to make Ireland & a lower class share the tax would facilitate its re-enactment with those who had hitherto been its sole bearers: the sentiment of the House of Commons was decidedly against exemptions: the proposal last December to carry the tax downwards raised no opposition: & if we were to think of opponents, what would their position be if they were able to say you perpetuate at once the odious equal rate and & [sic] the likewise odious exemptions.[1]

I said I was willing to propose whatever the Cabinet might decide on—except one thing, namely the breaking up of the basis of the Income Tax: that I could not be a party to & I should regard it as a high political offence: with this reservation I should follow their judgement but I strongly adhered to my whole plan, and I objected to the raising the additional spirit duty for Ireland to 1/- per gallon,[2] while I demurred to the abandonment of the exemption for Pensions on Life Insurances under the Income Tax.

Lord Aberdeen said you must take care that your proposals are not unpopular ones & I replied that it was after applying the test of popularity that I was convinced the Budget would be damaged and weakened by the withdrawal of these two points.[3]

We agreed to meet tomorrow: regarding the equal rate & Legacy duty as settled: & meaning then to settle the other points.[4]

12. T.

Wrote to E. Cardwell—Solr. General—D. of Wellington—H. Fitzroy—J.R. Hope Scott and minutes. Saw Ld Aberdeen—H.J.G.—The Speaker—E. Cardwell. 2¼–5. Cabinet. The Budget adopted. Wrote Mema. Worked on Treas. papers. H. of C. 5–9 and 10½–12¼. Spoke on two aggressive motions.[5] Read Hubbard on I. Tax.[6] Mem on Budget (E. C[ardwell]'s).

The Cabinet met again today to consider the subject of the Budget as to the points put into discussion yesterday viz. whether we should drop the extensions

[1] Views of Granville ('apprehensive'), Molesworth (favourable), Clarendon (favourable) and Newcastle (favourable), omitted.

[2] Cp. 20 June 43 and Buxton, i. 117.

[3] Details of legislative time-table omitted.

[4] Rest of mem. omitted; initialled and dated 11 April 1853; Add MS 44778, f. 84 ff.

[5] On duty on carriages, and public expenditure: *H* cxxv. 1040, 1049.

[6] See 31 Dec. 52.

of the Income Tax downwards & to Ireland together with the repeal of one half of the Soap Tax.

I quoted the returns which Mr. Baines[1] had supplied to me and which go to show that as matters now stand the class from £100 to £150 have gained six to seven per cent by that recent legislation of which the Income Tax has been the instrument while the class from £150 to £400 has gained but 1⅔ per cent.

Wood returned to his text of yesterday as did Graham & we got out into the open sea. Lord John started the notion of abandoning the extension downward but adhered closely to the extension into Ireland. We agreed that the remission on the Annuities should be in gross two millions. Ld. Lansdowne again suggested that a Spirit Duty & an Income Tax for Ireland together would constitute something like a breach of faith. Graham portended certain failure . . .[2]

Lord Palmerston drawing the distinction between the goodness of a plan & the practicability of carrying it said that he always thought Disraeli's Budget a very good plan, but then it could not be carried—and he thought we should be broken upon this plan. He however would accept the Budget provided we were not to be bound to dissolve or resign in the event of defeat upon such a point as the extension to Ireland or the extension downwards.

Lord John and I both said that such a question must be considered when the time came but clearly it would be open to the Govt. to take either course. If however said Lord John we were beaten on the question of differentiating the tax, then we should have to dissolve.[3]

Thus the whole Cabinet after finding that the suggested amendments cut against one another ended by adopting the entire Budget—the only dissentients being Ld Lansdowne, Graham, Wood, S. Herbert. Graham was full of ill auguries but said he would assent & assist. Wood looked grave & said he must take time.[4]

I have spoken this evening in confidence to Cardwell about the Budget; and he has suggested a new view of it, founded upon ideas somewhat distinct from those which have been discussed in the Cabinet.

His position is this. Impose the Succession Tax—and employ it, together with your present surplus, and with the approaching reduction of £620000 on the Three & a Quarter per Cents, 1. In reducing the Income Tax forthwith to 5¼d. 2. In reducing the Tea Duties when the means afforded by it will permit.[5] But impose no new Tax except the succession tax. Trust to the imposition of that tax together with the diminution of the Income Tax to 5¼d. And forego any idea of present remissions of indirect Taxation.[6]

This plan has the merit of great simplicity.

It would (probably) postpone all remissions of indirect taxation for two years: including even tea: but it would probably also obviate all opposition of a serious kind in the House of Commons which the new taxes and extensions may create—and it would offer inducement to pass the Income Tax unaltered in the shape of an immediate reduction of the rate for all to the point at which Mr. Disraeli put it for his favoured classes: a boon in itself, and valuable also as an earnest of the intention to put Parliament in a position to part with the tax altogether.

[1] Probably M. T. *Baines, then president of the poor law board.
[2] Further comments by them omitted.
[3] Further favourable comments omitted.
[4] Initialled and dated 12 April 1853; Add MS 44778, f. 98.
[5] Written over many deletions. [6] Statistics of this omitted.

It appears to me that this plan, although it is of course disappointing in several respects has on the whole greater recommendations as compared with its dangers than the less extensive modifications of the Budget which were discussed today.

It is inferior to the Entire plan in public justice: but its comparative safety will be determined by the question how far other elements than the simple consideration of public justice in a large sense sway the House of Commons.

I have stated in a note to Cardwell the view which I take of my own position relatively to this plan.[1]

13. Wed.

Wrote to E. Cardwell—T.G.—Sir A. Spearman—Mr J. Wood—Sir T. Fremantle—Ly Aylesbury—Archd. Garbett[2] and minutes. Saw Govr of Bank—Cardwell—Mr Parkinson—Robn. G—Ld Aberdeen—S. Herbert. Also Ld Abn. with Newcastle, & Argyll (who came in) on Cardwell's plan: wh expired.[3] Dined at Grillion's. C.s evening party afterwards kept me busy till ½ p. one. After wh, read French Report[4]—on I. Tax.

14. Th.

Wrote to Newcastle—Northcote—Fremantle—Sir C. Trevelyan—H. Fitzroy—S. Herbert—C. Pressly—& minutes. Read A[dam] Smith—Wilson's minute.[5] Saw Northcote—Mr Wood cum Mr Pressly & Mr Timm—Sir C. Trevelyan—Ld Aberdeen—do *cum* D. of Newcastle—H. of C. 4½–8¾ and 9½–12½. Spoke agt Gibson.[6] Beaten by 200:169. Our third time this week.[7] Very stiff work this: E. Ellice said Dissolution should be thought of: we agreed in the House to a Cabinet tomorrow at half past one: S. Herbert & Cardwell to whom I spoke inclined to Dissolution.

When I saw Cardwell on Wednesday [sc. Tuesday][8] night he expressed apprehension at our new Taxes & proposed to omit them all except the Legacy Duty with all our reductions of indirect taxation—lowering the Income Tax at once to 5¼d as an earnest of its future extinction.

I said I thought this a safer plan than the minor reductions of the Budget which had been discussed in the Cabinet.

And I advised him next morning to go and speak to Graham who had been so apprehensive.

He came back from Graham with an answer that he infinitely preferred Cardwell's plan to the decision of the Cabinet—to which however he would manfully adhere.

[1] Marked 'Secret'; initialled and dated 13 April [1853]; Add MS 44778, f. 106; doubtless so dated because written after midnight; journal entries and mem. below on 14 April confirm the talk must have been on 12 April. His diary dating of the Cabinets is correct; see *The Times*.

[2] Had succ. *Manning at Chichester.

[3] See next day.

[4] On the French Navy, in Add MS 44575, f. 1.

[5] Cp. 15 Mar. 53 n.

[6] Milner–*Gibson's motion to repeal advertisement duty: *H* cxxv. 1147.

[7] The gvnt. was also defeated in the Clitheroe election petition in 58:141 and on a resolution on Kilmainham hospital in 131:198; cp. *H* cxxv. 1032, 1074.

[8] Gladstone had muddled the days; he also below (15 Apr. 53) refers to Tuesday's cabinet as on Wednesday.

On this I went to Lord Aberdeen & stated the case to him with my own view of it & adding how I revolted from the idea of being the person to inveigle the Government or to drag it blindfold into needless dangers.

He agreed that those minor suggestions were botches of the plan and that this was more intelligible.

I told him I did not advise it but wished that it should be before the minds of some at least of my colleagues. The question was what to do? I advised sending for Newcastle. When he came he at once scouted the scheme as being even more dangerous than the Budget & without the compensating elements.

The Duke of Argyll came in & he took a similar view & stood for the whole Budget.

Lord Aberdeen or one of us remembered that in his opening speech he had declared that the especial mission of the Government he had formed would be to extend the commercial policy of Sir R. Peel: whereas Cardwell's plan was founded on foregoing indefinitely such extension.

Lord Aberdeen said he would *mention* the plan to Lord John: but that he thought it must be considered as at an end.

Today however another difficulty arose: Wood writes ominously as though he must resign if the Income Tax go to Ireland.

The 'Income Tax Committee' meet tomorrow morning, at half past ten, at Lansdowne House.[1]

15. Fr.

Wrote to Mr W.Ewart—T.G. Sir A. Spearman—Robn. G & minutes. Saw at noon Pressly & Timm on Inc. Tax: with a view to possible events. Cabinet $1\frac{1}{2}$–$4\frac{1}{2}$. Wrote memm. of it. H of C. $4\frac{3}{4}$–$7\frac{1}{4}$ and 10–1.[2] Saw J.N.G.—Mr Walter—The Speaker—Sir F. Baring—Mr Masterman—Sol. General. Dined at Ld Claud Hamilton's.

Today the Cabinet met at half past one to consider the effect of last night's division on the position of the Government.

Lord John stated what had occurred: adverted to the hostility of the radicals as exhibited in the tone of the debate: and stated or hinted an opinion that we must contract the Budget, take in a reef or two in consequence of what had happened, for safety's sake. He then produced a paper with which Wood had furnished him & which showed that we might drop the extensions of the Income Tax and the licences and on the other side reduce the Tax to 6d now & in two years to 5d, and also reduce the Tea Duties.

I stated that it appeared to me very doubtful whether the Budget could live in this House of Commons, whatever form it might assume: that even with such a perilous form I should look upon the whole Budget as less unsafe than a partial reduction; but that if reduction there must be I preferred the stringent contraction involved in Cardwell's plan. I pointed out the difficulties which we should have in dissolving some two months hence if beaten at an advanced stage of our financial measures: measures:[3] & raised the question whether it might not be wise even now to think of Dissolution.

[1] Initialled and dated 14 April 1853; Add MS 44778, f. 108.
[2] Voted for Jewish Disabilities Bill 3°: *H* cxxv. 1288.
[3] Written at top of new page.

Sir James Graham took the same view of the dispositions of Parliament: keen opposition, lukewarm support: the necessity which I had urged of a greater portion of party sympathy & connection to enable us to surmount the difficulties of a most hazardous & unusual operation.

But he did not appear to lean to Dissolution: and the elder members of the Cabinet generally declared themselves against it—Lord Palmerston, Lord Aberdeen, Lord Lansdowne. Newcastle too was against it. The objection taken of course was the want of a broad intelligible ground over & above the mere abstract merits of the ministry to justify the interruption by dissolution of the business of the Session.

Nor did they seem so confident of the strength of the Ministry in the country as Mr. Ellice who told me last night after the division that were he in the Cabinet he would certainly raise for discussion there the question of Dissolution—whether he might ultimately advise it or not.

Such being the opinion we went back to the position that we must have a Budget on Monday—but Clarendon, Herbert, & Palmerston joined the chorus of those who said the measure was too sharp upon Ireland. The idea was then started whether we should go the length of the entire remission of the consolidated annuities, and impose the Income Tax at 7d with the augmented spirit duty. Graham & Ld. Lansdowne were both inclined to this view: it found favour generally: and I felt that some excess in the mere sacrifice of money was no great matter compared with the advantage of so great an approximation to equal taxation.

Graham put to me pointedly the question whether I thought that viewing the temper of the House of Commons we could with the entire Budget overcome the feeling for differentiation, or safely go to the country on it? which resort all appeared to contemplate as a proximate contingency.

I said in reply that all my proposals had been adjusted with a view of overcoming the great difficulty of differentiation: & that speaking with great deference while I could not feel any security either in one alternative or another I thought the entire Budget safer than a reduced one for the House or the country and I felt that if we proposed it the name & fame of the Government at any rate would stand well.

Wood[1] seemed still rather to hang back: but the rest of the Cabinet now appeared well satisfied & we parted well resolved & certainly more likely to stand or fall by the Budget as a whole than we seemed to be on Wed[nesda]y. [Sc. Tuesday][2]

16. Sat.

Wrote to The Speaker (2)—Mr Pressly—and minutes. Saw Mr Wood with Mr Pressly—and Mr Timm—Sir C. Trevelyan—Mr Wilson—Mr Cook—Ld Aberdeen—Sir T. Fremantle. Cabinet 2¼–5½. A short drive to the Park with C. We dined at Stafford House—Lady Malmesbury's afterwards. Worked much & late on my Budget papers.

[1] 'on hearing from me that any surplus would be small Wood astounded the Cabinet by proposing that we should in that case ask for twelve months renewal of the Income Tax. Newcastle said we should be hooted: & the proposal fell stillborn': this added in the margin.

[2] Initialled and dated 15 April 1853; Add MS 44778, f. 112.

17. 3. S.E[aster]

St James (& Holy Commn. wh drew us there) mg. [1] Chapel Royal evg. Saw Newcastle—Herbert. MS of 1841 aloud in evg. Read Paradiso. But I was obliged to give several hours to my figures.[2] Wrote to the Speaker—Mr Pressly.

18. M.

Wrote minutes. Read Shakespeare (at nt.). This day was devoted to working up my papers & figures for the evening. Then drove & walked with C. Went at 4½ to the House. Spoke 4¾ hours in detailing the Financial measures: and my strength stood out well thank God.[3] Many kind congratulations afterwards. At 11 o'clock the Herberts & Wortley's came home with us & had soup & Negus.[4]

19. T.

Wrote to the Prince Albert[5]—Mr Cook—Lord J. Russell—V.C. Oxford—Chev. Bunsen—Ed D. News[6]—E. of Aberdeen—R. Phillimore—and minutes. Saw Pr. Fred. Schl[eswig] Holstein—Mr W. Russell[7]—Mr Jackson—Mr Bonham—Northcote—D. of Newcastle—Ld Granville—Ld Lansdowne—Goulburn—F. Charteris—E. Ellice. Read Thiers on Protection.[8] H. of C. 4¾–8 and 9½–1¼.[9] I received today innumerable marks of kindness: enough to make me ashamed. On Sunday that verse of the Psalms was as it were given me: 'O turn thee then unto me, and have mercy upon me: give Thy strength unto Thy servant, and help the son of Thine handmaid.'[10] But my life is wholly unworthy of these consolations.

20. Wed.

Wrote to Mr Wylie—Lady Peel (& copy)—Mr Gibson—Robn. G—Wm. Gladstone—E. of Aberdeen—Robt. Gladstone—J. W. Freshfield—Mr Panizzi—Archdn. Harrison—& minutes. Saw Mr Moffatt—Sir A. Spearman with Mr Coulson—Mr J. Wood with Mr Wilson—Presidents of Belfast & Galway Colleges[11]—Mr Calcraft.[12] H. of C. at 12. Levee at 2. Cabinet dinner

[1] See 9 May 54.
[2] In Morley, i. 468.
[3] His first budget: *H* cxxv. 1350. Full text in Bassett, *Speeches*, 183, notes in Add MS 44653, ff. 21–112.
[4] Cp. Morley, i. 468.
[5] Guedalla, *Q*, i. 103.
[6] Frederick Knight Hunt, 1814–54; physician and journalist; assistant editor of *Daily News* 1846, editor from 1851.
[7] William Russell 1800–84, 3rd s. of Lord William Russell; accountant general to court of Chancery 1839–73 and as such a commissioner for national debt reduction.
[8] L. A. Thiers, tr. M. de St. Félix, 'Speech on the commercial policy of France and in opposition to the introduction of free trade into France' (1852); delivered in 1851.
[9] Answered questions: *H* cxxvi. 33.
[10] Ps. lxxxvi. 16.
[11] Pooley Shuldman Henry, 1801–81, president of Queen's college, Belfast, 1845–79, and Edward Berwick, president of Queen's college, Galway, 1845 until he d. 1877.
[12] John Hales Calcraft, 1796–1880; liberal M.P. Wareham 1820–6, 1832–41, 1857–9.

at Ld Granville's. We discussed the Budget—Advertisement duty[1]—meeting in Downing St on Saty.—& were very merry. Lady Clarendon's party af[terward]s.

21. Th.

Wrote to Mrs Bennett—Sir T. Redington[2]—Rev. H. Hayman—Mr Pressly—Mr Phelps[3]—Mr Brooksbank[4]—Mr Coulson—Dr Briscoe—& minutes. Saw Adderley—Mr Trevor—Sir T. Redington—Sir A. Spearman—Mr Coulson—Ld Emlyn—Ld Ellesmere—Mr Tomline. H. of C. $4\frac{1}{2}$–$7\frac{1}{2}$ and $8\frac{1}{4}$–$10\frac{1}{2}$, also $11\frac{3}{4}$–$12\frac{1}{2}$.[5] Dined at Mrs Talbot's. Lady Ellesmere's in Evg. Our first breakfast: to some twenty.

22. Fr.

Wrote to Ld Palmerston[6]—Sir J. Walmsley—Mr Pressly—Mr Barlow—Mr Wood—Fremantle—D of Argyll—Sir J. Graham—Mr W. Brown—Mr Coulson—and minutes. Read Wilson's MS.[7] Saw Govr. of the Bank—Mr Gibson & Deputation (Advt. Duty)—Mr Franks. H. of C. $4\frac{1}{2}$–$8\frac{1}{2}$ and 9–$12\frac{1}{4}$. Spoke in answer to Kelly & carried the Stocks Commutation Bill thro' Committee.[8]

23. Sat.

Wrote to Mr Pressly—E. Cardwell (2) —Ld Aberdeen—G.C. Lewis—Mr Trevor—J.W. Parker—Mr Glyn—Mr Masterman—Mr Wilson—and minutes. Saw Mr Coulson—Sir A. Spearman—Principal of BNC—Mr Wilson—Mr Pressly—Attornies' Deputation—Albert Park Deputation.[9] Finished Wilson's MS. Cabinet $2\frac{3}{4}$–$6\frac{1}{4}$.[10] Dined at Mr Raikes Currie's to meet City notabilities. Called for Wms but did not succeed[R].

24. 4 S.E.

Whitehall Chapel mg Crown St Evg. MS. of 44 aloud at night. Saw S. Herbert—R. Cavendish. Wrote to Helen. Read the Pastor—Pitcairn[11]—A. Jones[12]—& divers tracts.

[1] Many pamphlets in this in Add MSS 44574–5.

[2] Sir Thomas Nicholas Redington, 1815–62; liberal M.P. Dundalk 1837–46, worked against famine 1847 as Irish poor law commissioner; K.C.B. 1849; secretary to board of control 1852–6.

[3] Joseph Lloyd Phelps, a clerk in a canal office, had written to protest against the revised income tax; he received an exhaustive reply; cp. Add MS 44374, ff. 251–8.

[4] Thomas Brooksbank, barrister and special pleader in Gray's Inn; probably the s. of T. C. (chief clerk in treasury 1834, d. 1850).

[5] Quarrelled with *Disraeli on spirit duties: *H* cxxvi. 163.

[6] See Guedalla, *P*, 88.

[7] Untraced MS by James *Wilson.

[8] *H* cxxvi. 318 ff.

[9] One requesting abolition of the attorney's certificate duty, the other proposing an Albert park in Finsbury; cp. *The Times*, 25 April 1853, 5 f.

[10] Note of resolutions agreed, Add MS 44636, f. 4.

[11] T. B. Murray, *Pitcairn: the island, the people, and the pastor; with a short account of the mutiny on the Bounty* (1853).

[12] Perhaps Alfred B. Jones, 'Observations on the diseases and loss of the teeth' (1853).

25. S.Mark.

Wrote to E. Cardwell—Ld Torrington—Mr C. Cowan[1]—T. S. Gladstone—E. Badeley—Sir T. Fremantle—H. Tufnell—Ld Ellenborough—G. Hudson & minutes. Saw Mr Greswell—Mr Glyn—Mr Warburton—Mr Goulburn—Mr Pressly—S. Herbert & others. Read Two Letters to an M.P.[2] H. of C. 4½–7½ & 8¼–12½. Consulted with the Speaker on the point of order as to Sir E. Lytton's amendment.[3] The dull debate augured well.

26. T.

Wrote to E. of Aberdeen—J. Wilson—Sir A. Spearman—Mr Litton—Rev. E. Hawkins—Mr C. Franks—A. Smollett[4]—Baron Bentinck[5]—& minutes. Saw J.N.G. & Rn. G—D. of Newcastle—H. Herbert[6] with Monsell[7] & Ball—Solr. General. Dined in B[erkeley?] Square. H of C. 4½–7½ and 10½–1 3/4.[8]

27. Wed.

Wrote to Mr Moffatt—Mr Goulburn—Ld Ellesmere—Sir W. Molesworth—Mr Meyrick—Sir A. Spearman—M[blank] and minutes. Dined with the Herberts: & at their evg party. Saw a sad case afterwards[R]. H. of C. 12¾–5. Sent up the Stocks Conversion Bill.[9] Walk with C. Read Brodie on Succn. Tax.[10]

28. Th.

Wrote to Mr Pressly—Mr Wilson—Sir J. Walmsley—J. Wood—Willy—Mr W. Williams MP.[11]—V. Pres Manchr. Comm[ercia]l. Assn.[12] and minutes. Saw Mr Trevor—Bp of Down & Connor[13]—Glass Deputation[14]—Mr Wilson—Mr Sadleir—Mr Wood—Mr J.D. Cook—and a body of Irish

[1] Charles Cowan, 1801–89, Edinburgh paper manufacturer and liberal M.P. Edinburgh 1847–59.
[2] Not found; cp., perhaps, 8 July 44.
[3] It damned the extended income tax as 'unjust and impolitic': *H* cxxvi. 454.
[4] Alexander Smollett, 1801–81, Edinburgh advocate and Peelite M.P. Dumbartonshire 1841–59.
[5] Adolphe, Baron von Bentinck, 1798?–1868, Dutch ambassador in London from 1851.
[6] Henry Arthur Herbert, 1815–66; Peelite M.P. co. Kerry from 1847; minor office 1857–8.
[7] William *Monsell, 1812–94; liberal M.P. co. Limerick 1847–74; convert to Rome 1850; president of board of health 1857, paymaster general 1866, 1871–3, under secretary for colonies 1868–70; cr. Baron Emly 1874; a member of the 'engagement'; cp. 23 Feb. 45n. and Add MS 44152, ff. 94–265.
[8] Spoke on South Sea Commutation Bill 3°: *H* cxxvi. 619.
[9] Ibid.: *H* cxxvi. 625.
[10] P. B. *Brodie, 'Tax on succession and burdens of land' (1850); succession duties as an alternative to income tax.
[11] William Williams, 1789–1865, radical M.P. Coventry 1835–47, Lambeth from 1850; known as 'Punch's Wiscount'.
[12] Malcolm Ross, who had sent a memorial supporting the budget; copy in Add MS 44528, f. 134.
[13] Robert Bent *Knox, 1808–93; prebendary of Limerick 1841, bp. of Down, Connor and Dromore, 1849, abp. of Armagh from 1886.
[14] Papers untraced.

members resp. Income Tax.[1] Also Ld J.R. & Sir J. Young thereon. H. of C. 4½–7½ and 9–12.[2] Read Brodie on Succession Tax—Inquiry into Debt.[3] I felt at length a good deal overset: & had recourse to blue pill at night.

29. Fr.

Wrote to Ld J. Russell—Mr Wilson—Mr Cowan—Lord Seymer[4]—MW Mayow—Mr Hadfield[5]—Mr H. Grant—and minutes. Read A. Stephens on Eccl Courts[6]—Raisin on Real Property[7]—Murray's Pitcairn. Saw Ld Granville—Mr Trevor—with them, Sir J. Graham & Ld Palmerston—Mr Barnes—J.N.G. I had only 6 or 6½ hours of business but was all the worse for it & repeated the Blue Pill—absenting myself from the H. of Commons.[8]

30. Sat.

Wrote to Ld Aberdeen—Sent for Hodgson who desired me to keep my bed & sleep as much as possible hoping I might thus be fit for work on Monday. So I had an idle day. Read Pitcairn (finished)—& Inquiry into Trade & Public Revenues—Set a few of my drawers in order: part of the Chaos wh I have not been able to look at since I took office. As usual, the doctor's verdict satisfied & approved all that C. had done for me.

May 1. 5 S E[aster]—SS. Philip & James.

All my Church today was in my room. Hodgson made a good report of me. Read Bp Van Mildert's Sermons[9]—Monro's Parish[10]—Joyce on Convocation.[11]

2. M.

Wrote to Cocks & Co—J. Wood—Mr Maclaurin[12]—Miss Brown—Christie & M.—E. Ellis[13]—Sir T. Carmichael—Mr J. Fergus[14]—Mr Bacon[15]—and minutes. Saw Mr H[odgson] again, who reported well. Saw Ld Abn.—Ld J. Russell—Sir J. Young—all without or agt. orders: but I refused all I

[1] The 1853 budget extended income tax to Ireland.
[2] Answered questions, then budget deb.: *H* cxxvi. 680.
[3] Cp. 25 Feb. 53. [4] Sc. Seymour.
[5] George *Hadfield, 1787–1879; anti-corn law leaguer and radical M.P. Sheffield 1852–74.
[6] A. J. Stephens, 'A letter to . . . Baron *Cranworth . . . on the constitution of the ecclesiastical courts' (1853); with appendix.
[7] Untraced.
[8] Thus missing the budget deb.: *H* cxxvi. 805.
[9] W. Van Mildert, *Sermons on several occasions, and charges* (1838); with a memoir by C. Ives.
[10] E. *Monro, *The parish:* [*a poem*] *in five books* (1853).
[11] A. J. Joyce, 'Last glimpses of convocation, showing the latest incidents and results of synodical action in the Church of England (1853).
[12] Probably Archibald Maclaurin, an Admiralty clerk.
[13] Copy on his dismissal from board of trade 1845 in Add MS 44528, f. 134.
[14] John Fergus, Kirkcaldy merchant and liberal M.P. Kirkcaldy 1835–7, for Fife 1847–59; d. 1865.
[15] George Peter Bacon, 1806?–78, proprietor and editor of the *Sussex Advertiser* from 1843; cp. Add MS 44374, f. 291.

could. Began the heavy task of correcting my Financial Statement. Read Inquiry into Public Revenues. H of C. 4½–5¼ and 10¼–2½. Voted in 323:252 for my Income Tax Resolution: a good division.[1] Yet what a muster of landed people for such an amendment![2]

3. T.

Wrote to Ld Granville. Saw Mr Wilson—Mr Barnes—F. Lawley. Mr Hodgson found me well on towards recovery. Read Burt on Separate Confinement[3]—National Miscellany.[4] Worked on correcting the proof of my Speech: I suppose it is from the Times: & very ill done, so as to entail extreme labour in making but a sorry affair of it.

4. Wed.

Wrote to W. Cowper[5]—Ld Provost of Edinb.[6]—Rev. J.C. Ward[7]—Sir C. Trevelyan—Hon A Gordon—JW Parker & Son—Sir C. Barry—J. Watts Russell—Sir F. Smith—E. Smith & Co,[8] and minutes. Read Burt on Sep. Confinement. Saw T.G.—Sir J. Young—F. Lawley. Dined with the Attorney General: then went to Lord Clarendons where the Cabinet remained till near 12.—Then for a moment to Norfolk House.[9]

5. Th. Ascension Day.

St James's mg—prayers only. Wrote to Sir A. Spearman—W. Monsell—Mr Hayter—Price (Robe)[10]—Mr A. Perceval.—Robn. G.—Lord Hatherton E. Cardwell—Ed. Fraser's Mag. and minutes. H. of C. 4½–5¾, 7–9, and 9¾–1¼.[11] Saw Mr Hodgson—Mr Kirk—Mr Wilson—Mr Muntz (Archer)[12]—Sir C. Trevelyan—A. Gordon. Read Mr Burt. My letters are now to be reckoned only by the hundred: the Priv. Sec.s are quite overwhelmed & we are obliged to get large fresh aid.

6. Fr.

Wrote to Lord Monteagle—Sir C. Wood—Rev Mr Champneys—Mr J. Wood—Rev Mr Hayman—A. Hayward—Horace Powys—W.F. Larkins

[1] *H* cxxvi. 1004.
[2] i.e. *Lytton's amndt., cp. 25 Apr. 53n.
[3] J. T. Burt, *Results of the system of separate confinement as administered at Pentonville prison* (1852).
[4] A literary periodical; John Armstrong, the editor had sent the first number.
[5] Cp. 23 July 27.
[6] Duncan *McLaren, 1800–86; Edinburgh draper; lord provost 1851–4; liberal M.P. Edinburgh 1865–81, when known as 'the member for Scotland'. Gladstone's letter is in J. B. Mackie, *Life of Duncan *McLaren* (1888) i. 320.
[7] sc. J. G. Ward; cp. 4 Apr. 30.
[8] Tailors in Old Broad street, City of London.
[9] The duke of Norfolk's town house in St. James's Square.
[10] Probably Price and Ball, tailors in the Strand, about a new chancellor's robe, *Disraeli having refused to part with the old; picture in Reid, *G*, 419.
[11] Row over Irish income tax: *H* cxxvi. 1193.
[12] Muntz was the intermediary in the patent purchase: cp. 17 Mar. 53n.

—A.S. Gladstone—H. Taylor—Maj. Cumming Bruce—Mr Duncan MP[1]—Sir A. Spearman—Mr Glyn MP—E. Cardwell—and minutes. H. of C. 4½–9¼ and 9¾–12¼: on the Budget.[2] Saw H.J.G.—Mr Wilson—Sir C. Trevelyan—Bp of Oxford—London Daily Press Deputation[3]—Mr A. Gordon—Sir S. Northcote. Read Burt.

7. Sat.

Wrote to D. of Newcastle—J. Wood (2)—Lord Chandos—Robn. G.—Sir W. Molesworth—Mr W. Kirk and minutes. 11½–1¼. Young, Redington, Pressly, & Timm, on I.T. Bill. Saw Ld Sefton with Ld Stradbroke—Ld Chancr.—A. Gordon—Ld Abn. At 1¼ went to the luncheon at Stafford House. Mrs Stowe's appearance had been unfavourably reported of; but it is not without mark & character.[4] I saw more however of Lady Stafford[5] whom I had not before known: & I was greatly charmed with her. Cabinet 3–4½. Off to Brighton at 5: where Mrs Denison kindly offers her house.[6] In evg worked on papers & letters—& read Moore's Journal.[7]

8. S.aft Ascension.

St Paul's mg & aft. Read Counter Theory (finished)—Joyce on Convocation—Denison's Charge[8]—Church Periodicals. Walk with C: & a day of much rest.

9. M.

Off to London at 9.55 after breakfast & a walk. Reached D. St before 12. Saw Sir A. Spearman—Sir C. Trevelyan—Messrs. Fox & Cobbett[9]—Mr Pressly come[10] Mr Timm on I. Tax. Settled list for my Birthday Banquet. H. of C. 4½–8½ and 9–1. Spoke agt. Palmer and voted in 276:201. We had not hoped so much.[11]

10. T.

Wrote to A.P. Saunders—Mr Cahill[12]—Sir C. Trevelyan—C. Pressly—Chev.

[1] George Duncan, 1791–1878, Dundee merchant and liberal M.P. Dundee 1841–57.

[2] Defended Irish income tax: *H* cxxvi. 1265.

[3] The proposed alteration of this duty encouraged a large number of petitions and deputations, listed in *PP* 1852–3, 'Index to the reports of the select cttee. on public petitions'.

[4] A formal welcome for Harriet Elizabeth Beecher Stowe, 1811–96, novelist, then on a tour of Europe. See 22 Aug. 54n.

[5] Lady Anne Leveson-Gower, *née* Hay-Mackenzie, 1829–88, m. 1849 as his first wife George Granville William, 1828–92, marquess of Stafford, 3rd duke of Sutherland 1861. She was a leader of London society and was cr. countess of Cromartie 1861.

[6] Rented for the summer.

[7] T. *Moore, *Memoirs, Journal and Correspondence of Thomas Moore, edited by . . . Lord John Russell*, 8 v. (1853–1856).

[8] G. A. Denison, 'The catechism of the Church of England the basis of all teaching in parish schools. A charge . . .' (1853).

[9] John Morgan Cobbett, 1800–77, 2nd s. of W.*; liberal M.P. Oldham 1852–65, and from 1872.

[10] Altered from 'cum'.

[11] Robert Palmer's motion to moderate schedule A income tax: *H* cxxvi. 1353.

[12] Edward Cahill, clerk in wages department of Admiralty.

Bunsen—E. Divett—Mrs H.A. Herbert[1]—Sir C. Wood—Duke of Argyll—Sir R. Mayne—Mr Hayter—Sir J. Young—E. Cardwell—and minutes.[2] Saw Mr Wilson—Sir S. Northcote—Mr Franks—Tufnell—Dined at Mrs Talbot's. H. of C. 4½–6¼ and 8½–10¾.[3] Then to the Opera.[4] On my way back I found I need not go to H of C. & took a turn thro' L[eicester] Square whence I fell into a convn. in Panton St: when followed the business with Wilson wh brought on the giving in[5] charge at the Stationhouse. These talkings of mine are certainly not within the rules of worldly prudence: I am not sure that Christian prudence sanctions them for such an one as me; but my aim & intention did not warrant the charge wh doubtless has been sent to teach me wisdom & which I therefore welcome[6]

11. Wed.

Wrote to Mr Finlaison—Ld Palmerston (2)[7]—Ld Chancellor—D. [of] Newcastle—Abp of York—Mr Hubbard—and minutes. Police Court at 10½.[8] The prisoner was remanded. Saw D[uke of] Argyll—Govr. Bank—Mr Wilson—Sir A. Spearman—Inspector Parke[9]—Newcastle—Ld Lansdowne—Cardwell. Rode: an adventure, after so long cessation. It is Johnnie's poney, a playful & nice tempered animal full of spirit. It is melancholy to think who shd. have been its burden.[10] Dined at Ld Chancellor's—Lady Clarendon's ball afterwards. 2–6 Four hours on Legacy Duty Bill: with D. of N[ewcastle], Graham, Bethell, Trevor, Earle,[11] & Thring: a hardheaded party.

12. Th.

Wrote to Sir J.E. Wilmot—Ld J. Russell—S. Herbert—Ed. M[orning] Herald[12]—and minutes. 10–11. 13 to Breakfast. Worked from 11 on Customs' Duties with Wilson Fremantle Cardwell & C[ustoms] Officers—from 2 on I.T. Bill with Mr Coulson Pressly & Timm. Saw Newcastle—Northcote—Bunsen. H of C. 4¾–7½ and 8–12½. Spoke near 2 h on Legacy Duty[13]—having to get it up during the previous I.T. Debate—a day of severe work; & I am again out of sorts.

13. Fr.

Wrote to Ld Mayor—and minutes. H. of C. 4½–7 and 8½–12¾: on Legacy

[1] Mary, da. of J. M. Balfour of Whittinghame, A.J.'s* grandf.; she m. Henry Arthur Herbert 1837 and d. 1866.

[2] Incl. a note to *Palmerston, in Guedalla, *P*, 90.

[3] Inspection of nunneries: *H* cxxvii. 79.

[4] Donizetti's *Lucrezia Borgia.*

[5] These two words written over two others.

[6] William Wilson, a Scot, was arrested for 'attempting to extort money' by threatening to expose Gladstone to the *Morning Herald* for speaking to a prostitute.

[7] Both in Guedalla, *P*, 91–4.

[8] Report in *The Times*, 12 May 1853, 5e; judgement was delayed until 13 May 1853.

[9] John Duke Parke, police inspector for the Piccadilly district, in charge of the Wilson case.

[10] i.e. John Gladstone, his deceased nephew.

[11] Thomas Earle, clerk in the inland revenue office.

[12] Robert Knox, d. 1859, edited *Morning Herald*, 1846–58.

[13] *H* cxxvii. 258.

Duty &c. The declining to divide was a mere shallow ruse but a good sign.[1] Mr Wilson, Sir A. Spearman, Mr Andersen,[2] Mr Hubbard, at 10½ to settle the Exr. Bonds notices.[3] The Customs' party 11–1¼: finished revising Resolutions. Then went to Marlb[orough] St to make my deposition for the committal of Wilson.[4] Back to see Mr Hodgson at 2½. Pressly at 3 on A[dvertisment] T[ax] Resolutions. Saw Northcote—Ld Aberdeen—Inspector Parke—Mr Goulburn—Mr Wood—Mr Moffatt—Mr Delane—Ld Aberdeen—R. Lowe. Read Cameron on E.I.[5]

14. Sat.

Wrote to V.C. Oxford—Capt. Harness[6]—Mr Heywood[7]—J.D. Cook—and minutes by the hundred. Read Ballot Weighed[8]—SS. Report.[9] Saw Mr Lefroy—Newcastle—Geo. Hope—Sir C. Trevelyan—Sol. General & the Legacy Duty Bill party from 9½ to 1½. Got off about five to Falconhurst:[10] we arrived at 7½ & spent a calm evening there with our most kind afflicted friend Mrs Talbot.

15. Whitsunday.

Markbeach[11] Ch. 11 A.M. (with H.C.) & 3 P.M. *Such* a congregation! the living fruit of the piety of the dead—& of the living too—it speaks much for all. read Jeune's Sermon[12]—Sinclair's Charge[13]—Bp Wordsworth's Report & Sermon—Hamilton's Letter[14]—Brecon Ch[15]—Rendu's Report.[16]

[1] *Disraeli intervened at the end of the deb. to defer opposition until the bill was published: *H* cxxvii. 370.

[2] Sc. W. G. Anderson.

[3] Cp. 23 May 53.

[4] Report in *The Times*, 14 May 1853, 8d. *Greville (15 May 1853) recorded that the 'Wilson affair . . . has almost entirely passed away already, not having been taken up politically' and noted the press's reticence.

[5] C. H. *Cameron and Sir E. *Ryan, 'A letter to the honourable the court of directors of the East India Company' (1850).

[6] (Sir) Henry Drury *Harness, 1804–83; secretary to railway commission 1846–50, commissioner of Irish works 1852–4; in Indian mutiny; directed Chatham dockyard 1860; K.C.B. 1873.

[7] James Heywood, 1810–97; Trinity, Cambridge, liberal M.P. North Lancashire 1847–57; campaigned for abolition of university theological tests.

[8] Possibly E. C. Whitehurst, 'The Ballot. A reply to S. *Smith and Lord J. *Russell' (1853).

[9] Charles *Wordsworth, *Report of the proceedings of the special synod of the united diocese of St. Andrews . . . with the sermon preached on that occasion by the bishop* (1853).

[10] Home of Mrs. J. Chetwynd-Talbot from 1850, by Edenbridge, Kent.

[11] Markbeech church, Edenbridge; Robert Shapland Hunt, of Exeter, Oxford, was the curate from 1852.

[12] F. *Jeune, 'The epistles written by the spirit of the living God' (1853); on II Cor. iii. 3.

[13] J. *Sinclair, 'Church questions of 1853. A charge, delivered to the clergy of Middlesex' (1853).

[14] W. K. *Hamilton, 'The cathedral commission. A letter to . . . the dean of Salisbury' (1853).

[15] 'Christ's college, Brecon, its past history and present capabilities considered, with reference to a bill now before parliament' (1853).

[16] See next note.

16. M.

Church at 10¼ AM. Wrote to Lord Chancellor—J.N.G.—Sir W. Molesworth —C. Pressly—Principal BNC—T.M. Gibson—M. Eugene Rendu[1] & some four score minutes. Read (on recommn.) the Heir of Redclyffe.[2] Drive, & walk, with C. & Mrs Talbot.

17. T.

Church 10¼ A.M. Wrote to Ld Monteagle—Ld Cowley—Ld Kinnaird—Sir C. Wood—Sir J. Young—Jos Hume—Mr Smollett—Robn. G (2)—Ld Aberdeen—Mr J. Wood—Ld Clarendon—E. Coleridge—Sir W. Molesworth —and minutes—as many as yesterday. My post of Whitmonday, a holiday, yielded some 70 letters. Drive with C. & Mrs Talbot: to Edles & Cowden.[3] Read the Heir of Redclyffe—The Eastern Question[4]—Stephen on N.S.W. Constn.[5]

18. Wed.

Wrote to Sir J. Graham—Ld Jocelyn—Sir T. Fremantle—Mrs Lane[6]— V.C. Oxford—Sir C. Trevelyan—Ld Belhaven—J.N.G.—Sir J. Pakington —H.J.G.—A.B. Cochrane[7]—Rev A. Whyte—Newcastle—and minutes— on the scale of former days. Also wrote on C[olonial] Ch[urch] Bill. Read Heir of Redclyffe—Maurel's Wellington.[8] Drove to South Park[9] for luncheon & saw Ld Hardinge.

19. Th.

Set off for London at 8¼ much the better thank God for my holiday. Reached D[owning] Street 10½. Wrote to G.A. Denison—O.B. Cole—Miss Vernon[10]— Mr Wilson—Sir C. Trevelyan (2)—and minutes. Succession Tax Meeting 1¼–4½. H of C. through the evening to 1 A.M.[11]—but away to ride ¾ hour— & dine.—Business then with many members of Parlt.—Saw T.G. [Read] Treasury papers.

20. Fr.

Wrote to W.M. Goalen—Sir J. Young—Provost of Oriel—R. Barker—

[1] Eugène Rendu, 1824–1903, French educationalist, author of *De l'instruction primaire à Londres dans ses rapports avec l'état social* (2nd ed., extended, 1853).

[2] Charlotte *Yonge's first success (1853).

[3] 4 miles SE. of Edenbridge.

[4] Perhaps 'The cross versus the crescent; or, the religious view of the eastern question' (1853).

[5] Sir A. *Stephen, 'Thoughts on the constitution of a second legislative chamber for New South Wales' (1853).

[6] The wife of Charles Lane, 1793?–1879; Queen's, Oxford; rector of Deal 1838–45, of Wrotham, Kent, from 1845. She had requested a position for a Mr. Berrington. Cp. Add MS 44528, f. 141 and 9 Oct. 54.

[7] Of Stourbridge; Gladstone hoped to sell him the remains of Oak Farm.

[8] Jules Maurel, *Le duc de Wellington* (1853).

[9] *Hardinge's seat 4 miles NW. of Tunbridge Wells.

[10] Probably Catherine, da. of 2nd Baron Vernon; she d. in 1867, aged 85.

[11] Spoke on misc. estimates: *H* cxxvii. 409.

J S Wortley—and minutes. Legacy Duty Synod 2–4½—I believe the last. Saw Mr C. Uppington & his daughter & paid them their money.[1]—Saw Inspector Parke—Jocelyn—& many members of Parlt. on business. H. of C. 4½–7½ and 8–12½. I.T. Bill read 2° in silence![2] Read 'Priestly Despotism in Wesl. Conf.'[3]

21. Sat.

Wrote to Lyttelton—Ld Aberdeen—C. Pressly—Jas Freshfield—W. Wilson[4]—Sir R. Murchison—Mr Hubbard—Inspector Parke—Jas Wilson—Sir A. Spearman—Cardwell—Rev. E.S. Foulkes—J.E. Elliot[5]—the Lord Primate[6]—E[arl of] Clarendon—Ld Monteagle—& minutes. Saw Sir A. Spearman—Ld Granville. Cabinet 3½–6. Settled the Corporation Tax. India begun.[7] Accomplished a third ride. Dined at Sir J. Johnstone's—Duchess of Argyll's afterwards.[8] Worked rather late.

22. Trin[ity]. S.

Whitehall Chapel 11 AM (H.C.)—Chapel Royal aft—MS of 42 aloud in evg. Called to find Mrs Nixon:[9] she was not to be seen. Wrote to Rev. E. Greswell—M.F. Tupper—Archd. Wilberforce—Mrs Nixon—Mr Mallaby.[10] Read Priestly Despotism—Br. Qu. R. on Mad Guyon—on Mortmain[11]—Wilberforce on H. Eucharist[12]—& Pamphlets.

23. M.

Wrote to Col. Harcourt—Sir C. Wood—Sir T. Fremantle—R. Barker—Sir A. Spearman—and minutes. Saw Sir A. Spearman—Ld Aberdeen—Mr Crawford—Mr Hayter—Mr Pressly with Mr Timm—Sir T. Fremantle—Mr Trevor—various M.P.s. Tea draft Deputation—& Raisins Deputation 12–2½.[13] H. of C. 4½–8½ and 9¼–1¼.[14] The Herberts dined. Read Dodd on Court of Arches.[15] These are rather anxious days as to our financial operations in the City, in connection with the Exchr. Bills coming due.[16]

[1] Cp. passage following 31 Aug. 53.
[2] And spoke on misc. estimates: *H* cxxvii. 468.
[3] Untraced.
[4] To the blackmailer, refusing to attempt to modify the official verdict; copy in Add MS 44528, f. 142. Gladstone later secured his early release.
[5] John Edmund Elliott, 1788–1862, 3rd s. of 1st earl of Minto; liberal M.P. Roxburghshire 1837–41, 1847–59; minor office 1849–52.
[6] J. B. *Sumner.
[7] See Conacher, 82.
[8] 27 Grosvenor Square and 4 Carlton House Terrace respectively.
[9] Mrs. Col. Nixon, of Dorset Place.
[10] Joseph Mallaby, attorney in Birkenhead.
[11] *British Quarterly Review*, xvii. 317, 420 (May 1853); on Upham's *Guyon* and on the select cttee's report on mortmain.
[12] R. I. *Wilberforce, *The doctrine of the holy eucharist* (1853).
[13] Papers in Add MS 44575, f. 91.
[14] Spoke on Income Tax Bill: *H* cxxvii. 515.
[15] E. Dodd, 'Reform your arches' (1853).
[16] Cp. PRO T. 29/551, f. 409. About £17m. worth of bills was due, and authorization was needed for further issues.

24. T. X

Wrote to Mr Goulburn—J. Griffiths—Ld Aberdeen—Mr Craufurd—Ld Torrington—J. Wood—Mrs Walond[1] (al[ias] Miss Fellowes)—Sir J. Young —Robn. G.—Mr W. Beaumont[2]—Mr A.K. Smith[3]—Provost of Oriel— and minutes—the correspondence continues extremely heavy. 2–4¼ P.M. Savings Bank Synod. Saw Mr Trevor—Sir A. Spearman—Mr Pressly— Mr Dawson[4]—Mr Conolly.[5] Gave my birthday dinner: 28 covers: in the drawingroom. Out afterwards to see the fireworks. Rode: Osborne joined me & told me many anecdotes. Read Dockyard Report.[6]

25. Wed.

Wrote to Ld Palmerston—Mr J. Ball—J.D. Coleridge—Mrs Cracroft—Bp of Oxford—Sir J. Young—and minutes. An appeal made to me at night went better than heretofore. National Debt Commrs. met 10½–11½. Saw Phillimore—Spearman—Ld Chancellor—Monsell—Trevelyan—Newcastle —Bp of Oxford—Pressly & Timm on Assessed Taxes 3–5. Rode in the Park. Read Ld Stanley on Church Rates—a memorable pamphlet.[7] Dined at S. Herbert's—Cabinet. The Church Rate & India questions after dinner: the latter stands strangely enough.[8]

26. Th.

Wrote to Rev. B. Wilson—R.M. Milnes—Dr Jacobson—Jas Watson—Sir J. Ramsden—Ld Belhaven—Mr Colvile—and minutes. Read 'Englishman' to Ld Derby.[9] Ten to breakfast. Saw W.R. Farquhar—Northcote—Mrs Malcolm—Sir W. Heathcote—Mr A. Gordon—Ld Arundel—Mr Pressly— Mr Kirk[10]—Mr Ball—Mr Bright—Mr Brocklehurst. H of C. 4½–6¾ and 9¼– 1½ on Church Rates. The second division 172:220 was ominous enough.[11]

27. Fr.

Wrote to Fremantle—Mr Malet—Ld Monck—Mr Price—Mr Wilson—and

[1] Probably a cousin of Sir T. Gladstone's wife.

[2] Wentworth Blackett Beaumont, 1829–1907, s. of T.W.*; liberal M.P. South Northumberland 1852–85, Tyneside 1886–92; cr. Baron Allendale 1906.

[3] Alexander Kennedy Smith, a mechanic; cp. Add MS 44375, f. 74.

[4] Probably Frederick Dawson, a treasury clerk.

[5] Thomas Conolly, 1823–76; tory M.P. Donegal from 1849.

[6] Report of select cttee. on dockyard appointments: *PP* 1853, xxv. 1.

[7] Lord E. H. S. *Stanley, 'The church-rate question considered' (1853); supports the exemption of dissenters from paying church rates.

[8] Cp. Add MS 44778, ff. 137–42 (written on 10 June); and Conacher, 82. 'Appealed to another' [?] here deleted.

[9] See 4 Dec. 52.

[10] William Kirk, 1795–1870; linen merchant and liberal M.P. Newry 1852–7, and from 1868.

[11] The second division was *Hume's amndt. to stop church rates and supply all anglican needs from the church commissioners' funds: *H* cxxvii. 646.

minutes. Scotch Spirit Deputn. at 1—Irish do ½ past 1.[1] Saw Mr Gledstanes[2]—Ld R. Grosvenor—Earl of Aberdeen. Mr Pressly with Mr Timm, on Inc. Tax. Mr Wood with Mr Dobson,[3] on Licences. H. of C. 4½–1¼ working I.T. Bill in Committee.[4]

28. Sat.

Wrote to Sir J. Young (2)—Sir A. Spearman—W.R. Farquhar—Ld Palmerston—Macaulay and minutes. Evening at home. Read Scott's Letter to Herbert[5]—Tasso, Ger. Lib.[6] Visited Christie's. Saw Mr Kennedy—Mr Hayter—Sir T. Fremantle—Sir C. Trevelyan. Cabinet 2¾–6¼.

29. 1 S.Trin.

Whitehall, & Chapel Royal. MS. of 47 aloud in evg. Walk with C. Saw Rev. Mr Wilson. Read Eclipse of Faith[7]—Joyce on Convocation[8]—Garbett's Letter to Bp of Chichester.[9]

30. M.

Wrote to D. of Newcastle—Mr Goulburn—Archd. Garbett[10]—Mr Fergus—Sir T. Fremantle—Sir H. Ward—Provost of Eton—Archdn. Clerke[11]—Sir C. Trevelyan—and minutes. H of C. 4½–1½—without leaving my place except in 2 divisions.[12] Saw Sir A. Spearman—Mr Pressly with Sir J. Young & Mr Timm 1–3¾—Mr Wood with Mr Dobson. This day my work touched 17 hours very nearly. Read a little Tasso.

31. T.

Wrote to Hon. A. Gordon—Ld Torrington—Mr C. Pressly—Sir T. Fremantle—D.T. Gladstone—S. Herbert—D. of Newcastle—Mr Hawes—Ld E. Bruce—Mr Peto—Ld Howard—Mr H. Baring—Mr Bouverie—& minutes. Saw Lyttelton—A. Gordon—Arbuthnot—Sir A. Spearman—J.E. Denison—& many MP.s on Inc. Tax Clauses & other matters—also J.N.G.—Sir J. Young. Read Pritchard on E. Courts.[13] Attended Pres. Civil

[1] Of Scottish and Irish distillers, cp. *The Times*, 28 May 1853, 6b.

[2] John Hampden Gledstanes, a merchant, of White Lion Court, Cornhill.

[3] Thomas Dobson, 1797?–1855, a surveying general examiner to inland revenue board, joint secretary there 1860–3; assistant secretary of excise 1856–60.

[4] *H* cxxvii. 719ff.

[5] Perhaps a letter to H. A. Herbert, M.P., then in correspondence on annuities, cp. Add MS 44528, f. 155.

[6] T. Tasso, *La Gerusalemme liberata* (? ed. of 1768).

[7] F.B., [H. *Rogers], *The eclipse of faith; or, a visit to a religious sceptic* (1852).

[8] Cp. 1 May 53.

[9] J. Garbett, 'What kind of synod does the Church of England require? A letter to the lord bp. of Chichester' (1853).

[10] Draft in Add MS 44375, f. 115.

[11] Charles Carr Clerke, 1798–1877; student of Christ Church 1814, canon 1846, subdean 1852; archdeacon of Oxford from 1830; chaired cttee. for Gladstone's election rival 1865.

[12] Income Tax Bill in cttee.: *H* cxxvii. 789.

[13] W. T. Pritchard, *Reform of the ecclesiastical courts* (1853).

Engineers 9 P.M.[1] Drive with C. H. of C. $4\frac{1}{2}$–$5\frac{1}{4}$ and 10–$2\frac{1}{2}$. Lord J.R. made I thought an imprudent speech highly galling to the R.C.s & loudly cheered by Tyrrell: the truths contained in it being of dangerous & insidious application.[2] Cabinet 2–$4\frac{1}{2}$.[3] Gazed with much pleasure on my Murillo: though I have some misgiving about *my* laying out so much money on a picture.[4]

Wednesday June One 1853.

Wrote to C. Baring Wall—Ld Lansdowne—A. Lockhart—Mr O'Flaherty[5] —H.J.G. (2)—Sir C. Trevelyan—Provost of Oriel—Fremantle, & minutes. Sixteen to dinner: & a large evening party.[6] Standing did my leg much harm. Saw Ld A. Hervey—Jas Freshfield—Sir J. Young—Sir A. Spearman —Mr Wilson—Mr Glyn. Also I had many conversations today on Ld J.R's speech of last night: e.g. with Charteris—Herbert—Osborne—Atty General —D. of Argyll. I called on Ld Abn. to report about it. Conv. with Mass[imo] d'Azeglio. Read 'Paradiso'.

2. Th.

Wrote to G. Burnett—P.A. Pickering—and many minutes. On account of my leg I staid in bed & worked there; Saw Pressly with Timm—another long bout on I.T.—Lord Dunraven—Mr Trevor. Rose at 3.—Saw the Cork Cutters Deputation.[7] H. of C. $4\frac{1}{2}$–$1\frac{3}{4}$: working Income Tax & Customs the whole night. A little stung once or twice: but very sorry for it immediately: would God that my conscience wrought equably.[8]

3. Fr.

Wrote to Mr V. Scully[9]—Col. Harcourt—Miss Fellowes—Ld Breadalbane[10] —C. Pressly—Ld J. Thynne—V.C. Oxford—Ld Belhaven—J.N.G.—Rev Mr Richards—Robn. G.—Rev. P.M. Smythe—Mr J.H. Forbes[11]—J.E. Gladstone and minutes. Saw Mr Griffiths jun[12]—Mr Longman—F R Bonham—Mr Trevor—Mr Hodgson (my doctor)—Newcastle. H of C. $4\frac{1}{2}$–$7\frac{1}{2}$. Then nursed myself by quiet, as the Indian debate continued through

[1] James Meadows *Rendel, 1799–1856; harbour and canal engineer; president of civil engineers 1852–3.

[2] *Russell, speaking on Irish ecclesiastical revenues, denied the Irish any just grievances: *H* cxxvii. 940.

[3] Cp. last n. on 25 May 53.

[4] A 'Virgin and Child', now at Hawarden.

[5] Anthony O'Flaherty, liberal M.P. Galway 1847–57.

[6] Report in *The Times*, 2 June 1853, 5e.

[7] Papers untraced.

[8] *H* cxxvii. 1037ff.

[9] Vincent *Scully, 1810–71; Irish barrister and liberal M.P. Cork 1852–7, 1859–65. A long letter on the budget, copy in Add MS 44528, f. 146.

[10] John Campbell, 1796–1862, 2nd marquess of Breadalbane 1834; lord chamberlain 1852.

[11] i.e. John Hay *Forbes; his judicial title of Lord Medwyn ended 1852.

[12] Probably the son of the Oak Farm agent.

the evening.[1] Read Greswell's Politian[2]—Upham's Guyon.[3] My darling Willy's birthday—God be with him: I would he were old enough to take my place & let me be out of this whirl which carries me off my balance.

4. Sat.

Wrote to J. Murray—Archd. Clerke—J.V. Cox[4]—Dr Jacobson—A. Williams—Mr Daniell—& minutes. Spent the morning in bed to nurse my erysipelas & my leg—working however. Cabinet 3–5½. Went with S. Herbert to the Trinity H[ouse] dinner. The Prince made his little Speeches admirably.[5] Read D'Inverness a Brighton.[6] Saw S. Herbert—Graham.

5. 2 S.Trin.

Remained in bed till 1½: drove out: rest of the day on the sofa. Prayers only for Church. Sermon aloud in Evg. Saw Mr Pollen.[7] Read Mad Guyon—Trabaud[8]—Ch. Periodicals.

6. M.

Wrote to Prov. of Oriel—Mr Roche MP—Mast[er of] University [College Oxford][9]—A. Robertson—T.F. Kennedy[10]—Mr Cowan—Baron Alderson—Mr J. Wood—Mr J. Fergus MP . . . . . . and minutes. Saw Mr Wilson—Mr Pressly with Mr Timm—Sir Alex. Spearman—Col. Mure. H of C. 4½–9—my last bout on the Income Tax. It went off at last amidst loud Cheers.—H. again 12–1¼.[11] Dined at Mrs Talbot's. Dissuaded Robinson from going further in evil [R]. Quelle en sera la fin? Dieu le sait.[12] My leg mends thank God with rest.

7. T.

Wrote to Earl of Aberdeen—Mr Pressly—Sir C. Trevelyan—Ld Granville

[1] *H* cxxvii. 1092.
[2] W. P. *Greswell, *Memoirs of Angelus Politianus, A. S. Sanazarius, Pelrus Bembus, H. Francastorius, M. A. Flaminius, and the Amalthei* (1801).
[3] T. C. Upham, *Life and religious opinions and experience of Madame de la Mothe Guyon; together with some account of the personal history and religious opinions of Fénelon, abp. of Cambray*, 2 v. (1847).
[4] Perhaps a pen-slip for John Edmond Cox, 1812–90; fellow of All Souls 1836; vicar of St. Helen's, Bishopgate, 1849–87; D.D. 1870; antiquarian and free-mason.
[5] Report in *The Times*, 6 June 1853, 5f.
[6] Not found.
[7] Probably John Hungerford Pollen, d. 1902; fellow of Merton, Oxford, 1842–52, proctor 1851; later became roman catholic.
[8] Probably *Recueil de romances nouvelles, composées par le sieur Marius Trabaud* (1827).
[9] Edmund Burke Roche, b. 1815; a distant relation of *Burke; radical M.P. Cork 1837–55.
[10] Thomas Francis *Kennedy, 1788–1879; whig M.P. Ayr 1818–34; paymaster of Irish civil service 1837–50; commissioner of woods and forests 1850–4, when dismissed by Gladstone; championed by *Russell in a great row with Gladstone June 1854–January 1855.
[11] Income Tax Bill 3° and later India, *H* cxxvii. 1208, 1230.
[12] 'What will be the end of it? God knows.'

—Mr Rowlett—Mr M. Smith[1]—Mr M'Cartney[2]—Ld Palmerston—and ... minutes. Bought a few books! Saw Mr A. Munro—Mr Mullins[3]—Mr Arbuthnot—Ld A. Hervey—Mr Monsell—Mr Trevor. No House. Drive with C. Dined with the Milnes's. Lady Clarendon's afterwards. Saw B[aron] Brunnow. Read La Reine Marg.[4] This was a day of some relaxation. Sworn in at Court of Exchequer: & settled a motion as Judge.[5]

8 X. Wed.

Off at 8¾ to Eton. Breakfast with the Provost. Attended the Speeches: inferior to the last I heard, & not better than in my time: conv. with the Prince on the Turkey question. Saw Willy: pale but come on. Off to Oxford in aftn. Arrived 4¼ PM. Made calls—& then went to the Chapterhouse [Christ Church] where the company[6] assembled for dinner. We sat down at 6½: and were out of the Hall before nine, speeches, applause (wh was tumultuous especy. for Ld Derby) & all. I then went to the Lecture Room & the Dean's & got off by the Train at 10. Reached Pall Mall 12¾. Reconnoitred for Robinson but was repelled by the entourage [R].

9 X. Th.

Wrote to Lord Advocate—Mr W. Baron—Sir T. Fremantle—Ld Wodehouse[7]—& minutes. H. of C. 4½–5½ and 10½–12. Finished Customs Duties: another sensible step onward with the Budget.[8] Saw Mr Wilson—Mr Freshfield—Mr Dickinson—Drove with the children to see Mrs Wadd, &c. —Read Rej. Addresses[9]—Huc's Travels. Wrote Mem. in Cabinet box on the proposal to erect three Colonial Archbishoprics.[10] Four only to breakfast. In evg saw Loader: & spoke with other two [R].

10. Fr.

Wrote to Sir T. Fremantle—E. Cardwell—W. Brown (2)—D. of Richmond —Dr Todd—Baron Alderson—Mrs Swinfen[11]—Ld Advocate & minutes.

[1] Martin Tucker Smith, 1803–80; liberal M.P. Midhurst 1831–2, Wycombe 1847–65; an East India Company director.

[2] George MacCartney, *né* Hume, b. 1793; tory M.P. for Antrim 1852–9.

[3] Probably Edward Mullins, notary and solicitor to Royal British Bank.

[4] Probably C. R. de Caumont de la Force, *Histoire de Marguerite de Valois, Reine de Navarre*, 2 v. (1749).

[5] Not reported in *English Reports*, 8 Exchequer 821; the chancellor customarily made a token appearance at the exchequer court, cp. W. S. Holdsworth, *History of English Law* (ed. 1956), i. 234.

[6] 'for' here deleted.

[7] John *Wodehouse, 1826–1902; 3rd Baron Wodehouse 1846; under-sec. foreign office 1852–6, 1859–61; ambassador to Russia 1856–8; lord privy seal 1868–70; colonial sec. 1870–4, 1880–2; Indian sec. 1882–5, 1886, 1892–4; foreign sec. 1894–5; cr. earl of Kimberley 1866. Cp. Add MSS 44224–9.

[8] *H* cxxvii. 1353.

[9] Cp. 19 Nov. 41.

[10] This sentence carried back (by a pair of ‡ signs) from foot of next p.

[11] Mrs Francis Swinfen, of 5 Connaught Square; probably the mother-in-law of *Peel's brothers Edmund and John.

Revised the proposals as to Advt. Duty & the Penny Stamp.[1] Saw Mr Glyn—Mr Wilson—Mr Tollemache[2]—Mr Arbuthnot—Mr Trevor—Lord Advocate—& others. H of C. 4½–7 and 7½–11. Progress again with the Budget.[3] Read Cardwell's Railway Report[4]—Court on I. Tax[5]—Wrote Cabinet Mem. on India.[6]

11. Sat. St Barnabas.

Wrote minutes. Saw Irish Depn. at 12—another at one—Mr Wood with Pressly & Timm—Cabinet 3–6½. Dined at Duke of Argyll's. Revised Stamp & Licence proposals.[7] Luncheon at Helen's to meet Mr Ramsay.

12. 3 S. Trin.

St Martin's H.C. 8½ AM—Whitehall at 11—Chapel Royal 5½. Walk with C. & children. MS. of 42 aloud at night. Read Mad. Guyon—Dr Duncan's Life[8]—Burges's Address to Farmers—Do Commentary.[9]

13. M.

Wrote to Ld Portman—Mr Timm—T.S. Gladstone—T. Jones (Asst. Barr[iste]r)[10]—Sir J. Fitzgerald[11]—Ld J. Russell—and minutes. House (except ½ h) 4½–1¾ on Succn. Duty &c.[12] Saw Mr Wilson—Mr Pressly with Mr Timm—Mr Wood *cum* Dobson—Northcote. Ventured to spend an hour in arranging some of my papers. Read Mad. Guyon.

14. T.

Wrote to Amn. Minister—Rev. Dr Jelf—Ld Shaftesbury[13]—Mr Hayter—Sir H. Verney—Rev W. West[14]—Mr Robert Gladstone—Mr Adderley—

[1] Add MS 44742, f. 148.

[2] John Tollemache Tollemache, 1805–90, tory M.P. South Cheshire 1841–68, West Cheshire 1868–72, cr. Baron Tollemache 1876; a progressive agriculturalist whose provision to tenants of 'three acres and a cow' originated that phrase.

[3] *H* cxxvii. 1380.

[4] Cp. Conacher, 119 n. 5.

[5] Major H. Court, 'A review of the income tax in its relation to the national debt' (1853).

[6] Cp. 2nd n. on 25 May 53.

[7] Cp. Buxton, i. 123–4.

[8] G. J. C. Duncan, *Memoir of Henry *Duncan, D.D., minister of Ruthwell, founder of savings banks.* (1848).

[9] G. Burges, 'Reflections on . . . the present spirit of the times in a letter to the freeholders of . . . Norfolk' (1819) and 'A commentary on the . . . commutation of tithes' (1838).

[10] Thomas Jones, barrister in the Middle Temple from 1845; specialised on N. Wales and Cheshire circuit.

[11] Sir John Forster *Fitzgerald, 1784?–1877, soldier, fought at Badajos 1812, lieutenant general 1841, general 1854, field marshal 1875; liberal M.P. co. Clare 1852–7; d. at Tours, the oldest officer in the service.

[12] *H* cxxviii. 62; notes on the deb. in Add MS 44742, f. 153. Also moved 2° Savings Bank Bill: *H* cxxviii. 124.

[13] Instead of 'Ld. Torrington'.

[14] Washbourne West, 1811–97, fellow of Lincoln from 1845, perpetual curate of All Saints, Oxford, from 1852; a record plural voter, with 23 votes in as many counties, recorded 17 tory votes at 1892 election.

and minutes. Off at 9½ to the Old Bailey to give Evidence in re W. Wilson.[1] Attended the drawing-room. Saw Newcastle—Ld Portman—Cardwell—Mr W. Brown. H of C. 4½–6¾ and 10–2.[2] Ten to dinner: incl. HJG, Jas Hope & Badeley.

15. Wed.

Wrote to Mr Roberts—Mr Goulburn—Mr W. Brown—Ld Shaftesbury—J. Tidd Pratt—Chas Robertson—D. [of] Newcastle—Mr C. Litchfield—Hon F. Charteris—and minutes.[3] H. of C. 12½–3 for Univ. Polls Bill—where I had to sit still & acquiesce in rather an absurd arrangement.[4] Saw the Speaker—Solr. General—Mr Freshfield—Mr Cobbett—Sir R. Inglis—Mr Roberts—Mr J. Wood—Mr Wilson—Mr Currie. Got on horseback again for an hour: my leg, well protected, just & only just admitting it. Attended the Queen's Ball but got back & to bed by about midnight. In the morning (9½–11) I had had to attend the Old Bailey. I made no statement in Wilson's case. Mr Bodkin's[5] speech in some points went beyond the exact truth in my favour; & I was mute though I made some small signs: but there was nothing that bore upon the prisoner, nor anything that misstated my motive & intention, nor could I by rule as I believed interpose had there been more adequate cause.[6]

16. Th.

Wrote to Mr Roberts—Madlle. L. Maur[7]—Scotts—Sir C. Trevelyan—V. Chancr. Oxford—Ld Torrington—and minutes. H. of C. 4¾–12½. Succession Duty Bill in Commee. &c.[8] Near 20 to breakfast. Saw Mr Haddan—Bp of Oxford—Ld Granville—Lord Duncan—Mr Gore—Judge Coleridge—D of Argyll—Newcastle. Succession Duty Synod 2½–4½. Read a little of Testa.[9]

17. Fr.

Wrote to Ld Verulam[10]—Fremantle—Ld Portman—J.R. Herbert[11]—Capt. Dillon[12]—Ld Torrington & minutes. H. of Commons 4½–3½ without any break except the Lobby on divisions: Succn. Duty, & Irish Spirits.[13] Saw Ld Aberdeen—E. Cardwell—Mr Haddan. Home in broad day.

[1] The case was delayed until the next day.

[2] Voted in 232 to 172 agst. the ballot: *H* cxxviii. 229.

[3] On rates of interest, Add MS 44742, f. 155.

[4] On polling arrangements: *H* cxxviii. 237.

[5] (Sir) William Henry *Bodkin, 1791–1874, K.C. 1826, Peelite M.P. Rochester 1841–7; assistant judge, Middlesex sessions 1859, kt. 1869; wrote on law.

[6] Wilson pleaded guilty, but sentence was delayed until the next day, when he got 12 months hard labour in the house of correction; cp. *The Times*, 16 June 1853, 7d and 17 June 1853, 7c.

[7] Unidentified; involved in rescue work?

[8] *H* cxxviii. 309.

[9] G. B. Testa, *Storia della guerra di Federigo Primo contro i communi di Lombardia*, 2 v. (1853).

[10] James Walter Grimston, 1809–95, 2nd earl of Verulam 1845.

[11] John Rogers *Herbert, 1810–90, portrait and historical painter; painted some of the frescoes in the house of lords.

[12] Reply to a begging letter, copy in Add MS 44528, f. 152.

[13] *H* cxxviii. 385.

18. Sat.

Wrote to Ld Verulam—J.W. Patten—Ld J. Thynne—Sir J. Young—Mr P. Erle[1]—Mr Pressly—H.J.G.—and minutes. Rode in aftn. Saw Mr Wood with Dobson—Pressly & Timm—Mr Trevor—Ld Canning—Mr Wilson—E.L. Robertson. Advt. Duty Deputation at 1.[2] Cabinet 3–6¼ (Licences, my share). Dined with the Wenlocks. Read Jamaica papers.[3]

19. 4 S.Trin.

Whitehall & Chapel Royal. MS of 46 on I Pet. V aloud at night. Went to Chev. Bunsen's at 9 to hear the wonderful Cologne singers.[4] Wrote to Judge Coleridge—Mr Freshfield.[5] Read pamphlets by Archdeacon Hale—Sedgwick—Bp of Argyll—Septuagenarius—Mr Brownlow Gray.[6] Also Mad. Guyon—Bp of Van Mildert.

20. M.

Wrote to Mr Trevor—Mr G.C. Glyn—Mr C. Cowan—and minutes. H of C. 4½–1½: on Succession Duty Bill &c.: beaten on Timber, but with doubtful issue.[7] Saw Mr Goulburn—Mr C. Trevor—Mr J. Wood—Mr Pressly with Mr Timm—Mr Wilson.[8]

21. T.

Wrote minutes. Read Viaggio orribile[9]—Dr Pusey's Evidence.[10] 7¾–6¼. Expedition to Chobhame where we saw the camp & review: a spectacle full of beauty & interest; in very pleasant company to boot.[11]

22. Wed.

Wrote to Mr Wilson—Judge Coleridge—Mr Pressly—Mr Litchfield—T.G. —Mr J. Richardson[12]—H.J.G. (& copy)—Mr Goulburn—Sir J. Young—

[1] Peter Erle, 1795–1877, barrister from 1821, Q.C. 1854; chief charity estate commissioner 1853–72; P.C. 1872.

[2] Cp. *The Times*, 20 June 1853, 5a.

[3] On legislative proceedings in Jamaica: *PP* 1852–3, lxv. 165.

[4] The Cologne Choral Union, on a tour of Britain.

[5] Starting the procedure for the reduction of Wilson's sentence; copy in Add MS 44528, f. 154.

[6] W. H. *Hale, 'Suggestions for the extension of the ministry . . .' (1853); J. *Sedgwick, 'Hints on the establishment of public industrial schools' (1853); A. Ewing, 'A letter to E. B. *Ramsay' on education (1853); Septuagenarius, 'Britain's wreck, or breakers ahead' (1853); S. B. Gray, 'The revival of Bp. *Berkeley's Bermuda College' (1853).

[7] The govt. was defeated by 3 votes; the clause was carried on 1 July 1853: *H* cxxviii. 465, 1129ff.

[8] Instead of 'Watson'.

[9] Possibly *Viaggio dei missionari Lombardi da Plymouth a Sydney* (1852).

[10] *Pusey refused to give evidence to the Oxford commission, whose legality he questioned; he gave it instead at length to the hebdomadal board's commission, cp. Liddon, *Life of Pusey*, iii. 381–6.

[11] A mock battle, in the presence of the court and the king of Hanover; cp. *The Times*, 22 June 1853, 5d.

[12] Jonathan Joseph Richardson, 1815–76; Peelite M.P. Lisburn 1853–63.

and minutes. H. of C. 5–6.[1] Cabinet dinner at Pembroke Lodge.[2] Saw Mr G. Glyn—Mr Gibson—Manchr. Sav. Bank Deputn.[3]—Newcastle. Visited the Woodburn Gallery at Christie's.[4] At night spoke with one seen formerly: & two strangers [R].

23. Th. X

Wrote to Ld Aberdeen—Sir C. Eastlake—Sir G. Clerk—E. Cardwell—Robn. G—H.A. Herbert—& minutes. H of C. 4½–8½ and 11–3 (A.M.)[5] Saw Sir S. Northcote—Mr Bonham—Sir G. Clerk—Mr Crafer. Succn. Duty meeting 3½–4½. Visited Christie's for a few minutes to see the Giorgione.[6] Twelve to breakfast: including Dr Wellesley who looked at my pictures &c. & gave me his judgments on them. Saw E.C.—not all right with me [R].

24. Fr X *St. John Baptist*

Wrote to C.G.—Hon J.W. Percy[7]—Sir C. Lemon—Col. Thwaites—E. of Aberdeen—E. Cardwell—Fremantle—& minutes. H of C. 6½–9¼ and 11¾–12½.[8] Saw Mr J. Coleridge—Mr Nicol[9] & Mr Holt[10]—Bonham—Sir C. Trevelyan—do with Mr G. Craufurd—Mr Hinton[11] & Mr Morley (Edn.)[12]—Sir S. Northcote—J.N.G. Rode. dined with the Herberts—& saw Robinson: but little hope there [R]. Settled Stamp Bill with Messrs. Pressly & Timm. Further meeting on Timber Clauses. Read Remarks on Treaty of 1786.[13]

25. Sat X

Wrote to Col. Mure—Sir D.J. Norreys—Mr Cureton—Mr Duncan—Robn. G.—Hon. C. Berkeley[14]—C.G.—Mr Nicol—& minutes. Rode—gallantly contesting it with the Rain. Saw Messrs. Holt & Nicol (and telegraphed to Sir G. Clerk)—Mr Trevor—Newcastle. Cabinet 2–5½. Read on Treaty of 1786. Dined with the Clarendons. Mrs Lowe's[15] afr. On my way home saw Robinson once more [R].

[1] *Inglis's Recovery of Personal Liberty Bill: *H* cxxviii. 534.
[2] *Russell's house, a mile south of Richmond Park. [3] No papers traced.
[4] The collection of Samuel Woodburn, 1785?–April 1853, a leading connoisseur, sold at Christie's in June 1853 and May 1854; cp. 17 Apr. 54.
[5] India Bill 2°: *H* cxxviii. 605.
[6] 'The adoration of the Virgin', in the Woodburn sale.
[7] Josceline William Percy, 1811–81, 2nd s. of 5th duke of Northumberland; tory M.P. Launceston 1852–9.
[8] India Bill: *H* cxxviii. 735.
[9] Henry Nicol, 1821–1905; treasury clerk 1849–60; superintendent county court dept. of the treasury, 1860–91.
[10] Unidentified.
[11] Probably John Howard *Hinton, 1791–1873; baptist minister of Devonshire Square chapel 1837–63; educationalist.
[12] Unidentified.
[13] 'Historical and critical remarks upon the tariff' (1787); on the Anglo–French treaty; attributed by *McCulloch to *Eden.
[14] Craven Fitzhardinge Berkeley, 1805–55, youngest s. of 5th earl of Berkeley; liberal M.P. Cheltenham 1832–47, 1848, 1852–55.
[15] Georgiana, *née* Orred, m. 1836 Robert *Lowe, 1st Viscount Sherbrooke. They then lived in Lowndes Square.

26. X *5 S.Trin.*

Chapel Royal mg, Bedfordbury Evg. MS on Gospel aloud—Read Wiseman's Review of Seymour[1]—Bennett's Life of Bogue[2]—Van Mildert—Mad. Guyon. Rain off at night: I went out: saw Williams: a barren interview I fear [R].

27. M.

Wrote to Mr C. Franks—Ld Canning—Ld Aberdeen—Mr V. Scully—Sir John Young—Mr Edw. Ellice—Bp of Argyll—Sir C. Wood—Mr Wilson—Mr W. Brown—Dr Jeune—and minutes. Wrote Mem. on Inc. Tax Irish clauses.[3] Saw Mr Goulburn—Mr Timm—Dr Bowring—Sir S. Northcote—Mr Trevor. H. of C. 4½–5¼ and 11½–1¼.[4] Drove with the children & Aunt Johanna. Also walked out for shopping. Walk at night likewise. O[5] Read Giannone's Confession of Faith[6]—Remarks on Tariff (finished)—Huc's Travels.

28. T. X

Poor Helen's birthday: may all be or become well with her. Wrote to Rev. C. Marriott—Earl Granville—C.G.—Anon. Clergyman (heu!)[7]—Ld Belhaven—Sir T. Fremantle—Mr Mitchell—Sir R. Murchison—Mr Trevor—Ld Belhaven (2)—Mr Tudway[8]—Mr C. Marriott—Mr Tollemache—S.H. Northcote. Saw E. Cardwell—Sir Geo. Clerk—Sir A. Spearman—Mr Wilson. Rode on horseback. Then attended the Baptism & banquet at the Palace.[9] In the Chapel I had a conv. with C. Wood about dogma. Of the visible objects of the evening, by far the most interesting was the King of Hanover.[10] There is such a depth of touching expression in his countenance as is rarely to be witnessed. Read Huc. Walk: & saw two, without profit [R].

29. X *St Peter. Wed.*

Ch Ch Broadway 6 P.M. Wrote to Rev. F. Teed—Mr Jas Wilson—Rev. R. Scott—Earl of Abn.—J. Griffiths—Sir A. Spearman—Ld Hardinge—Robn Gladstone—C.G.[11]—Christie & Manson—Scotts—and minutes. Cabinet 1¾–4½. Saw Bank of Ireland Deputation—Dublin Chamb.

[1] N. P. S. *Wiseman, 'Convents. A review of two lectures . . . by M. H. Seymour' (1852); reprinted from the *Dublin Review.*

[2] J. *Bennett, *Memoirs of the life of the Rev. David *Bogue, DD.* (1827).

[3] Add MS 44742, f. 157.

[4] India Bill: *H* cxxviii. 814.

[5] At end of a line of text, i.e. nothing found.

[6] P. Giannone, *Professione di Fede* (?1730).

[7] Had written to complain of govt. indifference to the colonial church; draft reply in Add MS 44742, f. 161.

[8] Robert Charles Tudway, 1808–55; sheriff of Somerset 1842; tory M.P. Wells from 1852.

[9] The baptism of *Leopold; cp. *The Times*, 29 June 1853, 5a.

[10] George V, 1819–78, *Victoria's first cousin; blinded 1833; succ. to throne 1851, deposed 1866.

[11] Some in Bassett, 101.

Commerce do[1]—Mr Franks—Mr Wilson—A. Kinnaird. Dined at Lord Wodehouse's. Tornando a casa fui accostato da 2 persone: coll'una andai da ella, ed ebbi lungo discorso: poco frutto [R][2]

30. Th.

Wrote to D. of Newcastle—C.G.—Sir J. Duckworth—Fremantle—Dr Jacobson—Scotts—Ld J. Russell—and minutes. Seven to breakfast. Attended the marriage of Louisa Neville at St James's.[3] Also the breakfast where I was called upon to propose the Bride & Bridegroom. Saw Bp of Oxford—Mr Trevor—Mr Wilson—Ld Colborne—J.N.G. Rode. Dined with J.N.G. H of C. 4½–5 and 10½–2½: voted in 322:140 for 2d r. India Bill.[4]

Fr. July One. 1853.

Wrote to Mr J.A. Smith[5]—Mr Henley—and minutes. C. returned from Hagley—Saw Mr Wood with Mr Pressly—Mr Goulburn—Sir A. Spearman—Mr Franks. Saving's Banks' Scots Deputn.[6] Railway Commee. 3–4. H. of C. 4½–12½: on Advt. Duty & Succession Bill.[7]

2. Sat.

Wrote to Mr Sotheron—Bp of Argyll—Mr Gamble[8]—Sir J. Young & minutes. Saving's Bank Meeting 12–1½.[9] Cabinet 2–6. Rode in the Park. Dined at Cardwell's.[10] Lady Derby's af[te]r. Saw Newcastle—Roundell Palmer—Oswald.

3. 6 S.Trin.

Whitehall mg & H.C.—Chap. Royal aft. Printed S[ermon] aloud in evg. Music. Walk with C. & the children. Read Upham's Guyon—Bennett's Bogue—Van Mildert—Chr. Remembr.[11]

4. M.

Wrote to Gov. B[an]k [of] Ireland[12]—Miss A. Harcourt—Mr Timm—W.K. Hamilton—Mr W. Brown—Mr Goulburn—Scotts—Ld J. Russell—and

[1] Papers scattered in Add MS 44577.

[2] 'On my way home, was accosted by two persons; went with one of them to her house, and had long conversation: with little fruit'.

[3] Cp. 22 Nov. 41.

[4] *H* cxxviii. 1074.

[5] John Abel Smith, 1801–71, partner in Smith, Payne and Smith, bankers, and whig M.P. Midhurst 1830–1, Chichester 1831–59, 1863–8.

[6] Supporting his Bill, with qualifications: Add MS 44577, f. 163.

[7] *H* cxxviii. 1090.

[8] Perhaps Richard Wilson Gamble, 1823–87, barrister at Irish bar 1851, county court judge for Armagh from 1880.

[9] Minutes by Gladstone in Add MS 44742, f. 164.

[10] Anne Cardwell, *née* Parker, m. 1838 Edward *Cardwell, the Peelite politician; she d. 1887.

[11] *Christian Remembrancer*, xxvi. 1 (July 1853); perhaps the review of books on metaphysics.

[12] John Barton; copy in Add MS 44528, f. 155.

minutes. H. of C. $4\frac{1}{2}$–$12\frac{3}{4}$ on Succession Duty Bill &c.[1] Saw Mr Arbuthnott—Mr Trevor[2]—Mr Wood—Mr Timm. Read Marmont on Turkey.[3]

5. T.

Wrote to Mr Muntz—D. of Newcastle—Mr W. Evans[4] and minutes. Rode out: & went in evg to Lady C. Harcourt's concert. Read Marmont. Saw Ld Aberdeen—Mr Hayter—Sir A. Spearman on Sav. Banks Bill—Malt Duties Depn.—Nat Debt Commr.—R. Phillimore—& others.

6. Wed.

Wrote to Ld A. Hervey—T.M. Gladstone—Ld Wilton—E. Cardwell—Mr Franks—Mr Hayter—& minutes. Saw Ld Canning—Sir A. Spearman & Mr Tidd Pratt—Mr C. Franks—Newcastle—Sir C.E.T[revelyan]. Cabinet $1\frac{1}{2}$–$4\frac{1}{2}$. Cabinet Dinner at Sir W. Molesworths. Holland House before & the Queen's Concert after it.

7. Th.

Wrote to V. Chancr. Oxford—Mr Gibson—Mr C. Trevor—Mr Duncan—Dr Jelf—and minutes. A breakfast of sixteen: the last of the year: Ly C[annin]g & Ly Waterford[5] came. Saw Mr Trevor—Mr Godley—Bp of Argyll—Archd. Harrison—Canon Blomfield. H. of C. 6–3 A.M. Succession Duty chiefly: finished the Committee on the Bill.[6] Home to tea & a little reading. C. had a dinner, wh I had hoped to attend.

8. Fr. X.

Wrote to Mr C. Cowan—Mr W. Brown (the Baltic affair)[7]—Govr. of Bank—Sir A. Spearman—Fremantle—Sir C.E. T[revelyan]—Mr Pressly & minutes. Rode to Fulham. Saw Ld Canning—Miss A. Harcourt—Ossulston & various members of P[arliamen]t. Read Huc. H of C. 6–$7\frac{1}{2}$ and 10–1.[8] Walk, afr.: little good [R].

9. Sat.

Wrote to Mr Jas Wilson—Mr Pressly—Mr J. Rowsell[9]—Sec. S.P.G.—Ld J. Russell—and minutes. Cabinet $1\frac{3}{4}$–5.—Rode. Saw Mr J. Wood—Fremantle. Dined at Holland House. Worked an hour on my private affairs & settled some bills & the like. Also worked on arranging letters.

[1] Spoke on Succession Duty Bill: *H* cxxviii. 1167.
[2] 'Govr Bank [of] Ireland' here deleted.
[3] A. L. F. V. de Marmont, *State of the Turkish empire*, tr. Sir J. M. F. *Smith (1839).
[4] A retiring admiralty clerk; Gladstone's reply, on pension: Add MS 44528, f. 155.
[5] Lady Louisa de la Poer Beresford, 2nd da. of Lord *Stuart de Rothesay; m. 1842 3rd marquess of Waterford and succ. to his estates when he d. 1859; she d. 1891. Cp. also 13 Feb. 36 n.
[6] *H* cxxviii. 1377.
[7] On the shipping of ice; copy of a very long letter in Add MS 44528, f. 163.
[8] India Bill: *H* cxxviii. 1433.
[9] Joel Rowsell, 1806–86; bookseller in Great Queen Street 1846–54, later in King William Street; a London eccentric.

10. 7 S.Trin.

Whitehall mg—Chap. Royal aft. Printed Serm. aloud. Walk with C. & the children. Saw M.E.G.—Duchess Dow[age]r of Beaufort. Read Whately's Evidence[1]—Pickering's Races of Man[2]—Nicolay's Letter[3]—Church Periodicals.

11. M.

Wrote to Molesworth—Ld Granville—& minutes. 5½–6½. Ld Ward's concert.[4] Walk by Hungerford[5] at night. Saw Bonham—J. Wood & Pressly—Mr Trevor—do with Sol. Gen. & Sir J. Graham—also with Mr R. Palmer—saw also Mr Spooner—Sir J. Walmsley—Robn. G.—J.N.G. Latin lesson to Stephen. Read Huc. H. of C. 6¾–7¾ and 8½–1.[6]

12. T.

Wrote to Sir T. Fremantle—Mr J. Wood—Sir A. Spearman—C.G. Reid—Mr Monsell—Ld Portman—T.M. Gladstone—Mr Jas Heywood—Mr C. Trevor—Mr Goulburn—Herries & Co.—and minutes. Latin lesson to Stephen. Saw Robn. G & Sir E. Perry[7]—Sir C. Trevelyan—Sir J. Walmsley & I[sle] of Man Depn.[8]—Mr Wood—Ld Granville—Mr Wilson. Rode 5–6. Reached H of C. in time to speak against time & prevent a defeat on the Malt Duties:[9] then dined with the Primate & was more than ever charmed with Lady Waterford's goodness & beauty. Read Huc.

13. Wed.

Wrote to Ld Aberdeen—Ld R. Grosvenor—Mr Oliveira—Ld Oranmore[10]—Ld Portman—Bp of Argyll—H. Glynne—Johnson Longden & Co—E. Cardwell—R. Phillimore—Chairm. Customs—S.H. Northcote—Mr Arbuthnot—Williams & Co and minutes. Saw Mr Gibson—Mr Trevor—Mr Vance[11] & Mr Grogan[12]—Lord Aberdeen & Sir J. Graham—Dr Jacobson—Ld Stanley—M. Masson.[13] Parlty. dinner: seventeen, one Peelite the rest

[1] R. *Whately, *Introductory lessons on Christian evidences* (1843).

[2] C. Pickering, *The races of man: and their geographical distribution* (1844).

[3] C. G. Nicolay, 'A proposal to establish a missionary college on the north-west coast of British America, in a letter to . . . Gladstone' (1853).

[4] He lived in Dudley House, Park Lane.

[5] Hungerford market, off the Strand.

[6] India Bill: *H* cxxix. 34.

[7] Sir Thomas Erskine *Perry, 1806–82, kt. 1841; chief justice of Bombay 1847–52; liberal M.P. Devonport 1854–9; member of council of India 1859–82; wrote on law and India.

[8] On Manx customs: cp. *The Times*, 13 July 1853, 5d.

[9] There was a govt. majority of four: *H* cxxix. 126.

[10] Dominick Browne, 1787–1860; liberal M.P. co. Mayo 1813–36; cr. Baron Oranmore in Irish peerage 1836.

[11] John Vance, 1808–75, Dublin merchant and tory M.P. there 1852–65, Armagh 1867–75.

[12] (Sir) Edward Grogan, 1802–91; barrister and tory M.P. Dublin 1841–65; cr. bart. 1859.

[13] Probably Victor Masson, 1807–?65; French publisher; on one of the juries at the 1851 exhibition.

Liberal: Lady Graham's[1] afterwards, & then walked. Latin lesson to Stephen. Drove with C. to Holland House aftn. party.

14. Th.

Wrote to Ld Granville—Mr Adderley—Sir W. Heathcote—and minutes. Five to breakfast. Latin lesson with Stephy. Saw Mr Trevor—J. Talbot. H. of C. 3–4. and 6–2 AM on Report of Succession Duty, &c.[2] Read Packet Committee's Report[3]—Huc's Travels.

15. Fr.

Wrote to Sir J. Graham—Mr G. Burnett—Ald[erma]n Neild[4]—Mr Masterman—Mr H. Currie[5]—Archdn. Marriott—& minutes. Saw Sir A. Spearman—Mr Pressly—Mr Spooner—Mr W.B. Hughes—Mr Wilson Patten—E. Cardwell—S. Herbert. Latin lesson to Stephen. Read Packet Report (finished)—Huc's Travels. H. of C. 3–4, 6–6½, and 9–12½.[6] Abortive attempt to ride: out at night—saw E.C., also two more persons [R].

16. Sat.

Wrote to Mr Goulburn—Robn. G.—Mr Gibson—Mr C. Franks—Mr Ewart—Mr Hayter—Ld R. Grosvenor (2)—Mr Pressly—Ld Aberdeen—Dr Bull—F.P. Walesby—Sir C. Barry—& minutes. Read Q.R. on Fiquelmont.[7] Saw Mr Craven—Mr Arbuthnot—Ld Granville—Cabinet 2–5. Rode: dined at Sir W. Molesworth's—the height of luxury:[8] Lady Westminster's afterwards. Worked on Channel Harbours—Col. Ch. papers.[9]

17. 8 S.Trin.

Whitehall mg & Ch. Royal aft.—Printed Serm. (Parker) aloud at night. Walk with C. Wrote to D. of Newcastle—Read Mad. Guyon—Lessons on Evidence (finished)—& that most extraordinary & moving narration of Mad. de La Valliére by Mad. de Genlis.[10]

18. M.

Wrote to C.G. Reid—Mr Goulburn—Dr Vaughan—E. of Aberdeen—&

[1] Lady Fanny Graham, *née* Callender, m. Sir John *Graham 1819; she d. 1857.

[2] Spoke on it: *H* cxxix. 215.

[3] On contract packets, *PP* 1852–3, xcv. 137.

[4] William Neild, chairman of the Manchester Savings Bank trustees; copy in Add MS 44528, f. 169.

[5] Henry Currie, 1798–1873; London banker and Peelite M.P. Guildford 1847–52; cp. 22 July 54.

[6] India Bill: *H* cxxix. 306.

[7] *Quarterly Review*, xciii. 128 (June 1853); on Count Ficquelmont 'The *Palmerston policy'.

[8] He was the only radical in the cabinet.

[9] *PP* 1852–3, i. 341.

[10] S. F. Brulart de Genlis, *Vie pénitente de Mme. de la Vallière . . . suivi de réflexions sur la miséricorde de Dieu* (1807).

minutes. H. of C. 4½–11 and 11¾–1½. Finished the Succession Bill, with good divisions.[1] Worked on priv. business ½ h. Saw Mr Trevor—Mr Lingen—Mr Hayter—F.R. Bonham—Ld R. Grosvenor—Sir A. Grant. Col. Ch. meeting C.O. 2¼–4¼. That subject is sorely complicated.[2] Read Duch. de la Valliére.

X *19. T.*

Wrote to Prince Albert (2)[3]—Mr Spooner—Sir W. Farquhar—Sir J. Walmsley—J.W. Patten—Ld Hardinge—and minutes. Read Duch. de La Valliére. H. of C. 3–4.[4] Saw Mr Goulburn—Sir A. Spearman—Mr Wilson—Mr Trevor—Sir Jas Matheson—Sir A.S. with Mr Coulson—Bps Salisb. & Oxf. with Sir J. Harding[5] on Col. Ch. Bill—Sir C. Trevelyan. Dined at Blackheath with the Haddos: and brought A. Kinnaird back with me. Visited E. Harrington [R]: with proof enough agt me, & with some little hope of good for E.H. Home late.

20. Wed.

Wrote to Sir J. Graham—Messrs. Dumbell & Callister[6]—Mr H. Currie—J.N.G.—Mr A. Hayward[7]—Sir G. Clerk—Provost of Eton: & minutes. Dined (Cabinet) at Sir J. Graham's: Atty. General's music & Colloredo Ball afterwards. Saw Mr Sotheron—Sir S. Northcote—Mr Arbuthnot—Mr H. Herbert—Mr Bruce—Mr Bramston—Sir W. James—Ld R. Grosvenor—Sir W. Molesworth—Ld A. Hervey—Ld Palmerston. Read Mad. de La Valliére. H of C. 12¼–3: we overthrew the Attornies & made a holocaust of the Advt. Duty.[8]

21. Th.

Wrote to Sir J. Graham—and minutes. Read Mad. de La Valliére: a wonderful book. Finished the Genlis part of it. H of C. 12–2 (Sav. Banks)—and 8¼–2¼: (Stamps &c.).[9] Rode. Saw Ld Aberdeen—Sir J. Graham—Mr Trevor—Solr. General—Mr Phillips—Sir S. Northcote—Mr Godley—Mr Wilson—Mr E. Ellice. 2½–4½ Visited Nat. Gall and Royal Academy: first time: it closes Saty.

22. Fr.

Wrote to Prince Albert[10]—Mr Divett—Bp of Oxford (2)—Mr J.H. Philipps[11]

[1] *H* cxxix. 398.
[2] The Colonial Church Regulation Bill, a private member's bill sponsored by tractarians; cp. Conacher, 103.
[3] In Guedalla, *Q*, i. 104.
[4] Edinburgh Annuities Bill: *H* cxxix. 440.
[5] Sir John Dorney Harding, 1809–68; privately tutored by T. *Arnold; advocate in doctors' commons 1837, advocate general 1852–62; kt. 1852.
[6] Unidentified.
[7] Had written to request the commissionership of charitable trusts; cp. Add MS 44528, f. 171.
[8] Govt. majority of 84: *H* cxxix. 484.
[9] Spoke on both: *H* cxxix. 534, 584.
[10] Guedalla, *Q*, i. 106.
[11] (Sir) John Henry Philipps (Scourfield), 1808–76, tory M.P. Haverfordwest 1852–68, Pembrokeshire from 1868; he took the name of Scourfield 1862 and was cr. bart. 1876.

—Sir W. Molesworth (2)—and minutes. H. of C. and H. of L. 5¾–8 and 10½–2½.[1] Saw Ld Aberdeen—Bp of Oxford—Bp of Salisbury—Sir J. Herschel[2] —Ld Lyttelton—Mr Wood—Mr Timm—Sir A. Spearman—Mr Arbuthnot —& MP.s. Dined with the Wortleys.

X *23. Sat.*

Wrote to Sir W. Farquhar—Mr Dyce—and minutes. Read Citn. Westr. on Land Tax[3]—R. Owen's Rational Quarterly.[4] Off to Eton Dinner at 1½. It lasted 3–6½. To Surly Hall & the boats afterwards. Willy well in all senses. Saw Lyttelton—Sir A. Spearman—Mr Wilson—Sir C. Trevelyan.

24. 9 S.Trin.

St George's mg & aft. Luncheon with the Harrises.[5] Visited the Coleridges at Eton. Music in Evg. Read Duch[esse] de La V[allière] Vie Penitente—& Letters—Archdeacon Williams's Charge.[6]

25. M. St James.

St George's Chapel 10½ A.M.—Wrote to M.F. Tupper—Mr Timm—Bp of Moray—Sir C. Wood—Mr Wilson—Mr R. Palmer—Mr Christopher—Mr G P Bacon—R. Phillimore—and minutes. Saw Ld Granville—E. Cardwell —Sir A. Spearman—Mr Jowett—Sir C. Trevelyan. Read Austin on Gold[7]— R.P. on the Russian question.[8] Came up from Windsor at 1½. H. of C. & H. of Lords 6 PM to 3½ AM—½ hour home for dinner. The Succession Duty was admirably well disposed of by 102:68 on Ld Derby's first amendment.[9]

26. T.

Wrote to Ld Palmerston—Mr Lefevre—Dr Forbes Winslow—Ld J. Russell—Rev Dr Richards—and minutes. H. of C. 3–4 and again at 6[10] Twelve to dinner—and evening party afterwards. Saw Mr Arbuthnot—Mr Oliveira—Mr Jowett—Sir A. Spearman—Ld Aberdeen—The Govr. of Bank resp. the liquidation of Minor Stocks next Jany.[11]—S. Herbert.

X *27. Wed.*

Wrote to Rev. N. Wade—Rev. J.H. Nicholls[12]—Rev W. Rawson—and

[1] India Bill: *H* cxxix. 657.
[2] Sir John Frederick William *Herschell, 1792–1871; astronomer; cr. bart. 1838; master of the mint 1850–4.
[3] 'The land tax, its origin, progress and inequality stated in a letter to the chancellor of the exchequer, . . . by a citizen of Westminster' (?1837).
[4] Three numbers only published, by Robert *Owen, socialist (1853).
[5] Cp. 20 Jan. 52 n.
[6] Probably an untraced charge by John Williams, archdeacon of Cardigan.
[7] W. Austin, 'On the immediate depreciation of gold and how to avoid loss' (1853).
[8] R. J. *Phillimore, *Russia and Turkey. Armed intervention on the ground of religion considered as a question of international law* (1853).
[9] *H* cxxix. 697.
[10] India Bill: *H* cxxix. 808.
[11] Draft proposals in Add MS 44742, f. 169.
[12] Jasper Hume Nicolls, 1819?–77; fellow of Queen's, Oxford, 1843–8; principal of Bishop's College, Lennoxville, Canada, ?1849; D.D. 1850.

minutes. H. of C. 12–1 and 5–6.[1] Read Carlyle's Latter Day Papers.[2] Saw Mr Wood & Mr Timm—Lambeth &c. Deputation[3]—Audit Commrs.—H. Fitzroy—Mr Saunders resp. Cab Licences & went with him to Somerset House[4]—Sir A. Spearman—A. Gordon—Earl of Aberdeen. Rode. Dined at Grillion's—& walked afterwards. Saw two persons: a very mixed retrospect [R].

28. Th.

Wrote to H. Fitzroy—Ld Aberdeen—Sir W. Molesworth—Mr Wilson—Mr Shelley—and minutes. Dined with the Wortleys. Saw Mr J. Wood—Fitzroy—Molesworth—Monsell—R. Palmer—& others. H. of C. 12–4 (S[outh] S[ea] Resolution) 6–7¾ and 10–3 A.M.[5]

29. Fr.

Wrote to Sir E. Wilmot (2)—Sir E. Filmer—Rev. J.L. Ross—and minutes. H. of C. 12–4 (spoke 1½ hour on Debt Conversion &c)—6–6½ and 8¾–2.[6] Took Willy who was interested. Saw Mr Wood—J.E. Denison—Sir A. Spearman—Mr Timm—Mr Jowett—D. of Newcastle with Sol. Genl (on Col. Ch. Bill)—Northcote—Sir C. Wood—The Speaker—Ld J. Russell. Read Huc.

30. Sat.

Wrote to Ld J. Russell—Mr Franks[7]—Rev Mr Jowett—Mr J. Wood—Mr W. Gladstone—Mr G F Bowen—& minutes. Saw Ld Canning—Mr Wood—Sig. Minghetti[8]—D. of Argyll. Dined with the Herberts. Lady Palmerston's afterwards. Rode. Cabinet 2–6.

31. 10 S. Trin.

St Martins H.C. at 8½—Whitehall 11—& Chapel Royal 5½. MS on St James aloud in evg. Walk with C. & Willy—Read Church Periodicals—Allen on State Churches[9]—La Valliére's Letters (finished)—Mad. Guyon.

Monday Aug. One. 1853.

Wrote to Johnson L. & Co—Mr W. M'Kay[10]—Mr Timm[11]—Lord Cowley—

[1] Misc. business: *H* cxxix. 831. [2] Cp. 18 Feb. 50. [3] Papers untraced.
[4] London cab drivers were on strike, 27 to 29 July 1853.
[5] Effectively winding up the South Sea stock: *H* cxxix. 890.
[6] *H* cxxix. 981. [7] Draft in Add MS 44375, f. 212.
[8] Marco Minghetti, 1818–86, Piedmont politician; a cousin of *Acton; Cavour's minister of interior 1860–2, finance minister 1862–4, ambassador to London 1868–9; prime minister 1873–6.
[9] John Allen, *State churches and the kingdom of Christ* (1853).
[10] Refusing him a post in the treasury; copy in Add MS 44528, f. 174.
[11] Draft in Add MS 44579, f. 1.

Mr Coulson—Count Sclopis[1]—Henry Tayleur—Robn. G—Mr Allen—J. Wood and minutes. Went to Lady Holland's & made it a cold dinner.[2] Saw Sir A. Spearman—Bp of Oxford—Messrs. Anstey & Rogers—Mr Coulson—Duke of Newcastle (very private)[3]—Mr Wood—Sig. Minghetti—J.E. Denison—Mr Delane. H. of C. at $12\frac{1}{2}$—then $7\frac{1}{4}$–$9\frac{1}{2}$ and 10–3 A.M.[4] Read Huc.

2. T.

Wrote to Mr Wilson—Archd. Marriott—Robn. G.—Bp of Exeter—Bp of Montreal—O.B. Cole—M.F. Tupper—Miss Amphlett[5]—H.J.G., (& copy)—Ld Dalhousie—Sig. Dassi—& minutes. H. of C. $6\frac{1}{4}$–$7\frac{3}{4}$ and $9\frac{1}{2}$–$2\frac{1}{2}$. Spoke on Col. Ch. Bill: to make the best of a mismanaged & a bad business.[6] Rode—also a little domestic business. Attended City Deputation. Saw Sir C. Wood—J.E. Denison. Read Rangabé on Oriental question.[7]

3. Wed.

Wrote to Northcote—Rev. R. Greswell—T.G.—Bp of Oxford—H. Tayleur—E.P. Bouverie—Gen. Anson[8]—Dr Harington—Mr Richards—Solr. General—& minutes. Saw Mr Divett—Mr Henley—Sir J.E. Wilmot—Mr Timm—Solr. General—Sir J. Pakington—Mr Pressly—Mr Jowett—Mr Philipps. H of C. 12–$2\frac{1}{2}$ & $4\frac{1}{2}$–6.[9] Rode with Willy: who wants practice but I hope this only. Dined at the Palace: the Queen was very gracious & I got upon Reform & the Crown Estates with the Prince.[10] Duchess of Inverness's afterwards.[11] Read Huc.

4. Th. X

Wrote to A. Spearman—Mrs Cracroft—Ld Palmerston—Mr A. Pellatt[12]—Gov. Cold B[ath] Fields Prison[13] . . . and minutes. H. of C. $12\frac{1}{4}$–$4\frac{1}{4}$, 6–$6\frac{1}{2}$

[1] Count Frederick Paul Sclopis de Salerano, 1798–1878; Piedmontese politician and historian; liberated Piedmont press laws 1848; senator 1849; 1st vice-president of Italian senate 1860.

[2] i.e. arrived late.

[3] Probably about *Newcastle's divorced wife.

[4] Merchant Shipping Bill 3°: *H* cxxix. 1115.

[5] Eliza Maria Anne Amphlett, da. of John Amphlett of Clent; she m. 1862 George Butler of Camberwell and d. 1882.

[6] *H* cxxix. 1211.

[7] I. G. Rizos Rankabes, *Τὰ Ἑλληνικὰ, ἤτοι Περιγραφὴ γεωγραφικὴ, ἱστορική, ἀρχαιολογική, καὶ στατιστικὴ της ἀρχαίας καὶ νέας Ἑλλάδος*, 3 v. (1853–5).

[8] George *Anson, 1797–1857, s. of 1st Viscount Anson; liberal M.P. Yarmouth 1818–34, South Staffordshire 1837–53; major general 1851; in India 1853–4, commander in chief there from 1855.

[9] Misc. business: *H* cxxix. 1214.

[10] *Albert was a strong supporter of *Russell's approach to a reform bill; cp. Martin, *Life of the Prince Consort*, iii. 29.

[11] Lady Celia Letitia Gore Underwood, 8th da. of 2nd earl of Arran, m. firstly 1815 Sir George Buggin who d. 1825, second 1830 1st duke of *Sussex, who d. 1843; she took her maternal surname of Underwood 1831, was cr. duchess of Inverness 1840 and d. 1873. Cp. *LQV* 1 series, i. 599ff.

[12] Apsley *Pellatt, 1791–1863; glass manufacturer and liberal M.P. Southwark 1852–7.

[13] George Laval Chesterton; requesting information on W. Wilson's conduct; copy in Add MS 44528, f. 176.

and $10\frac{1}{4}$–$3\frac{1}{4}$ A.M.[1] Saw Mr Timm—Mr Dyce—Mr Trevor—Sir J. Graham (resp. Bonham)[2]—Speaker—and others.[3] Rode—dined with the Wortleys.

5. Fr.

Wrote to Prince Albert & copy—E. Coleridge—Bp of Salisbury[4]—Sir J. Young—Ld Lyttelton—H. Tayleur—& minutes. H. of C. 12–4, 6–9, and $10\frac{1}{4}$–1.[5] Walk afr.—Rode—dined with the Herberts. Saw Sir R. Brooke—Sir A. Spearman—Mr Wilson. Household business.

6. X Sat.

Wrote to Prov. of Eton—Sir R. Brooke—Sir J. Herschel—Mr C. Franks—Dr Richards—Mr P. Erle . . . Dr Hawkins—Dr Ogle—& minutes. C. went off to Hagley. Cabinet $2\frac{1}{4}$–4. Dined at Mrs Wadds: most hospitably entertained. Saw Mr Jowett—Mr J. Wood—Govr. of Bank—Mr Mulvany,[6] with Sir C. Trevelyan—Lord Kinnaird—Northcote.—Saw E.C. in evg: who goes on well [R]. Io malamente.[7]

7. 11 S.Trin.

Chapel Royal & H.C. mg—Marg. Chapel evg. MS on Gospel aloud. Wrote to Bp of Brechin—Mr Wilson—H.E. Manning (and draft).[8] Read Mad. Guyon—Huc—Fulg. Manfredi[9]—Archdn. Sandford's Charge.[10]

8. M.

Wrote to Robn G.—D. of Newcastle—T.W. Philipps [sc. Phillips]—Warden of Winchr.[11]—E. Cardwell—C.G.—& minutes. Drove out for calls. Seven to dinner. Saw Mr Kane—Mr Wilson—J. Wood—Ld Aberdeen—Sir C. Trevelyan—Sir S. Northcote—Sir A. Spearman—The Speaker. H. of C. $12\frac{1}{2}$–$2\frac{1}{4}$, 3–$4\frac{1}{4}$, 6–9, and $10\frac{3}{4}$ to past 3 A.M.[12]

9. T.

Wrote to Sir J. Graham—S. Herbert—Williams & Co—Canning—G.

[1] Misc. business: *H* cxxix. 1252.
[2] About patronage for him, cp. Conacher, 132.
[3] Draft 'most private' on Frank Lawley's future, to Lady Wenlock in Add MS 44376, f. 9.
[4] In Lathbury, ii. 134.
[5] Spoke on South Sea annuities: *H* cxxix. 1404.
[6] Perhaps George F. *Mulvany; 1809–69, painter and keeper of Royal Hiberian Academy 1845, director of Irish national gallery from 1864.
[7] 'I, badly'.
[8] In Lathbury, ii. 287.
[9] F. Manfredi, ed. R. Gibbings, *Were 'heretics' ever burned alive at Rome? A report of the proceedings in the Roman Inquisition against Fulgenzio Manfredi, taken from the original manuscript* (1852).
[10] J. Sandford, 'A charge to the clergy and wardens of the archdeaconry of Coventry' (1852).
[11] Robert Speccott Barter, 1790–1861; tutor at New College 1815; warden of Winchester from 1822.
[12] Misc. estimates: *H* cxxix. 1451.

Burnett—Mr Dyce—C.G.—Mrs Wadd—& minutes. H. of C. 12–1 and 6–7¾.[1] Dined at Ld Hardinge's. Saw Mr Wilson—Mr Harrison—Mr Franks—Ld Abn. Drove out for calls. Read Huc. Worked on correcting Succn. Duty Speech.[2] Wrote Memm. on S.S. Co's Bill.[3] Saw E. Harrington at night: there is hope of good there: but the instrument! [R]

10. Wed.

Wrote to Ld Chancellor—H.J.G.—Mr Walpole—Sir J. Young—Ld Aberdeen—A.B. Hope—E. St Germans—J.D. Cook—H. Tayleur—C.G.[4]—Dss. of Sutherland—and minutes. Saw Northcote—Mr Wilson—Mr Trevor—D. of Newcastle—Sir J. Young—H.J.G.—Mr Lancaster—Ld Spencer—Ld A. Hervey—Sol. Genl.—Sir J. Graham. H of C. 12–2½.[5] Drove out for calls. Dined with the Herberts. Read Huc.

11. Th.

Up at 4.30 Reached Portsea[6] by S. Coast at 9: embarked in the Ld Warden by Mr Macgregor's[7] kindness & saw the magnificent spectacle admirably well. I felt the stroke of each gun firing in the 'action' on the opening in my[8] chest. We returned ashore at 5, & I reached Downing St soon after nine. H. of C. 10½–12.[9] Saw Molesworth.

12. Fr.

Wrote to D. Newcastle—Mr Hayter—Ld Chancellor—Scotts—Ld Palmerston (2)—H.J.G.—Ld Aberdeen[10]—Mr Pressly—Mr R.M. Fox MP.[11]—Mr Lancaster—C.G.[12]—Mrs Work[13]—Mr Harter[14]—and minutes. H. of C. 3¾–8¼.[15] Dined with the Herberts. Saw H. Wilberforce—Mr Greswell—Sir C. Trevelyan with Northcote—S. Herbert—Lord Chancellor—Mr Rogers—Mr Arbuthnot. Present[ed] to the Crown Princess Olga: a most striking person in manner & with great & indelible remains of uncommon beauty.[16] Dopo m[ezza] notte un passeggio: vidi due persone, delle quali una Francese: con questa mi sono intrattenuto per un'oretta [R].[17]

[1] Misc. estimates: *H* cxxix. 1560.
[2] Not published; cp. notes before 1 Sept. 53.
[3] Add MS 43070, f. 366; new clauses in Add MS 44579, f. 49.
[4] Part in Bassett, 102.
[5] Misc. business: *H* cxxix. 1598.
[6] Portsea Island, between Portsmouth and Langston harbours, strongly fortified, joined to mainland by railway bridge.
[7] Unidentified.
[8] Instead of 'the'.
[9] Misc. business: *H* cxxix. 1602.
[10] On papal aggression, some in Conacher, 173 and n.
[11] Richard Maxwell Fox, 1816–56; liberal M.P. co. Longford from 1847.
[12] Bassett, 102.
[13] Unidentified.
[14] James Collier Harter, Manchester merchant, about his visit there; cp. 10–14 Oct. 53.
[15] Spoke on land tax: *H* cxxix. 1707.
[16] Princess Olga Nicolajevna, da. of Tsar Nicholas I; she m. 1846 Charles I of Wurtemburg, 1823–91; he succ. as King 1864, supported Austria 1866, joined German empire 1871.
[17] 'Walk after midnight: saw two; one of them a Frenchwoman, with whom I talked for the best part of an hour.'

13. Sat.

Wrote to Mr Maguire—Dr Richards—Ld A. Hervey—Mr T.L. Hodges—Mr M'Donald—C.G.—Bannavie Inn[1]—Hutcheson & Co[2]—& minutes. H. of C. 12–1½. Framed & put through its stages a Land Tax Amendment Bill.[3] Saw Mr Pressly with Mr Timm—Sir T. Fremantle—Hop Deputation—Ld Aberdeen—H.J.G.—Mr Hayter—A. Munro. Visited Mr Munro's Studio. Sat to Claudet for Stereoscope likeness[4]—this is a truly wonderful device. Off at 5½ to the [Greenwich] Fish Dinner. Ld Palmerston as Chairman kept up the ball admirably well. Back with Newcastle: & went to Lady Palmerston's. Saw E.C. late [R]. Pretty well knocked up.

14. 12 S.Trin.

Chapel Royal mg. St Paol*ino* evg.[5] MS. of 42 aloud. Wrote to R.R. Madden—C.G.—Sig. Minghetti—H. Glynne. Saw Helen who came to luncheon. Read Madden's Savonarola[6]—Tracts by various persons. Dined with the Herberts.

15. M. X

Wrote to Mr Hayter—Sir J. Young (2)—Mrs Cracroft—Mr Munro—Dean Ramsay—Mr Herries—Mr Murray—C.G. Reid—S.H. Northcote—J.N.G.—Mr F. French MP.[7]—Mrs Wadd—Mr R M Fox MP.—Mr O. Higgins MP.[8]—Rev Mr Meredith[9]—Mr Bonham[10]—Mrs Fitzmaurice—Mr M. Blake MP[11]—Mr Bellew MP.[12]—Sir C. Wood—Stat[io]n M[aste]r Euston—C.G.—Statn. Mr., Crewe—Mr T. Keogh[13]—Sig. G.B. Testa[14]—Messrs. Cox & Shaw[15]—& minutes. Saw Mr Cunard[16]—Mr Coulson—Sir C. Trevelyan—E of Aberdeen—D. of Newcastle—Mr May[17]—Sir J. Young—Mr Hayter—Sir R. Mayne—H. Taylor. An hour's shopping. H. of C. 1¼–2½.[18] Dined at the

[1] See 19 Aug. 53.
[2] David Hutcheson and Co., steamship co., operating in Western Scotland.
[3] *H* cxxix. 1707; it went through all its stages that afternoon.
[4] Not found.
[5] Probably St. Paul's chapel in Great Portland Street.
[6] 'Upham's Guyon' here deleted; R. R. *Madden, *The life and martyrdom of Savonarola*, 2 v. (1853).
[7] Fitzstephen French, 1801–73; whig M.P. co. Roscommon from 1832.
[8] George Gore Ouseley Higgins, 1818–74, in Jamaican civil service, then liberal M.P. co. Mayo 1850–7.
[9] Perhaps Thomas Edward Meredith, ?1825–92; Corpus, Cambridge; curate in Shropshire 1849–52; naval chaplain 1852–67; vicar of Burley Down, Cheshire, 1867–82.
[10] Cp. 4 Aug. 53.
[11] Martin Joseph Blake, 1790–1861, liberal M.P. co. Galway 1833–57.
[12] Thomas Arthur Grattan Bellew, 1824–63; liberal M.P. co. Galway 1852–7.
[13] William Nicholas *Keogh, 1817–78; Irish barrister and liberal M.P. Athlone 1847–56; legal office for Ireland 1852–6; justice of common pleas 1856, tried Fenians 1865.
[14] Giovanni Battista Testa, Italian historian; had sent a copy of his book; cp. 16 June 53.
[15] Soap manufacturers; accepting, 'not without some scruple', a gift of scented soap; copy in Add MS 44528, f. 181.
[16] (Sir) Samuel *Cunard, 1787–1865; Canadian merchant; founded shipping firm 1839; cr. bart. 1859.
[17] i.e. T. Erskine *May.
[18] Misc. business: *H* cxxix. 1726.

French Ambassadors to celebrate the Fête Napoleon.[1] Saw M. Bishop [R] (6) Read Mad. Guyon.

16. T.

Wrote to Sir W. Molesworth—Mr Wilson—F.R. Bonham—C.G.—Sig. Dassi—Aunt J.—Sir A. Spearman—Ld J. Russell—& minutes. Fee Fund meeting at 2½. H. of C. 3–5.[2] Shopping &c another hour. Saw F.R. Bonham—Sir C. Trevelyan—Mr Wilson—Rt. G—Mr Gardner—HJG—Rob. M'Culloch—Granville—Canning. F. Lawley dined to talk over arrangements. Saw P. Lightfoot [R]. Conduct but very middling. Arranging & packing my things for the journey.

17. Wed.

Off by 9 AM Express. At Stafford staid to join C. who came for the 9.15. Reached Glasgow at 11½. Elderslie[3] after 12. Saw Cardwell. Read Carlyle's Life of Sterling.[4]

18. Th.

Wrote to Sir Wm. Molesworth. Read Robinson Crusoe. Cobden on Burmese War:[5] Drive to Glasgow. Renewed my old friendship with the Hagarts[6] who are here to meet us: and was very much struck with Mrs Speirs. Dinner party in Evg.

19. Fr.

Off at 7¼ to the Boat which took us by the Crinan [canal] to Oban Fort William and Corpach:[7] we slept comfortably at Banavie[8] & received much attention on the way. The Episc. Clergyman came to see me: Mr M'Lennan.[9] He had a request to make. Read Carlyle's Life of Sterling. The rain spoiled our view of & on from Oban: but we saw much grandeur among the mountains.

20. Sat.

On by Steam at 7.30 to Laggan[10]—by post to Glenquoich Lodge at 2.30.[11]

[1] Louis Napoleon's revival of Bonaparte's *fête*.
[2] Russia: *H* cxxix. 1760.
[3] Seat half a mile E. of Renfrew, of Archibald Alexander Spiers, 1840–68, liberal M.P. Renfrewshire 1865; his fa. Alexander d. 1844 having m. 1836 Eliza Stuart, da. of T. C. Hagart; she m. 1867 Edward *Ellice and d. *ca.* 1898.
[4] T. *Carlyle, *The life of John *Sterling* (1851).
[5] R. *Cobden, 'How wars are got up in India: the origin of the Burmese war' (1853).
[6] Cp. 16 May 28.
[7] On Loch Eil, 4 miles NW. of Fort William.
[8] At S. end of Caledonian canal, 2 miles NE. of Fort William.
[9] A. MacLennan, episcopal priest at Fort William from 1821.
[10] Locks on the Caledonian canal, 9 miles SW. of Fort Augustus.
[11] The seat of Edward *Ellice *fils*, on the north side of Loch Quoich, 25 miles NW. of Fort William.

The Glengarry drive exceedingly beautiful. The Western screen of mountains from G. Lodge really grand. Mr Ellice recd. us most kindly & walked me out. Finished C's Life of Sterling: a terrible & tragic book.

21. 13 S.Trin.

Prayers at noon in the dining room. Read the Ch prayers & MS. (of mine) in evg, in our own room. Wrote for the purpose. Read Taylor's Hist. Rel. Life in England[1]—Madden's Savonarola.

22. M.

Wrote to D. Newcastle—J. Woolley[2]—E. Clarendon—C.G. Reid—Rev. H. Caswall—Mrs Lane—Sir W. Heathcote—Mr O. Matthias,[3] & minutes. Out fishing: ride with Mr Ellice in evg. Music at night. Read Savonarola—Thackeray.[4] Lesson in Sallust to Willy. Late at night had notice of an expedition to the Glenelg Hills[5] early tomorrow.

23. T.

Up at 6¼ & away to Loch Hourn[6] down the fine pass—The hills exceeded all my expectation for both beauty & grandeur, to say nothing of Skye with Coreish[7] in the distance. We were out after deer until nine in evg: opposite Barrisdale & up Eastwards from over Loch Dhulochan.[8] Read Minghetti.[9]

24. Wed.

Another day after the deer from our excellent & merry quarters at Lochournhead.[10] The weather was lovely & the scenery improved greatly with the sun. I had but a snapshot at a hind. The ladies came down, & rowed up back to the Head. Willy remained by favour. Read Mr Wilson.[11]

25. Th.

A third Deer day beyond Arnisdale:[12] Willy accompanied Archie & me &

[1] J. J. *Tayler, *A retrospect of the religious life of England* (1845, enlarged ed. 1853).
[2] John *Woolley, 1816–66, headmaster of various schools 1842–52, first principal of Sydney University from 1852. Cp. 15 Sept. 53 and Lathbury, ii. 135.
[3] Octavius Mathias, d. 1864; Corpus, Cambridge, 1828; vicar of Horsford, Norfolk, 1829–51; rector of Christ Church, New Zealand, 1851–5; archdeacon of Akaroa from 1855.
[4] W. M. *Thackeray, *The English humourists of the eighteenth century* (1853).
[5] Running down to the sea, opposite the SE. end of Skye.
[6] A sea loch, running inland, dividing Glenelg from Knoidart.
[7] Loch Coruisk, below the Cuillin hills of Skye.
[8] A fresh water loch, 5 miles SW. of Barrisdale.
[9] His letter of 13 August 1853 from Long's Hotel, New Bond Street, in Add MS 44376, f. 40, or his book; cp. 15 Sept. 53.
[10] At the E. end of Loch Hourn.
[11] B. Wilson, *A letter to . . . Gladstone . . . on the new bill for the removal of Jewish disabilities* (1853).
[12] A village midway along N. shore of Loch Hourn.

tripped like a roe. We got milk & shelter at a shepherds. Near 3 hours to the Head from wind: three hours chiefly walking to a ten o'clock dinner & music in the evening. Wrote to F. Lawley & worked on papers.

26. Fr.

Wrote to F. Lawley—Ld Aberdeen—Mr M'Lennan—Mr Knowles—& minutes. Sallust with Willy. Sculled C. & gave W. a lesson in the art.[1] Read Taylor. Music in Evg.

27. Sat.

Wrote to Sir A. Spearman—G. Richmond—& min. Went down to Tomdoun[2] to drive for deer. Read Tayler—Caled C. Report.[3] Sallust with Willy. Daily conversations with Mr Ellice who is as full of experience as of shrewdness, & of hospitable kindness as either.

28. 14 S.Trin.

Din[in]g room prayers as last S.—Walked up the Quoich in aftn & to my great dissatisfaction missed our aftn prayers in our room: wh I read alone. Wrote MS. on Jer XII. 5. Read Tayler. Wrote to Miss Amphlett, & min[utes].

29. M.

Wrote to Mrs Chisholm[4]—H. Wilberforce—M. Loader[5]—& min. Read Tayler. Rifle practice mg—Grouse shooting &c. at Tomdoun aft. Music in evg. Conv. with Mr E[llice] as usual.

30. T.

Early breakfast & off with E. E[llice] to deerstalking. Bad winds: breakneck ground: my head weak, but much enjoyment of country nevertheless. A doubtful shot was all my performance. Back after 9.

31. Wed.

Wrote to Mr Severn—Wilson—Molesworth—& minutes. Read King's Geol.[6] Off at 8½ by land & water to Glen Shiel, Loch Duich, Loch Elsh: luncheon at Inverinate,[7] housed by the Kerrisons.[8] A most striking route & lovely day.

[1] 'Also in Sallust[?]' here deleted.

[2] On the Garry, 6 miles E. of Loch Quoich.

[3] *Report by the committee of negotiation appointed by the board of directors of the Caledonian Railway Company to confer with various guaranteed and preferential interests* (1851).

[4] Of Bridaig House, Dingwall; a distant relative, known for her piety; cp. 2 Sept. 53 etc.

[5] A rescue case, cp. 4 Oct. 53.

[6] D. *King, *The principles of geology explained, and viewed in their relations to natural and revealed religion* (1850, 4 ed., 1853).

[7] Lodge on N. shore of Loch Duich, 10 miles SE. of Lochalsh.

[8] Cp. 29 Jan. 37 n.

Memorandum.[1]

Agreed to be guardian to W.C. James's children May 10. 1852.

Trustee under O.B. Cole's marriage settlements—Ab. 1834.

Guardian to Earl of Lincoln's (now Duke of Newcastle's) children ab. 1844.

Trustee under Lady Wenlock's Will for her younger children—May 1852.

Engaged to pay C. Uppington £230 at any date after Jan 1, 1853. Paid 1853 by cheque on Scotts.[2]

[1] The next four sentences, under this heading, ruled off at the top of the back inside cover.

[2] These two sentences, lightly erased, written through the entries for 27 and 30 August 1853.

[VOLUME XVIII.[1]]

NO. 18.

SEPT. 1. 53 TO FEB. 24. 55.

Speeches Corrected but not published separately. 1853 Succession Duty 2 R.
1855. Explanations Feb. 23.[2]

Highlands.
Thursday Septr. One 1853.

We carried off our hosts the Kerrisons & made a most pleasant day's journey between driving boating & (for me) walking, by Plockton—Keshorne—Shieldag—Torridan—to Kinloch Ewe[3]: in about 10 hours. At Torridan I found a Cousin: at K[inloch] E[we] friends & acquaintances. Read Intr. to Vegetable Physiology.[4] Inn *rude* but good.

2. Fr.

Wrote to Aunt J.—Provost of Inverness[5]—Lady M'Kenzie (Kilcoy).[6] Morning Exp[editio]n after a merry breakfast to Loch Maree (ab 3 miles from Inn) Then to Achur Alt—Luichart H. to luncheon.[7]—& on to Dingwall[8] through a beautiful district. We put up at the National Hotel. Saw Mrs Chisholm—Mr Hutcheson[9]—& a Deputation from the Town Council.[10]

3. Sat.

Early breakfast & prayers at Mrs Chisholms. Then by mail at 8¼ to Dunrobin Castle.[11] Our most kind friend Mr Ellice parted from us at Tain.[12] We arrived about three: and the Duchess took us about the gardens and beach. The place is most striking, the welcome the kindest possible.

[1] Lambeth MS 1432, 70ff.
[2] Thus far, inside front cover.
[3] At SE. end of Loch Maree, 40 miles NWW. of Inverness.
[4] Published anonymously (1845).
[5] James Sutherland.
[6] Sarah Anne Philamena, *née* Parkes, m. 1844 Sir Evan Mackenzie of Kilcoy, 1816–83; 2nd bart. 1845.
[7] 17 miles W. of Dingwall.
[8] The county burgh of Ross and Cromarty, on the Cromarty Firth, 18 miles NW. of Inverness; His mother's birthplace.
[9] Of D. Hutcheson and Co., the steamship company.
[10] Offering him the freedom of the burgh, cp. Add MS 44579, f. 68 and 27 Sept. 53.
[11] Seat of the dukes of Sutherland, on the Moray Firth by Golspie, about 40 miles NE. of Dingwall; an eleventh-century house with many later additions.
[12] Sea port 25 miles NE. of Dingwall.

4. 15 S.Trin.

Prayers in our room; the two Lascelles cousins attending.[1] Pain then drove me to bed ab[out] noon; there being an apparent return of my erysipelatous inflammations.[2] Conv. with Willy on matters of Ch. polity & commission. Used powerful hot water applications. Read Wilson's Letter[3]—Upham's Guyon—Savonarola.

5. M to 8. Th.

These four days all spent in bed, under the careful hands of Dr Broomhall[4] while the sore was in process of 'maturation' with constant & sometimes sharp pain. Poultice bath & hot water applications were constantly used. The kindest messages came from the D. & Dss.—I read Savonarola—the Key to Uncle Tom's Cabin[5]—a remarkable work—and began Bulwer's 'My Novel'.[6] Also wrote (chiefly by C.s or Willy's hand) to Bp of Moray—Prov. Inverness—Scotts—E. of Aberdeen.

9. Fr. & 10. Sat.

Dr B[roomhall] opened the wound with the lancet—the probe showed it more than 1½ in. deep. He was very well pleased with the progress & I now seemed to have fairly turned the corner thank God. These days the Duchess came to visit me, & read to me: full of the utmost kindness & simplicity. Willy had had but one lesson in his Sallust. Wrote to [space for two names]. Read Bulwer's My Novel. Some return of appetite. The poulticing & baths continued.

11. 16 S.Trin.

C. & Willy read the Service. Read Upham's Guyon—Savonarola—pamphlets. Conv. with Willy. Progress continued.

12.

Up, & a little in the open air. Saw D. & Dss. Read My Novel. Wrote to Capt Turner[7]—Dr Goodford—Sir A. Spearman—Mr Rolls.[8] Made arrangements & wrote directions for Willy's departure.

[1] Probably Claud and Edwin Lascelles, (1831–1903, 1833–77) the two oldest of the nine children of Lady Caroline Georgiana Lascelles, who m. W. S. S. Lascelles 1828; her *sister m. the 2nd duke of Sutherland, cp. 10 Feb. 40.

[2] This illness kept him from visiting Haddo, where *Aberdeen hoped to persuade him to agree to *Russell's becoming prime minister; cp. Conacher, 173–4 and 4 Oct. 53.

[3] Cp. 24 Aug. 53.

[4] Thomas Taylor Broomhall, M.D. Aberdeen 1826; physician to the duke of Sutherland.

[5] H. B. Stowe, *A key to Uncle Tom's Cabin: facts and documents upon which the story is founded* (1853).

[6] E. G. E. *Bulwer [Lytton], *My novel; or, varieties in English life*, 4 v. (1851–2).

[7] Otherwise unidentified.

[8] Probably a further step in the case of J. H. Rolls, reinstated at the customs: cp. 18 May 44.

13. T.

Drove out with the Duchess & C.—Rapid progress now: the wound only 1 in by ½ in. It has been little short of a carbuncle. Read My Novel. We reluctantly parted with Willy off for Eton.

14. Wed.

Wrote to E. of Aberdeen. Drove & walked out with Dss. Today I ventured to dine & spend the evening with the family. I accomplished shaving on Sunday: & may thankfully record this eight or nine day's of bed illness as the longest since I had the scarlet fever at 9 or 10 years old. Read 'My Novel'.

15–17. Th–Sat.

Wrote (Fr[iday]) to Scotts—(Sat) Gadaléta [1]—C.G. Reid. (& min.) Finished 'My Novel'—Read Sydney Univ. Addresses [2]—Minghetti on Corn Laws [3]—Mancini on Machiavelli [4]—Raleigh on Govt.[5]—During these days I dined with the family—drove usually with Duchess & C.—shared in the evening music—But Dr B[roomhall] visited me daily & there was need: particularly as a new spot threatens & this day Sat. I was obliged to be much on my back & used ice applications. Stimulating ointment for the old wound now given up. C. had a threatening of being laid up yesterday: but is right today.

18. 17 S.Trin.

Read prayers (on my back) at noon. Walk with C. & Mr Gäbler.[6] Much lying up still needed. Treatment by ice externally. Read Savonarola—Upham's Guyon—A conv. with Dss. in evg on Sabbath observance—H.S. interpn.—& other matters of religion. Her spirit very good.

19. M.

Wrote to Dr Pusey—J.N.G.—Mr Hayter—Scotts—Mr R. Chance [7]—Mr H. Lees—Mr J. Griffiths—and minutes. Read Pennant's Tour [8]—Agric. Survey [9]—Sclopis, Relazioni [10]—Whitmore on Wine Trade.[11] Walk with C.—Singing in evg.

[1] O. F. Gadaleta had written a letter in Italian; cp. Add MS 44374, f. 243.

[2] 'Inaugural addresses, delivered on the occasion of the opening of the University of Sydney' (1852).

[3] M. Minghetti, *Della Riforma delle Legge Frumentarie in Inghilterra* (1846).

[4] Untraced work by P. B. Mancini, who published a book on Machiavelli in 1873.

[5] Sir W. *Raleigh, *The cabinet-council: containing the chief arts of empire, and mysteries of state* (1658).

[6] B. Gäbler, comparative philologist; later corresponded on classical museums; Hawn P.

[7] Robert Lucas Chance, 1782–1865; glass manufacturer, who supplied all the glass for the 1851 exhibition.

[8] T. *Pennant, *A tour in Scotland 1769* (1771).

[9] Perhaps the statistics on Scottish agriculture in *PP* 1852–3, ci. 163.

[10] Count F. Sclopis, *Delle relazioni politiche tra la dinastia di Savoia ed il governo britannico* (*1240–1815*) (1853).

[11] W. W. Whitmore, 'The wine duties' (1853).

20. T.

Wrote to Ld Stair[1]—R. Wilbraham[2]—minutes. Read Sclopis—Mignet's Marie Stuart.[3] Dr reported some progress: but I am still much on my back. A long & beautiful drive with D[uche]ss & Mr Loch to Loch Brora.[4] Music in evg.

21. Wed. (St Matth).

Wrote to Ld Aberdeen—T.S. Gladstone—Read Mignet's Marie Stuart. Walk to the seashore and exped[itio]n to see the Ondine.[5] Music in evg. Up to luncheon today. Drove through Rogart—a most remarkable district.[6]

22. Th.

Wrote to H.J.G. Dr reported much progress today—Went to the sea—visited Golspie school when I heard Homer creditably construed—The Ashburtons came: but we lost the Staffords[7] Seahams[8] & Vernons. Music in evg. Read Mignet.

23. Fr.

Wrote to Mr Arbuthnot—Bailie M'Kenzie[9]—D. of Argyll—Prov. Inverness—Earl Talbot[10]—Natl. H. Dingwall—J. M'Culloch & minutes. Read Mignet: a most sad & shocking history almost unrelieved in any quarter. Saw Dr B[roomhall] for the first time out of my room. Music in evg. Drive & walk in the Glen. Arrangements for departure. I can now walk freely without material discomfort.

24. Sat.

Wrote to Bp of Moray—Ld Prov. Glasgow[11]—Ld Mayor of London—& minutes. Read Mignet—Montaigne—Isolario (Venice).[12] Drive with C.

[1] North Hamilton Dalrymple, 1776–1864; 9th earl of Stair 1853.

[2] Roger William Wilbraham 1817–97; a treasury clerk; succ. to Delamere estates, Cheshire, 1885.

[3] F. A. M. Mignet, *Histoire de Marie Stuart*, 2 v. (1851).

[4] About 5 miles N. of Dunrobin, but accessible only by a detour along the coast. James *Loch, 1780–1855; as manager of the Sutherland estates depopulated Sutherlandshire; liberal M.P. St. Germains 1827–30, Wick district 1830–52. Gladstone wrote latin inscription for his tomb: Add MS 44747, f. 187.

[5] Probably a ship for evicted tenants emigrating; evictions were still occuring.

[6] The district by the rivers Brora and Fleet, largely depopulated by evictions by the Sutherlands; the village of Rogart is 7 miles W. of Golspie.

[7] i.e. the duke of Sutherland's eldest son; cp. 7 May 53 n.

[8] Mary Cornelia, da. of Sir John Edwards, bart., m. 1846 Viscount Seaham, 5th marquess of Londonderry; she d. 1906.

[9] Keith William Stewart MacKenzie of Seaforth, a bailie of Dingwall.

[10] Cp. 16 May 43.

[11] Robert Stewart, 1810–66; mine owner; lord provost 1851–4.

[12] B. Zamberti, Venetian humanist, *floruit* 1505, *Isolario* (n.d.).

25. S.18 Trin.

Prayers &c at noon in dining room. Ch. prayers at 6 in our own room. Wrote to Auth. Tusc[an] Persec[utio]n[1]—Mr Bonham—Ld Brougham—J. Willox[2]—Read Savonarola & Appces. (finished)—Upham's Guyon.

26. M.

Wrote to Mr G. Buckle[3]—R. Wilbraham—Landlord at Tain—do at Oban—do at Inverness.[4] Duchess of Suthd.—Lord Provost of Edinburgh—and minutes. Read Mrs Norton's Statement[5]—Smith's Poems.[6] 3–7. Journey to Tarbet H[ouse][7] 29 m. by Muckle Ferry. Most kindly received by Ld & Ly Stafford. Music in Evg.

27. T.

Wrote to Sir A. Spearman—Aunt J—Mr Suter[8]—Rob. Gladstone—Sir W. Farquhar—Mr Goulburn—Mrs Isab. Wilson[9]—& minutes. We were taken through the pretty Garden & grounds at Tarbet & went off at 11¼. At Dingwall, the freedom was presented & I spoke in ackn[owledgemen]t:[10] then a dinner with Mrs Chisholm. Reached Inverness (32 m. in all) at 5, went in a crowd to the Castle where freedom & speech came over again but with a large & warm audience.[11] Read Palmer on the Eastern Question.[12]

28. Wed.

Off at 6½ to the Canal[13] & at 7 to Oban which we reached before 8 in the evening passing for the last two hours through a tempest which made a very rough sea even of these landlocked waters. At the Caledonian [hotel] though it was crowded we did very well. Wrote to Agnes—Supt at Warring-

[1] An anonymous author, writing from Seeley's, Fleet Street publishers, had sent a pamphlet dedicated to Gladstone on the persecutions in Tuscany; copy in Add MS 44528, f. 186.

[2] John Willox of Edzell, by Fettercairn, had requested a treasury post; cp. Add MS 44528, f. 186.

[3] George Buckle, London engraver, probably engraving the Claudet, cp. 13 Aug. 53.

[4] Mrs. Addams of the Caledonian Hotel, Oban; George Cockburn of the Union Hotel, Inverness.

[5] One of the statements, on debt, in court or in *The Times*, made in 1853 by Mrs. C. E. S. *Norton; cp. her *Life* by J. G. Perkins (1909), 228–37.

[6] Alexander *Smith, Glaswegian, *Poems* (1853); including his 'Life drama' which caused a sensation.

[7] One of Sutherland's houses, by Kildary railway station, 15 miles NE. of Dingwall.

[8] Thomas George Suther, 1814–83; priest in Edinburgh 1837–55, in Aberdeen 1855–79; bp. of Aberdeen 1857.

[9] Possibly Isabella Wilson, lodging house keeper in Norton Street, London, involved in rescue work.

[10] Report of speech in N. Macrae, *The romance of a royal burgh* (1923), 190–3.

[11] Cp. Add MS 44579, f. 69.

[12] W. *Palmer of Magdalen, 'Remarks on the present aspect of the Turkish question' (1853); argues the inevitability of Turkish partition.

[13] The Caledonian canal, open since 1822.

ton. Read Quelques Mots sur la Question d'Orient[1]—Huc. Mr Brewster came on board & staid an hour. He is particularly pleasant.[2]

29. Th.

7–11½ Oban to Greenock, Paisley, & Drumlanrig:[3] train 1¼ hour late. The Duke [of Buccleuch] was still up. Read Huc. Somewhat sick in mg: but we both recovered after we were fairly clear of the swell.

30. Fr.

Chapel 9 A.M. Wrote to Ld Provost of Edinbro'.[4] In the forenoon & till 2 walked & drove about this noble place. Then joined the shooting party: being (D.G) quite equal to it in strength. We were 22 or 24 at dinner: not a show company but poor relations & the like, wh is so honourable to perceive in this princely position. The Duchess spoke as with a disembarrassed mind. I saw something of Lady Bath & liked her. Read Huc.

Saturday Octr. One 1853.

Chapel 9 A.M. Wrote (from Hn.) to H. Tayleur—R W Wilbraham—H. Lees. After breakfast at 10¼ we left for Thornhill:[5] where I fell in with an eccentric octogenarian farmer. At Carlisle we met the Seahams & came on to Warrington:[6] missed our cross train: fell in with W[ilson] Patten, dined at his house,[7] & reached Hawarden after[8] eleven: where we found the Talbots.

2. 19 S.Trin.

Church 11 A.M. (& H.C.) and 6½ P.M. Renewed acquaintance! with the children all well thank God & generally blooming. Walk with C. Read Upham's Guyon.

3. M.

Church 8½ A.M. Wrote to J. Lacaita—Robn. G—W.C. James—J.N.G.—Earl Talbot—W. Brown MP.—and minutes. Examined Hampton—Harvey—& MacCulloch himself resp. that family.[9] The poor Coachman seemed to come out well. Off by the Mail at night to London. Read Essay on Carlyle. My children—seeing J. Talbot—and the M'Culloch business brought me here instead of my going straight to London.

[1] Anon. pamphlet of this title published 1854; perhaps a work by J. G. Huc, author of *Histoire en vers de la guerre d'Orient* (1856), see next day.

[2] These two sentences at foot of next column.

[3] Seat since 1689 of the dukes of Buccleuch, 17 miles NW. of Dumfries, with a fine view of the Nith valley.

[4] In J. B. Mackie, *Life of Duncan *MacLaren* (1888), i. 320.

[5] The station for Drumlanrig, 14 miles NW. of Dumfries.

[6] Railway junction midway between Manchester and Liverpool.

[7] Bank Hall, by Warrington.

[8] Instead of 'about'.

[9] A servants' dispute, apparently involving M'Culloch's wife.

4. T.

Wrote to Bp of Argyll—C.G.[1]—Duke of Newcastle—Mrs MacCulloch.[2] Saw Mr Wilson—S. Herbert—Nat. Debt Commissioners.[3] My long pending conv. with Ld Abn. came off: & weighty enough it was.[4] After dinner I went out & saw M. Loader & E. Harrington [R]. I trust it it may please God at length to give me the complete self-mastery wh I ought so long ago to have attained. Worked upon arranging my papers.

5. Wed.

Saw Ld Devon—Mr Eyre—Mr J. Wood—Sir A. Spearman—Mrs MacCulloch, who made many charges agt. her husband. Mr Roberts—Ld Aberdeen—Scotts—Mr Brickwood. With Spearman I went fully into the question how to deal with Ex[cheque]r Bills & the January payments. Dined with Govr. Bank & discussed the same questions until midnight with him. Saw—[G.] Williams by accident [R]: & young Nunn[5] by apptt. Calls & shopping. Wrote to Mayor of Manchr.—Ed Times—Messrs. Wms. Chester—Ed M. Chron.—H. Tayleur—Mr P. Rose[6]—C.G. and minutes.

6. Th.

Wrote to D. of Newcastle—S. Herbert—Mr Saunders[7]—Mr G. Glyn—D.T. Gladstone—Mr J. Wood—Miss Law[8]—C.G. and minutes. Calls: every one out of town—incl. Mrs Norton. Saw Alick Wood—R. Phillimore—Mr Trevor—S. Herbert—Mr Wilson (on financial accts.) Dined with Herbert & spent the rest of the evening with Newcastle—on Cabinet matters.

7. Fr.

Wrote to Rev. R. Eaton[9]—Mr Tilsley[10]—Williams & Co—C.G.[11]—Nunn—Bp St. Andrews[12] and minutes. Dined with S. Herbert & evg. on this great Eastern question. At 10½ [a.m.] to Mr Saunders the dentist. Then saw Govr. Bank on Financial arrangements—Ld Courtenay—Mr Wilson with

[1] Extracts in Morley, i. 481–3, and Bassett, 103.
[2] The coachman's wife.
[3] The speaker; Sir John *Romilly, 1802–74, master of the rolls 1851–73, cr. Baron Romilly 1873; the governor of the bank of England; Sir Frederick *Pollock, lord chief baron of the exchequer court; William Russell, accountant to chancery court; and Gladstone himself.
[4] Cp. 4 Sept. 53 n.
[5] Joshua Nunn, probably an applicant for a position; cp. 11 Oct. 53.
[6] The s. of H. St. J. Rose who had suffered in Colin Robertson's bankruptcy and who had requested a treasury position for his son. Copy in Add MS 44528, f. 188.
[7] (Sir) Edwin Saunders, 1814–1901; dentist to *Victoria and Gladstone; first dentist to be knighted, 1883.
[8] Probably Elizabeth Sophia Law, 1818–88, sister of 1st earl of Ellenborough; she became a Franciscan nun.
[9] Richard Storks Eaton, Trinity, Dublin, 1830; curate of Little Bredy, Dorchester, 1833–49, rector of Compton Abbas, Dorset from 1849.
[10] Hugh Tilsley, of the inland revenue board.
[11] Some in Bassett, 103.
[12] Now Charles *Wordsworth.

Sir A. Spearman—Mr W. 2°—Cabinet 2–6.[1] Saw E. Collins accidentally, in evg [R]. Read (on the Turkish Empire) Annuaire des Deux Mondes.[2]

8. Sat.

Wrote to Gov & D[eputy] G[ov.] Bank—E. Cardwell—Mr J.C. Martin[3]—C.G.—Mr Goulburn—J.N.G.—Ld Prov. Edinb. & (dft)[4]—Mrs Barber & minutes. Saw Mr Glyn—S. Herbert—Mr Wood—Mr Russell & Mr Saunders—Mr Wilson—Commn. N. Debt met at 11. Cabinet 2–4¾: saw Ld Abn. afterwards: also A. Gordon.[5] St Mary's Ch Crown St 8½ P.M. Read Wheaton[6] & Annuaire.

9. 20 S.Trin.

St Martin's H.C. 8½ a.m.—St Philip's[7] at noon (finding Chapel Royal shut)—7 P.M. St Barnabas. Aunt J.s to tea afterwards. Wrote to Ld Prov. Edinbro (private)—also wrote out & sent my public letter (after showing it to Ld Abn.)[8]—Sir W.C. James—Rev. T.A. Powys.[9] Saw P. Lightfoot in evg by appt. [R]. Read Mad. Guyon (finished)—Reconstructed Liturgy—Bishop Spencers pamphlet[10]—Scots Ep. Mag.—Ch of Eng. Quart (Jan)—J. Tayler on Methodism.[11]

10. M.

Canning came on business & breakfasted. Off at 9½ Reached Manchester at 5¼. Bp of Oxford joined at Bletchley[12] & we had many matters to discuss. C. & Stephen joined at Crewe. We were most kindly received at Mr Harter's & the evening was spent with a large dinner & evening party of chief Manchester people. Read Tayler on Methodism. Bankes on Corfe Castle.[13]

11. T.

Wrote to Mr G. Burnett—Robn. Gladstone—Ld Prov. Edinbro.—Mr Jas Wilson—Joshua Nunn & minutes. The day (except being *seen* at the Exchange wh was very crowded & was even enthusiastic) was given to

[1] Cp. Conacher, 195–6.
[2] *Annuaire des deux mondes 1852–1853* (1853), 614; on 'La race Turco-Slave'.
[3] John Charles Martin, 1798?–1878; fellow of Trinity, Dublin, 1821–9; rector of Killeshandra, Kilmore, from 1831; archdeacon of Armagh 1854–66, of Kilmore from 1866.
[4] Add MS 44376, f. 84.
[5] Cp. Conacher, 199.
[6] H. Wheaton, *Elements of international law; with a sketch of the history of the science*, 2 v. (1836).
[7] In Granville Square.
[8] In J. B. Mackie, *Life of *MacLaren*, i. 321–2; accepting the freedom of Edinburgh; some bailies had opposed him on religious grounds.
[9] Thomas Arthur Powys, 1802?–71; fellow of St. John's, Oxford, 1819–31, rector of Sawtry St. Andrew, Huntingdonshire, from 1831.
[10] Untraced pamphlet by A. G. *Spencer, bp. of Jamaica.
[11] Cp. 21 Aug. 53.
[12] Railway junction on Oxford to Cambridge line.
[13] G. Bankes, *The story of Corfe castle and of many who have lived there* (1853).

sight seeing.[1] Mr Whitworths tool manufactory[2]—Mr Neild's Print-works[3] —the Free Library—Mr Brown's Warehouse. Dined at Mr Slaters.[4] Saw the Town Clerk[5] resp. tomorrows arrangements.

12. Wed.

Cathedral service 11 a.m. Saw the Church.[6] Then to the Inauguration of the Peel Monument[7] (a fine work) before a great assemblage—of *men* almost exclusively, & working men. There I spoke, to the cracking of my voice. Then to the Town Hall:[8] addresses from Corpn. & the two Chambers & a speech of 1¼ hour, wh was greatly helped by a singularly attentive & favourable audience. Then came the luncheon & toasts after it.[9] The Bp of Oxford laid a strong hand upon the company. Then a Deputation on Inland Bonding. Then to Mr Curtis's Machine Factory.[10] And a large dinner & evg. party at Mr Harter's wound up the day. Wrote to Ld Abn.[11]—R. Wilbraham.

13. Th.

We went off early to the Savings Bank & saw it.[12] Then to the Denton Consecration where the Bishop [of Oxford] preached a grand Sermon.

Then to luncheon where we were obliged to make speeches. Then to lay the foundation stone of new Schools where I had again to speak to an assembly of the *people*.[13] Then to Mr Walton's Factory to see the Card setting & other most curious machines.[14] Then to Broughton[15] & back to Riseholme where the Mayor (app[aren]tly a very amiable person) gave a large dinner party.[16] Home after midnight—having stopped to see the great Independent Chapel in Oxford Road by the way.[17]

[1] Report in *The Times*, 12 October 1853, 5f.

[2] The works of (Sir) Joseph *Whitworth, 1803–87, Manchester machine tool and armament manufacturer; cr. bart. 1869.

[3] Cp. 18 Jan. 43.

[4] William Slater, 1796–1889; solicitor in Manchester from 1820, later to the Liverpool–Manchester railway; the leading parliamentary solicitor of his day.

[5] (Sir) Joseph Heron 1809–89; Manchester town clerk from 1838; kt. 1869.

[6] The parish church of St. Mary, which became the cathedral when Chester diocese was divided in 1847.

[7] In front of the royal infirmary.

[8] Now replaced.

[9] He spoke on the Turkish question, cp. *The Times*, 13 October 1853, a–f; Morley, i. 483–4, Conacher, 206.

[10] Matthew Curtis, d. 1887, cotton machinery manufacturer, mayor of Manchester 1860–1, 1875–6.

[11] Cp. Morley, i. 483–4; Conacher, 206.

[12] Founded in 1818.

[13] Printed in 'The advantages of education. An address by . . . W. E. Gladstone' (n.d.? 1888).

[14] James *Walton, 1802–83, made many mechanical inventions, built largest card manufacturing works in the world at Haughton Dale, Lancashire, with Matthew Curtis 1853.

[15] Broughton New Hall, by Broughton; J. C. Harter's house.

[16] Rusholme, a suburb of Manchester.

[17] In Rusholme Road, just off Oxford Road.

14. Fr.

Off at 10½ to Sir E. Armitage's Cotton Mill:[1] an admirable specimen. Thence to the Salford Peel Park Library & Museum,[2] when Ld Stanley came to us. More speeches. To the Railway for the Train at one: where we bid good bye to our most kind hosts. Reached Hawarden with the Bp of O. & the Archdn. [Wilberforce] at 4 & set to writing.

Wrote to Sec. Manch. Free Library[3]—Robn. G—R. Wilbraham—Rev. T. Lund[4]—Alex Oswald and minutes. A party to dinner. The children thank God all well: & except Stephen all in *bloom.*

15. Sat.

Ch 8½ a.m. Wrote to Mrs Fitzmaurice—Jas Watson—Williams Deacon & Co—Jas Wilson—Sec. Lanc. & Carl. Co[5]—J. Wood—Willy—Sir D. Le Marchant[6] & minutes. Arranging books papers &c in the north room to wh I migrate.[7] Found an old wish of Lady Glynne's written with beautiful piety. 17 to dinner. Music in evg. Read on Slavery in Cuba.[8] Two hours walk with the Archdn. [Wilberforce] conv. on our difficulties: wh touch him very nearly. Also on H[oly] E[ucharist].

16. 21.S.Trin.

H[awarde]n Ch mg: also to the Confirmn.; where we had three servants, in the aftn.; & to Buckley in evg. Two more walks & discussions with the Archdn. Read his book on the H.E.:[9] & Connelly's "Coming Struggle".[10] Wrote to Walter James. Music in evg.

17. M.

Church 8½ a.m. Wrote to R.W. Wilbraham—Col Phipps[11]—Ld Granville—Dr Briscoe[12]—H. Tayleur—& minutes. Wrote Mem on Kensington Estate

[1] Sir Elkanah Armitage, 1794–1876, founded cotton spinning firm of Armitage and Co. 1827, mayor of Manchester 1846–8; kt. for his services against Chartists 1848.

[2] A large park purchased by public subscription in 1846: contains a bronze statue of *Peel by Noble.

[3] Edward Edwards, 1812?–86; librarian of Manchester Free Library 1850–58; catalogued library of Queen's, Oxford, 1870–80.

[4] Thomas Lund, 1805–77; fellow of St. John's, Cambridge, 1829–41, rector of Morton, Derbyshire, 1841–64, of Brindle, Lancashire, from 1864; wrote text-books on algebra.

[5] Samuel Edward Bolden, 1812–80; secretary of the Lancashire and Carlisle railway 1844; cattle breeder.

[6] Sir Denis *Le-Marchant, 1795–1874; sec. to B. of T. 1836–41; cr. bart. 1841; chief clerk to Commons 1850–71.

[7] Known as 'the temple of peace'.

[8] M. Torrente, *Slavery in the Island of Cuba* (1853).

[9] Cp. 22 May 53.

[10] P. Connelly, 'The coming struggle with Rome, not religious but political: or, Words of warning to the English people' (1852).

[11] (Sir) Charles Beaumont *Phipps, 1801–66, s. of 1st earl of Musgrave; lieut. colonel Scots fusiliers 1837; *Albert's secretary 1847, prince of Wales' treasurer 1849, his secretary 1864; K.C.B. 1858.

[12] Richard Briscoe, 1808?–90; fellow of Jesus, Oxford, 1831–66; D.D. 1845; vicar of Whitford, Flintshire, 1839–65, rector of Nutfield, Surrey, from 1865.

after working on the papers.[1] Read Calhoun[2]—Slavery in Cuba. Large dinner party: Music in evg. Walk with the Bp & Archdn. to discuss Court of Appeal, & other matters.

18. St Luke T.

Church 11 a.m. Agnes's birthday: God bless her: she leaves us nothing to wish but that she may grow up such as she is. Wrote to Lord Aberdeen—Willy[3]—Mr Higham—Sir J. Young—& minutes. Walk with Sir W. Heathcote—Also one with the Archdeacon. Read Calhoun—Britain's duty[4]—&c. Party & music in evg.

19. Wed.

Church 8½ a.m. Wrote to Mr Barker (2)—Mr Griffiths—Count Lavradio[5]—Miss Brown—W. Rigby—Scotts—W. Hancock—Jas Watson—Wms. Deacon & Co—R. Wilbraham—& minutes. Saw Mr Burnett—Mr W. Hancock—J. Phillips. Read Calhoun. Walk & conv. again at night with the Archdeacon. An interesting task but one of heavy responsibility.

20. Th.

Ch 8½ a.m. Wrote to Bp of Oxford (2)—A. Munro—R. Wilbraham—J. Wood—Lord Palmerston—J.N.G.—& minutes. Spent the morning on the Jelf & Maurice Correspondence.[6] Read also Calhoun—& Spectateur de l'Orient.[7] Walk with C.—Music.

21. Fr.

Ch 8½ a.m. Wrote to E. of Aberdeen—Kelso—Mr Chamberlain—J. Griffiths—Wms. Deacon & Co—J.G. Talbot—R.L. Chance—& memorandum on Smith's case (Cop Farm).[8] also minutes. Read Calhoun—Quarty. on a'Beckett—do on Louis XVII (pt.).[9] Saw Mr Burnett. Walk with S.R.G. & Calvert:[10] & at night music, & the pretty game with a silly name "Cockamaroo".[11]

[1] Add MS 44742, f. 170.
[2] Probably *Eulogies delivered . . . on the life and character of J. C. Calhoun* (1853).
[3] In Lathbury, ii. 150.
[4] Untraced pamphlet.
[5] Portuguese minister in London from December 1853.
[6] R. W. *Jelf drove J. F. D. *Maurice from his London chair for the supposed heterodoxy of his *Theological Essays* (1853). S. *Wilberforce had sent Gladstone the correspondence, cp. Wilberforce, ii. 209–16 and Add MS 44579, f. 75.
[7] Periodical ed. by R. Rangabé; see 27 June 50.
[8] Hawn P.; Smith had mismanaged the farm.
[9] *Quarterly Review*, xciii. 349, 387 (September 1853); A. P. *Stanley on *Becket's murder, *Croker on M. A. de Beauchesne, *Louis XVII*, 2 v. (1852).
[10] i.e. Frederick Calvert.
[11] Russian bagatelle.

22. Sat.

Ch 8½ a.m. Wrote to Earl of Aberdeen—H. Gabbitus[1]—Lord Steward—Robn. G—Officer G.P.O.—R. Wilbraham—Troppaneger[2]—J. Timm—Rev. Mr Brewer—Alick Finlay—Dss. of Sutherland and minutes. Read Birch's Pamphlet[3]—Quarty. on Louis XVII (finished)—Music & "the game in evg" Conv. with Calvert on Oxford Reforms.

23. 22 S.Trin.

Hn. Ch mg & aft. Walk with C. Read Gilbert on the Atonement[4] & made some way in R. Wilberforce's noble book. Left Hawarden at 9¼ & travelled all night to go to Windsor Castle where the Prince wants me on business.

24. M.

Reached Downing St before 6 a.m. & got a supplemental sleep. To Windsor by train at 2 P.M. Wrote to Ld Monteagle—Dr Pusey—Sir C. Trevelyan—Jas Watson—C.G.—Ed British Cabinet in 1853[5] and minutes. Saw Mrs Wadd—Scotts—Ld Clarendon—Newcastle—Ld Aberdeen—Read "The British Cabinet in 1853". Council at Windsor. Then two hours with the Pr. on Kensington Estate.[6] Then to Eton saw Willy & Coleridge. The Queen—very gracious in evg: spoke strongly for peace.

25. T.

St George's 10½ a.m.—& mg. prayers in the Castle. Wrote to C.G.[7] Read 'British Cabinet'. Wrote draft minutes on Kensington Estate & read it to the Prince:[8] who shewed me his minute on the Turkish question.[9] Saw Willy mg. & aftn—E. Coleridge—who described him well as centripetal)—Earl of Aberdeen—Clarendon—Col Grey—& 2 hours walk with Wellesley to the farm fowls dogs &c.

26. Wed.

Mg prayers—saw Willy—& away at 10.5. A long sitting with Ld Aberdeen on my way to D[owning] Street. Wrote to Sir C. Trevelyan—C.G.—E. Coleridge—Willy—H. Tilsley—C. Franks—Earl of Powis and minutes. Saw J.N.G.—Govr. of Bank—F.R. Bonham—Sir C. Trevelyan—Read Br. Cabinet—Evg. with G. Williams [R]. This is for future reflection.

[1] Unidentified; not the educationalist.
[2] A. Troppanegar had requested a customs appointment for his son.
[3] J. Birch, 'The Rev. [Archdeacon] C. Dodgson's new tests of orthodoxy' (1853).
[4] J. *Gilbert, congregationalist, *The christian atonement, its basis, nature, and bearings* (1834).
[5] Unidentified author of *The British cabinet in 1853* (1853).
[6] The profits from the 1851 exhibition were used to purchase an estate in South Kensington, today filled with museums; cp. Martin, ii. 445–6.
[7] Some in Bassett, 103.
[8] Add MS 44742, f. 176.
[9] A memorandum for the cabinet, dated 21 October 1853, in Martin, ii. 525–7.

27. Th.

Wrote to Lord Elgin—Mr Brickwood—Sir J. Young—R.W. Rawson—J. Nunn—Mr J. Wilson (3)—Mr W. Brown—Bp of Oxford—Robn. G.—Jas Watson—G. & Co—Mr Arbuthnot—Ld J. Russell—Sir C. Trevelyan—Lord Hardinge—and minutes. Saw Captain Elliot[1]—Lord Hardinge—Sir C. Trevelyan—Mr Franks—Govr. Bank—Mr Brickwood—S. Herbert. King's Coll Council 2–4½ on the Maurice affair wh went badly.[2] Worked on public papers all the evg to 12½.

28. Fr. SS.Simon & Jude.

Wrote (from Hawarden) to J. Phillips—Mr Panizzi—H. Tayleur—Jas Watson—Mr D. Gladstone—& minutes. Up at 4½ & left by 6 a.m. train Reached Hawarden[3] at 12½. Found all well. Read Br. Cabinet (finished)—La Veritè sur la Question de l'Orient.[4]—Colt on his Revolvers.[5]

29. Sat.

Stephen's croup broke up the night somewhat & I only rose to breakfast. Wrote to W.H. Lyttelton—H. Tilsley—Rev. Mr Watkin[6]—and minutes. Conv. with G. resp. Maurice & on Ch. of E. Read Maurice's last Essay &c[7]—Keshan's Ireland[8]—Phillimore's Russia & Turkey.[9] Walk with C.

30. 23 S.Trin.

Hawarden Ch mg.—Broughton aftn. Read Wilberforce on the H.E.—Thompson on the Atonement[10]—Anglo Maderensis[11] and Three Letters to Bp of London.[12]

31. M.

Wrote to Sir C. Trevelyan—Jas Watson—Ld Clarendon—Archd. Wilberforce—C. Litchfield—and minutes. Read Wilberforce on H.E.—Calhoun on the U.S. Govt.—Pope's Essay on Man. Walk with S.R.G. & L[yttelto]n. Games in evg. Saw Mr Burnett.

[1] Perhaps (Sir) Charles Gilbert John Brydone Elliot, 1818–95; captain 1841, commander at the Nore 1870–3; K.C.B. 1881.

[2] Cp. 20 Oct. 53 and n.

[3] Instead of 'home'.

[4] Possibly an earlier edition of Jacques Tolstoy's pamphlet (1855).

[5] S. *Colt, 'On the application of machinery to the manufacture of rotating chambered-breech fire-arms, and their peculiarities' (1853).

[6] John William Spiller Watkin, 1819?–1908; St John's, Cambridge; curate of Christ Church, Blackfriars, 1843–7, of St. George's, Hanover Square, 1847–8, rector of Shipbourne, Kent, 1858–75.

[7] Cp. 20 Oct. 53 n.

[8] D. Keshan, 'Ireland: an inquiry into the social condition of the country' (1853).

[9] Cp. 25 July 53.

[10] W. *Thomson, *The atoning work of Christ* (1853); *Bampton lectures.

[11] 'A letter to the bp. of London on the subject of foreign chaplaincies ... by Anglo-Maderensis' (1853); on the anglican chaplaincy in Madeira.

[12] Perhaps T. Harvey, 'Letters addressed to the bp. of London' (1845); also on foreign chaplaincies.

Tues. Nov. one 53. All Saints.

Hawarden Church 11 a.m. Wrote to Prince Albert—C. Ross—Sir J. Graham—Rn. G—Ld J. Russell—R. Wilbraham & minutes. Read Calhoun —Mill's Pol Ec.[1] N.Z. Year Book[2]—Sydney Univ. Correspondence—Medecin Malgré Lui.[3] Bagatelle in evg. Walk with C.

2. Wed.

Ch 8½ a.m. Wrote to Mr Arbuthnot—Mr G. Grant—Sir C. Trevelyan—W.C. James—Gerald Wellesley—W. Hancock. D of Newcastle—(& copy) and minutes. Went with Mr Burnett over the Shordley property which is in good condition.[4] Read Molieres Misanthrope—Calhoun's Works.

3. Th.

Ch 8½ a.m. Wrote to W. Hancock (& copy)—J. Griffiths—Sir C. Trevelyan —R. Wilbraham—C. Pressly—E. Breakenridge—C. Litchfield—J.G. Hubbard—Jas Watson—Lord Devon—J.E. Denison—Sir B. Brodie[5]—& minutes. Laid up in part today with another 'erysip. phlegmen'[6] Read Mill's Pol E.—Joseph's Lives of Criminals.[7]

4. Fr.

Wrote to Mrs Chisholm—Mrs Scott[8]—Bp of Aberdeen—Mrs Bennett—Rev. C. Marriott—R. Barker—Ld R. Grosvenor—and minutes. Read Mill—Calhoun—Drove with C. Saw W. Lyttelton—Preparations for departure.

5. Sat.

Off at 9½ to Liverpool. From thence to Seaforth where I spent 3 to 4 hours. Saw Burnett—Breakenridge—Rn. G—Mr Rawson—Dinner party at Court Hey in evg. Read account of Relations &c: attack on the Canterbury Committee: perhaps once & that unavoidably.[9] Wrote to D of Newcastle—Ld Holland—Ld St Germans—A. Panizzi[10]—Mr W. Grey[11] and minutes.

[1] Cp. 7 Jan. 53.
[2] *Hand-book for New Zealand, consisting of the most recent information* (1848).
[3] By Molière (1666).
[4] 4 miles S. of Hawarden.
[5] Sir Benjamin Collins *Brodie, 1783–1862; the court surgeon from 1832; cr. bart. 1834.
[6] The infection in his leg.
[7] H. F. Joseph, *Memoirs of convicted prisoners* (1853).
[8] Mrs. Scott of Clarencefield, Dumfries, had requested a post office position for her son.
[9] Perhaps a row about the New Zealand church constitution, cp. *Colonial Church Chronicle*, vii. 156 (October 1853).
[10] In Fagan, *Life of *Panizzi*, ii. 128.
[11] Probably William Grey, 1820?–72; Magdalen Hall, Oxford; principal of Queen's, St. John's, Newfoundland; curate of Milford, Surrey, 1860–5.

6. 24.S.Trin.

9½–6 Exp. to Seaforth—9 miles off. Seaf[orth] Ch, (& Holy C) mg 10½–1½. Ab 50 communicants: whole rail addressed at once: Ch half full below, less above; no responses; singing rather professional: sermon well meant, α–Church. But the occasion was one of interest to me. The memory of my ungodly childhood came thickly upon me. Others may look back upon that time as one of little strain: for me it offers nothing in retrospect but selfishness & sin. May the Eternal Priest absolve it and the Manhood wh has followed. I sat an hour & had luncheon with the Rawsons. Then to Waterloo, & saw Mr Jones & went to his church: better fabric, congrn., & service. In evg read Wilberforce on H.E.—Bp Edin's Charge[1]—Mr Jones's Sermon.

7. M.

Wrote minutes. Saw Breakenridge—H. Tayleur—Mr Moss—Mr Cunningham—Eden & Barrow[2]—Went over the place with Robn. Then visited the Great Hall[3] at Liverpool—& that singular phenomenon the very beautiful Unitarian Chapel[4]—Read Memoirs of Convicted Prisoners—finished. 5–11 Express to London. Took the book to E. H[arrington] thinking it might attract. But I did not turn it to account. Saw also E.C. [R].

8. T.

Wrote to Bp of Oxford—Sir J. Graham—Dr Jelf (2)—Ld Mayor—C.G.—Ld Steward—T.G.—Mr Hubbard—Mr Franks & minutes. Saw S. Herbert—Mr Wilson—Sir C. Trevelyan—Sir J. Graham—Ld Granville. Cabinet 2½–6½. Dined with the Herberts. Read Ed. Rev. on Church Parties (part)[5]

9. Wed.

Wrote to Dr Pusey—Ld St Germans—Dr Todd (M.D.)[6]—Lord Advocate—Mr Pressly—Sir J. Young—Mr E. Eyre—Mr Franks—C.G. Saw Mr Franks—Mr Wilson—Elcho[7]—Govr. & Dep. Govr. of Bank—Earl of Aberdeen—Banting—Granville & Cardwell. Off at 5¾ for Windsor Castle, Queen & Prince both very gracious: & conv. with much interest on the Eastern Question. Read Creasy on Constn.[8]

[1] C. H. *Terrot, *Charge to the clergy of the diocese of Edinburgh* (1852).
[2] William Barrow, a Liverpool solicitor.
[3] St. George's Hall, between the Assize courts.
[4] James *Martineau's new chapel in Hope Street, by T. D. Barry 1848–9; very early example of nonconformist gothic, now demolished.
[5] *Edinburgh Review*, xcviii. 273 (October 1853); review of W. Goode, *The divine rule of faith and practice* (1853).
[6] Robert Bentley *Todd 1809–60, physician; revolutionized treatment of fevers.
[7] On top of another name.
[8] Sir E. S. *Creasy, *The text-book of the constitution* (1848).

10. Th.

To Eton mg. Saw Coleridge—M. Van de Weyer—Wrote to E.A. Bowring—T.G. Willy—C.G.—J. Macgregor—Dr Jelf and minutes. Saw Sir C. Trevelyan[1]—Newcastle—Cabinet $2\frac{1}{2}$–$5\frac{1}{4}$. Back to Windsor—with Argyll & Molesworth—just in time for dinner & Henry V: rather heavily acted but with glorious parts in it. Wrote draft for H.O. to the Univ. Chancellors.[2]

11. Fr.

Prayers 9 a.m. & St George's $4\frac{1}{2}$ P.M. Wrote to Lord J. Russell—Mr Franks—Govr. Bank of E.—Mr Higham—Sec.El.Telegr.Co[3] and minutes. Wrote paper of propositions on the Eastern question.[4] Saw the Prince & reported for the Queen the Cabinet of yesterday: also on the Univ. & other matters. In evg the Queen renewed the Eastern subject to Molesworth & me. On Wedy. she mentioned the Czar's letter to her.[5] Saw Willy—Mr Coleridge—the Provost of Eton: & drove with C. to Dropmore.[6] Read Mem on Public accts.[7]

12. Sat.

Left the Castle after prayer & breakfast. Wrote to Mr E.A. Bowring—Dr Hook—Ld J. Russell—Mr Wilson—& minutes. 2–$3\frac{3}{4}$. Court of Exchequer to frame the Roll for Sheriffs.[8] Cabinet to $5\frac{3}{4}$. E[ast] I[ndia] Co's dinner $6\frac{1}{2}$.[9] Conv. in evg on my way [R]. Saw Graham—Granville—Ld Aberdeen—Ld J. Russell. Read Commissariat papers[10]—amended Univ. draft.[11]

13. 25 S.Trin.

St Matthews mg—Whitehall evg. Luncheon with the Wortleys. Saw J.N.G. Dined at Newcastles. Read Wilberforce (finished)—Ld A. Hervey (began)[12]

14.

C. off by 6 a.m. Train: a new reason in dear little Lena's broken arm. Wrote to Mr Apsley Pellatt—Jas Watson—Ld Palmerston—Bp of Exeter—Mr C. Litchfield (2)—Dr Jephson—Ld Lansdowne—J.E. Denison—Govr. of

[1] 'Grant', and another name, here deleted.

[2] The govt. had allowed time for the universities to prepare their own suggestions for reform; this letter, sent on 12 December 1853 under *Palmerston's name, called for information on these suggestions: *PP* 1854, i. 196.

[3] J. S. Fourdrinier; the electric telegraph company operated from 1846, between London and Paris from 1851.

[4] Add MS 44742, f. 186.

[5] In *LQV*, 1 series, ii. 559.

[6] Cp. 7 June 45.

[7] Untraced.

[8] The high sheriffs for the English and Welsh counties, excluding Middlesex and Lancaster, were nominated annually this day.

[9] Cp. *The Times*, 14 November 1853, 10c.

[10] The commissariat estimates for 1854–5 printed in February 1854 in *PP* 1854, xl. 127.

[11] Cp. 10 Nov. 53.

[12] Lord A. C. *Hervey, *The genealogies of our Lord* (1853).

the Bank—Mr Blamire[1]—E. of Clarendon—Ld Hardinge—Sir W. Molesworth—Robn. G—M.E.G.—and minutes. Dined with the Wortleys. Read Heathfield's Essays[2]—Tayler on Methodism.[3] Tried to find Bishop & failed [R]. Saw Ld Canning—Mr F. Scott—Mr Wilson—Mr Campbell—Mr Kennedy.

15. Tues.

Robn's. birthday: God bless him. Wrote to Mr G. Burnett—Capt. Synge[4]—Ld Canning—H. Readett—Rev. W. Rawson—C.G.—T.G. (& draft) Robn. G. & minutes. Saw Mr Monro—Ld Aberdeen—& Sir J. Graham—Calls & shopping. Dined with the Herberts. Sought Inn[ominata][5] 1. afr. but failed: saw Inn. 2.[6] & a new phase of human nature [R]. Read Constabulary Report & a variety of papers.[7]

16. Wed.

Wrote to E. Shaftesbury—Mr Fourdrinier—Lady A. Peel—Prince Albert—C.G.—J.G. Hubbard—Jas Watson—and minutes. Albert Park Deputn. at 2. Cabinet 3–5½. Dined at Ld Abns. Cab[ine]t Dinner. Saw Ld Lansdowne—Molesworth—Mr Wilson. Saw at nt. Whitnall: any good? [R] Read Tayler on Methodism.

17. Th.

Wrote to Sir C. Trevelyan—J. Hume—R. Neville—Pr. Albert—Miss Grosvenor[8]—C.G.—Ld J. Russell—& minutes. Read Cowell's letters to Sir F. Baring.[9] Saw Mr Nuster[10]—Sir C. Trevelyan—Mr Bowring—Mr Monsell—Elgin—Shopping. Saw Osborn (2°). Sought 1° but vainly [R]. Dined at Newcastle's.

18. Fr.

Wrote to Ld Chancellor (two)—T.G. (& draft)—Mr Thorn—Rev. S. Andrew—Sir C. Trevelyan—Molesworth—Ld J. Russell—T.W. Rathbone[11]—J.G. Hubbard—Ld Brougham—C.G.—Pr. Albert—and minutes. Saw

[1] William Blamire, 1790–1862; Christ Church; M.P. Cumberland 1831–6; tithe commissioner 1836–51, inclosure commissioner 1845–60. Copy in Add MS 44529, f. 2.

[2] R. Heathfield, *Contributions to the 'Postulates and Data', and other essays on finance, taxation, the gold discoveries, &c.* (1853).

[3] See 21 Aug. and 9 Oct. 53.

[4] Millington Henry Synge, 1823–1907; captain in royal engineers 1851, later major-general.

[5] i.e. a prostitute, name not yet known; cp. 18 Nov. 53.

[6] Cp. 17 Nov. 53.

[7] First and second reports of select cttee. on police: *PP* 1852–3, xxxvi. 1, 161.

[8] Victoria Charlotte, da. of Lord Robert Grosvenor; wrote to complain of pollution at Moor Park.

[9] Cp. 19 Jan. 44.

[10] Unidentified.

[11] Theodore Woolman Rathbone, 1798–1863; magistrate for Liverpool and Lancashire; member of leading Liverpool mercantile and philanthropic family.

Mrs MacCulloch—Govr. of Bank—Mr Goulburn—Mr Darley [1]—Mr Wilson—Sir C. Wood *cum* Sir C. Trevelyan—[Mrs.] E. Herbert—Dean Milman. Dined with the (Norwich) Stanleys. Read Tayler on Methm.—Ed. Rev. on Ch parties (finished). Saw Inn[ominat]a 1: name Wright [R].

19. Sat.

Wrote to Ld Lansdowne—E. Collins—Mr Jas M'Gregor—T.G. (& draft)—Sir C. Trevelyan—Mr Wilson—Mr G. Burnett—Sir C. Wood—Ld Hardinge—C.G. and minutes. Cabinet 2½–5. Saw Ld Lansdowne—Molesworth—Trevelyan—Palmerston—S. Herbert. Dined with the Woods. Saw E. Collins afr.: in low spirits—& no wonder [R]. Read Office Reports.

20. S.Pre Advent.

Chapel Royal mg. Titchfield St evg. Read Chr. Rem on H. Euch [2]—Gilbert on the Atonement [3]—Coleridge on Modernism [4]—Caswall on Scottish Ep. Ch.[5]—Hervey on Genealogies. Walked in evg.

21. M.

Wrote to J.D. Coleridge—T.G. & draft—Mr Dyce—Miss Wright.—Mr H. Brand [6]—Rev. S. Robins—Mr E. Ellice—C.G. and minutes. Went to the Soho French Play on speculation: rather a failure.[7] Saw Mr Pennelhouse [8]—Dr Armstrong [9]—Sir S. Northcote—Dr Bowring—Sir C. Trevelyan. Missed Wright, saw others [R]. Read Cowper's Task [10]—Spectateur de l'Orient [11]—Poor Law Office Report.[12]

22. T.

Wrote to Molesworth—Robn. G—J. Wilson—C.G.—Mr Higham [13]—& minutes. Worked a good deal on arranging letters & papers. Cabinet 2½–5½. Saw Trevelyan—do *cum* Northcote—Wilson. Saw Edwards [R]. Dined with the Herberts. Read Spect. de l'Orient—Tayler's Methodism—finished. Wrote minutes on the case of the Pavilion.[14]

[1] Probably John Richard *Darley, 1799–1884; Irish schoolmaster and priest; archdeacon of Ardagh 1866; bp. of Kilmore 1874.

[2] *Christian Remembrancer*, xxvi. 263 (October 1853); a review of *Wilberforce's *Eucharist*, cp. 22 May 53.

[3] Cp. 22 Oct. 53.

[4] H. N. *Coleridge, *Greek poets* (1834), 274: 'The women of the Odyssey discover occasionally a modernism and a want of heroic simplicity'.

[5] H. Caswall, *Scotland and the Scottish church* (1853).

[6] (Sir) Henry Bouverie William *Brand, 1814–92; liberal M.P. Lewes 1852–68, Cambridgeshire 1868–84, parliamentary secretary to treasury 1866; speaker 1872–84; cr. Viscount Hampden 1884, succ. as 23rd Baron Dacre 1890. Cp. Add MSS 44193–5.

[7] *Les Anglaises pour rire* at the Royal Soho theatre.

[8] Probably sc. Pennelthorne.

[9] Cp. 20 Apr. 49; he was about to be consecrated bp.

[10] Cp. 23 Sept. 48.

[11] Cp. 20 Oct. 53.

[12] Fifth annual report of the poor law board: *PP* 1852–3, i. 1.

[13] James Higham, assistant secretary to office for national debt reduction; son of S.?

[14] Not found; perhaps on the Pavilion theatre, burnt down 1856. Or Brighton?

23. Wed.

Wrote to Sir W. Farquhar—T.G.—Bp of Oxford—Sec. S.P.G.—Bp of Fredericton—O.B. Cole—Willy—J. Wood—T.G.—and minutes. Dined at Granville's. Saw Mr Hubbard—Sir C. Trevelyan—Mr Higham—S. Herbert —Molesworth—Ld Aberdeen. Cabinet 2½–6½. Reform discussed largely—amicably & satisfactorily—on the whole.[1] Worked on accounts. Saw Harrington—Edwards [R].

24. Th.

6–1 to Hawarden—Wrote to J. Wood—F. Lawley—Read Colton on Am. Church[2]—St Columba's Corresp[3]—Coningsby on Eastern Q.[4]

25. Fr.

Wrote to Ld Aberdeen—Mr Dyce—Mr Arbuthnot—Sir C. Wood—Mr Lacaita—Mr Bezzi[5]—Rev. Mr Brandreth[6]—Mr Higham—Ld Granville—and minutes. Church 8½ a.m. Saw Burnett—on Stephen's matters—& my own. I have found little Lena with her arm in a sling, rather pale, but very contented & well thank God. Read Report on Dec[imal] Coinage[7]—Colton on Amn. Church—Walpole's Letters to Mann Vol. I.[8]

26. Sat.

Ch 8½ a.m. Wrote to G. Bennett—S. Herbert—J.N.G.—Mrs Talbot—Mr Pressly—Ld Aberdeen—Sol. General & minutes. Read Report on Dec. Coinage—Colton on Amn. Church.—Walpole's Letters to Mann.

27. Advent Sunday.

Ch. mg & evg. Wrote a plan for Church Rates.[9] Read Thompson on the Atonement. Bp. of St Asaph's Charge.[10] Colton on Amn Church (finished)—Hardwick's Church History.[11]

[1] Cp. Morley, i. 490.
[2] C. Colton, *The genius and mission of the protestant episcopal church in the United States* (1853).
[3] In *Colonial Church Chronicle*, ii. (1848).
[4] Coningsby, pseud., 'The present crisis, or, the Russo-Turkish war and its consequences to England and the world' (1853).
[5] G. A. Bezzi, professor of Italian at King's College, London, until 1854. Gladstone supported Lacaita as his successor, copy in Add MS 44520, f. 6.
[6] William Harper Brandreth, 1813?–85; Christ Church; rector of Standish, Wigan, from 1841.
[7] Report of select cttee. recommending swift introduction of decimal coinage: *PP* 1852–3, xxii. 387. The origin of Plantagenet Palliser's great project when chancellor in *Trollope's political novels.
[8] H. *Walpole, *Letters . . . to Sir H. *Mann, . . . British envoy at the court of Tuscany*, 3 v. (1833).
[9] Add MS 44742, f. 193.
[10] T. V. *Short, *Charge delivered to the clergy of the diocese of St. Asaph, at the triennial visitation* (1853).
[11] C. Hardwick, *A history of the Christian church* (1853).

28. M.

Ch 8½ a.m. Wrote to Duke of Argyll—J. Wilson—J.E. Denison—J. Higham—Dr Jacobson—Jas Watson & minutes. Dined at the Rectory. Katie[1] slightly better. Read Dec. Coinage Report—Hor. Walpole's Letters —Pride & Prejudice—Plan of Reform[2]—Trevelyan on Superann[uatio]n.[3] Began Tasso with Agnes.

29. T.

Wrote to E. of Aberdeen—Jas Higham—Supt. Chester St[ation]. Mr. A.L.[4] —E. Coleridge—F. Lawley—& minutes. Italian lesson to Agnes. Latin to Stephen. Read Dec. Coinage Report—Trevelyans E.I. Evidence[5]—H. Walpole's Letters.—Pride and Prejudice.

30. Wed. St Andrew.

Ch 11 a.m. Wrote to Mr H. Maitland—S. Herbert (two)—D. of Argyll— Rector of Exeter—Mr Delane—Ld Chancellor—& minutes. Italian lesson to Agnes. Read Dec. Coinage Report—Report on Civil Service Organisation[6] —H. Walpole—Pride and Prejudice.

Thursday Decr. One 1853.

Wrote to Mr Arbuthnot—J. Watson—Lord Brougham—F. Lawley—Sir C. Trevelyan—J.N.G.—Mr Buchanan[7] and minutes. Church 8½ a.m. Tasso with Agnes. Latin with Stephy. Mr Godley came in evg: we sat rather late. Read Dec. Coinage Evid. (finished)—Nat. Gallery Report[8]—Pride & Prejudice.

2. Fr.

Ch 8½ a.m. Wrote to Sir W. Molesworth—Robn. G—E. Breakenridge—Mr J. Wood—Sir C. Trevelyan—E. of Aberdeen—Rev. J.H. Stewart—and minutes. Tasso with Agnes. Latin with Stephy. Read Nat. Gallery Report &c—H. Walpole's Letter—Pride and Prejudice. Walk with Godley.

[1] Henry Glynne's daughter; she d. February 1854.

[2] Perhaps T. Bannister, 'The suffrage nationalized' (1853); copy in Add MS 44579, f. 393.

[3] A printed memorandum, in Add MS 44579, f. 135.

[4] 'Mr. A.L.' of Greenwich had written a begging letter; draft reply in Add MS 44376, f. 190.

[5] Evidence of Sir C. *Trevelyan to select cttee. on Indian territories: *PP* 1852–3, xxviii. 121.

[6] The *Northcote–*Trevelyan report on the organization of the permanent civil service, dated 23 November 1853: *PP* 1854, xxvii. 1 and Add MS 44579, f. 139.

[7] Perhaps Andrew Buchanan, secretary to Russian legation in London.

[8] Report of select cttee.: *PP* 1852–3, xxxv. 1.

3. Sat.

Ch 8½ a.m. Wrote to Sir J. Graham[1]—Mr Wilson—M. Lyttelton—Mr Higham—H. Maitland—S.H. Northcote—& minutes. Tasso with Agnes. Latin with Stephy. Dined at the Rectory: discussed Pr[ide] & Pr[ejudice]—music in evg. Little Kate today D.G. seems out of danger. Read Turkish question Papers[2]—Walpole's Letters. Pride & Prejudice (Finished).

4. 2 S.Adv.

Ch 11 a.m. (H.C.) & 6½ P.M. Read Thomson on Atonement (finished)—Ch periodicals—Kenneth.[3]

5. M.

Ch 8½ a.m. Wrote to Jas Watson—Robn. G (2)—Sir T. Fremantle—J. Murray—Lord Hobart—J.N.G.—& minutes. Walk with C. Worked on accounts—(H[awarde]n residence & Clewer)[4] Saw Burnett—Tasso with Agnes—Read Q.R. on Oxford[5]—Milward on Dec. Coinage[6]—Lalla Rookh.[7]

6. T.

Ch 8½ a.m. Wrote to Sir T. Fremantle—Ld Aberdeen—Sir C. Trevelyan—Banting & Co—Mr J. Wilson (2)—J.E. Denison—Sir S. Northcote—& minutes. Bp of Oxford. Called on Mr Austin[8]—Tasso with Agnes—Latin (& walk) with Stephy. Dined at the Rectory—Music. Read Lalla Rookh—Q R. on Oxford (finished)—Tutors' Report on Professoriate.[9]

7. Wed.

Ch 8½ a.m. Wrote to Sir C. Trevelyan (2)—Mr R. Caparn—Mr Arbuthnot—Mr J. Higham—Ld J. Russell—Mr A. Whyte—Sir C. Hotham—F. Lawley—Maitland & Co—Rev. Mr Adams—Rev. W. Thomson[10]—and minutes. Tasso with Agnes. Latin with Stephen—Lady & C. Lyttelton dined—music in evg. Read Lalla Rookh. Packing & arranging for departure.

[1] Cp. Conacher, 317.

[2] Draft on the collective note to be signed in Vienna deploring Russo-Turkish hostilities: *PP* 1854, lxxi. 698.

[3] [C. M. *Yonge], *Kenneth; or the rear guard of the grand army; a tale* (1850).

[4] In Hawn P.

[5] *Quarterly Review*, xciii. 192 (June 1853); J. B. *Mozley on the Oxford commission.

[6] A. Milward, *The decimal coinage. A letter to* [*Gladstone*] *advocating . . . the issue of a five farthing piece* (1853).

[7] By T. *Moore (1817); cp. 29 July 39.

[8] Edward Austin, ?1824–*ca.* 60; Queen's, Oxford; curate of Broughton, Hawarden, 1853.

[9] 'Recommendations respecting the relation of the professorial and tutorial systems, November 1853'; n. 3. of the Oxford tutors' association's *Papers*. The association favoured moderate reform to remove abuses in the existing system with only slight increases in professorial power; it influenced Gladstone, usually through Woollcombe and Haddan, during the negotiations.

[10] William Thompson, 1795?–1854, principal of St. Edmund Hall, Oxford, from 1843.

8. Th.

Wrote various minutes. We left at 10.50. In Chester I saw Mr Barker on SRG.s matters. Reached Hagley at 5½. Read Godley's Article on N.S.W.[1]—Rejected Addresses.[2]

9. Fr.

Church 10 a.m. Wrote to Sir C. Trevelyan (3)—J. Murray—H. Maitland & Co—Mr W. Brown—Sir T. Fremantle—Mr J. Wilson—Mr Arbuthnot—H. Fitzroy—F. Lawley—and minutes. Saw W. Lyttelton resp. Maurice. Walk up Clent Hill.[3] Worked on Ital. Grammar for Meriel. Tasso with Agnes. Latin with Stephen. Read Chatterton[4]—Jortin's Erasmus[5]—Heywood on Oxford.[6]

10. Sat.

Wrote to T.A. Hope—Sir C. Trevelyan (2)—G. Burnett—Mr B. Oliveira—Sam Scott—Sir J. Shelley—Miss Weale—Ld Granville—Rev. Mr Lake—Rev. Mr Ffoulkes—A.S. Finlay—and minutes. Read Spackman on Currency[7]—Mill on do[8]—Child on Trade[9]—Sav. Bank Essay.[10] Tasso with Agnes—and Willy who is now to begin. Latin with Stephy. Music in evg.

11. 3.S.Adv.

Church 11 & 3 P.M. Conv. with Willy on m[orning] Sermon. Music in evg. Read Oxford (Hebd. Counc.) Report & Evidence[11]—Wilson's Bampton Lectures.[12]

12. M.

Ch 10 a.m. Wrote to V. Chance[llo]r Oxford—Sir T.G. (2)—Mr Jas Wilson—F. Lawley—Mr J.T. Bullock—Molesworth—H. Maitland & Co and minutes. Tasso with Willy & Agnes. Latin with Stephen. Walk with the party. Read Oxf. Evidence. Adone of Marino.[13]

[1] Untraced article by J. R. *Godley.

[2] Cp. 19 Nov. 41.

[3] A mile SE. of Hagley.

[4] T. *Chatterton, *His works, published by R. *Southey, with his life by G. Gregory*, 3 v. (1803).

[5] John *Jortin, *Life of Erasmus*, 2 v. (1758–60).

[6] J. Heywood, *The recommendations of the Oxford university commissioners, with selections from their report, and a history of the university subscription tests* (1853).

[7] W. F. Spackman, *The commercial barometer from 1845 to 1853, showing the operation of the present system of currency* (1853).

[8] J. S. *Mill, *Principles of political economy*, ch. xiii; cp. 4 Jan. 53.

[9] Sir J. *Child, *Brief observations concerning trade, and interest of money* (1668).

[10] Untraced.

[11] *Report and evidence upon the recommendations of her majesty's commissioners for inquiring into the state of the university of Oxford* (1853); produced by a hebdomadal board cttee.

[12] H. B. *Wilson, *The communion of saints, an attempt to illustrate the true principles of Christian union* (1851).

[13] G. Marino, *Adone* (1623).

13. T.

Ch 10 a.m. Wrote to Herr Halbreiten [1]—Mr J. Wood—Mr Arbuthnot—Dr Jelf—Sir W. James—Mr Lake—Mr J.M. Ludlow [2]—Mr White—Archd. Allen and minutes. Tasso with Willy (Agnes ill) Latin with Stephy. Walk with Charles [Lyttelton?]. Read Oxf. Evidence—Adone of Marino—U.S. Coinages Manual.

14. Wed.

Ch 10 a.m. Wrote to Lord J. Russell (2) [3]—A. Panizzi [4]—H. Maitland & Co—F. Lawley—Sir C. Trevelyan—Coles Child & minutes. Walk with Willy. Tasso with [blank] Latin with Stephy. (X) [5] Read Oxford Hebd. Evidence—Adone of Marino. Saw Mr Knight resp. Settlement & Rating.[6]

15. Th.

Church 10 a.m. Wrote to Dr Jacobson—F. Lawley—Worked on Oxford questions & prepared a draft of Scheme.[7] Tasso with Willy & Agnes. Read Oxford Evidence (finished)—and Adone of Marino.

16. Fr.

Off at 9. a.m.—astounded by a note from A. Gordon.[8] Reached Paddington at 3.15. D[owning] St at 4. Latin with Stephy on the way. Wrote to Rev. B. Jowett—H. Fitzroy—A. Gordon—Jas Wilson—Lady Wenlock and minutes. Dined at Mrs Stanley's to meet Archdeacon [J.C.] Hare—an introdn. wh has long hung fire. Saw A. Gordon—D. of Newcastle—After dinner went to the Admiralty $10\frac{1}{4}$–$1\frac{1}{2}$ where Ld A., N., Graham, & I went over the late events & considered the course for tomorrow's Cabinet.[9]

17. Sat.

Wrote to Mr Ellice & others—and minutes. Saw Northcote—resp. Oxford—S. Herbert—Mr J. Wood—Mr Briscoe (Jesus Coll.)—the Chancellor [10]—Newcastle—Mr Wilson—Cabinet $1\frac{1}{2}$–6. Dined at Canning's: then with N. till nearly 2 on the late occurrences & *C. versus C.*[11] Worked on my Oxford draft.[12]

[1] Probably Ulrich Halbreiter, 1812–77; painted religious subjects; lived usually in Munich.

[2] John Malcolm Forbes Ludlow, 1821–1911; barrister; Q.C. 1843; christian socialist and author.

[3] Part in Conacher, 334; on Oxford reform.

[4] On Poerio, in Fagan, *Life of* **Panizzi*, ii. 128.

[5] Meaning obscure; rescue work at Harwarden improbable.

[6] Perhaps (Sir) Frederick Winn Knight, 1812–97; tory M.P. Worcestershire 1841–85; minor office 1852, 1858–9; K.C.B. 1886.

[7] Marked 'Secret', the origin of the 1854 Act; Add MS 44742, f. 199.

[8] To announce *Palmerston's resignation; cp. Morley, i. 490.

[9] Cp. Conacher, 238. Version of this sentence in Morley, i. 490.

[10] Of Oxford University, Lord *Derby.

[11] *Clarendon had been very critical of Stratford *Canning, cp. Conacher, 164–5.

[12] Revised draft in Add MS 44742, ff. 205–33.

18. 4.S.Adv[ent].

Whitehall mg. (Ordination—the children appeared to be struck)—Ch[apel] Royal aftn.—& MS. for 3 S. Adv. aloud in evg. Wrote to Ld Abn.—and copy. Saw Panizzi—resp. Poerio—S. Herbert—Ld Aberdeen & Graham—H. Fitzroy (bis). My day was thus very much invaded—but for just cause. Worked much on Oxford scheme—Read divers.

19. M.

Wrote to Warden of Merton—Mr Grey—Provost of Oriel—Sir J. Young—Warden of Durham—H. Fitzroy—Ld Granville—C. Wood—Lord J. Russell[1]—Jas Wilson—Sir J. Graham—Ld Raglan—Ld Hardinge—and minutes. Cabinet 5–7. Saw Ld Aberdeen early in forenoon[2]—Fitzroy—Newcastle—Clarendon—resp. Lord P[almerston]—also Ld Hardinge—Herbert (who dined)—Jas Wilson—Irish Presbyt. Deputn. at noon.[3] Read Session of 52–3.[4]

20. Tuesd.

Wrote to Sir S. Northcote—J.H. Parker—Mr Arrowsmith—Ld Ellesmere—Ld J. Russell—and minutes. also Dft for I.T. letters. Double Italian lesson with Willy & Agnes. Eleven to dinner. Saw Mr Wilson—Ld Elcho—Turkish Minr.[5] & Namik Pacha[6]—Ld Aberdeen—C. Wood—H. Fitzroy—and in evg Mr Jowett—Mr Lake with Mr Rawlinson—resp. Oxford. Read Session 52–3. Arranged my Oxford papers.

21. Wedy.

Wrote to Ld Aberdeen—T.G—Sir C. Trevelyan—and minutes. Read Sir E. Wilmot on Reform[7]—Marshall on do[8]—Daubeny on Physical Science in Oxf[9]—Westgarth's Australia Felix.[10] Called on Ld Palmerston & sat an hour.[11] Saw also Sir W. Molesworth—C. Wood—Ld Aberdeen—Bp of Oxford. Partially confined with heavy cold. Tasso with Willy & Agnes. Sugar refiners &c. 1–2½.[12]

[1] Forwarding sketch of Oxford reform bill; fragment in Conacher, 335.
[2] Cp. Conacher, 225.
[3] Papers untraced.
[4] [E. M. Whitty], *History of the session 1852–3, a parliamentary retrospect* (1854); reprinted newspaper articles.
[5] Constantine Musurus, 1807–91; Turkish minister in Athens 1840, in Vienna 1848, in London 1851–6, ambassador in London 1856–85; given title of Pasha on Sultan's visit to London 1867. Report to Stratford de Redcliffe on proposals to support Turkey financially in Add MS 44376, f. 232.
[6] Turkish politician, in London to arrange the loan, cp. Guedalla, *P*, 96–7.
[7] Sir J. E. E. *Wilmot, *Parliamentary reform. A letter to R. Freedom on the re-distribution, extension, and purification of the elective franchise* (1854).
[8] Possibly W. Marshall, *Railway legislation and railway reform considered with special reference to Scottish lines* (1852, 2 ed., 1853).
[9] C. G. B. *Daubeny, 'Can physical science obtain a home in an English university?' (1853).
[10] W. *Westgarth, *Australia Felix; or, an account of Port Philip* (1847).
[11] In Morley, i. 490.
[12] Report in *The Times*, 22 December 1853, 6e.

22. Th.

Wrote to Maitland & Co—and minutes. Partially confined as yesty. Conclave on Army Rations 12–1½. Saw Trevelyan—Wood—Ld Panmure. Cabinet 2–7½—on Eastern question—Palmerston—& reform [1]—Newcastle & Herbert dined, & talked till 11½. Read Session of 1852–3. A day of no small matter for reflection.

23. Fr.

Wrote to Bp of Oxford—C. Pressly—Sir J. Harington—Robn. G.—Sir W.C. James—Mr Biscoe—H. Maitland & Co—Col. Mure—S. Herbert (2) [2] —J.D. Cook—Newcastle—& minutes. Saw Mr Gr. Berkeley [3]—J.D. Cook—Ld Granville—A. Gordon—D. of Newcastle—Jas Wilson—Sir C. Trevelyan —Ld Aberdeen. Tasso with Willy & Agnes. Ordnance Map Conclave 2–3½.[4] Read Session 52–3. 3½ hours on arranging papers & letters in evg.

24. Sat.

St Paul's Kn[ightsbridge] 9 P.M. Wrote to Williams Deacon & Co—S.R.G. —Jas Watson—Scotts—Chairman of Com. (S. Carolina Senate) [5]—Newcastle—St German's—Ld Stratford de R.[6]—Ld Ellesmere—Lady Macclesfield [7]—T.G.—Rev. C. Marriott—Robn. G.—Sir C. Trevelyan—and minutes. Sawr R. Phillimore—Sir C. Trevelyan—J.D. Cook—Mr Hayter—Ld Granville—D of Newcastle. 2–4 Ordnance Map Conclave. Read Session 52–3. Again about arranging.

25. S. Christmas Day.

Whitehall Chapel & H.C. mg. Broadway Evg. MS. of 41 aloud at night. Wrote to Bp of Moray—Rev. Mr Codd [8]—Mr J.D. Cook—Mrs Wadd. Saw Lord Aberdeen. Read Bp of O's Sermon [9]—Archd. Sinclair's do [10]—Codd on Diocesan Colleges—Biden [11]—Archd. Merriman's Journal.[12] (Health) calls at Mrs Wadd's—A. Robertson's &c.

[1] Cp. Morley, i. 490–1, and Conacher, 226, 242.
[2] Fragment in Conacher, 226–7.
[3] (Grenville) Charles Lennox Berkeley, 1806–96, 2nd s. of Sir G.C.*; liberal M.P. Cheltenham 1848–52, 1855–6, for Evesham 1852–5; whip 1852–6; parliamentary secretary of poor law board 1853–6; customs commissioner 1856–86.
[4] The treasury circular of 23 April 1853 on the scale of the survey had produced a mass of replies: *PP* 1854, xli. 190ff.
[5] Not found.
[6] Draft, on Namik Pasha, in Add MS 44376, f. 232.
[7] Lady Mary Frances, 2nd d. of 2nd marquess of Westminster; she m. 1842 as his 2nd wife Thomas Augustus Wolstenholme Parker, 1811–96, who succ. as 6th earl of Macclesfield 1850. She bore 11 children and d. 1912.
[8] Edward Thornton Codd, 1817?–78; St. John's, Cambridge; perpetual curate of Cotes-Heath, Staffordshire, 1844–59; vicar of Bishop's Tachbrook, Warwickshire 1859–77. Wrote 'A letter to the bp. of Lichfield on diocesan theological colleges' (1853).
[9] S. *Wilberforce, 'The deceitfulness of sin' (1853); on Heb. iii. 13.
[10] J. *Sinclair, 'Great Britain and America: a farewell sermon preached in St. Paul's Chapel, New York' (1853); on Psalm cv. 1.
[11] J. Biden, *Plain and practical sermons* (1853).
[12] N. J. *Merriman, R. Gray, ed., *The Kafir, the Hottentot, and the frontier farmer. Passages of missionary life* (1854).

26. M. St Stephen.

Westminster Abbey at 3 P.M. Wrote to Sir T. Fremantle—Robn. G—Sir J. Herschel—Mr Dyce—E. Cardwell—H. Lees—Mr Arbuthnot—Mr White —Rev. H.B. Barry—Mr Grogan—Mr Banting—& minutes. Saw Bonham—Ld Aberdeen—Dss of Sutherland (at S[tafford] House). Eleven to dinner: a family party. Worked on my private affairs afterwards. They will soon I hope begin to look tidy again, as far as depends on me. Read Recueil des Documens (on Russia).[1] Tasso with Willy & Agnes.

27. T. St John.

St Andrew's Wells St 5 P.M. Wrote to Lord J. Russell—S. Herbert[2]—Lord Chancellor—Ld Elcho—Rev. H. Mackenzie—and minutes. Worked most of the day on the Oxford question. Wrote Mem. on College Elections.[3] Latin lesson to Stephy—Tasso with Willy & Agnes. Saw J. Horton: middling [R].—Ld E. Bruce. Read Session 52–3. Recueil des Documens.

28. Wed. Innocents.

St Andrew's Wells St 5 P.M. Wrote to Mr G.F. Bowen—Mr Dyce—Dr Daubeny—Mr Roberts—Prov. of Oriel—Mr V. Scully—Sir S.R. Glynne—Mr Hume—Mr Jas Wilson—S. Scott—Jas Watson—H.J.G.—& minutes. Worked on private affairs & accts. Saw Ld Elcho—Mr A. Gordon—Mr C. Franks—Mr Hayter. Called for Osborne: but in vain [R]. Read Pasley on Dec. Coinage[4]—Recueil—Session 52–3. Latin with Stephy. Tasso with Willy & Agnes.

29. Th.

Wrote to Sir C. Wood—Rev Mr Jowett[5]—F. Lawley—Sir W. James—J. Higham—J.C. [sc. G.] Hubbard—Jas Watson—and minutes. 1–5½. Exp. to Windsor to attend Council. Business with Graham—Ld Aberdeen—Ld J. Russell—S. Herbert—Rev. C. Marriott 2½ h. on Oxford. In aftn. saw Osborne [R]: remember Hooker on the torch.[6] Herbert dined. The three elder children brought me presents & very nice letters.

The singular blessing of this year has been *health*. Without this among them I know not how I could have gone through its labours. It has not I grieve to say been a year of advance towards purity, taken as a whole: in some other particulars I would trust there may be gain: but again remember 'he that keepeth the whole Law'.[7] I sometimes please myself with thinking

[1] *Recueil des documents pour la plupart secrets et inédits* (1853); on Nesselrode.
[2] Some in Conacher, 243.
[3] Add MS 44742, f. 234.
[4] Sir C. W. *Pasley, *Observations on the expediency and practicability of simplifying and improving the measures, weights and money, used in this country, etc.* (1834).
[5] Cp. Conacher, 335 and draft in Add MS 44376, f. 252.
[6] Cp. 19 Nov. 52.
[7] Paraphrase of Proverbs, xxix. 18.

that this verse is a real joy to me: 'Thou hast set our misdeeds before Thee, our secret sins in the light of Thy countenance':[1] but even this may only be a deeper snare.

30. Fr.

Latin with Stephy. Wrote to Rev Mr Woodall[2]—W.C. James—Strahan Bates & Co[3]—Jas Wilson—E. Macdonnell—J.N.G.—J.N.G's Coachman—Mr J. Haywood[4]—Govr. of the Bank—Bp of Oxford—and minutes. Read Spectateur de l'Orient[5]—Marriott on College Statutes[6]—Latin lesson to Stephen. Saw Mr Pressly—Mr Reynolds with Mr Bowring—Ld Aberdeen. Read Biography of Disraeli[7]—Fraser for Jan[8]—Session 1852–3. Saw Collins (X) & another [R].

31. Sat.

Wrote to E. Brackenridge—J.A. Hope[9]—Bickers & Bush—Jas Watson—Wms. Deacon & Co—White & Co[10]—D of Newcastle—Jas Wilson—Senior Proctor[11]—G. & Co—Sir C. Trevelyan—G. Burnett—& minutes. Tasso with Willy & Agnes: a double dose. Saw Mr Goulburn on Univ. & finance—Went into the City—Read Recueil—Session 52–3 (finished)—B. Disraeli—Thistle & Cedar of Lebanon.[12] Worked on private affairs.

[1] Psalm xc. 8.

[2] Edward Harrison Woodall, of Oriel, Oxford; curate of Bainton, Yorkshire, 1838–9; rector of St. Margaret's, Canterbury, from 1841.

[3] Strahan, Paul, Paul and Bates, bankers at Temple Bar.

[4] sc. J. Heywood, M.P. and writer on Oxford; cp. 14 May and 19 Dec. 53.

[5] Cp. 20 Oct. 53.

[6] C. Marriott, *A few words on the statute for new halls, to be proposed to Convocation, . . . May 23* (1854).

[7] T. Macknight, *The right hon. Benjamin *Disraeli, a literary and political biography* (1854).

[8] *Fraser's Magazine*, xlix. 1 (January 1854), with articles on *Palmerston, *Derby, and London.

[9] Sir James Archibald *Hope, 1785–1871; served in Peninsula; major-general in Canada 1841–7; general 1859.

[10] Probably White and Borrett, cp. 21 Feb. 49.

[11] Drummond Percy *Chase, 1820–1902; fellow of Oriel 1842; senior proctor 1853; principal of St. Mary Hall from 1857.

[12] By Habeeb Risk Allah (1853).

Sunday Jan One 1854.

Circumcision.

Whitehall (H.C.) mg. Chapel Royal aft. Wrote to Bp of Oxford (2)—at great length—& to Rev B. Wilson. Read Wilson's Bampton Lectures[1]—Thistle & Cedar of Lebanon.

2. M. X

Wrote to Govr. of Bank—J.N.G.—Rev Mr Kennaway—S. Herbert—Colonel Phipps—Mr H. Rich . . . & minutes. Latin with Stephen. Tasso with Willy & Agnes. Saw Ld Canning—Sir C.E. Trevelyan (2) and (late) Lightfoot [R]—with very indifferent effect. Dined at Chev. Bunsen's to meet Count Portalis.[2] Read Minton's Reply to E.R.[3] Visited the Serpentine—or, in other words, London on the ice.

3. T.

Wrote to Ld Palmerston—Mrs Nimmo—Maitland & Co—E. Cardwell—Rev Mr Jowett—Mr J[ames] Loch—Mr Tidd Pratt—Mr J. Wood—Solicitor General—Sir J. Graham[4]—A. M'Culloch—Chairman of E.I. Co (2)—D of Newcastle—Sir J. Young—and minutes. Saw Ld J. Russell—Ld Abn.—Ld Hardinge. Cabinet 2–5¾. Tasso with Willy & Agnes. The Lytteltons dined. Finished Minton—Read Census (Religious worship) Report.[5] Put up & delivered parcel for Collins [R].

4. Wed.

Wrote to R. Blakey[6]—Ld Clarendon—Mr Jowett—and minutes. Another morning's work on the Oxford draft. Meeting N[ational] D[ebt] Commrs. at 2½. Latin lesson with Stephen & Tasso with Willy & Agnes. Saw Mr Hubbard—Mr Tidd Pratt—S. Herbert—Sir C. Trevelyan—do *cum* Mr Stephenson—G. Wellesley. Went by 6¼ Train to Windsor: C. kept back by prudence.[7] I was the only guest and thus was promoted to sit by the Queen at dinner. She was most gracious & above all so thoroughly natural. Read Sismondi[8]—Dryden.

[1] Cp. 11 Dec. 53.

[2] Baron Auguste Portalis, 1801–55; French lawyer and politician, wrote on church and state in 1846.

[3] S. Minton 'The evangelicals and "The Edinburgh": a reply to the article on "Church parties" . . .' (1853).

[4] On administrative reform: cp. Conacher, 232, 317–8.

[5] 'Religious worship, England and Wales', *PP* 1852–3, lxxxix. 1; the only official religious census ever taken of England and Wales.

[6] Robert *Blakey, 1795–1878; philosopher, angler and radical journalist; professor of philosophy at Queen's, Belfast, 1849–51.

[7] See 7 Jan. 54.

[8] See 22 June 54.

5. Th.

Two hours after breakfast with the Prince. Then went to London for 3½ h. Cabinet. Ret[urne]d to Windsor for dinner: & gave the Queen a report of the Cabinet.[1] Read Sismondi—Balliol papers.[2]

6. Fr.

Epiph[any] & C.G.s birthday. St George's Chapel 10½ A.M.—Off to London at 12.20. Drive &c. with C. Wrote to Sir J.S. Forbes—Mr J. Wood—Sir W.C. James—Jas Watson—Mr Goulburn—Mr Wall—Sir A. Spearman—S. Herbert—and minutes.[3] Tasso with Willy & Agnes. Saw Mr Jowett—Sir C. Wood—Sir C. Trevelyan—Mr Litchfield[4] & Mr Dwight.[5] Dabbled in China.[6] Read Palmer's Oxford Evidence[7]—Sismondi—Dryden—Ryley on Decimal Coinage.[8]

7. Sat.

Wrote to Ld Palmerston—The Queen—Mr Russell Ellice—Mr J.D. Cook[9]—Lord J. Russell—Mr Sadleir[10]—Mrs Herbert—& minutes. Trustees Nat. Gall. meeting 1–2. Latin lesson with Stephen. Saw Ld Aberdeen—D. of Newcastle—Mr Wilson—Mr Kennedy—Solr. General—F. Lawley. Cath. had alarms in the night of the coming event. In the aftn. they became decided: & at nine, to the beat of drum, she gave birth to a dear little boy, a pair for Henry.[11] The last stage was tedious & thus severe—even relatively to the usual meaning of the word in such matters: which God knows is serious enough. I had a dinner party going on at the moment: but F. Lawley kindly acted for me. Thanks be to God for the mercies of the day. Read King's Coll. Reform! Plan.[12] Worked a little on private affairs.

8. 1 S. Epiph.

Titchfield St (& H.C.) 11 A.M.—Chapel Royal aft—both times with Willy—MS. for Epiph aloud at night. C. & the baby going on perfectly well, thanks

[1] Probably verbal.

[2] In *Statutes of the colleges* (1853).

[3] On Oxford reform, see Conacher, 335–6.

[4] Samuel Litchfield, china dealer in Hanway Street.

[5] William Moss Dwight, extra treasury clerk 1809–36; assistant bill clerk 1836–54; senior clerk 1854–8.

[6] i.e. in adding to his porcelain collection.

[7] Roundell *Palmer on the Magdalen oath, see Ward, 167.

[8] E. Ryley, *Decimal coinage. A brief comparison of the existing system of coins and money of account, of that proposed by the decimal coinage committee, and of another system* (1853).

[9] 'Lord Aberdeen' here deleted.

[10] John Sadleir, 1814–56; liberal M.P. Sligo borough 1853–6; share forger and suicide; wrote to resign as a treasury lord: Add MS 44529, f. 28.

[11] Herbert John*, d. 1930; the Gladstones' last child; Eton and University, Oxford; fellow of Keble, Oxford; liberal M.P. Leeds 1880–5, West Leeds 1885–1910; under secretary of home office 1892–5, secretary 1905–10; chief liberal whip 1899–1905; governed South Africa 1910–14; cr. Viscount 1910.

[12] *Maurice's dismissal caused a working men's meeting in his support, which called for reform of the college; report in 'King's College and Mr. *Maurice by a barrister of Lincoln's Inn' (1854), 43.

to God. Wrote to Duchess of Sutherland—T.G.—M.F. Tupper—Robn. G.—Mrs Herbert—J.N.G.—Lady Glynne. Read Wilson's Bampton Lectures—Tupper's Ballads[1]—Maltby's Charge[2]—Williams's Statement[3]—& other pamphlets.

9. M.

Wrote to Solicr. General—Mr Arber[4]—Maitland & Co—Col. Phipps—Mr Jowett[5]—Ly. Grenville—H.J.G.—and minutes. Tasso with Willy & Agnes. Read Biogr. of Mr. Disraeli.[6] Saw Rev. Mr Jowett—Dr Bowring—W. Hampton (No 6)—Mr Wilson—Mr Haddan—Sir C. Trevelyan—Rev G. Williams—Ld Granville. Walked out for air at night. C.s troubles ab. nursing promise to be less, thank God. Last night & tonight I rubbed her to sleep. Worked 3 h. late at night on Oxford plan.[7] Explained to Willy the plan for his allowance.

10. T.

Wrote to Sir C. Trevelyan—Mr Hayter—Robt. Gladstone—Sir W. Clay—D. Newcastle—Robn. G—Rev Mr Kennaway—Rev Mr Lake—J.S. Brickwood—and minutes. Cabinet 2–5½. Saw Rev Mr Wall—Mr Russell Ellice—Ld J. Russell—Granville. Latin lesson with Stephen. Dined at Ld Granville's. Worked on Oxford plan.[8] Took Willy to Bickers's & elsewhere. Read Disraeli. This by numbers is usually about C.s hardest day: but matters went well: near two hours rubbing did good.

11. Wed.

Wrote to J.N.G.—E. Breakenridge—Mr Collison[9]—Ld Aberdeen (& dft)—E. Cardwell—Duchess of Buccleuch—Bp of Oxford—Bp of Moray—and minutes. Dined at Ld J. Russell's. Saw Mr Hayter—T.G. & his people—Ld Clarendon—Ld Lansdowne—Panizzi. Tasso with Willy & Agnes—a double dose (as we had none yesty.). Read Oriental Question Papers. Again employed in C.s matters—she had a less easy day but not from the old cause. Worked on private affairs—and on Oxford question.

12. Th.

Wrote to Sir C. Trevelyan—Ly Canning—Provost of Oriel—Solr. General—S.H. Northcote—Lyttelton—E. Cardwell—Dr Jeune—M.F. Tupper—Mr

[1] M. F. *Tupper, *A dozen ballads for the times about church abuses* (1854).
[2] E. Maltby, *A charge delivered to the clergy of the diocese of Durham* (1845).
[3] Untraced.
[4] Henry B. Arber, examiner in the public accounts audit department.
[5] Who had that day sent a draft University Bill, cp. Add MS 44743, f. 1.
[6] Cp. 30 Dec. 53.
[7] First draft of the Bill: Add MS 44743, f. 13.
[8] Second draft: Add MS 44743, f. 19.
[9] Frederick William Portlock Collison, 1814–89; fellow of St. John's, Cambridge, 1838–55; rector of Marwood, Devon, from 1853; had written on the Bill: Add MS 44377, f. 29.

Godley—Sir J. Herschel—G. Burnett—and minutes. Read the Disraeli Biography. Saw . . . Ld Monteagle—E. Cardwell—Mr Brickwood—Mr Tidd Pratt—S H Northcote—Sir C. Trevelyan—and Newcastle with Prov. of Oriel to dinner & conv. on Oxford. Latin with Stephen Tasso with Willy & Agnes. C. improving thank God. Cabinet 2½–4½: good. Wrote Mem. on Oxford.[1]

13. Fr. X

Wrote to Bp of Oxford—Sigr. Corti[2]—Rev H. M'Kenzie—Rev Mr Browne—Bp of Moray—Ld Lansdowne—Messrs. Holland[3]—Rev H B. Barry—and minutes. Tasso with Willy & Agnes. Also walk with Willy. At night he returned [to Eton]. I have never known him more satisfactory than in this vacation: his promise grows with growing years. C. again better. Saw Trevelyan—Mr Gardner. Dined with the Cannings. Saw Griffin [R]. Read Barry on Univ. Constn.[4]—Disraeli Biography.

14. Sat.

Wrote to Bp of Oxford—E. Cardwell (2)—Sir R. Inglis—Mr Sadleir—D[uche]ss. of Buccleuch—Mr Higham—Mr Hubbard—E Breakenridge—Chev Bunsen—F. Lawley—J.D. Cook—Sir C. Trevelyan—Sir J. Graham[5]—and minutes. Saw Sir S. Northcote—Sir Ch. Trevelyan (2)—F. Lawley. Tasso with Agnes. Latin with Stephen. My first ride, for ¾ hour. Dined with the Farquhars. C. still prosperous. Read Harrow Pamphlets[6]—& Disr. Biography.

15. 2 S.Epiph.

Chapel Royal mg: at home evg & some reading to C. I was detained by writing an article in the P. Albert case wh I took up to Mr Cook's: the result of a conv. with him.[7] Wrote to Mr Cook—Bp of Argyll. Saw Mr Lacaita—Mr Cardwell (Oxf.—2.)—Mr Cook. C. had an uncomfortable night: improved during the day. Read Fra Dolcino.[8]

[1] Add MS 44743, f. 119; cited in Conacher, 336. Also a long letter to *Russell on civil service entrance; extracts ibid. 321–2.

[2] Count Luigi Corti, secretary of Sardinian legation, had written on income tax; lengthy reply in Add MS 44529, f. 31.

[3] William Holland and Sons, cabinet makers in Piccadilly.

[4] H. B. Barry, *Remarks on the three proposals for reforming the constitution of the university of Oxford* (1854).

[5] On civil service entrance: extracts in Conacher, 319–20.

[6] 'A few words on the monitorial system at Harrow. By one who was once a monitor' (1854), and 'A reply to "One who was once a monitor"' (1854).

[7] The *Daily News* and the protectionists had accused *Albert of treason and of responsibility for *Palmerston's resignation. Gladstone's article, defending *Albert, was published next day in the *Morning Chronicle*; cp. Martin, ii. 538ff. and Add MS 44743, f. 121.

[8] L. Mariotti, *A historical memoir of Frà Dolcino and his times* (1853).

16. M.

Wrote to Lord J. Russell—J.D. Cook—Hon F. Lawley—Mr Gardner—E. Cardwell (2)—Mr J. Wood (2)—Sir F. Pollock—Dr Jacobson—Ld Galloway—Govr. of Bank—Bp of Oxford—Ld Ward—Mr Masterman—and minutes. Saw Mr Hayter—Mr Wood—Mr G.F. Bowen—R. Phillimore—E.L. Robertson—Mr Lacaita; & Ld Aberdeen—on matters highly interesting.[1] Latin with Stephen. Tasso with Agnes. Dined with the Cannings. Read Pamphlets on Ch. Rates, Cross v. Crescent, National Edn., and Sewell's Oxford Sermon.[2] Saw anon. unprofitably [R].

17. T. X

Wrote to Dss Sutherland—T.G.—J.N.G.—Rn. G—Rev. Mr Sandilands—Rev. E.M. Cole[3]—Mr W Brown MP.—Brothers (Circ)[4]—J. Griffiths—C. Greville—Ld Ellesmere—Sir J. Graham[5]—Sir C. Trevelyan—and minutes. Rode out. Worked on private affairs. Saw Sir C. Trevelyan—Dr Jacobson—Sir S. Northcote—Mr Wilson—S. Herbert. Latin lesson with S. Tasso with Agnes. Read Disraeli Biography—Treasury papers. Saw Fr[enchwoman]; sad, & strange [R].

18. Wed. X

John's birthday: all good to him. Wrote to Ld Palmerston—Mr Lowe—Rev A.P. Stanley—Ld Canning—Sir T. Fremantle—Sir C.E.T.[6]—Rev Prof. Wilson[7]—Sir C. Barry—D. of Newcastle—Rev Dr Vaughan—Mr J.D. Cook—Mr Jas Wilson (2)—and minutes. Saw Sig. Corti—Sir S. Northcote (2)—Mr Hubbard—Ld Lyttelton—G.F. Lewis—Sir J.E. Tennent—and late Car. with good words but only words good [R]. Latin with Stephen. Tasso with Agnes. Dined at Sir C. Wood's—Ly J. Russell's afterwards. Read Disr. Biogr—Treasury papers.

19. Th.

Wrote to Ld Palmerston—Mrs Bennett—Ld J. Russell (2)—Mr J. Wood—Ld Clarendon—Mr G. Williams—D. of Newcastle—Rev. W.W. Malet—Sol. General—Earl Granville—H.J.G.—Ld Cowley—Sir W. Molesworth—Canon Repton—& minutes. Bookbuying & other shopping. Saw Mr Griffiths—Mr A. & Lady M. Hope—Mr J.D. Cook—Mr D B Chapman—Lord Aberdeen. Rode for ½ hour. Ten to dinner: I made Northcote known to Ld Abn. I have rarely seen Inglis better. Finished the Disr. Biogr. Latin with Stephen. Tasso with Agnes. Read Treas. papers.

[1] On the Queen's view of his article, cp. Conacher, 271.
[2] W. *Sewell, 'Collegiate reform . . . preached before the university' (1853); on I John iv. 19. See also 17 May 53.
[3] Perhaps Edmond Hearle Cole, curate of Halwell and Beaworthy, Devon.
[4] i.e. a round-robin letter to his brothers.
[5] Cp. Conacher, 331.
[6] Against leakages to press: cp. Conacher, 325.
[7] H. B. *Wilson.

20. Fr.

Wrote to Solr. General—Robn. G—Govr. Bank—A.H.D. Troyte—Dr Molesworth—Sir C. Trevelyan—Rev D. Robertson—Lord J. Russell (a pamphlet?)[1]—Rev Mr Church—E. Cardwell—S.H. Northcote—Mrs Larkins—and minutes. Went book & china hunting. Latin with Stephen. Tasso with Agnes. Saw J. Talbot—Dr Acland. Had my little Stephen with me at dinner: conversations with him yesterday & today. At *length* he breaks down a little in the prospect of leaving home which before only seemed to kindle his manliness. He is a most dear boy. Read Northcote's Article[2]—Love v. Marriage (Phalansterian).[3]

This morning I lay awake till four with a sad & perplexing subject: it was reflecting on & counting up the numbers of those unhappy beings, now present to my memory with whom during now so many years I have conversed indoors or out. I reckoned from 80 to 90. Among these there is but one of whom I know that the miserable life has been abandoned *and* that I can fairly join that fact with influence of mine. Yet this were much more than enough for all the labour & the time, had it been purely spent on my part. But the case is far otherwise: & tho' probably in none of these instances have I not spoken good words, yet so bewildered have I been that they constitute the chief burden of my soul.[4]

21. Sat.

Wrote to S. Herbert—Dr Jacobson—Mr Unsworth[5]—Mr Clementson[6]—E. of Aberdeen—Dr Pearce[7]—Mr E M Cole—Dr Macbride—Count Walewski—Mr Tidd Pratt—Rev E.B. James[8]—E. Cardwell (2)—& minutes. Cabinet 2–6½. Saw Newcastle—Molesworth—Graham—Ld Abn. Also Car: better than before [R]. In the morning we dispatched dear little Stephy (with E. Talbot) to Torquay: a pure, gentle, & tender soul, with life & courage in him too. His future I am assured whether bright or not will be blessed.

22. 3 S.Epiph.

Chapel Royal mg & aft. MS. on Conv. St P[aul] aloud at night. Wrote on Theol.[9] Walk with Agnes to Aunt J.s. Read Q.R. on Chinese Rebels, their

[1] A twenty two page letter defending examinations for the civil service: Add MS 44291, f. 93 and Morley, i. 649.

[2] Untraced, unless that of December 1852, seen by Gladstone April 1853, in Add MS 44738, f. 72.

[3] A description of the Phalanstère, a working and recreational residence for 2,000 people, proposed by Fourier; cp. *Westminster Review* (April 1848), xlix. 125.

[4] He made a list of these cases, completed two days later; in Lambeth MSS.

[5] William and George Unsworth, foreign china dealers in Hanway Street.

[6] Perhaps William Clementson, Trinity, Oxford, 1847; vicar of Wymynyswold, Kent, 1877–80.

[7] Perhaps Samuel Pearce, surgeon, of Bethnal Green Road.

[8] Edward Boucher James, 1819?–92; fellow of Queen's, Oxford, 1842–58; proctor 1856; vicar of Carisbrooke from 1858.

[9] On charity, Add MS 44743, f. 128.

religion[1]—Wilson's B[ampton] L[ectures]—Bp Medley's Charge[2]—Report on Metrop[olitan] Ch[urches] F[und][3]—Clewer Statutes[4]—& Sundries.

23. M.

Wrote to Wms. Deacon & Co—S.R.G.—E.L. Robertson—Jas Wilson—Ld J. Russell—T.F. Kennedy—J. Kindersley[5]—R. Phillimore—Bp of Argyll—and minutes. Tasso with Agnes. Dined with the Wortleys. Saw J. Wortley—Sir C. Trevelyan—Ld Aberdeen—Mr Monsell (Ordnance Est[imates]).[6] Worked on Private business. Wrote Treas. Mema.[7] & read papers.

24. T.

Wrote to Ld Lansdowne—Mr J. Wood (2)—Mrs Lillicrap[8]—Robn. G.—Ld Chandos—Mr Kirk—Sir T. Fremantle—Ld Canning—and minutes. 12–2. P[rivy] C[ouncil] Ed[ucation] Comm[ittee] (Oxford). 2–6½ Cabinet. Stiff! Saw Granville—Newcastle. Tasso with Agnes. Raised the Catalogue of Friday Nt. to 112. Dined with the Herberts. Saw one, not sought, far gone [R]. Read Report on Religious Worship. Wrote contribn. to Q. Speech.[9]

25. Wed. Conv.St Paul. X

Wrote to Mr T.L. Hodges—Robn. G (2)—Mr G. Burnett—Jas Wilson—Mr Henderson—J. Bywater[10]—Mr W. Burns—Sir J. Young—Willy—Sir C. Trevelyan—Mr Lake—Dr Jacobson—Mr Jowett—Sir S. Northcote—E. Cardwell (2)—Rev H. M'Kenzie—Mr H. Chester and minutes. Worked on Oxford plan & papers:[11] also Treasury papers. Tasso with Agnes. Saw Lord Aberdeen *cum* Sir J. Graham—Ld Harrowby—Mr J. Wood—Mr Durham. Rode out: also china-hunting: missed service at Abp Tennisons.[12] Evg with C. Baby is really a pretty child: his health thank God perfect. Saw Osborne [R]: good words, nothing else good.

[1] *Quarterly Review*, xciv. 171 (December 1853).
[2] J. *Medley, 'A charge to the clergy of the diocese of Fredericton' (1854).
[3] The fund closed this year, with a report and address to *Blomfield, having raised £266,000; cp. *Memoir of C. J. *Blomfield* (1863), i. 250.
[4] The community at Clewer had drawn up a tentative rule, not finalized until 1863, cp. *The founders of Clewer* (1952), 27.
[5] Reply to George Herbert Kindersley, solicitor, on new law court buildings: Add MS 44529, f. 42.
[6] i.e. William Monsell.
[7] On civil service: Add MS 44743, f. 129.
[8] Possibly a connection of William P. Lillicrapp, furrier, of Davies St., Berkeley Square.
[9] Which mentioned, *inter alia*, economy, taxation, civil service and university reform: *H* cxxx. 3 and Add MS 44778, f. 163.
[10] Jane Bywater, a rescue case; cp. 12 Feb. 54 and introduction above, iii. xlv.
[11] Add MS 44743, f. 130.
[12] i.e. at Abp. *Tenison's (d. 1715) chapel in Regent Street.

26. Th.

Wrote to The Queen[1]—Mr Litchfield—Lord Aberdeen (2)[2]—Sir R. Inglis—Mr Oliveira[3]—& minutes. A third paragr. for the Queen's Speech. Went at 9½ to A. Robertson's funeral at Kensall Green. P.C. Ed[ucatio]n Committee 12–2. (Oxford). Cabinet 2¼–6¼.[4] Coasting trade—Civil service[5]—Answer to Brunnow. Thirteen to dinner. Saw Ld Abn.—Govr of Bank.

27 Fr.

Wrote to Sir C. Trevelyan—Mr Jowett—Mr Monsell—Mr Wilson—Mr Cardwell—Mr Oliveira & minutes. Saw R. Phillimore (Oxf)—Mr Hayter—Mr Knott (Oxf)[6]—Mr Geo. Glyn—Ld Abn.—Sir C. Wood—Sir J. Graham. Conclave on New Estimates 12½–2½.[7] Cabinet 2½–6½. Dined with the Clarendons. Read Dryden's Life.[8]

28. Sat. X

Wrote to Mr Cook—Govr. of Bank—Mr Wood—Sol. General—Mr Wilson—R. Phillimore—Mr Oliveira—Sir S. Northcote—Rev Mr Barry—Willy—G.F. Bowen[9]—and minutes. Saw Sir C. Trevelyan—Lord J. Russell—Mr C. Villiers—C. Villiers—Ld Lyttelton. Tasso with Agnes. China-hunting once more. Dined at Granville's. Saw Car—and Morgan (82) (took home) [R]. Cabinet 2½–6.

29. 4 S.Epiph.

Chapel Royal mg. Bedfordbury Evg. MS. on the day aloud at n[igh]t. Dined upstairs with C. Wrote to E. Cardwell—Lord J. Thynne—A. Gordon—Mr Mucklestone. Read Döllinger's Hippolytus[10]—Wilson's B[ampton] Lect. (finished)—Pusey's Sermons[11]—Newman's Univ. Lectures.[12]

30. M.

Wrote to Ld J. Russell—Rev. T. Carter—Ld Clarendon—E. Cardwell—Mrs Scott—Prince Albert—Ld Canning—J.R. Jeffery[13] and minutes. 2–4 China hunting in many shops—brought matters nearly to a close. Saw Mr

[1] Add MS 44743, f. 132; in Guedalla, Q, i. 108; cp. *LQV*, 1 series, iii, 10–11.

[2] Cp. Conacher, 248n.

[3] Draft, on wine duties, in Add MS 44377, f. 116; Oliveira soon moved a motion on them, cp. *H* cxxx. 672 (14 February 1853).

[4] On civil service; note of votes in Add MS 44778, f. 157.

[5] Cp. Add MS 44778, f. 157, and Conacher, 323.

[6] John William Knott, 1822?–70; fellow of Brasenose 1844–67; junior proctor 1853–4; vicar of St. Saviour's, Leeds, 1851–9, of East Ham, Essex, from 1866.

[7] Cp. Conacher, 253.

[8] Cp. 24 July 46.

[9] Copy, on fellowships, in Add MS 44377, f. 118.

[10] J. J. I. von Döllinger, *Hippolytus und Kallistus* (1853).

[11] E. B. *Pusey, *Parochial sermons*, 2v. (1852–3).

[12] Cp. 9 Apr. 52.

[13] James Reddecliff Jeffery, 1809–71; Liverpool and London draper; bankrupt 1871.

Wilson—Mr Bonham—Mr Litchfield—Rev. N. Wade—Lord A. Hervey—Speaker—Sir C. Trevelyan, and Mr W. *cum* Lord A. H[ervey]. Ld. J.R.s official dinner—Worked late—& walk. Saw one, a pitiable case [R]. Tasso with Agnes.

31. T.

Wrote to Sir T. Acland—Robn. G—Mr J. Higham—Hon A. Gordon—Sir C. Trevelyan—Mr Mozley—Dr Acland—Mr Haddan—Sir S. Northcote—Chev. Bunsen—Sol. General—Mr Kirk MP.—Ld Palmerston—and minutes. Saw T.G.—Sir T. Acland—Mr Hayter—Mr Bonham—JNG with T.G.—Mr Cardwell—Sol. General—Mr Baines. A short drive with C. H. of C. $3\frac{3}{4}$–8 and $8\frac{3}{4}$–$11\frac{1}{4}$.[1] Saw E. Collins who I believe goes on well: a source of real though I must add ill-deserved satisfaction [R].

Wednesday Feb. One 1854.

Wrote to The Lord Advocate—Sig. Corti—The Ld Chancellor—Mr Keates[2]—Rev. J.T. Tweed[3]—Mr Kennedy—Mr J.R. M'Culloch—S.R. Glynne—Junior Proctor[4]—R. Barker—Chev. Bunsen—H. Lees—Rev. Mr Rawson—and minutes. Cabinet dinner at Ld Abn's. Saw Mr Hayter—Mr Trevor—Mr Monsell—Mr Higham—Mr Wilson—Mr Drummond—Ld Chancellor—D. Newcastle—Ld Lansdowne—Ld Overstone—Rev D. Melvill. H. of C. 12–$1\frac{1}{2}$. Saw Mary [Lyttelton] & her fine infant:[5] & took C. upstairs there. Hanway St again.[6] Audit Board for the half year: only 114 sign. 108 mill[ion] £.[7]

2. Th. Purification

St. Mary's Crown St $8\frac{1}{2}$ P.M. Wrote to J. Wilson—Ld Granville—E. Cardwell—Rev. Mr Greswell—Pr. Albert—Sir S. Northcote—T.D. Acland——Mr A. Symonds—E. Cardwell—D. of Newcastle—Mr Wood, & minutes. Saw Mr Hayter—Mr Bonham—Mr Wilson—Do *cum* Ld Canning—Trevelyan—E. Cardwell—Sir J. Graham—Mr Wilson—and others. Read Symonds on the Civil Service[8]—Quetelet.[9] Worked on Treas. papers.[10]

3. Fr.

Wrote to S.H. Northcote—Ld A. Hervey—Sir J. Graham—Rev C. Marriott—Rev H. Mackenzie—Mr J. Fogg[11]—Bp of Tasmania—and minutes. Read

[1] Queen's speech: *H* cxxx. 3.
[2] Joseph Andrew Keates, Devon landowner who settled in Liverpool.
[3] sc. J. P. Tweed.
[4] J. W. Knott; copy in Add MS 44377, f. 153.
[5] Robert Henry Lyttelton, January 1854–1939; the Lytteltons' 6th s.; Trinity, Cambridge; solicitor and writer on cricket.
[6] For china shops, cp. 6 and 21 Jan. 54nn.
[7] See 21 Feb. 54.
[8] A. Symonds, *Papers relative to the obstruction of public business and the organization of the civil service* (1853); a privately printed plan for complete reorganization of the service.
[9] L. A. J. Quételet, probably his *Du système social* (1848).
[10] And spoke on the consolidated fund: *H* cxxx. 216.
[11] John Barratt Fogg, of Mold, Flintshire.

Farini Vol. IV—Acland's Letter on Oxf. Constn.[1] Saw Robn. G. Sir C. Trevelyan—Mr C. Gore[2]—S. Herbert—Sol. General—Mr J.J. Johnson.[3] Evening at home. Saw Horton: missed Loader [R].

4. Sat.

C. went to Churching at St Martin's 11.30 A.M. Wrote to Signor Farini—Count Corti—Lord J. Russell—J. Murray—Dss. of Sutherland—Ld Raglan—Ld Hardinge—Rev W. Rawson—Rev J.D. Browne[4]—Mr Hayter—S.H. Northcote—E. Cardwell—and minutes. Saw Ld Canning—Mr Wilson—Mr Oliveira—Holland & Co—Mr J. Murray—Sir C. Trevelyan. Cabinet $2\frac{1}{4}$–$6\frac{1}{2}$. Dined at Lord Palmerston's. Saw evg one piteous & one shocking & yet moving case [R]. Read Farini.

5. 5 S.Epiph.

Ch. Royal mg & H.C. with C.—St Mary's Cr[own] St evg. MS. for the day aloud at night. Saw T.M. Gladstone—Sir Jas Graham. Wrote to Rev. H.G. Liddell—Geo. Grant—A. Loader [R]. Read Vaughan on Oxford[5]—Ch Periodicals. The Duchess of Beaufort is dying: assuredly it will be in peace.[6]

6. M.

Wrote to T.M. Gladstone—J.N.G.—Mr Panizzi—Mr Jowett—Sir C. Trevelyan—and minutes. P.C. Educ. Comm. $12\frac{1}{4}$–2. Drove with C. to Hanway Street. At No 6 about books. Saw Mr Dyce—Ld Canning—Ld Duncan[7]—Mr Wilson—Mr Wade. Read Farini. Sought & missed 17 of Sat. evg. [R]. H. of C. $4\frac{1}{2}$–6.[8]

7. T.

Wrote to Mr Woollcombe—Ld Canning—Provost of Oriel—Dr Pusey—Dr Jacobson—Ld Aberdeen—J. Bywater—Rev. Mr Chamberlain—Sir C. Trevelyan—Chev. Bunsen—Mr J. Johnson—and minutes. Rode at 11

[1] (Sir) H. W. *Acland, 'A letter to . . . Gladstone . . . on the formation of the Initiative Board in the university of Oxford' (1854).
[2] Charles Alexander Gore, 1811–97; *Russell's private secretary 1830–4, 1835–9; commissioner of woods, forests and revenues 1839–85.
[3] Probably John James Johnson, 1812–90; barrister 1836; recorder of Chichester from 1863.
[4] John Denis Browne; Trinity, Dublin; vicar of Braintree, Essex, from 1852.
[5] H. H. *Vaughan, *Oxford reform and Oxford professors* (1854); a denunciation of *Pusey.
[6] She died in August that year.
[7] Adam Haldane-Duncan, 1812–67; styled Viscount Duncan until 1859 when he succ. as 2nd earl of Camperdown; whig M.P. Southampton 1837–41, Bath 1841–52, Forfarshire 1854–9.
[8] Parliamentary oaths: *H* cxxx. 273; cp. 25 May 54.

with S. Herbert. H. of C. $4\frac{1}{2}$–$7\frac{3}{4}$.[1] Saw Lord A. Hervey—W.M. Goalen—T.M. Gladstone—Mr Anderson—Sir C. Trevelyan—Ld Aberdeen—Mr Arbuthnot—Sir W. Heathcote—J. Bywater [R]. Evg at home: but went out late to deliver letters. Read Farini.

8. Wed. X

Wrote to Rev H. Wall—The Queen[2]—Col. Grey—Lord Raglan—C.A. Wood—Mr Law Hodges—& minutes. Rode at 11 with S. H[erbert]. House at 12—introduced Sir W. Heathcote & heard poor Hudson.[3] Conclave on Vote & Cons. Fund Charges. Cabinet $2\frac{3}{4}$–$6\frac{1}{2}$. Saw Ld Abn.—Rev Mr Rawlinson—Ld J. Russell—Dean Milman—Mr R. Lowe—Mr Blackett[4]—R. Phillimore. Dined at Molesworth's. Late saw Griffin: no real good I fear [R]. Read Oxf. Report (Colleges dft).[5]

9. Th.

Wrote to Rev H. Mackenzie—Robn. G.—Lord J. Russell—Mr Gore—Lady Northcote[6]—Lord Camoys[7]—Ld Clarendon—Maj. Moorsom—Sir C. Trevelyan—and minutes. Ride with S. Herbert. Saw Mr Bonham—Mr Hayter—W.M. Goalen—Bp of Oxford—Mr Wood—do with Sir J. Young—Lord Aberdeen. H. of C. $4\frac{1}{2}$–8.[8] Read Oxf. Report—Saw in evg. another such case as last week [R].

10. Fr.

Wrote to Ld J. Russell—Dr Jacobson—Rev. C. Marriott—Mr Rawlinson—Mr Jowett—Rev C. Marriott—Dr Pusey—Sir W. Heathcote—Prov. of Oriel—Ld Raglan—Ld Aberdeen (2)—The Queen—Ld Palmerston[9]—Dr Acland—Ld Granville. Rode with S. Herbert. H. of C. $4\frac{1}{2}$–8 & again at $12\frac{1}{2}$.[10] Saw Mr Wilson—Sir C. Trevelyan—Lord Monteagle—Sir C. Wood. Read Farini.

11. Sat.

Wrote to Rev Mr Lake—Rev Mr Rawlinson—Mr J. Wood—Govr. of Bank—Mr Wilson—Sir C. Trevelyan (2)—Dr Pusey—Mad. Gherardini[11]—

[1] Irish M.P.s corruption deb., in which *Duncombe denounced G. *Hudson for corrupting M.P.s: *H* cxxx. 337.

[2] In Guedalla, *Q*, i. 109.

[3] *Hudson's personal statement in self-justification: *H* cxxx. 342.

[4] Cp. 7 Apr. 52.

[5] The sections and sub-sections, on college statutes etc., of the royal commission: *PP* 1852 xii. 289.

[6] Lady Cecilia Frances Northcote, *née* Farrer, da. of 1st Baron *Farrer, m. S. H. *Northcote 1843 and s. 1910.

[7] Thomas Stonor, 1797–1881; 5th Baron Camoys 1839 on revival of the title by royal writ; took his seat as a baron of the reign of Richard II; lord-in-waiting 1846–52, 1853–8, 1859–66.

[8] Misc. business: *H* cxxx. 358.

[9] In Guedalla, *P*, 97.

[10] Election bribery: *H* cxxx. 405.

[11] Art collector; Gladstone bought her collection for the nation; cp. Add MS 43071, f. 53 and 20 Mar. 54.

Stephy—Mr Woollcombe—Mr Brown—Mr E. Ffoulkes—Mr J.D. Cook—and minutes. Saw Ld Canning—Mr Hodges—Mr G. Arbuthnot—Mr Anderson—Mr C. Litchfield—Ld Advocate—Ld J. Russell—Mr Moseley—Ld Ellesmere. Cabinet 2¾–6½. Dined with the Speaker: Lady Granville's afterwards. Rode with S. Herbert. Saw Farquhar who gave me the tidings that the Dowr. Duchess [of Beaufort] has sunk greatly & will soon be taken to her rest. A solemn but yet a joyous moment, she is *so* prepared.

12. Septua S.

St M. Magd. (and H.C.) mg. St M. Crown St (prayers) evg. MS on Ep. aloud at night. Wrote to Rev N. Wade—Mr Goldwin Smith. Saw Mr Cook—Alex. Goalen—Mr Greswell—Mr Liddell. Jane Bywater reported well of, is rescued, & goes to the St Barnabas Refuge: an issue very different from my deserts [R]. Read Faber's 'All for Jesus'[1]—Hawkins Sermon[2]—Randolph's Do[3]—and Tracts.

13. M.

Wrote to Sir C. Trevelyan—Dr Pusey—Mrs T. Goalen—C.A. Wood—Mr Arbuthnot—Mr Mozley[4]—Mr Haddan (2)—Ld J. Russell—Acctt. General[5] Rev D.T. Barry[6]—Mr Litchfield—Mr Meyrick[7]—Sir J. Young—and minutes. Read Farini. Saw Mr Lake—Dr Pusey (1.2.)—Mr G.W. Hope—Mr Hayter—R. Gladstone jun.[8]—Ld J. Russell—S. Herbert. Ride with S. Herbert. H. of C. 4½–8. Reform. A modest speech: a neutral reception: which would however have been bad if the Bill intrinsically considered had not been good.[9] Worked on Oxf. Scheme.

14. T.

Wrote to Provost of Oriel—Mr Dyce—Prince Albert—Prof. Hussey—Rev Mr Rawlinson—Sir C. Trevelyan—D of Newcastle—and minutes. H. of C. 4½–8.[10] Finished Farini. Saw Sir Wm. Heathcote—Vice Chancr. of Oxford—Prince Albert (11–12¾)—Mr Monsell—J.N.G. We got the sad news of Katie's death (the other little Catherine, following ours)[11] and at night had to receive poor Henry [Glynne]. Worked on Oxford.

[1] F. W. *Faber, *All for Jesus: or, the easy ways of divine love* (1853).
[2] E. *Hawkins, 'Christ our example' (1853); on Luke ix. 23.
[3] H. Randolph, 'The heavenly order' (1854); probably preached in Advent, 1853.
[4] Draft reply in Add MS 44377, f. 229.
[5] Sir John Thomas Briggs, 1781–1865; Sir J. *Graham's private secretary 1830; accountant general to the navy 1832–54; kt. 1851.
[6] David Thomas Barry; Trinity, Dublin; incumbent of St. Barnabas, Liverpool, 1853-7; sec. of C.M.S. in Lancashire.
[7] Frederick *Meyrick, 1827–1906; fellow of Trinity, Oxford, 1847; rector of Blickling, Norfolk, from 1868; canon of Lincoln 1869; ardent evangelical controversialist; cp. Add MS 44251.
[8] Robertson Gladstone, 1844–93; 4th s. of Gladstone's similarly named brother; a bachelor.
[9] *Russell introduced his Reform Bill: *H* cxxx. 491.
[10] Oliveira on wine: *H* cxxx. 672.
[11] i.e. Catherine Glynne following Catherine Jessy Gladstone.

15. Wed.

Wrote to Ld Granville—Ld Palmerston—Mr S. Laing—Mrs Bennett—Rev Mr Lake—Rev. H. Mackenzie—Mr Bickley[1]—Rev. Dr. Pusey—Mr G. Burnett—and minutes. Rode with S. Herbert. Saw Mr Henderson—Sir T. Acland. Cabinet dinner $7\frac{3}{4}$–$2\frac{1}{4}$ AM. Oxford $\frac{1}{2}$ hour: the rest war & its accompaniments. Wrote Draft reply to Ld Derby on Oxford Petition: and Mema. of arrangements for the transport of little Katie's remains to Hn.

16. Th.

Wrote to Solr. of Customs[2]—The Queen[3]—Sir T. Fremantle—Ld Aberdeen—Rev J.L. Ross—Sir S. Northcote—Mr Trevor—Sir W. Herries—Sir S. Glynne—Mr Wilson. Saw Sir C. Trevelyan—Governor of the Bank—Lord Harris—Mr T.M. Gladstone—The Solicitor General—The Solr. to the Customs—Sir A.Y. Spearman—Ld J. Russell *cum* Ld Palmerston[4]—Lord Hervey—Mr R. Palmer—D of Newcastle. Rode with S. Herbert. House 5–7.[5] Evg at home: but walked & saw one who I trust got more good than harm, if not much [R]. Read pamphlets on Currency—Eastern question—Law Courts—&c.

17. Fr.

Wrote to Dean of Ch. Ch.[6]—T.G.—Sir W. Heathcote—Dr Pusey—Sir W. Molesworth—Mr R. Palmer—Sir C. Trevelyan (2)—The Queen[7]—Mr Rawlinson—Ld Palmerston. Rode—H of C. $4\frac{3}{4}$–9 & 10–$12\frac{1}{2}$.[8] Saw Mr Allen—Ld A. Hervey—Solr. to Customs—Ld Aberdeen. Saw Manchr. Edn. Bill Deputation.[9] Read Ld Monteagle's Exchr. Memm.[10]

18. Sat.

The Baptism of our little Herbert took place at 12: in company with the 10th Lyttelton: may God's grace be with them.[11] Wrote to Ld Monteagle—Mr Liddell—Ld Lyttelton—Newcastle—Ld J. Russell—Robn. G.—Ld Aberdeen—Ld Stanley (Alderley)—Mr Oliveira—Sir C. Trevelyan—Sir J.E. Tennent—Sir T. Fremantle—Mr A. Oswald—Rev Mr Barrow[12]—Rev Mr Marriott—Mr J. Wood—Rev W. Scott. Saw Ld J. Russell—Sir J.

[1] Possibly Samuel Bickley, a broker at Lloyd's.
[2] Felix John Hamel.
[3] In Guedalla, *Q*, i, 111.
[4] On Oxford reform. Cp. Add MS 44743, ff. 143–9 and Conacher, 336–7.
[5] Bribery: *H* cxxx. 736.
[6] Copy in Add MS 44377, f. 245.
[7] *LQV*, 1s. iii. 12.
[8] *Layard started a deb. on Russia: *H* cxxx. 831.
[9] Lead by *Bright and Sir E. Armitage: *The Times*, 18 February 1854, 11 b; cp. 21 Feb 54n.
[10] On the pay office; cp. Add MS 44529, f. 55. *Monteagle was comptroller of the exchequer.
[11] This entry, like many of the names in this vol., in red ink.
[12] John Barrow, 1810–81; fellow of Queen's, Oxford, 1845–55; D.D. 1855; principal of St. Edmund Hall, Oxford, 1854–61; became a Jesuit 1864; wrote 'The case of Queen's college, a letter to . . . Gladstone' (1854).

Graham—Granville—Sir C. Trevelyan—Sir W. Herries—Solr. Genl. cum Ld J. Russell on Oxford Bill. Council at B. Palace 3–4¾. Read Barrow on Queen's Coll. Dined at Ld Lansdowne. Walk senza discorso notabile.[1]

19. Sex[agesim]a. S.

Whitehall mg: St M Crown St evg. Wrote MS on Ep. & read it aloud evg. Wrote to Mr Cook. Saw Mr Hallam—A. Gordon. Read Newman on Univ. Edn.—Clarke on Convocn.[2]—& divers pamphlets. Worked 2 h. at night on Oriental question Blue Books.[3]

20. M.

Wrote to Ld Chancellor—Miss Robertson—M. F. Tupper—Miss Halbreiter[4]—H.J.G.—and minutes. Read Hooper on Law School[5]—Magd. Coll. Statues[6]—Oriental question papers. Saw Mr Wilson—Mr G. Moffatt—Lord Aberdeen—Ld Stanley (Alderley)—Mr J. Wood—Mr S. Herbert. H. of C. 4¾–7 and 8½–2.[7]

21. T. X

Wrote to Mr M. Bernard—Mr J.D. Cook (2)—Ld J. Russell—Ld Aberdeen—Sir J. Graham—Mr Grogan—Paymr. General—Mr Delane[8]—Rev A.C. Wilson[9]—Col Harcourt—Rev J.M. Wilson[10]—Rev C. Marriott—Provost of Oriel—and minutes. Ride with Herbert. Dined with Lady Lyttelton. Read Barry on Constitn. for Oxford.[11] Saw Sir C. T[revelyan] with Anderson on Treasury reorganisation & public accounting—Solr. General on Oxford Bill—Mr Blackett—Mr Phinn.[12] Cabinet 2¾–5.[13] House 5–6¼. Saw Harrington in evg. [R].

[1] 'Walk, without conversation worth record'.
[2] J. B. B. Clarke, *Three letters, addressed to the clergy of the diocese of Bath and Wells, on the revival of convocation* (1854).
[3] *PP* 1854 lxxi; 1; correspondence on religious privileges in Turkey, up to January 1854.
[4] Daughter or sister of U. Halbreiter?
[5] J. J. Hooper, 'The establishment of a school of jurisprudence in the university of Oxford' (1854).
[6] Sc. 'Statutes'; cp. 4 Dec. 47.
[7] Russia: *H* cxxx. 917.
[8] Leaking details of the Oxford University Bill, copy in Add MS 44377, f. 256.
[9] Arthur Charles Wilson, 1826–1880; student of Christ Church 1845–54; headmaster of Basingstoke school 1870–3; rector of Dunston, Lincolnshire, 1873–6; vicar of Norton from 1876.
[10] John Matthias *Wilson, 1813–81; fellow of Corpus, Oxford, 1841, president from 1872; White's professor of moral philosophy 1846–74.
[11] H. B. Barry, 'A few words on the constitution to be submitted to the convocation of the university of Oxford' (1854).
[12] Thomas Phinn, 1814–66; barrister; liberal M.P. Bath 1852–5; counsel to board of stamps in the exchequer 1852, to admiralty 1854, 1863, secretary there 1855–7.
[13] 2° of the Manchester and Salford Education Bill to give rate aid to education: *H* cxxx. 1045.

22. Wed.

Wrote to Sir W. Herries—Rev C. Marriott—Mr Rawlinson—Ld Palmerston—Mr Wilson—Rev Mr Burgon.[1] Read Burgon's pamphlet—and other Oxford tracts. 14 to dinner: incl. Ld Stanley. Saw Duke of Newcastle—Baron Martini—Mrs Goalen—Mr Hoffay[2]—R. Phillimore—Ld Clarendon—Ld Aberdeen—Sir T.G.—J.N.G.—Ld Prov. Edinb.—J.W. Patten—Lord Ellesmere—Judge Coleridge—Sir Wm. Heathcote. House 12–12½.[3] P.C. Committee 12½–1½. Levee 2–3. Wrote Pol. Mema.

Lord Aberdeen sent for me today and informed me that Ld. Palmerston had been with him to say he had made up his mind to vote for putting off (without entering on the question of its merits) the consideration of the Reform Bill from the present year.

I said we could not go on with the Bill in a state of war: for after defeat on the 2d reading we could neither continue in office with honour, nor resign—to bring in a new ministry in a minority, which must probably first struggle, certainly then dissolve, & perhaps have a further struggle after the meeting of the new parliament, thus causing a partial interregnum when Govt. required all its strength, & running the risk of great evil in the event of disaster *between* two Parliaments: nor could we ourselves dissolve for kindred reasons.[4]

He said he would speak to Ld John; and seemed himself inclined to stop.

He then asked me whether I did not think he might himself withdraw from Office when we came to the Declaration of War. All along he had been acting against his feelings, but still defensively. He did not think he could regard the offensive in the same light, & was disposed to retire. I said that a defensive war might involve offensive operations & that a Declaration of war placed the case on no new ground of principle, did not create the quarrel but merely announced it, verifying to the world (if itself justifiable) a certain state of acts which would have arrived. He said all wars were called or pretended to be defensive. I said that if the war was untruly so called our position was false: but that the war did not become less defensive from our declaring it or from our entering upon offensive operation. To retire therefore upon such a declaration would be to retire upon no ground warrantable & cognisable by reason; it would not be standing on a principle, whereas any man would require a distinct principle to justify him in giving up at this moment the service of the Crown. He said how could he bring himself to fight for the Turks? I replied we were not fighting for the Turks, but we were warning Russia off the forbidden ground. That if indeed we undertook to put down the Christians under Turkish rule by force then we should be fighting for the Turks—but in this I for one could be no party. He said that if I saw a way for him to get out he hoped I would mention it to him. I replied that my own views of war so much agreed with his and I felt such a horror of bloodshed, that I had thought the matter over incessantly for myself. We stand I said upon the ground that the Emperor has invaded countries not his own, inflicted wrong on Turkey & what I feel much more most cruel wrong on the wretched inhabitants of the Principalities: that war had ensued and was raging with all its horrors: that we had procured for the Emperor an offer of honourable terms of peace

[1] John William *Burgon, 1813–88; fellow of Worcester, Oxford, 1864; dean of Chichester 1876; wrote, *inter alia*, 'Oxford reformers' (1854).

[2] Ernest Albert Hoffay, inspector of naval and military accounts at the audit office.

[3] Russia: *H* cxxx. 1113.

[4] More on reform omitted.

which he had refused: that we were not going to extend the conflagration (but I had to correct myself as to the Baltic) but to apply more power for its extinction: and this I hoped in conjunction with all the Great Powers of Europe: that I for one however could not shoulder the musket against the Christian subjects of the Sultan: and must there take my stand. (Not even I had already told him if he agreed to such a course could I bind myself to follow him in it). He said Granville & Wood had spoken to him in the same sense. I added that I thought S. Herbert & Graham probably would adhere.[1]

Ellice had been with him & told him J. Russell & Palmerston were preparing to contend for his place. He himself, deprecating Lord A's retirement, anticipated that if it took place Lord Palmerston would get the best of it & drive Lord John out of the field by means of his war-popularity though Lord John had made the speech of Friday to set himself up in this point of view with the country.

In consequence of what I had said to him about Newcastle he had watched him & had told the Queen to look to him as her Minister at some period or other: which though afraid of him (as well as of me) about Church matters, she was prepared to do. I said I had not changed my opinion of Newcastle as he had done of Lord John Russell: but I had been disappointed and pained at the recent course of his opinion about the matter of war.[2] Yes Lord Aberdeen replied: but he thought him the description of man who would discharge well all the duties of that office. In this I agree.[3]

23. Th.

Wrote to Earl Granville—Rev Mr Lake—Lady F. Hotham—Rev Mr Timins—Prov. of Oriel—Aunt J.—Mr J B Fraser[4]—Ld Palmerston—Mr Marriott—Solr. General—Sir W. Herries—Mr J. Wood—Mr B. Price & minutes. Saw Rev Mr Barrow—Scottish Est. Ch. Deputation[5]—Lord Aberdeen *cum* Ld J. Russell—Mr Hankey—Mr Deedes. Saw accidentally E. Collins & one of 19 in Park: who promised to fly [R]. Read Scots Schools Pamphlet[6]—Wildman on Convocation[7]—Gunmakers' Statement.[8]

This was a day of great anxiety about little Harry. He had in combination the three main symptoms which attend on complaints of the brain: sickness, torpor of the bowels, & drowsiness in a high degree. He also put his hands up to his face: Locock said at midday that if he was sick any more he shd. have 2 grains of calomel at once: & if he were not then relieved 'he should feel very unhappy about him'. But just at that very point, & between 5 & 6 he *was* greatly relieved: so that I went to the House (8½–10½) in the evg:[9] & to bed with a lightened heart.

[1] 'Perhaps Argyll & Molesworth & even others might be added' added in the margin.
[2] 'At my house last Wednesday he declared openly for putting down by force the Christians of European Turkey.'; added in the margin.
[3] Initialled and dated 22 February 1854; Add MS 44778, f. 167.
[4] James Baille *Fraser, 1783–1856; explored Himalayas and Persia.
[5] A presbyterian deputation: *The Times*, 24 February 1854, 7e.
[6] Perhaps J. Bryce, 'Public education in its relation to Scotland and in parish schools. A letter to . . . *Aberdeen' (1854).
[7] R. Wildman, *What is convocation?* (1853).
[8] Papers untraced.
[9] Scottish education deb., and spoke on Surrey electoral registration: *H* cxxx. 1151, 1198.

24. Fr. St Matthias.

Wrote to Mr Arbuthnot—Mr Horsfall MP.—Bp of Down & C[onnor]—Rev. Dr Hook—Sir J. Young—Mr Woollcombe—Mr Wilson (2)—Sir C. Trevelyan—Mr J. Wood—T.M. Gladstone—Mr Lucas MP. & minutes. H. of C. 5–7¼ and 10½–1¼.[1] 5 to dinner. Saw Sol. General—Sir T.G.—Sir A. Spearman—Mr Ellice—Lord A. Hervey—Ld Elcho. Read Cook on Scots Schools[2]—Hatsell on Supply.[3] Rode with Herbert: visited Mr Munro's Studio & saw his bust of Peel; the *best* head & face of him that I have seen.[4]

Harry had much uneasiness & fretfulness today: but Locock when he came was entirely satisfied finding ample cause for his state in the condition of the liver & bowels. God be praised for His great goodness.

25. Sat.

Wrote to Dr Pusey—Sir T. Fremantle—Mr J. Wood—Mr Wilson—Rev Mr Lake—Sir C. Trevelyan—& minutes. Rode with Herbert. Saw Archdn. Harrison—Solr. General on Oxford Bill. At Cabinet 2¾–6.[5] Dined with the Herberts & went to the Olympic: to see Wigan & Robson.[6] Worked after return. Read Mitchell on Newsp. Stamps.[7]

Thank God Harry continues to make progress & we are easy.

26. Quinqua[gesima] S.

St Martin's H.C. 8½.—St James's mg & evg. MS. on Ep. aloud at night. Cabinet 3–5. Saw Lord Aberdeen—Duke of Newcastle. Worked long on Oxford plan. Read Vaughan's Sermon[8]—Fra Dolcino.[9]

27. M.

Wrote to Lord J. Russell—Rev Mr Haddan—Mr Arbuthnot—Rev W. Thomson[10]—Mr T.M. Gladstone—Sol. General—& minutes. Rode in the forenoon. Cabinet at 3½. Got opinion of Edn. Commee. on Oxf. Constitn. Saw Sir S.H. Northcote—Mr Stephenson—Sir W. James—Solr. General—Lord J. Russell. H. of C. 5–7¼ and 10¼–1¼. Spoke on Small Arms Vote.[11] The Herberts dined: we discussed postponement of Reform & possible difficulties.

[1] Army estimates: *H* cxxx. 1283.

[2] J. *Cook, *Statement of facts regarding the parochial schools of Scotland* (1854).

[3] J. *Hatsell, *Precedents of proceedings in the house of commons*, 4v. (1818); iii, on lords, and supply.

[4] Colossal bust for the Peel memorial at Oldham.

[5] Cp. Conacher, 297.

[6] Alfred Sydney *Wigan, 1814–78; actor and lessee of the Olympic Theatre 1853–7, with Thomas Frederick *Robson, 1822–64, the greatest comic actor of the day. The plays were *The first night*, *The lottery ticket* and *The wandering minstrel*.

[7] Untraced pamphlet by Charles Mitchell, publisher of *Newspaper press directory*.

[8] Perhaps C. J. *Vaughan; *Personality of the tempter, and other sermons* (1851).

[9] Cp. 15 Jan. 54.

[10] William *Thomson, 1819–90; fellow of Queen's, Oxford, 1840, provost 1855–61; bp. of Gloucester 1861; abp. of York from 1862.

[11] Arguing for manufacture by machinery: *H* cxxx. 1423.

28. T.

Wrote to Mr D. Gladstone—Scotts—Mr T.B. Horsfall—Dr Locock—Sir C. Trevelyan—Mr W. Brown—Solr. General—Ld Palmerston—Mr C.H. Frewen[1]—Rev Mr Burgon[2]—Sir W. Heathcote—Rev. Jas Mozley—and minutes. Rode mg. Dined with the James's. Saw Solr. General on Oxford—Messrs. Wood Pressly & Timm on Budget preparations. Ld Palmerston on Cabinet matters. H. of C. $4\frac{3}{4}$–$7\frac{1}{2}$ and $10\frac{1}{4}$–$1\frac{1}{4}$.[3] Worked on house & personal accts.

Ash Wednesday March One 1854.

Whitehall Chapel 11 A.M. Wrote to Mr T.W. Rathbone—Mr R. Liddell[4]—Lord Hardinge—Rev G. Nugee[5]—Rev Mr Mayow—Rev Dr Hook—T.M. Gladstone—Herr Krüger[6]—Mr Anderson—Sir H. Ellis—Archdn. Harrison—Solr. General—Rev Mr Richards—Sir W. Herries—Sir C. Trevelyan—Rev G. Butler[7]—Lord Chancellor—and minutes. At a Cabinet today 3–6 we determined to postpone the Reform Bill to Ap. 27.[8] Saw Ld Chancr.—S. Herbert. Worked on Budget. Corrected Oxford proofs. Read Inst. of Justinian[9]—& De Imitatione [Christi].

2. Th.

Wrote to T.M. Gladstone—Rev Mr Lake—Recorder of London—Rev Mr Haddan—Bp of Oxford—Mrs Tyler—Mr Horsfall—Scotts—Lord Cowley—a variety of Oxford letters for tomorrow—and minutes. Ten to dinner. Saw S.H. Northcote—Lord Monteagle—Sir J. Young—Lord J. Russell—Bp of Oxford—Revenue Conclave at 3. Worked on Budget papers and materials. H. of C. $4\frac{3}{4}$–7 and 10–$11\frac{3}{4}$.[10]

3. Fr.

Wrote to Lord J. Russell—Child & Co—Ld Monteagle—R. Phillimore—V.C. Oxford (2)—Mr G. Smith—Dean of Ch. Ch.—Rev Mr Greswell—

[1] Charles Hay Frewen, 1813–78; tory M.P. East Sussex 1846–57; sheriff of Leicestershire 1866.

[2] Copy of long letter in Add MS 44377, f. 287.

[3] Opposed disclosure of newspaper circulations: *H* cxxxi. 140.

[4] Robert Liddell, 1808–88; fellow of All Souls 1831–6; vicar of Barking 1836–51, of St. Paul's, Knightsbridge, 1851; condemned for ritualism by consistory court 1855, partially reprieved by privy council, 1857.

[5] George Nugée, 1819–92; Trinity, Cambridge; curate of St. Paul's Knightsbridge, 1847–55; rector of Widley, Hampshire, 1858–72.

[6] Carl Wilhelm Krüger of Minden, 1797–1868; the National Gallery bought his collection this year; cp. 20 June 54.

[7] George *Butler, 1819–90; tutor at Durham 1848–51; curate of St. Giles', Oxford, 1854–6; vice-principal, Cheltenham college, 1858–65; principal of Liverpool college 1866–82; canon of Winchester from 1882; m. 1852 Josephine Elizabeth*, *née* Grey, the social reformer, who d. 1906.

[8] Cp. Add MS 44778, f. 175, and Conacher, 300–1.

[9] Justinian's *Institutiones* formed the introductory section of his *Digest* of Roman law.

[10] Spoke on Scottish ordnance survey: *H* cxxxi. 201.

Master Univy.—Rev Mr Rawlinson—Master Pembroke—Sir W. Heathcote—Provost of Oriel—Ld Palmerston—Ly Cottenham[1]—Sir W. Molesworth—Mr A. Miller—Sir C. Trevelyan—RM Milnes—Prince Albert—Mr Jowett—and minutes. Saw Sir S. Northcote—Mr C. Macaulay[2]—Sir Alex. Spearman—Mr Allen. Budget Conclave 2–3½. Sugar Refining do 3½–4½. H. of Commons 4¾–7½ and 9–10¼.[3] Pd 2d at a concert & walked round by Borough. Rode with Herbert. Read Oxford Pamphlets.

4. *Sat.*

Wrote to Sir T. Fremantle—J.D. Cook—Sir W. Heathcote—Ld J. Russell—Mr D.B. Chapman—Mrs T. Goalen—Mrs Cracroft—E. Cardwell—Ld Brougham—Ld Panmure—Mr Wilson (2)—Robn. G.—and minutes. Rode in the forenoon. Lady Palmerstons[4] at night. Saw Jocelyn—Ld Stanley—Mr Wilson—Mr Wood *cum* Pressly & Timm—Sir T. Fremantle—Sir A. Spearman—& busy with Budget figures & arrangements. Cabinet 2¾–6. Budget easily disposed of. Read MacCulloch—Dryden.

5. *1 S.Lent.*

Whitehall & H.C. mg: St Matthew's evg—MS. of 1840 aloud at night. Wrote to Ld Palmerston—Bp of Oxford. Read Fra Dolcino—All for Jesus[5]—Pamphlets & Ch. Mag. Worked on Budget a while after evg prayers.

6. *M.*

Wrote to Master of Pembroke—Rev Mr Rawlinson—and minutes. Cabinet 2–3½. Rode in forenoon. House 4½–11. Budget Sp. 2 hours: subsequent debate & passage of arms with Mr Disraeli.[6] Saw Ld Chancellor—Sir A. Spearman—Mr Wilson *cum* Messrs. Wood Pressly and Timm. Read Pulling on City of London[7]—Parker on Attornies.[8]

7. *T.*

Wrote to Sir J. Young—Rev H.B. Barry—Ld Ellesmere—Judge Coleridge—Dr Bull—Rev C. Marriott—Mr Grogan—Rev R. Greswell—Mr J. Wood—Mr Hayter—Robn. G—J. Carmichael[9] & min. Rode in the forenoon. Saw

[1] Caroline Elizabeth Pepys, *née* Baker, m. 1821 3rd earl of Cottenham; she d. 1868.

[2] Charles Zachary Macaulay, 1813–86; T.B.s* private secretary 1839–41; secretary of audit office 1854–65, chairman 1865–6.

[3] Postponement of Reform Bill: *H* cxxxi. 277.

[4] 4 Carlton Gardens.

[5] Cp. 12 Feb. 54.

[6] His second budget met a deficit of £2,854,000 by increasing income tax for half a year from 7d. to 10½d., with provision for further increase if war required it. Gladstone spoke very strongly against financing the war by borrowing: *H* cxxxi. 357; cp. O. Anderson, *A liberal state at war* (1967) 194–7 for the decline of this policy.

[7] A. Pulling, *père, The city of London corporation inquiry* (1854).

[8] R. A. Parker, *Remuneration of attorneys and solicitors* (1853).

[9] Liverpool merchant who had telegraphed support for increased war taxation; cp. 44529, f. 62v.

Sir S. Northcote—Sir C. Trevelyan[1]—Tyne deputation (at Admty.)—Rev Mr Jowett—Sir W. Heathcote—Messrs. Rawlinson, Haddan, & Marshall, from Oxford—of whom the two first, with Heathcote dined, to pursue our subject. Worked on Oxford papers.

8. Wed.

Wrote to Vice Chancellor—Mr Hext—Master of Univy.—Sir C. Barry—and minutes. Rode in the forenoon. H. of C. 12½–5¾.[2] Saw Mrs T. Goalen—J.N.G.—Sir G. Barry—Mr A. Gordon—Rev. Dr Jeune—Mr J. Wilson—Mr Divett MP.—Mr Wilbraham. Cabinet dinner at Lansdowne House: Countess Colloredo's afterwards. I spoke pointedly to *him*. Up till 4½ AM. working upon the Oxford Bill.

9. Th.

Wrote to Mr Rawlinson—Master of Univy.—Aunt J.R.—Rev P. Smythe—Sir W. James—Sir C. Trevelyan—Mr B. Harrison—E. Cardwell Rev. C. Marriott & minutes. Read Thomson on Queen's Coll.[3] H. of C. 5½–9.[4] Then dined with the Herberts. Council, & audience of the Queen resp. Crown Lands 3–4½. Dundee Deputation at 2.[5] Saw Sir S. Northcote—Mr Goldwin Smith (Oxford)[6]—Lord J. Russell (do)—Sir C. Trevelyan—Mr Allen (No 6.).

10. Fr.

Wrote to Ld Clarendon—Ld Stanley (Ald[erley])—Rev. G. Hext—Ld J. Russell—Sir G. Philips[7]—Mr W. Brown—Rev Mr Lawrence[8]—The Speaker—Rev Mr Perry—Sir A. Spearman—Govr. of Bank—& minutes. Rode in the forenoon. Saw Mr Wilson—Sir S. Northcote—Earl of Aberdeen—Sir C. Wood. Cabinet 2¾–4½. H. of C. 4½–5¾.[9] Evg at home: again worked on & corrected freely the Proof of Oxford Bill. Read M'Culloch on Wages.[10]

11. Sat. X

Wrote to Sir W. Heathcote (2)—Ld Aberdeen—V.C. Oxford—Ld J. Russell—Archdn. Harrison—H. Tayleur—Mr A.H. Wylie—G. Burnett—Mr M'Culloch—Mr Sotheron—Ld Granville—Judge Coleridge—Ld Ellesmere

[1] Cp. Conacher, 327.
[2] Succession to Real Estate Bill: *H* cxxxi. 467.
[3] W. *Thomson, 'An open college best for all, a reply to . . . John Barrow' (1854); cp. 18 Feb. 54.
[4] Ministers' money: *H* cxxxi. 552.
[5] Cp. *The Times*, 10 Mar. 54, 9c.
[6] Cp. 27 July 54n.
[7] Sir George Richard Philips, 1789–1883; liberal M.P. Steyning 1820–32, Kidderminster 1835–7, Poole 1837–52; 2nd bart. 1844.
[8] Alfred Lawrence, 1791–1874; Christ's, Cambridge; rector of Sandhurst, Kent, 1831–57.
[9] Introduced Exchequer Bills to raise £1,750,000: *H* cxxxi. 618.
[10] J. R. *McCulloch, *Essay on the circumstances which determine the rate of wages* (1826).

—Sir J. Awdry[1]—C.G.—and minutes. Saw Mr Cureton—Mr Wood *cum* Mr Pressly—Ld Granville—Sir A. Spearman—Ld Abn. St Mary's Crown St 8½ P.M. Rode in forenoon. C.G. went to Hagley. Saw Osborne: failed to see Lightfoot [R]. Worked on Treas. Papers at night. Read Fitzgerald's Address.[2]

12. 2 S.Lent.

Chapel Royal mg.—Brompton Ch (with Aunt J.) evg. MS of 42 aloud. Read Vie de Rancé[3]—Dolcino—Pusey's Sermons.[4] Wrote on the Temptation. Visited Aunt J.

13. M.

Wrote to Master of Univy.—Solr. General—Dr Jacobson—J. Rowsell—Rev. H.J. Dixon[5]—Herr Krüger—Rev. Dr Pusey—C.G.—Rev J.L. Ross—and minutes. Rode in the forenoon. H. of C. 4½–9½ and 10¼–12½ waiting for Finance Debate.[6] Saw Mr Wilson—Mr J. Dickenson[7]—Sir Wm Heathcote—Earl Granville—Solr. General—R. Lowe.

14. T. X

Wrote to Judge Coleridge—H. Tayleur—Archd. Harrison—V.C. Oxford—Ld Granville—Mr Muter[8]—Mr Dyce—and minutes. House of C. 4¾–6½.[9] Dined with the Herberts—Saw Mr Krüger—Dr Hessey[10]—Col. Thwaites—Sir C. Trevelyan—Sir A. Spearman—Ld Granville—S. Herbert—Goulburn—Cardwell—F. Lawley—and late Adel, 5 [R].[11] Read Townshend on H. of C.[12] Worked on Oxf. Bill.

15. Wed.

Wrote to Mr Dyce—Master of Pembroke—Dr Pusey—Ld Palmerston—Mr Wilson—Dr Molesworth—Ld J. Russell (two)—Mr Harcourt MP.[13]—Sir W. Heathcote, and minutes. Rode. Visited Christie's—Saw A. Oswald—Mr Greenwood—Herr Krüger—Mr G. Christie—Ld Elcho—Ld Abn.

[1] Sir John Wither Awdry, 1795–1878; fellow of Oriel, Oxford, 1820–30; judge in Bombay 1830, chief justice there 1839–41; urged colonial church reform, see Conacher, 102.

[2] J. E. *Fitzgerald, 'Address . . . at the opening of the first legislative council of the province of Canterbury, New Zealand' (1853).

[3] F. R. de Châteaubriand, *Vie de Rancé* (1844); the seventeenth-century Trappist.

[4] Cp. 29 Jan. 54.

[5] Henry John Dixon, b. 1814; University, Oxford; curate of Lurgashall, Sussex, from ?1842.

[6] Spoke on postage to Australia, and delayed the finance deb.: *H* cxxxi. 696, 756.

[7] Perhaps Joseph Dickenson, an inspector of coal mines.

[8] James Mutter, inland revenue office clerk.

[9] Property Disposal Bill: *H* cxxxi. 796.

[10] James Augustus *Hessey, 1814–92; D.C.L. 1846; headmaster of Merchant Taylors 1845–70; prebendary of St. Paul's 1860–75; archdeacon of Middlesex from 1875.

[11] Reading unclear.

[12] W. C. Townsend, *History of the house of commons, 1688–1832*, 2 v. (1843–4).

[13] i.e. G. G. Vernon-Harcourt, Peelite M.P. for Oxfordshire 1831–61; cp. 11 May 31n.

Dined at Herberts: Ly Clarendon's & Atty General's afterwards: but my head was stuffed with influenza. Worked on Oxf. Bill. Read Oxf. Law &c Suggestions.[1] C.G. returned.

16. Th.

Wrote to F.R. Bonham—Lord J. Thynne—Ld Aberdeen—E. Cardwell—J. Wood—J.E. Fitzgerald—Mr Booker MP[2]—Dr Hessey—Dr Pusey—Mr Wilson—Mr Horsfall—and minutes. Kept my bed for the forenoon. Arranged for circulating Oxf. papers & bill. Saw Ld J. Russell on Commn. Saw Sir C. Trevelyan—Ld Abn—Mr Hayter—Conclave on readjustment of Consol. Fund & Voted Charges. Worked on Bill Stamps & at last wrought out a scale wh I hope may do.[3]

17. Fr.

Wrote to Judge Coleridge—Mrs Wadd—Sir J. Harding—Robn. G.—Rev J.H. Hext[4]—and minutes. Rode in the forenoon. Read Townshend's Hist. of House of Commons. Saw Mr Hayter—Mr Shelley—Sir W. Heathcote—Mr Arbuthnot—Archdn. Harrison. H. of C. $4\frac{3}{4}$–$12\frac{1}{2}$ on Oxford Bill & Ways & Means.—A good start for the first-named: thank God.[5]

18. Sat.

Wrote to H. Tayleur—Sir T. Fremantle—Ld A. Hervey—Princ. St Alban Hall—Robn. G.—Ld Clarendon—Mr Delane—Lord J. Thynne—Mr Lefevre—Earl of Aberdeen—Bp of Ripon—Sir S. Northcote—and minutes. Saw Ld J. Thynne—Bonham—Mr Brown MP & Depn. of For[eign] Bill Stamps[6]—Mr Glyn—E. Bruce. Cabinet $2\frac{3}{4}$–6. Off at $6\frac{3}{4}$ to the Harris dinner.[7] Thence to the Speaker's Levee. Thence to Stafford House: & home before midnight. Read Townshend.

19. 3 S.Lent.

After breakfast Hamilton came & we entered upon his subject. He finally left me near three, & went to accept the Bishopric.[8] A new & auspicious day for the Church of England! Chapel Royal aft.—MS. of 53 on Gospel aloud. Wrote to Sir H. Dukinfield. Saw Lord Aberdeen—Ld E. Bruce—

[1] Sir J. W. Awdry, and Sir J. Patteson, 'Suggestions with regard to certain proposed alterations in the university and colleges of Oxford' (1854); on a law school.

[2] Thomas William Booker(-Blakemore), 1801–58, tory M.P. Herefordshire from 1850; added name of Blakemore 1855.

[3] 'Penny taxation' on foreign and colonial bills and contracts; cp. Buxton, *Finance and Politics*, i. 207 and Add MS 44529, f. 36v.

[4] John Hawkins Hext, 1810?–78; Exeter, Oxford; vicar of Morval, Cornwall, 1842–1858, of Highweek 1858–64, of King's Teignton, Devon, from 1858.

[5] Reviewed the main objections given in deb. against the Bill: *H* cxxxi. 943, 987.

[6] Cp. *The Times*, 20 Mar. 54, 8e.

[7] On his appointment to govern Madras; cp. ibid., 7c.

[8] W. K. *Hamilton was reluctant to become bp. of Salisbury (on the decease of E. *Denison) as he contemplated joining Rome; cp. Purcell, i. 531–2.

R. Cavendish—Sir W. James—Mrs Goalen. Read Hamilton's Sermon on Bp Denison[1]—Vie de Rancé.

I have been more overcome & overdone by this day than by any day's *labour* for a long time; and I cannot describe the end of it otherwise than as being stunned by God's mercy.

20. M.

St James's 8 A.M. Wrote to Mr G. Arbuthnot—Mr Moffat—Mr G. Burnett—Mr J. Wood—Govr. of Bank—Mr J. Wilson—Rev. E. Austin—Mr Raikes—Sir W. Molesworth—Mr Anderson—Mr J.E. Denison & minutes. Worked on Oxford Bill. Attended at Marlborough House to see the Gherardini models. Visited Mr Noble's Studio with Dss of Sutherland: much pleased there.[2] Saw Ld A. Hervey—Mr Arbuthnot—Mr Hayter—Sir W. Molesworth. H. of C. 4½–8 and 9½–12. Col[onial] Ch[urch] Bill 2d reading carried by 196:62. D.G.! I purposely sat mute.[3] Read Parl. (Budget &c.) Debates of 1793–6.[4]

21. T.

Wrote to
Rev. J.B. Mozley
R W Sewell[5]
H. Harris[6]
Bp of Ripon
Ld Monteagle
Master of Pembroke
E. of Aberdeen, & minutes.
Sir R. Inglis
Mr T.H. Baylis
Rev. E. King[7]
R. Stokes[8]
W.E. Jelf.
Govr. of Bank
Rev. T. Briscoe[9]

H. of C. 4½ 2¼. Spoke 1 h. in answer to Disraeli & others.[10] Saw Mr Anderson—Mr Litchfield—Sir C. Trevelyan—Mr Redgrave *cum* Mr Cole[11]—Sir T. Fremantle—Mr J. Wood—Scots Malt Spirit Deputation.[12] Read Mrs Norton's pamphlet.[13]

[1] W. K. *Hamilton, 'In the midst of life we are in death' (1854).
[2] Matthew *Noble, 1818–76; sculptor, chiefly of busts; studio in Bruton Street.
[3] *H* cxxxi. 1017.
[4] His speech next day discussed Pittite war finance.
[5] Presumably W. *Sewell.
[6] Henry Harris, 1818–1900; fellow of Magdalen, Oxford, 1850, vice-president 1853; rector of Winterton Basset, Swindon, 1858–97; theologian.
[7] Edward *King, 1829–1910; curate of Wheatley 1854–8; chaplain of Cuddesdon 1858–63, principal 1863; professor of pastoral theology, Oxford, 1873; bp. of Lincoln 1885; a strong tory and high churchman.
[8] Probably intended to read E. Stokes; Gladstone unnecessarily corrected the 'E' of King of note above.
[9] Thomas Briscoe, 1811–95; fellow of Jesus, Oxford, 1834–59; curate of Holyhead 1857, vicar there from 1868; chancellor of Bangor from 1877.
[10] Defended his income tax proposals: *H* cxxxi. 1161.
[11] Richard Redgrave of the department of practical art, and Sir Henry *Cole, 1808–82; sec. of dept. of practical art 1852–73; organized exhibitions; K.C.B. 1875. About the Gherardini collection.
[12] Led by Sir J. Anderson, M.P., *The Times*, 22 Mar. 54, 9e.
[13] Mrs. C. *Norton, 'English laws for women in the nineteenth century' (1854); cp. Add MS 44378, f. 191.

22. Wed. X

Wrote to J.E. Denison—Princ. St M. Hall—Mr Anderson—Ld Lansdowne—Mr Haddan—Mr Litchfield—Mr Meyrick—Lord Aberdeen—Rev O. Gordon[1]—Mr B. Price—& minutes. Saw Ld Aberdeen—Mr Ewart—Sir T. Fremantle—Sir C. Trevelyan—Sir A. Spearman—Mr Franks. Rode in forenoon. Attended the Levee. H of C. 12¼–1¾ for the Simony Bill.[2] Saw Car. Evg. [R].

23. Th.

Wrote to Mrs Wm. G.—Sir T. Fremantle—J. Lloyd Phelps[3]—Govr. of Bank—Prince Albert—Sir H. Willoughby[4]—Rev. W.E.C. Austin[5]—Bp of Ripon—E. Cardwell—Baron Cresswell[6]—T.M. Gladstone—Rev. H. Tripp[7]—J.N.G.—Ld Aberdeen—J.E. Denison—Rev. H. Harris—R. Palmer MP.—Major Graham[8]—Mr W. Brown MP.—Dr Hessey—and minutes. Also minute on Greek question. Also minute on the purchase of Burlington House.[9] Saw Sir C. Trevelyan—S. Herbert—Mr Williams MP.[10]—Mr Hayter—Mr Fortescue.[11] Dined with the Herberts. Read Disraeli's Bentinck.[12] H. of C. 4½–6½.[13]

24. Fr.

Wrote to Mr Anderson—Mr Wood—Profr. Donkin[14]—Robn. G.—Bp Moray & Ross—Mr Cook—Rev. C. Marriott—Prince Albert—Rev. T. Briscoe—Sir J. Graham—Ld J. Russell—Mr Monsell (2)—Ld Clarendon—Sir T. Fremantle—C.G.—and minutes. Rode in the forenoon. H. of C. 4½–6½ and 11–12¾.[15] Coming home at 10 found C. & M. suddenly brought

[1] Osborne *Gordon, 1813–83; student of Christ Church 1834–61, censor 1847–61; member of the tutor's association, of the Oxford commission 1877; rector of East Hampstead, Berkshire, from 1860. Cp. E. G. W. Bill and J. F. A. Mason, *Christ Church and reform 1850–1867* (1970), 36.

[2] *H* cxxxi. 1177.

[3] Draft on income tax in Add MS 44378, f. 250.

[4] Sir Henry Pollard Willoughby, 1796–1865; 3rd bart. 1813; tory M.P. Isle of Wight 1831–2; Newcastle-under-Lyme 1832–5, Poole 1841–7, Evesham from 1847.

[5] William Edmund Crawfurd Austin (Gourlay), 1822?–97; fellow of New college, 1840–63; rector of Stoke Abbott, Dorset, 1862-77, of Stanton St. John, Oxford, from 1878; added surname of Gourlay.

[6] i.e. Sir C. *Cresswell, judge of common pleas.

[7] Henry Tripp, b. ?1816; fellow of Worcester, Oxford, 1845–58; vicar of Denchworth, Berkshire, 1855–8; rector of Winford, Gloucestershire, from 1858.

[8] (Sir) Fortescue Graham, 1794–1880; *Victoria's A.D.C. 1854–7; K.C.B. 1865; colonel of marines 1866.

[9] It was bought in 1854 for £140,000 by the government, and became the home of sundry royal societies.

[10] Three at this time, probably Michael Williams, 1785–1858, miner and banker; liberal M.P. W. Cornwall 1853–8.

[11] 'Dined at home' [?] here deleted.

[12] Cp. 31 Jan. 40n., and 5 Feb. 52.

[13] Misc. business: *H* cxxxi. 1238.

[14] William Fishburn *Donkin, 1814–69; professor of astronomy at Oxford from 1842; worked with H. H. *Vaughan to extend power of professors 1852–4.

[15] Settlement and Removal Bill 2°: *H* cxxxi. 1274.

from Brighton by an alarming Tel. message about Lady Glynne. After cons[ultatio]n they decided on waiting for the early train. Saw Ld Shaftesbury—Sir A. Spearman—Mr Trevor—Mr G. Glyn—Govr. of Bank—Sir W. Heathcote—Ld Norreys—Mr Fortescue.[1] Read Mrs Norton.

25. Sat. Annunc[iatio]n.

Wrote to Mr Redgrave—Mr Cook—Ld Canning—Ld Norreys—W.S. Blackstone—Mr B. Price—Mast. of Pembroke—Mr H. Lees—Rev. W. Palmer—W.C. James—Rev. J.B. Mozley—C.G.—W.H.G.—Mr Dodd—Mr W. Brown—Ld J. Russell—Mr G. Arbuthnot—Rev W. Sewell—& minutes. Saw Mr Arbuthnot—Sir A. Spearman—S. Herbert—Mr Hincks. Cabinet 2¾–5¾. Lord Mayor's dinner. Returned thanks for H. of Commons.[2] Returned home to my work. Read Ed. Rev. on Stamps.[3]

26. 4 S.Lent.

Marg. Chapel & H.C. mg. Ch[apel] Royal with Agnes aft.—Conv. with her at dinner. MS of 43 aloud in evg. Read Mrs Norton's Statement—Taylor v. R. Wilberforce[4]—Vie de Rancé. Wrote to J.B. Mozley[5]—Solr. General—Mrs Norton—R. Wilberforce.[6] Saw Sir W. James—E. Collins [R].

27. M.

Wrote to Ld J. Russell—Ld Canning—Mr Rawlinson—Dr Hessey—Sir W. Farquhar—Mr Hayter—Rev. Mr Johnson—C.G.—Earl of Shrewsbury—Stephy—Rev. R. Owen—Robn. G.—Rev E. Coleridge—Sir S. Scott & Co (cancelled)—Sir W. Molesworth, and minutes. Rode in the forenoon.

Saw Bp of Oxford—Messrs. Myers[7] & Duncan—Sir A.Y. Spearman—Ld Advocate—Norreys—Ld E. Howard—Read Disraeli's Bentinck. H. of C. 4½–8¼ and 9–11½.[8] Cabinet 2½–4½.[9]

28 T.

Wrote to Dr Jacobson—Mr Hayter—Rector of Exeter—C.G.[10]—Mr H. Lees—and minutes. Rode in the forenoon. H. of C. 4¾–8 and 10–1. Spoke

[1] Chichester Samuel (Parkinson-)*Fortescue, 1823–98; liberal M.P. Louth 1847–74; junior treasury lord 1854–5, under-secretary for colonies 1857–8, 1859–65; added name of Parkinson, 1862; chief secretary for Ireland 1865–6, 1868–70; president of bd. of trade 1871–4; cr. Baron Carlingford 1874; privy seal 1881–5, president of council 1883–5; unionist 1886. Cp. Add MS 44121–3.

[2] Spoke on war finance; *The Times*, 27 Mar. 54, 8c.

[3] *Edinburgh Review*, xcviii. 488 (October, 1853); by Alexander *Russel.

[4] J. Taylor, 'An appeal to the . . . abp. of York on the uncondemned heresies of . . . *Wilberforce's . . . "Eucharist"' (1854).

[5] Draft in Add MS 44379, f. 1.

[6] Cp. D. Newsome, *The parting of friends* (1966), 381–2.

[7] Jacques Myers, otherwise unidentified.

[8] Message from the Queen announcing end of negotiations with Russia and start of 'active assistance' to Turkey: *H* cxxxi. 1352. Deb. on this delayed until 31 March 1854.

[9] On civil service reform, cp. Add MS 44636, f. 8.

[10] Bassett, 104.

on Dublin Commun[icatio]ns.[1] Cabinet $2\frac{1}{2}$–$4\frac{1}{2}$. Read Disraeli's Bentinck. Saw Sir S. Northcote—J.N.G.—Mrs Goalen—Ld Canning—MacCulloch (sick)—Mr Hamilton (M's doctor)[2]—Mr W. Brown. Col[onial] Ch[urch] conclave (Walpole, Sol. Gen., Phillimore, & Herbert) at night.

29. Wed.

Wrote to
Scott & Co
Rev Dr Hessey
H. Harris
W. Palmer
Mr Rintoul
Sir T. Fremantle
Ld Seymour
Dep Govr Bank[3]
Wms. Deacon & Co—
Ld Monteagle
Ld Canning
Robn G.
Provost of Eton
Mr Dyce
Earl Nelson
Mrs Goalen
C.G.[4]
Mr Marriott
Govr of Bank
G.F. Mathison
Pres[iden]t Varvogli.[5]
John Wood
Ld Granville
& minutes

Saw Mr Wood—Mr Arbuthnot—Sir A. Spearman—Mr Allen. Council B[uckingham] Palace 3–4.[6] Dined at Stafford House. Bunsen, Lacaita, Sir J. Macneill,[7] & conv. till midnight. Saw one going like a sheep to the slaughter [R]. Read Newmarch on Bills of Exchange[8]—Bank Correspondence.

30. Th.

Wrote to Lady C.N. Grenville—Mr G. Glyn—Dep. Govr. Bank—Mr Herbert RA.—Mr Masterman—Mr Redgrave—Rev. C. Marriott—Mr Greene MP.[9]—Rev. R. Hake[10]—C.G.—Mr Strutt MP.[11]—Sir A. Spearman—and minutes. Saw Mr Glyn—Dep. Govr. of Bank—E. Cardwell—Ld Seymour—Mr Allen—Sol Genl. Rode in the forenoon. H of C. $4\frac{1}{2}$–$7\frac{3}{4}$ and $8\frac{1}{4}$–$10\frac{3}{4}$.[12] Read Gilbart on Banking[13]—Disraeli's G. Bentinck—Thornton on Credit.[14]

[1] On the packet service to Ireland: *H* cxxxi. 1401.
[2] Perhaps Charles Thomas Hamilton, physician of Allsop Terrace, Regent's Park.
[3] Thomas Mathias Weguelin, 1809–85; Russian banker in London, deputy governor of England 1853–5, governor 1855–7; liberal M.P. Southampton 1857–9, Wolverhampton 1861–80.
[4] Bassett, 104.
[5] President of the Chamber of Deputies of Athens, which had passed a vote of thanks to Gladstone; cp. Add MS 44529, f. 74.
[6] Cp. Bassett, 104.
[7] Sir John *MacNeill, 1795–1883, br. of D.*; minister in Teheran 1836; chairman Scottish poor law board 1845–78.
[8] W. *Newmarch, *The new supplies of gold; facts, and statements* (1853), 107–19.
[9] 'Govr. of Bank' here deleted.
[10] Robert Hake, b. ?1822; chaplain of New college, Oxford, 1847–58; rector of St. George, Canterbury, 1866–9; vicar of Aylsham, Norfolk, from 1883.
[11] Edward *Strutt, 1801–80; liberal M.P. Derby 1830–47, Arundel 1851–2, Nottingham 1852–6; chancellor of duchy of Lancaster 1852–4; cr. Baron Belper 1856; a philosophic radical.
[12] Income Tax Bill 3°: *H* cxxxii. 81.
[13] J. W. *Gilbart, *The elements of banking* (1852).
[14] H. *Thornton, *Nature and effects of the paper credit of Great Britain* (1802).

31. Fr.

Wrote to Govr. of the Bank—Mr T. Lane Fox[1]—Miss Blackstone[2]—Mr Wynne MP.[3]—Mr H. Tayleur—Duke of Sutherland—C.G.—Provost of Eton—Ld Aberdeen (2)—T.M. Gladstone—J.R. Godley—Rev Mr Lawrence—Mr Miles MP.[4]—and minutes. Rode in forenoon. Dined with the Herberts. Saw Mr Wood—Mr Litchfield—Mr Trevor—S. Herbert (Ld J. R's letter).[5] H. of C. 4½–8 and 9¼–1.[6] Read Disraeli's Bentinck.

Sat. April One 1854. X

Wrote to Queen's Proctor[7]—Mr Wilson—Mr Arbuthnot—C.G.—Sol. General—Ld Elcho—Mr Goulburn—Mr Anderson—Sir W. Heathcote—& minutes. Saw Mr Goulburn—Sir S. Northcote—Mr Comm Gen Filder[8]—Sir C. Trevelyan—Bp of Oxford—Sir A. Spearman. Oxford Deputation with Ld JR.[9] Ld Adn. on state of the Govt. Dined with the Herberts. Lady Clarendon's afr.—Saw one late: notable [R].

2. 5 S.Lent.

Chapel Royal mg. St James's Evg. MS. of 41 aloud. Wrote to Mr Woodgate—Warden of New College. Saw Mrs Norton—Ld Brougham—Lady Wenlock—Ld Aberdeen—do *cum* Duke of Newcastle—S. Herbert & Geo. Hope. Read Vie de Rancè—Chr. Remembr.[10]—Woodgate, Dickinson, & Freeman on Oxford Reform.[11]

3. M.

Wrote to Rev. A.W. Haddan—Ld Londonderry—Mr Burnett—Ld Canning—Mr Chaplin—Dss. of Sutherland—Mr Neate[12]—Sir W. Heathcote—Mr C. Ross—Mr H.W. Hobhouse[13]—Mr C. Marriott—Rev A.P. Stanley—

[1] Thomas Henry Lane Fox, d. 1861; Christ's, Cambridge; vicar of Sturminster Newton, Dorset, from 1839.

[2] Jane Martha, sister of W. S. Blackstone; had asked for help for her brother; cp. Add MS 44529, f. 75 and 11 Nov. 28.

[3] William Watkin Edward *Wynne, 1801–80; antiquarian and tory M.P. Merioneth 1852–65.

[4] Cp. 21 June 34.

[5] *Russell threatened resignation on reform; cp. J. Prest, *Lord John *Russell* (1972) 365.

[6] Deb. on Queen's message on war with Russia: *H* cxxxii. 198.

[7] Francis Hart Dyke, 1803–76; 4th s. of Sir Percival Hart Dyke, 5th bart.; proctor 1825, Queen's proctor from 1845.

[8] William Filder, 1789–1861; assistant commissary general 1811, commissary general 1840; commanded commissariat in Crimea to end of 1855.

[9] Meeting with the professors, who requested extended powers; cp. E.G.W. Bill, *University reform in nineteenth century Oxford* (1973) 161.

[10] *Christian Remembrancer*, xxvii, (April 1854) on the census.

[11] H. A. Woodgate, 'University Reform' (1854); F. H. Dickinson and E. A. *Freeman, 'Suggestions with regard to certain proposed alterations in the university and colleges of Oxford' (1854); in reply to the Tutor's Association circular.

[12] Charles *Neate, 1806–79; fellow of Oriel, Oxford, 1828–79; Drummond professor of political economy 1857–62; liberal M.P. Oxford city 1857 (unseated), 1863–8.

[13] Henry William Hobhouse, 1791–1868; banker; liberal M.P. Hereford 1841–7.

Bp of Exeter—Mr Macaulay—Mr Anderson—and minutes. Saw Unitarian Dep[utatio]n resp. Oxford Bill[1]—[blank—] Mr Hayter—Sir W. Heathcote —Ld Chandos—Mr R. Palmer—Sir B. Hall—Provost of Eton—Mr Masterman & Depn. on Bill of Exchange Stamps. Rode in the forenoon. Attended the Court for the Addresses in aftn.[2] The P. of Wales stood by the Queen: his countenance modest & expressive, with the faintest shade of melancholy. H. of C. 6½–8 and 9½–12½.[3] Willy came home from Eton: C. from Hagley leaving Lady G. thank God easier. Yesterday was Harry's birthday & it passed without my thought, wh was sadly ungrateful. Read Mr Neate's pamphlet[4]—Disraeli's Bentinck.

4. *T.*

Stephen's birthday: God bless him. Wrote to Mr H. Drummond—Rev Mr Stokes—Dep. Govr. Bank—Mr Wilson—Mr Cardwell—Mr C. Neate— Mr G. Smith—Ld Canning (2)—Sir W. Herries—and minutes. Rode in the forenoon. H of C. 9¼–12½.[5] Saw Mr Dyce—Ld Londonderry—Mr Allen—Sir A. Spearman—Mr Wood—Mr Hayter—Mr Weguelin—C. Wood—Scotch Ed[ucatio]n Episc. Deput[atio]n at 1[6]—Nat. Debt Commrs. at 2—Mr Macaulay on Fellowships in evg.[7]

Went with the Duchess of Sutherland to the Gordon Squ. Church: which is very beautiful & suggested many things. It rouses sympathy, more than it gives satisfaction: even to the eye and ear.[8] Read D.'s Bentinck—Bp Gillies to the Lord Provost.[9]

5. *Wed.*

Wrote to Mrs Nimmo—Mr Hayn[10]—Sir S. Scott & Co—Mr Duncan—Ld A. Hervey—Ld Clarendon—Warden of New Coll.—Mr C. Neate—Sir J. Graham—Mr E.A. Freeman[11]—Williams & Co (Chester)—Robn. G. (2)—Dep. Gov. Bank[12]—Mr Allen—and minutes. Saw Mr Miles—Ld J. Thynne Sir C. Trevelyan—Mr Colvile—Sir A. Spearman—Mr Duncan—Mr Allen, and Mr Wood. Rode with Fitzroy—into the country! 1 h. 20 m. Cabinet dinner at the D. of Argylls. Lady Clarendon's afterwards.

[1] On the abolition of religious tests: *The Times*, 4 April 1854, 6f.

[2] Presentation of the lords' and commons' replies to the Queen's message announcing war: *H* cxxxii. 197, 217.

[3] Misc. business: *H* cxxxii. 326.

[4] C. *Neate, 'Objections to the government proposals for reforming the constitution of the university of Oxford' (1854).

[5] Dublin University Bill: *H* cxxxii. 376.

[6] No report found.

[7] On the Oxford Bill.

[8] Catholic Apostolic [Irvingite] Church, completed 1854, by J. R. Brandon.

[9] Untraced.

[10] Probably Watson Ward Hayne of Burchell and Hayne, London solicitors.

[11] Edward Augustus *Freeman, 1823–92; fellow of Trinity, Oxford, 1845; regius of professor of modern history from 1884; medievalist and violent controversialist. He wanted the Anglo-Saxon professorship statutes changed.

[12] Draft in Add MS 44379, f. 155.

6 Th. X

Wrote to Mr Jacques Myers[1]—Mrs Norton—Provost of Oriel—Mr Tufnell MP—Col. Harcourt MP—Ld Monteagle—Dep. Govr. Bank—and minutes. Rode in the forenoon. Attended the Elgin dinner.[2] Saw Mr Anderson—E. Cardwell—Sir J. Graham. With & through Mr A. I got (I hope) to the bottom of the question of Def[iciency] Bills & we have made a change good I trust for the public.[3] H. of C. 4½–6½ and 11½–12½. Spoke on the Stonor Committee.[4] Saw one late: of the more hopeful [R].

7. Fr.

Wrote to Sir W. Heathcote—S. Herbert—Warden of New Coll.—Mr Anderson—Dep. Govr. Bank[5]—Mr Randolph[6]—Archdn. Grant—Mr Hayter—and minutes. Rode in the forenoon. H. of C. 4½–2 A.M.—except ½ h. for dinner. Spoke 1 h on Oxford Bill.[7] Saw Sir C. Trevelyan—Lord R. Grosvenor—Mr Anderson—do *cum* Mr Greenwood.

8. Sat.

Wrote to Mr Monsell—Lord Monteagle—Mr J. Wood—Ct. Walewski—Sir J. Stephen—Ld Canning—Robn. G.—Dep. Gov. Bank—Mr R. Low—Ld Hatherton—Mr Hume—Sir C. Trevelyan—Rev. Mr Hackman—and minutes. Saw Sir C. Trevelyan—Rev Mr Church—Mr Napier[8] & Mr Hamilton—Col. Harcourt M.P.—Mr Anderson—Sir A.Y. Spearman. Cabinet 2¾–5¾. Important: & satisfactory.[9] Rode with Willy & J. Talbot. Read 'La Politique Anglo-Francaise.[10] Worked on Oxford &c.

9. Palm Sunday.

Whitehall Chapel mg: St James's Evg (prayers). MS of 46 aloud. Worked on Oxford Bill at night. Wrote to Dss of Sutherland—Mrs Norton. Read Rancé—Taylor's Article on Marriage[11]—Ludlow on Maurice's case[12]—Chr. Rem. Walk with C.

[1] Not further identified.

[2] Cp. *The Times*, 7 April 1854, 12e.

[3] A prolonged quarrel with the bank of England: he reduced quarterly payments to it to prevent excessive deficiency bill issues; the bank accused him of illegality and took private counsel when the law officers supported him. Statement of his case in Add MS 43071, f. 126.

[4] Controversy over the judicial appointment of Alban Charles Stonor, 1817–66, solicitor general in Van Diemen's Land 1850–4, accused of election bribery in Sligo: *H* cxxxii. 534.

[5] Draft in Add MS 44379, f. 179.

[6] John James Randolph, 1817?–99; student of Christ Church 1834–40; fellow of Merton from 1840, sub-warden 1846.

[7] Defending the 'gradual organisation of an efficient professorial system': *H* cxxxii. 768.

[8] (Sir) Joseph* Napier, 1804–82; barrister; tory M.P. Dublin university 1848–58; lord chancellor of Ireland 1858–9; cr. bart. 1867; defender of the Irish establishment.

[9] *Russell's Reform Bill was postponed *sine die*, with no pledge to reintroduce it; cp. Conacher, 305.

[10] Comte de Tegoborski, *De la politique anglo-française dans la question d'Orient* (1854).

[11] Cp. 3 Apr. 49.

[12] [J. M. Ludlow] 'King's College and Mr. *Maurice: No. 1' (1854).

10 M.

Wrote to Lord Aberdeen—Mr Dyce—Dep. Govr. Bank—Mr W. Brown—and minutes. Rode in the forenoon. H. of C. 4½–10. Col. Ch. Bill.[1] Read Disraeli's Geo. Bentinck. Worked on Oxf. Bill & nearly finished corrections. Saw Sir A. Spearman—Mr J. Wood[2]—Mr Dyce with Mr Redgrave—Dep. Gov. Bank. At ten H. heard from Ld J. with amazement that he had changed his mind & could not go on. 10–12 at Ld Abns with Newcastle Graham & Herbert determining on our course.[3]

11. T.

Wrote to Lord J. Russell—Rev. Jas Murray—Ld Canning—Solr. General—Sir C. Trevelyan—& minutes. Worked on Figures for Statement tonight, & on Oxford Bill. About two came a notice that the J.R. crisis was over. Saw Mr Dyce—Sir W. Heathcote—S. Herbert—Mr Anderson Mr Hankey—Mr Laing—Mr Glyn—Dss. of Sutherland came[4] with C. at night after the Palace.[5] H. of C. 4½–10¾. Spoke 1 h. on presenting the Balance Sheet.[6]

12. Wed.

Westmr. Abbey 10 A.M. Wrote to Dep. Govr. Bank (2)

Rev. Mr Lowe	Ld Aberdeen
B. Wilson	Sir J. Graham
Mr Marriott	Mr Monsell and minutes.

Rode in evening. Saw Lord Canning—Sir C. Trevelyan—Mr Anderson—Rev Jas Murray. Cabinet 3–6¼. Tasso with Willy & Agnes. Worked on the law case resp. Deficy. Bills. Read Disraeli's G. Bentinck.

13. Th.

Wstmr. Abby 10 A.M. and Titchfield St 5 P.M. Wrote to Ld Canning (2) Ld Powis—Ld E. Bruce—Ld Aberdeen—Granville—Jocelyn—Mr Hankey MP.—Dunlop MP.[7]—Count Walewski—Mr Geo. Bowyer MP.—Rev J.H. Timins—Col. Harcourt MP.—Dep. Gov. Bank—Solr. General—Sir C. Trevelyan—J.J. Randolph & minutes.

Rode in aftn. Visited All Saints Ch. the fine & (as Richmond said) living work of Mr Butterfield.[8] Saw Messrs. Wood Pressly & Timm 11½–1½ on the New Taxes.[9] Also Ld Aberdeen—Ld Granville. Read Disraeli's Bentinck.

[1] This time he spoke on it: *H* cxxxii. 810; cp. 20 Mar. 54.

[2] Instead of 'Wadd'.

[3] The Peelites expected *Russell's resignation on reform; *Aberdeen hoped Gladstone would lead the Commons; cp. Conacher, 307–8.

[4] Instead of 'called'.

[5] The duchess and Mrs. Gladstone had dined there.

[6] *H* cxxxii. 878.

[7] Alexander Colquhoun-Stirling-Murray-Dunlop, 1798–1870, liberal M.P. Greenock 1852–68; legal advisor to the free church party in the 1843 disruption.

[8] Cp. 4 July 45n.

[9] The start of preparations for the further budget of 8 May 1854; these included the issue of bonds on 21 April 1854 which Gladstone disingenuously claimed were not a loan; cp. *H* cxxxii. 1462–3.

14. Good Friday.

Westmr. Abbey 10 A.M. and Titchfield St 5 P.M. I was disappointed at finding no Communion in the Abbey: but perhaps it was better: for to-morrow I hope to have worked my way through much of my arrears, & then to be less pressed by this tumult of business wh follows & whirls me day & night, so that I cannot attain to recollection much less compunction. O venga il giorno.[1] Wrote to Lord J. Russell—Mr Anderson—Sir Jas Stephen—Rev. O. Gordon—Mast. of Pembroke—E. of Aberdeen—Dep. Gov. Bank—Mr Wilson—Sir W. Heathcote—Sir W. Molesworth, & minutes. Read Vie de Rancè. Worked down my mass of papers in arrear somewhat. visibly at length. Worked on Oxford Bill. MS. of 44 aloud to servants at night.

15. Sat. Easter Even.

Westmr. Abbey 10 A.M. and Titchfield St 5 P.M. Wrote to Lord J. Russell (2)—Mr Bromley[2]—Rev. C. Marriott—Sir J. Young—Rev. J.E.T. Rogers —Mr Panizzi—Mr E. Fellowes—Mr J. Myers—Mr G. Burnett—Mr J. Wood—Mr Williams MP.—J.N.G.—R. Phillimore (cancelled)—Sol. General—Ld Panmure—Rob. Gladstone—T.G.—and minutes. Saw Hollands[3] —Allen—Mr Anderson. Dined with Dow[age]r Ly Wharncliffe[4]—Worked on Oxford Bill. Finished Disraeli's Bentinck: a remarkable & interesting work. Read Grellier.[5]

16. Easter Day.

Chapel Royal & H.C. 12–3. St Andrews W[ells] St Evg: where I thought I saw poor Lady L[incoln] from far. MS. on I Cor XV aloud at night. Saw Panizzi—Wrote to Rev Dr Burgess[6]—Rev Mr Lowe—Rev E. Austin—Rev Mr Trevitt.[7] Read Vie de Rancé—Life of Chicheley[8]—Newman on Acad. Education.[9]

17. M.

Wrote to Lord Ellenborough—T.B. Macaulay—J.T. Delane—Rev. C. Marriott—Sir J. Young—Sir C. Trevelyan (2)—Ld Aberdeen—Sir W. Heathcote—Sol. General—Mast. of Pembroke—S.R. Glynne—Hon T.

[1] 'O may the day come'.

[2] (Sir) Richard Madox Bromley, 1813–65; secretary to commissioners for auditing public accounts 1848–Feb. 54; accountant general of the navy, 1854–63; commissioner Greenwich hospital from 1863; K.C.B. 1858.

[3] Perhaps William Simons Hollands, City architect.

[4] Lady Elizabeth Caroline Mary, da. of 1st Earl Erne, m. 1799 J. A. Stuart-Wortley-*Mackenzie, 1st Baron Wharncliffe; she d. 1856.

[5] J. J. Grellier, *The history of the national debt, from 1688 to the beginning of 1800* (1810).

[6] Henry *Burgess, 1808–86, nonconformist; anglican priest 1850; Ph.D. Gottingen 1852; incumbent of Clifton Reynes 1854–61, then vicar of Whittlesea; essayist.

[7] James Trevitt, b.? 1813; St. Alban's Hall, Oxford; perpetual curate of St. Philip's, Bethnal Green, 1852.

[8] O. L. Spencer, *Life of Henry *Chichelé, archbishop of Canterbury* (1783).

[9] Cp. 9 Apr. 52.

Mostyn[1]—C.G.—Dep. Gov. Bank (2)—Mr Greenwood, minutes and a long draft to Dep. Govr. Bank which kept me till hard on 4 A.M. with work on Acts &c.[2] Worked much on Oxford Bill. Saw Mr Anderson. Visited B. Museum & Woodburn's Gallery[3] (for public purposes)—managed a few cards & small *jobs* (fac cende).[4] Dined with the J.N.G's.

18. T.

Westmr. Abby 10 A.M. Wrote to Ld Clarendon—Ld J. Thynne—Rev Mr Stafford[5]—Ld Holland—Rev J.W. West[6]—C.G.—Supt. O[xford] W[orcester] W[olverhampton] Rr.—Mr Wilson—Ld J. Russell—Robn. G.—& minutes. Saw J.N.G.—Mr Anderson—Mr Greenwood—Dep. Gov. of Bank. Fired off my letter to the Bank with Greenwood's full approval. A festival of Justice: I wrote 18 cheques. Read Parl. Deb. & Pol. Ec. with a view to financial plan—also Coriolanus. Sought 3 but found none [R].

19. Wed.

Wrote to Mr W.R. Greg—Ld Clarendon (2)—Mrs Hagart—Sir C. Trevelyan —Ld Aberdeen—Rev. Mr Butler—A. Kinnaird—Mr Dunlop MP.—[7] G. Glyn MP—Sir A. Spearman—& minutes. Saw Mr Thornton—Mr Anderson—Trevelyan—Molesworth—Lord Granville. Came off at 4 & examined Cardwell's Synodalia[8] &c. on my way. Reached Hagley by Euston Express at ten. Read Quelque[s] Mots sur L'Orient[9]—Politique Anglo-Française. Lady Glynne stationary in health: more & more relieved in mental activity. C. well.

20. Th.

Wrote to Rev Mr Liddell—Rev H.E. Lowe[10]—Rev H. Hayman—S.R.G. —Mr T. Mostyn (with[11] copy)—& minutes. Read Quelque Mots—Ball. & Merton Statutes[12]—Further Papers resp. Civil Service. Up Clent Hill with C. & Harry.

[1] Thomas Edward Lloyd-Mostyn, 1830–61, eldest s. of 2nd Baron Mostyn; liberal M.P. Flintshire from May 1854.

[2] Challenging the legality of the bank's actions; cp. Add MS 44380, f. 7 and 6 Apr. 54n.

[3] Cp. 22 June 53.

[4] Obscure; perhaps *facienda*, things to be done.

[5] James Charles Stafford, 1794?–1873; fellow of Magdalen, Oxford, 1832–42; vicar of Dinton, Wiltshire, from 1841; cp. Add MS 44380, f. 21.

[6] A nonconformist; probably on the test clause of the Oxford Bill.

[7] The rest of the sentence is in pencil.

[8] Cp. 6 Aug. 42.

[9] Probably 'Quelques mots sur la lettre du czar (of January 1854) . . . et de la question d'orient au point de vue de sa popularité en France' (1854). Or see 28 Sept. 53.

[10] Draft in Add MS 44380, f. 35.

[11] Instead of 'and'.

[12] In *Statutes of the colleges of Oxford* (1853).

21. Fr.

Wrote to Mr Pennington[1]—Solr. of Customs—Mr Jas Wilson—Rev. J. Barmby[2]—Ld J. Thynne—Sir T.G.—and minutes. Saw Ld Ward & Mr Melvill on Oxford matters. A long, unsatisfactory, & app[aren]tly useless conversation with "Billy"[3] on the Athanasian Creed & what it involves. Read Anderson on Ex[cheque]r Memm.[4]—New College Statutes[5]—Scarron's Roman Comique[6]—& pamphlets.

22. Sat.

A day of rain at last: but got out with C. Read New Coll Statutes (finished) —Chadwick on Civil Service[7]—Pusey's Answer to Vaughan.[8]

23. 1 S.Easter.

Ch mg & aft. Out on the hill with C. Wrote to Sir W. Heathcote—Master of Pembroke—Dep. Govr. of Bank—Supt. Worcester Station—& minutes. Read Pusey's Answer (finished)—Bp of Exeters Pastoral Letter[9]—Vie de Rancé—Mansell on Maurice.[10]

24. M. X

Wrote to Sir C. Trevelyan—and minutes. Read All Souls Statutes[11]—Scotts Report on Royal Tombs.[12] On Clent Hill with C.—Off at 5 to town by express: Lord Ward was my Fellow traveller from Worcr. & we had much conversation. Willy met me at Euston & we had tea. Saw Lightfoot afterwards [R].

25 T. St Mark.

Wrote to Scotts—Sir W. Molesworth—Mr G.G. Scott—Rev M. Walcott[13] J. Griffiths—Supt. Worcr. Station—J. Wood—Sir T. Fremantle—G. Smith—Mr Anderson—Dr Jeune—Lord J. Russell—Cocks & Co—and

[1] George James Pennington, auditor of the civil list.

[2] James Barmby, 1822–97; fellow of Magdalen, Oxford, 1846–59; tutor at Durham 1860–75; principal of Hatfield's Hall, Durham, 1859–76; vicar of Pittington, Durham, 1875–94.

[3] i.e. William, Lord Ward.

[4] An MS.

[5] In *Statutes of the colleges of Oxford* (1853).

[6] By P. Scarron (1752).

[7] A paper prepared by E. *Chadwick in collaboration with J. S. *Mill, and sent to *Trevelyan, cp. S. E. Finer, *Sir Edwin *Chadwick* (1952), 481.

[8] E. B. *Pusey, *Collegiate and professional teaching and discipline, in answer to Professor *Vaughan's strictures, chiefly as to the colleges of France and Germany* (1854); cp. 5 Feb. 54.

[9] H. *Phillpotts, 'A pastoral letter to the clergy of his diocese, April 1854' (1854).

[10] H. L. *Mansel, *Man's conception of eternity; an examination of* [F. D.] **Maurice's theory of a fixed state out of time* (1854).

[11] In *Statutes of the colleges.*

[12] By (Sir) G. G. *Scott on tombs in Westminster abbey, of which he was surveyor.

[13] Mackenzie Edward Charles *Walcott, 1821–80; curate of St. Margaret's, Westminster, 1847–50, of St. James's, 1850–3; precentor of Chichester from 1863; ecclesiologist.

minutes. Saw Robn. G—Lord Aberdeen—Mr Hayter—Mr Arbuthnot—R. Phillimore—Dr Jelf—Mr Greenwood. 12–3¼: over Westminster Abbey with Lord J. Thynne and Mr Scott. Dinner party of fifteen. Worked late on Oxford Bill.

26. Wed.

General Fast.[1] Chapel Royal mg & aftn. Wrote to Sir W. Heathcote—Mr T.E. Brown[2]—Rev C. Marriott—Mr Marshall—Sir C. Trevelyan—and minutes. Wrote MS. on the day: & read it to family at night. Read Vie de Rancé.

27. Th.

Wrote to Mr Walker—Mr Greenwood—Dep. Gov. Bank (dft)[3]—Ld J. Russell—Mr Mozley—and minutes. Attended the Drawingroom. Saw Mr Arbuthnot—Mr Greenwood—Mr Price—Mr Anderson—Mr Greswell—Mr Goulburn—H. of C. 4½ 9¼ and 9¾–11¾.[4] Spoke on Oxf. Bill. Saw one not yet fallen & tried but sadly ill to save it [R]. Read Walcott's Wykeham.[5]

28. Fr.

Wrote to Sir C. Trevelyan—F. Lawley—Prince Albert—Ld Ward—Rev B. Jowett—Rev. J. Griffiths[6]—J. Griffiths—Rev Mr Rawlinson—Sir F.H. Doyle—Rev Dr Jelf—Lord Londonderry—Mr Rowl[and] Hill—Rev Mr Walcott—Mr Delapryme[7]—Mr Marriott—Mr Meyrick—Mr J.M. Knott. Saw Govr. of Bank—Dr Jeune—Granville—Clarendon—Mr Hankey—Mr A. Gordon—B[oard of] I[nland] R[evenue] Conclave 2–3. Cabinet 3–5. Dined at Mrs Talbot's. H. of C. 5–6½.[8] Saw one with little profit [R].

29. Sat.

Wrote to Mr Kennedy[9]—Mr Marriott—Mr Anderson—Mast. Pembroke—Mr T. E. Brown—Bp of Ripon—Sir J. Potter[10]—and minutes. Saw Mr Longden—Mr Glyn—Lord Canning—Mr Anderson—Mr Arbuthnot—J.N.G.—Lefevre. The Prince at B[uckingham] P[alace] 12–1 Cabinet 2¾–

[1] Proclaimed by the government; for the several fasts during the war, see O. Anderson, *A liberal state at war* (1967), 180–1.

[2] Thomas Edward *Brown, 1830–97; fellow of Oriel, Oxford, 1854–8; schoolmaster 1858–93; Manx dialect poet; cp. Add MS 44380, f. 88.

[3] Add MS 44380, f. 120.

[4] Oxford Bill in cttee: *H* cxxxii. 921.

[5] M. E. C. *Walcott, *William of Wykeham and his colleges* (1852).

[6] John *Griffiths, 1806–85; fellow of Wadham, Oxford, 1830–54, warden 1871–81; protested against *Tract XC*, 1841; keeper of the Oxford archives 1857; classicist.

[7] Charles Delapryme, 1815–99; barrister 1845; radical politician, though never an M.P.

[8] The war: *H* cxxxii. 998.

[9] To dismiss him for inefficiency and injustice; copy in Add MS 44529, f. 88. Cp. Magnus, 116 and 21 June 54 & 6 June 53.

[10] Sir John Potter, 1815–58; Manchester draper; mayor there 1848–51; kt. 1851; liberal M.P. Manchester from 1857.

$5\frac{1}{4}$. Academy $2–2\frac{3}{4}$ and $5\frac{3}{4}–10$ for the pictures & the dinner, at wh I had to speak.[1] Mrs Greene's afterwards. Bed 2 A.M.

30. 2 S.Easter.

Whitehall Chapel mg. St Andrew's Wells St Evg. MS. of 44 aloud at night. Wrote to F. Lawley—Lord John Thynne—W. Monsell MP.—Mr W. Smythe of Methven.[2] Saw Ld Granville—Sir W. James. Looked into the singular history of Balaam.[3] Read Sewell's Sermons[4]—Vie de Rancé.

Monday May One 1854. St. Philip & St. James

Wrote to Earl of Aberdeen—The Speaker—Rev Mr Hooper[5]—Mr Wilson—Miss H.J. Gladstone—Mr H. Raikes—Rev. R. Owen—Mr Jas Caird[6]—Mr Rawlinson—Dr Jeune—Dr Hessey—and minutes. Saw Ld J. Russell—Mr Arbuthnot—Sir A. Spearman. H of C. $5–12\frac{3}{4}$ working Oxford Bill.[7] C. & the children went to the Queens Ball wh I reluctantly missed. Read 'Bank in 1847'.[8]

2. T.

Wrote to Sir J. Young—Dr Briscoe—Rev. T. Buckley—Mr Greswell—Mr Wilson—Mr T.M. Gibson—& minutes. Saw B.I.R. Conclave—Sir A. Spearman—Do with Gov. & Dep. Gov. Bank—Do with *Di* and Mr Anderson—Col. Freestun M.P.[9]—Ct Walewski—Sir James Graham—Ld Palmerston—Ld Lansdowne. Rode in aftn. Opened my tenders for E. Bonds—a failure. I shall have rough weather: but this tries what a man is made of. I am sure a little trial is needed: & probably a little is as much as I am good for.[10] Mad. Walewski's in evg. Worked[11] on Finance.

3. Wed.

Wrote to Ld J. Thynne—Mr J.D. Cook—The Speaker—Mr J. Wilson—Mr Brock—Messrs. Overend—Granville—and minutes. Saw Mr Wilson—Mr Wood—Govr. of Bank—Sir A. Spearman. Cabinet $3\frac{3}{4}–4\frac{1}{2}$. The new taxes

[1] Supporting the use of public money for the arts: *The Times*, 1 May 1854, 12d.
[2] William Smythe of Methven, 1803–92; Perthshire landowner and railway director; convenor of the county.
[3] Probably E. W. Hengstenberg, *Dissertations on the genuineness of Daniel . . . and a dissertation on the history and prophecies of Balaam* (1848).
[4] W. *Sewell, *A year's sermons to boys*, 1st v. (1854).
[5] Francis John Bodfield Hooper, 1809?–88; rector of Upton Warren, Bromsgrove, from 1836; wrote on free trade, and Jews; cp. Add MS 44380, ff. 38, 161.
[6] (Sir) James Caird, 1816–92; Peelite M.P. Dartmouth 1857–9, Stirling burghs 1858–1865; economist and agriculturalist; K.C.B. 1882.
[7] In cttee., on the commissioner's names: *H* cxxxii. 1115.
[8] Untraced.
[9] (Sir) William Lockyer Freestun, 1804–62; fought as colonel in British legion for Carlists in Spain 1835–7, in Syria in regular army 1840–2; liberal M.P. Weymouth 1847–1859; kt. 1860.
[10] Cp. O. Anderson, 'Loans versus taxes: British financial policy in the Crimean war', *Economic History Review*, xvi. 315–16.
[11] 'pretty late, worked' here deleted.

proposed by me accepted—even with an addition.[1] Cabinet Dinner at S. Herbert's—C's evening party afterwards. Conv. with Tricoupi[2] & de Cetto[3]—also with R[oundell] Palmer—& with Sir C. Eastlake—& with J. Ball.

4. Th.

Wrote to Mr Hayter—Sir A. Spearman—Williams & Co (Chester)—Mrs T. Goalen—Rev Mr Haddan—Ld Panmure—Ld Palmerston[4]—Rev R. Owen—and minutes. H. of C. $4\frac{1}{2}$–$6\frac{1}{2}$; and $8\frac{1}{2}$–$12\frac{1}{2}$ on Oxford Bill.[5] Saw Sir W. Heathcote—G.G. Scott—Mr Uwins—Mr Hayter—Mr Anderson—Sir A. Spearman—Ld Aberdeen—Mr Horsman: with whom I had a late & curious conv. Read Emerton[6]—Bank in 47.

5. Fr.

Wrote to Ld Lansdowne—Mr Wilson—Ld Aberdeen (2)—Mr Glyn MP—Ld Granville—Sir Jas Hogg—Mr Arbuthnot—Sir J. Wood—Govr. of Bank—Ld Ward—J. Griffiths—H. Tufnell—Dr Jacobson—Judge Coleridge—Govr. of Bank—and minutes. H. of C. $4\frac{1}{2}$–$5\frac{1}{2}$ and $11\frac{1}{4}$–$12\frac{1}{4}$.[7] Saw Govr. of Bank—Sir A. Spearman—Mr Anderson—Mr Arbuthnot—[blank—] Merchant Taylor's Deputn.—Mr Glyn—Mr Denison. Worked on Financial papers—read C. Wood's Sp. of Ap. 47.[8] & kindred papers.

6. Sat.

Wrote to Govr. of Bank—Mr Greenwood—Ld Granville—Mr Fitzgerald—Ld Lyttelton—Bn. Alderson, & minutes. Cabinet 3–$6\frac{3}{4}$. It was determined that I should go through the whole case on Monday. Saw Sir A. Spearman—Mr Anderson—BIR Conclave on Resolutions. Rode. Dined at home—& worked till after 3 A.M. on Finance Hist. & figures.

7. 3 S.E[aster].

Whitehall & H.C. 11 AM. Chapel Royal aft. Saw JNG—R. Cavendish—Cardwell. Read Vie de Rancé. MS of 40 aloud at night. Worked much on Finance figures.

[1] The preparation for the supplementary budget of 8 May; cp. 6 May 54.
[2] Spiridion Tricoupi, 1791–1873; historian; Greek ambassador to Britain 1838, 1842–3, 1852–67.
[3] Baron de Cetto, 1795?–1879; Bavarian minister in London until 1872; in correspondence about Helen Gladstone.
[4] In Guedalla, *P*, 97.
[5] Defended the quality of Oxford tutors: *H* cxxxii. 1267.
[6] J. A. Emerton, *A letter to . . . *Russell on university reform* (1854).
[7] Supplemental naval estimates: *H* cxxxii. 1311.
[8] *Wood's speech, as chancellor, on deficiency bills, discussed by Gladstone in his speech on 8 May; cp. *H* xcii. 528, cxxxii. 1434.

8. M.

Wrote to The Speaker and minutes. Drove with C. in aftn. Saw Mr Anderson—Sir A. Spearman—Mr. B.B. Williams[1]—Mr Wilson. Finished the arrangement of my papers & figures—no small affair. H. of C. 4½–10¾. Statement 3½ hours. Every appearance favourable to our plan. Never had I more cause to feel the unutterable mercy of God, the strength of His sustaining arm, & the power of the vision of the great High Priest in Heaven ever offering Himself for us.[2] After H. went to Queen's Concert for the 2d Act:[3] & walked afterwards.

9. Tues.

Wrote to Govr. of Bank (2)—Mr Jos. Sandars—Ld J. Russell—Stephy—Mrs Uwins[4]—Ld Aberdeen—E. Cardwell—Sir Jas Hogg—& minutes. Saw Sir W. Farquhar—Sir A. Spearman—Mr Wilson—Mr Wood. H. of C. 4½–6½. Mr Disraeli made an astonishing error resp. the Malt Tax & gave us 1. a majority of 81, 2. the prestige of a substantive decision, 3. the advantage of an opponent's act of bad faith, at one & the same blow.[5] Bp of Oxford's breakfast. We discussed the Church Rate question with Macaulay: & afterwards the affair of Archdeacon Denison.[6] Saw pictures at Christie's. Dined at Ld Duncan's. Duchess of Sutherland's afterwards. Some progress with papers.

On most occasions of very sharp pressure or trial, some word of Scripture has come home to me as if borne on angel's wings: many could I recollect: the Psalms are the great storehouse: perhaps I shd. put some down now for the continuance of memory is not to be trusted.

1. In the winter of 37, Ps. 128. This came in a most singular manner but it wd. be a long story to tell.[7]
2. In the Oxford contest of 47 (wh was very harrowing) the verse 'O Lord God, Thou strength of my health: Thou hast covered my head in the day of battle'.[8]
3. In the Gorham contest, after the judgment: 'And though all this be come upon us, yet do we not forget thee; nor behave ourselves frowardly in thy covenant. Our heart is not turned back: neither our steps gone out of thy way. No not when thou hast smitten us into the place of dragons: & covered us with the shadow of death.[9]

[1] Benjamin Bacon Williams, 1796?–1870; stockbroker; had written on bonds; Hawn P.
[2] The supplementary budget increased the malt, sugar, and spirit duties, and income tax to 14d. Bond issues were also explained: *H* cxxxii. 1413; cp. 16 Aug. 54.
[3] Songs by Schubert and Donizetti.
[4] Sarah, m. 1851 Thomas *Uwins; wrote *Memoir* of him (1858).
[5] A procedural dispute in which *Russell was able to present several precedents for immediate raising of the malt tax, with discussion on it deferred: *H* cxxxiii. 46.
[6] He had resigned as examining chaplain to the bp. of Bath and Wells after a quarrel over the eucharist; sentence of deprivation was passed 1856, reversed 1857.
[7] See 8 Jan. 38.
[8] Ps. cxl. 7.
[9] Ps. xliv. 18–20.

On Monday 17 April 53 it was: 'O turn thee then unto me, & have mercy upon me: give thy strength unto thy servant, and help the son of thine handmaid'.[1]

Yes, the son of Thine handmaid.

Last Sunday it was not from the Ps. for the day: 'Thou shalt prepare a Table before me against them that trouble me: thou hast anointed my head with oil, & my cup shall be full'.[2]

The blessed, blessed Psalms! And yet I have alas! 'behaved myself frowardly in Thy covenant'!

10. Wed.

Wrote to Ben. Consolo[3]—Robn. G (3)[4]—Duke of Argyll—W.B. Gordon[5] Sir A. Spearman—W Brown MP.—E. Horsman MP.—Dr Jeune—Mr B B Williams—and minutes. Saw Mr Arbuthnot—Sir A. Spearman—Rode in aftn. Large dinner party: & evg party afterwards. The Bp of New Zealand came early & I got him to my dressingroom that I might not meet him among strangers. Everyone seemed delighted with him. Went early to Exhibn. & remained until ten.[6]

11. Th.

Wrote to Mr Beamish—Mast[er of] Pembroke—Sir F. Smith[7]—Sir J. Young—Scotts—and minutes. Rode in evg. 11 to breakfast: a very interesting party: & conv. afterwards on Dante with Lacaita. Saw Col. Freestun—Lord Aberdeen—Mr Wilson. H of C. $4\frac{1}{2}$–$5\frac{3}{4}$ and $6\frac{1}{2}$–$12\frac{1}{2}$ on Oxford Univ. Bill in Committee.[8] Worked on arranging papers—& arrear of corresp. now heavy. Read Sir F. Smith's Marmont.[9]

12. Fr.

Wrote to Mr Anderson—Mr Kinnaird—Archdn. Horn[10]—Mr Marriott—Govr. of Bank—Sir A. Spearman, & minutes. Rode in aftn. H. of C. $4\frac{1}{2}$–$5\frac{3}{4}$ and $10\frac{3}{4}$–2. Beaten on Scots Edn. Bill: 193:184.[11] Saw Mr Anderson—Mr Wood—Sir A. Spearman—Sir C. Trevelyan—Sir J. Graham—A. Kinnaird —Mr Cowan MP—Mr Crawfurd MP.[12] Read Sir F. Smith—Bank Debate of 1816.[13]

[1] Ps. lxxxvi. 16. [2] Ps. xxiii. 5.

[3] An Italian living in Brussels, had written on Naples. [4] Altered from '(2)'.

[5] Of the Union Bank, Workington; had written on stamps; cp. Add MS 44529, ff. 96, 103.

[6] Probably the royal academy exhibition, then open.

[7] i.e. Sir J.M.F. *Smith. [8] *H* cxxxiii. 178. [9] Cp. 4 July 53.

[10] Thomas Horn, 1800–74; archdeacon of Buckinghamshire 1845; rector of St. Thomas's, Haverfordwest, 1851–66.

[11] The deb. was adjourned for six months; a temporary measure was later passed: *H* cxxxiii. 232 and Conacher, 351.

[12] Edward Henry John Craufurd, 1816–87; edited *Legal Examiner* 1852; barrister 1854; liberal M.P. Ayr district 1852–74.

[13] On secrecy and political partiality of directors: *Parliamentary Debates*, xxxiii. 264 (14 March 1816).

13. Sat.

Wrote to Sir W. James—Rev G. Rawlinson—J. Graham—Mast. Pembroke—Rev. H. Tripp—Bp St Asaph—Sir T. Fremantle—and minutes. Rode in evg. Cabinet 3¾–6¾. Dined with the Wortleys. Saw A. Gordon—Sir A. Spearman—T.G. A bad account of Lady G[lynne] led C. in the morning to decide on going: & subsequently came a telegraphic summons. In evg saw one aet. 17 un sol fallo:[1] with hope [R].

14. 4 S.E[aster].

Lambeth Consecration of Bp of Sarum & H.C. This was indeed a great occasion. St A. Wells St in evg. MS on Gospel aloud. Wrote to Duke of Buccleuch—Mr Smyth of Methven—Ld Palmerston—A. Gordon. Saw Duke of Buccleuch—R. Cavendish—Rev. Mr Liddell—W. Lyttelton. Read Vie de Rancé—many Sermm. & tracts.

15. M.

Wrote to Ld Granville—C.G.—Ld J. Russell (2)—H. Tayleur—E. Cardwell—Ld E. Bruce—Robn. G. (2)—T.G.—Sir A. Spearman—and minutes. Saw Ld J. Russell—Sir C. Wood—Mr Wilson—J.N.G.—S. Herbert. Read Whewell[2]—Ex Fellow of Jesus[3]—Report of 1807[4]—Parl. Bank Debates. Received the news of Lady Glynne's release on Saturday. Her death is the emerging from a cloud not the entering into one. Worked on her accts. that I may close my stewardship in this department.

16. T.

Wrote to Dss of Sutherland—Cocks & Co—Rev. J. Rigaud[5]—H.J.G.—Lord J. Russell—Robn. G.—Solr General—Ld Aberdeen—Hon A. Gordon[6]—and min.[7] Saw Mr Wilson—Mr Anderson—Mr A. Gladstone—Sir A. Spearman. Off by Express 5.15 PM: reached Hagley at 10. Found all as I might have hoped. Read Dean of Hereford's Manual[8]—Brookbanks MS.[9]—Parl Debates of 94, 97 &c.

17. Wed.

Wrote to Sir J. Graham—Lord Aberdeen—F. Lawley—Duke of Buccleuch—Jas Wilson—Mr Anderson—R. Barker—and minutes. Walk on the hill

[1] 'one aged 17 who has only fallen once'.

[2] W. *Whewell, *Of the plurality of worlds. An essay* (1853).

[3] 'Thoughts on the proposed reform at Oxford as far as it affects Jesus College . . . by an Ex-Fellow' (1854); on the problems of Jesus and Wales.

[4] Second report of select cttee. on public expenditure of the Kingdom: *PP* 1807 ii. 379; on the bank—the prelude to the 1808 arrangement.

[5] John Rigaud, 1823?–88; fellow of Magdalen, Oxford, from 1849, dean 1850, bursar 1852, librarian 1874.

[6] Recommending C. T. *Baring for a see; fragment in Conacher, 373n.

[7] These two words in pencil.

[8] Presumably an MS of R. Dawes, 'Manual of educational requirements necessary for the civil service' (1856); with a preface and appendix.

[9] A legal opinion, perhaps on the bank row; cp. 21 Apr. 53.

with the family. We conversed partially on the arrangements of property &c. & with resp. to S.s affairs & his having made no will. Read Sir A. Stephen on NSW 2d Chamber [1]—Decimal Coinage [2]—Smith's Marmont—Phen[omena] of Industrial Life.[3]

18. Th.

Wrote to Lord Aberdeen—Mr Arbuthnot—Mr Anderson—Mr Panizzi—Mr Pressly—Sir A. Spearman—H. Tayleur. Walk on the hill. We pursued some of our conversations on family arrangements. Read Brooksbank's MSS—Sir F. Smith's Marmont—Ld L.s conversations with Napoleon.[4] We saw the coffin today.

19. Fr.

Wrote to Ld Ellesmere—Sir C. Wood—Mr J. Griffiths—Mr Geo. Bennett—Mr W. Brown—[blank—] & minutes. We went off at 11—& reached Hawarden at 6. I walked to St[ation] & from C[hester]. Wenlock, Ralph & Fred Neville came. Read Swift's Examiner—Perceval's Corresp. with the Bank.[5]

20. Sat.

Holy Commn. 8½ A.M. At 9¾ we left the Castle for the Funeral.

Wrote to Lord J. Russell—G. Burnett—Ld Granville—Miss Brown—Mr Burnaby—Mr Rawson—H. Tayleur—Robn. G.—Sir J. Graham—Solr. General—& minutes.

The funeral arrangements were simple & good. C. & M. with Lady L. fell in near the ch[urch]yard gate. We walked in procession from within the Park Gates. Some people were collected: but it was known that privacy was desired. It was a great contrast to think of between her long 20 years of wearing sorrow, and the time when she was the pride and flower of this sweet spot. May her spirit rest in Christ & joyfully wait His final coming.

Read Oliphant [6]—Swift's Examr. We dined at the Rectory.

21. 5 S.E.

Parish Church at 11 A.M. and 6½ PM. Wrote to Rev. J.O. Powell—Stephy—Rev. J.L. Ross—Archdn. Thorp—& minutes. Read Whewell's Plurality of Worlds.[7] Walk with C. We dined at the Rectory & soon after 9 I left for London. Reached D[owning] St. 4.50 A.M.

[1] Sc. Sir J.; cp. 17 May 53.

[2] Cp. 6 Jan. 54, or one of many current pamphlets on this.

[3] Anonymous (1854).

[4] W. H., 3rd Baron Lyttelton, 'Some account of Napoleon Bonaparte's coming on board the Northumberland . . . with notes of two conversations' (privately printed 1836).

[5] During the 1809–10 bullion controversy, which included the problem of war loan finance; cp. D. Gray, *Spencer *Perceval* (1963) 357–87.

[6] L. *Oliphant, *The Russian shores of the Black Sea in the autumn of 1852* (1853, expanded ed. 1854).

[7] Cp. 15 May 54.

22. M.

Wrote to Mr Moffatt—Ld J. Russell—Mr Labouchere—C.G.—& minutes. Saw Col. Maberly—Ld Granville—Sir A. Spearman—Mr Wilson—Mr Anderson—Govr. of the Bank—Sir J. Graham. Read Whewell's Book. H. of C. 4½–8¼ and 9–2. Spoke 1¼ hour in ans. to Baring (he was very effective) & Disraeli. Vote 290:186.[1] Went[2] to see Ld Braybrooke—& Lady Wenlock.

23. T.

Wrote to Mr Monsell—C.G.—Master of Pembroke—& minutes. Saw Ld Aberdeen—Ld Spencer—Hon & Rev. Geo. Spencer—Mr Anderson—Mr Wilson—Mr Pressly—Bp Oxford—Sol. General—Atty General—Adam Gladstone—Ld J. Russell—Sir C. Wood. Wrote Mem. on Swedish Subsidy.[3] H of C. 4¾–6½ and 9¾–10½.[4] Saw one afterwards: little or no good [R]. Read N[ew] S[outh] W[ales] Constn. Report & debate.[5] Rode in evg.

24. Wed.

Wrote to Dr Whitley[6]—Mr M. Prentice[7]—Solr. General—Dss of Sutherland—Rev J.L. Ross—Mr Horsfall MP—Mr E. Arnaud[8]—Ld Kinnaird—C.G.—and minutes. Saw Govr. of Bank—Mr Wilson—Mr Anderson—Sir A. Spearman—Sir C. Wood—Mr Dwight. Visited Aunt J. in evg. Cabinet 3–7. Rode a little in evg. Read N.S.W. Constn. Debate.

25. Th. Ascension Day.

Wrote to Mr B. B. Williams—Mr Busby[9]—& minutes. Saw Sugar Refiners Dep. 2–3. Sugar Importers 3–3¾.[10] Mr Anderson & Sir C. Trevelyan—Mr J. Wood & Mr Dobson—Mr Wilson—Ld J. Russell[11]—Solr. General. Whitehall Chapel & H.C. 11–1½. Dined at Stafford House. H. of C. 4½–7½ Spoke 1 h. & voted in 247:251 on Ld J.R.s Oaths Bill: wh Bill was from the first a great mistake of his & his only.[12]

[1] *Baring attacked the low interest policy of the govt., exposed the extent of exchequer borrowing, and moved an amndt. against further issue of short term exchequer bonds: *H* cxxxiii. 692.
[2] Instead of '23. T.'
[3] He was ready to hire Swedish mercenaries, but opposed a subsidy; cp. Anderson, *A liberal state at war*, 217.
[4] Church Rates Bill: *H* cxxxiii. 805.
[5] In 'Further papers relative to the alterations in the constitutions of the Australian Colonies': *PP* 1854 xliv. 1–74.
[6] Perhaps John Whitley, d. 1855; D.D.; chancellor of Killaloe from 1837.
[7] Reply on increased duties to Manning Prentice, Stowmarket brewer; cp. Add MS 44529, f. 99.
[8] Probably Elias Arnaud, d. 1860; collector of customs in Liverpool 1825–55.
[9] Perhaps Michael Horton Busby of City Road, London, furniture manufacturer.
[10] Both large deputations, the latter with twenty-two M.P.s: *The Times*, 26 May 1854, 7e.
[11] '(Oxf' here deleted.
[12] Bill for a new oath of allegiance: *H* cxxxiii. 885.

26. Fr.

Wrote to Ld J. Russell—and minutes. Rode in forenoon. C.G. returned evg. H. of C. $4\frac{1}{2}$–$8\frac{1}{2}$ and 9–$12\frac{3}{4}$: working Revenue Bills & Oxf. Bill.[1] Worked on amending Oxf. Bill. Saw The Solr. General (Oxf. B)—Lord Spencer—Mr Wilson with Sir T. Fremantle—Mr Romilly[2] with Sir C.T.—Sir A. Spearman—Sir W. Heathcote—Mr C. Trevor—E. Cardwell.

27. Sat.

Wrote to R. Phillimore—Attorney General—Mr Greenwood—Mr Rawlinson—The Speaker—Sir A. Spearman—Miss Doyle—Mr E. Eyre—& minutes. Cabinet $4\frac{3}{4}$–$7\frac{3}{4}$. Saw Mr Robarts (Proctor, at Doctor's Commons[3]—Mr Greenwood. Stafford House 3–$4\frac{3}{4}$ to hear the Cologne singers.[4] It was a great treat. Evg. at home. Read N.S.W. Constitn. Debate.

28. S.aft. Asc.

Whitehall mg—St James's Evg. MS of 42 aloud at night. Wrote to D. of Buccleuch—Mr W. Smythe—Mrs Talbot—Rev Mr Wray—Bp of Ripon—Dr Jelf. Saw Dean Ramsay—Duke of Buccleuch—Sir W. & Lady James. Read Vie de Rancé.

29. M.

Wrote to Mr Anderson—Mr Jowett—Sir T. Fremantle—Mrs Goalen—Mr Woodgate—Mr Cairns—Ld Ellesmere—J.G. Hubbard—H. Tayleur—Rev. R.W. Browne[5]—Ld Elcho—and minutes. H. of C. $4\frac{1}{2}$–$9\frac{1}{2}$ and 10–1. I tried to gather up some ends of the debate on the position of Min[iste]rs.[6] Saw Solicitor General—Mr Wilson—Mr Hayter—Mr Wood *cum* Mr Timm—Sir A. Spearman—Ld Spencer—Mr Hankey—Wilson Patten—Mr Hadfield MP. Read Senior's Journal.[7]

30. T.

Wrote to Sir J. Shelley[8]—Lord Ward—Ld Palmerston—Robn. G.—B.B. Williams—Pr. Albert—T.B. Horsfall MP—and minutes. Dined at Lady Wenlock's, Lord Lansdowne's afterwards. Saw Mr Griffiths *cum* Mr Burnett—R. Phillimore *cum* Mr Robarts—Mr Arbuthnot—Mr Shiffner[9]—Bp

[1] *H* cxxxiii. 1031.

[2] Edward Romilly, 1804–70; br. of John*; commissioner for auditing public accounts 1836; chairman of the audit board 1854–65; sheriff of Glamorgan 1869.

[3] Either Frederick or Nathaniel Robarts, both proctors and notaries in doctors'-commons.

[4] On a tour of England.

[5] Robert William Browne, 1809–95; priest 1834; professor of classical literature, King's college, London, 1835–63; prebendary of St. Paul's cathedral 1845–60, of Wells 1858–63, canon there from 1863.

[6] During the deb. on Bribery Prevention Bills: *H* cxxxiii. 1110.

[7] Cp. 12 June 52.

[8] Sir John Villiers Shelley 1808–67; 7th bart. 1852; liberal M.P. Westminster 1852–65.

[9] Probably (Sir) George Shiffner, 1791–1863; rector of St. Peter Westout, Lewes, 1818–48, vicar of Amport, Andover, from 1848; 3rd bart. 1859.

of Ripon—Ld Aberdeen—Ld Elcho—Ld John Russell—Solr. General—Mr Gregson[1] & Mr Crawfurd. Rode. Read Senior's Journal.

31. Wed. X

Wrote to Mr Goulburn—Sir A. Spearman—Mr Wilson—Mr Rawson—Mr Hubbard—Bp of N. Zealand—& minutes. Rode. Saw Archdeacon Harrison—Rev Mr Buckeridge[2]—Mr Arbuthnot—C. Wood—Ld Granville—Ld Lansdowne—Cabinet Dinner at Newcastle's. Read Molesworth on Orange River Sov[ereign]ty.[3]

Thurs. June One 1854.

Wrote to Sec. State Home Dep—Cocks & Co—Ed. Edinb. Advertiser—Mrs Goalen—Mr MacMahon MP[4]—Mr W. Forbes—Sir J. Graham—and minutes. Rode ½ hour. Saw Govr. of the Bank—Sir W. Heathcote—Sir C. Wood—C. Marriott—Mr Anderson—Mr Pressly *cum* Mr Timm—Sir A. Spearman—Ld Elcho—Duke of Newcastle—Ld Aberdeen—Gibson. Six to breakfast. H. of C. 5¾–8 and 8½–1½: on Oxf. Bill. We carried the new Halls by a majority of 205:113 which I hope will make them secure in the Lords.[5] Read Lords' Protests.

2. Fr.

Wrote to Mr Spottiswoode—Mr Phinn MP—Wm. Gladstone—Mr G. Smith—Solr. General—Ld Ripon—Mast. of Pembroke—H. Tayleur—Mast. of Balliol—Mrs Herbert[6]—Bp of Tasmania—E[arl] Granville—E[arl of] Clarendon—and minutes. Saw Mr Anderson—Mr Brickwood—Sir W. Heathcote. H. of C. 4½–8½ and 9–11: on Financial Bills.[7] Concert at the Palace afr. Read N.S.W. Debate.

3. Sat.

Willy's birthday: may God's blessing follow him. Wrote to Mr B. Harrison—W. Smythe—Mr W. B. Gordon—Cocks & Co (2)—Bp of St Asaph—G.F. Bowen—Duke of Buccleuch—Ed. Edin Advertr.—Govr of Bank—Judge Coleridge—& minutes. Worked on matters of Lady Glynne's Estate. Cabinet 2¾–4¾. Saw Mr Brickwood—R. Phillimore—Lyttelton—Mr

[1] Samuel Gregson, 1795–1864; liberal M.P. Lancaster 1847–8, 1852–64; chairman of East India and China association.

[2] George Buckeridge, fellow of Worcester, Oxford, master of St. John's hospital, Lichfield.

[3] Sir W. *Molesworth, 'Materials for a speech in defence of the policy of abandoning the Orange River Territory. May, 1854.'

[4] Patrick McMahon, 1813–75; liberal M.P. co. Wexford 1852–65, New Ross 1868–74; junior counsel in Tichborne case 1872–3.

[5] The clause gave some members of convocation the right to open private halls of residence: *H* cxxxiii. 1187.

[6] Cp. 18 June 54.

[7] Spoke on Consolidated Fund Charges Bill: *H* cxxxiii. 1258.

Anderson. Went off to Windsor at 5½. Evening at the Deanery—Read Scott—Moltke's Russian campaigns.[1] Found Willy flourishing & happy.

4. *Whits[unday].*

Breakf. with the Provost. Eton Chapel mg: heard the Bp of NZ.s noble sermon: The Holy Communion followed. St George's aftn. Dined with the Provost. Read Milman[2]—Dowding.[3]

5. *M.*

Clewer Chapel[4] 4¾ PM. Wrote to Townsend & Robarts—Cocks & Co—Scott & Co. Breakfast at Coleridge's. Luncheon with the Provost: met Pistrucci there. Much with the Bishop. Back to London at 5.50: after visiting the House of Mercy at Clewer. Read Moltke—La Russie et ses Accusateurs.[5] Sought for Lightfoot & Osborne but without effect [R].

6. *T.*

Wrote to Judge Coleridge—Mr C. Trevor—Ld J. Russell—Sir C. Eastlake—Robn. G (2)—Mr E. Palmer—Sir W. Heathcote—Mr Anderson—Ld Courtenay—S. Herbert[6]—Sir J.E. Tennent—Mr J. Wood—Ed Blackwood's Mag[7]—Mr Crosfield—Ld Palmerston—Ld Monteagle—Hon A Gordon and minutes. Saw Sir A. Spearman—Ld Overstone—Lord F. Kerr. Worked on Lady G's Estate affairs: & made up Inventory. Visited De Bammeville's collection at Christie's.[8] Saw Osborne: poco di bene [R].[9] Read Moltke—Contes de la Reine de Navarre[10]—Blackwood on Oxf. Bill.[11]

7. *Wed.*

Wrote to D. of Sutherland—Mr Anderson—Ld J. Russell—Mr A. Gordon[12] & minutes. Lacaita's Lecture at Stafford House 3–4¼.[13] Saw Sir C. Eastlake & Co resp. the De Bammeville Pictures—Earl of Aberdeen—S. Herbert—Mr Arbuthnot—Govr. of the Bank—Judge Coleridge—G.C. Lewis—D. of

[1] H. C. B. von Moltke, *The Russians in Bulgaria and Rumelia in 1828 and 1829*, tr. Lady Duff Gordon (1854).

[2] Perhaps H. H. *Milman, *History of Christianity*, 3v. (1840), cp. 26 Feb. 40; not his *History of Latin Christianity*, cp. 27 Aug. 54.

[3] W. C. Dowding, *Religious partizanship, and other papers* (1854).

[4] Attached to the Clewer House of Mercy, by Windsor. See introduction, above, iii.xlv.

[5] L. d'Estramberg, *La Russie et ses accusateurs dans la guerre d'Orient* (1854).

[6] Cp. Conacher, 387.

[7] John *Blackwood, 1818–79; edited his *Edinburgh Magazine* from 1845; his firm, founded 1852, published George *Eliot.

[8] The collection of Italian paintings by E. Joly de Bammeville, sold at Christie's on 12 June; many bought by the national gallery.

[9] 'little good'.

[10] Cp. 31 May 47.

[11] *Blackwood's Edinburgh Magazine*, lxxv. 507 (May 1854).

[12] Cp. Conacher, 406–7.

[13] A lecture on Italian literature to a society audience, cp. C. Lacaita, *An Italian Englishman* (1933) 64.

Argyll—H. Powys. Dined with Govr. of Bank. Rode in aftn. Read Stonor Report.[1]

8. Th.

Wrote to Dean of Carlisle—Canning[2]—and minutes. Council at B. Palace: audience of Prince Albert.[3] Visited the De Bammeville Pictures at Christie's with C. Saw Ld Aberdeen[4]—A. Gordon—Lord J. Russell—Duke of Newcastle—Ld Granville—Mr Thackeray[5]—Ld Canning—Sir A. Spearman—Mr Goldwin Smith[6]—Mr Lacaita—Mr Dyce—Mr Moffatt MP.—Attorney General—Mr Green (Ir:)[7]—Mr Hayter. Saw also Bishop [R]. H. of C. 6½–8½ and 9½–12¾.[8]

9. Fr.

Wrote to Lord Lyndhurst—Mr Moffatt—G[reat] W[estern] Railway—H. Tayleur—Ld Stanley (Ald[erley])—C.A. Wood—Ed. Blackwood—Holland—Ld Aberdeen[9]—Ld Overstone (2)—Sir W. Molesworth—& minutes. Saw Govr. of the Bank—Duke of Newcastle—Lord Aberdeen—Ld Torrington *cum* Mr Wood—Irish Distiller's Deputn.—Horatio Nelson Deputn.[10]—Mr Wilson—Sir J. Graham—R. Phillimore—E. Cardwell—Mr Trevor—J. N. G.—J. Wood—Ld Stanley (Alderley). Levee 1¾–2¾. H. of C. 4½–6½ and 9¾–12½ on Estimates.[11] Read Ruskin on Pre Raphaelism.[12] Dined with the Jameses.

10. Sat.

Wrote to Prince Albert—Ld Aberdeen—Sir C. Trevelyan—Bp of Oxford—Chev. Bunsen—Mr Meyrick—Mr Griffiths—Mr C. Trevor—Col. Harcourt—Ld Ward—Ld J. Russell—Sir J. Young—Mr M'Mahon MP.—and minutes. Saw Sir A. Spearman—Govr. of the Bank—Sir C. Trevelyan—Ld Lansdowne—Christie—Duke of Newcastle—and F. Lawley.[13] 1½–5½ with S. Herbert to the opening of the Crystal Palace.[14] The aerial character of the fabric is marvellous: but the effect too cold to the eye. The music was extremely fine. Dined at Ld Spencer's. Saw Berkeley—not unhopeful [R]. Read Preraphaelism.

[1] *PP* 1854 vii. 681; cp. 6 Apr. 54.
[2] Extract in Conacher, 407–8.
[3] This council established the secretaryship of state for war; cp. *LQV*, 1s, iii. 42–3.
[4] Fragment in Conacher, 408.
[5] Probably the novelist, though no confirmation found.
[6] See 27 July 54n.
[7] Unidentified.
[8] Spoke on misc. estimates: *H* cxxxiii. 1282.
[9] One name here deleted.
[10] The Nelson Memorial Fund requested a civil list pension for *Nelson's da. Horatia; many documents in Add MS 44381.
[11] Spoke on them, including the Kennedy affair: *H* cxxxiii. 1323.
[12] By J. *Ruskin (1851).
[13] The start of the scandal; cp. 10 Jan. 47n. and Magnus, 116.
[14] Opened by *Victoria on its new site at Sydenham.

11. St Barnabas & Trin[ity] S[unday].

Chapel Royal (Dr Hook) mg & St M[ary] Crown St Evg. MS for St Barn. aloud. Saw Sir W. Molesworth—Earl of Aberdeen—R. Cavendish—Lady Wenlock with C. & others resp. F. L[awley]. Read de Rancé[1]—& various Sermons & pamphlets. Also saw one of little hope [R].

12. M.

Wrote to Master E. Litton[2]—G. Christie—Rev. J.O. Powell—Cocks & Co —Sir W.C. James—Dr Twiss—W.S. Blackstone—Solr. General—Rev Mr Wayte—and minutes. Rode. H. of C. 4½–9½ and 10½–1½. A good divn. about Stamps.[3] Saw Mr Wilson—Mr B. Harrison—Mr Craufurd M.P.—Sir W. Molesworth—Governor of the Bank—Sir C. Trevelyan—Mr Timm—Mr C Villiers.

13. T.

Wrote to Bp St Asaph—J. Griffiths—Ld Aberdeen (2)—Ld Granville—Mr Hadfield MP—Mr Uwins—Ld Clarendon—Robn. G.—Willy—and minutes. Rode—mg. H. of C. 4½–8 and 8¾–12½.[4] Read Gregson[5]—Univ. meeting—Moltke. Saw Ld Harrowby (Oxf. Bill)—Governor Higginson—Lord Spencer—Duke of Argyll—Granville—Sir W. Heathcote—Molesworth —Mr Kirk M.P.

14. Wed. X

Wrote to Lord Ward—Mr Slaney[6]—Sir T. Fremantle (2)—Rev A. Barry —Ld Clarendon—Hon A. Gordon—Mr W. Brown MP—Mr Timm (with Memm.)—Mr Hadfield—J. Blackwood[7]—W.D. Seymour MP[8]—T.B. Horsfall MP—and minutes. Rode, aftn. Saw Govr. of Bank—Sir A. Spearman—J.N.G.—Mr Cureton—Ld Ellesmere. Cabinet dinner Sir C. Wood's. Ld Ellesmere's afterwards—to see him about O.C.[9]—Saw Horton afterwards [R].

15. Th.

Wrote to Ld Aberdeen—Mr Kirk MP.—Rev Mr Stoky[10]—Mr Uwins—

[1] Cp. 12 Mar. 54.

[2] Edward Litton, 1787–1870; master in Irish chancery from 1843.

[3] Spoke on Stamp Duties Bill; the govt. majority was 22: *H* cxxxiii. 1362.

[4] The ballot, and church temporalities: *H* cxxxiii. 117.

[5] Perhaps T. G. Gregson, 'Speech . . . on the state of public education in Van Diemen's Land' (1850).

[6] Robert Aglionby *Slaney, 1792–1862; liberal M.P. Shrewsbury 1826–35, 1837–41, 1847–52, 1857–62; chaired commissions on education and health; advocated rural and economic reform.

[7] A row; copy in Add MS 44381, f. 132.

[8] William Digby *Seymour, 1822–95; liberal M.P. Sunderland 1852–4, Southampton 1859–65; recorder of Newcastle from 1854; censured for commercial transactions 1859.

[9] *Ellesmere was first head of the executive commission established by the Oxford Act.

[10] Sc. Edward Stokes.

Govr. of Bank—Mr Anderson—& minutes. H of C. 4½–10¾ & 11¼–1¾ on Oxford Bill &c.[1] Seven to breakfast. Saw Rev. Mr Wayte—Mr Wilson—Sir A. Spearman—R. Phillimore.

16. Fr.

Wrote to Chev. Bunsen—J.L. Ross—Mr G. Smith—J. Wood (2)—Col. Harcourt MP.—Master of Pembroke—and minutes. H. of C. 4½–1¼ working Oxf. Bill—wh got a great blow.[2] Saw Ld Torrington—Ld Aberdeen—Sir A. Spearman—Mr J. Wood. Read div[ers]a.

17. Sat.

Wrote to Miss Conway—J. Myers—Ld R. Grosvenor—and minutes. Cabinet 3–6¾. Rode. Read Senior's MS Journal. Saw Sir T. Fremantle—Earl of Aberdeen—Hon A. Gordon—Mr Phinn. Called for Berkeley—but failed as twice before [R]. 12–2 meeting at D. of Buccleuch's about Trin. College [Glenalmond].

18. 1 S.Trin.

Whitehall mg. St Paul's Kn[ightsbridge] aftn:[3] where I went to be godfather to S. Herbert's little boy (Wm. Reginald).[4] Wrote to Lord Aberdeen—C. Greville. Saw Mr Goulburn—Mr Hallam. Invited to dinner at the Palace where were the King of Portugal & Duke of Oporto: to my no small dissatisfaction.[5] Read Mrs Bennett on Leopardi[6]—Archd. Harrison on Church Rates[7]—Theologia Germanica.[8] Saw one late on my way home [R].

19. M.

Wrote to Sir W. Heathcote—Mr Hatchell[9]—D of Buccleuch—G. Smith—Master of Pembr.—Sir T. Fremantle—& minutes. Rode mg. W.I. Loan opened—at 2 PM. Saw Sir A. Spearman—Govr. & Dep. Govr. Bank—Mr G.E.H. Vernon—Mr Wilson. H of C. 4½–9 (Oxford Bill) & 10½–1 (Supply &c).[10]

[1] Spoke on it: *H* cxxxiv. 183.

[2] An additional clause to protect closed scholarships for certain schools was carried by R. *Palmer: *H* cxxxiv. 281.

[3] W. J. E. *Bennett's church.

[4] William Reginald Herbert, 3rd s. of S.*, lost at sea on H.M.S. Captain, 1870.

[5] Pedro V, 1837–61, king of Portugal 1853, and his brother, Louis Philippe, 1838–89, duke of Oporto, who succ. as Louis I 1861.

[6] Probably an untraced MS or article by Mrs. A. R. Bennett, his cousin.

[7] B. *Harrison, 'The church rate question, and the principles involved in it. A charge . . .' (1854).

[8] Ed. by F. Pfeiffer, tr. by S. *Winkworth with a preface by C. *Kingsley (1854).

[9] John Hatchell, 1783–1870; K.C. 1835; solicitor general for Ireland 1847–50, attorney general 1850–2; liberal M.P. Windsor 1850–2; commissioner of Dublin insolvent debtors from June 1854.

[10] Spoke on the first: *H* cxxxiv. 342.

20. T.

Wrote to Earl of Aberdeen—Mr Worsley—T.S. Gladstone—Col. Harcourt—Mr Hayter—Mr Oliveira—and minutes. Rode, mg. H of C. 6[1]–12¾ on the case of Baron de Bode &c.[2] Went 2–3 with C.G. to see the Krüger & other pictures at the National Gallery.[3] Read Daubeny's Lecture[4]—Saw Earl of Aberdeen—Sir A. Spearman *cum* Govr. Bank—Solr. to the Treasury—Decimal Coinage Deputn.—Mr C. Greville (2)—Mr Hayter—J.N.G.

21. Wed.

Wrote to Prov. Oriel—Goldwin Smith—H.B. Barry—Ld J. Russell—Ld Stratford—Ld Palmerston—D of Buccleuch—and minutes. H. of C. 2–6. Spoke on Church Rates and voted in 209:182 agt. Sir W. Clay's Bill.[5] Saw Govr. of the Bank (2)—Ld J.R. *cum* Solr. General on Oxford Bill—Mr Anderson—E. Cardwell. Worked on Oxford Bill. Dined at the Trinity House—Ld Ellesmere's afterwards. Read Kennedy's Pamphlet. Poor fellow.[6]

22. Th.

Wrote to Govr. of Bank—Mr S.W. Wayte—E. of Aberdeen—G. Smith (2)—Sir C. Trevelyan—T. Briscoe—E. Cardwell—Jas Wilson—Mast. Pembroke—Rev H. Drury[7]—Robn. G.—and minutes. Rode, aft. Read Sismondi,[8] late. Wrote Memm. on the campaign.[9] Saw Govr. of the Bank—Mr Jos. Napier—Hon A. Gordon—Mr Anderson—Sir R. Bethell—Mr Hadfield MP.—Mr Macgregor MP.[10] H. of C. 6¼–8 and 8½–1½. Spoke agt. Mr Heywoods Clause & voted (1) in 162:251, (2) in 205:196.[11]

23. Fr. X

Wrote to Mr Shelley—H.J.G.—Hon A. Gordon[12]—Scotts—Judge Coleridge—Mr Dyce—& minutes. Rode, mg. H. of C. 4½–7¼ on Oxford Bill: & again

[1] Instead of '6½'.

[2] Spoke on the case of de Bode, claimed to be a British citizen, whose property had been confiscated by the French govt. in 1793: *H* cxxxiv. 419.

[3] Cp. 1 Mar. 54.

[4] C. G. B. *Daubeny, 'Address on the completion of the arrangements for receiving the Fielding herbarium' (1853); cp. also 21 Dec. 53.

[5] Church Rates Abolition Bill: *H* cxxxiv. 448.

[6] T. F. Kennedy, 'Letter to Lord John Russell . . .' (1854); on his dismissal; cp. 29 Apr. 54.

[7] Henry *Drury, 1812–63; lecturer at Caius, Cambridge, 1838–9; vicar of Bremhill, Wiltshire, from 1845; prebendary of Salisbury from 1855; archdeacon of Wiltshire 1863; wrote on the church.

[8] J. C. Simonde de Sismondi, *Études sur les sciences sociales* (1836–8); cp. 23 Sept. 54.

[9] Urging despatch of sufficient force to take Sebastopol, in Guedalla, *P*, 97; cp. Conacher, 452n.

[10] James M'Gregor, 1808–58; Liverpool banker; chairman S.E. railway 1848; tory M.P. Sandwich 1852–6; cp. 13 July 54.

[11] *H* cxxxiv. 543. Heywood's clause to remove the subscription to the thirty nine articles at matriculation (one of the barriers to dissenters) was carried; his clause waiving oaths when taking degrees was rejected.

[12] Cp. Conacher, 392.

in evg.[1] Saw Duke of Buccleuch—R. Phillimore—Sir A. Spearman—Mr Wilson—Attorney General. Saw one (Fr.) late [R]. Dined at Mr Moffatt's.

24. Sat. St Joh.Bapt.

Wrote to Ld Braybrooke—Judge Coleridge—Mast. Pembroke—Rev. L. Bagot[2]—Mr G. Smith—Mrs T. Goalen—Rev T. Briscoe—Mr W. Smee—Rev S.W. Wayte—Prov[ost of] Oriel—Williams & Co (Ch[este]r)—Mr G. Burnett—& minutes. Cabinet 3–6½.[3] Rode, afterwards. Saw Hon A. Gordon—Lord A. Hervey—Mr Jas Wilson—Mr J.A. Roebuck. Evg at home—Read [blank].

25. 2 S.Trin.

Whitehall mg St James's evg. Wrote to Prov. Oriel—& copy. MS of 42 aloud at night. Saw Ld Abn.—called to see Helen but failed. Read Sir R. Peel on Dissrs. Adm[issio]n in 1834[4]—Ld A. Hervey[5]—Mental Prayer[6]—Life of Ld Cobham[7]—Sermons.

26. M.

Wrote to Ld J. Russell—Mr W. Grogan[8]—Mast. Pembroke—Mr Marriott—Abp of Armagh—Mr Napier—Mr J. Williams (Chester)[9]—Scotts—Robn. G.—Rev Mr Jowett—Provost of Oriel and copy—and minutes. Rode, mg. Saw Mr Ellice M.P.—Mr Denison M.P.—Mr Goldwin Smith—Sir C. Wood—Sir W. Heathcote—Read Moltke. H of C. 4½–9 and 11¾–12½.[10] Saw Wolf. (52) [R].

27. T.

Wrote to Sir W. Heathcote—Mr G. Butt[11]—Signor Manin[12]—Mr J.H. Law—Sir C. Trevelyan (2)—Mr Wood—Sir W. Molesworth—Mr Wilson—Mr Craufurd MP—Mr Gibson R.A.[13]—& minutes. Rode, aft. Dined at Lady Wenlocks. Saw Mr B.B. Williams—Mr Wilson—Ld Harrowby. Read

[1] *H* cxxxiv. 615.

[2] Lewis Francis Bagot, 1814?–70; Christ Church; rector of Leigh, Staffordshire, from 1846.

[3] On dissenters; memorandum in Add MS 44636, f. 12.

[4] *H* xxii. 702.

[5] Cp. 13 Nov. 53.

[6] Untraced.

[7] A. M. Brown, *The leader of the Lollards, his times and trials* (1848).

[8] William Grogan, house and estate agent in Conduit Street.

[9] Perhaps John Deakin Williams, builder.

[10] Spoke on Fund Charges Bill: *H* cxxxiv. 697.

[11] George Medd Butt, 1797–1860; barrister 1830, bencher Inner Temple 1845; Peelite M.P. Weymouth 1852–7.

[12] Daniele Manin, 1804–57; Venetian; demanded Italian independence from 1838; headed Venetian republic 1848–9, when he surrendered to Austria. Cp. 1 July 54.

[13] David Cooke Gibson, 1827–56, artist in Edinburgh 1844–52, in London from 1852; exhibited at Academy 1855–7.

Mahon's Hist.[1] H of C. at $3\frac{3}{4}$ and $10\frac{3}{4}$–$12\frac{1}{4}$. Another abstract resolution, & passed (most reluctantly on my part) with our consent![2] Walk afr.

28. W. X

Helen's birthday. All good be with her. Wrote to Sir W. Heathcote—Mr G. Smith—Mr Buckeridge—Prov. Oriel—Duke of Buccleuch—Robn. G.—Bp of Aberdeen—Lyttelton—Rev Mr Haddan—and minutes. Rode, mg. Saw Sir C. Wood—Sir A. Spearman—Earl of Aberdeen—Mr Wilson—D. Newcastle—Lord J. Russell—D. Argyll. Comm[ittee] Ed[ucatio]n P.C. 12–1. 3–$4\frac{3}{4}$ attended Mr Lacaita's Lecture, & saw the Pictures a little.[3] Cabinet dinner at Pembroke Lodge[4]—returned at 1 cold. Walk. ma.[5] Read La Guerre d'Orient.[6]

29. Th.

Wrote to Mr Prescott—W. Gladstone—J.G. Hubbard—T. Weguelin—K.D. Hodgson[7]—D. of Newcastle—Messrs. Scott—Robertson G.—Mast. Balliol—Sig. Manin.—Sir A. Spearman—Mrs Bennett—& minutes. Rode, aftn. Read Maynooth Debate—Russia and Europe.[8] Saw Mr Greene M.P.—Sir W. Heathcote—Rev. Mr Haddan—Mr Wilson—Hon A. Gordon—Sir J. Graham. H of C. $12\frac{1}{4}$–$1\frac{1}{2}$, $6\frac{1}{4}$–11, and 12–$1\frac{1}{2}$ on Oxford Bill and other subjects. I was vexed at failing to qualify the mischief of Palmer's Clause: & at the mode of withdrawal of the Col[onial] Ch[urch] Bill.[9]

30. Fr.

Wrote to Mast. Pembroke—Mr Bright—E of Aberdeen (2)—G.W. Hope—Govr. of Bank—Mr Rawlinson—Ld Chancellor—Sir W. Molesworth—[three blank spaces] and minutes. Read Mahon's Hist. &c. Saw Mr [H.] Roberts—Sir A. Spearman. Fighting against a heavy headach & strong chill all day.

Sat. July One. 1854.

A night & day of fever and headach with much physic: it won in the aftn. Seven to breakfast, to meet Manin. He too is wild.[10]...While C. was out I had an ill timed visit of N[ewcastle] & S. H[erbert] as messengers from Cabinet. Hodgson in evg.—No food.

[1] P. H. *Stanhope, *History of England from the peace of Utrecht to the peace of Versailles, 1713–83*, 7 v. (1836–54).
[2] Collier's motion on the law of partnership: *H* cxxxiv. 752.
[3] Cp. 7 June 54.
[4] The famous 'sleeping cabinet' at *Russell's house in Richmond Park.
[5] 'but' (Italian). Usually used by Gladstone in book margins to indicate disagreement.
[6] Cp. 5 June 54.
[7] Kirkman Daniel Hodgson, 1814–79; partner in Baring brothers' bank; director of bank of England 1849–78, deputy governor 1862, governor 1863–4; liberal M.P. Bridport 1857–68, Bristol 1870–8.
[8] Instead of 'Turkey'. 'Read Maynooth Debate' here deleted.
[9] *H* cxxxiv. 888; for *Palmer's clause, see 16 June 54 n.
[10] The last five words underlined with dots.

2. Sund.(3 Trin.)

Another day of fever & much discomfort: the head still *incapable* of any thought without violent effort. Hodgson thrice. No food.

3. M.

The fever off: and a rash appeared. Much more comfortable but very weak: cd. hardly stand. About midday ate an egg. In evg appetite began to return. Saw Bp of Oxford.

4. T.

Rash more fully out: decided chicken-pox. General health much better: appetite good. Dictated letters to Earl of Clarendon—Earl of Besborough[1] —Mr Wilson—Lord Sydney.[2] Also began Hide & Seek.[3]

5. Wed.

An entirely sleepless night M–Tues but a fair day followed: last night better. Saw Canning 11–2 on the Oxford Bill. Read Hide and Seek. All going on well on improving. But I am hideous beyond description: & it is hard to think how one can ever get back within the conditions of visibility.

6. Th.

All going well thank God. Read 'Hide and Seek'. Saw Ld Ellesmere—Mr Hayter (Oxf. Bill)—Captain G[ladstone]—Bishop of Oxford—Lord Canning.

7. Friday.

Admirable report from H. of Lords about the Oxford Bill through the evg. They made a beautiful piece of Parliamentary work of it.[4] Saw Bp of Oxford—Lord Canning. Read Hide & Seek (finished). Hodgsons reports of me continue excellent: I am to move tomorrow.

8. Sat.

Wrote to Scott & Co—Mr H. Lees. Saw Mr Wilson—and others. Set a few matters to rights below. Off at 4 PM. to Falconhurst: where Mrs T[albot] actually *keeps* house to let in the leper.[5] Felt at once the influence of change of air. Read Chr. Rem. on Voltaire & Johnsoniana.[6]

[1] Cp. 3 July 36 n.
[2] John Robert Townshend, 1805–90, 3rd Viscount Sydney 1831; household office 1841–6.
[3] By W. Wilkie Collins, just published.
[4] Despite *Derby's opposition, the bill had a fairly smooth course, cp. Conacher, 343.
[5] Cp. 14 May 53.
[6] *Christian Remembrancer*, xxviii. 171; review of L. F. Bungener, *Voltaire and his times* (1854).

9. 4 S. Trin.

mg & evg prayers at home alone. Read the Western World revisited[1]—Sermons in Glass[2]—Jewish Emancn.[3]—& Sermons. Got out a little, on foot & driving.

10. M.

Wrote to Dr Pusey—Rev Mr Rawlinson—Ch. Justice Pollock[4]—Mr W. Brown MP.—Rev. Dr Moberly—Mr J.S. Brickwood—and minutes. Better on my feet today & more with the party. Read Finlay's Gk Empire Vol 2[5]—Mahon's Hist of England—& Gisborne's Essay on Cattle & Sheep.[6]

11. T.

Wrote to Banting & Sons—Rev. D. Gladstone—Mrs Bennett—Sir A.Y. Spearman—Attorney General—Master of Pembroke—Rev Archer Gurney[7]—and minutes. Saw Ld Canning on Oxford Bill.[8] Read Finlay's Byz. Empire—Mahon's Hist. Engl.—Disraeli's Memoir of his Father & Cur. Literature.[9] Drove with Mrs T[albot]. C. & M. My progress good: a scouring by blue pill &c. last night.

12. Wed.

Wrote to Sir T.G.—Provost of Oriel—Rev C. Marriott—Mr F.C. Sharpe[10]—Mr Wilson MP—Mr T.S. Gladstone—Sir Geo. Grey MP.—Mr A.M. Dunlop—Sir Jas Graham—Mr Hume MP.—Mr T.A. Hope—and minutes. Read Keble on Adm[issio]n of Diss[ente]rs[11]—Thomson on Intt of Money[12]—Mahon's Hist of Engl.—and Hubbard on Currency.[13] Rain nearly all day.

13. Th.

Ch. 10¼ A.M. Saw Mr Hunt—S.R.G.—Drove early. Wrote to Mr A.A.

[1] By H. Caswall (1854).
[2] Untraced.
[3] Untraced.
[4] i.e. Sir J. F. *Pollock.
[5] G. *Finlay, *History of the Byzantine and Greek empires, 716–1453*, 2 v. (1854).
[6] T. *Gisborne, *fils*, *Essays on agriculture* (1854); the first, reprinted from the *Quarterly Review*.
[7] Archer Thompson *Gurney, 1820–87; barrister 1846; priest 1849; curate of Holy Trinity, Exeter, 1849–58, of Llangunider, Brecon, 1882–3; chaplain in Paris 1858–71; minor poet.
[8] He was in charge of it in the lords.
[9] I. *D'Israeli, *Curiosities of literature* [14 ed., with a review of the life & writings of the author, by his son], 3 v. (1849).
[10] Of St Martin's le grand, London, sending him £5 to be given to W. Wilson, the blackmailer, on his release from gaol; cp. Add MS 44529, f. 116.
[11] J. *Keble, *A few very plain thoughts on the proposed admission of dissenters to the university of Oxford* (1854).
[12] J. Thomson, *Tables of interest at 3, 4, 4½ and 5 per cent . . . showing the exchange on bills* (1768); often reprinted; or similar tables by W. T. Thomson (1853); cp. 17 July 54.
[13] Cp. 23 Jan. 44.

Watts [1]—Lord Carlisle [2]—Dr Twiss—Rev Mr Fowle [3]—Mr Pollard Urquhart—Mr Jas Macgregor MP—Duchess of Buccleuch—Lord John Russell—Sir S. Scott & Co—Archdeacon Harrison—and minutes. Read Mahon's Hist—Hubbard on the Currency. Drives mg & aftn.

14. Fr.

Canterb. Cathl. 3 P.M. Wrote to Sir Geo. Grey—C.G—Mr Grogan—Ld Aberdeen—and minutes. Left Falconhurst at 10: came to Canterbury at 1¼ & remained till 6, chiefly in examining with Archd. Harrison the Cathedral & its accompaniments: which are indeed rich & rare. Saw Canon Stanley [4] also on the Oxford Bill. At 6 drove over with the Jameses to Betteshanger [5] through a very fine agricultural district. A happy evening there was disturbed by a summons to London: for another J. R[ussell] crisis! [6]

15. Sat.

Wrote to Ld Monteagle—Rev Mr Rawlinson—Ld Abn.—and minutes. Saw Earl of Aberdeen *cum* Sir Jas Graham—Hon A. Gordon—Rev Mr Adams—Earl Granville. Cabinet 3¼–6¾. Out at Bettishanger in the morning to see the Ch & place: off to Sandwich at 9½: reached London at 2. Dined at home. In evg saw E. Collins [R].

16. 5 S.Trin.

Ch Ch Broadway & H.C. mg. Ch. Royal aftn.—MS of 47 for S. 4. aloud at night. Walk with C. & children. Wrote to Willy. Read Rancé (maxims) [7]—Caswall's Western World—Wilberforce's Sermons & Charge on Holy Commn. [8] Saw Mr Hodgson.

17. M.

Wrote to Ld Monteagle—Willy—D of Newcastle—T.G.—Robn. G.—Earl Granville—Mr Dunlop—& minutes. H. of C. 4¾–7 and 9¾–10½. [9] Read La Guerre d'Orient (finished)—Russia & Europe (finished)—Thomson on Dec. Coinage. [10] Saw Sir C. Trevelyan with Sir A. Spearman—Mr Monsell—Duke of Newcastle—Govr. of the Bank—Milnes Gaskell. Saw Louis aet. 15 (and missed seeing Wolf) [R]: how deeply sad! Meeting of MP.s 1–3½. No

[1] Alaric Alexander *Watts, 1797–1864; edited newspapers and periodicals until bankrupt, 1849; clerk in inland revenue 1853; given civil list pension 1854; poet and literary editor.

[2] Cp. 13 Oct. 32.

[3] Probably Fulwar William Fowle; Merton, Oxford; rector of Allington, Wiltshire, from 1816.

[4] i.e. A. P. *Stanley.

[5] 4 miles W. of Deal.

[6] Following an attack by *Disraeli; cp. Conacher, 358–9.

[7] A. J. Le Bouthillier de Rancé, *Maximes chrétiennes et morales* (?1699).

[8] R. I. *Wilberforce, *Sermons on the holy communion* (1854) and cp. 23 Sept. 44.

[9] War office: *H* cxxxv. 317.

[10] W. T. Thompson, *Decimal numeration and decimal coinage* (1854).

two speakers agreed: & I shd. have said the whole was very chaotic: but the whips are satisfied. The meeting was not in favour of any party or section of Govt. in particular. No two persons quite agreed: but a bad spirit was shown by Mr Vernon Smith(!) Mr Horsman & Mr Bright.[1]

18. T.

Wrote to Provost of Oriel—Sir W. James—Mr G A Hamilton—Robn. G.—Ld Monteagle—The Queen—D of Newcastle (2)—Dr Pusey—E.T. Williams[2]—Scotts—Ld Palmerston—Ld Braybrooke—Attorney General—H. Tayleur—Rector of Exeter—and minutes.[3] Rode, aftn. Saw Ld Granville—Duke of Newcastle—Sir A. Spearman—Rev. R. Daniell—Earl of Aberdeen—Sir C. Trevelyan—Mr Wilson—Ld A. Hervey—Hon F. Lawley—Mr A. Gordon. H of C. 8½–11. Spoke, & beaten, on Greene's Printing Committee.[4] Lady V. Sandars's Concert afr.[5] Then worked on Lady G[lynne]'s Estate accounts. Read 'Un Mot sur Les Aff. d'Orient'.[6]

19. Wed.

Wrote to Mr Rawlinson—J.N.G.—Mrs Malcolm—Ld Wodehouse—Archdn. Harrison—S. Herbert—Ld Londonderry—and minutes. Rode aftn. Saw Mr Grogan (H[ouse] Agent)—Mr Hayter—Mr Wilson—Lord Monteagle—Mr F. Lawley (resp S. Australia &c)[7]—Sir Geo. Grey—D of Newcastle. 10 to breakfast Bp of N.Z. Parliamy. & Official dinner party of 13. Conv. with Ld R. Clinton[8] about F. Lawley, very encouraging. Read Finlay. Cabinet 12½–5½.

20. Th.

Wrote to Ld Lansdowne—Scotts—Sir A. Spearman—Mr Roebuck—Bp of Brechin—Mr Wilson—E. Cardwell (2)—Rev H.E. Lowe—Rev H. Pritchard[9]—F. Lawley—Mast. Balliol—E. Granville—Stephen E.G—Willy—Ld Canning—and minutes. Worked on accounts & papers. Saw Maj-Gen Sir F. Smith—Mr Timm—Mr Lawley—Mr R. Greswell—Mr Greenwood—Robn. Gladstone—Lord Lansdowne—D. of Argyll—Attorney General. Rode, aftn. Read Universities & the Ch.[10] H. of C. 5½–6½ and 9¼–2.[11]

[1] A meeting in Downing Street of government supporters to consider its position; cp. Conacher, 359.

[2] Edmund Turberville Williams, ?1817–85; Exeter, Oxford; vicar of Caldecot, Monmouthshire, from 1841; copy, on a post, in Add MS 44529, f. 118.

[3] And wrote to Willy on God, in Lathbury, ii. 151.

[4] Greene's motion for a select cttee. on parliamentary printing: *H* cxxxv. 405.

[5] Lady Virginia Frances Zerlina, da. of 2nd marquis of Headfort; m. 1850 Joseph Sandars, Peelite M.P. Yarmouth 1848–52, who d. 1893; she d. 1922.

[6] Not found.

[7] His appointment there as governor, soon rescinded.

[8] Lord Robert Renebald Pelham-Clinton, 1820–67, 6th s. of 4th duke of Newcastle; Peelite M.P. North Nottinghamshire 1852–65.

[9] Henry Pritchard, 1820?–57; fellow of Corpus, Oxford, from 1847; proctor 1852.

[10] [C. *Hardwick], *Universities and the Church of England, by a Cambridge man* (1854).

[11] Bribery Bill; spoke on stamp duties: *H* cxxxv. 489.

21. Fr.

Wrote to Rector of Exeter—J. Amery—Mr G. Sanders—Mr Pressly—Scotts—Mr Anderson—J.N.G.—Mr Senior—G. Burnett—Sir J. Young—Mr Glyn—Lady Shelley—Ld Granville—& minutes. Saw Lord Aberdeen—Lord J. Russell—Lord Granville—Sir A. Spearman—Mr Anderson—Sir C. T[revelyan] cum Mr A. & Mr Shelley—Mr Wood. Rode, aftn. Read Tayler's Hist. of Taxn.[1] Wrote Memm. on Vote of Credit.[2] H of C. 6–7½ and 9¼–1.[3]

22. Sat. X

Wrote to Ld Canning—Mrs Goalen—Freshfields—and minutes. At 2¼ we went off by train to Mr Currie's at West Horsley:[4] & rode through the woods & on the downs. Saw Ld Granville—Mr Grogan—Mr Pressly—F. Lawley. Read Aretino's Ragionamenti[5]—Taylor's Hist Taxation—W. Indn. on Sugar Duties.[6]

23. 6 S.Trin. X

West Horsley Ch mg & aft. Wrote to Dr Pusey. Read Wilberforce's Sermons—Caswall's W[estern] W[orld] revisited[7]—Whewell's Plur[ality] of Worlds.[8] Walk with Mr Currie & the rest. The intendeds are an excellent couple & may they have every blessing.[9]

24. M.

Wrote to Hon A. Gordon[10]—Sir C. Trevelyan (2)—Bp of Brechin—Mr Fortescue—Mast. Balliol—and minutes. Returned to London 1–3¼. Saw Sir A. Spearman—Duke of Argyll—Mr F. Scully MP.[11]—Mr Wilson—Robn. G. H. of C. 6–8 and 9¼–1¾: watching the debate.[12] Read Aretino Rag. (an evil book, an extraordinary picture)—Manzoni's Adelchi[13]—Whewell's Plur. of Worlds. 7 to dinner.

[1] By W. Tayler (1853). [2] Not found. [3] Bribery Bill: *H* cxxxv. 497.
[4] Henry Currie's seat 5 miles SW. of Leatherhead.
[5] Cp. 27 Dec. 43 and 24 July 54.
[6] Perhaps 'Case of the British West Indies stated by the West India Association of Glasgow' (1852) or 'Some considerations on . . . the West India Colonies . . . by a West Indian' (1823).
[7] Cp. 9 July 54. [8] Cp. 21 May 54.
[9] Emily, H. Currie's da., m. August 1854 Charles Henry Wyndham A'Court (Repington), 1819–1903, nephew of 1st Baron Heytesbury and br.-in-law of S. *Herbert; M.P. Wilton 1852–5, then assistant controller of national debt office; took surname of Repington 1855.
[10] Cp. Conacher, 418.
[11] Francis Scully, 1820–64; barrister 1841; liberal M.P. Tipperary 1847–57.
[12] Govt. motion, supported by a message from the Queen, for a vote of credit of £3m.: *H* cxxxv. 598.
[13] By A. Manzoni (1822).

25. T. St James.

Wrote to Robn. G.—Ld Palmerston—[blank—] Scotts: V. Chancellor—Mr Pressly—and minutes. Rode, mg. Read Whewell's Plur. of Worlds. Saw Ld Canning—The Queen's Proctor—Mr Arbuthnot—Bishop of Oxford—Mr Wilson MP—Mr Anderson—Earl of Clarendon—J.N.G.—Lord Aberdeen—whom I found deeply wounded.[1] Worked on letters & papers. H. of C. 12½–1½, 6–8, and 10–12¾. Herbert's Speech put all right.[2]

26. Wed.

Wrote to Robn. G.—Rev Mr Marshall—Mr Burr—Rev Mr Stokes—Scotts—Rev Mr Tweed—& minutes. Rode mg.—Audit meeting. Cabinet dinner: settled to reintroduce a Publ. Rev. &c Bill.[3] Saw Sir Jas Graham—Mr Gregson M.P. Mr W. Brown M.P.—Mr Pressly—Mr Anderson. H of C. 3–6.[4] Read Senior's Journal—Whewell's Plur. of Worlds. Went with Dss. of Sutherland to the Academy—lighted up.

27. Th.

Wrote to Lady Beauchamp[5]—Mr Headlam—& minutes. Worked on the Oxford Bill. H of C. 2–4 and 6–1. All our points carried by good majorities: & a day of storm ended in sunshine.[6] Saw Sir A. Spearman—Mr Wilson—Mr Goldwin Smith—Read Senior's Journal. Rode. G[oldwin] Smith shared my early dinner.[7]

28. Fr.

Wrote to Mr Gibbon—Prov. of Oriel—Mr E. Ball MP[8]—Sir A. Spearman—F. Lawley (2)—Rev C. Marriott—A. Gordon[9]—Ld J. Russell[10]—Mr Dalyell—V.C. Oxford (& copy)[11]—Dr Hessey—& minutes. Prepared reasons of Dissent to Lords Amendments Oxf.[12] Saw Mr Grogan (signed)—Ld Canning *cum* Sir J. Young & Mr Wood—Mr Wood—Duke of Newcastle—Mr Arbuthnot—Mr Hadfield MP.—Mr Wilson—Sir Geo. Grey—Mr Jas

[1] In general, by attacks on his leadership by coalition supporters; in particular, by Gladstone's refusal to defend him the previous day, cp. Conacher, 413–8.

[2] *H* cxxxv. 716.

[3] An earlier bill had been altered by the lords; the second bill's 2° was on 2 August: *H* cxxxv. 1174.

[4] Misc. business: *H* cxxxv. 789.

[5] Catherine, *née* Otway, m. 1st Henry Murray, 2nd, as his 2nd wife, in 1850, John Reginald Lygon Pyndar, 3rd Earl Beauchamp, 1783–1853; she d. 1875.

[6] Lord's amndts. to Oxford Bill dealt with, and money voted to purchase Burlington House: *H* cxxxv. 827.

[7] Perhaps this was the occasion of which Goldwin *Smith wrote in *My memory of Gladstone* (1904), 3; he may have conflated this day with 9 May 54 or 8 June 54—or both.

[8] Edward Ball, 1793–1865; tory M.P. Cambridgeshire 1852–63; a strict reactionary.

[9] Fragment in Conacher, 418.

[10] Fragment ibid. 378–9.

[11] Sent copy of final form of the Oxford Bill, cp. Add MS 44381, f. 265.

[12] A cttee. had been set up to draw up reasons for rejecting some lords' amndts. to the Oxford Bill: *H* cxxxv. 863.

Wortley—Mr Hayter. H. of C. 12–2, 7–8 and 10–3.[1] Read Senior's Journal.

29. Sat.

Wrote to Rev Mr Meek—Freshfields—Sir G. Grey—Bp of Brechin—Mr Holt[2]—Sir A. Spearman—Ld J. Russell—& minutes. Cabinet 3–5. Went to No 6 to arrange my books a little. Read Senior's Journal. Off at 5.30 to Clifden:[3] where we had a most pleasant evg: sculled on the river, the first time for many many years. Saw Robn. G—Jas Wortley—Mr Grogan—Sir C. Trevelyan.

30. 7 S.Trin.

Eton Chapel mg where we again heard a noble Sermon from Bp of NZ—but one to make me deeply ashamed. Saw the Provost—Coleridge, who gave me a delightful acct. of Willy—& F. Lawley on his matters, wh stand *well* in ref. to these vile reports.[4] We got no aftn Ch. Read Wilberforce—Brodie's Psychol. Inquiries[5]—D. of Argyll read to us in evg from In Memoriam.[6] Wrote to F. Lawley.

31. M.

Read N.B.R. on Morality of Public Men—& on Murchison.[7] Drove to Burnham Beeches[8] & saw the most perfect sylvan scenery. Returned to London with our most kind hostess[9] $3\frac{3}{4}$–$5\frac{1}{2}$. House 6–8, and $9\frac{1}{4}$–$2\frac{1}{2}$ on Supply &c. Saw F. Lawley—& (on his matter)—Jas Wortley—Sir G. Grey—Mr G.C. Glyn.

Tuesday August One X *1854.*

Wrote to Mr H.A. Bruce—Ld Beauchamp—H.J.G.—Aunt J.—Mr Wood—Ld J. Russell—Ld Aberdeen—D[owage]r Countss. Beauchamp—Mr Grogan—Sir W. Molesworth—Mr C.A. Wood—Bp of Salisbury—Ld Lyttelton—& minutes. C.G. went to Broadstairs with the children.[10] Read Whewell's Plur. of Worlds, Quarty. & Blackwood. Saw J.N.G—Robn. G—both—A. Gordon—Sir A. Spearman—Mr Anderson—Mr B.B. Williams—Ld J. Russell—Mr Wilson—Ld Besborough—Mr D. Seymour[11]—Ld

[1] Bribery Bill: *H* cxxxv. 911.

[2] George Holt, 1790–1861; Liverpool cotton broker; arranging for Westcott to paint Gladstone for the city; cp. Add MS 44529, f. 123v. and 27 Nov. 54.

[3] Cp. 15 June 48.

[4] But see 2 Aug. 54 etc.

[5] Sir B. C. *Brodie, *Psychological inquiries*, i. (1854).

[6] Cp. 23 June 50.

[7] *North British Review*, xxi. 505, 544 (August 1854); on *Harcourt, and a review of Sir R. I. *Murchison, *Siluria* (1854).

[8] $2\frac{1}{2}$ miles NE. of Maidenhead.

[9] 'at' here deleted.

[10] On the coast, 2 miles NE. of Ramsgate.

[11] i.e. W. D. *Seymour.

Aberdeen. Visits: saw Bishop [R] & another meeting with the Law Officers Sir A. Spearman Mr Anderson Mr Greenwood & Mr Wilson resp. Deficiency Bills issue.[1]

2. Wed. X

Wrote to Rev A. Rankin—Mr Chadwick[2]—C.A. Wood—and minutes. H of C (principally) 12¼–6.[3] Rode in evg. Saw A. Gordon—Mr Wood—Chicory Deputation—Attorney General—Arranged some[4] papers. All went well till at 7½ when I came in F. Lawley came to me & made his sad confession. The evening was chiefly spent in considering with him, with J. Wortley, & later with Wortley and his brothers what should be done. I also saw Ld Aberdeen upon it who did not think it a case for the Cabinet.[5] Saw Bishop again [R]—better or less bad.

3. Th.

Wrote to Mr Moffatt—Mr Lefevre—Ld Besborough—R W Wilbraham—D of Newcastle—Sir A. Spearman & minutes. A night of storm & morning[6] of floods. H of C. at 12½ and 3—again 6–11 and 11½–2. Saw Attorney General—Mr Anderson *cum* Sir C. Trevelyan—Sir E. Dering[7]—Mr Wilson. Early in the forenoon I went to Ld J.R., N., & Sir G. Grey to meet on Lawley's matters: and also begged[8] Wenlock & J. Wortley to probe him further that we may at length know our ground. We met in the afternoon again at my house when it was determined that Grey should make a statement & offer a Commee. if desired. It was a day of much distress & anxiety: mitigated as far as it could be by the considerate kindness of the House. I took part in the debate, & was afterwards occupied with the Publ. Revenue Bill.[9]

4. Fr.

Wrote to Mr Anderson—Rev E. Stokes—Mast. Balliol—J. Wood—Sir C. Trevelyan—Sir J. Graham—Ld Clarendon—Sir R. Mayne—Ld St Germans—G.K. Rickards—Solr. General—R. Wilbraham—Dr. Lady Wenlock—and minutes. Saw S. Lawley & Jane[10]—Mr J. Wood—Mr Arbuthnot—S. Herbert—Sir J. Graham—Manchr. Beersellers Deputn.—A. Gordon—Mrs

[1] Cp. 6 Apr. 54 n.

[2] (Sir) Edwin *Chadwick, 1800–90; utilitarian; secretary to poor law commissioners 1834–46; member of health board 1848, pensioned off July 1854; kt. 1888.

[3] Spoke on Stamp Duties Bill 3°: *H* cxxxv. 1057.

[4] Instead of 'arranging'.

[5] Lawley had been gambling with the funds.

[6] Instead of 'day'.

[7] Sir E. C. Dering was Peelite M.P. East Kent 1852–7, 1863–8, and d. 1896. Cp. 23 Nov. 38 n.

[8] Instead of 'urged'.

[9] Sir G. *Grey announced that Lawley's appt. to govern South Australia was cancelled. Gladstone praised Lawley's abilities and defended his support for the original appt.: *H* cxxxv. 1252. He soon resigned as private secretary (see 3 Dec. 54 n.).

[10] i.e. Jane Stuart-Wortley.

Wadd—Mr. & Mrs Heywood[1]—A. Kinnaird. Today was like not a calm but a void after a storm: & the solitude of my Priv. Secretary's room which has been like a mill for 18 months was very melancholy. Dined with the Herberts. Pressure begins for F.L.s immediately abandoning his office as Private Secretary. This again makes me sad, to part from the unhappy. Dined with the Herberts. H of C. 3–4, 6–8¼ and 10½–12½.[2]

5. Sat.

Wrote to Mr J. Freshfield—J.N.G.—Sir W. Molesworth—Ld Meath—Dr. Css. Beauchamp—H. Fitzroy—Sir T. Fremantle—and minutes. Read H. of C. Orders &c. Cabinet 2½–4¾. H. of C. 2–2½.[3] Saw Mr Grogan—Mr Wilson—Ld Granville—Mr Wood & Mr Pressly. Off at 5.30 to Polesden[4] where we found the Bp of NZ. the C. Herveys[5] Mr Trench[6] & Mr Lorrell:[7] an excellent party. We sat till 12.

6. 8 S.Trin.

Great Bookham Ch[8] mg & aft. H.C. in mg. Bp preached both times. A day of excellent converse. Read Wilberforce—Bickersteth's Life & Correspondence.[9]

7. M.

Wrote to Jas Watson—Mr Meyrick—Ld J. Russell—and minutes. Watching the cricket in wh Willy distinguished himself. Walk with the Bishop—also with Farquhar. Read Talbot case.[10] Off at 7½: reached D[owning] St 9½.

8. T.

Wrote to D of Newcastle—Sir J. Young—E. of Aberdeen—Mr Lucas[11]—Dean Ramsay—Sir B. Hall—Sir C. Barry—Mr Hume—Rev D. Robertson—Robn. G.—W.S. Lindsay[12]—Rev H. Glynne—Mr W. Grogan—Sir W. James—Sir C. Wood—and minutes. Saw Ld Aberdeen (on Speech &c.)—H. Glynne—Robn. G—Mr Westcott—Mr Wilson—Stephen & F.C. Lawley.

[1] Mr. and Mrs. A. M. Heywood of London and Liverpool; correspondence until 1885 in Hawn P.

[2] Canada Bill: *H* cxxxv. 1319.

[3] Misc. business: *H* cxxxv. 1361.

[4] Polesden Lacy, 2½ miles NW. of Dorking, Surrey; seat of Sir W. R. Farquhar.

[5] Lord Charles Amelius Hervey, 1814–80, 5th s. of 1st marquess of Bristol; Trinity, Cambridge; rector of Great Chesterford, Essex, from 1839; m. 1839 Harriet Charlotte Sophia, da. of 1st earl of Harrowby; she d. 1899.

[6] i.e. R. Chenevix *Trench; cp. 13 Aug. 54.

[7] Unidentified.

[8] 2 miles SW. of Leatherhead.

[9] T. R. *Birks, *A memoir of the rev. Edward *Bickersteth*, 2 v. (1852).

[10] 'A report of the judgment, delivered by Dr. [J.] Radcliffe in the case of Talbot v. Talbot' (1854); an ecclesiastical dispute.

[11] Probably Frederick *Lucas, 1812–55; barrister 1835; become a roman catholic 1830, started *The Tablet* 1840; liberal M.P. co. Meath from 1852.

[12] William Schaw Lindsay, 1816–77; founded shipping firm; liberal M.P. Tynemouth 1854–9, Sunderland 1859–65; historian of merchant shipping.

Dined with the Heywoods. H of C. 2–7½. Spoke on O'Flaherty's case.[1] Saw Osborne & another afr. [R]

9. Wed.

Wrote to Ld Torrington—G. Arbuthnot—J.F. Fortescue[2]—Mr Erle—Rev Mr Stokes—C.G.—Smith Child[3]—Sir G. Grey—W.S. Lindsay—Robn. G.—Dow[age]r Ly. Lyttelton—and minutes. Rode, aftn.—Finished Whewell. Saw Bishop of Salisbury—Governor of the Bank—Mr Arbuthnot—Mr Moffatt MP. Saw R. Berkeley—hopeful [R]. H. of C. (spoke on Finance of the year) and Cabinet 12–3¾.[4] Began review & arrangement of letters and papers.

10. Th.

Wrote to Ld Granville—Mrs Selwyn[5]—Sir A. Spearman—Mr J.D. Cook—Bp of London—W.R. Farquhar—Mr Harrison—Ld Palmerston—Mr T. Young[6]—Ld Ellesmere—C.G.—Mr A.B. Cochrane—G. & Co—Sir C. Trevelyan—Jas Watson—and minutes. Rode in aftn. Saw Mr Wilson—Mr Arbuthnot—Sir C. Trevelyan—Dean Ramsay & Dr Hannah[7]—Lord Canning—Sir J. Shelley. Missed seeing Wolf [R]. Finished Fra Dolcino. Continued my work upon letters books papers &c. H. of C. at 3. P.M.[8]

11. Fr. X

Wrote to Sir J. Johnstone—Jas Wilson—Ld Aberdeen—Mr C. Gore—Ld Mahon—J.N.G.—Mrs Spring[9]—C.G.—& minutes. H. of C. at 3.[10] Worked on my papers books letters &c. Saw Goldbeater's Deputation[11]—Mr Anderson—Mr Arbuthnot—Rev. D. Robertson. Went to Aunt J. Memm. on Kennedy's Office—Cabinet Dinner Ld Lansdowne's 8–12. Saw Woolfe [R]: of whom I may think with shame.

12. Sat.

Wrote to Mr Hayter—F.C. Lawley—Scotts (2)—Rev D. Robertson—W.C. James—Bickers—Master of Balliol—Rev G. Nugee—Sir J. Graham—

[1] Not on the floor of the House, or unreported: *H* cxxxv. 1409.

[2] Probably John Faithful Grover Fortescue, ?1787–1868; rector of St. Giles's, Colchester, 1813, of Snoreham, Essex, 1849–65.

[3] (Sir) Smith Child, 1808–69; tory M.P. North Staffordshire 1851–9, West Staffordshire 1868–74; cr. bart. 1868.

[4] *H* cxxxv. 1490.

[5] Sarah Harriet, da. of Sir John *Richardson, m. 1839 G. A. *Selwyn.

[6] Thomas Young, receiver general of the Post Office, demanded compensation for retirement; cp. Add MS 44529, f. 128v.

[7] John *Hannah *fils*, 1818–88; fellow of Lincoln, Oxford, 1840; rector of Edinburgh Academy 1847–54; D.C.L. 1853; principal of Trinity College, Glenalmond, 1854–70, vicar of Brighton 1870–87; theologian.

[8] Misc. business: *H* cxxxv. 1533.

[9] Wife of an army officer, had written to complain of increased taxation; Add MS 44529, f. 129.

[10] Writs: *H* cxxxv. 1537.

[11] No report found.

C M Lushington—Ld C. Hervey—Mrs Osborne[1]—W.T. Hamilton[2]—and minutes.[3] Worked on bills and letters—Read Hales's Appeal[4]—Report on Spirit of Wine[5]—Westgarth.[6] Saw Sir A. Spearman (& I hope we have got the outline of a good plan for the N[ational] D[ebt] Commn. money)[7]—Sir C. Trevelyan—Mr Roberts—Mr Grogan—F. Lawley—Bid goodbye, reluctantly, to Mrs Higginson. Off at 3 for Ramsgate & Broadstairs arrived at 8 merrily escorted from the terminus.

13. 9 S.Trin.

Ch mg & evg. Conv. & Examn. on Gospel with the three elder children. Walk with C. Read Aspinall's Sermons[8]—Wilberforce's do—Bp Forbes on Nicene Creed[9]—Mayow's Tract.[10]

14. M.

Wrote to Sir C. Trevelyan—Mrs Cooper[11]—W. Hampton—Lord Hatherton—Lord J. Thynne—Mr Arbuthnot—F.C. Lawley—Ld Ellesmere—Ld Aberdeen—Ld Stanley (Ald[erley])—Mr Meyrick—Mr J. Griffiths—Mr J. Walker—and minutes. We all bathed. Tasso with Willy & Agnes. Read Westgarth's Austr. Felix.[12] Worked on Commissariat papers: & plans for next Session.

15. T.

Wrote to Sir A. Spearman—Mr G. Smith—Ld Harrowby—Rn. G.—Jas Watson—G. & Co—Mr Grogan—and minutes. Worked on Finance. And on Lady G's resid. Estate. Tasso with W. & A. Read Westgarth—Trench on Words.[13] Bathed early.

16. Wed.

Wrote to Jas Wilson—Mast. Balliol—J.R. Godley—and minutes. Bathed. Saw Sir W. James. At Ramsgate with Willy. Read Westgarth—Trench—Tasso with Willy & Agnes. Began that most odious task: correcting the proof report of a speech (May 8).

[1] Probably Emily Charlotte, *née* Grenfell, m. 1834 Sydney Godolphin *Osborne, 1808–89, rector of Durweston, Dorset, 1841–75; worked at Scutari; courtesy title 1859.
[2] Of the mint; had sent a gift: Add MS 44529, f. 129v.
[3] Parliament was this day prorogued.
[4] Untraced.
[5] *PP* 1854, lxv. 739; report of imports and exports of wines and spirits.
[6] Cp. 21 Dec. 53.
[7] Details in Add MS 44743, f. 92.
[8] J. *Aspinall, *Parish sermons* (1854).
[9] Cp. 5 Dec. 52.
[10] M. W. Mayow, 'War. A few words to soldiers and sailors called to active service, with short prayers for their private use' (1854).
[11] Refusing to intercede with bp. of London for her husband, W. M. Cooper, in a dispute: Add MS 44529, f. 131.
[12] Cp. 21 Dec. 53.
[13] Cp. 11 Dec. 52.

17. Th.

Wrote to E. of Aberdeen—F. Lawley—Sec. Scots Union Co.—J.N.G.—Freshfield—H. Glynne—W.S. Lindsay MP.—Jas Wilson—Rev Mr Stokes—Gladstone & Co—Mr Arbuthnot—Scotts—Mr J. Higham—and minutes. Bathed. Walk with Willy. Tasso with W. & Agnes. Read Westgarth—Mackinnon's Hist. of Civilisation.[1] Worked on proofs of speech.

18. Fr.

Wrote to Mr Waddington[2]—Prof. Huber[3]—Mr Wilson—Sir B. Hall—Sir J.E. Wilmot—Mr Mackinnon[4]—& minutes. Tasso with W. & Agnes—Bathed as usual with the boys. Saw Mr Newell[5]—Miss Eden—who has much to say & says it freely.[6] Read Westgarth—Trench—Worked on N.D. Comm. Finance.

19. Sat.

Wrote to Mr Hansard—Lord Ch. Hervey—Fr. Lawley—Bp N. Zealand—E. of Aberdeen—Mr T.H. Griffiths—Robn G—and minutes. Finished the odious task of correction. Saw Archdn. Harrison. Read Westgarth (finished) and Trench on Words. Bathed with the boys.

20. 10 S.Trin.

Church mg (with H.C.) and evg. Read Wilberforces Sermons on H.C.—Dobbin's Sermon[7]—Began some daily work with Willy with a view to his Confirmation. Begun a paper with a view to assisting him.

21. M.

Wrote to Rev. F. Meyrick—F. Lawley—R. Wilbraham—Mr Mackinnon—Lord C. Hervey—Mr Wilson—Lady Ellesmere—Mr Jones—and minutes. Bathed with the boys: also walked with them: explored Margate. Conv. with Willy for Confirmn. Read Finlay's Byzantine Empire. Trench on Words, Tasso with W. & A.

22. T.

Wrote to Freshfields—J.N.G.—Sir A. Spearman—Sir J.S. Forbes—Sir C.

[1] W. A. *Mackinnon, *On public opinion in Great Britain and other parts of the world* (1828), rewritten as *History of civilization* (1846).

[2] David Waddington, 1801–?63; railway constructor; tory M.P. Maldon 1847–52, Harwick 1852–7.

[3] Victor Aimé Huber, 1800–69; German philanthropist and cooperative leader; wrote on English universities; cp. 23 May 44.

[4] William Alexander *Mackinnon, 1789–1870; historian and liberal M.P. Dunwich 1830–1, Lymington 1831–52, Rye 1852 (void on petition), 1853–65.

[5] Christian Frederick Newell, Clare, Cambridge, incumbent of Broadstairs, Kent, from 1850, author of *The crisis and its duties* (1854).

[6] Emily *Eden, da. of 1st Baron Auckland; novelist and traveller in India; she lived at Eden Lodge, Broadstairs, and d. 1869.

[7] Small deletion here. O. T. Dobbin, 'The sabbath of heaven' (1849); on Heb. iv. 9.

Trevelyan—Mr G. Smith—Mast. Pembroke—Mr Jer. Briggs[1]—Mr Jos. Durham—and minutes. Walk by the sands(?) to Ramsgate. Bathed with the boys. Tasso with W. & A. Read Finlay's Byz. Empire[2]—Mrs Stowe's Tour[3]—Trench on Words (finished).

23. Wed.

Wrote to Mr Reynolds—Sir C. Trevelyan—Mr Grogan—Bp of Salisbury—Mr Anstey—Judge Coleridge—Mr Binger—Sir W. Farquhar—Mr L. Evelyn[4]—Mr Anderson—Mr Jas Watson—Mr Jones—& minutes. Bathed with the boys. Read Mrs Stowe—Finlay's Byz. Empire. Mrs Talbot came. Walk with C. Willy taken ill: & we had to fetch the doctor in the night. In the morning I had a conv. with him for confirm[atio]n.

24. Th. St.Barthol.

Wrote to J. Walker—J. Griffiths—E. of Aberdeen—Mr Barrow—R. Campbell[5]—Mr Jones—H. Glynne—and minutes. Read Mrs Stowe—Ruskin on Crystal Palace.[6]

But this became a day of great anxiety. The sickness did not give way to remedies. At 4 Mr Walter[7] apprehended Asiatic Cholera, the exhaustion was so great, the extremities also being cold and the appearance about the eyes bad. A mustard emetic wh he administered removed his fears as to the contents of the stomach, and proved to be the turning point as to its action. Dr Acland[8] came before six and felt the case to be still very anxious as one of diarrhoea only. Medicine however was withheld to give rest & an interval to nature, & a little arrowroot with brandy was given wh the stomach retained. Sleep came on at 7 lasted till midnight, was resumed after another portion of arrowroot & brandy had been administered & lasted another five hours—leaving to us a cheerful and blessed dawn, very different from the last.—We found the illness, unknown to us, was really very sharp on Tuesday.

25. Fr.

Wrote to Mr Arbuthnot—Mr Wilson—Bickers & Bush—W. Hampton—Bp of Salisbury—and minutes. Dr Acland again came in the morning & joined Mr Walter in consultn. but all was bright through the day though much weakness & need for care remains. Read A. Stanley on Black Prince (aloud

[1] Replying to a complaint about legislation: Add MS 44529, f. 131.
[2] Cp. 10 July 54.
[3] H. B. Stowe, *Sunny memories of foreign lands* (1854) describes her meeting with Gladstone on 7 May 53.
[4] Cp. 18 July 40.
[5] Perhaps Robert James Roy Campbell, London banker.
[6] J. *Ruskin, *The opening of the Crystal Palace considered in some of its relations to the prospects of art* (1854).
[7] Odiarne Coates Walter, medical officer at Broadstairs.
[8] i.e. H. W. *Acland.

to Willy)[1]—Finlay's Hist. Much with Willy: & altogether it was an unsettled day but of great joy. Walked with J. Talbot to Ramsgate: drive with C. & Mrs T.

26. Sat.

Wrote to Mast[er of] Pembroke [Oxford]—S. Herbert—Ld Aberdeen—Mr Grogan—Mr W. Mayow[2]—F. Lawley—Mr Lacaita—Dr Acland—Sig. Ferrari[3]—J.N.G.—Mr Freshfield—G. & Co—Marq. Dragonetti—and minutes: Willy again much better. Read Review of the Session[4]—A. Stanley's Essays. Drive with C. in search of Ebbe's Fleet: wh we did not *quite* find today.[5] Dr Acland again came in mg.

27. 11 S.Trin.

St Peter's Ch mg: Broadstairs aft. Wrote to Mr Wilson—minutes. Read Milman's Latin Xty (began)[6]—Wilberforce's Sermons—Stanley's Augustine. Willy came down for a little in the evg.

28. M.

Dear Lena's birthday: she is good, sensible, & gentle: full of hum & promise: may the light of God's countenance continue to shine on her. Wrote to Rev A P Stanley—Mr Pressly—Lord Steward—Mr Wilson—Mr L. Jones[7]—Mr Arbuthnot—Rev. Ld C. Hervey—Sir C. Trevelyan—Sir A. Spearman, & minutes. Finished Stanley's Essays—read Milman. Bathed. Drive with C. & the children. Saw Miss Eden in evg.

29. T. X

Off at 9¾ by Margate and Tilbury[8] to London. Wrote to Johnson L[ongden] & Co—F. Lawley—Jas Watson—Mr Barrow—Mr Stephenson—C.G.—Ld Harrowby—K. M'Kenzie[9]—Sec. Tithe Redn.—and minutes. Saw Rev. Mr Rowsell—Mr Anderson—Mr Arbuthnot—Mr Pressly—Sir A. Spearman—Sir Jas Graham. Also saw Horton (hopeful) and another [R]. Read Milman's Lat. Xty.

30. Wed.

Wrote to C.G.—E. Coleridge—Bp of Oxford—Sir A. Spearman—Ld St Germans—Johnson L & Co—& minutes. Saw Sir C. Trevelyan—Sir A.

[1] A. P. *Stanley, *Historical memorials of Canterbury. The landing of Augustine; the murder of Becket; Edward the Black Prince; Becket's shrine* (1855); an MS or proof.
[2] Cp. 24 Dec. 29.
[3] i.e. Francesco Ferrara.
[4] Cp. 19 Dec. 53.
[5] Cp. 6 Sept. 54.
[6] H. H. *Milman, *History of latin christianity*, 6 v. (1854–5).
[7] Possibly Lewis Jones, tailor, of Jarvis and Jones in Conduit Street, off Regent Street.
[8] On the Thames, 22 miles E. of London.
[9] Unidentified.

Spearman—Mr Clifford. 12¾–6¼ to Osborne[1] by Southampton & East Cowes. I felt the change of climate very sensibly. Read Milman. The Prince desired me to stay over till Friday. Conv. with Clarendon.

31. Th.

Wrote to Mr L. Jones—C.G. Read Milman—Diezel on Russia.[2] 11½–1½ with the Prince—on various matters: art, metropolis improvements, & finance. Joined the Queen's driving party to Newport.[3] Walk with Clarendon to the Prince's Farm: Saw Col. Phipps. Suleiman Pacha[4] dined: French with a Turk's cap. After dinner he was shrewd & diverting at the Queen's table in a high degree. Made a slight analysis from Milman.[5]

X *Friday Sept One 1854.*

Wrote to C.G.—Mr Stephenson—Ch. Pope[6]—Mr G. Berkeley—Sir J. Young—& minutes. Left at 10 with Clarendon. Came to London at 3: but by special train. We had much conv. especially on Cabinet management & Legislation, & on Finance. Saw D. of Newcastle—Sanders (Dentist)—Mr Young—Govr. of Bank. Read Diezel. Preparations for dividing & packing books. Saw Osborne X.

2. Sat.

Wrote to Jas Watson—Sir A. Spearman—Sir B. Hall—R. Wilberforce—Mr Wilson—Prince Albert—Mr G. Glyn—Messrs. Cocks—& minutes. Read Milman—Fraser's Magazine.[7] Saw Sir C. Trevelyan—Mr Arbuthnot. Packed 5 to 600 Volumes in the morning. 12.10–4 to Ramsgate: met C. Walk with her. Found all well thank God: but a sad sorrow in the news of Archdn. Wilberforce's resignations.[8] Worked on Sav. Bank accounts.

3. 12 S.Trin.

B[road]stairs Ch mg & evg. Conv. on the Gospel with the children. Walk with C. Read Wilberforce's Sermons (finished)—Milman's Hist.

4. M.

Wrote to Bp of Sodor & Man—L.A. Jones[9]—Bp of Oxford[10]—Mr Meyrick —Mr Wykeham Martin—Mrs Talbot—E. of Aberdeen—and minutes.

[1] Royal residence designed by *Albert, 1 mile SE. of Cowes on the Isle of Wight; *Victoria d. there. The house was given to the nation by *Edward VII.

[2] G. Diezel, tr. F. Rowan, *Russia, Germany, and the Eastern question* (1854).

[3] Capital of the Isle of Wight, 5 miles S. of Cowes.

[4] A visiting diplomat.

[5] Not found.

[6] A London printer.

[7] *Fraser's Magazine*, l (September 1854); articles on the ministry, Persia, and the war.

[8] Anticipating legal proceedings, he resigned all his anglican preferments on 30 August.

[9] Lewis A. Jones, treasury clerk 1834–57; first class clerk 1857–68; superintendent 1868.

[10] On R. I. *Wilberforce, in Newsome, *The parting of friends*, 402.

Bathed with the boys. Tea on the shore beyond N. Foreland. Read Milman —Fraser's Magazine—Goulburn's Financial Statement of 1846[1]—Tasso with W. & Agnes.

5. T.

Wrote to Mr Masterman—Jas Wilson—Sir J. Herschel—J.N.G.—S.R. Glynne—H. Glynne—W. Hampton—& minutes. Bathed with the boys. Walk with C. Tasso with W. & Agnes. Read Milman—Ph. Chasles' Etudes[2] —We went to tea with Miss Eden: and saw a large portfolio of her singularly beautiful & happy drawings.

6. Wed.

Wrote to Jas Wilson—Robn. G—W. Smythe (Methven)—John Lefevre—Rev W.W. Malet—Mr Anderson—& minutes. Bathed with the children. Read Milman. Walked (7 m) to Ebbe's Fleet St Augustine's landing place.[3] A disturbed night: as afterwards appeared from harvest bugs on the stubbles.

7. Th.

Wrote to J.G. Hubbard—Sir C. Trevelyan—& minutes. Read Milman. Bathed in forenoon. An attack of nettle-rash sent me to bed; wh in the evg became much aggravated.

8. Fr.

Wrote (perforce) to Earl of Aberdeen[4]—Mr H.R. Reynolds—Law Officers —and minutes. Read Milman. A day of really acute suffering—relieved in the course of the night by action of the bowels.

9. Sat.

Wrote to Scotts. Read Milman. Saw C.A. Wood. In the evening I had increased relief from further medicine & ate a little. Stephen came.

10. 13 S.Trin.

Morning prayers in my bed. Walked slowly to St Peter's[5] in aftn. Still under physic but all doing well. Read Bp Forbes—Milman. Wrote to R. Cavendish, & min. Saw Wood—S.R.G.

[1] H. *Goulburn, 'Financial statement . . . May 29, 1846.'

[2] V. E. Philarète Chasles, *Études sur la littérature et les mœurs de l'Angleterre au xixe siècle* (1850).

[3] On Pegwell Bay, 3½ miles SW. of Ramsgate; also traditional landing place of Hengist and Horsa.

[4] To refer bank of England dispute to cabinet; cp. Conacher, 382.

[5] St. Peters church, St. Peter's 2 miles NW. of Broadstairs.

11. M.

Wrote to J.G. Hubbard (draft)—Lyttelton—Sir A. Spearman—J.N.G.—Mr Anderson—Scotts—R. Cavendish—Jas Watson—F. Dickinson—Jas Wilson—W. Hampton—& minutes. Tasso with the children. Read Milman. Walk & drive with Willy & S.R.G. Went to see R.C. St Augustine's at Ramsgate:[1] also Ch. Ch. hard by.[2] Two conversations with Willy: one on R.C. Ch., and one on use & division of time: both satisfactory. Saw Miss Eden. Began to correct Speech of May 22.

12. T.

Wrote to Ld J. Russell—Sir T.G.—R. Wilbraham—Mr W. Brown—Sir A. Spearman—Mr Pressly—Mr H F Stephenson—Mr W. Smythe—Mr K. M'Kenzie—Mr Hayter—& minutes. Corrected Speech of May 22. Bathed with Willy. Walk with C: we discussed the whole Hampton case.[3] Worked upon papers. Read Milman. Tasso with W. & A.

13. Wed.

Wrote to
Govr. of Bank (see 11 Sept.)
(Quarterly Letter)[4]
Mr Anderson—Sir C. Trevelyan—Earl of Aberdeen—Rev. R.W. Whitford—Bishop of Oxford—Rev R.I. Wilberforce—Sir T. Gladstone—& minutes. Bathed as usual. Saw Miss Eden (whom we much regret to leave)—Rev Mr Newell. A day of settling, paying, and packing. Read Milman (finished Vol II.)

14. Th.

Wrote to Mr Roberts[5]—Bp of Moray—Mr Hayter—and minutes. Read Finlay's Greek Empire—Jane Eyre[6]—M. Gore on the Crimea.[7] Off at 2½ on foot by St Peters (Vicarage)[8] to Bettishanger[9] wh I reached in pouring rain a little before six. C. & the party came an hour later. A kind reception & a happy evening.

15. Fr.

Wrote to Lord Aberdeen—Sir J. Graham—Solr. General—R. Wilbraham—W Hampton—Rev Mr Rowsell—& minutes. Drive with the James's to

[1] On the west cliff at Ramsgate, the masterpiece of A. W. N. *Pugin, whose house, the Grange, was built nearby in the same gothic style.
[2] The anglican church.
[3] i.e. the butler and his wife, to whose second child Gladstone was godparent.
[4] The quarterly statement of returns from the bank; cp. Sir J. Clapham, *The bank of England* (1944), ii. 251–4 and App. F.
[5] i.e. Henry Roberts, cp. 19 Nov. 52.
[6] By C. *Brontë (1847).
[7] M. *Gore, *Description of some of the principal harbours and towns of the Krimea* (1854).
[8] Cp. 10 Sept. 54.
[9] Sir W. C. James's house 4 miles W. of Deal.

Mungeham Walmer & Deal.[1] We saw the Duke [of Wellington]'s room: & found the Duchess of Buccleuch. Conv. with James on our Church Fund & larger matters. Read Jane Eyre. Dinner party in evg.

16. Sat.

Wrote to Lord Aberdeen—Sir J. Young—J.G. Hubbard—Mr Entwistle—Ld D. Stuart—and minutes. Read Jane Eyre—Word in Season (on culture of Wheat)[2]—Laurie on Dec. Coinage.[3] Rode with James to see Barfreston Church[4] (but his own is a sight too) and the noble old Fredville Oak.[5] Organ in evg.

17. 14 S.Trin.

Bettishanger Church mg & evg. Walk with W. James to the Schools. Read De Imit[atione Christi]—Lord A. Hervey—Wrote to Wilbraham—Sir C. Trevelyan.

18. M.

Off at 9½ to Sandwich[6] & Canterbury: where with C. I again went over the Cathedral & then visited St Augustine's[7] & St Martin's.[8] We returned at 4.20. Read Jane Eyre. Lord Hardinge dined & we had much conv. on the army & the war.

19. T.

Wrote to Lord J. Russell—Rev Mr Butler—Lyttelton—J.G. Hubbard—Mrs Scott—Ld Aberdeen—Ld A. Hervey—Mr Bright MP—& minutes. Finished Jane Eyre a very remarkable but jarring book. Reached D[owning] St. 2.20. Saw Sir A. Spearman—Mr Wilson—& Conclave on Defic[ienc]y Bills & Bank. Worked on Treas. papers. Arranging books & letters at night.

20. Wed.

Wrote to Mr Grogan—Brown Shipley & Co[9]—Mrs Laurie[10]—Rev Mr

[1] Mongeham and Walmer are seats respectively 2 miles SW. and 1½ miles SSW. of Deal; *Wellington d. at the latter, the official residence of the warden of the cinque ports.

[2] [Samuel Smith], 'A word in season; or how the corngrower may yet grow rich, and his labourer happy' (1849); several subsequent editions.

[3] J. Laurie, *Decimal coinage. A practical analysis of the comparative merits of one pound and tenpence as the ruling integer of a decimal currency for the United Kingdom* (1854).

[4] A small Norman church, 6½ miles NNW. of Dover.

[5] In Fredville Park by Barfreston; 36 ft. in girth, reputedly planted before 1066.

[6] One of the cinque ports, 5 miles SW. of Ramsgate.

[7] To the E. of the cathedral; once a monastery, in the nineteenth-century a missionary college.

[8] ¾ miles E. of the cathedral; contains some pre-Saxon remnants.

[9] Liverpool Anglo-American merchant bankers; (Sir) W. *Brown, M.P., was the senior partner; cp. Add MS 44378, f. 157.

[10] Mary Laurie, wrote to thank Gladstone for letter on her dead husband; cp. 16 Sept. 54.

Richards—Coutts & Co—Marg. Campana [1]—Lady Napier [2]—Sir C. Barry—Mr Wilson—Sir W. James—& minutes. Saw Mr Brickwood—Mr Pressly—Lord Aberdeen—Mr Wilson—Mr Roberts—Sir C. Trevelyan—F.C. Lawley. Worked on my books at No 6. Also on Lady G's Estate matters and my own private papers.

21. Th.

Wrote to Dean Saunders—Mr Pressly—Mr Wilson—Sir W. Molesworth—J.N.G.—Ld Chancellor—M Tupper—Govr. Bank (dft) & minutes. Saw Lord Aberdeen *cum* Sir J. Graham—4–6. Law Officers cum Mr Wilson 2–4. —F. Lawley—Sir A.Y. Spearman—Hampton (on his matters)—Mr Wilson. Shopping & books. St James's Ch. 7 P.M. Read Gov. Barkly's Jamaica tour.[3] Arranging papers & for departure.

22. Fr.

Wrote to Clarendon—Mr Hubbard—Mr Hayter—Mr Harrison (F.O) [4]—Mr Pressly—Sir J. Graham—Mr Wilson—D of Newcastle & minutes. Read Somerville Phys. Geogr.[5]—Marmont's Turkey [6]—Sismondi.[7] Saw Govr. of Bank—Mr Wilson—Mr Fox—Mrs Talbot—Mr Durham—Mr King (Commr.).[8] Off at 2¾ for Audley End [9] where we arrived at six. Willy bid us goodbye at the Station. We were most kindly received.

23. Sat.

Service (short) in Chapel at 9½. Wrote to Earl of Aberdeen—Lady Canning—Mr Wilson—R. Cavendish—Dean of Peterb.—Miss Brown—Mr J. Durham—Rev. W. Selwyn—Sec. E. Co. RR.[10]—and minutes. Saw Mr Herbert. We drove to Chesterford,[11] walked, & sat a good deal with Ld Braybrooke. A round game in evg. Read Somerville—Sismondi—Etudes Sociales.

24. 15 S.Trin.

Saff[ron] Walden Ch (a noble one)[12] mg. Littlebury aft.[13] Walk with Ld Braybrooke. Read Ld A. Hervey[14]—Milman on the Atonement.[15] Examined the very extraordinary Psalter here: valued at £300.

[1] Wife of A. Fabio Campana, 1815–82; Italian composer and singing teacher; lived in London from 1850.

[2] Elizabeth, *née* Johnstone, grandda. of earl of Hopetoun, m. 1816 William John, 9th Baron Napier, she d. 1883.

[3] Probably *PP* 1854, xlii. 79; Sir H. Barkly's report of the Jamaican economy.

[4] T. R. Harrison, printer to the foreign office.

[5] Mary *Somerville, *Physical geography*, 2 v. (1848).

[6] Cp. 4 July 53.

[7] Cp. 22 June 54.

[8] Probably Charles King, commission agent, of Friday Street, Cheapside.

[9] Cp. 15 Nov. 41.

[10] To arrange the journey.

[11] On the river Granta, 3½ miles NNW. of Saffron Walden.

[12] Perpendicular in style.

[13] 1½ miles NW. of Saffron Walden.

[14] Cp. 13 Nov. 53.

[15] R. *Milman, *The love of the atonement: a devotional exposition of the fifty-third chapter of Isaiah* (1853); and wrote at length to R. I. *Wilberforce, in Newsome, *The parting of friends*, 382–3.

25. M.

Service 9½. Wrote to Sir A. Spearman—Robn. G.—Mr O'Neill Daunt[1]—and minutes. Read Somerville—Sismondi. We went to shoot partridges & hares. Saw Ld C. Hervey. Read Somerville—Sismondi.

26. T.

Ld B[raybrooke] accompd. me early towards the railway & I came to Ely[2] with Ld C. H[ervey] at 11. Morning service there; the Cathedral nave filled with Militia afterwards. We went over the Church with Selwyn; its beauty is hardly to be described. On with C. to Peterborough[3] at 2.15. Afternoon service there: saw the Cathedral: it has much of simple grandeur but loses by the windows. We were most kindly entertained at the Deanery. Read Somerville—Sismondi.

27. Wed.

Cathedral 10 A.M. Made up a packet of minutes & letters. Off at 11.10 to Retford[4] & Manchester. reached Worsley[5] at 5¾. Read as yesterday & Ld Ellesmere's Address.[6] Singing in evg. Much delighted & surprised by the place.

28. Th.

Wrote to Sol. General—Ld C. Hervey—Sol. Treasury—Jas Watson—J.G. Hubbard—W C James—V.C. Oxford—Wm. Smythe—Murray (Union Bank Ed[inburgh])[7]—W. Selwyn—Ld Palmerston, & minutes. Read Sismondi—Acct. of Railway Commee. Proceedings in 1825: one of the most curious records of the age.[8] We visited the Patricroft works & (more remarkable still) their *owner*.[9]

29. Fr.

Wrote to Ld Chancellor—Sir C. Wood—Dr Macbride—Ld Monteagle—R. Wilbraham—H. Glynne, & minutes. Read Ed. Rev. on Teatotalism[10]—Mrs Somervile [sic]—Ely Cathedral Hand Book.[11] Walk with Lord E[llesmere] mg—with him & the ladies aftn.

[1] William Joseph O'Neill Daunt, 1807–94; radical M.P. 1832–3; *O'Connell's secretary; leading disestablishmentarian.

[2] Cathedral town 15 miles NE. of Cambridge.

[3] Cathedral town 43 miles NE. of Northampton.

[4] East Retford, 18 miles NW. of Newark.

[5] Ellesmere's seat, 6 miles NW. of Manchester.

[6] F. *Egerton, 1st earl of Ellesmere, *Address to the Royal Geographical Society of London* (1854).

[7] R. R. Murray, a teller.

[8] Select cttee. on the Liverpool and Manchester Railroad Bill, which discussed rival merits of canals and railways; cp. E. Richards, *The leviathan of wealth* (1973), 59ff.

[9] Iron works 5 miles W. of Manchester founded and run by James *Nasmyth, 1808–90, inventor and engineer.

[10] *Edinburgh Review*, c. 43 (July 1854); on 'Teatotalism, and laws against the liquor trade'.

[11] *Hand book to the cathedral church of Ely. With engravings* (1852).

30. Sat.

Wrote to Ld Lansdowne—Ld Canning—Mr Wilbraham—Mr Wilson—Sir T. Fremantle—Mr Anderson—Mr Greenwood & minutes. Walk with Ld E[llesmere] to see his second Church.[1] Singing in evg. Read Mignet's Charles V [2]—Sismondi—M'Culloch's Russia & Turkey.[3]

Oct 1. 16 S.Trinity.

Church 10½ (and H.C.) mg—3½ aft. Wrote to Willy [4]—Mr Wilson—& minutes. Walk with Lord & Lady E. Read Ld A. Hervey—Mignet's Charles V—Thorp's Charge [5]—Hutchins's Sermon.[6]

2. M.

Wrote to Govr. of Bank (with draft) [7]—Ld Aberdeen—Ld Clarendon—Mr Wilson—Sir A. Spearman—R. Wilbraham—& minutes. Off at 12½: Ld & Ly E. went with us to Patricroft. We were all in great joy about the flood of news from the Black Sea.[8] Saw Mr Barker in Chester—Unpacking &c. at Hawarden. Read Report on Public Houses.[9]

3. T.

Church 8½ A.M. Wrote to Bp of Oxford—R. Wilberforce—Sir J. Graham—Robn. G—Mr E. Sharpe [10]—and minutes. Saw Mr G. Burnett 2 h—and settled the new book cases or rather bookholders with [David] Bailie. Unpacked 3 boxes the first fruits of the 5000 vols that are to come here: my Divinity & Literature. Walk with S. to Dee Cottage. Read Public Houses Evidence—Mrs Somerville.

4. Wed.

Church 8½ A.M. Wrote to Ld Palmerston [11]—Mr D. Conner [12]—Atty. General—Ld Canning—Lady Canning—Mrs Talbot—& minutes. I reflected on Wilberforce's case & wrote a short draft with a view to it.[13] I find myself

[1] He owned the livings of Ellenbrook, Walkden-Moor and Worsley.

[2] F. A. M. Mignet, *Charles Quint: son abdication, son séjour et sa mort au monastère de Yuste* (1854).

[3] J. R. *McCulloch, *Russia and Turkey* (1854); an extract from his *Geographical dictionary* (1841).

[4] On confirmation, in Lathbury, ii. 153–6.

[5] T. Thorp, perhaps 'Charge at the visitation, in July 1843', or an untraced later one.

[6] G. Hutchins, 'The Church of England identified with the primitive Church of Jerusalem; a sermon' (1845); on Acts xvi. 31.

[7] In Add MS 44381, f. 167.

[8] The allied victory at the battle of the Alma, fought on 20 September 1854.

[9] Recommending a uniform system of licencing by magistrates: *PP* 1854, xiv. 231.

[10] Edmund *Sharpe, 1809–77, railway designer and constructer; cp. Add MS 44529, f. 157v.

[11] In Ashley, *Palmerston*, ii. 68, and Guedalla, *P*, 99. Cp. Morley, i. 494.

[12] Daniel Conner, 1798–1880, of Manch House, Cork, had written on Dunmanway Union; cp. Add MS 44529, f. 154.

[13] He became a roman catholic in Paris on 1 Nov. 1854.

under a very formidable responsibility & can but hope I am in the line of duty. Up late. Read Milman (began V. 3.)—Public Houses Evidence. Walk with Stephen. Saw Mr E. Sharpe 2½–4½ on LCS. RR.—Mr Griffiths (Ch[urch] w[arde]n).[1]

5. Th.

Wrote to E. Breakenridge—Rev. H. Ffoulkes—R. Wilbraham—Captain G. —Sir A. Spearman—Mr E. Sharpe (with incl.)—Mr Masters Smith[2]—and minutes. Walk with J. Talbot. Read Publ. H. Evidence—Cargill on Act of 44[3]—Stansfeld on Monetary Panics.[4] Worked on LCSRR. affairs.[5]

6. Fr.

Church 8½ A.M. Wrote to Govr. of Bank (sign.)—Mr Forshall[6]—E. Cardwell —Mr Anstey—Hatchards & minutes. Read Publ. H. Evidence—Stansfeld to Cobden[7]—do on Monetary Panics. Walk with S. & J. Talbot. Wrote on Currency.

7. Sat.

Confined to bed by an attack of incipient diarrhoea. Wrote (by C) to Mr E. Sharpe—Sir C. Trevelyan—read Stansfeld (finished)—Publ. H. Ev. (1853). Saw R. Wilberforce in evg: but only on Oxford & general matters theological & other.

8. 17 S.Trin.

Church 3 P.M. My morning was occupied (in bed) perforce with matters of business. Wrote to Mr Anderson (Q[uarterly] Acct.)—Mr Wilson—Sir T. Fremantle—Robn. G—& minutes. Morning prayers alone. Read Woodward's S.[8]—Hardwicke's Hist[9]—Ch. periodicals. Walk with R.W. & in aftn. some two hours with him on the Roman argument.

9. M.

Wrote to E. Breakenridge—Jos. Martin—D[10] of Newcastle—R Wilbraham —Rev C. Lane[11]—Sir A. Spearman—& minutes. At the Church resp. the

[1] Richard Griffiths, of the village.

[2] William Masters Smith, 1802–61; sheriff of Kent 1848; tory M.P. West Kent 1852–7; a strong protectionist.

[3] W. Cargill, 'The currency' (1845); discusses 1844 Bank Act.

[4] H. Stansfeld, *The Currency Act of 1844, the cause of the panic of October 1847, and the generator of monetary panics periodically* (1854).

[5] It needed an independent terminus; Gladstone later unwillingly agreed to help to promote one, while still chancellor: Add MS 44529, f. 197.

[6] Josiah *Forshall, 1795–1863; secretary to British Museum 1828–50; chaplain to Foundling Hospital from 1829; cataloguer and editor.

[7] H. Stansfeld, *A letter to Richard *Cobden . . . on our protective and restrictive currency laws* (1850).

[8] Perhaps F. B. Woodward, *Sermons preached in St. Stephen's chapel, Dublin* (1850).

[9] Cp. 27 Nov. 53.

[10] Unidentified.

[11] Probably Charlton Lane, perpetual curate of St. Mark's, Kennington, Surrey; rural dean of Southwark, 1854.

Organ. Morning & evg. much conv. with R. W[ilberforce] on the English case. Began to write to Graham on Currency in evg. Up to 12, and lost my sleep in consequence. Read Fenn on the Funds.[1]

10. T.

Rose at 11: heavy cold & hoarseness, the new *turn* of Saturday's attack. Wrote to Sir J. Graham—R. Wilbraham—Mr Woodard—Ld Talbot de Malahide[2]—J. Griffiths—and minutes. Again to the Ch. where we carried the placing of the organ *along* the Church. Today I had only a shorter convn. with W[ilberforce] on the case of the English Church. Read 'Faut-il une Pologne?'[3]

11. Wed.

Wrote to V.C. Oxford—Mr T. Rathbone—Solr. General—Mr Godley—Robn. G—Mr Anderson—Mr Greenwood—Sir F. Rogers—& minutes. Read Mrs Somerville.[4] But now indeed most of my reading time is absorbed in the wonderful details of the Battle of Alma & its sequel.[5] Rose at midday. Resumed conv. with W.; on his dogmatic work (*ἔργον.*)[6] Walked with C.

12. Th.

Wrote to Bp of Moray—Mr Panizzi—Rev Mr Burgess—Mr Anderson—Ld Canning—J.N.G.—Hon A. Gordon—and minutes. Read Mrs Somerville—Publ. Houses Evidence. R. Wilberforce went. He leaves me in doubt & fear tho' not without hope; and with a sense how ill I have done my part. Singing in evg.

13. Fr.

Wrote to R. Wilbraham—Solr. General—C. Pressly—and minutes. Also worked at calcul[atio]ns on the harvest & wrote part of a letter on them.[7] Sat or stood rather to Mr. Munro for a bust: of wh I am rather ashamed, but the act is not spontaneous.[8] Saw Mr Burnett. Worked on my books, a part of the new cases havg come home. Read Somerville—Publ. H. Evidence.

14. Sat.

Ch 8½ A.M. Wrote to D. of Newcastle—J. Sandars—Ed. Guardian[9]—Ld Panmure—Mr E. Sharpe—R. Wilbraham—Overends—and minutes. Sat

[1] C. Fenn, *A compendium of the English and foreign funds, and the principal joint stock companies* (1837).

[2] James Talbot, 1805–83; court office 1863–6; succ. as 4th Baron Talbot de Malahide 1850.

[3] By M. Mochnacki, tr. V. Budgenski (1854).

[4] Cp. 22 Sept. 54.

[5] *PP* 1854, ix. 477, and many press reports.

[6] 'work' again.

[7] See next day.

[8] Exhibited at Royal Academy 1855.

[9] Marked 'Immediate'; draft on the 'magnificant harvest', signed 'Ruricola', in Add MS 44381, f. 192, printed in *The Guardian*, 18 October 1854, 800; but see Sir J. Clapham, *The bank of England*, ii. 222.

long to Mr Munro. Worked on books: over 700 vols now lodged. Rode with a party. Read Somerville—Canadian Resignation [1]—Oriental question papers.[2]

15. 18 S.Trin.

Ch. mg & evg. Wrote to Mr Wilson—minutes. Spent my day on R. Wilberforce's sad & saddening book.[3] Conv. with C. Wynne on Oxford Bill & its consequences.

16. M. X

Church 8½ A.M. Sat to Mr Munro. Finished Wilberforce's Book on Church authority: it froze my blood. Off at 4½ for the Express to London. D[owning] St (late) at 12½. Read Hutchinson's Massachussetts.[4] Saw Blanchard [R]—& another.

17. T.

Wrote to Bank of E. (draft)—Agnes—Willy—Bp of Oxford—Mr Hayter—C.G. Saw Mr J. Wood—Mr Sandars—Mrs Lindsay [5]—Ld Aberdeen—S. Herbert. Dined with the Granville's. Saw Bishop—of wh I hope good might come [R]. Worked on my books & packed some 500 to 600.

18. Wed.

Wrote to C.G.[6] and minutes. Also B. of Engd. (letter).[7] 1–5¾. Journey to Windsor & back for Council: some Cabinet on the way. Saw Willy (at Windsor)—Sir J. Graham—C. Wood—Mr J. Wood—Mr Wilson. Worked on books & made my packings up to about 900. Read Central America papers (part) [8]—Ashworth on the Preston Strike [9]—the (Canada) Hincks & Bowes suit.[10]

19. Th. X

Wrote to Mr J.A. Smith—Mr Rich—Sir J. Potter—Mr Masterman—Mr Durham—Sir J. Young—Mr Brotherton—Maj. Graham—Rev. J E Glad-

[1] Of the *Hincks ministry; cp. 18 Oct. 54.
[2] *PP* 1854, lxxii. 213ff.
[3] *An inquiry into the principles of church authority* (1854); his last book.
[4] T. *Hutchinson, *The history of the province of Massachusetts bay, from 1749 to 1774* (1828).
[5] A volunteer nurse for the Crimea; cp. Bassett, 104.
[6] In Bassett, 104.
[7] Draft in Add MS 44381, f. 206.
[8] Probably trade returns: *PP* 1854–5, xxxix. 145.
[9] H. *Ashworth, *The Preston strike, an enquiry into its causes and consequences* (1854); the Preston mill-workers strike in December 1853 was not broken until May 1854.
[10] *Hincks and John Bowes, mayor of Toronto, were accused of railway contract corruption, cp. Sir F. *Hincks, *Reminiscences*, 356.

stone—Miss Nightingale [1]—Mr Roberts—Thos Foster [2]—Sir C. Anderson [3] —Ld Panmure—C.G.—Hon G. Talbot—Sir W. James—Rev. F. Oakeley—Ld Cowley—Solr. General—Rev Mr Row and minutes. Saw Miss Chambers (2) [4]—Mr Wood cum Mr Pressly—Mr Sandars—Sir C. Trevelyan —Mr Wilson—Mr Roberts—W. Hampton—Mr Wm. Gladstone—Mr Anderson. Sought but missed Collins [R]. Saw Wolf, & one other [R]. Finished Central Ama. papers. read Chr. Remembrr. Began to write what may become a letter to R. Wilberforce.[5]

20. Fr.

Wrote to Sir C. Trevelyan—Rev. Mr Burgess—Mr J. Wood—Sir C. Barry—Mr Wilson—Sir W. Molesworth—Scotts—Mr A. Russel (Ed. Scotsman) [6]—Bp N. Zealand—Mr J. Wood—Sir A. Spearman—and minutes. Carlton in Evg. Saw R.J. Phillimore—Mr A. Durham—D. of Newcastle—Sir Jas. Graham—Sir A. Spearman—Mr Wilson—Mr Holland—Mr Allen—Ld Aberdeen. Wrote minute on B.I.R. vacancy. Read De Quincy's Autobiograph. Sketches [7]—Macaulay's Report on Indian Service Examn.[8] Worked on books at No 6.

21. Sat.

Up at 5 & by train at 6¼ to Hawarden (met by C. in Chester) at one. Wrote to Robn. G.—and R. Wilberforce (with copy).[9] Read The Lost Prince.[10] Sat to Mr Munro.

22. 19 S.Trin.

Ch mg. & evg. Wrote to Willy—(meaning of life, and use of Time.) Read Ld A. Hervey (finished)—Life of Channing [11]—M'Kenzie's Sermon [12]—Remarks on Origin of Evil.[13] Walk with C.

[1] Florence *Nightingale, 1820–1910, founder of nursing. *Herbert asked her on 15 October to go to the Crimea; she left London on 21 October, after correspondence with the treasury; cp. E. T. *Cook, *Life of Florence *Nightingale* (1913), i. 157.

[2] Thomas Campbell Foster, 1813–82; barrister; parliamentary reporter for *The Times*; failed to become M.P.; recorder of Warwick from 1874.

[3] Sir Charles Henry John Anderson, 1804–91; 9th bart. 1846; sheriff of Lincolnshire from 1851; antiquarian and ecclesiologist.

[4] Miss J. J. D. Chambers, on sisterhoods of mercy.

[5] Cp. 21 Oct. 54.

[6] Alexander *Russel, 1814–76; ed. of Scottish newspapers, of *The Scotsman* from 1848; anti-clerical and anti-protectionist.

[7] T. *De Quincey, *Autobiographic sketches*, 2 v. (1853–4) from *Selections grave and gay, from writings published and unpublished*, 14 v. (1853–60).

[8] Published as *The Indian civil service. by . . . T. B. *Macaulay, . . . Lord *Ashburton, the Rev. . . . H. *Melvill, B. *Jowett, and . . . the Speaker* (1855).

[9] Draft in Add MS 44381, f. 212.

[10] J. H. Hanson, *The lost prince; facts leading to prove the identity of Louis XVII and Eleazar Williams* (1854).

[11] Cp. 21 Mar. 52.

[12] H. *Mackenzie, 'The mission of the Scottish episcopal church; a charity sermon' (1854); on Col. iv. 5.

[13] Untraced.

23. M.

Ch 8½ a.m. Read The Lost Prince—Ld Carlisle's Diary.[1] Went with Henry over the Sandycroft works.[2] Sat to Mr Munro. Planned & ordered the rest of my new bookcases.

24. T.

Wrote to Sir A. Spearman—Sir J. Young—Mr E. Sharpe—Rev. N. Wade—J.N.G.—Robn. G—and minutes. Read The Lost Prince—Lord Carlisle. Sat to Mr Munro. Rode with Agnes & a party. Church 8½ a.m.

25. Wed.

Church 8½ a.m. Wrote to R. Wilberforce (Eheu!) and copy—Robn. G.—E. Sharpe—Supt. G.W. Goods Station—Mr Hayter—Mr Wilson—Mr Wood—Atty General and minutes. Read Ld Carlisle—Owen Jones on Colour in Statuary[3]—The Lost Prince. Busy about arrangements with Mr Munro—also George's money arrangements. Last sitting to Mr. M. who left us in the Evg. Walk with G. to St. John's.[4] Worked on my books.

26. Th.

Ch 8½ a.m. Wrote to R. Wilbraham—Mr G. Patton—Mr Wilson—Mr C. Paskin—J.G. Talbot—Sir C. Trevelyan & minutes. We dined at the Rectory. Rode with Agnes & her cousins. NB. Mazy promises admirably. Read Ld Carlisle. Finished arranging the 2d batch of books.

27. Fr.

Ch 8½ A.M. Wrote to[5] Mr Grogan—Mr Wilson—Mr Higham—Fremantle—R. Phillimore—and minutes. Saw Burnett (SRG). Tasso with Agnes. Walk with L[yttelto]n. Read the Lost Prince—Ld Carlisle—Childe Harold.[6]—Zeal without Innovation.[7]

28. Sat. SS.Simon & Jude.

Church at 11 A.M. Wrote to Ld Aberdeen—H. Tayleur—J.N.G.—Sir W. Molesworth—S.E.G.—& minutes. Read the Lost Prince (finished)—Ld Carlisle's Diary—his Lecture on Pope.[8] Singing.

[1] G. W. F. *Howard, Lord Carlisle, *Diary in Turkish and Greek waters* (1854).
[2] The estate improvements by the Dee, 1½ miles NE. of the castle.
[3] O *Jones, *An apology for the colouring of the Greek court in the Crystal Palace* (1854).
[4] St. John's church, Hawarden; J. E. Troughton was the curate.
[5] 'Sir C. Trevelyan' here deleted.
[6] By *Byron (1812–18).
[7] By [James Bean] (1808).
[8] G. W. F. *Howard, *Lectures and addresses, in aid of public education; including a lecture on the poetry of *Pope* (1852).

29. 20 S.Trin.

Ch. mg & aft. Read (Parker) Liturgical Offices[1]—Overton's Apology[2]—Heylyn's History[3]—Rogers on the Articles.[4]

30. M.

Church 8½ A.M. Wrote to Mr Hayter—Rev. F. Fowke—Mr Wilson—Ld Elcho—Capt. Robertson[5]—Mr Wood—Mr Greenwood—Mr Godfrey—Mr M'Culloch—Duke of Newcastle—Sir C. Trevelyan—G.W. Goods Sup[intenden]t—& minutes. Walk to C's ride. Tasso with Agnes. Lady L[yttelto]n & a party dined. Singing in evg. Read Ld Carlisle (finished)—Childe Harold—Public Houses, Evidence.[6]

31. T.

Ch. 8½ A.M. Wrote to E. of Clarendon—S. Herbert—W. Hampton—J. Tombs[7]—Sir J. Herschel—Rev. E. Hawkins—Mr Pressly—Mr Jas Wilson. —and minutes. Read Publ. H. Evidence—Willis's Canterb. Cathedral[8]—Childe Harold—Civil Service Papers.[9]

Wed Nov.1.1854.All Saints.

Church 11 A.M. Wrote to D of Newcastle—Dr Pusey—Dr Steinbein[10]—Mr Higham—Dean Ramsay—Mr Glyn—and minutes. Rode with Meriel & Agnes. Read Civil Service Papers—Clarke's Travels[11]—Calcolo Decidozzinale[12]—Childe Harold—Willis's Canterbury Cathedral.

2. Th.

Ch. 8½ A.M. Wrote to Sir C. Trevelyan—Sir J. Graham—R. Wilbraham—Rev. G. Forbes—Mr Goulburn—Dr Jeune[13]—Sir T. Fremantle—Duchess of Sutherland—and minutes. Tasso with Agnes. Dinner party: singing. Mr [E.] Austin told me of his conversation with poor R.I. W[ilberforce]. Read Royer's Narrative[14]—Civil Service Papers—Willis's Canterb. Cathedral (finished).

[1] *The two liturgies A.D. 1549 and A.D. 1552 with other documents* . . ., ed. J. Ketley for the Parker Society (1844).

[2] J. *Overton, *The true churchmen ascertained or, an apology for those of the regular clergy of the establishment who are sometimes called evangelical ministers* (1801).

[3] Cp. 9 Dec. 40.

[4] T. *Rogers, *The catholic doctrine of the Church of England, an exposition of the thirty nine articles* (1607, 1854).

[5] To refuse to recommend Captain H. L. Robertson to *Dalhousie, as he had done so already: Add MS 44529, f. 172v., 174v.

[6] Cp. 2 Oct. 54.

[7] John Tombs, a builder, of Warwick Street, Golden Square.

[8] R. *Willis, *Architectural history of Canterbury cathedral* (1845).

[9] 'Reports of Cttees. of Inquiry into Public Offices': *PP* 1854, xxvii. 33.

[10] Of Stuttgardt; had sent a book by Schübler on banking: Add MS 44529, f. 167.

[11] E. D. *Clarke, *Travels in various countries of Europe, Asia and Africa*, 6 v. (1810–23).

[12] Untraced.

[13] '(2)' here deleted.

[14] A. Royer, *English prisoners in Russia, a personal narrative of the first lieutenant of H.M.S. Tiger* (1854).

3. Fr.

Wrote to Mr J. Travers—J.N.G.—Ld Chancellor—J. Lacaita—Sir J. Herschel—Mr Slaney—Atty. General—and minutes. Church 8½ A.M. Read Royer's Narrative—Ed. Rev. on Macaulay's Speeches—on Army—and on Railway Policy &c[1]—Civil Service Papers.

4. Sat.

Ch. 8½ A.M. Wrote to Master of Pembroke—Robn. G.—D. of Richmond[2]—Mr Patton—D. of Newcastle—Sir C. Trevelyan—and minutes. We dined at the Rectory. Walk with G., S., & Godley. Read Royer (finished)—Civil Service Papers—Ed. Rev. on Ch. Rates[3]—Harford on Currency.[4]

5. 21 S.Trin.

Ch mg (H.C.) & evg. Read Hickes's Devotions, & Preface[5]—Overton's Apology—Canning's Memoirs.[6] Walk with C.

6. M.

Ch 8½ A.M. Wrote to D of Newcastle—Ld Elcho—Mr W. Grogan—W. Brown—& minutes. Read Civil Service Papers—Publ. Houses Evidence—Burns's Letters[7]—Demosthenes, Phil[ippic] I. Tasso with Agnes—Ride with Agnes—called on Mr Ffoulkes.

7. T.

Ch. 8½ A.M. Wrote to Earl of Aberdeen—Robn. G.[8]—W.C. Robertson[9]—Mr Wilson—W. Crawford—Mr Goulburn—Rev J. Bramston—Hampton—Mr Whatman[10]—Sir C. Trevelyan—and minutes. Organ consultation with Church. Called on the Brewsters. Dinner party—& singing. Read Publ. H. Evidence—Burns's Letters.

8. Wed.

Ch. 8½ A.M. Wrote to R. Wilbraham—Mr Glyn—Capt. Robertson—Sig. C. Lieto[11]—S.H. Northcote—Sir J. Herschel—Dean Ramsay—and minutes.

[1] *Edinburgh Review*, c. 420, 490, 534 (October 1854).

[2] Charles Gordon-*Lennox, 1791–1860; fought in Peninsula; succ. as 5th duke of Richmond and Gordon 1819; paymaster-general 1830–4; president of Royal Agricultural Society from 1845.

[3] *Edinburgh Review*, c. 305 (October 1854).

[4] Untraced.

[5] G. *Hickes, *Devotions, in the ancient way of offices, with psalms, hymns* (1701).

[6] Cp. 22 Oct. 54.

[7] *Reliques of Robert *Burns, consisting chiefly of original letters*, ed. R. H. Cromek (1808).

[8] Part in Morley, i. 494.

[9] Had applied for a distributorship of stamps.

[10] James Whatman, 1813–87; Eton and Christ Church; liberal M.P. for Maidstone 1852–7, 1865–74, for West Kent 1857–9.

[11] Casimeiro di Lieto; Italian correspondent, letters missing in Hawn P.

Read Demosth. Phil I.—Publ. H. Ev. & Report (finished)—Burns's Letters. Saw Mr Barker—Mr Cooper (of Jamaica).[1]

9. Th.

Ch. 8½ A.M. Wrote to Rev. A. M'Lennan[2]—Ld Harris—and minutes. Arrangements for departure. 2–11¼ to D[owning] St. by Birmingham. Worked on my books. Read Sclopis[3]—Memoirs of Fox.[4] Conv. with C.

10. Fr.

Wrote to Ld Braybrooke—C.G.—Bp of Argyll—C. Marriott—& minutes. Saw Mr Timm—Sir C. Trevelyan—Mr Bowring—Sir W. Molesworth. Cabinet 3½–6½.[5] Dined with the Wortleys. Worked 3½ hours on my books. Read De Quincey Autobiogr. Sketches—Fox's Corresp.

11. Sat.

Wrote to Atty. General—Mr Macnab[6]—T.B. Horsfall—Dr Jeune—Mr Keat[7]—C.G.—T. Foster—& minutes. Worked on books 2½ h. Sent off Batch No 3. Cabinet 2½–6. Saw Mr Wood—Dr Jacob—Snell & Co—Hon A. Gordon—S. Herbert. Dined with the Herberts. Saw Bishop [R]. Read Fox's Corresp.

12. 22 S.Trin. X

Marg. Chapel & H.C. mg. Ch. Royal aftn. Read the Dispatches.[8] Wrote to Lady Braybrooke—C.G.[9]—Archdn. Brooks. Dined with Lady W[enlock]: first meeting since the F. L[awley] catastrophe. Read Bp London's Charge (deplorable)[10]—Bp of Gloucesters[11]—Chr. Rem. on Liguori—on Convocation[12]—Ch. Periodicals.

13. M.

Wrote to Dr Pusey—Ld Canning—Duke of Richmond—Robn. G (2)—Ly M. Farquhar—Rev. H. M'Kenzie—Rev. Ld C. Hervey—Ld Talbot de Malahide & minutes. Worked at No 6. 2–4 Court of Exchr. for the roll of

[1] Not further identified.
[2] Episcopal incumbent at Fort William from 1821.
[3] Cp. 19 Sept. 53.
[4] R. Fell, *Memoirs of the public life of the late . . . Charles James *Fox* (1808).
[5] To consider the war; cp. Bassett, 105.
[6] H. MacNab had sent a Fife newspaper clipping on Kennedy.
[7] George Keat, army instrument maker in High Holborn.
[8] On the war, perhaps those on colonial attitudes to it: *PP* 1854–5, xxxvi. 735.
[9] Cp. Bassett, 106.
[10] C. J. *Blomfield, 'A charge delivered to the clergy of the diocese of London' (1854); he was probably upset by the bp.'s uncompromising anti-ritualism (p. 47).
[11] J. H. *Monk, 'A charge to the clergy of the diocese of Gloucester and Bristol . . . in August and September 1854'.
[12] *Christian Remembrancer*, xxviii. 401, 369 (October 1854); on Liguori's theology, and 'A letter to a convocation man, 1697'.

Sheriffs: under 12 Ric 2! c. 2.[1] Saw D. of Buccleuch (Trin Coll)—Mr Whatman—No 6[2]—Montagu Villiers[3] (Mr Reid)—S. Herbert. Read Arnold's Lectures.[4] Dined with the Herberts. C.G. came up. Cabinet 4–6½.

14. T.

Wrote to Rev H. M'Kenzie—S.E.G.—Jas Freshfield—G.C. Glyn—Count Cavour—Sig. Sacchi (& draft)[5]—Capt Robertson—S.H. Northcote—Mr Moffatt—Ld J. Russell, & minutes. Saw Mr Wilson. Worked on book & house arrangements. Dined with the Herberts. Saw one: miserabile [R].[6] Read Fox—Papers on restriction of trade with Russia.[7]

15. Wed.

Wrote to Wm. Brown—Dr Worthington—J.N.G.—Bp of Salisbury—& minutes. Saw Bp of Oxford (breakf &c.)—Governor of the Bank—Duke of Newcastle—Earl of Aberdeen—Mr Jas Freshfield—Mr G.C. Glyn—Overends—in the City.[8] Mr Wood *cum* Mr Timm. Book buying: Leslie,[9] & Petheram. Read Report of 47–8 on Commercial Distress[10]—Jacob's Sermon—Latter's do.[11]

16. Th. X

Wrote to Mr G. Burnett—Agnes G.—Ed. M. Chronicle—A.W. White[12]—Ed. Times—J. Murray—E. of Clarendon—and minutes. Saw M.F. Tupper—Sir A. Spearman—Earl of Aberdeen—Mr C. Franks—Mr H. Roberts—R. Phillimore. Saw one: miserabile [R]. Read Remusat on Protm.:[13] Bank Act of 1694.[14]

17. Fr.

Began to use in the family Bp Hamilton's excellent War prayer.[15] Spent the morning chiefly in framing a plan of House Tax.[16] Wrote to H. Glynne—Mr Pressly—and minutes.[17] Saw Sir J. Graham—S. Herbert—Ld Granville.

[1] Cp. 12 Nov. 53. [2] i.e. checking his house in Carlton Gardens. [3] i.e. H. M. *Villiers.
[4] Cp. 22 Oct. 42. [5] Terenzio Sacchi, Italian author; cp. Add MS 44382, f. 273.
[6] 'Unhappy woman'; a rescue case. [7] *PP* 1854, xxxix. 144, lxvi. 116 and vi. 225.
[8] The phrase 'in the City' bracketed with the last 3 names.
[9] John Leslie, theological bookseller in Great Queen Street.
[10] The select secret cttee. found it 'not expedient to make any alteration in the Bank Act of 1844': *PP* 1847–8, viii. 7.
[11] G. A. Jacob, 'Connexion between true religion and sound learning. A sermon' (1853) and 'A sermon' (1854), on Prov. xxiv.
[12] Probably (Sir) Arnold William White, 1830–93; London solicitor from 1857; solicitor to the Queen from 1864; kt. 1887.
[13] C. de Remusat, 'Des Controverses au sein du Protestantisme', *The Globe* (1829), reprinted in *Critiques et Études Littéraires*, i. 402 (1859).
[14] The act establishing the bank of England; its charter, then expiring in 1855, was also first granted that year.
[15] In W. K. *Hamilton, 'Prayers, which in the present distress may be used' (1854).
[16] He had decided that further increase in income tax would be socially unjustifiable, and was therefore, because of his hostility to borrowing, thrown back on further indirect taxation; cp. O. Anderson, *A liberal state at war*, 203.
[17] One on war commissariat cited from Add MS 44744, f. 82, in Conacher, 490.

Read Fox's Memoirs—Debates of 1772 on Subscription[1]—Cabinet 3–6¼. Stamp of Newsp. Dined with the Herberts.

18. Sat.

Wrote to Mrs Herbert—G. Burnett—Bp of Sarum—Dr Baylee[2]—Rev Mr Haddan—Robn. G.—Lyttelton—and minutes. Cabinet 3–6¼. Stamp (newsp.) settled—Central Ama.—indirect Russian trade. Saw Mr Leslie—Mr Rob. Hook[3]—Sir T. Fremantle—Lord Canning—Mr Pressly—Mr Panizzi—Duke of Newcastle. Dined with the Cannings. Read Remusat on Protestantism.

19. 23 S.Trin.

St Paul's (Kn[ightsbridge]) mg—and H.C.—Chapel Royal Evg. Wrote to Bp of Oxford (2)—A Panizzi—Hon Mrs Stanley.[4] Read King's Greek Church[5]—Brevint on Sacrament & Mass.[6]

20. M.

Wrote to Ld Canning—J. Moss—Duke of Argyll—Robn. G.—G.E.H. Vernon—and minutes. Dined with the Herberts: we met Mrs Maude.[7] Saw Stamped Press Deputn.—Omnibus Deputation[8]—Mr J. Christy[9]—Sir A. Spearman—Attorney General—Mr Wilson—Earl of Aberdeen—Ld Chancellor—Mr Wood *cum* Mr Timm. read French Savings Banks[10]—Fox's Memoirs.

21. Wed.

Wrote to Robn. G.—Lord Aberdeen—J. Moss—Rev. Dr Jacob[11]—Rev Mr Nunn—and minutes. Cabinet 3–6¼. Read Ch. &c. Debates of 1772, 3. Saw Bp of Salisbury (he breakfasted & spent the morning)—Mr E.N. Brown—Archdn. Thorp—Duke of Newcastle. Evg at home: much ransacking & sorting of papers & pamphlets.

[1] On clerical petition to be relieved from subscription to the articles: *Parliamentary history*, xvii. 245.

[2] Joseph *Baylee, 1808–83; founder and first principal of St. Aidan's, Birkenhead, 1856–71; vicar of Shepscombe from 1871.

[3] Banker; a partner in Herries, Farquhar, Davidson, Chapman & Co.

[4] Ellen, da. of Sir J. H. Williams, bart., m. 1832 William Owen Stanley, 1802–84, the twin of 2nd Baron Stanley of Alderley; he was whig M.P. Anglesey 1837–47, Chester 1850–7, Beaumaris 1857–74. She d. 1876.

[5] J. G. *King, *The rites and ceremonies of the Greek church in Russia* (1772).

[6] D. *Brevint, *The depth and mystery of the Roman mass* (1684).

[7] Probably Catherine Mary, *née* Bisshopp, who m. 1853 (Sir) Frederick Francis Maude, 1821–97, who was badly wounded in the Crimea; fought in Afghanistan 1878–9; K.C.B. 1879; she d. 1892.

[8] Cp. *The Times*, 21 November 1854, 6e.

[9] Perhaps J. T. Christy, Bond Street hatter.

[10] Untraced; doubtless in preparation for the deputation.

[11] Edwin Jacob, 1794–1868; Corpus, Oxford; D.D. 1829; vice-president of King's College, Fredericton, New Brunswick, 1829–60.

22. Th.

Wrote to Agnes—Mr Craufurd MP.—Sir T.G.—Sir C. Eastlake—O.B. Cole —Mr H. Farrer[1]—M. Villiers—and minutes. Saw Mrs Watkins (HJG.s)[2]—Duke of Newcastle—S. Herbert—C. Ross—Mr Pressly—Mr Anderson—Sir C. Trevelyan—Bp of New Zealand—J. Griffiths—Earl of Aberdeen—F. Lawley. Dined with the Herberts—Worked on books & pamphlets. Read Whittemore(!) on Louis Napoleon.[3]

23. Th.

Little Mazie's birthday: God bless the darling. Wrote to Mr T.M. Gibson—Mr J. Wood—Mrs Herbert—Mr R. Barker—Mr W Crawfurd—and minutes. Dined with the Herberts. Worked 2½ hours on books, mg. Commissariat Conclave 2¾–6. Saw Duke of Newcastle—Mr Roberts. Read Fox's Memoirs —History of Offices[4]—Exchequer Debate of 34.[5]

24. Fr.

Wrote to my Mary—T. Foster—J. Hume MP.—Ld Courtenay—and minutes. Cabinet 3¼–6¼.[6] Opened three measures. Worked on my books. Saw Mr Leslie—Lord Courtenay—Mr Wilson. Dined with Mrs Talbot. Read Fox's Memoirs—Bank Acts.—Wrote Mem. on Finance of N.D. Commrs.[7] and corrected Draft of Bill.

25. Sat.

Wrote to Ld Courtenay—C.A. Wood—Sir J. Herschel—and minutes. Dined with the Herberts. Conv. on Miss Stanley.[8] Finished & sent off my books. Saw Mr H.L. Reid[9]—Mr P. Westcott[10]—Sir G. Grey—Sir C. Eastlake—Mr S. Herbert—Sir A. Spearman—E. of Aberdeen (J.R. again!)[11] Educn. Commee. P.C. 12¾–2½. Worked on arranging papers & the like.

[1] Probably T. H. *Farrer; cp. 3 Mar. 36.

[2] i.e. Helen Jane Gladstone's companion.

[3] W. M. Whittemore, 'The seventh head; or Louis Napoleon foreshadowed by prophecy' (1853); prophesying, from Revelation xii., his overthrow of the Turks, and his fall in 1864.

[4] Untraced.

[5] *H* xxii. 193.

[6] It agreed on a special parliamentary session, to start on 12 December.

[7] In Sir J. Clapham, *The bank of England* (1944), ii. (app. F).

[8] Mary Stanley, 1814–79, sister of A.P.*; selected first nurses for Crimea; nursed there, quarrelling with F. *Nightingale; became roman catholic 1856; worked in Lancashire distress 1861.

[9] Unidentified.

[10] Philip Westcott, 1815–78, of Liverpool; portrait painter in London from 1850. Cp. 27 Nov. 54.

[11] *Russell wanted *Palmerston rather than *Newcastle at the new war office; the acrimonious correspondence was circulated; cp. Conacher, 497–9. But see Gladstone's comments on the ministry in *EHR*, ii. 288 (1887).

26. Pre-Advent.

St James's mg. Bedfordbury evg. Saw Ld Courtenay (appt)—Miss Stanley 2 h. on the R. Communion. Wrote MS on Gospel & read in evg. Read Brevint—Victoria Eccl. proceedings[1]—Clark & Melvill's Sermons.[2]

27. M.

Wrote to Mr Brickwood—Sir J. Young (2)—Solr. General (2)—Ld Wodehouse—Mr Monsell—Bp of Oxford—W.R. Farquhar—V.C. of Oxford—J.G. Hubbard—Ld Courtenay—Sir A. Spearman—Ld Monteagle—M. Guizot—Ld Chancellor—Rev Mr Hawker—Commrs of Sewers,[3] & minutes. Saw Mr C.A. Wood—Messrs. Scott—Mr Westcott (sat two hours)—Mr S. Herbert—Sir C. Anderson—Jane Wortley (resp. Col. Stuart).[4] Read Ld A. Hervey on Metaphysics[5]—Rogers on St Thos Charterhouse[6]—Pulling on Lond. Corpn.[7]—Fox's Memoirs.

28. T.

Wrote to Mr Delane—R. Barker—A.P. Stanley—Willy—Ld Monteagle—P. Westcott—J.G. Hubbard (2)—C.A. Wood—Sir A. Spearman—Sir G. Grey—my Brothers—Robn. G.—Dr Pusey, & minutes. Saw Ld Canning—Mr Anderson—Ld Kinnaird—Newspapers Anti Stamp Depn.[8]—Mr Wood cum Mr Timm—Mr Goulburn—Mr Monsell—Mr Arbuthnot—Ld Aberdeen (Q Speech & Legisln.)—Ld Granville. Walk: & saw one [R]. Read Fox's Memoirs—Dundas Correspondence.[9]

29. Wed.

Wrote to A. Oswald—J.R. Hope Scott—J.D. Cook—Rev Mr Humphreys—Mr Brown—Ld J. Russell—C.A. Wood—Mr Trevor—J.N.G.—Mr Timm—& minutes. Dined with Mrs Talbot. Saw Earl of Aberdeen—J.G. Hubbard—Sir J. Graham—Solr. General—Mr Hayter—Mr Arbuthnot—Mr Westcott (sat 2 h.) Read the Dundas & Napier Correspondence (finished)—Wilson on Banking.[10] Worked on books.

[1] *PP* 1854–5, xxxviii. 1; Victorian petitions for a royal veto of the new constitution, which allotted £50,000 of public funds for religious purposes.

[2] Probably F. Clark, *Plain sermons for country congregations* (1839), and Henry *Melvill, *A selection from . . . lectures* (1853), or one of his many earlier sermons.

[3] To complain about smells in Downing Street: Add MS 44529, f. 182.

[4] Perhaps John Ramsay Stuart, 1811–89; lieutenant colonel 1854; served in Crimea; general 1868; commander in Scotland 1875.

[5] Lord A. C. *Hervey, 'Metaphysics. A lecture delivered to the Bury Young Men's Institute' (?1854).

[6] W. *Rogers, 'The education prospects of St. Thomas Charterhouse. A letter to . . . *Russell' (1854).

[7] Cp. 27 Nov. 54.

[8] Cp. *The Times*, 29 November 1854, 7f.

[9] Cp. 18 Mar. 52.

[10] James *Wilson, *Essays on capital, currency and banking* (1847).

30. Th. St. Andrew

Wrote to A. Oswald—Ld Aberdeen (2)—W Brown MP—Sir A. Spearman—Robn. G—Mr J.G. Hubbard—Bp of Oxford—and minutes. Cabinet 3–5¾. Read Twisleton[1]—Sir J. MacNeil.[2] Saw Mr J. M'Lennan[3]—Mr Wilson—Leighton (Binder). Off to Windsor at 5¾. The Queen could speak of nothing but the army. The Prince said of the last J.R. letter as described by me it was 'shameful'.[4]

Friday Dec.One 54.

Wrote to Lord Chancellor—Canning—Mr H. Lindsay—Mr W. Witts[5]—Supt. LSWRR[6]—Hon H Fitzroy—J.G. Hubbard—and minutes. Read Twisleton (finished)—Sir J. MacNeil. Saw Bp of N. Zealand—Mrs Coleridge—E. of Aberdeen—Sir C. Trevelyan—Mr Wilson. Cabinet 3–5½:[7] & back to Windsor. Evening conv. much as yesty.: with the Prince also resp. Cambridge.

2. Sat.

St George's 10½ A.M. Migrated to the Bp of NZ's.[8] Walk with him & Dr Goodford, for Eton matters. Dinner party at Coleridge's. Saw Dean of Windsor—Sir J. Patteson (E.C.'s).[9] Read 'Progress of Russia in the East' (finished).

3. Adv.Sunday.

Eton Chapel mg, when Bp NZ again preached a very noble Sermon. Windsor Ch in evg: he preached then also. Walk with him, & most of the spare hours in his society: we conversed on the Ch at home & in the Colonies.[10] At his desire I spoke a little to Willy my godson.[11] Saw Coleridge about (my) Willy—Bp NZ—& Private Secretary.[12] Wrote a letter, & also a paper of suggestions, for Willy: who not being well remains with us at Windsor. Read Bp of Oxford's Charge.[13]

[1] E. T. B. Twistleton, 'Evidence as to the religious working of the common schools in Massachusetts' (?1854).

[2] Cp. 22 May 43.

[3] Possibly John M'Lennan, London instrument maker.

[4] Cp. 25 Nov. 54 n.

[5] Of Church Street, Westminster, had accused Hampton of dishonesty: Add MS 44529, f. 187.

[6] Lewis Crombie was secretary and superintendent of the London and South Western Railway.

[7] To approve plans for expansion of the army; cp. Conacher, 509.

[8] Fund-raising in England 1854–5; lived by Eton.

[9] i.e. at E. Coleridge's Eton house.

[10] He had returned to England to obtain power to sub-divide his diocese; on his return to New Zealand four bps. were consecrated 1855.

[11] Cp. 6 May 40.

[12] Coleridge recommended (Sir) Robert George Wyndham *Herbert, 1831–1905; Eton and Balliol; fellow of All Souls from 1855; Gladstone's private secretary 1855; colonial secretary of Queensland 1859; member of legislative council and first prime minister there 1860–5; permanent under-secretary for colonies 1871–92; K.C.B. 1882.

[13] S. *Wilberforce, *A charge to the diocese of Oxford, at his visitation* (1854).

4. M.

Off at 10.25 to London: shopping &c. there. Wrote to H.J.G.—A. Oswald—Sir A. Spearman—Mr Hayter—F.C. Lawley—J. Heywood—Bp of Oxford —W. Brown MP—Mr Anderson—Mr J. Wood—Sir J. Graham—& minutes. Dined with the Herberts. Saw Mr J. Griffiths—Ld Canning—S. Herbert—A. Gordon. Cabinet 3–5¼: strange enough.[1] Read Meyrick's Sermon[2]—Garbett's Charge[3]—Fremantle on Civil Service.[4]

5. T.

Wrote to Willis (bookseller)[5]—Mr Lefevre—Mrs Hampton—Mr Thornely —Mr Twisleton—Lt Gladstone[6]—Mr Brickwood—Dr Jeune—Sir A. Spearman—and minutes. Dined with Mrs Blackwood.[7] Saw divers [R]. Saw Mr Wilson. Read Creasy's Hist of the Ottoman Turks.[8] Worked on my books No 6.

6. Wed.

Wrote to Sir C. Eardley—Mr Willis—Mr Hopkinson—Mr Glyn MP.—Rev. R. Greswell—Mr Tombs—Sir A. Spearman—and minutes. Worked upon my books at No 6. Saw E. Cardwell—Mr Willis—Ld Aberdeen *cum* Sir J. Graham—resp. 'crisis'[9]—Sir W. Molesworth—Sir Culling Eardley. Pyx P.C. Commee. 9½ A.M. Cabinet dinner at Ld Abns. It deserves a Memm.[10]

7. Th.

Wrote to J. Murray—E. of Abn. (draft) (stopped)[11]—S. Herbert—S H Northcote—E. Saward[12]—E. Cardwell—J.S. Brickwood—A. Oswald—Mr Hayter—Rev W. Malet—C.A. Wood—J.G. Hubbard—Mr Goulburn (2). Saw R. Phillimore—Mr Wilson—Sir A. Spearman—Mr Greswell—Mr S. Herbert—Mr A. Gordon—E. of Aberdeen. Dined with Goldsmith's Co: toasts afterwards.[13] Worked on books D[owning] St. Saw 2 [R].

[1] A discussion of *Russell's war office proposals; cp. Conacher, 497.
[2] F. *Meyrick, *Two sermons preached before the university, May 29, and Nov. 5; with an appendix* (1854); on Deut, viii. 11 and Acts ix. 1.
[3] J. *Garbett, *A charge, delivered at Chichester* (1854).
[4] MS from T. F. *Fremantle.
[5] George Willis, bookseller with several shops in the Covent Garden area.
[6] Charles Alexander Gladstone, 1834–55, cousin, son of David; in 15th regiment, Bengal.
[7] Eliza, *née* Dupré, m. 1803 John Blackwood, uncle of 4th Baron Dufferin; she d. 1860.
[8] Sir E. S. *Creasy, *History of the Ottoman Turks*, i. (1854).
[9] The war office crisis; that evening Aberdeen, Palmerston and *Russell all offered to resign; cp. Argyll, i. 509–10.
[10] On the war office, Add MS 44778, f. 188; fragment in Conacher, 498.
[11] Ibid., f. 192; and ibid. 498n.
[12] Refusing him a clerkship: Add MS 44529, f. 192.
[13] No report found.

8. Fr.

Wrote to Jas Watson—Ld Hardinge—Sir C. Eardley—B. Quaritch—Sir T. Fremantle—Rev Mr Church—Sir J. Herschel—Mr Wilson—W. Monsell—and minutes. Went to Lady Ln. for tea. Saw Earl of Aberdeen—Ld J. Russell—Sir J. Graham—Mr Wilson—S. Herbert. C.O. meeting at 1 & 2½. Cabinet 3–5½.[1]

9. Sat. X

Wrote to Ld Canning—Rev T. James—Mr R. Herbert—Earl of Abn.—Sir C. Trevelyan—C.G.—& minutes. C.G. went off early: to Willy's confirmation (after all it was by the hands of Bp of NZ) & Hawarden. I prayed for him but indifferently. Saw Mr Wilson—Sir C. Trevelyan—Ld Chancellor—Earl of Aberdeen. Cabinet 3–6¾. 1½ h. on the Kennedy affair: a strange & again a childish scene.[2] Saw A. Harington [R]. Read Creasy's Ottoman Turks.

10. 2S.Adv.

Chapel Royal mg and St James's (prayers) evg. Wrote to Rev. F. Meyrick—Sir J. Clark—Rev. E. Coleridge—Dr Pusey. Read Calixtus Pref. to Cassander[3]—Marsden's Hist[4]—Sir C. Eardley's devastated Prayer Book[5]—Meyrick's Sermon (2)[6]—&c. A round of (meant to be charity) calls. Dined with the Herberts.

11. M.

Wrote to Mrs Herbert—Ld J. Russell—Rev W. Scott—D of Newcastle—Rev S. Hawtrey[7]—R. Barker—Jas Watson—C.G.—& minutes. Attended Ld J.R.s official dinner.[8] Saw one [R]. Saw Sir A. Spearman—Mr J. Wood—Mr Wilson—Mr Arbuthnot—Newsp. Stamp (Postal arrangements) Conclave 11–2½—Mr Hayter—Sir J. Graham. Read Creasy.

12. T.

Wrote to Mr Rawson—C.G.—Mr Marriott—E.A. Bowring—& minutes. Read 'Thirty Years of Foreign Policy'.[9] Saw Mr Wilson—Ld Courtenay—J.N.G.—Lord Aberdeen—C.A. Wood. H. of C. 4–2½ (7–8½ home). The attack went off in smoke.[10]

[1] To consider the Queen's speech; cp. Conacher, 500.

[2] Cp. Conacher, 377ff, 501, 530–1.

[3] *Geo Cassandri de communione sub utraque specie dialogus, una cum aliis superiore seculo scriptis et actis eodem facientibus Geo. Calixtus collegit et edidit* (1642).

[4] J. B. *Marsden, *The history of the early Puritans* (1850) and *The history of the later Puritans* (1852).

[5] Sir C. E. *Eardley, *The book of common prayer . . . slightly altered* (1854).

[6] Cp. 4 Dec. 54.

[7] Stephen Thomas Hawtrey, 1809–86; Trinity, Cambridge; curate at Windsor 1844–51; head maths master at Eton 1851–71.

[8] The eve-of-session dinner, held at the foreign office.

[9] [T. *Macknight], *Thirty years of foreign policy; a history of the secretaryships of . . . *Aberdeen and . . . *Palmerston* (1855).

[10] *Pakington and *Layard's attack on the Queen's speech: *H* cxxxvi. 105.

13. W.

Wrote to Ld Courtenay—Sir J. Young—Mr Bentley—C.G.[1]—Ld A. Hervey—and minutes. H of C. 12¼–3: spoke on Report of Address.[2] Dined with the Herberts. Saw Mr Hayter—Mr Wilson—Mr Fitzgerald *cum* Sir C.T.—Mrs Herbert. Read 30 Years of F. Policy. Saw one [R].

14. Th.

Wrote to Rev Mr Rawson—Ld Lansdowne—Robn. G—Mr Gibson RA.—C.G.—D of Newcastle—Sir G. Grey—and minutes. H of C. 4¼–6¼.[3] Saw Sir A. Spearman (2)—Sir C. Trevelyan—Mr E.A. Bowring—Lord Elcho—Sir A. Gordon. Saw Garden (50) [?R]. Read Rev. Deux Mondes on Banking[4]—30 Years F. Policy—Creasy's Hist. Ottoman Turks.

15. Fr.

Wrote to E. of Aberdeen—Mr W. Forbes—T. Macknight[5]—Robn. G.—J.H. Parker—C.G.—& minutes. H of C. 4½–6½.[6] Dined with the Herberts. Saw E. of Aberdeen—do *cum* Sir J. Graham—Bp of Sodor & Man—J.N.G. Packed most of the last batch of books. Read Cox on Br. Commonwealth[7]—Macknight on For. Policy.

16. Sat. X

Wrote to Mr Wilson—Lord Hardinge—Rev Mr Wayte—Sir J. Young—C.G.[8]—Mr Craufurd MP—Mr H. Cox[9]—and minutes. Cabinet 3¾–6½. Saw Sir F. Doyle—Lord Canning. Saw Berkeley—M. Dumin [R].[10] Finished & sent off the last batch of cases from No 6. Read Creasy—and Macknight—also Æn. Bk IV.

17. 3 S.Adv.

St Mary Magd. mg & H.C.—St James's (prayers) evg. Read MS on Ep. aloud. Wrote to M. Dumin. Saw do in evg: agreed on a letter home [R]. Read Calixtus—Westerton's Popish Practices &c[11]—Miss Stanley on Sisterhoods.[12] Saw Ld Abn. with Sir J. Graham. Wrote Mem. about Kennedy: &

[1] In Bassett, 106.
[2] Defended govt.'s handling of 'the great game of war': *H* cxxxvi. 232.
[3] Stalled on newspaper stamps: *H* cxxxvi. 302.
[4] *Revue des Deux Mondes*, 2nd series xviii. 792 (1854); 'Les finances de la guerre, ressources financières de la Russie', by L. Tegoborski.
[5] Thomas *MacKnight, 1829–99; liberal editor and author; cp. 12 Dec. 54.
[6] The war: *H* cxxxvi. 378.
[7] H. Cox, *père*, *The British commonwealth: or a commentary on the institutions and principles of British government* (1854).
[8] In Bassett, 107.
[9] Homersham Cox, 1821–97; barrister from 1851, judge 1871–93; cp. two notes above.
[10] A rescue case; see subsequent days.
[11] C. Westerton, *Popish practices at St. Paul's, Knightsbridge* (1854); a reply to *Blomfield, with notes.
[12] Mary Stanley, *Hospitals and sisterhoods* (1854).

vented my overflowing disgust at the conduct of Ld J. & the degradation of the Cabinet.[1]

18. M. X

Wrote to S. Herbert—C.A. Wood—Ld Aberdeen—Rn. G—Ld Duncan—C.G.[2] Miss Doyle—Mad. Dumin[3]—M. Azeglio—and minutes. Saw Sir A. Spearman—Ld Aberdeen—do with D. of N. Sir J.G. & S.H. to consider the Kennedy case. Saw Mr Wilson—Mr Brown MP.—Sir G. Goodman M.P.[4]—Mr A. Gordon. Saw Berkeley (=Morgan)—M. Dumin [R]. H of C. 4¼–5¾ & at 8.[5] Read Creasy—Macknight.

19. T.

Wrote to Mr M. Leverson[6]—Mr Wilson—Wm. Gladstone—C.G.[7]—Lady Meath—Robn. G.—J.W. Cowell[8]—Baron de Cetto—B.B. Williams—and minutes. Saw Mr Wilson—Marq. Azeglio—E. of Aberdeen—Ld Duncan—Mrs Herbert—Sir J. Graham. Worked on my books. Cabinet 2½–4. House 4¼–7¼ and 10–1¾. Voted in 241:202 for 2d r[eading] For[eigners] Enlistment Bill. I never before heard the announcement of a majority in wh I had myself voted with such doubtful (if indeed doubtful) feelings.[9] Read Macknight (finished): also Nicicisia [sic] Thucyd B VI.[10]

20. Wed.

Wrote to Mr Peto—Ld Palmerston—Rev E. Hill—Rev. D. Robertson—Mr Colnaghi—S.H. Northcote—C.A. Wood—J.G. Hubbard—C.G.[11]—Rev R W Brown—Rev Dr Jeune—and minutes. Dined with the Herberts. H. of C. 12–1½ & 3–6. Spoke on Cons[olidated] Fund Resolution.[12] Saw Ld Duncan cum Ld Adv[ocate]—Mr Fitzgerald—J.N.G.—Sir W. Molesworth—S. Herbert. Read Australian papers—Alexander on Dec[ima]l Coinage.[13] Sat up late to write Memm. on Australian *Veto.*[14]

[1] Untraced; ? destroyed.
[2] In Bassett, 108, marked 'Secret'.
[3] Probably the mother of the rescue case of the previous day.
[4] Sir George Goodman, 1792–1859; Leeds woolstapler; first and four times mayor of Leeds; kt. 1852; liberal M.P. Leeds 1852–7.
[5] Spoke on tax paid by serving officers: *H* cxxxvi. 461.
[6] Montague Leverson of London, had sent suggestions on how to run the exchequer: Add MS 44529, f. 198.
[7] Bassett, 108.
[8] John William Cowell of Gloucester terrace had written on new bank note issues: Add MS 44529, f. 198.
[9] He thought it would be 'a relief to be beaten, after the state to which our internal relations have come' (Bassett, 109). Had spoken earlier on officers' legacy duties: *H* cxxxvi. 502.
[10] Thucydides, *History of the Peloponnesian war*, book vi., on Nicias, general in the Sicilian expedition, 415, put to death 413.
[11] Bassett, 109.
[12] *H* cxxxvi. 618.
[13] J. Alexander, 'Suggestions for a simple system of decimal notation and currency, after the Portuguese model' (1854).
[14] Supporting abolition of imperial veto on local affairs; printed for cabinet: Add MS 44585, f. 79.

21. Th.

Wrote to E. of Aberdeen—Rev B. Wilson—Sir W. Molesworth—Sir C. Wood—Rev Mr Brown—C.G.—Wm. Gladstone—T.G.—Sir T. Fremantle —Mr Wilson—& minutes. Sat to Mr Westcott. Saw Sir A. Spearman—Mr Hubbard—Mr C.A. Wood—Lord Aberdeen *cum* S. Herbert—Sir W. Molesworth—Mr Wilson. Cabinet $2\frac{3}{4}$–$4\frac{1}{4}$.[1] H of C. $5\frac{1}{4}$–7.[2] Saw divers [R]. Read Creasy. Worked on books.

22. Fr.

Wrote to Tathams—C.G.—Freshfields—Ld J. Russell—Mr Goulburn—& minutes. H of C. under orders to speak $4\frac{1}{4}$–$6\frac{3}{4}$ & $7\frac{1}{2}$–$1\frac{3}{4}$: but it was not required.[3] Saw Mr Wood—Sir A. Spearman—Ld Granville—Mr Arbuthnot —Mr Wilson—Lord Aberdeen—Mr Owen.[4] Saw M. Dumin [R]—Read Creasy (finished V. 1.).

23. Sat.

Wrote to Me. Dumin & copy[5]—Miss Eden—Sir S. Scott & Co—J.G. Hubbard—and minutes. Cabinet $2\frac{3}{4}$–$4\frac{1}{4}$.[6] Off by Express to Hawarden. Arrived at midnight: all well D.G. Saw Mr Wilson—Mr R. Herbert—Mlle. Dumin [R]—and others. Set to work on my books.

24. 4 S.Adv.

Hawarden Ch. mg & evg. Read Rogers on the Articles[7]—Litton on the Church.[8] Much delight with the children.

25. Xmas Day.

H[awarde]n Ch mg (H.C.) & evg. Willy knelt at the altar between his Mother and me. Seldom I believe has a fairer and purer heart offered its first fruits to God. In the aftn. I walked with him & spoke of the Holy Eucharist. As for me I was troubled during the morning about my feud in the Cabinet: brute passions were in my mind with the thought of the new-born Christ, even as the animals in the stable where He lay: but at the Altar the Son of God came to me and bid them be still.

Read Litton—Rogers. We dined with H. at the Rectory. Put a few books away.

26. T. Saint Stephen.

Ch 11 A.M. Wrote to Earl of Aberdeen[9]—Robn. G.—Ld Chancellor. Set

[1] On the deteriorating war situation; cp. Argyll, i. 514.
[2] Foreigners Enlistment Bill: *H* cxxxvi. 746.
[3] The same: bill passed, despite *Bright's great speech; session ended: *H* cxxxvi. 794.
[4] In pencil. [5] In pencil.
[6] Discussion of *Argyll's military proposals; cp. Argyll, i. 515.
[7] Cp. 29 Oct. 54.
[8] E. A. Litton, *The church of Christ, in its idea, attributes, and ministry* (1851).
[9] One sentence in Conacher, 380.

to work in earnest with my books aided by Willy and Stephy: in a chaos of some 2000. Saw Mr Burnett. Read Shirley[1]—Monti's Basvilliana.[2]

27. Wed. St John.

Church 11 AM. Again worked much of the day on my books. Saw Robn. who came over to speak of several matters of business. Wrote to Lord Hardinge —M. Dumin—Ld Chancellor—Robn. G.—Sir F. Doyle & minutes. Read Shirley—Basvilliana (finished).

28. Th. H. Innocents'.

Church 11 A.M.

A third bout carried me through most of the work of arranging books: the number I have here must be over 5000. Walk with Willy to St John's. Arranged with Bailie for more book-room. Read Shirley. Wrote to V. Chancr. of Oxford—Ld Aberdeen—& minutes. My evening closed with a short retrospect & examn.

29. Fr.

Church 8½ A.M. Resumed work on my books more moderately. Wrote to R. Phillimore—Mr T.L. Holt[3]—Mr Dalyell—Rev N. Woodard—Anderson —and minutes. Read Alfieri's Misogallo[4]—Monti, Poesie[5]—Memoirs of Bp Watson[6]—Shirley. Walk with S.R.G.

During the year now fully added to my life the mercies of God have been as abundantly showered upon me as at any former time. Especially should we be most thankful that during the time of pressure we have been spared all anxiety about the children's health. Willy's short illness came at the time of greatest freedom. And in matters other than health all I trust goes well.

In looking back over the stained course of my life, I have cause to feel yet more keenly my[7] need to escape before long from a sphere of so much temptation so sorely oppressing me. I refer particularly to the sins of wrath, impurity, & spiritual sloth. The first[8] of them seems to toss me like a tempest. Of the next I can only hope it has not been more flagrant. But as to the last I feel its bonds to be heavier than ever. It seems as if my ordinary occupations left to me none of the nerve requisite for most of the forms of self-discipline: as if I lay exhausted & smitten down, waiting to be recruited, & able to do nothing for the discipline of soul or body in the times given me

[1] By Charlotte *Brontë (1849); cp. 14 Sept. 54.

[2] V. Monti, *La Basvilliana* (1793).

[3] Thomas Littleton Holt, 1794?–1879; journalist and campaigner against advertisement duty; was refused compensation for govt. prosecution of unstamped press: Add MS 44530, f. 5.

[4] V. Alfieri, *Il Misogallo. Prose e rime* (1799).

[5] By V. Monti, 2 v. (1800).

[6] J. *Bunting, *Memorials of the late Richard *Watson, including the funeral sermon* (1833).

[7] Instead of 'the'.

[8] Instead of 'former'.

for recreation from sheer want of strength.—Now these things are realities: & as in the sight of God I fondly trust that the desire which I have expressed to "escape because of the stormy wind and tempest"[1] is to grow to ripeness and to bear its fruit when He shall signify to me that the hour is come.

30. Sat.

Church 8½ A.M. Wrote to R. Wilbraham—Robn. G.—Rev. J. Cazenove[2]—Mr Wilson—Bp St Andrew's—Rev G. Trevor & minutes. Read Yates &c. on Dec. Coinage[3]—Watson's Memoirs—Alfieri's Misogallo—Monti's Aristodemo[4]—Shirley (finished Vol I.). Walk with S.R.G.

31. S. after Xmas.

H[awarde]n Ch. mg (with H.C. to which Willy also spontaneously went) and evg. Wrote to S. Herbert. Read Bp Fowler's design of Xty[5]—Watson's Memoirs—De Rancy, Maximes[6]—St Leo, Sermones[7]—Litton on the Church.

At night I heard the bells ring in the New Year: a solemn sound, telling us that the great clock of Time has tolled once more. O mighty stream we cannot arrest thee but we can load our little vessel as it floats on thy bosom with good fruits of holy living; God being our helper.

The end of this year has been joyously marked by Willy's going to the altar. My most special pang is the growth of sloth in my spirit: my increasing repugnance to pain, discomfort, inconvenience, & even effort: as if the brain said 'I cannot.' But I hope for better days & better things.

[1] Psalm iv. 8.

[2] John Gibson Cazenove, 1821–96; Brasenose, Oxford; sundry curacies 1846–52; tutor at Cumbrae college 1854–67, provost 1867–75; dean of St. Mary's cathedral, Edinburgh, from 1878.

[3] By James *Yates; perhaps a draft of 'Narrative of the origin and formation of the international association for obtaining a uniform decimal system' (1856).

[4] By V. Monti (1786); a tragedy.

[5] E. *Fowler, *The design of Christianity* (1671).

[6] Cp. 16 July 54.

[7] In Migne, *PL*, lvi.

WHERE WAS HE?

1848–1854

The following list shows where the diarist was each night; he continued at each place named until he moved to the next one.

4 February	1848	Hagley
7 February		London
16 May		Birmingham
17 May		London
13 June		Dropmore
16 June		London
22 August		Hagley
11 September		On ship
12 September		Perth
13 September		Fasque
23 October		Edinburgh
24 October		Perth
25 October		Fasque
29 December		Dalkeith
2 January	1849	Fasque
24 January		On train
25 January		London
26 January		Oxford
1 February		London
3 April		Hagley
11 April		London
23 June		Eastbourne
25 June		London
13 July		On ship to France
14 July		On train through France
15 July		Posting through France
16 July		Marseilles
19 July		Sailing to Genoa
20 July		Sailing to Leghorn
21 July		Sailing to Civita Veccia
22 July		Rome
23 July		Posting to Naples
24 July		Naples
26 July		Sailing to Civita Veccia
27 July		Sailing to Leghorn
28 July		Sailing to Genoa
29 July		Posting to Milan
30 July		Milan
31 July		Como
1 August		Lecco
2 August		Laveno
3 August		Domodossola
4 August		Posting across Alps
6 & 7 August		Posting to Paris
8 August		Posting to Amiens
9 August		London
23 August		Hawarden
22 September		London
25 September		Hawarden
2 October		On ship
3 October		Fasque
17 October		Haddo House
20 October		Fasque
4 December		Kinnaird
5 December		Fasque
8 January	1850	Edinburgh
9 January		Fasque
28 January		Carlisle
29 January		Northampton
30 January		London
9 February		Hagley
18 February		London
2 March		Hagley
6 March		London
12 April		On train
13 April		Fasque
16 April		On train
17 April		Brighton
23 April		London
27 April		Brighton
29 June		Eton
1 July		London

2 August	Hagley
12 August	Hawarden
15 August	London
17 August	Hawarden
30 August	On ship
31 August	Fasque
23 September	On train
24 September	Hawarden
30 September	Grove Park, Warwick
2 October	London
7 October	Hawarden
13 October	On train
14 October	London
18 October	On ship
19 October	Paris
25 October	Moulins
26 October	Roanne
28 October	Lyons
29 October	Chambèry
30 October	Modane
31 October	Susa
1 November	Turin
4 November	Genoa
7–9 November	On ship
10 November	Naples
18–22 February 1851	Sailing to Marseilles
23–4 February	Posting through France
25 February	On train from Paris
26 February	London
9 April	Paris
10 April	London
16 April	On train
17 April	Fasque
30 April	Glenalmond
2 May	Fasque
7 May	London
1 August	Hagley
11 August	Hawarden
12 August	Hagley
18 August	London
20 August	Hagley
28 August	On train
29 August	Fasque
23 October	Glenalmond
24 October	Fasque
29 October	Haddo House
1 November	Fasque
26 December	Lancaster
27 December	Liverpool
28 December	Hawarden
15 January 1852	Clumber
19 January	Eton
20 January	Cuddesdon
22 January	Oxford
26 January	London
1 May	Blackheath
3 May	London
20 June	Windsor
21 June	London
7 July	Bristol
9 July	Tenby
12 July	St. David's
13 July	Carmarthen
14 July	Builth
15 July	Hereford
16 July	Shrewsbury
17 July	Hawarden
8 September	St. Asaph
11 September	Hawarden
12 October	London
13 October	Hawarden
19 October	Liverpool
20 October	On train
21 October	London
22 October	Oxford
26 October	Hawarden
4 November	London
11 December	Hagley
13 December	London
25 December	Hawarden
27 December	London
1 January 1853	Hawarden
8 January	London
12 January	Windsor
15 January	London
26 January	Oxford
29 January	Moor Park, Rickmansworth
31 January	London
29 March	Wilton
2 April	London
7 May	Brighton
9 May	London
14 May	Falconhurst, Kent
19 May	London
23 July	Eton

17 August		Elderslie, Renfrewshire
19 August		On ship
20 August		Glenquoich
2 September		Dingwall
3 September		Dunrobin
27 September		Inverness
28 September		Oban
29 September		Drumlanrig
1 October		Hawarden
3 October		London
10 October		Manchester
14 October		Hawarden
23 October		On train
24 October		Windsor
26 October		London
28 October		Hawarden
5 November		Liverpool
7 November		London
9 November		Windsor
12 November		London
24 November		Hawarden
8 December		Hagley
16 December		London
4 January	1854	Windsor
6 January		London
19 April		Hagley
24 April		London
16 May		Hagley
19 May		Hawarden
21 May		London
3 June		Eton
5 June		London
8 July		Falconhurst, Kent
14 July		Betteshanger, Kent
15 July		London
22 July		West Horsley
24 July		London
29 July		Cliveden
31 July		London
5 August		Polesden
7 August		London
12 August		Broadstairs
29 August		London
30 August		Osborne
1 September		London
2 September		Broadstairs
14 September		Betteshanger, Kent
19 September		London
22 September		Audley
26 September		Peterborough
27 September		Worsley
2 October		Hawarden
16 October		London
21 October		Hawarden
9 November		London
30 November		Windsor
4 December		London
23 December		Hawarden

DRAMATIS PERSONAE

An index to the whole work will appear in the concluding volume, together with a bibliography of Gladstone's reading as recorded in the diary. Meanwhile readers may be helped by this list of biographical notes, most of which refer to the first occasion of mention in the diary. A plain date indicates a first mention in the diary text, usually with a footnote at that date; a date with 'n' (e.g. 27 Oct. 48n) indicates a mention in a footnote to a person or event noticed by the diarist on that day.

This list covers the years 1840–1854 and must be read together with that at the end of volume two, which deals with 1825–1839. People mentioned in that list are not repeated here. Readers who wish to identify a person mentioned in the diary, but who is not in this list below, should refer to the previous list. The exceptions are names that occur in the first two volumes but are more fully identified by a footnote in volume three or four; these are marked † following their date, in the list below. A few cross-references from this list are to names in the volume two list. Names mentioned on the fly leaf of an MS volume of the diary are marked (f.l.) with the nearest date. To increase the list's usefulness as a guide to identification, priests, the largest occupational group in these volumes, have their initials prefixed by *Rev.*, *bp.* etc., and some other occupations have been briefly indicated.

People with double-barrelled, or particuled, surnames appear under the last part of the name, except that names in M' and Mc are under Mac, Irish names in O' are under O, and D'Arcy, D'Arsonval, D'Orsey and D'Urban are under D.

Rulers and royal dukes are given under their regal or Christian names. Other peers, and married women, are listed under their surname, with cross-references from their titles and maiden names.

Titles, given in italics in this list, are ignored in its alphabetical order, which is that of surnames, followed by full forenames, of which only the initials appear. Names of firms follow other similar surnames, e.g. Williams, Deacon & Co. follows the other Williams's.